Designing Forms for Microsoft Office InfoPath and Forms Services 2007

Microsoft .NET Development Series

John Montgomery, *Series Advisor*
Don Box, *Series Advisor*
Martin Heller, *Series Editor*

The Microsoft .NET Development Series is supported and developed by the leaders and experts of Microsoft development technologies including Microsoft architects. The books in this series provide a core resource of information and understanding every developer needs in order to write effective applications and managed code. Learn from the leaders how to maximize your use of the .NET Framework and its programming languages.

Titles in the Series

Brad Abrams, *.NET Framework Standard Library Annotated Reference Volume 1: Base Class Library and Extended Numerics Library*, 0-321-15489-4

Brad Abrams and Tamara Abrams, *.NET Framework Standard Library Annotated Reference, Volume 2: Networking Library, Reflection Library, and XML Library*, 0-321-19445-4

Keith Ballinger, *.NET Web Services: Architecture and Implementation*, 0-321-11359-4

Bob Beauchemin and Dan Sullivan, *A Developer's Guide to SQL Server 2005*, 0-321-38218-8

Don Box with Chris Sells, *Essential .NET, Volume 1: The Common Language Runtime*, 0-201-73411-7

Keith Brown, *The .NET Developer's Guide to Windows Security*, 0-321-22835-9

Eric Carter and Eric Lippert, *Visual Studio Tools for Office: Using C# with Excel, Word, Outlook, and InfoPath*, 0-321-33488-4

Eric Carter and Eric Lippert, *Visual Studio Tools for Office: Using Visual Basic 2005 with Excel, Word, Outlook, and InfoPath*, 0-321-41175-7

Mahesh Chand, *Graphics Programming with GDI+*, 0-321-16077-0

Krzysztof Cwalina and Brad Abrams, *Framework Design Guidelines: Conventions, Idioms, and Patterns for Reusable .NET Libraries*, 0-321-24675-6

Len Fenster, *Effective Use of Microsoft Enterprise Library: Building Blocks for Creating Enterprise Applications and Services*, 0-321-33421-3

Sam Guckenheimer and Juan J. Perez, *Software Engineering with Microsoft Visual Studio Team System*, 0-321-27872-0

Anders Hejlsberg, Scott Wiltamuth, Peter Golde, *The C# Programming Language*, Second Edition, 0-321-33443-4

Alex Homer and Dave Sussman, *ASP.NET 2.0 Illustrated*, 0-321-41834-4

Joe Kaplan and Ryan Dunn, *The .NET Developer's Guide to Directory Services Programming*, 0-321-35017-0

Mark Michaelis, *Essential C# 2.0*, 0-321-15077-5

James S. Miller and Susann Ragsdale, *The Common Language Infrastructure Annotated Standard*, 0-321-15493-2

Christian Nagel, *Enterprise Services with the .NET Framework: Developing Distributed Business Solutions with .NET Enterprise Services*, 0-321-24673-X

Brian Noyes, *Data Binding with Windows Forms 2.0: Programming Smart Client Data Applications with .NET*, 0-321-26892-X

Brian Noyes, *Smart Client Deployment with ClickOnce: Deploying Windows Forms Applications with ClickOnce*, 0-321-19769-0

Fritz Onion with Keith Brown, *Essential ASP.NET 2.0*, 0-321-23770-6

Fritz Onion, *Essential ASP.NET with Examples in C#*, 0-201-76040-1

Fritz Onion, *Essential ASP.NET with Examples in Visual Basic .NET*, 0-201-76039-8

Ted Pattison and Dr. Joe Hummel, *Building Applications and Components with Visual Basic .NET*, 0-201-73495-8

Scott Roberts and Hagen Green, *Designing Forms for Microsoft Office InfoPath and Forms Services 2007*, 0-321-41059-9

Dr. Neil Roodyn, *eXtreme .NET: Introducing eXtreme Programming Techniques to .NET Developers*, 0-321-30363-6

Chris Sells and Michael Weinhardt, *Windows Forms 2.0 Programming*, 0-321-26796-6

Dharma Shukla and Bob Schmidt, *Essential Windows Workflow Foundation*, 0-321-39983-8

Guy Smith-Ferrier, *.NET Internationalization: The Developer's Guide to Building Global Windows and Web Applications*, 0-321-34138-4

Paul Vick, *The Visual Basic .NET Programming Language*, 0-321-16951-4

Damien Watkins, Mark Hammond, Brad Abrams, *Programming in the .NET Environment*, 0-201-77018-0

Shawn Wildermuth, *Pragmatic ADO.NET: Data Access for the Internet World*, 0-201-74568-2

Paul Yao and David Durant, *.NET Compact Framework Programming with C#*, 0-321-17403-8

Paul Yao and David Durant, *.NET Compact Framework Programming with Visual Basic .NET*, 0-321-17404-6

For more information go to www.awprofessional.com/msdotnetseries/

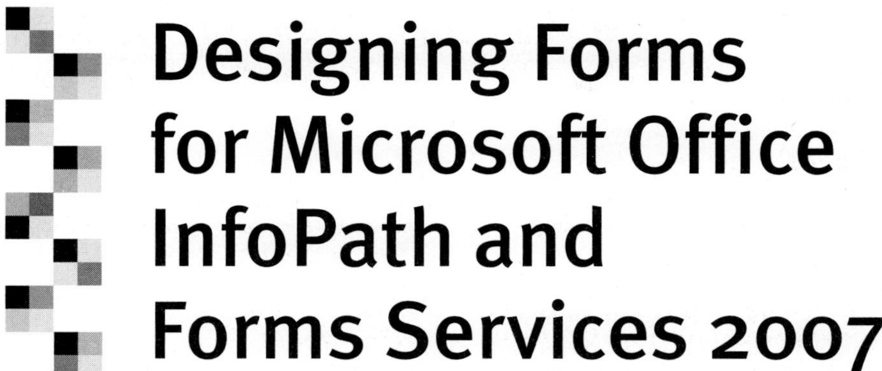

Designing Forms for Microsoft Office InfoPath and Forms Services 2007

- Scott Roberts
- Hagen Green

Addison-Wesley

Upper Saddle River, NJ • Boston • Indianapolis • San Francisco
New York • Toronto • Montreal • London • Munich • Paris
Madrid • Capetown • Sydney • Tokyo • Singapore • Mexico City

The publisher offers excellent discounts on this book when ordered in quantity for bulk purchases or special sales, which may include electronic versions and/or custom covers and content particular to your business, training goals, marketing focus, and branding interests. For more information, please contact:

U.S. Corporate and Government Sales
(800) 382-3419
corpsales@pearsontechgroup.com

For sales outside the United States please contact:

International Sales
international@pearsoned.com

This Book Is Safari Enabled

The Safari® Enabled icon on the cover of your favorite technology book means the book is available through Safari Bookshelf. When you buy this book, you get free access to the online edition for 45 days.

Safari Bookshelf is an electronic reference library that lets you easily search thousands of technical books, find code samples, download chapters, and access technical information whenever and wherever you need it.

To gain 45-day Safari Enabled access to this book:

- Go to http://www.awprofessional.com/safarienabled
- Complete the brief registration form
- Enter the coupon code: VSGW-MG3I-HA8Z-53IW-GDKU

If you have difficulty registering on Safari Bookshelf or accessing the online edition, please e-mail customer-service@safaribooksonline.com.

Visit us on the Web: www.awprofessional.com

Library of Congress Cataloging-in-Publication Data

Roberts, Scott, 1969–

Designing forms for Microsoft Office Infopath and forms services 2007 / Scott Roberts, Hagen Green.

p. cm.

Includes bibliographical references and index.

ISBN 0-321-41059-9 (pbk. : alk. paper)
1. Microsoft InfoPath. 2. Business—Forms—Computer programs. I. Green, Hagen. II. Title.

HF5371.R63 2007

651'.29028553—dc22

2006036478

ISBN 0-321-41059-9

Text printed in the United States on recycled paper at Courier in Stoughton, Massachusetts.

First printing, February 2007

*To my wife, Andrea, and my two sons, Sean and Bradley.
It is due to your constant love and support that I was able to complete this project. Thank you for always being there for me no matter what project I undertake. I love you all a million times more than you could ever possibly know.*

—Scott

To Jaime, my love and my life, for putting up with my two jobs and helping me stay strong through the end. And to my parents, Stuart and Christine, for their perseverance in love and for being the best parents anyone could ask for.

—Hagen

Contents at a Glance

List of Figures xxi
List of Tables xlvii
Foreword li
Preface lv
About the Authors lxv

PART I Designing Forms 1

1 **Introduction to InfoPath 2007 3**
2 **Basics of InfoPath Form Design 25**
3 **Working with Data 85**
4 **Advanced Controls and Customization 155**
5 **Adding Logic without Code 215**
6 **Retrieving Data from External Sources 241**
7 **Extended Features of Data Connections 297**
8 **Submitting Form Data 327**
9 **Saving and Publishing 397**
10 **Building Reusable Components 431**
11 **Security and Deployment 455**
12 **Creating Reports 553**
13 **Workflow 613**
14 **Introduction to Forms Services 665**

PART II Advanced Form Design 727

15 Writing Code in InfoPath 729

16 Visual Studio Tools for Microsoft Office InfoPath 2007 833

17 Advanced Forms Services 865

18 Hosting InfoPath 965

19 Building Custom Controls Using ActiveX Technologies 1037

20 Add-ins 1073

21 Importers and Exporters 1115

Appendix: Further Reading 1149

Index 1157

Contents

List of Figures xxi
List of Tables xlvii
Foreword li
Preface lv
About the Authors lxv

PART I Designing Forms 1

1 Introduction to InfoPath 2007 3
What Is InfoPath? 3
InfoPath 2003 7
InfoPath 2003 Service Pack 1 12
InfoPath 2007 17
What's Next? 24

2 Basics of InfoPath Form Design 25
Getting Started 25
What Is a Form Template Anyway? 26
Design a Form Template Dialog 27
Creating a New Blank Form Template 30
Designing the Layout of Your Form 34
Using the Layout Task Pane 34
Color Schemes 39

Using Controls 41

Standard Controls 43

Repeating and Optional Controls 49

File and Picture Controls 67

Creating Multiple Views 73

Advanced Formatting 76

Control Formatting 78

Format Painter 79

Formatting Multiple Controls 80

What's Next? 83

3 Working with Data 85

Getting Started 85

Data Binding 86

Creating the Data Source Automatically 86

Understanding Data Source Details 93

Data Source Field and Group Properties 95

Name Property 95

Data Type Property 98

Cannot Be Blank Property 101

Repeating Property 102

Default Value Property 106

Data Source Details 108

Manually Editing the Data Source 110

Adding Nodes 116

Moving Nodes 119

Deleting Nodes 121

Referencing Nodes 122

Starting with Your Own Data Source 124

Advanced Data Binding 137

Understanding Data Binding 138

Design-Time Visuals 149

Editing Default Template Data 151

What's Next? 154

4 Advanced Controls and Customization 155

Getting Started 155

Advanced Controls 156

Hyperlink 156

Expression Box 158

Vertical Label 163

Scrolling Region and Horizontal Region 164

Choice Group, Repeating Choice Group, and Choice Section 167

Repeating Recursive Section 171

Custom Controls 173

Control Properties 174

Data Tab 176

Display Tab 182

Size Tab 189

Advanced Tab 193

Creating Master/Detail Relationships 198

Advanced Customizations 204

Editing Default Values 204

Customizing Commands 210

What's Next? 213

5 Adding Logic without Code 215

Getting Started 215

Conditional Formatting 215

Data Validation 222

Adding Data Validation to a Form Template 223

Pattern Matching 227

Rules 229

Logic Inspector 235

What's Next? 240

6 Retrieving Data from External Sources 241

Getting Started 241

Data Connections 242

Why Do We Need Them? 242

Conceptually Understanding Data Connections and Data Sources 242
All Data Connections Are Not Created Equal 244
Creating a Data Connection 245
XML Files 247
Databases 256
Setting Up a Connection to a Database 257
Integrating the Database Connection into the Form Template 268
Web Services 273
What Is a Web Service? 273
Creating a Simple Web Service Using Visual Studio 2005 274
Using the Simple Web Service 279
InfoPath Web Services 280
Web Service Repository 291
SharePoint Libraries and Lists 292
What's Next? 296

7 **Extended Features of Data Connections 297**
Getting Started 297
Extended Features of Web Services 298
Searching with UDDI 299
ADO.NET Web Services 300
Secondary Data Source Binding 307
Designing the Form Template 307
Filling Out the Form 310
Offline Mode Query Support 312
List Box Controls Connected to Secondary Data Sources 316
Showing Secondary Data in a List Box Control 317
Using the Main Data Source for List Box Items 321
Filtering List Box Items 323
What's Next? 325

8 **Submitting Form Data 327**
Getting Started 327
Why Submit? 328
Using the "Form-Only" Model to Disable Save 329
Issues with Data Validation and Submitting Forms 331

Submitting Forms 334
Introduction to Submit Data Connections 334
What Submit Method Is Best for My Form Template? 335
Submitting via E-Mail 337
Submitting to a Database 341
Submitting to a Web Service 344
Including Text and Child Elements Only 358
XML Subtree, Including the Selected Element 361
Entire Form 362
Submitting Digitally Signed Form Data 365
ADO.NET `DataSet` Submit 369
Designing a Form Template with a Dataset 370
Filling Out the Dataset Form 375
Submitting to a SharePoint Library 377
Submitting to a Web Server via HTTP 380
Custom Submit Using Form Code 383
Custom Submit Using Rules 384
Submitting to a Hosting Environment 391
Submit Options 392
What's Next? 395

9 Saving and Publishing 397
Getting Started 397
Saving and Publishing a Form Template with InfoPath 398
Network Locations 400
SharePoint or Forms Services 404
E-Mail 413
Installable Form Templates 417
Common Conveniences 420
Saving Templates as Extracted Source Files 421
Previewing Form Templates 424
With Sample Data 426
With User Roles 427
Domain Simulation 428
Saving Form Data 429
What's Next? 430

10 Building Reusable Components 431

Getting Started 431

Designing a New Template Part 432

Template Part Design Mode 434

Using a Template Part 438

Adding a Template Part to the Controls Task Pane 438

Inserting a Template Part into a Form Template 442

Updating Template Parts 447

Updating a Form Template That Contains the AddressBlock Template Part 449

Locating All Template Parts That Need to Be Updated 451

Customizing Existing Template Parts 452

What's Next? 454

11 Security and Deployment 455

Getting Started 455

Introduction to InfoPath Security 456

InfoPath Security Levels 458

Designing Security into Form Templates 459

Restricted Security Level 460

Domain Security Level 467

Automatic Security Level 482

Full Trust Security Level 484

Trust and Designer Lockdown 499

Trust Center 499

Designer Lockdown 504

Digital Signatures 507

Using Digitally Signed Data in Forms 509

Allowing Only One Signature 527

Using Independent Signatures (Co-signing) 531

Setting Up Counter-Signatures 532

Digital Signatures in the XML Data and Schema 533

Information Rights Management 538

Permission on Form Templates 539

Permission on Forms 542

Permission with Document Libraries 548
What's Next? 552

12 Creating Reports 553
Getting Started 553
Merging Forms 554
Merging Forms in InfoPath 555
Design Recommendations for Merging Forms 561
Customizing Merge Behavior in Design Mode 564
Custom Merge XSL (Advanced) 580
Printing 586
Print Views 586
Headers and Footers 589
Multiple View Printing 592
Word Print Views 596
Print Views in Browser-Enabled Forms 603
Exporting Forms 605
What's Next? 612

13 Workflow 613
Getting Started 613
User Roles 614
Creating User Roles 616
Determining a User's Role When Filling Out a Form 620
User Roles in Action 621
Role-Based Views 631
Workflow with Microsoft Office SharePoint Server 2007 634
Workflow with InfoPath E-Mail Forms 643
Designing and Using InfoPath E-Mail Forms 644
Creating Rules for InfoPath E-Mail Forms 648
Storing Received Forms in Outlook Folders 650
Filling Out an InfoPath E-Mail Form 652
Sorting, Grouping, and Filtering Responses 656
Merging and Exporting InfoPath E-Mail Forms 657
Customizing E-Mail Support for a Form Template 660
What's Next? 663

14 Introduction to Forms Services 665

Getting Started 665

What Is InfoPath in the Browser? 666

Why Use the Browser? 668

What Is Forms Services? 669

Installing and Configuring Forms Services 671

Installing Forms Services 673

Configuring Forms Services 675

Is Forms Services Installed? 677

Publishing a Form Template to Forms Services 678

Getting Familiar with Browser Forms 682

Creating a New Form 682

Toolbar 683

Controls 688

Supported Web Browsers 690

Designing a Browser-Enabled Form Template 690

Design Once 692

Design Checker 693

Browser-Enabled Forms without the Design Checker 701

Designing Browser-Enabled Template Parts 701

Getting Familiar with the Browser Form Experience 701

SharePoint Integration 705

Document Libraries 705

Site Content Type 709

Data Connections 710

Data Connection Libraries 711

Security and Data Connection Libraries 713

Filling Out Browser Forms 714

Configurations Supported by Forms Services 715

URL-Based Options 716

Mobile Support: Smart Phone and PDA 720

Mobile Compatibility 722

Filling Out a Mobile Form 725

What's Next? 726

Part II Advanced Form Design 727

15 Writing Code in InfoPath 729

Getting Started 729

Writing Code Behind a Form 730

Settings Related to Adding Code 732

Adding Code to a Form Template 737

Filling Out and Debugging a Form with Code 738

The InfoPath Object Model 741

Form Events 742

XML Data Events 744

Using `XPathNavigator` Objects 777

Registering Event Handlers 780

Script and the Custom Task Pane 782

Programming InfoPath . . . in Action! 790

The MOI Consulting Request Form 791

Filling Out the MOI Consulting Request Form 792

Designing the MOI Consulting Request Form 797

What's Next? 832

16 Visual Studio Tools for Microsoft Office InfoPath 2007 833

Getting Started 833

What Is VSTO? 834

Bringing InfoPath into Visual Studio 835

Installing VSTO 836

Designing a Form Template with VSTO 836

Start Designing a Form Template 837

The VSTO Design Experience 843

The VSTO Feature Set 853

Missing Features in VSTO 861

Previewing a Form in VSTO 863

What's Next? 864

17 Advanced Forms Services 865

Getting Started 865

Controls and Browser Optimizations 867

Postback Settings 871

The Update Button 872

Designing Accessible Forms 874

Form Code 875

Executing Form Code in the Browser 876

Circumventing Browser-Enabled Limitations 878

Detecting the Browser or the InfoPath Client 883

Form Code Compatibility with Forms Services 884

SharePoint Integration 885

Advanced Publishing 888

Managing Form Templates 904

Configuring InfoPath Forms Services 906

Configuring Shared Services and Providers 907

Filling Out a Form on a SharePoint Page 928

Data Connections 929

Data Connections Administration Settings 931

Centrally Managed Connection Library 936

Authentication Considerations 943

E-Mail Data Connections 948

Performance Tips and Best Design Practices 950

Form Template Deployment 951

Views 952

Form Code 953

Reduction of Form Postbacks 953

Data-Heavy Features 954

Data Connections 956

Form View State 956

Miscellaneous Performance Tips 957

Performance Monitoring 958

Health Monitoring 962

What's Next? 963

18 **Hosting InfoPath 965**

Getting Started 965

Hosting Scenarios 966

Document Information Panel 966

Creating an InfoPath Host Application 977

Creating an InfoPath Host Application in .NET 979

Host to InfoPath Communication 990

Handling Events from the Form 1001

Using the Host Property 1004

Submitting a Form to the Host 1007

Hosting the InfoPath Form Control in a Web Browser 1011

Host to InfoPath Communication 1020

InfoPath to Host Communication 1028

What's Next? 1036

19 **Building Custom Controls Using ActiveX Technologies 1037**

Getting Started 1037

Installing and Using ActiveX Controls 1038

Adding an ActiveX Control to the Controls Task Pane 1038

Property Pages 1047

Building Custom Controls for InfoPath Using ActiveX 1049

Building an ActiveX Control for InfoPath Using C++ 1049

Building an ActiveX Control for InfoPath Using C# 1061

What's Next? 1072

20 **Add-ins 1073**

Getting Started 1073

Introduction to COM Add-ins 1074

`IDTExtensibility2` *Interface 1075*

Adding User Interface Items 1076

Building a COM Add-in for InfoPath 1076

`OnConnection` *Method 1079*

`OnStartupComplete` *Method 1083*

Event Handlers for Loading a Form 1088

Copy and Paste Button Event Handlers 1090

Custom Task Panes 1093

Creating a Custom Task Pane 1093

Writing Add-ins and Custom Task Panes Using VSTO 2005 SE 1105

Implementing a Managed Add-in 1105

Adding a Custom Task Pane in a Managed Add-in 1108

Managing InfoPath Add-ins 1111

What's Next? 1114

21 Importers and Exporters 1115

Getting Started 1115

Built-in Form Importers 1116

Importing a Form into InfoPath 1119

Fixing the Imported Form 1125

Post-Import Warnings 1126

Creating Your Own Form Importers and Exporters 1128

InfoPath Import/Export Framework 1128

How Post-Import Warnings Work 1140

Importing Form Data 1142

Data Importer Framework 1142

`IInfoPathDataImporter` *Interface 1143*

What's Next? 1148

Appendix: Further Reading 1149

Index 1157

Figures

FIGURE P.1: *Open With Form Template dialog* lviii

FIGURE P.2: *Dialog shown when InfoPath cannot find the Visual C# project with the form code* lx

FIGURE 1.1: *Controls task pane in InfoPath 2003* 8

FIGURE 1.2: *Data Source task pane in InfoPath 2003* 9

FIGURE 1.3: *Insert Layout Table toolbar item* 13

FIGURE 1.4: *Tables toolbar* 13

FIGURE 1.5: *Fill Out a Form dialog in InfoPath 2003 SP1* 17

FIGURE 1.6: *Filling out a browser-enabled form template in Internet Explorer* 18

FIGURE 1.7: *Getting Started dialog* 21

FIGURE 1.8: *Design a Form Template dialog* 22

FIGURE 2.1: *Getting Started dialog* 27

FIGURE 2.2: *Design a Form Template dialog* 28

FIGURE 2.3: *New blank form* 33

FIGURE 2.4: *Layout task pane* 35

FIGURE 2.5: *Employment application form template with title added by using Table with Title* 36

FIGURE 2.6: *Merge and split cells category of the Layout task pane* 37

FIGURE 2.7: *Employment application form template with cells for first and last names* 38

FIGURE 2.8: *Employment application form template with a row for address information* 38

FIGURE 2.9: *Color Schemes task pane* 40
FIGURE 2.10: *Controls task pane* 42
FIGURE 2.11: *Employment application form template after adding standard controls* 46
FIGURE 2.12: *Section control selected in design mode* 47
FIGURE 2.13: *Preview of the employment application form* 48
FIGURE 2.14: *Employment application form template with Optional Section controls* 50
FIGURE 2.15: *Optional controls when previewing the form* 51
FIGURE 2.16: *Optional controls after clicking on the link, Click here to insert* 51
FIGURE 2.17: *Context menu for the Optional Section control when filling out a form* 52
FIGURE 2.18: *Employment application form template with Repeating Section control* 53
FIGURE 2.19: *Repeating Section control when previewing the form* 54
FIGURE 2.20: *Context menu for Repeating Section control when previewing the form* 54
FIGURE 2.21: *Three instances of the Repeating Section control inserted into the form* 55
FIGURE 2.22: *Insert Repeating Table dialog* 57
FIGURE 2.23: *Repeating Table control in design mode* 57
FIGURE 2.24: *Change To menu* 58
FIGURE 2.25: *Repeating Table control after changing from a Repeating Section control* 58
FIGURE 2.26: *Repeating Table control when previewing the form* 60
FIGURE 2.27: *Horizontal Repeating Table control in design mode* 61
FIGURE 2.28: *Horizontal Repeating Table control when filling out a form* 62
FIGURE 2.29: *Insert Master/Detail dialog* 63
FIGURE 2.30: *Master and detail controls in design mode* 63
FIGURE 2.31: *Master/Detail control in the application review form when filling out a form* 64
FIGURE 2.32: *Master/Detail control showing more applicant data* 64
FIGURE 2.33: *Binding design-time visual showing the name of the control* 65
FIGURE 2.34: *List controls in design mode* 66
FIGURE 2.35: *List controls when filling out a form* 66
FIGURE 2.36: *Multiple-Selection List Box control when filling out a form* 67

FIGURE 2.37: *File Attachment control in design mode* 68
FIGURE 2.38: *File Attachment control when filling out a form* 68
FIGURE 2.39: *File Attachment control with résumé file attached* 69
FIGURE 2.40: *File Attachment control commands* 69
FIGURE 2.41: *Insert Picture Control dialog* 71
FIGURE 2.42: *Picture control when filling out the form* 72
FIGURE 2.43: *Picture control with picture inserted* 72
FIGURE 2.44: *Ink Picture control that contains text entered with a Tablet PC stylus* 73
FIGURE 2.45: *Views task pane* 74
FIGURE 2.46: *Add View dialog* 75
FIGURE 2.47: *View Properties dialog* 75
FIGURE 2.48: *Font task pane* 77
FIGURE 2.49: *Selected Text Box control* 78
FIGURE 2.50: *Format Painter on the Standard toolbar* 79
FIGURE 2.51: *Format Painter cursor* 80
FIGURE 2.52: *Text Settings tab in the View Properties dialog* 83

FIGURE 3.1: *Clicking on a control in the view to select the bound control in the data source* 87
FIGURE 3.2: *A Hyperlink control bound to* `field1` *in the data source, with a link to the text of* `field1` 88
FIGURE 3.3: *Warning dialog when changing the name of a data source field or group for a published form* 97
FIGURE 3.4: *Data type validation error that occurs when a field contains invalid data* 100
FIGURE 3.5: *Warning when saving a form with validation errors* 100
FIGURE 3.6: *Validation error for the cannot be blank property, delineated by a red asterisk* 102
FIGURE 3.7: *Repeating* `field4`*, which is bound to the Numbered List control and repeats in* `group1` 104
FIGURE 3.8: *Airline form with default value for* `FlightType` *as* `"Roundtrip"` 106
FIGURE 3.9: *The default value calculation button* 107
FIGURE 3.10: *The Insert Formula dialog, with a formula that sets this field's default value to today's date plus 45 days* 107

FIGURE 3.11: *Data source details for the* `FlightType` *field bound to the option buttons in the airline form* 108

FIGURE 3.12: *Label for the node* `PurposeOfVisit`*, created when inserting the control into the view* 118

FIGURE 3.13: *Move Field or Group dialog used to move an existing field or group* 119

FIGURE 3.14: *Validation error that appears when opening a form created before the* `FlightType-FlightDate` *node swap* 121

FIGURE 3.15: *Setting the* `Employee` *group to repeat and reference itself* 123

FIGURE 3.16: *Filling out the MOI Company's employee information form* 124

FIGURE 3.17: *Design a form from an existing XML document or schema instead of creating the data source from scratch* 125

FIGURE 3.18: *Selecting the location of an XML document or schema* 125

FIGURE 3.19: *Choosing whether to include data from a selected XML file as the form template default data* 127

FIGURE 3.20: *The first prompt when starting from an ambiguous schema* 129

FIGURE 3.21: *Disambiguating the data source by using the Edit Settings dialog* 130

FIGURE 3.22: *Prompt that appears when starting from a schema with multiple top-level elements* 131

FIGURE 3.23: *The Type drop-down menu, with an option for adding a complete XML Schema or XML document* 134

FIGURE 3.24: *Data source created from the XML document* 136

FIGURE 3.25: *Text Box Binding dialog that appears when Automatically create data source is disabled or Change Binding is used from a control* 139

FIGURE 3.26: *Changing binding via the context menu by right-clicking on any control that can be bound* 140

FIGURE 3.27: *Context menu of most popular control bindings* 143

FIGURE 3.28: *Dialog that results from clicking More on the menu shown in Figure 3.27* 143

FIGURE 3.29: *Inserting* `field1` *in the data source* 144

FIGURE 3.30: *An absurd control nesting:* `Attribute` *contains* `DocumentElement`*, which contains* `Attribute` 145

FIGURE 3.31: `NumberOfChildren` *attribute field, which is bound to both the Optional Section and the Drop-Down List Box inside of the Optional Section* 146

FIGURE 3.32: `NumberOfChildren` *attribute is nonexistent in the form and XML data* 147

FIGURE 3.33: `NumberOfChildren` *attribute field inserted in the form and XML with a default value of 1* 147

FIGURE 3.34: *A simple repeating field:* `field1` 147

FIGURE 3.35: *Three controls multiply bound to* `field1` 148

FIGURE 3.36: *Critical design-time visual on an unbound Text Box control* 150

FIGURE 3.37: *Edit Default Values dialog, which offers the quickest way to edit data source defaults* 152

FIGURE 3.38: *Cutaway of the Edit Default Values dialog when Choice exists in the data source* 153

FIGURE 4.1: *Insert Hyperlink dialog* 157

FIGURE 4.2: *Select a Field or Group dialog* 157

FIGURE 4.3: *Hyperlink control in design mode* 158

FIGURE 4.4: *Insert Expression Box dialog* 159

FIGURE 4.5: *Insert Formula dialog after choosing a field* 159

FIGURE 4.6: *Insert Formula dialog after checking the Edit XPath checkbox* 160

FIGURE 4.7: *Insert Function dialog* 160

FIGURE 4.8: *Repeating Table control for expenses* 161

FIGURE 4.9: *Data source for the expense report example* 161

FIGURE 4.10: *Insert Formula dialog after inserting the* `sum` *function* 162

FIGURE 4.11: *Expense report form during preview* 163

FIGURE 4.12: *Insert Vertical Label dialog* 164

FIGURE 4.13: *Vertical Label control* 164

FIGURE 4.14: *Scrolling Region control in design mode* 165

FIGURE 4.15: *Application review form with Scrolling Region when filling out the form* 166

FIGURE 4.16: *Horizontal Region controls in design mode* 167

FIGURE 4.17: *Choice Group control in design mode* 168

FIGURE 4.18: *Employment application form with Choice Group control* 170

FIGURE 4.19: *Default Choice Section with context menu commands* 170

FIGURE 4.20: *Employment application form after replacing the default Choice Section* 170

FIGURE 4.21: *Repeating Recursive Section in design mode* 172

FIGURE 4.22: *Repeating Recursive Section when filling out the employee information form* 173

FIGURE 4.23: *Properties dialog for the Text Box control* 175

FIGURE 4.24: *Dialog that warns about data loss when changing field names* 177

FIGURE 4.25: *Binding design-time visual for the* `FirstName` *Text Box control* 178

FIGURE 4.26: *Integer Format dialog for Whole Number (integer) data types* 179

FIGURE 4.27: *Field for minimum salary desired formatted as currency* 179

FIGURE 4.28: *Properties dialog for the Optional Section for the minimum salary desired* 181

FIGURE 4.29: *Display tab of the Text Box Properties dialog* 183

FIGURE 4.30: *Placeholder text in a Text Box control* 184

FIGURE 4.31: *Display tab for the Rich Text Box control* 186

FIGURE 4.32: *Insert Picture dialog* 187

FIGURE 4.33: *Size tab of the Text Box Properties dialog* 189

FIGURE 4.34: *Text Box control with inner text not aligned to outer text* 190

FIGURE 4.35: *Text Box control with inner text aligned to outer text* 191

FIGURE 4.36: *Properties dialog for resizing multiple controls* 192

FIGURE 4.37: *Advanced tab for the Hyperlink control* 193

FIGURE 4.38: *Advanced tab of the Text Box Properties dialog showing the Input recognition section* 194

FIGURE 4.39: *Input Scope dialog showing standard input scopes* 196

FIGURE 4.40: *Input Scope dialog showing custom input scopes* 197

FIGURE 4.41: *New Input Scope dialog showing Phrase List option* 197

FIGURE 4.42: *Sample data source for the Master/Detail example* 200

FIGURE 4.43: *Master/Detail tab for a Repeating Table set as the master control* 200

FIGURE 4.44: *Master/Detail tab for a Repeating Section set as a detail control* 202

FIGURE 4.45: *Master/Detail control when filling out a form* 204

FIGURE 4.46: *Section Properties dialog for an Optional Section control* 205

FIGURE 4.47: *Edit Default Values dialog for an Optional Section control* 206

FIGURE 4.48: *Repeating Section Properties dialog* 207

FIGURE 4.49: *Section Properties dialog for a Repeating Section fragment* 208

FIGURE 4.50: *Repeating Section Properties dialog showing three sections—*`Apples`*,* `Oranges`*, and* `Bananas` 209

FIGURE 4.51: *Filling out the grocery shopping list* 209

FIGURE 4.52: *Section Commands dialog used to customize commands* 210

FIGURE 4.53: *Default commands for a Choice Section when filling out a form* 212

FIGURE 5.1: *Conditional Formatting dialog* 216
FIGURE 5.2: *Conditional Format dialog* 217
FIGURE 5.3: *Conditional Format dialog with multiple conditions* 219
FIGURE 5.4: *Conditional Format dialog with condition, where* `StockPrice` *is less than or equal to $18.00* 220
FIGURE 5.5: *Conditional Formatting dialog with one condition* 220
FIGURE 5.6: *Conditional Format dialog specifying the four conditions needed to set the background color to yellow* 221
FIGURE 5.7: *Conditional Formatting dialog showing all three conditions* 222
FIGURE 5.8: *Data Validation dialog* 223
FIGURE 5.9: *Validation tab on the Field or Group Properties dialog* 224
FIGURE 5.10: *Data Validation condition builder* 225
FIGURE 5.11: *Inline alert for a data validation error* 225
FIGURE 5.12: *Full error description for a data validation error* 226
FIGURE 5.13: *Data Validation dialog listing two conditions to validate the total number of guests* 227
FIGURE 5.14: *Data Entry Pattern dialog* 228
FIGURE 5.15: *Red asterisk error* 228
FIGURE 5.16: *Custom pattern* 229
FIGURE 5.17: *Adding or modifying an existing rule so that four actions are always run when the form is submitted* 230
FIGURE 5.18: *Specifying the action for a rule to run when a user clicks the Button control* 231
FIGURE 5.19: *Entry points and structure of the Rules feature* 232
FIGURE 5.20: *Dialog displayed when an action on a rule fails to execute when the user fills out the form* 234
FIGURE 5.21: *Form template for the Logic Inspector sample* 236
FIGURE 5.22: *Logic Inspector showing the logic for the entire form template* 237
FIGURE 5.23: *Detailed view of the* `DataValidation` *node* 239

FIGURE 6.1: *Relationships between a form and its external data sources* 243
FIGURE 6.2: *Design a Form Template dialog, the starting point for creating a main query connection* 245
FIGURE 6.3: *Creating a secondary query connection for a form template* 246
FIGURE 6.4: *Data to fill into a form and save to Sample.xml, to be read later by using an XML file adapter* 248

FIGURE 6.5: *Entering the file location to use when creating a secondary connection to XML data* 249

FIGURE 6.6: *XML file connection settings to opt in or out of including the data as a file in your template* 249

FIGURE 6.7: *Final page of the Data Connection Wizard for an XML file* 251

FIGURE 6.8: *Data Connections dialog after finishing the XML file Data Connection Wizard* 252

FIGURE 6.9: *Data Source task pane showing secondary data source* 253

FIGURE 6.10: *Clicking on the Button to query the* `Sample` *data connection* 254

FIGURE 6.11: *Data Connection Wizard when creating a new database connection* 259

FIGURE 6.12: *Connecting to SQL Server after clicking Select Database* 260

FIGURE 6.13: *Select Database and Table dialog* 261

FIGURE 6.14: *Database connection's data source structure showing the added* `Customers` *and* `Orders` *tables* 262

FIGURE 6.15: *Adding the* `Orders` *child table to the* `Customers` *parent table* 262

FIGURE 6.16: *Defining a relationship between the child and parent tables* 263

FIGURE 6.17: *Sort Order dialog for setting three levels of sorting order* 265

FIGURE 6.18: *Edit SQL dialog, which allows hand-editing of the query statement used by InfoPath to create the data source* 267

FIGURE 6.19: `Customers` *secondary data source* 268

FIGURE 6.20: *A nested database table (*`Orders`*), which is hard to represent when the parent table (*`Customers`*) is in the view as a Repeating Table* 270

FIGURE 6.21: *Our rendition of displaying the* `Customers` *and* `Orders` *data* 271

FIGURE 6.22: *Preview of the modified form layout with Northwind customers and orders data* 272

FIGURE 6.23: *New Web Site dialog with a template for an ASP.NET Web service* 274

FIGURE 6.24: *Part of the browser-friendly test page when navigating to the Web service* 278

FIGURE 6.25: *Browser test form for the* `SaveItem` *Web service method* 280

FIGURE 6.26: *Entering an address to the WSDL* 281

FIGURE 6.27: *List of methods from the Web service that can be used to receive data* 283

FIGURE 6.28: *Setting up the parameter to the* `SaveItems` *Web service method, which involves selecting which data source node provides its value* 284

FIGURE 6.29: *Choosing the data source node to submit to the* `SaveItems` *method* 285

FIGURE 6.30: *InfoPath design mode after finishing the Web service Data Connection Wizard* 286

FIGURE 6.31: *Querying and submitting our Web service form during preview* 287

FIGURE 6.32: *Designing the TerraServer form using the* `GetTile` *Web service method* 290

FIGURE 6.33: *Querying the TerraServer for a section of the San Francisco Bay near Highway 80* 291

FIGURE 6.34: `Pictures` *library on Windows SharePoint Services* 293

FIGURE 6.35: *The libraries and lists available for querying from the SharePoint server* 293

FIGURE 6.36: *Choosing which fields from the SharePoint list you want to use for the data connection* 294

FIGURE 6.37: *Filling out the music and photos form* 295

FIGURE 7.1: *Searching for Web services by using UDDI in InfoPath* 300

FIGURE 7.2: *Creating a typed dataset from our* `Customers` *and* `Orders` `SqlDataAdapter` *objects* 304

FIGURE 7.3: *The Visual Studio schema editor* 305

FIGURE 7.4: *Adding a relationship to the* `Customers` *and* `Orders` *tables in the dataset* 305

FIGURE 7.5: *Secondary data source–bound controls allow for little customization* 308

FIGURE 7.6: *Form after querying the XML file secondary data connection* 310

FIGURE 7.7: *Enabling query support for offline mode when adding or modifying a secondary data connection* 313

FIGURE 7.8: *Configuring a form template for offline mode queries* 313

FIGURE 7.9: *InfoPath global cached queries setting* 315

FIGURE 7.10: *Error dialog shown if querying an external data source fails when filling out the form* 315

FIGURE 7.11: *Error dialog that results from clicking Try to Connect in Figure 7.10 if the data connection is unavailable* 316

FIGURE 7.12: *Grocery list form template, unchanged, from Chapter 4* 318

FIGURE 7.13: *Drop-Down List Box Properties dialog* 319

FIGURE 7.14: *Selecting a secondary data source node from the XML file connection that provides data for the List Box entries* 319

FIGURE 7.15: *Filling out the grocery list form when the items are retrieved from a data connection* 320

FIGURE 7.16: *Using the main data source to provide data for a List Box control* 321
FIGURE 7.17: *Adding a note-taking capability to our grocery form* 322
FIGURE 7.18: *Filling out the form after we've added the note-taking feature* 322
FIGURE 7.19: *Specifying a filter to show only grocery items from a selected category* 324
FIGURE 7.20: *Filling out the grocery form with category filters* 325

FIGURE 8.1: *Dialog asking the user whether to save or submit the form* 329
FIGURE 8.2: *Settings for enabling and disabling certain features for users, such as the ability to save a form* 330
FIGURE 8.3: *The first view of the job application form* 332
FIGURE 8.4: *The last page of the job application form* 333
FIGURE 8.5: *Dialog about the submit error that occurs when the user clicks the Submit button after not filling in a name in the first view* 333
FIGURE 8.6: *Submit Options dialog, the starting point for enabling submit* 335
FIGURE 8.7: *First page of the Data Connection Wizard for setting properties of the e-mail sent when users submit the form* 338
FIGURE 8.8: *Configuring the attachment options for submitting via e-mail* 340
FIGURE 8.9: *Dialog prompt in which the user must click Send in order to submit a helpdesk request* 341
FIGURE 8.10: *Specifying whether your form only receives data, only submits data, or does both with a Web service* 346
FIGURE 8.11: *Selecting a Web service method for submit* 348
FIGURE 8.12: *Design mode after finishing the Data Connection Wizard for submitting data to a Web service* 348
FIGURE 8.13: *Error dialog that results when submitting a form with validation errors that are in the current view* 349
FIGURE 8.14: *Student sign-in form during preview* 350
FIGURE 8.15: *Dialog confirming that submit succeeded* 350
FIGURE 8.16: *Student sign-in form showing the instructor's Class Information view with default data* 352
FIGURE 8.17: *Designing the sign-in form view* 354
FIGURE 8.18: *Configuring conditional formatting to hide the* `LateReason` *section if the start time is later than now* 354
FIGURE 8.19: *Setting custom data validation to make the* `Reason` *field required when the* `LateReason` *section is visible* 355

FIGURE 8.20: *Defining parameter mappings for Web service submit* 356
FIGURE 8.21: *Tardy Johnny signs in to Philosophy 101* 357
FIGURE 8.22: *Debugging the Web service by using Visual Studio* 359
FIGURE 8.23: *Debugger paused at our breakpoint* 360
FIGURE 8.24: *Data source for the student sign-in form* 362
FIGURE 8.25: *Parameter mappings dialog configured to submit the entire form* 363
FIGURE 8.26: *Dialog that gives the user a chance to digitally sign a form before continuing with submit* 367
FIGURE 8.27: *Controlling whether or not to display the prompt shown in Figure 8.26* 368
FIGURE 8.28: *Configuring change tracking for an ADO.NET dataset Web service* 371
FIGURE 8.29: *Setting up a parameter mapping for a* `DataSet` *object* 372
FIGURE 8.30: *Data source representative of a dataset structure* 373
FIGURE 8.31: *Designing the view of the form receiving and submitting an ADO.NET* `DataSet` *object* 374
FIGURE 8.32: *Filling out a dataset form template with default data* 375
FIGURE 8.33: *After querying the form shown in Figure 8.32* 375
FIGURE 8.34: *Error that results from trying to modify dataset form data after submit* 376
FIGURE 8.35: *Configuring SharePoint document library submit for the student sign-in form* 378
FIGURE 8.36: *Submit Options dialog configured to submit to a SharePoint document library* 379
FIGURE 8.37: *SharePoint document library that contains submitted form data* 380
FIGURE 8.38: *Submit Options dialog for Web server submit via HTTP* 381
FIGURE 8.39: *Setting the destination option to use an ASP.NET page* 381
FIGURE 8.40: *Setting up submit using rules* 385
FIGURE 8.41: *List of rules that run when the form is submitted* 386
FIGURE 8.42: *Actions for the actual submit to the Web services* 387
FIGURE 8.43: *Expression shown in a popup message when a student signs in late to class* 387
FIGURE 8.44: *Dialog that appears when Johnny signs in tardy* 388
FIGURE 8.45: *Dialog that appears when submit with rules fails on a secondary connection* 390
FIGURE 8.46: *Dialog shown when submit using rules fails on the main submit connection* 391

FIGURE 8.47: *Generic success dialog for the main submit connection* 393
FIGURE 8.48: *Generic failure dialog for the main submit connection* 393
FIGURE 8.49: *Advanced section of the Submit Options dialog* 393

FIGURE 9.1: *InfoPath prompt that appears when choosing Save or Save As for a new form template* 399
FIGURE 9.2: *First page of the Publishing Wizard, offering a variety of publishing options* 400
FIGURE 9.3: *Publishing a MeetingRequest template to a Web server via a "backdoor" network share* 401
FIGURE 9.4: *Specifying the users' access path* 402
FIGURE 9.5: *Error dialog that appears when opening a form from a path that is not the access path* 403
FIGURE 9.6: *Flowchart for determining whether the form template publishes to a SharePoint server or a Forms Services site* 404
FIGURE 9.7: *Specifying a server location for publishing to a SharePoint site or Forms Services site* 406
FIGURE 9.8: *Choosing whether to publish the form template to a SharePoint document library or a site content type* 406
FIGURE 9.9: *Saving the template somewhere on the SharePoint server when creating a site content type* 407
FIGURE 9.10: *Wizard page showing promoted properties from the template's data source, which appear as columns in SharePoint libraries and lists* 408
FIGURE 9.11: *Form library on SharePoint* 409
FIGURE 9.12: *Adding site content types to a document library* 410
FIGURE 9.13: *Selecting a field from the data source to promote* 411
FIGURE 9.14: *First wizard page for publishing a form to e-mail recipients* 414
FIGURE 9.15: *Promoting properties to make them available as columns in Outlook* 415
FIGURE 9.16: *Resulting e-mail in Outlook after finishing the Publishing Wizard for e-mail* 416
FIGURE 9.17: *First page of the Publishing Wizard for creating an installable form template* 418
FIGURE 9.18: *Choosing a location to save the Installer file* 418
FIGURE 9.19: *Final page of the Publishing Wizard when creating an installable form template* 419

FIGURE 9.20: *Browse For Folder dialog for selecting a location to save template source files* 422
FIGURE 9.21: *Dialog warning that appears when saving source files to a folder that already contains existing source files* 423
FIGURE 9.22: *Configuring preview settings* 426
FIGURE 9.23: *Error message that results from attempting to open a form that was saved while previewing* 429

FIGURE 10.1: *Address block section of the MOI employment application form* 432
FIGURE 10.2: *Data source for the address block template part* 433
FIGURE 10.3: *Design a Form Template dialog with Template Part option selected* 433
FIGURE 10.4: *Design Tasks pane when designing a template part* 434
FIGURE 10.5: *Address block after pasting it into the view* 437
FIGURE 10.6: *Add or Remove Custom Controls dialog* 439
FIGURE 10.7: *Add Custom Control Wizard's Select a Control Type page* 439
FIGURE 10.8: *Add Custom Control Wizard's Select an InfoPath Template Part page* 440
FIGURE 10.9: *Add Custom Control Wizard's Custom Control Added page* 441
FIGURE 10.10: *Custom category of the Controls task pane after adding the AddressBlock template part* 441
FIGURE 10.11: *AddressBlock template part inserted into a blank form* 444
FIGURE 10.12: *AddressBlock template part with cascading Combo Box controls* 448
FIGURE 10.13: *Template Part Properties dialog* 449
FIGURE 10.14: *Design-time visual shown on the new AddressBlock template part* 450
FIGURE 10.15: *More details for the new template part* 450
FIGURE 10.16: *Design Checker task pane showing template parts that need to be updated* 452
FIGURE 10.17: *Template Part Properties dialog after changing name and ID* 453

FIGURE 11.1: *Configuring security and trust settings for a form template* 459
FIGURE 11.2: *Form Template Properties dialog for setting the form ID* 460
FIGURE 11.3: *Error dialog when opening a restricted form template that attempts to query an external data source* 461
FIGURE 11.4: *Setting an access path, which is not required when publishing a restricted form template* 463

FIGURE 11.5: *Cache conflict that occurs when a different version of the same form template is opened* 464

FIGURE 11.6: *Getting Started dialog showing form templates in the InfoPath cache* 465

FIGURE 11.7: *Resource Files dialog, which shows files accessible by all form templates* 466

FIGURE 11.8: *Internet Explorer Web content zones, each of which has its own security level* 469

FIGURE 11.9: *Settings for defining the local intranet zone* 470

FIGURE 11.10: *Security prompt for cross-domain data access* 474

FIGURE 11.11: *Office Configuration Tool security settings for InfoPath* 477

FIGURE 11.12: *Error dialog that appears when a domain form is not opened from its access path and the published template is unavailable* 480

FIGURE 11.13: *Opening a domain form whose access path doesn't match the .xsn location, but the form template exists at the originally published location* 481

FIGURE 11.14: *Entering a domain for the template when previewing the form* 482

FIGURE 11.15: *List of any settings or features resulting in the form template being at domain trust level* 484

FIGURE 11.16: *Security and Trust tab of the Form Options dialog* 485

FIGURE 11.17: *Trusted root certification authorities for the current user* 488

FIGURE 11.18: *Security and Trust category settings for signing a form template* 489

FIGURE 11.19: *Selecting a certificate to use for digital signing* 490

FIGURE 11.20: *Creating a self-signed certificate for code signing* 490

FIGURE 11.21: *General tab of the Certificate dialog, which shows whether the publisher of a certificate is trusted* 491

FIGURE 11.22: *InfoPath prompt that appears when a signed template's CA isn't trusted* 492

FIGURE 11.23: *Error that occurs when opening a full trust form template that is neither digitally signed nor installed* 494

FIGURE 11.24: *Error that occurs when attempting to remove an installed form from the dialog* 495

FIGURE 11.25: *Trusted Publishers category of the Trust Center dialog* 500

FIGURE 11.26: *Add-ins category of the Trust Center dialog* 501

FIGURE 11.27: *Dialog for adding and removing COM add-ins* 502

FIGURE 11.28: *Privacy Options category of the Trust Center dialog* 503

FIGURE 11.29: *Enabling protection to discourage users from changing your form template* 504

FIGURE 11.30: *Warning dialog that appears when users attempt to change a protected form template* 505

FIGURE 11.31: *Disabling InfoPath design mode as an administrative policy* 506

FIGURE 11.32: *Configuring digital signatures for a form template* 509

FIGURE 11.33: *Our sample MOI Consulting performance review form* 510

FIGURE 11.34: *Setting up the template to allow signing the entire form* 512

FIGURE 11.35: *Filling out the MOI performance review before using a digital signature* 514

FIGURE 11.36: *Digital Signatures dialog, which tracks who has signed this form* 514

FIGURE 11.37: *Selecting what form data to sign* 515

FIGURE 11.38: *Clicking the Sign button to apply a digital signature to the form* 515

FIGURE 11.39: *Additional Information dialog, which shows exactly what you're signing before you sign it* 516

FIGURE 11.40: *Digitally signed form with read-only controls* 518

FIGURE 11.41: *Error dialog that appears when trying to change signed form data* 518

FIGURE 11.42: *Friendly reminder that the form being opened is digitally signed* 519

FIGURE 11.43: *Choosing whether or not to show a notification when signed forms are opened* 520

FIGURE 11.44: *Setting up the Personal Information part of the view for partial signing* 523

FIGURE 11.45: *Creating a new set of signable data (partial signing) on a Section control* 524

FIGURE 11.46: *Setting up digital signatures on a Section control* 526

FIGURE 11.47: *Signing the "Info" set of signable data when filling out the form* 527

FIGURE 11.48: *Using the Select the Data to Sign dialog opened by clicking the Digital Signatures button* 527

FIGURE 11.49: *Signing a set of signable data when filling out the form* 528

FIGURE 11.50: *Form showing that the set of signable data has been signed* 529

FIGURE 11.51: *Signature Details dialog for a signed Section control* 530

FIGURE 11.52: *Form showing that Robert co-signed John's review rating* 531

FIGURE 11.53: *Permission button on the Standard toolbar* 539

FIGURE 11.54: *Defining IRM permission on a form template (top checkbox) and forms (lower checkbox)* 540

FIGURE 11.55: *Dialog about verifying credentials when opening a form template* 541
FIGURE 11.56: *Restricted permission for user Dana while designing a form template* 541
FIGURE 11.57: *Specifying permission during design mode to apply when the form is filled out* 543
FIGURE 11.58: *Specifying permission for the current form while filling it out* 544
FIGURE 11.59: *Form Permission task pane* 545
FIGURE 11.60: *Permission dialog after clicking the More Options button* 546
FIGURE 11.61: *Enabling Information Rights Management on the SharePoint Central Administration site* 549
FIGURE 11.62: *IRM settings for a document library* 550

FIGURE 12.1: *Weekly status report form* 555
FIGURE 12.2: *Merge Forms dialog* 556
FIGURE 12.3: *Merge Forms dialog showing the Views menu* 557
FIGURE 12.4: *Weekly status report document library in Merge Forms view* 558
FIGURE 12.5: *Merge error dialog for forms with a schema that doesn't match the target form* 558
FIGURE 12.6: *Merged status report form* 559
FIGURE 12.7: *Data source for the status report form template* 561
FIGURE 12.8: *Weekly Status Report view in the weekly status report form template* 563
FIGURE 12.9: *Team Status Report view for merging multiple status report forms* 564
FIGURE 12.10: *Rules and Merge tab on the Field or Group Properties dialog* 566
FIGURE 12.11: *Advanced tab of the Repeating Section Properties dialog* 567
FIGURE 12.12: *Merge settings error dialog* 567
FIGURE 12.13: *Merge Settings dialog for the* `StatusReports` *repeating group node* 569
FIGURE 12.14: *Merge Settings dialog with merge customizations* 572
FIGURE 12.15: *Merge Settings dialog for the* `EmployeeInformation` *node* 573
FIGURE 12.16: *Team status report after merging three status reports* 574
FIGURE 12.17: *Merge Settings dialog for the* `Summary` *node* 575
FIGURE 12.18: *Merge Settings dialog for the* `Summary` *node after customizations are complete* 577
FIGURE 12.19: *Merge Settings dialog for the* `ThisWeek` *node after customization* 577
FIGURE 12.20: *Merged team status report after all customizations are complete* 578

FIGURE 12.21: *Advanced tab of the Form Options dialog* 579
FIGURE 12.22: *Field or Group Properties dialog after specifying a custom merge XSL in the manifest* 582
FIGURE 12.23: *Create Print Version dialog* 586
FIGURE 12.24: *Printed team status report* 587
FIGURE 12.25: *Print Settings tab of the View Properties dialog* 588
FIGURE 12.26: *Header format dialog* 590
FIGURE 12.27: *Header format dialog after adding* `Team` *field and date* 591
FIGURE 12.28: *Team status report with header and footer information* 591
FIGURE 12.29: *Sales Report view* 592
FIGURE 12.30: *Merged sales report data* 593
FIGURE 12.31: *Print dialog* 593
FIGURE 12.32: *Print Multiple Views dialog when filling out a form* 594
FIGURE 12.33: *Print Multiple Views dialog in design mode* 595
FIGURE 12.34: *XML Structure task pane in Microsoft Office Word* 598
FIGURE 12.35: *Word document used to generate the Word print view XSL* 599
FIGURE 12.36: *Word Print Views dialog* 600
FIGURE 12.37: *Choosing the path and file name from the Add Print View for Word Wizard* 601
FIGURE 12.38: *Specifying the Word print view name in the Add Print View for Word Wizard* 602
FIGURE 12.39: *Filling out the Team Status Report view in the browser* 604
FIGURE 12.40: *Print View button on the Forms Services toolbar* 604
FIGURE 12.41: *Team Status Report view shown as a print view in the browser* 605
FIGURE 12.42: *Export To menu item expanded* 606
FIGURE 12.43: *Choosing the type of data to export* 607
FIGURE 12.44: *Choosing the forms from which to export data* 608
FIGURE 12.45: *Status report data exported to Microsoft Office Excel* 608
FIGURE 12.46: *Export to Excel Wizard after choosing to export only the data from a specific table* 609
FIGURE 12.47: *Selecting the data to export* 610
FIGURE 12.48: *Sales data exported to Microsoft Office Excel* 611
FIGURE 12.49: *Open and Save tab of the Form Options dialog* 612

FIGURE 13.1: *Manage User Roles dialog* 616
FIGURE 13.2: *Add User Role dialog* 617

Figure 13.3: *Select Users dialog* 618
Figure 13.4: *Manage User Roles dialog after adding a few roles* 620
Figure 13.5: *Open and Save tab of the Form Options dialog* 622
Figure 13.6: *Selecting User's current role as the qualifier in the Condition dialog for rules* 623
Figure 13.7: *Rule dialog after setting the condition and action* 623
Figure 13.8: *Rules for Opening Forms dialog after adding all rules* 624
Figure 13.9: *Preview tab on the Form Options dialog* 625
Figure 13.10: *Preview drop-down toolbar menu* 625
Figure 13.11: *Selecting the* `UserRole` *field that corresponds to the* `TeamName` *field in the secondary data source* 628
Figure 13.12: *Insert Formula dialog after adding a calculated default value* 628
Figure 13.13: *Specifying a user role in the condition for data validation* 630
Figure 13.14: *Conditional Format dialog after changing the condition to use a user role* 631
Figure 13.15: *Manage User Roles dialog after adding "Team Manager" and "Sales Manager" roles* 632
Figure 13.16: *Conditional Format dialog after adding conditions for manager roles* 633
Figure 13.17: *Rule dialog after adding a rule to switch to the Team Status Report view* 634
Figure 13.18: *Add a Workflow page* 637
Figure 13.19: *Customizing the Travel Request Approval workflow* 638
Figure 13.20: *Workflow initiation e-mail message* 639
Figure 13.21: *E-mail task requesting approval of the travel request* 639
Figure 13.22: *Travel Request form showing the Workflow Task message bar* 640
Figure 13.23: *Workflow dialog* 641
Figure 13.24: *Workflows dialog* 642
Figure 13.25: *Food survey form template* 646
Figure 13.26: *Choosing which properties to make available in Outlook folders* 647
Figure 13.27: *Sending the form to a list of e-mail recipients* 647
Figure 13.28: *Rules Wizard showing the rule specific to InfoPath forms* 648
Figure 13.29: *Choose InfoPath Form dialog* 649
Figure 13.30: *Create New Folder dialog after selecting InfoPath Form Items* 650
Figure 13.31: *Folder properties dialog after clicking on the InfoPath Forms tab* 651
Figure 13.32: *Team Lunch folder showing "Food Preference" column* 652

FIGURE 13.33: *InfoPath e-mail form in Outlook's reading pane* 653
FIGURE 13.34: *Filling out an InfoPath e-mail form* 653
FIGURE 13.35: *Submit dialog when submitting an InfoPath e-mail form* 654
FIGURE 13.36: *Mail Options task pane* 655
FIGURE 13.37: *Team Lunch folder showing responses to the food preference survey* 656
FIGURE 13.38: *Team Lunch folder grouped by food preference* 657
FIGURE 13.39: *Expense Reports InfoPath form folder* 659
FIGURE 13.40: *InfoPath actions context menu* 659
FIGURE 13.41: *E-Mail Attachments tab in the Form Options dialog* 661

FIGURE 14.1: *Filling out the status report form in InfoPath* 667
FIGURE 14.2: *Filling out the status report form in the browser by using Forms Services* 667
FIGURE 14.3: *Message indicating that a feature cannot be used in a browser-enabled form template* 670
FIGURE 14.4: *Message indicating that a feature can be used in a browser-enabled form template but is not active in the browser* 671
FIGURE 14.5: *Choosing the type of server to install* 674
FIGURE 14.6: *SharePoint database configuration settings for a farm* 675
FIGURE 14.7: *Choosing to publish to Forms Services via the Document Library option* 679
FIGURE 14.8: *Last page of the Publishing Wizard before clicking the Publish button* 681
FIGURE 14.9: *Last page of the Publishing Wizard after clicking the Publish button* 682
FIGURE 14.10: *Toolbar shown when filling out a form in the browser* 684
FIGURE 14.11: *Configuring toolbars for a browser-enabled form template filled out in the browser* 685
FIGURE 14.12: *Saving a form in the browser* 686
FIGURE 14.13: *Editing a Rich Text Box control in the browser* 689
FIGURE 14.14: *Commonality of InfoPath and Forms Services feature sets* 692
FIGURE 14.15: *MOI Consulting feedback form* 694
FIGURE 14.16: *Compatibility settings in the Form Options dialog* 695
FIGURE 14.17: *Errors and messages in the Design Checker after making the feedback form template browser-compatible* 696

FIGURE 14.18: *Browser-compatibility message within the Digital Signatures category under the Form Options dialog* 696
FIGURE 14.19: *Remake of the Overall Satisfaction table without vertical text* 699
FIGURE 14.20: *Filling out the MOI Consulting feedback form in the browser* 702
FIGURE 14.21: *Promoted properties in a form library* 706
FIGURE 14.22: *Converting an InfoPath data connection to use a server-defined data connection file* 712
FIGURE 14.23: *Filling out the status report form on a Pocket PC device* 721
FIGURE 14.24: *Repeating Section control with three items in a mobile form* 723
FIGURE 14.25: *Editing the first row from the mobile form shown in Figure 14.24* 723
FIGURE 14.26: *Mobile form toolbar with the Pocket PC Internet Explorer toolbar showing below it* 724

FIGURE 15.1: *Programming category in the Form Options dialog* 732
FIGURE 15.2: *Confirmation dialog shown before removing code* 733
FIGURE 15.3: *Upgrading code from a form template compatible with InfoPath 2003* 733
FIGURE 15.4: *Programming options, which are saved as defaults for all new form templates* 736
FIGURE 15.5: *VSTA development environment* 737
FIGURE 15.6: *EventBubbling sample, which shows `Site` and `Sender` node names as events bubble up the data source* 746
FIGURE 15.7: *MOI Consulting morale event scheduler form in design mode* 750
FIGURE 15.8: *Password dialog prompt* 751
FIGURE 15.9: *Custom error message that appears when a `Changing` event handler is canceled* 755
FIGURE 15.10: *Error that occurs when calling unsupported OM during the `Changing` event* 756
FIGURE 15.11: *Show Error Message dialog* 767
FIGURE 15.12: *Supporting entry of last and first names in a Repeating Table control* 769
FIGURE 15.13: *MultipleNotifications sample form in design mode* 775
FIGURE 15.14: *One of the notifications when adding underline to a rich text (XHTML) field* 776
FIGURE 15.15: *Setting up a custom task pane in the Form Options dialog* 785
FIGURE 15.16: *Filling out the CustomTaskPaneInterop sample form* 787

FIGURE 15.17: *Welcome view of the MOI Consulting request form* 791
FIGURE 15.18: *Dialog that results when the Time-sensitive / Critical request type is selected* 793
FIGURE 15.19: *Dialog that appears when form errors exist in the current view* 793
FIGURE 15.20: *Informing the user that signing is required to continue* 794
FIGURE 15.21: *Dialog that appears after using the Click here to sign this section link in the MOI request form* 795
FIGURE 15.22: *Request Details view of the MOI Consulting request form* 795
FIGURE 15.23: *Confirm view of the MOI Consulting request form* 796
FIGURE 15.24: *Thank You view of the MOI Consulting request form* 797
FIGURE 15.25: *Main data source for the MOI Consulting request form template* 801
FIGURE 15.26: *Error dialog that appears when user attempts to open an existing MOI request form* 808
FIGURE 15.27: *Dialog for clearly presenting to the user any form errors* 811
FIGURE 15.28: `GetSubAreas` *secondary data source* 821
FIGURE 15.29: *Request Details view* 825
FIGURE 15.30: *Finding the* `xmlToEdit` *and* `ActionType` *capability of a structurally editable control* 828
FIGURE 15.31: *Setting up the form's main submit to use code* 830

FIGURE 16.1: *Visual Studio's New Project dialog* 837
FIGURE 16.2: *Structure of a VSTO InfoPath project* 838
FIGURE 16.3: *Design a Form Template dialog in VSTO* 839
FIGURE 16.4: *Dialog informing that VSTO never modifies an existing form template* 840
FIGURE 16.5: *VSTO environment while designing a form template* 843
FIGURE 16.6: *Design Tasks task pane in VSTO* 844
FIGURE 16.7: *InfoPath controls in a list view* 846
FIGURE 16.8: *InfoPath controls as icons* 846
FIGURE 16.9: *Microsoft Office InfoPath category options in the VSTO Options dialog* 850
FIGURE 16.10: *Notification for managed code errors, which makes debugging easier* 851
FIGURE 16.11: *Quick Find in VSTO* 854
FIGURE 16.12: *Resource Files dialog used in InfoPath and VSTO* 858
FIGURE 16.13: *Visual Studio 2005 refactoring tools* 859
FIGURE 16.14: *InfoPath Tables toolbar, which is not available in VSTO* 861

Figure 17.1: *Design Checker messages from the MOI feedback form template* 867
Figure 17.2: *Controls targeted by the messages in the Design Checker for the MOI feedback form template* 868
Figure 17.3: *Postback settings for a control in a browser-enabled form template* 871
Figure 17.4: *Customizing toolbar buttons for a browser-enabled form template* 872
Figure 17.5: *Configuring a Button control to use the Update Form option for a browser-enabled form template* 873
Figure 17.6: *Accessibility control settings* 874
Figure 17.7: *Our own message box* 879
Figure 17.8: *Publishing to Forms Services a form template that requires administrator approval* 890
Figure 17.9: *Specifying a path during publishing to save a form template requiring administrator approval* 891
Figure 17.10: *Administration links for Forms Services* 893
Figure 17.11: *Upload Form Template page* 894
Figure 17.12: *Manage Form Templates page* 896
Figure 17.13: *Choosing a site collection and Web application for activation* 897
Figure 17.14: *Activating a form template on the Site Collection Features page* 898
Figure 17.15: *Forms Services Admin tool authored by using the admin object model* 901
Figure 17.16: *Some settings for configuring InfoPath Forms Services* 906
Figure 17.17: *Configuring the session state shared service* 908
Figure 17.18: *Administrative session state thresholds* 910
Figure 17.19: *Quiescing error that frustrated John when creating a status report form* 913
Figure 17.20: *Configuring to quiesce a form template on the Quiesce Form Template page* 914
Figure 17.21: *Status of a quiescing form template* 914
Figure 17.22: *Fully quiesced form template* 915
Figure 17.23: *Quiesce tool authored by using admin object models* 919
Figure 17.24: *Diagnostic Logging administration page* 926
Figure 17.25: *Global administrative data connection settings for Forms Services* 932
Figure 17.26: *The Convert Data Connection dialog* 938
Figure 17.27: *Connection Options dialog when modifying a server-based connection* 939
Figure 17.28: *Uploading to the centrally managed connection library* 940

FIGURE 17.29: *Passing NTLM credentials for data connections with InfoPath and Forms Services 944*

FIGURE 17.30: *Settings on the Managing the Web Service Proxy page 947*

FIGURE 17.31: *Configuring Forms Services form session state 957*

FIGURE 17.32: *Adding performance counters for templates activated with InfoPath Forms Services 959*

FIGURE 17.33: *Microsoft Operations Manager Operator Console 962*

FIGURE 18.1: *Document properties dialog in Word 2003 967*

FIGURE 18.2: *Document Information Panel in Word 2007 967*

FIGURE 18.3: *Document Information Panel dialog 968*

FIGURE 18.4: *SharePoint Document Properties page 969*

FIGURE 18.5: *Document Information Panel Settings page 970*

FIGURE 18.6: *List of content types in the Data Source Wizard 971*

FIGURE 18.7: *InfoPath form template based on the Document content type after adding the Assigned To column in SharePoint 972*

FIGURE 18.8: *Data source for the Document content type 974*

FIGURE 18.9: *Customized Document Properties view for editing standard document properties 975*

FIGURE 18.10: *Publishing the new form template as a Document Information Panel template for SharePoint 975*

FIGURE 18.11: *Document Information Panel showing the Document Properties–Server view 976*

FIGURE 18.12: *Document Information Panel showing the Document Properties view 976*

FIGURE 18.13: *Word document showing the Document Information Panel and the* `Author` *property in the body of the document 977*

FIGURE 18.14: *Visual Studio Toolbox after adding the InfoPath* `FormControl` *control 980*

FIGURE 18.15: *IP Insurance application after adding Combo Box and GroupBox controls 984*

FIGURE 18.16: *IP Insurance application after loading the auto insurance form 986*

FIGURE 18.17: *Standard toolbar for the IP Insurance application 991*

FIGURE 18.18: *Submit Options dialog with Hosting environment as the destination 1008*

FIGURE 18.19: *Copying the physical path for the SharePoint root site collection from IIS Manager 1013*

FIGURE 18.20: *Opening the SharePoint site by using the file system path* 1014
FIGURE 18.21: *Solution Explorer after adding the XmlFormView folder and MyPage.aspx Web form* 1015
FIGURE 18.22: *Toolbox after adding the* `XmlFormView` *control* 1016
FIGURE 18.23: *Hosting the life insurance form in MyPage.aspx* 1019
FIGURE 18.24: *Adding the* `Initialize` *event handler in the host page for the* `XmlFormView1` *control* 1023
FIGURE 18.25: *Host page handling the form submit by sending a custom response* 1030
FIGURE 18.26: *Clicking the Validate Form button shows a dialog box message in the browser* 1034
FIGURE 18.27: *State of the life insurance form while the dialog box still has focus* 1034

FIGURE 19.1: *Add Custom Control Wizard showing the* `Microsoft UpDown Control` *6.0 (SP4) selected in the list of ActiveX controls* 1039
FIGURE 19.2: *Specify Installation Options page of the Add Custom Control Wizard* 1040
FIGURE 19.3: *Specify a Binding Property page of the Add Custom Control Wizard* 1041
FIGURE 19.4: *Specify an Enable or Disable Property page of the Add Custom Control Wizard* 1043
FIGURE 19.5: *Specify Data Type Options page of the Add Custom Control Wizard* 1044
FIGURE 19.6: *Specify Data Type Options page showing the Field (element with custom data type) option* 1046
FIGURE 19.7: *Properties dialog for the* `Microsoft UpDown Control` 1048
FIGURE 19.8: *Stock Properties page of the ATL Control Wizard for the* `Simple InfoPathActiveX` *control* 1052
FIGURE 19.9: *Color property page for the SimpleInfoPathControl object* 1054

FIGURE 20.1: *New Project wizard showing the Shared Add-in project template type* 1077
FIGURE 20.2: *Selecting InfoPath as the supported application in the Shared Add-in Wizard* 1078
FIGURE 20.3: *Data flow for the FormUtilities add-in* 1080
FIGURE 20.4: *Form Data View task pane* 1094
FIGURE 20.5: *New Project wizard showing the InfoPath Add-in project type* 1106
FIGURE 20.6: *TrackBar task pane* 1111
FIGURE 20.7: *Trust Center dialog showing the Add-ins tab* 1112
FIGURE 20.8: *COM Add-ins dialog* 1113

FIGURE 20.9: *Warning dialog shown after an add-in causes a serious error* 1114
FIGURE 20.10: *Disabled Items dialog* 1114

FIGURE 21.1: *MOI Consulting expense report form created in Word* 1118
FIGURE 21.2: *Import Wizard page for selecting the importer to use* 1120
FIGURE 21.3: *Import Wizard page for selecting the file to import* 1120
FIGURE 21.4: *Import Options dialog for importing Word documents* 1121
FIGURE 21.5: *Import Options dialog for importing Excel workbooks* 1122
FIGURE 21.6: *Final page of the Import Wizard* 1123
FIGURE 21.7: *Expense report form after importing into InfoPath* 1124
FIGURE 21.8: *Change To Repeating Table dialog* 1126
FIGURE 21.9: *Registry key structure for importers and exporters* 1129
FIGURE 21.10: *Export Wizard showing a custom exporter* 1131
FIGURE 21.11: *Importer/exporter process flow* 1133
FIGURE 21.12: *Import Form Data dialog* 1143

Tables

Table 2.1: *Starting Points for Form Design* 30

Table 2.2: *Data Requirements for the MOI Consulting Employment Application* 32

Table 2.3: *Design Tasks Pane* 34

Table 2.4: *Standard Controls* 45

Table 2.5: *Controls That Support Applying Font to All Controls* 82

Table 3.1: *Icons Shown in the Data Source Task Pane for Various Types of Data Source Nodes* 87

Table 3.2: *InfoPath 2007 Controls and Their Binding Behaviors* 89

Table 3.3: *XML Data and Schema That Match Before Changing a Field or Group Name* 96

Table 3.4: *Mismatched XML Data and Schema After a Name Change* 96

Table 3.5: *How Data Source Operations on a Published Form Template May Affect Saved Forms* 97

Table 3.6: *Data Types Available in InfoPath Design Mode and Their Value Ranges* 99

Table 3.7: *Sample Form XML Data with and without a Repeating Container* 104

Table 3.8: *Data from Table 3.7, but with Updated Node Names for Readability* 105

Table 3.9: *InfoPath Controls and the XML Schema Created "Behind" the Data Source in the XSD File* 111

Table 3.10: *Designing a Music Collection Form's Data Source with and without Attributes* 117

Table 3.11: *Analyzing Nodes' Namespaces Relative to Their Immediate Ancestors* 136

Table 3.12: *Control, Node, and Other Unrelated Properties That Change or Get Reset After Rebinding* 141
Table 3.13: *The Behaviors of Various Controls When Multiply Bound to* `field1` *While Filling out the Form* 148
Table 3.14: *Design-Time Visual Icons That Appear Over Controls to Indicate Potential Binding Issues* 149
Table 3.15: *When Design-Time Visuals Appear on Controls* 150

Table 4.1: *Controls That Support Input Scope* 195

Table 5.1: *Actions Available for a Rule* 233

Table 6.1: *Types of Main and Secondary Data Query Connections* 246
Table 6.2: *Descriptions of the Web Service Methods Used in Listing 6.1* 277

Table 7.1: *Available and Unavailable Features for Secondary Data Sources* 309

Table 8.1: *Unsupported Database Data Types for Submit* 343
Table 8.2: *Differences between the Receive and Submit Data, Submit Data, and Receive Data Wizards* 346
Table 8.3: *Matrix of Submit Possibilities among Fields, Groups, and the Include Setting* 362
Table 8.4: *Structure of the* `Customers` *Table for the MOI Consulting Firm* 369

Table 9.1: *Persistence of Publishing Options in the Form Definition (.xsf) File* 421
Table 9.2: *Disabled Commands When Previewing a Form* 425

Table 10.1: *List of Features Not Supported by Template Parts* 435

Table 11.1: *OM Security Level Definitions* 472
Table 11.2: *Form and IE Security Level Impacts on OM Security Level* 473
Table 11.3: *CAS Permission Set for* `LocalIntranet` 496
Table 11.4: *Permissions Granted and Denied to a User Given a Form Template in Design Mode* 539
Table 11.5: *Mapping of Default SharePoint Roles to IRM Permissions* 551
Table 11.6: *Direct Mapping of SharePoint Permissions to IRM* 552

TABLE 12.1: *Default Merge Actions Based on Node Type* 560
TABLE 12.2: *Merge Customizations Available for Each Node Type* 570
TABLE 12.3: *List of Available Separators in the Merge Settings Dialog for Rich Text Fields* 576
TABLE 12.4: *Merge Actions in the Aggregation Namespace* 584
TABLE 12.5: *Merge Attributes Available for Merge Actions* 584

TABLE 13.1: *Workflows Included with Microsoft Office SharePoint Server 2007* 635

TABLE 14.1: *Controls Supported in Forms Services* 688
TABLE 14.2: *Matrix of Browsers Supported for Use with Forms Services* 691
TABLE 14.3: *Form Features That May Automatically Communicate with the Server* 704
TABLE 14.4: *SharePoint Permissions and How They Apply to Forms Services* 707
TABLE 14.5: `OpenIn` *Parameter Values with Brief Descriptions* 717

TABLE 15.1: *Programming Languages and Available InfoPath Object Model Versions* 731
TABLE 15.2: *Form Events Exposed by InfoPath* 743
TABLE 15.3: *Invalid Object Model Calls During XML Events* 757
TABLE 15.4: *Examples of Advanced XPaths for Registering XML Event Handlers* 782
TABLE 15.5: *Types of Data Connections and Their Commonly Used Properties and Methods* 823

TABLE 16.1: *InfoPath-Specific Commands in VSTO* 848
TABLE 16.2: *InfoPath Controls' Behaviors on Double-Click* 852
TABLE 16.3: *Commonly Used Code Snippets* 860

TABLE 17.1: `IsBrowser` *and* `IsMobile` *Values in Various Environments* 884
TABLE 17.2: *Object Model Classes, Events, Properties, and Methods Not Implemented by Forms Services* 886
TABLE 17.3: *Full List of stsadm.exe Commands Specific to Forms Services* 899
TABLE 17.4: *New and Existing Form-Filling Sessions During Quiescing and Quiesced Status* 914
TABLE 17.5: *Commands for stsadm.exe Specific to Quiescing* 918

TABLE 17.6: *Administration OM on the* `FormTemplate` *Object Specific to Quiescing* 918

TABLE 17.7: *Forms Services Errors That May Appear in the Windows Event Log* 921

TABLE 17.8: *Forms Services Warnings That May Appear in the Windows Event Log* 923

TABLE 17.9: *Complete List of InfoPath Forms Services Performance Counters* 960

TABLE 18.1: *InfoPath Form Control Methods* 981

TABLE 18.2: *InfoPath Form Control Properties* 983

TABLE 18.3: *Commonly Used Properties of the* `XmlFormView` *Control* 1017

TABLE 18.4: *All Properties of the* `XmlFormView` *Control (Includes Properties from Table 18.3 but No Inherited Properties)* 1026

TABLE 18.5: *Properties and Methods Not Available to the ASP.NET Host Page* 1027

TABLE 18.6: *Events the ASP.NET Host Page May Not Sink* 1028

TABLE 19.1: *Field or Group Types* 1045

TABLE 19.2: *Interfaces and Properties That Controls Should Implement to Work Well in InfoPath* 1050

TABLE 19.3: `InfoPathControl` *Interface Methods* 1059

TABLE 20.1: `IDTExtensibility2` *Interface Methods* 1075

TABLE 20.2: *Application Events Available to COM Add-ins* 1082

TABLE 20.3: `CreateCTP` *Parameters* 1097

TABLE 20.4: `CustomTaskPane` *Methods, Properties, and Events* 1098

TABLE 21.1: *String Values to Be Added Under Each LCID Key* 1130

TABLE 21.2: *Methods of the* `IFormTemplateConverter2` *Interface* 1133

TABLE 21.3: *Methods of the* `IConversionManager` *Interface* 1134

TABLE 21.4: *Method of the* `IConversionManager2` *Interface* 1134

TABLE 21.5: *Parameters for the* `Import` *and* `Export` *Methods* 1136

TABLE 21.6: *Methods of the* `IInfoPathDataImporter` *Interface* 1144

TABLE 21.7: *Print Settings Supplied to the Data Importer* 1144

TABLE 21.8: *Controls Included in the Controls Collection* 1145

TABLE 21.9: *Properties of the* `IInfoPathViewControl` *Interface* 1147

Foreword

Designing Forms for Microsoft Office InfoPath and Forms Services 2007 is written by two distinguished members of the InfoPath product team who designed, implemented, and tested many of the core features of the product. I was delighted when I learned that Scott Roberts and Hagen Green had decided to share their experience this way: Scott was deeply involved in the creation of the Forms Design experience in InfoPath, while Hagen provided deep contributions to the creation of InfoPath Forms Services.

This book is an excellent hands-on introduction to Microsoft Office InfoPath, which represents a revolutionary leap in XML editing technologies and a new paradigm for gathering business-critical information. A wide variety of audiences will appreciate the information provided in this book: Information workers will learn how to design InfoPath forms without requiring development skills, and developers will learn how to add custom business logic to their forms and integrate them deeply to other applications.

Workers everywhere generate content that contains valuable data every day—in e-mail messages, status reports, and the like. But they also spend an inordinate amount of time searching for that same information when they need to reuse it. When, and if, they find it, they often spend even more time rekeying the relevant data into another document. Why hasn't technology made it easier to gather and integrate all this content we generate? The problem is that many of the documents we use for everyday business processes aren't amenable to automation. While data capture and validation has been a core component of traditional forms for some time, the technology needed to automatically gather, say, valuable data from a text document hasn't been available. This is the core vision that led to the creation of InfoPath.

What's interesting and unique about InfoPath is the type of information it allows people to gather. InfoPath lets organizations design and edit what people in my field call "semistructured" documents, or documents that have regions of meaning, in the same way that columns in a database have meaning. While the program provides great design and editing capabilities for traditional forms such as purchase orders and equipment requests, what's innovative is that InfoPath squarely targets information that historically has been more difficult to capture, such as business-critical data contained in sales reports, inventory updates, project memos, travel itineraries, and performance reviews. The XML community has been trying to build a tool like InfoPath for a long time. XML is about creating documents in which the content is delimited, or set apart, by tags that explain the meaning of each piece of content. With XML, documents can become a source of information as rich as a database, enabling search, processing, and reuse. InfoPath has been built from the ground up to understand XML. The underlying structure of the information in an InfoPath template is described using a *schema.* A schema describes how the data is constructed, in the same way that a blueprint describes how a building is constructed. Because InfoPath understands XML, customers can define their own business-specific schema using the latest XML standards.

Numerous industries, including financial services, insurance, governments, and healthcare organizations of all sizes, are using custom-defined XML schemas to create documents with regions of meaning that are specific to their business. This allows them to reuse content across productivity applications and across other kinds of tools such as databases, workflows, and server processes. Across the world, government administrations are creating XML schemas that can represent important data related to their citizens: records such as birth certificates, housing permits, or registrations to public programs. It is important for such constituencies to enable the capture of this data by using tools that are interoperable and can reach any platform. It is in this context that the importance of the new functionalities of InfoPath 2007 and InfoPath Forms Services can be understood: Business processes are extended beyond the firewall by enabling users to complete forms by using Web browsers such as Internet Explorer, Mozilla Firefox, and Safari or by using HTML-enabled mobile devices. Another way to collect information in an interoperable and standardized way is to capture XML data by e-mail. InfoPath 2007 enables the user to gather information using e-mail messages and to complete forms without leaving the familiar Office Outlook 2007 environment.

The XML community, which I am proud to be part of, worked on and implemented such scenarios for a very long time, but what makes InfoPath unique is how easy it is to design and deploy such forms and templates. With our vision of enabling millions of users to create and use XML information, it was extremely important to make sure that the design of the forms can be done easily without writing code while allowing experienced developers to add advanced functionality when necessary. You will learn in this book how to easily design forms by using the drag-and-drop interface of InfoPath and, for example, how to add Information Rights Management to help protect forms from inappropriate usage. If you are a developer, you will learn, for example, about the new functionality of InfoPath that enables you to use form template libraries and to add to a form prebuilt template parts that include sophisticated data connectivity features. You will also learn how to use InfoPath 2007 in conjunction with Visual Studio 2005 to incorporate InfoPath 2007 with other preexisting applications.

Microsoft's long-term vision for InfoPath is really the vision behind Microsoft's overall Web services strategy: to make it easy to create, access, and share XML data between different systems on a network. InfoPath is the first end-user product that gives information workers the capability to exploit XML and Web services. Enjoy the book!

Jean Paoli
General Manager, Interoperability and XML Architecture, Microsoft Corporation
Cocreator of the W3C XML 1.0 Recommendation
Cocreator of Microsoft Office InfoPath

Preface

It Just Makes Sense

Over the past ten years, Extensible Markup Language (XML) has become more widely used than ever before as a means of transferring data between applications and even between organizations. XML provides a standard protocol with which these applications and organizations can communicate. Using XML Schema, a company can define a standard structure for its data that can then be used across multiple departments and organizations. This structured data enables developers to easily create applications that can communicate with each other without much effort.

In addition, most organizations use forms in one way or another, whether to enter a purchase request, submit expense report information, or track weekly status. If you look at a typical form, you will notice that the form itself is structured unlike a typical freeform document created in an application such as Microsoft Office Word 2007. In these freeform documents you can type anything you like in any way that you choose. Although a form may contain sections that allow you to enter freeform text such as comments, most of your typical forms are highly structured. Fields in the form usually require you to enter specific types of data such as sales numbers or costs. Since XML defines a structured data format (which can contain some unstructured elements) and forms are highly structured with bits of freeform data, it makes sense to tie together forms and XML data. Once a user has filled out a form that is connected to XML data, the data can easily be incorporated into back-end processes that understand the structure of the XML data for that form. So, this fits one of the main purposes of XML—tying together multiple processes using a standard protocol.

Since building forms based on XML just makes sense, many software developers want to create forms-based applications to collect data and store it as XML. However, until a few years ago, this was a tedious and time-consuming process. Developers had to use tools such as Microsoft Visual C++, C#, or Visual Basic .NET and write sometimes a tremendous amount of code to create a forms application. Often, forms applications share similar functionality, such as spell checking, calculations, and data validation. In order to share this functionality across multiple forms applications, software developers needed to create code libraries in order to reuse their code. This worked fine when sharing the code within the same department or company. However, developers across multiple companies were likely going to duplicate the same work unless, of course, companies purchased these libraries from a third-party vendor.

Developing forms applications in this way is not something that typical information workers can do. Usually this type of coding is reserved for advanced software developers. Another disadvantage of this approach is that different forms applications usually have different user interfaces. Each time a user fills out a form, he or she may need to learn a different set of commands and menu items. This learning curve costs the company time and money.

About five years ago, Microsoft recognized the need for a common tool to build forms based on XML technologies. Existing XML-based tools required a thorough understanding of XML, so most information workers had trouble understanding how to use them. Also, most information workers do not know how to write code and, therefore, could not easily use development tools such as Microsoft Visual Studio. Therefore, it just made sense to create a tool that developers and information workers could use to create forms based on XML and that users could use to fill out those forms. That tool is InfoPath. (In Chapter 1, we'll tell you exactly what InfoPath is all about and introduce you to the extensive feature set included in this application.)

Looking at the wealth of features included in InfoPath, especially those added in InfoPath 2007, it also just made sense to create this book. This book is titled *Designing Forms for Microsoft Office InfoPath and Forms Services 2007* for a reason. It's all about designing forms using InfoPath 2007, as we're sure you have figured out by now. This book will teach you everything you need to know about creating forms using InfoPath 2007 and probably a few things you never thought you needed to know.

Who Should Read This Book

Whether you are an information worker who has created only a few forms in Word or a software developer who is familiar with more advanced coding concepts, if your intention is to learn how to design InfoPath forms, this book is for you. This book will talk about not only the basics of designing forms but also such advanced concepts as writing managed code for InfoPath. As long as you have an understanding of basic form concepts and a desire to learn, you are in the right place. If you want to learn everything you can about InfoPath 2007, you have found the right book.

How This Book Is Organized

This book contains two parts. Part I is all about designing forms in InfoPath. No prior coding experience is required to understand the concepts, so both information workers and developers can use Part I to learn the basics of InfoPath form design. Many chapters build on previous chapters and become slightly more advanced as you progress. For example, in Chapter 4 we discuss advanced controls and customization, but by Chapter 6 we show how to pull external data, such as from a Web service, into your forms. By the time you finish reading Part I, you should know everything you need to know to design an InfoPath form for the InfoPath client application or for the browser without having to write any code.

Part II is about advanced form design. In this part of the book we talk about using more advanced form design techniques, including how to write code for InfoPath. These chapters are geared mainly toward software developers who have some basic coding experience. However, if you are an information worker and you have completed Part I of this book, the second part may interest you as well. In Part II, we talk about such topics as the InfoPath object model (Chapter 15), advanced topics regarding InfoPath Forms Services (Chapter 17), and ways to host InfoPath (Chapter 18).

Conventions Used in This Book

We use a few typographical conventions throughout this book. **Bold** text indicates key topics or terms. The names of features shown in the user interface, such as menu items, appear in *italic* text.

Information that pertains to InfoPath Forms Services is clearly displayed as features in the text. These tips will let you know when certain InfoPath features work differently in browser forms or don't work at all.

Samples

Almost every chapter in this book has one or more samples, which you can download from the Addison-Wesley Web site for this book. Sometimes the samples are InfoPath form templates (.xsn) files, which is the case throughout Part I. In order to use these form templates, you first need to open them in InfoPath design mode and resave them to a local folder. (This will make more sense after you start reading Part I.) Trying to open the form template in order to fill it out without first saving it will result in an error.

Some samples include form (.xml) files in addition to form templates. To open the forms, first open InfoPath, and then open the XML file using the standard *Open* dialog (i.e., click on the *On My Computer* link from the *Getting Started* dialog.) The first time you open one of the sample forms, the dialog shown in Figure P.1 will be displayed. This dialog allows you to choose the form template associated with the form you are trying to open. The text of the chapter indicates the correct form template to use. After you

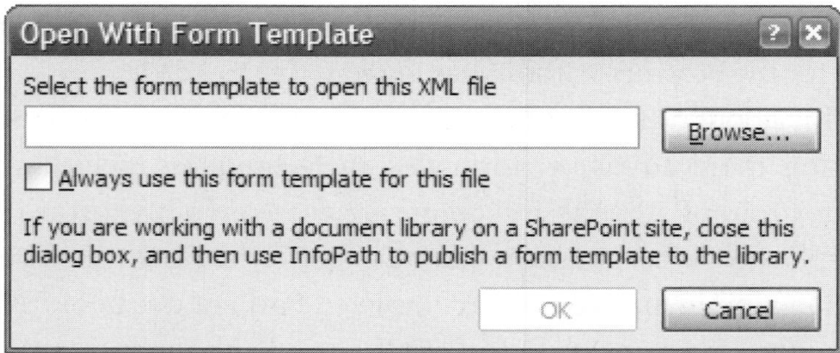

FIGURE P.1 Open With Form Template dialog

choose the form template, click the checkbox *Always use this form template for this file.* After the form is opened, immediately save it. This will prevent you from having to choose the form template each time you open the form.

Some sample form templates define one or more data connections. For these samples to work properly, the external data source must exist. To see if a form template depends on a data connection, go to the *Data Connections* menu item under the *Tools* menu while in design mode. Since there are many types of data connections, we'll describe how to set up each one to successfully preview the form.

- XML document: If the XML (.xml) file exists within the form template (under the *Resource Files* menu item on the *Tools* menu), there is nothing you need to do. If the XML file is external to the form template, you will need to click the *Modify* button on the *Data Connections* dialog to point to your copy of the XML file. You can find the file within the samples for a given chapter.
- Database: A database connection depends on a SQL Server or Access database. If the sample uses a SQL Server database, you must have SQL Server installed and have administrative rights to the SQL Server instance. For an Access database, the chapter will include an Access database (.mdb) file. For either case, click the *Modify* button on the *Data Connections* dialog to update the data connection to point to your database to restore the connection.
- Web service: To use a Web service, you must have Internet Information Services (IIS) 6.0 or higher installed on your computer. The ASP.NET 2.0 ISAPI Web extension must be enabled, and ASP.NET should be configured to render .aspx pages. Copy the Web service code from the sample and paste it into a new ASP.NET Web service project in Visual Studio 2005. If you don't have Visual Studio, you can still create the Web service by creating a text file with extension .aspx within an IIS virtual directory. Check to see if the Web service code requires read or write access to specific directories; you can grant access to those directories or simply update the code to use directories of your choice. Before using the Web service with InfoPath, try navigating to the Web service by using a Web browser on the local machine. Once the Web service works outside of

InfoPath, you can click the *Modify* button in the *Data Connections* dialog to change the Web service connection from the sample to point to your own Web service.

- SharePoint library or list: The prerequisite to using samples with a SharePoint library or list connection is a Microsoft Office SharePoint server. If you have a SharePoint server, ensure you have at least reader rights if the connection is only reading data. Likewise, if the sample form template submits to a SharePoint library, you must have contributor or higher privilege. Ensure the library or list upon which the form template depends actually exists on the server. To use your library or list, edit the connection to point to your server and select the appropriate library or list.

In Part II of this book, most of the samples include code. Those samples that require you to perform special actions (or actions in a specific order) to build the samples include ReadMe.txt files that explain what you need to do.

For sample form templates that include form code, you must do the following. First, find the sample form template (.xsn) and archive (.zip) files with the same name. Extract the archive to a location on your computer by right-clicking on the .zip file and selecting *Extract All.* Next, open the form template in design mode as you would for samples without form code. Select the *Microsoft Visual Studio Tools for Applications* (VSTA) menu item under *Tools* and then *Programming.* If InfoPath cannot find the VSTA project, the dialog shown in Figure P.2 appears. Click the *Browse* button to navigate to the *Visual C# Project* (.csproj) file within the extracted folder. Once the

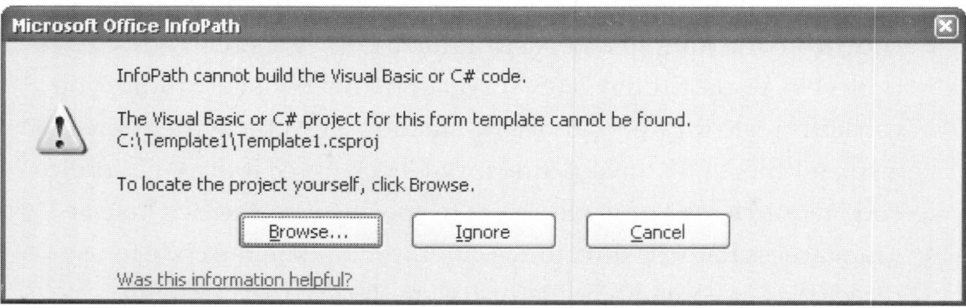

FIGURE P.2 Dialog shown when InfoPath cannot find the Visual C# project with the form code

Microsoft Visual Studio Tools for Applications window appears, hit F5 to fill out the form while previewing it. The debugger will be automatically attached, so any breakpoints or unhandled exceptions halt form execution.

Some samples in Part II require references to the interop assemblies for InfoPath. In order to set a reference to the correct interop assemblies, open the *Add Reference* dialog in Visual Studio and browse to the install location for Microsoft Office 2007. (This is usually C:\Program Files\Microsoft Office\Office12.) Then, locate the ipeditor.dll file and select it. This will include the Microsoft.Office.Interop.InfoPath interop assembly that you need as well as a few assemblies that aren't needed. In order to be able to install the samples, you will need to remove the references to the ADODB, MSHTML, and MSXML2 assemblies. Some samples use the Microsoft.Office.Interop.InfoPath.Xml assembly. You can also locate this assembly in the install location for Office 2007.

Some code snippets that you see within chapters may differ from the code in the sample. Due to space constraints, brevity in code may have resulted in reformatting or removal of comments or error-handling code that are not required to understand the sample. Regardless, the functionality of the code itself remains unaffected. Note that the code included with the sample form templates is not considered production quality. The code samples, not to mention the form templates themselves, have not been subjected to the rigorous testing you would expect from a company such as Microsoft.

Acknowledgments

The process of writing a book is never a one-person job (or two-person job, in this case). There are always many different people involved in the writing of a book, from the publisher to the reviewers to the product team whose product we are writing about. Therefore, we extend heartfelt thanks to the following people.

First, we want to thank the entire InfoPath product team. Without the InfoPath team and the wonderful application that is InfoPath, this book wouldn't exist. Next, we thank our editor, Joan Murray, who has guided us throughout the 15 months it took to make this project a reality. Also, the following people from Addison-Wesley played a key role in the process: Kim Boedigheimer, Curt Johnson, Eric Garulay, and Jessica D'Amico. We also thank our copyeditor, Chrysta Meadowbrooke, who did an outstanding job; our project manager, Kathy Glidden; and our project editor, Tyrrell Albaugh.

Next, from the InfoPath team, we thank our Development Manager, Paul Lorimer, for coordinating the InfoPath review process and for providing general support and guidance. Thanks to our Test Manager, Brad Thompson, and our managers Laurent Mollicone (development) and Rodrigo Lode (test) for their support throughout this project. To Jean Paoli, whose vision made InfoPath a reality, we extend our gratitude.

We thank our reviewers on the InfoPath team: Dragos Barac, Andrew Begun, Ned Friend, Jun Jin, Nathaniel Stott, Mike Palmer, Balbir Singh, and Willson Raj David. Thanks for ensuring that the technical content was accurate. We also thank our external reviewers (those who are not members of the InfoPath team): Pedro Serrano, Joe Kunk, and Susan Ramlet.

In addition, many other people helped us along the way, whether with technical information or advice on what topics would be most useful to readers.

- Dragos Barac helped us with user roles, workflow, and hosting. We extend a special thank you to Dragos, who went out of his way on many occasions to help us. In fact, he reviewed most of our chapters and provided extremely valuable feedback. Dragos, we thank you very much for the contribution you have made to the success of this book.
- Eilen Hao helped us understand workflows in Microsoft Office SharePoint Server.
- We extend our thanks to the following people for their help with InfoPath hosting: Petru Moldovanu, David Airapetyan, Yael Peled, DeVere Dyett, Gary Hsu, Balbir Singh, and Alnur Ali.
- Nathaniel Stott gave us his help with InfoPath e-mail forms.
- For providing us with information about workflow, we thank Ned Friend, Noah Edelstein, and Michael Dalton.
- For helping us with COM and managed add-ins, we thank Petru Moldovanu, Frank Mueller, and David Vierzba.
- We thank Mike Palmer, Andrew Begun, Silviu Ifrim, Eric Korn, and Nima Mirzad for their help with the InfoPath object model.
- Jeff Bienvenu and Aparna Suripeddi shared their knowledge of Information Rights Management.

- Mary Smith provided pointers to the Office Customization Tool.
- Without Travis Rhodes and Nick Dallett, we couldn't have included topics on the data connection library, centrally managed connection library, and Universal Data Connection (UDC) files.
- Natalie Eason helped set up and convey all sorts of information on Visual Studio Tools for Office (VSTO).
- The InfoPath XML Schema guru, Phyllis Lai, offered her insight on data source intricacies.

Hagen would like to thank Scott for his mentorship throughout writing this book. He is not only a role model but also a great personal friend. I could not have asked for a better coauthor as well as coworker. Scott, thank you for all you have taught me in authorship.

Scott would like to thank Hagen for his dedication and persistence throughout the long and difficult process of completing this project. Your hard-working attitude and easygoing nature make you a joy to work with. We started this project as close personal friends and made it through all the tough times unscathed.

Last, but certainly not least, we'd like to thank our families. Scott thanks his wife, Andrea, and his two sons, Sean and Bradley, for being so supportive during the 15 months it took to write this book. Without you three, life would have been much more difficult during this time. Hagen thanks his girlfriend, Jaime, for being by his side throughout one of the biggest undertakings of his life. Hagen also thanks his parents, Christine and Stuart, for their constant encouragement and support, especially his dad for being his biggest fan and the first to preorder this book!

Feedback

After you read this book, we would love to hear what you think about it—both positive and negative. This will help us improve future revisions. Also, feel free to send us any questions you may have. We would be happy to help. To contact us, simply send us an e-mail at DesigningIPForms@hotmail.com. If you have a question, either Scott or Hagen will reply as quickly as possible. We hope that you enjoy the book and that it makes the process of designing InfoPath form templates much easier.

About the Authors

Scott Roberts is a Senior Development Lead in the InfoPath team at Microsoft Corporation. Scott has been a developer on the InfoPath team since the initial inception of the product and was one of four developers who worked on the prototype for what later became the InfoPath form template designer. Now Scott leads a team of developers who are responsible for various features in InfoPath, including template parts and custom controls implemented with ActiveX, the built-in InfoPath controls, and the Word and Excel importers, to name a few. Scott is also the author of *Programming Microsoft Internet Explorer 5* (Microsoft Press, 1999) as well as many technical articles and publications. In his spare time, Scott enjoys spending time with his wife, Andrea, and two sons, Sean and Bradley. He also enjoys physical fitness and a style of martial arts called Tang Soo Do.

Hagen Green is a Software Design Engineer in Test II with the InfoPath team at Microsoft Corporation. He has been with the team since the advent of XDocs, the codenamed predecessor of InfoPath. Hagen has worked on InfoPath features such as the designer platform, XSL support, Web services and datasets, and most recently on InfoPath Forms Services. Hagen has also recorded Webcast talks on advanced InfoPath features, and he contributed the InfoPath chapter to *Visual Studio Tools for Office* (Addison-Wesley, 2006). When he's not working, Hagen spends his time running marathons, cycling, mountain biking, rock climbing, and skiing. He also is an avid reader, enjoys tracking the stock market, and looks forward to more writing in the future.

PART I
Designing Forms

1 Introduction to InfoPath 2007

What Is InfoPath?

The rapid adoption of XML-based technologies over the past decade has precipitated the need for a tool that helps end users interact with and share XML data. On August 19, 2003, as part of the Microsoft Office System 2003, Microsoft shipped a new application created to fill that need—Microsoft Office InfoPath.

InfoPath may be one of the least known yet most appropriate platforms for gathering data in the Microsoft Office suite of applications. But InfoPath's popularity has been on a sharp rise. Anyone from an information technology (IT) manager tracking a purchase request workflow to little Johnny tracking his music collection can benefit from what InfoPath offers. Before InfoPath, programs such as Word, Excel, or Access may have been used for these tasks. There is nothing wrong with using any of these other programs to build forms. However, none of these applications were built with forms in mind, so they don't provide the ease of use and power that InfoPath has when it comes to creating a form based on XML data. The goal of this book is to make you an expert InfoPath form designer. Whether you are a novice, an information worker, an experienced developer, or anyone in between, you have found the right book to help you get the job done with InfoPath 2007.

You may be wondering why Microsoft created this new tool. Doesn't Microsoft already have other form design tools such as Word, Excel, and

Visual Basic .NET, to name a few? While it is true that you can build forms with these tools, none of them are based solely on XML technologies, nor were they created exclusively to edit XML data. Both Word and Excel can interact with XML data, but they do not offer structural editing of the XML data to the extent that InfoPath does. Visual Basic .NET requires you to have at least a basic understanding of application development. InfoPath does not require you to be a developer in order to build a form. Anyone who has experience using Word can create a form in InfoPath.

Thanks to the familiar Microsoft Office user interface (UI), ramp-up time to productivity is minimal. Users with little or no programming experience can use InfoPath in design mode to create form templates. InfoPath users can also fill out forms based on those templates. Since InfoPath was designed (no pun intended) to be used by almost anyone with little or no training, form designers have all the tools needed to deliver form templates that are easy to use. Of course, if you are a developer, you may also want to customize your form templates, for example, by writing script or managed code using InfoPath's extensive object model (OM).

Using InfoPath in design mode, you can rapidly build form templates that interact with XML data and XML Schema (XSD) with little or no code required. Then users can open InfoPath to fill out forms based on the form templates you created. Because InfoPath is a Microsoft Office product, the UI is as familiar to users as Word 2003. In fact, InfoPath provides a lot of the same features as Word (e.g., spell checking, rich text editing), so filling out forms in InfoPath is as easy as drafting a document in Word. The main difference is that when users are filling out an InfoPath form, they are actually editing XML data.

Form Templates and Forms

Form template: The blueprint for a form, which you create in InfoPath design mode. Many forms that are unrelated in content can be created with the same form template. The form template defines the look-and-feel and functionality of a form.

Form: An instance of a form template that users fill out by using InfoPath.

However, the value of InfoPath goes way beyond its ability to edit XML data directly. In fact, its usefulness as a data-gathering and management tool is one of the most powerful aspects of InfoPath. Also, because the InfoPath form templates you create can be based on industry-standard XML Schemas and integrated with Web services, data stored in InfoPath forms can be integrated with existing processes in your organization and across other organizations.

Let's look at an example. Say that you run a sales organization. You have an existing database that contains customer and sales data. Your sales manager wants you to create two different forms—one for salespeople to input customer information and another for them to input sales data. Before InfoPath, there were many ways to create these forms. However, since the data comes from a back-end database, all of these methods involved writing some code. And you would typically have to duplicate this code from one form to the next.

With InfoPath, creating these forms is much easier. InfoPath allows you to create form templates that connect to existing databases or Web services, thus removing the need to write code to access the data. This part is done for you. InfoPath also allows you to easily merge the data gathered in these forms so that you can create aggregate reports for upper management. Again, InfoPath enables you to do this without writing any code at all, unlike other form tools. InfoPath includes an extensive OM, so it's highly customizable. Using InfoPath, you can enable almost any scenario you can dream up.

As your business needs change, so should your software. InfoPath is designed to cater to these ever-changing data collection needs. Built on World Wide Web Consortium (W3C) standards, XML and its associated technologies help InfoPath deliver on its promises. A few of the greater benefits of XML include the following:

- Provides a semistructured data format
- Is human readable
- Is easy for programs to process
- Works across disparate systems

Technologies encompassing XML include Extensible Stylesheet Language Transformations (XSLT) for transforming the XML to another format such as HTML, XML Path Language (XPath) for selecting specific parts of the XML data for processing, and XSD for defining precise rules for how the XML structure and data should look. InfoPath seamlessly incorporates each of these technologies into the experience of designing and filling out forms. For example, thanks to XSLT, one of the most important benefits of using InfoPath is the ability to separate data from how it is displayed. With the drag-and-drop UI of the InfoPath design mode, you can completely change the look-and-feel of a form without changing the underlying data that is saved when a user fills it out. Another advantage is being able to merge data from multiple forms. This is especially useful when creating a report, for example.

As we mentioned, InfoPath offers a plethora of built-in features geared toward collecting data that would require custom code in other form design tools. With InfoPath, for example, you can use data validation and conditional formatting to ensure that users enter valid data before the form is submitted to your back-end databases or Web services. You can also design your forms to collect only the data you need. Traditional forms include many parts that don't apply to everyone. For example, employment applications often contain sections relevant only to people with college degrees. However, these forms have to include sections for this information since the forms are static by nature. These forms may contain instructional text such as "If you chose Yes for question 5, please enter more information here. Otherwise, skip to question 6." With InfoPath, you can design dynamic forms that contain the additional sections only if needed. Using our example, when a user chooses Yes to question 5, a section of the form that wasn't visible suddenly becomes available. Also, the static employment application may not provide enough room to fill in a complete employment history. In this case, users must either not include the additional information or provide it on an additional form. With InfoPath forms, your users can fill in as much data as they need since your forms can be built to grow dynamically. When your users need more space to fill in additional data, the form can expand to meet their requirements.

These are just a few aspects of InfoPath that makes it a more powerful tool for XML-based forms than other applications. We will talk about these benefits and more throughout this book. First, however, we'd like to give you an overview of the evolution of InfoPath through three successive versions—InfoPath 2003, InfoPath 2003 Service Pack 1, and InfoPath 2007. This will not only give you some insight into the product's background but also introduce you to several of its features.

InfoPath 2003

To provide reasonable context for discussing new InfoPath features, let's look at the different versions of the product and what each brings to the table. Version 1, officially released as InfoPath 2003 on August 19, 2003, is Microsoft's inception into the XML forms and data collection markets. As such, it bundles competitive features to allow for a rich form experience. This section recaps the highlights of InfoPath 2003.

The InfoPath design mode is all about creating nice-looking forms that include basic functionality. The design surface, or view, is similar to that of Microsoft Word. The content of the view flows from left to right, top to bottom, and serves as the presentation layer for the form's data. Absolute positioning, such as what PowerPoint offers, would make InfoPath form design cumbersome when accommodating different resolutions and monitor sizes. Therefore, **layout tables** are used instead as the positioning paradigm of choice—equivalent to that of many professional Web sites. Tables offer a familiar and flexible option when demanding pixel-by-pixel, picture-perfect parity.

For those of us with a less than acute sense for visual design, **color schemes** spice up even the most boring forms. A single click on the *Bright Blue* color scheme adds a subtle blue color theme to parts of your form template's controls and layout tables. If you don't care for the effects of *Bright Blue,* you can choose another scheme at your convenience at any time. Color schemes more dramatically affect Repeating Table controls more than other controls. The header and footer backgrounds, text, and table borders comply with the current theme.

InfoPath 2003 introduced a general set of controls for inclusion in forms. Figure 1.1 shows the *Controls* task pane. As you would expect, the InfoPath design mode includes controls such as Text Box, List Box, Drop-Down List Box, Check Box, Bulleted List, Numbered List, Plain List, Option Button,

FIGURE 1.1: Controls task pane in InfoPath 2003

and Button. The Section, Optional Section, Repeating Section, and Repeating Table controls support InfoPath's structural editing features. These editing features allow the end user, while filling out the form, to modify the structure of the XML data as the XML Schema allows. Structural editing is what makes InfoPath such an attractive offering compared with its alternatives. The Hyperlink, Expression Box, Picture, and Rich Text Box controls round out the controls available in InfoPath 2003.

We mentioned earlier that the data and the presentation layers are two disparate concepts. We've already discussed the presentation layer, but we haven't yet focused on the data. When we refer to "data," we really mean "data and structure." XML consists of hierarchical elements that may or may not contain text content. The definition for the XML structure is bounded by the rules of the XML Schema. (We will talk more about XML

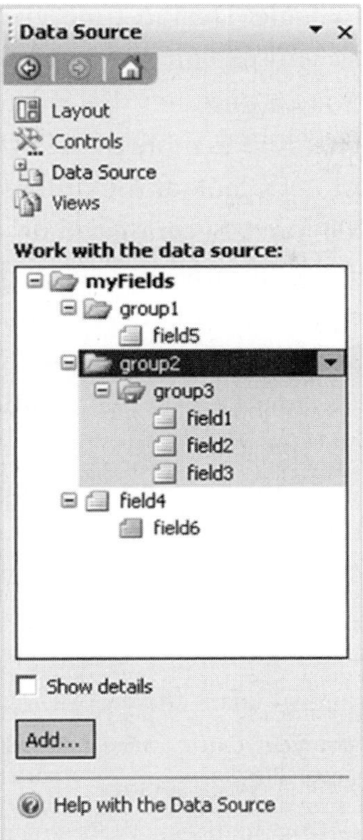

FIGURE 1.2: Data Source task pane in InfoPath 2003

Schema in Chapter 3.) InfoPath abstracts away the XML Schema details through the *Data Source* task pane (DSP; see Figure 1.2). The DSP is a design-mode feature that shows what the XML Schema allows. If you don't have an XML Schema lying around, there's no need to worry. InfoPath automatically builds the XML Schema as you insert new controls onto the designer view. Inserting a control into the form may create either a **field** or a **group** in the DSP. This process populates the DSP based on which controls are selected. The newly inserted controls are **bound** to the newly created data source. The word **binding** describes the connection between what the user sees and what data is stored behind the scenes. We'll talk more about binding in Chapter 3.

Binding sounds easy, right? It is—for most situations. But due to the flexibility of hooking up any data source to any controls, getting into odd binding dilemmas is inevitable. **Design-time visuals** are icons displayed on your form controls as you design your form template. These visuals serve as handy reminders to a designer that the form may be broken. We will discuss this versatile feature in more detail in Chapter 3.

Besides the visual zest, let's look at the different ways to pull external data into an InfoPath 2003 form. **Secondary data sources** are used to connect to databases, SharePoint libraries or lists, and Web services. Say your car registration form template has a Drop-Down List Box control containing all 50 states in the United States. When creating your form template, you could enter each state manually when creating the list items for the control, but it's probably easier to point the Drop-Down List Box control to an existing database. SharePoint servers are somewhat ubiquitous in high-tech small business. Pulling a real-time list of manager names or part numbers into your form allows it to always be up to date with no intervention on your behalf.

Web services have created a growing sensation throughout the Internet community for the last several years. Any popular search engine will yield innumerable results when you query for Web services. Ironically, many search engines also expose a Web service for you to do the searching. InfoPath supports connecting to these Web services without you, as the form designer, writing a single line of code. All you need to know is where the Web service resides. So forget about details like the Web Service Definition Language (WSDL), input parameters, and output parameters that you would need to understand if using other form tools. However, if you wish to deal with those aspects of the Web service using InfoPath 2003, you can access them by writing script code against the InfoPath OM.

The InfoPath OM in version 2003 is designed as a programmatic extension to many features provided in the InfoPath UI and some features that are not. The OM is not a superset but rather a supplement to the functionality available from the UI. To access the OM in InfoPath 2003, you could choose to write either JScript or VBScript in the Microsoft Script Editor (MSE). MSE is the Microsoft Office–bundled development environment of choice for scripting languages. InfoPath even has an extensive help system built into MSE that provides on-demand, context-sensitive help while scripting InfoPath objects.

So let's say that we've made the final touches on our new InfoPath form template by adding some JScript code using MSE. We're all ready to roll the form template out to our team. It's time to **publish** our form template. Publishing is a short process to deploy the form template to a location accessible by users. A few steps through a wizard is all it takes to properly put your template on a network file share, SharePoint site, Web server, or other shared location.

We've exhausted our brief talk of the InfoPath design mode for now. Let's peek at some of the important features you can find while filling out a form. As mentioned earlier, the UI is instantly familiar. You can expect the standard Microsoft Office set of features, such as cut, copy, and paste; a dizzying array of font formatting options; spell checking; find and replace; and clip art (to name a few).

What's so special about InfoPath? It sounds a lot like Word in many ways. However, InfoPath has two key advantages: An InfoPath form uses XML data, and InfoPath offers data validation, which is not found in Word. If you are an application developer, you will appreciate the tight integration between XML data type validation and the InfoPath UI. You can think of data validation as a way to guide your users to format their input as you determine. For example, if you want a phone number, you could easily use a text box that accepts any text the user types. But with data validation, you can disallow a phone number if it's not ten digits or has non-numeric characters. InfoPath's validation model is also extensible by using the InfoPath OM and writing custom form code.

A popular way to make your form template more interactive is to use **conditional formatting.** Take an expense report form that adds up prices from a list of items purchased during a business trip. You can design the form template so that if the sum of expenses is more than $1,000, the text for the total value will change from a calm black to an attention-getting bold red. Conditional formatting can be used throughout your form template to not only change fonts but to show and hide regions of your form as well.

It's great to have your users happily filling out your forms. But how do you make sense of the data saved in XML files? InfoPath has convenient, built-in reporting features to bring together data for you and your users. The first of these reporting functions is form merge. When a user selects multiple saved forms, InfoPath aggregates the data from each saved form into a single new one. A common use for this feature is rolling up status reports for the boss. InfoPath also exposes custom form merging for advanced developers by allowing them to write their own custom XSLT. InfoPath 2007 greatly improves this customization experience by supporting custom merge actions in design mode. We will discuss this in more detail in Chapter 12.

Another way to report InfoPath form data is to export it to Excel. Sometimes InfoPath may not be the best environment to do complex spreadsheet functions like pivot tables. Exporting the data to Excel is a simple click away, and you can customize the process by exporting specific parts of the data. Once data is exported to Excel, you can create pivot tables and charts to help you analyze the data. Since InfoPath is a powerful data-gathering tool, reporting options such as form merging and export to Excel help round out the story for bringing data together in a useful way. We will talk more about exporting form data to Excel in Chapter 12 as well.

InfoPath 2003 Service Pack 1

Even before InfoPath 2003 was out the door, InfoPath 2003 Service Pack 1 (SP1) was under construction; it was finally released on July 27, 2004. Convenience features, such as a table-drawing tool and the Format Painter, were added in SP1. Integration was introduced or enhanced, such as Web service support for ADO.NET DataSet objects. New controls, such as the File Attachment and Master/Detail controls, were added. Finally, InfoPath was also made more robust by adding features like crash recovery while filling out a form. Even if the computer doesn't crash, there's always the possibility that a power outage may occur (or the battery may die on your laptop). If you didn't think it could get any better, InfoPath 2003 SP1 was available as a free upgrade on the Web and fully backward compatible with 2003.

In tune with the numerous enhancements you would expect from a new release, InfoPath 2003 SP1 provided a much richer design experience. A lot of features that were already available in other Microsoft Office applications were integrated into InfoPath 2003 SP1. The new *Insert Layout Table*

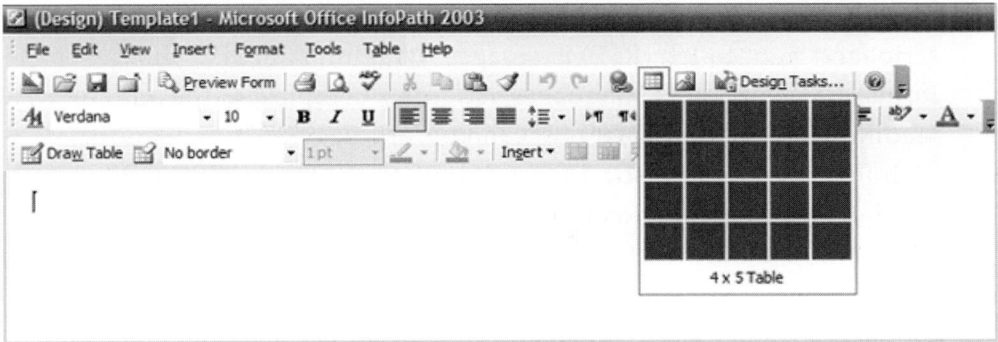

FIGURE 1.3: Insert Layout Table toolbar item

button (available on the *Standard* toolbar, as shown in Figure 1.3) enables you to quickly insert a table with as many as five columns and four rows.

Another tool that was added in SP1 to make table creation easier is the new *Tables* toolbar (Figure 1.4). This toolbar, which includes a table-drawing tool that can be turned on by clicking the *Draw Table* button, simplifies the process of creating tables tremendously. Using the table-drawing tool, you can easily draw a table any way you want without having to use the *Insert Table* dialog. The *Tables* toolbar also allows you to quickly and easily change various properties of any table, such as borders and shading. Considering that most InfoPath forms rely heavily on table layout, these tool improvements were welcome additions.

FIGURE 1.4: Tables toolbar

Another very useful tool added in SP1 is the **Format Painter.** You may already be familiar with this tool since it's also available in other Microsoft Office applications, such as Word. This tool allows you to quickly copy formatting from one part of the form template's view to another. You can select text or a control and copy its formatting to other text or another control in the form template.

The new table tools and the Format Painter are just two of the many features added to InfoPath 2003 SP1 in response to customer feedback. There are many more features that were added as well. Another feature added in response to feedback from international markets is support for complex script and right-to-left (RTL) languages. With InfoPath SP1, you can create forms that work with languages requiring complex script and/or RTL reading such as Arabic, Hebrew, Chinese, and so on.

InfoPath 2003 SP1 also added a slew of new controls to the *Controls* task pane. As with the other features added to improve the design experience, the decision about which controls to add in SP1 was based solely on customer feedback. (We will talk about each of these controls in more detail in Chapters 2 and 4.) The following controls were added in InfoPath 2003 SP1:

- Master/Detail
- File Attachment
- Choice Group
- Repeating Choice Group
- Choice Section
- Recursive Section controls
- Scrolling Region
- Vertical Label
- Ink Picture
- Custom controls

One of the most exciting additions to the *Controls* task pane was the support for custom controls. As of InfoPath 2003 SP1, you can use ActiveX technologies to build your own custom controls for InfoPath. We will talk about this in more detail in Chapter 19. (Support for custom controls has been expanded in InfoPath 2007 to include the ability to build controls without code. We'll talk more about this in the next section of this chapter and in Chapter 10.)

Data source enhancements, such as support for choice and recursion, were added in conjunction with the new Choice Group and Recursive Section controls. Customers clearly use industry-standard XML Schemas with choice constructs. As a result, InfoPath 2003 SP1 fully supports the XML Schema choice element and the Choice control that binds to it. Recursion is also very common in real-world XML Schemas. Recursion is when a schema element can contain itself. For example, a schema describing a hierarchy of employees can be described only by using recursion (since an employee can have employees under him or her). The Recursive Section control naturally supports recursion by allowing you to insert the same item as a child of itself. In SP1 there is no extra burden on the form designer to get this working properly, but in InfoPath 2003 it was a bit of a technical hurdle.

One of the most useful features introduced for nondevelopers in SP1 was the **Rules** feature. Overwhelming customer feedback was clear: Too many seemingly simple things required writing script. For example, showing a dialog or changing views required a few lines of script. With rules, setting up your form template to show a dialog is a few button clicks away. A more complex scenario would be to switch views, submit to a database, and set the value of a field—all in one rule and without code! Introducing rules to the masses meant less programming and more form function.

Creating a rich, functional form template is sufficient until you realize that your one form template does not fit all users. Sometimes data in the form shouldn't be shown to specific users. Imagine a form that tracks top issues, and each issue has a checkbox to set the entry as private. With InfoPath 2003 SP1, you can assign users to private and public **roles** and, in combination with conditional formatting, decide whether or not to show private data based on the current user role.

When it comes to trusting the data in a form, little can supersede the security offered by **digital signatures.** Highlights such as nonrepudiable partial signatures, cosigning, and countersigning allow the form template designer a greater level of freedom while not sacrificing the concept of "secure by default." Factor in the extended programmability support for digitally signed forms, and you have a complete solution for protecting form data.

Arguably one of the most anticipated features in the SP1 release was the introduction of **managed code** support. With the world buzzing about .NET, customers could not wait to get their hands on the free Visual Studio Toolkit plug-in. Along with managed code support, a revised and expanded programming interface, or object model was included. In Chapter 15 we will introduce you to the new InfoPath 2007 OM.

Not only can InfoPath simplify the creation of forms but, as mentioned earlier, since InfoPath forms are based on XML, they can be integrated easily into existing business processes and workflows. By using InfoPath with Microsoft Office SharePoint Server or Outlook, you can quickly build workflow processes in a fraction of the time it would take with other forms development tools. We will talk in more detail about workflow in Chapter 13.

With the growing popularity of Tablet PCs, it seems only natural that InfoPath would include support for these devices. InfoPath 2003 included limited support for Tablet PCs that was expanded in SP1. In design mode, the Ink Picture control enables you to include sections in your form template that are exclusively for handwriting with the Tablet PC pen. When editing the form, all controls support an ink-entry mode that allows you to write in them with your Tablet PC pen. Your writing will then be converted to text. While in ink-entry mode, InfoPath supports many of the same gestures to edit and correct text you may already be familiar with.

SP1 also brought enhancements in form template deployment. InfoPath 2003 made it very difficult to send form templates by e-mail for users to fill out. Form template designers had to jump through a few technical hoops to get it to work properly. It was also inconvenient for recipients as well. The addition of **e-mail publishing** in SP1 opened up the potential for anyone with an e-mail address and InfoPath to fill out a form. Deploying a form template via e-mail is only a quick click away. Once a template is deployed via e-mail, users can open the e-mail message in Outlook and start filling out the form.

In addition to enabling you to build more elaborate form templates, new features also enhance the process of filling out forms. One very useful new feature is the *Fill Out a Form* dialog (now called the *Getting Started* dialog in InfoPath 2007). This dialog, shown in Figure 1.5, gives you a starting point for editing forms and a central location for managing them. Using the dashboard, you have easy access to forms you've filled out before by clicking the *Recently Used Forms* link in the left-hand side of the dialog. You can also add forms to your list of favorites by clicking the *Add to Favorites* link on the right-hand side and keep track of your favorites via the *Favorites* link on the left. You can download forms from Office Online by clicking the *Forms on Office Online* link or design a new or existing form template by clicking either the *Design a Form* or *Design this Form* links. This new dialog greatly simplifies the process of creating, filling out, and managing forms.

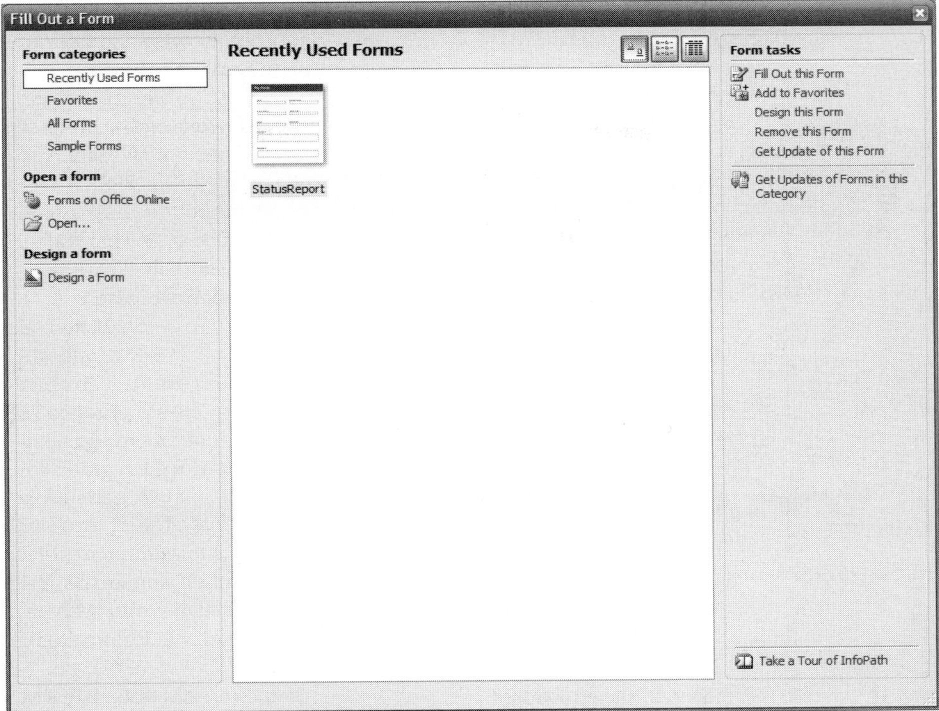

FIGURE 1.5: Fill Out a Form dialog in InfoPath 2003 SP1

InfoPath 2007

The next wave of Office products (the 2007 Microsoft Office system) includes the next version of InfoPath—InfoPath 2007. As with previous versions, all feature additions in InfoPath 2007 were based on customer feedback. InfoPath 2007 not only includes improvements in the core client application but also finally satisfies the number one customer request—the ability to fill out forms without having to install the InfoPath client application on every user's computer. To satisfy this request, InfoPath 2007 introduces a sister product called InfoPath Forms Services.

InfoPath Forms Services brings reality to the ultimate deployment story: publishing your InfoPath form template to the Web. Anyone anywhere, on any device, can now fill out your form. Feedback dictated the InfoPath Forms Services would need to reach UNIX users running Mozilla, Mac OS folks with Safari, and even always-on-the-go businesspeople with

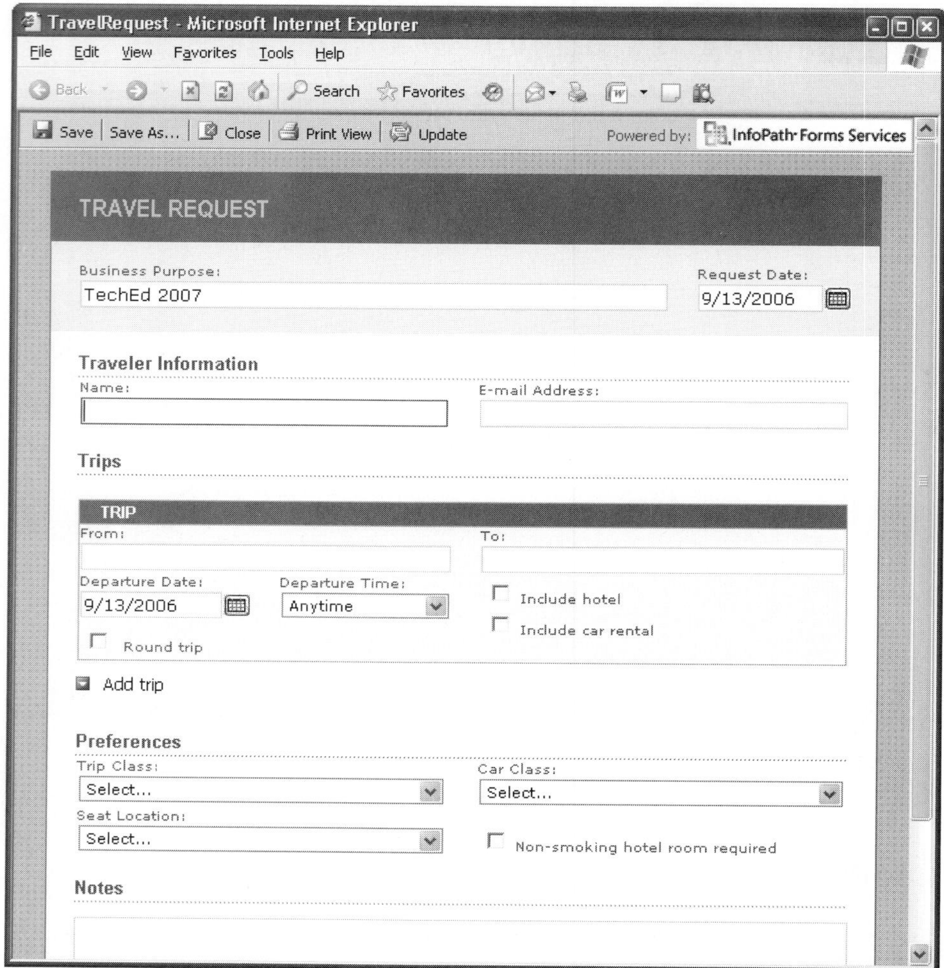

FIGURE 1.6: Filling out a browser-enabled form template in Internet Explorer

their HTML-enabled PDAs and smart phones. Forms are filled out in full fidelity with data validation, conditional formatting, and even custom form code, to name a few features. (Figure 1.6 shows an InfoPath form being filled out in a browser.)

The key to making InfoPath Forms Services successful was to maintain as much compatibility as possible with the InfoPath client application. As a result, most form templates created with the InfoPath client can simply be reused "as is" in Forms Services. The InfoPath client application helps support the few limitations of InfoPath Forms Services by offering two modes: InfoPath-only or browser-enabled form templates. There are no restrictions in the InfoPath-only mode. In the browser-enabled mode, some features that are not supported (either in full or in part) are disabled or removed from the InfoPath design mode UI. When designing a new form template, you choose whether to design a client or browser-enabled form template. However, you are free to change it at any time. To support switching from an InfoPath-only to a browser-enabled form template, the design mode offers the **Design Checker,** which reports form features added during InfoPath-only mode that are incompatible with InfoPath Forms Services. (We'll discuss the Design Checker in Chapter 14.) The Design Checker also helps maintain compatibility with InfoPath 2003 SP1 if your users are not all using InfoPath 2007 yet.

You can expect your browser-enabled forms to behave similarly in InfoPath Forms Services as you would with the InfoPath client application. All conditional formatting, data validation, rules, multiple views, digital signatures, security settings, and most controls are respected. There are so many similarities between the InfoPath Forms Services and the InfoPath client application that it's a more interesting conversation to discuss what the InfoPath Forms Services *does not* support.

Due to the InfoPath form architecture and the tremendous flexibility in form configuration, some of the more advanced features of the InfoPath client are not supported. For example, forms with script are not supported. Managed form code works as expected, but showing UI, such as a message box, by calling methods in the InfoPath or Windows Forms object models, is not. Another major difference between InfoPath and Forms Services is the behavior of data connections. The security model of data connections is more restrictive with browser forms. A complete discussion of browser-supported features can be found in Chapters 14 and 17.

InfoPath Forms Services is built on top of the rich capabilities of the SharePoint Server 2007 platform, which includes Windows SharePoint Services. You can harness the full power of SharePoint sites, document libraries, lists, and other SharePoint-specific features. The SharePoint Server package adds portal features such as Workflow Services and Enterprise Search. Partially filled forms in the browser can be saved to a form library and ultimately submitted to a SharePoint document library, for example. Administrators can configure InfoPath Forms Services settings from the command line, but the SharePoint Central Administration site offers a more user-friendly option for doing so.

A favorite feature for Web designers is the ability to host a browser-enabled form as a control in a Web page. Since Forms Services is implemented as an ASP.NET control, Web design gurus familiar with ASP.NET will have no problem incorporating forms into their existing Web infrastructure. Various events exposed from the form control serve as liaisons between the control and the hosting page. This helps tie your form intimately into the overall design and experience of your Web page.

The InfoPath Forms Services package is meant not as a replacement but rather as a complement to filling out forms with the InfoPath client. The relationship between Forms Services and the InfoPath client application can be compared to the relationship between Outlook Web Access (OWA) and the Outlook client application. OWA tries to do the job of the Outlook client on the Web but offers fewer features than the Outlook client application; for example, OWA lacks offline and client-only mail rules. As with OWA and Outlook, when the InfoPath client is available, you would prefer to use it over the server due to the fact that the InfoPath client provides a richer set of features. Even with the advancements in browser and Web technology, it is nearly impossible to do the same things in a Web browser as you would in the InfoPath client. However, most people don't really notice what is missing when they use a browser-enabled form. Limitations aside, InfoPath Forms Services is a truly remarkable advancement for creating ubiquitous InfoPath forms.

In addition to meeting the number one customer request with Microsoft InfoPath Forms Services, the InfoPath team also responded to feedback about the InfoPath client application by adding many new features.

The first change you may notice when opening InfoPath 2007 for the first time is that the *Fill Out a Form* dialog has changed slightly. First of all, it's now called the *Getting Started* dialog, as shown in Figure 1.7. A few items have been rearranged, and a list of the most recently used and created forms appears on the left to give easy access to those forms.

Next, when you click on the *Design a Form Template* link in the *Getting Started* dialog, you will notice another new dialog—the *Design a Form Template* dialog (Figure 1.8). Just as the *Getting Started* dialog greatly simplifies

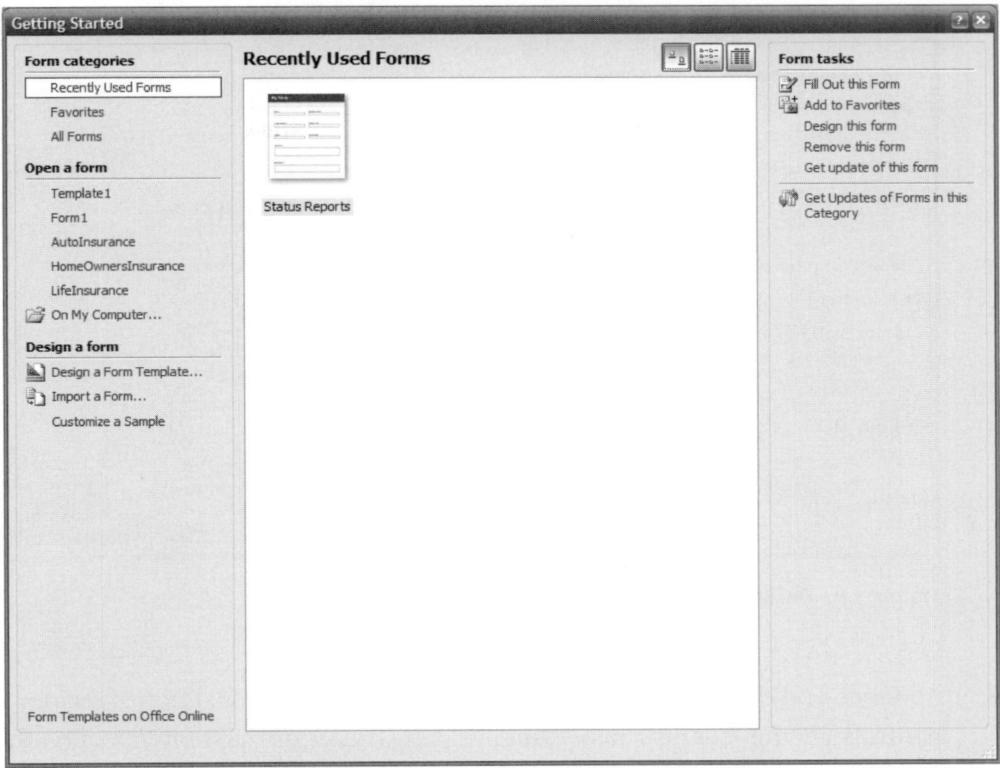

FIGURE 1.7: Getting Started dialog

the process of filling out forms, the *Design a Form Template* dialog does the same for designing forms. From this dialog, you can choose what type of form to design and the data source for your form design. (The different types of form designs will be discussed in more detail throughout this book. Data sources will be discussed further in Chapter 3.)

From the *Design a Form Template* dialog, you can also choose to customize one of the sample form templates installed with InfoPath or to download form templates from Office Online. From this dialog you can also import a form from another application or open a recently used form template. With InfoPath 2007, you can import forms from Word or Excel or download other importers from third-party vendors. (Form importers are discussed in more detail in Chapter 21.) As you can see, the *Design a Form Template* dialog is extremely useful for managing your form templates.

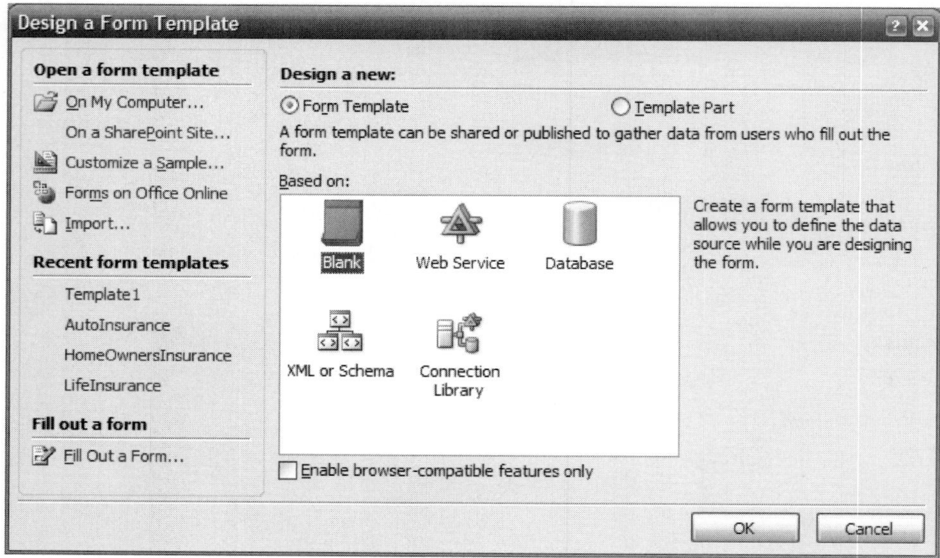

FIGURE 1.8: Design a Form Template dialog

Once you design a form in InfoPath 2007, you might next notice the new controls in the *Controls* task pane. Again, based on customer feedback, InfoPath 2007 added new controls—the Combo Box, the Horizontal Repeating Table, the Multiple-Selection List Box, and the Horizontal Region—which will all be discussed in Chapters 2 and 4. However, the most exciting addition in terms of controls is the ability to create custom controls with no code. InfoPath **template parts** allow you to create custom controls that are aggregates of existing controls already built into the InfoPath design mode. In addition, you can add rules, calculations, data validation, and even secondary data sources to template parts you design, thus creating reusable components with no code required. (Template parts are discussed in detail in Chapter 10.)

Another appealing addition to InfoPath 2007 is integration with Outlook. **InfoPath e-mail forms,** as the feature is called, enables users to fill out forms in the body of an e-mail instead of having to open the InfoPath client application. InfoPath's deeper integration in Outlook will be discussed in detail in Chapter 13.

Some of the other additions to the InfoPath client application are not as obvious. Many performance improvements enhance the usability of

InfoPath. Several long operations now offer progress dialogs that can be canceled. Also, cases where multiple dialogs used to be displayed now show only one.

A few more of the many feature additions include Information Rights Management (IRM), date calculations, support for read-only views, bound fields in headers and footers, and better support for offline forms.

In addition to the new features for form template designers and form users, many features were added specifically for developers. The first notable addition is integration of the InfoPath design mode into Visual Studio Tools for Office (VSTO). Now the design experience is completely integrated into Visual Studio 2005. Such InfoPath design-time features as the *Controls* and *Data Source* task panes are now toolbars in Visual Studio. Visual Studio integration will be discussed at length in Chapter 16.

As we mentioned earlier, InfoPath 2003 initially included support for scripting and offered the Microsoft Script Editor as the environment for writing script code. InfoPath 2003 SP1 included support for managed code through the Microsoft Office InfoPath 2003 Toolkit for Visual Studio .NET. And, as we just mentioned, InfoPath 2007 includes full integration with Visual Studio. But what if you just want to enhance your forms a bit without installing Visual Studio or resorting to script? Well, now you can do that with Visual Studio Tools for Applications (VSTA). With VSTA, you can use managed code anywhere you would have used script in InfoPath 2003 and SP1. We will talk more about VSTA in Chapter 15.

Another cool feature addition geared toward developers in InfoPath 2007 is support for add-ins. Developers can write their own add-in components using the Component Object Model (COM) or managed code. These add-ins enable you to control or modify InfoPath's behavior and add functionality that does not exist in the core InfoPath client application. Since add-ins are supported by other Microsoft Office applications, developers can write code once that will work across applications. The addition of add-ins also makes it possible for InfoPath (and other Microsoft Office applications) to provide support for Custom Task Panes, which allow you to add your own rich content to a task pane built into the core application. (These Custom Task Panes are different than the HTML custom task panes included in InfoPath 2003.) Add-ins will be discussed in Chapter 20.

As you can probably tell just from this introduction, InfoPath contains a very rich set of features just in the InfoPath client application (not to mention all the features available in InfoPath Forms Services). In Chapter 18, we will talk about how it is now possible to take advantage of these form-editing features in your own application. Many developers have asked for the ability to host InfoPath since InfoPath 2003 was released. With InfoPath 2007, it is now possible to add rich form editing to your own applications by reusing InfoPath. This is such a popular scenario that other Microsoft Office applications have taken advantage of this feature. Word, Excel, and PowerPoint now show their document properties in a **Document Information Panel** that is actually an InfoPath form. The Document Information Panel includes all the features you have come to expect from an InfoPath form. In Chapter 18, we will show you how you can add these features to your own application.

What's Next?

You may be thinking, "With the many features available in InfoPath, where do I start?" That's a good question. The answer obviously depends on your level of expertise. If you have no experience with InfoPath, start at the beginning. Part I is all about designing form templates from scratch and assumes you have no prior knowledge of InfoPath. Starting with Chapter 2, we will walk you through very basic form design. Each chapter in Part I may assume knowledge of and build on previous chapters. By the time you finish Part I, you can consider yourself an expert form designer and will be able to create complex form templates from scratch with no code.

If you are an application developer and already know a bit about InfoPath, feel free to skim over Part I and then jump right into Part II, where we'll talk about advanced form design. We'll discuss adding code to your InfoPath form templates (both script and managed code), using advanced features of InfoPath Forms Services, creating add-ins, hosting InfoPath, creating custom components with ActiveX, and much more.

So, now that you know a little about InfoPath and where to go next, let's get started.

2

Basics of InfoPath Form Design

Getting Started

In Chapter 1 you learned a little about the basic purpose of InfoPath and got a small glimpse of the features available in this form tool. Now it's time to start digging in. In this chapter, you will learn about the basics of designing an InfoPath form. We will talk about the various ways to create forms as well as the common features you will use in most forms. In the next few chapters, you will learn about more advanced form design concepts, such as data binding and advanced controls.

You can run InfoPath in two modes: design mode and fill-out-a-form mode. The design mode is that which you use to design form templates and is the mode we will work in for most of this book. The fill-out-a-form mode is the mode that InfoPath runs in when users fill out a form and is also the mode that InfoPath is in when you initially start the application, even before you open a form.

> **TIP Changing the Start Mode**
>
> In order to change the mode that InfoPath starts in, you can use the `/design` command-line parameter when running InfoPath (e.g., `infopath.exe /design`).

What Is a Form Template Anyway?

Before we start designing a form, let's talk about what a form template is. A form template provides the blueprint on which users fill out forms. When talking about designing a form, we are actually referring to the form template. In this book, we will use the phrases "designing a form template" and "designing a form" interchangeably. When talking about designing the form or form template, we will be referring to InfoPath running in design mode. Obviously, when we talk about filling out a form, we are referring to the fill-out-a-form mode. In this case, the user is actually filling out a form based on a form template. Think of it this way—there is one form template upon which multiple unique forms can be filled out. The form template is, therefore, the blueprint used to create new forms of that type.

But what exactly is a form template? A form template in InfoPath is a collection of data, views, resources, and a manifest stored in a cabinet (CAB) file, which is a compressed file format somewhat like a ZIP file. InfoPath uses the .xsn file extension for form templates. The data resides in the underlying data source, which, as its name implies, is the source of the data. This data source could be an XML file, Web service, database, or SharePoint list, for example, where the data entered into the form is stored. In this case, this data source is referred to as the main data source since it is the main source of the data for the form. In a form template, there is always a main data source where the user-entered data is stored.

In addition to the main data source, the form can contain one or more secondary data sources. These secondary data sources can be used to populate different parts of the form, such as a drop-down list of cities and states. (The main data source can also be used to populate different parts of the form.) We will talk in great detail about data and data sources in Chapters 3 and 6.

The form template also contains at least one view, which provides a way to visualize the data. This part of the form template contains the layout for the form and any controls into which users enter data. We will talk about layout and controls in this chapter and in Chapter 4. The form template may actually contain multiple views based on the data source so you can present the underlying data in many ways. For example, you may want to create different views of the data for different languages or to present part of the data in one view and the rest in other views.

The form template can also contain various resources. These could be pictures you add to your form or any other type of file you want to store with the form template. Static pictures added to the form are automatically added to the form template as resources. Other resources can be added to the form using the Resource Manager, which is available through the *Resource Files* menu item on the *Tools* menu in design mode.

Finally, the form template contains a form definition file, sometimes referred to as a manifest. This manifest contains all the information about the form template, such as which files and resources, special editing behaviors (e.g., spell checking, auto-complete), and other data-centric features (e.g., rules and calculations) are included in the template.

Let's start designing our first form template by talking about how to use InfoPath in design mode.

Design a Form Template Dialog

When you start InfoPath, the first thing you see is the *Getting Started* dialog (Figure 2.1). On the left-hand side of this dialog toward the bottom is the

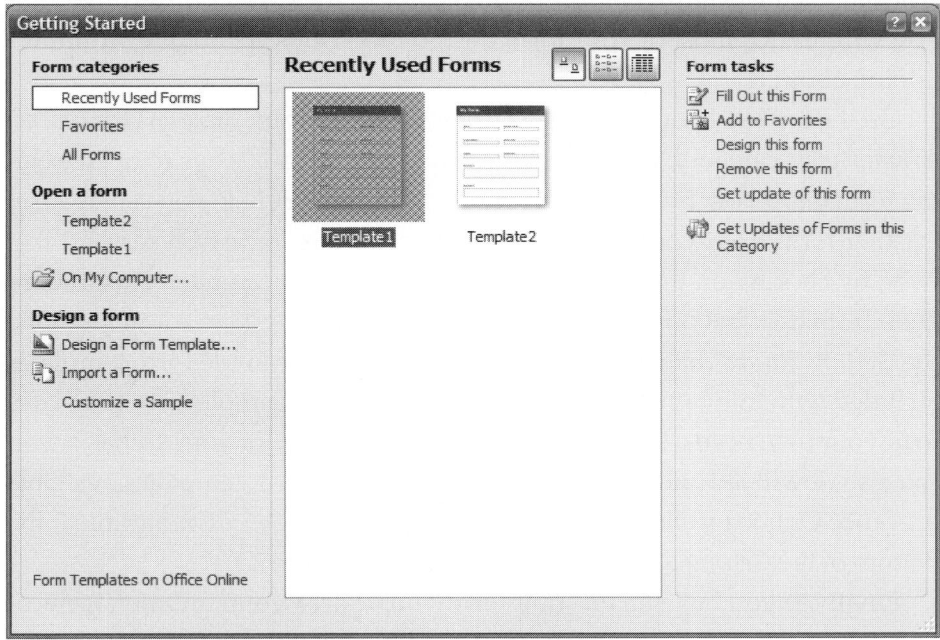

FIGURE 2.1: Getting Started dialog

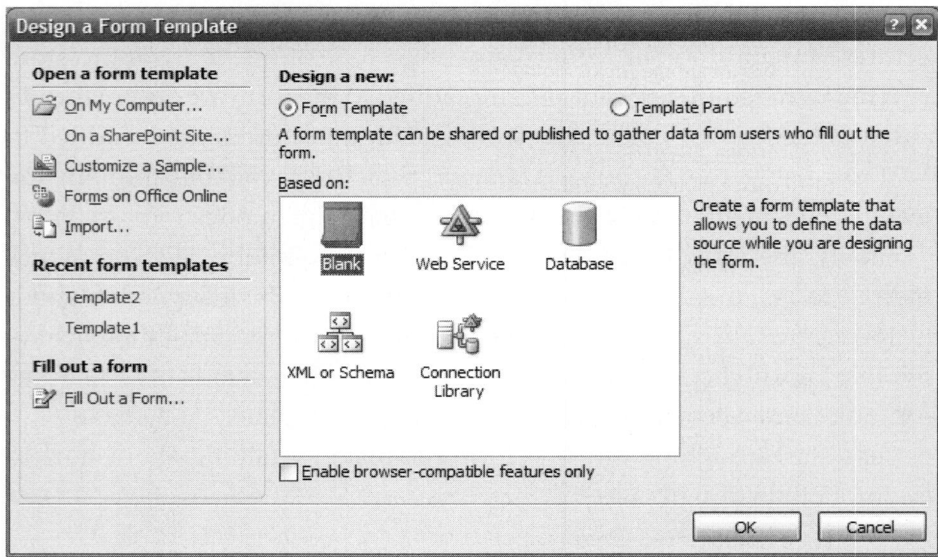

FIGURE 2.2: Design a Form Template dialog

Design a Form Template link, which, when clicked, opens the *Design a Form Template* dialog (Figure 2.2). Since this dialog is the common starting point you will use for most of your form design tasks, let's spend a few minutes talking about it.

On the top left-hand side of the *Design a Form Template* dialog is the *Open a form template* category, which provides you with various ways to open existing form templates. By clicking on the *On My Computer* link, you can open an existing form from your computer, a network share, or a Web server. Likewise, by clicking on the *On a SharePoint Site* link, you can open a form template from a SharePoint site. When you click on the *Customize a Sample* link, the *Getting Started* dialog reopens and shows the five sample form templates included with InfoPath 2007. You can customize these sample form templates to fit your own needs. If none of the samples will work for your scenario, you can also download and customize one of the many form templates available on Office Online by clicking on the *Form Templates on Office Online* link at the bottom of the *Getting Started* dialog, as shown in Figure 2.1.

Finally, if you have an existing form you've created in another application such as Word or Excel that you would like to migrate to InfoPath, you can click on the *Import* link on the *Design a Form Template* dialog. (This link is also available from the *Getting Started* dialog but is named *Import a Form* there.) InfoPath 2007, by default, includes two form importers—Word and Excel. InfoPath also provides a form importer framework that allows third parties to create their own form template importers. (We'll talk more about form importers and also show you how to create your own in Chapter 21.)

The next category on the left side of the *Design a Form Template* dialog is *Recent form templates.* This category lists the most recent form templates you have designed. The forms listed in this category will most likely be the ones you design the most. The final category on the left, *Fill out a form,* contains only one link, which will take you back to the *Getting Started* dialog.

TIP Changing the Number of Recent Form Templates

By default, the last four form templates you designed will appear in the list of recent form templates on the *Design a Form Template* dialog. You can change the number of form templates listed by opening the *Options* dialog, which is available on the *Tools* menu. On the *General* tab of this dialog, you can turn off the recently used file list or change the number of files listed. Note, however, that this will affect all the places in the product that have a list of recently used files (such as the *Getting Started* dialog), not just the *Design a Form Template* dialog.

When you are designing a form from scratch, you will be most interested in the category called *Design a new,* which takes up the entire right-hand side of the *Design a Form Template* dialog. From here, you can choose exactly what you want to design—either a form template or a template part. (Template parts are discussed in detail in Chapter 10.) Most of the time, you will want to choose the default option, which is to design a form template. From there, under the *Based on* section of the dialog, you can choose how you want to start designing your form. Table 2.1 lists the different available starting points.

Finally, at the bottom of the *Design a Form Template* dialog is a checkbox for enabling browser-compatible features only. This allows you to design a form that users can fill by using a Web browser, without requiring them to have the InfoPath client application installed. Of course, in this case, you

TABLE 2.1: Starting Points for Form Design

Starting Point	Purpose
Blank	Creates a new blank form. InfoPath will automatically create the underlying data source as you insert controls.
Web Service	Creates a new form template from a Web service. The underlying XML data structure comes from the Web service definition.
Database	Creates a new form from an existing Microsoft SQL Server or Access database. The underlying data source is inferred from the structure of the database.
XML or Schema	Creates a new form template from an existing XML file or XML Schema. If you specify an XML file, the underlying XML data structure for the form template will be inferred from the structure of the XML. If you specify an XML Schema file, the underlying XML data structure comes from the schema file itself.
Connection Library	Allows you to browse a Microsoft Office server for a data connection that you can use as the basis for your form template.

must publish your form template to a server that has InfoPath Forms Services installed. (InfoPath Forms Services is discussed in Chapters 14 and 17.)

Before we can talk about some of the more advanced ways to design forms, such as from a Web service, database, or other data source (which we'll talk about more in Chapter 6), it's important to understand the basics of form design. What better way to understand the basics than to create a form from scratch.

Creating a New Blank Form Template

Let's create an employment application form that prospective employees can use to apply for a position at the fictional MOI Consulting Corporation, a company that offers software consulting services. Creating this form template from scratch is very easy. The first thing you should always do before creating a form is to define your requirements. We recommend you do this for all the form templates you design. Doing so will make designing them much easier. You should define not only the intention of your form but also the layout and data structure. Let's go through the requirements process briefly for the employment application form. (We will demonstrate this only for this form. For samples in the following chapters, we will assume that the requirements have been defined ahead of time.)

The first thing we should define for our employment application form is our requirements specification. Our requirements specification should include a basic high-level summary of what the form will do, such as the following: The MOI Consulting employment application enables prospective employees to apply for open positions throughout the company. The user of the form will be able to search and apply for one or more jobs across the company. When applying for a position, the prospective employee will enter pertinent information, such as name, address, and phone number. The form will require that the user attach a résumé when applying for a job.

As you can see, the high-level summary broadly defines what the form will do. In reality, your requirements specification will likely contain much more detail, including drawings of the form layout. For this sample, we'll design the layout of the form template as we go. However, we do want to define the data requirements for our form ahead of time. Doing so now will make it much easier for us to decide which controls should be included in the form template and, ultimately, what type of data will be stored in the underlying data source. Typically, when you define your data requirements, you will also define the type of data (e.g., string, decimal, currency, date, and so on). The data requirements for the MOI Consulting employment application are defined in Table 2.2, which also indicates whether the data is displayed by the form or input by the user. (A typical employment application may contain much more data than this. However, for the purposes of this sample form, we are collecting only a limited amount of data.)

TABLE 2.2: Data Requirements for the MOI Consulting Employment Application

Data Item	Data Type	Source/Description
First name	String	User
Last name	String	User
Phone number	String	User
E-mail address	String	User
Street address	String	User
City	String	User
State	String	User
Postal code	Number	User
Country	String	User (chosen from a list of countries)
Minimum salary desired	Currency	User
Position name	String	Form (displays the position names for the user to choose from)
Position ID	Number	User (stored in the form data when the user chooses a position name, which corresponds to a position ID)
Position description	Formatted text	Form (read-only data based on the position ID)
Comments	Formatted text	User
Résumé	File or hyperlink	User

Now that we've defined our requirements and the data we want to collect, let's create our form template. From the *Design a Form Template* pane shown in Figure 2.2, just click on the *Blank* icon in the *Based on* section of the dialog, and then click the *OK* button. InfoPath then switches into design mode and presents you with a new blank form, as shown in

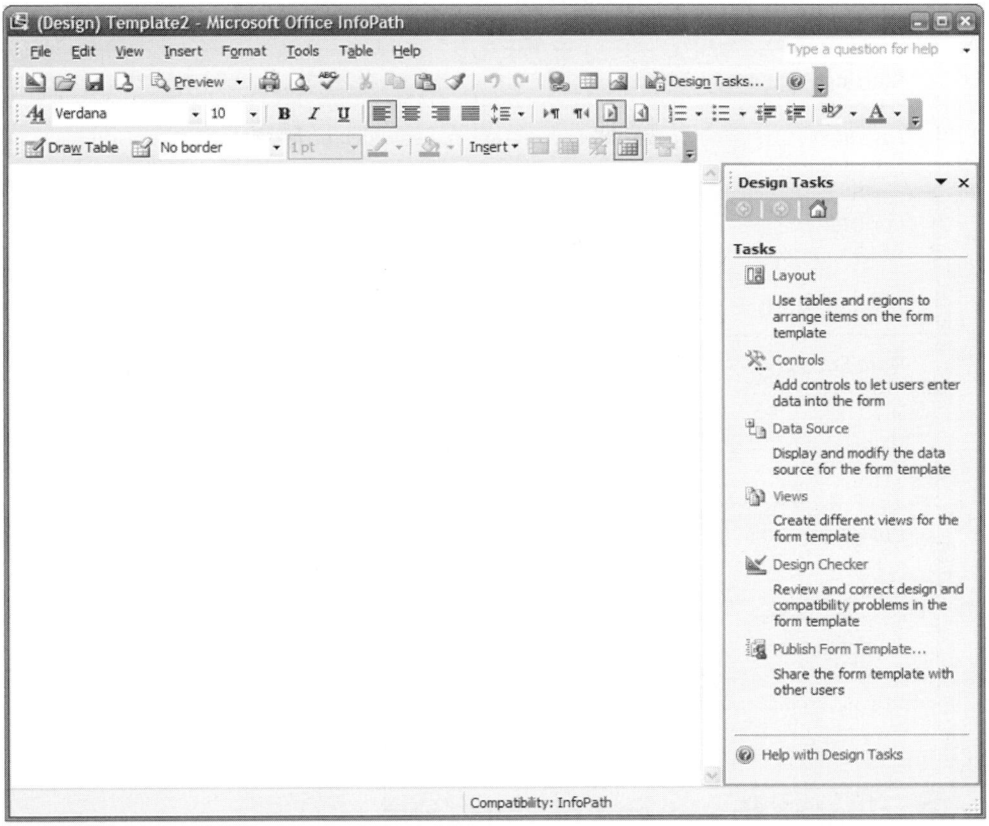

FIGURE 2.3: New blank form

Figure 2.3. As you can see, on the right side of InfoPath in design mode is the *Design Tasks* task pane. This task pane lists all the common tasks you will perform when designing a form. Each of these is listed in Table 2.3. Typically, when you design a form using InfoPath, you will follow each of the tasks in the *Design Tasks* pane in order. This is especially true if you are designing a new form. In certain cases, however, you may choose to perform one or more tasks multiple times or some tasks not at all. To the left of the *Design Tasks* pane is an empty area called the design surface or view. The design surface is where you set up the form's layout and place the controls into which users will enter data when filling out the form.

TABLE 2.3: Design Tasks Pane

Starting Point	Purpose
Layout	Opens the *Layout* task pane, which provides layout controls you can use to arrange and organize your form template.
Controls	Opens the *Controls* task pane, which provides many different form controls you can add to your form. These controls allow users to add data when filling out the form. The controls can also be used to group other controls.
Data Source	Allows you to modify the data source behind the form template directly. (See Chapters 3 and 6 for more on data sources.)
Views	Opens the *Views* task pane, which allows you to add other views to your form template and to switch between existing views.
Design Checker	Opens the *Design Checker* task pane, which shows you warnings and errors in your form template and helps you correct them. (See Chapter 14 for more on the Design Checker.)
Publish Form Template	Starts the Publish wizard, which enables you to make your form template available so users can create forms.

Designing the Layout of Your Form

Using the Layout Task Pane

Since the first thing you normally will do when designing an InfoPath form is design its layout, the first task shown in the *Design Tasks* pane is *Layout*. Clicking on this link opens the *Layout* task pane (Figure 2.4). When you open this task pane, you will notice that most of the actions involve tables, which are the main design construct used in InfoPath to lay out text and controls in your form templates.

The *Layout* task pane makes the process of designing the layout of your form much easier by giving you a few common table formats that you can

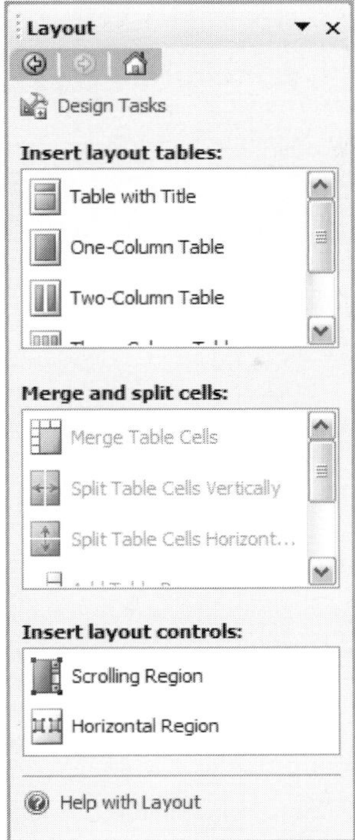

FIGURE 2.4: Layout task pane

insert into your form template. For example, if you click on the *Table with Title* icon, a table with two rows is inserted into the form template. The first row of this table is where you insert the title for your form. The second row is where you insert the rest of your form content. We gave our sample form the title "MOI Consulting Employment Application," as you can see in Figure 2.5. You can also click on one of the other icons to insert a one-, two-, or three-column table. Clicking on *Custom Table* lets you create a table with as many as 63 columns and 100 rows. Using these tools, you can insert many separate tables or nest tables within each other to create an intricate form design.

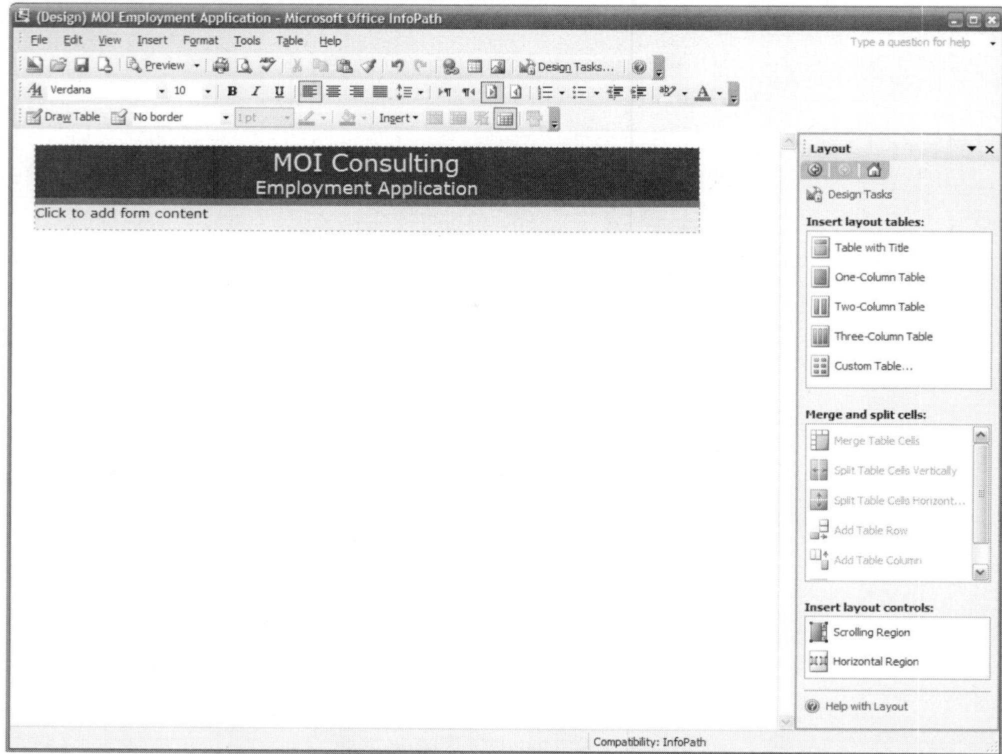

FIGURE 2.5: Employment application form template with title added by using Table with Title

Gridlines

By default, when InfoPath is in design mode, layout tables have dashed borders, which are called **gridlines.** These borders show up only in design mode and not in fill-out-a-form mode. Their purpose is solely to show you the boundaries of the table rows and columns. You can hide the gridlines by clicking on the *Hide Gridlines* button in the *Tables* toolbar. This enables you to see how the form will look when the user is filling it out. When gridlines are hidden, you can click on the *Show Gridlines* button to show them. If you want your layout tables to have borders when users fill out the form, set up borders in the *Borders and Shading* dialog, which you can access from the *Format* menu (or the context menu for the table) when the insertion point is within the table.

Once you insert the basic structure for your form and place the insertion point inside one of the tables (by clicking inside the table), the *Merge and split cells* section of the *Layout* task pane becomes active, as shown in Figure 2.6. (The *Merge Table Cells* item becomes active only if you select multiple table cells.) This section of the *Layout* task pane allows you to customize your layout tables by doing such things as merging and splitting cells or inserting more rows or columns. (These actions are also available through the *Table* menu and *Tables* toolbar, as well as many other commands that will help you customize your layout.) Since we know our data requirements, let's use the commands in the *Merge and split cells* section of the *Layout* pane to customize the table we inserted earlier.

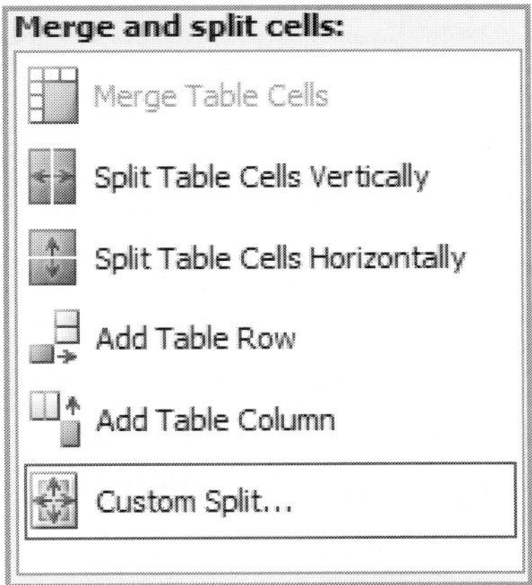

FIGURE 2.6: Merge and split cells category of the Layout task pane

You can place the cursor inside the second row of the layout table by clicking where it says *Click to add form content*. We know from Table 2.2 that we want to give the user a place to enter his or her name. Since we are storing the name in two parts—last name and first name—we will need to have two places in the form for the user to enter this information. Therefore, we want to split the second row of our layout table into two cells—one for the first name and one for the last name. (Of course, splitting the row into two cells isn't a requirement for the user to be able to enter data, but it will make the form look a little better.) To split the row into two cells, click on *Split Table Cells Vertically* in the *Layout* task pane. Finally, so that the user knows what data to enter, let's add instructive text to each cell. Figure 2.7 shows the results of these changes.

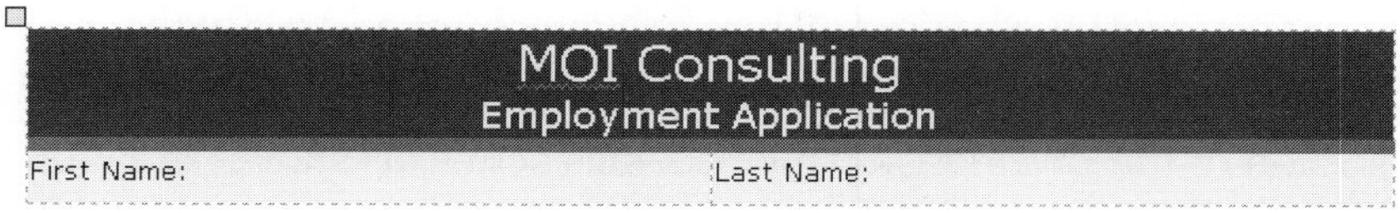

FIGURE 2.7: Employment application form template with cells for first and last names

> **TIP Selecting the Entire Table**
>
> In Figure 2.7, you may notice a small square in the upper-left corner of the layout table that becomes active when you place the insertion point inside the table. If you click on this square, the entire table becomes selected. Note that if you are designing a form to work with an RTL language, the square will be in the upper-right corner of the table.

Next, let's add a new row so that we can insert controls to allow the user to enter address information. To add a new row, place the insertion point in the last row of the table and then click on the *Add Table Row* command in the *Layout* task pane. When you add the new row, you'll notice that it looks exactly like the row above it—it has two cells. However, we want just one cell so that the user has a lot of space to enter the address. In order to make this row only have one cell, we need to merge the two cells. To do this, the cells to merge must be selected. If you have just inserted the row, all cells in the row should be selected. If not, then just move your mouse to the left of the row (until the cursor becomes an arrow) and click to select all cells in the current row. Next, click *Merge Table Cells* in the *Layout* task pane.

Now that the cells are merged, add some descriptive information about what the user will enter in this part of the form, in this case, the address (Figure 2.8). You may want to format this new text to make it look nice.

FIGURE 2.8: Employment application form template with a row for address information

Even though you should plan the layout of your form template ahead of time, you will probably refine the layout as you perform other form design tasks. Also, as new requirements arise, you will have to change the look-and-feel of your form. InfoPath provides all the tools you need to easily customize your layout by using the *Layout* task pane, the *Table* menu, and the *Tables* toolbar. Since much of the layout of our employment application form will depend on controls we want to use for data entry, we'll continue to change the layout throughout this chapter.

One final category of the *Layout* task pane that we should note before moving on is the *Insert layout controls* section. The two items in this section of the task pane pertain to layout but are more akin to controls, so we will talk about them in Chapter 4.

Color Schemes

If you are creating the sample form template as you read this chapter, when you inserted a layout table with a title, you may have noticed that the title row is dark blue and the rest of the table is light blue. Certain types of form content, such as layout tables and Repeating Table controls (which we'll talk about later in this chapter), use color schemes to help you design better-looking forms. Color schemes help you make your forms a bit more exciting by adding color. If you choose colors that are in the active color scheme, you can be sure that the colors will match. In InfoPath 2007, the default color scheme is *Blue,* but it's very easy to change it to something that suits your tastes. To do so, just open the *Color Schemes* task pane (Figure 2.9) by clicking on the *Format* menu and then *Color Schemes.* Next, click on one of the color scheme palettes in the task pane. It's as easy as that. The layout tables and Repeating Table controls change to use the colors in the new scheme. Since it's so easy, you can experiment with different color schemes until you find the one you like best.

> **TIP Accessing the Design Tasks Pane from Anywhere**
>
> If at any time you wish to return to the *Design Tasks* task pane, click on the *Design Tasks* menu item from the *View* menu. Alternatively, if you have opened any of the task panes from the *Design Tasks* pane, you can just click on the *Design Tasks* link at the top of that pane.

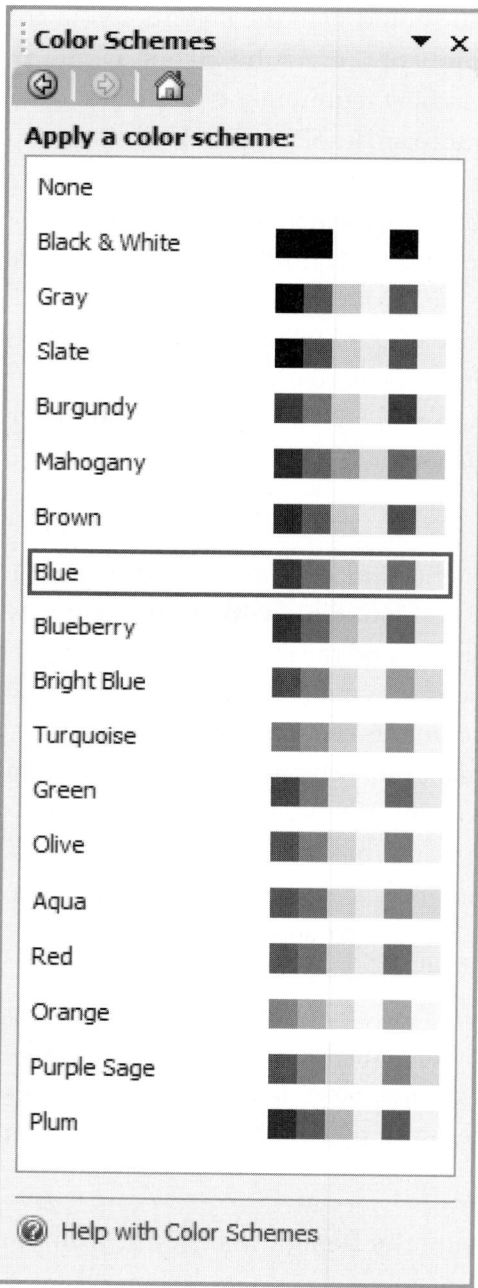

FIGURE 2.9: Color Schemes task pane

Using Controls

Once you've designed the layout of your form, you'll want to give your users a way to enter data. Therefore, the next step is to add controls. InfoPath includes many controls you can use for various purposes, such as allowing users to type in formatted or unformatted text, retrieving data from a database, or grouping multiple controls. There are many ways to insert controls into your form; by far, the easiest is to use the *Controls* task pane (Figure 2.10). Open this task pane by clicking on the *Controls* link in the *Design Tasks* pane. InfoPath provides so many controls that they are grouped into different categories to help you find them. We will describe the basic controls in this chapter but will postpone our discussion of the advanced controls until Chapter 4.

Forms Services

Some controls are not available when designing browser-enabled forms.

From the *Controls* task pane, you can insert a control into your form in one of two ways. The first way is simply to click on the control in the *Controls* task pane. This will insert the control at the current location of the insertion point in the design surface. The second way is to drag the control from the task pane into the design surface. Using the second method, you have a little more control over where the control is inserted. In this case, you don't need to first move the insertion point to the location where you want to insert the control.

When you insert a control, no matter how you've done it, InfoPath does a few things behind the scenes. First, a view representation of the control is created. This view representation is the visual aspect of the control. In other words, it's what the user sees. Next, for most controls, if the *Automatically create data source* checkbox is checked in the *Controls* task pane (which it is by default when designing a blank form), InfoPath creates fields or group elements in the data source. These fields or groups result in XML Schema

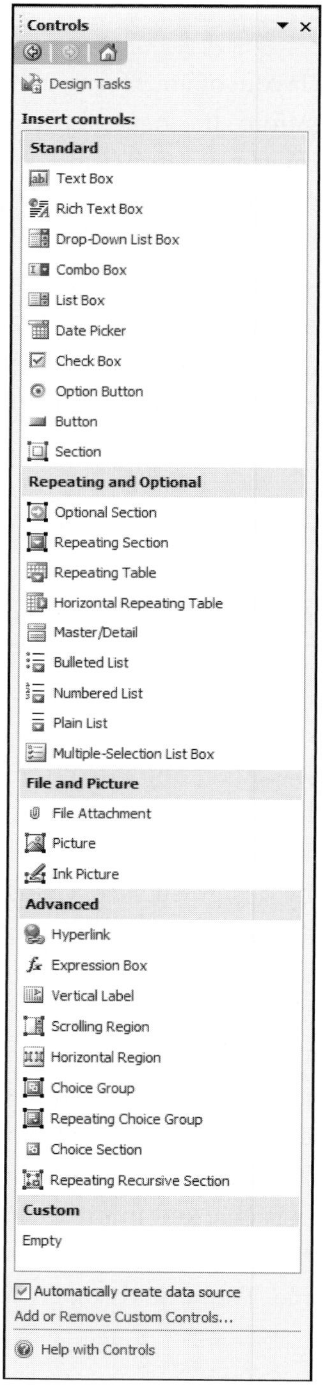

Controls
Design Tasks
Insert controls:
Standard
Text Box
Rich Text Box
Drop-Down List Box
Combo Box
List Box
Date Picker
Check Box
Option Button
Button
Section
Repeating and Optional
Optional Section
Repeating Section
Repeating Table
Horizontal Repeating Table
Master/Detail
Bulleted List
Numbered List
Plain List
Multiple-Selection List Box
File and Picture
File Attachment
Picture
Ink Picture
Advanced
Hyperlink
Expression Box
Vertical Label
Scrolling Region
Horizontal Region
Choice Group
Repeating Choice Group
Choice Section
Repeating Recursive Section
Custom
Empty
Automatically create data source
Add or Remove Custom Controls...
Help with Controls

FIGURE 2.10: Controls task pane

constructs when the form template is saved. The exact schema constructs created are determined by the type of control inserted. (We will talk in detail about what schema is created for each control in Chapter 3.) Finally, InfoPath may or may not add information about the control to the form definition file (manifest). As we mentioned earlier, this manifest information tells InfoPath various things about the control, such as whether or not the control supports spell checking or auto-complete and what to do when inserting a new instance of the control.

We can tell which controls we want to use in our form simply by looking at the data we want to collect and the data type of each item (refer back to Table 2.2). Of course, we may want to use other controls as well in order to group controls or to present additional data to the user, such as a list of open positions to choose from. Each control in the *Controls* task pane has a default data type associated with it. (The full list of default data types for each control is listed in Chapter 3; see Tables 3.2 and 3.6.) Therefore, we can use our data requirements to help us decide which controls to use.

Now that you have a basic understanding of InfoPath controls and what is happening under the hood, let's take a look at each of the controls in each category in the *Controls* task pane and start adding the controls we need to our employment application form.

Standard Controls

The controls in the *Standard* category are the controls you'll use most often. You should be familiar with these basic form input controls if you've ever filled out a form in Word or an HTML form on the Web. Table 2.4 lists all the standard controls, a description of each one, and the type of data each is associated with by default. (Chapter 3 will go into more detail about the XML Schema constructs associated with each control and also how to change the default data type.) All of these controls are pretty straightforward, so we won't talk about each one in detail. However, we will use most of these controls in our employment application form, so you will get a chance to see them in action.

Type-Ahead Support in List Box Controls

InfoPath users have often requested the ability to look up items in the Drop-Down List Box, List Box, and Combo Box controls by typing the first few letters of the item they are looking for. In InfoPath, you can typically look up items based on the first letter but no more.

If you install Windows Internet Explorer 7, InfoPath will support full type-ahead. This means that you can type as many characters as you need until you find the entry you are looking for. (For the Combo Box control, this works only when the list box is displayed.)

Forms Services

The Combo Box control is not supported in browser-enabled forms.

As you can see in Table 2.4, each control in the *Controls* task pane has a specific purpose and behavior. Some controls have the same purpose but differ only in the way they appear in the view (e.g., the Drop-Down List Box displays only one item, while the List Box displays multiple items).

Let's start adding controls to our employment application form. Looking back at Table 2.2, where we listed the data requirements for the form, we see that, for the most part, we want to collect simple data items such as strings and numbers. Therefore, most of our controls will likely be from the *Standard* category in the *Controls* task pane. First, let's add the controls to our form template that correspond to the name of the potential employee. Since the data for the first and last names is simple text, we will insert Text Box controls into the form template for each of them. Looking back at Figure 2.8, you can tell from the descriptive text (or labels) where to insert each Text Box control.

Next, let's add controls to allow the user to enter a phone number and e-mail address. We will add these controls in a new row right below the first and last name controls. As mentioned earlier, we can use the *Layout* task pane or the *Table* menu to insert a new row into the layout table.

Table 2.4: Standard Controls

Control	Description	Default Data Type
Text Box	Enables basic text entry. This is the control you will use most often.	Text (string)
Rich Text Box	Allows the user to enter formatted text and other rich form content, such as tables, lists, hyperlinks, and pictures.	Rich text (XHTML)
Drop-Down List Box	Displays a list of items from which the user can choose. Only one item is displayed at a time.	Text (string)
Combo Box	Works the same as the Drop-Down List Box but also allows the user to enter his or her own value. This control acts like a Text Box and Drop-Down List Box combined.	Text (string)
List Box	Displays a list of items just like the Drop-Down List Box but can display multiple items at a time. The user can choose only one item from the list.	Text (string)
Date Picker	Allows the user to enter a date, time, or both (depending on the underlying data type) or to choose a date from a calendar. By default, only a date can be entered. In Chapter 3 we will show you how to change the data type for a control.	Date
Check Box	Displays multiple options for the user to choose. For example, you might use multiple Check Boxes to allow the user to choose topics of interest. Using this control, the user can choose multiple items at a time.	True/false (Boolean)
Option Button	Works the same as the Check Box but allows the user to choose only one option at a time from a group of options. For example, you may use two Option Buttons in your form to ask the user a yes/no question. You want your user to choose only yes or no but not both.	Text (string)
Button	Performs an action, such as submitting the form, querying a database, executing a rule, or running form code. (Each of these topics is covered later in the book.) The Button control does not store any data in the form.	None

continued

TABLE 2.4: Standard Controls (*continued*)

Control	Description	Default Data Type
Section	Groups other controls in a logical way. Any control in the *Controls* task pane can be inserted into a Section control. This enables you to group controls in the view and fields and/or groups in the data source that logically fit together.	Group (i.e., container)

Finally, we want to add controls to allow the user to add address information. Since a person's address has multiple components—street address, city, state (or province), postal code, and country—we need to use multiple controls to allow the user to enter this data. However, since all of this data logically belongs together, we also want to group the controls in the form. To do so, we'll use a Section control. Also, we'll add another layout table with a title inside the Section control in order to lay out the controls neatly. For most of the address data, we'll use mainly Text Box controls. However, we will use a Combo Box control for the country. MOI Consulting usually receives applications from people in only a few countries but will accept them from any country. A Combo Box control allows the potential employee to choose his or her country from a list or to enter it manually if it doesn't exist in the list. (Figure 2.11 shows the employment application form template in design mode after adding these controls.)

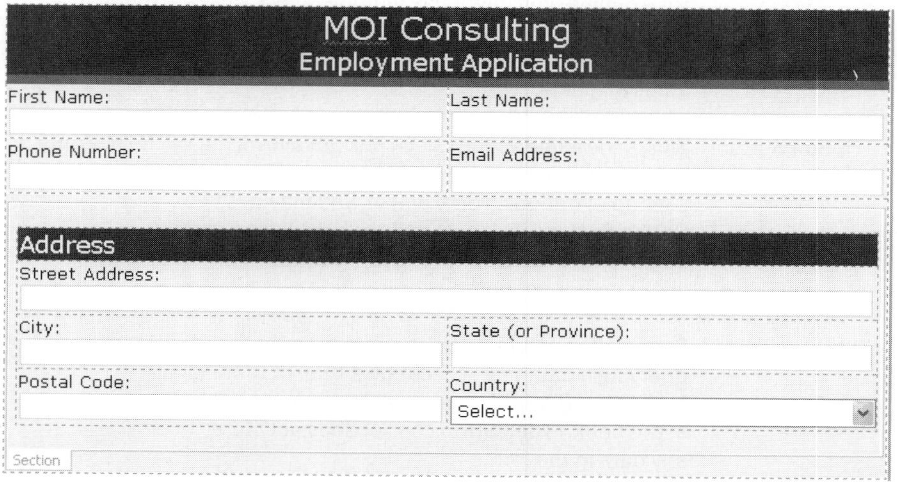

FIGURE 2.11: Employment application form template after adding standard controls

> **NOTE Why Use a Section Instead of a Layout Table?**
>
> As we mentioned, Section controls can be used to logically group other controls in the view. However, you may think that layout tables have the same effect. While it is true that layout tables do logically group controls in the view, layout tables are not connected to data in any way. Section controls, on the other hand, *are* connected to data. As you will learn in Chapter 3, the data type to which Section controls are bound is a container. This container data type is used to group other data in the data source as well.

Notice in Figure 2.11 the tab at the bottom that contains the word *Section* and the border surrounding it. This is called a **design-time visual.** You've already seen some of the design-time visuals available in InfoPath—the gridlines for the layout tables. Since the Section control is a simple container control whose sole purpose is to group other controls, it doesn't have any borders by default. Therefore, in design mode there is a design-time-only border and tab so you can see the logical boundaries of the control. This visual does not exist in fill-out-a-form mode. Not only is this design-time visual useful for designing your form, it's also functional. When you click on the tab at the bottom of the control, the Section control becomes selected (Figure 2.12). This will be quite useful when we talk about more of the advanced features of controls in Chapter 4. You will also notice yet another design-time visual in the upper corner of the Section control that says *group1.* This design-time visual gives you information about the data source for the control, so we will talk more about this one in Chapter 3.

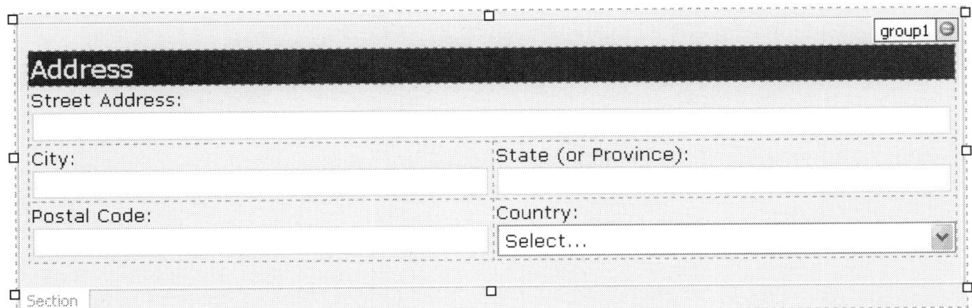

FIGURE 2.12: Section control selected in design mode

Now that we've created quite a bit of our form, it's time to test it. In general, it's a good idea to test your form template at various points during the design in order to address any issues with the layout or behavior of the form. When testing your form, you obviously want to use the form in the same way your users will. You may be thinking that the most obvious way to do this is by saving the form template and then filling it out. While that is true, there is an easier way. While in design mode, InfoPath allows you to preview your form by clicking the *Preview* button on the *Standard* toolbar or by clicking on the *File* menu, then *Preview,* and then *Form.* Previewing your form while in design mode runs your form in almost exactly the same way as if you had saved the form template and then filled it out normally. When previewing, you can quickly test your form template at any point during its design. We'll talk in more detail about different ways to preview forms as we continue designing our form in this chapter.

Figure 2.13 shows our form while previewing. You can see that the form looks a little different than it does in design mode. For instance, the design-time visuals aren't displayed, nor are the gridlines.

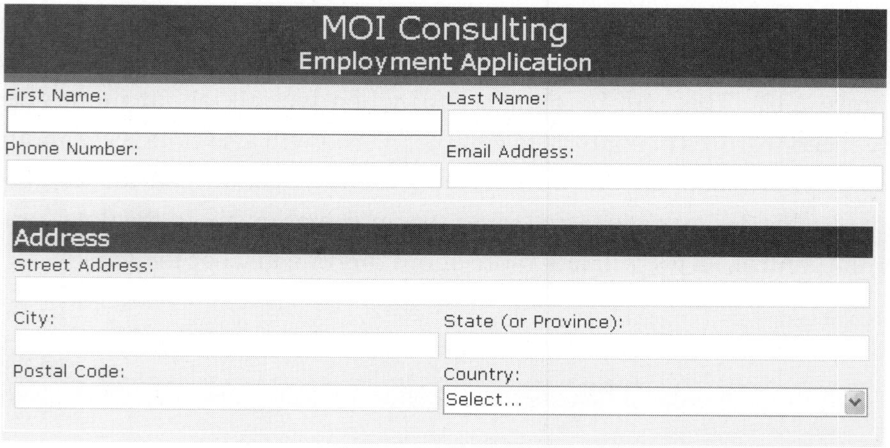

FIGURE 2.13: Preview of the employment application form

Forms Services

It's not possible to preview a browser-enabled form in the browser because previewing such a form must use the InfoPath application. To see the form in the browser, you need to publish the form to an InfoPath Forms Services–enabled server. Chapters 9 and 14 explain how to publish to InfoPath Forms Services.

Repeating and Optional Controls

Let's return to designing our employment application form. Looking back at Table 2.2 again, we see that there are still more data items we want to collect. For example, we want to allow the user to enter the minimum salary he or she would like and any additional comments. Let's say that we won't require users to indicate the minimum salary desired or to add comments. Since this is the case, we want to use optional controls for this data. Also, we want to allow users to apply for multiple jobs at the same time. Therefore, data that relates to different positions could be entered multiple times. In order for the user to enter these data items, we have to add repeating controls to our form. Let's look at the repeating and optional controls available to you when designing a form template. As we learn about each of them, we can decide which ones we want to use in our employment application form.

Optional Section Control

The Optional Section control is like a Section control in that it is a container for other controls and text. You can put as much text and as many other controls in it as you like. The advantage that the Optional Section has over the normal Section is that you can use it for data that users of your form are not required to enter. The Optional Section and its associated data are not inserted into the form until the user chooses to do so. For example, in our employment application form, we want to give the user the option of entering additional comments. For this data, we will use a Rich Text Box control so the user can enter formatted data. However, to make the comments optional, we will put the Rich Text Box inside an Optional Section. Since the minimum salary desired is also optional, we will place a Text Box for the salary in a separate Optional Section. We are using two Optional Section controls instead of one because the user may wish to add comments but no salary information or vice versa. The result of adding these controls is shown in Figure 2.14.

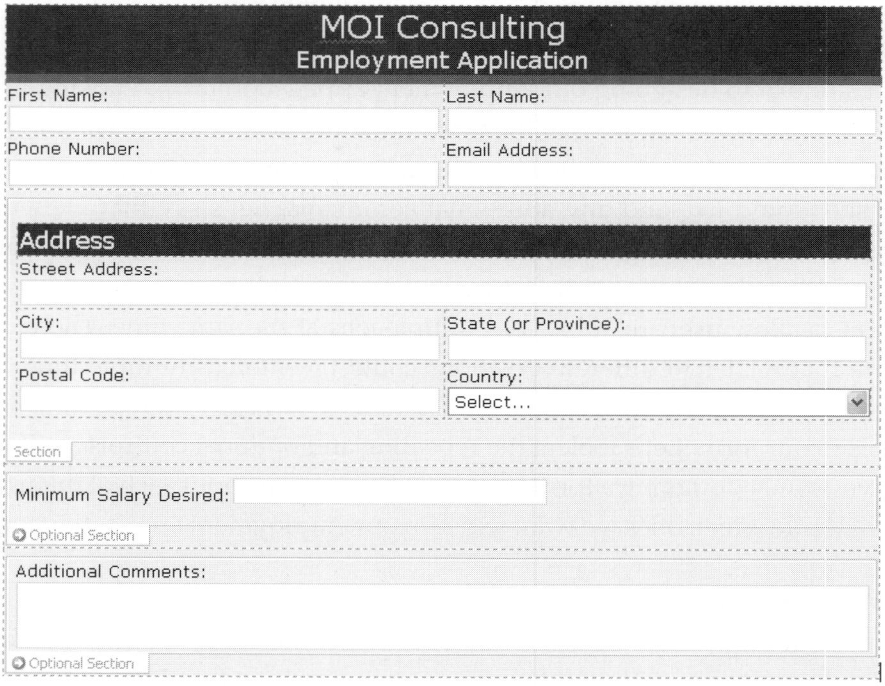

FIGURE 2.14: Employment application form template with Optional Section controls

Let's preview our form again to see how the Optional Section controls behave. Figure 2.15 shows the part of the form that contains these controls when users fill out a form. Each of the Optional Section controls simply shows a link that says *Click here to insert.* (Obviously, that text isn't very descriptive. In Chapter 4, we'll show you how to customize it.)

FIGURE 2.15: Optional controls when previewing the form

Remember, as we mentioned in Chapter 1, the underlying structure of an InfoPath form's data source is XML. Each control in your form, therefore, equates to some XML content in the underlying document. When you open a form that contains an Optional Section, no underlying XML content pertains to that control until you click on the *Click here to insert* link. That also means that no matter how many controls you put inside an Optional Section, there is no XML structure for those controls until you click on the *Click here to insert* link. When you click on one of the links in our employment application form, the contents of the Optional Section are shown, and the underlying XML structure is created for the Optional Section and the controls it contains. (Exactly what XML structure is created will be described in Chapter 3.) Figure 2.16 shows the two Optional Section controls in our form after clicking on each of the links.

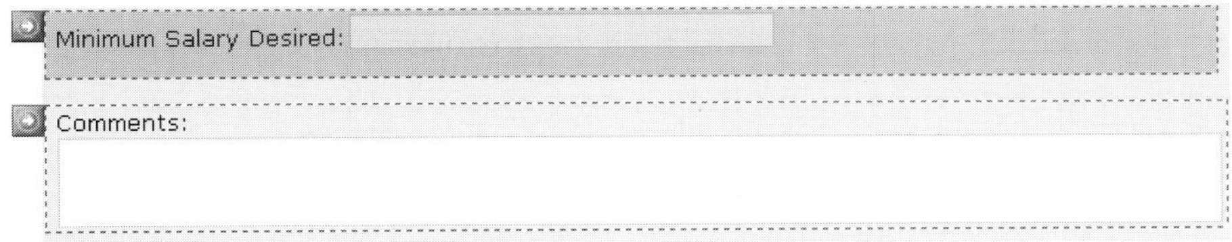

FIGURE 2.16: Optional controls after clicking on the link, Click here to insert

Control Behavior and Structural Selection When Filling Out a Form

Now that you know a bit about the Optional Section control, it's a good time to talk about special behaviors shared across multiple controls when filling out a form. Looking at Figure 2.16, you may notice two interesting details. First, an icon on the left side of the Optional Section control appears after we've inserted the control by clicking the *Click here to insert* link. This icon designates what type of control it is—Optional Section, Repeating Section or

Repeating Table, or File Attachment (which we'll talk about in this chapter). This icon is quite useful in another way as well. Clicking on the icon brings up a context menu that contains control-specific commands. (You will also see this same context menu if you right-click anywhere inside the control except inside another control nested within it.) Figure 2.17 shows the context menu that appears when you click on the icon for the Optional Section control. In Chapter 4, we'll show you how to customize the commands on this menu.

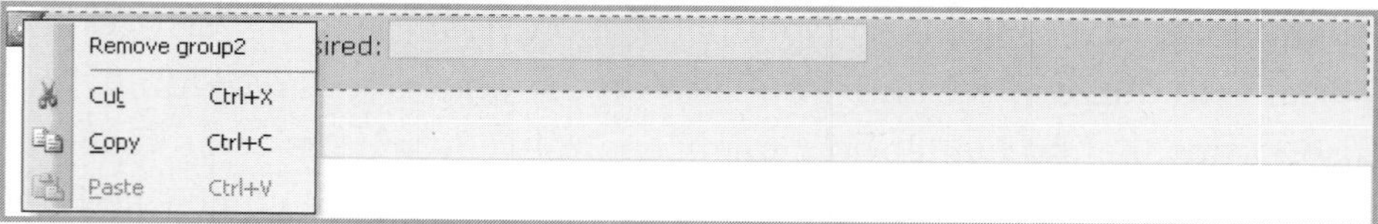

FIGURE 2.17: Context menu for the Optional Section control when filling out a form

The second interesting detail in Figure 2.16 is that the first Optional Section control is highlighted while the second is not. When filling out a form, the repeating and optional controls support a type of selection known as structural selection. This means that when you click on the Optional Section control, for example, you select the Optional Section and all of the controls it contains. Any action you then perform on the Optional Section, such as removing it by using the context menu or the Delete key, is also performed on controls inside the Optional Section. This may seem obvious, but remember that when you are filling out a form, you are editing XML data. When you delete the Optional Section control, you delete the underlying XML data associated with it. The deletion of the XML data causes all of the controls inside the Optional Section and the Optional Section itself to be removed. This concept becomes even more interesting when using repeating controls, which we'll talk about next.

Repeating Section Control

The Repeating Section control is yet another container control like the Section and Optional Section controls. Therefore, it can contain text, tables, and other controls, even other Repeating Sections. The main difference is that, when filling out the form, this control allows you to insert multiple instances of the Repeating Section and all its contained controls. Remember that one of the requirements of the form template we are designing is to be able to apply for multiple positions at once. Looking back at Table 2.2, we can see that the data items for position name and position ID will need to repeat. It makes sense, then, to use a Repeating Section control that contains a Drop-Down List Box control so the user can choose a position to apply for, a Rich Text Box control for the description of the position, and a Check Box so the potential employee can apply for a specific position. (The description of the position will be based on the position chosen by the user. Since this description cannot change, the Rich Text Box containing the text will be read-only. In Chapter 4, you'll see how to make a control read-only.)

Figure 2.18 shows our form template after we've added the Repeating Section control and the other necessary controls. Notice that, again, we are

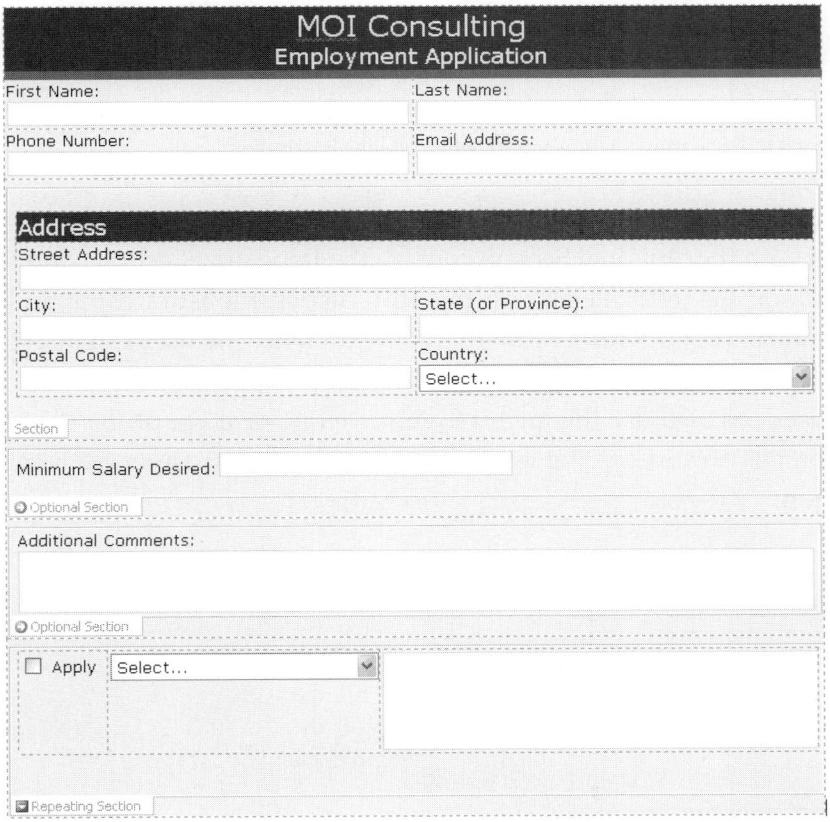

FIGURE 2.18: Employment application form template with Repeating Section control

using a layout table to position the controls within the Repeating Section. We've also resized the controls so that the data entered by the user will fit a little better. (To resize a control in design mode, just click on the control to select it, click on one of the resize handles, and drag the control until it is the right size. Chapter 4 will show you other ways that you can resize controls.)

Once again, it's time to preview our form to see how it looks and to test the new functionality. Since all we've done is add the Repeating Section control, let's focus on testing that part of the form. Figure 2.19 shows the Repeating Section part of the form while previewing the form.

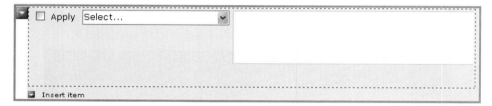

FIGURE 2.19: Repeating Section control when previewing the form

As with the Optional Section control, the Repeating Section control has an icon on the left. Clicking on this icon displays a list of commands for this control (Figure 2.20). From this context menu, the user can insert new instances of the Repeating Section in order to apply for additional jobs. The user can also use this menu to remove one or more of the Repeating Section controls in case he or she no longer wants to apply for a specific position.

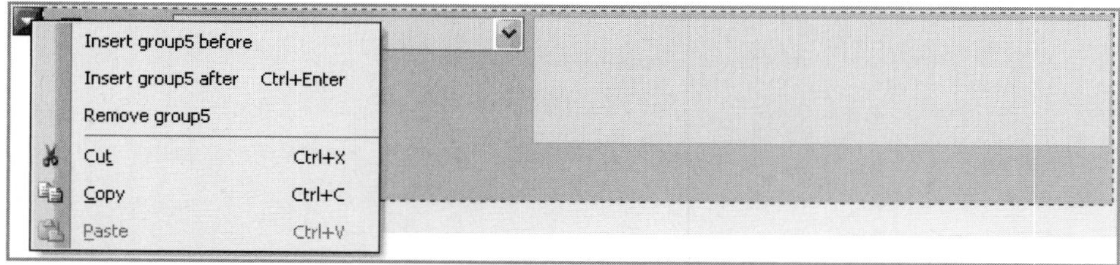

FIGURE 2.20: Context menu for Repeating Section control when previewing the form

In addition to using the context menu, there are two other ways to insert new Repeating Section controls when filling out a form. You can click on the Repeating Section (which structurally selects the control) and then hold down the Ctrl key while pressing Enter. Or, if you prefer, you can click on the *Insert item* link below the Repeating Section control. In all cases, each time you insert an item, a new Repeating Section and the controls it contains are added to the form—both in the view and in the underlying data source. Figure 2.21 shows three instances of the Repeating Section control inserted into the form. When these controls are added, new XML data is inserted into the underlying document as well.

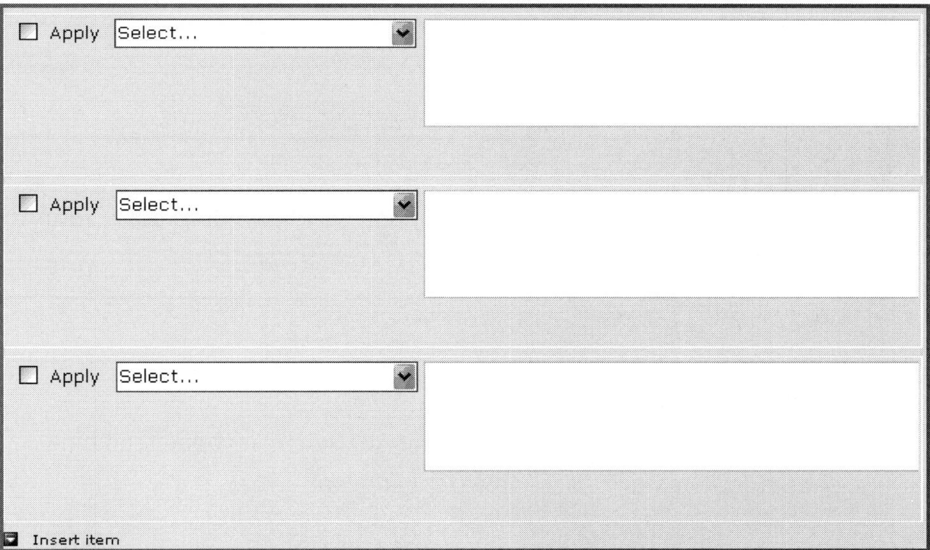

FIGURE 2.21: Three instances of the Repeating Section control inserted into the form

Forms Services

Removing an Optional Section or Repeating Section control or a row in a Repeating Table control in a browser-enabled form prompts for confirmation since the action cannot be undone!

TIP An Easier Way to Remove a Repeating Control

We mentioned that you can click on the context menu for a Repeating Section and then remove the control. There is an easier way. You can just press the Delete or Backspace keys to do the same. This applies to all repeating controls when you're filling out a form. Also, if you hold down the Shift key while clicking on a repeating control, you can select multiple controls (or rows if you are doing this in a Repeating Table control) at once. Any action you take for the repeating control, such as inserting or removing it, will apply to all the selected controls. For example, if you select three controls and then choose one of the *Insert* commands from the context menu, three new instances of that repeating control will be inserted into the form. Likewise, if you press the Delete key while all three instances are selected, all three will be removed from the form.

Forms Services

Selection of multiple controls is not supported when filling out a form in the browser.

Forms Services

When filling out a form in the browser, the Alt+Delete keyboard combination shortcut will remove a section or repeating table row.

Repeating Table Control

The Repeating Table control is very similar to the Repeating Section control—it is a container for other controls that allows a user to insert one or more instances of the data when filling out a form. The main difference between the Repeating Table and Repeating Section controls is the way they look. (We'll explore some other differences in the next few chapters.) You've already seen the Repeating Section control, which looks a lot like the Section control. The Repeating Table control, as you might imagine, looks like a table. When you insert a Repeating Table control while designing a form

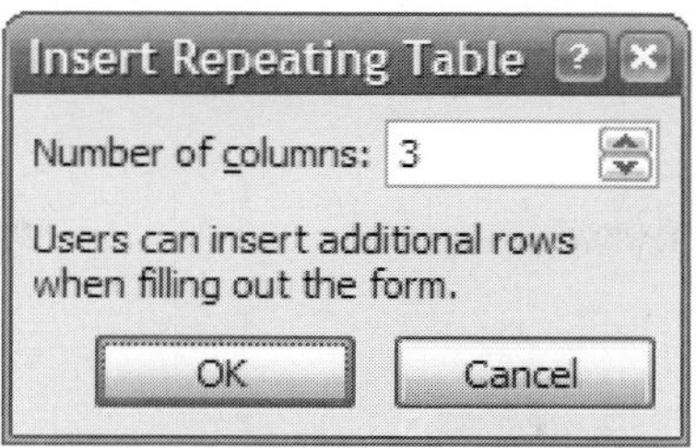

FIGURE 2.22: Insert Repeating Table dialog

template, you are presented with a dialog that allows you to choose the number of columns you want to insert into the Repeating Table initially (Figure 2.22).

If you choose the default of three columns, you will see the Repeating Table shown in Figure 2.23. When you insert this control, you will notice that it supports color schemes, just as layout tables do. The color scheme is reflected in the first row, the header row, in which you can add column headings.

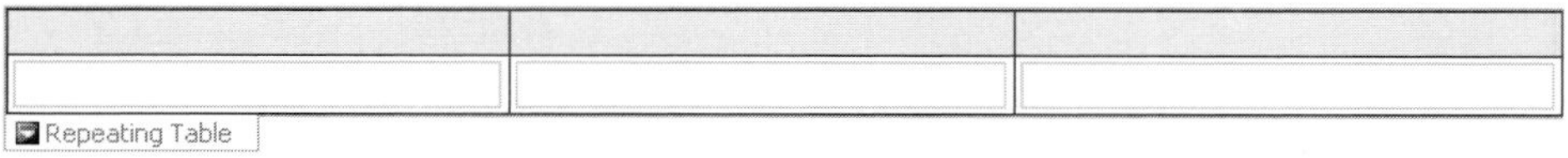

FIGURE 2.23: Repeating Table control in design mode

The Repeating Section and Repeating Table controls are so similar that you can change one control to the other. (In order to do so, however, the Repeating Section control, and its underlying data, must contain other controls.) Let's do that in our employment application form. Changing the Repeating Section control that contains the job information to a Repeating Table is very simple. First, right-click on the *Repeating Section* tab at the bottom of the control (or anywhere inside the control, except on another control). When you do, you will see a context menu. On the context menu is a fly-out menu called *Change To.* If you hover the mouse over that fly-out menu (or click on it), you will see a choice of controls to which you can change the Repeating Section (Figure 2.24).

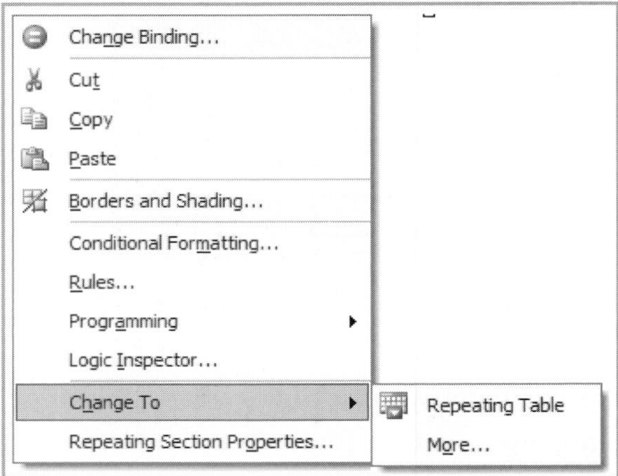

FIGURE 2.24: Change To menu

In our case only one control is shown—Repeating Table. Clicking on the *Repeating Table* menu item on the *Change To* menu will change the Repeating Section to a Repeating Table (Figure 2.25).

Field 12	Field 13	Field 14
☐		

Repeating Table

FIGURE 2.25: Repeating Table control after changing from a Repeating Section control

Notice that all the controls inside the Repeating Section were retained. However, we lost the label next to our Check Box control. When you change from a Repeating Section to a Repeating Table, all the labels inside the Repeating Section are removed. However, labels are added to the header row for each column. In Figure 2.25, you can see that the labels are "Field 12", "Field 13", and "Field 14". You may be wondering where these labels come from. These labels are the names of the data fields associated with the controls. For now, you can consider these to be the names of the controls. In Chapter 3, we'll talk more about the data source and how controls are mapped to fields. In Chapter 4, we'll show you how to change the control name through the properties dialog for a control.

Change To Menu Item

You can use the *Change To* menu item for most controls. (It's not available for the Choice Group and Choice Section controls nor for controls that aren't directly connected to the data source, such as the Button and Expression Box controls.) However, you can't change one control to any other type of control that exists. The type of data item in the data source that the current control is associated with determines the controls it can be changed to. You can change a control only to another one that supports the same data type. (We will talk more about what data types each control supports in Chapter 3.) Notice on the *Change To* fly-out menu shown in Figure 2.24 that, in addition to the *Repeating Table* option, there is also a *More* menu item. Clicking on this menu item displays a dialog that shows additional items. The options shown on the *Change To* menu above the *More* menu item are the ones that make the most sense. The controls shown when you click on the *More* menu item are those that will work in terms of data type but may not be the most sensible choices.

Notice in Figure 2.25 that our Drop Down List Box control (which was previously inside the Repeating Section control) was changed to a Text Box in the Repeating Table control. When changing from one type of container control to another, InfoPath replaces the inner controls as well. When this happens, InfoPath chooses the default control for the type of data that the original control is associated with. In this case, the Text Box control is the default for the string data type. Changing this back to a Drop-Down List Box control is easy—just right-click on the Text Box control, go to the *Change To* menu, and then click on *Drop-Down List Box*. Let's change the Text Box to a Drop-Down List Box, change the column headers in our Repeating Table to be more descriptive, and resize the columns in the Repeating Table (we don't need as much space without the label in the first column). Then, let's preview the form again and test it by adding a few rows. Figure 2.26 shows the result, which looks very similar to the original since we were using a layout table inside the Repeating Section. (In many cases, it makes sense just to use

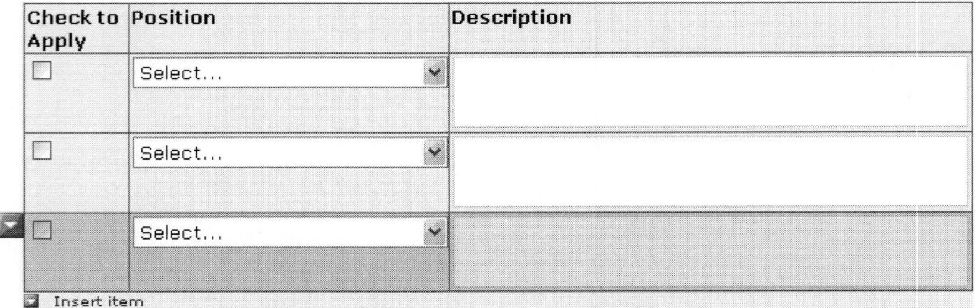

FIGURE 2.26: Repeating Table control when previewing the form

a Repeating Table control from the start.) The only noticeable differences when using a Repeating Table instead of a Repeating Section with a nested layout table are that the Repeating Table has a header row and borders are turned on by default. Layout tables have borders turned off by default.

Horizontal Repeating Table Control

The Horizontal Repeating Table control was added in InfoPath 2007 to support table structures that flow from left to right (and, in some cases, right to left) instead of top to bottom. One example of this is a form where the data entered is based on the calendar year. In this form, you would enter data for January. Then, when February comes around, you insert a new column to the right and enter the data for February. It makes sense to use a Horizontal Repeating Table in this case. You may say, "Why not just add 12 columns to the form initially?" Remember that one of the advantages of using InfoPath is that you need to enter only the amount of data you need. You can save time and effort by not adding all the columns to your form initially and allowing users to enter them as needed. This is exactly the reason behind the Repeating Table control. However, since the Repeating Table control flows from top to bottom, it makes sense to have one that flows left to right. Let's take a quick look at the Horizontal Repeating Table control.

Forms Services

Horizontal Repeating Table controls are not supported in browser-enabled forms.

When you first insert the Horizontal Repeating Table when designing a form template, similar to the Repeating Table, you are presented with the *Insert Horizontal Repeating Table* dialog. However, in this case, you choose the number of rows inserted into the table. (This makes sense since this table is flowing horizontally instead of vertically. In this case, rows are more like columns.)

After clicking *OK* in the dialog, the Horizontal Repeating Table control is inserted into the view (Figure 2.27). You may notice that this control isn't exactly the same as a Repeating Table. In fact, this control is not just a table but a conglomeration of other controls. Inserting this control inserts a two-column layout table, which we'll call the outer layout table in this discussion. The first column contains another layout table, which is used for the row headers, much like the Repeating Table control's column headers. The second column of the outer layout table contains a Repeating Section control, which contains another layout table for positioning a set of Text Box controls.

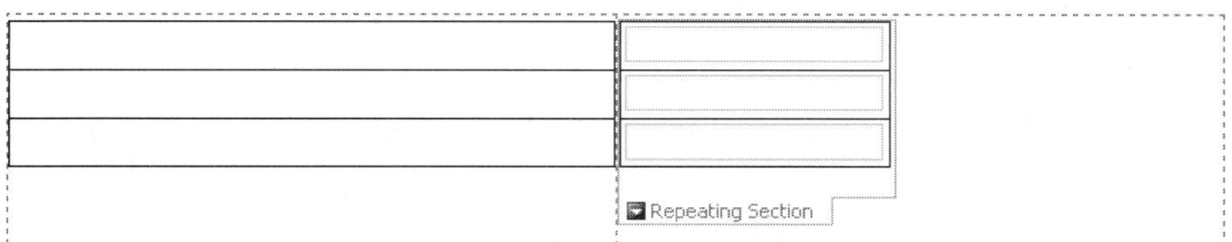

FIGURE 2.27: Horizontal Repeating Table control in design mode

When filling out a form containing a Horizontal Repeating Table control, each time the user clicks the *Insert item* text to insert a new instance of the control, the Repeating Section control will flow from left to right within its table cell. Once the control reaches the right side of the layout table cell, the next Repeating Section will be inserted on the next line. In this way, you can use the size of the second column in the outer layout table to control how the inner Repeating Section controls flow and wrap. Figure 2.28 shows the control when filling out a form after three instances of the control have been inserted. The third instance has wrapped to the next line. Of course, you can move the header layout table and the Repeating Section outside of the outer layout table (e.g., by cutting and pasting the controls) so that the Repeating Section controls can flow from left to right without wrapping at all.

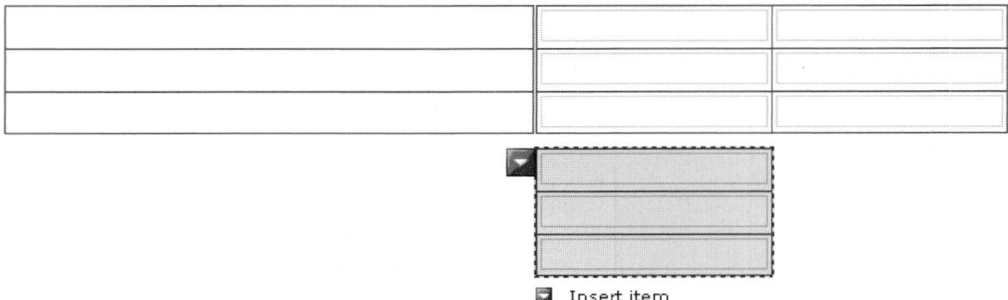

FIGURE 2.28: Horizontal Repeating Table control when filling out a form

Master/Detail Control

The Master/Detail control is very useful for viewing large amounts of data. For example, let's say that you are a hiring manager at MOI Consulting and you want to look at all the applicants' information and the jobs they have applied for. This data, which comes from the employment application form, would normally be stored in a database. Therefore, it makes sense to create an application review form in InfoPath to view this data. Using a Master/Detail control, you can create a streamlined form that first displays a limited set of information about all the applicants. Then, when you select an applicant, more extensive information is shown. This way, you don't need to show all the information for every applicant all at once.

Forms Services

The Master/Detail control is not supported in browser-enabled forms.

The Master/Detail control is another control that is an aggregation of other controls. In this case, the Master/Detail control is actually two controls—a master control and a detail control. Only a Repeating Table can be used as the master control. However, either a Repeating Section or a Repeating Table can be used as the detail control. By default, when you insert the control from the *Controls* task pane, the detail control is a Repeating Section. When you first insert the control, you will see the *Insert Master/Detail* dialog (Figure 2.29).

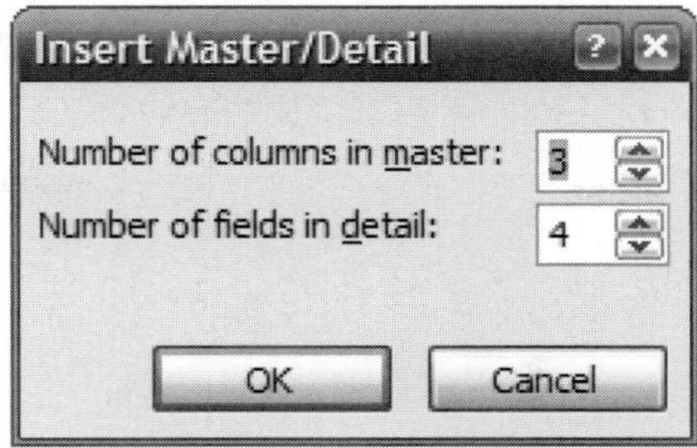

FIGURE 2.29: Insert Master/Detail dialog

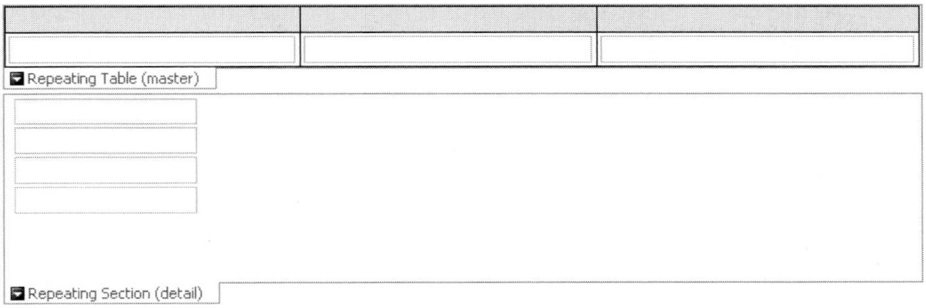

FIGURE 2.30: Master and detail controls in design mode

You can choose the number of columns in the master control and the number of fields in the detail control. Figure 2.30 shows the result.

The only visual difference between these controls and the normal Repeating Table and Repeating Section controls is the text displayed in the design-time visuals. The master contains *(master)* in the text and the detail contains *(detail)*. The other difference, not immediately evident, is that these controls are connected. By default, when you insert these controls, they both act on the same data in the underlying XML. When you change the data in the master control, for example, the data changes are reflected in the detail control. (In Chapter 4, we'll discuss other ways to create master and detail relationships for controls that do not act on the same data in the underlying data source.)

Let's look at an example of how the Master/Detail control works when filling out a form. Figure 2.31 shows the Master/Detail control using hypothetical applicant data. We've selected the first row in the master table, which corresponds to an applicant named John Smith. In the master table, you see a

Last Name	First Name	Phone Number
Smith	John	555-1234
Doe	Jane	555-4321

Insert item

Smith
John
555-1234
jsmith@smith.com

Insert item

FIGURE 2.31: Master/Detail control in the application review form when filling out a form

subset of the data including the applicant's last and first names and the phone number. In the detail control, you see the same data and a little more—the e-mail address. If you then select the second row in the master table, you will see the data pertaining to Jane Doe in the detail section.

Although we see some of the same data in the detail section as in the master table, there's no reason that this has to be the case. We can easily remove fields from the detail section and add new ones. Figure 2.32 shows the

Last Name	First Name
Smith	John
Doe	Jane

Insert item

Phone Number: 555-1234
Email Address: jsmith@smith.com
Minimum Salary Desired: 45,000

Address
Street Address: One Circle Way
City: Cincinnati
State (or Province): OH
Postal Code: 45211
Country: United States

Positions Applied

Position ID	Position Name	Description
1011	Senior Software Engineer	Experienced Software Engineer needed for start-up company specializing in software services.
2024	Systems Engineer	Systems Engineer who has experience with Web servers needed to install and maintain backend Windows servers.

Insert item

Insert item

FIGURE 2.32: Master/Detail control showing more applicant data

Master/Detail control when filling out a form with some modifications. This time, to make things more interesting, we've removed the phone number from the master table and added more controls to the detail section for the address, minimum salary desired, and positions applied for—all data that came from the employment application form. The application review form shown in Figure 2.32 is closer to the real-world form we would use to view all the applicants that have filled out the employment application form.

TIP How to Tell a Control's Name

In the Master/Detail control, by default there are certain controls in the detail section that act on the same data as those in the master table. How do you tell which controls are acting on the same data? In design mode, you can use another type of design-time visual called a binding visual. This visual tells you the name of the control. This is actually the name of the data item to which the control is connected in the underlying data source. To see the name of the control, just hover your mouse over the control. When you do, you will see the visual shown in Figure 2.33. Using the name of the control, you can tell which control in the detail section acts on the same data as another control in the master table. (We will talk more about these binding visuals and the type of information they convey in Chapter 3.)

FIGURE 2.33: Binding design-time visual showing the name of the control

Bulleted List, Numbered List, and Plain List Controls

In many cases, as we're sure you've noticed by now, InfoPath provides some controls that act on the same data but look different in the design surface of the form. You have already seen this with the Repeating Section and Repeating Table controls. They act on the same type of data but look a lot different in the view. The same could be said of three other controls in the *Controls* task pane—the Bulleted List, Numbered List, and Plain List controls. These controls all act on repeating data like the Repeating Section and Repeating Table controls do, but in a slightly different way: The list controls are not container controls. In other words, you can't insert other controls inside of them.

Instead, the list controls allow you to insert multiple instances of one data type instead of multiple instances of a container (which may contain multiple other controls). You can think of these list controls as being like a repeating Text Box or Rich Text Box. In a Text Box control, you enter one type of data—usually a string or a number. The same is true with the list controls. The only difference is that you can insert multiple instances when filling out a form.

Another difference is that these controls all look like lists when a form is filled out. If you have ever created a list in Word, for example, you know what to expect. Figure 2.34 shows the list controls in design mode, and Figure 2.35 shows them with some data when filling out a form. The main difference between the three list controls lies in how they look. From top to bottom in Figure 2.35, the first control is a Bulleted List, the second a Numbered List, and the third a Plain List. With the Plain List control, if you don't have any data in the form, it's hard to tell that the list control is there. It's not until you position the insertion point inside the Plain List control that the first list item becomes highlighted so you know that you can insert data. Therefore, it is sometimes helpful to add a border to the Plain List control so users will know where to insert data when filling out the form.

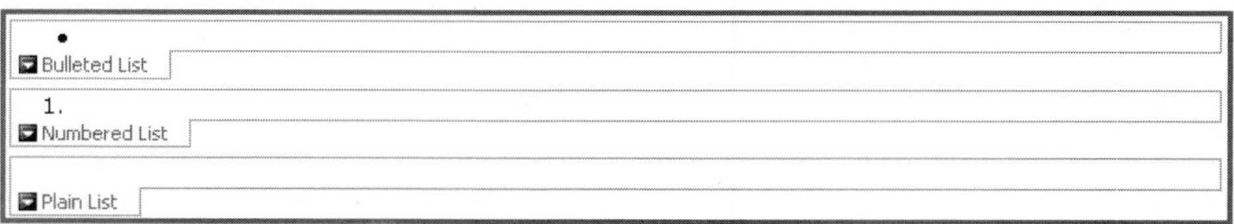

FIGURE 2.34: List controls in design mode

- Item 1
- Item 2
- Item 3

1. Item 1
2. Item 2
3. Item 3

Item 1
Item 2
Item 3

FIGURE 2.35 List controls when filling out a form

Multiple-Selection List Box Control

The Multiple-Selection List Box control is another new control for InfoPath 2007. Like the Drop-Down List Box, Combo Box, and List Box controls, this control allows you to present a list of items to the user. However, the main difference is that the user can choose more than one item at a time. Therefore, the Multiple-Selection List Box is more like the list controls in the way it stores data, although conceptually it's still a List Box. Figure 2.36 shows this control in fill-out-a-form mode after adding it to the form template and then adding a few list items. (In Chapter 4, we'll show you how to add list items to this control.) Notice that there is space in the last line for the user to add an item to the list. In this way, the Multiple-Selection List Box control is sort of like a repeating Combo Box control in that users can choose items from the list or enter their own. (By default, the additional space for users to enter their own items is not active. You can turn this on by selecting this option in the properties dialog for this control. We will talk more about properties dialogs for controls in Chapter 4.)

Forms Services

The Multiple-Selection List Box control is not supported in browser-enabled forms.

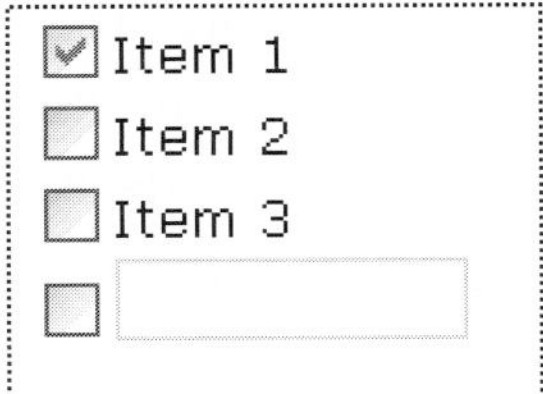

FIGURE 2.36: Multiple-Selection List Box control when filling out a form

File and Picture Controls

Following the *Repeating and Optional* category in the *Controls* task pane is the *File and Picture* category. From the name, you can probably guess what types of controls it contains. Specifically, there are three controls in this category. We'll talk about each one of them in turn.

File Attachment Control

The File Attachment control enables users to attach almost any type of file to your form. However, files that are deemed unsafe cannot be attached to the form by default. The list of files that cannot be added to a form is the same as the list of file types that cannot be attached to an e-mail message. (For more information about the File Attachment control and the blocked file types, see the MSDN article "Attaching Files in InfoPath 2003," which is available on the MSDN Web site. You can find a reference to this article in the Appendix.)

The File Attachment control is fairly straightforward to use. Since we want to allow our users to attach a résumé to the employment application form, let's add a File Attachment control. First, we add a row above the Optional Section control that contains information about the minimum salary desired. Then, we insert a File Attachment control into this row. Figure 2.37 shows the resulting File Attachment control.

FIGURE 2.37: File Attachment control in design mode

Let's preview the form and see how the File Attachment control works when filling out a form. Figure 2.38 shows the File Attachment control when filling out a form. As you can tell from the help text inside the control, you can click on the control to attach a file. In our case, users are going to attach a résumé, so let's test this part of the form by doing the same.

When you click on the File Attachment control, InfoPath shows the *Attach File* dialog, which is very similar to the *Open File* dialog you have seen countless times in many different applications. From this dialog, you

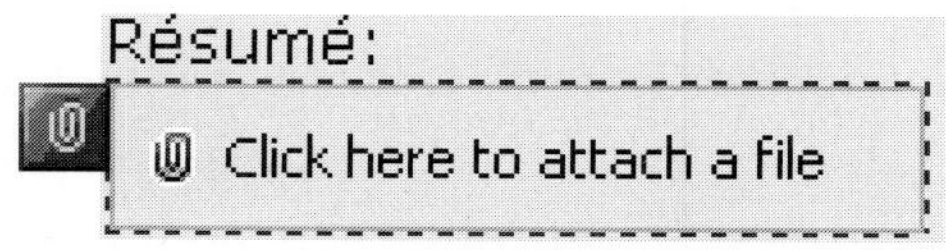

FIGURE 2.38: File Attachment control when filling out a form

can choose the file you want to attach. Once you attach a file, the File Attachment control changes to show information about the file. Figure 2.39 shows that the attached file is My Resume.docx, which is a Microsoft Office Word Document (using the new Word 2007 file format) and is 9.21K in size.

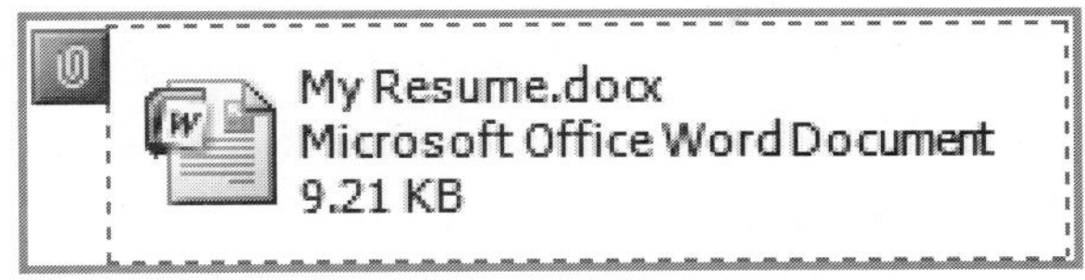

FIGURE 2.39: File Attachment control with résumé file attached

At this point, once the file is attached, you can click the icon on the left to see a list of commands that apply to this control (Figure 2.40). From here, you can attach a new file, open the current file using the application associated with it (you can also double-click on the File Attachment control to open the file), save the attached file to a location on your local machine or a network share of your choice, or remove the control from the form completely. (Pressing the Delete key while the File Attachment control is selected will also remove the file from the form.) You can use other commands to cut, copy, and paste.

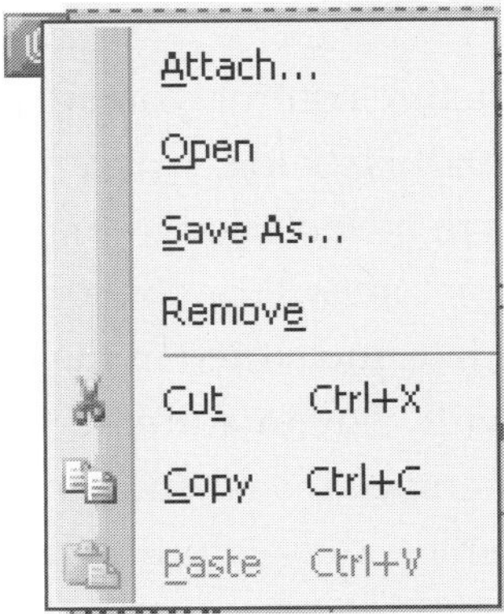

FIGURE 2.40: File Attachment control commands

Note that any changes you make to the file after opening it from this menu will not be saved to the form automatically. In fact, the file opens as a read-only file, so you must save it to a new location if you've made changes. If you wish to update the form with the changed document, after you save the file to another location, you must remove the current file from the form and attach the new version.

> **TIP XML Format for the Attached Files**
>
> When you attach a file to a form, the original file is converted to a textual representation of the binary format of the file. InfoPath uses base64 encoding to convert the binary format of the file to text that can be saved in XML. In addition to the base64-encoded data, InfoPath adds information to the data about the file—type of file, size, and so on. A discussion of the format of attached files is included in the article "Attaching Files in InfoPath 2003," available on the MSDN Web site. (This article is referenced in the Appendix.)

Picture Control

The Picture control is much like the File Attachment control. However, the Picture control is specifically tailored for pictures, whereas the File Attachment control works with any type of file. The File Attachment control will show you details about the attached file; the Picture control will show you the picture itself.

When you insert the Picture control, you are presented with the dialog shown in Figure 2.41. From this dialog, you can choose whether you want pictures inserted by users to be included in the form or attached as a link. With the first option, the picture will be converted to a textual representation of the binary picture data and stored in the underlying XML. With the second option, the form will contain a link to the original location of the picture. From the user's perspective when filling out a form, the behavior for both options is the same—the picture will be displayed in the form view. However, be careful. If you choose the link option, and your users are sharing the filled-out form, they all must have access to the original location of the attached picture or they will not be able to see the picture in the form.

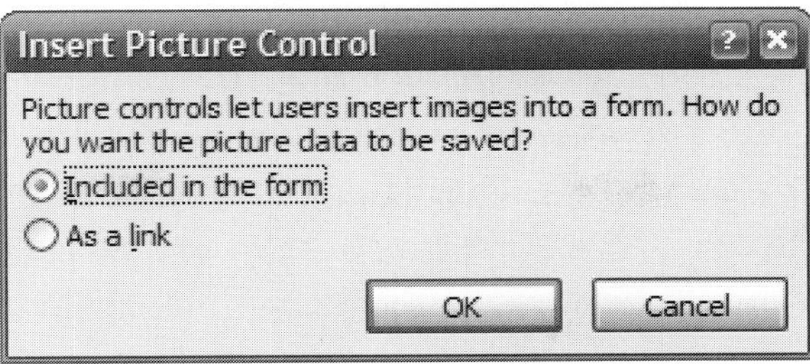

FIGURE 2.41: Insert Picture Control dialog

Forms Services

The Picture control is not supported in browser-enabled forms.

TIP Gotcha: Inserting Large File Attachments and Pictures Included in the Form

Be careful if you use a File Attachment control or if you use a Picture control with the option to include the picture in the form. Some file attachments and pictures can be quite large. Adding large picture files to a form can bloat the underlying XML since the picture data is converted to a textual representation of the binary data. If the underlying XML data becomes too large, performance of your form can degrade significantly. The File Attachment control will warn users if they try to attach a file larger than 1MB. The Picture control will not warn users in this case. If you expect your users to attach pictures that are larger than 1MB, consider choosing the option for linking to the picture when you insert the Picture control in your form template.

Figure 2.42 shows how the Picture control looks when filling out a form. As with the File Attachment control, helpful text tells the user to click on the control to insert a picture. Clicking on the control opens the *Insert Picture* dialog, which is similar to the *Attach File* dialog for the File Attachment control. However, by default, this dialog opens in the My Pictures folder for the current user.

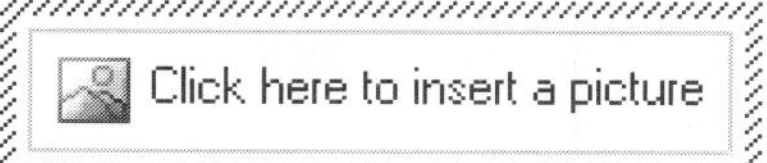

FIGURE 2.42: Picture control when filling out the form

FIGURE 2.43: Picture control with picture inserted

When a user inserts a picture, he or she will see the picture in the form, as shown in Figure 2.43. To change the picture, the user can click on the Picture control again and choose a new image.

Ink Picture Control

The Ink Picture control is one of the ways that InfoPath supports designing forms to be filled out with Tablet PCs. Users can write in the Ink Picture control with the Tablet PC stylus. Figure 2.44 shows the Ink Picture control after a user wrote in the control while filling out a form. In Chapter 4 we'll talk about another feature included in InfoPath to support designing forms for the Tablet PC.

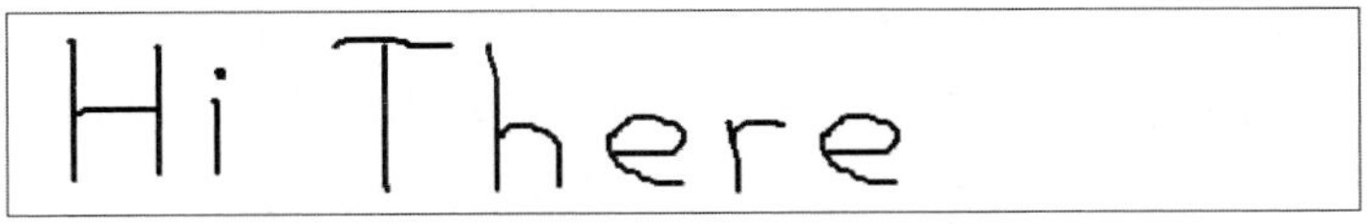

FIGURE 2.44: Ink Picture control that contains text entered with a Tablet PC stylus

---

Forms Services

The Ink Picture control is not supported in browser-enabled forms.

When designing a form template that uses the Ink Picture control, you will most likely design and test your form on a normal Windows PC. When you initially insert the Ink Picture control and then preview, the control may not work. Tablet PC systems contain all the necessary components needed to support inking into the Ink Picture control. However, normal Windows PCs running Windows XP, Windows Server, or Windows Vista do not include these components by default. Therefore, if you are designing and testing a form template on a normal Windows PC and you wish to include the Ink Picture control, you must install the Microsoft Windows XP Tablet PC Edition Software Development Kit. (You can find a reference to this SDK in the Appendix.) This kit will install all the components needed to test the Ink Picture control on machines that are not Tablet PCs.

Creating Multiple Views

Everything we've talked about so far in this chapter involves one view. Remember that a form template is a collection of data, views, resources, and a manifest. By default, when you design a new form template, it has only one view. A view is just a way to visualize the underlying data source. In other words, you insert text, layout tables, and controls (connected to the underlying data source) in a view so users who fill out forms based on your form template have some way to enter data. Users of your form have no knowledge of the underlying data source. To them, the view is the form.

Having only one view in a form template is usually sufficient. However, what if you want to use the same underlying data source but provide different views of the data? For example, you may want to design a form template to be used in different countries. The underlying data source is the same, but the text in the view should be in the language of the person filling out the form. Or, what if you want to create a form template where employees see one view of the data and managers see more? You could always design multiple form templates. However, that's a tad cumbersome. Since the underlying data source is the same but only the view of the data differs, it makes sense to use multiple views.

Adding multiple views to your form template is easy. Just click on the *Views* link on the *Design Tasks* pane or click on the *Manage Views* menu item on the *Views* menu. In either case, the *Views* task pane opens (Figure 2.45).

FIGURE 2.45: Views task pane

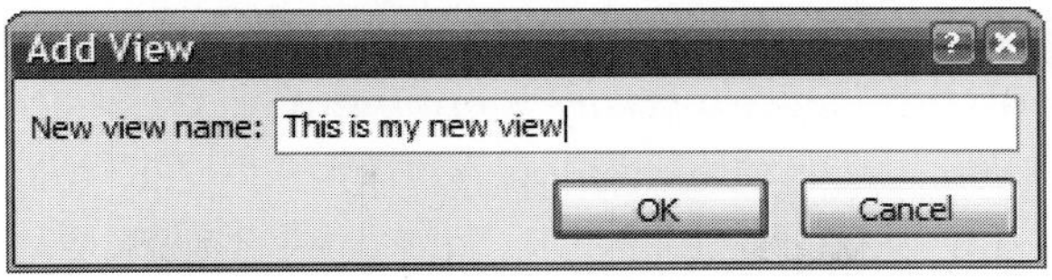

FIGURE 2.46 Add View dialog

In this task pane, you can add a new view by clicking on the *Add a New View* link at the bottom. Doing this opens the *Add View* dialog (Figure 2.46), in which you can enter a name for your new view. After clicking the *OK* button, your new view is added to the list of views in the *Views* task pane.

From the *Views* task pane, you can also customize the properties for your views. First, select a view in the list of views in the task pane. Then, you can either double-click on the name of the view or click on the *View Properties* button at the bottom of the task pane. In either case, the *View Properties* dialog opens, as shown in Figure 2.47. (If you want to open the

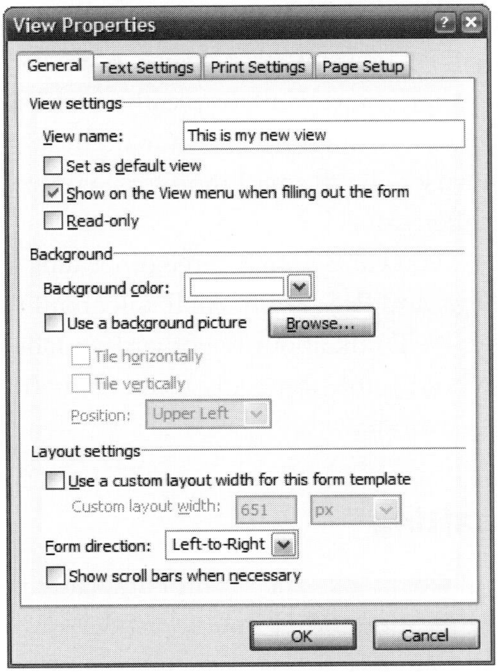

FIGURE 2.47: View Properties dialog

View Properties dialog for the current view without going to the *View* task pane, just click on the *View Properties* menu item on the *View* menu.)

From the *General* tab in this dialog, you can change many of the basic properties for your view. For example, you can set the view as the default, which means that this view will be the first one your users see when they open your form. You can also specify whether or not to show the view on the *View* menu when filling out the form. Typically, you would want to show it, but in some cases, you don't. For example, you may want to control when the user switches to a different view. Perhaps you want to change a view when the user clicks on a button or adds specific data to the form. (We'll talk about how to do this in Chapter 5 when we talk about rules.)

In this dialog, you can also set whether or not to make the view read-only. Let's says that you want to have one view used by data entry personnel and another used by those who have permission only to view the data. In that case, you would use a read-only view where none of the data can be changed. Its sole purpose is to allow users to view the data but not change it.

The other properties on the *General* tab are fairly self-explanatory. You can add a background color or picture to your view, for example. You can also specify a custom width for your form. By default, the view width for your form template is set by InfoPath. You can, however, change this value to something other than the default. Typically, the default width should suffice, but sometimes you might want to make it larger or smaller. For example, if all your users have small monitors, you may want to set the default to some smaller value.

From Figure 2.47, you can see that three other tabs are available—*Text Settings, Print Settings,* and *Page Setup.* We'll talk about the *Text Settings* tab later in this chapter. We'll talk about the other two tabs later in this book. But now, let's talk about some of the advanced formatting operations you can perform in design mode.

Advanced Formatting

As we mentioned in Chapter 1, one of InfoPath's advantages is that it's a Microsoft Office application. So, if you've used Word before, InfoPath's user interface should already be familiar to you. In fact, in InfoPath you can format text in pretty much the same way as you would in Word. In

Word 2003, for example, to format a string of text as bold, you would select the text with your mouse and then press the *Bold* button on the *Standard* toolbar. Or, you could open the *Font* dialog from the *Format* menu and then choose *Bold* from the *Font Style* list. InfoPath provides the same formatting options as in Word. In InfoPath, however, you use the *Font* task pane (also available on the *Format* menu), as shown in Figure 2.48. In addition to basic text formatting, InfoPath also has a few advanced formatting options, which we'll talk about next.

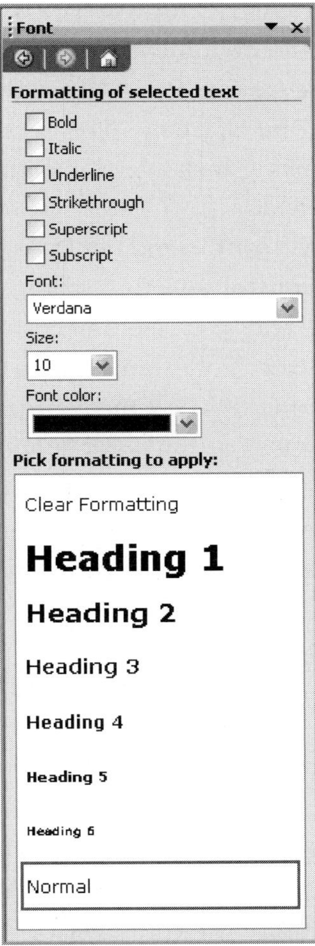

FIGURE 2.48: Font task pane

ntrol Formatting

fore we can dive into the more advanced formatting features, it makes sense to review the basics of control formatting, including control selection. If you have used InfoPath before, you may want to skip this section. (However, you may still learn something new if you read it.) If you are new to InfoPath, read on.

As we just mentioned, you can select and format text in InfoPath the same way you do in other Office applications. But how can you format a control so that the text entered by your users is always underlined, for example? Well, that's just as easy. One way you can do this is by first selecting the control as you would do for text: Click to the right or left of the control and drag your mouse cursor. Then choose the format you want from the *Formatting* toolbar or *Font* task pane. This is called **text selection.** However, selecting a control using text selection formats not only the control but also the surrounding text.

If you want to format the control and not the surrounding text, you must use what is aptly named **control selection** so you are selecting just the control and nothing else. The way you select a control depends on the type of control you are trying to select. For example, for a simple noncontainer control, such as a Text Box, you can select the control by simply clicking on it. The square boxes that appear at the corners and sides of the control, as shown in Figure 2.49, tell you that the control is selected. These square boxes, called **grab handles,** can also be used to resize the control. Click on one of them and then drag the control to the desired height and width.

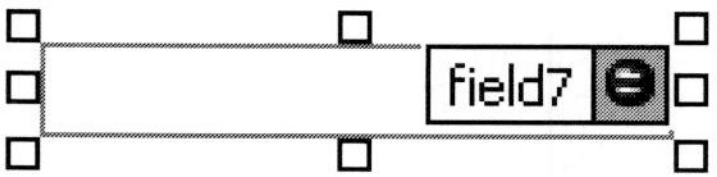

FIGURE 2.49: Selected Text Box control

To select a container control, such as a Section, you must click either on the border of the control or on the tab at the bottom (refer back to Figure 2.12). Clicking anywhere else inside the container control will place the cursor inside the container itself. (This is a convenience feature that allows you to quickly place your cursor inside the container and add text and other controls.) Finally, for layout tables, you can select an entire table by clicking the small square box at the upper-left corner of the table (refer back to Figure 2.7).

Whether you use text selection or control selection, once you have selected the control, you can usually format it exactly as you would text. However, a couple of controls behave differently, which, at first, may catch you off-guard. When you select a Rich Text Box control, for example, none of the standard font styles (e.g., bold, italic, underline) are available. This is because the Rich Text Box can contain formatted text. If you could specify bold text for the Rich Text Box control, for example, users of your form would not be able to add text that was not bold. Other controls, such as the Picture and Ink Picture, may support only some formatting or none at all, depending on the type of data they are associated with. Some other controls, such as ActiveX controls (which we'll talk about in Chapter 19), may not support formatting at all.

Format Painter

Now that we've reviewed the basics of formatting, let's talk about a few InfoPath features that make your life easier when it comes to formatting text or controls. The first is the **Format Painter.** If you are an avid Word user, you are familiar with this tool. This feature gives you a way to copy the formatting of text or a control in the form template to other text or controls. The Format Painter, in fact, isn't limited to design mode. If you include a Rich Text Box control in your form, users can use the Format Painter when filling out that part of the form.

The Format Painter is available on the *Standard* toolbar and looks like a paintbrush (Figure 2.50). To use it, select the text or control whose formatting you want to copy (or, for text, simply place your cursor within the formatted text), and then click on the paintbrush toolbar button. The cursor changes to a paintbrush (Figure 2.51) to indicate that InfoPath is currently in Format Painter mode. Next, just select the text or control to which you want to copy the formatting. The formatting that was present on the text or control you originally selected is copied to the new text or control.

FIGURE 2.50: Format Painter on the Standard toolbar

FIGURE 2.51 Format Painter cursor

As we mentioned earlier, not all controls support all types of formatting. The Format Painter can apply only the types of formatting that a control supports. (And for some controls, no formatting can be copied to them.)

Using the Format Painter can make formatting tasks much easier. However, what if you want to copy formatting to multiple strings of text or multiple controls? How can you do that without constantly clicking on the paintbrush toolbar button? If you double-click on that button instead of just single-clicking on it, InfoPath will remain in Format Painter mode until you press the Esc key. Once in this mode, the original formatting will be copied to all the text and controls you select. This makes the process of copying formatting from one part of the form to another that much easier. Another way to easily copy formatting is to use shortcut keys. Just as you can copy and paste text using Ctrl+C and Ctrl+V, respectively, you can copy and paste formatting using Ctrl+Shift+C and Ctrl+Shift+V.

Formatting Multiple Controls

As we mentioned, the Format Painter allows you to copy existing formatting from one part of the form to another. This is great if you have some preexisting formatting in your form. What if you want to set the formatting for controls in your form template but don't have any existing formatting in your form yet or you want to set only a few format styles? If you want to set the formatting styles for a single control, you can just select it and set the formatting as we described earlier. However, what if you want to do this on multiple controls at the same time? There is a very easy way to do this, which most new InfoPath users don't know—just select multiple controls at once and then format them.

You can easily select multiple controls by using text selection, but that will include all surrounding text. What if the controls you want to format aren't next to each other but, instead, are spread throughout the form template? In that case, you can actually use multiple control selection. To select multiple controls at once, first select one control using the correct selection method for that type of control, as discussed earlier. Then, hold down the

Ctrl key while selecting other controls. If you try to select a control that is already selected, that control will be deselected. Once you have selected all the controls you want to format, just format them as you would had you selected a single control.

Of course, when you apply formatting to multiple controls at once, only those formatting styles that a control supports will be applied. In some cases, if one of the controls you selected doesn't support any formatting, the formatting styles in the *Formatting* toolbar and *Font* task pane may be completely disabled. Just unselect the control that doesn't support the formatting styles and format that control separately (if it supports formatting at all).

You may be thinking that this is great. You can easily format multiple controls at once. But what if you want all your Text Box controls, for example, to be formatted the same way every time a new one is inserted? A little-known feature included in InfoPath design mode allows you to do this—*Apply Font to All Controls.* When you select a control, such as a Text Box, two new, previously hidden, menu items appear on the *Format* menu—*Apply Font to All Text Box Controls* and *Apply Font to All Controls.* (The name of the first menu item will change depending on the type of control you've selected.) Note that these menu items appear only for controls that support this feature, as shown in Table 2.5.

These menu items are very similar to the Format Painter in that they allow you to copy the formatting from the currently selected control to other controls in the form template. However, the menu items enable you to do this more quickly. When you select *Apply Font to All Text Box Controls* from the *Format* menu, the formatting styles from the currently selected Text Box control are copied to all the Text Box controls in the form template. When you select *Apply Font to All Controls,* the current formatting is copied to all controls (that support this feature) in the form template.

But, wait, there's even more. InfoPath remembers the formatting styles you copied. If you select *Apply Font to All Text Box Controls,* the next time you insert a Text Box control, it will be formatted with the same styles. If you choose *Apply Font to All Controls,* all newly inserted controls listed in Table 2.5 will be formatted the same way. Those controls that do not support this feature will not be formatted when you insert them from the

TABLE 2.5: Controls That Support Applying Font to All Controls

Control Name
Text Box
Rich Text Box
Date Picker
Drop-Down List Box
Combo Box
List Box
Bulleted List
Numbered List
Plain List
Expression Box
Multiple-Selection List Box

Controls task pane. In addition, just like the other formatting features, when a control is inserted, it will be formatted only with the formatting styles that it supports.

What if you want to set the default formatting styles for a control or you want to change the default styles after you have set them using the *Apply Font to All Controls* feature? Clicking on the *View Properties* item on the *View* menu opens the *View Properties* dialog, as we mentioned earlier. On the *Text Settings* tab (Figure 2.52), you can set or change the default formatting for controls that support this feature. Just as when you selected one of the *Apply Font to All Controls* items in the *Format* menu, the formatting styles set in the *Text Settings* tab will apply to any newly inserted controls of that type. If you save the form template, InfoPath will remember these settings the next time you open it. (These settings are specific to each form template. When you open a new form template, the settings for the previous form template do not apply.)

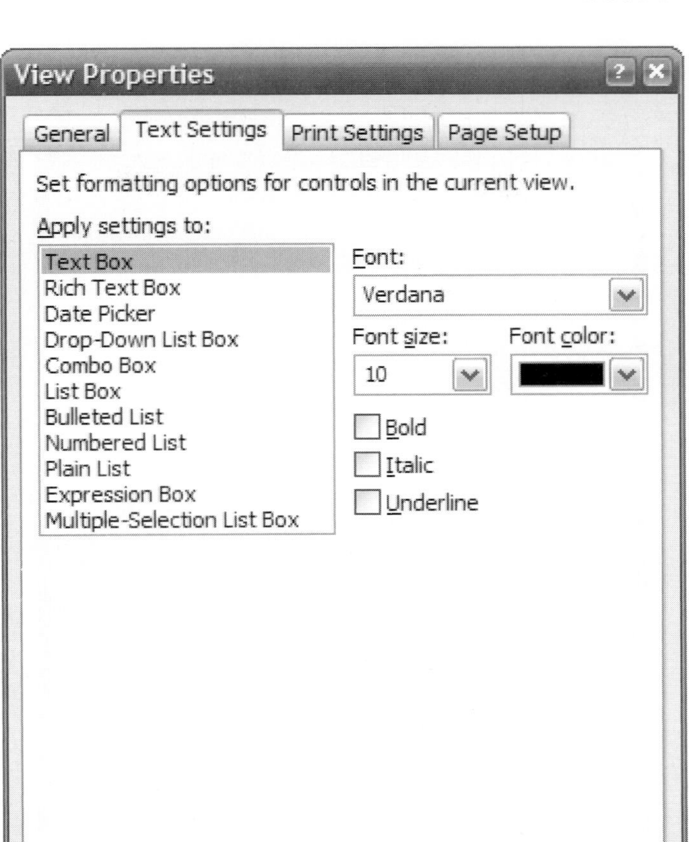

FIGURE 2.52: Text Settings tab in the View Properties dialog

What's Next?

In this chapter, you learned a little about form templates and saw how to create one from scratch. You learned how to design the layout of your form and how to include controls so users can enter data into your form. You also learned about multiple views and some of the advanced formatting features available in InfoPath. In the next chapter, you'll learn all about data. We'll talk about some of the data-centric features available in InfoPath and how controls are connected to the underlying data source.

What's Next?

3

Working with Data

Getting Started

In the last chapter, you learned about some of the basic features of InfoPath design mode that allow you to add visual flair to your forms. A visually pleasing and well-laid-out form may win accolades from your users; however, a form is not ultimately useful if it doesn't gather the data in the format you need. In this chapter, you will learn about a form template's data source by examining the *Data Source* task pane. Now that you know a little about controls, we'll show how they link to the data source through a mechanism called **data binding**. Recall that the data source is the behind-the-scenes XML that is created as users fill out your form and is used when saving or submitting the form.

We will also talk in depth about the various properties available on data source fields and groups. We'll consider the implications of changing data source properties and how it may affect your form template. Some of the properties we'll review include name, data type, cannot be blank, repeating, and default value.

Once you know about the ins and outs of data binding and data source properties, the next step is working with the data itself. We'll show you how to define two types of default data in your form: static and calculated. **Static default data** is always the same for each new form created from the form template. Most airline Web sites, for example, default to a round-trip instead of one-way ticket when planning a new flight. **Calculated default data** is determined by inputs from the environment (such as date and time or user name) or by other form data.

We'll also talk about how to alter the data source by using the *Data Source* task pane. We'll discuss operations such as *Add, Move, Delete,* and *Reference* and show how they can be used when designing your forms. We will allude to XML Schema details and call out some "gotchas" along the way to enrich the dialogue.

To start, let's first delve into how InfoPath controls hook up with XML behind the scenes.

Data Binding

Creating the Data Source Automatically

Do you remember what you did when designing your first InfoPath form? Most first-time users find their way to the *Controls* task pane and figure out how to insert controls into the view. We think it's because there's a big, empty view and folks want to fill it in with interesting "stuff." Most people dragging in controls likely don't realize that each newly inserted control creates a corresponding data source entry. We will talk in depth about how InfoPath creates the data source entry later in this chapter.

To see the data source in design mode, click on the *Data Source* menu item on the *Design Tasks* pane (as described in Chapter 2) or the *View* menu. Clicking on a control in the view will simultaneously select the data source node to which the control is **bound** (as shown in Figure 3.1; a sample called Binding is included with the samples for this chapter on the book's Web site). InfoPath 2003 and InfoPath 2003 Service Pack 1 have a *Data Source* context menu item that appears when you right-click on a bound control. Version 2007 does not have this option, however, since customer feedback indicated it was underused.

For each new control, InfoPath automatically creates one of two types of data source nodes. (A **node** is XML lingo for the smallest unit of valid, complete structure in a document. For more information about data source nodes, see "XML Schema Part 2: Datatypes Second Edition," referenced in the Appendix.) A **field** holds text data such as a string like `Monday` or a number like `100`. A field can also be referred to as a **leaf node**. (Picture an

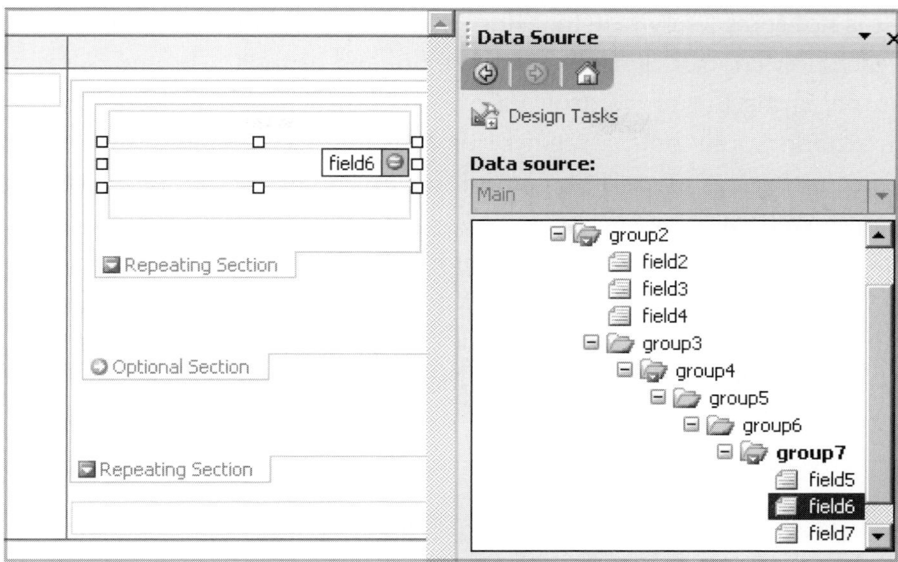

FIGURE 3.1: Clicking on a control in the view to select the bound control in the data source

upside-down tree where each leaf is at the lowest level and the root is at the top.) A field is represented in the data source by a document icon. The other type of node in the data source is a **group,** which is shown as a folder icon. (Groups can be compared to the branches on our tree.) Table 3.1 shows both the field and group icons. A group, or container node, cannot directly contain text data. Rather, a group can include fields or groups under itself. Given these two types of nodes, a data source can have many groups and fields in a hierarchical tree structure. The root is the top-most group of the tree. See Figure 3.7 later in this chapter for an example of such a data source.

TABLE 3.1: Icons Shown in the Data Source Task Pane for Various Types of Data Source Nodes

Node Type	Field (Element)	Field (Attribute)	Group
Nonrepeating			
Repeating		Field (Attribute) cannot repeat.	

It is not completely true that InfoPath creates a node in the data source for each new control: Some controls are not and cannot be bound. A prime example is the Button control. Inserting a Button does not create a data source node. Some controls are hybrids; they might be bound to a leaf node, but not always. A Hyperlink control, for example, may be inserted with a simple Web address, such as `http://www.awprofessional.com`. Or a Hyperlink can be bound to the data source, that is, the Hyperlink would link to the text of the leaf node to which it's bound. Figure 3.2 shows a Hyperlink bound to a data source field with the value `http://myHyperlinkText`. (This sample file, called Hyperlink, is included with this chapter's samples.)

FIGURE 3.2: A Hyperlink control bound to `field1` in the data source, with a link to the text of `field1`

Table 3.2 shows a full list of InfoPath 2007 built-in controls and their binding behaviors.

A common misconception when designing a form is that deleting a control from the view will also delete the data source node to which the control is bound. InfoPath is smart and helps you create new controls, but it doesn't want to assume too much and remove data source nodes that might be critical to the operation of your form. Deleting nodes automatically whenever a control is deleted could cause problems later when you try to use InfoPath's many data-centric features. To get around the so-called

TABLE 3.2: InfoPath 2007 Controls and Their Binding Behaviors

Control	Binding Behavior	Data Source Node	Comments
Text Box	Bound	Leaf node	
Rich Text Box	Bound	Leaf node	Binds to the XHTML data type.
Drop-Down List Box, Combo Box, List Box	Bound	Leaf node	
Date Picker	Bound	Leaf node	Usually binds to the date and time data types.
Check Box	Bound	Leaf node	Can bind to any type, typically Boolean.
Option Button	Bound	Leaf node	Usually many Option Button controls are bound to the same node because each Option Button has its own assigned value that, when selected, changes the bound node's value.
Button	Unbound		
Section, Optional Section	Bound	Container node	
Repeating Section, Repeating Table, Horizontal Repeating Table	Bound	Repeating container node	
Master/Detail	Bound	Single repeating container node (with both the master and detail controls bound to this repeating node); or can use two container nodes (one for master and the other for detail)	Best to think of this control as a special behavior between two container-bound controls. Note that Repeating Table as master and Repeating Section as detail is the default

continued

TABLE 3.2: InfoPath 2007 Controls and Their Binding Behaviors (*continued*)

Control	Binding Behavior	Data Source Node	Comments
			when Master/Detail is inserted. However, you can change the detail control to be a Repeating Table instead of a Repeating Section.
Bulleted List, Numbered List, Plain List, Multiple-Selection List Box	Bound	Repeating leaf node	
Picture	Bound	Leaf node	Picture data can be saved into the form as base64Binary, or a link to the image resource location is stored as a string.
File Attachment, Ink Picture	Bound	Leaf node	Binds to the base64Binary data type.
Hyperlink	Bound or unbound	Leaf node, if bound	Either the display text and/or the link itself can be bound or unbound.
Expression Box, Vertical Label	Bound, unbound, or multiply bound	Any node or set of nodes, if bound	Binding can be defined manually, which may or may not point to data source node(s).
Scrolling Region, Horizontal Region	Unbound		Appears to behave like a container control but isn't bound. Scrolling Region allows for a grouping of many controls within a specific area.
Choice Group	Bound	Virtual Choice Group	A virtual Choice Group is not a real item in the XML but is represented in the data source as a special *(Choice)* node.

Table 3.2: (*continued*)

Control	Binding Behavior	Data Source Node	Comments
Repeating Choice Group	Bound	Virtual repeating Choice Group	Similar to Choice Group.
Choice Section	Bound	Container node immediately under a virtual Choice Group	Choice sections may exist only within a Choice Group.
Repeating Recursive Section	Bound	Repeating recursive container node	

problem of inserting too many controls and then having to fix up the data source after the fact, consider these alternatives.

1. Design the data source first through the *Data Source* task pane. Then design the view by inserting data source nodes as controls. This is the reverse process from first dragging in controls. We discuss creating data sources manually in "Manually Editing the Data Source" later in this chapter.
2. Design the view, but with *Automatically create data source* (the checkbox at the bottom of the *Controls* task pane) unchecked. You will explicitly create each data source node as you insert each control. This might help prevent rampant control inserting!

> **NOTE** **Manually Cleaning Up Extra Data Source Nodes**
>
> In a later section of this chapter, "Manually Editing the Data Source," we show how to remove fields and groups by using the *Data Source* task pane.

Should you still decide to create the data source by inserting controls with *Automatically create data source* enabled, the data source fields and groups will have default names such as `field1` and `group1`. There are advantages in naming your data source nodes properly instead of keeping generic names. The foremost benefit is human recognition. You can look at the data source (even a saved .xml form in a text editor like Microsoft Notepad) and clearly understand its structure as well as what it means. It's also an alternative way to determine whether you've missed something such as including a field for customer feedback. Other advantages include easier long-term form template maintenance, reusability of the data source in other form templates, and your peace of mind when InfoPath prevents someone from saving or submitting the form because `CustomerName`, instead of `field52`, cannot be empty. Throughout the remainder of the chapter, we'll use descriptive names for our data source fields and groups.

If you're stuck designing an existing form template with a data source of generic names, there are quick ways to update the node names. You have two possibilities; your choice will depend on whether you're a mouse clicker or keyboard junkie.

1. Mouse: Double-clicking a data source node brings up the *Field or Group Properties* dialog. Default focus is on the *Name* text box, so simply type the new node name and dismiss the dialog.
2. Keyboard: Clicking a node in the data source and then hitting F6 puts focus on the node you clicked. Use the Up and Down arrow keys to move around the data source. Hit the Enter key to get to the *Field or Group Properties* dialog and type the new name. After closing the dialog, hit F6 again to restore focus to the *Data Source* task pane. InfoPath always shifts focus to the view unless you explicitly hit F6 to put it on the task pane.

It's nice to know ahead of time that the data source doesn't support undo, or redo for that matter. Any data source change is said and done the moment you do it. To revert your changes, you will need to reverse them manually. You might choose to occasionally save your form template with a different name to snapshoot your data source. This is especially helpful when you're carrying out many data source changes.

Understanding Data Source Details

You don't need to know very much about controls to understand the data source, so let's shift gears to talk about data source details. To help you master the data source and its many options, we should discuss XML Schemas. Learning the intricacies of XML Schemas is critical to becoming an InfoPath expert. During our discussions we'll make superficial references to schema concepts without getting into too many details since, of course, this isn't a book about XML Schemas.

In Chapter 1, we said that InfoPath generates semistructured documents. Semistructured documents are a midpoint between unstructured and fully structured. An unstructured document is the content of this text: freeform with no forced boundaries. Alternatively, a fully structured document defines every allowable input and offers little or no flexibility for user-defined data.

A fully structured document may look like this:

```
<Title>Designing Forms for Microsoft Office InfoPath
and Forms Services 2007</Title>
<Author>Roberts</Author><Author>Green</Author><ISBN>123456</ISBN>
<Genre>Developer</Genre><Subject>InfoPath</Subject>
```

A fully structured document, such as the XML snippet shown above, allows for very little flexibility since specifics such as `Author`, `ISBN`, `Genre`, and `Subject` are all specifically requested. In contrast, a semistructured document could be as such:

```
<Title>Designing Forms for Microsoft Office InfoPath and Forms Services
2007</Title>
<Author>Roberts,Green</Author><ISBN>123456</ISBN>
<Description>Developer-oriented InfoPath book on designing form templates
with the latest version of the forms designer and filler.</Description>
```

The difference between the fully structured and semistructured documents is flexibility in the `Description` field. The `Genre` and `Subject` fields are included in the `Description` in a freeform format. You can see that the semistructured document allows for some additional flexibility in comparison to the fully structured version.

Before we continue, let's establish a vocabulary so our understanding of upcoming topics is mutual. A **node** is a generic XML-specific term to describe the smallest unit of data in XML. A node in the InfoPath data source during design mode can be one of these types: **element** or **attribute**. (There are others not shown by InfoPath—such as comments and processing instructions—but those XML details are beyond the scope of this chapter.) When speaking about the **data source**, there can be several different meanings:

- What is shown in the design-mode *Data Source* task pane
- The XML behind the scenes when filling out a form
- External data that InfoPath queries to import data

Typically the context of the term should make it clear to which definition we are referring.

Since elements and attributes are nodes, how do fields and groups fit into the picture? Fields and groups are InfoPath-specific concepts that map to XML. To recap, a field is an element node that can hold text data the user enters. A group cannot hold text data. When an element can hold text data we call it a leaf node since it cannot contain a group. Likewise, since a group can further contain groups and fields, it is considered a container node.

Let's close up this terminology session with a final comparison: elements and attributes with fields and groups. Comparing these terms is attempting to bring together XML with InfoPath, so there isn't exactly a one-to-one mapping, as you'll see. A field can be an element or attribute. InfoPath delineates the two in data source details by showing *Field (element)* or *Field (attribute).* (An element and attribute are both shown in Figure 3.25 later in this chapter.) Here's where it gets confusing: A group is also an element. The obvious but critical difference between *Field (element)* and *Group* is that a field is a leaf node and a group is a container node. Table 3.1 earlier in this chapter shows the icons InfoPath displays in the *Data Source* task pane during design mode to differentiate between fields and groups.

Element and Attribute Fields in XML

An element in an InfoPath form's XML data is represented by an opening and closing tag and may contain data, such as **<my:field1>**hello **</my:field1>**. An attribute can also hold data but must reside on an element, such as <my:field1 myattribute="hello">hello again </my:field1>.

Data Source Field and Group Properties

Name Property

Double-clicking on an item in the *Data Source* task pane yields a dialog to modify the node's properties. The first property, which we discussed earlier in the chapter, is the field or group name. This name is also conveniently accessible from the bound control's properties dialog despite it being a property of the data source (this is discussed further in Chapter 4). The field or group name is simply a way to reference data that is held behind the field itself. If you've ever written source code to program a computer, the name is synonymous with a variable name. A variable can be referenced, its data assigned to, and so on; so too can a data source field. As you might know, changing a node name is very easy to do: Just type in a new, unique name. But exercise caution before changing a field or group name if your form template has been published. If you change a node name and republish the form to the same location, there's a possibility that forms created from the previously published version will either no longer open or open but with data loss. Let's take a closer look at why this happens.

NOTE Changing Field or Group Names Can Break Existing Forms

If saved forms already exist based on your form template, changing field or group names in the data source may cause data loss when upgrading the form to the new template data source.

TABLE 3.3: XML Data and Schema That Match Before Changing a Field or Group Name

XML Form Data	Form Template Schema
A	A
B	B
C	C

For a form to be successfully opened, the XML data in the form must agree to the rules and requirements of the form template schema. For example, a schema could define fields `A`, `B`, and `C`, as shown in Table 3.3. Therefore, all forms created from this template using this schema will have fields `A`, `B`, and `C`. Whenever a form is saved and reopened, you could reasonably expect all three fields would exist in that form's XML. What if, between the time someone saves and reopens the form, you open the form template in design mode and change the data source by renaming leaf node `B` to `D`? Table 3.4 shows this change in the form template schema. Depending on your template's setting for handling *Version Upgrade* (which is automatic by default), the form will either open with the data missing from field `B` (the default case) or not open at all with an error message about validation errors (field `B` was found, but expected field `D`). The version upgrade feature setting is found in the *Form Options* dialog's *Versioning* category.

TABLE 3.4: Mismatched XML Data and Schema After a Name Change

XML Form Data	Form Template Schema
A	A
B	*D*
C	C

At the time you might introduce a potentially breaking change when designing a published form template, InfoPath will prompt you. Figure 3.3 shows the warning dialog. If you absolutely must change a published

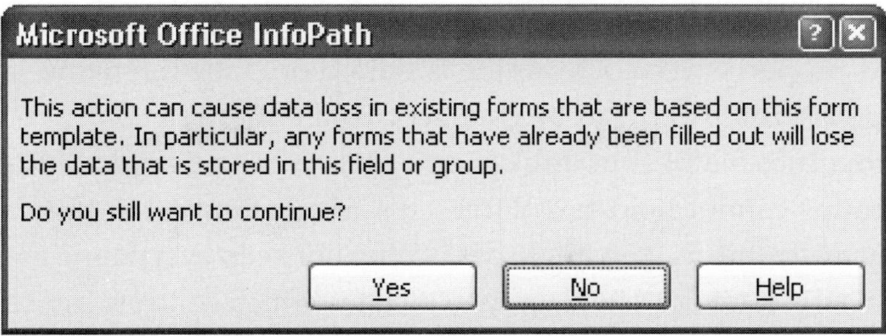

FIGURE 3.3: Warning dialog when changing the name of a data source field or group for a published form

template's data source, ensure the change is forward compatible. Table 3.5 lists data source operations and how they may affect published form templates with version upgrade set to automatic (the default setting). If the upgrade mode was set to *Do nothing,* data loss cases in Table 3.4 would instead be breaking changes. A breaking change with version upgrade set to *Do nothing* will cause previously created forms to fail to open. We recommend that you do not change the setting for this reason alone. The information in Table 3.5 also assumes that all data source changes are done using InfoPath and not via hand-editing or an external tool to edit the schema directly. (Specifically, the nodes in question are never required and, when repeating, have no upper bound.)

TABLE 3.5: How Data Source Operations on a Published Form Template May Affect Saved Forms

Data Source Operation	Data Loss?
Delete node	Yes, if the form has the node.
Insert node	Never.
Change node name	Yes, if the form has the node.
Change nonrepeating to repeating	Never.
Change repeating to nonrepeating	Yes, if the form has more than one instance of the node.

Data Type Property

The next property we will examine is data type. Like the name property, data type is visible and can be changed from either the control or bound node properties dialog. But unlike name, data type will apply only to fields since groups cannot hold text. First, let's understand what the data type property really means. You might ask: "Why not keep everything as string?" The answer is twofold. The data type dictates which controls can be bound to the field in question. Strings happen to be the most control-compatible data type, but you can never bind a string field to a Rich Text Box control, for example. On the contrary, you could bind a Picture (or even Ink Picture) control to a string field (instead of the expected base64 type). But it would be unfortunate if you mistakenly also bound a Text Box control to that same field. Garbage text will appear in the Text Box if a picture is selected. (Multiple binding, where two or more controls are bound to the same node, is discussed in the "Design-Time Visuals" section later in this chapter.) Thus it's imperative to use the most appropriate data types for your data source fields so bindings such as a Text Box control to picture data don't happen.

Similarly to changing the name property, changing the data type of a field on a previously published form template can break or cause data loss on old forms. Think twice when "tightening" the restrictions on a field's data type. If an age field was a string, and you changed it to whole number on a formerly published template, any forms that didn't exactly use a number will be broken or have lost that data if reopened. Examples of breaks would be an age field with any of these values: `"18 1/2"`, `"18.5"`, or `"18 years, 6 months"`.

Choosing appropriate data types for your fields will help keep user-entered data relevant. Table 3.6 looks at each data type and what it buys in terms of validation. (You can find a full quick reference guide to XML Schema data types on the World Wide Web Consortium site [referenced in the Appendix], on which the information in Table 3.6 is based.)

It's always a good idea to keep your data types as strict as possible when you first design your form. If the data type is too strict, loosening it up will never break existing forms. Looking for more comprehensive validation than just data type? We discuss declarative data validation in Chapter 5.

TABLE 3.6: Data Types Available in InfoPath Design Mode and Their Value Ranges

Data Type	Allowed Values
String	Any text data
Rich text (XHTML)	HTML (i.e., well-formed XML)
Whole number (integer)	–2147483648 to 2147483647
Decimal (double)	63-bit floating point type, or a legal literal (0, –0, INF, –INF, NaN)
True/false (Boolean)	TRUE, FALSE, true, false, 0, 1, {blank}
Hyperlink (anyURI)	Uniform Resource Identifier (URI); see the World Wide Web Consortium on naming and addressing referenced in the Appendix for details
Date	Calendar date, in the form YYYY-MM-DD
Time	An instant of time that occurs every day; based on the ISO 8601 format
DateTime	A specific instant of time, in the form YYYY-MM-DDThh:mm:ss±hh:mm; based on the ISO 8601 extended format
Picture or File Attachment (base64)	Base64-encoded binary data
Custom (complexType)	Custom data

When users fill out the form, data source fields help users adhere to the data type by passively informing them of errors. Data types such as string, XHTML, and complexType do not validate because the nature of those data types are freeform. However, all other data types discourage user input in some way. The word "discourage" accurately describes the user experience when entering invalid data. The data is allowed to be entered, but as the user changes focus, the control shows a thick red hashed border signaling a problem. Hovering over or giving focus to the control shows a

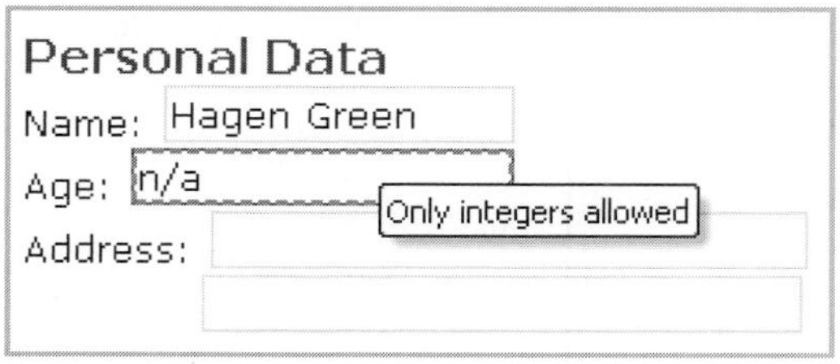

FIGURE 3.4: Data type validation error that occurs when a field contains invalid data

Forms Services

Browser-enabled form templates also show validation, but tool tips are not used. Instead, a box appears above the control with the validation error message. Additional details are available if the error message text appears as a link. Clicking the link opens a dialog with additional details. You can also hit Ctrl+Shift+I to show the dialog.

tool tip with the specific validation error (Figure 3.4). In this case, only integers are allowed.

Data type errors always prevent users from submitting the form if submit functionality is enabled. (Submit is discussed at length in Chapter 8.) Even if a data connection, which can send data to an external system, submits a single field that is valid at the time of submit, it is still not allowed. (Chapters 6, 7, and 8 provide more information on data connections.) Despite submit not scoping the validation only to the specific data in the form to be submitted, the entire data source must be free of validation errors for submit to happen. Unlike submit, a form can be saved with validation errors only after the user accepts a daunting warning message (Figure 3.5).

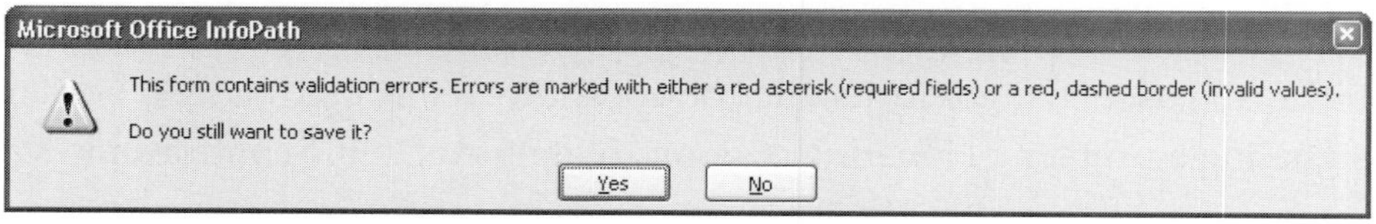

FIGURE 3.5: Warning when saving a form with validation errors

Forms Services

Browser-enabled form templates in the browser do not warn when saving a form with validation errors. Submit will fail, however, if the form contains errors.

Data types have no bearing on whether or not a field requires filling out. Even though technically an empty integer field does not make sense, it is allowed. Astute readers may argue that the XML Schema integer type is not satisfied by an empty value. This argument is undoubtedly true. Since InfoPath is meant to be a user-friendly and flexible tool, it leverages the XML Schema `nillable` feature. When a schema defines a node to be `nillable`, it allows an empty value for the node to be a valid value in addition to the data type constraints. Some schema data types do not make sense with `nillable` such as string since an empty string is valid by definition.

Cannot Be Blank Property

To manage whether or not a field is valid as empty, use the *Cannot be blank* checkbox on the *Field or Group Properties* dialog. In our discussion about data types, we said that some data types add `nillable` to the schema definition for a given node. Checking *Cannot be blank* will remove `nillable`. Doing so enforces the classical definition of those XML Schema data types. Types where `nillable` does not make sense will respond differently in the schema to the cannot be blank property. A string, for example, actually changes to a custom InfoPath-defined data type called `requiredString`. This custom type is similar to a string but adds a minimum length constraint through XML Schema's `minLength` feature. The schema that InfoPath generates for this custom type is shown in the code below. Figure 3.6 shows an example of using the cannot be blank property when filling out the form.

```
<xsd:element name="field1" type="my:requiredString"/>
<xsd:simpleType name="requiredString">
    <xsd:restriction base="xsd:string">
    <xsd:minLength value="1"/>
</xsd:restriction>
</xsd:simpleType>
```

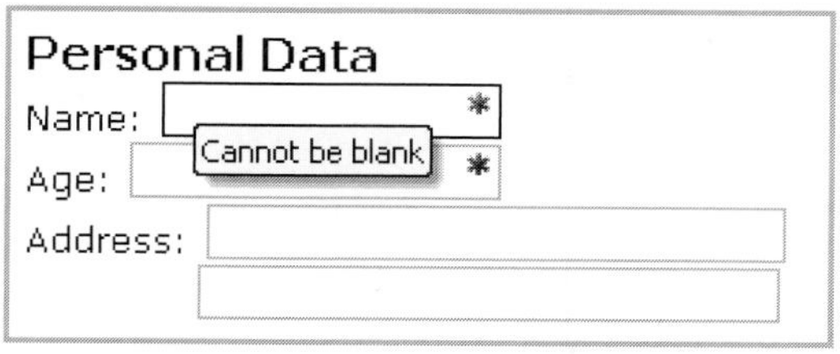

Personal Data
Name: * Cannot be blank
Age: *
Address:

FIGURE 3.6: Validation error for the cannot be blank property, delineated by a red asterisk

Fields that cannot be blank are treated similarly to validation errors but with a different visual cue. Notice that the warning message in Figure 3.6 equally addresses empty and invalid fields as needing attention.

> **TIP Extracting the XML Schema from a Form Template**
>
> To see your form template's XML Schema(s), select *Save as Source Files* from the *File* menu in design mode. The XML Schema file name extension is .xsd. You can view the file in an application that can render schemas such as Visual Studio .NET, or simply open it in a text editor like Notepad. You can find more information about *Save as Source Files* in Chapter 9.

Repeating Property

So far we've looked at the following properties of a node: name, data type, and cannot be blank. The next property we'll discuss, which applies equally to leaf and container nodes but not attribute nodes, is repetition. Why is repetition necessary? Repetition lets a form designer gather more than one of a specific piece of data when a user fills out the form. Say a form collects the names of participants in a bicycling ride. Without repetition, the names would need to be entered into a single Text Box control bound to a field. A special delimiter character could separate the names. We wouldn't want to maintain that list! Can't we just create more fields instead? The approach of using multiple fields does not work because you don't know ahead of time how many participants will show up. You could group first letters of last names across multiple Text Box controls and fields, but we're still back into the same problem. Repeating fields and groups solve these maintenance nightmares by making many items of data easy to manage.

Any nonattribute node in the data source can repeat except for the top-level node, per XML standards. (The top-level node in an XML document is formally known as the document element.) When a field or group is blessed with the ability to repeat in InfoPath, it does not mean it must repeat. To understand what repeating really means, we again turn to the form template's XML Schema definition. When a node is defined in a schema, you have the option to specify the minimum (`minOccurs`) and maximum (`maxOccurs`) number of times it can appear. InfoPath, by design, always creates fields and groups with their minimums equal to `"0"`. This means the node need not appear in the XML. By default when filling out the form, any field or group can be deleted (assuming the user interface provides a way to do so, such as an Optional Section control). The maximum of a nonrepeating node is `"1"`. This gives each node a simple binary behavior: It exists or it doesn't. When the *Repeating* checkbox in the *Field or Group Properties* dialog is checked, InfoPath modifies the maximum number of times the node is allowed to appear to be `"unbounded"`. This value is understood by XML Schema to mean there's no limit to how many times the node may appear, until you run out of memory on your computer! Since the minimum is still `"0"`, a Repeating Section control, for example, could be completely removed from the form even though the schema classifies it as repeating.

Let's look at how repeating nodes appear in the data source and peek at the form XML when filling out their corresponding controls. We'll use a Numbered List control for our repeating field example. Figure 3.7 shows the data source and repeating `field4`. Notice that `group1` is the immediate container of `field4`. `group1` was inserted for us when we dragged in a Numbered List control. InfoPath always inserts a group above a repeating node whenever you insert a new repeating control into the view. To justify the existence of this extra node, Table 3.7 shows a comparison of XML data where `group1` does and does not exist. As you can see, the clear benefit of this container node is that it helps to better organize the data into a hierarchy. An advantage of hierarchical data (over a flat structure) is grouping of similar data under a common parent for organizational purposes.

Earlier we discussed naming our fields and groups with real names instead of the default names InfoPath assigns. To not be hypocritical, we

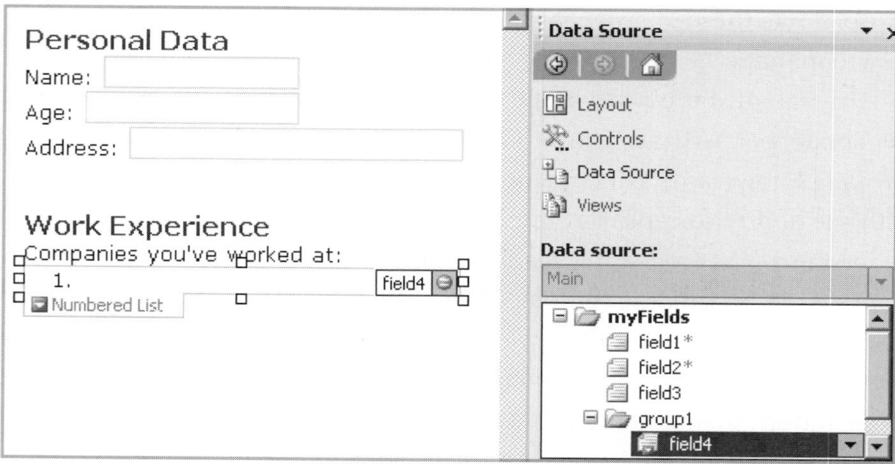

FIGURE 3.7: Repeating field4, which is bound to the Numbered List control and repeats in group1

TABLE 3.7: Sample Form XML Data with and without a Repeating Container*

Sample Data Based on Figure 3.7	Same Sample Data, but without group1
<my:myFields> <my:field1>John Smith </my:field1> <my:field2>26</my:field2> <my:field3>1 Microsoft Way </my:field3> **<my:group1>** *<my:field4>Microsoft* *Corp.</my:field4>* *<my:field4>Self-employed* *</my:field4>* *<my:field4>Education:* *Research</my:field4>* **</my:group1>** </my:myFields>	<my:myFields> <my:field1>John Smith </my:field1> <my:field2>26</my:field2> <my:field3>1 Microsoft Way </my:field3> *<my:field4>Microsoft Corp.* *</my:field4>* *<my:field4>Self-employed* *</my:field4>* *<my:field4>Education:* *Research</my:field4>* </my:myFields>

* Repeating data is italicized.

will rename our repeating field to something that makes sense. For naming the repeating field as well as the container node, we're constrained by what XML allows us to name a node: It must begin with an alphabetic character or underscore and may contain alphanumeric characters, underscores, hyphens, and periods. Let's rename `field4` to be `Employer`. What about renaming `group1`, the container node? A best practice for naming containers is to use the plural name of the repeating node name. In this case, `group1` would change to `Employers`. It makes sense, too. `Employers` can hold many instances of `Employer`. Table 3.8 shows the node names updated from Table 3.7.

TABLE 3.8: Data from Table 3.7, but with Updated Node Names for Readability*

Sample Data Based on Figure 3.7	Same Sample Data, but without the **Employers** Container
<my:myFields> <my:field1>John Smith </my:field1> <my:field2>26</my:field2> <my:field3>1 Microsoft Way</my:field3> **<my:Employers>** *<my:Employer>Microsoft* *Corp.</my:Employer>* *<my:Employer>Self-* *Employed </my:Employer>* *<my:Employer>Education:* *Research </my:Employer>* </my:Employers> </my:myFields>	<my:myFields> <my:field1>John Smith </my:field1> <my:field2>26</my:field2> <my:field3>1 Microsoft Way </my:field3> *<my:Employer>Microsoft* *Corp.</my:Employer>* *<my: Employer>Self-* *Employed</my:Employer>* *<my:Employer>Education:* *Research </my:Employer>* </my:myFields>

* Repeating data is italicized.

Since repeating groups work in fundamentally the same ways as repeating fields, we won't spend time discussing them.

Cannot be Blank Property versus Optional

It's a perfect time to touch on a point of potential confusion between a field marked as cannot be blank and an optional field. When you select the *Cannot be blank* checkbox, it means that if the field exists, it cannot be empty. When a field or group is optional, that is, it is defined in the schema as having a `minOccurs` of `"0"`, it is possible to delete the field or group when filling out the form and it will not exist in the data. So a field set as cannot be blank can coexist with a node being optional, but the cannot be blank property works only when the node exists in the data. Note that the cannot be blank property applies only to leaf nodes, while the state of being optional can apply to any node including groups.

Default Value Property

Static Default Values

The last major property you should know about a data source node, specifically a field, is its default value. Default values help make your form easier to fill out by saving time and lessening the possibility of confusing your users. Let's explain by using the airline Web site example mentioned earlier. The company could set the default values as a round-trip flight and a normal meal preference. Users could change those values if they want something different, but otherwise they wouldn't need to do anything further to fill in those portions of the form. Figure 3.8 shows a form that replicates the airline Web site. (The sample file is called Airline.)

> **TIP Show Data Source Details**
>
> Check *Show Details* on the *Data Source* task pane to show each leaf node's data type and default value, if specified. Calculated default values are not shown.

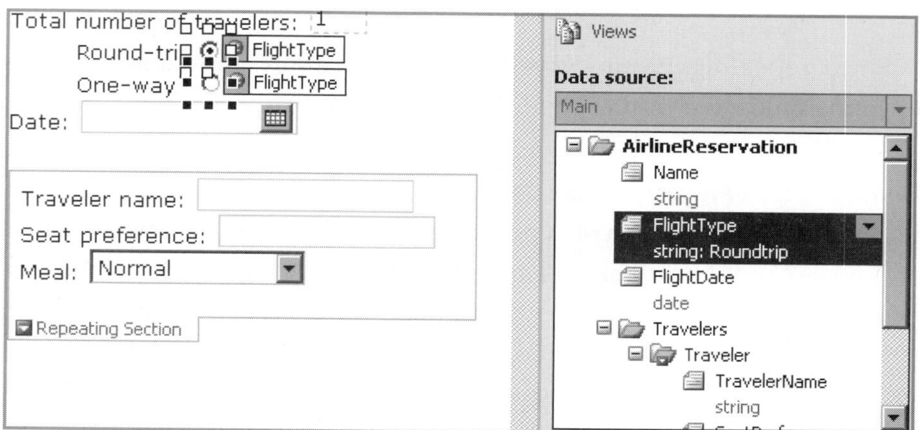

FIGURE 3.8: Airline form with default value for `FlightType` as `"Roundtrip"`

Calculated Default Values

Let's tackle a more challenging problem with default values. The airline's marketing department tells us that, on average, flights are scheduled 45 days ahead of time. They want the Date Picker control to default to this "sweet spot" date to make the form easier for people to fill out. You might think that custom code would need to be written to implement this functionality. It is possible to write script or managed code to do this, but it's much easier when using calculated default values. Clicking the insert formula button (Figure 3.9) will show the *Insert Formula* dialog (Figure 3.10). We'll talk more about the *Insert Formula* dialog in the next two chapters. Clicking on the *Insert Function* button shows a series of categories; one of them is *Date and Time*. Two functions give us the tools we need to get the date (`today`) and add 45 days (`addDays`). Notice that when you choose the `addDays` function, you'll get the following:

```
addDays(double click to insert field, double click to insert field)
```

By using the function `today()` in one of the `double click to insert field` parameters and typing the value `"45"` in place of the other, you'd make the marketing people very happy.

FIGURE 3.9: The default value calculation button

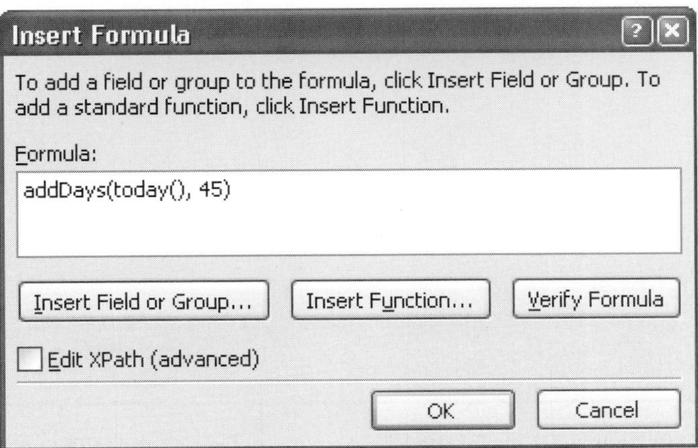

FIGURE 3.10: The Insert Formula dialog, with a formula that sets this field's default value to today's date plus 45 days

Data Source Details

Let's tie up our conversation about data source nodes by visiting the *Details* tab on the *Field or Group Properties* dialog. Figure 3.11 shows the dialog for the node bound to the Option Buttons in which we set `"Roundtrip"` as the default value. Notice that so far we've discussed all of the properties listed except for one: namespace. We won't get into too many details, but a namespace is an XML concept by which nodes are classified. For example, most of the XML data in the manifest.xsf file belongs to the `xsf` namespace, which is `http://schemas.microsoft.com/office/infopath/2003/solutionDefinition`. You can discover this for yourself because the elements in the XML are prefaced with `xsf` and a colon before the element name. Likewise, when creating a new form template using InfoPath, the schema associated with that template is in its own unique namespace. Forms created from that specific form template will always have its XML data in that namespace. In this case, the dialog in Figure 3.11 shows the namespace for our form template to be

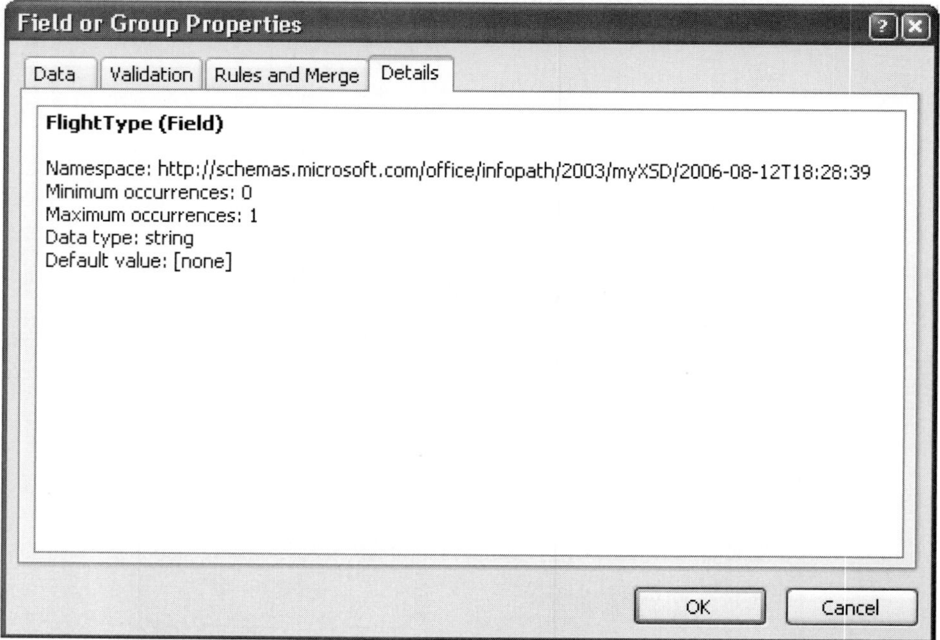

FIGURE 3.11: Data source details for the `FlightType` field bound to the option buttons in the airline form

`http://schemas.microsoft.com/office/infopath/2003/myXSD/2006-08-12T18:28:39`. We'll talk more about namespaces in the data source (and their corresponding prefixes) later in this chapter.

Enough talk about XML Schemas. Let's materialize these concepts by revealing the actual structure of the data. Since you're already familiar with the airline form and its data source, its schema will be easier to understand. Listing 3.1 shows the schema for the airline form template.

LISTING 3.1: XML Schema for the Airline Form Template

```
<?xml version="1.0" encoding="UTF-8" standalone="no"?>
<xsd:schema targetNamespace=". . ." xmlns:my=". . ."
xmlns:xsd="http://www.w3.org/2001/XMLSchema">
<xsd:element name="AirlineReservation">
   <xsd:complexType>
      <xsd:sequence>
         <xsd:element ref="my:Name" minOccurs="0"/>
         <xsd:element ref="my:FlightType" minOccurs="0"/>
         <xsd:element ref="my:FlightDate" minOccurs="0"/>
         <xsd:element ref="my:Travelers" minOccurs="0"/>
      </xsd:sequence>
      <xsd:anyAttribute processContents="lax"
      namespace="http://www.w3.org/XML/1998/namespace"/>
   </xsd:complexType>
</xsd:element>
<xsd:element name="Name" type="xsd:string"/>
<xsd:element name="FlightType" type="xsd:string"/>
<xsd:element name="FlightDate" nillable="true" type="xsd:date"/>
<xsd:element name="Travelers">
   <xsd:complexType>
      <xsd:sequence>
         <xsd:element ref="my:Traveler" minOccurs="0"
         maxOccurs="unbounded"/>
      </xsd:sequence>
    </xsd:complexType>
</xsd:element>
<xsd:element name="Traveler">
   <xsd:complexType>
      <xsd:sequence>
         <xsd:element ref="my:TravelerName" minOccurs="0"/>
         <xsd:element ref="my:SeatPreference" minOccurs="0"/>
         <xsd:element ref="my:MealPreference" minOccurs="0"/>
      </xsd:sequence>
   </xsd:complexType>
</xsd:element>
<xsd:element name="TravelerName" type="xsd:string"/>
<xsd:element name="SeatPreference" type="xsd:string"/>
<xsd:element name="MealPreference" type="xsd:string"/>
</xsd:schema>
```

The schema may appear overwhelming at first, but it is quite simple to parse. The data source fields and groups you've seen in previous examples are in bold. If you're wondering why some of the elements appear to be duplicates, it's because some instances are simply element declarations, while others are implementations of the elements. Declaring an element differs from using that element; the latter is accomplished through a `ref`. It is possible in XML Schemas to declare and use an element simultaneously, but it is programmatically more efficient for InfoPath to maintain a schema (such as this) where declarations and usage are exclusive.

An example of a declaration is the `Name` element as an `xsd:string`. Because all declared elements are top level (i.e., their parent is the `xsd:schema` element), a reference to an element declaration is necessary to actually use that element. Recall our earlier discussion on the minimum and maximum number of times a node can appear. All nodes declared in this schema have the `minOccurs="0"` designation. This means they need not appear. Can you find the one node that is repeating?

Now that we've seen a sample schema for the airline form, we can better understand what schema is automatically created for each new bindable InfoPath control. Table 3.9 maps each control to the schema that is created. The name in bold is the node actually bound to the control we insert.

To look at the form template schema for yourself, along with the handful of other files that make up the form, use the *Save As Source Files* option from the *File* menu.

Manually Editing the Data Source

Many forms are created through inserting controls into the view. With what we've reviewed in the section "Understanding Data Source Details," you can easily dive into the *Field or Group Properties* dialog to alter basics like name, data type, repeating, cannot be blank, and default value. In this section, we go beyond the node basics and look at the data source as a whole. We'll show you intermediate data source concepts that fall into two categories. The first category involves data source intricacies rather than the properties of a specific node. In the second category, we'll show you how to do things with the data source that InfoPath won't do automatically or doesn't fully explore. By the end of our discussion, you should

Table 3.9: InfoPath Controls and the XML Schema Created "Behind" the Data Source in the XSD File

Control	Schema	Comments
Text Box, Drop-Down List Box, Combo Box, List Box, Option Button	`<xsd:element name="field1" type="xsd:string"/>`	

Rich Text Box	`<xsd:element name="field1">`
	`<xsd:complexType mixed="true">`
	`<xsd:sequence>`
	`<xsd:any minOccurs="0"`
	`maxOccurs="unbounded"`
	`namespace=http://www.w3.org/1999/xhtml`
	`processContents="lax"/>`
	`</xsd:sequence>`
	`</xsd:complexType>`
	`</xsd:element>`
		This is the formal definition of XHTML in XML Schema. The attribute named `mixed` means there can be both elements and text. `xsd:any` allows any nodes in the namespace (nodes such as `a`, `font`, and `div`).

Check Box	`<xsd:element name="field1"` `type="xsd:boolean"/>`	
Date Picker	`<xsd:element name="field1" nillable="true"` `type="xsd:date"/>`	The `nillable` attribute means this field can be empty and still be valid.

Section, Optional Section	`<xsd:element name="group1">`
	`<xsd:complexType>`
	`<xsd:sequence/>`
	`</xsd:complexType>`
	`</xsd:element>`
		The empty `xsd:sequence` element means `group1` has no child nodes.

continued

TABLE 3.9: InfoPath Controls and the XML Schema Created "Behind" the Data Source in the XSD File (*continued*)

Control	Schema	Comments

Repeating Section	`<xsd:element name="group1">`
	  `<xsd:complexType>`
	    `<xsd:sequence>`
	      `<xsd:element ref="my:group2"`
	      `minOccurs="0"`
	      `maxOccurs="unbounded"/>`
	    `</xsd:sequence>`
	  `</xsd:complexType>`
	`</xsd:element>`
	`<xsd:element name="`**`group2`**`">`
	  `<xsd:complexType>`
	    `<xsd:sequence/>`
	  `</xsd:complexType>`
	`</xsd:element>`
		Control is bound to `group2`, which is the optional and repeating node. `group1` is simply a wrapper.

Repeating Table, Horizontal Repeating Table	`<xsd:element name="group1">`
	`<xsd:complexType>`
	    `<xsd:sequence>`
	      `<xsd:element ref="my:group2"`
	      `minOccurs="0"`
	      `maxOccurs="unbounded"/>`
	    `</xsd:sequence>`
	`</xsd:complexType>`
	`</xsd:element>`
	`<xsd:element name="`**`group2`**`">`
	  `<xsd:complexType>`
	    `<xsd:sequence>`
		`group2` is repeating with `group1` as a wrapper and `field1, field2`, and `field3` as children.

	<xsd:element ref="my:field1" minOccurs="0"/> <xsd:element ref="my:field2" minOccurs="0"/> <xsd:element ref="my:field3" minOccurs="0"/> </xsd:sequence> </xsd:complexType> </xsd:element>	
Master/Detail	(See comments.)	The master control is a Repeating Table, and the detail control is a Repeating Section.
Numbered List, Bulleted List, Plain List, Multiple-Selection List Box	<xsd:element name="group1"> <xsd:complexType> <xsd:sequence> <xsd:element ref="my:field1" minOccurs="0" maxOccurs="unbounded"/> </xsd:sequence> </xsd:complexType> </xsd:element> <xsd:element name="**field1**" type="xsd:string"/>	Repeating field1 is wrapped by group1.
File Attachment, Picture, Ink Picture	<xsd:element name="**field1**" nillable="true" type="xsd:base64Binary"/>	

continued

TABLE 3.9: InfoPath Controls and the XML Schema Created "Behind" the Data Source in the XSD File (*continued*)

Control	Schema	Comments

Choice Section, Choice Group	`<xsd:element name="group1">`
	`<xsd:complexType>`
	`<xsd:`**`choice`**` minOccurs="0">`
	`<xsd:element ref="my:group2"`
	`minOccurs="0"/>`
	`<xsd:element ref="my:group3"`
	`minOccurs="0"/>`
	`</xsd:choice>`
	`</xsd:complexType>`
	`</xsd:element>`
	`<xsd:element name="`**`group2`**`">`
	`<xsd:complexType>`
	`<xsd:sequence/>`
	`</xsd:complexType>`
	`</xsd:element>`
	`<xsd:element name="`**`group3`**`">`
	`<xsd:complexType>`
	`<xsd:sequence/>`
	`</xsd:complexType>`
	`</xsd:element>`
		`group1` is a Choice Group with `group2` and `group3` as the mutually exclusive choices.
		
		Note that a Choice Section cannot exist outside of a Choice Group.

Repeating Choice Group	`<xsd:element name="group1">`
	`<xsd:complexType>`
	`<xsd:`**`choice`**` minOccurs="0"`
	`maxOccurs="unbounded">`
	`<xsd:element ref="my:group2"`
	`minOccurs="0"/>`
	`<xsd:element ref="my:group3"`
	`minOccurs="0"/>`
	`</xsd:choice>`
		Same as Choice Group, but the choice is repeating.

<table>
<tr><td></td><td></xsd:complexType>
</xsd:element>
<xsd:element name="group2">
<xsd:complexType>
  <xsd:sequence/>
</xsd:complexType>
</xsd:element>
<xsd:element name="group3">
<xsd:complexType>
  <xsd:sequence/>
</xsd:complexType>
</xsd:element></td><td></td></tr>
<tr><td>Repeating Recursive Section</td><td><xsd:element name="group1">
<xsd:complexType>
  <xsd:sequence>
    <xsd:element ref="my:group2"
    minOccurs="0"
    maxOccurs="unbounded"/>
</xsd:sequence>
</xsd:complexType>
</xsd:element>
<xsd:element name="<b>group2</b>">
  <xsd:complexType>
    <xsd:sequence>
      <xsd:element ref="my:group2"
      minOccurs="0"
      maxOccurs="unbounded"/>
      </xsd:sequence>
  </xsd:complexType>
</xsd:element></td><td><code>group2</code> is recursive (it references itself), while <code>group1</code> is a wrapper. The first instance of <code>group2</code> is not bound, but the second instance is bound.</td></tr>
<tr><td></td><td></td><td></td></tr>
</table>

have a high level of confidence when creating, editing, and customizing your data source with InfoPath's design mode.

There are four actions you can take to shape and customize a data source: add, move, delete, and reference. Two of the four, move and delete, may be destructive to previously created forms. Add and reference are incremental change operations that will not break old forms because the newly added nodes are optional in the template's XML Schema.

Adding Nodes

InfoPath automatically adds nodes for you when you insert a control with *Automatically create data source* enabled. However, there are some kinds of nodes that InfoPath will never create automatically. Attribute nodes, for example, are introduced into the data source only by adding them manually. Five data types InfoPath will never automatically assign to a node are whole number, decimal, time, date and time, and custom. Moreover, there is a convenient advantage in designing the data source manually instead of inserting controls into the view.

To add an attribute, right-click on any node (with the exception of *(Choice)* or an existing *Field (attribute)*) and select *Add*. On the *Add Field or Group* dialog that appears, set the *Type* drop-down to *Field (attribute)*. Once added, an attribute node has the same icon in the data source as a *Field (element)*, but its coloring is dark blue. Attributes are always added to schema as optional despite the XML Schema standard allowing for prohibited (may never exist) or required (must always exist) attributes. An attribute called `myAttribute`, when added to the `myFields` group of the data source, manifests itself in the XML Schema as:

```
<xsd:attribute name="myAttribute" type="xsd:string"/>
<xsd:element name="myFields">
   <xsd:complexType>
      <xsd:sequence/>
      <xsd:attribute ref="my:myAttribute"/>
      <xsd:anyAttribute processContents="lax"
       namespace="http://www.w3.org/XML/1998/namespace"/>
   </xsd:complexType>
</xsd:element>
```

In an XML form it looks like:

```
<my:myFields my:myAttribute="this is the attribute's value"
xmlns:my=
http://schemas.microsoft.com/office/infopath/2003/myXSD/2005-09-
08T05:16:00
xml:lang="en-us">
```

Attributes are similar to elements but do not allow the rich text or custom data types and cannot be repeating. The use of attributes is likely a choice of either style or necessity. If you really want a highly structured data source, using attributes allows another level of hierarchy under a field node. For example, say you create a form template to keep track of your music collection. You may have a repeating element field called `title`. Data tidbits like musician, genre, and duration might be attributes on the field. Your choice to use attributes depends on personal preference and external requirements. (See Table 3.10 for a comparison of the data source structures.) For example, using attributes is a necessity when your form's data source will ultimately be submitted to a Web service, or other back-end process, that has strict requirements for the shape of the submitted data.

TABLE 3.10: Designing a Music Collection Form's Data Source with and without Attributes

With Attributes

```
<music>
   <titles>
      <title musician=''
      genre=''
        duration='174'>
        title goes here
      </title>
      <title musician=''
      genre=''
        duration='174'>
        title goes here
     </title>
  </titles>
</music>
```

Without Attributes

```
<music>
   <titles>
      <title>
         title goes here
      </title>
      <musician></musician>
      <genre></genre>
      <duration>174</duration>
   <title>
        title goes here
      </title>
      <musician></musician>
      <genre></genre>
      <duration>174</duration>
   </titles>
</music>
```

Attributes are at a disadvantage, compared to elements, with the data types they can be assigned. Since attributes can hold only text content, data types that require XML data cannot be used. Rich text is off limits because it's composed of XHTML node data. Custom is a user-defined data type that could contain XML nodes. Other data types are supported by attributes in the same way as an element. You can expect features such as data validation, conditional formatting, and rules (all discussed in Chapter 5) to work similarly with attributes as with elements. After all, a *Field (attribute)* is a *Field (element)*, right?

InfoPath assigns the most appropriate data type to a field node when you insert a control that can hold text, such as a Text Box. Given this behavior, you should consider changing the data type of the nodes InfoPath creates as you see necessary. For example, if you use a Text Box control in a form to ask for the number of checked luggage items, a whole number will help you validate the input much better than a string. Declarative validation can be used to further restrict the input to allow, say, numerical digits zero through three. We discuss declarative data validation in Chapter 5.

Another key benefit of adding nodes to the data source yourself (versus inserting a new control first) is the convenience of auto-generated labels. A label is not a special control, but just text followed by a colon and a space inserted before the control in the view. To get such a label, simply insert a field from the data source into the view. (See Figure 3.12; the sample file is called LabelNodeNameInView.) Alternatively you can right-click on a data source field to select the type of control to insert; or you can drag and drop

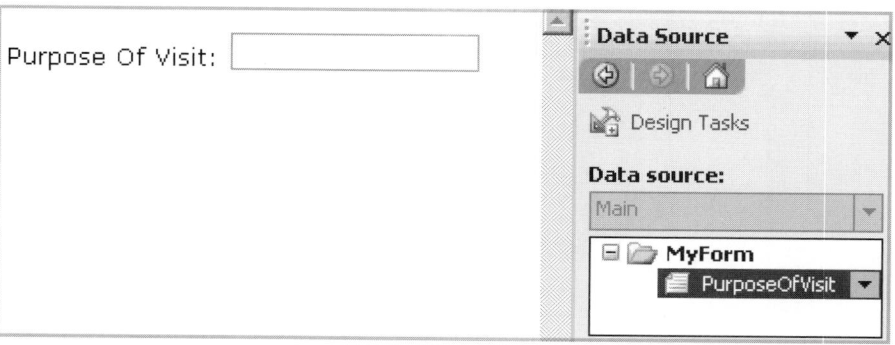

FIGURE 3.12: Label for the node `PurposeOfVisit`, created when inserting the control into the view

with the right mouse button to a specific place and choose from the menu of compatible controls that pops up. By default, InfoPath creates friendly label names. A friendly label detects the `PascalCased` or `camelCased` capitalization in the node name and adds appropriate spaces. So a node name like `TravelerSeatPreference` or `travelerSeatPreference` creates the friendly label "Traveler Seat Preference". In case you prefer not to have labels created or don't like the friendly labels, switches such as *Create labels for controls automatically when adding from data source* and *Convert field or group names into friendly names* are available on the *Form Options* dialog's *Design* tab.

Moving Nodes

The second operation you can perform on a data source node is move. Moving a node does not change the field or group declaration. Instead, it moves the reference (which is the field or group shown in the *Data Source* task pane) to another suitable location, as you specify in the *Move Field or Group* dialog (Figure 3.13). If the move is simply one or two nodes away from its

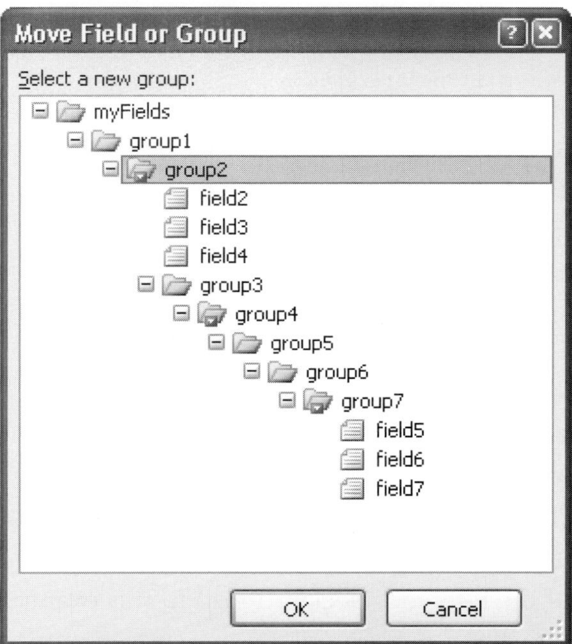

FIGURE 3.13: Move Field or Group dialog used to move an existing field or group

current position, consider using *Move Up* or *Move Down.* Moving a node up or down from its current physical position in the data source is very easy to do: Right-click on the node and select *Move Up* or *Move Down.* To move a node further than just up or down one, use the *Move* command instead.

Let's walk through moving `field3`. You can see in Figure 3.13 that `group2` is selected by default; this is because `group2` is the immediate parent node of `field3`—the node we elected to move. The dialog will let you move a node to any compatible location in the data source. The rules regarding where you can move a field or group are similar to the rules for creating them. Remember that when you move a node, you're moving it under the group node selected in the dialog. (Attributes fields can be moved under element fields in addition to groups.)

To understand why you would want to move a node, take another look at the airline form schema shown earlier. Notice that `xsd:sequence` contains references to fields and groups. The `sequence` is important in that the references must be ordered; otherwise, the form will not validate against the schema. Let's look at the `AirlineReservation` document element in Listing 3.2.

LISTING 3.2: The AirlineReservation Document Element

```
<xsd:element name="AirlineReservation">
   <xsd:complexType>
      <xsd:sequence>
         <xsd:element ref="my:Name" minOccurs="0"/>
         <xsd:element ref="my:FlightType" minOccurs="0"/>
         <xsd:element ref="my:FlightDate" minOccurs="0"/>
         <xsd:element ref="my:Travelers" minOccurs="0"/>
      </xsd:sequence>
      <xsd:anyAttribute processContents="lax"
       namespace="http://www.w3.org/XML/1998/namespace"/>
   </xsd:complexType>
</xsd:element>
```

This schema fragment defines the `AirlineReservation` group to contain four nodes. (We don't know from looking at this fragment whether the references are fields or groups. To figure it out, we'd need to see the definitions for each of the reference declarations.) In this example, the `my:Name` node must come before `my:FlightType`, which must appear before `my:FlightDate`, and so on. Whenever the form is submitted or saved, this node order is defined in that data. Say your network server administrator requires the order of the data to be Name, FlightDate, FlightType, and then Travelers. You could simply swap the FlightDate node with the FlightType node by using the *Move* command. Despite this being a seemingly trivial operation, moving a field or group may break old forms. Since the data is defined in a sequence, changing the sequence will cause older forms that have another sequence of data to fail schema validation. When someone tries to reopen a form with a bad sequence of data, the form will fail to load and will display an error message such as the one shown in Figure 3.14.

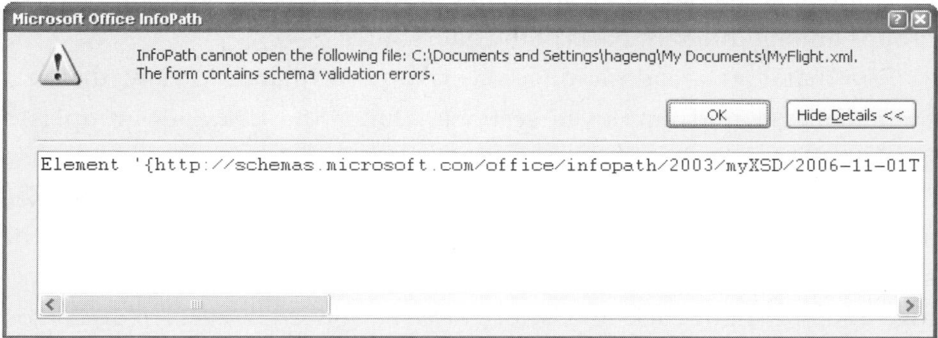

FIGURE 3.14: Validation error that appears when opening a form created before the FlightType-FlightDate node swap

There are very specific exceptions when moving a node will not break your form. These cases are limited to when a node is moved to a different place under the same parent and will work only when under a choice (or an xsd:all) construct in the schema. In fact, this is a special case. Expect most move operations to break (or cause data loss) in existing forms.

Deleting Nodes

There is nothing new to learn about deleting a field or group except to reiterate that it will break or cause data loss for old forms. Deleting a node does what you'd expect: It deletes the node and all of its children nodes (and so on). The *Move* node operation discussed in the last section is implemented as a combination of using *Delete* followed by *Add*, so you can now apply the concepts from *Add* and *Delete* to your understanding of *Move*.

Referencing Nodes

The last data source operation we have not yet discussed is *Reference*. A reference occurs when a declared node is actually used or instantiated. All of the nodes you can see in the *Data Source* task pane are actually references of declared nodes in the schema. A node is declared only once, but it can be referenced as many times as you want. When you use the *Reference* operation, it appears as if a physical copy of the node were created at the new location (which is the target of the reference, as you specify in the *Reference Field or Group* dialog). *Reference* comes in handy when you share fields or groups among different parts of the data source.

Say that you are designing a yearly performance review that has both manager and employee sections. Under the `Manager` group is a group called `PersonalInformation`, which holds fields such as `Name`, `SocialSecurityNumber`, `Birthdate`, and `Address`. Since you need the same information under the `Employee` group, would you re-create the same group and fields? Not any more, now that you know about referencing! You can right-click and select *Reference* on `PersonalInformation` under the `Manager` group and then select the `Employee` group as the target. The result is what you want: a duplicate copy of `PersonalInformation` under `Employee`.

Recursion

Another useful feature of the *Reference* operation is the ability to enable a recursive relation between groups, otherwise known as recursion. Recursion in XML occurs when a node references itself directly or indirectly. For example, direct recursion happens when `NodeA` references `NodeA`. An example of indirect recursion is `NodeA` referencing `NodeB`, which, in turn, references `NodeA`.

Let's see when you could take advantage of recursion. Take an InfoPath form that tracks the MOI Company's employee information from CEO down to all nonmanagement employees. How can you effectively abstract the MOI Company's hierarchy in the data source? Let's lay out our assumptions.

- One or more employees will not have a manager (e.g., CEO).
- If an employee has a manager, he or she will have exactly one manager.
- An employee may have zero or more employees working directly under him or her.

To model the MOI Company's employee ladder, we'll use direct recursion. First, create your data source for a single MOI employee's information. Next, set the `Employee` group to repeat and then reference to itself (right-click on the `Employee` group, select *Reference,* and select the `Employee` group in the resulting dialog), as shown in Figure 3.15.

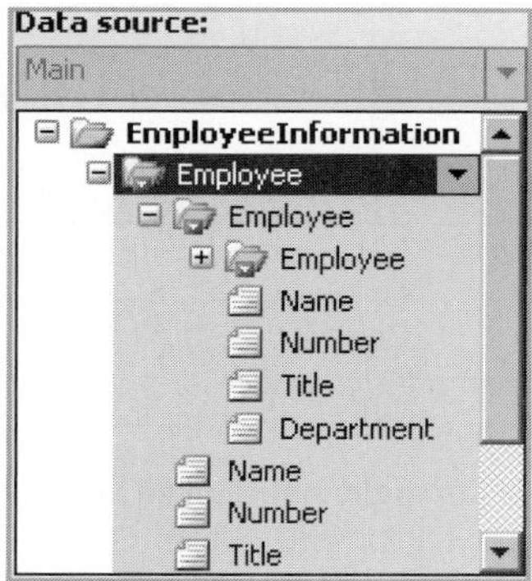

FIGURE 3.15: Setting the `Employee` group to repeat and reference itself

If you simply insert the `Employee` group into the view as a Repeating Recursive Section (which is the default choice), users will see something similar to Figure 3.16 when filling out the form. The form nicely models the company's infrastructure and is intuitive to use. That was the quickest form template we've ever designed—all while being very useful! (The sample is called EmployeeInformation.)

Forms Services

Recursive data sources are supported in browser-enabled form templates, but recursive controls are not.

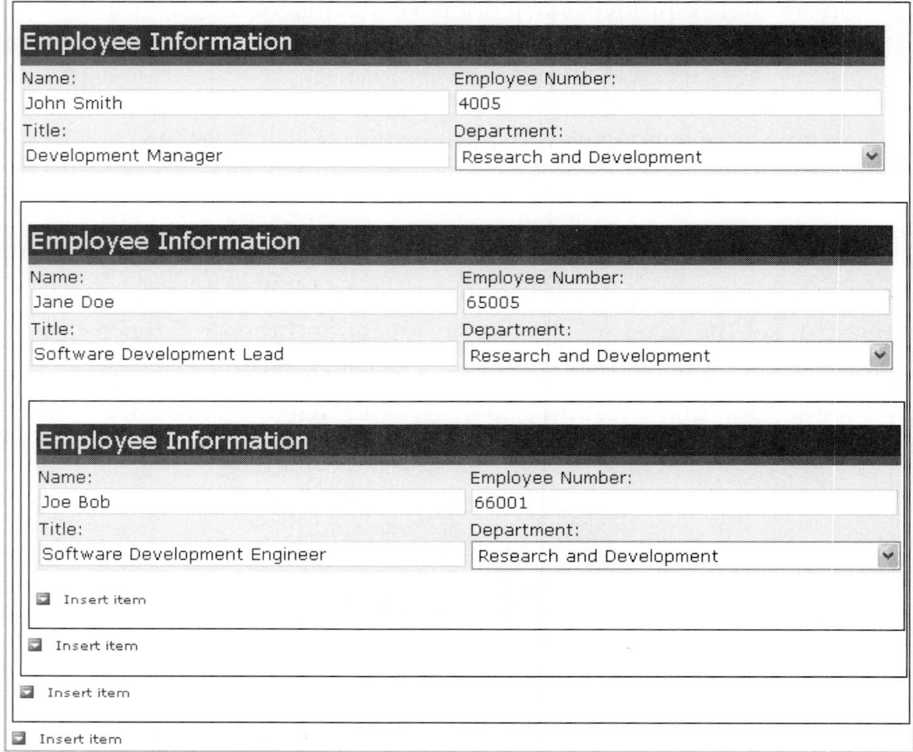

FIGURE 3.16: Filling out the MOI Company's employee information form

Starting with Your Own Data Source

Until now we've assumed that you're creating a new, blank form. Starting from blank allows you to take full advantage of the built-in capabilities of data source editing. If you're familiar with XML Schema, you might have already realized that InfoPath's data source features cover no more than about 25% of the total features available with schemas. This seeming lack of support in design mode for creating these schemas from scratch does not mean InfoPath can't support them! However, it's important to remember that InfoPath is not meant to be a schema design tool, but rather a forms designer and filler. Nevertheless, when designing a new form, you can choose to start from XML or schema instead of blank, as shown in Figure 3.17.

After you select *XML or Schema,* the dialog shown in Figure 3.18 prompts you to select a file of type .xml or .xsd for InfoPath to use to create a form

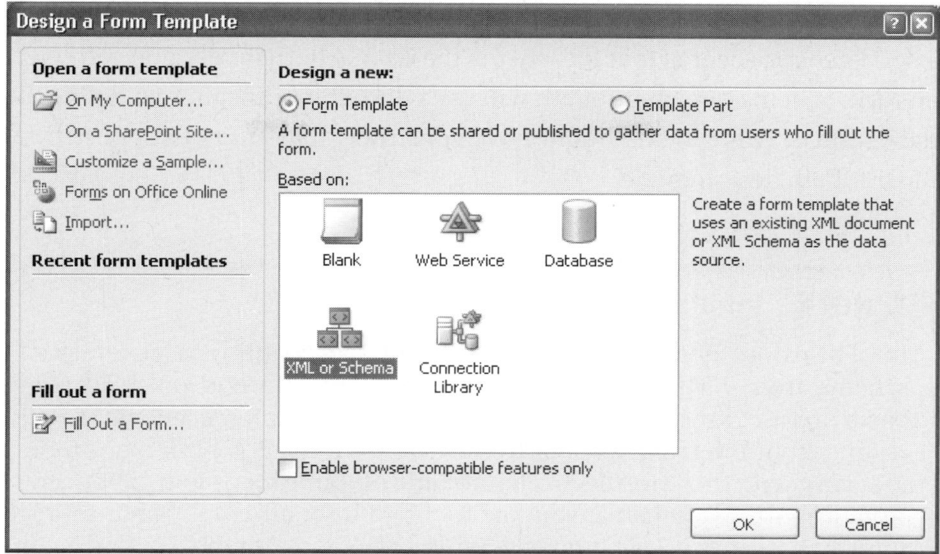

FIGURE 3.17: Design a form from an existing XML document or schema instead of creating the data source from scratch

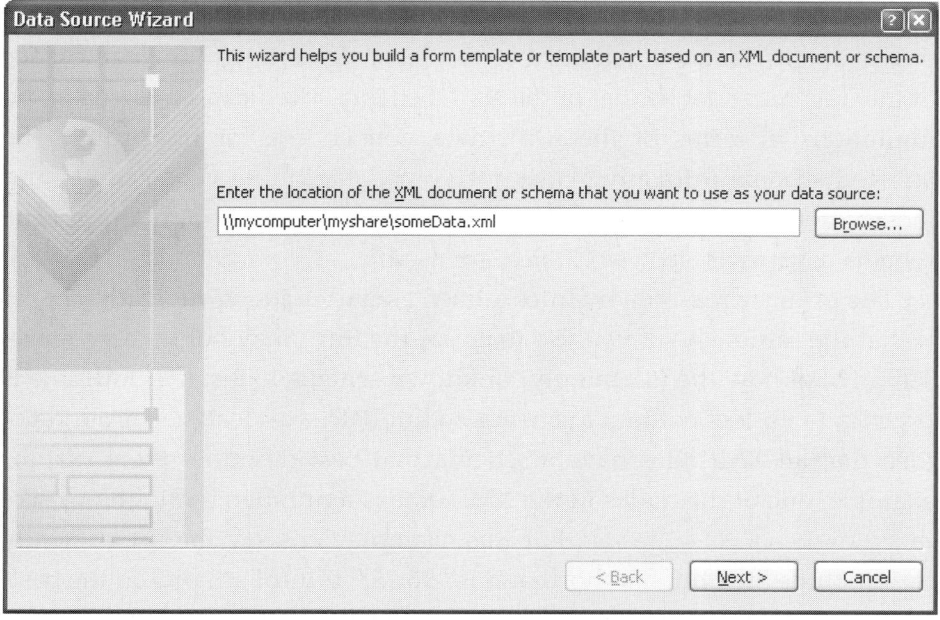

FIGURE 3.18: Selecting the location of an XML document or schema

template. If you choose an XML file, InfoPath uses its own algorithms to infer a generic schema that loosely fits the data. Alternatively you can select an XML Schema, which InfoPath will use without modification to define the data source. This schema might have constructs that are not supported by the InfoPath design mode.

> **NOTE** InfoPath Schema Inference
>
> InfoPath does not use the .NET XSD Inference utility to generate a schema from XML data. Since InfoPath cannot depend on .NET for basic product functionality, it implements its own inference logic. Your results from inferring schema from XML with the XSD Inference tool will vary with those results from InfoPath. Nothing stops you, however, from importing a schema from the tool into InfoPath. MSDN has more information on the XSD Inference utility (referenced in the Appendix).

Starting from XML Data

To start from an XML file, it must have well-formed XML data, and that XML data cannot be a schema. By definition, this means the data must have a single document element or top-level element, and the namespace of the data must not be that of the XML Schema specification. There are no limitations in terms of the XML data you choose for importing. The inferred schema InfoPath creates for your data will be very general and loosely defined, meaning all data types are strings and not many special schema constructs, such as Choice, are used.

The primary reason why InfoPath isn't smarter about inferring schema is that the sample XML you use to create the form may not be very representative of how the (seemingly) unknown schema looks. (An XML file is practically useless without a schema, so InfoPath was designed around the idea that all XML files have a schema that best describes them.) If, for example, one of the nodes in the XML data is a number, it might look like this: `<date>06.05</date>`. For this example, let's say the user actually meant "June 5th" but his shorthand is "06.05." If InfoPath picked the best-fit schema, this `date` field would be interpreted as a decimal (double) data type! Attempting to open a different form with a date that didn't look like a decimal value would fail to open. Since a single XML sample cannot encapsulate the many variations of possible data, the InfoPath-inferred schema is very general. When starting from an XML file, the data source is editable (i.e., you can change node names and data types, add or remove nodes, and so on), so it's a good idea to tighten up the data source when designing the form template.

When starting from XML, a prompt (Figure 3.19) asks whether or not you want to use the XML data in the file you selected as the default data for the form template. This means every new form created from the form template will have the data from this XML file. The *No* button has focus by default since this option is rarely used, but when you're dealing with a large amount of data, clicking *Yes* can save you a lot of time!

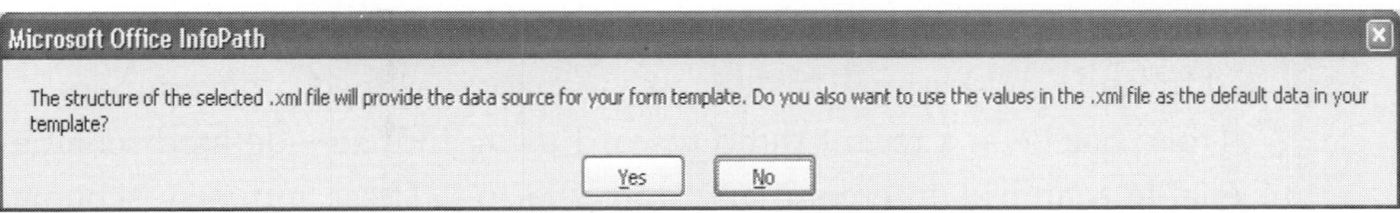

FIGURE 3.19: Choosing whether to include data from a selected XML file as the form template default data

Inferring XML and XML Schema

You may encounter a rare situation where an XML file is interpreted as a schema or an XSD is understood by InfoPath as an arbitrary XML file. When evaluating the chosen file, InfoPath looks at the content of the file instead of its extension. If the file content is valid XML, its root element is called `schema`, and its namespace is `http://www.w3.org/2001/XMLSchema`, InfoPath thinks it's a schema. Any other XML data is said to be arbitrary XML in which a schema will be created. An exception is what appears to be an XML file, but within the data there is an embedded schema, otherwise known as an inline schema. Inline schemas are not supported, with the main reason being that they're uncommon. A workaround is to manually separate the schema in its own file for consumption by InfoPath.

Starting from XML Schema

A common enterprise scenario is creating a new, blank form starting from XML Schema. However, many companies may already use or can generate a schema via another system, such as Microsoft BizTalk Server and popular customer relationship management (CRM) software, or they might already have access to a schema. One of the biggest worries for a company actually using an industry schema is the great deal of custom developer work and potential long-term maintenance costs involved in creating an in-house application. (An industry schema is an XML Schema definition that many companies may share to conform to a standard, e.g., to communicate inventory orders with suppliers.) Before InfoPath, there was no easy way to effectively put the schema to use in an organization. This story has changed now that InfoPath consumes schemas to create meaningful forms that fully exploit their definitions. Also, the overhead required to maintain such a form is orders of magnitude lower, and the form can be easily developed by an IT professional instead of a team of seasoned programmers.

There has been a recent trend toward using industry-defined schemas to enable seamless intercompany data sharing. These industry schemas define taxonomies that are consistent across disparate companies. Even small businesses can now use these industry-defined schemas to help propel themselves into the mainstream line of business. This is all achievable without a custom programmer. InfoPath primarily exists for the purpose of making XML available to the masses without them necessarily understanding the core technologies and implementation details. As we mentioned in Chapter 1, InfoPath not only ties together existing back-end systems but also introduces a Microsoft Office–standard interface already familiar to a majority of end users.

To begin designing a form template from an existing XML Schema, simply follow the same steps as you'd use to start from an XML file. InfoPath will respect your schema definition and its constraints. Even imported and included references in the schema you select will be added to the form template automatically.

InfoPath disallows editing via the *Data Source* task pane in the design mode. This behavior is a curse and a blessing: Your custom schema stays pure as it was probably intended to be, yet making changes is not as convenient. The reason InfoPath locks the schema is actually due to the schema definition itself! The schema you chose does not have an extensibility mechanism to allow new schema to be added. We'll touch a little more on this later.

Starting from schemas allows a form template designer to select very complicated and intricate schemas. These schemas may have constructs you couldn't generate yourself in the *Data Source* task pane. A strong grasp on XML Schema fundamentals is helpful for understanding more complex schemas.

Potential Complications of Starting from XML Schema

There are some unique and rare cases when InfoPath will not be able to directly consume your custom XML Schema. These cases occur when your schema is ambiguous and a data source could not be properly created due to the ambiguity. Figure 3.20 shows the dialog InfoPath will use to ask for your input. If you aren't sure how to disambiguate your schema properly, simply click *Accept Settings* and do not change the default data source choices. If your data source ends up being incorrect after you accepted or edited the data source settings, go back and try different data source settings.

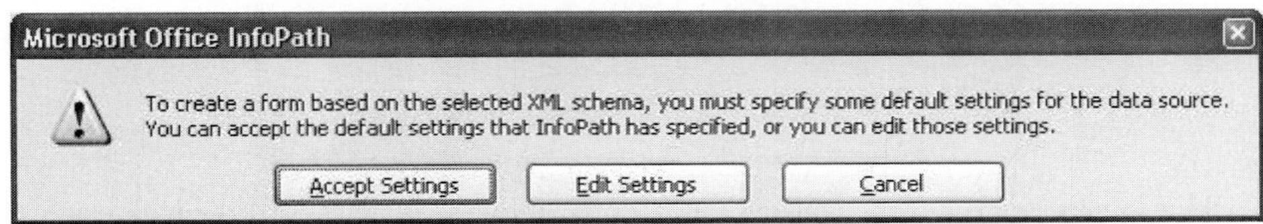

FIGURE 3.20: The first prompt when starting from an ambiguous schema

The schema in Listing 3.3 is ambiguous because of the nested repeating sequences shown in **bold**.

LISTING 3.3: An Ambiguous Schema

```
<?xml version="1.0"?>
<xsd:schema xmlns:xsd="http://www.w3.org/2001/XMLSchema">
   <xsd:element name="TopLevelElement">
      <xsd:complexType>
         <xsd:sequence minOccurs="2" maxOccurs="4">
         <xsd:sequence minOccurs="3" maxOccurs="5">
            <xsd:element name="b" type="xsd:string"/>
         </xsd:sequence>
         </xsd:sequence>
      </xsd:complexType>
   </xsd:element>
</xsd:schema>
```

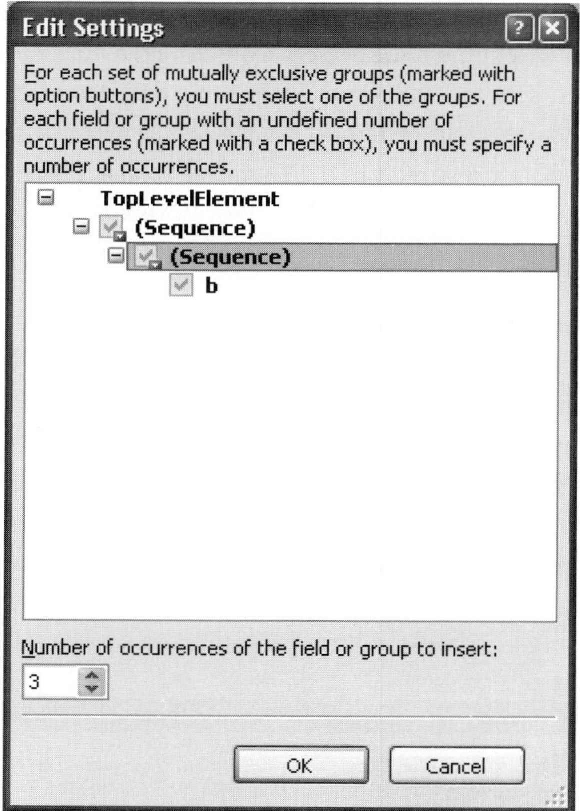

FIGURE 3.21: Disambiguating the data source by using the Edit Settings dialog

We admit that the *Edit Settings* dialog (Figure 3.21) is not very intuitive. However, the chances you will encounter this dialog are quite small. We believe that if you do, it means the schema you are designing against is intricate or was poorly written.

Forms Services

Forms based on disambiguated schemas cannot be used in the browser as a browser-enabled form template.

Another case you are more likely to encounter is starting from a schema with multiple top-level elements. InfoPath will prompt for which document

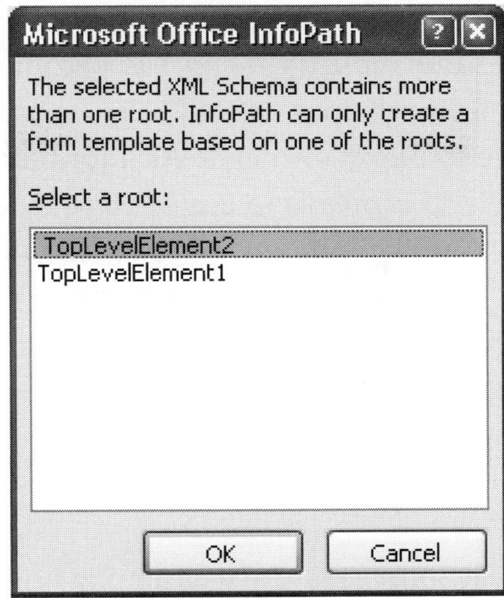

FIGURE 3.22: Prompt that appears when starting from a schema with multiple top-level elements

element it should use to create the data source (Figure 3.22). Remember that a valid XML data source has only a single top-level element. A schema can define more than one top-level element, as shown in Listing 3.4. (Ellipses hide irrelevant schema structure.)

LISTING 3.4: A Schema with Multiple Top-Level Elements

```
<?xml version="1.0" . . . ?>
<xsd:schema . . . xmlns:xsd="http://www.w3.org/2001/XMLSchema">
   <xsd:element name="TopLevelElement1">
     . . .
   </xsd:element>
   <xsd:element name="TopLevelElement2">
     . . .
   </xsd:element>
</xsd:schema>
```

Since `TopLevelElement1` does not reference `TopLevelElement2` and vice versa in the schema shown in Listing 3.4, it has multiple top-level elements. A schema has multiple top-level elements if and only if the top-level elements do not reference each other.

Schemas defining multiple top-level elements aren't uncommon in industry. This happens when merging multiple schemas into a single schema or even when a single schema serves more than a distinct, targeted purpose. Say two companies in the same industry merged to become one company; they could literally merge their schemas as well. Also, some tools may generate schemas with multiple top-level elements. As a form designer, if you aren't sure which of the top-level elements to use, it's best to ask people who gave you the schema. If this isn't an option, the next action is to design multiple form templates—one template per top-level element. The downside to this approach is that InfoPath keeps a copy of the schema in each form template, so if you had to change the schema file it would be necessary to manually update each form template individually.

Convert Main Data Source

The Convert Main Data Source feature was among one of the more sought-after additions to design mode. Before this feature was available, starting from an existing XML Schema meant you were stuck with that exact schema forever (unless, of course, you did some serious surgery by manually editing the form template's files; however, a mistake would render your form broken in design and edit modes). If it weren't for Convert Main Data Source, we would have an appendix section dedicated to the tedious process of updating your template! The entry point for this feature is on the *Tools* menu as *Convert Main Data Source*.

If your form template started life from blank, XML, or XML Schema, you can convert the data source to another XML or XML Schema file. There is no such idea as converting to blank. Doing so is equivalent to deleting all top-level fields and groups in your data source. The convenience of converting to another XML or Schema offers benefits in scenarios such as the following.

- Your customer initially sent you the wrong schema, so you need to design against the updated version.
- One or more of your requirements has changed since beginning development on the form template, and thus the schema you started with is no longer accurate.
- You found a more complete or descriptive XML file than you were designing against. Instead of adding the fields and groups manually, you can convert.

The first two are the most common scenarios. The first one is trivial to carry out. However, there is more difficulty involved when you need to modify the schema but also carry out the updates yourself. Since the data source is locked, your changes cannot happen in design mode. You will need to manually change the schema outside of InfoPath before being able to perform the main data source conversion. As always, make a backup of your schema before attempting any changes.

Visual Studio (2003 and later versions) has a convenient graphical schema editor. You could make changes (or even create a new schema) by using Visual Studio and then run the conversion to import the updated (or new) schema. This is the preferred way to update the schema file. A second way to update the schema is to open it for editing in InfoPath by adding an `xsd:any` extensibility element. (In a moment, we will talk about how an `xsd:any` looks.) The last way to update a fixed data source is to open the schema in a text editor such as Notepad and hand-edit the file yourself. This is potentially dangerous but is the most precise way to get desired results. We cannot recommend hand-editing files within an InfoPath form template.

When you run Convert Main Data Source, all controls in the view try to maintain their binding. Other features try to maintain their integrity as well. InfoPath has a set of binding heuristics in which it performs the following high-level algorithms.

- Ignore namespaces when matching node names.
- Ignore virtual schema nodes such as `sequence` and `choice`.
- Maintain integrity of default data, rules (discussed in Chapter 5), and validation features.

Among the features not automatically updated are user-defined XPaths (XPath is a language to select data from an XML file) on a control like an Expression Box, custom form code, any auxiliary files (such as a custom task pane HTML file, which is discussed in Chapter 15), and hand-edited references. Ensure that you have a backup of the form template before running a schema conversion. Sometimes a conversion may have unintentional side effects if your template is highly customized. You may not realize the damage until you run a full test of filling out your form and check the saved or submitted XML data. Since conversion is a one-way street (no undo), you'll want to provide your own safety net.

> **WARNING** Converting to Ambiguous Schema
>
> You cannot convert to an ambiguous schema. If you start from such a schema, InfoPath will prompt you to disambiguate the data source, but converting will fail with the following message: "InfoPath was unable to add or modify the data connection or data source. The wizard will now close. Details: The selected XML Schema cannot be used because it contains a structure that InfoPath does not support."

Yet another reason behind Convert Main Data Source is the desire to update a form template based on data from an Access database, a SQL Server, or a Web service. A major scenario for this type of conversion is preparing a form template to use a live server farm instead of an internal test server.

What if after creating a complex form template starting from blank, you learn from your customer about a schema they want to use for only a portion of the data source? Don't go through the work of manually creating the data source to match the schema! There's a feature in the *Add Field or Group* dialog nestled in the *Type* (not *Data type*) drop-down menu called *Complete XML Schema or XML document*, as shown in Figure 3.23. When selected, the dialog

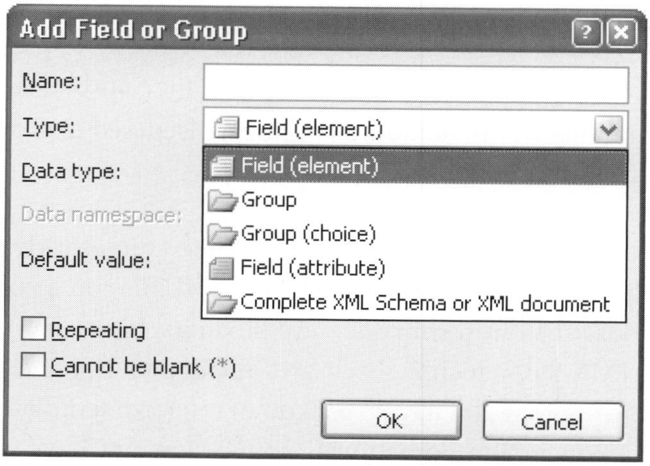

FIGURE 3.23: The Type drop-down menu, with an option for adding a complete XML Schema or XML document

shown earlier in Figure 3.18 appears. This is the same dialog used in many places throughout InfoPath design mode when choosing an XML document or schema. After selecting a schema, you will see it appear in the data source in the location you chose. After adding the schema, you can move, reference, or delete it as you would any other data source node; however, you cannot make changes within it. This is consistent with the experience you'd have if you were starting the form template from that schema alone.

> **WARNING** Ambiguous Schemas Cannot Be Added
>
> You cannot add a schema into your data source if it is ambiguous. You will receive this error message: "The XML Schema you selected cannot be added because it contains structures that InfoPath cannot completely support without simplifications."

Namespaces in the Data Source

Occasionally you will notice a prefix on some of the fields or groups in the *Data Source* task pane. These prefixes appear as `ns1:`, `s0:`, `my:`, or other letters and numbers followed by a colon. The node with the prefix is telling you it is in a different namespace than its ancestors in the data source. Recall that a namespace is the way in which XML classifies nodes. Rich text, for example, is in the `http://www.w3.org/1999/xhtml` namespace. This specific namespace is referenced by the namespace prefix `xhtml`. The namespace prefix name is irrelevant as it's defined and associated with the namespace in the XML file. For hungry eyes, open an XML file and search for `xmlns` to find namespace and alias associations.

Let's create a new form template from a simple XML file to demonstrate how namespaces are revealed in the data source. Let's start with the following XML data. Create a new text file using Notepad and transcribe this data. Then save the file with a .xml extension on your computer.

```
<?xml version="1.0"?>
<my1:a xmlns:my1="namespace1">
  <my2:a my3:b="attribute" xmlns:my2="namespace2" xmlns:my3="namespace3"/>
  <my1:c>some text</my1:c>
</my1:a>
```

TABLE 3.11: Analyzing Nodes' Namespaces Relative to Their Immediate Ancestors

Node Name	Namespace	Namespace Prefix	Prefix Shown in Data Source?
a	namespace1	my1	No, the top-level data source node prefix is never shown. To see the namespace, visit the *Details* tab on its *Field or Group Properties* dialog.
a	namespace2	my2	Yes, my2:a is in a different namespace than my1:a.
b	namespace3	my3	Yes, attribute my3:b is in a different namespace than my2:a.
c	namespace1	my1	No, since my1:c is in the same namespace as its immediate ancestor my1:a.

There are four data source nodes in this XML document: a, a, attribute b, and c. How can we have two nodes with the name a? Remember that namespaces classify nodes. It's best to think about a node not in terms of its name, but rather in terms of both its name and namespace. Table 3.11 shows how these data source nodes map to namespaces and prefixes and when the prefix is shown in the *Data Source* task pane. Figure 3.24 shows the resulting data source from the XML document shown above.

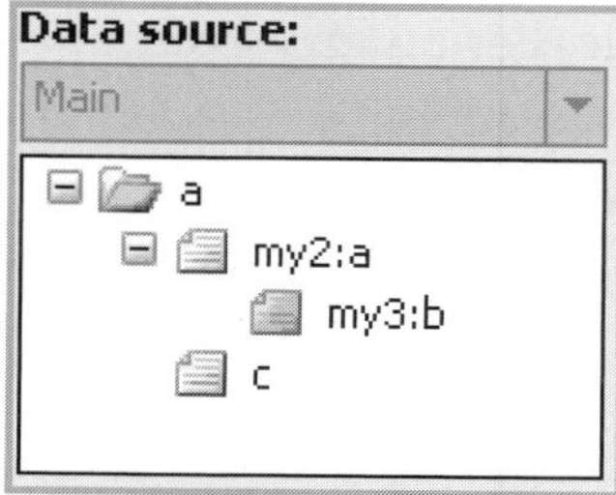

FIGURE 3.24: Data source created from the XML document

We've seen in this chapter that when you start from a custom XML Schema, the data source is locked. The full truth is not that InfoPath locks the schema itself. The real issue is that the schema you chose does not allow for extensibility. In other words, if the proper schema extensibility mechanisms exist, some or even the entire data source is editable in design mode. Let's look at the simple editable schema shown in Listing 3.5.

LISTING 3.5: A Simple Editable Schema

```
<?xml version="1.0"?>
<xsd:schema xmlns:xsd="http://www.w3.org/2001/XMLSchema">
   <xsd:element name="OpenNode">
      <xsd:complexType>
         <xsd:sequence>
            <xsd:any namespace="##other" minOccurs="0"
             maxOccurs="unbounded"/>
         </xsd:sequence>
      </xsd:complexType>
   </xsd:element>
</xsd:schema>
```

The key in this example is the `xsd:any` schema construct. This is not specific to InfoPath per se but is understood in XML to mean "anything can go in this place." If you have an existing schema where you want parts to be open for editing in design mode, you can hand-edit the schema in a basic text editor. Add the `xsd:any` element within each compositor you want to enable editing: `xsd:sequence`, `xsd:choice`, or `xsd:all`.

Actually, the above example will allow for anything except new attributes. XML Schema always segregates elements and attributes, hence the nuance. To also open the schema for attributes, you need to add the following within the `xsd:complexType` node (outside of the compositor):

```
<xsd:anyAttribute processContents="lax" namespace="##other"/>
```

We will not discuss the specifics of the `xsd:any` or `xsd:anyAttribute` nodes as that conversation is schema-specific and can be found on the W3 Schools Web site (referenced in the Appendix). For InfoPath purposes, even expert schema hackers don't need to know more than what we've presented in this conversation about enabling the data source for editing.

Advanced Data Binding

We're going to take a step back from data source details and see how designing your data source can affect which controls you can use and even how you lay them out in the view. You can skip this entire section if you can follow one guideline: Design the view with all controls first and never modify the data source again. In our opinion, that's nearly impossible to do for any real-world form. In other words, you should not skip this part of the chapter! In the real world, things in the data source will change as you design different parts of your form template and into the future as new requirements emerge. Or if you prefer, as many people do, to design the view first and then go back and fix up the data source—this part is for you!

We mentioned that you can skip this part if you can follow that one guideline. That's because InfoPath will insert a control only if its binding is not potentially broken. If a properly bound control is already in the view, many actions you can take when modifying the data source could break that binding. It's possible for you to break the binding because InfoPath does not require the form template to be in a pristine state. InfoPath will guide you to create a well-functioning form template, but the form designer has the fine-grained control to ultimately override and break the form template. So if you insert a control (whether the node is created or preexisting), the binding will be correct. However, you can move, reference, delete, or modify any of the node's properties as you wish. Any of these actions might affect the binding between the control and the data source node. InfoPath does not (nor should it) automatically fix the way you set up your view to accommodate changes in the data source. Changing a data source field or group after it is bound can lead to problems if a change is made that the binding does not support. But you can count on InfoPath to get the binding correct when you first insert a control (from either the *Controls* or *Data Source* task panes.)

Understanding Data Binding

First, let's describe what it means to bind a control to the data source. The literal definition of the word "bind" is to tie together. Without controls, we could not display the form data. Without the data, controls would forever be empty. When a control or data source node (it works both ways) is bound, a connection is forged between what the user sees while filling out the form and the XML data behind the scenes. Let's take a closer look at what happens when you're designing a form and inserting controls.

1. The data source node is created that matches the control type you're inserting.

2. A new control of the type you chose is inserted in the view.
3. Binding is established between the control and the data source node.

We already discussed data source nodes, which covers the first step. The second step is trivial since the control is simply created. The third step is implicit when inserting a new control. If you unchecked the *Automatically create data source* checkbox and inserted a new control into the view, steps 2 and 3 would still happen, but you would be prompted to select a data source node for binding. Figure 3.25 shows the dialog prompt.

> **TIP Choosing a Data Source Node for Binding**
>
> You aren't constrained to choose an existing node for binding a control. Right-clicking on a node in Figure 3.25 brings up *Add* and *Reference* operations.

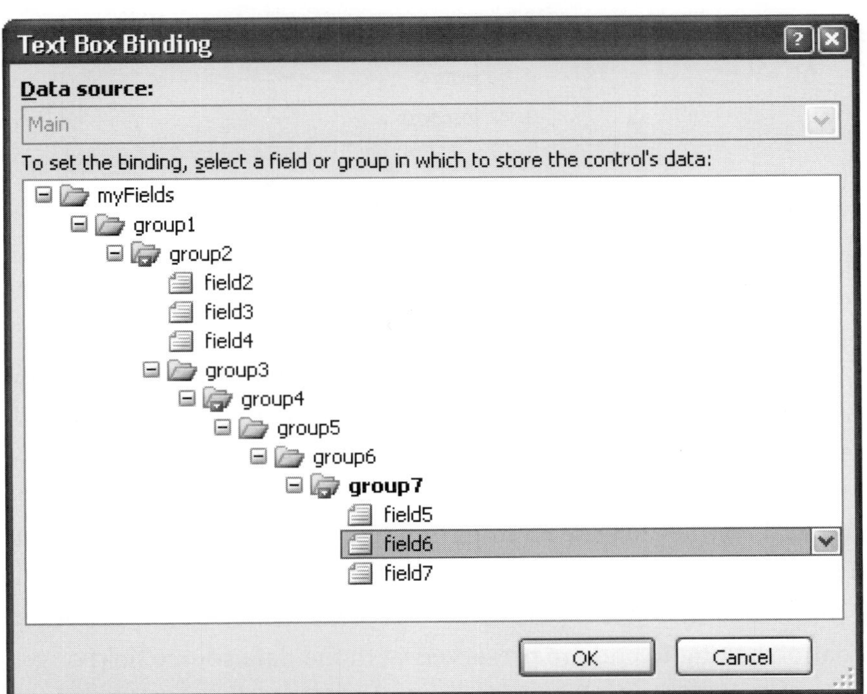

FIGURE 3.25: Text Box Binding dialog that appears when Automatically create data source is disabled or Change Binding is used from a control

Changing Control Binding

Another way to access the dialog shown in Figure 3.25 is to right-click a control and select *Change Binding* from the context menu, as shown in Figure 3.26. The dialog from Figure 3.25 allows you to select any node that is compatible with the control. In general, controls that hold text data bind to fields, while container controls, such as Sections, bind to groups. We will soon see that this isn't a hard-and-fast rule, but it's reassuring to know it's followed about 90% of the time.

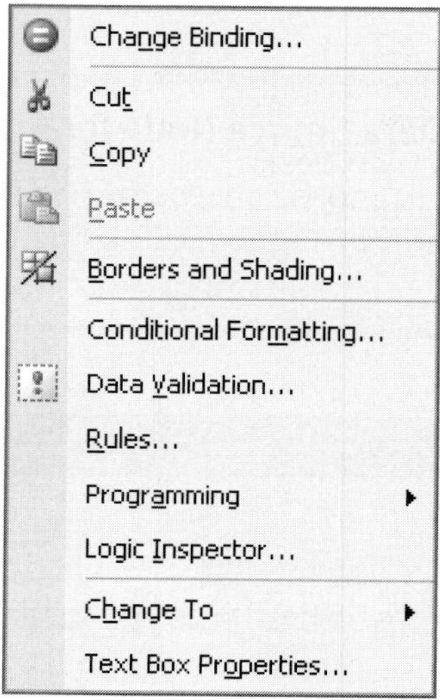

FIGURE 3.26: Changing binding via the context menu by right-clicking on any control that can be bound

Changing binding is a convenience for leaf controls such as Text Boxes but can end up being quite cumbersome for container controls. When changing binding, InfoPath maintains all of the control's properties. Some control properties are lists of names and values (for List Box), cannot be blank, and conditional formatting, to name a few. Keep in mind that the node has its own set of properties, some of which are exposed in the control properties dialog. Properties such as field name, data type, and data validation belong to and are preserved with the data source field or group. When rebinding, control properties are kept with the control, while the node properties for that control can change depending on which field or group you choose for binding. Table 3.12 has a complete list of node and

TABLE 3.12: Control, Node, and Other Unrelated Properties That Change or Get Reset after Rebinding

Control properties	List Box entries Conditional formatting Size (size, padding, margins, alignment) Accessibility (name, tab index, access key, screen tip) Placeholder text (applies only to leaf controls) Control formatting (bold, italics, etc.) Value when selected (for Option Button and Check Box controls) Data type formatting (for numerical and date visual formatting; applies only to numerical and date/time data types) Header and footer (for Repeating Table controls) Filter data criteria Insert button and hint text (for repeating controls) Input scope
Node properties	Merge action Cannot be blank Data validation Rules (see Chapter 5) Data type Field name Rich Text Box options and formatting Input recognition (available only on leaf controls) *Edit Default Values* settings (but only if the *Edit Default Values* dialog setting is selected to be *To all occurrences of this section* or *To all the data rows in the table;* applies only to insertable and deletable container controls)
Independent (apply only to container controls that are insertable and deletable)	ViewContext is determined at bind-time and will be different each time the control is rebound. (ViewContext is an advanced, seldom-used property. It's useful when writing form code for disambiguating a multiply bound data source node.) *Customize Commands* settings are lost on rebinding. *Edit Default Values* settings are lost if the *Only when the user inserts this section* or *Only to the rows the user inserts* option button is selected.

control properties so you can better understand the sometimes foggy separation between controls and data.

Rebinding a container control should be avoided if you have many controls within the container. Rebinding will automatically unbind all controls within the container. This is more of an annoyance than a convenience since you'll need to go through and rebind each of the unbound controls. Having the contained controls become unbound was a design decision due to the user-model problems encountered during scenario testing with changing binding. Should you need to change container binding, we recommend that you instead delete the old control and insert the correct container from the *Data Source* task pane. If you had controls within the old control, you can copy and paste them into the new control.

> **TIP Reverting Rebinding**
>
> Rebinding is an undoable operation.

Customizing New Bindings

We've talked about inserting controls directly from the *Controls* task pane, inserting nodes from the *Data Source* task pane, changing control binding, and changing the type of a control if it was already inserted into the view. Did you know you can choose what control to insert based on a specific field or group? It's pretty easy to do: Instead of using the left mouse button to insert a data source node into the view, use the right mouse button. When you release the mouse button to drop the new control, a menu of the most popular control bindings appears (Figure 3.27).

The menu list will vary depending on two factors: node selected and location (or context) of the drop. The list is abridged if too many options are available. For all options, click the *More* menu item, which results in the dialog shown in Figure 3.28.

You can probably guess that a field node was used for the example shown in Figures 3.27 and 3.28, but you should also know that this field is a child of a repeating group. However, take a closer look at a couple of the entries in these figures. It may strike you odd that *Section with Controls* is

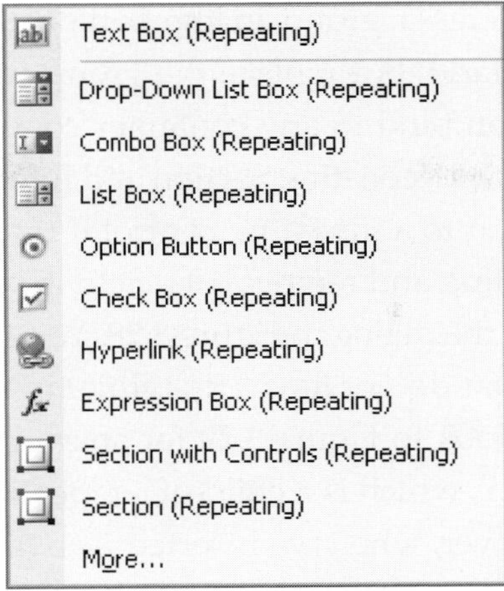

FIGURE 3.27: Context menu of most popular control bindings

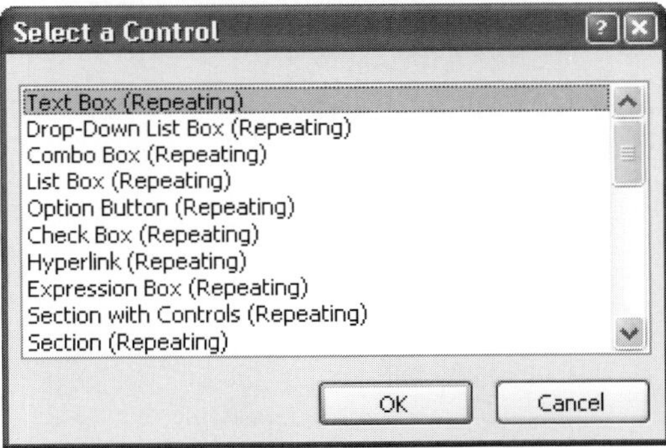

FIGURE 3.28: Dialog that results from clicking More on the menu shown in Figure 3.27

offered as a binding choice for a field node. What does it mean to insert a field as a Section with Controls?

There's a subtle connection between fields and groups (as an InfoPath concept) and nodes (in XML terms). Recall our discussion about the schema that InfoPath generates for us: All data source nodes are optional. This includes fields and groups. In terms of a node being optional, is there really a difference between a field and a group? Not really! The field is either in the XML or it's not. The same is true for a group, of course. You may be able to easily visualize an Optional Section control being inserted and deleted, which inserts and deletes a group in the behind-the-scenes XML. Now imagine the same scenario, but replace the group with a field. Any fields (attributes included) can bind to any container controls (except those that require repetition, such as Repeating Section and Repeating Table; however, a *Field (element)* can bind to a repeating control if the node repeats). This is one way to allow inserting and removal of a field in your data source.

Let's scroll down in the dialog of Figure 3.28. You'll see we can even bind our node to controls that do not have *(Repeating)* in their names. But what does this mean? Let's look to Figure 3.29 for answers. In this specific case, we have inserted `field1`, which is a child of a repeating group (`group2`), in the data source. Moreover, when we inserted `field1` into the view, we did not insert it inside its parent (the existing Repeating Section) in the view. InfoPath adds *(Repeating)* to the control options because it automatically inserts the repeating parent (which happens to be a Repeating Section) for us. If we choose a control name that didn't have *(Repeating)* appended to its name, InfoPath binds the inserted control to the first instance of the repeating data. Alternatively, if we just dropped `field1` into the Repeating Section, we would not be offered any *(Repeating)* options since we are already in the proper context of its repeating parent.

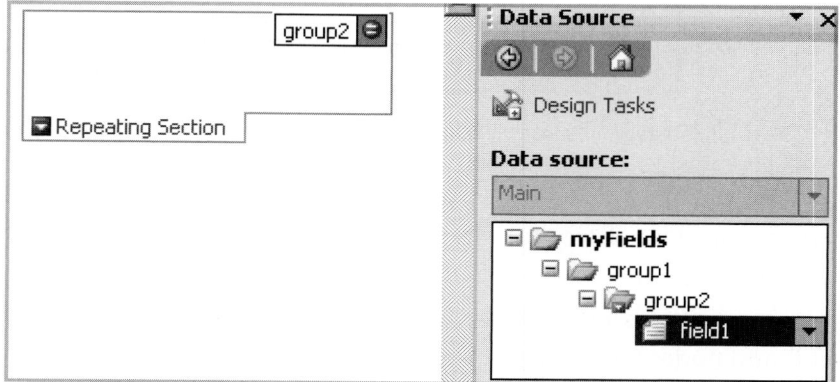

FIGURE 3.29: Inserting `field1` in the data source. The context of a drop affects available control binding options.

Odd Bindings

Let's reflect on the scenario we just talked about for a moment: InfoPath allows us to insert a node into the view without its parent node as well? Sure! That's the beauty of separation between the data and the presentation by the view. You can insert any node into the view and put it anywhere! Let's take an absurd example just to show you what we mean. Consider a simple data source of the document element and an attribute, as shown in data source of Figure 3.30.

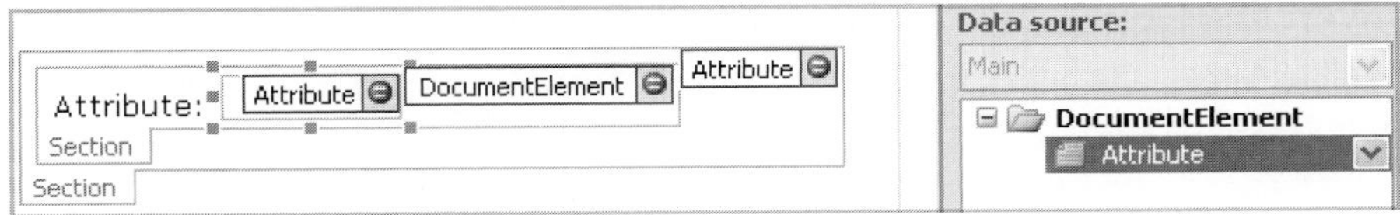

FIGURE 3.30: An absurd control nesting: `Attribute` contains `DocumentElement`, which contains `Attribute`

We inserted controls from the *Data Source* task pane in Figure 3.30. We call this sample absurd because there is no rationale for an attribute to be bound to a Text Box control inside of the document element (bound to a section) that is also inside the attribute (again, but as an Optional Section!). However, this sample shows you that odd bindings can be done, and InfoPath is very flexible in allowing them. This sample (called AbsurdBinding) exhibits the exclusive natures of the view and data source and shows how plasticity in binding opens up the door to creativity—the sky's the limit!

Multiple Binding

Let's swing to a more practical side of binding and control usage. For example, let's take a minimalist approach to our data source where we want the XML node only if it has data when filling out the form. Expanding on our earlier airline form example, say that you want the `NumberOfChildren` field in the data source to appear in the XML if the field is filled out. Otherwise, the node should not appear at all. This node can be either an element or attribute field in the data source. It doesn't matter which we choose since they are both optional (`minOccurs="0"` in the schema).

Let's use an attribute and check the *Cannot be blank* box in the attribute's properties dialog. Inserting the attribute from the data source into the view as an Optional Section with Controls allows this field to be removed and inserted by the user. The *Cannot be blank* setting on the data source node has no bearing on inserting and removing the Optional Section. The setting applies only when the field actually exists (when the Optional Section is inserted). The default control inside of the Optional Section is a Text Box. However, we prefer a Drop-Down List Box, so we use the *Change To* command (as discussed in Chapter 2) on the context menu of the control to convert to a Drop-Down List Box. Figure 3.31 shows the result.

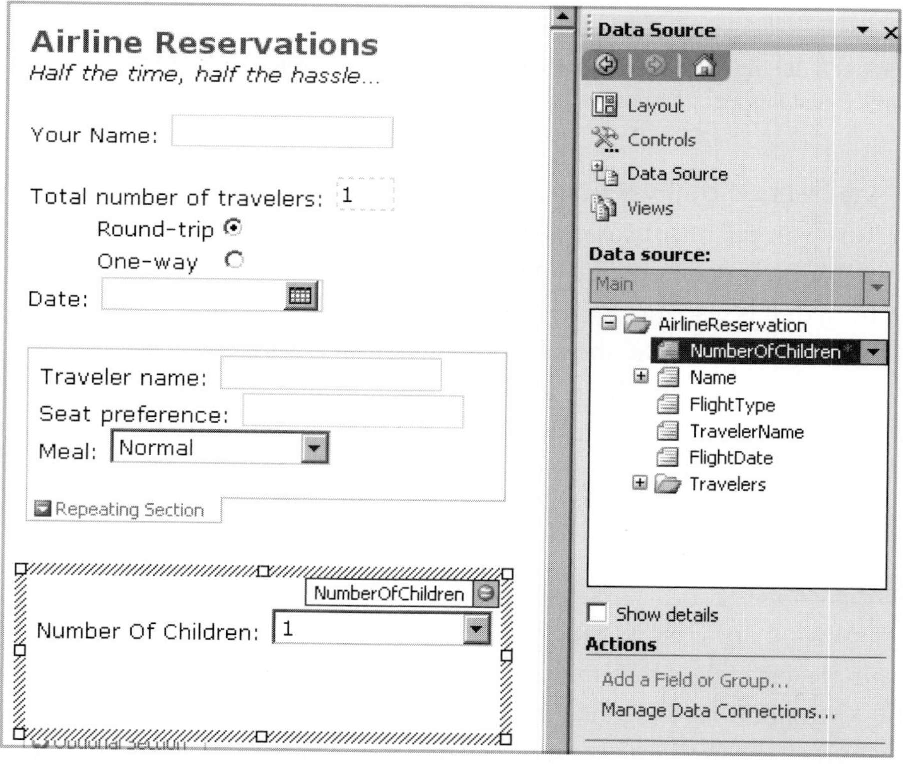

FIGURE 3.31: `NumberOfChildren` **attribute field, which is bound to both the Optional Section and the Drop-Down List Box inside of the Optional Section**

When filling out the form (Figure 3.32), the attribute is not inserted because we used an Optional Section, which removed the attribute from the default form. (If we wanted to include the Optional Section by default in new forms, the Optional Section properties dialog has an option button

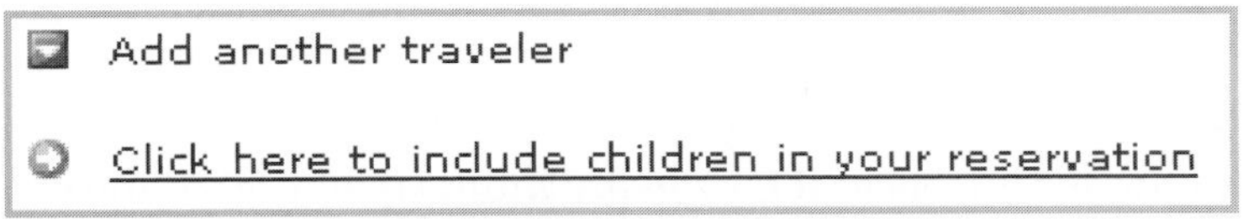

Add another traveler

Click here to include children in your reservation

FIGURE 3.32: `NumberOfChildren` **attribute is nonexistent in the form and XML data**

labeled *Include the section in the form by default.* This feature is discussed in Chapter 4.) Clicking the link to include children in our reservation inserts the Optional Section with the Drop-Down List Box as expected. You can see the inserted controls in Figure 3.33.

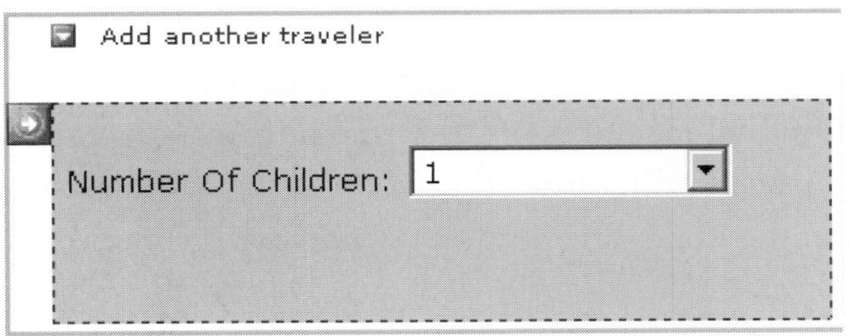

FIGURE 3.33: `NumberOfChildren` **attribute field inserted in the form and XML with a default value of 1**

Some Details of Multiple Binding

Let's take a seemingly odd scenario to help you understand the effects of design-mode binding when filling out a form. We have the data source shown in Figure 3.34. The view, a snippet of which appears in Figure 3.35,

FIGURE 3.34: **A simple repeating field:** `field1`

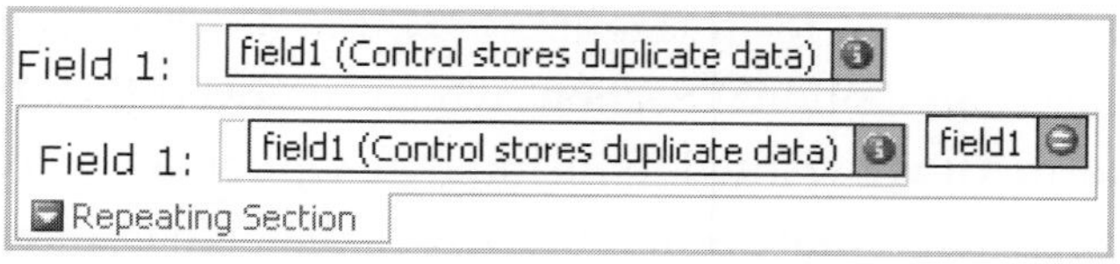

Field 1: field1 (Control stores duplicate data)
Field 1: field1 (Control stores duplicate data) field1
Repeating Section

FIGURE 3.35: Three controls multiply bound to `field1`

has three controls: a Text Box and a Repeating Section with a Text Box inside. All three controls in the view are multiply bound to the same node: `field1`. What happens to `field1` as we fill out the form? Table 3.13 explains the form behavior based on the state of the Repeating Section.

We can best convey the implications of multiply bound controls by explaining Table 3.13. When the Repeating Section is removed, so is `field1`—and it's removed altogether from the XML when filling out the form. When a control is bound to a node that doesn't exist, the control is made read-only and can not be filled in until that node is reinserted. If you insert one Repeating Section, the two Text Boxes mirror each other since they are bound to the exact same node: the first instance of `field1`. When inserting additional instances of the Repeating Section, each instance will bind to the corresponding repeating node in the XML. However, the Text Box outside of the Repeating Section will always be bound to only the first

TABLE 3.13: The Behaviors of Various Controls When Multiply Bound to `field1` While Filling out the Form

Repeating Section Instances	Single Text Box Displays	Repeating Section Text Box Displays
0	Control appears but is empty and read-only.	Control does not exist.
1	User-entered data (e.g., blue).	User-entered data (e.g., blue).
2 or more	User-entered data (e.g., blue). (This value is always the same as the user-entered data from the first instance of the Repeating Section's Text Box.)	User-entered data (e.g., green).

instance of `field1`. Remember that how you set up your controls does not matter; ultimately what matters is the data in the form XML. In this case, the Text Box outside of the Repeating Section is redundant because it just replicates the data in the first instance of the Repeating Section's Text Box. Table 3.13 is consistent with our findings.

Design-Time Visuals

Figure 3.35 shows circular icons with the letter "i" on the upper-right of the Text Box controls. On screen, these icons appear in blue. Some of these icons, otherwise known as design-time visuals (or just visuals for the purpose of this conversation), are shown in design mode even when you're not hovering the mouse over the controls! To get information on why the visual is appearing, hover your mouse over the corresponding control. You can get additional details and suggestions for fixes by right-clicking the control and choosing *More Details.* You might encounter three types of visuals: normal, informational, and critical. Table 3.14 shows the icons for these visuals. Additional visuals are shown with the Design Checker feature, which we will discuss in Chapter 14.

Table 3.14: Design-Time Visual Icons That Appear Over Controls to Indicate Potential Binding Issues

Normal Visual	Informational Visual	Critical Visual

Normal visuals are representative of typical bindings, so there's nothing new to discuss.

Informational visuals remind you that their controls exhibit a nonstandard binding but that the binding itself is fine. There is no action necessary on your part if the visual appears due to the intended design of your form. The visual icon itself is harmless, will not affect your form layout, and does not reveal itself when users fill out the form. Unfortunately, there is no option to hide or remove visuals.

A more important visual is quite noticeable and critical in nature: the red exclamation point ("!"). When this visual appears, it most likely means the associated control will not work or store the proper data when users fill

TABLE 3.15: When Design-Time Visuals Appear on Controls

Informational Visual Reason	Critical Visual Reasons
More than one control in the same view is bound to the same node (also known as multiple binding).	Data source is missing. Data type is not compatible with the control. Control is repeating, but data source doesn't repeat.

out the form. You can hover over the control or use the *More Details* option to gain insights into the binding problem. Most times, fixing a critical visual involves changing the control's binding or one of the bound node's properties. Table 3.15 lists common reasons why a visual may appear.

> **NOTE Option Buttons and Multiple Binding**
>
> Multiple binding is actually expected with some controls, such as Option Buttons, so information visuals are not shown in those cases.

> **NOTE Check Box and Option Button Do Not Show Visuals**
>
> Small controls such as Check Box and Option Button will never show visuals unless you hover the mouse over them. This helps avoid disrupting your form development when using small controls.

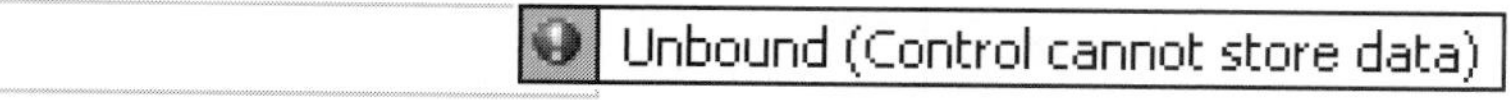

FIGURE 3.36: Critical design-time visual on an unbound Text Box control

Figure 3.36 shows the case of a critical visual appearing when the data source is missing. That is, a control exists in the view, but it is not bound to a node in the data source. We refer to this as an unbound control. Such controls are not very useful because they are read-only at runtime and never can be filled in. You can rebind an unbound control or simply delete it from the view. (Some controls are always unbound and can never be bound. Therefore, these controls usually will not show design-time visuals. These controls include Button, Scrolling Region, Vertical Label, Expression Box, and Hyperlink if it does not point to a data source field.)

TIP Showing All Visuals

When a dialog is open that relates to the data source as a whole, such as the *Default Value* menu item from the *Tools* menu, all controls will expand their visuals messages as if you were hovering over them. This is a quick way to see all messages without individually hovering over each control in the view.

NOTE Buttons in the Form Template Definition (.xsf) File

There is an `xsf:unboundControls` region in the InfoPath form definition (.xsf) file, but it tracks only Button controls. This is necessary for associating Button clicks with various actions, such as submitting the form or executing custom form code. Other unbound controls are not tracked in this region since they aren't functional to the form.

Editing Default Template Data

In this chapter we've looked at how to set simple default data on fields. The entry points have been through a control's properties or *Field or Group Properties* dialogs. We've set default data such as `"1"` for the `NumberOfChildren` field and `"Roundtrip"` as the default trip type. We could continue the lengthy process of setting default values by individually going to each control or *Field or Group Properties* dialog, but what if you had a form with literally hundreds of fields? For tasks en masse, the *Edit Default Values* dialog (Figure 3.37) is your best friend. Conveniently available from the *Tools* menu (under the *Default Values* item), this dialog displays the entire data source in a fashion similar to the *Data Source* task pane. Unlike the *Data Source* task pane, the *Edit Default Values* dialog is geared for quickly editing default values, selecting whether a node is included or excluded, and specifying how many times a repeating node exists when a repeating field or group is selected (which is not shown in Figure 3.37). Remember that since this dialog controls default values, the settings apply only to new forms created from the form template. Let's look at the *Edit Default Values* dialog to understand how it works.

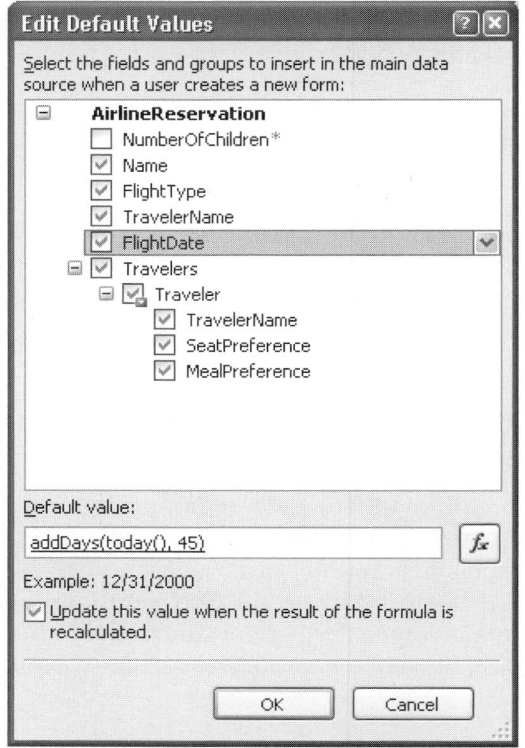

FIGURE 3.37: Edit Default Values dialog, which offers the quickest way to edit data source defaults

This dialog displays the data source in its entirety and, as you can see, it's easy to set the default value. To quickly set multiple default values, use the up and down arrows along the side to traverse to an item, then hit a single Tab key or the Alt+D access key to send focus to the *Default value* text box so you can fill in the value. To get back to the data source nodes, hit Shift+Tab or Alt+S.

Unchecking a checkbox adjacent to a node name, or hitting the Spacebar key, removes the node from new forms. Some nodes may already be removed in your form. In our airline form, the `NumberOfChildren` field does not exist at first and is inserted when a user clicks the *Click here to include children in your reservation* link to insert the Optional Section. If you decide to uncheck a node in the *Edit Default Values* dialog, be sure it can be inserted when filling out a form. Should a leaf control not have a node when filling out the form, it will be read-only. The user experience could be quite frustrating if there's no way to enter data into the control. If you must remove a field bound to a leaf control from the data source, a best practice is to bind the missing node to an Optional Section. Then bind a leaf control of your choice to the same node and put it inside of the Optional Section. We used this multiple-binding technique earlier with the `NumberOfChildren` attribute field.

If your data source has a Choice construct, the nodes under the Choice (known as "children of the Choice") are represented as option buttons instead of checkboxes, as shown in Figure 3.38. Since only one child of the Choice can exist at any given time, you can select which child exists in new forms. Users filling out the form can replace the default option with another of their choosing.

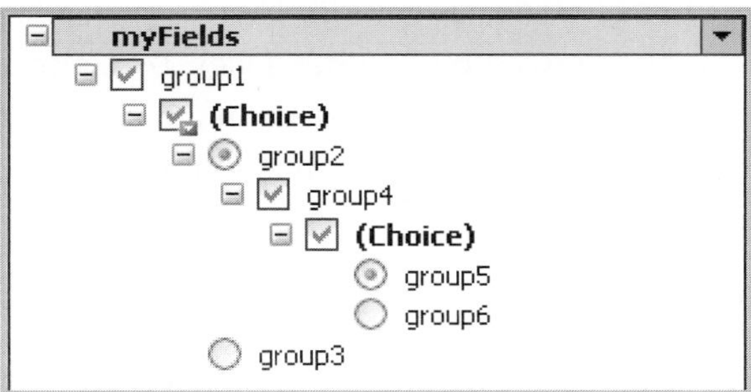

FIGURE 3.38: Cutaway of the Edit Default Values dialog when Choice exists in the data source

Repeating nodes have the customary blue square with white triangle icon overlay. To quickly insert new instances of a repeating node, hit the Insert key. To remove more than one instance of a node, hit the Delete key. For each inserted instance of a repeating item, you can expand its children nodes and continue to set default values. Each instance of a repeating node can have different default values if you wish.

Double-clicking any item reveals that data source node's details, including namespace, minimum and maximum occurrences, data type, and default value. As an alternative to double-clicking, you can also hit Alt+Enter to get to the data source node details. Should you need some details of data source nodes but don't want to spend time digging into each one, try hovering the mouse over each item. A tool tip will appear with a brief synopsis of that node.

Similar to what we see in control and *Field or Group Properties* dialogs are the *Default value* text box, *Insert Formula* button, *Example* sample data, and *Update this value when the result of the formula is recalculated* checkbox. Depending on what item is selected, these items may be enabled or disabled and may contain values set previously (either here or elsewhere). Anything you change in this dialog will be reflected throughout your form template after you click the *OK* button. *Cancel* will discard any changes you made since opening *Edit Default Values.*

Unlike the *Data Source* task pane, the *Edit Default Values* dialog is resizable and always obeys the mouse roller. Scrolling with the mouse roller makes for quick viewing of the overall data source structure and offers a viable alternative to task pane navigation. There's even a fast way to get to the dialog: Hit Alt+T followed by another T key. By centralizing common data source editing operations and the speed in which you can access them all in one place, you can be more productive while designing your form.

What's Next?

This chapter covered the core data source essentials for designing a form. Specifically, we discussed working with data in the *Data Source* task pane, setting data source field and group properties, binding controls to data source nodes, starting from blank versus existing XML Schema, interpreting design-time visuals, setting default values, and handling default data fragments. Each of these topics ties together, making InfoPath a superb data-centric platform for designing and filling out forms. In the next chapter, we discuss advanced controls as well as ways to customize controls by changing their properties. Then in Chapter 5, we introduce two major data-centric features that build on many of the concepts in this chapter: data validation and rules.

4

Advanced Controls and Customization

Getting Started

In Chapter 2, you learned the basics of designing forms in InfoPath 2007, including how to use layout tables to position text and controls in your form. You also learned quite a bit about the many different controls that are available for you to add to your form, including controls that enable you to collect and display data and controls that enable you to group other controls in the form. In Chapter 3, you learned all about data binding and how controls are connected to the underlying data source.

In this chapter, we're going to dive deeper into a few advanced control concepts that will expand on what you learned in Chapters 2 and 3. We'll complete our discussion of controls by talking about the advanced controls included in InfoPath design mode and, briefly, about custom controls you can add to the *Controls* task pane. Not only will we show you how to change the look and behavior of controls by setting control properties but we'll also show you some of the more advanced controls and control features. Let's get started by talking about the advanced controls available in the InfoPath design mode.

Advanced Controls

In Chapter 2, we introduced most of the controls available in the *Controls* task pane. However, we didn't talk about the advanced controls. The controls listed in the *Advanced* category of the *Controls* task pane include those that you will typically use less often or that are associated with complicated data structures. Therefore, we have deferred our discussion of these controls until now. Although you may use them less often, you may find that these controls can be invaluable, depending on the types of scenarios you are trying to fulfill. Let's talk about each of these controls briefly so you have a good understanding of them all.

Hyperlink

By now, we're sure you are intimately familiar with hyperlinks. Hyperlinks are used so ubiquitously throughout most applications that it only makes sense that InfoPath would include not only support for textual hyperlinks but also a Hyperlink control. You may wonder why we need a control to show hyperlinks. Think of it this way. Let's say that you want to include a hyperlink in your form, but you want it to change depending on other data entered into the form or on a link you've stored in a database (so you can easily change the link without having to change all the form templates that reference it). To do so, you need the Hyperlink control. The Hyperlink control allows you to pull either the hyperlink URL and/or the text displayed to the user from the underlying data source itself.

When you insert the Hyperlink control, the first thing you see is the *Insert Hyperlink* dialog (Figure 4.1). By default, you can type in the values for *Address* (under *Link to*) and *Text* (under *Display*) for the hyperlink. After you type in the necessary data and click the *OK* button, a normal hyperlink is inserted into the form. In this case, the hyperlink is not a control—it's just a typical, familiar hyperlink.

Instead, if you click the *Data source* radio button for either the *Link to* or *Display* values in the *Insert Hyperlink* dialog, you can choose from where in the underlying data source you want these values to come. Once you click on one of the *Data source* radio buttons, the *Select XPath* button becomes

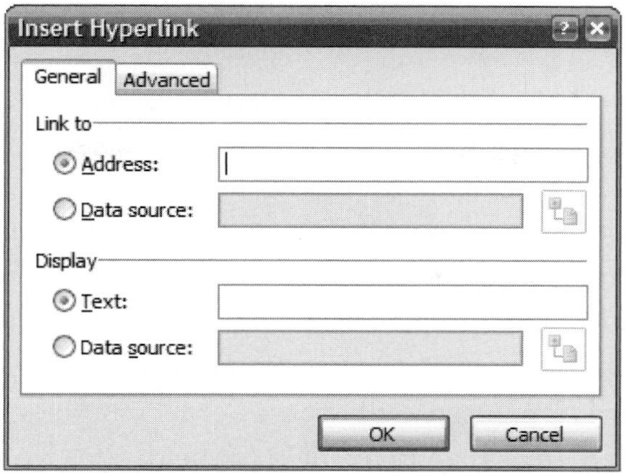

FIGURE 4.1: Insert Hyperlink dialog

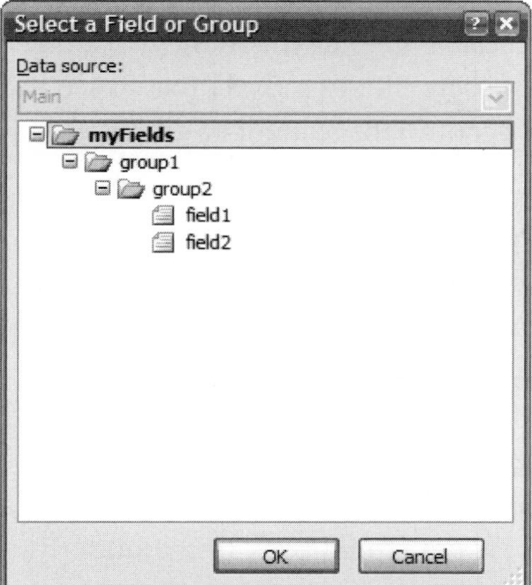

FIGURE 4.2: Select a Field or Group dialog

enabled. (The button to the right of the *Data source* text box is called the *Select XPath* button, as shown in the tool-tip text that appears when you hover your mouse over the button.) If you click on either of these buttons, the *Select a Field or Group* dialog appears (Figure 4.2). From this dialog you can then choose from where in the data source you want the value to come.

FIGURE 4.3: Hyperlink control in design mode

Once you have chosen a data field from the *Select a Field or Group* dialog, the Hyperlink control is inserted, as shown in Figure 4.3. This control has a dashed border just like layout tables do. Also, just as with layout tables, this dashed border indicates that the border is visible in design mode only. When filling out a form, users will not see borders for this control. In fact, in that mode when there is data in the field (or fields) that you chose from the *Select a Field or Group* dialog, the Hyperlink control appears as a normal hyperlink. Of course, you can always explicitly set visible borders for the Hyperlink control by selecting the control in design mode and then clicking on the *Borders and Shading* menu item on the *Format* menu. If you explicitly add a border, when users fill out a form, they'll see the hyperlink looking more like a Text Box control that cannot be edited.

Expression Box

The Expression Box control might be considered one of the more advanced controls in the *Controls* task pane. This control allows you to include expressions in your form that contain constant values or calculations that could involve XPaths that point to fields or groups in the underlying data source. Other controls can contain calculations and constant expressions as well, but the Expression Box differs from other controls in that the data in the Expression Box is not stored back to the underlying data source. The data used in an expression can come directly from the data source, but the main purpose of the Expression Box is to perform calculations on other data in the data source and to display the results in the form. For example, you may want to use an Expression Box to calculate and display the sum of all the expenses in a repeating table.

When you insert an Expression Box, the first thing you see is the *Insert Expression Box* dialog (Figure 4.4). In this dialog, you can enter an XPath expression by hand or click on the *fx* button (also called the *Edit Formula* button) to build the expression.

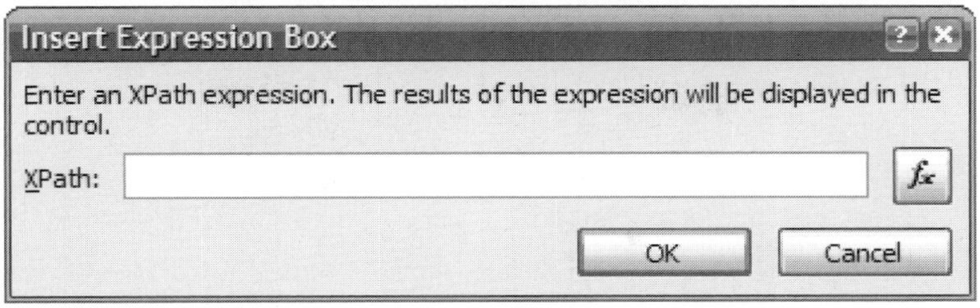

FIGURE 4.4: Insert Expression Box dialog

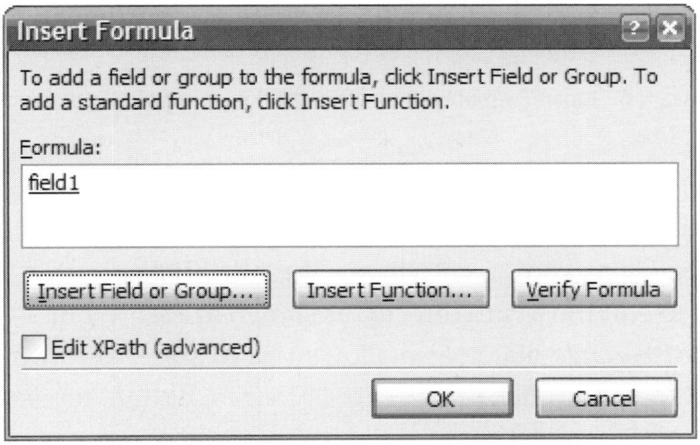

FIGURE 4.5: Insert Formula dialog after choosing a field

When you click on the *Edit Formula* button, the *Insert Formula* dialog (Figure 4.5) opens. This dialog should look familiar to you from Chapter 3. In this dialog, you can enter the formula by hand, choose fields or groups from the data source, or choose functions to include in your expression.

Clicking on the *Insert Field or Group* button in the dialog opens the familiar *Select a Field or Group* dialog that you've seen before. From this dialog, you can choose a field or group from the underlying main data source (or a secondary data source). Choosing a field from the data source inserts the name of the field into the *Formula* box in the *Insert Formula* dialog. Figure 4.5 shows the *Insert Formula* dialog after we chose a field named `field1`. Notice that the name of the field is underlined. This indicates that if you double-click on the underlined name (or select it and press Alt+I), the *Select a Field or Group* dialog will be reopened with this field selected in the data source

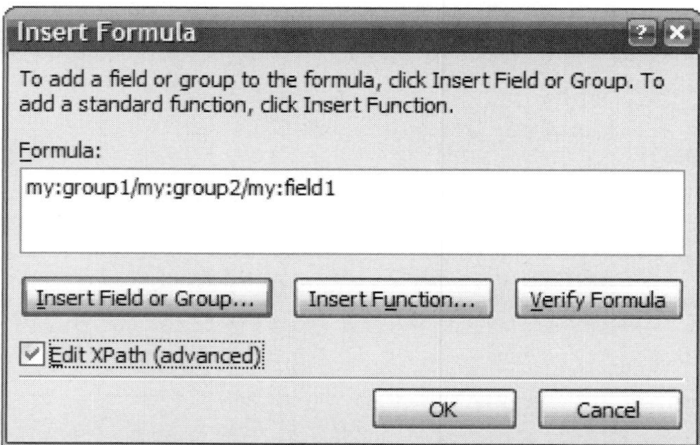

FIGURE 4.6: Insert Formula dialog after checking the Edit XPath checkbox

tree. The underlined name also indicates that the *Insert Formula* dialog is showing you the abbreviated version of the XPath for this field. If you click the *Edit XPath* checkbox, you will see the full XPath for that field, which allows you to edit the XPath directly, as shown in Figure 4.6.

The *Insert Formula* dialog also allows you to insert one or more built-in functions. When you click on the *Insert Function* button, the *Insert Function* dialog opens (Figure 4.7). From this dialog, you can choose one or more

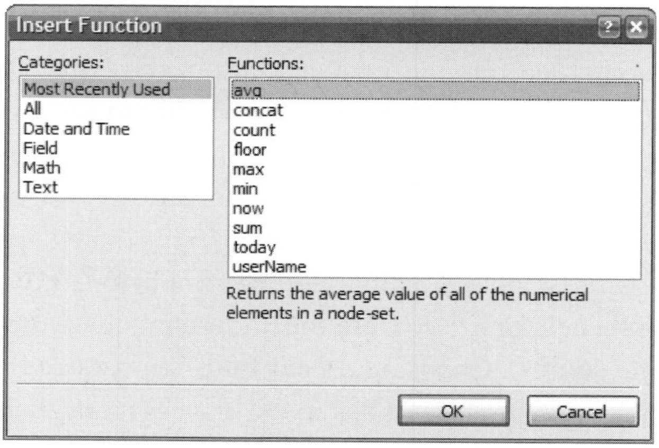

FIGURE 4.7: Insert Function dialog

functions from the different function categories—*Date and Time*, *Field*, *Math*, or *Text*. Functions that you use most often are listed in the *Most Recently Used* category.

Let's look at an example of a common way of using the Expression Box control. Say that you have an expense report form. In this form is a Repeating Table in which you enter the description and cost of each expense. At the bottom of the Repeating Table, it's only natural to provide the total of all expenses. This is an ideal place to use an Expression Box. Figure 4.8 shows this Repeating Table with the Text Box controls bound to the

Expense	Cost Expenses
ExpenseDescription	ExpenseCost

Repeating Table

FIGURE 4.8: Repeating Table control for expenses

`ExpenseDescription` and `ExpenseCost` nodes. Figure 4.9 shows the data source for this example. (This sample, ExpenseTotalCalculation, is included with the samples for this chapter on the book's Web site.)

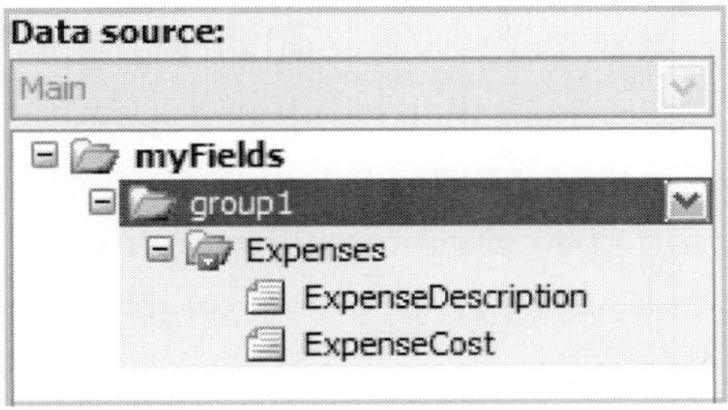

FIGURE 4.9: Data source for the expense report example

Notice in Figure 4.8 that we added a footer row to the table. You can add a footer row by using the *Display* tab of the properties dialog for the Repeating Table. In the second column of the footer row, we're going to add an Expression Box control that will be used to calculate the sum of all the `ExpenseCost` fields. When inserting the Expression Box, we click on the *Edit Formula* button, then click on the *Insert Function* button, and then

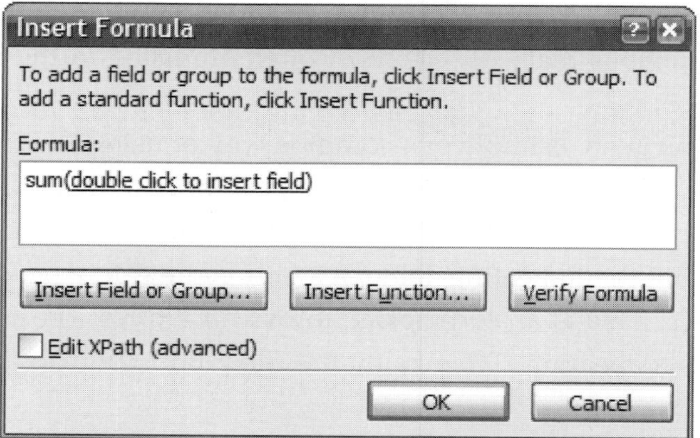

FIGURE 4.10: Insert Formula dialog after inserting the `sum` function

choose the `sum` function from the list. After we close the *Insert Function* dialog, the *Insert Formula* dialog looks like that shown in Figure 4.10.

In Figure 4.10, notice the text *double click to insert field* inside the parentheses next to the function. If a function requires additional parameters, it will include this help text. Double-clicking on the instructional text opens the *Select a Field or Group* dialog, which allows you to choose a field to pass to the function. (Instead of double-clicking, you can select the instructional text and press Alt+I.) In this case, we want to pick the `ExpenseCost` field. For the `sum` function and many of the other mathematical functions, you typically want to pick a field that is either repeating by itself or is in a repeating context in the data source. If you choose a field that is not repeating, the calculation won't be very interesting. In this case, the `ExpenseCost` field is a child of the `Expenses` group node, which is repeating

Finally, after completing our formula, we can click on the *Verify Formula* button to ensure that there are no errors in our expression. After we verify the formula and correct any errors (there shouldn't be any at this point), we click on the *OK* button to insert the Expression Box control into the form. (If you decide you want to change the expression after you have inserted the control, you can do so from the properties dialog for the Expression Box. We'll talk about control properties later in this chapter.)

The inserted control looks very similar to the Hyperlink control shown in Figure 4.3. Like the Hyperlink, the Expression Box has a dashed border that is purely for design purposes; by default, the Expression Box has no borders when users fill out a form.

Let's preview our form and test it. After we enter a few expense items, the form looks like that shown in Figure 4.11. The three expense items add up to a total cost of $215.55. (We've added some data formatting to the Text Box and Expression Box controls to show the costs as currency with two decimal places.) As you can see, the Expression Box control can be very useful for doing calculations such as this.

Expense	Cost
Dinner	$75.55
Taxi	$15.00
Hotel	$125.00
	$215.55

Insert item

FIGURE 4.11: Expense report form during preview

Vertical Label

The Vertical Label and Expression Box controls are virtually the same. The main difference is that the Vertical Label is used to display text vertically in the form and is not connected to data in the data source in any way. (The Vertical Label is especially useful for forms in Asian languages where text tends to flow vertically.) These two controls are so similar, in fact, that you can even change the Expression Box to a Vertical Label and vice versa through the properties dialog for each of these controls.

Forms Services

The Vertical Label control is not available in browser-enabled forms.

Insert Vertical Label

Enter the text to be displayed in the control.

Text:

Note: Users cannot edit this text in the form.

OK Cancel

FIGURE 4.12: Insert Vertical Label dialog

FIGURE 4.13: Vertical Label control

When you insert the Vertical Label control, you first see the *Insert Vertical Label* dialog (Figure 4.12). You can then insert the text you want to display vertically. Note that this text is static and cannot be edited by users of your form. Once you insert the text and click the *OK* button, the Vertical Label control is inserted into the form (Figure 4.13). Once again, the dashed borders tell you that by default, users will see no borders for this control when filling out a form.

Scrolling Region and Horizontal Region

Back when we talked about the *Layout* task pane, we briefly mentioned two layout elements that are a lot like controls—the Scrolling Region and the Horizontal Region. These two layout elements are so much like controls that they exist in both the *Layout* and *Controls* task panes. Like the other layout elements, these two controls are not connected to data in the form;

their purpose is strictly to help you enhance your form's layout. Therefore, these controls are very simple.

Forms Services

The Scrolling Region and Horizontal Region controls are not supported in browser-enabled forms.

The Scrolling Region is much like the Section control in that you can include other controls inside it. In fact, in design mode the Scrolling Region, as shown in Figure 4.14, looks almost the same as the Section control. The main difference, besides the fact that the Section control is connected to data and the Scrolling Region control is not, is that the Scrolling Region includes a vertical scrollbar that becomes active if the content of the region goes beyond the region's height boundaries. (You can also set up the Scrolling Region to scroll horizontally, which we'll show you how to do later in this chapter when we talk about control properties.)

FIGURE 4.14: Scrolling Region control in design mode

The Scrolling Region is particularly useful when used with repeating controls that have large amounts of data. For example, you can use the Scrolling Region with the detail control of the Master/Detail control in order to make your data easier to deal with. In Chapter 2, we designed a form that would allow a user to view information about all the potential employees and the positions for which they applied. If an applicant applies for 50 positions, for example, the form could grow quite large. We

Last Name	First Name
Smith	John
Doe	Jane

Insert item

Phone Number: 555-1234

Email Address: jsmith@smith.com

Minimum Salary Desired: 45,000

Address

Street Address: One Circle Way

City: Cincinnati

State (or Province): OH

Postal Code: 45211

Country: United States

2024	Systems Engineer	Systems Engineer who has experience with Web servers needed to install and maintain backend Windows servers.
1012	Junior Software Engineer	Junior Software Engineer needed to write code exactly to specifications.
1013	Senior Software Engineer	Senior Software Engineer needed to review code written by junior Software Engineer.

Insert item

Insert item

FIGURE 4.15: Application review form with Scrolling Region when filling out the form

can use the Scrolling Region control to make this data more manageable in the view. Figure 4.15 shows this same form from the user's perspective, but with the Scrolling Region added to the form template. (We've added a border to the Scrolling Region so users can easily see the boundaries of the control when filling out the form. This sample form template is called ApplicationReviewForm.)

The Horizontal Region is pretty much the same as the Scrolling Region. The main difference is that you can place multiple Horizontal Region controls horizontally on the same line in the form, as shown in Figure 4.16. The Scrolling Region, however, allows you to place only one control on a line at a time. Like the Scrolling Region, the Horizontal Region is a container control, meaning that it can contain other controls. And, just like the Scrolling Region, the Horizontal Region is not connected to data in the underlying data source as other container controls such as the Section are. Although the Horizontal Region doesn't have scrollbars turned on by default, you can

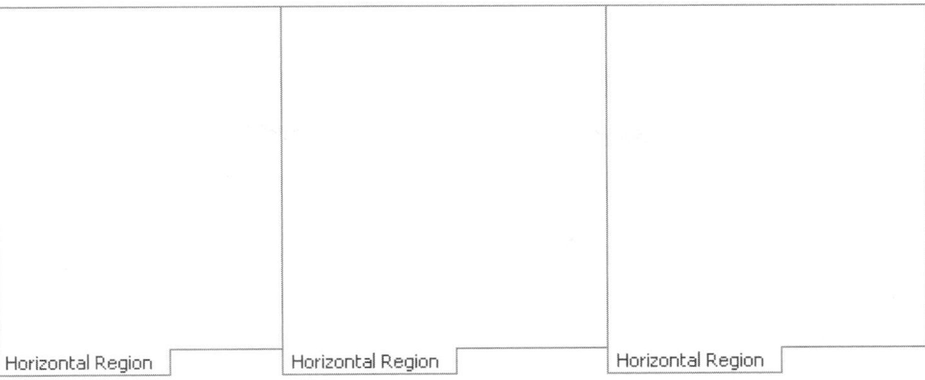

FIGURE 4.16: Horizontal Region controls in design mode

specify that you want it to have vertical or horizontal scrollbars or both, the same way as you can for the Scrolling Region, as we'll show you later in this chapter. You can also make a Horizontal Region act more like a Scrolling Region by opening the properties dialog for the Horizontal Region and unselecting the *Enable horizontal layout* option in the *Display* tab.

Choice Group, Repeating Choice Group, and Choice Section

The next three controls in the *Advanced* category of the *Controls* task pane, as well as the Repeating Recursive Section that follows, are the most complicated in terms of the type of data to which they are bound. To fully understand the choice controls, it helps to have an understanding of the underlying Schema associated with these controls. Therefore, you may want to review the schema for the choice nodes discussed in Chapter 3. Even if you don't have a thorough understanding of the schema constructs behind the choice controls, you can still derive a lot of benefit from using these controls.

Forms Services

Choice controls are not supported in browser-enabled forms.

As you might imagine from the names of these controls, you can use them to give the user a choice between entering different types of data in the form. For example, let's look again at our employment application form. In that form, we ask the user to attach a résumé to the form. However, instead of attaching an actual file, the user may want to provide a hyperlink to a résumé on a Web site. To allow the user to choose between attaching a file and inserting a hyperlink (but not both), we can use the Choice Group control. The Choice Group control is another one of those composite controls like the Repeating Table or Horizontal Repeating Table.

When you insert the Choice Group control, you actually insert multiple controls at once, as shown in Figure 4.17. First, there is the outer Choice Group container. Can you see something special about this control that you've seen before? Since the control has a dashed border, the borders don't appear by default when a user fills out a form that contains this control. This container control, however, is a bit different than other container controls. First, it's not really a control. Wait, it looks like a control, doesn't it? Yes, but it's really considered a virtual control whose sole purpose is to group Choice Section controls while in design mode. (A virtual control is connected to a virtual node in the data source and does not exist in the view when the form is filled out.)

The other difference you will notice about this control when you try to use it is that it can contain only Choice Section controls. You can't put any other control inside it. In fact, when you try to insert a Text Box control directly into the Choice Group control, InfoPath automatically puts the Text Box in a Choice Section control for you. If you try to insert anything but a Choice Section control inside the Choice Group other than from the *Controls* task pane, such as by copying and pasting a Text Box, InfoPath will give you an error message.

FIGURE 4.17: Choice Group control in design mode

The Choice Section control is very similar to a Section control—it is a container control that contains other controls and is connected to data in the underlying data source. The one main difference between a Choice Section and a Section control is that the Choice Section can exist only inside a Choice Group. So, for example, if you try to drag and drop a Choice Section outside of a Choice Group, you will receive an error.

As you've seen, when you insert a Choice Group, it contains two Choice Section controls by default. The *Controls* task pane also includes a Choice Section control in case you would like to add more choices to your Choice Group. However, if you click on the Choice Section control in the *Controls* task pane and your insertion point is not inside a Choice Group in the view, the Choice Section control will automatically be wrapped inside a Choice Group. As we mentioned, this is due to the fact that Choice Section controls can only exist inside a Choice Group control.

Now that we know all about the Choice Group and Choice Section controls, let's go ahead and add a Choice Group control to the employment application form we started in Chapter 2. This Choice Group control will allow users to choose between attaching a file and inserting a hyperlink. To do that, we'll first insert a Choice Group control into the form. Since we want attaching a file to be the default option, we'll move the existing File Attachment control into the first Choice Section control. By default, when you insert a Choice Group control, the first Choice Section in the group is the default, as indicated by the text of the design-time visual at the bottom of the control. In Chapter 3, we showed you how to change the default choice. (In addition to moving the File Attachment control in the view, you'll also want to move the node to which the File Attachment control is bound in the data source to be a child of the correct group node to which the Choice Section is bound. To find the correct group, click on the Choice Section control to select it, and then open the *Data Source* task pane. The correct node in the *Data Source* pane will be selected automatically.)

Next, we'll insert a Text Box control that can be used to insert a link to a résumé on a Web site. (We use a Text Box control instead of a Hyperlink control because a Hyperlink control is used only to view data, not to enter it.) Figure 4.18 shows the results of these changes.

As we mentioned, by default, when filling out the form, the user sees only the default Choice Section that contains the File Attachment control. The user

FIGURE 4.18: Employment application form with Choice Group control

can click the Choice Section icon on the left of the control and replace the current Choice Section with the second one, as shown in Figure 4.19. (Note that `group7` and `group8` are the names of the data items in the data source to which the Choice Sections are connected. Later in this chapter, we'll show

FIGURE 4.19: Default Choice Section with context menu commands

you how to change those names to something more descriptive.) Figure 4.20 shows this part of the form after replacing the default Choice Section with the second one, which allows the user to insert a URL for his or her résumé.

FIGURE 4.20: Employment application form after replacing the default Choice Section

The Repeating Choice Group control is not much different than the Choice Group control. The main difference is that, like the Repeating Section control, you can insert multiple Choice Sections of a particular type. For example, let's say that you want to allow the user of your form to not only attach a file but also supply a URL. If you want to support this scenario when users fill out your form, you should use the Repeating Choice Group control. This control is really like a combination of the Choice Group and Repeating Section. When a user fills out a form that contains this control, he or she can insert multiple instances of one type of Choice Section (e.g., multiple résumé files) or replace one Choice Section with another (e.g., if the user decides to include a URL instead of a résumé file.)

Repeating Recursive Section

Forms Services

Recursive controls are not supported in browser-enabled forms.

The Repeating Recursive Section is, by far, the most complicated control in terms of the type of data structure to which it is bound. This control allows you to insert multiple instances of the same data structure within the current Recursive Section control when filling out a form. Whenever you have multiple instances of the same data structure within each other, this is referred to as recursion.

For example, let's say that you are a manager and you want to design a form in which you can store all information about your employees (e.g., name, employee number, title, and so on). Some of your employees may be managers, so you want to store information about their reports as well. Since a manager is an employee and the people on his or her team are also employees, the data is recursive. It makes sense to use a Repeating Recursive Section for this form. (In Chapter 3, we showed the schema for a Repeating Recursive Section; see Table 3.9.)

Look at Figure 4.21, which shows the employee information form with a Repeating Recursive Section. (We've added a border to this control to make the hierarchy more pronounced when filling out the form. This form is in EmployeeInformation with the samples for this chapter.) As you can see, the Repeating Recursive Section is basically a Repeating Section that can contain other controls. In fact, we've added a layout table and

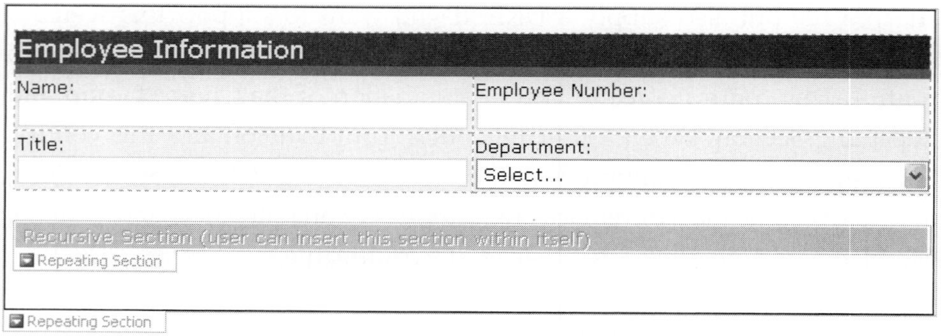

FIGURE 4.21: Repeating Recursive Section in design mode

some controls to the Repeating Section so that employees can enter their employee information. However, one difference between the Repeating Section and the Repeating Recursive Section is the existence of an inner Repeating Section that looks sort of strange. This inner Repeating Section is sort of gray with the text *user can insert this section within itself.* This strange-looking Repeating Section is called the **Recursive Section.** In design mode, this section simply indicates that this control is recursive. Anything you place within the outer Repeating Section will be duplicated within it at least once. If you remove the inner Recursive Section, the Repeating Recursive Section control is no longer recursive.

To see this control in action, look at Figure 4.22, which shows how the Repeating Recursive Section looks when a user fills out the form. From the form, you can see that John Smith is a Development Manager. Jane Doe is a Software Development Lead who reports to John Smith. Joe Bob is a Software Development Engineer who reports to Jane Doe. The Repeating Recursive Section allows you to create hierarchies of similar data structures very easily. The example shown in Figure 4.22 is very simple, however. The Repeating Recursive Section allows you to insert multiple instances of the data at any level. So, you could insert many other employees at John's, Jane's, or Joe's levels.

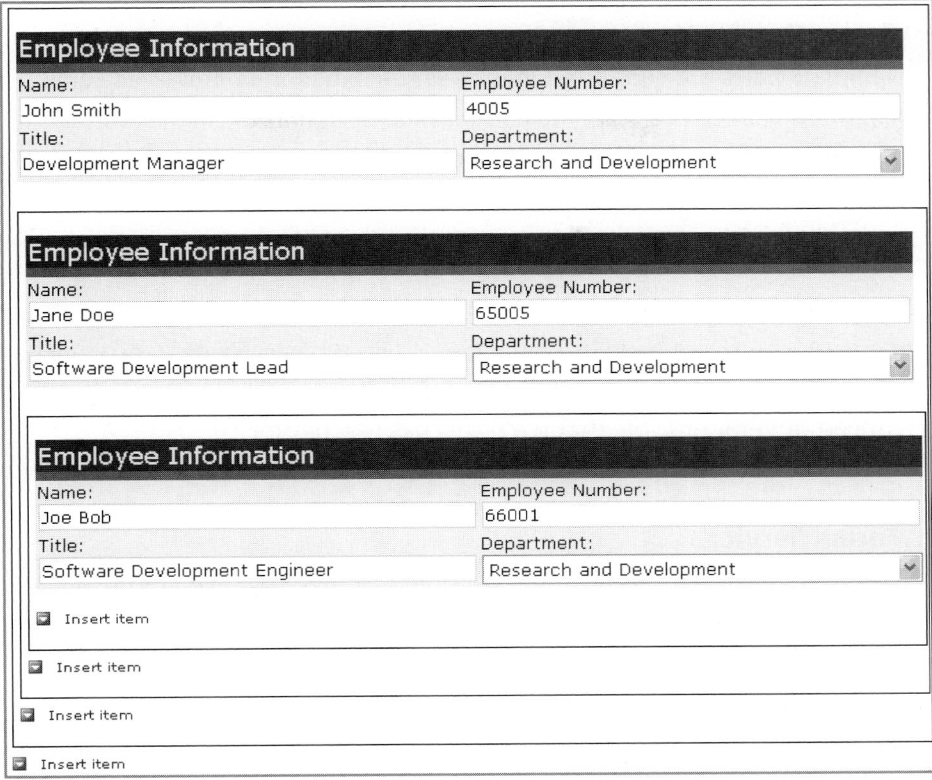

FIGURE 4.22: Repeating Recursive Section when filling out the employee information form

Custom Controls

The final category in the *Controls* task pane is the *Custom* category. This category allows you to add controls you have created yourself or have obtained from another form designer or developer. InfoPath supports two types of custom controls—template parts and ActiveX controls. Template parts provide a way for you to build your own custom controls using the InfoPath design mode. These template parts are basically an aggregation of other InfoPath controls and features. They support most features that are available to you when designing a form template except form code. We will talk in great detail about template parts in Chapter 10.

Forms Services

Template parts are supported in browser-enabled forms. However, some controls included in a template part may not be supported in the browser. Design-Time visuals display on controls that are not supported when designing a browser-enabled form.

Custom controls implemented by using ActiveX technologies are those you create by writing code in Visual C++, Visual Basic, Visual C#, or Visual Basic .NET, for example. Building custom controls with ActiveX is an advanced developer topic that we'll discuss in Chapter 19.

Forms Services

Custom ActiveX controls are not supported in browser-enabled forms.

Control Properties

In Chapter 2, we talked about how to format controls, which is one way you can customize the properties of a control. In addition to formatting, controls in the InfoPath design mode offer a wide array of other, more interesting properties you can set to customize your form template.

There are different ways to access the properties of a control. The first thing you must do before you can access control properties is to select the control. (We talked in detail about control selection in Chapter 2.) If you have selected a Text Box control, for example, you can then access the control properties by selecting the *Text Box Properties* menu item on the *Format* menu. You can also just hold down the Alt key and then press Enter. Double-clicking on the control is yet another way you can access the properties for a control. (For a container control such as a Section or Repeating Table, you can double-click on the tab at the bottom of the control or on any of the borders of the control.) In all these cases, whether you click on the menu item, use the access key, or double-click on the control, the properties dialog for the control opens. Figure 4.23 shows the properties dialog for the Text Box control.

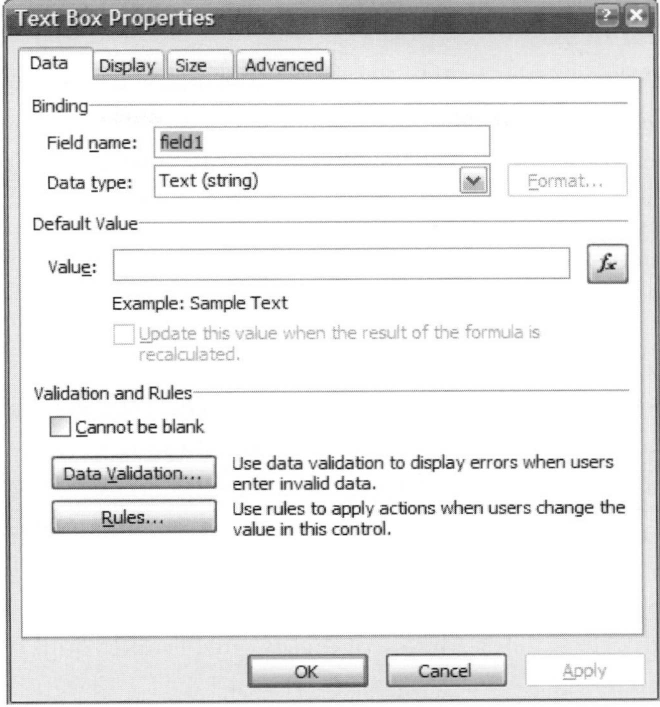

FIGURE 4.23: Properties dialog for the Text Box control

Even though the properties dialog is similar for all controls, each control has its own set of properties specific to that control. For now, let's concentrate on the similarities. We'll talk about some of the differences later in this chapter. You'll notice that the properties dialogs for most controls contain four tabs at the top of the dialog—*Data, Display, Size,* and *Advanced.* Some controls have only a couple of these tabs, and a few controls have only one or more than four. We'll talk about each of these tabs in detail, including additional tabs you may see in the control properties dialogs. When we talk about each tab, we will discuss the corresponding control properties in detail. However, we won't mention every single property that exists in the control properties dialogs. There are just too many to list. This gives you an opportunity to explore the properties dialog for each control and learn about those properties we haven't mentioned.

Forms Services

On some tabs of various control properties dialogs, you may see a peach-colored box with an "i" surrounded by a blue circle or an "x" with a red circle. These boxes describe anomalies specific to browser-enabled forms, such as incompatibilities or a degraded user experience.

Data Tab

As you may have guessed from the name of this tab, the *Data* tab is where all the properties related to data are exposed. The *Data* tab exists only on the properties dialogs for controls bound to data in some way. Therefore, controls such as the Button, Hyperlink, Expression Box, Vertical Label, Scrolling Region, and Horizontal Region do not have a *Data* tab in their properties dialogs. Instead, these controls either do not have this tab at all or have a *General* tab that contains general properties for that control. Just open the properties dialog for one of these controls and you'll immediately notice the difference.

When the *Data* tab is present on a properties dialog, it contains a *Binding* section at the top of the tab. This *Binding* section is where you specify how the control is bound to the underlying data source. In Chapter 3, we talked about how controls are bound to data. In addition to the *Field or Group Properties* dialog we discussed in Chapter 3, the *Binding* section of the *Data* tab is another place you can specify how a control is bound to the underlying data source.

The main property that specifies how the control is bound to the data source is the field name. (In the case of a container control, this property is called the group name.) If you are creating a new blank form template, when you first insert a control, the node to which the control is bound is given a default name. For controls that collect or display data to the user, such as Text Box, Drop-Down List Box, and Date Picker, the control is bound to a field whose name is `fieldX`, where `X` is replaced by a number that is incremented each time one of those types of controls is inserted (e.g., `field1`, `field2`, and so on). For container controls, the name of the control begins with `group` (e.g., `group1`, `group2`, and so on). You can change the name of the field or group in the underlying data source by using the *Field or Group Properties* dialog or the *Data* tab of the control's properties dialog.

Let's look at the employment application form template we started to create in Chapter 2. This form template contains many different controls, each of which has a generic name created by InfoPath when the control was inserted. It would make sense for us to change the names of the control to better describe the data to enter. For example, the Text Box control that will accept the user's first name has a control name of `field1`. The Text Box for the last name is called `field2` since it was inserted into the form right after the first name Text Box. When you look at the underlying data source, the names `field1` and `field2` don't tell you anything about the data the user will enter into the form. So, let's go ahead and change the names of these fields to `FirstName` and `LastName`, respectively. (We'll leave it up to you to go through the rest of the sample form and change the names of other fields to something more descriptive.)

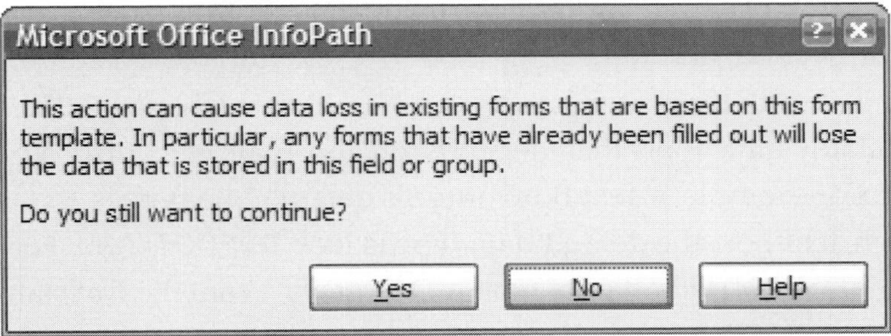

FIGURE 4.24: Dialog that warns about data loss when changing field names

Since you've previously saved the form template, when you change the name of the Text Box, you will see the warning dialog shown in Figure 4.24. This dialog is warning you that, if users have already filled out forms based on your form template, changing the control name may cause you to lose data. If you are still in the initial design phase for your form template and users aren't currently using it to fill out forms, it's safe to change the field name. If users have filled out forms based on your form template, you could cause them to lose their data if you make this change. In general, it's a good practice to set the names of your fields and groups before you allow users to start filling out forms based on your form template.

As we talked about in Chapter 3, InfoPath in design mode uses design-time visuals to give you information about controls. One bit of information that the design-time visuals give is the name of the field or group to which a control is bound. When we changed the name of the Text Box used for entering the user's first name in the properties dialog for the control and then committed the change by clicking the *OK* or *Apply* buttons, the design-time visual also changed to reflect the new control name, as shown in Figure 4.25.

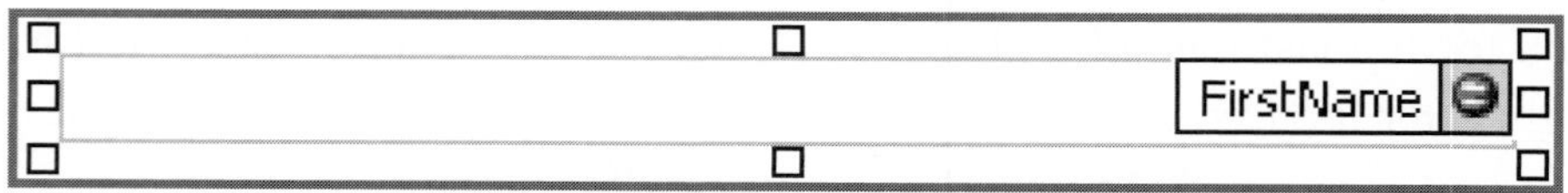

FIGURE 4.25: Binding design-time visual for the `FirstName` Text Box control

In addition to the name of the control, you can also change the data type in the *Data* tab just as you can in the *Field or Group Properties* dialog. (Of course, this property doesn't apply to container controls, so it doesn't exist on the *Data* tab of the properties dialog for controls such as Section, Repeating Section, and Repeating Table.) When you insert a control while designing a blank form template, as we discussed in Chapter 3, the control has a default data type that depends on the type of control you have inserted. For example, a Text Box control's default data type is *Text (string).* For a Rich Text Box, the default data type is *Rich Text (XHTML).* For a Date Picker control, the default data type is *Date (date).* From the *Data* tab on the properties dialog, you can change the data type to something other than the default for most controls. (The Rich Text Box control doesn't support any other data type except *Rich Text (XHTML),* so this property is disabled on the *Data* tab of its properties dialog.)

Let's look again at the employment application form. In that form template, we added a Text Box control in which the user could enter the minimum salary desired. When we inserted this Text Box, the default data type is *Text (string),* as you will see when you look at the *Data type* field in the *Data* tab. Since the user will enter a salary figure, it would make sense to change the data type to one of the number types and then format the data as currency. In the case of our employment application, we don't want the user to enter decimal data, so let's change the data type to *Whole Number (integer).* (There may be a few users who want to specify a minimum salary of $45,000.20, but we think that not allowing them to add the additional 20 cents is okay.)

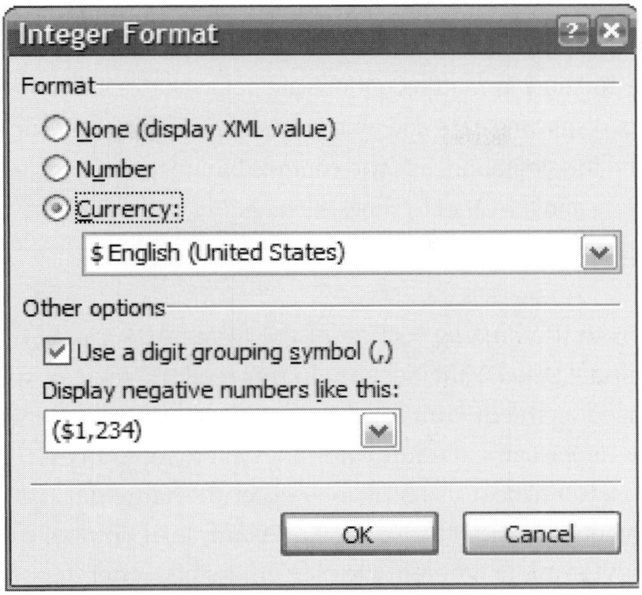

FIGURE 4.26: Integer Format dialog for Whole Number (integer) data types

Once you change the data type to something other than *Text (string)*, the *Format* button next to the *Data type* field becomes enabled. When you click on this button, the *Integer Format* dialog opens (Figure 4.26). The format options available in the *Integer Format* dialog depend on the type of data for the control. In this case, since the data type is *Whole Number (integer)*, three options are available—*None (display XML value)*, *Number*, and *Currency*. By default, for the *Whole Number (integer)* type, the formatting type is *Number*. In Figure 4.26, we have changed the formatting type to *Currency*. Now, when we preview the form and enter a salary figure into the Text Box for the minimum salary desired, when we tab out of the control, the value is automatically formatted for currency (Figure 4.27).

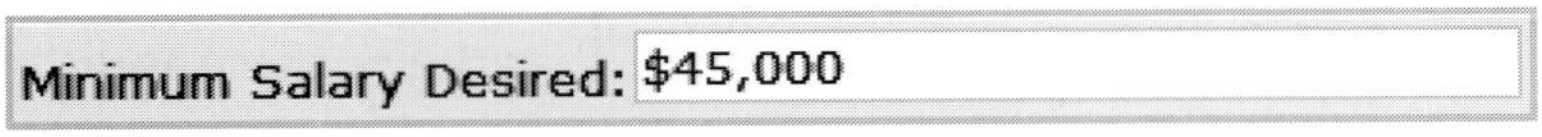

FIGURE 4.27: Field for minimum salary desired formatted as currency

Forms Services

Some date and time formatting options are not available in browser-enabled forms. Also, displaying date and time in the same control isn't supported. To work around this limitation, use two controls bound to the same field: one to show the date and the other to show the time.

In addition to the *Binding* section of the *Data* tab, some of the properties dialogs contain a *Default Value* section. In this section, you can specify a value that will be used as the default for the control when a user begins filling out the form. (This is the same default value we talked about in Chapter 3.) This is particularly useful if most users usually enter the same data into the control and only a few enter a different value. For example, if you have created a status report form template wherein the user enters his or her department name, if this form is usually filled out by people in your department and only rarely by those in another department, you could include your department name as the default value for the department name Text Box.

The *Data* tab for most of the properties dialogs of several controls, such as the Text Box and Drop-Down List Box, contains another section called *Validation and Rules.* (In some cases, it's called just *Validation.*) This section of the *Data* tab allows you to include instructions to InfoPath about how to validate the data entered into the control. We'll discuss the topics of data validation and rules in Chapter 5.

If you open the properties dialog for a container control that is connected to data such as a Section or Optional Section, you will notice that the *Data* tab looks a bit different than in the properties dialog for the standard controls. Let's look at the properties dialog for the Optional Section that stores information about the minimum salary desired (Figure 4.28). At first it may strike you as being odd that the title of this dialog is *Section Properties* even though you opened the dialog for an Optional Section control. The reason for this is quite simply that the Section and Optional Section controls are basically the same control. The main difference is whether or not the control is included in the form by default when a user initially fills out the form. Remember that an Optional Section and the contents within it are not included in the underlying XML of the form until the

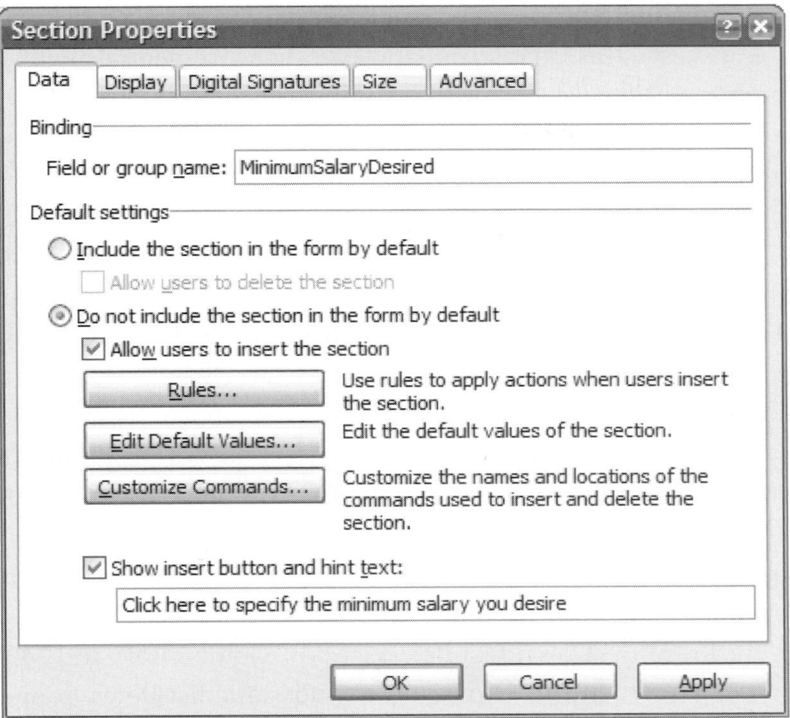

FIGURE 4.28: Properties dialog for the Optional Section for the minimum salary desired

user inserts the control by clicking on the *Click here to insert* link. However, a Section control is included in the underlying XML by default when the form is opened. You can actually change a Section to an Optional Section, and vice versa, through the *Default Settings* section of the properties dialog for these controls.

Notice in Figure 4.28 that *Do not include the section in the form by default* is selected. If you select *Include the section in the form by default* and click the *Apply* button, the Optional Section will change to a Section control. (In fact, the design-time visuals for the control, specifically the text shown in the tab below the control, will change to reflect the fact that this control is now a Section instead of an Optional Section.)

When you've chosen *Do not include the section in the form by default,* three buttons become enabled—*Rules, Edit Default Values,* and *Customize Commands.* We'll discuss the *Edit Default Values* and *Customize Commands* options later in this chapter when we talk about advanced customization. The *Rules* button is discussed in Chapter 5. However, here we should mention one other property in the *Data* tab for this properties dialog. Back in Chapter 2, we talked about the *Click here to insert* button that appears for Optional Sections when a user fills out a form. (This button is titled *Insert item* for Repeating Sections and Repeating Tables.) The default text for this button is not very descriptive in most cases. Luckily, you can change this text by using the properties dialog. You can also choose to turn it off if you decide you don't want it in your form for whatever reason. In Figure 4.28, notice that we customized the hint text so that users know they can click the button to insert the minimum salary they desire.

As you can probably tell based on the two types of properties dialogs we've talked about so far, InfoPath offers several ways that you can customize your controls. The *Data* tab is, in fact, the most diverse tab included in the properties dialogs. Each control has at least a few options that are different than other controls. For example, the *Data* tab of the properties dialogs for the Drop-Down List Box, List Box, Combo Box, and Multiple-Selection List Box controls allow you to add static list items or specify a location in a data source from which to retrieve the list items. (We'll talk about these options in Chapter 7.) Obviously, these options don't apply to the Text Box or Section controls, so they are not present in their properties dialogs. The main point is that there are many different properties available on the *Data* tab of the various properties dialogs for controls. In fact, there are too many to describe each one here in detail. We encourage you to explore the *Data* tab in the different properties dialogs in order to learn more. For now, we'll turn our attention to another common tab in the properties dialog—the *Display* tab.

Display Tab

As its name implies, the *Display* tab includes properties that allow you to customize the way a control is displayed. As with the *Data* tab, the *Display* tab contains different properties depending on the type of control with which it is associated. However, the *Display* tab is not quite as diverse as the *Data* tab. In fact, the *Display* tab on the properties dialogs for most controls contains only one item, the *Conditional Formatting* button, which we'll talk about in Chapter 5.

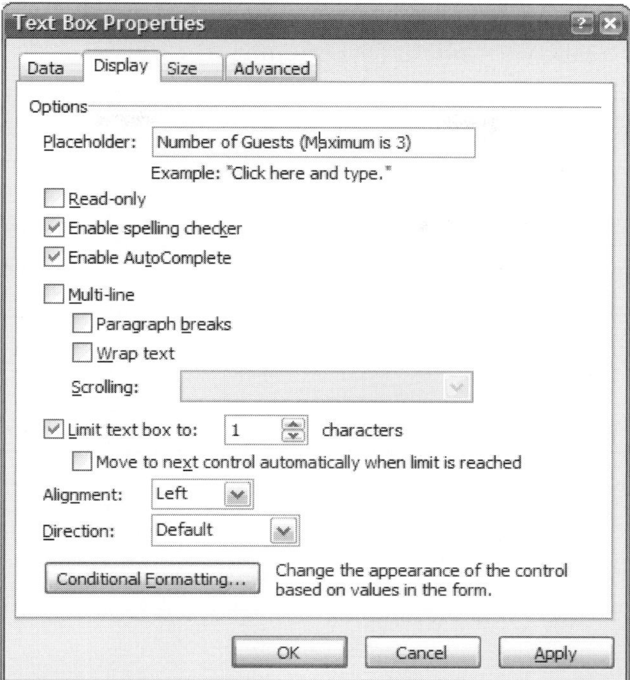

FIGURE 4.29: Display tab of the Text Box Properties dialog

Let's look at a couple of controls that have interesting options in the *Display* tab of their properties dialogs. The Text Box and Rich Text Box have several display properties that can be customized. Figure 4.29 shows the *Display* tab of the properties dialog for a Text Box control.

Most of the checkboxes in the *Display* tab shown in Figure 4.29, such as *Read-only, Enable spelling checker,* and *Enable AutoComplete,* are self-explanatory. Some of the others warrant further explanation. The *Placeholder* field in this dialog allows you to insert descriptive text so your users know what you want them to insert. For example, in this Text Box control, a user enters the total number of guests he or she is bringing to a party. You may want to provide more information, such as the fact that the maximum number of guests each user can bring is three. Adding the text "Number of Guests (Maximum is 3)" to the *Placeholder* field will help users understand what you expect. If you close the dialog by clicking the *OK* button and then preview your form, the placeholder text will be added to your Text Box, as

Number of Guests:

Number of Guests (Maximum is 3)

FIGURE 4.30: Placeholder text in a Text Box control

shown in Figure 4.30. While filling out the form, when you click in the Text Box, the entire placeholder text becomes selected. If you start typing at this point, the placeholder text will be replaced with whatever you enter in the Text Box.

Forms Services

Placeholder text and spelling checker features are not available when users fill out a form in the browser.

You can set another interesting property in the *Display* tab by using the *Multi-line* checkbox. This property is useful if you want your users to be able to enter multiple lines of text. Normally, you would use a Rich Text Box control for this. However, in some cases, it is useful to use a Text Box instead of a Rich Text Box. One obvious reason is that you may not want your users to enter formatted text. It is possible to restrict a Rich Text Box to unformatted text, but the Text Box control offers a few properties that the Rich Text Box does not, such as *AutoComplete.* So, whenever you want to take advantage of all the features offered by a Text Box control but also want to allow your users to enter multiple lines of text, just click the *Multi-line* checkbox.

Forms Services

The *Multi-line* property is available on a browser-enabled form, but the *Paragraph breaks* and *Wrap text* settings are automatically enabled. These settings cannot be changed. Additionally, the *Scrolling* drop-down menu is disabled with *Show scroll bar when necessary* as the default setting.

When you select the checkbox next to the *Multi-line* option, both the *Paragraph breaks* and *Wrap text* checkboxes become selected as well. (It is possible at this point to uncheck one of these options in order to customize this property even further.) The *Paragraph breaks* property allows you to insert line-break characters into the text by pressing the Enter key. (If the data type of the node to which this Text Box is bound is not *Text (string),* the *Paragraph breaks* checkbox is not available.) The *Wrap text* property will cause the text to wrap to the next line when the text length exceeds the width of the control. (Normally, text will not wrap and will, therefore, extend past the viewable area of the control. Then you must place the cursor inside the Text Box and move it to the left or right in order to see the rest of the text.) For both of these properties, you can choose from the corresponding drop-down list box how you want scrolling to be handled when the text becomes too long for the control. You could always show scrollbars, for example, or only when needed. You can scroll automatically when typing or expand the control to show all the text. (Note that the scrollbar options apply only to the Rich Text Box control. The Text Box control will always expand to show all the text.)

There is another interesting property available in the *Display* tab for the Text Box properties that allows you to limit the number of characters that can be entered into the control. When you select the *Limit text box to* checkbox, you can enter the maximum number of characters you want to allow your users to enter into the Text Box control. (If you previously selected the *Multi-line* checkbox, this property is not available.) In this example, since the maximum number of guests allowed is three, users should enter only one character into this Text Box control. Therefore, we'll set this property to *1.* In addition, when you select the *Limit text box to* checkbox, the checkbox *Move to next control automatically when limit is reached* also becomes enabled. This property will force the cursor to move to the next control once the limit is reached. This option is especially useful for forms filled out by data entry personnel who must enter data very quickly. Advancing to the next field when the limit in the previous field is reached will make the task of filling out many forms go much quicker.

The *Alignment* drop-down list box allows you to specify the text alignment within the Text Box. If you have installed support for right-to-left languages in the *Regional and Language Options* dialog in the *Control Panel* and you have added a right-to-left language, the *Direction* drop-down list box allows you to choose the direction of the control. This property will set the direction to either left-to-right or right-to-left for this specific control. If you choose *Default*, the direction of the control matches the direction of the control's parent if the control is inside a container control (such as a Section) or the form template if it is not. Changing the direction in the properties dialog for a control allows you to specify that parts of your form flow from left to right while others flow from right to left, for example. This may be useful if you are creating a form template where parts of the form will be filled out using a right-to-left language.

Of course, there is one other item in the *Display* tab for the Text Box properties—the *Conditional Formatting* button. As we mentioned earlier, we will talk about this in Chapter 5. For now, let's look at some of the display properties available for a few other controls.

Figure 4.31 shows the *Display* tab for the Rich Text Box control. This tab looks very similar to the one for the Text Box control, but there are a few noticeable differences. A few checkboxes stand out. The first is the *Character formatting* checkbox. This option specifies whether or not users of your form

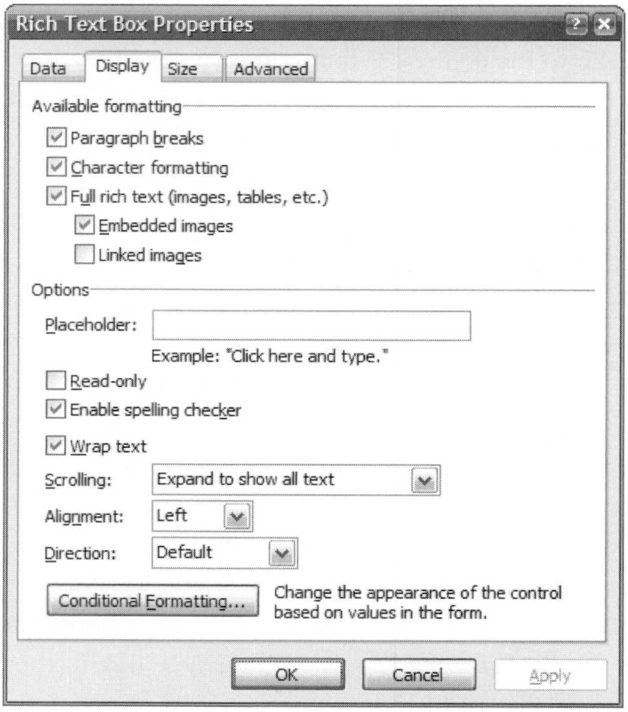

FIGURE 4.31: Display tab for the Rich Text Box control

can format text (e.g., bold, italic, underline) in the Rich Text Box control. By default, this option is turned on. Unchecking this option also unchecks the *Full rich text* option since full rich text editing depends on character formatting. As you probably guessed by the text in the dialog, the *Full rich text* checkbox allows you to control whether or not the user can insert images, tables, hyperlinks, and other rich text features into the Rich Text Box control.

Below the *Full rich text* option are two dependent checkboxes—*Embedded images* and *Linked images*—which allow you to control whether or not the user can insert embedded or linked images, respectively. These options are disabled if the *Full rich text* option is not checked. By default, only the *Embedded images* option is selected. When a user fills out a form, inserting an embedded image into a Rich Text Box control includes the picture data in the form XML. That means that when the user saves the form, the picture is base64 encoded and then saved as text in the XML. Inserting a linked image includes a link to the image (in the form of a URL) in the XML.

If you select only one of these checkboxes—*Embedded images* or *Linked images*—users will insert the image as they normally would. InfoPath will look at these options to determine how to save the data. However, if you choose both options, users must specify how they want InfoPath to insert the image. Figure 4.32 shows the *Insert Picture* dialog, which was opened

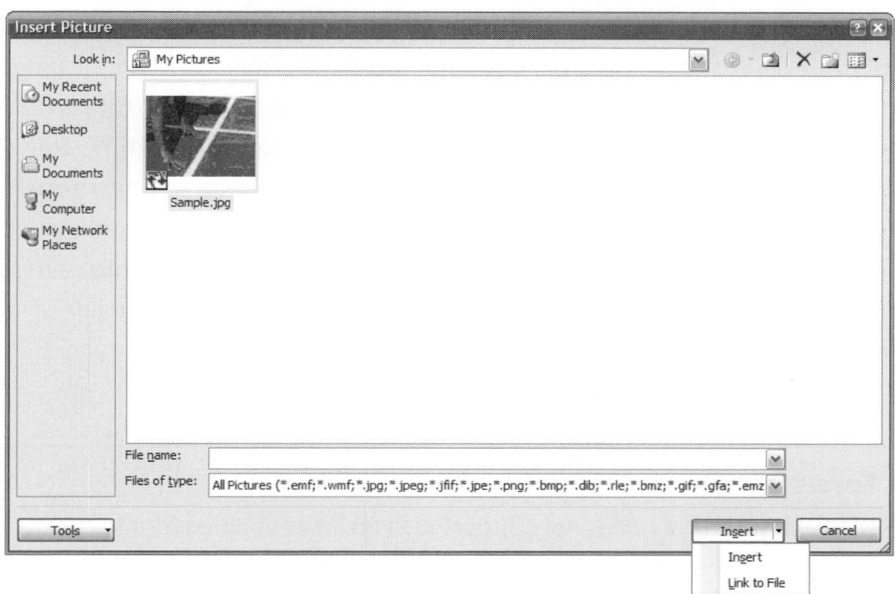

FIGURE 4.32: Insert Picture dialog

by first clicking on the *Insert* menu, then *Picture*, and finally *From File* while the cursor is inside a Rich Text Box with both the *Embedded images* and *Linked images* options turned on. You'll notice in Figure 4.32 that the *Insert* button has a drop-down menu with additional options. One of these is *Link to File*. Choosing this menu item inserts the image as a link. (Note that if users insert a clip art image from the *Picture* menu, the picture is always inserted as an embedded image.)

Forms Services

When you're designing a browser-enabled form, the *Display* tab for the Rich Text Box control has an additional checkbox labeled *Enable browser-compatible settings* only. When this box is checked, every checkbox in the *Available formatting* region is checked and disabled except for *Embedded images*. Embedding of image data is never allowed when filling out a form in the browser.

Other controls offer various options in their *Display* tabs. For example, as we mentioned earlier, it's possible to change the Expression Box control to a Vertical Label and vice versa. To do so, simply open the properties dialog for either one of these controls and click on the *Display* tab. Then, to make the control flow vertically (or not), simply select the *Display text vertically* checkbox. Also, you can add or remove scrollbars for the Scrolling Region and Horizontal Region controls by changing the scrollbar settings from the *Display* tab on the properties dialogs for these controls. We encourage you to explore the *Display* tabs on the properties dialogs of all the controls to see what they have to offer. For now, though, let's turn to another tab of the properties dialog—the *Size* tab.

Forms Services

Displaying vertical text is not supported in browser-enabled forms.

Size Tab

The purpose of the *Size* tab should be fairly obvious from its name. From this tab you can set the size of a control. This tab exists on the properties dialog for every control except three—the File Attachment, Hyperlink, and Recursive Section (which is part of the Repeating Recursive Section control). This tab contains all the properties that have something to do with setting the size of a control.

Take a look at Figure 4.33, which shows the *Size* tab of the Text Box control's properties dialog. The Text Box control is one case where all the size properties are enabled on the *Size* tab. (Not all controls support all size properties. For those controls that don't support certain properties, those features are either disabled on the *Size* tab or not present at all.) On the *Size* tab, you can change the height and width of the control. Obviously you can also change the height and width by resizing the control with the

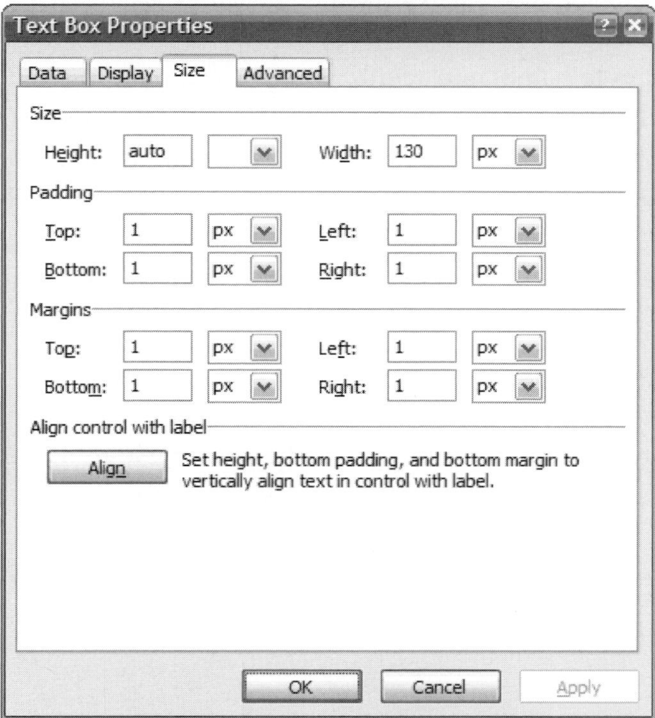

FIGURE 4.33: Size tab of the Text Box Properties dialog

mouse. However, using the *Size* tab allows you to set the height and width to precise measurements. Also, you can change the units in which the height and width are stored. By default the size values are in pixels, but you can change the units to inches or centimeters, for example.

As well as specifying precise measurements, you can choose to set the height and width to a percentage. In this case, the actual size of the control is based on the size of the container control that the control is in or the view surface if the control is not inside a container control. For example, let's say that you have a Text Box control inside a Section and the Section is 500 pixels wide. If you specify that the width of the Text Box is 50%, the actual size of the Text Box will be 250 pixels initially. If you then change the size of the Section control, the Text Box will grow to match. In this case, the width of the Text Box will always be 50% of the width of the Section. In addition to percentage height and width, you can also specify *auto,* as you can see in Figure 4.33. When you set the height or width to *auto,* the size of the control is based on the size of its content. For a Text Box, this means that the size will be based on the text within it.

In addition to height and width, you can add **padding** and **margins** to the control. Padding adds space inside the control, while margins add space outside the control. You can set the values of the padding and margins properties using the same types of values as height and width (including percentages). However, you can't set these values to *auto.* If you try to, the value will be reset to the previous value when you close the dialog.

Setting Text Alignment

At the bottom of the *Size* tab for the Text Box control, you will notice the *Align* button. Pressing this button sets the padding and margins to values that will make the text within the Text Box line up with the text outside the Text Box. (More specifically, this button aligns the baseline of the text inside a control to the baseline of the text outside the control.) For example, Figure 4.34 shows a Text Box control from the user's perspective when

Text outside the Text Box
Text inside the Text Box

FIGURE 4.34: Text Box control with inner text not aligned to outer text

filling out a form. In this case, the Text Box has a border that is $2\frac{1}{4}$ points wide. Notice that the text inside the Text Box is higher than the text outside of it.

Now, let's click the *Align* button. Doing so in this case sets the bottom padding to 0 pixels and the bottom margins to –4.5 points. Figure 4.35 shows the same Text Box control after applying this change. Now the text inside the control lines up with the text outside of it.

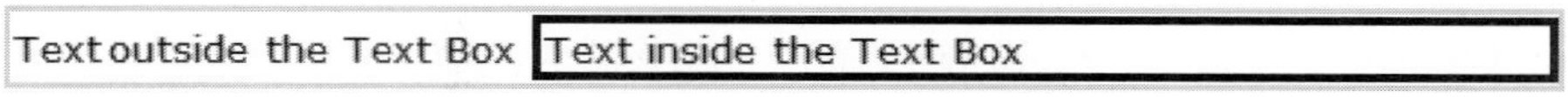

Text outside the Text Box | Text inside the Text Box

FIGURE 4.35: Text Box control with inner text aligned to outer text

We should note a couple of things about this feature. First, and most important, is that in order to determine the values for bottom padding and bottom margin that are needed to align the text, InfoPath takes a few things into account, including the font size set on the control as well as the size of the border. Since the font size set on the control is important, the font size of the text outside of the control must be the same. If the font sizes are different, the text inside and outside of the control will not line up correctly. The second important thing to note about this feature is that it's not available for all controls. It is available on only a few controls that can contain text—Text Box, Rich Text Box, Date Picker, and Expression Box. (This feature is not available for the Combo Box control even though you can type text into that control.)

Resizing Multiple Controls

As we mentioned, there are two way to resize controls. The first and easiest way to resize a control is to use the mouse. After selecting a control, just click on one of the square grab handles and drag the control to the correct size. But did you know that you can easily resize multiple controls at once using this method? To do so, select all the controls you want to resize by holding down the Ctrl key and clicking on each control. Then, just resize one of the controls as you normally would. All the selected controls will be resized by the same amount. However, not all controls can be resized. The File Attachment control is one such control. Therefore, if you select a Text

Box, a Rich Text Box, and a File Attachment, you won't be able to resize any of them. In that case, just unselect the File Attachment control by holding down the Ctrl key and clicking on the File Attachment. Then you will be able to resize the other controls.

Resizing multiple controls this way is certainly useful. However, what if you want to set the size of all the selected controls to 50%? Or what if you want to set the margins or padding on multiple controls (or use the alignment feature) at the same time? That's just as easy. After you have selected all the controls whose size properties you want to change, just open the properties dialog as you normally would. When you do this, a properties dialog with only the *Size* tab opens (Figure 4.36). In this case, a Text Box and a Drop Down List Box were selected together. Since the Drop Down List Box control doesn't support all the size properties, those that aren't supported are disabled. This *Properties (Multiple Selection)* dialog allows you to

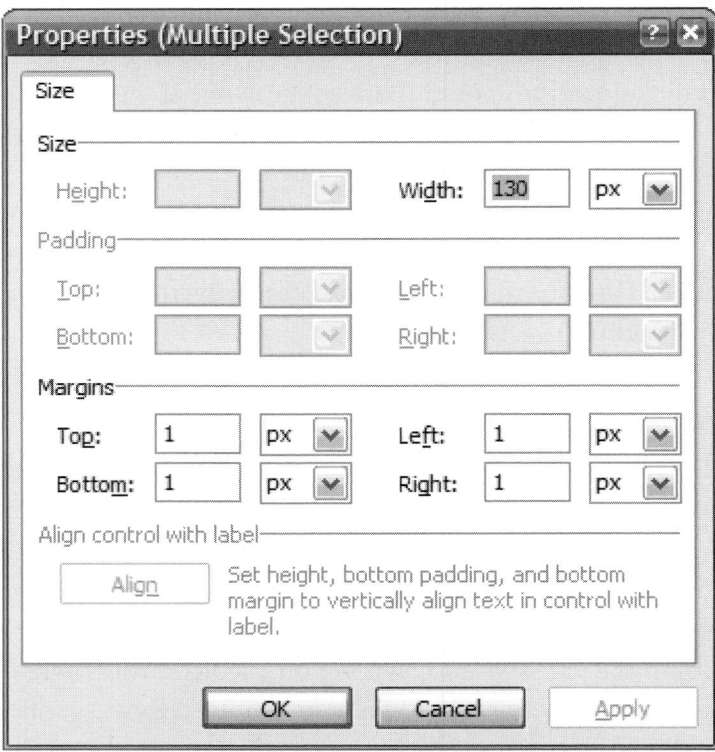

FIGURE 4.36: Properties dialog for resizing multiple controls

change only those properties supported by all the selected controls. This means that, if one of the controls you selected doesn't support resizing at all (such as a File Attachment control), all the properties in this dialog will be disabled.

Advanced Tab

The final tab that is common to almost every control is the *Advanced* tab. (The only control whose properties dialog doesn't have an Advanced tab is the Recursive Section control, which is part of the Repeating Recursive Section control we talked about earlier.)

The *Advanced* tab contains only a few options in most cases. Let's look at one of the simplest cases—the Hyperlink control. Figure 4.37 shows the *Advanced* tab for the properties dialog of the Hyperlink control. In this case, there are only three properties you can change—*ScreenTip*, *Tab index*, and *Access key*.

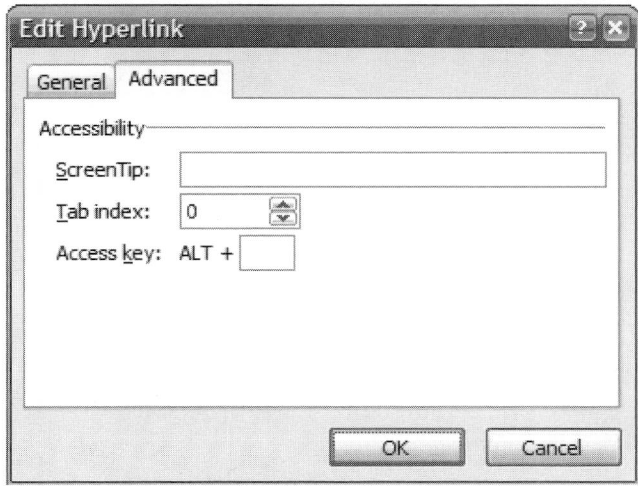

FIGURE 4.37: Advanced tab for the Hyperlink control

In the *ScreenTip* text box, you can specify the text that should be shown when the user of your form hovers the mouse cursor over the control. This allows you to include helpful text to tell the user what to do. Incidentally, this property is used by accessibility tools such as screen readers to give more information to users who have visual impairments.

The *Tab index* property allows you to specify how the focus moves from one control to another when the user presses the Tab key while filling out the form. If you set all controls to the same tab index (such as *0*, which is the default), the focus moves from control to control in the order in which the controls are laid out in the form. This property allows you to change that default behavior so that focus moves in an order other than the way the controls are laid out. Typically, getting the tab index correct can be difficult, so we suggest that you keep the default value of *0* for all your controls.

Finally, the *Access key* text box allows you to set a keystroke that, when the user combines it with the Alt key while filling out a form, causes the focus to move directly to that control. This is especially useful if you expect users to have to make frequent changes to the same control or if you want to make your controls accessible to users who have disabilities.

Those controls that accept handwriting or speech input, such as the Text Box and Rich Text Box, also include an *Input Scope* button in the *Advanced* tab, as shown in Figure 4.38. (Table 4.1 lists all the controls that support

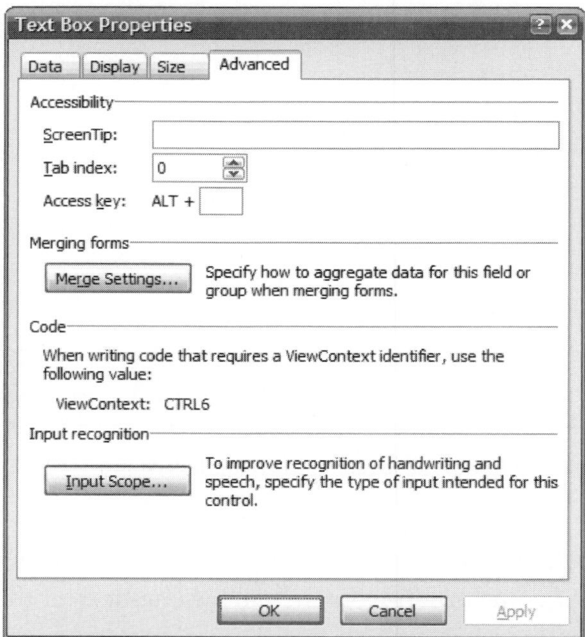

FIGURE 4.38: Advanced tab of the Text Box Properties dialog showing the Input recognition section

Table 4.1: Controls That Support Input Scope

Text Box
Rich Text Box
Date Picker
Combo Box
Bulleted List
Numbered List
Plain List
Multiple-Selection List Box

specifying the **input scope.**) The *Input Scope* button is useful if you are designing forms to be filled out on Tablet PC devices. This feature helps improve the recognition of handwriting or speech input. It does this by allowing you to specify what type of content you expect in this control. Recognition of nonkeyboard input can never be 100% accurate. However, using the *Input Scope* button to specify what type of input you expect can help handwriting and speech recognizers do a better job of recognizing user input into these fields.

To specify an input scope, just click the *Input Scope* button. When you do, the dialog shown in Figure 4.39 appears. From there, you can choose one of the standard input scopes from the list. The default option in this list is *None (use field type).* If you leave the default, the recognizer will use the data type of the node to which the control is bound in order to recognize the user input.

You can choose one of the other standard types to help improve input recognition. For example, one of the standard input scopes (which you can't see in Figure 4.39) is *IS_NUMBER*. This input scope tells the recognizer that you expect the input to be a number. So, if the user writes a "5" that looks like an "S," the recognizer will be able to convert the written text correctly

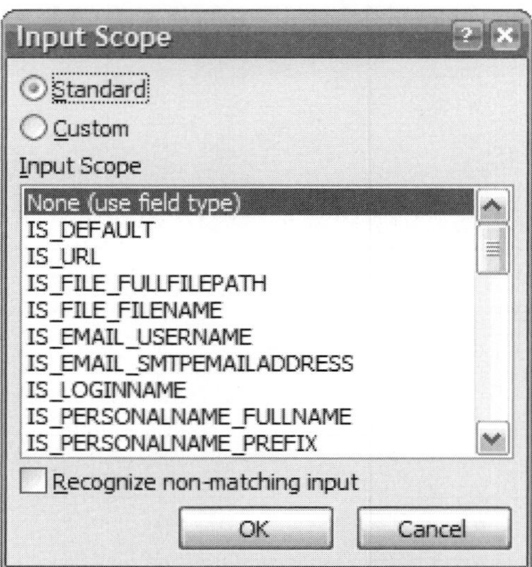

FIGURE 4.39: Input Scope dialog showing standard input scopes

to the number 5. For more information about the standard input types, take a look at the `InputScope` enumeration in MSDN, which is referenced in the Appendix.

The *Input Scope* dialog also has a checkbox, *Recognize non-matching input.* This option specifies whether or not the input scope you chose should restrict the recognizer to match the specified pattern or simply bias the recognizer toward the pattern. By default, this option is unselected, which restricts the recognizer to the pattern you specify.

If none of the standard input scopes work for your scenario, you can define your own. When you select the *Custom* option button, the dialog changes, as shown in Figure 4.40. This dialog shows a list of all the input scopes you have defined.

To add your own custom input scope, just click the *New* button, which will open the *New Input Scope* dialog shown in Figure 4.41. Here you can define your input scope by specifying a *Phrase List* or a *Regular Expression.* The *Phrase List* option is simply that—a list of phrases that will be used to

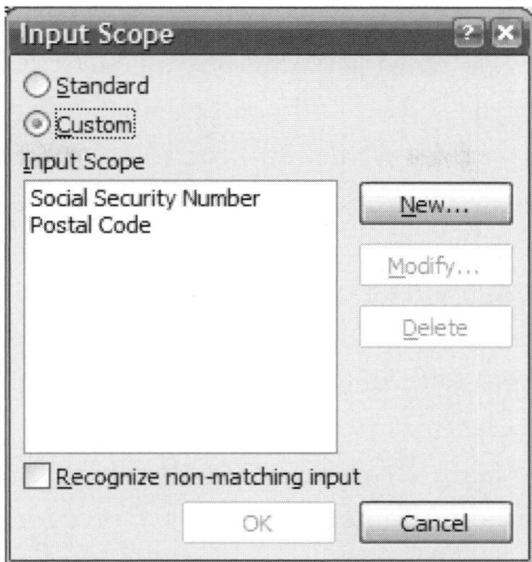

FIGURE 4.40: Input Scope dialog showing custom input scopes

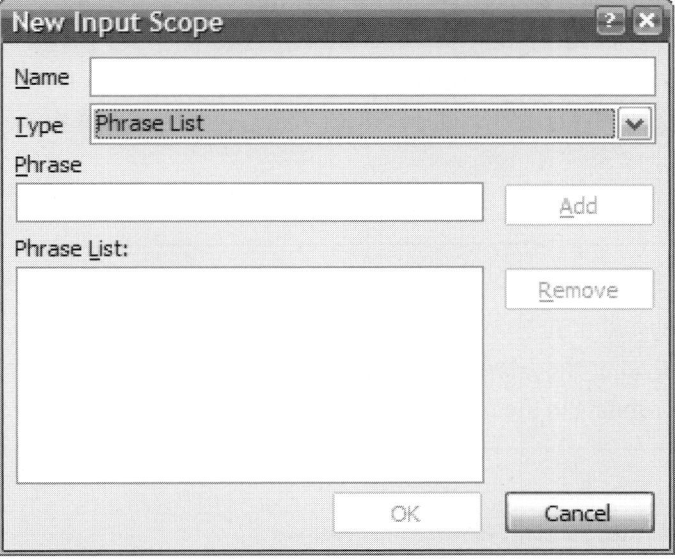

FIGURE 4.41: New Input Scope dialog showing Phrase List option

restrict or bias the input recognizer. These phrases can include a single word or more than one word separated by a space. (Note that before you can enter a list of phrases, you will need to enter a name for your custom input scope.) When a user writes into the form (or uses speech recognition), the recognizer will use the phrase list to help it recognize the input.

If you choose the *Regular Expression* option, you can enter your own regular expression that will be used to restrict or bias the input recognizer. (You can find the regular expression syntax for the input scope under the "Custom Input Scopes with Regular Expression" topic in MSDN, which is referenced in the Appendix.)

The Input Scope feature can be very valuable if you design form templates that will be used on Tablet PC devices. However, a complete discussion of this feature is outside the scope of this book (pun intended). For more information about Tablet PC recognition and the Input Scope feature in general, see the "Programming the Tablet PC" section in MSDN, which is referenced in the Appendix.

Input Scope is a fairly advanced feature, which is exactly why it exists on the *Advanced* tab. The *Advanced* tabs for some other properties dialogs do contain a few other items besides what we've talked about so far, such as the *Merging forms* and *Code* sections. We will talk about these properties in Chapters 12 and 15, respectively.

Forms Services

When designing a browser-enabled form, most controls have a *Browser forms* tab adjacent to the *Advanced* tab. This tab configures settings specific to forms running in the browser. We'll explore the details in Chapter 17.

Creating Master/Detail Relationships

Forms Services

Master/detail relationships are not supported in browser-enabled forms.

All the tabs in the properties dialogs we've discussed so far are common to most controls. There is one additional tab available in the properties dialogs for the Repeating Section and Repeating Table controls—the *Master/Detail* tab. In Chapter 2, we introduced the Master/Detail control. This control actually inserts two controls into your form—a Repeating Table and a Repeating Section. The Repeating Table control is designated as the master control, and the Repeating Section is the detail control. Using the Master/Detail, you can streamline the way you present data to your users. The master control shows a subset of the data, while the detail control shows an expanded set of data—the details. Each of these controls is bound to the same group node in the underlying data source when you insert the Master/Detail into the form. This is great, but what if you want to establish a master/detail relationship for a Repeating Table and Repeating Section that are not bound to the same group node? Or what if you want to establish a master/detail relationship for a Repeating Table and Repeating Section that already exist in your form template? Well, you can do that by using the *Master/Detail* tab.

Let's look at an example. Say that you have a list of salespeople in your organization. Each salesperson has one or more items that he or she is responsible for selling to your customers. You want to design a form that will allow you to enter and view sales figures for each of the salespeople in your organization. These requirements just scream for a Master/Detail control. In this case, using your previous experience designing relational databases, you decide to store the personal data for each salesperson (e.g., salesperson ID and name) under one group node in the underlying data source and the sales figures under another. Each of these group nodes contains a salesperson ID that you can use to link the salesperson data to the sales data for that salesperson. (Figure 4.42 shows the data source for this example.) Based on this design, it's not possible to use the default Master/Detail control that exists in the *Controls* task pane. Instead, you must create your own master/detail relationship.

First, you must open the *Data Source* task pane and insert a Repeating Table that is bound to your `SalesPeople` group node. (As explained in Chapter 3, you can do this by dragging the `SalesPeople` group node into the design surface and then choosing *Repeating Table* from the menu.) Then, do the same for the `Sales` group node, but this time choose *Repeating Section with Controls* instead.

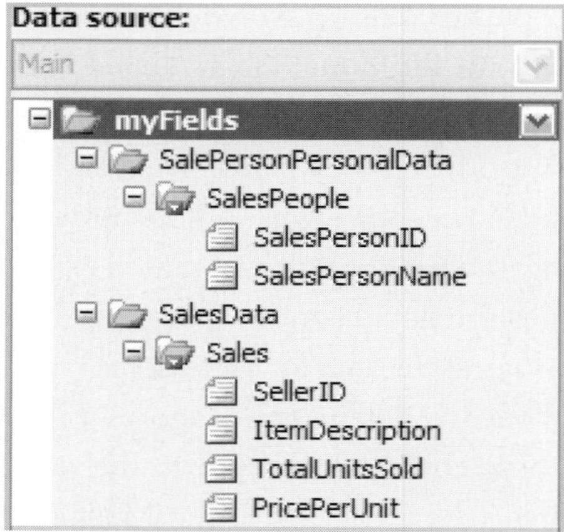

FIGURE 4.42: Sample data source for the Master/Detail example

Once you've inserted these two controls, open the properties dialog for the Repeating Table and click on the *Master/Detail* tab. Since this control contains the personal data for each salesperson, we are going to designate it as the master control. Doing so is very easy—just click the *Set as master* option button. Then, specify an ID to use to identify this master control. Later, this ID will be used to link a detail control to the master. In this example, let's just specify the ID for the master control as `SalesPersonData`. (Figure 4.43 shows the *Master/Detail* tab after designating the Repeating Table as the master.)

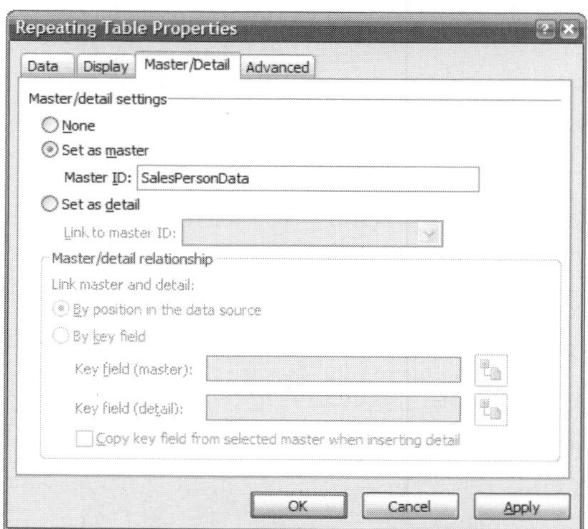

FIGURE 4.43: Master/Detail tab for a Repeating Table set as the master control

Design-Time Visuals for Master/Detail Controls

When you initially create a master/detail relationship using the *Master/Detail* tab instead of inserting the control from the *Controls* task pane, the master control will show a warning design-time visual before you specify the detail control. Don't be alarmed. This expected warning is intended to alert you in cases where you have deleted a detail control connected to a master. This is just a warning, so the control will still work correctly even if you never specify the detail control.

However, after you have established the master/detail relationship, if you delete the master control, the detail control will show an error design-time visual. This case is an error instead of a warning due to the fact that having a detail without a master is not usually what you intend. (As with other design-time visuals, you can choose *More Details* from the context menu for a control that shows a warning or an error to see more information about the problem, including suggested remedies.)

Once you've set the Repeating Table as the master control, you'll want to set the Repeating Section you inserted as the detail control. As with the master, you set the Repeating Section as the detail control by using the *Master/Detail* tab. Figure 4.44 shows the *Master/Detail* tab for the Repeating Section. (One thing to note in Figure 4.44 is that you can't use a Repeating Section as a master control. However, it is possible to use either a Repeating Section or a Repeating Table as the detail control.) In order to set this control as the detail, you must first select the *Set as detail* option. Then, from the *Link to master ID* drop-down list box, choose the ID of the master control to which you want to link this detail control. In this case, we've chosen `SalesPersonData`. Next, in the *Master/detail relationship* section of this tab, specify how the detail control is linked to the master. By default, when you insert a Master/Detail control from the *Controls* task pane, since both controls are bound to the same group node in the data source, the detail control is linked to the master by position in the data source. This basically means that, when a user fills out a form that contains a Master/Detail

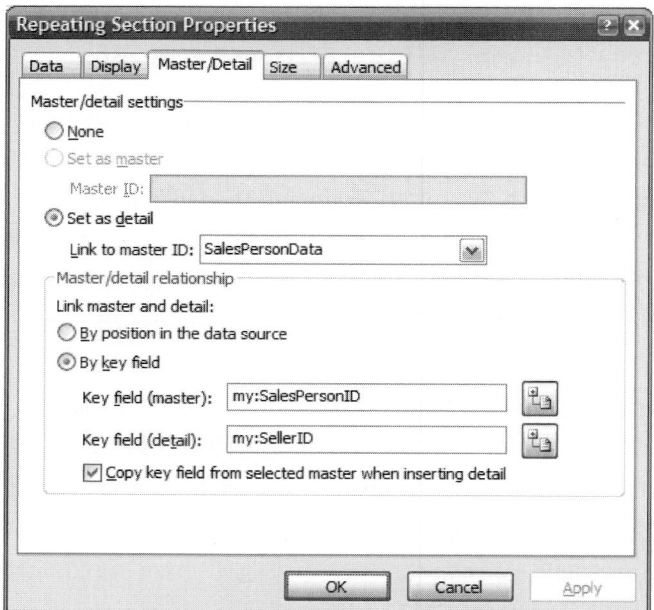

FIGURE 4.44: Master/Detail tab for a Repeating Section set as a detail control

control, the first master control in the form is linked to the first detail control, the second master to the second detail, and so on.

For our example, since the Repeating Table is bound to the `SalesPeople` group node and the Repeating Section is bound to the `Sales` group node, we want to select the *By key field* option. This option allows us to link the detail control to the master by using two fields from the data source. In database terminology, these are the keys we'll use to join the two groups. In this case, we have linked the detail to the master by using the ID of the salesperson. (The data source does not permit us to have two fields with the same name. Therefore, we have named one `SalesPersonID` and the other `SellerID`. Even though they are named differently, these two fields will contain the same data—the ID of the salesperson.) Linking the detail to the master by the salesperson ID means that, when a user filling out the form selects a salesperson from the master control, the sales data for the salesperson with the corresponding ID will be shown in the detail control.

When you link a detail control to a master control by using a key field, the *Copy key field from selected master when inserting detail* checkbox at the bottom of the Master/Detail tab becomes enabled and is selected by default. This option is particularly useful when inserting new records in the detail control. When this option is selected and the user inserts a new detail item when filling out the form, the data from the key field in the master control is copied to the corresponding key field in the detail. If you uncheck this option, it is possible to easily get into a situation where the user can't insert a new detail item when filling out the form.

For example, say that you have a row in the master that has a salesperson ID of 123, and that salesperson has no sales. If you have unchecked the *Copy key field* option, the user won't be able to insert any sales details for this salesperson. This is because the detail control is linked to the master control by a key field. When the user tries to insert a new detail item, the key field for that detail is initially empty. Since the key field is empty, it doesn't match the currently selected item in the master, so the new detail item is not shown. However, if you have selected the *Copy key field* option, when the user inserts the new detail item, the data from the key field of the currently selected master item is copied to the corresponding key field of the detail. Now the key fields match, and the new detail item is shown. Due to the difficulty in dealing with these issues, we recommend that you leave the *Copy key field* option selected when linking a detail control to a master control using a key field.

Now that we've established the master/detail relationship, let's take a quick look at this sample by previewing the form. (The form template for this sample is called MasterDetail.) Figure 4.45 shows our Master/Detail control in action. Here we have two salespeople listed in the master control. Since we've selected the second salesperson in the master control, all the sales data for the salesperson whose ID is 321 is shown as details.

If you download this sample and look at it in the InfoPath design mode, you'll notice that we pulled together a couple of concepts that we've talked about so far. We are using a Scrolling Region for the detail control in order to make the data easier to maintain. We are using an Expression Box to calculate the total sales from the units sold and price per unit figures. Also, we've changed the data types for many of the controls and added data formatting (e.g., currency) based on the type of data being displayed.

As we've mentioned earlier and as you can see from this example, you can make large forms really easy to use by combining the Master/Detail and Scrolling Region controls.

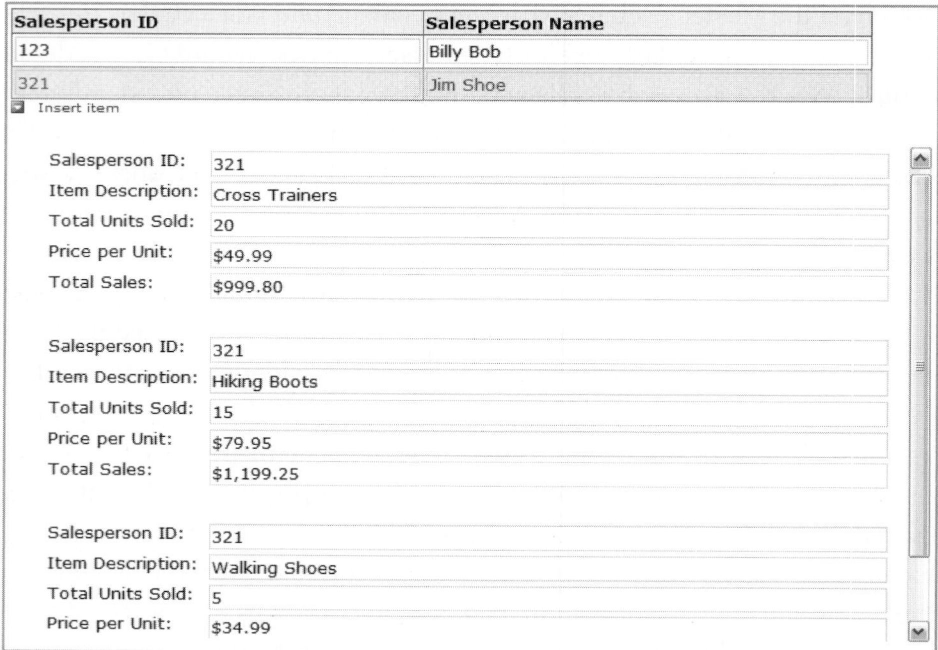

FIGURE 4.45: Master/Detail control when filling out a form

Advanced Customizations

In addition to the many customizations you can make to a control that we've discussed so far, there are a number of advanced customizations you can do. You can change the default values for a control or customize the menu commands shown for certain controls. Let's take a quick look at these more advanced customizations.

Editing Default Values

In Chapter 3, we talked about how to edit the default template data by using the *Edit Default Values* dialog. Another way to edit the default template data is available from the properties dialog for certain container controls. But wait—how do control properties affect the options available for the data source? This is a great question that can be answered only by understanding the integration between the view and the data source. Recall that when designing a form template, InfoPath creates data source nodes that are optional in the XML Schema (`minOccurs` is `"0"`; `maxOccurs` is `"1"`). Just because a node is optional doesn't mean it can be removed or inserted when filling out the form. To allow this behavior, the optional node must be bound to a control that can be inserted and deleted, such as Optional Section, Repeating Table, Repeating Section, (Repeating) Recursive Section, Horizontal Repeating Table, and Choice Section. Enabling this otherwise dormant behavior adds the ability to set default data, among other custom options, that is specific to the control but applies to the data.

Let's look at an Optional Section's properties dialog, for example, to see these features in action. We'll first look at the *Edit Default Values* button in the *Section Properties* dialog (Figure 4.46). This button is essentially similar to the *Default Values* item on the *Tools* menu. However, when you open the *Edit Default Values* dialog by clicking the button in the properties dialog, the data source is scoped to the node to which this Optional Section is

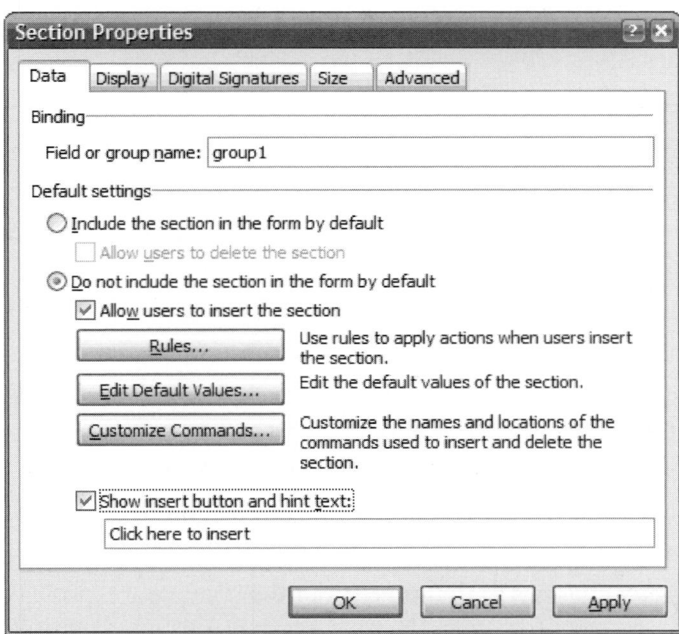

FIGURE 4.46: Section Properties dialog for an Optional Section control

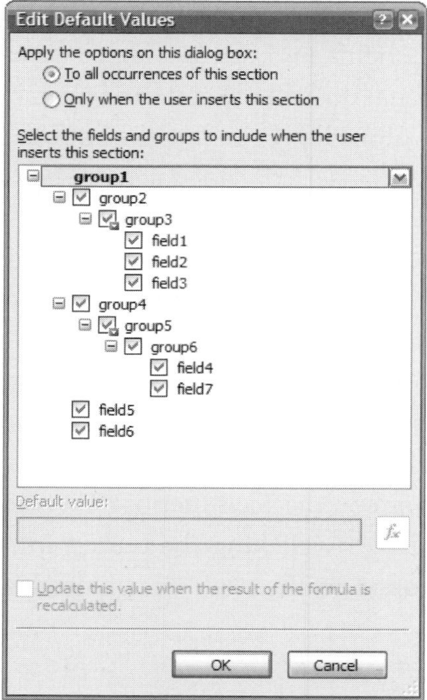

FIGURE 4.47: Edit Default Values dialog for an Optional Section control

bound, as shown in Figure 4.47. In this case, the Optional Section is bound to the `group1` node.

Any changes you make to the scoped data source in Figure 4.47 will mirror to the main data source. There really is no difference, but that's only because the first of two option buttons is selected. The first option button is labeled *To all occurrences of this section.* In English, this means that any default data you enter in this data source tree will exist as default data for the form as well as default data when this control is inserted. That's right: There are two types of default data. The default data inserted when a user inserts a control while filling out the form uses a predetermined **XML fragment.** When you select the first option button, the data in the fragment associated with this control is mirrored to the form default data and vice versa. That is, with the first option, any changes in default data under the `group1` node will be used when a form is created and when a row is inserted. This coupled nature of the form and fragment data (i.e., the form and fragment data staying in sync) seems to be the default behavior that most users generally expect.

> **NOTE XML Fragments**
>
> An XML fragment refers to a subtree of a complete XML data source. The fragment itself is still valid XML data, but it may not semantically make sense when it stands alone.

The second option button, *Only when the user inserts this section,* may make sense despite the confusing terminology used on the first option button. When you select this option button, the setting applies to the data source fragment that is used only when this control is inserted. This setting does not affect the form data used to create new blank forms. Since the form data is now decoupled (or disassociated) from the fragment data, the default values used when creating a new blank form are different than when you insert the control.

Setting fragment default data for other insertable and deletable container controls is similar. However, another dimension is added specifically when working with XML fragments for Repeating Section controls. There is no obvious entry point to the *Edit Default Values* dialog from the *Repeating Section Properties* dialog, as shown in Figure 4.48. Instead, this dialog allows

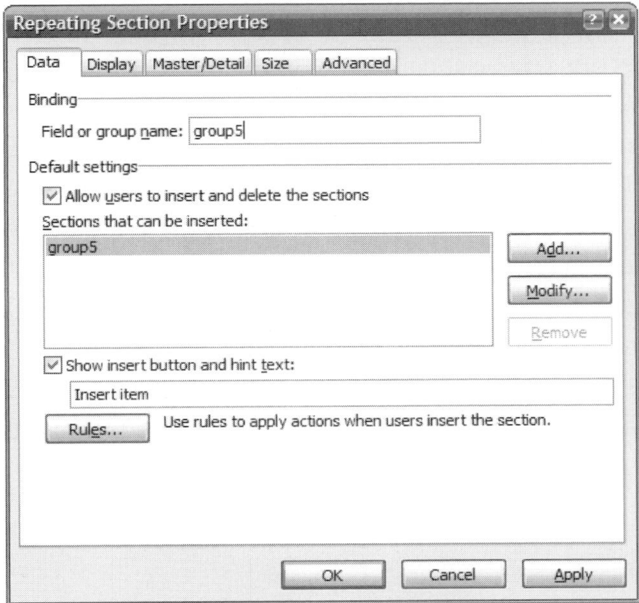

FIGURE 4.48: Repeating Section Properties dialog

you to define multiple fragments, each distinguished by a name. By default there is a single (form-coupled) fragment.

Clicking either the *Add* button or the *Modify* button opens the dialog shown in Figure 4.49, which has the familiar entry points we have seen on the Optional Section's properties dialog.

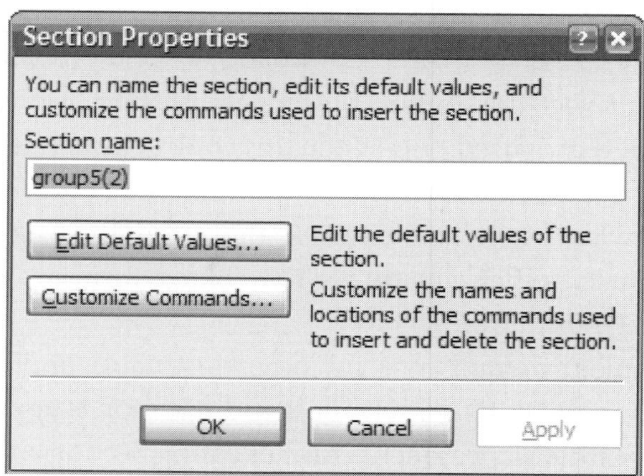

FIGURE 4.49: Section Properties dialog for a Repeating Section fragment

Repeating Section controls support this list of fragments (more generically, a list of sections, to be consistent with the title of the dialog) because it enables a form designer to further customize the form for quicker filling out. Let's create a grocery list form that can take advantage of this feature. We'll modify the first Section name to be `Apples`. When modifying the `Apples` fragment, we want to decouple it from the template by selecting *Only when the user inserts this section* because we don't want `Apples` to exist by default in new forms. Then we create two Sections (for a total of three) in the *Repeating Section Properties* dialog; each Section name is the data we want to use for that fragment. Figure 4.50 shows the properties dialog after adding the three sections. The effect of creating these fragments is shown in Figure 4.51. (This sample is named GroceryShoppingList.)

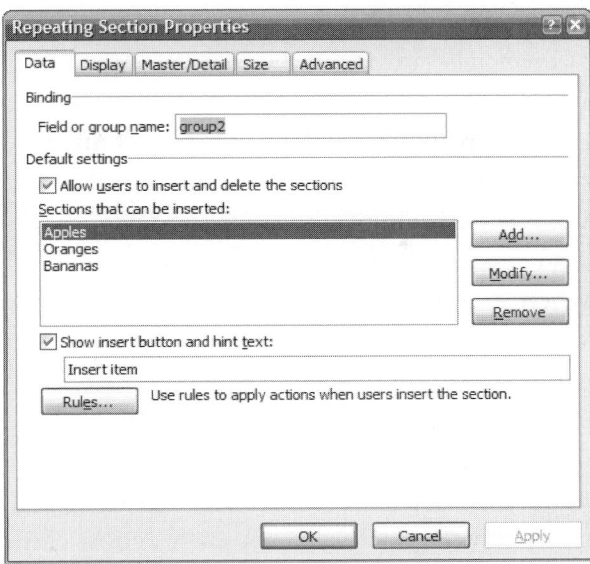

FIGURE 4.50: Repeating Section Properties dialog showing three sections—`Apples`, `Oranges`, and `Bananas`

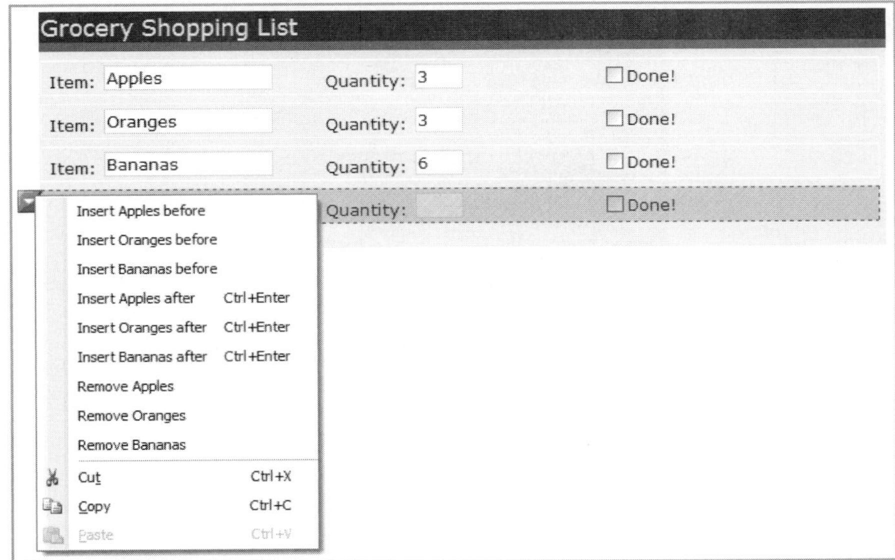

FIGURE 4.51: Filling out the grocery shopping list

Customizing Commands

The *Customize Commands* buttons in the dialogs shown in Figure 4.46 and Figure 4.49, when clicked, open the *Section Commands* dialog shown in Figure 4.52. In this dialog you can change the text of menu commands for a container control. This is also where you can control where and how the fragment data is inserted when filling out the form. By default, all commands use text such as *Insert group2 above,* where *group2* is the name of the bound node when a control has a single fragment or the name of the Section in the case of multiple fragments for a Repeating Section. So there's no need to customize fragment commands unless you want to change the default command text or alter its locations. The commands shown in Figure 4.51 when filling out the grocery shopping form use the default command text and locations. Of the various actions you can carry out on a Repeating Section control, for example, each action can have multiple entry points, such as an InfoPath menu or the *Insert Section* context menu, as shown when filling out the form in Figure 4.51. The location of each command is determined by the *Section Properties* dialog when designing the form.

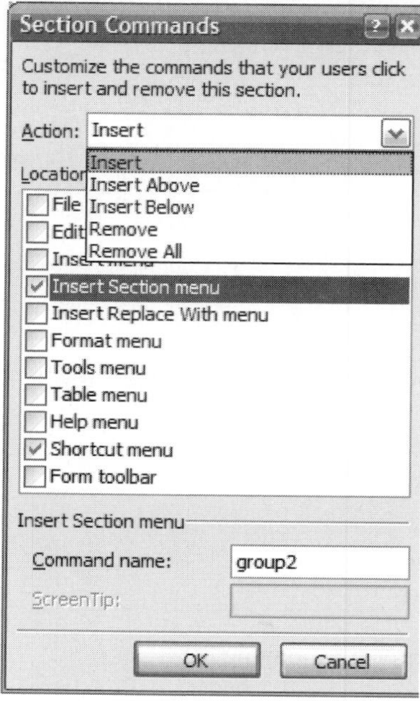

FIGURE 4.52: Section Commands dialog used to customize commands

Exposing a command for inserting or removing a fragment (such as *Insert above*) does not mean it can be used at any time. The command will be disabled unless the context is correct for it to be used. For example, say that a data source has two group nodes—`group1` and `group2`. In the view, a container control bound to `group2` is inside of a container control bound to `group1`. When a user fills out the form, commands to insert `group2` will be shown on the *Insert* menu but will be disabled if `group1` doesn't already exist. Exceptions to this rule are the *Shortcut, Insert Section,* and *Insert Replace With* menus, where the commands will not appear at all unless they are available. (The *Shortcut* menu is also known as the context menu.)

TIP Assigning a Shortcut Key to a Command

To assign a shortcut key, such as Alt+A, to your custom command, just add an ampersand (&) before any character in the *Command name* text box. Then you can use that character in conjunction with the Alt key (e.g., Insert &Bananas), which allows you to execute the command much faster. The best place to use this technique is on the *Form* toolbar, which is always visible. (The *Form* toolbar is a custom toolbar you can add to your form by checking this option in the *Section Commands* dialog.) Places where access keys do not work are on the *Shortcut, Insert Section,* and *Insert Replace With* menus. Be careful not to assign the same key as one of the top-level menu items or your shortcut key will not work.

The *Action* drop-down in Figure 4.52 reflects actions that apply specifically to the type of control you're working on. The actions listed in this figure are from a Repeating Section, a Recursive Repeating Section, and a Repeating Table. An Optional Section has only the *Insert* and *Remove* actions. A Choice Section, on the other hand, has *Insert, Remove,* and *Replace With.* Finally, a Choice Section inside a Repeating Choice Group offers the same actions as those shown in Figure 4.52 plus the *Replace With* action.

Of all the actions available, *Remove All* is never selected by default. This is because it isn't used very often, but it is very useful in some cases. For example, if your form receives a lot of data from a database, you might want to enable *Remove All* to allow users to quickly clear that data. A convenient place to show *Remove All* can be on the *Shortcut* menu, where it's safely hidden unless a user brings up the context menu on the control.

Actions like *Insert* and *Remove* are straightforward. Let's briefly discuss what some of the other actions mean. Two of the other actions are *Insert Above* and *Insert Below*. You might ask, "Insert above and below what?" Remember that when your custom commands for this control are shown to the user, a control must be selected; otherwise, the command won't show. That is, there is always a context for the action. Think of it as "Insert above the control instance the user has selected."

A Choice Section control's *Replace With* action is actually quite tricky in its function and is best explained with an example. Let's say we have Choice Section controls A, B, and C. You know that because this is a Choice Group control, only one Choice Section of the Choice Group can exist at any time. So either A or B or C can be in the form at a given moment. Let's assume that A is the default choice in the form. When we show the context menu for A, it will say *Replace with B* and *Replace with C* (Figure 4.53). What if B was in the form? Its context menu would show insert commands for A and C. As you can see, when you display the context menu for a Choice Section when filling out the form, the menu shows commands for all Choice Sections under the same Choice Group (except, of course, the Choice Section that is already inserted).

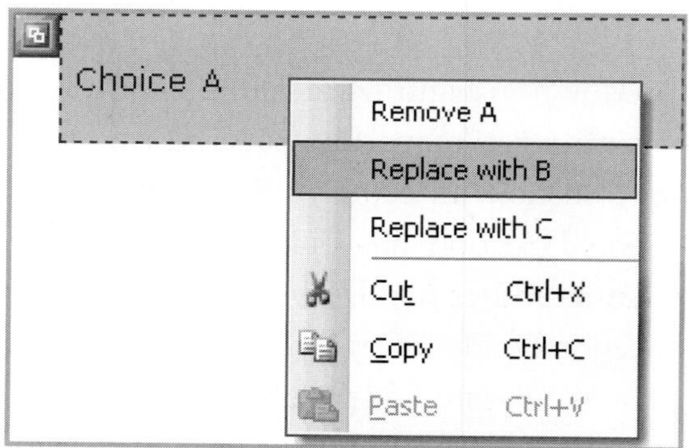

FIGURE 4.53: Default commands for a Choice Section when filling out a form

What's Next?

In this chapter, we've rounded out our discussion about controls. You learned about the advanced controls available in InfoPath in design mode that you can add to your form template in order to do some fairly complex operations. You've also learned how to customize your controls through control properties. Now you can design intricate form templates. In the next chapter, we'll expand our discussion of form design even further by showing you how to add logic to your form templates without having to ever write a line of code.

5 Adding Logic without Code

Getting Started

In the last chapter, you learned about the advanced controls available in the InfoPath design mode as well as some advanced customizations you can do. In this chapter, we'll dive into some of the more advanced design features you can use to add business logic to your form templates without writing any code at all. We'll not only talk about conditional formatting, which is a control-centric feature, but we'll also talk about data-centric features such as data validation and rules that happen to be exposed through the properties dialogs for controls. Those features act on the data in the underlying data source but also have an affect on controls. Let's start by talking about conditional formatting, which is a feature that is available for most controls.

Conditional Formatting

In Chapter 4, we talked about properties dialogs for controls and the different tabs that appear, including the *Display* tab. Conditional formatting is the one feature that appears in the *Display* tab for almost every control. In fact, the Hyperlink, Scrolling Region, and Horizontal Region controls are the only ones that don't support this feature. However, the properties dialog isn't the only way to access it. Once you select a control, you can access the *Conditional Formatting* dialog from the *Format* menu or the context menu for the control.

Conditional formatting allows you to format a control (e.g., bold, italic, underline) based on a set of conditions. However, this feature allows you to do more than just format the control. You can also hide the control, disable it, or make it read-only. (The available options depend on the type of control.) You can also use this feature to do such things as hide a certain row in a Repeating Table or color it green, for example, based on a set of conditions. In some cases, such as with Repeating Tables, Repeating Sections, and Optional Sections, you can even prevent users from inserting or deleting instances of the control based on conditions you specify. (In some cases, such as for a Rich Text Box control that doesn't support all types of formatting, certain options will be disabled.)

Let's set conditional formatting on a Text Box as an example. To specify conditional formatting for a Text Box, the first step you must take is to open the *Conditional Formatting* dialog from the *Format* menu. (Of course, as we mentioned, you can also open this dialog by clicking the *Conditional Formatting* button in the *Display* tab of the properties dialog or from the context menu.) When you click on the *Conditional Formatting* menu item on the *Format* menu, the dialog shown in Figure 5.1 opens. At first, this dialog doesn't look very interesting. Later, after we add a few conditions, this dialog will display all the conditions and their corresponding actions.

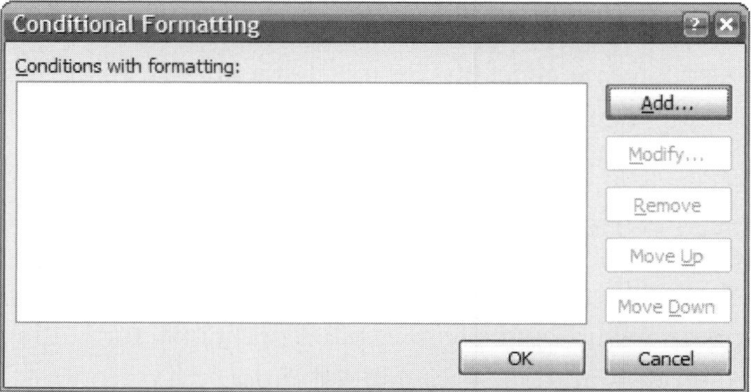

FIGURE 5.1: Conditional Formatting dialog

To add conditions to the *Conditional Formatting* dialog, just click on the *Add* button, which opens the *Conditional Format* dialog (Figure 5.2). Use this

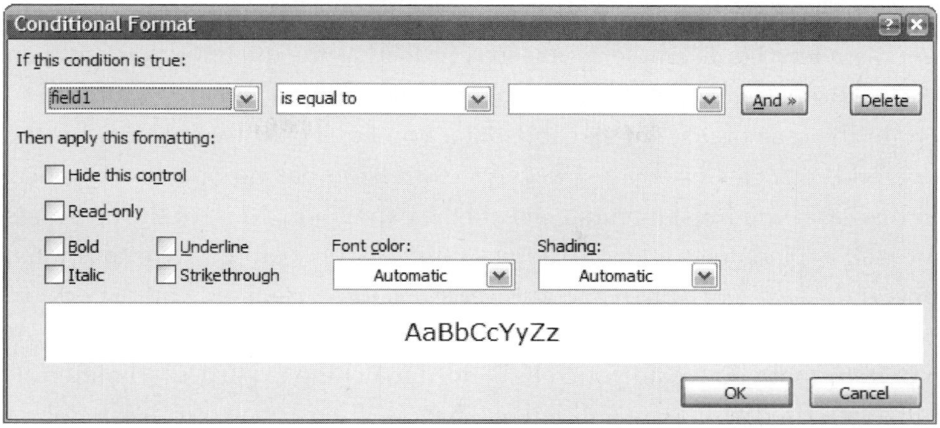

FIGURE 5.2: Conditional Format dialog

dialog to specify your conditions and what to do if the condition is true when the user fills out the form. At the very top of the dialog is the section where you specify your conditions. You can specify one or more conditions to be evaluated when the user fills out the form. Each condition usually consists of three parts—a qualifier, an operand, and a value.

You choose the qualifier from the leftmost drop-down list box in the condition section of this dialog. The qualifier can be one of four values—a field, an expression, the user's current role, or a set of signable data. By default, the field to which the control is bound is listed as the qualifier. You can choose a different field by clicking on *Select a field or group* from the qualifier drop-down. When you do so, the familiar *Select a Field or Group* dialog is displayed, from which you can choose a field as the qualifier. If you choose *The expression* from the qualifier drop-down, you can add your own expression as the condition. In this case, there is no operand drop-down, only a value field for you to enter your expression. The *User's current role* qualifier allows you to base the condition on the current role of the user. (We'll discuss user roles in Chapter 13, so we won't go into much detail here.) Finally, you can base your condition on a set of signable data. A set of signable data is created when you add a digital signature to a Section control, which we'll talk about in Chapter 11.

The second drop-down in the *Conditional Format* dialog lets you choose the comparison operand for your condition. Depending on the qualifier you select in the first drop-down, there could be many operands to choose from or only a few. For example, if you select a field as the qualifier, you can then choose from many operands, such as *is equal to, is blank, is not present,* and so on. In the case of a set of signable data, you have only two choices for the operand: *is signed* or *is not signed.* An expression has no operand because, in this case, you must manually create the expression. Most of the operands are self-explanatory and are things you've seen before. Two additional operands—*matches pattern* and *does not match pattern*—allow you to perform conditional formatting based on a preset pattern, such as a phone number, or a pattern that you create yourself. Pattern matching is particularly interesting when used with data validation, so we will postpone our discussion of pattern matching until later in this chapter.

The third drop-down allows you to enter a value that will be evaluated along with the qualifier and operand. If you have specified a field as the qualifier, the value drop-down will allow you to choose many options, such as text, a number, a date, or a time. Which options are available depends on the data type of the field to which the control is bound. For example, a Text Box control bound to a string field will show all the options just mentioned in the value drop-down. If the Text Box is bound to a whole number field, you won't be able to choose the options to enter text, a date, or a time. When you choose one of these options, the drop-down list box converts to a text box, which allows you to enter the data you wish to use when evaluating the condition. In addition to entering a value, you can choose to select a field or group whose value will be used in evaluation. You can also choose to enter a formula. Choosing the *Use a formula* option from the value drop-down opens the familiar *Insert Formula* dialog (discussed in Chapters 3 and 4), which allows you to build a formula to use in the condition.

If you want to specify more than one condition, use the *And* button. Clicking this button inserts a new condition. When the new condition is inserted, a new drop-down appears for the previous condition (Figure 5.3). This drop-down allows you to specify an operator to use to join the two conditions. You can choose either *and* or *or* as the operator. Obviously, choosing *and* means that all conditions must apply, and *or* means that either one or another condition must apply. When you specify multiple conditions, keep in mind that the conditions are evaluated from top to bottom.

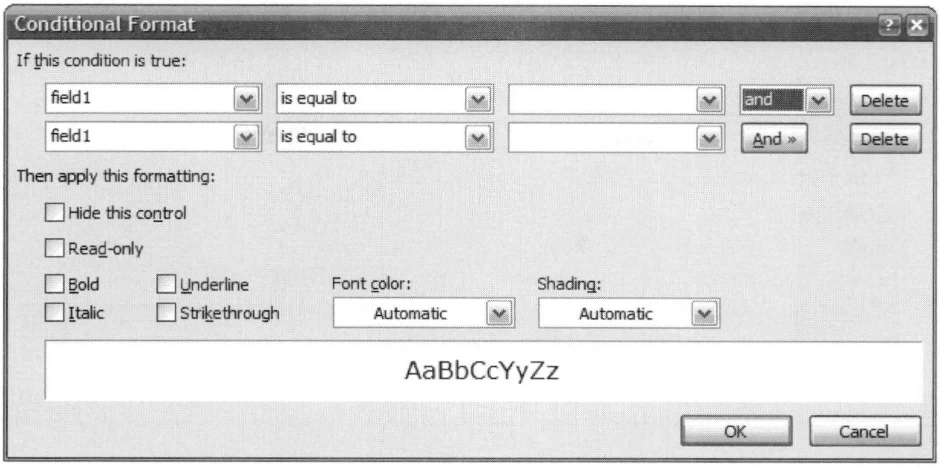

FIGURE 5.3: Conditional Format dialog with multiple conditions

Let's look at an example that will tie together these concepts and make this easier to understand. Let's say that we have a Text Box control that will be used to track the value of your favorite stock. You purchased the stock at $20.00 per share. You obviously want to make money on your investment, but you don't want to hold onto the stock forever. Therefore, if the share price is $25.00 or more, you want to sell. But you also don't want to lose too much money. So, if the share price is $18.00 or less, you want to sell then, too. In this scenario, you can apply conditional formatting to your Text Box control so that you can see at a glance whether or not you should sell or hold. If you sell, you also want to be able to easily tell whether or not you are going to lose money.

First, let's add one condition to the *Conditional Format* dialog that will add a background color of red to the Text Box if the value of one share of stock is less than or equal to $18.00. (Note that the condition doesn't actually contain the dollar sign.) Figure 5.4 shows the *Conditional Format* dialog with this condition. (You'll have to trust us that the shading is set to red since we can't show the color in this and the following figures. To see the entire set of formatting in all its glory, open the ConditionalFormatting form template included with the samples for this chapter on the book's Web site.) Note that we changed the name of the field to `StockPrice` so

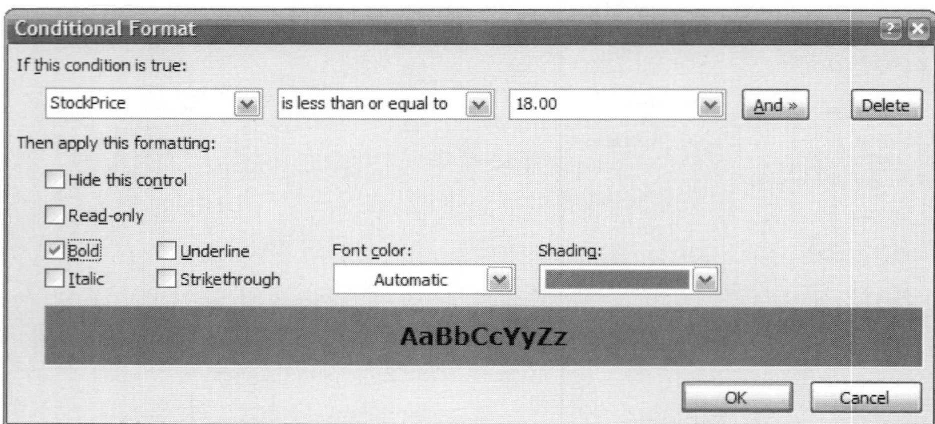

FIGURE 5.4: Conditional Format dialog with condition, where `StockPrice` is less than or equal to $18.00

that it's more descriptive. We also decided to format the value as bold text so that it really stands out.

After you close the dialog by clicking the *OK* button, the condition is added to the initial *Conditional Formatting* dialog (Figure 5.5).

Next, let's add a similar condition that will set the background color of the Text Box to green if the value of `StockPrice` is greater than or equal to $25.00. We add that condition the same way we did the first one except that

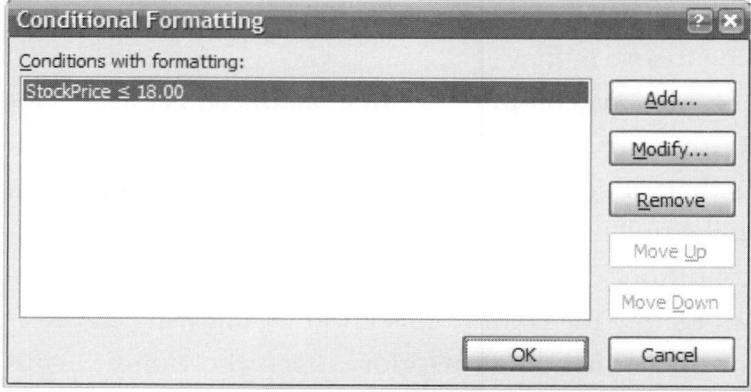

FIGURE 5.5: Conditional Formatting dialog with one condition

we choose green as the shading value. Also, we will set the text to italic in this case instead of bold, just to make things interesting.

Finally, let's set the background color to yellow if the value of `StockPrice` gets within $1.00 of either $18.00 or $25.00 so we'll know that it's almost time to sell. To do this, we'll have to specify four conditions in the *Conditional Format* dialog. The first two conditions specify that the value is greater than $18.00 and less than or equal to $19.00. The second two conditions specify that the value is greater than or equal to $24.00 and less than $25.00. The background color is set to yellow if either of these two sets of conditions applies. Figure 5.6 shows the *Conditional Format* dialog after adding the four conditions. Notice that the first two and last two conditions are connected by using the *and* operator. These two sets of conditions are joined by using the *or* operator. So, the outcome is that the background color of the Text Box is set to yellow if the stock price is between $18.00 and $19.00 or between $24.00 and $25.00.

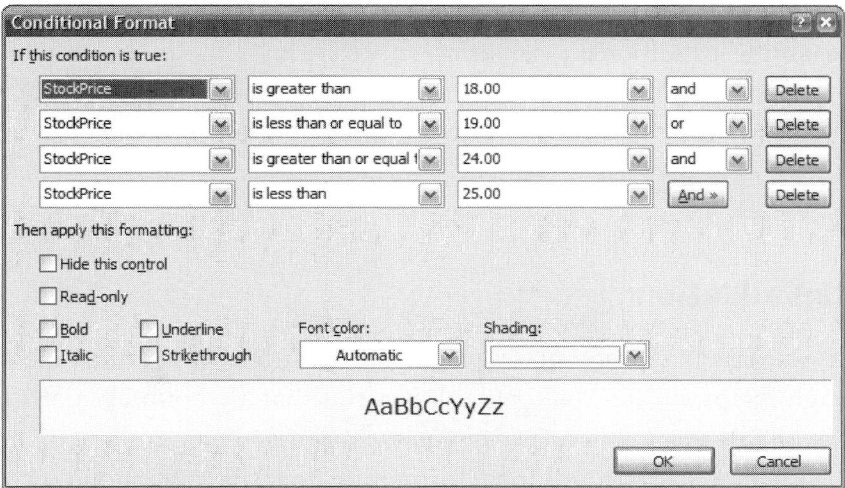

FIGURE 5.6: Conditional Format dialog specifying the four conditions needed to set the background color to yellow

Once you've added all these conditions, the *Conditional Formatting* dialog will list them (Figure 5.7). Just like the conditions you specify in the *Conditional Format* dialog, the list of conditions in the *Conditional Formatting* dialog are evaluated in the order they are listed. You can change the order in which the conditions are evaluated by using the *Move Up* and *Move Down* buttons.

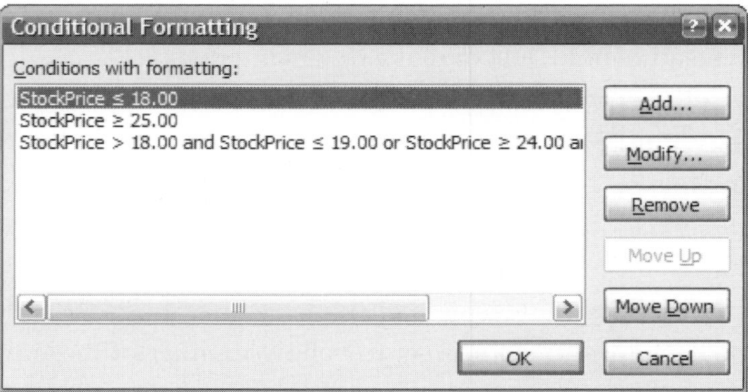

FIGURE 5.7: Conditional Formatting dialog showing all three conditions

By now, you can see all the cool things that are possible with conditional formatting. As we mentioned, in addition to formatting a control, you can hide or disable it or, in the case of Repeating Tables, Repeating Sections, and Optional Sections, you can prevent users from inserting or deleting rows. For example, conditional formatting is very useful with Repeating Tables—you can set the formatting for an entire row (or even hide or block row insertion) in the table based on the values entered into that row or in another part of the form. Conditional formatting is a very powerful feature. We hope you are already seeing ways you can put it to use.

Data Validation

Data validation is another one of those data-centric features exposed through the properties dialog for all controls that are bound to data. (It is also available through the *Field or Group Properties* dialog for a node in the data source.) As with conditional formatting, for data validation you specify one or more conditions that will determine whether the data entered by the user when filling out a form is valid. These conditions could be based on such things as preestablished business rules for your department or company. Data validation is a step beyond XML Schema data type validation such as simply defining *Whole Number* or *Date,* which we talked about in Chapter 3. With data validation, you can define a range of allowable whole numbers or restrict the selected date to be within a prescribed threshold, for example. Data validation behaves like its lesser data type validation cousin in that it's passive in its approach. Only after data is entered in the control and the user tabs or clicks away does it take effect. Its nonintrusive nature allows you, as a form designer, to be very liberal in how many data validation conditions you define.

When a user of your form enters data that violates one of your validation conditions, the node in the underlying data source is tagged with an error. This tag triggers a visual error for all the controls bound to that node in the current view. This means that controls present in other views may have errors. Since data validation happens at the data source level, sometimes a node can be tagged with an error but not be bound to a control in any views. Having a node not bound to a control might sound bizarre, but it's used quite often. Particularly, unbound nodes can be used as a temporary location for data or a hidden field for submitting data. Notwithstanding uses for unbound nodes, you should exercise caution when using data validation on nodes to which the user may not have access, such as read-only controls or unbound nodes.

Adding Data Validation to a Form Template

You can add data validation conditions for a field node in multiple ways. One way is by clicking on the *Data Validation* button in the *Data* tab of the properties dialog for a control. Clicking on this button opens up the dialog shown in Figure 5.8.

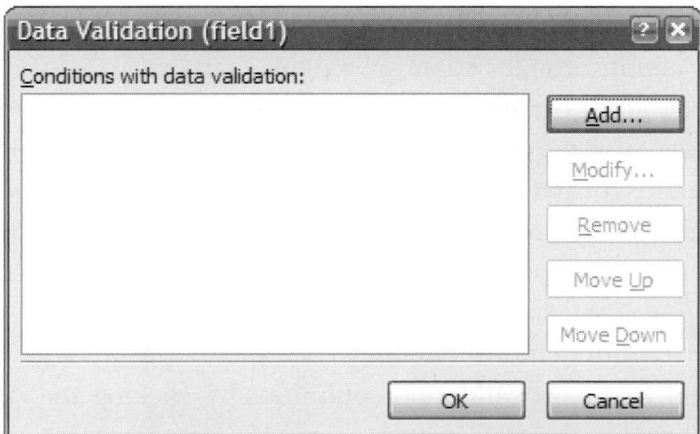

FIGURE 5.8: Data Validation dialog

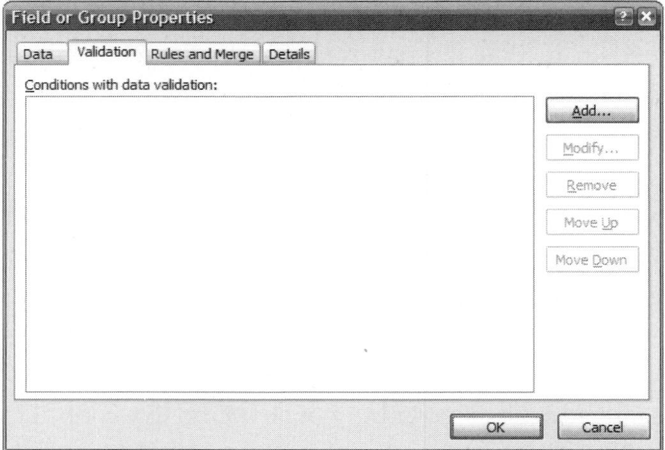

FIGURE 5.9: Validation tab on the Field or Group Properties dialog

The second way you can add data validation conditions is through the *Validation* tab of the *Field or Group Properties* dialog (which we talked about in Chapter 3) for a field node. The *Validation* tab (Figure 5.9) is basically the same as the *Data Validation* dialog (Figure 5.8). In both cases, the *Data Validation* dialog and the *Validation* tab will both list all the validation conditions you add. One thing to note about the data validation feature is that it is available only for field nodes in the data source. This means that the *Data Validation* button will be available in the properties dialog only for controls that are bound to fields. Also, the *Validation* tab will be enabled in the *Field or Group Properties* dialog only for field nodes in the data source. This feature is also not available for any node in a secondary data source. (You'll learn more about secondary data sources in Chapter 6.)

Let's look at an example. Say that you've created a form template to help you plan a party. (The sample we are about to create is called PartyPlanner.) In this form template, you have a Text Box control in which users will enter the total number of guests they are going to bring to the party. In this case, you want to make sure that the total number of guests is greater than zero (you can't have negative guests) and less than ten. This is the perfect place to add data validation.

Let's add two data validation conditions by clicking the *Add* button. Figure 5.10 shows the dialog after we entered one condition. This dialog is, basically, the same condition builder you saw earlier when we talked

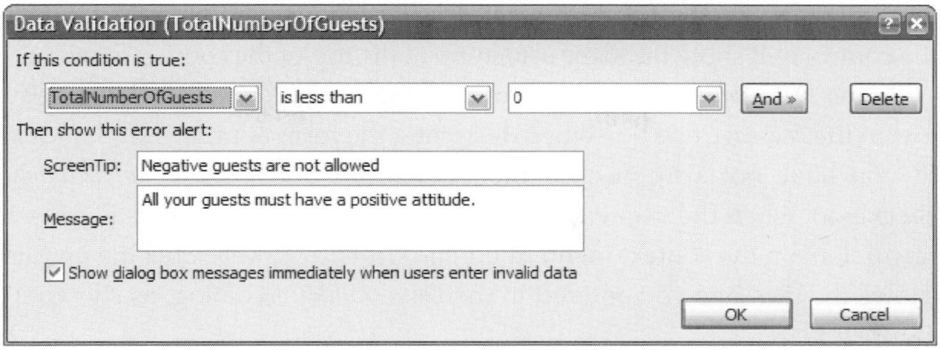

Data Validation (TotalNumberOfGuests)
If this condition is true:
TotalNumberOfGuests | is less than | 0 | And » | Delete
Then show this error alert:
ScreenTip: Negative guests are not allowed
Message: All your guests must have a positive attitude.
Show dialog box messages immediately when users enter invalid data
OK | Cancel

FIGURE 5.10: Data Validation condition builder

about the *Conditional Format* dialog. However, in this case, instead of being able to specify different formatting to use when a condition is true, you can specify how to display an error when the user enters data that violates one of the conditions. Figure 5.10 shows that we've added a condition to handle the case when a user enters a negative value into the Text Box control bound to the `TotalNumberOfGuests` field.

When the user enters a negative value, we can handle this error in one of two ways. When you first open the dialog, the checkbox next to *Show dialog box messages immediately when users enter invalid data* is unselected. This indicates that only the screen tip you enter into the *ScreenTip* text box will be displayed. If you leave the checkbox unchecked, the user will see a thick red dashed border around the control when a validation condition has been violated (Figure 5.11). Hovering the mouse over the control will show the

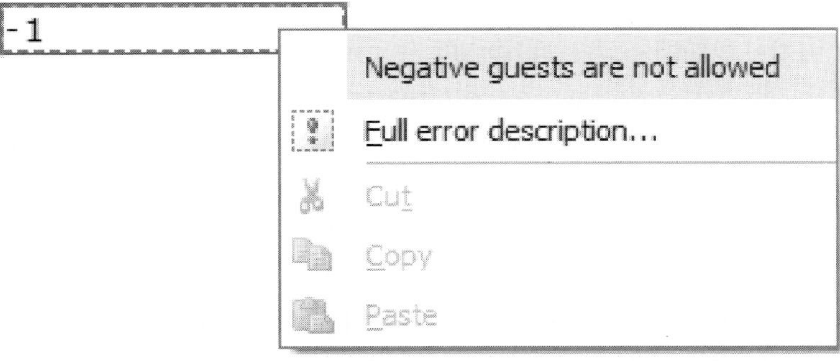

FIGURE 5.11: Inline alert for a data validation error

ScreenTip text you specified in the *Data Validation* dialog. Right-clicking on the control will show the same screen tip at the top of the context menu.

In the *Data Validation* dialog shown in Figure 5.10, you can also specify text in the *Message* text box when designing the form template. In that case (if you have not also checked the *Show dialog box messages immediately* checkbox), when the user enters a negative value, he or she will also see a menu item on the context menu titled *Full error description.* Clicking on this shows the message you entered in the *Data Validation* dialog, as shown in Figure 5.12.

FIGURE 5.12: Full error description for a data validation error

Forms Services

The action *Show dialog box messages immediately when users enter invalid data* is available for browser-enabled forms, but users will see the message immediately only if they view the form in InfoPath, not with a browser. The same form in the browser will not immediately show the dialog.

Back in the *Data Validation* dialog, if you now select the checkbox at the bottom of the dialog, as we have already done in Figure 5.10, when the user enters invalid data, the same dialog shown in Figure 5.12 will immediately be displayed without the user having to select the *Full error description* menu item from the context menu.

In addition to the condition that ensures the user can't enter a negative number of guests, you'll also want to add a condition to handle the case where the total number of guests is greater than or equal to ten. Once you

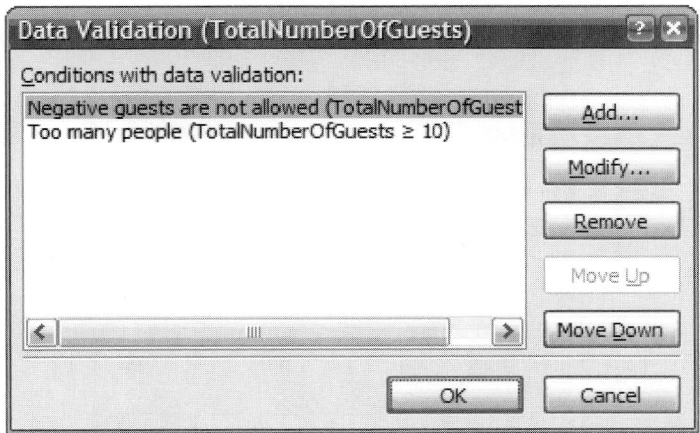

FIGURE 5.13: Data Validation dialog listing two conditions to validate the total number of guests

do that, the two conditions will appear in the list of conditions in the *Data Validation* dialog, as shown in Figure 5.13. As with the *Conditional Formatting* dialog, the conditions will be evaluated in the order they are listed in the dialog, so be aware of this fact when you add new conditions.

Pattern Matching

One of the more interesting uses of data validation is for pattern matching. Let's say that in the party-planning form template you have a Text Box control in which the user can enter his or her phone number so you can get in touch if there's a change of plans. Let's also say that you are storing the party-planning data in a database and you then use some back-end process to create a report of all the potential attendees. Your back-end process depends on the phone number being in a specific format. Therefore, you want to ensure that the phone number entered by the user is in the correct format. You can use pattern matching along with data validation for this.

Let's see how we can put pattern matching to use in this example. First, we'll add a data validation condition as usual. For this case, in the condition builder in the *Data Validation* dialog, we'll choose *does not match pattern* as the comparison operand for the condition. When you choose this operand and then click on the drop-down button for the value drop-down

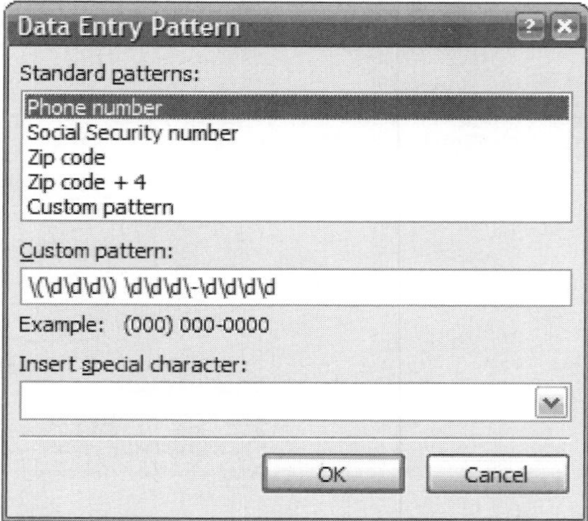

FIGURE 5.14: Data Entry Pattern dialog

list box, the only option is *Select a pattern.* Clicking on this item opens the *Data Entry Pattern* dialog (Figure 5.14).

The first pattern in the list of standard patterns is *Phone number,* which is exactly what we need. Now, after we close this dialog and add an error message to display when the condition is invalidated, if the user of the form enters a value into the Text Box that doesn't match this phone number pattern, he or she will receive an error. You'll notice in this case, when you first preview or fill out the form, that if the Text Box control is initially empty, a red asterisk will appear in the upper corner, as shown in Figure 5.15. This

FIGURE 5.15: Red asterisk error

error visual indicates that the Text Box cannot be empty. This is because you have specified a pattern that the data must match. Empty data doesn't match the phone number pattern. However, this error is different than the user entering invalid data, so InfoPath uses a red asterisk to indicate the error instead of the typical red dashed border.

One other thing you should note in Figure 5.14 is that you can add a custom pattern. The custom pattern can be any regular expression of your choosing. Each of the standard patterns is, in fact, implemented by using a regular expression. When you click on any of the standard patterns in the *Data Entry Pattern* dialog, you will see the corresponding regular expression listed in the *Custom pattern* box. You can follow the standard patterns when building your own custom pattern. You can also choose any of the special characters from the *Insert special character* drop-down list box in the dialog. As you can see, the *Data Entry Pattern* dialog is sort of a miniature regular expression builder.

For example, let's say that you want to create a custom pattern that matches a string that contains ten characters that are either "a" or "b". You can do so by entering the custom pattern shown in Figure 5.16.

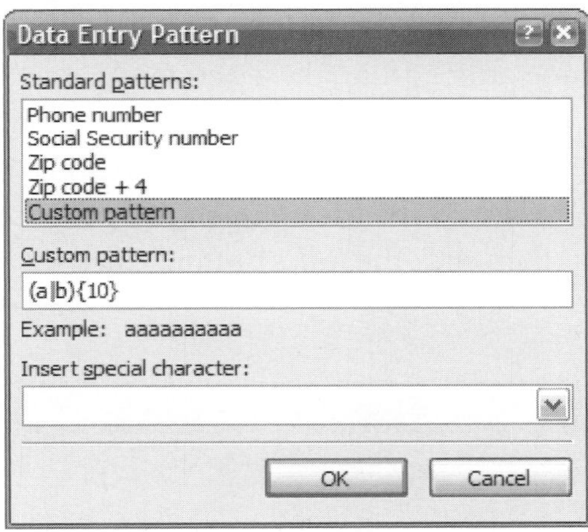

FIGURE 5.16: Custom pattern

Data validation is the next best thing to writing code to precisely validate the integrity of user-entered data. In fact, validating data declaratively is preferred to writing form code since it is less prone to bugs and easier to maintain. With some practice, you can create very powerful data validation constraints to ensure the data entered in your form is valid. In the long term, data validation will save you time and money since you no longer need to send forms back to your users because they weren't filled out properly the first time.

Rules

The Rules features is yet another data-centric feature available in the *Data* tab of the properties dialog for most controls (via the *Rules* button) and through the *Field or Group Properties* dialog (via the *Rules and Merge* tab). (This feature is also available by right-clicking on a control and then clicking on the *Rules* menu item.) Rules make it easy for you to create more interactive forms without having to write form code. A rule simply defines an action (or actions) to be performed based on some user action or condition.

An example of a rule action may be as simple as showing a dialog when the user clicks on a Button control in the form. Or you may want to set one field's value based on data entered into another field. You can even string together a series of actions in a single rule. For example, when the user clicks a Button control in the form, you could query a data connection, set a field's value, show a dialog box, and then open a new form. Figure 5.17 shows the *Rule* dialog after adding these actions.

Creating a rule is quick and easy. Let's create a simple form that shows a dialog when a Button control is clicked. After creating a new blank form, insert a Button control into the view. Open the properties dialog for the Button control, and then click the *Rules* button. Click the *Add* button to add

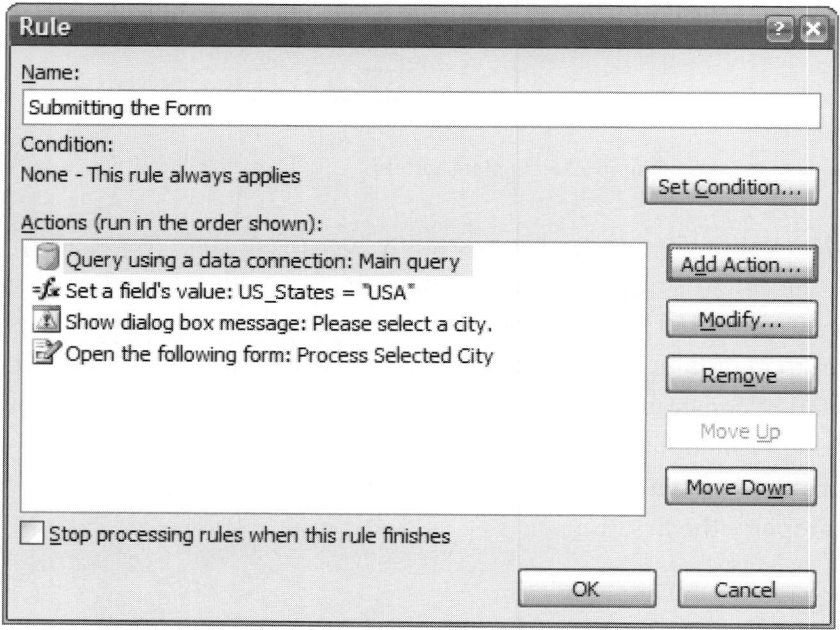

FIGURE 5.17: Adding or modifying an existing rule so that four actions are always run when the form is submitted

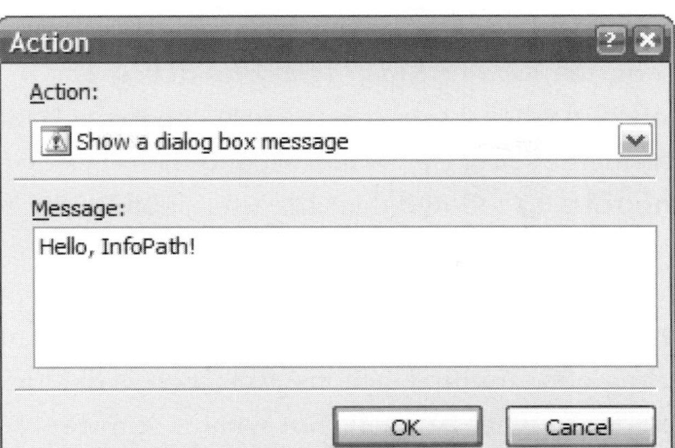

FIGURE 5.18: Specifying the action for a rule to run when a user clicks the Button control

a rule, and then click the *Add Action* button. This opens the dialog shown in Figure 5.18. Next, choose the default action, *Show a dialog box message,* and type in the text "Hello, InfoPath!" When you fill out the form and click the Button control, a dialog box displays your message. That's how easy it is to create a rule to show a message to your users. (This sample is called Rules-SimpleExample.)

Forms Services

Showing dialog boxes is not supported in the browser for browser-enabled forms.

You can easily see that a rule takes care of some useful actions, but when does a rule actually get executed? Similarly to form code, they are run when an event occurs either in the form or data source. Rules have an opportunity to run when a Button control is clicked (as seen in our example), the form is opened or submitted, and any data source is changed. We will learn more about form and data source events in Chapter 15.

Since rules are executed based on data source changes, an entry point to define rules is available on any data source node with the exception of the

(Choice) group and fields and groups within a recursive structure. The *Rules and Merge* tab on the *Field or Group Properties* dialog has the *Rules* entry point. To set up rules when a user opens a form, go to the *Form Options* dialog via the *Tools* menu, select *Open and Save,* and then click on the *Rules* button. For setting rules to follow when the user submits the form, use the *Submit Options* dialog, which is also found on the *Tools* menu.

As you can tell from Figure 5.19, which shows the entry points in the user interface for the Rules feature, all four entry points allow for multiple rules. A single rule can define multiple actions. An action is the lowest level of a rule where you define what happens. But what if you want to split up the actions so only some of them run under specific conditions? Actions are not conditional by themselves, but a rule itself can be conditional, as the *Set Condition* button in the *Rule* dialog implies (refer back to Figure 5.17). Setting conditions for a rule involves the condition builder that you've seen when we talked about conditional formatting and data validation.

Using multiple rules is the only way to handle error cases and bail out. For example, say that you define a set of rules for submitting a form. If the user didn't check the "I agree to all of the terms and agreements" checkbox in your form, the form should not be submitted. Moreover, you'd like to be very blunt and tell the user that he or she didn't agree to the terms in the form. You can do all of this in a single rule. If the checkbox in your form is

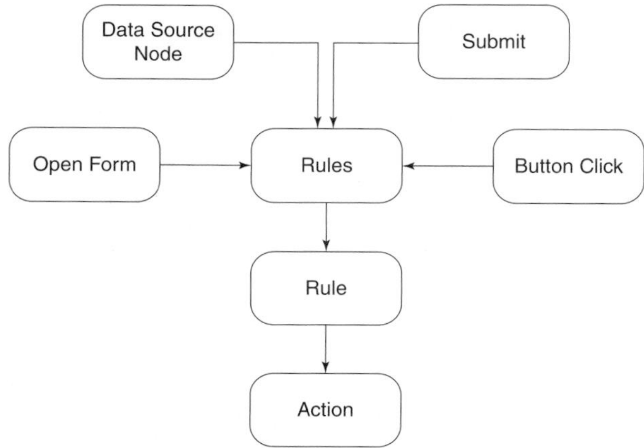

FIGURE 5.19: Entry points and structure of the Rules feature

indeed checked, the next rule can submit the form. But in order to prevent the next rule from submitting the form if the user didn't indicate agreement, you can check the *Stop processing rules when this rule finishes* checkbox shown at the bottom of the *Rule* dialog. If the condition is true (i.e., the checkbox in your form is checked and, therefore, the node to which it is bound is `"TRUE"`), this rule is run (a dialog is shown), and no other rules for this node are run. You can picture the *Stop processing rules* checkbox as a short circuit for a predefined chain of rules.

To get a better idea for the scope of what rules can do for your form, see Table 5.1 for a list of supported actions. More than one action can be associated with a given rule.

TABLE 5.1: Actions Available for a Rule

Rule Action	Description
Show a dialog box message	Shows a dialog box with a static text message.
Show a dialog box expression	Same as above, but the text is dynamically generated by an expression.
Set a field's value	Sets the value of any field in the main or a secondary data source. The value can be static or come from another main or secondary data source field.
Query using a data connection	Invokes a query data connection (see Chapter 6).
Submit using a data connection	Invokes a submit data connection (see Chapter 8).
Open a new form to fill out	Creates a new blank form based on the specified form template.
Close the form	Closes the current form. There is an option to prompt the user for saving if the form has not been saved. This action is available only from a Button control.
Switch views	Changes the current view to the specified view. This action is not available during data source changes because views cannot be changed while the data source is changing. Typically you'll use this action on a Button click.

Forms Services

The *Open a new form to fill out* rule action does not apply to browser-enabled forms.

Forms Services

The *Close the form* rule action has an option to prompt the user if changes haven't been saved yet. Browser-enabled forms do not allow for prompting.

Rules, despite being very useful when designing a functional form, are not always guaranteed to work properly. As a form designer, you should be aware of errors that may occur from executing actions. For example, the server for a data connection may not be available, so a query or submit to that server will fail. Or when opening a new form to fill out, that form may not actually exist. Figure 5.20 shows what happens when a rule action fails. If this dialog appears, the remaining actions of the current rule and the rules after the failed rule are not run. Unfortunately, there is not much you can do in rules to detect or react to error cases. Only writing form code will offer a finer grain of control.

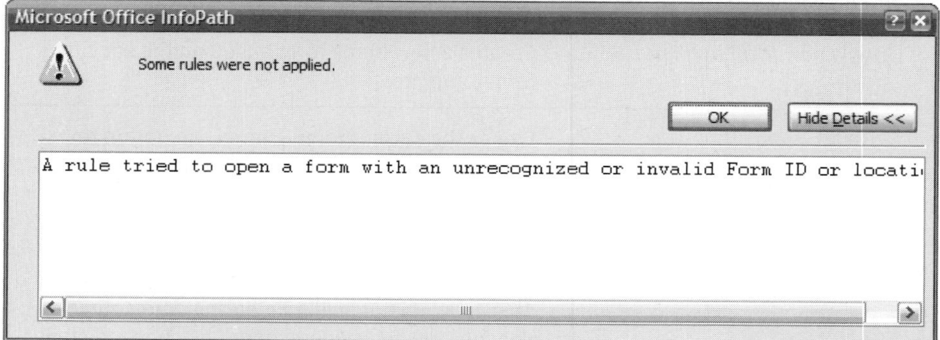

FIGURE 5.20: Dialog displayed when an action on a rule fails to execute when the user fills out the form

Forms Services

When a rule fails to execute, the *Form Warning* dialog appears, allowing the user to choose *Continue* or *Start Over. Continue* does not terminate the form-filling session but stops processing the rules involved in the failure. *Start Over* has the same effect as filling out a new instance of the form template.

At times, rules can appear to be more powerful than the user filling out your form. When using the *Set a field's value* action, a read-only Text Box control can be assigned a value! This might sound weird at first, but don't forget about the ever-important separation between the view and the data source. Since the Rules feature is data-centric, it should not surprise you that it operates directly on the data source. A Text Box control that is read-only is simply a restriction of that specific control in the view. Since the user must pass through the view layer before getting to the data source, it appears as if the node is read-only, but it is not. (If a node itself is read-only, an action to set its value will fail.) When we shift our discussion to writing form code in the advanced chapters, the distinction between the view and data gets much clearer.

Logic Inspector

Adding data validation, calculated default values (which we talked about in Chapter 3), and rules to your form templates enables you to build very complex forms in a short amount of time. However, what happens when something goes wrong? Or what if you are given a form template to maintain that you have never seen before? How do you determine what data validation, calculated default values, and rules are included in the form? In these cases, if the form template is even slightly complex, includes many nodes in the data source, and/or uses these features quite extensively, finding the root of the problem could be very difficult.

In order to make the process of diagnosing problems a little easier, InfoPath includes a tool called the **Logic Inspector** that you can use while in design mode. The Logic Inspector allows you to view all the logic in your form template or for a specific field or group in the data source very quickly. The Logic Inspector will show you information about the data validation, calculated default values, rules, and form code (which we'll talk about later in the book) that you've added to your form. It will also show you dependencies between different fields or groups in the form template.

For example, let's say that you've specified a calculated default value for a Text Box control bound to a field named `Greeting`. The value of this field is built by concatenating the string `"Hello"` with a name the user enters in another Text Box that is bound to a field called `Name`. The Logic Inspector will show you that the calculated default value for the `Greeting` field depends on the value entered in the `Name` field. If you delete the `Name` field and later discover that the value for the `Greeting` field is not working correctly, you can quickly look at the Logic Inspector to find out what is wrong.

Looking at a more extensive example should make this clear. Let's say that we have a form template whose view and data source look like those shown in Figure 5.21. (This sample is called LogicInspector.) In this form template, we have a data source with four fields. In the view, we have four Text Box controls bound to each of the nodes in the data source. The `DataValidation` field uses data validation to ensure that the value entered into the Text Box is greater than 0 and less than 10. The `CalculatedDefaultValue` field has a calculated default value that concatenates `"Hello"` with the name entered in the Text Box bound to the `Name` field. A Button control in the view can be used to validate the input to the Text Box bound to the `DataValidation` field. The Button control uses rules to determine whether the data is valid. In the case of each rule, two actions will occur: (1) Show a dialog box message telling you whether or not the value is valid, and (2) set the value of the `Result` field to

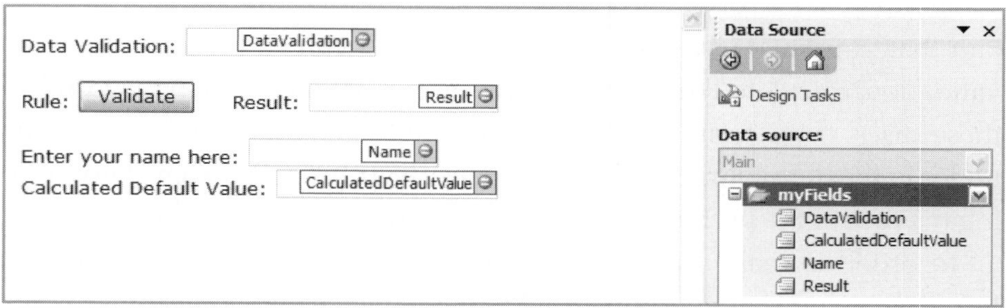

FIGURE 5.21: Form template for the Logic Inspector sample

either "Invalid!" or "No Errors", depending on the validity of the value the user entered. (Obviously, you can validate the input by using data validation. This example is included for illustrative purposes only.)

Now, let's look at the Logic Inspector to see what it can tell us about the logic in the form template. To show the logic for the entire form, click on the *Logic Inspector* menu item from the *Tools* menu while in design mode. When you do, the dialog shown in Figure 5.22 opens. The *Logic Inspector*

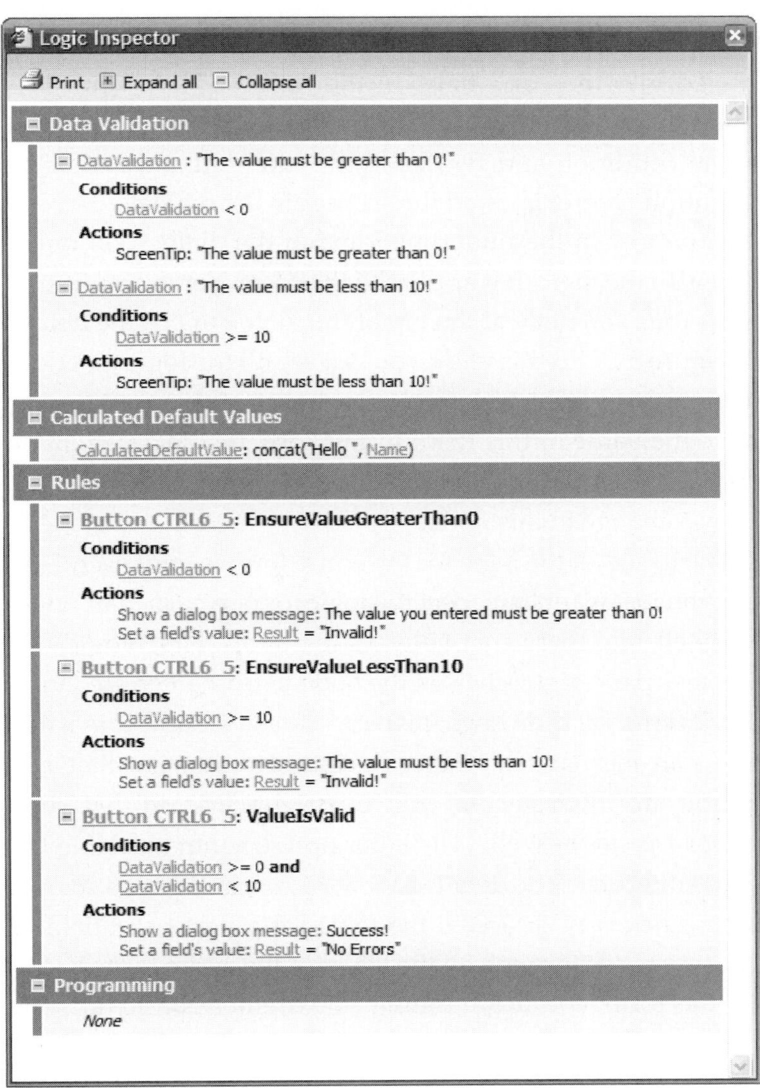

FIGURE 5.22: Logic Inspector showing the logic for the entire form template

dialog is divided into four categories: *Data Validation, Calculated Default Values, Rules,* and *Programming*. Each section lists all the logic associated with each category. (Obviously, the *Programming* section is going to be empty right now since we haven't talked about form code yet.)

In the *Data Validation* section, you can see all the conditions we specified on the field and the actions to perform when the condition is true. Under the *Calculated Default Values* section, you can see that the value of the `CalculatedDefaultValue` field is set by using the `concat` function. In this case, the `concat` function will concatenate the string `"Hello"` with the name entered into the `Name` field. In the *Rules* section, you can see that we specified three different rules for the Button control in the view. Each rule has one condition and two actions. Note that since there are three rules, the Button control is listed three times in the dialog.

Clicking on any of the underlined text in the dialog will open a more detailed view of the logic that applies to that item. For example, clicking on the `DataValidation` node at the top of the dialog opens the detailed view shown in Figure 5.23. In this view, you can see all the logic that depends on this field, logic that will be triggered by a change to this field, and logic that may change the value of this field. In this case, the data validation that is set on the `DataValidation` node both depends on this node and will be triggered by a change to this node.

Being able to see all the logic for the entire form is very useful. However, sometimes you just want to inspect the logic for one particular node. That is possible as well, and there are two ways to do this. First, you can open the *Data Source* task pane, right-click on the node you are interested in, and then click on *Logic Inspector.* (The Logic Inspector isn't available for virtual nodes, however.) As an alternative, if there is a control in the view that is bound to the node you are interested in, you can right-click on that control and choose *Logic Inspector* as well. (The latter option is not available for Button controls.) In either case, the detailed view shown in Figure 5.23 opens. This gives you a quick way to access the logic for a particular field or group without having to sift through all the logic for the entire form.

Unless the form you are building is extremely basic, at some point you're bound to add data validation, calculated default values, and rules

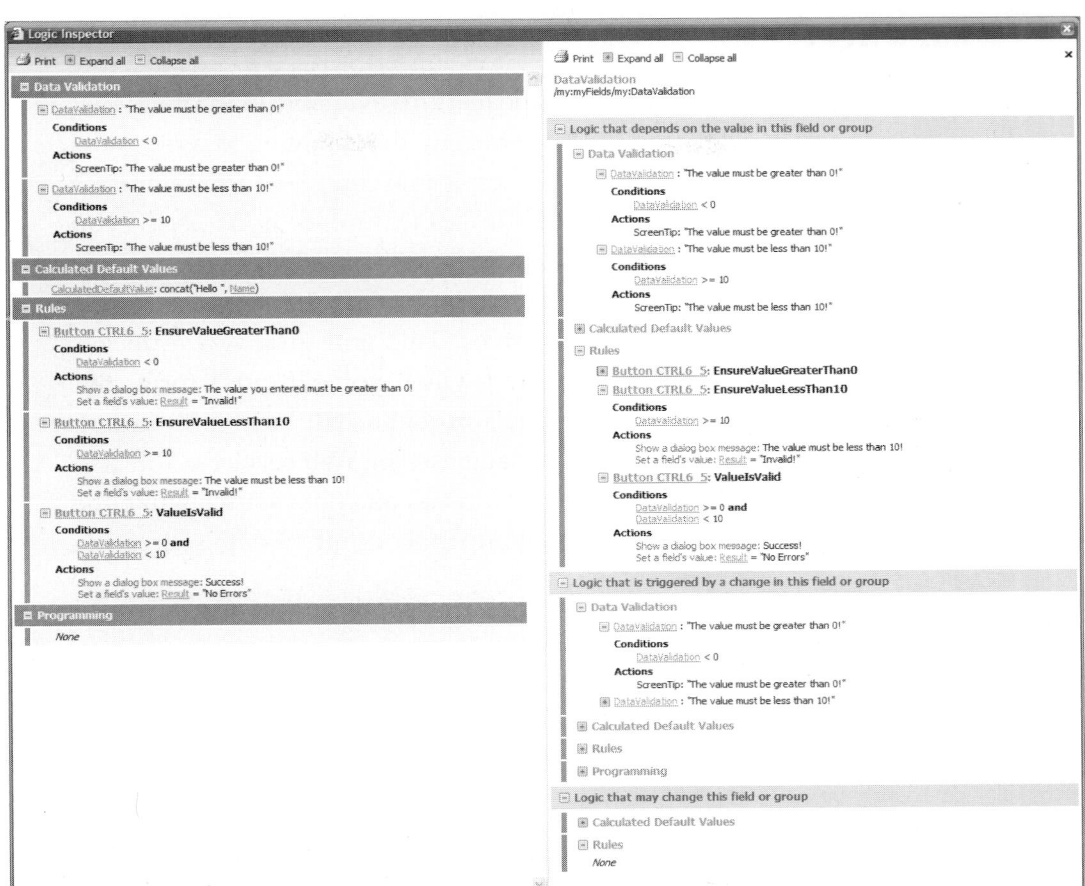

FIGURE 5.23: Detailed view of the `DataValidation` node

to your form template. (And, after you finish reading this book, you'll probably want to write some form code as well.) In fact, we would venture to say that most of your form templates will include one or more of these features. You might also be tasked with maintaining a form template created by somebody else. In this case, you might know nothing about the logic in the form template when you are first given this task. Whether you are trying to diagnose an issue with logic you created or just want to see all the logic in a form template you need to maintain, the Logic Inspector can make your job much easier.

What's Next?

In this chapter, you've learned about the features available in InfoPath that allow you to add business logic to your form without having to write code. At this point, you should be able to design some complex form templates that put many of InfoPath's advanced design features to good use. If you stopped reading now, you certainly would know enough to be dangerous. However, from here, things only get better. In the next chapter, we're going to talk in great detail about data sources. This will give you a deeper understanding about what is happening when you fill out a form. But that's not all. After reading the next chapter, you will be able to design form templates that are connected to databases or Web services. You will also be able to connect controls in your form to one data source while the data entered by the user is stored in a completely different data source. So, read on.

6

Retrieving Data from External Sources

Getting Started

In the last several chapters, we talked about working with data and controls. We learned all about the main data source, including fields and groups, their properties, and how they hook up with controls through binding. In this chapter, we'll apply that knowledge to discuss **secondary data sources**. Like the main data source, secondary data sources also hold data but cater to different form design needs. We'll walk through some scenarios that use secondary data sources and show you how easy it is to incorporate them in your form designs.

Talking about data sources won't make much sense, however, without first going over **data adapters**. Specifically, we are referring to data that is external to a form template's resource files (the *Resource Files* dialog, which manages internal form template files, is discussed in Chapter 2). Examples of external data sources include an XML file on a network share, a database in a corporate server farm, or even a Web service living on the Internet. For instance, say that you have a list of products changing on a daily basis. Instead of editing your form template every day, the data can be received dynamically from your company's database each time your form is opened.

The job of a data adapter is to get data from, say, a database, and then put that data into the main or a secondary data source. A data adapter is the mechanism that enables external data to flow into your form. Collectively, the data adapter and associated data source are known as a **data connection**. As its name suggests, the data connection gets data from an external data source and brings it into the form.

Data Connections

Why Do We Need Them?

A data connection is what InfoPath uses to connect to external data sources (or endpoints), beyond the form template, when users fill out the form. For the purposes of this chapter, we discuss only those data connections that pull, or query, data from an external source into the form. Submit connections, which push data to an external data source, are discussed in Chapter 8. There are four types of **query data connection** endpoints that InfoPath knows how to communicate with: XML files, databases, Web servers via Web services, and SharePoint servers. A form template can be set up with any number of data connections of any type. And just because a form template defines a data connection does not mean it actually uses it when the form is being filled out. As we progress in our discussion, it will be evident how this works.

In this chapter, we'll discuss each connection type so you can understand what it does and how to set it up. We'll also show examples of their use in some sample forms.

> **TIP Query Connection Lingo**
>
> A data connection is a concept that resides in an InfoPath form template. That is, we say a form template "defines a query data connection," for example, to get customer addresses. When filling out the form, the form is said to "query (or execute) the data connection" when it uses the connection to retrieve data.

Conceptually Understanding Data Connections and Data Sources

Before we get into details on how to set up a data connection when designing a form template, let's get a bird's-eye view of what happens conceptually when a query data connection is created. Creating a data connection establishes a potential channel of communication between the InfoPath form and an external data source. It is a "potential" channel because when a data connection is defined, it may not actually be used when filling out a form. If it is used, InfoPath requests data from the endpoint. Assuming the data successfully gets transferred via the channel, InfoPath will store the received data in a location for use by the form. The location is always a data source, but it isn't necessarily the main data source! InfoPath creates a secondary data source to temporarily hold the received data—saving or submitting the form does not include this data, which disappears when the form is closed. Figure 6.1 shows the relationships between the form and data sources. The bubbles around the form represent sources of external data, while the lines represent channels of data for requests and responses.

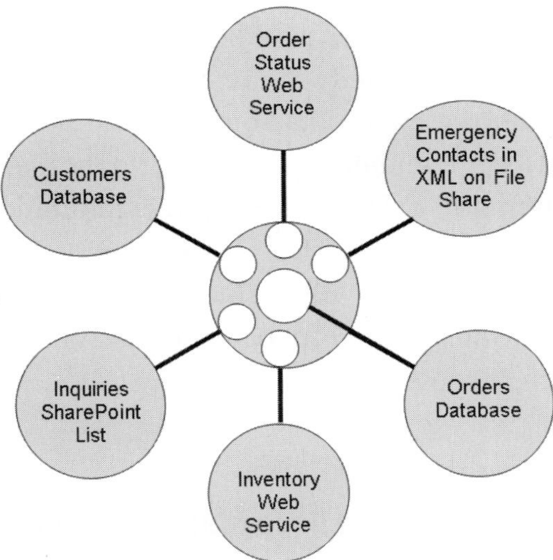

FIGURE 6.1: Relationships between a form and its external data sources

The data received from the connection can also be persisted with saved or submitted data. The only way InfoPath supports the persisting of data is if the data resides in the main data source. Remember that the main data source is ultimately what is submitted or saved when your users fill out the form. To clearly save queried data from an endpoint, InfoPath would need to take the received data and plop it right into the main data source. This is indeed what happens at a high level, and Figure 6.1 shows this with the connecting line between the orders database and the main data source.

All Data Connections Are Not Created Equal

As we jump into talking about the various types of data connections, it's important to understand that all data connections of the same type may not be the same. Different connections of the same type with similar end-points can exhibit different behaviors when you're designing and filling out a form with InfoPath. To better inform you on how to design data-rich forms, we highly recommend you keep the following in mind (and we will mention it again as well) as you continue: Many features around a form's data connection will behave differently depending on whether the connection is hooked up to the main data source or a secondary data source.

Each data adapter may have its own nuances around exactly what is different when it's connected to the main or a secondary data source, so, unfortunately, we cannot give you a blanket guideline for all connections. However, it's good to remember that the main data source can have only one query connection associated with it. And you must decide whether to use a connection on the main data source as the first step when you're designing a new form template. For example, only the main data source can be used to submit to a database. Keep this in mind as you gather the data requirements to design your form. (See Chapter 2 for details on gathering form requirements.) You will see that in the grand scheme of designing your form, allowing only one query connection on the main data source shouldn't be much of a restriction at all.

Technicalities of Main and Secondary Data Connections

The main data connection, if one exists (which is determined on the *Design a Form Template* dialog when you first create the form template), pulls external data into the main data source. The main data source holds the underlying form data that the user will ultimately save or submit. A secondary data connection also pulls external data, but into an auxiliary (or secondary) data source. Secondary data sources are physically separate from the main data source. Unlike the main data source, secondary data sources are not saved with the form data; in fact, their lifetime is that of the form-filling session.

Creating a Data Connection

Main Connection

To create a main query connection, you need to design a new form template (template parts do not support creating against a connection; they're discussed in Chapter 10). To design a new form template based on an external data source—that is, to use a data connection with the main data source—select one of these three *Based on* options in the *Design a Form Template* dialog (Figure 6.2): *Web Service, Database,* or *Connection Library.* We'll soon learn why the *XML or Schema* option does not create a connection.

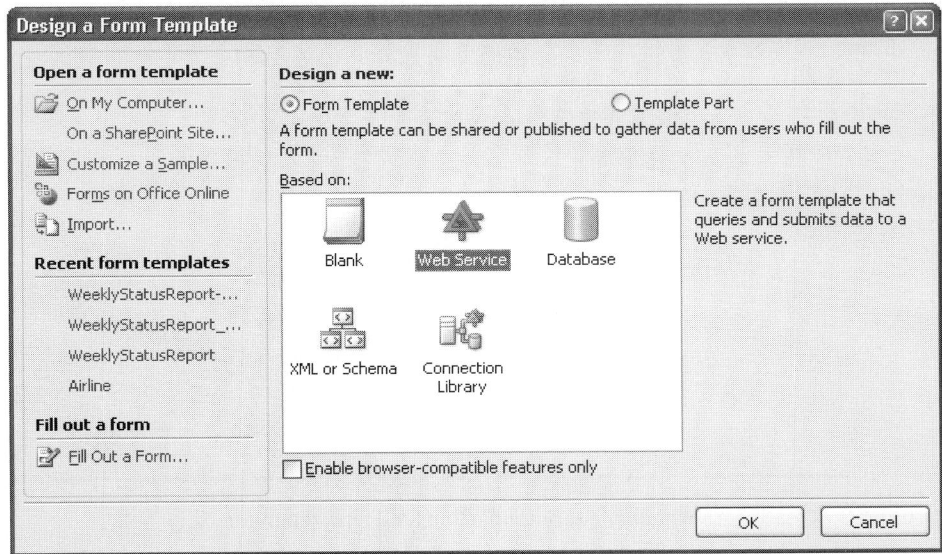

FIGURE 6.2: Design a Form Template dialog, the starting point for creating a main query connection

Secondary Connection

You create a secondary query connection while designing a form template instead of at the beginning as with the main connection. At any time while designing a form template, go to the *Data Connections* menu item on the *Tools* menu. (Later in this chapter, Figure 6.8 shows the resulting dialog.) After clicking *Add* to create a new secondary connection, choose *Create a new connection to receive data.* (A *Data Connection Library* option is also available, but we will introduce it in Chapter 14 and discuss it at length in

Chapter 17.) At this point, you decide which type of connection you need (as shown in Figure 6.3), depending on the external data source.

Table 6.1 shows the choices for main and secondary query data connections.

Now that you're familiar with how query data connections generally work, let's jump into details and examples for each of the connection types.

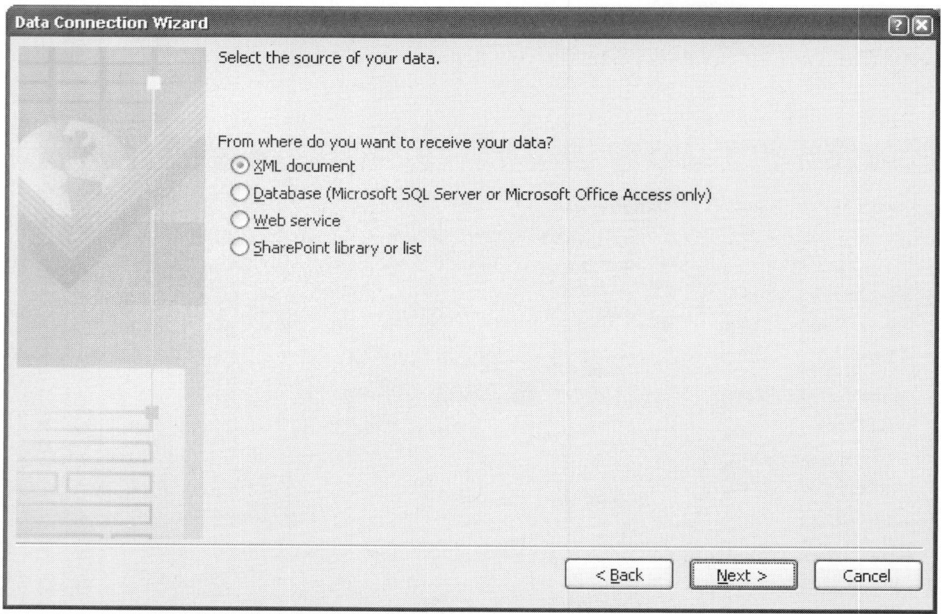

FIGURE 6.3: Creating a secondary query connection for a form template

TABLE 6.1: Types of Main and Secondary Data Query Connections

Data Source	Connection Types
Main	Database Web service Connection library
Secondary	XML document Database Web service SharePoint library or list Connection library

XML Files

With XML becoming a ubiquitous file format throughout the world, how can you quickly and easily get data from any XML file and incorporate it into your form? Use the **XML file data adapter**, of course! The purpose of this adapter is to read an XML file that can reside almost anywhere and to pull its data into a secondary data source for your form to use. The XML file used for the connection can come from your computer, a file share, or an HTTP or FTP site. You could even use an ASP or ASP.NET page to dynamically generate XML data on the fly! If XML exists somewhere, InfoPath can consume it, assuming the user filling out the form has been granted access.

WARNING XML File Permissions

Be mindful of permissions related to users accessing the XML file you designate when it's not included as a resource file in the form template. The user's Windows credentials are used to access the file. The same credentials are propagated to a Web server unless anonymous access is enabled. If the user doesn't have access to the XML data, your form will show an error message and will be missing that connection's data. Ensure all potential users have access to any endpoint data.

Forms Services

Connecting to an XML file on the local computer or using a UNC path (such as \\mycomputer\myshare) is not allowed and will fail in Forms Services when the connection is executed. To access an XML file that is not included in the template, we suggest keeping the file in a SharePoint document library accessible via HTTP.

The XML file adapter is available only for secondary data connections. The main data source has no concept of an XML adapter because it doesn't really need it. Since InfoPath already has the ability to open an existing XML file when you want to fill out any previously saved form, an adapter doesn't really make sense. But if you wanted to copy some data from an external XML file directly to the main data source, you could use rules for simple copying or write custom form code to orchestrate a complex copy scheme. Copying data from a secondary data source to the main data source is generic functionality any adapter can potentially leverage.

Let's jump into an example that shows off the abilities of the XML file adapter. First, we'll design a very simple form template that you'll fill out to create the external data source. Starting with a new blank form, simply insert a Bulleted List control and save the template. Fill out the form based on the template you just saved by adding the list items shown in Figure 6.4. Save this form to your desktop as Sample.xml. (This file is available with the samples for this chapter on the book's Web site. A sample called BulletedList-Items also was used to create this XML file.)

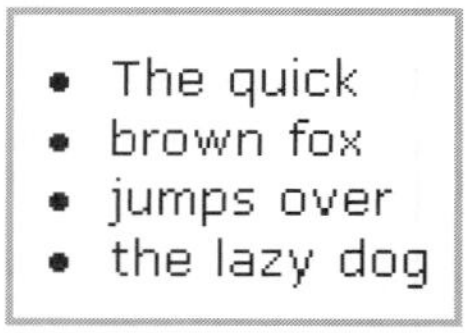

- The quick
- brown fox
- jumps over
- the lazy dog

FIGURE 6.4: Data to fill into a form and save to Sample.xml, to be read later by using an XML file adapter

Now let's design another new blank form template, but this time the template will be used to read the data we saved in the previous example. Instead of inserting controls, go to the *Data Connections* item on the *Tools* menu. Click the *Add* button on the *Data Connections* dialog and then select the *Receive data with an XML document* option for the source of your data. When prompted for the file location, as shown in Figure 6.5, point to the Sample.xml file you previously saved on the desktop. The *Resource Files* button is used to select an XML file that is already included in the form template.

The next dialog (Figure 6.6), despite looking simple, has a pivotal effect on this connection's settings. The first option, *Include the data as a resource file in the form template or template part,* will pull in the XML data when you click the *Next* button and save it in a file that's kept with the form template. The file would then be accessible through the *Resource Files* dialog (available

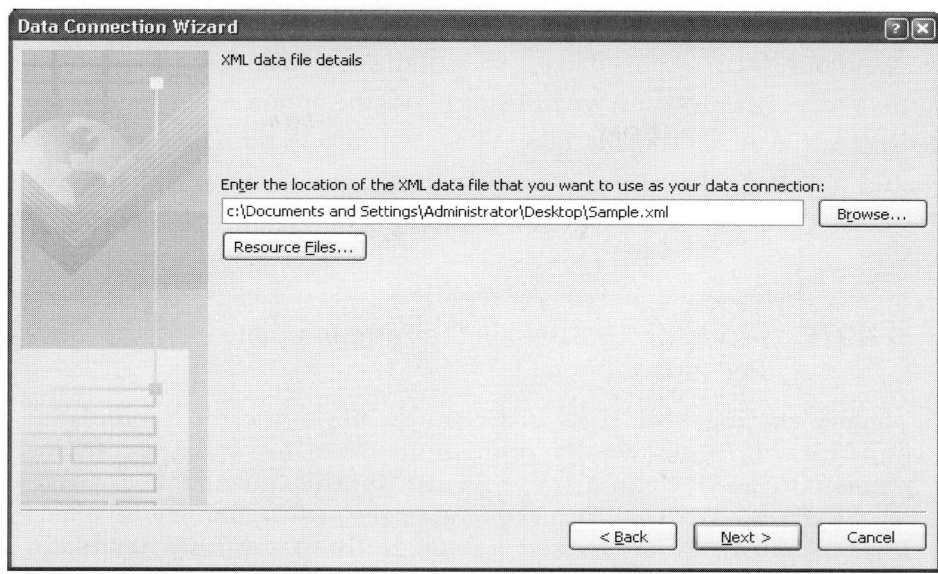

FIGURE 6.5: Entering the file location to use when creating a secondary connection to XML data

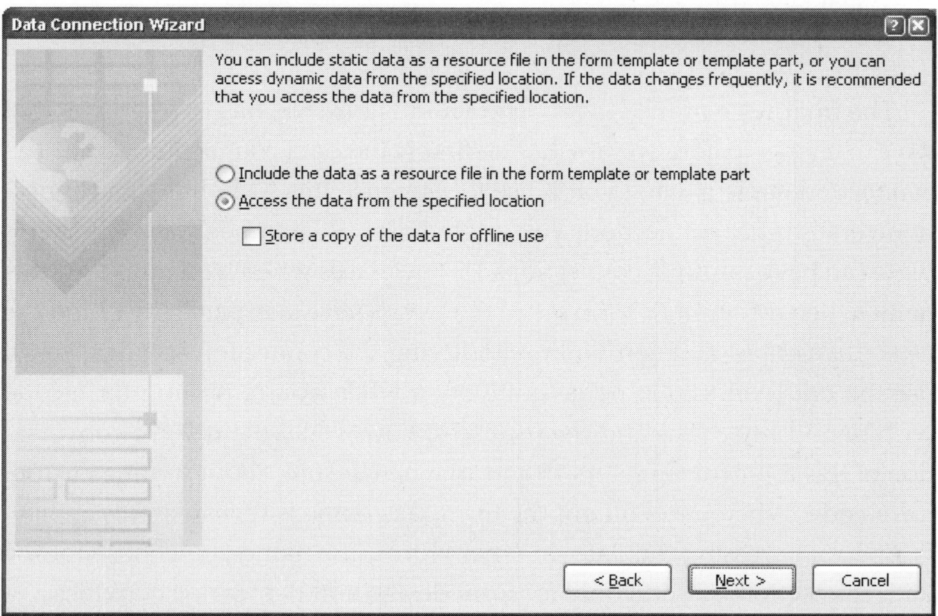

FIGURE 6.6: XML file connection settings to opt in or out of including the data as a file in your template

from the button in Figure 6.5 as well as the *Tools* menu in design mode). Since we want our XML data to be live, that is, if the data is updated we want our form to reflect the updates, we instead choose the option *Access the data from the specified location.* The checkbox to *Store a copy of the data for offline use* should not be checked. This is for the cached query feature, which we will discuss in Chapter 7 when we cover the topic of offline query support.

NOTE Including XML Data in the Form Template Resource Files

When including XML data as a resource file in the form template, InfoPath will try to keep the original file name. For example, if you pointed to \\MyComputer\MyShare\MyData.xml and chose the *Include the data as a resource file in the form template* option, a file called MyData.xml would be added automatically to the form template resource files. If the XML data comes from a Web site with characters such as slashes and question marks that cannot be used in a file name, InfoPath will attempt to use a base file name. For example, http://MyServer/MyData.aspx?Type=1 would yield a file with resource name MyData.aspx.

The final page of the wizard, shown in Figure 6.7, has two settings that we can change before we finish. The first is the data connection name. The connection name is what you'll use to reference this XML file data connection versus other connections you might have. (Remember that a form template can have multiple connections.) Some places where you might see this name when designing a form are in the *Data Source* task pane, rules, and the *Data Connections* dialog if you're modifying the connection settings. You'll use the data connection name quite often when you're writing form code with data connections and data sources; however, we'll reserve conversation of this topic for Chapters 15 and 16 when we talk about writing custom form code. When users fill out the form, this name is revealed only if there is an error accessing the data. In other words, the name you choose for the data connection is useful only for form design and debugging activities.

The checkbox *Automatically retrieve data when form is opened* enables this XML data adapter to get the data when the user opens the form (either new

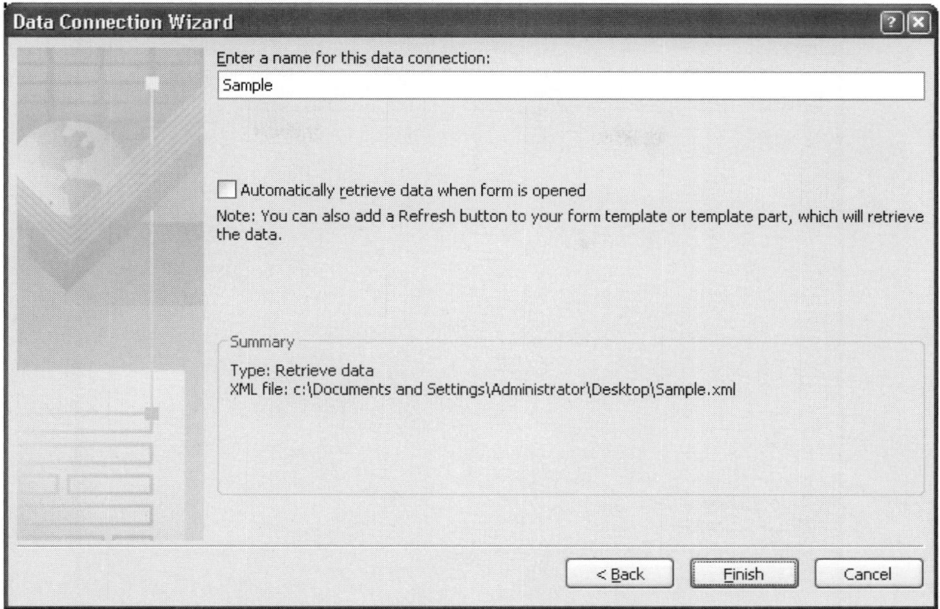

FIGURE 6.7: Final page of the Data Connection Wizard for an XML file

or existing), but before the form is shown. This is convenient for external data that never changes, such as a list of states used in a Drop-Down List Box. (We'll go into details when talking about List Box controls using data from secondary data sources in Chapter 7.) If you do not want the data to be queried automatically, which is the behavior we want in our sample form, you can query it on demand through a rule. We will set up a rule to query the XML file using this data connection in a moment. Click *Finish* to complete the creation of the data connection.

NOTE Automatically Retrieve Data Once or More

Checking the *Automatically retrieve data when form is opened* checkbox shown in Figure 6.7 does not mean you cannot requery this data connection later. You can requery (also known as **refresh**) the data via a rule, for example, at any time.

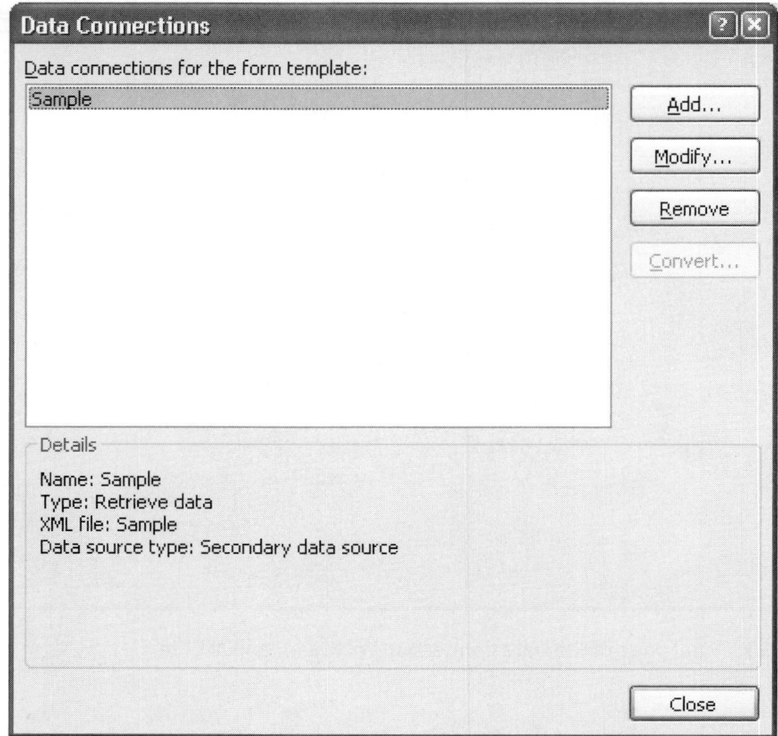

FIGURE 6.8: Data Connections dialog after finishing the XML file Data Connection Wizard

After clicking *Finish,* you can see the data connection we just created in the *Data Connections* dialog (Figure 6.8). The *Details* region shows the major settings for the connection. The *Details* region is helpful when you have many data connections listed and can't quite recall their specifics. You'll also notice that this dialog is the general entry point for configuring query data connections for both main and secondary data sources. You can add, modify, and remove connections from this dialog. However, if a main data source connection exists, it cannot be removed. We will find out why when we look at submit database connections in Chapter 8.

Now that we've created the XML file secondary data connection, let's design the visual aspects of our form template and see how to use the XML file data. At first, you'll notice nothing has visually changed in the form. Since a data connection is not visually represented, you might forget that

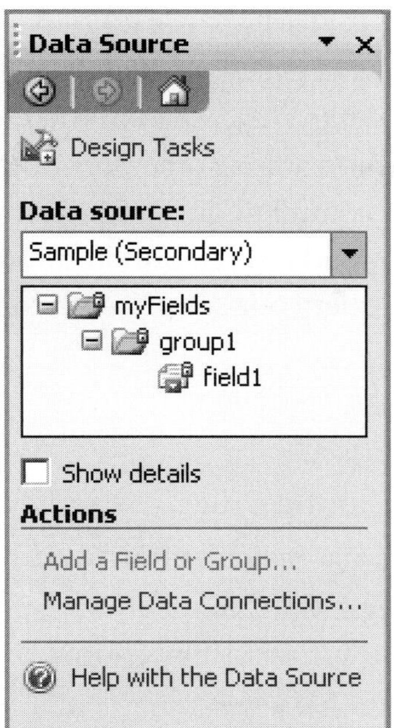

FIGURE 6.9: Data Source task pane showing secondary data source

it's even there! Obviously, one way to tell is to go back to the *Data Connections* dialog. Instead, let's go to the *Data Source* task pane (Figure 6.9). The *Data source* drop-down menu will have a new item, namely, *Sample (Secondary)*. This is the secondary data source that was created when we finished creating our XML file data connection. Notice that this data source has the same name as our data connection and that it is a secondary data source instead of the main one. The data source itself may look strikingly similar to the main data source—that's because InfoPath uses the same logic to create the data source for secondary sources as it does for primary sources. Unlike the main data source, secondary data sources are never permitted to be edited since the structure of the data source is directly correlated with the external data.

Let's insert the `field1` repeating field into the view as a Bulleted List. This can be easily done by right-clicking `field1` in the *Data Source* task pane. The Bulleted List is now bound to the secondary data source. (We'll learn more about secondary data source binding in a moment.) Try previewing the form.

Does nothing show up? That's because we chose not to query the data connection automatically when we worked in the dialog shown in Figure 6.7. Then how do we get our data? We learned in Chapter 5 that we can use the Rules feature on a Button click, among other form and data source events. For now, we can use a Button control to query the data via the data connection. Close the preview window and insert a Button control from the *Controls* task pane. Let's create a rule to query our `Sample` data connection.

1. Go to the *Button Properties* dialog.
2. Click on the *Rules* button.
3. Click the *Add* button to add a rule.
4. In this rule, click the *Add Action* button to add the query action.
5. Select the *Query using a data connection* action. The `Sample` data connection should be automatically chosen since it's the only data connection in the form template.
6. Click *OK* to close all open dialogs.

You could rename the Button control's label by using the *Button Properties* dialog if you want, but we'll leave ours labeled with the default name "Button." Let's preview again. This time, we still don't have any data. But clicking on the Button control will query the data connection and show the data from the Sample.xml file, as seen in Figure 6.10. If you see the *Microsoft Office InfoPath Security Notice* dialog, click the *Yes* button to continue. (A sample called QueryXmlFile is included with the samples for this chapter.)

FIGURE 6.10: Clicking on the Button to query the `Sample` data connection

Data Connections and Security Notices

You may wonder what the *Microsoft Office InfoPath Security Notice* dialog is and why it appeared (if it did) when you clicked the Button control to query the data connection. This dialog is meant to warn users of your form that InfoPath is connecting, on their behalf, to data at a different location than where the form is located. Since we are designing our own forms with our own connections, this warning is simply stating the obvious. We'll learn more about this cross-domain security prompt dialog in Chapter 11.

Let's do a quick demo to show you the power of query data connections. Keep the preview window open as shown in Figure 6.10. (Or you can minimize the preview window instead.) We want to go back and edit the Sample.xml file. Double-click on the Sample.xml file on the desktop to open it for editing, and then remove, say, the last line: "the lazy dog." After removing that text, save the form. Switch back to the form with the data connection as shown in Figure 6.10, then click the button again. Poof, the last item in the bulleted list disappears!

You might have noticed that you cannot insert or remove rows in the secondary data source after clicking the button. We'll investigate why this is the case, along with a series of other observations, in Chapter 7 when we discuss secondary data source binding.

XML or Schema for the Main Data Source

We mentioned that choosing *XML or Schema* for the main data source doesn't lead to creating a data connection. This is because the data in the chosen XML file is used simply to create the form template's main data source. (Optionally, it can also provide the form fields' default values.) Selecting an XML file for the main data source is a one-time operation. Likewise, if a XML Schema is selected, it just defines the structure of the data source.

Databases

One of the most sought-after connection scenarios is to get data from a database. The ubiquity of databases has exploded in the last decade, mostly due to the rapid growth of the Web. Why not leverage the existing data in these storage silos? Say, for example, that the MOI Consulting Corporation's customer service department is still using a console application via a legacy system to connect to the company's database. Why not use an InfoPath form instead? The benefits of using XML-based form technology and the well-known user interfaces of Microsoft Office are just a couple of reasons. Thus a database is a perfect and powerful complement to what InfoPath already offers.

InfoPath supports natively connecting to SQL Server 2000 (and later) as well as Access databases. To talk to a database, InfoPath uses Active Data Objects (ADO), which is a standard protocol for communicating with a database. InfoPath's database adapter uses ADOXML, which is an extension of ADO used to track changes and send update diffgrams to a database. A diffgram is used by ADO to communicate changes (such as inserts, updates, and deletions from the client) and to replay the set of actions (on the server) given some data. We'll look more closely at the database submit connection in Chapter 8.

NOTE Connecting to Databases Other Than SQL Server and Access

You cannot connect directly to Oracle databases or use ODBC or OLE DB connections, for example, but there are viable workarounds to enable such connections. The best option is to use a Web service that can talk to such a database through ADO.NET. However, if you don't (or can't) set up a Web service for this purpose, try creating an Access-linked table to connect to the database table you want to query.

Forms Services

Forms Services uses the `System.Data.OleDb` .NET Framework classes to communicate with databases.

Setting Up a Connection to a Database

When setting up the database connection, you can choose from a variety of ADO connection methods to talk with a SQL Server or Access database. These access mechanisms include DSN-less, ODBC DSN (for Access only), OLE DB, or even a Data Link file (with file extension .udl). InfoPath uses the My Data Sources folder in My Documents, so it's easy to create a new connection with Microsoft Office's built-in data source wizards. In particular, the +Connect to New Data Source and +New SQL Server Connection ODC files, when double-clicked, launch a wizard that helps you create an Office Data Connection file (also called an ODC file) to the database without a need to know details on creating an ADO connection string. The connection string itself can use standard security (where the credentials are stored in the form template) or a trusted security connection. If you set up a connection string with a user name and password, InfoPath will ask if you're sure you want to save that sensitive information with the form template to which others will inevitably have access. Typically, you will not want to bundle the credentials in the form unless, of course, that database user has very limited access. Your best bet for high security is to use a trusted connection. Details on connecting to a SQL Server or Access database are beyond the scope of this book.

> **NOTE** Office Data Connection Files
>
> ODC files contain information on how a computer connects to a data source. This file is not specific to InfoPath but general to Microsoft Office as a whole. Other Microsoft Office applications such as Excel and Access also use ODC files.

> **WARNING** Embedding SQL Server Login Credentials
>
> If you use SQL authentication to connect to your database, InfoPath will warn you that the user name and password are stored in plain text within the form template definition (.xsf) file. We do not recommend embedding credentials. Use a trusted connection whenever possible.

A database data connection is one of the few connections that can be used on the main data source. It can also be used as a secondary connection and, therefore, with a secondary data source. Designing a form (i.e., the main data source) against a database involves the same steps as creating an equivalent secondary data connection version, with the exception of submit. Secondary query data connections do not support submit. However, it's important to realize that a database connection on the main data source always includes both query and submit; they are inseparable, although they seemingly appear as two separate adapters in the *Data Connections* dialog. In this chapter we will focus only on the database query connection. Submitting to a database will be briefly discussed in Chapter 8. As a result, we'll begin with an example using a secondary data connection.

> **NOTE** Secondary Database Connections
>
> Secondary database connections only allow for receiving data. So only the main data connection can submit, but there's a caveat! The main connection cannot be only submit. For a main database connection, query and submit always come together and are inseparable. (There are ways to discourage submit or query functionality on a main database connection, but they're as simple as not visually showing Button controls to allow such actions.)

Since we'll introduce many new InfoPath-specific concepts with this example, and to minimize distractions with a complicated scenario, let's take the classic `Customers` and `Orders` tables in the Northwind database. (If you aren't familiar with the Northwind database, imagine a database for tracking your customers and their orders: a table for customers and another for their orders.) The Northwind database is available on most SQL Server installations, so it's easy for you to follow along if you'd like.

We start by creating a new blank form. Next, let's add the secondary connection by using the *Data Connections* dialog, electing to *Create a new connection to receive data*, and selecting *Database* (refer back to Figure 6.3).

The Data Connection Wizard for a database connection (see Figure 6.11) is quite visually different than the one we used for the XML file connection. From this single dialog, we can perform the following actions to configure this data connection.

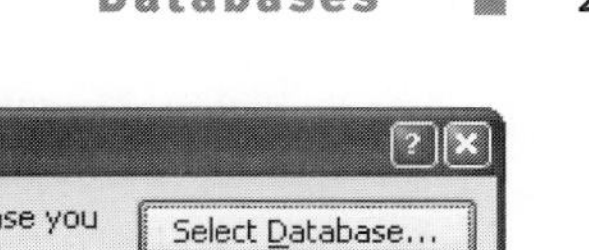

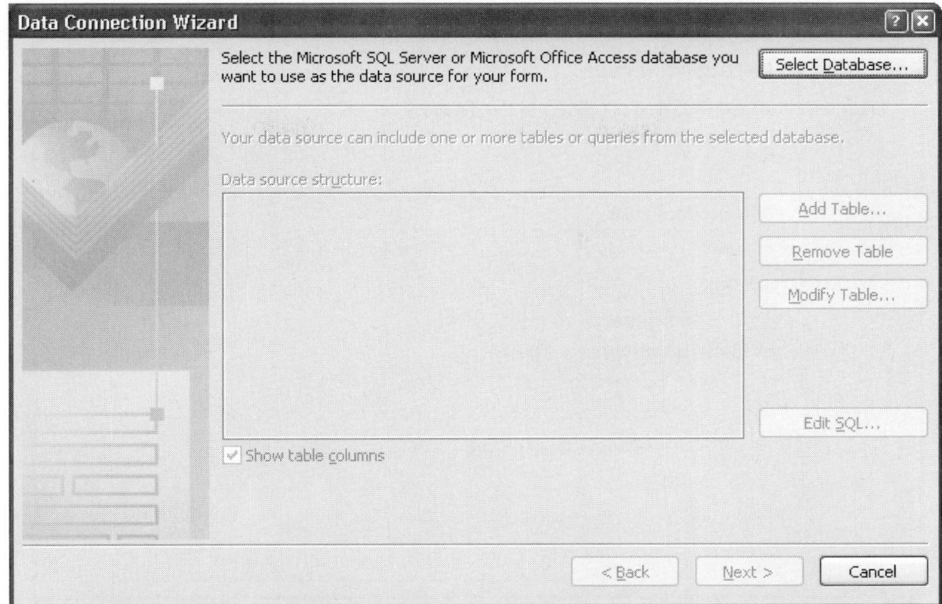

FIGURE 6.11: Data Connection Wizard when creating a new database connection

- Select a database to connect to (and create a connection if one doesn't exist).
- Add, remove, or modify tables used in the query.
- Selectively add or remove columns from tables in the query.
- Define relationships between columns in two or more tables.
- Edit the SQL query used by InfoPath to get the data from the database.

Let's show off these features by first selecting a database. Clicking *Select Database* shows the My Data Sources folder where we can create a new SQL Server connection. The result of creating a new SQL Server connection is an ODC file that InfoPath will use to create the InfoPath data connection to the database. Our computer's name is localhost.com, so that's what we'll connect to, as shown in Figure 6.12. We're using Windows Authentication, which means InfoPath will use the credentials of the user filling out the form to open the database connection when a query occurs. Don't forget to ensure that your users will have access! If you prefer to use a specific SQL user name and password, consider that those credentials will be visible to anyone who has access to your form template.

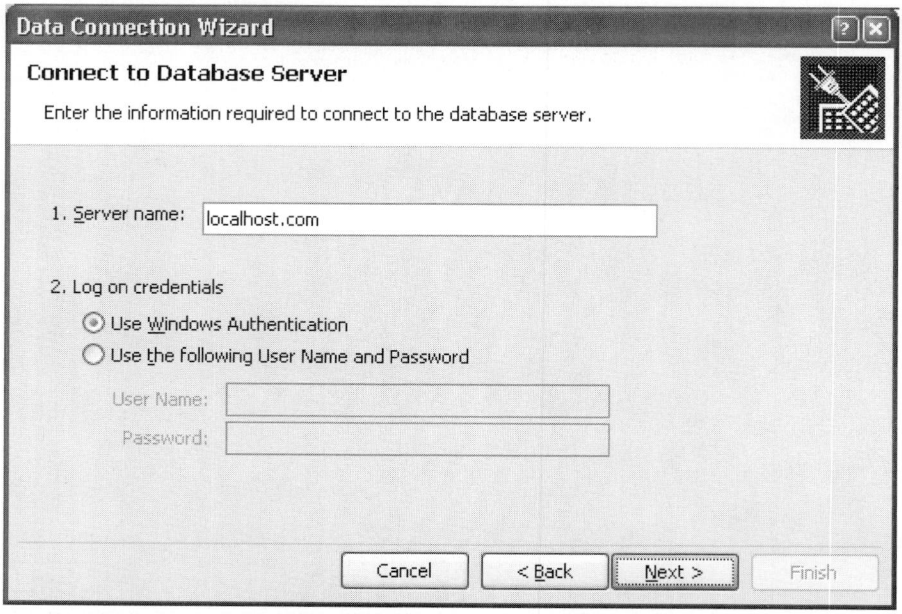

FIGURE 6.12: Connecting to SQL Server after clicking Select Database

WARNING **My Data Sources versus InfoPath Data Connections**

Don't get mixed up between a My Data Sources connection and an InfoPath data connection! *New SQL Server Connection* and *Connect to New Data Source* specifically create new ODC files in your My Data Sources folder in My Documents. InfoPath uses ODC files to define a database data connection from which your form can receive data.

After you configure the connection in the dialog shown in Figure 6.12, move on to the next part of the wizard, which prompts you to pick a database and a specific table or view (Figure 6.13). In our case, we want to pick the Northwind database and use `Customers` as the primary table. If you don't check the *Connect to a specific table* option, InfoPath will prompt you (unless there is a single table or view) to pick a table or view before using the ODC you create. For the purposes of a secondary query data connection where we do not submit, using a view is fine. Using a database view for the

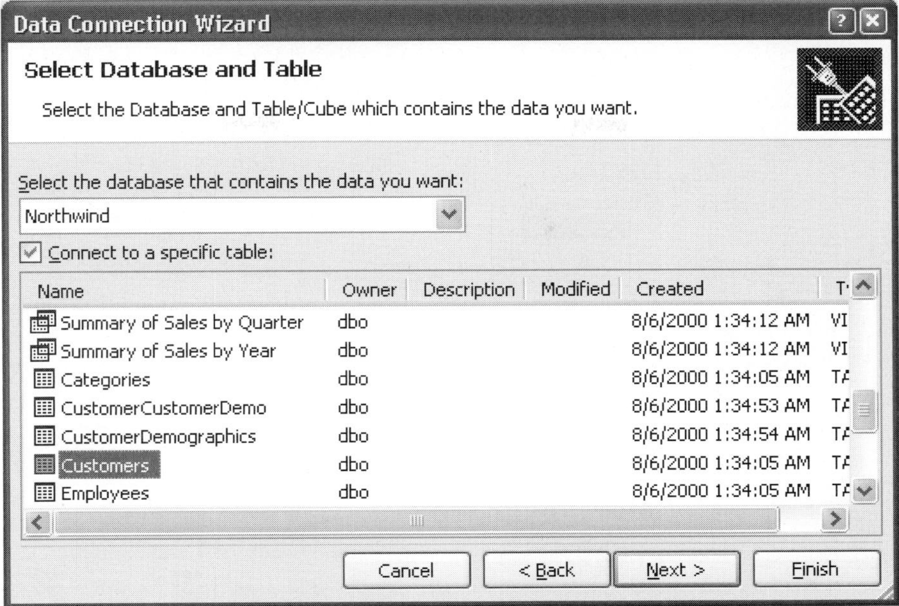

FIGURE 6.13: Select Database and Table dialog. Choose the Northwind database and the `Customers` table. The top two items in the list are database views instead of tables

connection is not preferred if the changes to that data are to be submitted. Clicking *Next* shows the last page of the wizard, which lets you set the ODC file name, a description, a friendly name, and search keywords. Since these are sole properties of the ODC file itself that InfoPath won't ever use, we won't go into details on their functions. For all practical purposes, you can click *Finish* on the *Select Database and Table* dialog in Figure 6.13.

When the Data Connection Wizard is completed, InfoPath shows an abstract representation of the data source in the *Data source structure* section (Figure 6.14).

Before we finish, we want to add the Northwind `Orders` table as a child table to the `Customers` table. This is very simple to do. The first step is to click *Add Table* to open the *Add Table or Query* dialog (Figure 6.15), and select the `Orders` table.

The next step is to define a relationship between the tables. Figure 6.16 shows the dialog for adding relationships. You must have at least one relationship to add a table and associate it to the existing tables in the data

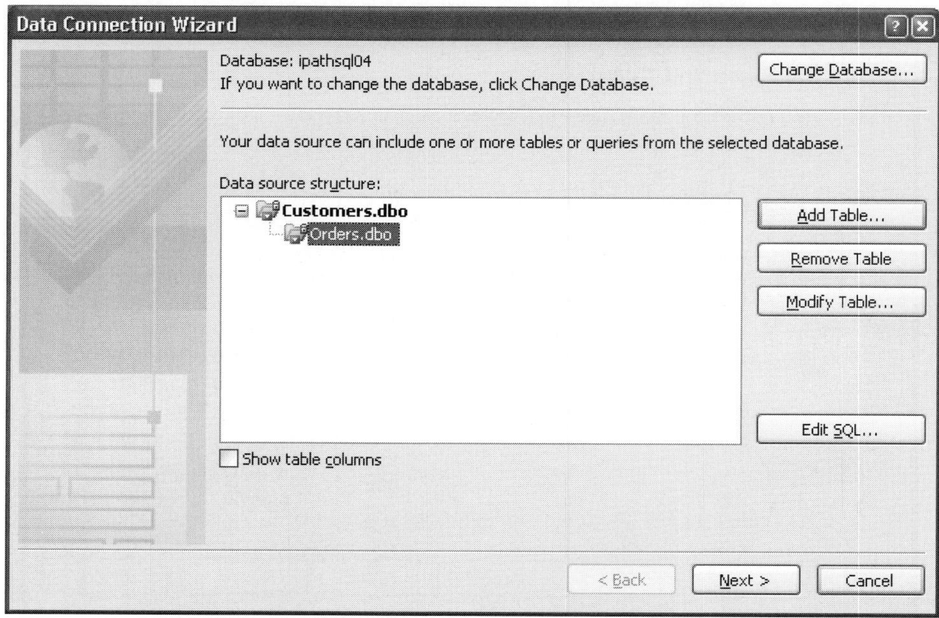

FIGURE 6.14: Database connection's data source structure showing the added `Customers` and `Orders` tables

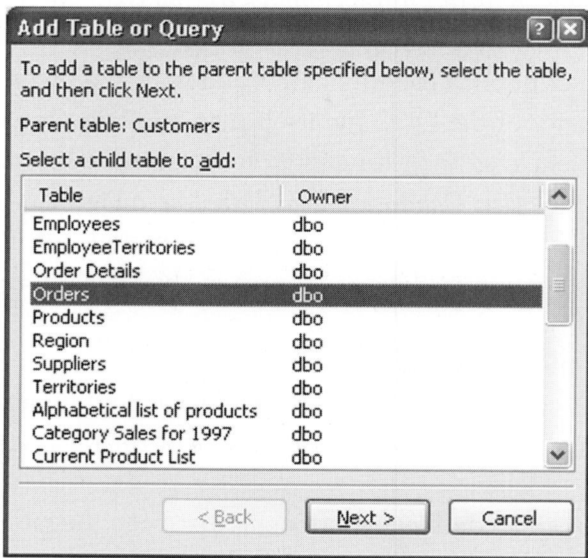

FIGURE 6.15: Adding the `Orders` child table to the `Customers` parent table

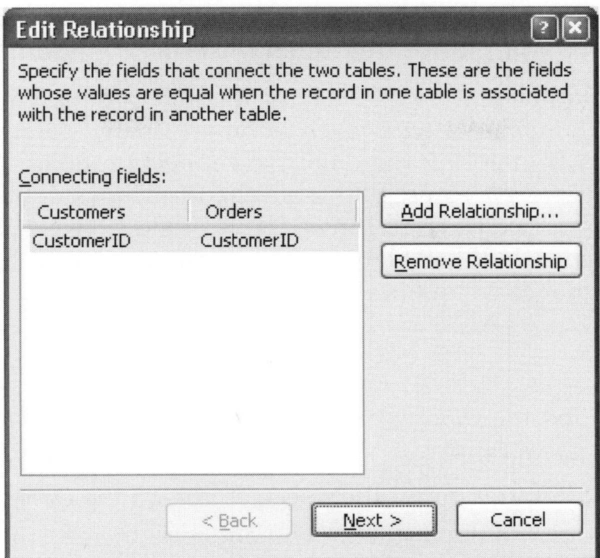

FIGURE 6.16: Defining a relationship between the child and parent tables. Some relationships are automatically defined for you

source. InfoPath tries to be helpful by automatically adding relationships between fields (i.e., table columns) with the same names. (In a moment, we'll see how to manually define and edit relationships.) In this case, the `CustomerID` fields exist in both the `Customers` and `Orders` tables, so that relationship is already defined. You will want to add other relationships as you see necessary to ensure the integrity of data between tables. New relationships are added as the last step before a new table is added. The final result, after adding both the `Customers` and `Orders` tables, is shown with a collapsed structure in Figure 6.14.

Using the *Show table columns* checkbox is similar to expanding the groups in the data source. All fields (i.e., table columns) of the tables are shown under their respective tables. Similar to the *Edit Default Values* dialog discussed in Chapter 3, the checkboxes adjacent to each field let you decide whether or not you want to include the field in this database query connection. Some checkboxes may be checked and disabled. This means the associated field(s) is either a primary key in the database table or is participating in a relationship with another table and must be included in the query.

TIP Form Performance Degrades with Large Amounts of Data

Some table columns may contain a large amount of data. This is especially true with SQL data types such as binary, image, nvarchar, text, and varbinary. If querying the database connection takes a prohibitively long time when you're filling out the form, consider analyzing the data that is queried. Deselecting a "large" field or two (when *Show table columns* is enabled) in Figure 6.14 can make a significant difference in performance when filling out the form.

When we added the `Orders` table, it was simply a matter of clicking *Add Table* and selecting the `Orders` table. If you have two or more tables, adding a table will add it under the selected table in the *Data source structure* section. By default, the last table you added is the one that will have selection. Changing selection is easy: Just click the item in the *Data source structure* section.

We'll leave adding yet another table—`Order Details`, as a child to the `Orders` table—as an exercise.

To further customize the data received by our database connection, the *Modify Table* button plays a pivotal role. This button is the entry point for two different actions: setting sort order and modifying table relationships. To better clarify the *Modify Table* button's behavior, the button text should actually read "Sort Order" when the top-level table is selected and "Edit Relationship" when any other table is selected. Modifying the parent table allows for multiple levels of sorting on returned records when the data connection is queried.

In our example, `Customers` is the top-level table, so selecting it and clicking *Modify Table* shows the dialog in Figure 6.17. Here we can determine potentially three levels of sorting order. At each level you can set the order for a specific field and choose *Ascending* or *Descending*. If you're familiar with SQL queries, note that this sorting is accomplished by using the `ORDER BY` clause followed by `DESC` or `ASC`. In our sample, we'll first sort by `ContactName` *(Ascending)* and then by `City` *(Descending)*.

Our next topic is to dive into the SQL statement itself to see how InfoPath generates the query text and uses it to create the secondary data source. Unfortunately, this sorting capability is not available through the

FIGURE 6.17: Sort Order dialog for setting three levels of sorting order

InfoPath user interface on child tables since the *Modify Table* button shows the *Edit Relationship* dialog. If you wanted to implement sorting on child tables, you could edit the SQL statement for yourself.

TIP Allowing Multiple Records to Be Displayed in a Form

Checking the box *Allow multiple records from this table to be displayed in the form,* shown in Figure 6.17, modifies the XML Schema created by InfoPath to accept multiple items back from the database table. If you expect only a single item to be returned, you can uncheck this box. It's important to remember that if you do not check the box and multiple items are returned, a structural validation error will occur and the query will be canceled. It's fine if you check the box and only one item is returned, however.

WARNING Can't Finish with Bad Sorting Conditions

The *Finish* button may be disabled in the *Sort Order* dialog if you have a sorting condition that doesn't make sense. For example, it will be disabled if you sort by the same field name more than once.

Let's now look at the *Edit SQL* button shown in Figure 6.14 and what we can do with it. Clicking it shows a plain dialog with a lot of text (Figure 6.18). Any changes you make in this dialog will attempt to be parsed by InfoPath to re-create the data source structure shown in Figure 6.14. If you make this **shape query** invalid through your own edits, you may receive one of these warnings or errors:

- Bad SQL
- Cannot create data source structure
- Column or table names do not adhere to XML naming standards

It's highly recommended that you use the *Test SQL Statement* button in the *Edit SQL* dialog to ensure that your SQL query is valid and that data is properly returned from the database. If you don't validate the SQL statement in this dialog, it will happen anyway when you click the *Next* button shown in Figure 6.14. So if you're making any modifications to the SQL query, we highly recommend that you save time and test it first. If you receive a warning about the column or table names not adhering to XML node name rules, you can ignore it, however, because the invalid characters (such as spaces) will be automatically replaced with underscores by InfoPath to create the data source.

Since our current query is getting all customers and orders from the database, there will be way too much data and will take too long for the data connection to finish. As a result, let's modify our query to give us just the first three customers and all of their orders. Toward the beginning of the SQL statement, replace `{select "CustomerID"` with `{select` **`TOP 3`** `"CustomerID"`. (The **bold** text is what you're adding to the query.) When you click *OK* to the *Edit SQL* dialog, you will receive a warning that the SQL statement cannot be represented as a tree view. This is simply a warning and will not affect the outcome of our data connection. As you can see, sometimes warnings are okay to ignore, assuming you test your form and ensure that your modification works as expected. In a moment when we open the form in preview, only three customers (and many more orders) will appear instead of almost one hundred customers (and who knows how many orders)!

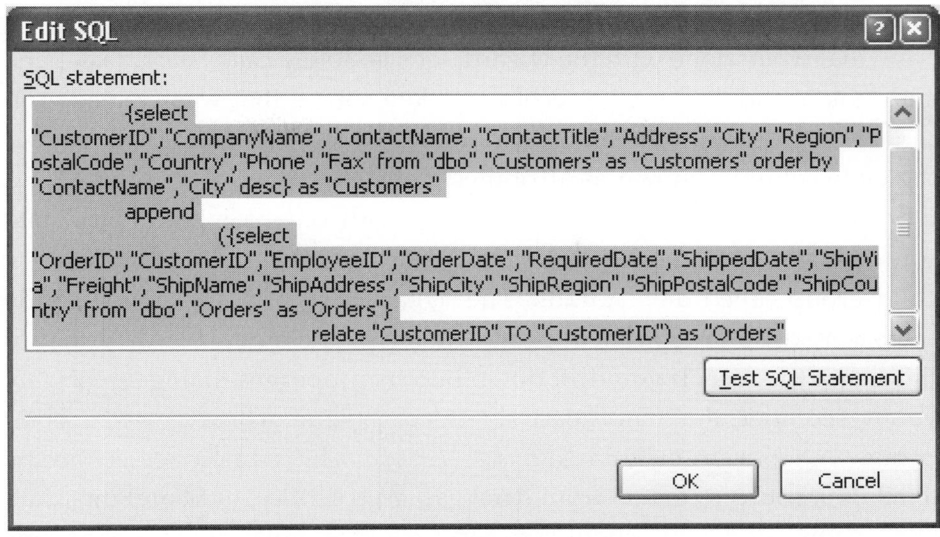

FIGURE 6.18: Edit SQL dialog, which allows hand-editing of the query statement used by InfoPath to create the data source

To find out more information about the ADO `Shape` command, its syntax, and usage, please see the "How to Use the ADO SHAPE Command" Microsoft Knowledge base article Q189657 (http://support.microsoft.com/kb/q189657).

After your database connection is set up as you'd like and you are ready to finish, click on the *Next* button shown in Figure 6.14. In the next step of the Data Connection Wizard, do not select the option *Store a copy of the data in the form template.* This option enables offline query support, which we'll talk about in Chapter 7.

The last page of the wizard is similar to that of the XML file data connection shown in Figure 6.7, except that the default name of the connection is usually the name of the primary table. In our case, since the SQL Query could not be successfully parsed by InfoPath, the name defaults to `Secondary Data Source`. Let's change it to `Customers`. The fact that the query could not be parsed is not a problem as it affects only InfoPath's attempt to guess at a default connection name. This time, let's leave the *Automatically retrieve data when form is opened* checkbox checked (which is the default setting).

Integrating the Database Connection into the Form Template

Now that we're done with the wizard, let's go to the *Data Source* task pane and look at the `Customers` secondary data source that was created. You can see in Figure 6.19 that tables are represented as repeating groups and the table columns shown as attributes. Let's look at the data source for a moment and point out the peculiarities with database secondary data sources. First, you'll notice the document element is `myFields` and has one child group called `dataFields`. The `myFields` group appears to be the same `myFields` group that appears when creating a new blank form, but this is not the case. If you drill down into its properties dialog *Details* tab, you'll see that the namespace is `http://schemas.microsoft.com/office/infopath/2003/dataFormSolution`. This namespace is specific to all data sources created from database, Web service, or SharePoint data connections. (We'll talk about Web service and SharePoint list connections later in this chapter.) As you might remember from Chapter 3, the namespace prefix (when an alias, or short name, followed by a colon exists in the field or group name) is not shown when the field or group in question is in

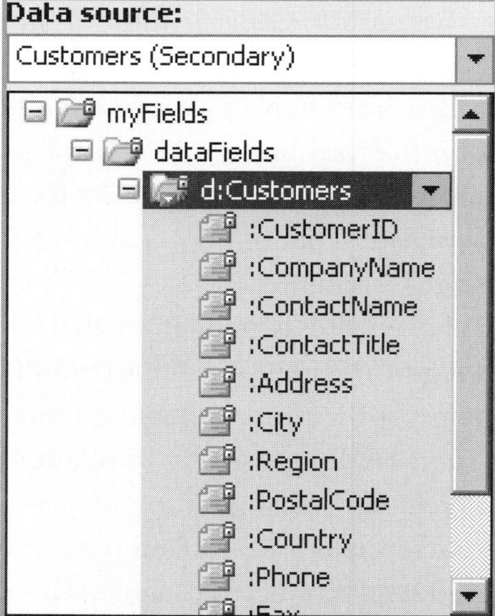

FIGURE 6.19: `Customers` **secondary data source**

the same namespace as its parent. That means `myFields` and `dataFields` are in the same namespace.

The tables themselves, represented as repeating groups, are in a different namespace altogether. To find out what namespace the `d` alias represents, you can again peek at the *Details* tab in the `d:Customers` group properties dialog. The namespace is `http://schemas.microsoft.com/office/infopath/2003/ado/dataFields`. The "ado" string in the namespace references the database data connection, which is internally known to InfoPath as the `ADOAdapter` in the solution definition (.xsf) file. This name is also used programmatically when we write custom code using the InfoPath object model.

Last are the table columns themselves, which are shown as attributes in the data source. Database data sources, by design, always represent columns as attributes. The data types associated with attributes nicely map to database data types. For example, XHTML (or rich text) can never be a data type in a database. Likewise, attributes don't support rich text. But you're probably wondering why each of the attribute fields in the data source is prefaced with a colon, yet no alias exists before the colon. Since the colon is shown on the attribute fields, it means their namespaces are different than the repeating groups (tables) in which they're contained. So what's the new namespace? None. That's right: Data source fields and groups may belong to the "no namespace" crowd. This is a feature of XML namespaces. The fact that there is no namespace does not affect any functionality whatsoever. Think of no namespace as just any other namespace! Moreover, since this secondary data connection will never submit, there is no concern about whether or not a server will accept this data in a particular namespace. (You will learn in Chapter 8 that submitted data must adhere to the restrictions of the endpoint, which includes the namespace of the data.)

NOTE SQL Server 2005 XML Data Type

InfoPath is not compatible with database table columns that have an XML data type. To interact with an XML column, consider connecting to the database by using ADO.NET through a Web service. See Chapter 7 for a full discussion of using ADO.NET and Web services with InfoPath.

As we did with the XML file data connection example, let's insert controls to create the view. We'll insert the top-level table, `d:Customers`, as a Repeating Section with Controls. We would have inserted it as a Repeating Table, but it's difficult to get the nested `Orders` table to display properly since you'd need to pick a specific column in `Customers` for the `Orders` table. You can easily see this problem in Figure 6.20, where we inserted `d:Customers` as a Repeating Table. (This sample file is called CustomersOrders.)

FIGURE 6.20: A nested database table (`Orders`), which is hard to represent when the parent table (`Customers`) is in the view as a Repeating Table

We'll change the `Orders` Repeating Section (which is inserted by default with the `d:Customers` Repeating Section) to a Repeating Table control, which is a good choice for database connections since the external data source is naturally tabular. Using a Repeating Table for the `d:Customers` table results in a nested `Orders` Repeating Table in the last column of the `d:Customers` table. This layout is not optimal for most uses, so we've modified the layout a bit for this example, as shown in Figure 6.21. (This sample file is called CustomersOrders2.)

Customer (ID)

Company Name:	Contact Name:
Contact Title:	Address:
City:	Region:
Postal Code:	Country:
Phone:	Fax:

Order ID	Customer ID	Employee ID	Order Date	Required Date	Shipped Date	Ship Via	Freight	Ship Name	Ship Address	Ship City	Ship Region	Ship Postal Code	Ship Country

Repeating Table

Repeating Section

FIGURE 6.21: Our rendition of displaying the `Customers` and `Orders` data

> **TIP Master/Detail Control**
>
> The Master/Detail control is designed for scenarios where a one-to-many relationship is defined, such as with our `Customers` and `Orders` tables. We leave it as an exercise for you to try using a Master/Detail control instead of nesting repeating controls.

Next step is to preview the form. Since the data connection we created is set to retrieve data when the form is opened, we should immediately see the `Customers` and `Orders` data. If you receive a *Microsoft Office InfoPath Security Notice* dialog, answer *Yes* to the prompt. We'll discuss this dialog in Chapter 8. Figure 6.22 shows the result.

If any data in the `Customers` or `Orders` tables were to change, we would need to close and reopen the form to retrieve them. The data connection is queried only when the form is loaded, so the data in the secondary data source is static for the duration of the form session. If we wanted the ability to requery the database for the latest data without reopening the form, we could add a Button control that uses a rule to perform the query.

Microsoft Office InfoPath

Close Preview

File Edit View Insert Format Tools Table Help

Type a question for help

Customer (ID ALFKI)

Company Name: Alfreds Futterkiste
Contact Title: Sales Representati
City: Berlin
Postal Code: 12209
Phone: 030-0074321

Contact Name: Maria Anders
Address: Obere Str. 57
Region:
Country: Germany
Fax: 030-0076545

Order ID	Customer ID	Employee ID	Order Date	Required Date	Shipped Date	Ship Via	Freight	Ship Name	Ship Address	Ship City	Ship Region	Ship Postal Code	Ship Country
10,64	ALFKI	6	8/2	9/22/1	9/2/1	1	29.46	Alfred	Obere S	Berlir		12209	Germany
10,69	ALFKI	4	10/	10/31/	10/13	2	61.02	Alfred	Obere S	Berlir		12209	Germany
10,70	ALFKI	4	10/	11/24/	10/21	1	23.94	Alfred	Obere S	Berlir		12209	Germany
10,83	ALFKI	1	1/1	2/12/1	1/21/	3	69.53	Alfred	Obere S	Berlir		12209	Germany
10,95	ALFKI	1	3/1	4/27/1	3/24/	1	40.42	Alfred	Obere S	Berlir		12209	Germany
11,01	ALFKI	3	4/9	5/7/19	4/13/	1	1.21	Alfred	Obere S	Berlir		12209	Germany

Customer (ID ANATR)

Company Name: Ana Trujillo Empare
Contact Title: Owner
City: México D.F.
Postal Code: 05021
Phone: (5) 555-4729

Contact Name: Ana Trujillo
Address: Avda. de la Constit
Region:
Country: Mexico
Fax: (5) 555-3745

Order ID	Customer ID	Employee ID	Order Date	Required Date	Shipped Date	Ship Via	Freight	Ship Name	Ship Address	Ship City	Ship Region	Ship Postal Code	Ship Country

Opening form...

FIGURE 6.22: Preview of the modified form layout with Northwind customers and orders data

> **TIP Sorting and Filtering Data**
>
> InfoPath does not allow for sorting the data while filling out the form. If you want to add sorting in the server layer, it should be added to the SQL statement while setting up the data connection. Otherwise, you can write custom form code to sort the data—we'll visit the topic of form code (and show a sorting example) in Chapter 15. Filtering, on the other hand, can be set up while designing the form template. Chapter 7 looks at how to filter list data, which can also be done for Repeating Tables and Repeating Sections.

Web Services

What Is a Web Service?

A Web service is one of the richest external data sources to which InfoPath can connect. If you have little experience with Web services, the next few sections should be a quick review. Otherwise, you can skip reading until after we create a simple Web service in Visual Studio 2005.

When we talk about a Web service, we are specifically referring to a software component that runs on a Web server. The component is defined by the Web Service Definition Language (WSDL), which is a W3C published protocol. (Details on the protocol are beyond the scope of this book. MSDN is recommended as an in-depth reference on Web services specifications; see the reference listed in the Appendix.)

To use a Web service data connection in InfoPath, the form uses the URL of the Web service in which you want to connect. For example, Microsoft TerraServer has a Web service at http://terraserver.microsoft.com/TerraService2. asmx. As you can see, the URL of the Web service endpoint appears somewhat similar to other Web pages you may visit in a Web browser. The distinguishing factor in the URL for this Web service is the ".asmx" file extension. The ASMX file is the actual Web service endpoint. This is the URL InfoPath uses for query and submit operations against the endpoint.

To create a Web service data connection while designing a form, InfoPath requires the WSDL URL. This is because a WSDL exposes the underlying Web service's public interfaces, including methods, input parameters, and output types. Typically you can simply append "?wsdl" to the endpoint URL to get the WSDL. For the TerraServer Web service, visiting http://terraserver.microsoft.com/TerraService2.asmx?wsdl yields its WSDL. A WSDL, despite being XML, is really not meant for human consumption unless you are familiar with its intricacies. Due to its complexity, there are tools available on the Web to help you easily decipher WSDL content. As you will see in our upcoming example, InfoPath helps you to easily understand what methods (and even each of their parameters, if any) are available from a given Web service WSDL. However, InfoPath is not very good at revealing the output types until you finish creating the data connection.

Creating a Simple Web Service Using Visual Studio 2005

To follow along with the text and create a Web service in Visual Studio 2005, your computer must meet the following prerequisites:

- Visual C# 2005
- Visual Web Developer 2005
- Internet Information Services (IIS) 6.0 or later with ASP.NET enabled (that comes with .NET Framework 2.0)
- FrontPage 2002 Server Extensions (installable through the *Add/Remove Windows Components* button)

We'll start with creating a new Web site in the Visual Studio Start page. This is the default page that appears when Visual Studio 2005 is opened. (Note that this is configurable, so your results may vary.) Click on the *Web site* link adjacent to the *Create* label, which is located in the *Recent Projects* (upper-left) region.

The *New Web Site* dialog appears with a list of templates (Figure 6.23). We want to choose the *ASP.NET Web Service* template. For this example,

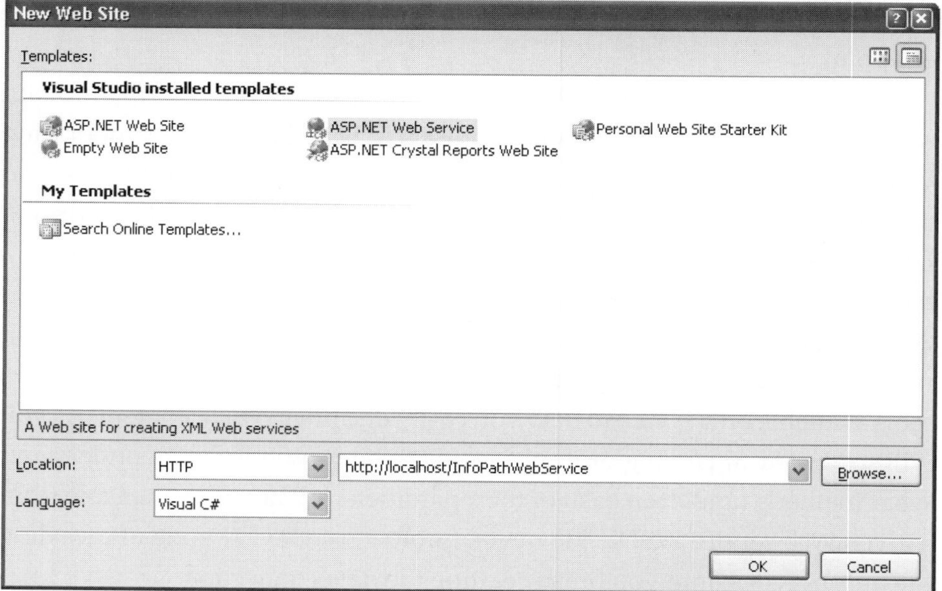

FIGURE 6.23: New Web Site dialog with a template for an ASP.NET Web service

we're assuming that the Web server is on the same machine as Visual Studio; thus, we'll create our Web service via HTTP directly to http://localhost/InfoPathWebService. This address is not the address of the Web service, however. It is simply the Web site that will be created for the Web service. This will become clear when we eventually use the Web service. After you click the *OK* button, it will take a few moments to create the site. If a prompt appears about ASP.NET not being installed, Visual Studio will offer to install it for you.

Once the site is created, Visual Studio opens the Service.cs file, which shows the code that defines the Web service. A single method called `HelloWorld` already exists, courtesy of the ASP.NET Web service template we selected. Feel free to experiment with `HelloWorld` before continuing with the next step.

Let's add our own Web service method. We will eventually design a form against this Web service to see how it works in InfoPath. Below the `HelloWorld` method, we'll want to add our own code. The C# code snippet in Listing 6.1 includes the `HelloWorld` method to show the relative placement of the new methods.

The code in Listing 6.1 adds a class-wide private variable and three public methods below `HelloWorld: FilePath, GetSavedItems, SaveItem`, and `SaveItems`, respectively. Collectively, this new code enables the Web service to get and set data for a specific file on the server. Since a Web service is intrinsically stateless, meaning that it does not remember the data you sent after it finishes executing, this code creates a very rudimentary storage system. Table 6.2 contains a summary of each method and what it does.

> **WARNING** Sample Code Is Not Production-Ready
>
> The code we added in this Web service is potentially dangerous from a security standpoint and should never be used in production. In production code, we would want to restrict access to the Web service through IIS, check all input parameters, and limit the file size and amount of data that can be sent to our `Save` methods. Our code serves only as an example to help you understand Web services and how InfoPath works with them.

LISTING 6.1: Writing Code for the Web Service Sample

```
[WebMethod]
public string HelloWorld()
{
    return "Hello World";
}
private string FilePath = System.IO.Path.Combine(
    Environment.GetEnvironmentVariable("TEMP"),
    "SavedItems.txt");
[WebMethod]
public string[] GetSavedItems()
{
    using (System.IO.StreamReader reader =
       new System.IO.StreamReader(FilePath))
    {
       string fileData = reader.ReadToEnd();
       return fileData.Split('\n');
    }
}
[WebMethod]
public void SaveItem(string item)
{
    SaveItems(new string[] { item });
}
[WebMethod]
public void SaveItems(string[] items)
{
    using (System.IO.StreamWriter writer =
       new System.IO.StreamWriter(FilePath))
    {
        foreach (string item in items)
        {
            writer.WriteLine(item);
        }
    }
}
```

You might be wondering how this code creates, or shapes, the Web service. Each public method with the `[WebMethod]` attribute above the definition is directly exposed via the Web service. The `GetSavedItems` method, for example, is called with no parameters and returns an array of strings. On the other hand, the `SaveItems` method accepts an array of strings but returns nothing. We will not spend more time reviewing the sample Web service code since Table 6.2 dissects and explains its parts. If you are not familiar with C#,

TABLE 6.2: Descriptions of the Web Service Methods Used in Listing 6.1

Item	Description	Purpose
`FilePath`	Private class-wide variable. Not available directly from the Web service.	A string variable that has the full file path to SavedItems.txt in the Windows temporary folder.
`GetSavedItems`	Public method exposed in the Web service.	Gets all of the data in SavedItems.txt. Each line is put in its own string by splitting the data by line breaks (new lines) in the file.
`SaveItem`	Public method exposed in the Web service.	Calls `SaveItems`. This method exists so we can test our Web service in the browser.
`SaveItems`	Public method exposed in the Web service.	Creates and overwrites the SavedItems.txt file. Each string parameter is written as a line in the file. We overwrite the file because, as you will see, InfoPath submits all of the data each time. If we appended content to the file, the data would be duplicated on each submit.

you can also create a Web service in other programming languages as supported by the .NET Framework and ASP.NET. The implementation details of a Web service do not matter to a client application (such as InfoPath).

TIP Debugging Your Web Service Project in Visual Studio

Visual Studio may warn you that debugging is not enabled. Visual Studio will fix the problem for you by choosing the *Add a new Web.config file with debugging enabled* option. You might also encounter an issue where debugging is unable to start. To fix it, you must enable Integrated Windows Authentication in Internet Information Services. Documentation on "IIS Authentication" is available on MSDN (as referenced in the Appendix).

To better understand how a Web service method is made available to a client such as InfoPath, let's see what the WSDL looks like. Recall that a WSDL is generated to describe a specific Web service definition. Before getting the WSDL, we'll first select the *Start Debugging* option on the *Debug* menu in Visual Studio. This option starts the default browser and navigates to the Web service default page (Figure 6.24). This page is auto-generated by ASP.NET for Web browsers. A true Web service client like InfoPath does not use this page. To get the WSDL, which is simply an XML file, click the *Service Description* link in the upper-right part of the page. Notice that "?WSDL" (which is not case-sensitive) is appended to the existing "Service .asmx" page URL.

Service
The following operations are supported. For a formal definition, please review the Service Description.
GetSavedItems
HelloWorld
SaveItem
SaveItems

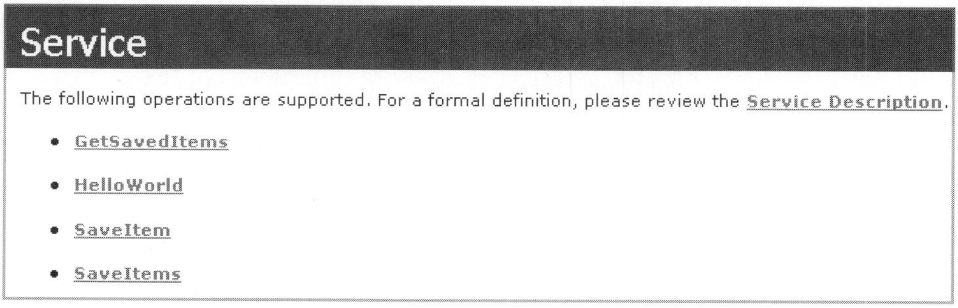

FIGURE 6.24: Part of the browser-friendly test page when navigating to the Web service

The WSDL is quite a large and incomprehensible XML document. If you use your browser's *Find* functionality to look for all instances of, say, `HelloWorld`, you will find almost a dozen occurrences. The most interesting parts are within the `wsdl:types` node, one part of which is shown below. These parts are schema fragments that define the input parameters and output types for the `HelloWorld` Web service method. A client such as InfoPath uses this information to construct the data source when a data connection is created for a Web service. In this case, the `HelloWorld` element is the input parameter; `HelloWorldResponse` is the output. An empty `complexType` element defines a parameterless method, while the response contains an optional string node called `HelloWorldResult`. So the `HelloWorld` method takes no parameters and returns a string, as shown in Listing 6.2.

Listing 6.2: The HelloWorld Definition in the Web Service WSDL

```
<s:element name="HelloWorld">
  <s:complexType />
</s:element>
<s:element name="HelloWorldResponse">
  <s:complexType>
       <s:sequence>
          <s:element minOccurs="0" maxOccurs="1"
                    name="HelloWorldResult" type="s:string" />
       </s:sequence>
  </s:complexType>
</s:element>
```

> **TIP Who Uses a WSDL, Anyway?**
>
> A WSDL is not meant for human consumption, but rather is used as an interface definition for computer programs that intend to connect to the Web service.

Using the Simple Web Service

Now's the time to use the Web service we created! Let's go back to the Web service default page shown in Figure 6.24 and click on the `SaveItems` method. A page appears that lets you test the method and also shows the choices you have for invoking it outside of the browser. Unfortunately, you'll notice that the `SaveItems` method does not allow for testing because "The test form is only available for methods with primitive types as parameters." Since this method has a string array (which is not a primitive type) for a parameter, we are restricted from using it in this browser test form. Now you understand why we have a `SaveItem` method that uses a primitive type! Try using that method instead by going back and clicking on the `SaveItem` link. The test form is now available with an input field into which you can enter a parameter value, as shown in Figure 6.25. Type in any data such as "banana" and click the *Invoke* button. The blank page that appears is the method response. A blank page is expected since `SaveItem` has no response; thus you see the empty page, which you can now close.

It's just natural that we now use the `GetSavedItems` method to see if our data was stored properly. Since the method takes no parameters, a click

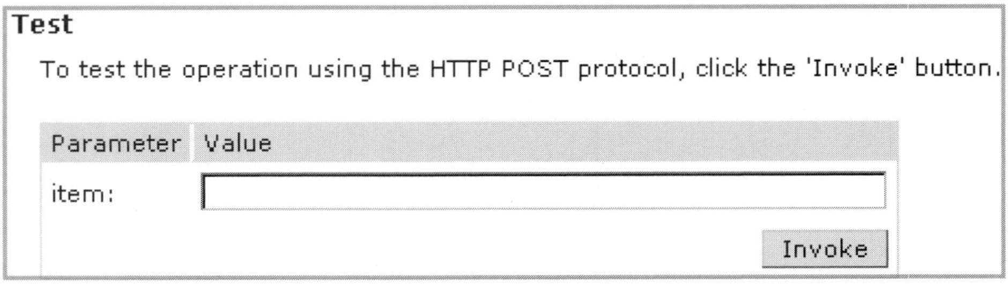

Test

To test the operation using the HTTP POST protocol, click the 'Invoke' button.

Parameter	Value
item:	

Invoke

FIGURE 6.25: Browser test form for the `SaveItem` Web service method

on the *Invoke* button returns the XML data shown in Listing 6.3. This response is exactly the data that a client application like InfoPath would receive when querying this Web service endpoint.

LISTING 6.3: Web Service Response from Running GetSavedItems

```
<?xml version="1.0" encoding="utf-8" ?>
<ArrayOfString
   xmlns:xsi=http://www.w3.org/2001/XMLSchema-instance
   xmlns:xsd=http://www.w3.org/2001/XMLSchema
   xmlns="http://tempuri.org/">
   <string>banana</string>
   <string />
</ArrayOfString>
```

TIP The Web Service Test Page

The test page is meant to be used by the Web service developer on the server itself for debugging and rudimentary testing. If the same page is accessed from a different computer, it shows the message "The test form is only available for requests from the local machine."

InfoPath Web Services

The next step is to use InfoPath with our Web service sample. But unlike the browser test form shown in Figure 6.24, a true Web service client like InfoPath can reside on any computer (including the same computer) with access to the Web server. Let's jump into InfoPath; however, this time we'll create a main data connection to our Web service. Creating a main data connection uses the same Data Connection Wizard as secondary connections, so it's a very similar process.

Instead of designing a new blank form, we'll choose to design a form from a Web service. Next, we are asked whether we want to receive data, submit data, or both. Since our Web service has save methods as well as get methods, we'll want to do both so we can submit to those methods that save data and receive from `GetSavedItems`. Since we're choosing to receive and submit data, we're really setting up two separate connections: Web service query and Web service submit data connections. This is one of the only cases when InfoPath sets up two separate connections simultaneously.

On the next page of the Data Connection Wizard we are prompted for the location of the Web service. Remember that this dialog is really asking for the WSDL location (as shown by the example text in Figure 6.26). The location to your WSDL is usually going to start with "http://" and typically includes "?WSDL" appended to the Web service address. But you don't need to add "?WSDL" to the address since InfoPath will do it for you if the first attempt to get the WSDL fails. Please disregard the *Search UDDI* button for now. UDDI is a topic for discussion in Chapter 7.

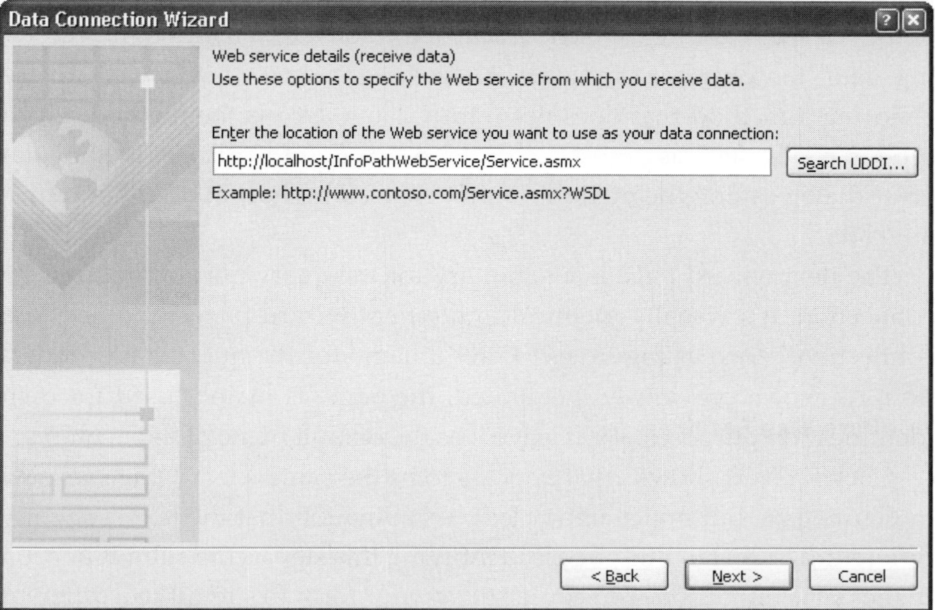

FIGURE 6.26: Entering an address to the WSDL

WSDL Portability

Remember that a WSDL is simply XML and can exist as a file even on your local computer's disk drive. Since WSDL encapsulates the physical Web service address, it is a portable definition and can exist autonomously.

NOTE Displaying the Web Service Method Description

The *Description of operation* section in Figure 6.27 displays the Web service method description from the WSDL. This description comes from the `Description` property of the `WebMethod` attribute in the Web service code. In this case, no description exists in the Web service code.

On the next page (Figure 6.27), we're presented with the list of all methods available from our Web service. You should recognize the method names from the code we wrote earlier using Visual Studio. Since this step of the wizard is asking us to choose an operation (i.e., a method) for receiving data, the obvious candidate is `GetSavedItems`. If you were to try choosing a method that does not return data (`void` is the method return type in code), such as `SaveItem` or `SaveItems`, InfoPath would show an error dialog saying the method cannot be used because it does not return any data.

The next wizard page is a summary for the query portion of our data connection. It's visually identical to the final wizard pages of other data connections, such as Figure 6.7. Enter a name for the query data connection. As we've previously mentioned, the name is mainly used for own identification purposes. We'll leave it as the default name of `Main query`.

Clicking *Next* shows what appears to be the same wizard page we saw in Figure 6.26. But notice upon closer examination that the text is slightly different. The text in this page is identifying this step as the submit portion of the data connection. You could set up your form to submit to a different server than the one from which you receive data. But as you may have

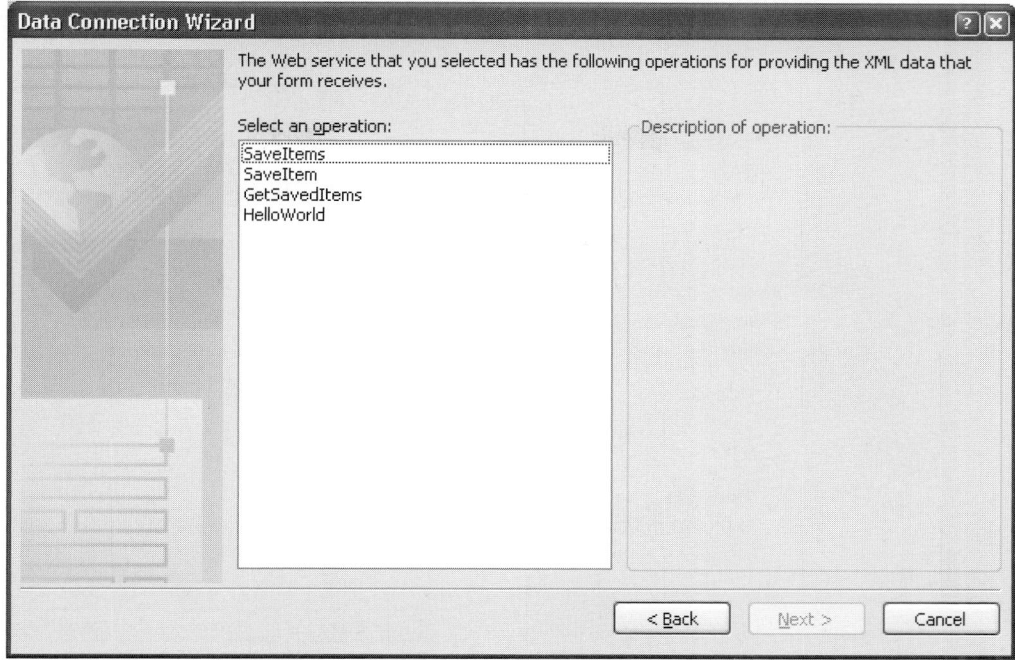

FIGURE 6.27: List of methods from the Web service that can be used to receive data

guessed, the Web service we created has both receive and submit methods. The URL we used in the receive data part of the wizard is conveniently copied for us automatically, so we don't need to do anything on this page but click *Next*. Most Web service data connections use the same server or Web service for receiving and submitting data, but it isn't a requirement and won't affect the behavior of the form or data connections.

Another strikingly familiar dialog appears on the next page. The only difference between this wizard page and that shown in Figure 6.27 is the text: This page is for submit and the previous one was for query. For submitting data, the `SaveItems` method is the clear choice. We do not want to use `SaveItem` because it was created for the sole purpose of using the browser test page. Moreover, we aren't losing any functionality (as you may have inferred from the code implementation of `SaveItem`) since `SaveItems` can still accept a single item.

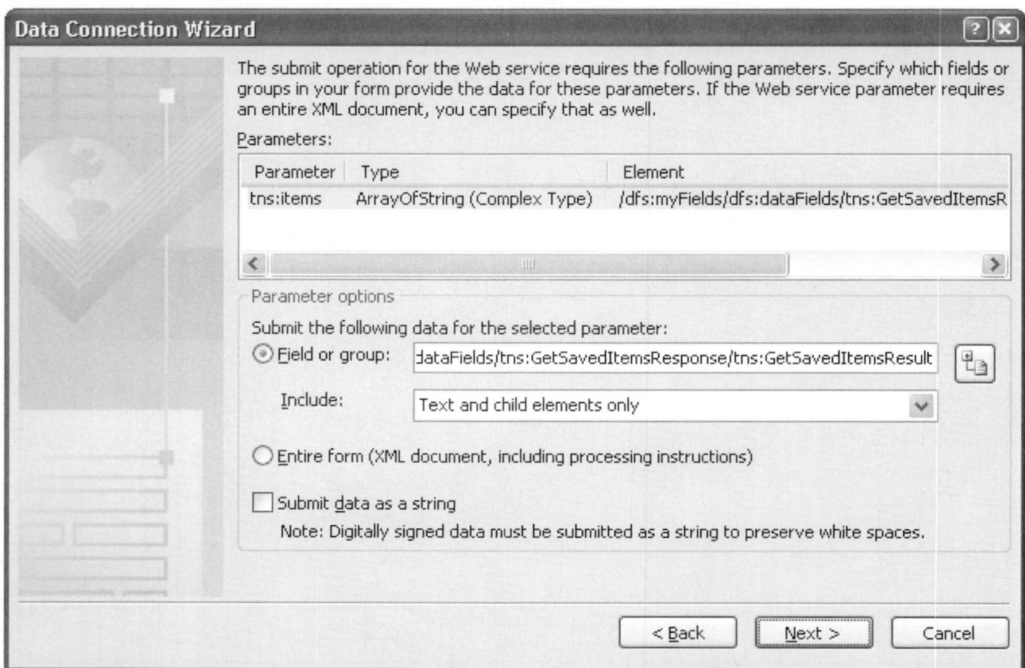

FIGURE 6.28: Setting up the parameter to the `SaveItems` Web service method, which involves selecting which data source node provides its value

The next page, shown in Figure 6.28, is specific to submit and at first may appear quite complicated. There are indeed many options available, but for now we'll use only its basics features to get your feet wet. This page is telling us that the `SaveItems` method has one parameter called `items`, which is of the type `ArrayOfString`.

For submit to work properly, we need to select the data source node that InfoPath will use for the parameter when submit occurs when filling out the form. To select the data source node, click on the button adjacent to the *Field or group* text box. The *Select a Field or Group* dialog appears for selecting a node; see Figure 6.29 for proper node selection. Figure 6.28 shows the resulting dialog after choosing the `GetSavedItemsResult` group. For now we'll just say that the `GetSavedItemsResult` node represents the `ArrayOfString` type that the `SaveItems` method expects. The discussion on mapping submit parameters with data source nodes is presented

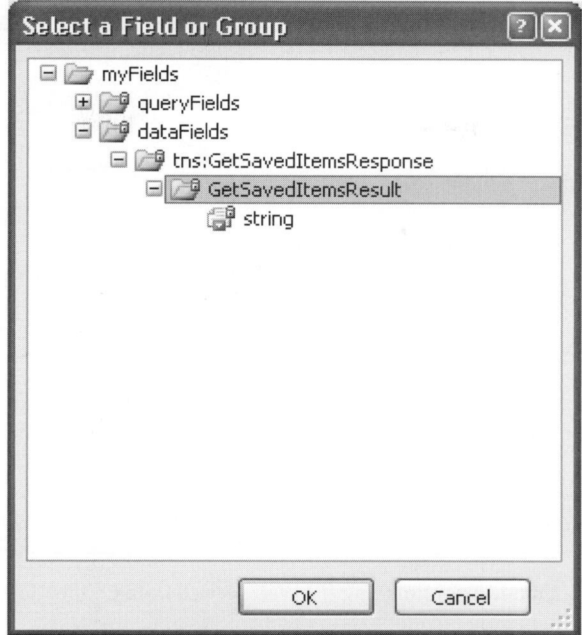

FIGURE 6.29: Choosing the data source node to submit to the `SaveItems` method. The data source is based on the query Web service data connection

in Chapter 8. We're done with this page and the submit connection, so click *Next* to continue to the final page of the wizard.

> **NOTE Submit Functionality**
>
> Chapter 8 further explores various submit scenarios and how to customize submit functionality.

It's no surprise that the final page of the Data Connection Wizard for submit is identical in appearance to the final page for query. Let's leave the data connection name as `Main submit` and click *Finish* to end what may have been the longest wizard session you've ever had! As shown in Figure 6.30, InfoPath design mode appears with some content already in the view to help guide you in creating your form based on your Web service connection. (The sample file is named BasicDataFormTemplate.)

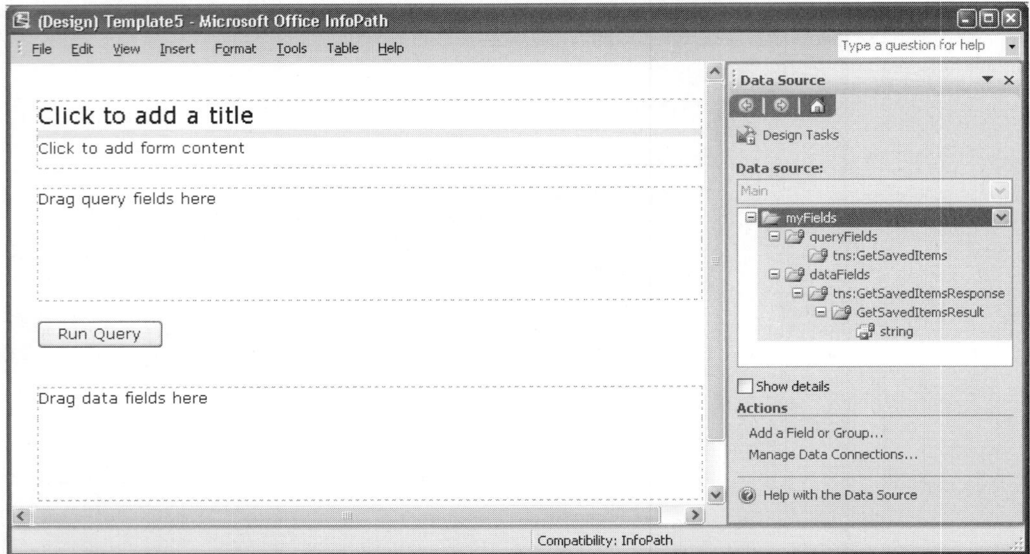

FIGURE 6.30: InfoPath design mode after finishing the Web service Data Connection Wizard

The precanned items in the view shown in Figure 6.30 exist only for your convenience. You may remove or repurpose them without harming your form. The regions labeled *Drag query fields here* and *Drag data fields here* are simply suggestions that you need not follow. For now, we can insert the data source field named `string` into the view as a Bulleted List, although you can use any other compatible control. The control can be inserted anywhere in the view. For this example, we'll insert it in the *Drag query fields here* region (even though the node we're inserting is really under a data field element) so it will visually appear at the top of our form.

The data source shown in Figure 6.30 is fully expanded. Do you recognize the structure of the data source? It came from the Web service query data connection that hooks up to the `GetSavedItems` method. InfoPath created the `myFields`, `queryFields`, and `dataFields` nodes, but the rest came from the WSDL! (If you want to verify this for yourself, open the WSDL again in a Web browser and search for any of the nodes' names in the data source.) Since the `GetSavedItems` method has no parameters, we have no field nodes in the `queryFields` group. It isn't necessary to insert the `GetSavedItems` group since there are no fields that contain data.

NOTE Why Is the Field within `dataFields` Named `string`?

You may wonder why the field returned from the `GetSavedItems` method is called `string`. The straight answer is because `string` is the name of the node in the WSDL. But who assigned this terribly vague name to this node in the WSDL? ASP.NET auto-generates the WSDL based on your Web service code. All it knows is that the return type of the method is a string, but return types don't get a name like parameters do. Thus the design of ASP.NET is such that the field simply gets the name `string`.

We've finished designing a very basic Web service form, so let's take it for a spin by previewing it. (This sample is called WebServiceQuerySubmit.) When the form opens, the first thing you want to do (after dismissing a security dialog, should it appear) is click the *Run Query* button. You should see "banana" in the list, or whatever data you entered into the test form back in Figure 6.25. Let's add two new items to our list—"apple" and "orange"—to round out our grocery list of fruit. But to send these to the `SaveItems` Web service method, we need to invoke submit. To do so, click the *Submit* button in the *Standard* toolbar, as shown in Figure 6.31.

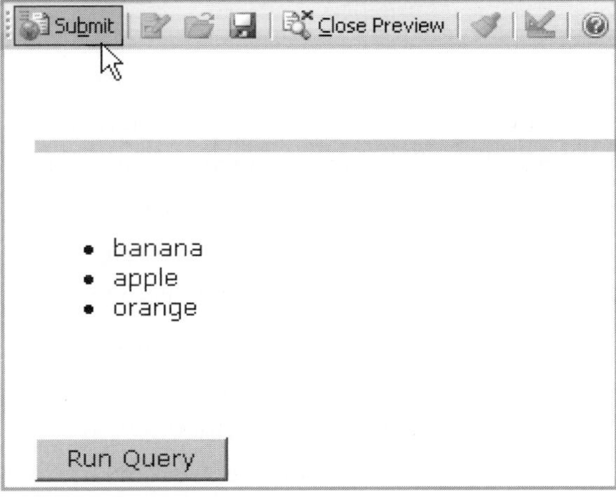

FIGURE 6.31: Querying and submitting our Web service form during preview

Web Service Compatibility with InfoPath

You will find that most Web services work fine during configuration in design mode as well as while users fill out the form. But some will pose problems—especially in design mode. InfoPath's support for Web services is built on top of a slightly modified version (specifically for the Microsoft Office family of products) of the SOAP Toolkit version 3.0. For those curious readers, SOAP historically stood for Simple Object Access Protocol; that acronym has since been deprecated, but the name "SOAP" remains. The Toolkit is a software application programming interface (API) used by Microsoft Office products to implement Web service functionality. Despite the great variety of Web services supported by the Toolkit, not all are supported by InfoPath.

We won't go into the numerous types of Web services, but the two most common ones are document/literal and RPC/encoded. The first part of each type, document or RPC, is called the binding style. The second part is called the use, which is either literal or encoded. Since this book is not about Web services, we will not discuss further details about Web services, SOAP, or WSDL. InfoPath supports only document/literal Web services. Supporting this type of Web service was a big gamble, not only for InfoPath but also for Microsoft as a whole. As of this writing, the number of document/literal services is growing while the number of RPC/encoded services is on a decline. Most Web services providers have agreed to support only the document/literal format in the future since it's a less complicated format and is easier to support from a client perspective.

What if you're stuck with a Web service that InfoPath doesn't support, such as one that is RPC/encoded? We've recommended to customers that they create what's called a proxy Web service that would live in the middle tier between InfoPath (the client) and the unsupported Web service (the server). The basic idea is to create a Web service using a program, such as Visual Studio, that supports RPC/encoded Web services. A Web reference can be made to the unsupported Web service from your proxy Web service, thus establishing data flow from the proxy to the unsupported Web service. The final step is to create a data connection against the proxy Web service using InfoPath. You can find more information on creating a proxy Web service at www.developer.com (as referenced in the Appendix).

If you're having problems getting a Web service working in InfoPath design mode, ask yourself the following questions to help you diagnose the issue.

- Can you see the Web service test page by using your browser?
- If you're trying to create a query data connection, does the method you select return any data?
- If you're trying to create a submit data connection, does the method you select accept input parameters?
- Does the Web service have an invalid inline Schema (in the `wsdl:types` section)?
- Do you have appropriate permissions to access the Web service endpoint?

Using the TerraServer Web Service in InfoPath

Have you used Microsoft's TerraServer Web site? Born as a Microsoft Research project, TerraServer is one of the world's largest map databases containing aerial photographs. It is a free service easily accessed from http://terraserver.microsoft.com. In our opinion, one of the coolest features of the TerraServer project is its Web service. The TerraServer team has a page dedicated to its Web services at http://terraserver.microsoft.com/webservices.aspx, including a white paper and full documentation on the (freely available!) public methods.

Let's use InfoPath to connect to the Microsoft TerraService .NET Web service (as the TerraServer team likes to call it) to get map data. Start by designing a new form template based on a Web service. We want only to receive data for this example. The Web service WSDL address is http://terraserver.microsoft.com/TerraService2.asmx. We'll select the `GetTile` method, which returns a 200-by-200-pixel image as base64Binary, which will bind to InfoPath's image control. After inserting the `dataFields` and `queryFields` group nodes into the form and adding some spice, we get something similar to Figure 6.32. (The sample file is called TerraServer.)

Let's preview this form by clicking the *Preview* button on the toolbar. Without needing to understand the intricacies of the TerraServer Web service, you can simply use the following values in the `queryField` controls and click the *Run Query* button. Accept any security prompts that appear.

FIGURE 6.32: Designing the TerraServer form using the `GetTile` Web service method

Figure 6.33 shows the result. As a little bonus, we recommend switching the Theme value from 2 to 4 and running the query again.

Theme = 2
Scale = Scale16m
Scene = 10
X = 173
Y = 1307

> **NOTE Security Prompt When Using a Data Connection**
>
> InfoPath protects the user by prompting him or her before connecting to an external data source. Since InfoPath actually connects with the current user account, the user must be informed. The external server is listed in the prompt. While the user should probably not allow a connection to http://evilhacker.com, the TerraServer service is safe.

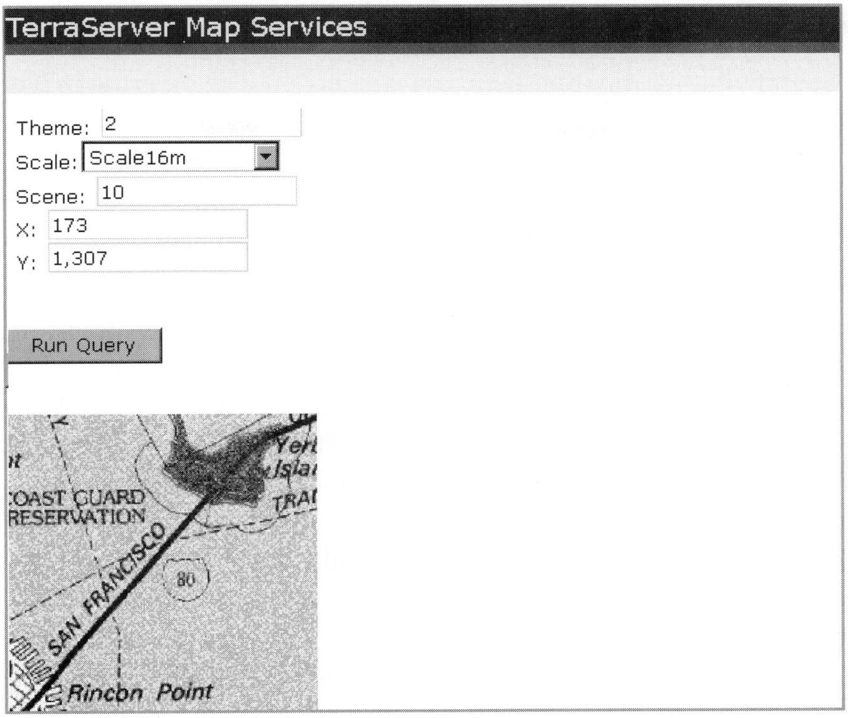

FIGURE 6.33: Querying the TerraServer for a section of the San Francisco Bay near Highway 80

Web Service Repository

Are you looking for a repository of Web services? We recommend looking at the XMethods Web site. (See the reference in the Appendix.) This site has a few hundred Web services with topics ranging from anagrams to radio station finders and even has a Web service that will dial a phone number and verbally articulate the text you send!

Other Web service resources are also available at your disposal. Simply use your favorite engine to search the Web for "Web services" and you're likely to find numerous references.

> **NOTE Using UDDI to Search for Web Services**
>
> In Chapter 7, we look at UDDI and how to use it to search for Web services.

SharePoint Libraries and Lists

The SharePoint libraries and lists data connection leverages the rich array of SharePoint Web services. The connection queries data from any Windows SharePoint Services library or list and, similar to other secondary data connections, puts the results into a secondary data source. You may ask why we wouldn't just use a Web service data connection to talk with SharePoint's Web services. The problem lies in the Web service WSDL. Most of SharePoint's methods return an undefined set of data. In the WSDL, this appears as a required `xsd:any` schema element. InfoPath is not very graceful in handling required `xsd:any` elements because they are wildcards and have no concrete definition. Thanks to the SharePoint data connection, InfoPath is smart enough to infer the data structure from the Web service and disregard the pesky `xsd:any`.

SharePoint connections are supported only as secondary data sources. This is because the list data is always read-only and never takes input parameter. If you wanted to upload an item to a document library (which could essentially add metadata to the list you're querying), you could use the SharePoint document library submit connection. We discuss this connection in Chapter 8.

We have our personal set of photos on a SharePoint picture document library. The SharePoint Web site isn't very helpful for easily tracking which pictures we have and how long each one has been there. In Chapter 3 we designed a form that tracks our music collection. Why not just use the same form to keep abreast of our photo gallery? (If we wanted to get creative, we could try to set up our form to associate pictures we have taken at some of our favorite bands' concerts!) Figure 6.34 shows the `Pictures` library on our SharePoint site.

Creating a SharePoint library or list connection is one of the easiest connections in InfoPath to set up. We're starting by adding a data connection in our music collection form template (which you can find in this chapter's samples as MyMusicAndPhotos); however, you can easily follow our steps while designing any form template. When creating a secondary SharePoint connection to receive data, we select the *SharePoint library or list* option button in the Data Connection Wizard. The next wizard page asks for your SharePoint server's Web site address. After we enter the address and click

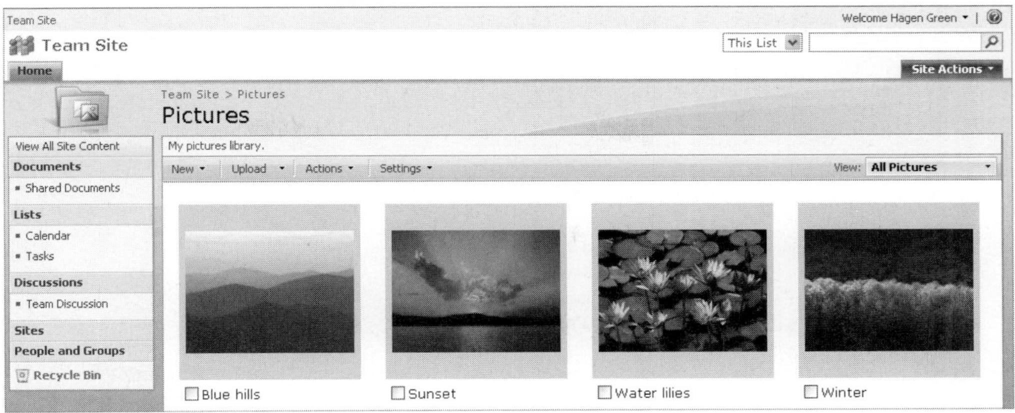

FIGURE 6.34: `Pictures` **library on Windows SharePoint Services**

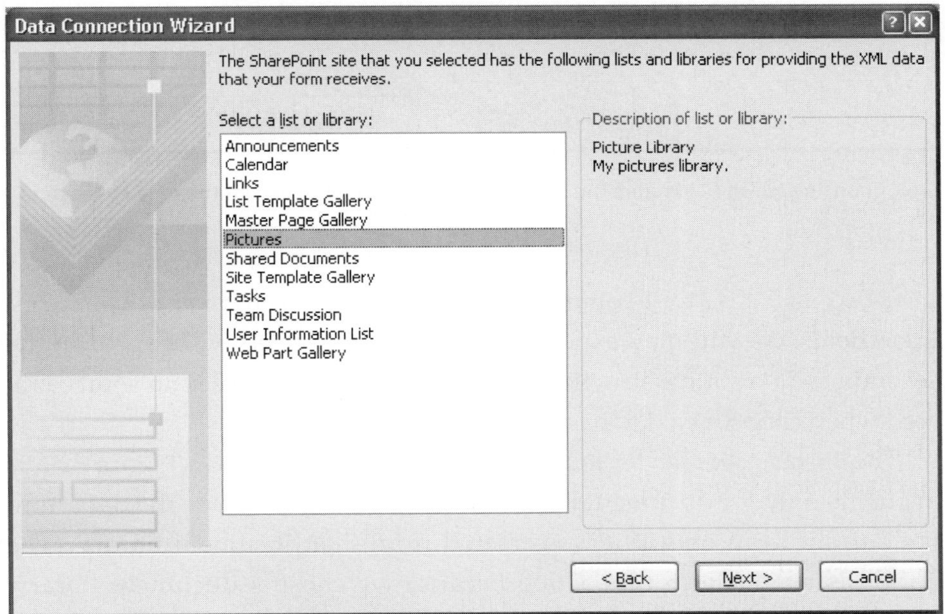

FIGURE 6.35: The libraries and lists available for querying from the SharePoint server

the *Next* button, all of the lists and libraries on the selected SharePoint server are revealed (Figure 6.35).

Let's select the `Pictures` document library, and go to the next wizard page (Figure 6.36). All properties from that library or list are available for your choosing. In the `Pictures` library, we choose the `Created`,

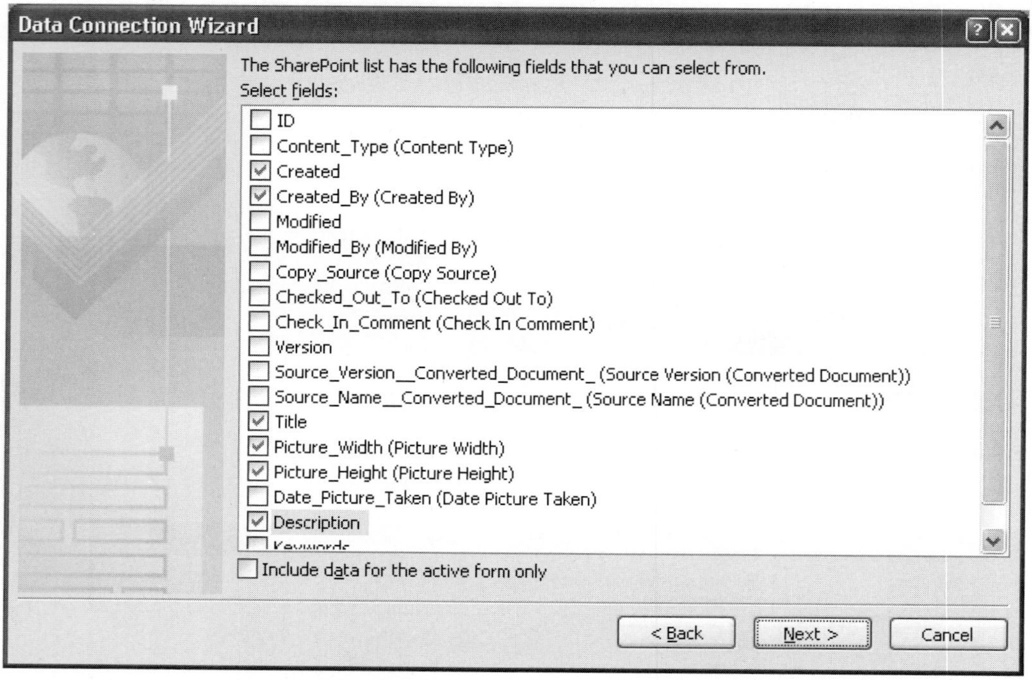

FIGURE 6.36: Choosing which fields from the SharePoint list you want to use for the data connection

Created_By, Title, Picture_Width, Picture_Height, and Description fields. As you may expect, the fields you selected will appear in the secondary data source structure as attributes—similar to a data source created when choosing a database.

The *Include data for the active form only* option shown in Figure 6.36 is available only for document libraries. Its function is to show the data from the current form only if it was created from that document library. (The option is available in this dialog because we chose a document library; however, selecting it doesn't make sense since we cannot create forms in this Pictures library.) It is possible to create a form from a document library when you publish a form template to a SharePoint form library. Publishing to SharePoint is discussed in Chapter 9.

After finishing the wizard, we inserted the repeating Pictures group from the secondary data source into the view. Since we're retrofitting the

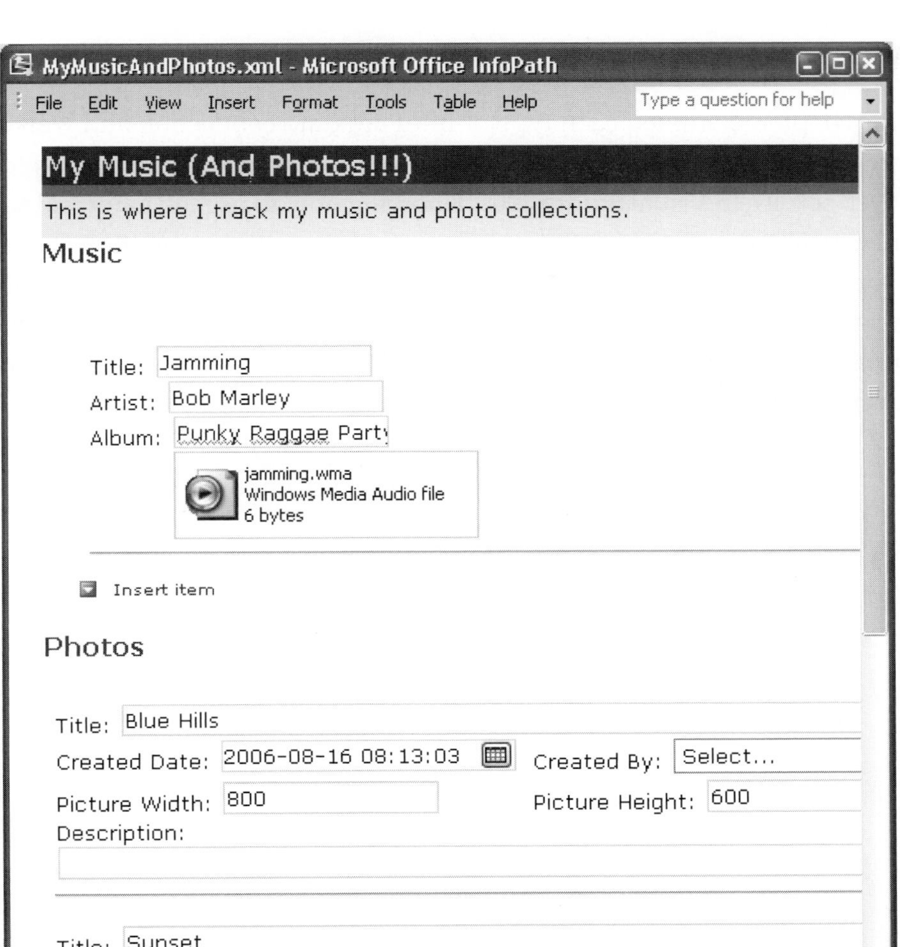

FIGURE 6.37: Filling out the music and photos form. The list of photos comes from the `Pictures` library on SharePoint

music-tracking form template with photo tracking, we can insert the `Photos` Repeating Section under the `Music` Repeating Section that is already in the view. Figure 6.37 shows the result when previewing the form. (This sample form is also called MyMusicAndPhotos.)

What's Next?

This chapter examined each type of InfoPath data connection and walked through examples of usage. We also learned how to set up, create, and test a Web service in Visual Studio 2005. Knowing how to use the main and secondary data sources via data connections, you have the foundation needed to proceed to the next chapter, which delves into extended features involving data connections. You'll learn about extended data connection and secondary data source features that will help you design more useful and functional forms.

7 Extended Features of Data Connections

Getting Started

In the preceding chapter, we talked about getting data from external data sources. There are four types of data connections that retrieve data: XML file, database, Web service, and SharePoint list or library. For each type of connection, we walked through an example and showed how to incorporate the resulting secondary data source into your form template.

Moving forward into this chapter, we'll build on what we already discussed about data connections and step into more advanced features. Starting with Web services, we'll talk about searching and discovering publicly available Web services by using **Universal Description, Discovery, and Integration (UDDI)**. Next, we'll discuss how to use Visual Studio to create methods that query and return data from a database with **ADO.NET**—yet another technology that works with Web services.

We used and learned a little about secondary data sources in the prior chapter, but in this chapter we'll extend our knowledge to reveal some strikingly different aspects compared to the main data source. The differences exist both when designing the form template and when filling out the form. Features such as spell checking and auto-complete differ when used with secondary data sources rather than the main data source. What you'll learn about secondary data sources will empower you, as a form designer, to make better decisions on how to incorporate them into your templates.

We've come to use and even depend on data connections throughout our forms. But what happens when someone is filling out your form offline? If you have several data connections that get data from various sources, they will not be available. Or will they? With **offline mode query support** for data connections, InfoPath remembers the data queried from the external data source. This feature, when enabled, unblocks users so they can continue filling out your forms even without the dependent network connection.

Finally, we'll see how to use secondary data sources to **populate the List Box family of controls**. (We will collectively refer to the Drop-Down List Box, Combo Box, and List Box controls as "List Box controls" in this chapter.) This is a common form design pattern used to get data from an external data source, such as a database, and to offer options in your form. In real-world forms, such a design pattern typically yields a large list of items (e.g., states and provinces). We'll also discuss how to filter the items in a List Box control if you want to narrow the options shown when users fill out the form. A neat use of **filters** is in the cascading Drop-Down scenario: A user selects a specific category, which filters another List Box to include only the items belonging to that category.

Extended Features of Web Services

In the last several chapters, we've learned about Web service connections and how InfoPath consumes their data. In this section, we'll take the next step by looking at two Web service–specific technologies that make using Web services more discoverable and useful in real-world situations. First, we'll talk about searching Web services by using UDDI. The ability to share and search Web service definitions fosters a growing and collaborative public community. The second extended topic on Web services is the use of ADO.NET to connect to a database. ADO.NET is a flexible and viable alternative to traditional database connections. Instead of connecting directly to a database, ADO.NET adds a middle-tier Web service to abstract the database through the Web service interface. We'll provide a sample to guide our discussion.

Searching with UDDI

It's not expected that you'll be able to create every Web service for your form template design needs. Sometimes your form might have a data-gathering requirement or need a capability that is not easily achievable. Such cases may include adding instant messaging or receiving stock quote prices. It may be hard to believe, but many Web services are freely and publicly available! Creating a stock quote service, for example, may not be something you want to take (or even have) the time to try to implement yourself. Welcome to UDDI. UDDI was originally designed as an XML-based system that maintains a registry of Web service endpoints intended for use by businesses. But now public UDDI servers are available to the general public on the Internet.

There are two ways to search UDDI: by service or by provider. The service is the name of the Web service method. The provider, meanwhile, is the entity offering the Web service. Unless you know the registered name of the company or individual who is providing the service, your best bet is to search by service name.

> **TIP UDDI Servers**
>
> The UDDI server is prepopulated with Microsoft's public UDDI server address. If your company has its own UDDI server, you can enter its URL and search it instead.

When you're creating a Web service connection, clicking on the *Search UDDI* button brings up the *Search Web Service* dialog (Figure 7.1). Let's say that we need to receive the MOI Consulting Corporation's stock price to display in our InfoPath form. We can search for services that contain the name "stock," as shown in Figure 7.1. Since UDDI is neither regulated nor monitored, many of the search results you receive may not work or be compatible with InfoPath.

Some Web services may not seem to work after you select them in the *Search Web Service* dialog, either when designing a form template or filling out the form. If you aren't sure why a Web service doesn't work, you may want to review the section about Web service compatibility with InfoPath in Chapter 6.

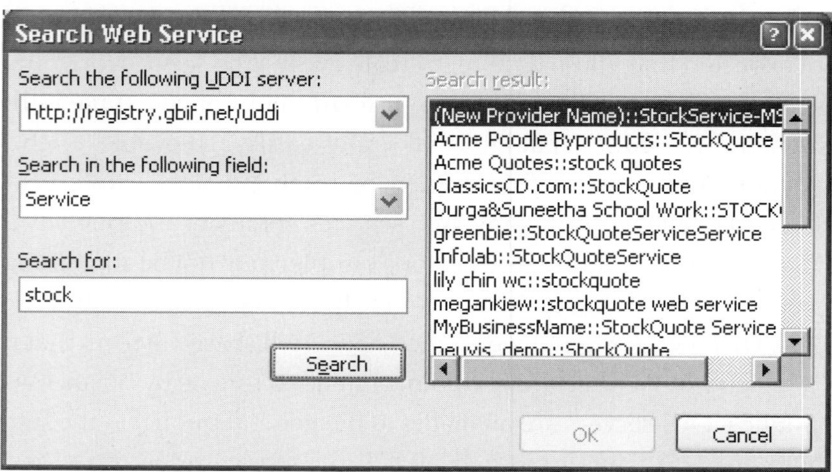

FIGURE 7.1: Searching for Web services by using UDDI in InfoPath

ADO.NET Web Services

InfoPath behaves differently when working with ADO.NET with a Web service. If you aren't familiar with ADO.NET, you can learn about it from an overview on MSDN (referenced in the Appendix). In summary, ADO.NET is a .NET framework library for connecting to data sources such as SQL Server, Oracle, or any other OLE DB and even generic XML data sources. With ADO.NET, you can retrieve, modify, and update the external data source by using a .NET data connection (such as a `SqlConnection`), a .NET data adapter (like the `SqlDataAdapter`), and a `DataSet`. A benefit of using ADO.NET over older technologies like ADO is its ability to encapsulate database tables, relationships, and constraints in a `DataSet` object that is portable and serializable (meaning the object is flattened into a stream for saving or sending).

Any InfoPath Web service query connection that returns a dataset is handled differently than other Web service connections. First, the `DataSet` object requires a special deserialization (opposite of serialization, to reinstate the object) algorithm. InfoPath is able to automatically detect a dataset and carry out a set of transparent operations to get the database data into the data source. Second, InfoPath respects many of the relationships and constraints defined in the dataset. For example, take the customers and orders scenario we used in the previous chapter with the database data connection.

A dataset could define the same relationship we used in Chapter 6, where we defined relationships for the database connection. The dataset could also ensure that the `CustomerID` and `OrderID` fields are unique and auto-incremented when new rows are added. Finally, when a dataset (in InfoPath) is submitted to a Web service method that accepts a `DataSet` object as a parameter, InfoPath properly handles the serialization for you behind the scenes. Theoretically, you could design a form against a dataset returned from a Web service and never really know it!

Typed and Untyped DataSets

There are two types of `DataSet` objects: typed and untyped. A typed dataset has a known schema, whereas an untyped dataset is essentially a wildcard. MSDN discusses the differences and how to create both versions in an introduction to `DataSet` objects (referenced in the Appendix). Creating an untyped dataset almost always requires less upfront work than a similar typed version.

When designing a form template against a Web service that returns a `DataSet` object, it is beneficial to use a typed dataset. InfoPath extracts the known schema when creating the data connection and uses it to create the data source. If an untyped dataset is returned by a Web service method, InfoPath will automatically query the Web service for an instance of the `DataSet` object and assume that the schema associated with that returned dataset is what will always be returned by the Web service. This design heuristic was instated because designing a form template implies that the schema will not change. If your dataset schema happens to change due to either a lapse in time or specific input parameters, the received data will fail schema validation, resulting in an error dialog and no data returned to the form.

TIP Submitting Dataset Data

A dataset from the main data source can be properly submitted to a Web service. Secondary data sources can receive a `DataSet` object but do not track changes, so they cannot be properly submitted back to the Web service. Using the main data source is a necessity if you want to submit your data back to the Web service for updating the database. The main data source performs change tracking (an ADO.NET requirement) and serializes the dataset automatically upon submit.

Example Customers and Orders Web Service

Our database data connection from Chapter 6 linked the Northwind database `Customers` and `Orders` tables. We'll do the same in this example, however, this time we'll use a Web service that exposes an ADO.NET dataset to get the same table data. The prerequisites for following along in this example are the same as for the Web service sample in Chapter 6: Visual C# and Web Developer 2005, Internet Information Services 6.0 or later with ASP.NET, and FrontPage 2002 Server Extensions.

We begin in Visual Studio and can actually reuse the existing Web service we created in Chapter 6. (We encourage you to review that chapter if you haven't already.) Recall that in Chapter 6 we created a Web site at http://localhost/InfoPathWebService. Open the InfoPathWebService project in Visual Studio, and then you're ready to go. In this sample, we don't need to write very much code. That's because we can leverage the many useful wizards in Visual Studio for connecting to and working with data.

To create the `SqlConnection`, `SqlDataAdapter`, and even the `DataSet`, we turn to the Visual Studio Designer features to auto-generate source code. It will save us time, instead of learning the ins and outs of objects we don't really need to understand in much detail. To enter the Designer, right-click on *Service.cs* under the *App_Code* folder and select *View Designer.*

We will add components to our class by dragging them from the Toolbox. Under the *Data* section in the Toolbox, we'll start by inserting a `SqlDataAdapter`. (If it's not listed, you can add it by right-clicking and selecting *Choose Items.*) When the `SqlDataAdapter` is inserted, the Data Adapter Configuration Wizard begins. On the first page, you want to create a connection, which is very similar to what we did for the database connection in the preceding chapter. Recall that we used the Northwind database in Chapter 6, so you may already have the connection defined in the most recently used drop-down. If so, you can reuse that connection.

The next wizard page asks for a command type. In other words, it wants to know whether to auto-generate SQL statements or use (and create) stored procedures. For this example, it's nonintrusive to use SQL statements—the first option.

Then the wizard asks what data from the database you want to select. Using the Query Builder, it's easy to select the `Customers` table from the list of tables and, after clicking *Close*, to select *All Columns* to add the columns to the table. For this `SqlDataAdapter`, we want to choose only the `Customers` table. If we chose the `Orders` table in addition to the `Customers` table, the wizard would not be able to auto-generate insert, update, or delete commands. After adding the table, we suggest that you add the query modifier `TOP 3` between the `SELECT` and `Customers` parts of the query. As we did in Chapter 6, adding the `TOP 3` query modifier will limit the size of the returned data to a reasonable payload.

The last wizard page shows a summary of what the wizard automatically set up for our `SqlDataAdapter`. You can see that the wizard took care of a lot of busy work. If you aren't convinced, look at the Service.cs code and notice the vast amount of auto-generated source!

We aren't done yet, however, since we still need to create another `SqlDataAdapter` for the `Orders` table as well as create the `DataSet` object. To do so, proceed through the same set of steps we used to create the `Customers` data adapter (but this time the connection you created will already exist in the connection drop-down on the first wizard page). After using the Query Builder, add `where CustomerID='ALFKI' or CustomerID='ANATR' or CustomerID='ANTON'` at the end of the `Orders` SQL statement. This is a temporary way to get only the orders for the top three customers we're selecting. (The proper way to match the orders with their customers would be to use a join query between the tables; however, since we are learning about ADO.NET with InfoPath and not the SQL query language, we will work with a simple example.)

After generating both `SqlDataAdapter` objects, you might want to consider renaming them from their default names of `sqlDataAdapter1` and `sqlDataAdapter2`. Right-click on one of the `SqlDataAdapter` objects and select *Properties*. Changing the *(Name)* property modifies the adapter name that you will see in the Designer view as well as what we'll eventually use to reference the adapter in our Web service code.

Now that we have created our adapters, the next step is to create a typed dataset. It's easy to create a typed dataset by using Visual Studio as it automatically takes care of writing dozens of lines of code that we would otherwise need to write. To begin, right-click on one of the `SqlDataAdapter` objects in the Designer view and select *Generate DataSet*.

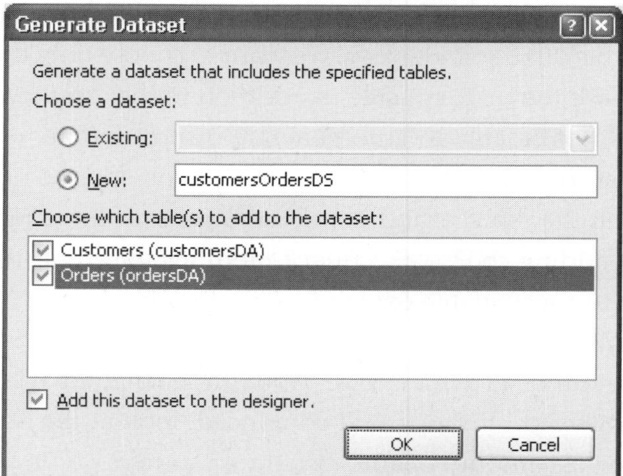

FIGURE 7.2: Creating a typed dataset from our `Customers` and `Orders` `SqlDataAdapter` objects

As shown in Figure 7.2, be sure that both tables, `Customers` and `Orders`, are selected. We can call this new dataset `customersOrdersDS`. Adding the dataset to the Designer is optional but is convenient in case you want to modify its properties later. Notice that the dataset that appears in the Designer view is called `customersOrdersDS1`. This is because the typed dataset class name is `customersOrdersDS` and the instance object created for us simply has a `1` appended to the class name.

The last step before writing code is to properly set up the relationships between the `Customers` and `Orders` tables. You can associate these tables by using the schema editor specifically for `DataSet` objects. To get to the schema editor, double-click on the `customersOrdersDS.xsd` file in the Solution Explorer. The schema editor appears similar to that shown in Figure 7.3.

The relationship between the `Customers` and `Orders` tables is established by right-clicking on the child (`Orders`) table and selecting *Relation* from the *Add* fly-out menu. Figure 7.4 shows the resulting dialog. The physical connection between the tables shows that a relationship exists.

We prefer to enable the *Nested Relation* option because the data will return in a hierarchical format (the `Orders` data is contained within the `Customers`

FIGURE 7.3: The Visual Studio schema editor

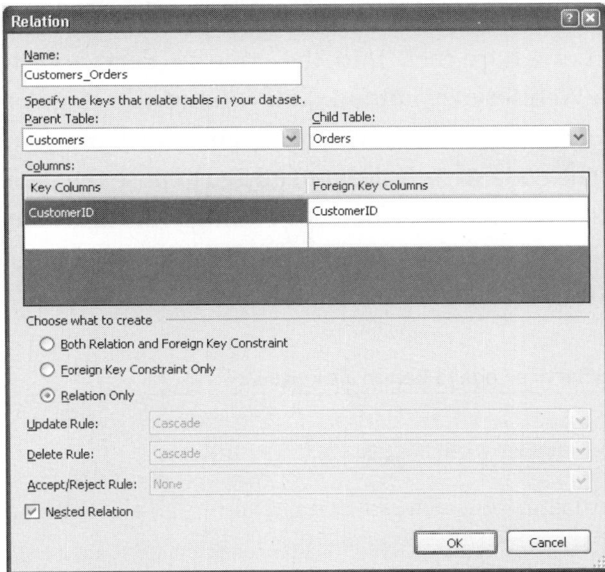

FIGURE 7.4: Adding a relationship to the `Customers` and `Orders` tables in the dataset

data) instead of flat (`Customers` and `Orders` data are not physically nested but are related by their primary and foreign keys). InfoPath is able to cascade update and delete operations to nested records only when the parent table changes. Unfortunately, the same features are not available when the data is flat. InfoPath will instead show an error dialog if you attempt cascading.

Cascading Updates and Deletes

Cascading occurs when a parent and child have a relationship and the dataset is configured to cascade changes. A relationship between tables is defined by a primary key on the parent table and a foreign key on the child tables. A change in the parent primary key, with cascading updates enabled, would also update all children foreign keys. Likewise, a cascading delete would remove all children table rows when the associated parent row is purged.

We're finished using the Visual Studio Designer to set up our ADO.NET components. Let's hop back into the code in Service.cs to expose our dataset from a Web service method. You will notice a large private method called `InitializeComponent`, which contains much of the auto-generated wizard code. The code we are about to add to expose the dataset (shown in Listing 7.1) can be added anywhere, but it might be easiest to add it immediately above the `InitializeComponent` method (which is below where we left off writing the `SaveItems` method).

LISTING 7.1: Web Service Code to Return a `DataSet`

```
[WebMethod]
public customersOrderDS GetDataSet()
{
    customersDA.Fill (customersOrdersDS1);
    ordersDA.Fill (customersOrdersDS1);
    return customersOrdersDS1;
}
```

We're almost finished. Before we can use this Web service, the `InitializeComponent` method call must be uncommented. (Visual Studio creates the project with it commented by default.) If you fail to uncomment this method call, the code generated by the wizard to initialize the objects we created in the Visual Studio Designer isn't executed. The

`InitializeComponent` call is at the top of the source code and is commented out with a double forward slash. Simply remove the two forward slashes and hit F5 to run. Click on the `GetDataSet` link and run the method by using the *Invoke* button.

Since the process is similar to the Web service we used in the previous chapter, we'll leave it as an exercise for you to create a query Web service data connection to receive the `Customers` and `Orders` dataset.

Secondary Data Source Binding

For each of the data connection examples in Chapter 6, we simply inserted controls from secondary data sources while designing our forms and saw them populated with data when previewing. Until now, our intentional focus has been on each of the data connections themselves. But we haven't yet explored secondary data source–bound controls and how they differ from controls bound to the main data source. To effectively use secondary data sources and their associated connections, it is important for us to account for these differences when designing, as well as editing, our forms.

Forms Services

Secondary data source binding works similarly in a browser form as in InfoPath.

Designing the Form Template

Let's go back for a moment to our XML file data connection example from the previous chapter and call out behaviors specific to secondary data sources. Start by designing the form and bringing up the *Bulleted List Properties* dialog for the Bulleted List that is bound to the secondary data source (Figure 7.5). The first thing you will notice is that almost everything in the dialog, at least on the *Data* tab, is disabled! This is because these settings do not make sense for controls bound to secondary data sources. The node name and data type (the latter isn't displayed in the *Bulleted List Properties* dialog) are predetermined by the external data source. A default value

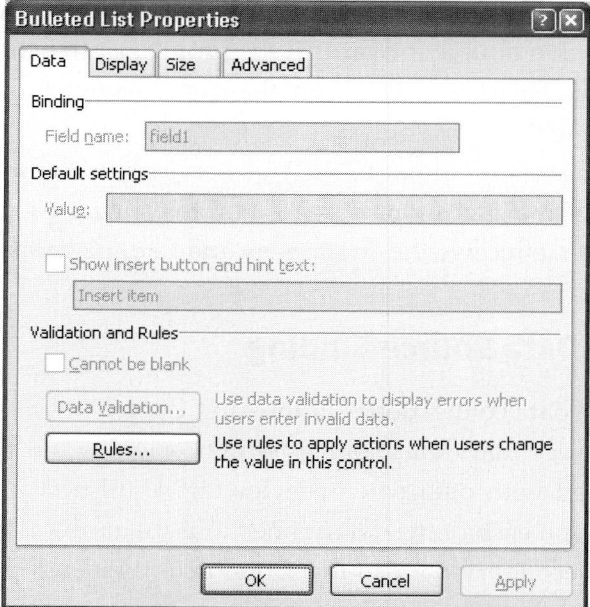

FIGURE 7.5: Secondary data source–bound controls allow for little customization

clearly doesn't make sense because the data is queried "live" from the endpoint. The *Show input button and hint text* checkbox is disabled because secondary data sources always disallow structural editing. **Structural editing** is the ability to insert and remove data source fields and groups via controls when filling out the form.

Recall from Chapter 1 that structural editing is the ability to add or remove items from your form. Such functionality is provided by Optional Section and Repeating Section controls. Due to the nature of secondary data sources being connected to query-only data adapters, there's no need for users to have the ability to insert or remove items from secondary data sources. Don't forget that data in secondary data sources is never saved, so user edits don't make much sense beyond the ability to provide query parameters, as you saw in the Web service data connection example.

Let's take another look at the *Bulleted List Properties* dialog from Figure 7.5. Alas, the rules feature is enabled! The Rules feature is the only data-centric feature allowed for any secondary data source field or group. The behavior is similar to that for rules on main data source fields and groups.

The *Display* tab has its own limitations. As they don't provide much value, features such as spell checking and auto-complete are not configurable for secondary data sources, but they are both always enabled. Conditional formatting, alternatively, is fully supported on secondary data sources and actually comes in quite handy when presenting information from data connections to the user. (See Chapter 5 for the discussion on conditional formatting.) Other options in the *Size* and *Advanced* tabs are available, with the exception of the *Merge Action* option. Form merging is specific to the main data source; you can find details in Chapter 12.

There should be no surprises when we look at the *Field or Group Properties* dialog for a secondary data source node. No options are available on any tabs, with the exception of rules. The *Details* tab on the node properties dialog may offer some helpful information, but as we will soon see, validation is not an issue to consider with secondary data sources. Table 7.1 presents the full list of supported and unsupported features for secondary data source–bound controls.

TABLE 7.1: Available and Unavailable Features for Secondary Data Sources

Available Features	Unavailable Features
Data formatting (for numeric data types) Rules Conditional formatting Accessibility (screen tip, tab index, access key) Input scope All size and alignment options Read-only Multiline (text wrapping) Paragraph breaks (only if read-only is enabled)	General node properties (name, data type, default value, cannot be blank, repeating) Auto-complete Spell checking Data validation Structural editing options (*Click here to insert, Edit Default Values, Customize Commands*) Rich text options Form-merging options

Filling Out the Form

To best understand how secondary data sources work when you're filling out a form, let's continue with the XML file data connection we created in the preceding chapter. Figure 7.6 shows how the form looks after querying the XML data.

FIGURE 7.6: Form after querying the XML file secondary data connection

The first thing you may notice is that it's possible to edit the data in the Bulleted List. However, try to insert or delete a row. It cannot be done. This is because secondary data sources do not allow for structural editing. For comparison and contrast, try to edit the data in the Sample.xml form again to see how you can remove and insert rows in the Bulleted List. (Recall that the Sample.xml form is the form we created in Chapter 6 to provide data for the XML file data connection.) One of the only ways for a user to change the structure of a secondary data source is to query the data connection. There are other ways to edit a secondary data source; however, they rely on the form designer to write custom form code to directly modify the secondary data source at a low level.

> **NOTE Secondary Data Connection Query**
>
> A query of a secondary data connection will overwrite the contents of its secondary data source. So clicking the Button control shown in Figure 7.6 clears any changes you might have made to the data (without warning!).

Data Validation

We've hinted several times that data validation need not concern you with secondary data sources. Since these data sources are temporary, ensuring their validity is not only unnecessary but also downright expensive in terms of computer resources. So no matter what type of data connection fills a secondary data source, the received data can be absolutely anything, and InfoPath will not complain. Case in point: When a secondary data connection isn't configured to receive data when the form opens, the associated data source is actually empty—and that's completely fine!

We know from Chapter 5 that there are two kinds of validation. In Chapter 5, we learned about data type validation. The other kind of validation is structural validation, which we'll talk about in a moment. Data type validation ensures, for example, that if a field is a whole number, any letter characters will cause a validation error (revealing itself as a visual error on the control). This is not the case with secondary data sources since data types are not enforced when a user fills out the form. Data types are still helpful when you design your form since, for example, if you use a whole number type, you can format the numerical value by using data formatting. Likewise, inserting a node with the date data type would insert a Date Picker by default. If a feature such as data formatting is enabled but the input value to the control doesn't match the data type needed, the feature will simply not apply itself. The effect is similar to the main data source but without the validation errors.

In addition to data type validation not being available, structural validation is also disabled but actually less of an issue. Structural validation focuses on the XML Schema constraints around inserting and removing nodes in the corresponding XML data source. Because UI-based structural editing (e.g., *Click here to insert*) cannot be enabled on secondary data source–bound controls, users don't even have an option to insert or delete any items. One of the only ways a secondary data source can insert or remove data is by querying via its data connection. If we created a secondary query connection to the `GetSavedItems` Web service method we worked with in Chapter 6, only requerying the connection could change the number of items shown. Obviously, the number of items could change only if someone submitted an update with more or fewer entries. And the ability to insert and remove items by using the UI is restricted to the main data source. In Part II of this book, you will learn how to write custom form code that inserts and removes items in the data source using the `XPathNavigator` object. These concepts could also be applied to secondary data sources as an alternative to structurally modifying their underlying data.

Offline Mode Query Support

One of the bigger customer requests from InfoPath users has been the ability to fully use their forms without an Internet connection, that is, in an offline mode. While InfoPath minimally supported the concept of offline forms in its first version, it has continually improved through version 2007. A form has always had the ability to work offline since the form template is cached on the local computer during its first use. But just because basic forms seem to work offline doesn't mean that all forms work properly without a connection.

During the course of Chapter 6, we saw how critical external data sources can be in the functioning of a form. Since many real-world forms heavily rely on their data connections, it would follow that InfoPath bolsters the concept of working with external data offline. Thanks to offline mode support for secondary query connections, there is no longer a need to write complicated form code to smoothly bring a rich offline experience to your form.

Forms Services

Offline query support does not apply to a browser-enabled form template running in the browser. A server running Forms Services can never really be considered offline.

Offline queries are supported on all secondary data connection types: XML document, database, Web service, and SharePoint list. But offline query support is not enabled by default when setting up a secondary data connection, as you can see in Figure 7.7. You may recognize this dialog from our earlier exercises when setting up XML file and database connections.

In addition to enabling offline query support for specific connections, there are two global settings for offline configuration. One setting controls the

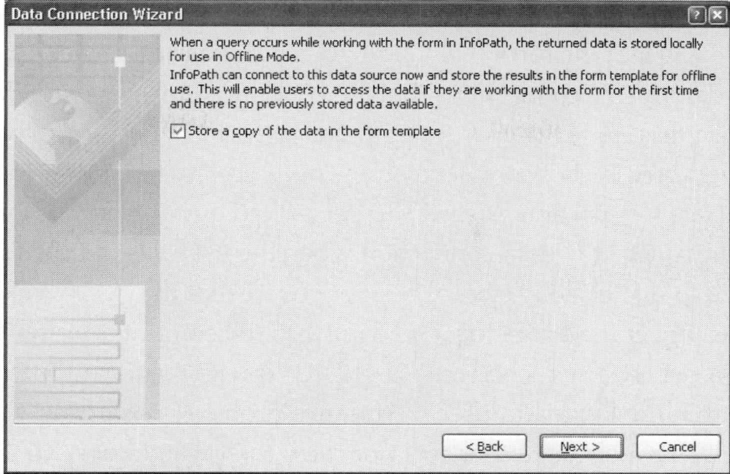

FIGURE 7.7: Enabling query support for offline mode when adding or modifying a secondary data connection

caching of queries at the form template level. The other setting is truly global as it controls whether or not InfoPath itself will cache form queries altogether.

You can set up offline query behavior for your form template in the *Offline* category under the *Form Options* item in the *Tools* menu (Figure 7.8). The first checkbox, *Allow users to fill out this form if data is unavailable,* essentially enables

Form Options
Category:
Open and Save
Offline
E-Mail Attachments
Property Promotion
Digital Signatures
Security and Trust
Preview
Programming
Versioning
Compatibility
Advanced
Offline
When a query occurs while working with the form in InfoPath, the returned data is stored locally for use in Offline Mode.
Allow users to fill out this form if data is unavailable.
Data may be unavailable because the form cannot connect to data sources successfully and no offline data is available.
Store data returned from queries so it can be used in Offline Mode.
Stored queries do not expire
Stored queries expire after this number of days: 3
OK
Cancel

FIGURE 7.8: Configuring a form template for offline mode queries

offline query support for this form. Despite the text being longwinded, the main caveat is that the form will fail to open if there is no cached query data for secondary query connections that are configured to *Automatically retrieve data when form is opened.* (Recall that the *Automatically retrieve data when form is opened* checkbox is shown when setting up a secondary query connection with the Data Connection Wizard.) To get cached query data, the form must successfully query the data connection when the user fills out the form. You don't need to do anything special besides ensure that the query happened at least once. The cached query is stored only on the computer from which the form was opened. The cached data is not stored with the form XML data, but rather within the logged-in user's Windows profile. Transferring your form from one computer to another will not carry the cached query to the target computer.

The second option shown in Figure 7.8 determines how long a cached query can be saved on a specific computer. The time span is measured from the last successful query. This setting does not actually change when InfoPath recaches the query data—that happens every time the query is successful when filling out the form. We recommend that you choose a setting that is consistent with the lifetime of the external data source. For example, not setting an expiration makes sense if you're dealing with a list of states in the United States, which should not change any time soon. But if the form is pulling part numbers from a catalog of inventory, you may want to consider setting an expiration of 30 days or fewer, for instance. Setting an expiration is virtually guesswork on your end (as you don't know how much time users spend offline before going online and refreshing the cached data), so a form could have outdated or invalid data. If the form is supposed to be submitted to a back-end process such as a Web service, the check for valid data could be performed in the Web service itself. We will talk more about submitting forms in Chapter 8.

The truly global setting for all InfoPath cached queries, not just those specific to a form template, is the master for controlling offline mode. The global offline setting is found in InfoPath's advanced settings. To get to the advanced settings (Figure 7.9), go the *Options* menu item on the *Tools* menu and then click on the *Advanced* tab. The *Cache queries for use in Offline mode* checkbox globally enables or disables cached query support in InfoPath. Even if you already have cached queries from your form templates, the

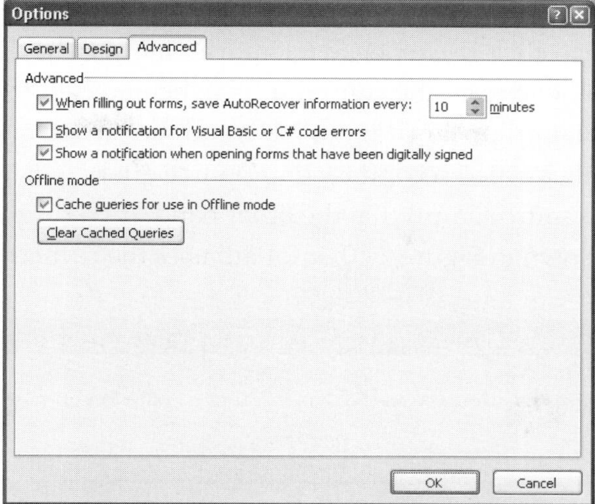

FIGURE 7.9: InfoPath global cached queries setting

cached data will not be used unless this checkbox is enabled. The *Clear Cached Queries* button deletes the saved queries that you may already have on your computer. Cached queries are saved on your computer within the same folders that house the InfoPath form template cache in your Windows user profile.

As a user fills out a form, a secondary data connection may fail at any time. Some connections may query at the time a form is opened, while others could query on a button click or any change to the form's main data source. At the moment the query fails, the dialog shown in Figure 7.10 allows the user to choose between the *Work Offline* or *Try to Connect* options. Clicking the *Show Details* button reveals the data connection name and the precise error. (Remember that the connection name is revealed only in an error dialog during an error and only when the form is being filled out!)

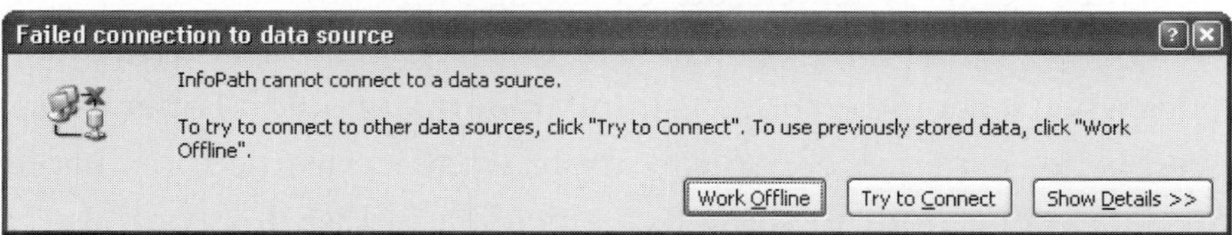

FIGURE 7.10: Error dialog shown if querying an external data source fails when filling out the form

If *Work Offline* was not the default button, we think most people's reactions would be to click *Try to Connect*. Unfortunately, if the data connection really isn't available (e.g., the computer is not connected to the network), another error dialog appears (Figure 7.11), and the cached query data is not used. As a result, a failed secondary data source query will leave the target secondary data source empty. On the other hand, if *Work Offline* is selected in the dialog shown in Figure 7.10, InfoPath uses the cached query data.

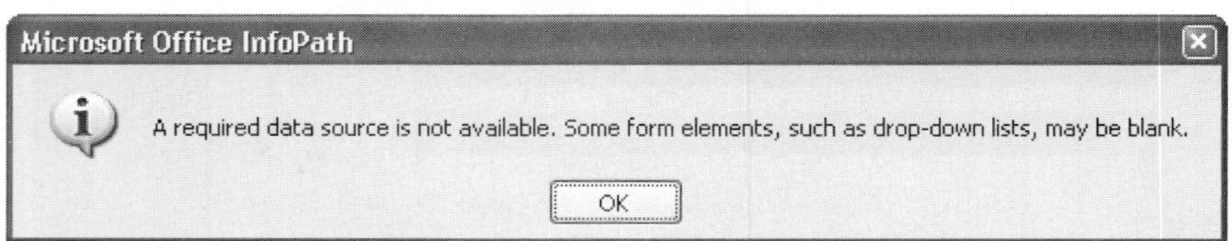

FIGURE 7.11: Error dialog that results from clicking Try to Connect in Figure 7.10 if the data connection is unavailable

Offline cached queries are very helpful for using forms on the go when a connection to the external data sources isn't always available. But it's advised to use cached queries sparingly since your users will be filling out your forms with potentially old data. If the external data does not change very often, the secondary connection cache will tend to be more relevant. There is an additional concern about a secondary query connection populating the list in a List Box control. But before talking about that potentially problematic issue, let's first look at the handy features that List Box controls offer to your form template designs.

List Box Controls Connected to Secondary Data Sources

As you surf the Web, either for pleasure or business, sites all over the Internet depend on data. Whether you're reading the news, booking a flight, or checking your e-mail, the content you care about most is dynamic and updates when it should. Who says InfoPath forms shouldn't offer the same or even better experience? We can apply what we learned in Chapter 6 about data connections to show dynamic data in List Box controls. Let's continue with a simple example that can be much improved: the itemized grocery list form template we used in Chapters 4 and 6. (The sample called

GroceryShoppingList is included with the samples for this chapter available for download from the book's Web site.)

Showing Secondary Data in a List Box Control

In Chapter 4 we created a grocery list form for explaining XML fragments and the *Edit Default Values* dialog. In the form template, we created an XML fragment for each item we could potentially want on our list: `Apples`, `Oranges`, and `Bananas`. This data served the example just fine, but in real life it's not plausible to continually update the form template for new items craved by our taste buds. Instead of using XML fragments or even adding or removing items manually from the List Box items, we'll create an XML file data connection from which the List Box will dynamically get its items.

> **Using a Data Source to Populate a List Box Control**
>
> The type of data connection we use to dynamically populate List Box items is irrelevant. Remember that all query data connections create a secondary data source. We could use any other data connection instead of an XML file and still yield similar results. XML files are easy to create for sample purposes, so you can follow along if you wish.

Let's create the XML file we'll use for our data connection. You can simply enter the text from Listing 7.2 into Notepad and save it with the file extension .xml on your computer. (You can also find this text in the GroceryItemsData sample file.)

Listing 7.2: Grocery Items to Use in an XML File to Populate a Data Connection

```
<GroceryItems>
   <GroceryItem name="Apples" category="fruit"/>
   <GroceryItem name="Bananas" category="fruit"/>
   <GroceryItem name="Oranges" category="fruit"/>
   <GroceryItem name="Carrots" category="vegetable"/>
   <GroceryItem name="Celery" category="vegetable"/>
   <GroceryItem name="Beets" category="vegetable"/>
   <GroceryItem name="Mixed Beans" category="canned"/>
   <GroceryItem name="Canned Corn" category="canned"/>
   <GroceryItem name="Olives" category="canned"/>
</GroceryItems>
```

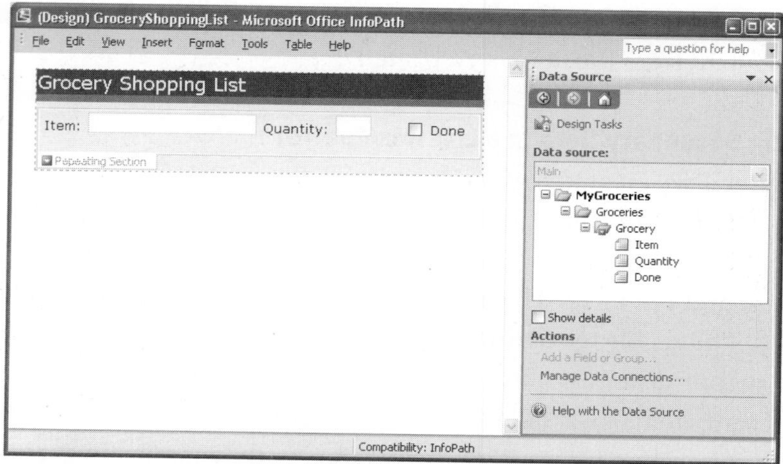

FIGURE 7.12: Grocery list form template, unchanged, from Chapter 4

After creating the XML file, we'll want to create a new data connection—but not quite yet. Before we add the connection, Figure 7.12 shows what the main data source and corresponding view for the grocery form look like from Chapter 4. To prepare for the data connection, let's change the "Item" Text Box to a Drop-Down List Box.

The next step is to create the data connection, but we will not add it as we have done before from the *Data Connections* menu item from the *Tools* menu. Instead, let's go to the *Drop-Down List Box Properties* dialog (Figure 7.13), which supports adding data connections and using repeating items from their secondary data sources.

Under the *List box entries* section in the dialog, there are three choices. By default, a List Box uses entries that are manually entered into the dialog. Since we want to get data from a secondary data source, we'll choose the *Look up values from an external data source* item. Clicking the *Add* button launches the familiar Data Connection Wizard for setting up a receive data connection. You can also choose to use a data connection library. Since our external data is in an XML file, continue stepping through the wizard and use the default settings to finish creating the connection.

After we create the connection, the properties dialog in Figure 7.13 will have the newly created connection selected in the *Data source* drop-down. However, we still need to complete the *Choose the repeating group or field where the entries are stored* section. This means we need to select the proper data source node in the secondary data source from which the List Box will

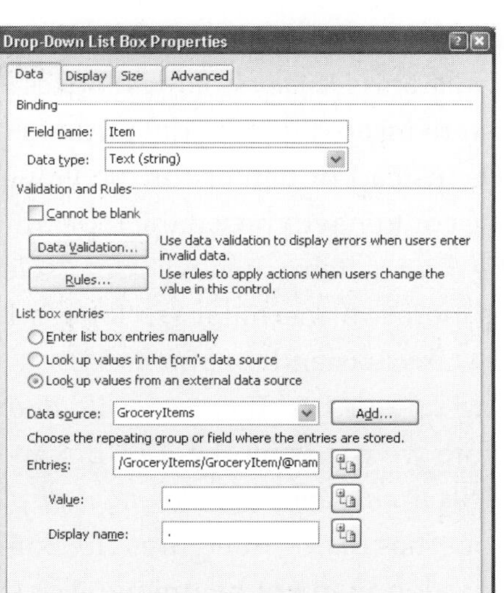

FIGURE 7.13: Drop-Down List Box Properties dialog

get its items. The data source node itself or any of its parents must be repeating. In our case, we'll select the `name` attribute field by using the button adjacent to the *Entries* field in the properties dialog. Figure 7.14 shows the data source node we selected for *Entries*.

Since we chose an attribute field, the properties dialog is smart enough to know that this is the field we want to use for both the visual display

FIGURE 7.14: Selecting a secondary data source node from the XML file connection that provides data for the List Box entries

name and the value that's used in the XML data. That is why there are periods in both the *Value* and *Display name* text boxes in Figure 7.13. Say, for a moment, that we were instead getting data from a database and wanted to use numerical IDs instead of names for the value saved in the form's XML. In that case, we could have chosen the repeating `GroceryItem` field in Figure 7.14 for the *Entries* item; then we could select different fields for *Value* (which would point to the database table's ID field) and *Display name* (pointing to the table's friendly name field).

We're done setting up our List Box to get its items from our XML file data connection. Before we try using this List Box in our form, we should quickly mention the *Show only entries with unique display names* checkbox at the bottom of the properties dialog in Figure 7.13. Sometimes the items you get from a data connection may not be unique. For example, say that you can query a list of meals for dinner at some restaurant over the course of a year. Since sometimes the same dinner will be served more than once in a year (due to its popularity), querying the restaurant for its meals will return duplicate names. If you prefer to not have duplicate entries in your List Box, you'll want to select the *Show only entries with unique display names* option.

Let's preview the form and see how the Drop-Down List Box behaves when you fill out the form. (The sample file's name is GroceryShopping-List2.) As you fill out the form (see Figure 7.15), remember that the Drop-Down List Box control is still bound to the main data source despite getting its data from a secondary source. So if you were to save the form, each of

FIGURE 7.15: Filling out the grocery list form when the items are retrieved from a data connection

the items you selected in the Drop-Down List Box controls would be remembered. The data connection is merely providing the list of items in the control as there is no binding association between the secondary data source and the Drop-Down List Box.

Using the Main Data Source for List Box Items

Another neat feature of List Box controls is their ability to pull data not only from secondary data sources (as we just saw) but also from the main data source! As you know from Figure 7.13, a List Box requires that you select a node that is repeating or has a repeating parent. Instead of selecting a node from a secondary source, let's just choose the main data source. For our grocery form, we enjoy the ability to track what groceries we need in addition to how many and whether or not we're done buying them. However, we also want the ability to take notes on some of the food we buy. Say that the apples look a little bit ripe; we want to note that we should eat them sooner rather than later.

We'll continue designing the form template by adding a Repeating Table control with two columns at the bottom of the view. (A file named GroceryShoppingList3 is included with the samples for this chapter.) Let's change the first Text Box to a List Box and go to its properties dialog. This time we select the *Look up values in the form's data source* so we can get the list of grocery items that have been added to the form as it's being filled out. For the entries, we'll select the `Item` node, as shown in Figure 7.16.

FIGURE 7.16: Using the main data source to provide data for a List Box control

Figure 7.17 shows how the form template looks after we've finished adding and formatting the Repeating Table control.

Figure 7.18 shows how the form with our new notes feature looks when we fill it out. The items in the List Box for note taking are dynamically added as we add items to our grocery list.

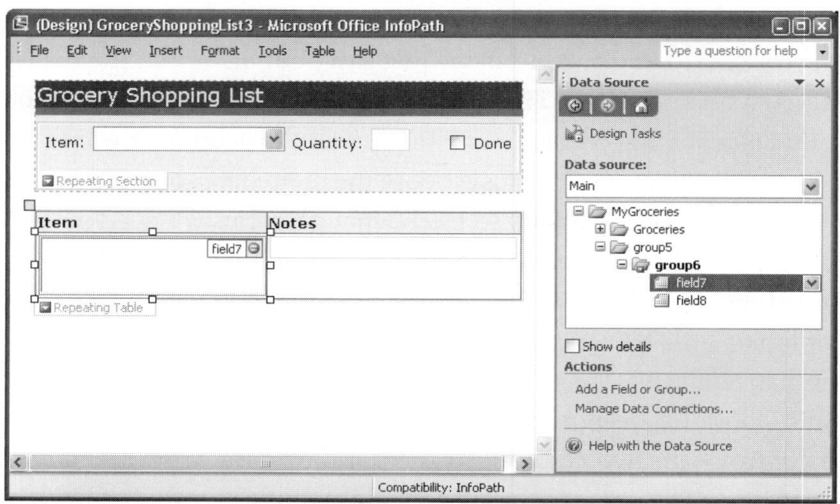

FIGURE 7.17: Adding a note-taking capability to our grocery form

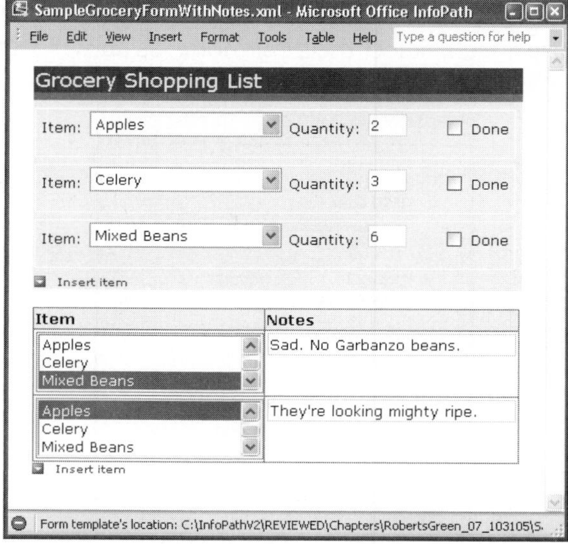

FIGURE 7.18: Filling out the form after we've added the note-taking feature

Filtering List Box Items

You can imagine that the XML file (or whatever the external data source might be) that holds all of the possible grocery items could be quite large. It could get so large that finding your item in the List Box could be a lengthy task! How can we keep the form useful and easy to use even when there are hundreds of possible grocery items to choose from? Filtering is the answer to "too much data" problems, especially when it's displayed directly to the user in a control such as a List Box or Drop-Down List Box.

Forms Services

Filtering items in List Box controls is available in browser-based form templates. However, filtering data on a Repeating Table or Repeating Section control is not supported.

When we created our sample XML file for the `GroceryItems` data connection, each grocery item had two attribute fields (as shown in Figure 7.14): `name` and `category`. Since items are categorized, we can filter the returned data by category. Let's see how we can adopt our form to use a category filter when selecting a grocery item. First, we'll need to insert a new Drop-Down List Box control that will display the list of categories and act as the filter. (Inserting this control will also add a field into the main data source. We should rename the node to `filter` in the data source so we can recognize it later.) We'll want to set up this Drop-Down List Box similarly to the Drop-Down List Box shown in Figure 7.13, but instead of selecting the `name` node for the *Entries* value, we want the `category` node. Since getting the categories from the grocery items will return duplicate entries, we can enable the *Show only entries with unique display names* checkbox.

We've now added a mechanism that the user can interact with to choose the filter he or she wants. But filtering won't actually work yet since we haven't set it up. Since we want to filter the Drop-Down List Box that shows all of the grocery items, that is where we need to apply the filter. To add the filter, go to the *Drop-Down List Box Properties* dialog for the `Items` node. This is the same properties dialog we saw in Figure 7.13. Click on the button adjacent to the *Entries* text box, and then click on the *Filter Data* button at the bottom of the dialog that opens after you click the *Entries* button. Let's add the filter such that *category* and *is equal to* are the selected options. This means we want to show items in this Drop-Down List Box only when its category is equal to something. The "something" we're looking for is the node bound to the Drop-Down List Box we added earlier, where users will select the category to use for filtering. The node is this example is called `filter`, and it exists in the main data source. Figure 7.19 shows the result of setting up the filter.

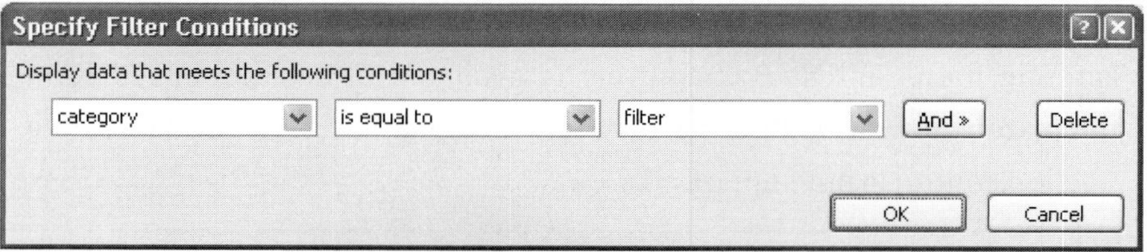

FIGURE 7.19: Specifying a filter to show only grocery items from a selected category

> **TIP Dealing with Duplicate Items in a List Box**
>
> Enable the *Show only entries with unique display names* checkbox to remove duplicates from List Box (including Drop-Down List Box) controls.

After clicking *OK* in all of the dialogs opened while creating the filter, we can preview the form again. By default, there are no items in the Drop-Down List Box to select a grocery item! That's because we haven't yet selected a filter. After selecting a filter from the *Filter by category* Drop-Down List Box, a list of grocery items that belong to the selected category are revealed. Figure 7.20 shows the form being filled out. (GroceryShoppingList4 is included with this chapter's samples.)

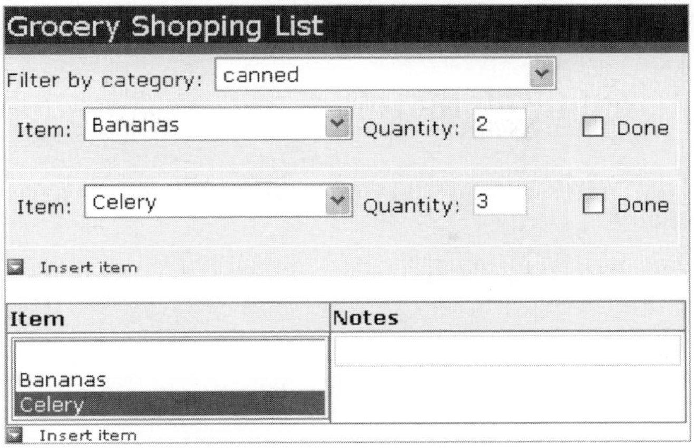

FIGURE 7.20: Filling out the grocery form with category filters

What's Next?

In this chapter, you learned about extended data connection features that help your forms work with external data. Features such as offline mode query support and List Box controls showing secondary data enable rich form-filling experiences without writing complicated code. The next chapter ties up everything we've learned since the beginning of the book as we explore form submit options. What mechanisms does InfoPath offer for collecting users' form data? Should the form submit or just save? We'll answer these questions and many more in the next chapter.

8

Submitting Form Data

Getting Started

Since the beginning of the book, we've showed how to design forms by taking advantage of numerous rich features in InfoPath. With all this ability to create and deploy a form template (we'll talk about the latter in the next chapter), are we forgetting about the actual purpose of the form in the first place? Ask yourself *why* you're creating a form. Some answers might include "to add a new work order to my database," "to send a status report to my manager," or "to get employment applications from candidates." In all of these situations and for most forms, you need to get data back from the forms your users fill out. The data in the form needs to go *somewhere*. In this chapter, we'll address how to get data out of your form and into an external data source of your choice.

To facilitate the process of getting data from your forms, we'll look at **submitting forms**. Submit, as you may have guessed from the last few chapters, is a member of the InfoPath family of data connections. Like query data connections, **submit data connections** can send data to many different types of endpoints. There are many configurable options for submitting data, especially around Web service submit connections. By the end of the chapter, you'll be able to confidently determine whether and how you want users to submit their form data.

Why Submit?

Instead of using submit to get data from your form, why not just have users save their form somewhere? There are a few problems with just saving the form as a method of submitting data.

First, how do you communicate that workflow to your users? Do you include a text blurb at the top of your form that gives precise instructions? Or do you send out accompanying instructions through e-mail? How do you ensure people will follow your instructions? It's a messy situation from a workflow and process perspective.

Second, simply saving the form does not enforce that the form is properly filled out. Even with any number of pending errors in the form data, the user is still allowed to save. Saving the form (using the *Save* or *Save As* menu items) should be limited to times when the user cannot finish the form in one sitting and thus saves a draft on his or her computer for continuation at a later time.

The third problem with saving, instead of submitting, is that you have no control over the saved file or the "drop box" (e.g., a network path where files can be saved). Since you're just counting on people saving a file somewhere, that file can be anything they want to copy over. It could be a huge movie file when you just wanted a small .xml file! And since you want everyone (assuming there is more than one person filling out your form) to save their forms somewhere, that means each person must have at least write access to that location. So files can be overwritten by anyone. If read access is enabled, anyone can look at other people's form data and even identify to whom that data belongs.

As you can see, many issues, both social and technological, limit the usefulness of saving form data. Submitting forms by using InfoPath mitigates these problems. Users no longer need to worry about what they must do to finish filling out the form because you've designed the form such that clicking a submit button, similar to a browser-enabled form template, is the clear last step. Also, you, the form designer, can sleep soundly because InfoPath submit enforces that your form is fully filled out with no validation errors. Moreover, since the drop box is now a database, Web service, or SharePoint site, there are many more layers of security that a perpetrator must penetrate to do any harm.

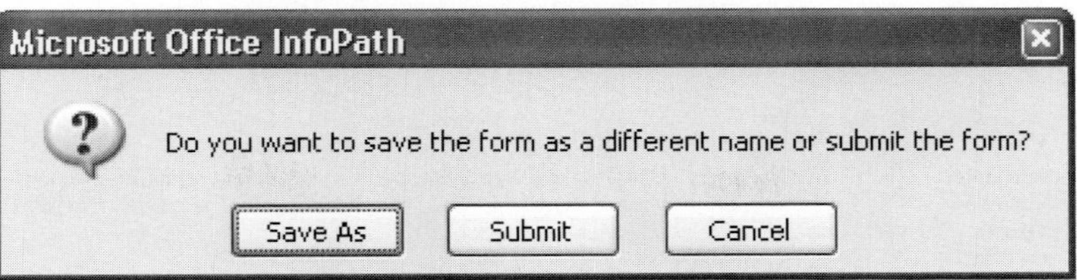

FIGURE 8.1: Dialog asking the user whether to save or submit the form

Sometimes hitting Ctrl+S to save is a nervous habit. When a user saves a form that has submit enabled, InfoPath asks if he or she really meant to save or would rather submit (Figure 8.1). This reiterates the final purpose of the form: to submit data to a data source. This dialog also helps to reveal the fact that the form supports submit if that wasn't clear to the user from the form's design.

Forms Services

A browser-enabled form template running in the browser does not use the dialog shown in Figure 8.1 when the user saves the form.

In some cases, you may never want users to save your form and only want the data submitted. Aren't most Web forms like that? Sure, some of them allow you to "come back later," but the majority of Web-based forms are simple enough that they can be filled out in a single sitting. There are also other reasons why you might want to prevent users from saving the form, for example, if the XML contains sensitive data or if the external data source to which the form submits, such as a SharePoint library, can support multiple submits. Let's see how we can disable save in the next section.

Using the "Form-Only" Model to Disable Save

The "Form-only" model, as its name suggests, is a series of design-time settings geared to make your template run most like a form—in the strict sense of the word. That means some InfoPath-specific features that are not critical for filling out forms can be disabled for a specific form template.

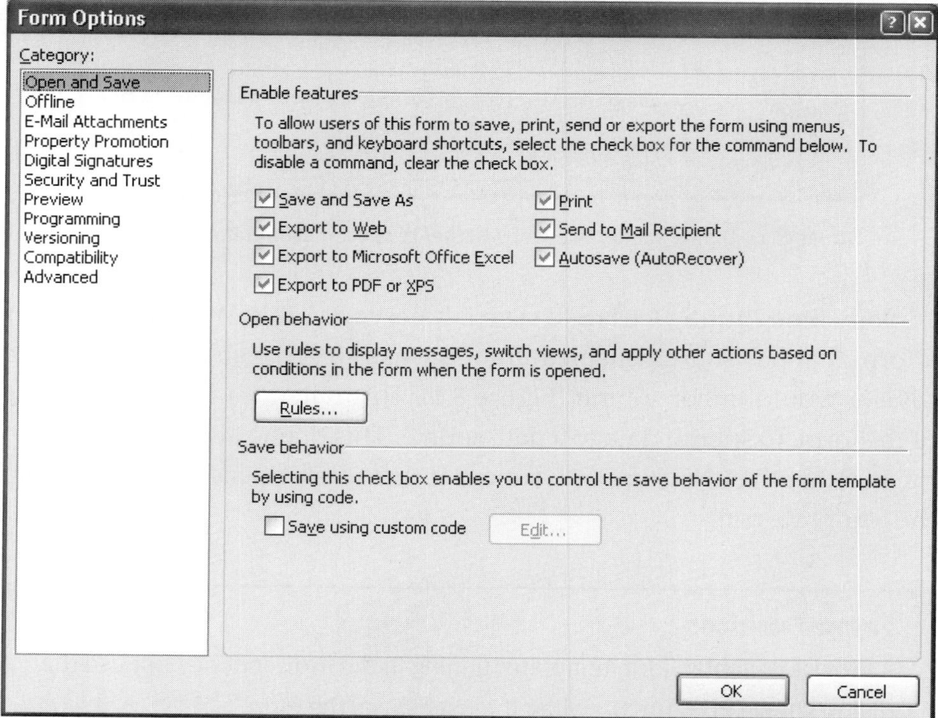

FIGURE 8.2: Settings for enabling and disabling certain features for users, such as the ability to save a form

To access the "Form-only" features, go to the *Form Options* dialog on the *Tools* menu in design mode and click on the *Open and Save* category. Figure 8.2 shows the corresponding dialog. The checkboxes at the top (in the *Enable features* section) control settings such as allowing users to save, print, or send forms to a mail recipient. By default, all features are enabled. When you uncheck a feature, its corresponding entry points will be disabled when users fill out the form, so they will not have access to that feature.

Forms Services

To disable *Save* and *Save As*, among other options, use the *Browser* category on the *Form Options* dialog to exclude commands on the browser form's toolbar.

> **WARNING** **Disabling a Feature Does Not Turn It Off**
>
> Disabling a feature means that all entry points (from the user's perspective) are disabled. However, you can still invoke the feature by using custom form code. Some features, such as Autosave, are not accessible via form code. We'll review InfoPath programmability in the advanced chapters of this book.

Unchecking the *Save and Save As* item in a form that supports submit might be helpful to guide a user away from save and toward submit. The decision to disable save depends largely on your form design and user scenario. Remember that if you decide to go ahead with disabling save, there is no way the user can override it when filling out the form. The only way to reenable save is to come back to the *Open and Save* tab to check the box. But the form can't change dynamically while it's being filled out, so if you restored the ability to save, it wouldn't happen until the form template was reopened (which would load the latest form template with save enabled).

Issues with Data Validation and Submitting Forms

We've learned all about data validation in previous chapters and how it helps to keep our form data as we intended. But we also know that validation errors aren't "hard errors." That is, just because there's an error doesn't mean the user can't keep filling out other parts of the form. The form is allowed to be in a so-called indeterminate state for as long as the user chooses. One of the few motivations behind a user actually fixing validation errors in a form is so he or she can submit. Submitting a form is the only action that requires the data to be free of validation errors.

Before you go retrofitting your forms with all sorts of validation, we want you to keep in mind a couple form design problems surrounding submit. Failure to check for these potential problems could contribute to user confusion or completely block the form from ever being submitted. What we're about to discuss relates to how data validation operates solely on the data while the user can see only what's in the form's views.

The first issue involves a form template that has multiple views and could confuse or even block the user upon submit. Take a job application

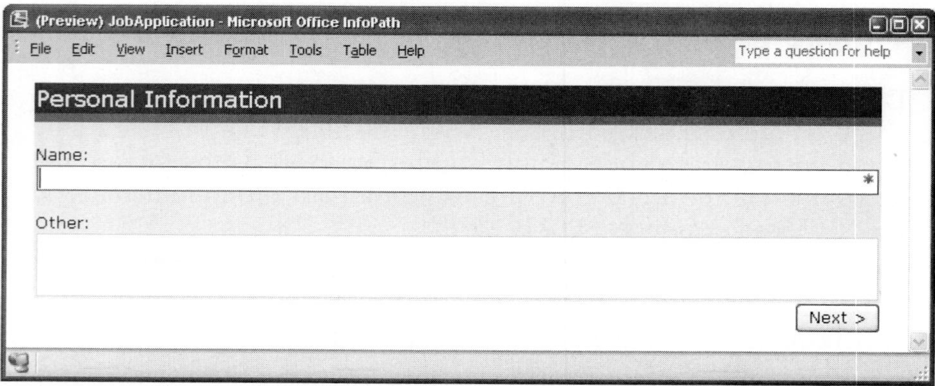

FIGURE 8.3: The first view of the job application form

form, for example. (A sample named JobApplication is included with the samples for this chapter on the book's Web site.) Say that it has three views: personal information, resume, and references. The form is set up such that the default view is the personal information view (Figure 8.3), and a *Next* button at the bottom of the view takes you to the next view—résumé. The same process happens for moving from the résumé view to the references view. Instead of a *Next* button, the references view has a *Submit* button. Because the form designer wants to enforce the workflow of the form, she unchecked the *Show on the View menu when filling out the form* checkbox in all views' properties dialogs. As a result, the user cannot go back to a previous view after clicking *Next*.

Say that a user forgot to fill out the *Name* text box on the personal information view. This field is required, as shown by the asterisk on the far right in Figure 8.3. By the time the user gets to the last page to submit, he's not only confused but also stuck! Figure 8.4 shows the last view of the form where submit happens after clicking the *Submit* button. There's no way to go back to fix the validation error on the first page.

Figure 8.5 shows the error the user will receive. Notice that the dialog text shows the node name with the validation error. It helps to use descriptive data source node names!

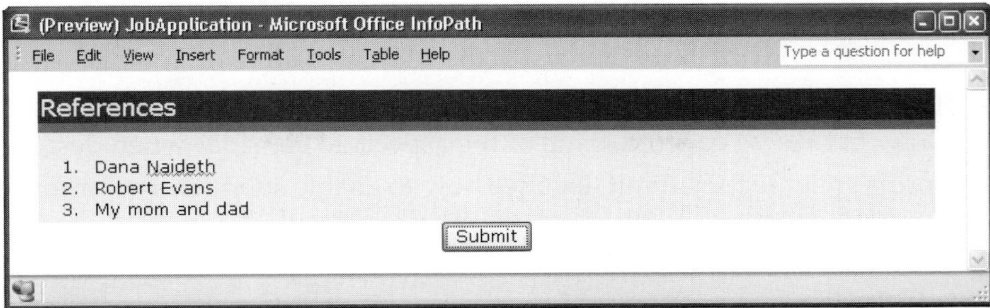

FIGURE 8.4: The last page of the job application form

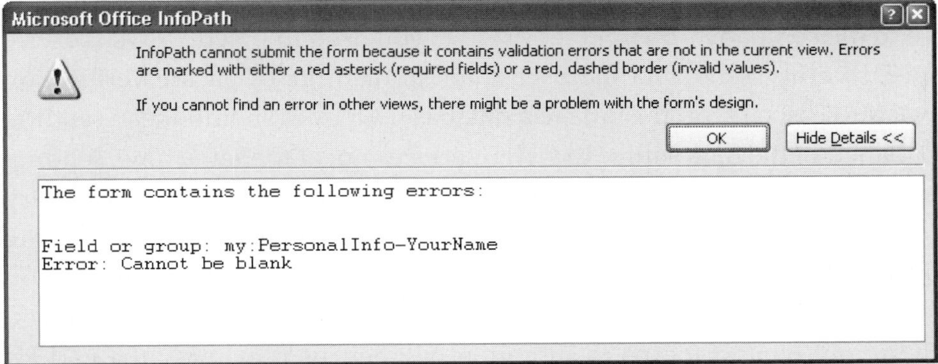

FIGURE 8.5: Dialog about the submit error that occurs when the user clicks the Submit button after not filling in a name in the first view

Forms Services

When submit fails because of validation errors, a browser alert dialog is shown similar to Figure 8.5. If more than one validation error prevents submit in a browser-enabled form template, only the first error is shown.

The error text in Figure 8.5 brings us to the second form design issue: validation errors existing on data source nodes that do not exist in any view. Since data validation works at the data source level, there is a chance that you could set data validation on a field that you never inserted in the view. Whether or not the field is meant to be in the view depends on your form design. Regardless, it's a best practice to not set validation constraints on data that is not exposed directly to the user in an editable control. (Also be sure that the control isn't read-only!)

Now that we've covered some of the aspects to consider when designing forms suitable for submit, let's see how to enable submit for your form templates.

Submitting Forms

Before setting up a form for submit, you should consider an important question: What does it mean to submit the form? Does the form data just go to the company's SharePoint site? Do you need to first do a Web service query, verify some data the user entered, then finally (if the verification was successful) send the data to a database? Or does submit mean sending only half of the data source to a Web service and, at the same time, sending an e-mail to your team? As you can see, the concept of submit is very loosely defined. However your form submit ends up, it is the finalizing action of filling out the form. By the time a user submits the form, you should have collected all of the data you need from him or her. Once you figure out what it means to submit, it will be trivial to apply the various techniques we talk about in this section to meet your submit goals.

Introduction to Submit Data Connections

There are eight different ways to set up submitting your form. Five of those ways actually send data directly to a storage medium such as a database. The other three are extensible mechanisms that can be highly customized. The extensible submit mechanisms can be set up to send the form data to storage media as well.

We begin with the submit data connections that communicate directly to a back-end store: e-mail, database, Web service, SharePoint library, and Web server via HTTP. Next we'll brush over the customization offered by three advanced ways to submit: by using form code, using rules, and submitting to the hosting environment.

The entry point for setting up submit for a form template begins with the *Submit Options* item on the *Tools* menu. The *Submit Options* dialog is the springboard for most discussion in the rest of this chapter.

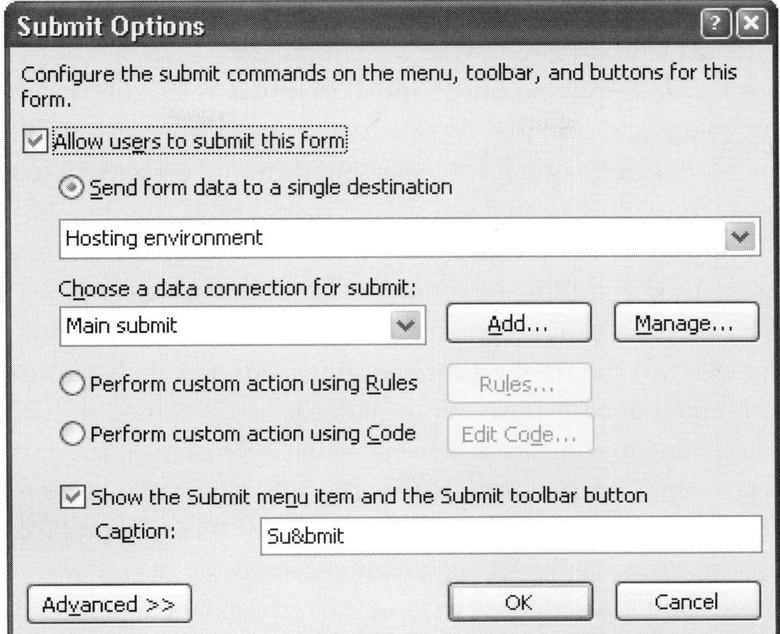

FIGURE 8.6: Submit Options dialog, the starting point for enabling submit

> **TIP Assign a Submit Keyboard Shortcut**
>
> The caption for the *Submit* menu and the toolbar button can be easily changed or even removed by using the *Caption* text box or adjacent checkbox, respectively, toward the bottom of the dialog. The ampersand (&) character makes the next letter an access key for the *Submit* button. Figure 8.6 shows that hitting Alt+B when filling out the form will trigger submit.

Forms Services

Using an access key on a *Submit* toolbar button is not supported in the browser.

What Submit Method Is Best for My Form Template?

Before we discuss submit details, we want to provide a quick overview of submit configurations that may be most appropriate for your situation.

That way you can jump straight to the specific submit topic to help you move forward with designing your form template.

Choosing the right kind of submit is usually a quick and easy process, assuming that you know how you want to finalize a user's form-filling session. For most forms, submit is the last interaction the user will have with your form template. As you'll see in later parts of this chapter, the process of submitting the form performs a multitude of actions, including validating data, sending or saving the form data, and closing the form. We'll postpone discussion on validating the data and closing the form until later in this chapter when discussing submit options. For now, let's figure out the kind of submit that best suits your form needs.

The first thing to consider when choosing a type of form submit is what you want submit to mean. In other words, when a user clicks the *Submit* button in your form, what is that supposed to do? It may sound like a silly question, but a form template can do almost anything during submit. One of the more common actions is to send the form data to a database or to a person via an e-mail attachment. If you simply need to send your data somewhere for storage, one of these submit connections should suffice:

- E-mail
- Database
- Web service
- SharePoint document library
- Web server (HTTP)
- Hosting environment (when hosting an InfoPath or browser-enabled form)

Sending the data as e-mail is typical for small survey-style forms. Say that you designed a quick form asking your coworkers what they want to eat for lunch today. Sending such a form template via e-mail is a lightweight process to efficiently receive responses. On the other hand, you wouldn't want dozens of technical design specification forms to all be sent to an e-mail inbox. More likely, you'd want them saved to a database for efficiently storing and indexing spec data. Alternatively, you may have a Web service for processing your form data. As you have learned in previous chapters, Web services provide a great deal of flexibility and customization.

In some organizations, Windows SharePoint Services plays a core role in data collection and collaboration. InfoPath supports SharePoint by allowing form data to be submitted to a document library. If you instead have a custom ASP or ASP.NET page for processing your form data, you'll want to choose a Web server (HTTP) for submitting the form. Finally, when hosting an InfoPath form (either the InfoPath program or in the Web browser), you'll most likely want to submit to the hosting environment. This type of submit informs the hosting program that the form is being submitted so it can respond accordingly.

In some form templates, submitting the form may be a more complicated matter. Instead of sending data to a particular location, you may want to just save the form on a network share, for example. There are several ways to define a custom submit: using rules or using code (see the option buttons in Figure 8.6). When you use rules to submit, the submit action itself is defined by the set of rules you establish. With rules, you can do many things, such as show a dialog, switch views, and execute data connections to query or submit data. If rules do not suffice for your form submit needs, the ultimate freedom and flexibility in submit is using code. You can write whatever custom form code you'd like to carry out your form template submit. We'll examine how to write form code in Chapter 15.

Now that you have a high-level understanding of submitting forms in InfoPath, let's look at each submit connection in more detail.

Submitting via E-Mail

Submitting via e-mail is the easiest way to set up submit for a form. It's relatively straightforward to set up and works with any form security setting (restricted being the least privileged). If you just need a quick and painless way to let your users send the form, and e-mail is an appropriate medium, then you're on easy street!

To allow your users to submit the form as e-mail, begin by visiting the *Submit Options* dialog. Next, enable the *Allow users to submit this form* checkbox (refer back to Figure 8.6). From the *Send form data to a single destination* drop-down, select *E-mail*. It may appear that you're done, but clicking the *OK* button in the dialog yields an error: "You must select a data connection for submitting data through e-mail. To create a new data

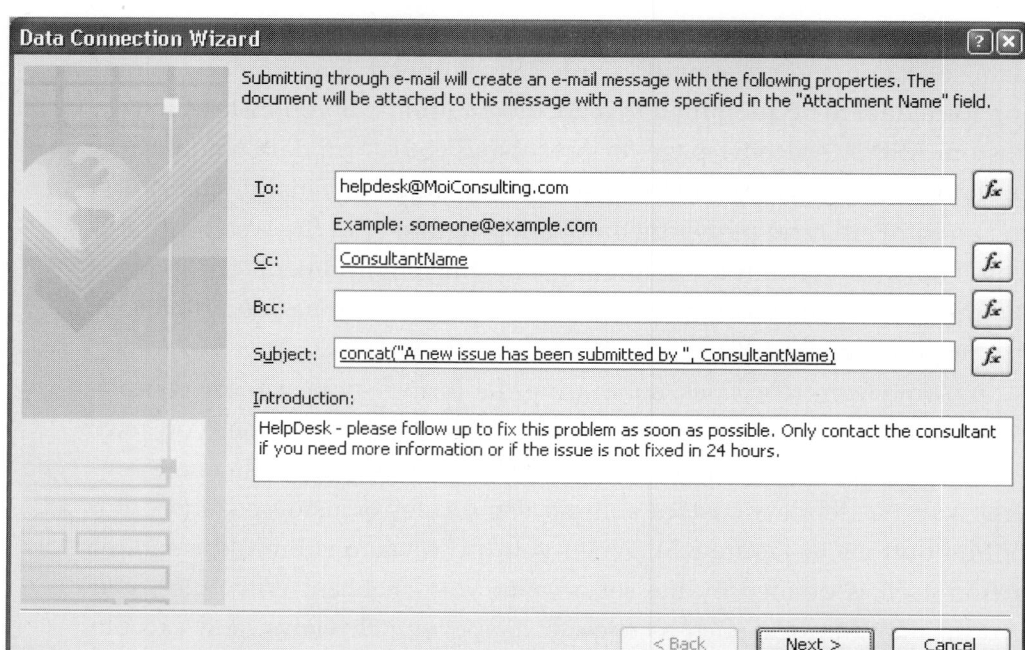

FIGURE 8.7: First page of the Data Connection Wizard for setting properties of the e-mail sent when users submit the form

connection, click Add." Click the *Add* button to create a new submit e-mail connection. Figure 8.7 shows the dialog that appears when you click *Add*.

For this example, we've created a form that lets our in-house consultants send technical issues to the MOI Consulting IT department. (The file for this sample is called EmailSubmit.) The form consists of fields that ask for the consultant's name and the specific problem. Whenever a user fills out the form to submit a technical issue, the e-mail is sent to helpdesk@MoiConsulting.com, and the consultant is carbon copied. For easy categorization in our e-mail client, we've included the consultant's name in the e-mail subject. Since the name of the consultant is in the form data, we use the `concat` function to combine a string (`"A new issue has been submitted by"`) with the field data. These settings, as well as the static introduction, which is included at the top of the sent e-mail but not seen by the user filling out the form, are shown in Figure 8.7.

> **TIP Formulas for E-Mail Properties**
>
> Instead of using static values (such as the To e-mail fields in this sample), you can use a formula to calculate a dynamic value. Formulas may be used on any fields, except the *Introduction* field, by clicking the formula button immediately to the right of the text box. As an example, we used the consultant name as a dynamic value for the carbon copy field of the e-mail.

Forms Services

When sending e-mail from a browser in a browser-enabled form, the e-mail introduction will always be prepended by "[Submitted by user@MoiConsulting.com]", where "user@MoiConsulting.com" is the user's authenticated credentials on the Windows domain. If credentials aren't available or anonymous access is enabled on the site, the e-mail address is replaced by "Anonymous".

The next wizard page, as shown in Figure 8.8, configures whether and how the form is attached to the e-mail. The first setting, which is not selected by default, sends an e-mail without any attachments. The e-mail body contains the current view (which is similar to the *Export to Web* feature that is always available when filling out the form). The second setting is more comprehensive than the first. Actually, it is similar to the first but tacks on the form (.xml) file as an attachment. The default value in the *Attachment name* text box is "Form", but you can choose another name by using the formula builder or simply typing in a static name. The formula builder lets you choose one or more form fields and even calculate names. In Figure 8.8, we've chosen to use the `concat` function to combine the consultant's name, which comes from the form data, and the date with a hyphen in between. If consultant Jack Smith submitted this form on June 5 to report a network outage issue, the e-mail would appear to the helpdesk inbox with the subject "Jack Smith-2006-6-5".

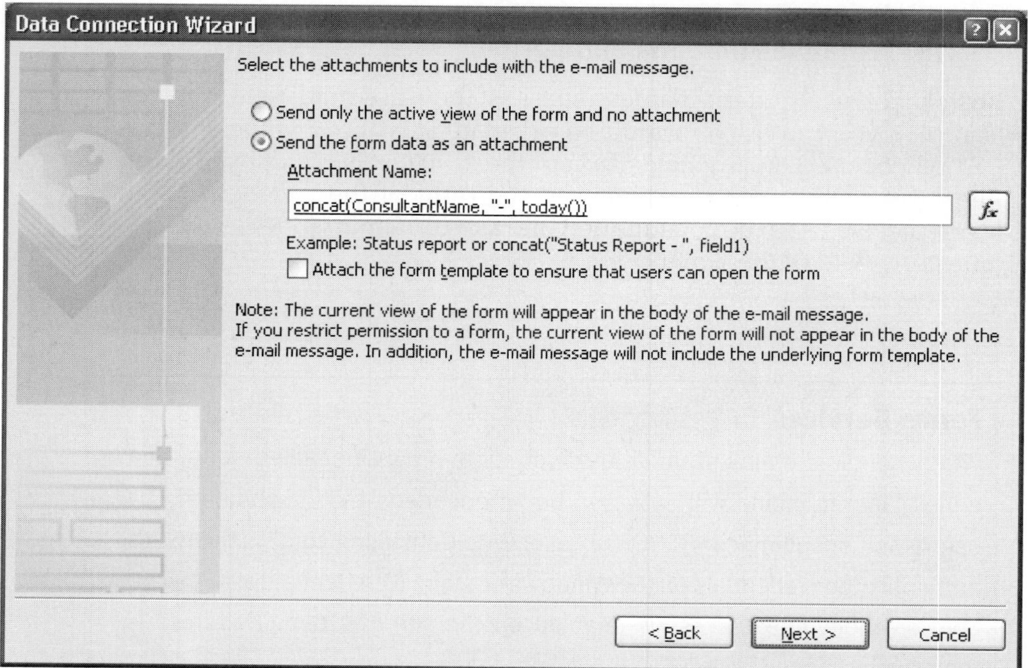
Data Connection Wizard
Select the attachments to include with the e-mail message.
Send only the active view of the form and no attachment
Send the form data as an attachment
Attachment Name:
concat(ConsultantName, "-", today())
Example: Status report or concat("Status Report - ", field1)
Attach the form template to ensure that users can open the form
Note: The current view of the form will appear in the body of the e-mail message.
If you restrict permission to a form, the current view of the form will not appear in the body of the e-mail message. In addition, the e-mail message will not include the underlying form template.
< Back
Next >
Cancel

FIGURE 8.8: Configuring the attachment options for submitting via e-mail

If the e-mail will be submitted to users who do not have access to the form template location, you will want to enable the *Attach the form template to ensure that users can open the form* option. If you're not whether sure your users will have access, it's a safe idea to attach the template. However, if your form template is too large to send via e-mail, you may want to consider a better way to share the template. Or you could consider a different type of submit for your form.

As with anything good in life, such as e-mail submit, there's always an associated (and sometimes hidden) cost. Downsides to using e-mail submit include both a hard prerequisite and user intervention. Without Outlook 2007, e-mail submit is not possible. Users trying to submit a form without Outlook 2007 will receive an error message explaining the requirement. Assuming that your users have Outlook 2007, when they submit, they will receive a dialog confirming the e-mail submit on their behalf

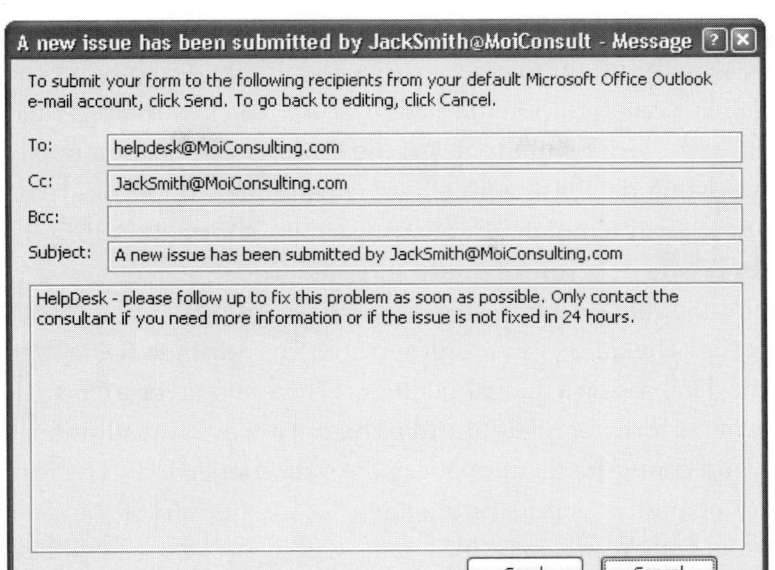

FIGURE 8.9: Dialog prompt in which the user must click Send in order to submit a helpdesk request

(Figure 8.9). Unfortunately, there is no way to suppress the dialog. It's a security feature so that forms can't maliciously send arbitrary e-mails on your behalf. Remember that there could be custom code behind the form that calls submit at any time. Without a prompt, you wouldn't know when e-mail is being sent. We'll see how to use custom code with data connections in the advanced chapters of this book.

Forms Services

Browser-enabled form templates in the browser do not show the dialog from Figure 8.9. Instead, the e-mail is sent without confirmation. Submit via e-mail will fail, however, unless the e-mail settings are set up in Windows SharePoint Services. Details are in Chapter 17.

Submitting to a Database

Submitting to a database isn't possible through a secondary data connection. In other words, a connection to submit to a database cannot be added via the *Data Connections* dialog while you're designing a form template. The only way to submit to a database is to initially design your form template against a database. On the *Design a Form Template* dialog when you're creating a new form template, select the *Database* option. You must already have an existing database with tables, constraints, and so on. When creating the new form template, InfoPath uses the information from the database to build the data source query and data fields.

Within the data source, there are two groups: `queryFields` and `dataFields`. The `queryFields` group contains attribute fields that will be sent to the database on a query operation. (There should be a *Query* button in the view of the form template already. You can always add additional Button controls and configure them to query the data connection.) The result from the query operation populates the `dataFields` portion of the data source with results. If there are no results, items within `dataFields` will be empty.

> **TIP Main Database Connections Can Always Query and Submit**
>
> When you're creating a main database connection, query and submit are always available. The only way to suppress either query or submit (or both) is to remove all entry points from the form template. Even if you remove the *Submit* toolbar button (which we talk about later in this chapter) and all Button controls in the view, the connections are still present in the form template.

Submitting data with a form template based on a database connection is easy. The simplest way is to click the *Submit* toolbar button when filling out the form. The `dataFields` portion of the data source is transformed into `UPDATE` and `INSERT` statements and sent to the database for processing. There is really no configuring of database submit since the structure of the database tables dictates the data that can be submitted.

There are occasions where a database data connection is set up, but submit isn't enabled. In fact, the last page of the Data Connection Wizard will notify you that data cannot be submitted to the database. You will see the following within the *Summary* portion: "Submit status: Not allowed—One or more of the columns in the data source has a large binary data type such as text, ntext, hyperlink, or image. Large binary data types are not supported."

TIP Pay Attention to the Wizard

Pay careful attention to the last page of the Data Connection Wizard for a database connection. You should always look for the *Submit status* label to ensure submit will work properly. If it's not successful, you may want to fix your database and try creating the form template again.

TABLE 8.1: Unsupported Database Data Types for Submit

Database Product	Unsupported Data Type

Access 2003	`Memo`
	`OLE object`
	`Hyperlink`

Access 2007	`Memo`
	`OLE object`
	`Hyperlink`
	`Attachment`

SQL Server 2000	`text`
	`ntext`
	`image`
	`hyperlink`

SQL Server 2005	`text`
	`ntext`
	`image`
	`hyperlink`
	`nvarchar(MAX)`
	`varbinary(MAX)`
	`varchar(MAX)`
	`xml`

Table 8.1 lists Access and SQL Server data types in which InfoPath cannot submit data. To work around these data type limitations, you will need to change the data type of the column in the database table. If you do not have access or are unable to change the data type of unsupported column(s), you may need to use a Web service with an ADO.NET `DataSet` object to update your data. (When switching to Web services and ADO.NET, it's preferable to switch the entire database connection—both query and

submit—to use a Web service. You can easily do so by using the *Convert Main Data Source* option from the *Tools* menu.)

We created a database connection in Chapter 6, so you already know the steps to get it up and running. Now that you have some details on submitting data to databases, you are well prepared to create your own connections directly to databases using InfoPath.

Forms Services

InfoPath Forms Services does not support submitting data to a database. To enable submit to a database, consider using a Web service with an ADO.NET `DataSet`. We talked about querying a `DataSet` in Chapter 7. We continue that discussion in this chapter while discussing how to submit data by using ADO.NET.

Submitting to a Web Service

In Chapter 6, you learned how to design a Web service by writing C# code in Visual Studio 2005. Creating a query data connection to the Web service required only a few easy steps through the Data Connection Wizard. In this chapter, we'll leverage our knowledge from the past two chapters to talk about submit data connections with Web services.

Recall from Chapter 6 that we set up a submit connection when using the `SaveItems` Web service. This method facilitated the saving of grocery items in the form. In this chapter, you'll learn a lot more about setting up submit and dive into the details that can help you select the precise data and send it to the data source of your choice.

Main Submit

If you're familiar with Web services, or even if you're not, you might be struggling with the difference between Web service query and submit data connections. What does it mean to *query from* instead of *submit to* a Web service? In the Web service world, there are no such concepts; the Web service is simply invoked. There is no real major difference in the technical details between the ways query and submit work in InfoPath. The only difference in either case is what InfoPath does with the response from the

Web service. In the query case, clearly, we care about the data returned from the Web service, so InfoPath puts the data into the `queryFields` data source nodes (as we saw in Chapter 6). For submit, the form is simply shipping form data off to an external data source. There may not be a Web service response anyway (i.e., the return type on the Web service method may be `void`). Even if there is returned data, InfoPath does not specifically care and, in fact, ignores it completely.

When Is Submit Considered Successful?

When InfoPath submits data to a Web service, the operation is deemed successful if the Web server (not the Web service) returns a regular HTTP response status code. Note that HTTP status codes are used in all HTTP communication (the protocol on which Web services are built). This includes any response in the 200 range of values. A list of status codes for HTTP version 1.1 is found at the World Wide Web Consortium (see the reference in the Appendix).

There are two ways to set up a main data source submit connection. One way is by choosing the *Receive and submit data* option when designing a new form based on a Web service. The other is by instead selecting *Submit data.* Figure 8.10 shows these options. You might naturally think that the *Submit data* option uses the same wizard steps as the *Receive and submit data* option. This is not the case, however. Table 8.2 compares the list of wizard steps for each type of Web service setup.

You'll notice that the chief difference between *Receive and submit data* and *Submit data* is that you do not select parameter mappings when you choose the *Submit data* option. The parameter mappings page is where you define what form data is sent to which Web service parameters. (We'll look at that dialog in the next section.) When designing a form that is submit-only, InfoPath creates the form data source based solely on the submit Web service method parameters. When setting up a receive-and-submit form, InfoPath uses only the receive Web method's input parameters and output type to generate the data source. So when it comes time to set up the submit

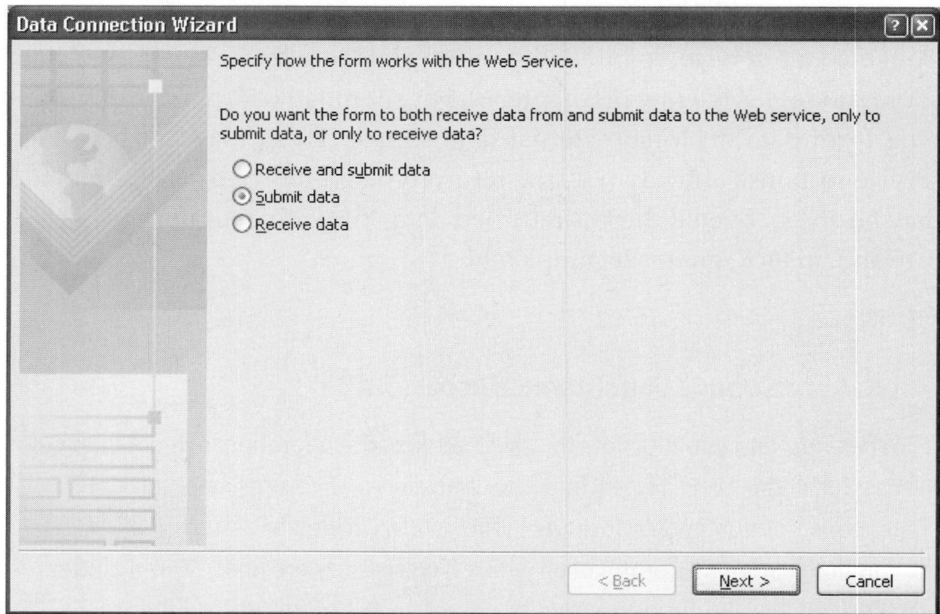

FIGURE 8.10: Specifying whether your form only receives data, only submits data, or does both with a Web service

TABLE 8.2: Differences between the Receive and Submit Data, Submit Data, and Receive Data Wizards

Wizard Page	Receive and Submit Data Wizard	Submit Data Wizard	Receive Data Wizard
Receive data WSDL location	✓		✓
Select query operation	✓		✓
Main query connection name	✓		✓
Submit data WSDL location	✓	✓	
Select submit operation	✓	✓	
Select parameter mappings	✓		
Main submit connection name	✓	✓	

portion in the Data Connection Wizard, the data source is already created, and thus the need for an additional step asking, "What form data source nodes are to be sent to the Web service when submitting?"

> **WARNING** **Data Connection Wizard on a Submit-Only Main Connection**
>
> When designing a submit-only form, you might wander back into the *Data Connections* or *Submit Options* dialogs. If you care to modify the `Main submit` data connection (the one created when you first designed your form template), you will end up stepping through the Data Connection Wizard again. However, this time, you will encounter the wizard page that asks you to select parameter mappings. This page's settings will be empty, and you will be required to set the mapping at this time. Read on to the next section to learn how to set the mappings properly.

To show how easy it is to create a submit-only form, let's design a student sign-in form for the local city college. (The file for this sample form template is called StudentSignIn.) We'll start by designing a new form template based on a Web service. Since a sign-in form just needs to send data, we can create a submit-only form; we choose *Submit data* from the dialog shown in Figure 8.10. The Web service WSDL is located on the local computer (localhost). (We'll look at the Web service definition in the next section.) Next, we choose the method we want to submit to, as shown in Figure 8.11: `StudentSignIn`.

The final wizard page shows the default submit connection name (`Main submit`) with a summary of the connection details. Clicking *Finish* takes you to the *Data Source* task pane in design mode (Figure 8.12).

Let's take a moment to understand the data source and how it was created from a submit data connection. First, every other data connection we've created so far has had a query connection. As a result, the `queryFields` group exists in those data sources. Since we do not have a query connection in this example, there is no `queryFields` group. Instead, the parameters of the Web service method are mapped to nodes under the `dataFields` group. The `studentId` and `studentName` fields correspond to the `StudentSignIn` Web method with integer parameter `studentId` and string parameter `studentName`.

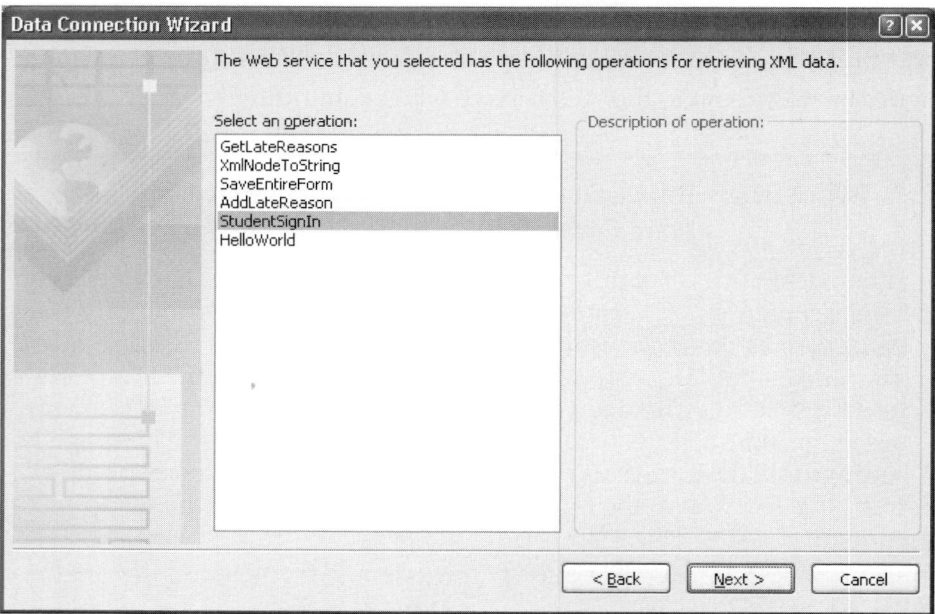

FIGURE 8.11: Selecting a Web service method for submit

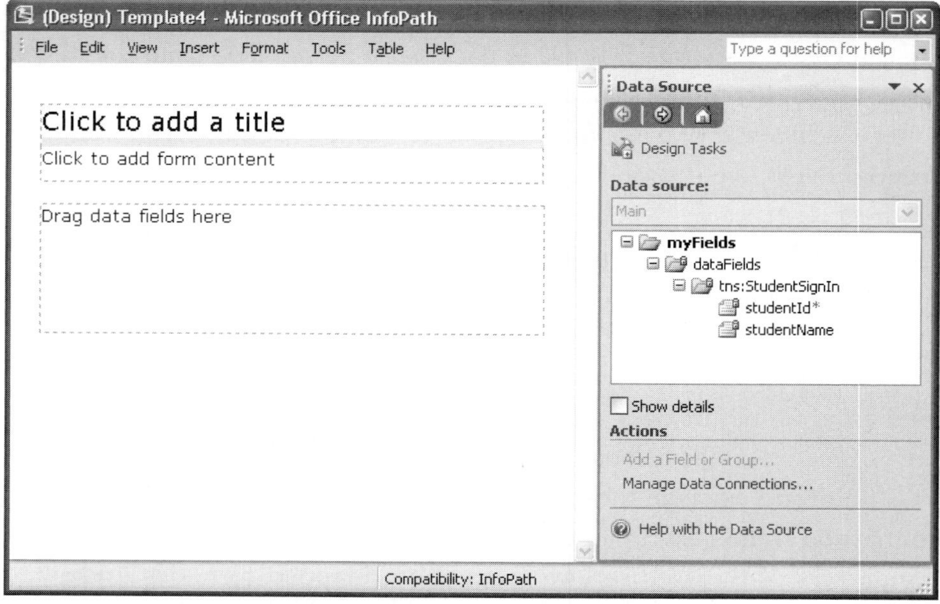

FIGURE 8.12: Design mode after finishing the Data Connection Wizard for submitting data to a Web service

Returning Data from a Web Service

The `StudentSignIn` Web method returns `void`, which means there is no return data. Despite `void` being the typical return type for methods meant to be used for submitting data, this may not always be the case. A Web method you decide to use for submit in a form could still return some data. An InfoPath submit data connection will discard any returned data from a Web service. Submit success or failure, as mentioned earlier, depends on the HTTP status return code.

After inserting the `studentId` and `studentName` fields into the view and doing a little spicing up (of course), we can preview the form to test it. When the form opens in preview, click on the *Submit* toolbar button (in the *Standard* toolbar) or the *Submit* menu item on the *File* menu. Since the `studentId` field is not filled out, it causes a validation error in the form, resulting in the dialog shown in Figure 8.13.

FIGURE 8.13: Error dialog that results when submitting a form with validation errors that are in the current view

This is similar to the validation error we saw in the job application form near the beginning of the chapter. However, in this case, we can fill in the `studentId` field by entering a number in the text box for the student ID. Figure 8.14 shows how the form looks when you preview it. The *Submit* button in the toolbar submits the form using the main Web service data connection.

Once the form is properly filled out and submitted, a submit success dialog confirms the submission (Figure 8.15). In this form, the only field that cannot be blank is `studentId`. In real forms, most fields in the data

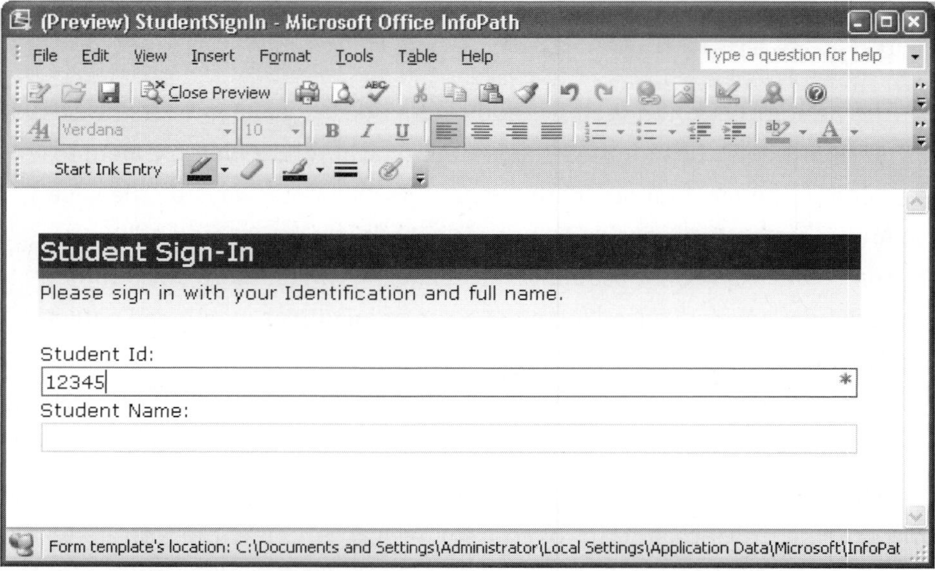

FIGURE 8.14: Student sign-in form during preview

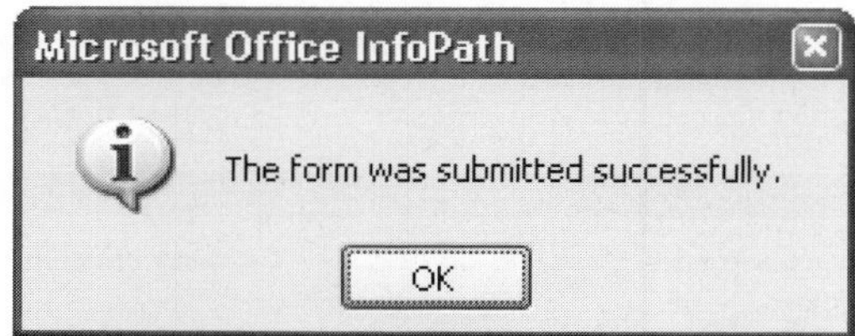

FIGURE 8.15: Dialog confirming that submit succeeded

source may not be allowed to be blank, and you may want to perform further validation on the input data. In our simple sign-in form, for example, we may want to connect to the student database and verify that the student ID and name actually exist. Moreover, it would also be logical to validate that the ID is associated with that student name.

A flexible way to implement these checks would be to use a Web service that can read from the database using ADO.NET. (Refer to Chapter 7 for more about ADO.NET with Web services.) The Web service could accept the necessary input parameters, read and check the data from the database, and finally return a Boolean—`true` if a match is made, `false` otherwise.

Your form could have data validation to check that the Web service does return `true`. If the value is `false`, a validation error will occur and the form will not be allowed to be submitted until the error is remedied.

Partial Submit

It's utopian to think that students will all be signed in before class starts. The reality is that many students (who always seem to be the same students!) are late. We want to track who is late, and how late, for each class. To implement this mechanism into our form, we'll want to include a view where the instructor can enter class information, including the start time. We'll add some logic to our existing form so that if the student submits the form after the class start time, we'll ask why he or she is late. The time checking will happen in InfoPath, not the Web service, so we don't need to count on a submit method to do the validation for us. But Web services will be used to query `GetLateReasons` and submit to `AddLateReason`, as shown earlier in Figure 8.11. (The sample form template is called StudentSignIn2.)

Understanding HTTP Status Codes and Submit

If the submit Web service was sent the class date and time as one of its parameters, it (instead of InfoPath) could figure out whether the student's sign-in is tardy by comparing against the current date and time. However, since we don't receive data from submit, we'd need to force submit to fail somehow. Recall that InfoPath uses the HTTP return status code to determine whether or not the submit was successful. One of the few ways to get the Web service to return a non-200-series status is by explicitly failing in the Web service code. For example, the Web service could throw an exception in a specific case. ASP.NET then sets the HTTP status to some value in the 500 range (typically 500), which means an "Internal Server Error" happened.

We start by creating another view that holds class information. To add class information to our data source, let's add a group called `ClassInformation` and add child fields to hold the data. The controls we insert into the *Class Information* view are editable by default. This view should be used only by the instructor. (In Chapter 13, you'll learn how to use roles with workflow, which enables this scenario.) On the *Student Sign-In* main view, we want to show the class data as read-only. That way a student cannot modify it during sign-in. Figure 8.16 shows our new view and the updated data source.

> **TIP Settings for Data Formatting**
>
> The start date and start time in the *Class Information* view are bound to the same data source field. To separate the date from the time for a single piece of data, we used data formatting to filter the data. The entry point to formatting data types, such as Integer and DateTime, is the *Format* button on the control's properties dialog.

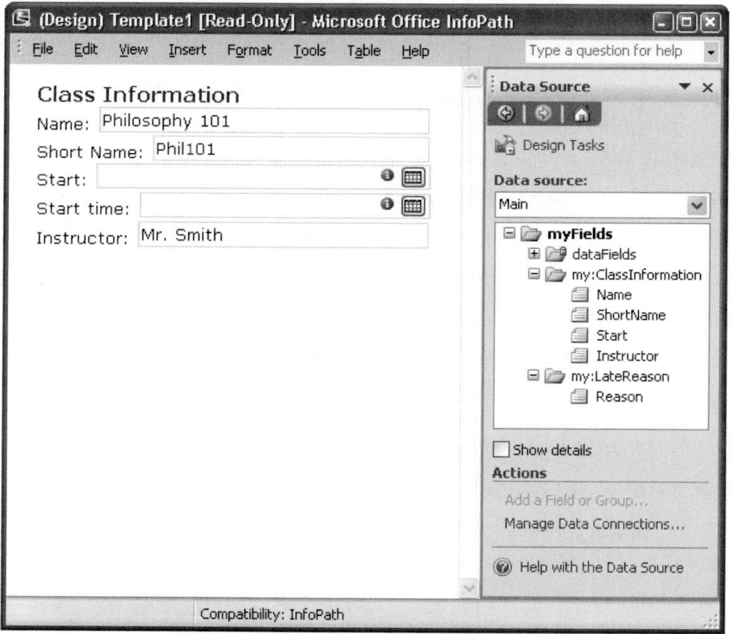

FIGURE 8.16: Student sign-in form showing the instructor's Class Information view with default data

Main Data Source Extensibility and Web Services

A form based on a Web service or database does not have an editable data source. However, it is possible to add field and group nodes immediately under the document element. Adding nodes will always create them in the `my` namespace, as you can see in Figure 8.16. To update or change the data source associated with the main data connection, use *Convert Main Data Source* (discussed Chapter 3), which is available on the *Tools* menu.

TIP Make Your Controls Fit the Data

Wondering how to get Expression Box controls to be exactly as wide as the data they contain (except for the title)? While in the *Size* tab of a control's properties dialog, type "auto" in the *Width* size text box. Once you select *OK* or *Apply,* the control will horizontally shrink to the size of the enclosed text. Don't be alarmed if the control collapses to be very narrow! This appears to happen if there's no text within the control when designing the form template. When a user fills out the form, all auto-width Expression Box controls automatically widen to accommodate their text.

Next, let's add logic to the form to detect whether the sign-in is tardy. If it is, we'll require the student to enter a reason when filling out the form. As you can see from Figure 8.16, in preparation for this requirement, we added a `my:LateReason` group and a `Reason` field to the data source. We've also inserted controls for these data source nodes into the view, as shown in Figure 8.17. (A sample file is called StudentSignIn3.)

The control that holds `LateReason` should appear only when the student is late, that is, when the value of the `Start` field (under the `Class-Information` group) is earlier than the current time. We can use conditional formatting on the `LateReason` section to accomplish this task. Figure 8.18 shows the formatting settings for the section.

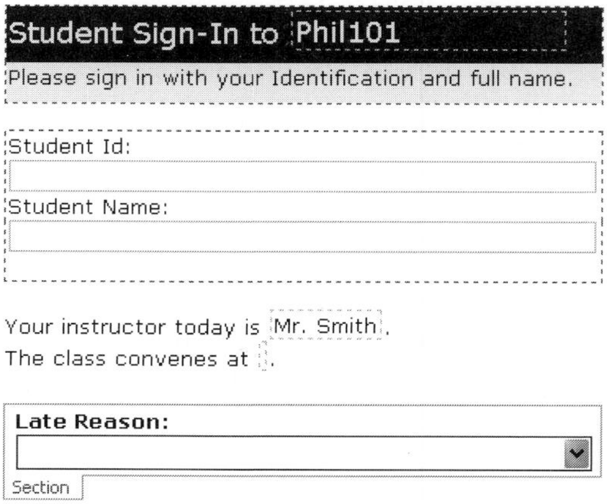

Student Sign-In to Phil101

Please sign in with your Identification and full name.

Student Id:

Student Name:

Your instructor today is Mr. Smith.
The class convenes at .

Late Reason:

Section

FIGURE 8.17: Designing the sign-in form view

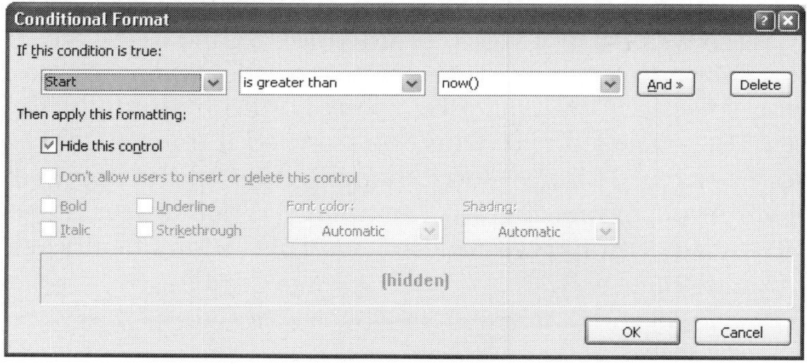

FIGURE 8.18: Configuring conditional formatting to hide the `LateReason` section if the start time is later than now

> **TIP Aligning Control Text with Adjacent Text Labels**
>
> When users fill out your form, does the text within your Expression Box controls not line up properly with the adjacent label text? In design mode, click the *Align* button on the *Size* tab of any control that can hold text. See Chapter 4 for more about alignment.

Now that we're showing the `LateReason` section when the student signs in late, we need to enforce that the student must fill out the `Reason` field explaining why he or she was late. Otherwise, the tardy student could submit the form without filling out the LateReason section. Your first reaction might be to set the *Cannot be blank* setting on the Reason field. This will put the form into a permanently bad state for all nontardy students; the same state, in fact, that we talked about at the end of the validation section earlier in this chapter. All on-time students would get submit errors similar to the one shown in Figure 8.5 because a data source field that isn't in the view is blank and, as a result, invalid. The real solution in this case is to use custom data validation.

Let's add custom validation on the Reason field. The logic in Figure 8.19 is somewhat opposite to that of conditional formatting: the Reason field must be filled out when the class started before now. If we set this up properly, the conditional formatting and custom validation will work nicely together. The Reason field is required to be filled in only when the LateReason section is shown. What we really wouldn't want (and it would be a bad bug with our form) is to require the Reason field to be filled in when the LateReason section is not visible. Another bug would be if we never let the tardy student satisfy the validation error. (Sure he or she is late, but let's not be mean.) We'll allow the validation error to subside only if the Reason field is not blank.

To complete the LateReason section and the Reason field, we need to get the list of late reasons from the GetLateReasons Web service method. To do so, we go to the Reason field's *Drop-Down List Box Properties* dialog and select the *Look up values from an external data source* option.

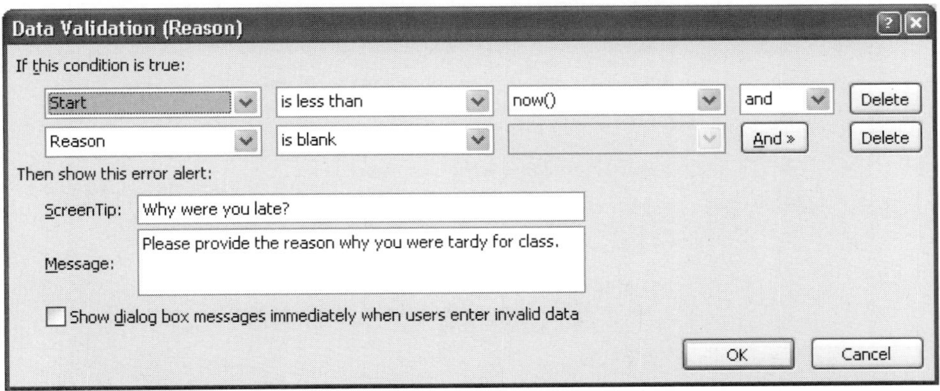

FIGURE 8.19: Setting custom data validation to make the Reason field required when the LateReason section is visible

We're pretty much finished with our form logic, but we're not done with the form yet. What are we doing with the `LateReason` field? The Web service we're currently submitting to accepts only the `studentId` and `studentName` fields (as we saw in Figure 8.12), so we'll need to modify the Web method to accept another parameter: `lateReason` as a string. Our Web service method used to look like this:

```
public void StudentSignIn(int studentId, string studentName)
```

Now we add another parameter, resulting in:

```
public void StudentSignIn(int studentId, string studentName, string
lateReason)
```

(Don't forget to rebuild your Web service!)

As we know from the previous data connection chapters, InfoPath will not automatically update its schema definition of the Web service. To accommodate for this external change, let's go to the *Data Connections* dialog on the *Tools* menu and modify the `Main submit` connection. Going through the dialog is a breeze since everything is already filled out, that is, until we get to the parameter mappings page of the Data Connection Wizard (Figure 8.20).

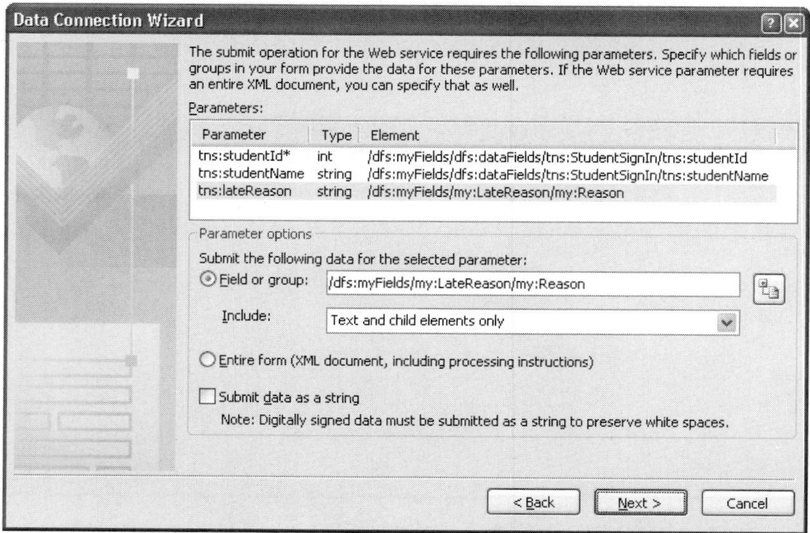

FIGURE 8.20: Defining parameter mappings for Web service submit

> **NOTE The Convert Main Data Source Option Is Only for Query**
>
> When we updated the main data connection for submit, why didn't we use the *Convert Main Data Source* option from the *Tools* menu? Submit is a second-class citizen compared to receive/query data connections. Unfortunately, converting the main data source is restricted to query connections.

Since the `StudentSignIn` method now takes three parameters, we need to define what data source nodes will be sent to each of these parameters when the form is submitted. We designed our form from the original (two-parameter) `StudentSignIn` Web method, so the first two parameters already exist under the `dataFields` group (as children under the `Student-SignIn` group). The third parameter should be mapped to the `Reason` node we recently created under the `LateReason` group. Notice that as you select a parameter in the *Parameters* section at the top of the dialog, the *Parameter options* region updates accordingly. This allows each parameter to have its own parameter options (i.e., the parameter options do not apply to all parameters, but rather to each parameter individually). The results will look similar to Figure 8.20. In the next few sections, we'll go into detail on the parameter options available to further customize your submitted data.

Now the form works precisely as we wanted (Figure 8.21). Nothing will change for on-time students; however, those lucky enough to be tardy must

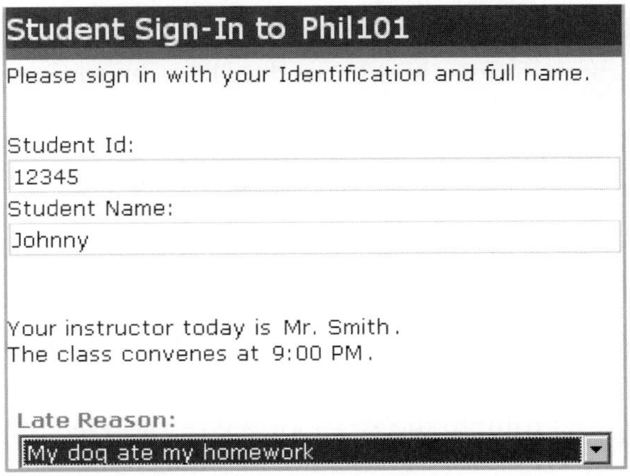

Student Sign-In to Phil101
Please sign in with your Identification and full name.
Student Id:
12345
Student Name:
Johnny
Your instructor today is Mr. Smith.
The class convenes at 9:00 PM.
Late Reason:
My dog ate my homework

FIGURE 8.21: Tardy Johnny signs in to Philosophy 101

select a late reason before submitting. We've decided not to allow students to add new reasons via the `AddLateReason` Web method. In a real-world student sign-in form, you may want to design another form template specifically for managing the list of late reasons students can select from the Drop-Down List Box control.

Submit Parameter Options

Let's go back to the parameter mappings dialog shown in Figure 8.20. Say that we instead had a Web service method that saved the class information entered by the instructor before students start signing in. To begin, we'll create a new Web service method that takes any XML data as a single parameter. (Note that this isn't very safe to do in practice without taking appropriate validation and security measures.) The method also returns that XML data as a string, but since we're submitting in InfoPath, the returned data is discarded. Our Web service method is defined as the following:

```
[WebMethod]
public string XmlNodeToString(System.Xml.XmlNode node)
{
    return node.OuterXml;
}
```

Including Text and Child Elements Only

Let's continue from where we left off with the student sign-in form. Instead of changing our existing main connection for submit, we can simply add a new submit connection! From the *Data Connections* dialog, add a new connection to submit data to a Web service. As before, we'll use the Web service on our local computer containing the Web method called `XmlNodeToString` that we just defined. On the parameter mappings page, let's select the `ClassInformation` group from the main data source. Notice that for the *Include* drop-down, we're keeping the default option of *Text and child elements only.* Leave all other settings on the dialog as they are, and continue to finish the wizard. We will now be submitting the `ClassInformation` group to the `XmlNodeToString` Web method.

> **TIP Mapping Parameters to Any Data Source**
>
> When selecting a field or group from the data source to map to a submit parameter, you aren't limited to the main data source. If you have query data connections in your form, their associated secondary data sources can be selected in the *Data source* drop-down in the *Select a Field or Group* dialog.

We just added a new submit data connection, but remember that it's different than the main submit connection that still exists. To call our new submit connection when filling out a form, we can use a Button control to invoke a rule. We can put the Button anywhere in the form, but it makes the most sense in the *Class Information* view. Finally, we appropriately labeled the Button as *Submit Class Information.*

It's time to test our new partial submit connection. Since the code in the Web service method is useless (and we can't see the data returned from submitting), we're going to set a breakpoint on the only line in the Web method. Set a breakpoint in Visual Studio by putting your cursor on the line of code where you want to stop execution and hitting F9. To actually hit the breakpoint, you need to be actively debugging the Web service. This is also easy to do: Just hit F5 in Visual Studio to "run" the project—this should open your Web browser and navigate to the .asmx test page. You can be sure you're actively debugging the code when *(Running)* is shown in the title of the Visual Studio window, as seen in Figure 8.22. If you want,

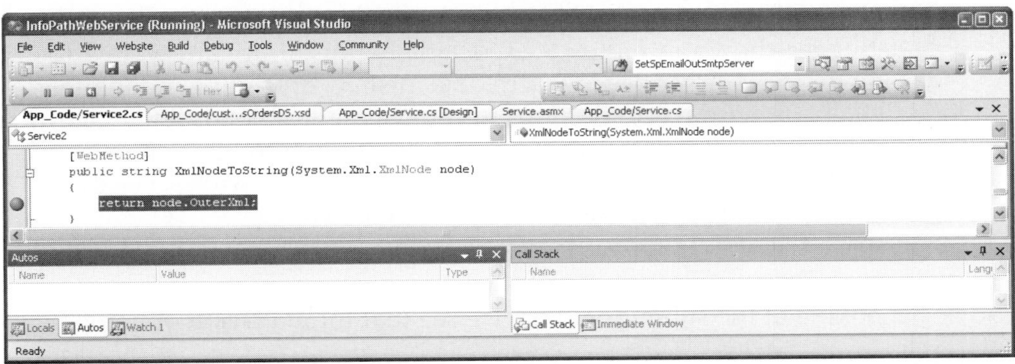

FIGURE 8.22: Debugging the Web service by using Visual Studio

the browser can be minimized since we'll be using InfoPath, not the test page, to call the Web service method.

Going back to InfoPath, let's preview the form and click the *Submit Class Information* button that we added to the *Class Information* view. (If you can't submit your form because of validation errors, go to the main view and fix any errors. Then try to submit again.) When submit happens, the Visual Studio window will appear on top of the InfoPath preview window with the breakpoint line highlighted, as shown in Figure 8.23. The *Autos*

```
[WebMethod]
public string XmlNodeToString(System.Xml.XmlNode node)
{
    return node.OuterXml;
}
```

FIGURE 8.23: Debugger paused at our breakpoint

tab at the bottom left of the screen has `node.OuterXml`. This is the XML data submitted by InfoPath to the Web service. The XML data is as follows:

```
<my:Name xmlns:my=\"http://schemas.microsoft.com/office/
infopath/2003/myXSD/2005-11-19T19:05:48\">Philosophy 101</my:Name>
```

Without the namespace data, it's much easier to read:

```
<my:Name>Philosophy 101</my:Name>
```

> **NOTE** **InfoPath Web Service Connection Timeouts**
>
> Did InfoPath show an error while you were in the Visual Studio debugger shown in Figure 8.23? That's because InfoPath waited too long for the Web service to return data. Instead of waiting indefinitely, all Web service data connections time out after 30 seconds if there is no response. This timeout is configurable, but only through custom code that can be added to your form. Specifically setting a Web service connection timeout is demonstrated in Chapter 15.

Looking at the submitted data, we see that InfoPath sent only the `Name` field under the `ClassInformation` group. So setting the *Include* drop-down to *Text and child elements only* (the default) sends only the first child node of the group you selected. If you wanted to select a field instead of a group node, you would see that only the text of the selected field is sent. What if you wanted to send the entire `ClassInformation` group and all of its children nodes (not just `Name`) to the Web service?

XML Subtree, Including the Selected Element

To send the entire data source selected in the *Field or group* item in the Data Connection Wizard's parameter mapping page (refer back to Figure 8.20), we can choose the *XML subtree, including the selected element* option. This setting is available on the *Include* drop-down. It's easiest to reuse the student sign-in form, and we can simply modify the newly created submit data connection from the last section. To modify the data connection, go to the *Data Connection* item on the *Tools* menu and click *Modify* when the proper connection in the *Data connections for your form* list box is selected. After modifying the connection's *Include* selection to be *XML subtree, including the selected element*, we can go back to preview and test the submit connection again.

This time, when submitting by clicking the *Submit Class Information* button, we get different data appearing in the Visual Studio debugger (with namespaces removed for clarity):

```
<my:ClassInformation>\n\t\t<my:Name>Philosophy101</my:Name>\n\t\t
<my:ShortName>Phil101</my:ShortName>\n\t\t<my:Start>
2005-11-22T16:12:55</my:Start>\n\t\t<my:Instructor>
Mr. Smith</my:Instructor>\n\t</my:ClassInformation>
```

The `\n` and `\t` characters are newline and tab characters, respectively. Replacing these entities makes the submitted XML much clearer:

```
<my:ClassInformation>
    <my:Name>Philosophy101</my:Name>
    <my:ShortName>Phil101</my:ShortName>
    <my:Start>2005-1122T16:12:55</my:Start>
    <my:Instructor>Mr. Smith</my:Instructor>
</my:ClassInformation>
```

This XML data matches up perfectly with the data source (Figure 8.24) that we'd expect to be submitted given our data connection settings. Table 8.3 summarizes InfoPath submit behaviors for fields and groups projected over the *Include* setting.

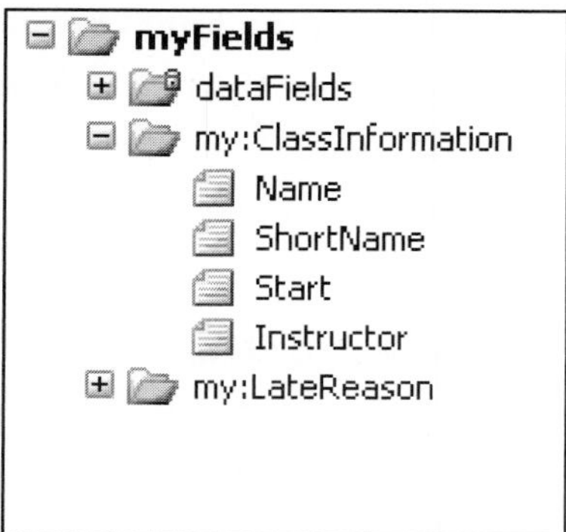

FIGURE 8.24: Data source for the student sign-in form

TABLE 8.3: Matrix of Submit Possibilities among Fields, Groups, and the Include Setting

Parameter Options	*Text and Child Elements Only*	*XML Subtree, Including the Selected Element*
Field	The text value of the selected field	The entire field node (which includes the text value)
Group	The first child element of the selected group	The group node itself and all of its children

Entire Form

Sometimes you will want more flexibility to handle the form data in the Web service. For example, say that you change your mind and no longer want `ClassInformation`, but instead care about the `LateReason` group. Instead of relying on InfoPath to filter and send precisely the data source you want, why not just send the entire form to the Web service? It's a bad idea if your data source is humongous; sending more data over an Internet connection means a slower submit experience, especially for dialup connections. However, if your form data source is of a manageable size (you'll need to determine what "a manageable size" means through testing), it is a good option.

> **TIP Increase Form Performance by Limiting the Amount of Submitted Data**
>
> If you must submit the entire form, try to limit the size of the data source to something reasonable. Form features such as the number of inline (not linked) pictures, file attachments, and recursive data can quickly increase the size of submitted data.

To submit the entire form, simply select the *Entire form (XML document, including processing instructions)* option button in the *Parameter options* section, as shown in Figure 8.25. An incisive reader might ask why we couldn't just use the *Field or group* option, select the `myFields` top-level group, and

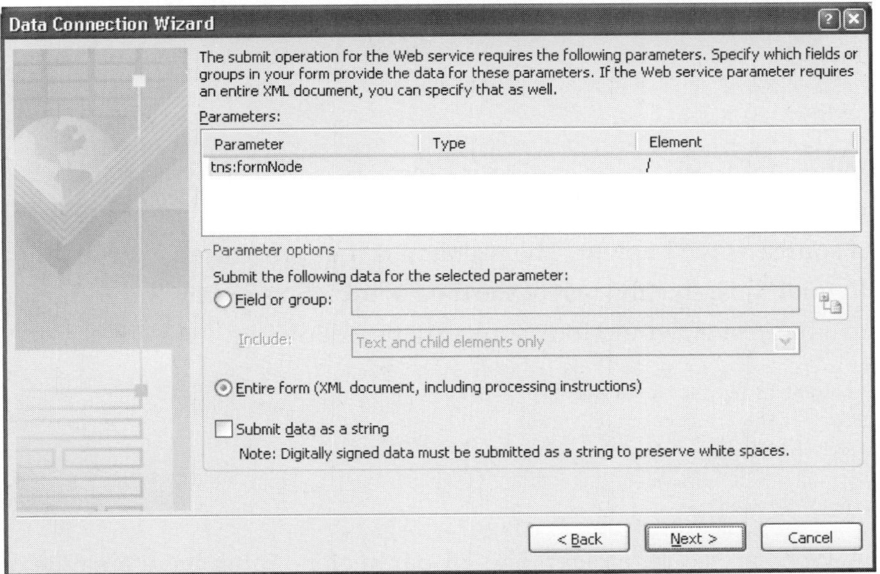

FIGURE 8.25: Parameter mappings dialog configured to submit the entire form

set the *Include* item to be *XML subtree.* The motivation behind using *Entire form* is that the XML processing instructions are sent along with the form data to the Web method parameter. If you're submitting to a Web service that saves the submitted form data to an XML file and you plan to open it in InfoPath, it is essential that you include processing instructions. Without one of the two processing instructions you'll find in an InfoPath .xml file,

Windows cannot properly associate the file with InfoPath. This disassociation is visually obvious because the .xml file icon will look not like an InfoPath file but rather like a generic .xml file that is usually opened by Internet Explorer. Should the other processing instruction not exist, InfoPath will be unable to determine which template should open the form.

XML Processing Instructions

A processing instruction is a special type of XML element that should appear (if any exist) as the first element(s) in an XML document. You can identify processing instructions in an XML file by the `<?` and `?>` delimiters that enclose the processing instruction's data. (Try opening any InfoPath form XML file in a text editor, such as Notepad, to look for its processing instructions.)

When InfoPath sends the entire form to a Web service parameter, it cannot simply send the processing instructions followed by the rest of the data source as we know it. The problem is that processing instructions are XML nodes just like the rest of the data source. So sending the entire form, from a high level, would look similar to the following:

```
<? Processing-instruction1 ?>
<? Processing-instruction2 ?>
<my:myFields>
   . . .
</my:myFields>
```

A Web service parameter, like all parameters, must have a single top-level element. But in our high-level XML snippet, there are three top-level items: two processing instructions and `myFields`. How, then, does InfoPath send the processing instructions? The trick is to wrap the processing instructions and document element (in this case, `myFields`) with an arbitrary top-level node. Submitting the entire form to a Web service parameter will always send a `dfs:IPDocument` node that contains the actual entire form, including processing instructions. In this case, the general practice of putting processing instructions at the top of an XML document is violated. However, it's the only way to send all of the form data as XML data. Also, it's very easy to handle this in the Web service logic. Simply use the `InnerXml` property of the `XmlNode` that receives the entire form. The `InnerXml` property is precisely the entire form you want as it strips off the arbitrary top-level wrapper. The entire document, when sent as a parameter to a Web service, looks like the following XML data:

```
<dfs:IPDocument xmlns:dfs=" . . .">
      <? Processing-instruction1 ?>
      <? Processing-instruction2 ?>
      <my:myFields>
         . . .
      </my:myFields>
</dfs:IPDocument>
```

A sample Web service that will save the InfoPath form data to a temporary file (with a .tmp extension) is shown in Listing 8.1. This code assumes that the entire form is submitted to the Web service since it is stripping off the top-level wrapper node. Figure 8.25 shows the parameters mapping dialog configured to use this code. (Notice that the parameter is `formNode`, which matches the `SaveEntireForm` parameter name.)

LISTING 8.1: Web Service Code to Save the Entire Form

```
[WebMethod]
public void SaveEntireForm(System.Xml.XmlNode formNode)
{
   string tempFile = System.IO.Path.GetTempFileName();
   using (System.IO.StreamWriter writer =
       new System.IO.StreamWriter(tempFile))
   {
       if (formNode != null)
           writer.Write(formNode.InnerXml);
   }
}
```

Submitting Digitally Signed Form Data

With security and privacy being top technological issues of this day and age, it is no surprise that many companies won't settle for anything less. In Chapter 11, we'll talk about the details of setting up form security and deploying secure forms. For now, let's assume our form is set up properly so users can digitally sign some or all of the form data. Without the need to discuss details, we can briefly explain how you can properly submit digitally signed data.

Sending digitally signed form data to an external data source such as a Web service isn't as easy as simply sending the data you want. As we'll find out in Chapter 11, there are two data source–specific characteristics associated with signed form data. In addition to sending the specific data source fields and groups to an external data source, the following must also be included:

1. The associated XML signature
2. Preserved XML content, including white space

If either of these two requirements is disrespected, InfoPath will detect the form as tampered because the digital signature hash of the form won't match the data. Even white-space characters (e.g., tab, newline) are nodes in XML! As a result, it's critical to maintain data integrity when transmitting the form data. However, a slight problem may exist when sending XML data: the sending or receiving entities (InfoPath, the Web service code, or any other software in between) may decide to reformat the XML for efficiency or even laziness in their serialization implementations. **Serialization** is a process in which data is packaged into a convenient transferable format. As you can see, and without going into too many more details, we cannot ultimately rely on sending the XML data as is. In a moment, we'll learn how to remedy this problem.

The most common scenario for sending digitally signed data is to submit the entire form (which may be completely signed or just partially signed, it doesn't matter). But as we saw a moment ago, we cannot just send the XML form data. The way to send XML data to a Web service without worrying about any data being changed is to send it as a string. This form of serialization happens within InfoPath, but it's a lossless serialization that's guaranteed to not change the shape of the original data source. And since we're transferring a string literal from InfoPath to the Web service, we can rest assured that the string's exact value is preserved. What do we need to do in the Web service code to support this? It's quite simple. Now that we're submitting a string instead of XML, we can change the `XmlNode` parameter to `string`.

> **WARNING** Be Careful with Signed XML Data
>
> After receiving signed XML data from InfoPath as a string in your Web service method, be very careful if you decide to load that XML string into an `XmlDocument` or Document Object Model (DOM). If you must load the data into an `XmlDocument`, for example, ensure that it will preserve all white space and not modify its data. Any modification to the data will render the form signature invalid.

Let's talk about how to set up a Web service submit connection on a form that has digitally signed data. When configuring the parameters mapping dialog (refer back to Figure 8.25), you'll want to select both the *Entire form* option as well as check the *Submit data as a string* checkbox. Consider the note text below the checkbox ("Note: Digitally signed data must be submitted as a string to preserve white spaces") to be a friendly reminder for future reference!

Forgot to Sign? In the beginning of the chapter (and as shown in Figure 8.1), we discussed how InfoPath helps guide the user to submit a form if he or she attempts to save it. Similarly, InfoPath also sways the user to sign the form if he or she didn't already do so before attempting to submit. The user will be reminded about signing only when filling out a form that allows the form data to be digitally signed. Figure 8.26 shows the prompt that appears when a user submits an unsigned form in that situation. Notice that the *Yes* button has focus by default, so hitting Enter or Return on the keyboard will automatically show the signing dialog.

To configure whether or not you want the prompt shown in Figure 8.26 to appear to your users, use the related checkbox on the *Form Options* dialog's

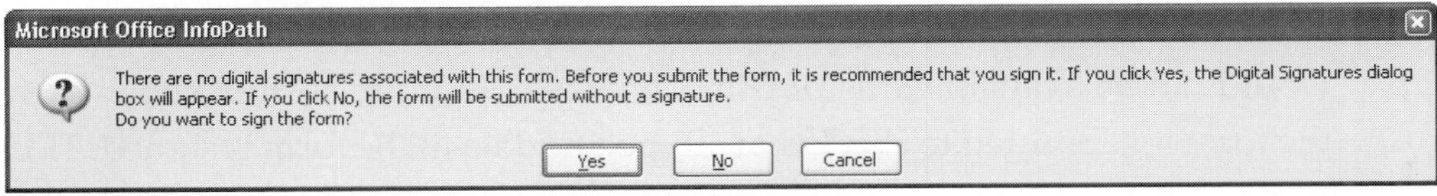

FIGURE 8.26: Dialog that gives the user a chance to digitally sign a form before continuing with submit

Forms Services

Browser-enabled form templates do not allow for signing the entire form. Since the *Prompt user to sign the form if it is submitted without a signature* checkbox is associated with signing the entire form, it's not an available option.

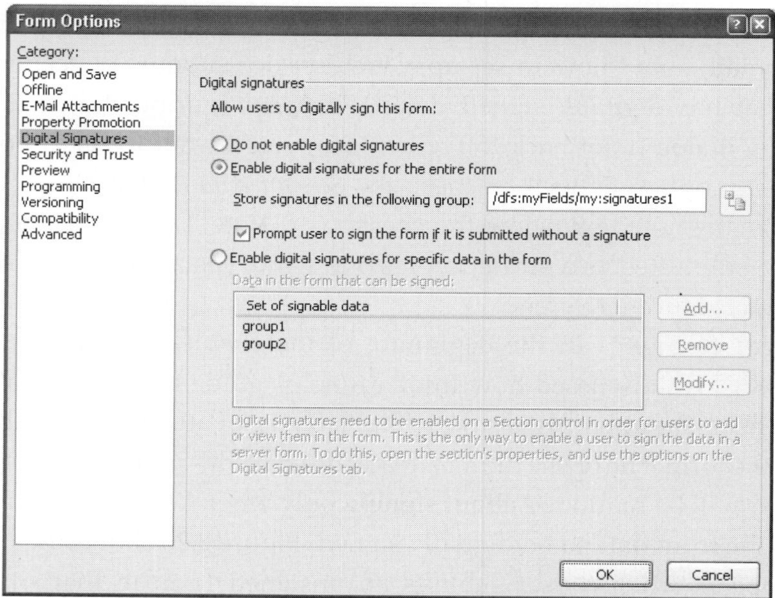

FIGURE 8.27: Controlling whether or not to display the prompt shown in Figure 8.26

Digital Signatures tab (Figure 8.27). Note that you can show the prompt only if digital signatures are enabled for the entire form. If instead you wanted to select the *Enable digital signatures for specific data in the form* item, this option would not be available. It is possible, however, to write custom code when the form is submitted to check that all specific data in the form is signed. This is a complex scenario that you should be able to implement after understanding the material presented in Chapter 15 when we discuss writing custom form code.

We'll learn all about digitally signing form data in Chapter 11.

ADO.NET `DataSet` Submit

In Chapter 7, we learned how to create a Web service by writing some C# code that returns an ADO.NET `DataSet`. In this chapter, we'll bring closure to this topic by showing an end-to-end example of designing a form to receive and submit (update) the back-end data. We'll focus more on the submit portion of the exercise not only because it's the main topic of this chapter but also because it's not as straightforward as other submit connections.

> **TIP Submitting `DataSet` Form Data**
>
> A `DataSet` object can only be submitted from the main data source. Secondary data sources can receive a `DataSet` object but do not track changes, so they cannot be submitted back to the Web service. Using the main data source is a necessity if you want to submit your data back to the Web service for updating the database. The main data source performs change tracking (an ADO.NET requirement) and serializes the `DataSet` object automatically upon submit.

For our back-end data, we'll use a customers database similar to the Northwind example from Chapter 7. But this time, the customers will be those from the MOI Consulting firm. We created a new database called `MOIConsulting` with table `Customers`. Table 8.4 outlines the database structure.

TABLE 8.4: Structure of the `Customers` Table for the MOI Consulting Firm

Column Name	Data Type	Comments
`CustomerID`	Integer	Primary key
`Name`	Varchar (string)	
`Email`	Varchar (string)	
`PendingOrders`	Integer	
`CustomerLogo`	Binary (base64)	Holds picture data; allows null

For this example, we already created a `SqlDataAdapter` and a `SqlConnection` and also generated a `DataSet` called `MOI_Customer_Dataset` by using Visual Studio 2005. (See Chapter 7 for the general steps to follow.) Listing 8.2 shows the Web service code to get and update the `DataSet`, respectively.

LISTING 8.2: Web Service Code to Get and Set the `DataSet` Object Data

```
[WebMethod]
public MOI_Customer_Dataset GetMoiCustomers()
{
   sqlDataAdapter1.Fill(moI_Customer_Dataset1);
   return moI_Customer_Dataset1;
}
[WebMethod]
public void SetMoiCustomers(MOI_Customer_Dataset customerData)
{
   if (customerData.HasChanges())
   {
      sqlDataAdapter1.Update(customerData.Customers);
   }
}
```

Designing a Form Template with a Dataset

Since dataset change tracking is supported only on the main data source, as we discussed in Chapter 7, we'll create a new form based on a Web service that will receive and submit data. Next, as we do for all Web service connections, we enter the location of the Web service WSDL. The next page of the Data Connection Wizard, shown in Figure 8.28, presents the *Include change information when submitting data* option. Without this checkbox enabled, the dataset would not be properly serialized to a diffgram format when submitted to a Web service. As a result, the dataset would be submitted in a raw XML format. Since the `SetMoiCustomers` code snippet in Listing 8.2 accepts a `DataSet` object as a parameter, InfoPath must submit a properly serialized diffgram when the user is filling out the form. Thus this checkbox must be checked. Submitting raw XML to a Web service method that accepts a `DataSet` object will not properly update the database and may even cause unintended side effects like duplication of data.

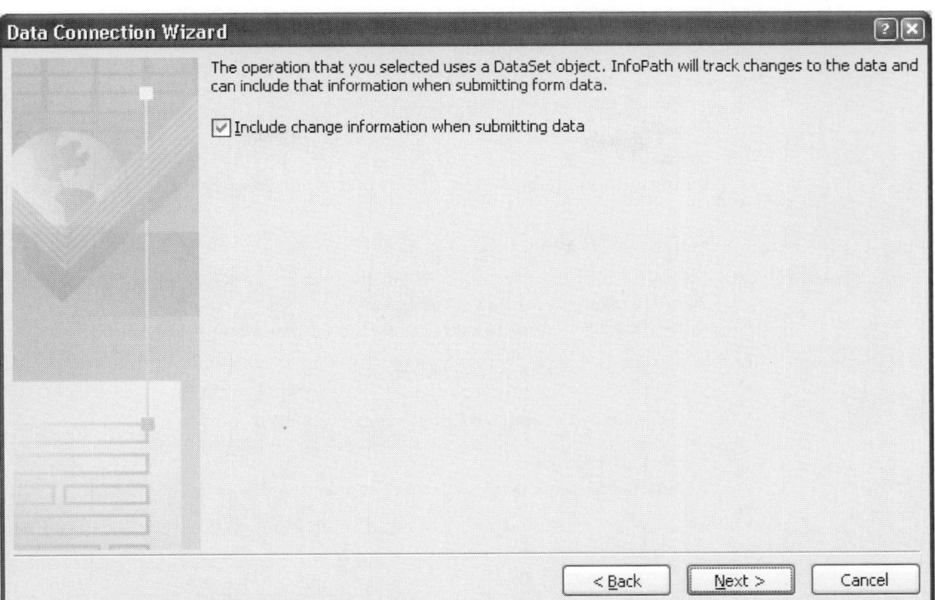

FIGURE 8.28: Configuring change tracking for an ADO.NET dataset Web service

Forms Services

Change tracking is not supported in browser forms. As a result, the raw XML data is sent to the Web service instead of a diffgram. The Web service will need to accept XML (such as an `XmlNode` object) and manually parse the changes to apply to the database.

The next few wizard steps include the final page for setting up the receive data connection, locating the WSDL file for the submit connection, and selecting the `SetMoiCustomers` Web service method. Finally, we get to the step where the wizard asks us to set up parameter mappings (Figure 8.29).

As you can see in Figure 8.29 by the *Type* being set as *(Complex Type)*, the parameter mapping step does not tell you that the `tns:customerData` parameter is a `DataSet` object. Actually, there is no good way to know it's a

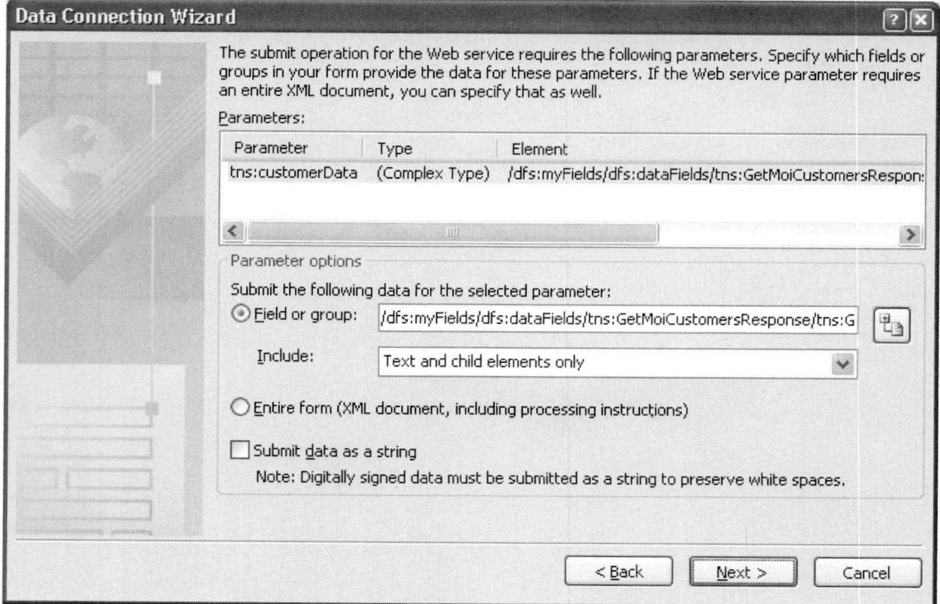

FIGURE 8.29: Setting up a parameter mapping for a `DataSet` object

dataset without looking at the Web service source code or WSDL. Well, there is another way, but it's just to go ahead and click the button adjacent to the *Field or group* text box to select a data source node. Expanding the data source in the *Select a Field or Group* dialog (Figure 8.30) might yield some hints that you're working with a dataset instead of some arbitrary data structure.

The data source in Figure 8.30 has telltale signs of a dataset. First and most easy to see is the repeating virtual (`Choice`) group. The other sign is the single group (or many groups for multiple tables) under the (`Choice`) group, which contains only fields. To find the root of the dataset itself, look no further than the immediate parent of the repeating (`Choice`) group: `ns1:MOI_Customer_Dataset`. In this case, we made it easy since the dataset node has the name "Dataset" in it. That's only because we used that name for the `SetMoiCustomers DataSet` object parameter. But we could have called it anything.

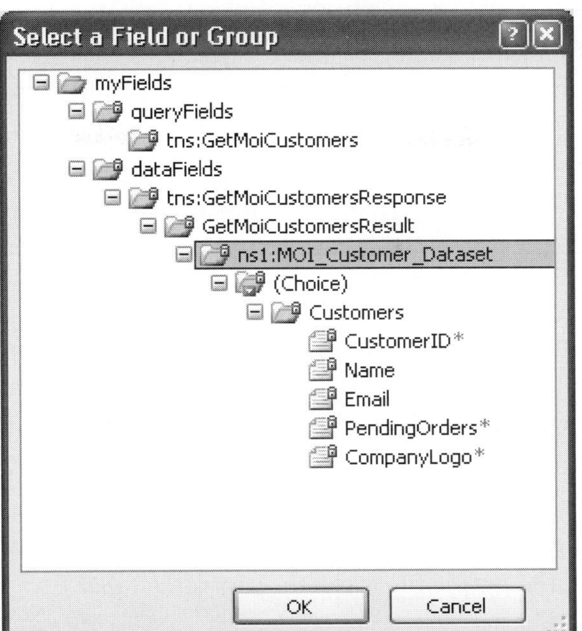

FIGURE 8.30: Data source representative of a dataset structure

Why are we discussing the root of the dataset and how to recognize it? That's the node that must to be selected when mapping a dataset parameter. As expected, Figure 8.30 has the correct dataset root node selected. When the dataset root node is properly mapped to a submit parameter, InfoPath will perform the proper serialization to create a diffgram when the form is submitted. Picking any other node in the data source will only send the raw XML data. The other *Parameter options* settings in Figure 8.29 do not affect dataset serialization as long as the correct `DataSet` object is selected as the group to submit.

> **NOTE Only One Dataset at a Time**
>
> InfoPath supports only a single dataset in the main data source. If more than one `DataSet` object is detected in the Web service WSDL when you're designing the form, InfoPath will warn that only one can exist at any given time when a user fills out the form.

Forms Services

Browser-enabled form templates in the browser do not track changes, so there's no diffgram serialization. As a result, it's not critical to choose the dataset group in the *Select a Field or Group* dialog shown in Figure 8.30. If the dataset is chosen, its content is submitted as plain XML data.

After you finish the wizard, the view is prepopulated similarly to starting with any other Web service connection: a table with a header, a region for query fields, a *Run Query* button, and a region for data fields. The data source for the form is exactly that shown in Figure 8.30. We'll take a simple approach to designing the view by including the data in a Repeating Table as well as inserting Button controls for querying and submitting. Figure 8.31 shows the view. (A sample file is called AdoNetDataSet.)

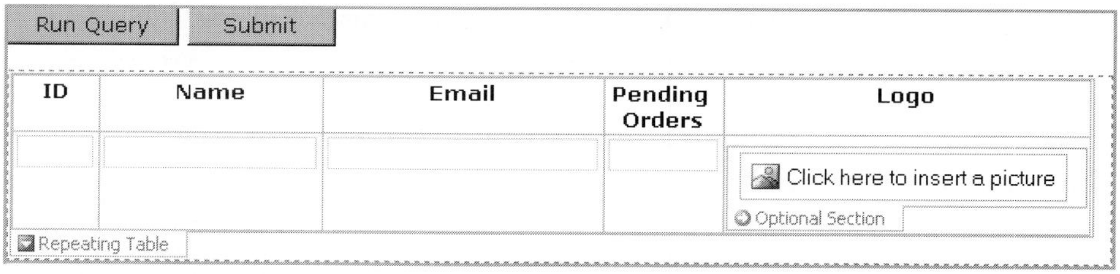

FIGURE 8.31: Designing the view of the form receiving and submitting an ADO.NET `DataSet` object

WARNING Null Values Translate to Missing Nodes

Use caution in designing your form when ADO.NET pulls data from a database that allows null values in a table column. A null value in a given row means that the control is not editable because there is no node in the data! Columns that can have null values should be inserted as an Optional Section with Controls. That way a user can insert the Optional Section to be able to edit that field. If there were no Optional Section for the "Logo" column in Figure 8.31, a picture could never be inserted if that value were null in any database table row.

Filling Out the Dataset Form

Now that our form is ready to go, let's preview and see what happens when we query and submit the data. When the form opens in preview, it will show a single, empty row in the `Customers` table (Figure 8.32).

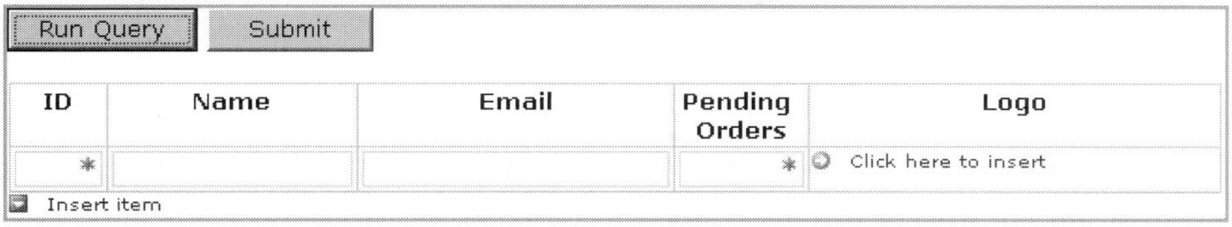

Run Query | Submit

ID	Name	Email	Pending Orders	Logo
*			*	Click here to insert

Insert item

FIGURE 8.32: Filling out a dataset form template with default data

In a real-world form, you could set up a rule to query the main data source when the form is opening. For now, we'll just click the *Run Query* button. Figure 8.33 shows the results from query.

Run Query | Submit

ID	Name	Email	Pending Orders	Logo
1	Food Corporation	food@food.com	4	
2	Computer Corp.	pc@computer.com	2	
3	Catering, LLC	catering@catering.com	0	

Insert item

FIGURE 8.33: After querying the form shown in Figure 8.32

TIP Primary Key Field in Form Templates

When designing a front end to database data, you typically wouldn't show the primary key column as we're doing in our example. Simply deleting the "ID" table column when designing the form will visually hide it from your users.

Let's try changing some data and submitting the form. Give the Catering, LLC customer a single pending order, and then click either of the *Submit* toolbar or view buttons. Then pretend that, just a moment ago, you also found out that Computer Corporation has only one pending order, not two. But when you try to update the field to be "1" from its current value of "2", an error appears (Figure 8.34). The dataset-specific data source is completely read-only after a successful submit operation.

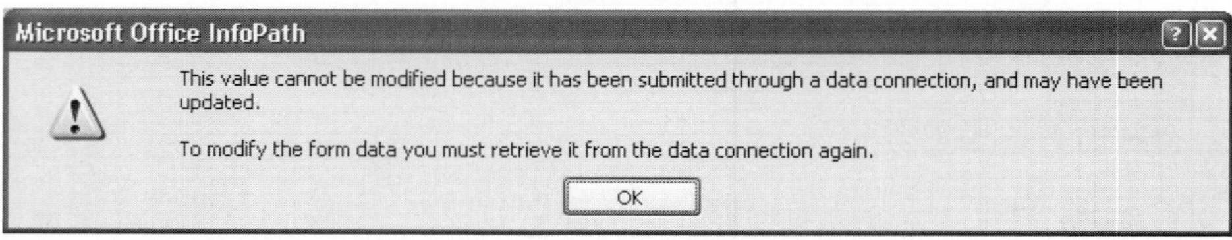

FIGURE 8.34: Error that results from trying to modify dataset form data after submit

Since ADO.NET submit packages the changes from the `DataSet` object as a diffgram and sends it off to the Web service, many things could have happened to our submitted data. The Web service method that we use for submit could have decided to further process the `DataSet` object by adding, removing, or modifying the data before sending it to the back-end database. Furthermore, the database itself may have triggers or may assign default or key values to any of the inserted data. If you want to submit the dataset data again, query first, and then you can make changes and submit again. You can create a rule (on the *Submit Options* dialog) that performs the data connection submit and then immediately does a query so that the user filling out the form doesn't need to manually requery the data.

Additional behaviors of ADO.NET `DataSet` objects and InfoPath are discussed in Chapter 7. For more information, a comprehensive article on using `DataSet` objects in InfoPath is on MSDN (see the reference in the Appendix; despite being specific to InfoPath 2003, the validity of this article carries over to InfoPath 2007).

Submitting to a SharePoint Library

Submitting a form to a SharePoint server is arguably one of the most useful out-of-the-box submit scenarios for InfoPath. SharePoint brings many rich and collaborative features to InfoPath forms, such as a central location to share data, orchestrate workflows, and manage alerts, to name a few highlights. To leverage these features among many others, the entire form XML must be uploaded to a document library. The SharePoint submit connection not only uploads the entire form to a library but also helps to maintain a homogeneous document library. A homogeneous library contains filled-out forms based on a single common form template. When form data is based on the same template, it is possible to perform operations in SharePoint, such as merging, across all items in a library. Let's now look at InfoPath-specific functionality that supports submitting to a SharePoint document library.

Setting up SharePoint submit is quite similar to what we did with e-mail submit. Three settings define the submit connection: a SharePoint document library, a file name, and a checkbox that indicates whether existing files can be overwritten. The document library and overwrite setting cannot be changed, but the form name can be generated by using a formula. (The target document library actually can be changed while the form is filled out, but doing so requires custom form code. See Chapter 15 for

SharePoint Document Library Submit

In reality, the SharePoint submit connection isn't doing anything new. Users can already save their forms to any SharePoint document library to which they have access. Obviously, the advantage with this SharePoint connection is the combination of submit with save to a document library.

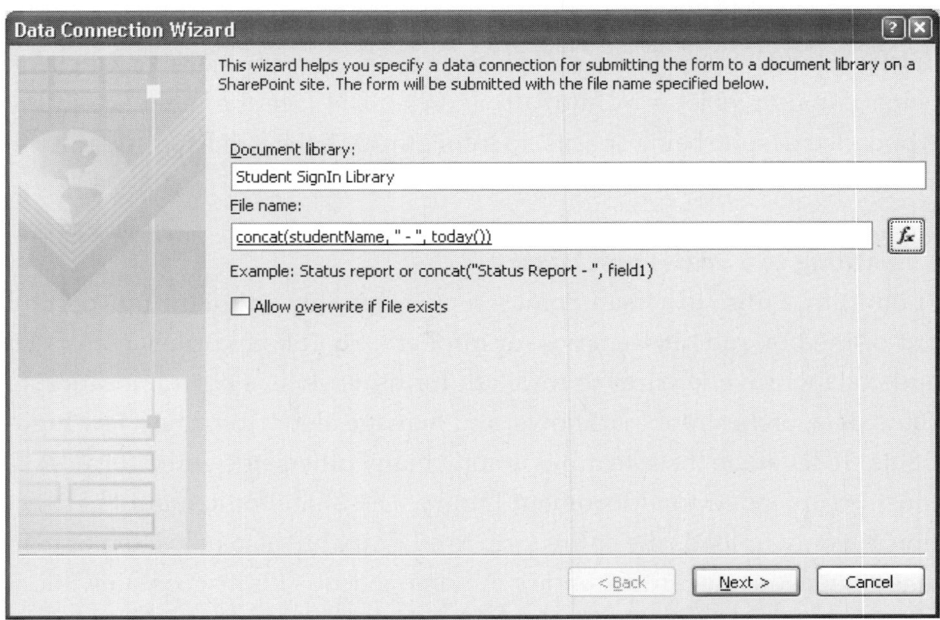

FIGURE 8.35: Configuring SharePoint document library submit for the student sign-in form

details on programming InfoPath.) Figure 8.35 shows these settings. (This sample is called StudentSignIn-SharePoint.)

Our example for submit to SharePoint will be to change the main submit on the student sign-in form. Instead of sending the form data to the Web service, we'll send it to a SharePoint document library specifically for sign-ins by students. Unlike changing a main query (when you can use *Convert Main Data Source*) or secondary data connection (when you can use *Modify* from the *Data Connections* dialog), submit is not as straightforward to reconfigure. Despite the main submit connection listed on the *Data Connections* dialog, we'll want to use the *Submit Options* dialog shown in Figure 8.36.

When you open the dialog, the *Send form data to a single location* drop-down should have *Web service* still selected from our earlier submit examples. The first step is to change it to *SharePoint document library.* As a result, the *Choose a data connection for submit* item becomes disabled. This happens because no SharePoint library submit connection exists in the form template. Clicking the *Add* button will jump us into the Data Connection Wizard for a SharePoint library submit connection. We already have a

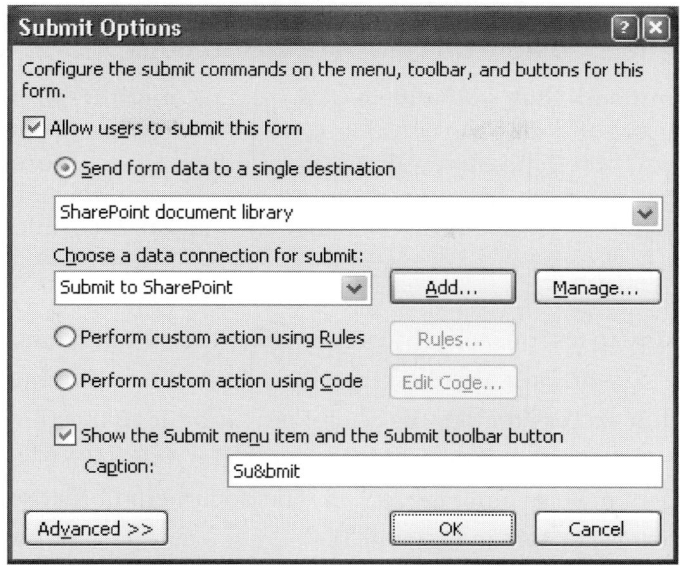

FIGURE 8.36: Submit Options dialog configured to submit to a SharePoint document library

SharePoint server with a newly created document library called `Student SignIn Library` that will hold the form submissions. We expect that each student who signs in will do so at most once in a day. (Each instructor will have his or her own library per class.) If an instructor wanted to use the same library for all classes, the *File name* item could be made more complicated by including more information from the `ClassInformation` group (such as `Name`, `ShortName`, `Start`, and `Instructor`; shown earlier in Figure 8.16). Finally, we do not want to allow overwrites. If this form were instead tracking attendance and were filled out by the instructor, it would make sense to allow overwriting in case the form needed to be resubmitted.

The next wizard page is the summary page that lists the connection details we entered in the dialog shown in Figure 8.35. After we click *Finish,* the Data Connection Wizard closes, and the *Submit Options* dialog is back in front, as shown in Figure 8.36. That's it! We've switched from using a Web service to a SharePoint submit connection! Notice, however, that the `Web Service Submit` connection still exists in the list on the *Data Connections* dialog. Since the data connection isn't being used, you can delete it.

> **WARNING Delete Unused Data Connections**
>
> We recommend that you delete stale data connections, primarily because users of your form could look into the template to get connection information that you might not want others to see. Moreover, it's a best practice for security to not expose connection information since it gives hackers specific knowledge that an external data source exists.

We're ready to test our form by previewing it. Assuming that all required fields in the sign-in form are filled in, we can click the *Submit* button. When we receive the success dialog, the SharePoint submit connection has saved the entire form to the document library with the name we assigned from the *File name* item shown in Figure 8.35. The document library with sample submitted forms appears in Figure 8.37.

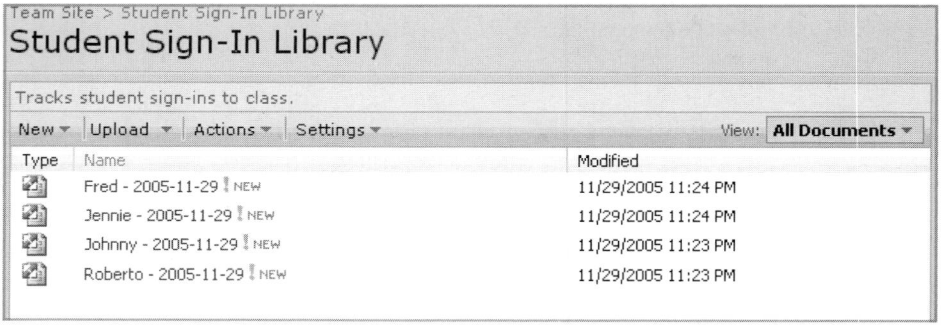

Team Site > Student Sign-In Library

Student Sign-In Library

Tracks student sign-ins to class.

New ▾ | Upload ▾ | Actions ▾ | Settings ▾ View: All Documents ▾

Type	Name	Modified
	Fred - 2005-11-29 ! NEW	11/29/2005 11:24 PM
	Jennie - 2005-11-29 ! NEW	11/29/2005 11:24 PM
	Johnny - 2005-11-29 ! NEW	11/29/2005 11:23 PM
	Roberto - 2005-11-29 ! NEW	11/29/2005 11:23 PM

FIGURE 8.37: SharePoint document library that contains submitted form data

Submitting to a Web Server via HTTP

One of the least complicated InfoPath submit scenarios is Web server via HTTP. Not to be confused with Web service submit, HTTP submit simply uses a `POST` operation to send the entire form's data to the server. Setting up Web server submit is limited to the main submit connection, so it is not possible to use it as a secondary submit or even with rules (as we'll discuss in a moment). In fact, InfoPath does not formally consider Web server submit a data connection. Let's set it up for the student sign-in form to see for ourselves.

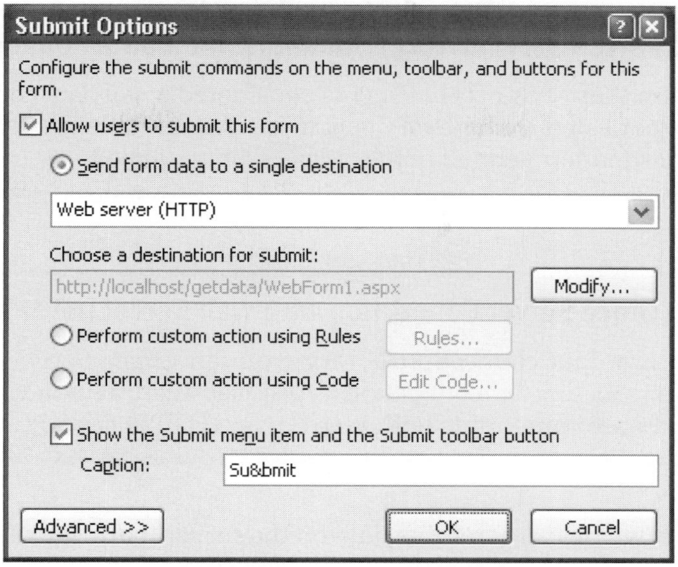

FIGURE 8.38: Submit Options dialog for Web server submit via HTTP

To submit the form to a Web server via HTTP, we'll start by going to the *Submit Options* dialog (Figure 8.38).

The only configuration option for Web server submit is a location. Changing the *Send form data to a single destination* item to *Web server (HTTP)* allows you to also set the *Choose a destination for submit* option. However, the *Choose a destination for submit* option does not allow you to type in a destination. To do so, click the *Modify* button, which lets you enter a server or use a data connection library, as shown in Figure 8.39. (This sample is called StudentSignIn-HTTP.)

FIGURE 8.39: Setting the destination option to use an ASP.NET page

NOTE Web Server (HTTP) Submit Is Not a Data Connection

Submit to a Web server (HTTP) is not considered a real data connection since it's not listed in the *Data Connections* dialog. Rather, it's simply a submit destination defined in the *Submit Options* dialog.

TIP Office Server Connection with Web Server (HTTP) Submit

If you use a data connection library from an Office Server connection, only `XmlSubmit` connection types classified as `ReadWrite` or `WriteOnly` are compatible with Web Server (HTTP) submit.

How can we properly receive data on the server that's sent using HTTP submit? You can use an ASP (.asp) or ASP.NET (.aspx) page to get the posted data. The request data will contain the entire form data source (the same data that would be in an XML file if the form data was saved). By loading the posted data into an `XmlDocument` or Microsoft Core XML (MSXML) DOM, you can get anything from the data source, such as field values. The logic in your ASP or ASP.NET page may use some of the form data to make decisions on what to do. For example, you might have Option Button controls in the form that the ASP page uses to determine how to send confirmation of the submission: e-mail, pager, home phone, or snail mail.

TIP How Web Server (HTTP) Submit Works

There may be a misconception that Web server (HTTP) submit saves a file to a Web server's virtual directory. In fact, this is not true. If you set up a virtual directory that allows for write permission (and the target physical directory also allows write for the appropriate users), submitting to http://Server/VirtualDirectory will appear to succeed from InfoPath, but in reality the submission never happened. The server will return an HTTP 405 error—Resource not allowed—to InfoPath. If you're wondering why InfoPath claims submit succeeded, it's because InfoPath only cares about the HTTP status code. Anything that's not in the 500 series of codes is considered a success.

The snippet shown in Listing 8.3 is code behind an ASP.NET page with server-side C#. The page gets the posted data from the submit request and sends it back as the response in an HTML page.

LISTING 8.3: ASP.NET Page Load Event Handler to Read Data Submitted by the Web Server (HTTP) Connection

```
private void Page_Load(object sender, System.EventArgs e)
{
    Response.Write("<html><body><head><title>Thanks for
       submitting!</title></head><body>");
    System.Text.Encoding encoding = System.Text.Encoding.UTF8;
    byte[] buffer = Request.BinaryRead(Request.TotalBytes);
    string strBuffer = encoding.GetString(buffer);
    Response.Write("You submitted: <p>" + strBuffer);
    Response.Write("</body></html>");
}
```

Secure Submit with HTTPS

Enabling HTTP Security, or HTTPS, is as simple as using an HTTPS address when you would otherwise use an HTTP address. (Secure Submit with HTTPS is not considered another data connection on its own, but is just a variant of the Web Server (HTTP) adapter.) The result is a secured communication stream between InfoPath and the server when a user fills out a form. HTTPS, however, is not limited to Web server (HTTP) submit. The HTTP Security protocol can be used with any HTTP-friendly data connection, such as Web service and SharePoint, to name a few.

Assuming that you have properly set up and tested the server for an operational HTTPS connection, just point InfoPath to that address. There is no additional setup or configuration.

Custom Submit Using Form Code

So far, submitting an InfoPath form has come to mean that some or all of the form data is being sent to an external data source. But submit doesn't necessarily mean that data needs to go anywhere! Case in point: submit using form code.

The idea behind submit using form code is the following: When the user submits the form, some code that you have written starts running. This code can do pretty much anything the form allows (in terms of security). For example, this code can use other data connections in the form, use its own custom mechanisms to talk to an external or local data source, or even do absolutely nothing! It's up to you. To enable submitting with custom code, select the *Perform custom action using Code* option button on the *Submit Options* dialog. (The *Submit Options* dialog is shown earlier in Figure 8.38.) To go ahead and add or edit code for submit, click the *Edit Code* button.

Editing Code with InfoPath

To edit code in C# or Visual Basic .NET, the following components are prerequisites: .NET Framework 2.0, Microsoft Core XML (MSXML) 6.0, and Visual Studio Tools for Applications (VSTA), which is an optional component with an InfoPath installation.

Custom submit with form code always succeeds unless the code sets a status flag to signify failure. However, if the form code fails unexpectedly (e.g., an unhandled exception is thrown by the code), submit will fail automatically.

We'll postpone further discussion until Chapter 15, where we'll show a form code submit example. However, we wanted to briefly introduce the concept of calling custom code from submit since it is an important consideration in complex form design.

Custom Submit Using Rules

Submitting with custom code isn't the only way to customize submit. What if you just don't know how or don't want to write code? Well, you shouldn't have to! Thanks to submit using rules, you can define a custom series of form and data source actions when the user submits the form.

To show the usefulness of rules as a submit mechanism, let's again revisit the student sign-in form. We added an additional submit data connection (called `Web Service Submit`) in the "Submit Parameter Options" section earlier in this chapter. But we had already defined a `Main submit` connection! If you recall, `Main submit` sent the student sign-in data, while `Web Service Submit` sent the `ClassInformation` group. What if, instead of having two separate kinds of submits, we wanted to coalesce them into a single submit action? With rules, it's easy! (The sample file is called StudentSignIn-Rules.)

Begin by going back to the *Submit Options* dialog and enabling the option button for *Perform custom action using Rules* (Figure 8.40).

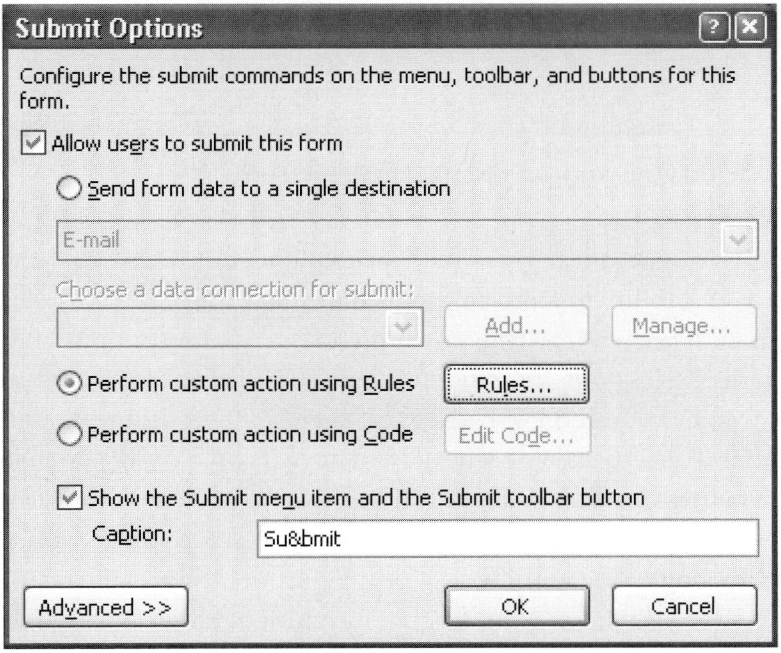

FIGURE 8.40: Setting up submit using rules

Then click on the adjacent *Rules* button. The *Rules for Submitting Forms* dialog will appear (Figure 8.41).

We have a choice of adding either two rules or a single rule to do the actual submits to the Web services. If we add two rules, each rule will have a single action to submit each of the connections: One will submit using `Main submit` and the other will submit with `Web Service Submit`. Alternatively, we could just use a single rule that has two actions. The advantage

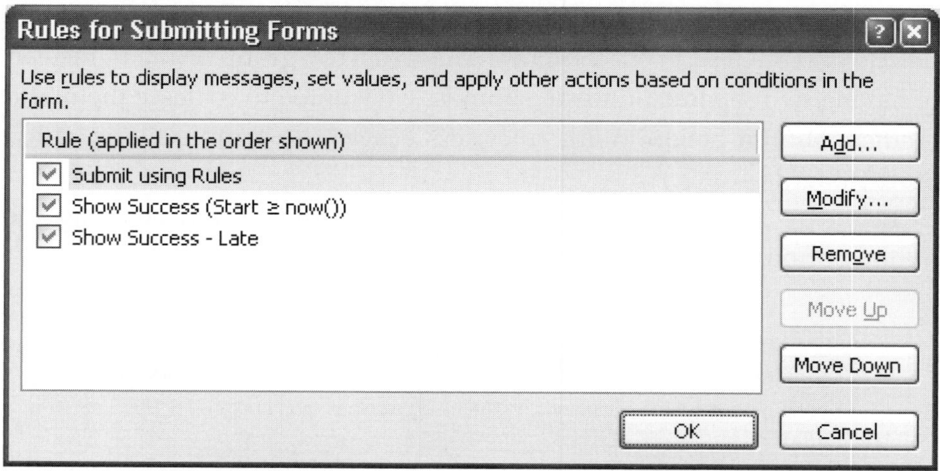

FIGURE 8.41: List of rules that run when the form is submitted

of using two separate rules is that each rule can have its own condition as well as the ability to stop running subsequent rules in the list shown in Figure 8.41. If we want to trigger submit on `Main submit` only under specific conditions, say, if the student signing in is tardy, but we want to always trigger submit on `Web Service Submit`, then using separate rules is essential. This is because each rule can have its own condition that determines whether or not it runs. But in our case, we always want to submit both connections simultaneously without any restrictions in condition. So we'll add a single rule with two actions; Figure 8.42 shows the result.

After submitting, we want to give the student either positive or negative feedback depending on whether or not they signed in on time. To do so, we add two more rules, as shown in Figure 8.41. The first of the two new rules checks whether the current time is earlier than the class time. If that's the case, the rule shows a "Thanks for being on time" message and stops processing rules. We want to stop processing rules so the "Show Success—Late" rule doesn't run. Otherwise, if the student is not on time, the "Thanks" message is skipped. In this case, we show a dialog box expression that's set up to show the student's name with a somewhat reprimanding message. This is accomplished by using a formula for the Expression Box, as shown in Figure 8.43.

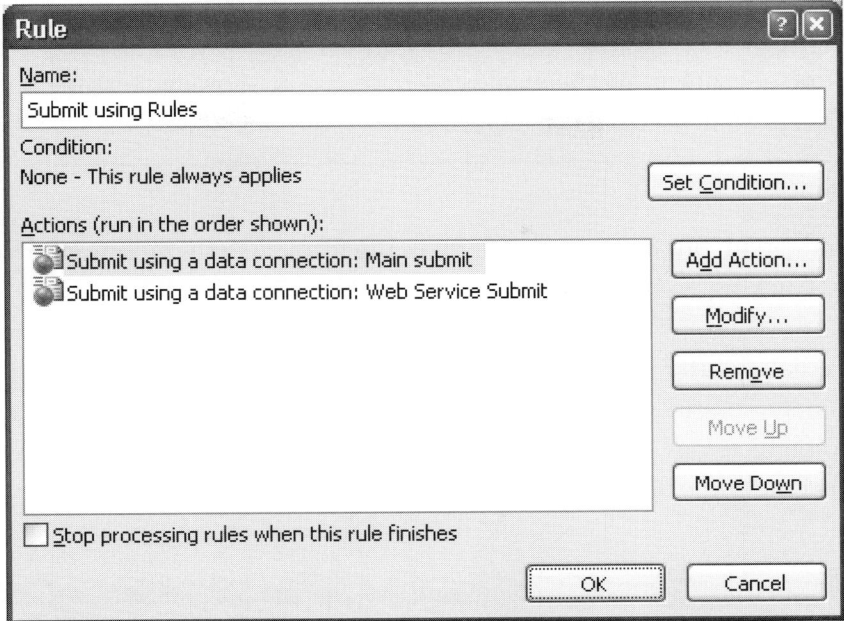

FIGURE 8.42: Actions for the actual submit to the Web services

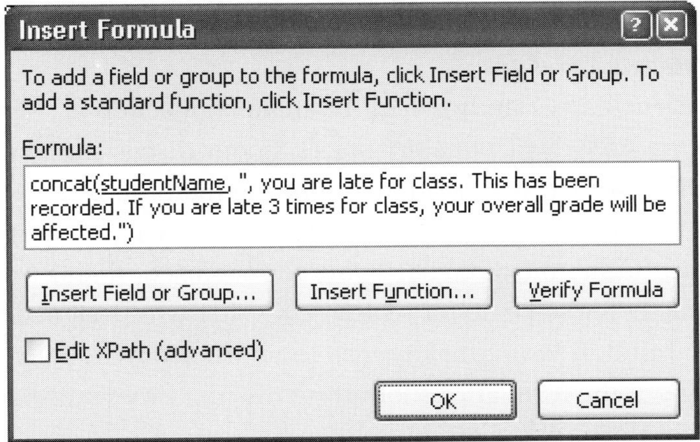

FIGURE 8.43: Expression shown in a popup message when a student signs in late to class

Forms Services

Browser-enabled form templates do not support showing message box dialogs when filled out in the browser.

Time to fill out the form! We'll fill in the form such that Johnny is late to class. Clicking *Submit* will take a moment to send the data to both Web services. Then, as we had set up, the warning in Figure 8.44 appears. Immediately after clicking *OK* to this dialog, the generic dialog that indicates a successful submit appears. We'll learn how to customize or even completely remove this generic dialog in the "Submit Options" section toward the end of this chapter.

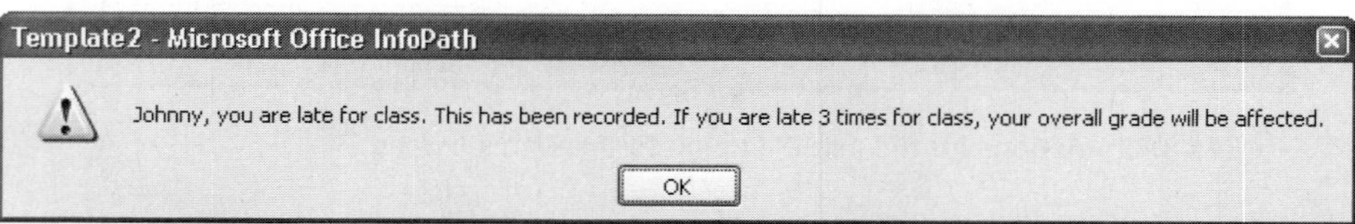

FIGURE 8.44: Dialog that appears when Johnny signs in tardy

ADO.NET Datasets and Rules

Rules are particularly handy when the main connection is a Web service submitting an ADO.NET `DataSet` object. In our discussion of submitting an ADO.NET dataset, we mentioned that the main data source becomes read-only (i.e., any changes to the data are forcefully rejected by InfoPath) after a successful submit. But what if your form is just updating a database—which is exactly the scenario for which ADO.NET was designed? With this question in mind, it won't make sense to your users why they can't continue filling out the form after submitting the first time. But there's a way to remedy this form-filling pitfall: rules to the rescue!

In our earlier example of the MOI Consulting `Customers` dataset, we had two separate operations corresponding to two buttons in the view: query and submit. If submitting the form requires a subsequent query operation to let the user continue editing the form data, why not just do it automatically? By going to the *Submit Options* dialog, we can change from submitting to a Web service to instead using rules. All we need is a single rule with two actions. The first action will submit the `Main submit` data connection. The second simply runs the `Main query` data connection. Now when a user submits the data, he or she can continue editing the form and no longer receive the pesky requery warnings shown back in Figure 8.34.

> **WARNING Query May Not Get Newly Submitted Data**
>
> It is not always guaranteed that running a query after a submit will return the same data the user had immediately before the submit! What if, for example, a dataset query took a string parameter that allowed filtering. Then the user added a record (e.g., a new row) that did not fall within the current query filter. If submitting the form did a submit operation and then requeried with the same query filter, the record the user just added would not appear. This could be confusing since the user might think his or her newly submitted data never made it to the back-end database, when indeed it did. If you use rules to requery submitted data, ensure that the query returns the same data that was shown before submit.

Disadvantages with Rules

Despite the ability to highly customize submit with rules, it does have some disadvantages. The main weakness with rules, in general, is the inability to gracefully deal with error handling. For example, what if one of the two data connections in our first rule had a problem and didn't submit properly? If the first connection failed, the second connection would never get a chance to submit because all subsequent actions and rules are skipped on failure. There are two different cases when submit with rules can fail: main submit and secondary submit connections.

In the case of failure when running rules on a secondary connection, the dialog box in Figure 8.45 appears (but without the details opened by default). The error message "Some rules were not applied" is not helpful to the user. The details might have more information, such as Figure 8.45 shows, but this dialog may still confuse an InfoPath novice filling out your form.

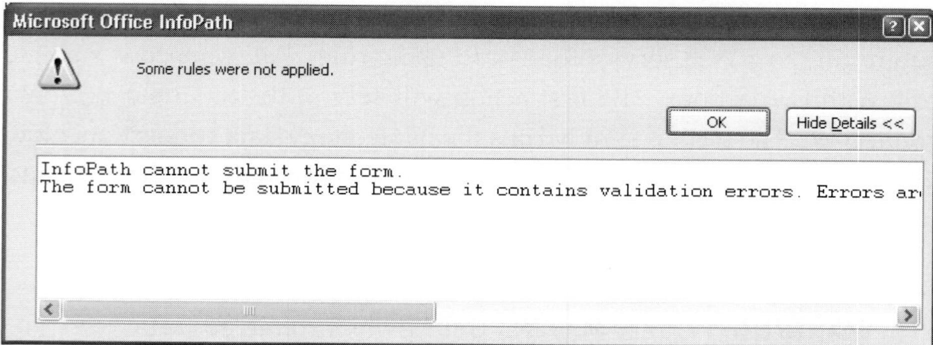

FIGURE 8.45: Dialog that appears when submit with rules fails on a secondary connection

TIP No Error Handling for Rules

Rules do not allow for you to handle errors. In other words, if a rule fails when the user is filling out the form, there is nothing you can do in the form design to change that experience. If error handling is integral to your form, you may want to consider using custom submit in form code. Form code allows you complete control and the ability to fine-tune form behavior should an error occur.

Recall that a **main submit connection** is the data connection listed in the *Submit Options* dialog and is invoked by using the *Submit* button in the toolbar or the menu, or a Button control whose *Action* item is *Submit.* In contrast, a **secondary submit connection** is listed in the *Data Connections* dialog (similar to the main submit) but not in the *Submit Options* dialog. It is run by using arbitrary rules or with custom form code, for example, using a Button control with a rule to submit a data connection.

Forms Services

Failing to submit while filling out a form in the browser results in the *Form Warning* dialog.

Alternatively, when the rule performing the custom submit fails when the main submit connection fails, InfoPath shows a more helpful dialog (Figure 8.46). At least saying "InfoPath cannot submit the form" is the top-level error message, unlike the error shown for the secondary submit failure. As you can see, using a main submit data connection gives a better initial error message compared with that of secondary submit. Let's hope it means fewer calls for help from your users!

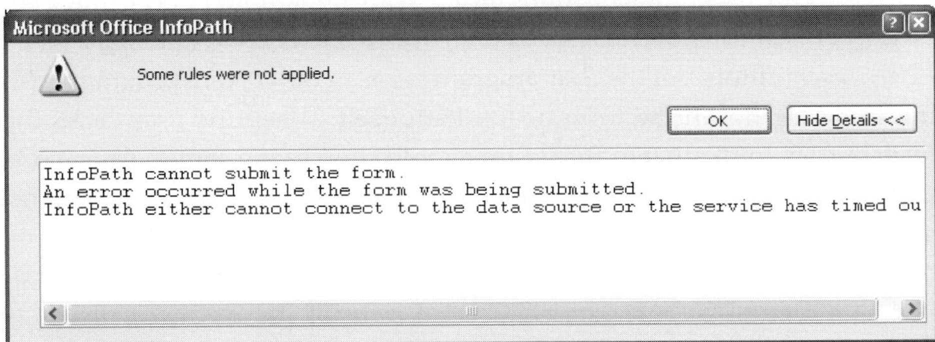

FIGURE 8.46: Dialog shown when submit using rules fails on the main submit connection

To help remedy any confusion around failures when using rules, you may want to provide a *Help* button in your form. If you use a button in the view as the primary means to submit your form, you could place an adjacent *Help with Submit* button that could show a dialog with helpful information on how to prepare a form for submit and what to do if problems arise.

Submitting to a Hosting Environment

In Chapter 18, we'll learn about hosting InfoPath—both in a Windows application and in a browser for Forms Services. But it's worth mentioning now that the "Submit to Host" data connection is a critical component when hosting InfoPath. It is the only way for InfoPath to call into the hosting environment while the form is being filled out.

Forms Services

Browser-enabled form templates support similar hosting concepts as InfoPath, but the actual implementation differs. Hosting an InfoPath, as well as a browser-based form, is discussed in Chapter 18.

Take a custom stockbroker program that allows Wall Street traders to efficiently fill orders and communicate with floor traders. The InfoPath form gets a list of available floor traders from a database and has a *Chat with Floor Trader* button. But the chat program exists in the custom program hosting InfoPath, not in the form or InfoPath itself. When the user clicks the form button, InfoPath tells the hosting application to run some custom code that the hosting application provides. In this case, the chat program begins, and the name of the floor trader with whom to chat is provided by the form.

The name "Submit to Host" is a little misleading. The feature is classified as a type of submit data connection in InfoPath; however, its use is much more generic than our perception of traditional form submit. You'll find that using "Submit to Host" is the only way to tell the hosting application that the form has been completed and that the hosting application should take control. Clearly this understanding transcends any typical submit of form data.

There are exciting opportunities behind hosting InfoPath using both the InfoPath program and Forms Services. Hosting allows Windows applications and Web sites to easily leverage the powers of form filling. The "Submit to Host" connection is unquestionably an important piece of the puzzle. Since it's classified as a submit connection, we felt that it must be mentioned in this chapter to complete our discussion. Hosting InfoPath, however, is an advanced scenario that inevitably requires writing custom C# or Visual Basic .NET code. In Chapter 18, we'll take a thorough look at how to design a form that is hosted as part of a custom program or Web page.

Submit Options

Every time we've used main submit when filling out forms in this chapter, some variation of the heartwarming submit success dialog appears (such

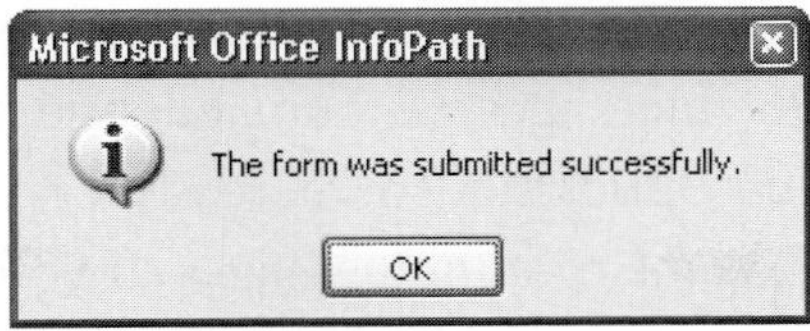

FIGURE 8.47: Generic success dialog for the main submit connection

as the one shown in Figure 8.47). Does this dialog not do your form justice when it's submitted? For example, do you prefer to thank your users or even give them your contact information for follow-up correspondence?

Likewise, is the standard failure dialog (Figure 8.48) what you want your users to see when submit fails? Wouldn't it be helpful to tell them

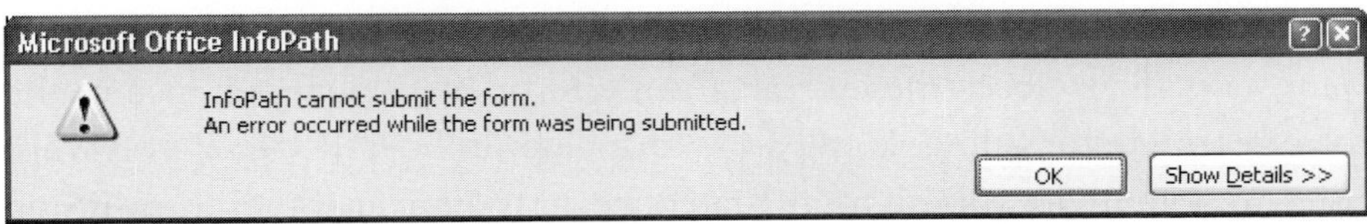

FIGURE 8.48: Generic failure dialog for the main submit connection

who to contact or, if there is a known issue, to try again later? All this and more is possible through the *Advanced* section in the *Submit Options* dialog.

To start customizing these dialogs, go to the *Submit Options* item from the *Tools* menu. By default, the generic messages are used because the *Show a success or failure message* checkbox is enabled (Figure 8.49). By checking

FIGURE 8.49: Advanced section of the Submit Options dialog

the *Use custom messages* box, you can override the default submit messages. But when overriding the messages, you must define messages for both the *On success* and *On failure* options. Also, there is no option to use form data (like using a formula) for the custom messages. If you wanted to use some form data in your message, you could use rules (as we did in the previous example) or custom submit through form code and show the dialogs yourself.

The *After submit* option is a very important setting for finalizing the form-filling experience for your users. What you choose will depend on the purpose of your form. The possible actions are *Close the form, Create a new blank form,* and *Leave the form open*. The default setting is for the form to remain open. But many times you'll want to choose *Close the form* to clearly let the user know that he or she is done. If your form is purely a repetitive data entry mechanism, the convenient option would be to *Create a new blank form*. This closes the current form and opens a new instance of the form template for filling. Finally, the form should be left open if you want users to potentially submit more than once, or if there are other form-filling duties to finish before the user manually closes the form.

WARNING Post-Submit Actions

The *After submit* setting takes effect only when the form is successfully submitted. If there is a submit error, the post-submit action will not occur. If the *Show a success or failure message* checkbox is not checked and submit fails, it will do so silently. A user may interpret a silent submit as a success and might close the form. If he or she didn't save the form, the entered data is lost.

It's important to recognize that the setting for *Show a success or failure message* is independent from the *After submit* action. When your form is submitted successfully, it could, for example, just close right away. To enable this submit behavior, the *Show a success or failure message* setting should be unchecked and *After submit* set to *Close the form*. Not showing a message in other *After submit* settings may not be helpful, however. Actually, other settings may confuse your users since they may not be sure whether the form really was properly submitted.

Forms Services

Closing a form in the browser will take the user back to the associated SharePoint library or Web page before he or she started to fill it out. Alternatively, you can also specify a URL for browser redirection after the form is closed.

As you can see, figuring out how you want your form to submit could be as or even more important than other aspects of form design. We recommend that you thoroughly test your form by replicating real situations that your users will experience. By iterating over the general form design, you can come up with a natural flow to the form-filling experience while keeping it aesthetically pleasing.

What's Next?

By now you should feel comfortable in designing a form for submitting data. As we've seen throughout this chapter, there are numerous options at your fingertips that can customize the user experience. Once you design a few forms and start playing with submit, you will become more accustomed with main and secondary submit behaviors. You will also gain a better understanding of how you want to process the submitted data on the server.

Until now, we've discussed how to use various InfoPath features to design powerful form templates. In the last few chapters, we learned about getting data into and out of forms from external data sources. But without publishing your form template, nobody can use your form! In the next chapter, we'll hit a landmark in the book: publishing your masterpiece so the world can fill out your form. After finishing the next chapter, you will have completed the basic lifecycle of InfoPath form template development.

9

Saving and Publishing

Getting Started

We've come to a point in this book where you have learned many ins and outs of InfoPath. However, we haven't covered a final yet critical part of designing a form: deployment.

Without deployment, you can't effectively distribute your form. We will look at various ways you can deploy, or **publish**, your form template. Publishing is the means of preparing a form template so users can fill it out. There are four ways to publish, depending on how users access your template:

- Saving to a network location
- Uploading to a SharePoint or Forms Services site
- Sending via e-mail
- Creating an installable form for redistribution

Each mechanism has its own set of advantages and disadvantages. As we review choices for publishing your template, you will come to understand which publishing choices are right for you.

After we talk about publishing, we'll touch on how to save your form template as an extracted set of form files. The *Save As Source Files* option is not a variation of publishing. Rather, it's a dismantling of your form template into its individual files for saving on your computer. We'll talk about various motivations and uses for the *Save as Source Files* option later in the chapter.

Another feature we've been using since Chapter 2 is **preview**. In this chapter, we'll share some settings and miscellaneous tips we think you'll find helpful. We'll show you how to better test filling out your form by simulating specific user conditions that are otherwise not easily attained by other means.

Saving and Publishing a Form Template with InfoPath

You've worked long and hard to create a stunning form template that streamlines business operations and cuts overhead by leaps and bounds. But all of the great work is just sitting on your computer! To get your form out to your audience, the template must be deployed at a location where all your users have access. Time for the big question: Should you save or publish?

We learned a little about saving in Chapter 2. As you already know, InfoPath creates an .xsn file that contains the various components (the .xsf form definition file, XML files, XML Schemas, XSL views, and so on) of the form template. Think of saving as a way to preserve an "original copy" of your form template that can be used for future upgrading. Every time you save the template, you're updating the original. The purpose of saving a form template somewhere is really for your personal use and further development. Other people should not fill out forms based on that template since you might decide to make changes that break existing forms, to change the form template location, or to remove the template. Also, others simply might not have access to the saved location (e.g., if it's on your personal computer). So the question we posed about whether we should save or publish does not make sense! Saving and publishing go hand in hand, as we'll see in a moment.

Publishing a form template basically takes a copy of your original form template and puts it in a new location. But there is more: Publishing is the way to make your form template available to your users for filling out.

Let's see what happens when you try to save a newly created form template for the first time. Click on the *Save* or *Save As* menu item under the *File* menu. The dialog shown in Figure 9.1 appears. As we discussed, publishing

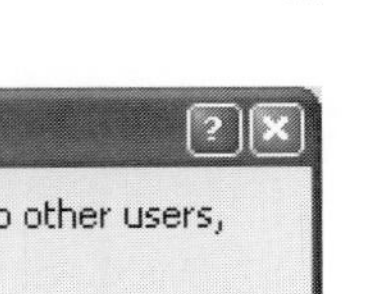

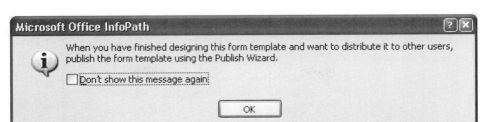

FIGURE 9.1: InfoPath prompt that appears when choosing Save or Save As for a new form template

means you are ready to share this template for people to fill out. (Choose the *Publish* menu item on the *File* menu below *Save* and *Save As*.) *Save* and *Save As* simply imply that you want to update your own personal copy of the form template that will (we hope), at some point in the future, be published.

> **NOTE Saving Comes with Publishing**
>
> If you choose to publish instead of save, you are forced to save anyway if you haven't done so already. If the template has been previously saved but is not up to date, it is saved again automatically at the end of the Publishing Wizard.

When choosing somewhere to save your form, the location really does not matter. We suggest saving the form template on a private and backed-up location for safekeeping. Privacy may especially be a concern if your form template has managed form code. The form's source code could be exposed to malicious users who can use that knowledge to hack your form. We'll learn more about adding form code to your template in Chapter 15.

The Publishing Wizard, whose first page appears in Figure 9.2, includes helpful utility options such as putting your form template on a SharePoint or Forms Services–enabled site, sending it via e-mail, or even creating an installable template. In case you're not sure which deployment method to use or why you would choose one over another, let's examine each one individually. To help guide a decision on how to publish your form template, try to answer the following four questions. As we discuss the ways a form template can be published, we'll touch on how these questions may apply.

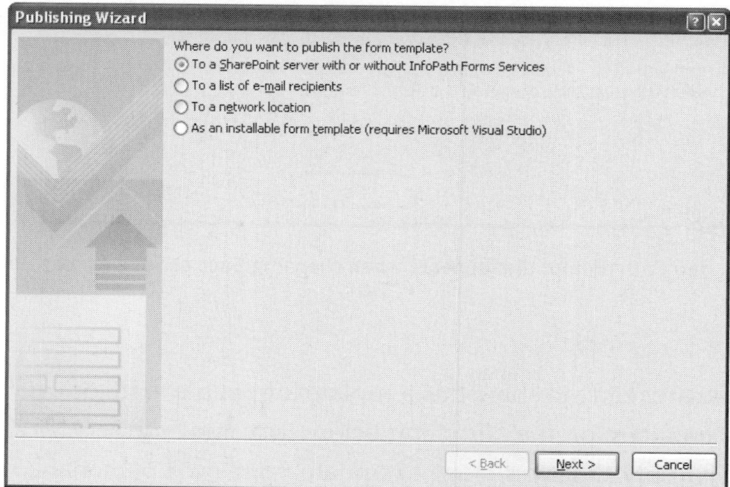

FIGURE 9.2: First page of the Publishing Wizard, offering a variety of publishing options

1. Do all of your users have the InfoPath client installed?
2. Will your form template be updated frequently?
3. Do all of your users have access to the same network?
4. Does your form use features that require full trust permissions?

Network Locations

The most fundamental option is to publish your form template on a network location, including shared folders or Web servers. This type of deployment is very basic because the form template XSN file is simply copied to the publish location. Publishing to a network location is convenient when everyone who will use your form has access to the file share and the InfoPath client installed.

If you elect to choose the *To a network location* deployment option (on the wizard page shown in Figure 9.2), the next page asks for the publish location and the form name. This page (Figure 9.3) accepts publish locations of all types, including local file (C:\folder\form.xsn), network (\\mycomputer\share\form.xsn), HTTP (http://mycomputer/mysite/form.xsn), FTP (ftp://mycomputer/mysite/form.xsn), and other file-based protocols. The form name is used to identify the form template as well as contribute to the form ID, which is a unique namespace given to the form XML data. In this example, we'll publish a form to our Web server at http://mycomputer:81/mysite/MeetingRequest.xsn. However, since we don't have access to

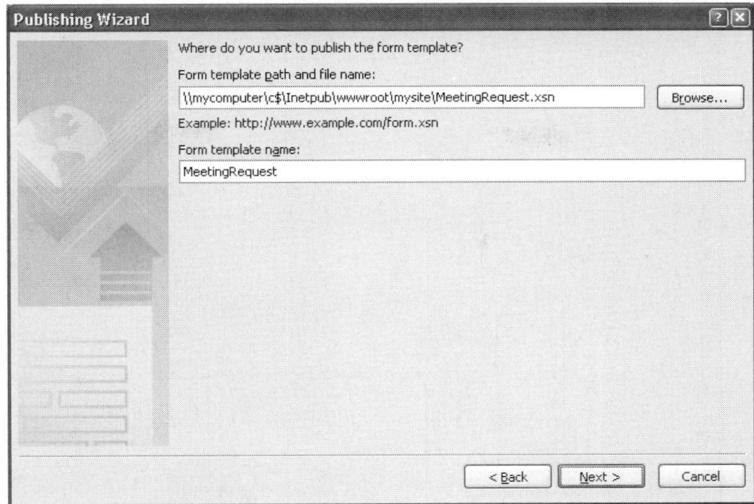

FIGURE 9.3: Publishing a MeetingRequest template to a Web server via a "backdoor" network share

write directly to this HTTP location, we'll use a "backdoor" file path to get to the physical location of that HTTP address: \\mycomputer\c$\Inetpub\wwwroot\mysite\MeetingRequest.xsn, as shown in Figure 9.3. (You can find the MeetingRequest form template in the samples for this chapter on the book's Web site.)

> **TIP Location for Publishing the Form Template**
>
> If you don't know the path where you want to publish the form template, use the *Browse* button adjacent to the *Form template path and file name* text box.

The last step before we finish the wizard is entering the users' access path, the location where users will go to create a new form from the template. In our example, the path is shown in Figure 9.4 as http://mycomputer: 81/mysite/MeetingRequest.xsn. Note that the access location is different from the path where we published. InfoPath needs to know where users will be opening the form because it grants slightly elevated (instead of restricted) permissions when a form is opened from the location where it was originally published. This security feature ensures that a form template

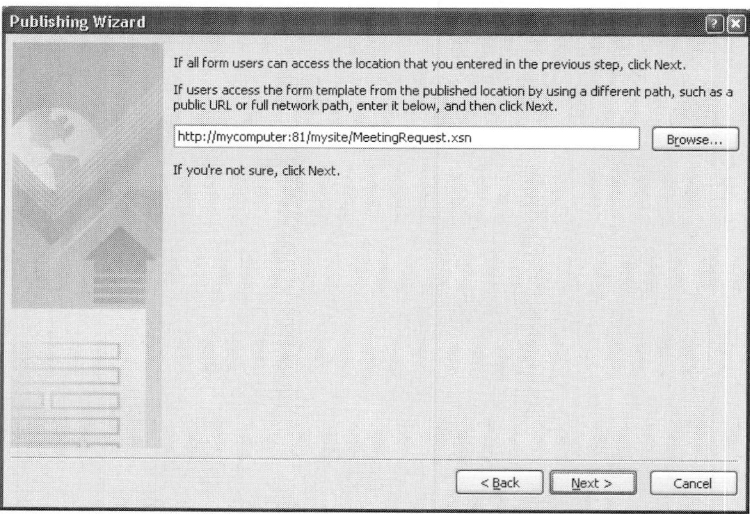

FIGURE 9.4: Specifying the users' access path

can't be distributed and opened from any location with high privileges. We'll talk more about InfoPath security in Chapter 11.

> **WARNING** Use Standard Paths for Publish Locations
>
> When publishing to a file share such as \\mycomputer\myshare\Form.xsn, the access path will typically be the same as the publish path. But be careful if you have mapped network drives such as Y: mapped to \\mycomputer\myshare. If you had such a mapping, it's okay to use Y:\Form.xsn as the publish location, but it would not work for the access path since your users may not all have \\mycomputer\myshare mapped to the same Y: drive letter.

The last page of the Publishing Wizard is a simple summary of the form name, publish path, and access path. Once you click the *Publish* button at the bottom of the wizard page, the actual process of publishing begins. If there are any errors in writing the form template to the publish path you specified, they will appear now. Since the access path is used only when users fill out the form, it is not possible to detect an error until the form is filled out. If there was an error in entering the access path, InfoPath will not grant the form any privileges, and an error dialog may appear similar to

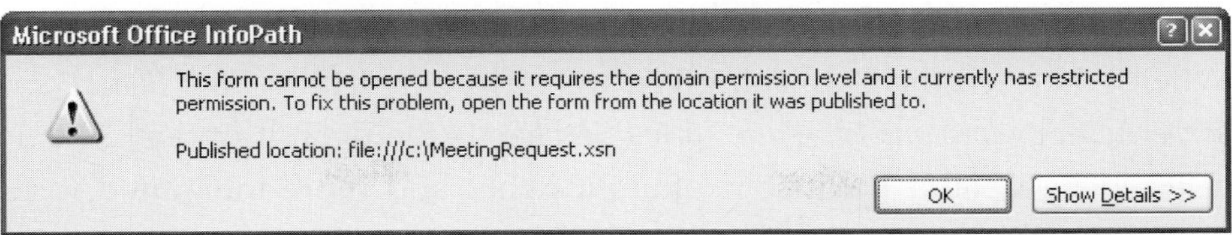

FIGURE 9.5: Error dialog that appears when opening a form from a path that is not the access path

that shown in Figure 9.5. This error will appear only for those forms that require elevated privileges, such as when using external data connections.

Forms Services

Attempting to fill out a browser-enabled form template that doesn't have sufficient permissions will fail with a *Form Error* dialog. The error message is similar to that shown in Figure 9.5.

> **TIP Insufficient Security Privilege Error**
>
> A quick fix to the error shown in Figure 9.5 is to move the form template to the physical location listed in the error. In this case, the form template must exist in C:\ with the name MeetingRequest.xsn. Another quick fix is to open the form template directly in design mode and preview it. The correct (and long-term) fix for this problem is to republish the form template to a location of your choice.

After you successfully publish, two convenience options become available for you to use as the Publishing Wizard closes. You can select *Send the form template to e-mail recipients* or *Open this form from the published location.* Sending the template via e-mail creates a new e-mail message with the form template as an attachment. This option may be unavailable if Outlook 2007 is not installed. If you choose to open the form instead, InfoPath will open the form as it would if a user were filling it out. It's always a good idea to try filling out your form from the published location to ensure all is well. If you select an option in the last page of the Publishing Wizard, clicking *Close* on the page carries out the selected option.

SharePoint or Forms Services

When you open the Publishing Wizard for the first time, *To a SharePoint server with or without InfoPath Forms Services* is the default option. This is selected by default because it offers a richer and more integrated form experience than any other type of publishing.

Nestled in the *To a SharePoint server with or without InfoPath Forms Services* option exists a duality: the ability to publish either to a SharePoint server or to a Forms Services site. The exact behavior depends on whether you selected the *Enable browser-compatible features only* option (a checkbox in the *Design a Form Template* dialog; you can also change the *Compatibility* setting to *Design a form that can be opened in a browser or InfoPath* by using the Design Checker) and whether the SharePoint site supports Forms Services. The flowchart in Figure 9.6 shows how the form template needs to be enabled for a browser as well as published to a SharePoint site running Forms Services to fill out forms in a Web browser. Determining whether the form template publishes to a SharePoint server or Forms Services site depends on whether the template is browser-enabled and whether Forms Services is provisioned on the target SharePoint server.

Let's look at a few compelling reasons to use SharePoint deployment over others. When a form lives on a SharePoint site, you and your users will greatly benefit from the many points of integration between InfoPath

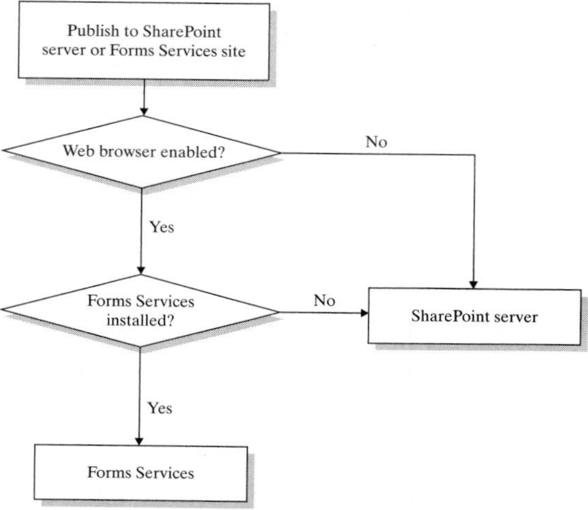

FIGURE 9.6: Flowchart for determining whether the form template publishes to a SharePoint server or a Forms Services site

and SharePoint. One attractive feature is that a form library is specifically created for the template. The library acts as a repository for holding forms created from the published template. Since we're working with a SharePoint library, we also get the benefits of property promotion, property demotion, alerts, RSS feeds, exporting of promoted data to a spreadsheet, and merging of forms in the library. We'll talk about merging forms in SharePoint in Chapter 12. You can find more information about SharePoint-specific features such as alerts and RSS feeds on MSDN blog sites (referenced in the Appendix).

You can see that publishing to a SharePoint site (when Forms Services is not enabled or the form is not browser-enabled) allows for a greater degree of collaboration than other publishing options. It also makes it quick and easy for you to update your form template without much of a hassle. However, unless your SharePoint site has a presence on the Internet, users of the form will need to be able to connect to the network where the SharePoint server is hosted. Note that once the form is opened from a specific computer, its template is cached for future use. (This applies to any form template you may open, not only those published to SharePoint.) So, deploying to SharePoint does not mean the user always needs access to that server for the form to open. But without connectivity to the server, the user will be unable to save back to the form library. Similarly, all of the benefits of using SharePoint are available only when there's connectivity to the site.

Let's walk through publishing a template to a new SharePoint library. Before entering the Publishing Wizard, ensure that the form template compatibility is set to *InfoPath.* This ensures we're publishing to a SharePoint site and not a Forms Services site. You can see the compatibility setting and change it by using the *Design Checker* item on the *Tools* menu. Once you're ready to use the Publishing Wizard, proceed by selecting the *To a SharePoint server with or without InfoPath Forms Services* option and clicking the *Next* button. This is where you enter the address of the site collection of the SharePoint server. A default site collection exists at the base server address, so we'll just use http://mycomputer (which may not be the local computer), as shown in Figure 9.7. (You can find details on site collections in SharePoint by reading the Microsoft TechNet Web site referenced in the Appendix.)

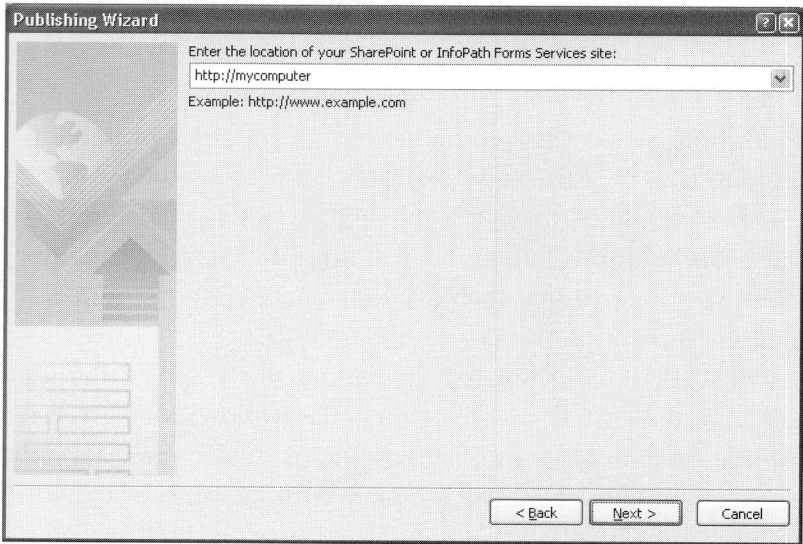

FIGURE 9.7: Specifying a server location for publishing to a SharePoint site or Forms Services site

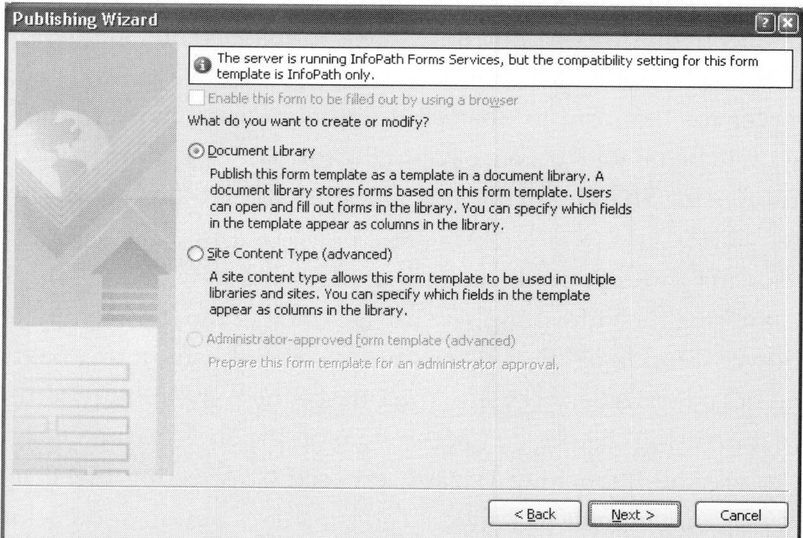

FIGURE 9.8: Choosing whether to publish the form template to a SharePoint document library or a site content type

The next wizard page (Figure 9.8) asks if you want to create a document library or a site content type. If you plan to use only a single library for managing forms, the *Document Library* option is for you. There will be an absolute address that everyone (who has the proper permission) can use, such as http://mycomputer/myformtemplate, to access the form library. If, on the other hand, you plan to reuse this form template across multiple libraries or lists, the *Site Content Type* option is a better choice.

On the next wizard page, you can choose whether to create a new document library (or site content type) or update an existing one. Updating is handy when you want to upgrade an existing form template with a newer version. Since we are publishing a new template, we'll create a new document library. If you chose a site content type in the last wizard page, the dialog will look the same but some text will read "site content type" instead of "document library."

The next step in the wizard contains two text fields: *Name* and *Description*. The name is the identifier you want to assign to the newly created document library (or site content type). We'll use the name `MeetingRequests`. When navigating to this library in a browser, the address would look like http://mycomputer/MeetingRequests. The description simply gives more information about the purpose of the library. The description appears when you browse document libraries in SharePoint as well as in the previous wizard page, where form libraries that can be updated are listed with their descriptions.

If you decided to create a site content type instead of a document library, the next wizard page you'll see, which is specific to site content types, asks for a location to save the template to (Figure 9.9). It's recommended that

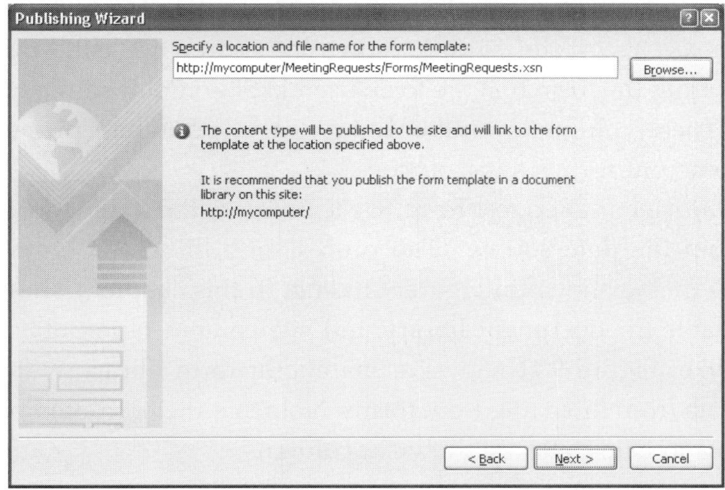

FIGURE 9.9: Saving the template somewhere on the SharePoint server when creating a site content type

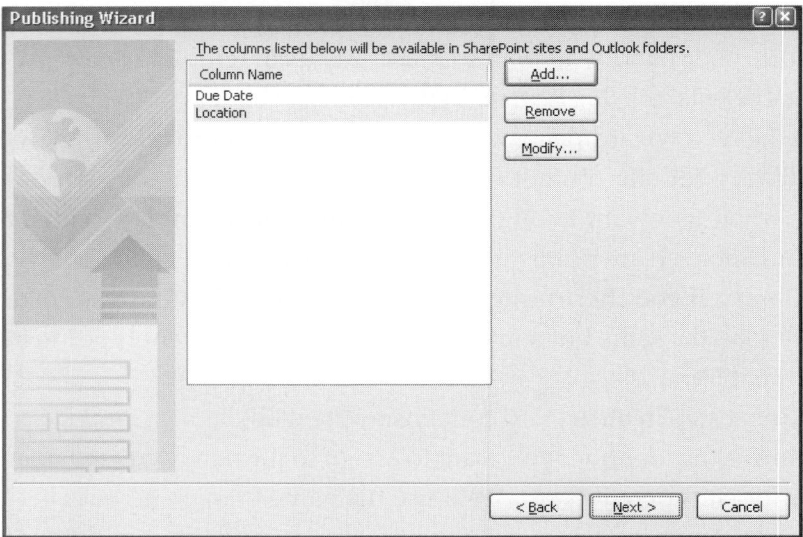

FIGURE 9.10: Wizard page showing promoted properties from the template's data source, which appear as columns in SharePoint libraries and lists

you use the default path; however, you can save the template anywhere on the same server. (InfoPath will not allow you to save the template on a different server.) Remember that publishing as a site content type does not mean the template is actually used anywhere. It simply means the content type is available for use on that SharePoint site. We'll show you how to use a site content type on a SharePoint site momentarily.

The next page of the wizard, shown in Figure 9.10, asks you to select columns from the form that are to be used in SharePoint sites and Outlook folders. These columns, commonly known as **promoted properties**, are fields from your form's data source.

For our MeetingRequest form, we'll promote the `When` and `Location` fields from the data source. (The process of adding a column includes using the dialog shown in Figure 9.13 later in this chapter.) These options are available for document library and site content type published templates alike. Figure 9.11 shows a SharePoint form library with the promoted data from three filled-out forms. Note that the promoted properties, Location and Due Date, are shown as columns.

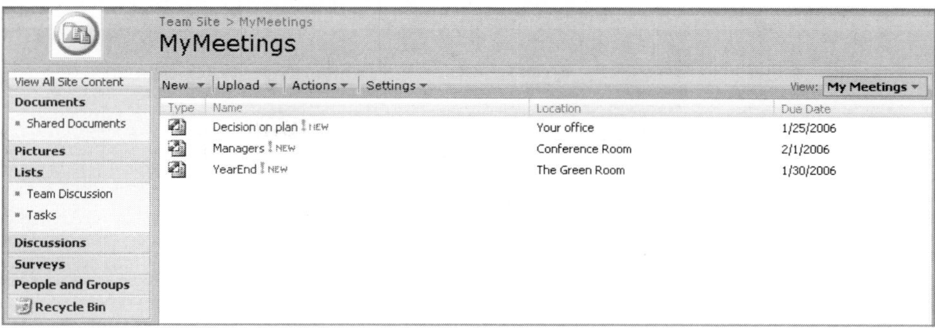

FIGURE 9.11: Form library on SharePoint

In the Publishing Wizard, after you've selected all the properties you want to promote as columns in the document library, clicking *Next* takes you to the final page, where you verify three pieces of information:

- The document library name you want to create (`MeetingRequests`)
- The document library location (http://mycomputer/MeetingRequests)
- The status of Forms Services on the SharePoint site (either enabled or disabled)

Using a Published Site Content Type on a SharePoint Site

To use a site content type published form in any document library after you've finished the publishing process, start by going to that library in a browser. Next, visit the *Document Library Settings* page. If you don't see a *Content Types* section on the settings page, you need to enable *Multiple Content Types* by clicking on the *Advanced settings* link. Under the *Content Types* section, click the *Add from existing site content types* link. This takes you to the *Add Content Types* page (Figure 9.12). Adding site content types will allow you to create new items of those types in that document library. Also, any promoted properties are revealed as columns in the document library. You've now added form-filling capabilities to an arbitrary document library, and you can repeat this process for any library on the SharePoint site!

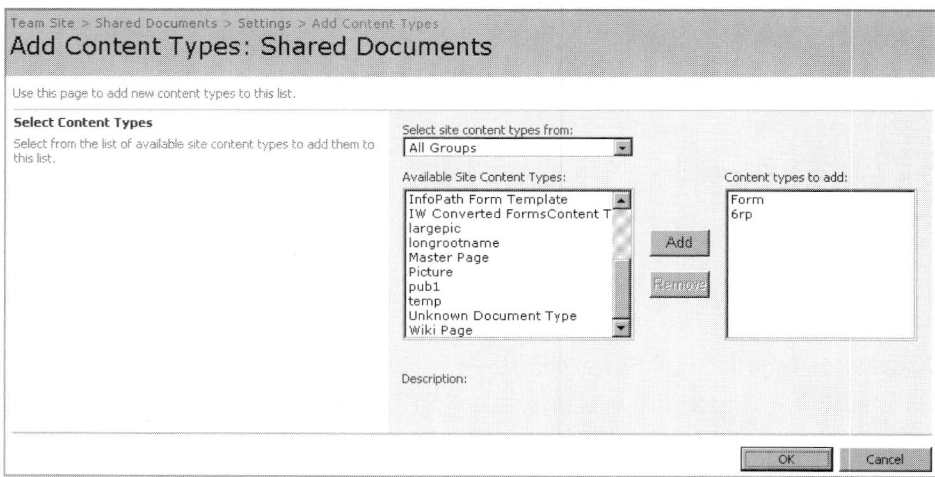

FIGURE 9.12: Adding site content types to a document library

Property Promotion

SharePoint libraries and lists hold data. SharePoint libraries hold files of data, while lists hold data as records, similar to a database. No matter what kind of data you're working with, certain properties of that library or list data can be shown to the user. When working with InfoPath XML files, you can instruct SharePoint to extract specific fields from the form data. These fields are selected during the publishing process and are listed in the wizard page shown in Figure 9.10.

> **TIP Property Promotion Outside the Publishing Wizard**
>
> Promoted properties can be added, removed, and modified without going through the Publishing Wizard. You'll find the entry point in InfoPath design mode on the *Form Options* dialog under the *Property Promotion* category.

There are a handful of options at your disposal when promoting a new property. First, you want to select any field or repeating group. In our meeting request template, we selected the `When` and `Location` fields from the data source. We will want to see this data without needing to open the form; the values of these form fields will be shown in columns of the library. The

Use a SharePoint Site Column from this group drop-down lists, of course, all of the site content types! Once you select a group, the *Display name* drop-down is populated with the columns for that content type. Beyond the site content types and their associated columns, the *(None: Create new column in this library)* group is always available, which lets you define your own custom column name specifically for this library. Figure 9.13 shows the `When` data source field promoted as Due Date. This means the `When` field value is shown in the document library with its column heading as Due Date.

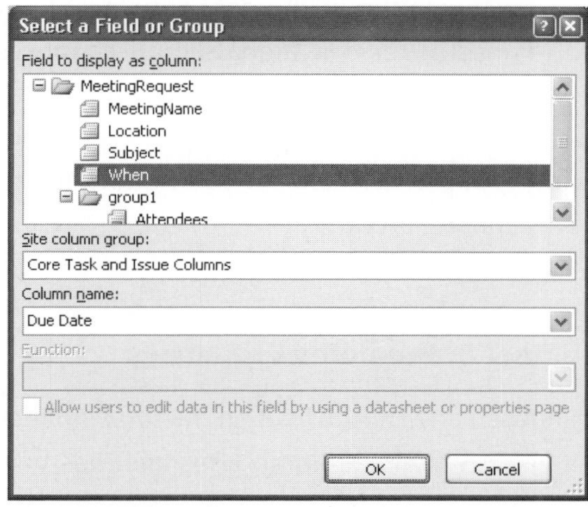

FIGURE 9.13: Selecting a field from the data source to promote. The display name (Due Date) can be set independently from the node name (`When`).

TIP Promoting Properties with Site Content Types

Using a form template as a content type in a library is more useful than just allowing that form to be filled out. If the form has promoted properties, they can be added as columns in the library that contains that form as a content type.

The *Function* drop-down is enabled in only two cases: when selecting a node with the rich text (XHTML) data type or when selecting a repeating field or any of its descendents. For rich text, the plaintext function is available in the *Function* drop-down list box. Its purpose is to strip out the HTML, leaving only the text data. Since SharePoint columns support only plain text, this function allows rich text to be used as a promoted property. The other functions (first, last, count, and merge) appear in the *Function* drop-down list box when a child field of a repeating group, or a repeating field itself, is selected. The first function, as its name suggests, promotes only the first item if there is more than one. The last function predictably exhibits the opposite effect of first. The count function gets the total number of items that exist in the repetition. This could be useful, for example, for the `Attendees` repeating field (which is hidden within the `group1` group in Figure 9.13) in our meeting requests form, as shown in the data source of Figure 9.13. Finally, the merge function is useful for concatenating all instances of a repeating field into a single value. Since each concatenated value (of a repeating field) is not really separated from the next value, the merge function is not often useful. If a repeating group is selected for promotion, the only useful function (and all that is available) is count.

Maximum Number of Promoted Properties

InfoPath 2003 imposed an artificial limit on the total number of promoted properties for a given SharePoint library. This limit has been removed in InfoPath 2007, allowing for any number of promoted properties. There is a limit of 40 promoted properties when promoting in Outlook, however.

The last feature to discuss in Figure 9.13 (which is actually disabled in this instance) is the *Allow users to edit data in this field by using a datasheet or properties page* checkbox. This long-winded name also goes by the technical designation of **property demotion**. Despite its derogatory demeanor, it's actually one of the most useful features of property promotion! Whereas property promotion is the exposure of field data in SharePoint library or list columns, property demotion lets you modify that promoted data in the column itself directly through SharePoint. This is a very useful and convenient feature since you don't need InfoPath to use it, but it doesn't come without a catch.

One of the downsides to editing a demoted property is the lack of data validation when the value is changed. This means if the demoted field has one or more validation constraints, such as if it's an integer data type, it's silently bypassed with property demotion. As you know from previous chapters, InfoPath fails to open forms with validation errors. Therefore, it's critical that you check the *Allow users to edit data in this field by using a datasheet or properties page* option only for fields with simple data types such as string. Also, you should ensure that there is no declarative validation on the demoted field. Likewise, check that the other declarative validation in your form template does not reference a demoted field. Furthermore, any calculations, rules, or form code (which we'll discuss in Part II of this book) associated with demoted fields are never run when demoted values are changed. Due to these inherent risks, we advise that you use property demotion with caution.

The *Allow non-validated editing on Windows SharePoint Services (Advanced)* checkbox is not available for all fields. Only fields that subscribe to a simple data type (such as string, integer, Boolean, and so on) and those that do not repeat or are not under a repeating field or group are eligible. When property demotion does not apply for a selected data source node, the checkbox is disabled.

Forms Services

If your form template is browser-enabled and a SharePoint server is running Forms Services, you are ready to publish a form for use in a Web browser! Clearly, this method of publishing is superior if some of your users do not have the InfoPath client application installed. For those who have the InfoPath client, forms opened from Forms Services can still open in the client. We'll discuss Forms Services in Chapter 14.

E-Mail

One of the more convenient ways to deploy a form template is to drop it into your users' e-mail inboxes. Templates that are well suited for e-mail deployment typically are smaller in size, are quick to fill out, and have a submit data connection so everyone's form data can get saved in a central location. Recipients of your e-mail do not require Outlook 2007. But since InfoPath and Outlook integrate quite nicely (as we'll see in Chapter 13), there is a richer experience awaiting those with an Outlook 2007 e-mail client.

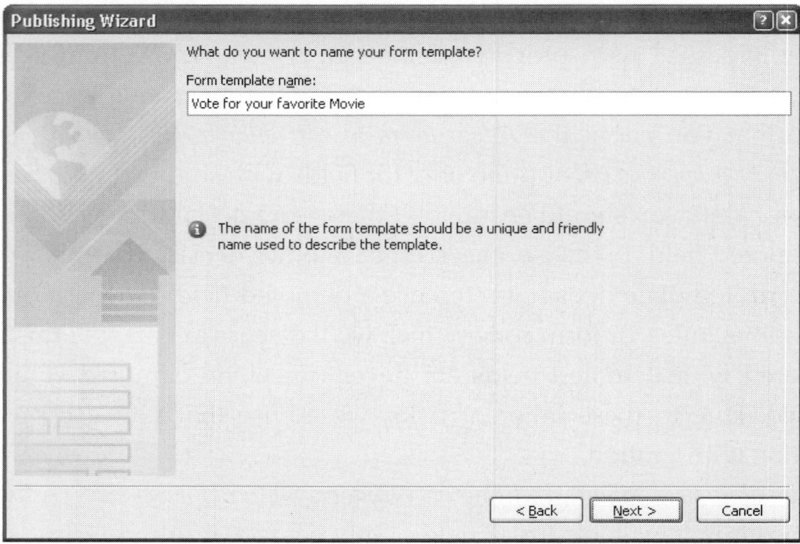

FIGURE 9.14: First wizard page for publishing a form to e-mail recipients

To initiate e-mail deployment, select *To a list of e-mail recipients* in the Publishing Wizard (refer back to Figure 9.2). The next wizard page asks for a form template name (Figure 9.14). This name is not used as the name of the template attached to the e-mail. (The attachment file name is the one you chose when saving the template before publishing.) Instead, the name you enter in the text box shown in Figure 9.14 is used as the form name and part of the ID; it also appears in the subject line of the e-mail. "Form name" is overloaded in this case, since the real form name (as well as the form ID) property can be set in the *Form Properties* dialog from the *Properties* menu item on the *File* menu.

> **TIP E-Mailed Forms in the Recently Used Forms List**
>
> What happens when a user wants to fill out an e-mailed form template but can't find the original e-mail? If the user already opened the form template once, it appears in the *Recently Used Forms* section on the *Getting Started* dialog shown when InfoPath first opens. That way, the user can fill it out over and over without having the original e-mail. The *Getting Started* dialog is discussed in Chapter 2.

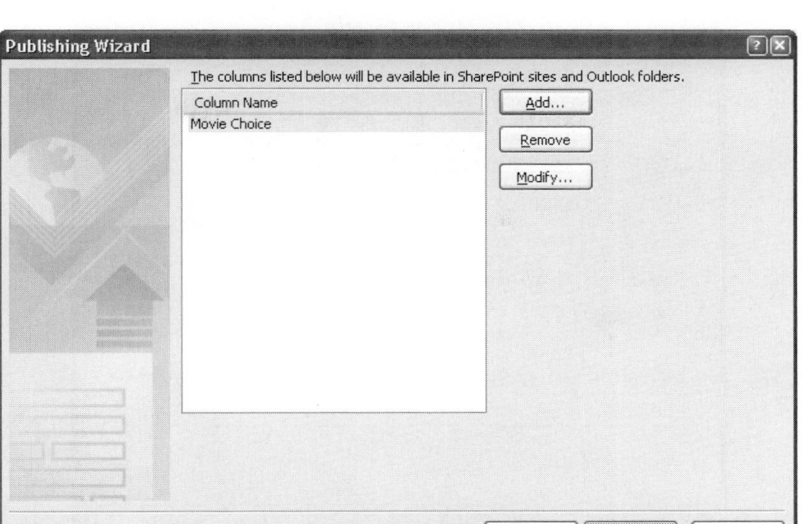

FIGURE 9.15: Promoting properties to make them available as columns in Outlook

The next page in the wizard asks for promoted properties (Figure 9.15). This is the same page we saw when publishing to a SharePoint site or Forms Services. Promoted properties are available as columns in Outlook for forms submitted via e-mail and when used with an InfoPath form folder. Since this topic is tangential to publishing via e-mail, we'll suspend discussion until Chapter 13.

The next page in the wizard simply offers advice for how to handle forms received in e-mail. It mentions that in order for promoted properties to work correctly in Outlook, an InfoPath form folder must be created. After you click the *Publish* button, an e-mail opens in Outlook, as shown in Figure 9.16. The form template is attached to the e-mail, although it may not visually appear to be the case.

There are a couple of restrictions when publishing via e-mail. The first restriction is that e-mailed templates may not request anything but restricted permissions. The Publishing Wizard will disable the *Next* button if *To a list of e-mail recipients* is selected but the form requests higher privileges than restricted. You can find a permissions setting in the *Form Options* dialog from the *Tools* menu in the *Security and Trust* category. Any data connections accessing another domain (i.e., one computer to another), for example,

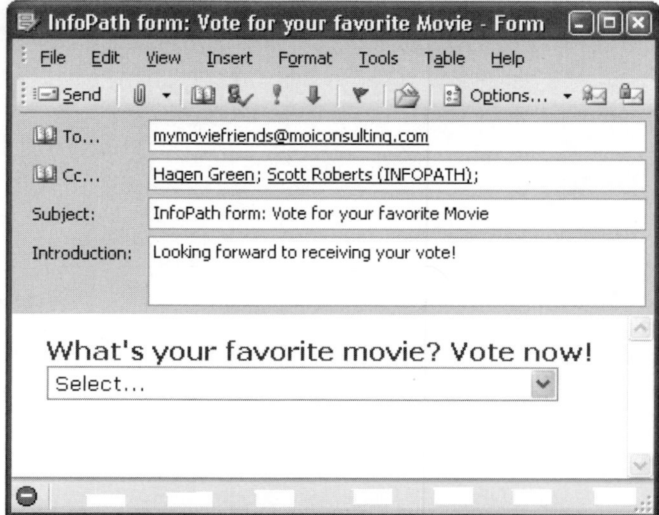

FIGURE 9.16: Resulting e-mail in Outlook after finishing the Publishing Wizard for e-mail

require domain trust permissions. We'll learn more about security and trust settings as well as what features require various levels of permissions in Chapter 11. Conveniently, enabling submit through an e-mail data connection does not require domain trust. So an easy way to get feedback from your e-mailed form template is to use an e-mail data connection that sends mail back to you!

The final restriction is that the form template must have at least an access path or form ID. The form template is even allowed to have both. But if neither the access path nor form ID is present, publishing via e-mail is blocked with an error message. The access path should always and automatically exist in your form template. It may not exist, however, if you published a template without an access path and then used that published copy to continue designing your form. The form ID can be modified from the *Properties* dialog on the *File* menu, but that's not really necessary because it will already have a name that uniquely identifies your form template. It is allowed to have an empty form ID, but this is disallowed by e-mail deployment when the access path is also empty. You can find additional information about the access path and form ID form properties in Chapter 11.

Installable Form Templates

Why do we need an installable form template option when we can use other deployment methods? An installed template has several advantages over other publishing types. First, it's the only easy way to distribute a full trust form template. Moreover, an installable template can be easily removed via the Windows *Add/Remove Programs* dialog. We'll look at what it means to be full trust as an InfoPath form template in Chapter 11, but for now consider a full trust form template as powerful as the InfoPath program in which it's running. But publishing an installable form template does not mean your template must be full trust; it can be set to any trust level. This deployment type in particular (over other deployment types) caters to form templates with the highest privileges.

Forms Services

Forms Services does not allow installable form templates. Digitally signed form templates, on the other hand, are acceptable for high privileges.

The wizard option for creating an installable form template is available only if you have Visual Studio .NET, 2003, or 2005 installed. If you do not have Visual Studio on your computer but still want to create an installable form template, consider using the Form Registration Tool (RegForm.exe) that comes with the InfoPath Software Development Kit (SDK). You can find information about RegForm.exe and the link to download the SDK on MSDN.

In the Publishing Wizard, the *Company Name* and *Language* text boxes shown in Figure 9.17 are settings specific to the Microsoft Installer file and not the form template. The company name is used in the default install path of the Installer program. In this case, when a user runs the Installer, the path would be C:\Program Files\MOI Corporation\[Template File Name]\ where "C" is the drive letter where the Program Files directory exists and "[Template File Name]" is the file name of the saved form template file. The Installer program supports many languages from which you can choose on this wizard page: Chinese (Simplified), Chinese (Traditional), English, French, German, Italian, Japanese, Korean, and Spanish. The language of the Installer

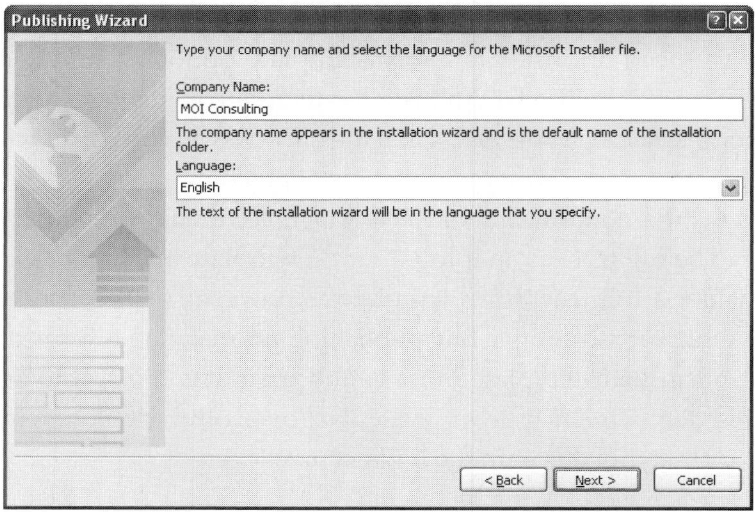

FIGURE 9.17: First page of the Publishing Wizard for creating an installable form template

is completely independent from the language or settings of the form template or InfoPath itself.

The next wizard page, shown in Figure 9.18, asks where to create and what name to give the Installer file. In our case, we chose to save to the C:\ root directory simply for the purposes of this example. However, in real

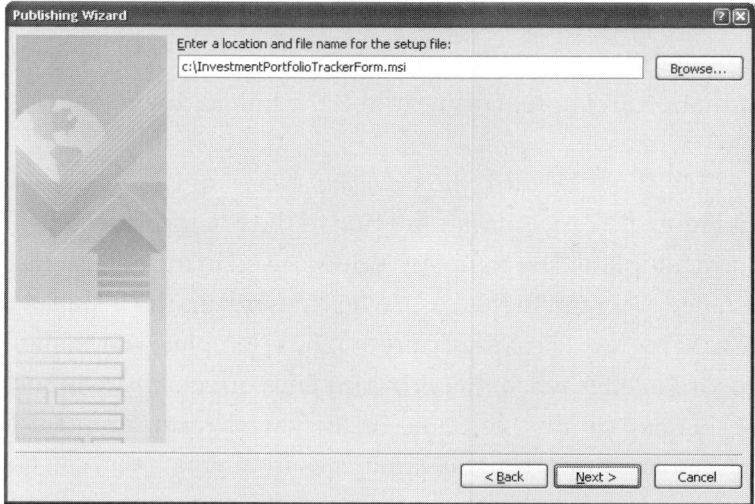

FIGURE 9.18: Choosing a location to save the Installer file

deployments, you can save wherever you want—a network share, an HTTP site—or you can even attach the saved Installer (.msi) file to distribute via e-mail. After you create the Installer file, you can move it as you wish since its function is autonomous from its location.

On the final page, shown in Figure 9.19, the wizard makes it clear that we're just about finished. Before clicking *Publish,* you'll want to review the details to ensure nothing was mistyped. Once you click *Publish,* InfoPath calls into Visual Studio with specific commands to build an Installer file. This process could take anywhere from five seconds to over a minute for a large form template with many resource files. If you're interested in the details of how InfoPath uses build scripts with Visual Studio to build an Installer package, an MSDN article listed in the Appendix explains the process.

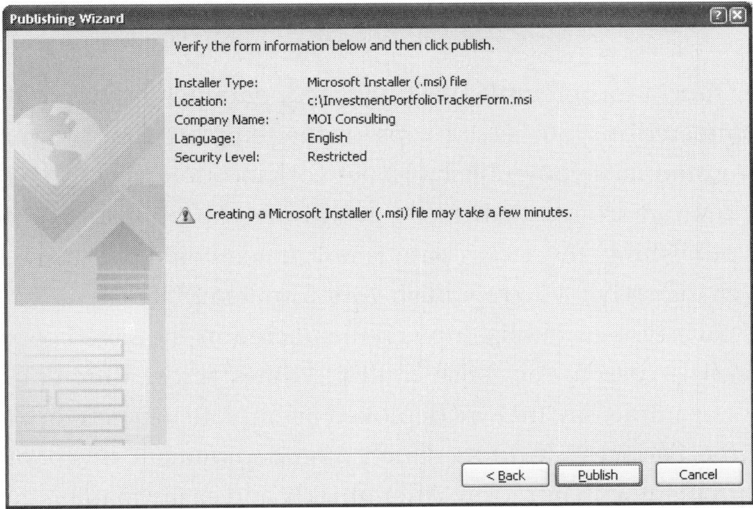

FIGURE 9.19: Final page of the Publishing Wizard when creating an installable form template

> **NOTE Processing Time Is Linear with Form Template Size**
>
> Creating a Microsoft Installer file is timely because InfoPath carries out many actions behind the scenes, such as generating a project with auto-generated code and building the project using Visual Studio. The larger your form template (including resources), the longer it will take Visual Studio to package all of the content.

Let's briefly take an about-face to review a few reasons why you would not want to publish your form as an installable template. If you plan to regularly update the template and redeploy as an installable form template again, using an installable form template is not the best option. Each time a user receives a new version of the template to install, the old installed template must first be removed before installing the new template. If you need a form with full trust permissions that receives updates, consider signing the form template with a digital signature and deploying to a shared location, such as a network share or SharePoint library. Chapter 11 covers the topic of digitally signing a form template.

Common Conveniences

Now that we've gone over each way you can publish a form template, let's briefly acknowledge some of the conveniences built in to the Publishing Wizard.

Every time a form template is published, parameters from publishing are remembered in your saved copy of the template (not the published one). For example, if you publish to a network location, the form name and publish location are recalled for the next time you publish. For network location publishing, the access path is not remembered because it is most likely to change when you republish your form template.

Since each type of publishing is remembered in the saved copy of the template, it is easy to republish multiple times across different publish types. For example, say that we deployed a template to a network location and a Forms Services site. Immediately after deployment, one of our users found a problem with our form. After quickly and easily making the necessary changes, we need to redeploy the template. Going through the Publishing Wizard twice (once for network location and another for Forms Services) is painless since all of the data we previously entered into the wizard is already populated.

Table 9.1 contains samples of XML that are saved in the form definition (.xsf) file to remember data entered into the Publishing Wizard. The XML added to the form definition file to remember publishing data is not included in the actual published template because including that information poses a potential security issue as it discloses facts your users do not need to know to use the form.

TABLE 9.1: Persistence of Publishing Options in the Form Definition (.xsf) File

Publishing Type	Persisted Data in the Form Definition File
Network location	<xsf2:share formName="Meeting Request" path="\\mycomputer\c$\Inetpub\wwwroot\mysite\MeetingRequest.xsn" accessPath="http://mycomputer:81/mysite/MeetingRequest.xsn"></xsf2:share>
SharePoint server or Forms Services site	<xsf2:wss path="http://mycomputer/MeetingRequests" name="MeetingRequests" description=""></xsf2:wss>
E-mail	<xsf2:mail formName="Vote for your favorite Movie"></xsf2:mail>
Installable form template	<xsf2:install path="C:\Investment PortfolioTrackerForm.msi" companyName="MOI Consulting" language="ENG"></xsf2:install>

Saving Templates as Extracted Source Files

We've learned about *Publish, Save,* and *Save As.* Why is there yet another way to save a form template? As an advanced feature, *Save as Source Files* isn't meant for the mainstream form designer. Its usefulness is limited unless you know what you're doing. The purpose of the feature is to explode the form template .xsn file into its individual files. An advanced user might want to extract individual files such as a view (.xsl) or XML Schema (.xsd) file for use outside of InfoPath. Recall from Chapter 2 that an .xsn file is simply a compressed Microsoft cabinet file (.cab) with a different file extension name. InfoPath expands this cabinet file into a folder of your choice.

To see the form files in your form template, select *Save as Source Files* from the *File* menu while designing a form. Figure 9.20 shows the resulting *Browse For Folder* dialog, which allows you to select a target folder for the form files. The behavior of this dialog is quite peculiar. There is no browse functionality as there is in the *Save As* dialog. Instead, you can only navigate your computer and network places. Even so, the navigation capabilities of this dialog are very limited and not user friendly. Sometimes it's

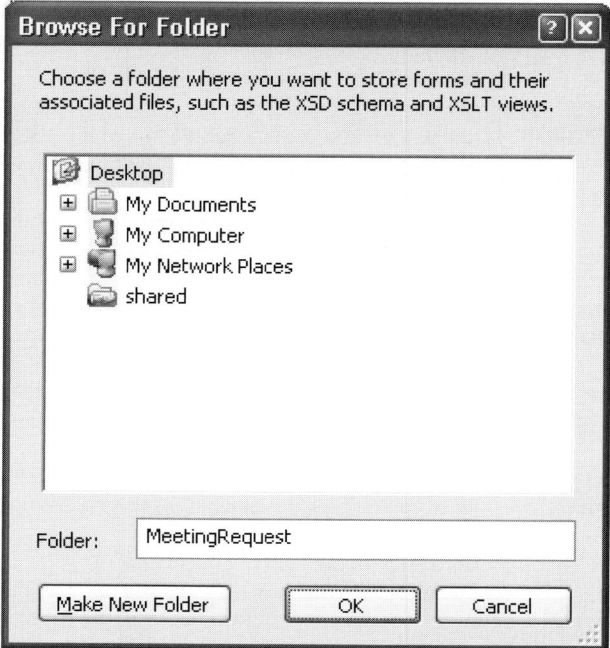

FIGURE 9.20: Browse For Folder dialog for selecting a location to save template source files

easier to just type a full path in the *Folder* box. The *Folder* box accepts local and network paths. HTTP and other non-UNC protocols are not allowed.

> **TIP Use Windows Explorer to Browse**
>
> Instead of using the dialog shown in Figure 9.20 to determine where you want to save your template files, we recommend you use Windows Explorer to find the location. Once you find the folder you want, copy the path from the *Address* bar in Explorer and paste it into the *Folder* text box in the *Browse For Folder* dialog.

Once you find the location where you want to save, the name shown in the *Folder* text box will be the folder where the form files are placed. In Figure 9.20, the form files will be saved in a folder called MeetingRequest on the desktop. But the MeetingRequest folder does not exist! A handy convenience of this dialog is the ability to select a location (such as the desktop, but it could be almost any folder) and manually type a folder name in which you want the files saved. The *Make New Folder* button offers the same functionality, but it's somewhat redundant if you just type in your own folder name and click *OK*. If you select or type a folder name that already contains form files, a prompt warns that some files may be overwritten (Figure 9.21).

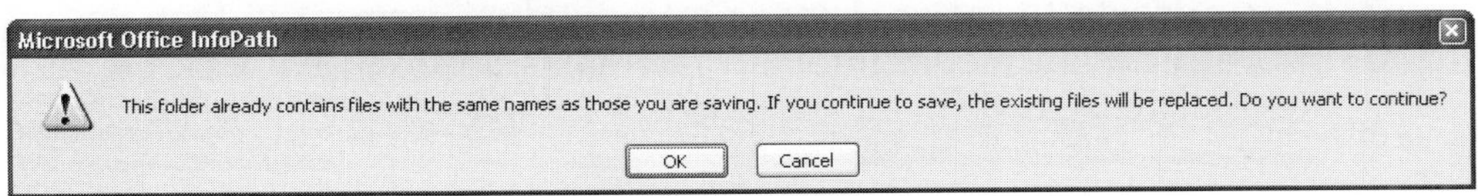

FIGURE 9.21: Dialog warning that appears when saving source files to a folder that already contains existing source files

The *Save as Source Files* feature is useful for a couple of reasons. The first use of the source files is for informational and educational purposes. Since the form files such as the form definition (.xsf), view (.xsl), and XML Schema (.xsd) files are just XML, they can all be opened in any simple text editor. You can browse through the files to learn about XML-related technologies as well as how InfoPath uses them for designing and filling out forms. For example, in Table 9.1 we revealed XML data that is saved in the form definition (.xsf) file to remember your publishing preferences. Many other form template settings reside in this file. In fact, you can double-click the .xsf file to fill out the form. Moreover, right-clicking on the .xsf file is equivalent to right-clicking on a .xsn template. You can right-click on any .xsf or .xsn file and select *Design* from the context menu to quickly jump into designing that form template.

Forms Services

Forms Services cannot deploy an extracted source files form template. Only a published form template (.xsn) file can be consumed.

The second reason to save the source files to a folder is to modify them outside of InfoPath design mode. This is not a recommended practice unless you know exactly what ramifications your changes will have on your form.

Carelessly changing form files outside of design mode may corrupt the template. As a result, InfoPath would no longer be able to open the form. If you must make a change to form files outside of design mode, it's always a good idea to first make a backup.

> **TIP Design Mode Locks Form Template Files**
>
> If you decide to make changes to individual form files, first close InfoPath design mode. InfoPath maintains an exclusive lock on all files that are actively being designed.

> **TIP Form Template Files Are Cached**
>
> Did you make a change to a file and then notice the change didn't show up when filling out the form? Since InfoPath caches the form files, it updates the cache only if the .xsf file has been updated. To do so, simply open the .xsf file in any text editor and save so that its modified date and time stamps are updated.

Previewing Form Templates

We all know that previewing lets us see what it's like to fill out our forms. Since Chapter 2, we've clicked the *Preview* button on the *Standard* toolbar. It's merely a convenience to jump into filling out your form from design mode. Filling out the form during preview is designed to mimic a user's form-filling experience. Actually, a few extras available while previewing make it very easy for you to simulate different user environments to help test your form.

If previewing is so similar to filling out a form, how do you know whether you're in preview or actually filling out the form as an end user? A preview window always starts with *(Preview)* in the title. Moreover, a few commands in the menus and toolbars are disabled. Table 9.2 has a complete list of entry points that are always unavailable while you're previewing a form.

InfoPath allows for only one preview window instance per form template. You can preview a form template as often as you'd like, but multiple preview windows cannot exist simultaneously for a single form template.

TABLE 9.2: Disabled Commands When Previewing a Form

Location	Disabled Commands
File menu	*Fill out a Form* *Design a Form* *Open* *Import Form Data* *Permission* (fly-out items) *Send to Mail Recipient*
Tool menu	*Design this Form*
Task Pane	*Fill out a form*

You can design as many form templates as you wish, and you can have separate preview windows for each template in design. But if you are in the midst of previewing a form, then go back to designing that same form (without closing the preview window), and then decide to preview again, the existing preview window is recycled.

The preview feature has an associated set of command-line parameters. They are used internally by InfoPath, VSTA, and VSTO when previewing a form. For example, when you preview from VSTO, the infopath.exe program is called with specific parameters so InfoPath knows to open for previewing the form. You never really need to use the command-line parameters directly yourself since InfoPath design mode, VSTO, and VSTA take care of automatically passing command-line arguments to InfoPath for you.

In the next few sections, we'll look at preview-specific features and how they help you design better forms. To access the dialog where most of these features are configured, go to the *Preview* menu fly-out on the *File* menu and select *Preview settings.* (An alternative entry point is the *Form Options* menu item on the *Tools* menu.) Figure 9.22 shows the resulting dialog.

Forms Services

Browser-enabled form templates cannot be previewed in the browser. To see a form rendered in the Web browser, publish the form to a server running Forms Services and bring up the form in the browser.

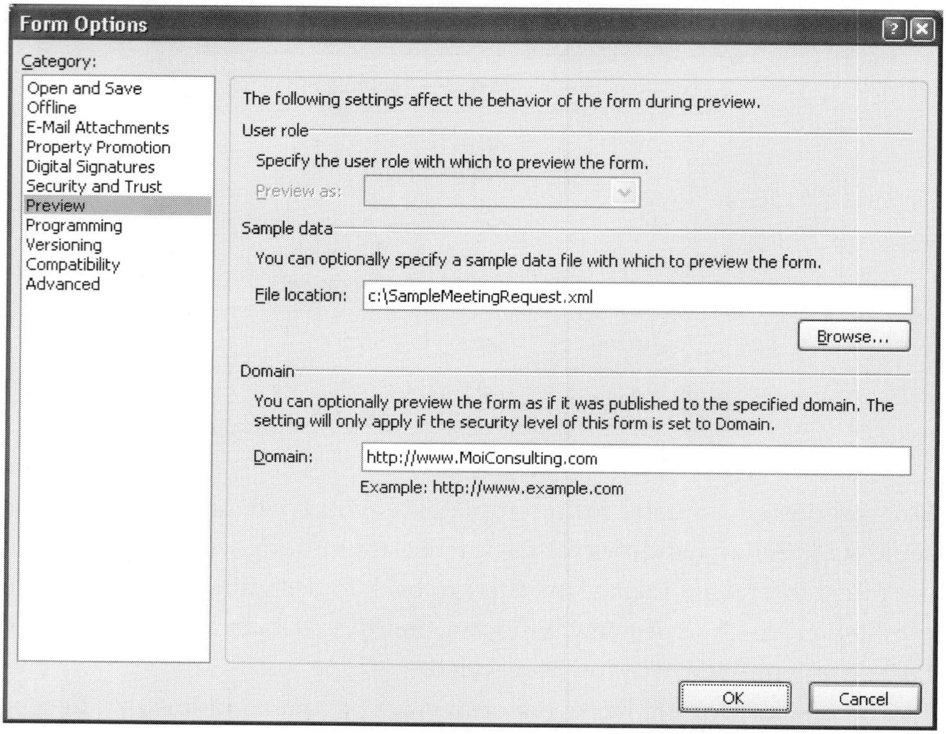

FIGURE 9.22: Configuring preview settings

With Sample Data

So far, we've always previewed forms with the default form data. This means that when you preview, you're seeing exactly what your users will see when they create a new, blank form. But isn't it more interesting when the form has some real-world data? Since InfoPath forms can dynamically change size and shape as your users insert rows and enter large amounts of data, you'll want to check that your form layout still looks reasonable. Another effect of testing with nondefault form data is that your form may behave differently if you have rules, roles, conditional formatting, data validation, or other data-centric InfoPath features. Therefore, it's imperative that you test your form well throughout its design so your users don't call you later to complain!

To specify a sample data file to use when previewing your form, visit the *Preview* category on the *Form Options* dialog (Figure 9.22). You can use the *Browse* button or type any path (including network and HTTP-based locations) in the *File location* text box. The text box does not validate that the file exists, so if you manually enter a path, make sure you don't mistype it.

> **NOTE Preview Options Are Persisted**
>
> After clicking *OK* in the *Preview* category of the *Form Options* dialog, your preview settings will always apply for the life of the form template. The settings are saved in the form definition (.xsf) file. Publishing removes this persisted information from the published version of the form template.

Are you at a loss for how to create a sample data file? Easy! Just preview your form, fill it out as you wish, and then save it. (We'll talk about saving during preview soon.) Recall the saved file location when you set the sample data *File location* in preview settings.

If you're using a sample data file that contains sensitive information, or you just don't want others to know what file you're using for testing your form, you have no need to worry. Publishing your form removes the sample data file path from the form definition file.

With User Roles

Without giving away too much, we'll gently introduce how to use a role when previewing your form. (For a full discussion on the definition of a role as well as how and when to use one, see Chapter 13.) The general purpose of a role is to customize the form-filling experience. As you'll see in a moment with an example, using roles in your form can be a critical part of its design. But there's no good way to simulate a person with a specific role filling out your form. You could ask a person with that role to help you test your form. But that's not a realistic expectation if you're dealing with multiple roles. If you're designing a form for a customer, it's probably not even possible (nor is it professional!) to ask for such help.

Forms Services

User roles are not supported in browser-enabled form templates.

Say, for example, that you're designing a form that shows a grocery market's entire inventory. Your form has two views: one for checkers (a read-only list of inventory) and one for managers (a read-write version). You set up two roles that model those two types of users. Checkers are not allowed to modify inventory, so they should not be given access to the managers' view. Let's assume that you've set up your form appropriately to restrict the checkers' access to the managers' view. How do you know everything in your form works as expected? Preview with a role!

By default, the *Preview as* drop-down on the preview options page (refer back to Figure 9.22) is disabled. This means that when you preview the form, it will run with no specific role. This is the default preview behavior unless you set a role. The *Preview as* drop-down is enabled when you define one or more user roles for the form template. (See Chapter 13 to learn how to add user roles.) When you preview with a role that isn't the default role, the form role will be explicitly set to the selected role.

> **WARNING Previewing with a User Role Is Not Impersonation**
>
> Previewing with a user role does not mean that you are impersonating that user or set of users. In other words, the InfoPath preview window is not running under other Windows credentials. The InfoPath application always runs in the context of the logged-in Windows user. Using roles is simply an InfoPath-specific concept and does not change the security context in which the form is executing.

Domain Simulation

The last preview setting to discuss is the *Domain* option. To fully take advantage of this setting, we highly recommend that you first learn about the InfoPath security model by reading Chapter 11.

Most forms rely on the ability to get and send data to different places. For example, a common scenario is a user submitting a form to your Web service or database. Many times these external data sources are not on the same server as the published form. In this situation, your form template needs extra permissions to talk to the external data source. As a result (and unless your form is full trust), your form will prompt the user, asking whether this communication is allowed to happen. Actually, any time your form attempts to send data to a computer that isn't where the template is published, the user could get a security prompt or simply be denied. To help you check the security implications of using a published form from a specific location, you can use the *Domain* text box shown in Figure 9.22.

Previewing your form in a domain will surface some security and prompting issues as if the form were actually published in that domain. If your form is set to domain trust (see Chapter 11 for more on trust levels) and you know where your form will eventually be published, it is a very good idea to set the preview domain and leave it enabled for the duration of designing your form. The *Domain* text box accepts file:/// (e.g., C:\folder), http:// and https://, and UNC (e.g., \\myserver\myshare) locations, which nicely correspond to the most common publish locations.

Similar to the sample data file location, the remembered domain is removed in published form templates.

Saving Form Data

A drastic new capability in InfoPath 2007 is the ability to save during preview. In previous versions of InfoPath, the *Save* command was unavailable—and for a good reason. Previewed forms, now that they can be saved, can never be reopened on their own. (There is a way to reuse them, but it involves using the Relink tool found in the InfoPath SDK. See the Appendix for a link to the InfoPath Team Blog, which has more information about relink and using the Relink tool.) Attempting to reopen a saved preview form results in an error dialog (Figure 9.23) because the form is not associated with a template.

One use for a saved preview form is as a sample data file to use while you're previewing a form (as we discussed earlier).

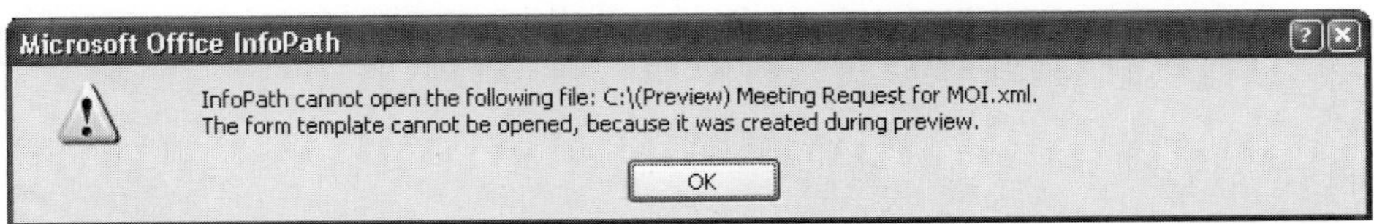

FIGURE 9.23: Error message that results from attempting to open a form that was saved while previewing

NOTE Associating Previewed Forms with Form Templates

You're probably wondering why forms saved while previewing can't be properly associated with the template. The answer is simple: Previewing always works on the unpublished form template from design mode. Since design mode represents a template in a transient state, the preview form is linked to the template, which resides in a temporary location. The temporary template is supposed to be deleted after you close the InfoPath application. Sometimes you'll notice that you can still reopen the preview form. This is fallout due to InfoPath being unable to immediately delete the temporary template. But you shouldn't depend on this behavior as it's nondeterministic.

What's Next?

Congratulations! We've come to a point where you can confidently design and deploy a form template. In the last chapter, you learned how to set up the form to submit data. Put it all together, and you've got what it takes to design InfoPath forms for many different situations. We encourage you to take the next step by finding a form to design in InfoPath. Think of paper forms you use every day in business. Or surf the Web to find plenty of examples that could benefit from an InfoPath rendition. But don't expect to be able to create an exact replica (in functionality) of a form yet. We have yet to cover many scenarios and advanced InfoPath features.

We inevitably previewed (no pun intended) a few topics that are coming up in future chapters, such as user roles and form security. As we dive into more detail about these topics, it may be helpful to keep this chapter handy for quick review of some of these concepts.

10 Building Reusable Components

Getting Started

At this point in the book, you not only know how to design form templates that look nice but you can also take advantage of most of the basic (and some not so basic) features available when using InfoPath in design mode. Now you can create professional-looking forms in no time. However, over time, as you create more and more form templates, you may find that many of them are very similar or share a lot of the same constructs.

For example, several of your form templates may contain sections used to collect address information from the user. It would be pretty tedious to have to add the same address block to each of your form templates, especially if there is no difference in this data from one form template to another. You could simply copy the controls and layout from the view and paste them into another form template. This would work fine for the view aspects of the form. However, what about the data structure, rules, calculated default values, data validation, and data connection information that you may have added to your form template? How do you copy these settings from one form template to another? Using copy and paste, this just isn't possible.

There is another way to share different parts of a form template in multiple form templates. With InfoPath 2007, you can build custom components that can be reused in one or more of your form templates. This means that you can create your own components or reuse ones created by third-party software providers.

You can create reusable components in two ways. The first is to write ActiveX controls in C++, Visual Basic, C#, or any COM-aware programming language. Creating controls this way requires you to put on your developer hat and write quite a bit of code. Since this is an advanced topic, we'll talk about this in the advanced section of this book in Chapter 19.

Fortunately, there is a second way to create custom components in InfoPath, one that doesn't require you to write even one line of code. These custom components are called **template parts**. As their name implies, template parts are parts of a form template. More specifically, template parts group pieces of a form template into a component that can be reused in multiple form templates. These custom components, which include controls, data structure, and many of the design features you've learned about so far (such as rules and data validation), enable you to quickly and easily reuse common design features across as many form templates as you choose. Let's jump right in and see how easy it is to create one of these components.

Designing a New Template Part

Designing a template part is just as easy as designing a new blank form. In fact, you design a template part the same way you would design a form template. Let's look at an example. Let's say that you work in the IT department at the MOI Consulting Corporation. MOI has a mandate that all forms that collect address information should follow a standardized format and data structure for that part of the form. Figures 10.1 and 10.2 show the format and data structure, respectively. (These figures should look very familiar to you since this is the address block from the MOI employment application form we used in earlier chapters.) Until now,

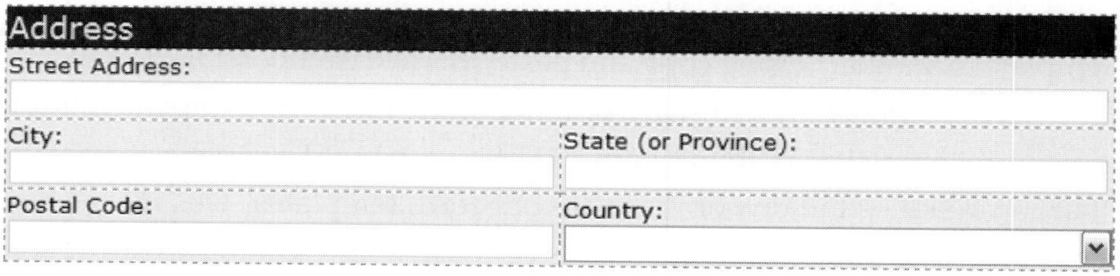

Address
Street Address:
City:
State (or Province):
Postal Code:
Country:

FIGURE 10.1: Address block section of the MOI employment application form

FIGURE 10.2: Data source for the address block template part

everybody at MOI who has created a form has either had to recreate this part of the form template from scratch or copy an existing form template and remove all the nonrelevant parts. Being the innovative form designer that you are, you figure out a way to make this process easier for everybody in the company—you create an address block template part. Let's look at the process for creating this component.

The first step (after starting InfoPath, obviously) is to open the *Design a Form Template* dialog as you normally would when designing a new form template. One thing you'll do differently, though, is to select the *Template Part* option at the top of the dialog, at which point the dialog changes to look like the one shown in Figure 10.3. Notice that the *Based on* section of the dialog looks a bit different. Only the *Blank* and *XML or Schema* options appear. This is because when designing a template part, you can either create a new

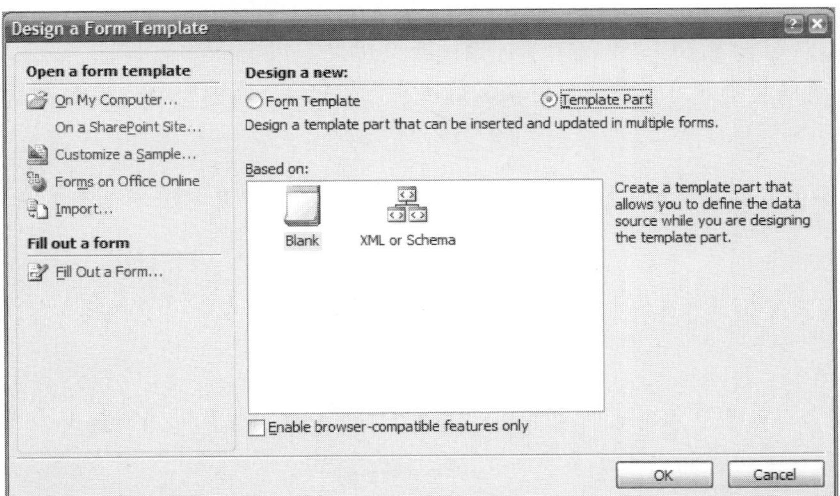

FIGURE 10.3: Design a Form Template dialog with Template Part option selected

blank template part or base it on an existing XML file or schema. It's not possible to base your template part on a Web service, database, or connection library as you can when designing a form template.

Since MOI Consulting has a required data structure for address blocks in forms, it seems natural that you would want to create your template part based on an existing schema. However, if you don't have an existing schema or you want to create one for your address block, you can create a new blank template part. So, let's select the *Blank* option from the *Based on* section of the dialog and then click the *OK* button. When you do so, InfoPath opens in design mode with a completely new template part that contains nothing in the view or data source. We'll add controls to the view next, which will also create the data structure we require for this address block template part.

Template Part Design Mode

When you open InfoPath in design mode when designing a template part, at first everything looks the same as it does when designing a normal form template. However, as you look around you will notice subtle differences. For example, if you look at the *Design Tasks* task pane (Figure 10.4), you'll notice that it doesn't contain all the design tasks that it normally does when you are designing a form template—the *Views* and *Publish Form Template* tasks are missing.

To understand the reason behind this difference, it's important to understand the concept of design targets. Whenever you open InfoPath in design

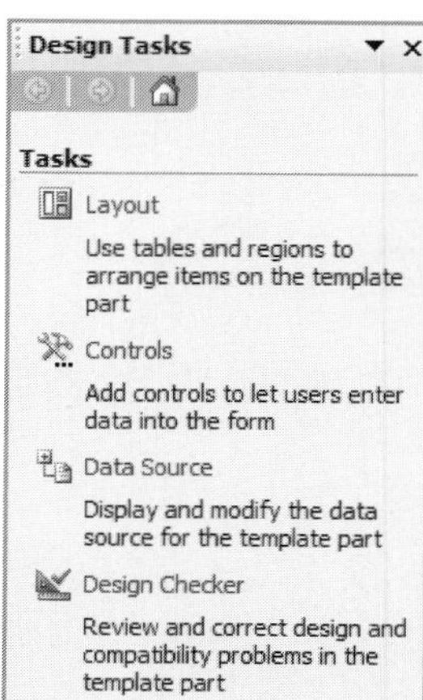

FIGURE 10.4: Design Tasks pane when designing a template part

mode, it can have one of two targets—form template or template part—which correspond to the option buttons with the same names in the *Design a Form Template* dialog. (Of course, in each case, you can specify that the form template or template part is browser-enabled. We will discuss this more in Chapter 14 when we talk about browser forms.) When you are targeting a form template, all the InfoPath design-mode features are available. When you are targeting a template part, only a subset of the design-mode features (those supported by template parts) are available.

For example, a template part can have only one view. So, the *Views* task pane is not available in the *Design Tasks* pane (or anywhere else, for that matter). As with the tasks in the *Design Tasks* pane, the entry points (e.g., menus, dialogs, and so on) for any features that are not available in template parts will be hidden. Table 10.1 lists all the features that are not supported by

TABLE 10.1: List of Features Not Supported by Template Parts

Unsupported Feature	Description
ActiveX controls	ActiveX controls, which we will talk about in Chapter 19, are not supported in template parts.
User roles	User roles available from the *Tools* menu are not supported by template parts.
Information Rights Management	IRM is not supported.
Digital signatures	Digital signatures cannot be added to the entire form or to the Section or Optional Section controls.
Multiple views	Only one view is supported in template parts.
Word print views	Since you cannot create multiple views, you also cannot create a print view for use in Word.
Print settings	Print settings are specific to a form template and cannot be included in template parts.
Page settings	Page settings are not supported for the same reason that print settings are not supported.
Changing the view name	The view that a template part is inserted in is defined by the form template and not the template part. So, it doesn't make sense to change the view name for a template part.

continued

TABLE 10.1: List of Features Not Supported by Template Parts *(continued)*

Unsupported Feature	Description
Background pictures for the view	As with the view name, the background picture is set by the form template. However, setting the background color from the *View Properties* dialog is supported, and the color chosen there will be used as the background color for the template part itself when inserted.
Form code	Code (script or managed) is not supported in template parts.
Publishing	You do not publish template parts as you do form templates. Saving a template part has the same effect as publishing in this case.
Printing multiple views	Since multiple views aren't supported, printing multiple views is also not supported.
Color schemes	Color schemes are defined by the form template in which a template part is inserted. Template parts will honor the color scheme of the form template.
Form Options dialog	Many options on the *Form Options* dialog pertain to form templates only. Therefore, the menu item for this dialog is hidden.
Designing a template part from a data connection	You can design only a blank template part or one from an XML file or schema. You can add a secondary data connection after creating the template part, however.
Form submit	It is not possible to define the submit behavior for a form template in a template part. This is controlled by the form template itself.
Form merging	It is not possible to define the merge actions for nodes in a template part. The merge actions must be specified in the form template. (Merging forms is discussed in Chapter 12.)
Form export	It is not possible to export a template part as you can a form template.
Mixed namespace editing	If you create a template part from a fixed schema, you cannot add new nodes to the schema. This is because template parts don't support mixed namespaces in the schema.

template parts and, therefore, won't be available in design mode when designing a template part.

Now that you've opened InfoPath in design mode to design a template part, the experience should be very familiar since you've designed a form template before. So, let's create our address block component. As we mentioned, the address block we want to create is the same one used in the MOI employment application form. So, to make things a little easier, let's just copy all the controls and layout from the view in the employment application form and paste them into the view of the template part we are creating. To do this, open the employment application form we created back in Chapter 2 (which is available with the samples for Chapter 2 on the book's Web site), select the *Address* Section control by clicking the design-time visual tab for the Section control and then press Ctrl+C to copy it. Then go to the template part and paste the controls and layout into the view for the template part.

After you paste, you'll notice that all the controls have error design-time visuals, as shown in Figure 10.5. This is because when you copy controls

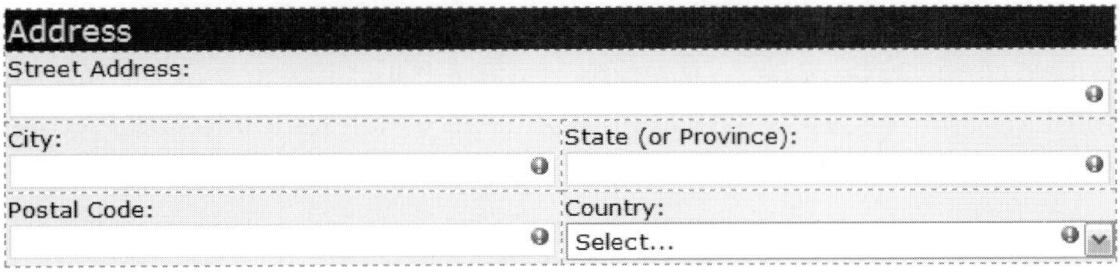

FIGURE 10.5: Address block after pasting it into the view

from one form template and paste them into another, only the view features are copied. None of the data bindings are preserved. (In fact, none of the data-centric features, such as data validation, calculated default values, and so on, are copied.) However, this is pretty easy to fix. First, you have to create the data structure shown in Figure 10.2. (If you need a refresher about how to create the data structure manually, see Chapter 3.) Once the data source is created, all you have to do is right-click on each control and choose the *Change Binding* option. Then from the binding dialog, choose the node to which you want to bind each control. (Of course, as you learned earlier, you can also create the data structure right from the binding dialog.)

Once you've changed the bindings for each of the controls, you have a fully functional template part that you can use in any form template. But before you can reuse this component in other form templates, you have to save it. In terms of what you do, saving a template part is no different than saving a form template. However, when you save, InfoPath will give the template part the .xtp extension instead of the .xsn extension used for form templates. This will be important later when you try to locate template parts to reuse. When you save the template part, the name you give the file will be the name you'll use when you install the template part into your *Controls* task pane, which we'll show you how to do next.

You've created your first template part, so let's put it to use. (In the last chapter, you learned about publishing form templates. You don't actually publish template parts as you do form templates. Saving a template part is analogous to publishing it in this case.)

Using a Template Part

Once you have a template part—whether you created it yourself as we just did or you are reusing one created by somebody else—you can add it to your *Controls* task pane so that you can use it just like any of the built-in InfoPath controls. Let's look at how you can install template parts so they can be inserted into your form templates.

Adding a Template Part to the Controls Task Pane

Reusing the address block template part in your own form template is easy. First you must create a new form template or open an existing one in design mode. Then open the *Controls* task pane. At the bottom of the task pane is a link titled *Add or Remove Custom Controls.* Clicking on this link opens the *Add or Remove Custom Controls* dialog (Figure 10.6). From this dialog, you can add or manage all your custom controls, whether they are template parts or ActiveX controls. If you've never added a custom control before, this dialog will be empty. However, once you add a control or two, each control name will appear in the *Custom controls* list box. (Figure 10.6 shows the *Add or Remove Custom Controls* dialog after adding the Address-Block template part.)

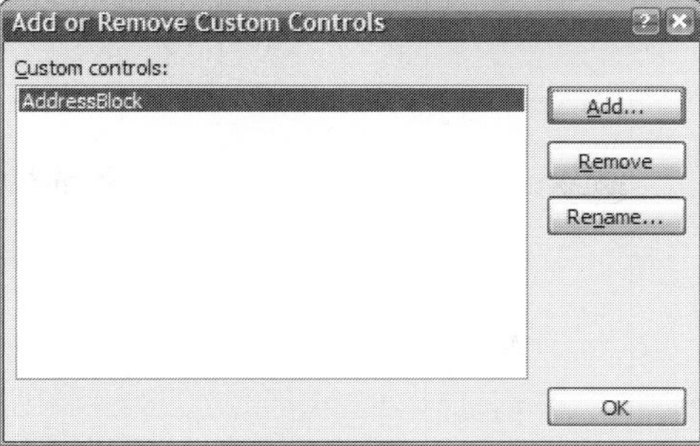

FIGURE 10.6: Add or Remove Custom Controls dialog

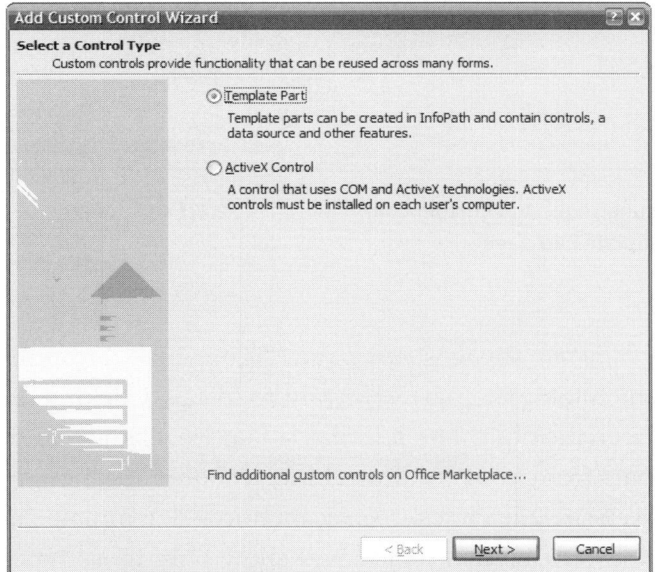

FIGURE 10.7: Add Custom Control Wizard's Select a Control Type page

In order to add a custom control, just click on the *Add* button, which will start the Add Custom Control Wizard. When you first start the wizard, the *Select a Control Type* page appears (Figure 10.7), from which you choose the type of control you want to insert into the *Controls* task pane.

As we've mentioned, InfoPath supports two types of custom controls—template parts and ActiveX controls. Since we are going to add a template part (and this option is the default), click the *Next* button, which will open

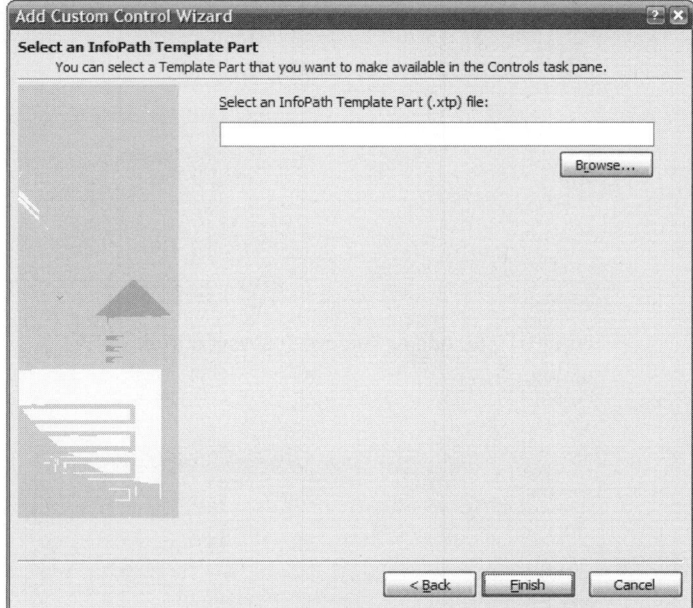

FIGURE 10.8: Add Custom Control Wizard's Select an InfoPath Template Part page

the *Select an InfoPath Template Part* page (Figure 10.8). From this page you can select which template part you want to install. Clicking on the *Browse* button will open the typical *Browse* dialog that we all know and love. Select a template part from your local machine, a shared location, a SharePoint site, or any Web site you choose. As we mentioned, template part files have an extension of .xtp, so this dialog will show only those types of files by default.

Once you choose the template part you want, click the *Open* button in the *Browse* dialog, and then click the *Finish* button after the dialog is closed. The *Custom Control Added* wizard page appears (Figure 10.9). As you can see, template parts have an icon and a version number associated with them. InfoPath automatically sets the version number and increments it each time you save the template part. We'll show you a little later in this chapter how to change the icon for the template part.

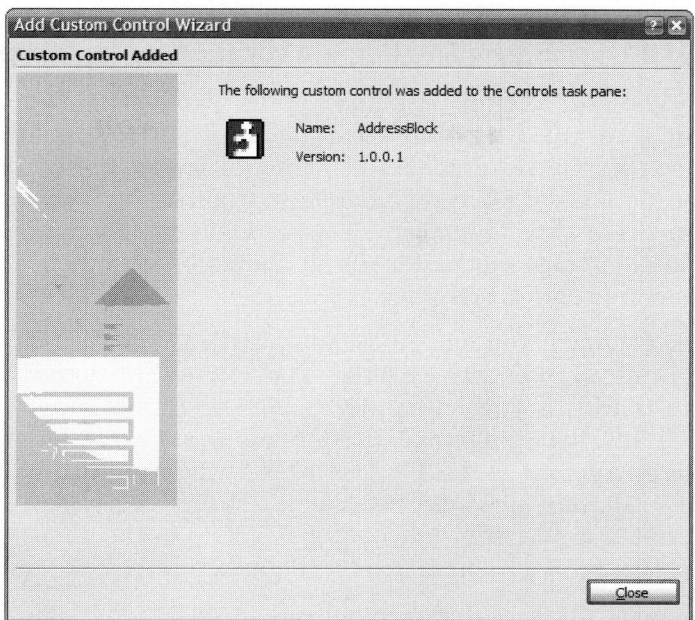

FIGURE 10.9: Add Custom Control Wizard's Custom Control Added page

Once you click the *Close* button on the *Custom Control Added* page of the wizard, the name of the template part is added to the list of custom controls in the *Add or Remove Custom Controls* dialog, as we shown earlier in Figure 10.6. Once you close this dialog, the template part is added to the *Custom* category of the *Controls* task pane (Figure 10.10). Once the template part appears in the *Controls* task pane, you can insert it into your form template just like any of the built-in controls supplied by InfoPath.

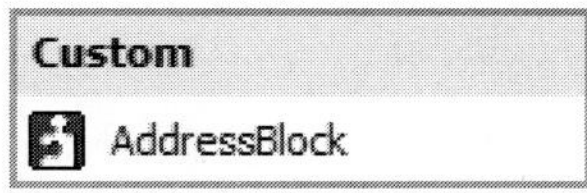

FIGURE 10.10: Custom category of the Controls task pane after adding the AddressBlock template part

NOTE Specifying an Alternate Location for Template Parts

When you add a template part to your *Controls* task pane, the component is installed on your computer in the following directory on Windows XP: C:\Documents and Settings\<*username*>\Local Settings\Application Data\Microsoft\InfoPath\Controls (where C:\ is your system drive and <*username*> is your login name). When you start InfoPath in design mode, it loads all the template parts from this location into the *Controls* task pane.

However, what if you want InfoPath to automatically retrieve template parts from an alternate location? Those who are designated as the administrator for your computer (which might be you) can create a registry key that points to an alternate location for template parts. This registry key is HKEY_CURRENT_USER\Software\Microsoft\Office\12.0\InfoPath\Designer. Create a string value called `IPCustomControlsFolder` under that key that points to the alternate location from where InfoPath should load the template parts.

There are a couple of things to note about this, though. First, this path can be only to a folder on your local machine or on a network share. Internet URLs won't work. However, if you want to place your template parts on a Web site, you can use folder mirroring to create a share that points to an Internet address. (You can do this by creating a new Network Place in Windows that points to the URL.) Second, if any of the template parts in the alternate location have the same template part ID as one already installed on you computer, each time you open InfoPath in design mode you will receive an error stating that the template part is already installed. In that case, the template part(s) from the alternate location will not be installed in the *Controls* task pane.

Inserting a Template Part into a Form Template

Once you install a template part by using the Add Custom Control Wizard, you can use it in any form template you create. Let's take a look at what happens when you insert a template part into a form template. As we mentioned, once the template part is in your *Controls* task pane, you can use it just like any of the other built-in controls—you can click on it in the task pane to insert it into the view, drag it into the view, or open the *Data Source* task pane and bind it to any field or group just as you can with the built-in InfoPath controls. If you insert your template part into a form template that has the *Automatically create data source* option set in the *Controls* task pane and you've created a blank template part (not one based on an XML file or schema), the data structure specified by the template part will be inserted into the form template. (We'll talk more about this shortly.)

If, instead, you open the *Data Source* pane to bind your template part to existing data in a form template, the data structure you can bind the template part to will depend on how the template part is defined. For example, look at the data structure for the AddressBlock template part in Figure 10.2 again. This template part is associated with a group node that has five fields below it. Therefore, you can bind the AddressBlock template part only to a group node that has at least five field nodes as children. If there are more than five child nodes, the first five nodes are used and the remaining nodes are ignored.

However, those first five nodes must match the data structure defined by the template part. Also, the data types of the nodes must be compatible with the data types to which you are trying to bind the template part (e.g., string and whole number data types are compatible but whole number and XHTML are not). Also, all template parts include at least one top-level group node. Therefore, in order to bind a template part to data in a form template, the data structure you are binding to must start with a group node. (Note, however, that it's not necessary for the field names in the form template to match the names of the fields in the template part itself.)

If you right-click on a group node in the *Data Source* task pane that fits the requirements just mentioned, the AddressBlock template part will be available. If you click on a group node that has only four children, for example, then the AddressBlock template part will not be available. (Note that template parts have a lower priority than the built-in control types. Therefore, to bind a template part to a node in the *Data Source* task pane, you may have to click on the *More* menu item on the context menu when you right-click on a node in the *Data Source* task pane. You will find template parts in the *Select a Control* dialog, which is opened from this menu item.)

Now, let's insert our AddressBlock template part into a new form template and see what's happening behind the scenes. Figure 10.11 shows this template part after inserting it into a blank form. As you can see, it looks a little different than the address block shown in Figure 10.1. In this case, the entire address block is inside a Section control. Since template parts are custom components, they are always contained within a Section control.

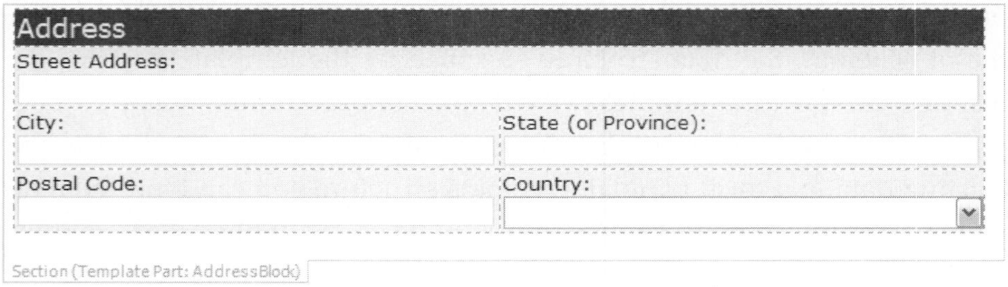

Address
Street Address:
City:
State (or Province):
Postal Code:
Country:
Section (Template Part: AddressBlock)

FIGURE 10.11: AddressBlock template part inserted into a blank form

This helps InfoPath treat the template part as a component, which is necessary for such things as updating existing parts. (You'll see why this is needed later in this chapter.)

Identifying a Template Part in the View

Template parts are very easy to identify because they are always contained within Section controls. The design-time visual for the Section control for a template part contains text that identifies it as a template part. The name of the part is also included in the design-time visual, as you can see in Figure 10.11. (Take a look at the tab at the bottom of the Section control.)

Once the template part is in the view, the contents of the template part (e.g., controls, calculated default values, data validation, and so on) all become part of the form template you are designing. In other words, once inserted into the form template, the template part is no longer a component treated as one atomic unit. You are free to move controls around in the view (or delete them); change rules, data validation, and calculated default values; change the data structure; and so on.

However, since the template part is no longer an atomic unit, you cannot delete everything added to the form template when you inserted the template part with one simple delete operation. (*Undo* won't help in this regard, either.) If you want to remove everything you added, you have to delete every item individually—the controls (which can all be deleted by deleting the template part Section control as long as you haven't moved any controls outside of it), the data structure, and so on.

As you can see, template parts provide you with an easy way to share and reuse aspects of your form, but they are not atomic controls such as a Text Box or Date Picker. In fact, template parts are more like the compound built-in controls such as the Master/Detail or Horizontal Repeating Table.

When you insert a template part into the view from the *Controls* task pane, how the data binding for the template part is handled depends on how it was originally created. If it was created as a blank template part, when you insert it into a form template, InfoPath treats it like one of the built-in controls. If your form template into which you have inserted a template part was created based on a blank form template or your form template is based on an open schema, not only are the controls inserted into the view, but the underlying data structure is created as well. If you designed your template part based on an existing XML file or schema, when you insert the template part into a form template, you will be asked to choose the group node to which the template part should be bound. (Of course, in either case, if you insert a template part into a form template that is based on a fixed schema, you will always be asked to choose the group node to which the template part should be bound. You must bind the template part to a group node since the component is always wrapped in a Section control, as mentioned earlier.)

Since our AddressBlock template part was created from scratch, when you insert it into a form template that allows editing of the data source, a group node containing five field nodes will be inserted into the main data source. As with other controls, where in the data source this group node is inserted depends on the current data source context in the view when you insert the control. For example, if the insertion point is inside a Repeating Section control in the view when you insert the AddressBlock, the group node for this template part will be inserted as a child of the repeating group node to which the Repeating Section is bound.

In addition to creating the data structure, when a template part is inserted, any calculated default values, rules, data validation, or data connections associated with the component are incorporated into the form template as well. When you insert a template part into a blank form template, this just means that these items are added to the new form template. However, if you are inserting a template part into an existing form template, you should be careful. Be particularly careful if you are binding it to a node that has calculated default values or data validation associated with it already or if your template part has rules and/or data connections associated with it and you have previously inserted it into the same form template.

> **NOTE** Issue with Data Connections When Inserting Multiple Instances of the Same Template Part
>
> If you have a template part that contains a data connection, when you insert multiple instances of that template part into a form template, all prior instances lose their connection to the secondary data source. For example, let's say that you created a template part that contains a Drop-Down List Box control that gets its list items from a secondary data source. When you insert two instances of that template part into a form template, the second instance retains its connection to the data source, but the first instance loses the connection. That means that, when a user fills out the form, the first instance of the Drop-Down List Box will have no list items, but the second one will. In this case, you have to reset the list items by opening the properties dialog for the Drop-Down List Box and specifying that the list items come from the same secondary data source as the second instance of the template part you inserted into the form template.

When you insert a template part, if you are binding it to an existing node that has calculated default values or data validation, the existing values and data validation will be replaced. If the values and data validation were created when you previously inserted this template part and you haven't made any changes, this shouldn't cause a problem. If you have made changes, though, you will lose those changes when you insert the template part. (This is a good reason to make regular backups of your form templates.) You will be warned about the fact that you might lose some of your changes ahead of time and will be given the option to cancel. However, the warning helps only if you know ahead of time that you have made changes to these items in the form template, which you may not know if you're maintaining an existing form template, for example. You can use the Logic Inspector as explained in Chapter 5 to determine whether there are calculated default values and data validation associated with a node.

If your template part has rules and data connections associated with it and you have previously inserted this template part into the form template, when you insert it again, those rules and data connections will also be replaced. However, in this case, only those rules and data connections associated with this particular template part will be replaced. Those from other template parts will not be affected. The main point here is to be careful and to know what calculated default values, rules, data validation, and data connections exist in your form template. Also, if you are modifying an existing form template, it's always a good idea to make a backup copy before you make any changes.

Template Parts with No Controls

It's possible to create a template part that contains no controls whatsoever. You may want to do this, for example, in order to reuse a particular data structure, complicated rules, or calculated default values. However, even though the template part contains no controls in the view, when you insert it into a form template, it will still contain a single Section control. You can delete that Section control from the view if you like. However, if you do so, there will be no way for you to update existing form templates with new versions of the template part.

Updating Template Parts

Let's say that your IT department has finally completed the AddressBlock template part and distributed it to the entire company. It has been six months, and now hundreds of form templates use this address block. Form template designers love this component because it saves them a lot of time and energy. Instead of having to add the address block to their form templates manually, they can now just insert the AddressBlock template part and their work is done.

However, users have been complaining that it's cumbersome to have to type the city and state every time they use a form that collects address information. They would like to choose this data from a list of cities and

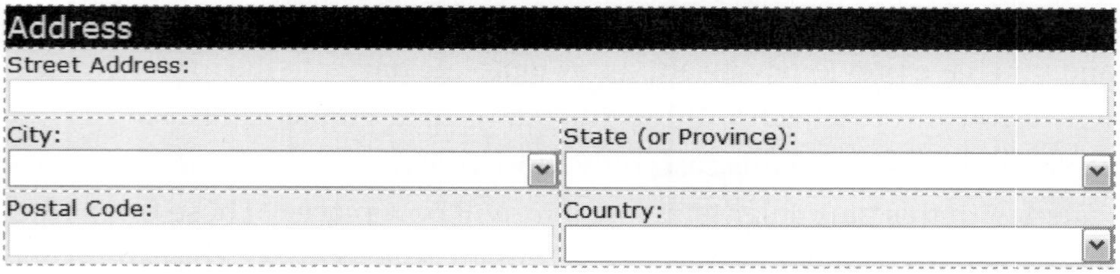

Address
Street Address:
City:
State (or Province):
Postal Code:
Country:

FIGURE 10.12: AddressBlock template part with cascading Combo Box controls

states. The designers in the IT department have graciously decided to make that change to improve the usability of forms throughout the company. They have updated the AddressBlock template part to replace the two Text Box controls for city and state with two cascading Combo Box controls—one that contains the state and another that shows the cities in the chosen state. (Also, the list of states will depend on which country is chosen from the country Combo Box. See Chapter 7 if you need a refresher about how to implement cascading List Box controls in a form template.) Figure 10.12 shows the new version of the AddressBlock template part after making these changes.

The other piece of feedback the IT department has received, this time from the form template designers, is that the AddressBlock component uses the default icon for all template parts. This makes it difficult to quickly differentiate between multiple template parts in the *Controls* task pane. So, the designers in the IT department decide to change the icon as well. Let's walk through how to do this.

To change the icon, first open the *Template Part Properties* dialog for the template part (Figure 10.13). You can open this dialog by clicking on the *Properties* menu item on the *File* menu while designing the template part. From this dialog, you can change the name of the template part, the ID, and the icon associated with the template part. The name and ID are generated automatically the first time you save your template part. (We'll change these later in this chapter.) The icon is set to a default icon for all template parts. The dialog in Figure 10.13 shows the *Template Parts Properties* dialog after changing the icon.

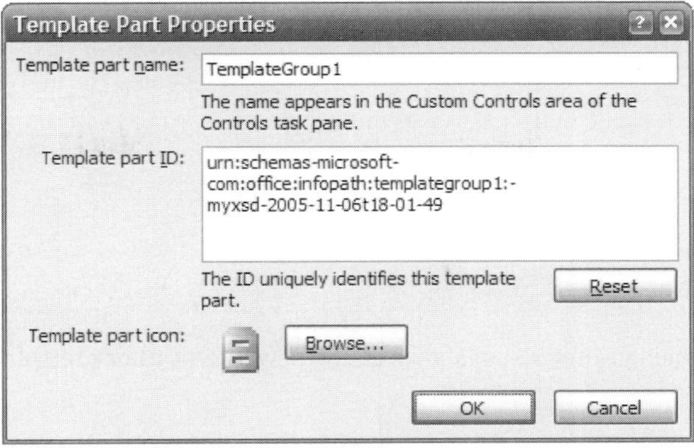

FIGURE 10.13: Template Part Properties dialog

Updating a Form Template That Contains the AddressBlock Template Part

Once the designers in the IT department have completed all the necessary changes to the AddressBlock template part, they tell all the form template designers in the company that a new version of the AddressBlock is available. As a form template designer, you want to take advantage of these changes. You also want an easy way to update the form templates that use existing AddressBlock template parts. It could be quite tiring to open each form template and search for all the template parts in every view before you can update them. Fortunately, there is an easier way to do this. You do have to open each of the form templates, but, once you do, you can update all instances of the AddressBlock throughout the form template (even across multiple views).

The first thing you must do is install the new AddressBlock. You install the new template part the same way you did the first time you installed the component. (If you have previously set up a repository of template parts using the registry key we talked about earlier, this step isn't necessary. In that case, InfoPath will load the new template part automatically.) Once you install the new version of the AddressBlock template part, all the existing AddressBlock components in the form template will now have a warning design-time visual, as shown in Figure 10.14. This visual simply alerts you to the fact that there is a new version of this component. When you see this design-time visual, if you then right-click on the tab at the bottom of

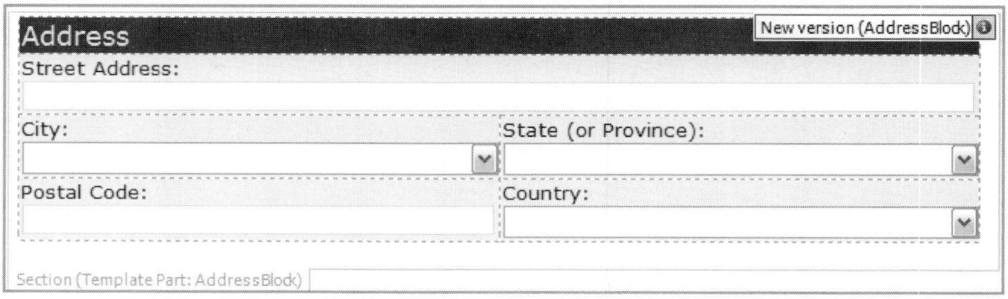

Address
New version (AddressBlock)
Street Address:
City:
State (or Province):
Postal Code:
Country:
Section (Template Part: AddressBlock)

FIGURE 10.14: Design-time visual shown on the new AddressBlock template part

the Section for the template part, you can choose *Update* from the context menu. This will update all the template parts of that type throughout your form template, even in different views. This is quite useful if you have a form template that uses many instances of the same template part.

In addition to the *Update* context menu item, you will see a *More Details* menu item on the context menu. Clicking on this item opens the dialog shown in Figure 10.15, which will give you more information about why there is a warning design-time visual on this Section control. You can then choose to update all AddressBlock template parts in the form template by clicking the *Update* button.

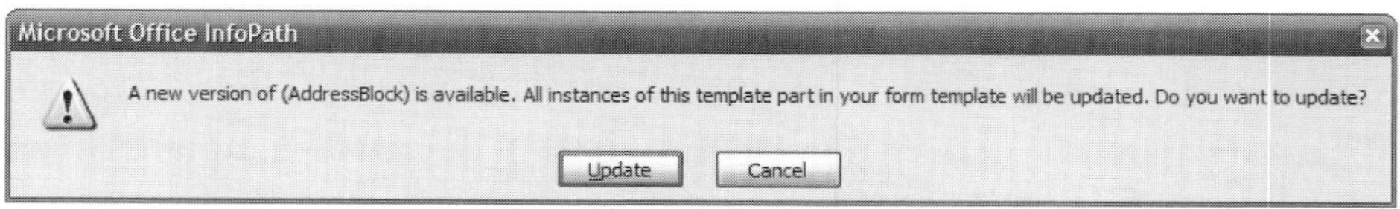

FIGURE 10.15: More details for the new template part

As we mentioned earlier, when you insert a template part into a form template, it's no longer an atomic component. The controls contained in the template part become part of the current form template. You are free to move the controls around or delete them entirely. However, when you update a template part, the component will be reinserted. That means that view changes are lost. For example, let's say that you deleted the city Combo Box from the template part. When you update the template part, the city Combo Box will be reinserted. (If you have previously moved pieces of the template part around in the view, those items will remain in the view.)

Also, when you update template parts, any view changes will be incorporated into the current form template, as will any calculated default values, rules, data validation, or data connections associated with the template part. When you update a template part that contains these features, as is the case when inserting a template part into an existing form template, any existing values, rules, data validation, or data connections will be replaced, as we talked about earlier, and not simply appended to the form template. In addition, in the case of updating an existing template part, if the component has any conditional formatting associated with it, those conditions and actions will also be replaced. Of course, when you update your template part, you will be warned that you may lose this data, but that won't help you if you've spent hours making those changes to your form templates in the first place. So, as we mentioned earlier, it's always a good idea to back up your form template before you update a template part.

Locating All Template Parts That Need to Be Updated

As you can tell, updating all template parts is relatively easy. However, what if you want to identify all the template parts that need to be updated not only in the current view but also in every view of your form template? You may, for example, want to inspect all instances of a template part before you choose to update them all so that you can determine whether there are any customizations (e.g., conditional formatting, rules, and so on) that you want to save. Locating all template parts that need to be updated is relatively easy as well.

First, go to the *Design Tasks* pane by clicking on the menu item of the same name on the *View* menu. Then, click on the *Design Checker* link in the task pane. This opens the *Design Checker* task pane (Figure 10.16). The *Design Checker* task pane provides you with a way to check your form template for various types of issues. This includes updates needed for template parts as well as many other items (which we'll talk about in more detail in Chapter 14).

Notice that a warning appears in the *Design Checker* task pane shown in Figure 10.16. (There will be one warning for each template part in the form template.) This warning tells you that there is an AddressBlock template part in the form template that needs to be updated. If you click on the warning text in the task pane, the template part that needs to be updated will be

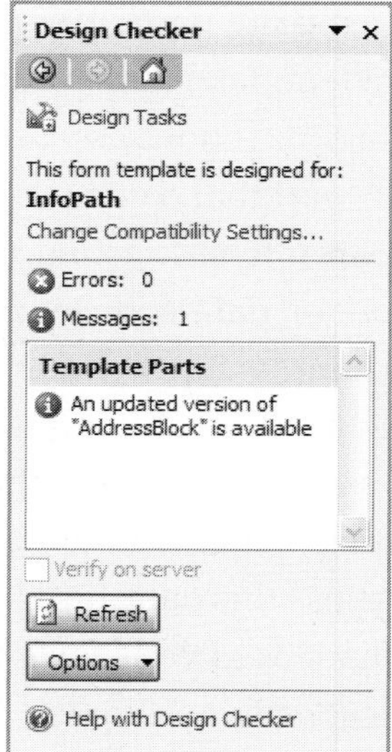

FIGURE 10.16: Design Checker task pane showing template parts that need to be updated

located. If the component is in the current view, it will simply be selected. If the component is outside of the viewable area of the current view, the view will be scrolled to show it. If the template part is in another view, the view will be switched to that view and the template part will be selected. Once you've located all the instances of the template part that need to be updated, and you've determined that it's okay to update them, you can then right-click on one of the components and update the current template part and any other template parts of this type by clicking the *Update* menu item as you normally would.

Customizing Existing Template Parts

Now that you know how to use template parts in your form templates, the next thing you'll probably want to do is go out to the Web and find some interesting template parts that you can reuse. There is no doubt that, when you do, you'll want to modify an existing template part in some way. For example, you may want to add your company logo, change or add some data validation, change the name of the template part, or simply change the icon.

Customizing an existing template part is very easy. When you find the template part you want to change, the first thing you'll probably want to do is download it to your computer (and pay for it if it isn't free). Then, you just open it in design mode in InfoPath as you would for any other template part. Once you make the changes you want, the next thing you'll obviously want to do is save. However, when you save, at this point you haven't created a new template part. All you've done is update an existing one. That means that if you then distribute this component to your users who happen to be using the original one, when they install your component and open a form template that uses the original one, they will be warned by InfoPath that an update is needed.

Maybe this is what you want. It is more than likely, though, that this isn't what you intended. Instead, you probably wanted to create a completely new template part based on an existing one. The one thing to remember is that a template part has an ID that uniquely identifies the component. (Refer back to Figure 10.13.) When you create a new template part, this ID is generated automatically for you. When you customize an existing part and save it, the ID does not change. Therefore, in order to create a new template part, you must change the ID. (It's also a good idea to change the name as well. In fact, when you change the name of the template part the ID is automatically changed. This is one easy way to create a new template part based on an existing one.) Figure 10.17 shows the *Template Parts Properties* dialog again, but this time after we changed the name and ID of the template part.

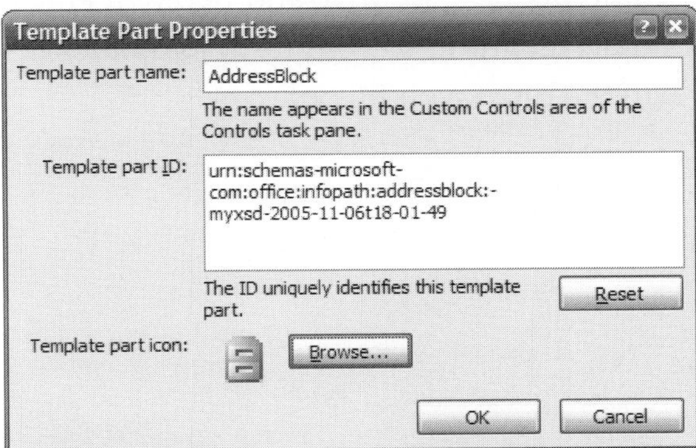

FIGURE 10.17: Template Part Properties dialog after changing name and ID

The name is simply a string and can be any name you choose. The ID is a Uniform Resource Name (URN) that uniquely identifies the template part. As you can see from Figure 10.17, the URN contains the name of the template part, the date, and the time, which helps to uniquely identify the template part.

If you want to create a new template part, you must change this URN. For example, you could change the name part of the URN and the date and time by hand. (You'll notice that when you change the name of the template part, the ID changes as well, but not vice versa.) If you decide that you want to regenerate the template part ID based on the new name you entered, just click the *Reset* button. Once you change the URN and save, you have a completely new template part. (Of course, since it's possible to manually edit the template part ID in the *Template Part Properties* dialog, it is also possible to enter the ID of an existing template part. This is only useful if you want to overwrite an existing part and not create a new one.)

What's Next?

In this chapter, you learned how to create your own components. Now you can not only design professional form templates but also create components that can be reused in other form templates. Template parts make designing form templates much easier and also give you a way to ensure consistency across the form templates in your organization.

In the next chapter, we'll talk about two of the final steps involved in designing a form template—security and deployment. We'll discuss how you can add digital signatures to your form templates in design mode and how you can sign the forms you fill out.

11 Security and Deployment

Getting Started

Every chapter until now has introduced new InfoPath functionality. As you continue progressing through this book, you'll notice that subsequent chapters address more advanced and challenging topics. Yet the progression into advanced feature sets means we're exposing more powerful elements you can incorporate into your form templates. This newfound power is not without its limits, thanks to InfoPath security and trust. Security is what your users will expect from InfoPath to protect themselves and their form data. Trust is a component of security that establishes a relationship between your form template and your users. Welcome to the world of **Trustworthy Computing**. We'll discuss what this means to you as the designer of form templates, as well as what it means to the users of your forms.

Next, we'll look at ways to discourage and even disable InfoPath's design mode. Locking down design mode can apply to a specific computer or even be used as a Windows domain policy for an entire corporate network. Disabling InfoPath's design mode, among other customizations, is made possible by using the Office Customization Tool (OCT). The OCT replaces the Office Resource Kit (ORK) from Office 2003.

We'll also talk about how you can enable users to secure the data they enter into a form by using **digital signatures**. Being able to digitally sign the data in a form is essential for business workflow processes. If you want to ensure that a form was filled out by a specific individual and hasn't been tampered with, digital signatures are your answer. We'll look at a few important aspects of digital signatures, such as the underlying technologies, and we'll touch on some legal implications.

The last topic of this chapter is **Information Rights Management**—otherwise known as **IRM**. The purpose of IRM is to restrict access to your form templates as well as the filled-out forms. You can limit access to specific users and even discourage features such as copying and printing. We look at advantageous uses of IRM and how you can leverage it in your deployments.

In the end, security is a necessary evil. It can hinder a developer from doing whatever he or she wants as well as impede the resulting program (or form) from having free rein over a computer. Restricting the power a program has over a computer is ultimately in the best interest of the users. To grant the developer and resulting program additional privilege on the user's computer, the developer is burdened with convincing his or her users that the program is trustworthy. This typically involves several things, such as gaining a reputation within the community and digitally signing the distributable. We'll learn about similar burdens for developing more powerful InfoPath form templates in this chapter. But keep in mind the ubiquity of personal computers. People use them for everything from e-mail to banking. Guaranteeing a user's identity and making sure that data is exposed only to the intended recipients are actions more important now than ever before. Understanding InfoPath security is in everyone's best interests.

Introduction to InfoPath Security

Inherent to any enterprise development platform such as InfoPath is the notion of Trustworthy Computing (TWC). But Trustworthy Computing is not a new concept. It has been a strict guiding principle in how Microsoft develops software and runs its business for several years now. (See Microsoft's TWC initiative Web site, referenced in the Appendix.) Without going into all of the aspects of TWC, we'll touch on the first two pillars relevant to InfoPath and form template design: security and trust.

There are two major perspectives to consider when designing and using trustworthy software. From the design point of view, how much trust must the program (as written by the developer) request to operate properly? Does it really need to talk over the network, and if so, to whom is it talking? Must the program read from or write to your computer's hard drive? These questions are answered, in part, by the distributor and by the reputation of the developer, as well as the various operations the program requests to perform.

The second perspective on trustworthy software comes from the standpoint of the program's end user. He or she should have the ability to control how much permission (e.g., for accessing the network or hard drive) a given program may be granted. Ultimately, the user should have the final word in granting or denying the program its rights. Only when a user can completely understand the security requirements of a program and have the final decision on what is permissible does Trustworthy Computing, in terms of a security vision, become reality.

Granting permission is the onus of the user. This can happen in many different ways, and the user may not even know he or she is giving permission! For example, when you're logged in as the administrator on your computer, you're giving any program you run full privileges to do whatever it wants. When you installed InfoPath on your computer, for example, you implicitly trusted that the setup files were really from Microsoft and not someone pretending to be Microsoft. You also trusted that the setup program does only what is advertised, namely, it installs the InfoPath program and support files but nothing else.

NOTE Installing InfoPath as an Administrator

You need to be an administrator to install InfoPath on your computer, but you don't need to be an administrator to run InfoPath itself. Those unfamiliar with security may not realize it, but many users run as administrators all the time! It's surely easy to do whatever you want as an administrator, but you expose much more surface area and increase the chances of attack, especially when downloading and running software from unknown publishers. The best security practice is to run as a Windows user with the least possible privileges to accomplish what you need to do on your computer. Escalation of privilege, such as running as an administrator, should be selective and minimal.

Moving from the scenario of trusting software and running programs on your computer, we can apply an equivalent philosophy to InfoPath and form templates. Consider InfoPath as your computer (specifically, the operating system) and form templates as programs you can run. Like Windows, InfoPath has built-in security measures to constrain a form's privileges while it's being filled out. Windows is quite a sophisticated product; so, too, is its security model. There are entire books dedicated to addressing the topics that encompass Windows security. However, explaining the InfoPath security model will take only a part of this chapter since its scope is obviously limited to filling out forms. Let's look at how design decisions you make and features used while designing your form templates influence the level of security (i.e., permission) necessary for the forms to work properly.

InfoPath Security Levels

As we just mentioned, there are two sides to Trustworthy Computing: that of the developer who *requests* permission and that of the user who *grants* permission. As form template designers, it is our job to determine how much permission we need to request from our users. Ideally we'll ask for exactly the permission the form template will need. But if we ask for too little permission, our form template may not work properly. Or if it does seem to work, it will fail at specific points if it doesn't have proper permission. We could always ask for the highest level of permission. However, users might not want our form template to run with so much authority. Even if they do, there would still be some limitations in how we could distribute our form templates. To be successful in deploying feature-rich form templates that users can trust without question, it's imperative to understand the intricacies surrounding InfoPath security levels.

We'll start by talking about the developer's perspective and the implications of security settings on form template design. Our discussion will help you understand when and why you'll need a specific security level for a given form template. Furthermore, we'll see the teeter-totter effects that security level settings have on form deployment and how they impact end users.

Designing Security into Form Templates

All InfoPath forms must run in one of three security levels: restricted, domain, or full trust. There is also an automatic setting that is enabled by default, but we'll talk about that later. Figure 11.1 shows the form security settings. We will refer to this figure throughout the chapter.

There's another aspect of form template security that helps determine how to assign the proper level of security. InfoPath uses two form template properties, among other factors, to help evaluate the best security level for a form: the **form ID** and the **access path**. The form ID is a unique way to identify a specific form template. (Select the *Properties* menu item under the *File* menu to see the *ID* text box that displays the form ID.) It's formatted as a Uniform Resource Name (URN) and is constructed from the prefix `urn:schemas-microsoft-com:office:infopath:` followed by the form

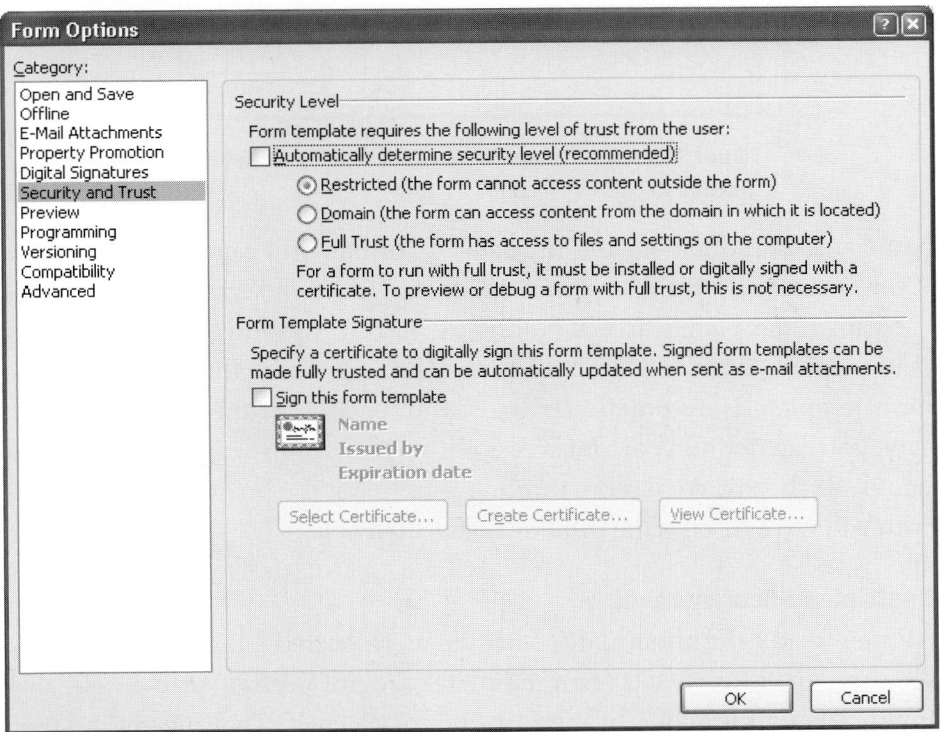

FIGURE 11.1: Configuring security and trust settings for a form template

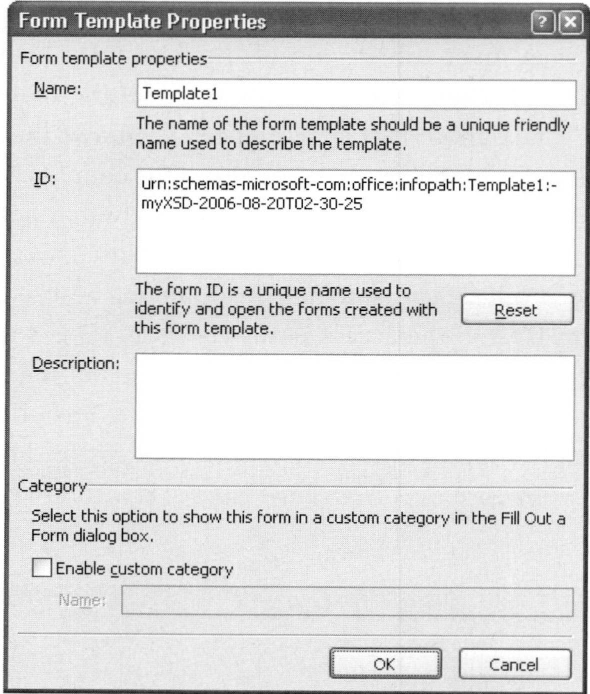

FIGURE 11.2: Form Template Properties dialog for setting the form ID

name and a unique date and time stamp format. You can modify the form ID in the *Form Template Properties* dialog, as shown in Figure 11.2.

A form template's access path is a Uniform Resource Location (URL) that people will use to fill out the form. The access path for an unpublished form template is automatically the saved location of the template. However, you can define a custom access path when publishing the template, as you'll see shortly. We'll more thoroughly explain the purpose of this access path when we discuss the different security levels.

Restricted Security Level

All new blank form templates start life as restricted—the lowest possible security level. Restricted form templates are not permitted to access anything outside the scope of the form template itself. That means the template must be completely self-contained. The downsides of restricted-level security are not without their upsides. As we'll soon see, restricted form templates are the easiest of all template security levels to deploy.

NOTE Security and Form Filling

Security levels do not apply during design time. That is, all InfoPath features are at your disposal as a designer regardless of the security level setting. Only when you preview or fill out a form are security restrictions in effect.

When you first think about restricted form templates, you may wonder about the effects on data connections. The mere presence of a data connection in your form template does not prevent your form from opening. (Unless, of course, the connection performs a query when the form loads.) There will be an error, however, the moment an attempt to use a data connection occurs. Figure 11.3 shows an example of such an error. You can see that InfoPath lazily evaluates some features of a form as it is being filled out.

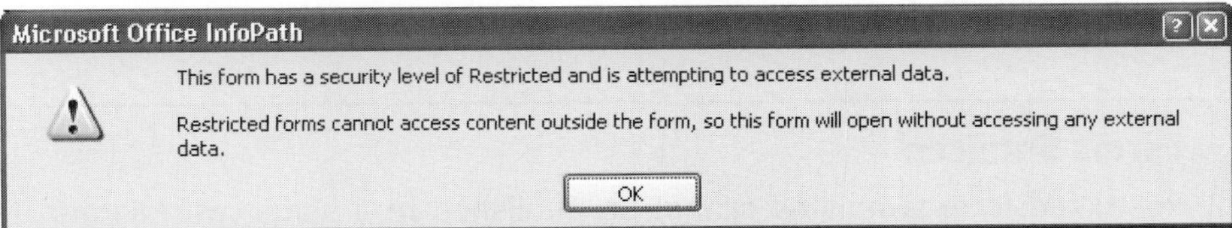

FIGURE 11.3: Error dialog when opening a restricted form template that attempts to query an external data source

Forms Services

Data connections, when running in Forms Services, require domain trust for "on-box" connections. Any connections that go "off-box" require full trust permission. Alternatively, domain trust form templates can still be used with "off-box" connections when using the Data Connection Library (DCL) or Centrally Managed Connection Library (CMCL). The DCL and CMCL features are discussed in Chapters 14 and 17, respectively.

Security Level Is Requested On Demand

It is still possible to open and use a form template that steps beyond its security boundary. However, any specific form features that depend on an elevated security level will fail with an error dialog. A data connection is only one example.

Deploying Restricted Form Templates

One of the big wins you gain by designing a restricted form template is its flexibility in deployment. In Chapter 9, we discussed the e-mail data connection and how it requires restricted permission. (This is the only case in which InfoPath blocks using a feature in design mode if the form template has too much privilege!) To understand why e-mail deployment requires restricted permission, it helps to understand how InfoPath handles opening restricted form templates.

Forms Services

Restricted form templates cannot be published to a server with Forms Services. The Publishing Wizard automatically elevates the privileges of a template if it is browser-enabled.

We told you in Chapter 9 that deploying a form template to users requires the process of publishing. But we didn't mention a slight detail: The access path does not matter when you publish a restricted template. Figure 11.4 shows the page of the Publishing Wizard where you set the access path. The primary reason why the access path doesn't matter is because restricted form templates can be opened from any location. There are absolutely no constraints on where a restricted form template can be opened from, including e-mail, a network share, or anywhere else you can imagine. So there's no need to republish a restricted template if you want to move its location; you can just move it! Because a restricted template cannot, by definition, have any form code or data connections, it is always considered to be safe.

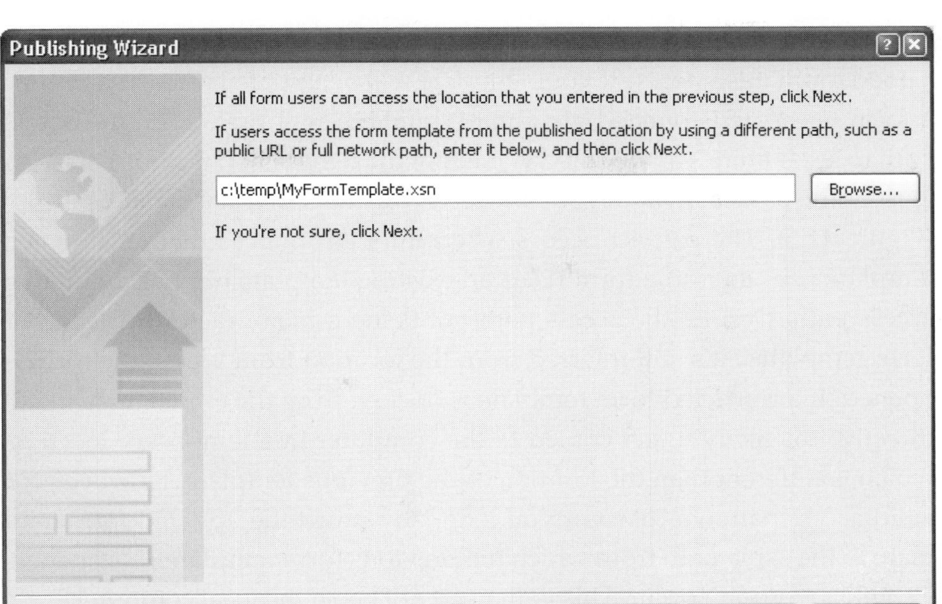

FIGURE 11.4: Setting an access path, which is not required when publishing a restricted form template

> **WARNING** Using the Access Path to Automatically Get Updates
>
> Restricted form templates do not require an access path. However, without a real access path, restricted templates forego the ability to automatically update themselves on a user's computer. When opening a form template, InfoPath checks the original publish location (i.e., the access path) and downloads the latest form template if the current one is out of date. If the access path is invalid, InfoPath silently skips the update.

> **NOTE** Restricted Flexibility
>
> Domain and full trust forms do not enjoy the freedom of mobility of restricted forms.

Given the flexibility bestowed on restricted form templates, they are also a good mechanism to use if your template will be updated often. Every time a form template is opened via e-mail, InfoPath will first check the access path to see if there's an updated version of the template. If there is no access path or the path is invalid, you may receive a *Form Template Conflict* prompt (Figure 11.5). The conflict occurs when InfoPath notices that an updated template uses the same form ID as an existing template but has a different access path. Despite the access path not being a major factor in restricted form templates, it's still inferred from the location from where the form is opened. If a restricted form template is opened from the e-mail attachment directly, it is likely to get copied to the computer in a temporary location, which is different than the location of the previous template. However, if a valid access path was used or you manually saved the updated form template to the same path from which the previous form template was opened, a conflict wouldn't occur. This path need not be on the local computer.

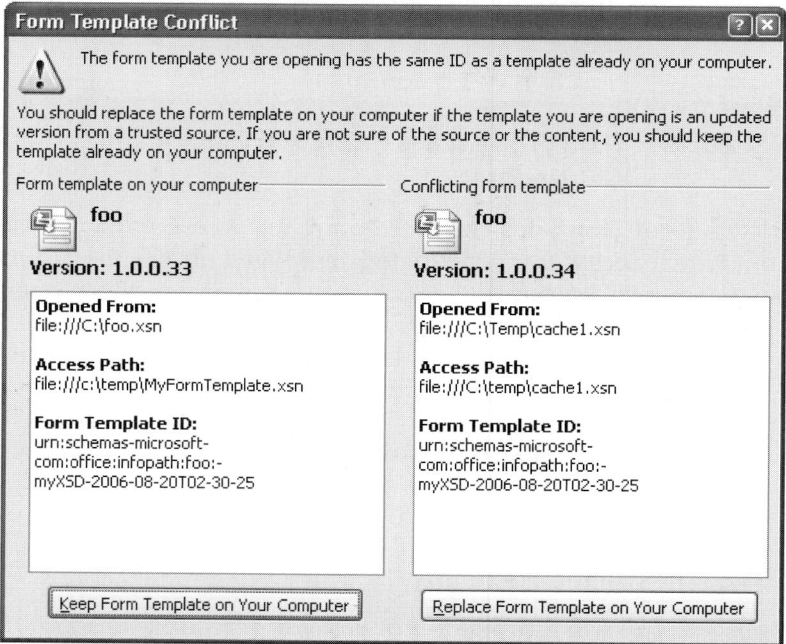

FIGURE 11.5: Cache conflict that occurs when a different version of the same form template is opened

> **WARNING** Access Paths on Restricted Form Templates
>
> Even publishing a restricted form with a blank access path can cause conflicts. InfoPath always infers an access path even when one doesn't exist in the template. The inferred path is the physical location of the restricted form being opened. So it's recommended that the access path on restricted form templates be properly set to a shared location that is accessible by all of your users.

Whenever InfoPath successfully opens a form template, it's cached (i.e., a copy is saved) in a permanent location for the current Windows user. The *Getting Started* dialog that we looked at in Chapter 2 shows all cached form templates when the *All Forms* link is selected (Figure 11.6). The *Remove this form* link on the right side of the dialog deletes the template from the cache.

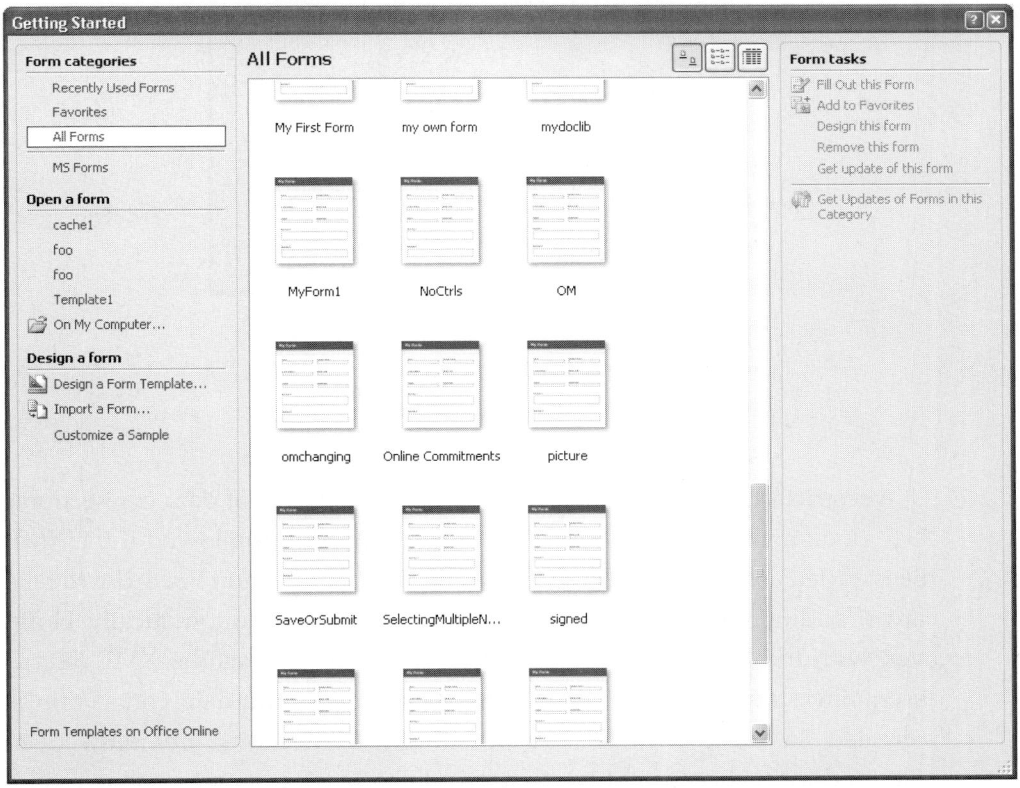

FIGURE 11.6: Getting Started dialog showing form templates in the InfoPath cache

A form conflict happens when a newly opened form has the same form ID as a cached form.

More Restrictions with Restricted Forms

We mentioned earlier that a restricted form cannot use any resource that is not listed in the form definition (.xsf) file. A resource can include any file that composes the form template (manifest.xsf, template.xml, myschema.xsd, view1.xsl, and so on) or those added manually in the *Resource Files* dialog (shown in Figure 11.7). We discussed the *Resource Files* dialog back in Chapter 2.

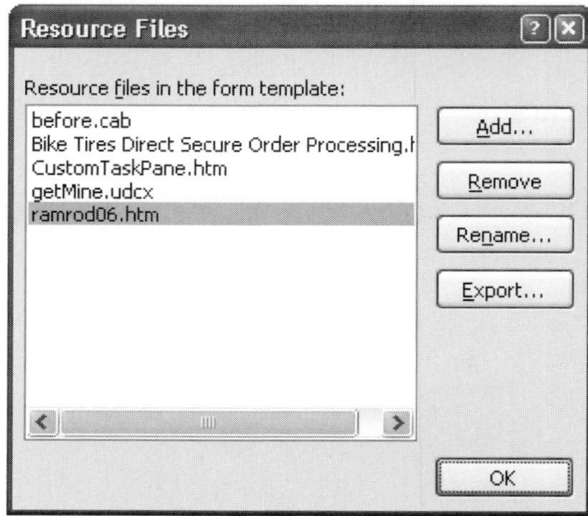

FIGURE 11.7: Resource Files dialog, which shows files accessible by all form templates

A restricted form template can have only two types of data connections: XML document and e-mail. An XML data connection is allowed if the XML file is added as a resource to the form. The Data Connection Wizard will take care of adding the XML file to the *Resource Files* dialog automatically. However, with the XML file as a part of the form, this means the XML data is essentially static and will never be updated unless the data connection is recreated in design mode. E-mail submit connections are allowed in restricted forms because of two reasons. First and foremost, sending e-mail does not transmit your credentials to connect to a potentially rogue computer.

Other data connections like Web service and SharePoint list, for example, may connect to the external data source with your identity, depending on your Internet Explorer security settings and the security zone of the target data connection. E-mail uses Outlook to send a message, so InfoPath is using software that you already trust and have configured on your computer. Second, submitting via e-mail requires explicit user intervention. When submit is initiated, a dialog appears from Outlook asking the user to click the *Send* button to send the mail. Due to an Outlook security feature, this dialog always appears when another program requests that an e-mail be sent. There is no way to suppress or bypass this security mechanism.

Domain Security Level

Domain forms are a giant step up for data access scenarios. With domain security, unlike restricted security, forms could have the ability to use resources across different domains. But what, exactly, defines a domain? The answer is more involved than you might think. Essentially, with domain security, the form template does not need to be self-contained and, unlike restricted forms, can access data outside of the form template. There are several different types of domains, otherwise known as zones, each with its own rules of engagement. What follows is an explanation of, first, what mechanisms contribute to the classification of a form as domain security, and second, how to determine what type of domain, or zone, into which a form falls. As we learn the types of domains, we'll also see what InfoPath-specific features are either enabled or disabled when a form runs in a specific domain.

A domain form is primarily identified by its published URL, more formally known as its access path (shown in the Publishing Wizard; refer back to Figure 11.4). We discussed the access path to a limited extent earlier in this chapter, but it becomes a central player with domain security forms. We can assert that all domain trust form templates must have access paths, but there is a single important exception: a form template published to a SharePoint site. (Form templates published to a SharePoint site do not have access paths. Such a template determines its access path to be the location from which the form template was opened.) Without an access path, a non-SharePoint domain form template will fail to open (as we'll discuss soon in the section about moving forms; see Figure 11.12).

But just because a form template has an access path does not mean it is a domain trust form. The difference lies in the form's explicit security level. You can see (as well as change) the security level by visiting the *Security and Trust* category on the *Form Options* dialog, as shown earlier in Figure 11.1. Even if the security level of the form template is automatically determined, either the *Restricted* or *Domain* option button will still be selected despite being disabled. Note that this setting simply classifies a template as restricted, domain, or full trust. You cannot actually choose the type of domain security the form will receive. The type of domain trust is strictly associated with the form's security zone.

Access Path Details

The access path is defined in the form definition (.xsf) file as the `publishUrl` attribute on the `xDocumentClass`. If the `publishUrl` attribute does not exist, the form doesn't have an access path. (The only exception is a form template published to a SharePoint site; then `publishUrl` is determined dynamically by the location from which the form template was opened.) Such could be the case for restricted form templates.

Once it's established that a form template is domain trust, the next step is to determine its **security zone**. The concept of a security zone is inherited from the Internet Explorer (IE) Web content zone model. In IE, each Web content zone has associated security settings that are clearly identified and could be modified.

WARNING Security Settings Spillover

Changing the security settings for IE may directly affect InfoPath security settings as well.

InfoPath shares the same Web content zones and even classifies locations using the same logic as IE. But where IE applies its *Security level for this zone*

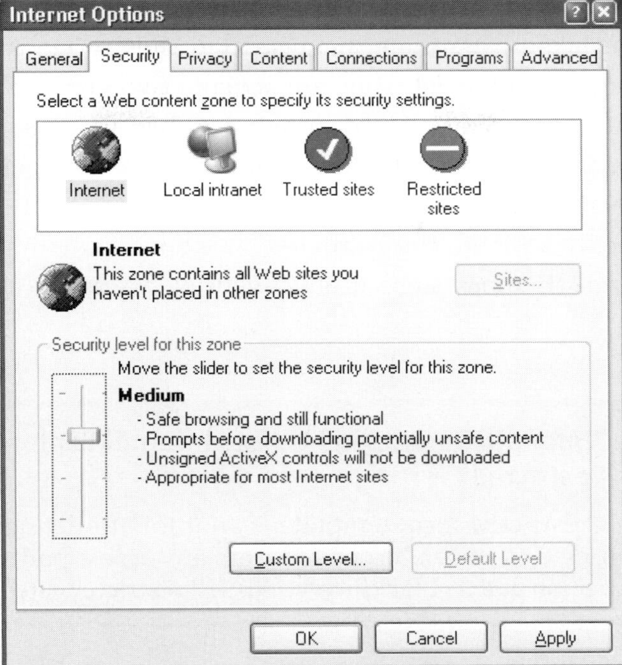

FIGURE 11.8: Internet Explorer Web content zones, each of which has its own security level

settings (as shown toward the bottom of Figure 11.8), InfoPath forms are subjected to other settings. We'll discuss those settings in a moment as we go through each IE zone. Let's see how InfoPath access paths are classified into the following IE Web content zones: restricted sites, local intranet, Internet, and trusted sites. Another security zone also exists, the local machine zone (or LMZ), although it is not explicitly shown in Figure 11.8.

> **NOTE Domain Trust Is Most Common**
>
> Most real-world form templates fall into the domain trust category. It's a natural balance between the restricted and full trust settings (as we'll see in the next section) that allows your form to carry out most mainstream operations. Unlike restricted form templates, a domain form template does not need to be self-contained. It is allowed to communicate outside its boundaries to the same domain or sometimes even to other domains, depending on the form's zone.

Restricted Sites Zone

You might mistakenly associate this restricted sites zone with InfoPath's restricted form security level. They are actually two very different topics. It's important to know that if a form template has an access path whose server is listed in the IE restricted sites zone, the form will never be allowed to open. A URL can exist in the *Restricted sites* list only if an administrator explicitly adds it. The restricted sites zone is naturally the most restrictive of all IE zones since it effectively blocks any communication with the site.

> **NOTE** **"InfoPath Restricted" Is Not "Internet Explorer Restricted"**
>
> Recall that a restricted form template is an InfoPath-defined security level. A restricted form can be opened from any access path, unless, of course, the access path is blacklisted in the IE restricted sites zone.

Local Intranet Zone

The local intranet zone classification defines lax security settings compared to other zones, with the exception of the trusted sites zone. Sites in the local intranet zone include three somewhat broadly inclusive categories, as defined by the settings shown in Figure 11.9. The first option is *Include all local (intranet) sites not listed in other zones.* This is a catchall for all sites that are not

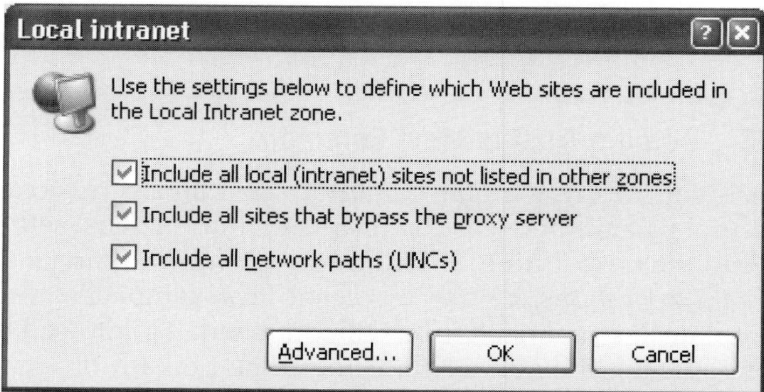

FIGURE 11.9: Settings for defining the local intranet zone

considered Internet sites and also are not trusted or restricted sites. The second option is *Include all sites that bypass the proxy server.* Since the proxy server acts as the gateway to Web sites outside the local network, this setting is yet another catchall for intranet sites. Finally, *Include all network paths (UNCs)* allows for locations such as \\MyComputer\MyShare\default.html to qualify as intranet content.

Local intranet forms, in fact, are one of the most common types of forms you'll find in a corporate environment. That's because forms and their data are often shared throughout an organization. Typically a SharePoint server, or some other central server, will act as the host for InfoPath forms. In smaller organizations that may not have a SharePoint server, a file server can also do the trick. In that case, the form can be published to a UNC network path by using the *To a network location* option on the first page of the Publishing Wizard. The ubiquity of the local intranet zone makes it an important zone to understand in terms of InfoPath security.

What does the local intranet zone mean for InfoPath? Generally, this zone impacts form security in three major areas, by determining whether or not custom ActiveX controls (marked unsafe for scripting) are allowed to be created in form script, whether cross-domain data access is enabled and to what extent, and what object model (OM) security level is available to custom form code. (Note that our conversation about ActiveX technology refers to objects in script code and not InfoPath custom controls.) We'll mainly concentrate on cross-domain data access in this chapter, but it's also important to understand the impact of the local intranet zone when using ActiveX objects through form script. Keep in mind that ActiveX objects can be used only with scripting languages and not with managed code. Also, do not confuse InfoPath template parts (see Chapter 10) with ActiveX custom controls (specific to programming, not just InfoPath; see Chapter 19 for more about custom ActiveX controls for InfoPath) as they're completely different mechanisms.

ActiveX controls are classified as either safe or unsafe for scripting. The classification is predefined by the author of the ActiveX component and cannot be modified. Creating an ActiveX object in form script requires the `CreateObject` method (VBScript) or the `new ActiveXObject` (JScript) methods.

The OM security level is a different concept than the form security level settings. It's based on a numeric system but was designed to be in step

TABLE 11.1: OM Security Level Definitions

OM Security Level	Description
0	Any form can access corresponding OM properties and methods through form code. There are no restrictions.
1	Reserved for future use.
2	Forms with code running in the same domain as the currently opened form can access level 2 OM properties and methods.
3	Only code belonging to a full trust form can access level 3 OM properties and methods.

with the form security model. There are four OM security level settings, but only three are actually used, so they map out nicely to our three form security levels: restricted, domain, and full trust. Table 11.1 introduces the OM security levels. The OM security levels classify the InfoPath OM into three groups: Level 0 includes OM properties and methods with least restrictions and is available to any form template; level 2 corresponds with domain trust and offers a majority of the functionality available in the OM, which satisfies most scenarios; and level 3 is the highest level and is used exclusively with fully trusted templates. (Level 1 is the currently unused level just mentioned.)

The OM security level is set as a direct result of the form template security level. Table 11.2 shows the various OM levels and how they correspond to all form security settings.

TIP OM Security Level Can Be Set for Template with Managed Code

The code behind a template can be granted higher privileges than the form security level would otherwise allow. This is accomplished by using the `InfoPath Form Templates` code group.

TABLE 11.2: Form and IE Security Level Impacts on OM Security Level

Form Security Level	IE Security Zone	OM Security Level
Restricted	Anything but restricted sites	2, otherwise 0
Domain	Restricted sites	0
Domain	Internet	2; with default cross-domain IE settings, accessing another form through the OM is denied
Domain	Local intranet	2, cross-domain is prompted
Domain	Local machine zone (LMZ)	Same as local intranet
Domain	Trusted sites	2
Full trust	Anything but restricted sites	3

As you can see from Table 11.2, a domain trust form in the local intranet zone can access only level 2 of the OM on itself. This means the form template can access OM that specifically relates to the current form (i.e., the form where the code is running) belonging to that template. Accessing another currently opened form using the OM is denied. In Part II, we'll explain in more detail what OM properties and methods are available in each security level. Furthermore, custom ActiveX controls (marked unsafe for scripting) are disallowed in the local intranet zone. If you try to instantiate the `FileSystemObject`, for example, an error will result. This is discussed in more detail in Chapter 15.

Finally, the benefit we've all been waiting for: cross-domain data access. InfoPath will prompt the user at the time the data access actually occurs. For example, querying or submitting to a Web service will open the dialog shown in Figure 11.10. Cross-domain security prompts will usually appear only once per user session, that is, the specific duration that a form is being filled out. Another security prompt may arise during

FIGURE 11.10: Security prompt for cross-domain data access

form filling if code behind the form template attempts to access another domain that hasn't already been prompted and approved. This prompt, such as Figure 11.10, lists every known server to which each of the form's data connections (not just the one currently attempting to run) may connect. This prompt may reappear suddenly for other servers if form code accesses other domains.

Forms Services

Browser-enabled form templates running in the browser do not prompt the user before executing an off-box data connection. This is because such a form template or its connection (through the use of a server-defined data connection file) is fully trusted. Data connection files are discussed in Chapters 14 and 17.

Internet Zone

The beloved Internet zone is where we do most of our everyday Web surfing. It's also the place that we least trust, besides the restricted sites zone. Due to the public and unregulated nature of the Web, an evil hacker could run an InfoPath form on your computer quite easily. The question isn't about whether a form from the Internet *can run* on your computer; it's about what an Internet-based form *can do* when it runs on your computer. This follows the security concept of defense in depth, where one assumes that a malicious form *will* run on your computer and that any security mechanisms in place to prevent such a form from running can and will be inevitably circumvented.

We started the domain trust section stating that domain trust forms offer a big win over restricted forms because of enabled data access scenarios. However, this isn't completely true. Domain forms that live in the Internet zone are subjected to a very strict security level. In fact, they are functionally equivalent in most ways to restricted forms. As a result, the same rules for restricted forms apply to Internet zone domain forms. Unsafe ActiveX custom controls and cross-domain data access are both explicitly disallowed by default IE settings, but these can be changed. Similarly, OM security level 2 is granted for OM running against the current form. This means only properties and methods classified as level 2 are allowed to be called by form code on the current running form itself. The only capability an Internet domain form has over a restricted form is same-domain data access. Say, for example, that a domain trust form is available at http://www.moiconsulting.com/forms/broker.xsn. The form can use data connections that connect anywhere on http://www.moiconsulting.com but cannot go elsewhere, such as other domains.

Unfortunately, there is no option to get more security clearance from an Internet zone form unless users add your form's access path to their trusted sites zone in IE. The only other alternative is to step up to the full trust security level. But deploying a full trust form isn't as simple as just flipping the switch to the *Full Trust* option shown earlier in Figure 11.1. Shortly, we'll look at the implications of creating a full trust form template.

InfoPath Uses Some Internet Explorer Settings

You can modify individual Web content zones in Internet Explorer by clicking the *Custom Level* button in the *Internet Options* dialog (refer back to Figure 11.8). InfoPath respects some settings in the resulting *Security Settings* dialog. For example, under *Miscellaneous*, you can modify cross-domain data access for the Internet zone (on the *Access data sources across domains* setting) from *Disable* to *Enable* or *Prompt*. Clearly, we do not advise anyone to loosen up security settings for a given zone. Our intention is to point out that InfoPath respects specific IE settings surrounding security.

Restricting Internet Domain Forms through the OCT

Network administrators may want to be able to dictate a blanket level of security for their organization. Microsoft Office offers a solution through the Office Customization Tool (OCT). InfoPath participates in the OCT, in one way, by letting an administrator restrict users opening forms in the Internet zone. To disable the opening of any forms from the Internet zone, an administrator can simply open the OCT and set the *Disable opening of solutions from the Internet security zone* policy.

To run the OCT, insert the original CD or DVD from which you installed the 2007 Microsoft Office system. Instead of simply running the setup.exe program from the disc, open a Windows command shell and navigate to the directory where setup.exe is located. Run `setup.exe /admin` to open the OCT. The OCT window will appear similar to that shown in Figure 11.11.

Forms Services

OCT settings do not apply to browser-enabled form templates in the browser.

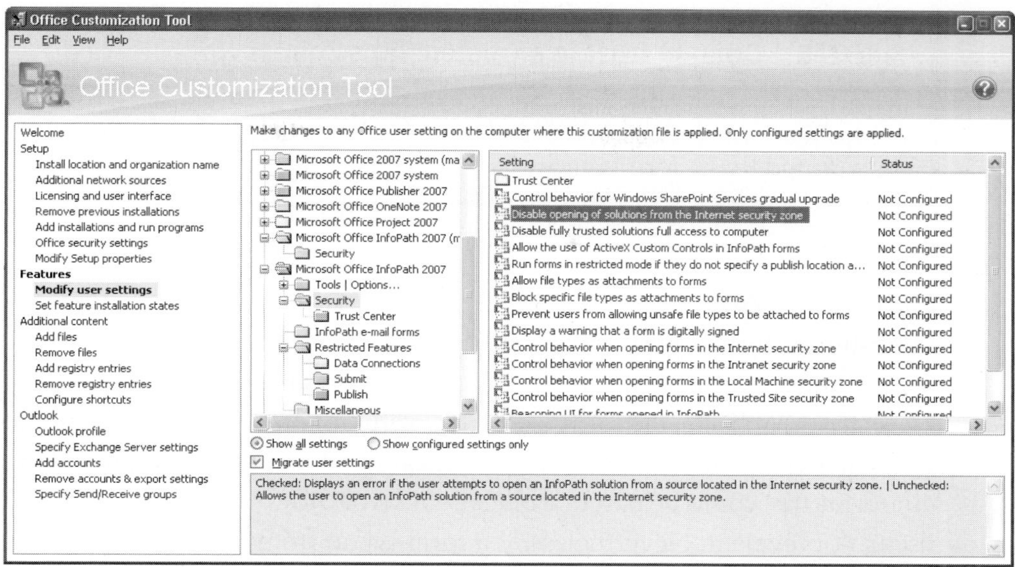

FIGURE 11.11: Office Configuration Tool security settings for InfoPath

Trusted Sites Zone

As you may have guessed, the trusted sites zone offers the highest level of trust for domain forms. When compared to other IE Web content zones for domain trust, the trusted sites zone loosens up many security constraints.

If you need one or more of the following, a trusted sites form will fit the bill:

- ActiveX custom controls not safe for scripting
- Cross-domain data access
- No security prompt (such as Figure 11.10) for cross-domain access
- OM security level 2 access

As we know, it's not possible to publish a form template directly to a trusted sites zone. InfoPath automatically, with help from IE, classifies forms according to their published zone. For a form to open in the trusted sites zone, the user of the form must add the URL of the form template (.xsn) file to the trusted sites list. But use caution when adding a site to the trusted sites list, as IE will trust all content from that site!

> **NOTE** Domain Trust in a Trusted Sites Zone Is Not Full Trust
>
> A domain form in a trusted sites zone is similar to a fully trusted form, except that only level 2, instead of level 3, OM properties and methods are granted to the form's code.

Local Machine Zone

Publishing a form whose access path is a local computer path is not a very compelling scenario for InfoPath. Since such a form isn't accessed through a file share or Web site, the form would be useful for only someone using that particular computer. Since InfoPath is ideal in a business setting for filling out forms that could be part of a bigger data workflow environment, private use isn't prevalent. Nevertheless, if a form is run from your computer, it is not allowed free reign. In fact, the level of security may surprise you.

Two types of domain forms can run in the local machine zone (LMZ): those form templates that are installed and those that are not installed. Unlike InfoPath 2003, installed domain templates do not have more permission than templates that are not installed in the LMZ. LMZ form templates, when filled out, are forced by InfoPath to run in the local intranet zone and are sandboxed to a randomly generated domain. The motivation behind locking down these templates is due to the inherent security risk when using the Web.

For example, an unknowing user could download and open a form without understanding that he or she just gave that form a whole lot more permission than just opening it straight from the Web would do. Even form templates installed by running a Microsoft Installer program are locked down despite a heavyweight installation process requiring administrator privileges. As all security-conscious users should know, one doesn't blindly run any script or executable program without completely understanding where it came from and what it does. But given the bad habits of some users who click *OK* and *Open* to almost every prompt (not to mention those who may also unknowingly run everything as a system administrator), it becomes very important for InfoPath to protect all of its users from malicious hackers and their evil intentions.

Forms Services

Installable form templates (.msi files) cannot be directly used with Forms Services. The alternative is to use a digitally signed template.

> **NOTE** Creating an Installable Form Template
>
> Chapter 9 talks about how to create a Microsoft Installer (.msi) file for a form template by using the Publishing Wizard to publish an installable form template.

Moving a Published Domain Trust Form

When a domain trust form is published, you go through the Publishing Wizard to enter the template's name, the physical location to which to save the template, and (on the last page) the access path. Until now, we've understood that domain templates are immobile. In other words, if you wanted to move a published form template, you'd need to republish the form to the new location. This is fine for moving a template around a network or Web site, but what if you wanted to e-mail the template? How would you publish a domain form to accomplish such a feat? As it turns out, this is pretty easy, although there is a caveat.

Before we learn how to move a domain form without republishing, let's first see how InfoPath attempts to open form templates in general. When a template is opened for filling, InfoPath first checks to see whether it already knows about the form in its cache. It does so by performing the following three lookups when a form is opened:

1. An attempt to match the form ID with one in the fully trusted form templates collection
2. An attempt to match the access path with a form template in the cached form templates collection
3. An attempt to match the form ID with a form template in the cache checked in step 2

We'll learn more about fully trusted templates a bit later, so the first step doesn't apply to us right now. However, notice that for steps 2 and 3 the access path and form ID, respectively, are checked against the cache. InfoPath caches every form template that is opened on your computer, so once you fill out a form, the template can be physically moved anywhere and will still open for you. But moving a published template is not recommended since users who have not yet opened the form (and don't have it in their caches) will be unable to open it. Figure 11.12 shows the error dialog that appears when a form template is moved before having being opened and cached by a specific user.

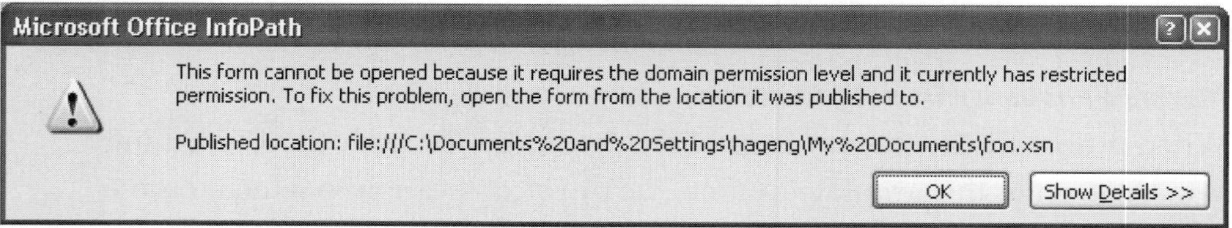

FIGURE 11.12: Error dialog that appears when a domain form is not opened from its access path and the published template is unavailable

> **NOTE InfoPath Form Template Cache**
>
> The InfoPath form template cache exists at <HomeDrive>:\Documents and Settings\<UserName>\Local Settings\Application Data\Microsoft\InfoPath.

You can circumvent the error shown in Figure 11.12 by copying the published template instead of moving it. This means the template at the originally published location still exists. Before performing the three match attempts just mentioned, InfoPath first checks to see if the form exists at its published access path. If it does, it proceeds with the three match attempts. If not, then InfoPath will ignore the form template you opened and simply try to use the template at the access path. Since the access path could be any location (such as a Web server on the Internet), InfoPath first asks if the user wants it to try to connect to that server and get the template. In

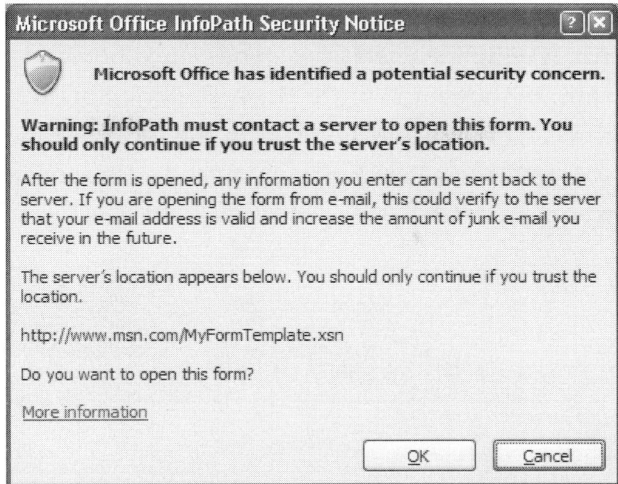

FIGURE 11.13: Opening a domain form whose access path doesn't match the .xsn location, but the form template exists at the originally published location

Figure 11.13, the original form template access path is http://www.msn.com/MyFormTemplate.xsn, but the template was copied elsewhere and opened from that copied location.

> **TIP Move a Form Template by Republishing**
>
> Copying a form template does not change the copied template's access path or form ID. As a result, InfoPath can still open copied templates if the original is available at its access path.

Simulating a Publish Domain for Testing

Grasping the security model for domain forms can be a perplexing and frustrating ordeal. And the worst part is that problems, if any, may not appear until you deploy your template and users start using your form. Fortunately, there are settings to configure preview to simulate the form template as published to a specific location. When you preview your form, it will behave as if it were being opened from the faux publish location you specify.

Start by going to the *Preview settings* item from the *Preview* fly-out menu on the *File* menu. A region labeled *Domain* has a text box that allows you to enter any domain, as shown in Figure 11.14. The domain http://MyServer entered in Figure 11.14 will put the form in the local intranet zone when previewed. If this URL were listed in your trusted sites zone, it would open in that domain zone instead.

Domain

You can optionally preview the form as if it was published to the specified domain. The setting will only apply if the security level of this form is set to Domain.

Domain: http://MyServer

Example: http://www.example.com

FIGURE 11.14: Entering a domain for the template when previewing the form

> **TIP Testing Your Form Template with Artificial Domains**
>
> When previewing with an artificial domain in preview settings, be sure to fully test your form. We recommend testing around data connections, roles, custom task pane, form code, or any other features that may have specific permission or data access requirements.

Automatic Security Level

We mentioned that all form templates begin life as restricted forms. This setting is chosen by the *Automatically determine security level (recommended)* feature, which is enabled by default on all form templates. The setting is a checkbox on the *Form Options* dialog when the *Security and Trust* category is selected.

The task of this automatic setting is to smartly select the appropriate security level for the form template. As a result, most form designers won't need to worry at all about the security settings of their form since they're taken care of behind the scenes. This is probably fine for the majority of form templates. But as we'll see in a moment, it's not appropriate for all form designs.

The auto-selecting security level feature was designed to select the lowest possible security level. It accomplishes this feat by analyzing specific features used in your form's design. The minimal security is chosen based on the highest level requested by any feature. But the maximum security level that the automatic feature can select is domain. Full trust will never be automatically selected, for three reasons. First, InfoPath cannot detect many features that require full trust permission, such as specific properties or methods used in custom form code. Moreover, some reasons why a form could be full trust require the template designer to make subjective decisions (e.g., to hide cross-domain security prompts). Second, even if the automatic feature could choose full trust, the form cannot be deployed as full trust without some additional preparatory work done by the form designer. (We'll discuss details in the next section on full trust.) Third, and most importantly, assigning a maximum level of full trust to a form template should be left as a final decision to the form designer. We'll see in the next section that there are more implications than meets the eye.

Having any of the following features in your form will bump up the security level to domain from restricted when *Automatically determine security level (recommended)* is checked:

- Custom task panes
- Form code (including script or managed code)
- Database, Web service, or SharePoint query or submit connections
- XML document data connections (when the XML file is not included in the form template)
- HTTP submit
- Custom ActiveX controls
- Roles
- Rules that open a new document

Forms Services

Browser-enabled form templates are bumped up to domain trust when a Rich Text Box control is inserted into a view.

TIP What Features in Your Form Template Need Domain Trust?

What if your form template is at the domain security level, but you aren't sure which features require domain security? One trick is to attempt to publish the form to a list of e-mail recipients. The Publishing Wizard will contain a *Details* link that, when clicked, opens a dialog (as shown in Figure 11.15) that includes all features that make the form require domain-level security.

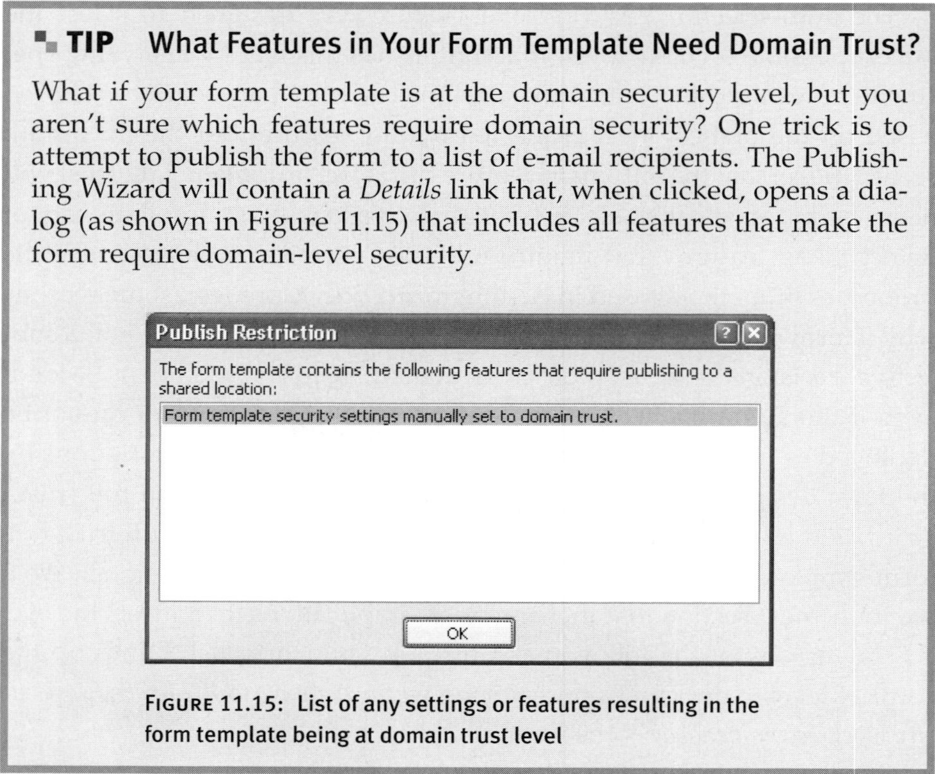

FIGURE 11.15: List of any settings or features resulting in the form template being at domain trust level

Full Trust Security Level

The full trust security level defines the most privileged and powerful classification of InfoPath forms. Running a form as full trust gives that form capabilities similar to those of a Windows program (such as InfoPath itself). With that kind of power comes many niceties that other security levels either don't support or support only after prompting the user. But as with all powerful form features, they don't come without sacrifice: full trust form templates are more cumbersome to deploy and maintain than forms of other trust levels.

A full trust form has one major advantage that other forms do not: access to security level 3 OM properties and methods. We'll leave details for Part II of this book, but we can quickly mention that level 3 OM is very powerful and could be used maliciously by a form. For example, level 3 OM allows you to manipulate InfoPath's toolbars, save the form to any location, and even quit the InfoPath application! As you can tell, it wouldn't be safe to allow just any form to have these capabilities. Other benefits over domain trust forms include having no prompts on cross-domain data access as well as allowing unsafe custom ActiveX controls unrestricted access.

Forms Services

Some level 3 OM properties and methods in InfoPath are unavailable when you design a browser-compatible form template. Details are covered in Chapter 17.

It's easy to design a full trust form template. At any time, simply go to the *Form Options* dialog shown in Figure 11.16, deselect the automatic trust setting, and select the *Full Trust (the form has access to files and settings on the computer)* option button. Surprisingly, it's even easier to test your full trust form! InfoPath 2007 lets you preview your full trust form as, well, full trust! InfoPath 2003 did not allow the same luxury. All it takes is a click on the *Preview Form* button. The experience of filling out your full trust form with

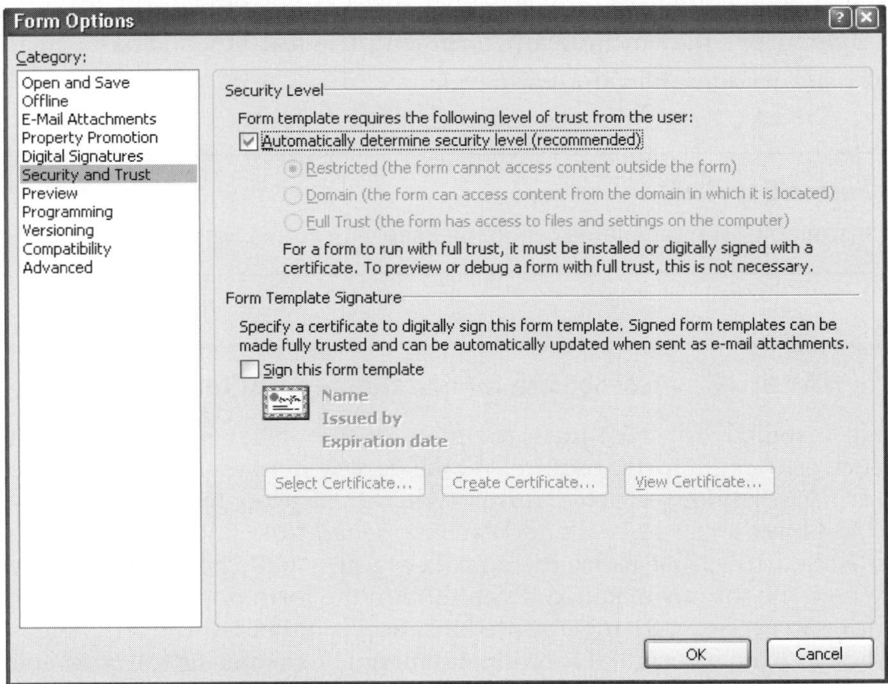

FIGURE 11.16: Security and Trust tab of the Form Options dialog

preview will be very similar to filling out the form. (Of course, some features are not available when previewing the form. See Chapter 9 for details.)

Previewing the form with full trust is fine and in fact recommended for ease of use during development and basic testing. However, don't forget that the form template will eventually need to be deployed so your users can use it. There are two very different ways to deploy a full trust template. Let's explore each option so you can determine which one better fits your form-designing needs.

Deploying an Installable Template

One way to deploy a full trust template is as an installable form. This means you'll distribute a single executable to your users that they will, as administrators, install onto their computers. In Chapter 9, we alluded to full trust forms when we discussed publishing a form as an installable form template. Following the steps to create a Microsoft Installer (.msi) file generates the final product that you can distribute. Your users then run the installer program to properly register the template on their systems. After a successful installation, the full trust form is ready to use like any other form. Installable form templates may include any form template features, such as a custom task pane, resource files, and form code.

Forms Services

Installable form templates cannot be used with Forms Services.

WARNING Access Path for Installable Form Templates

An installed full trust form template does not have an access path such as domain forms require. Yet the deployment model for full trust forms is unlike restricted forms (where restricted forms essentially don't have an access path and can be opened from anywhere). For an installed full trust form, the so-called access path is determined by where the form is installed. Even though the form doesn't technically have an access path, the installed location is upheld. If the template is moved from its original location, it will not be opened as full trust and may not open altogether.

After publishing your full trust form template as an .msi file, the next step is to get the file to your users. It need not be copied to a user's machine to run (it can be run from anywhere), and as a single file it's easy to manage. Since the .msi file uses the standard .NET setup program, the user can choose where to install the form template.

Installed Form Templates Are Listed in the Registry

When a template is registered, InfoPath stores some information in the registry. The registry hive location is at `HKEY_LOCAL_MACHINE\SOFTWARE\Microsoft\Office\InfoPath\SolutionsCatalog`. It stores key values such as original location (where the template is registered), seed caption (the template form name), and version.

After installing a form template, it can be used only from that location. The InfoPath *Getting Started* dialog, discussed in Chapter 2, has convenient links to registered forms in the *All Forms* category. If the form template is updated, the user will need to reinstall the template to get the updated version.

Deploying a Digitally Signed Template

Another way to publish a fully trusted form template is by digitally signing the form template (.xsn) file. Unlike an installable form template, a digitally signed (or just signed, for short) template need not be registered. This means there is no script or install program to run before a form can be filled out, yet you still get all of the same full trust benefits available with installed forms!

Forms Services

A fully trusted form template can be digitally signed and deployed to Forms Services.

To digitally sign your form template, you'll need to first get a code-signing certificate from a trusted certificate authority (CA). A code-signing certificate is issued to you by a trusted CA that is, in effect, guaranteeing to your customers that you are who you say you are. This gives your customers a high sense of trust that they're working directly with your products and services. How, then, do users (like us) know which CAs can be trusted to issue certificates and have sound policies and business practices? Most users may not have the time or even the know-how to determine who can be trusted. As a result, Microsoft has done much of the legwork for us by including a list in Windows of CAs it considers to be trusted. This list is called the Trusted Certificate Store (TCS). The TCS can be updated in two ways: automatically by Microsoft (when you use Windows Update) and manually. You can manually update the TCS when you encounter a certificate published by an untrusted CA (i.e., the publisher is not in your TCS). Some operating systems, such as Microsoft Windows XP, will show an *Untrusted Root Authority* dialog, which allows you to add that CA to your TCS.

You can view the TCS on your computer by going to the Microsoft Management Console (run `mmc` at the command line) and adding the Certificates standalone snap-in to the Console Root for My User Account. The TCS is listed under the Trusted Root Certification Authorities folder, as shown in Figure 11.17. This list comprises Microsoft's trusted CAs as well as those you have manually added via the *Untrusted Root Authority* dialog.

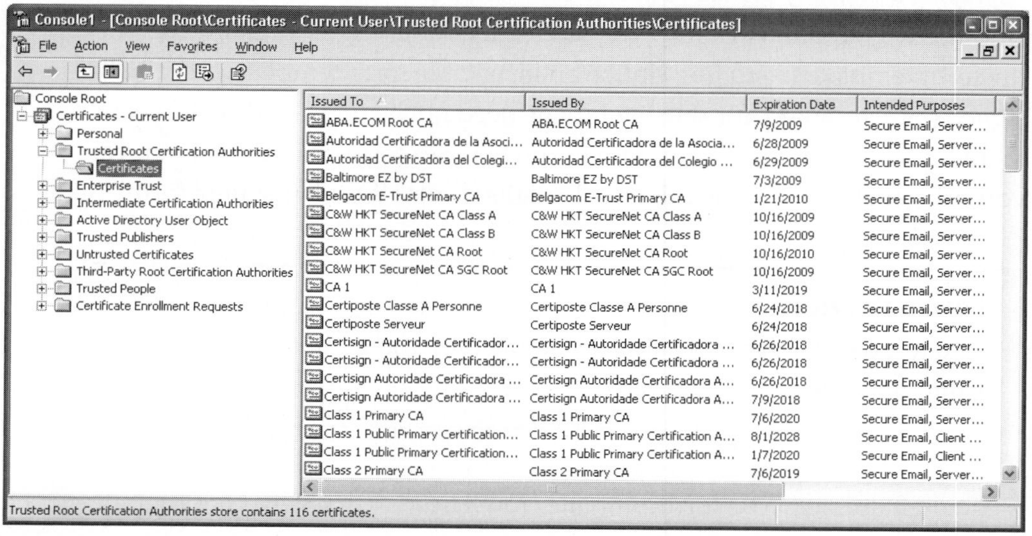

FIGURE 11.17: Trusted root certification authorities for the current user

If you want to remove a CA in the TCS, simply right-click on an entry and select *Delete.*

TIP List of Trusted Publishers

A list of trusted publishers is also available through InfoPath's Trust Center. You can access the Trust Center from the *Tools* menu. We'll discuss the Trust Center later in this chapter.

There are many CAs from whom you can get a certificate. For testing purposes, it's even possible to create your own self-signed certificate. If you're on a corporate Windows network, a Windows Server running a certificate service (which acts as a trusted CA for the entire Windows domain) can generate and distribute certificates. A widely accepted certificate is one published by a globally trusted authority such as a reputable company like VeriSign. The companies and organizations listed in the TCS are good starting points for finding a CA.

Now that you know a little about certificates, let's see how to sign an InfoPath form template. In this example, we'll show you how to generate and use a self-signed certificate. You can start with a new blank form template or opt to use any existing form template. Once you open the template in design mode, go to *Form Options* on the *Tools* menu and select the *Security and Trust* category. To enable signing, click on the *Sign this form template* checkbox, as shown in Figure 11.18.

FIGURE 11.18: Security and Trust category settings for signing a form template

The next step is to select a certificate to use for signing. Clicking the *Select Certificate* button will show the *Select Certificate* dialog, which lists the certificates issued to the current user (Figure 11.19).

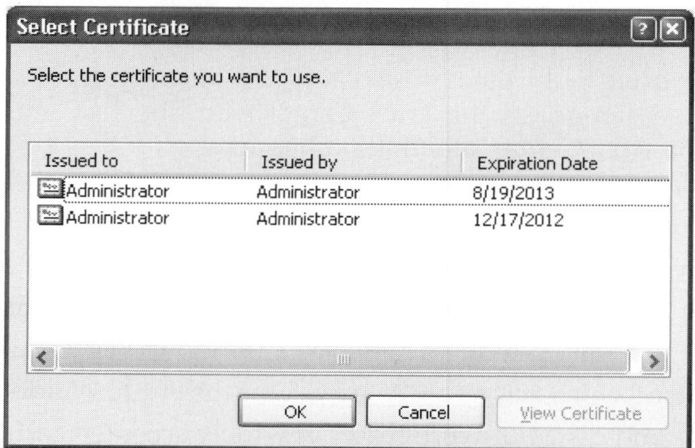

FIGURE 11.19: Selecting a certificate to use for digital signing

If no certificates appear in this dialog, you can use the *Create Certificate* button to generate a self-signed code-signing certificate. InfoPath creates a self-signed certificate as a personal certificate for the current user. Figure 11.20 shows the certificate details you'll see before you click *OK* to proceed with generation.

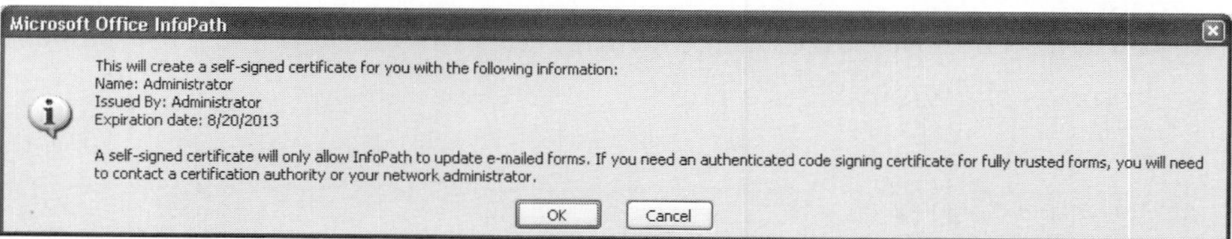

FIGURE 11.20: Creating a self-signed certificate for code signing

TIP Code-Signing Certificates Sign Form Templates

Only certificates that are intended for code signing are accepted for signing an InfoPath form template. The *Create Certificate* button creates a self-signed code-signing certificate. When you request a real certificate from a CA, be sure to mention that it will be used for code signing.

If you created a self-signed certificate, it will now appear in the *Select Certificate* dialog. Once you select this certificate, you've successfully signed your form template! You'll see some information about the certificate such as *Name, Issued by*, and *Expiration date* on the *Form Options* dialog. You can find complete details of the certificate by clicking the *View Certificate* button, which opens the dialog shown in Figure 11.21. This is the same dialog you'll see when you double-click a certificate in the Microsoft Management Console (shown earlier in Figure 11.17).

FIGURE 11.21: General tab of the Certificate dialog, which shows whether the publisher of a certificate is trusted

> **NOTE** Trusting Untrusted Certificates
>
> Notice that the self-signed certificate we created by clicking the *Create Certificate* button is not trusted. To make the certificate trusted, go to the Microsoft Management Console and click on the Certificates folder that contains the certificate. Drag the certificate from the Certificates folder under the Personal folder and drop it in the Certificates folder under the Trusted Root Certification Authorities folder.
>
> Trusting self-signed certificates is essentially meaningless because the whole point of a certificate is that it's corroborated by a third party like VeriSign. Furthermore, publishing form templates with self-signed certificates is a bad idea since not all of your users will automatically trust such a certificate as they would a real trusted certificate.

Now that we can see how easy it is to sign a form template, what's the end-user experience when filling out such a form? InfoPath will not automatically open a signed template unless its CA is trusted. Trusting a signed InfoPath form template is conceptually similar to trusting any other signed file, such as an e-mail message or Word document. For a form template to be granted fully trusted privileges, the publisher of the certificate must be listed in the TCS. This means that once you trust a given publisher, its certificate will be trusted not only when found on any form templates but also when associated with any program on your computer that uses certificates. Figure 11.22 shows the prompt shown when you open a template signed by an untrusted publisher. Clicking the *Open* button will temporarily grant trust to the publisher and certificate, but only for this session. Clicking *Trust*

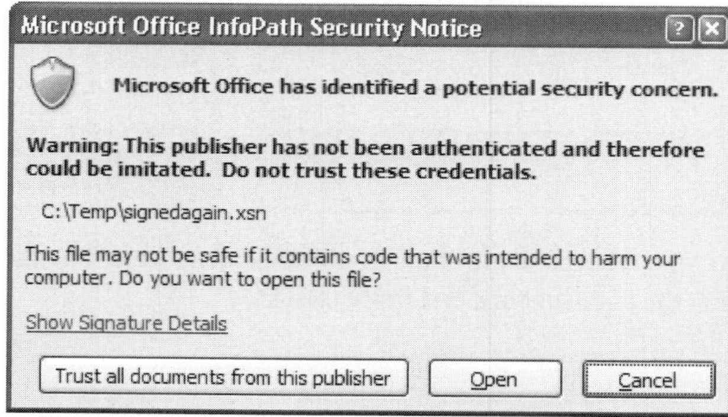

FIGURE 11.22: InfoPath prompt that appears when a signed template's CA isn't trusted

all documents from this publisher will add the publisher of this certificate to the TCS of your Windows user account automatically.

Sometimes the *Trust all documents from this publisher* button is disabled. This happens when the certificate issuer cannot be identified and, as a result, the certificate could be forged or faked. If you still want to add the certificate's publisher to the TCS, click the *Show Signature Details* link. This shows the *Certificate* properties dialog similar to that in Figure 11.21, but with an *Install Certificate* button adjacent to the *Issuer Statement* button. Clicking the button to install the certificate walks you through the Certificate Import Wizard, which takes care of adding the publisher to the TCS. Subsequently filling out forms with a certificate from this CA will not raise the prompt because the publisher is now trusted.

Similar to an installed form template, a digitally signed template does not have an access path but instead uses the form ID. But unlike an installed or registered template, a signed template, thanks to the use of the form ID and not an access path, is not associated with a specific location. As a result, signed templates are more like restricted templates since they can be opened from anywhere without limitation.

Updating a signed form template is a trivial operation. Since InfoPath caches all templates opened by a given user, it can detect when a newer version of an existing template is opened. If your users can double-click on an updated .xsn file that you send out, they will automatically start using the updated template version. The cache will also be updated with the newly opened version of the template.

NOTE **Why Digitally Sign?**

There are more reasons to digitally sign a form template than to just get full trust form permission. For example, domain trust templates deployed via e-mail have the ability to be auto-updated when they're signed. Moreover, signing a template, no matter what the trust level, guarantees the users of the template that it came from the specified publisher and has not been modified by another party. These guarantees are the direct benefits of using certificates rather than the result of any InfoPath-specific behaviors. You can learn all about digital signature certificates and Authenticode (Microsoft's solution allowing certificates to sign software) on MSDN, as referenced in the Appendix.

Full Trust Form Template Errors

When a full trust form template is opened that is neither digitally signed nor installed, an error dialog appears, as shown in Figure 11.23. The entire details message reads: "The form template is trying to access files and settings on your computer. InfoPath cannot grant access to these files and settings because the form template is not fully trusted."

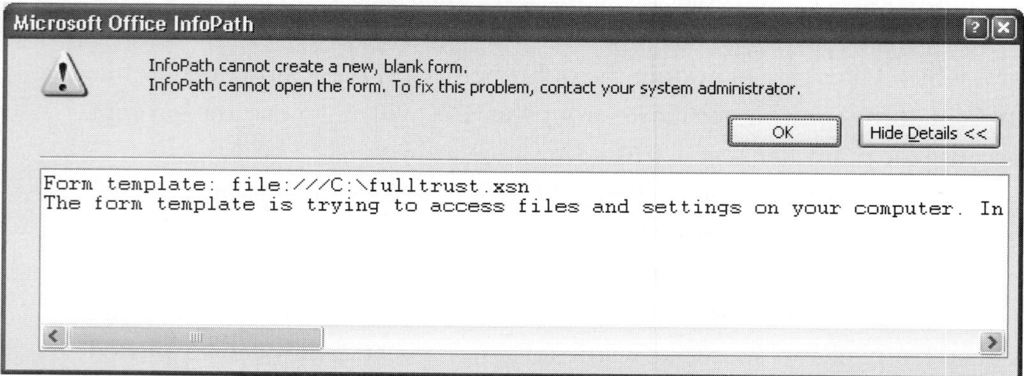

FIGURE 11.23: Error that occurs when opening a full trust form template that is neither digitally signed nor installed

Another error may surface when your users try to manage their form templates in the InfoPath *Getting Started* dialog (shown earlier in Figure 11.6). By default, there are three items listed under the *Form categories* section: *Recently Used Forms, Favorites*, and *All Forms.* (You'll also notice another category in Figure 11.6 labeled *MS Forms*; this is a custom form category.) An installed form template, even if it was never opened, will appear in the *All Forms* category. Users may be accustomed to clicking the *Remove this form* link in the *Form tasks* section of the dialog if they no longer want to keep seeing or using that form. Trying to remove an installed template will result in an error dialog, as shown in Figure 11.24.

The details portion of Figure 11.24 explains that to properly remove the form, you must first uninstall it. An installed form template can be removed by using *Add/Remove Programs* in the Windows Control Panel. Only after you successfully uninstall the template will it cease to exist in the list of form templates on the *Getting Started* dialog.

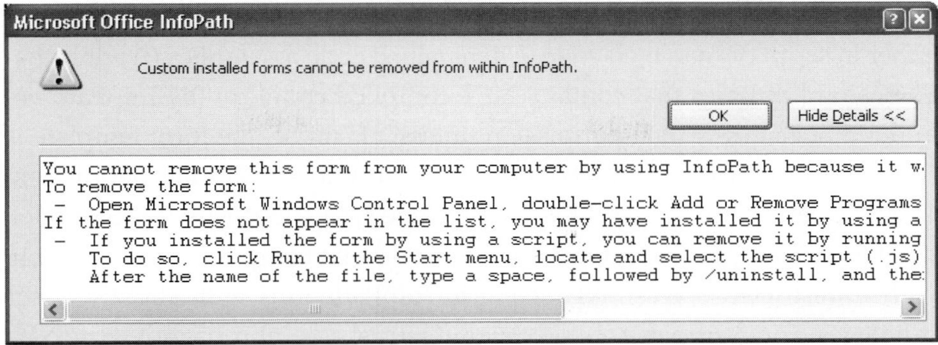
Microsoft Office InfoPath

Custom installed forms cannot be removed from within InfoPath.

OK | Hide Details <<

You cannot remove this form from your computer by using InfoPath because it w
To remove the form:
 - Open Microsoft Windows Control Panel, double-click Add or Remove Programs
If the form does not appear in the list, you may have installed it by using a
 - If you installed the form by using a script, you can remove it by running
   To do so, click Run on the Start menu, locate and select the script (.js)
   After the name of the file, type a space, followed by /uninstall, and the

FIGURE 11.24: Error that occurs when attempting to remove an installed form from the dialog

Restricting Full Trust Forms

By now, you know that a full trust form template is a powerful device. It's best to approach a full trust form with caution before running it on your computer. It helps to know who published the template and what the publisher claims the form is supposed to do. A malicious full trust form could do many types of harm if run; for example, it could steal files from your computer or try to take your machine to its knees by consuming all memory resources. In this section, we'll look at a few simple ways to prevent or limit unauthorized access to your computer by a rogue full trust form.

Forms Services

Since they run on the server, fully trusted form templates in the browser do not have access to your local computer.

Full trust form templates run with essentially the same credentials and access as the user running InfoPath. As a result, the potential for harm goes up with the level of access of the logged-in user. For example, running your computer with administrative privileges is the most risky proposition. An obvious way to limit potential damage is to run InfoPath under a user account with nonadministrative rights. An alternative to logging in as an administrator is to use the *Run As* command in Windows. This is accomplished by right-clicking on the INFOPATH.EXE program in the OFFICE12 installation directory and running the program as another user.

The most potentially dangerous type of form template has custom code, either in script or managed code. All managed code assemblies (Application Extension [.dll] files that contain .NET compiled code) run by InfoPath are granted `LocalIntranet` permission unless, of course, the form template is full trust, in which case the code is also run with `FullTrust` permission. This is a permission defined by .NET's Code Access Security (CAS) model. Unlike regular .NET programs that run on your computer in `FullTrust` with unrestricted access, .NET code in InfoPath runs with slightly lesser privileges. For example, a `LocalIntranet` trust assembly cannot write data to any data stores, such as a local hard disk. Table 11.3 shows the exact permission set for the `LocalIntranet` permission. Specific access to resources

TABLE 11.3: CAS Permission Set for `LocalIntranet`

Resource	`LocalIntranet` Permission Set
Execute code	Yes
User interface	Unrestricted
File system	Isolated storage: isolated by user but no quota File dialog: can access data in files chosen by the user
Network	Can make connections to share or site of origin only; can access DNS
Printing	Programmatic access to the default printer and to other devices if allowed by the user
Environment	`USERNAME` environment variable
Reflection	Public reflection; can emit types
Registry	None
Database	None
Win32 APIs or COM objects	None

Source: Excerpt of Figure 1 in "Find Out What's New with Code Access Security in the .NET Framework 2.0," Mike Downen, *MSDN Magazine*, November 2005, http://msdn.microsoft.com/msdnmag/issues/05/11/CodeAccessSecurity/default.aspx. Reprinted with permission.

under `LocalIntranet` permission can be changed by using CAS. More information on CAS is available on MSDN (as referenced in the Appendix).

NOTE **CAS and Form Code Permission**

While we claim that the code of a form template will receive `LocalIntranet` or `FullTrust` permission, this is not always true. The truth is that permission granted to form code by the .NET runtime ultimately depends on how CAS is configured.

`InfoPath Form Templates` Group

An administrator of a computer can use the Code Access Security Policy Tool (caspol.exe; included in the .NET Framework tools) to modify the security policy for one or more form templates. You can find caspol.exe on your computer by going to the Administrative Tools folder and selecting *Microsoft .NET Framework 2.0 Configuration*. To grant specific permission to a form template, add a new code group under any *Runtime Security Policy* item (e.g., *Enterprise, Machine, User*) with the name `InfoPath Form Templates`. When creating the code group, caspol asks you to specify the exact conditions for applying the permission and to define the permission itself. Additional details on caspol are beyond the scope of this book. You can find more information on MSDN (as referenced in the Appendix).

Arguably the more dangerous of the two types of form code is script. But for script to be effective in harming a computer, it must be able to create and use ActiveX objects. Either VBScript's `CreateObject` or JScript's `ActiveXObject` will create a new ActiveX object for the script to use. If an ActiveX object is marked by its author as safe for scripting, any form template with script can use the object. Alternatively, if an ActiveX object is unsafe for scripting, InfoPath will not allow script to instantiate or use that object unless the form security level specifically allows for unsafe ActiveX objects. Domain templates in the trusted sites zone and all fully trusted form templates are granted rights to instantiate and use unsafe ActiveX objects.

Before you open a template that is granted such privileges, we recommend that you first open it in design mode and inspect the script.

Finally, the most effective way to protect yourself from fully trusted forms is simply to not run them. Instead of painstakingly opening every template in design mode to see what trust level it requests (and what if you forget sometimes?), you can let InfoPath do that work for you automatically. One of the purposes of the Trust Center is to provide a master switch for allowing or disallowing fully trusted forms to run on your computer. You can find the *Show Trust Center* entry point under the *Tools* menu. At the bottom of the *Trust Center* dialog (shown in Figure 11.25 in the next section), you can see the *Allow fully trusted forms to run on my computer* checkbox. By default, the checkbox is enabled, which allows fully trusted form templates.

APTCA Allowable List

APTCA (`AllowPartiallyTrustedCallersAttribute`) is a .NET programming concept for allowing partially trusted code to call into strong-named (i.e., full trust) assemblies. InfoPath 2007 contains a list of public key tokens corresponding to strong-named assemblies that can be called by a form template. If a template attempts to call into an assembly that's not on its allowable list, InfoPath will display an error message and immediately close the form.

Public key tokens that are ECMA International standard–approved as well as tokens common to Microsoft products are already on InfoPath's APTCA list. The purpose of this APTCA list is to block elevation-of-privilege attacks, where a form template with domain trust exploits a known security issue in a common assembly, such as one in the global assembly cache (GAC).

As a result of this APTCA allowable list, some form templates that worked fine in InfoPath 2003 may not run in InfoPath 2007. To resolve the problem, identify the offending assembly and check the form template code for proper usage. If you want to allow referencing of an assembly not already on the allowable list, add a new `DWORD` with the public key token to the registry at `HKEY_LOCAL_MACHINE\SOFTWARE\Microsoft\Office\12.0\InfoPath\Security\APTCA`.

Trust and Designer Lockdown

Trust Center

The Trust Center is a collection of settings that relate to the security and privacy of the end user. If you use another Microsoft Office 2007 application such as Word or Excel, for example, you may have already encountered a similar *Trust Center* dialog, although each application may slightly customize its appearance. In InfoPath, there are three main categories in the *Trust Center* dialog: *Trusted Publishers, Add-ins*, and *Privacy Options*. The *Trusted Publishers* category manages the certificates for digitally signed and fully trusted form templates. The *Add-ins* category lets you set up and configure COM add-ins. Finally, the *Privacy Options* category determines whether InfoPath will send and receive data to and from Microsoft to help improve its products and your experience. None of the categories involve form-specific settings; rather, they're application-wide items that affect the behaviors of all form templates. You can find the *Trust Center* menu item under the *Tools* menu.

Forms Services

Trust Center settings do not apply to Forms Services.

TIP Trust Center Is Always Available

The Trust Center is available during both designing and form-filling sessions.

Trusted Publishers Category

Earlier in the chapter we talked about full trust permission and how to sign your form template with a digital signature. We showed the Microsoft Management Console and went over how to add and use the Certificates snap-in. Instead of going through the trouble of using another program like the Microsoft Management Console, you can have InfoPath present only the information you need in a simple dialog.

Recall that a trusted publisher is a CA whom you decided to trust. When you open a digitally signed form template, the dialog shown earlier in Figure 11.22 may be displayed. When this dialog appears, it means that the certificate used to sign the form template is not from a trusted publisher. Only if you click the *Trust all documents from this publisher* button will InfoPath add the untrusted publisher of that certificate to the list of trusted publishers. In turn, that trusted publisher will then appear in the *Trusted Publishers* list shown in Figure 11.25. Clicking the *View* button will show the *Certificate* dialog (refer back to Figure 11.21), which offers the same data shown in the columns of the *Trusted Publishers* section plus an engrossed level of detail that most users find unnecessary. The *Remove* button removes the CA from the list of trusted publishers.

The *Prior Trusted Sources* list might not appear in your copy of InfoPath. It is shown only if you've upgraded from a previous version of Microsoft Office. In any case, InfoPath does not honor the list of prior trusted publishers. Only

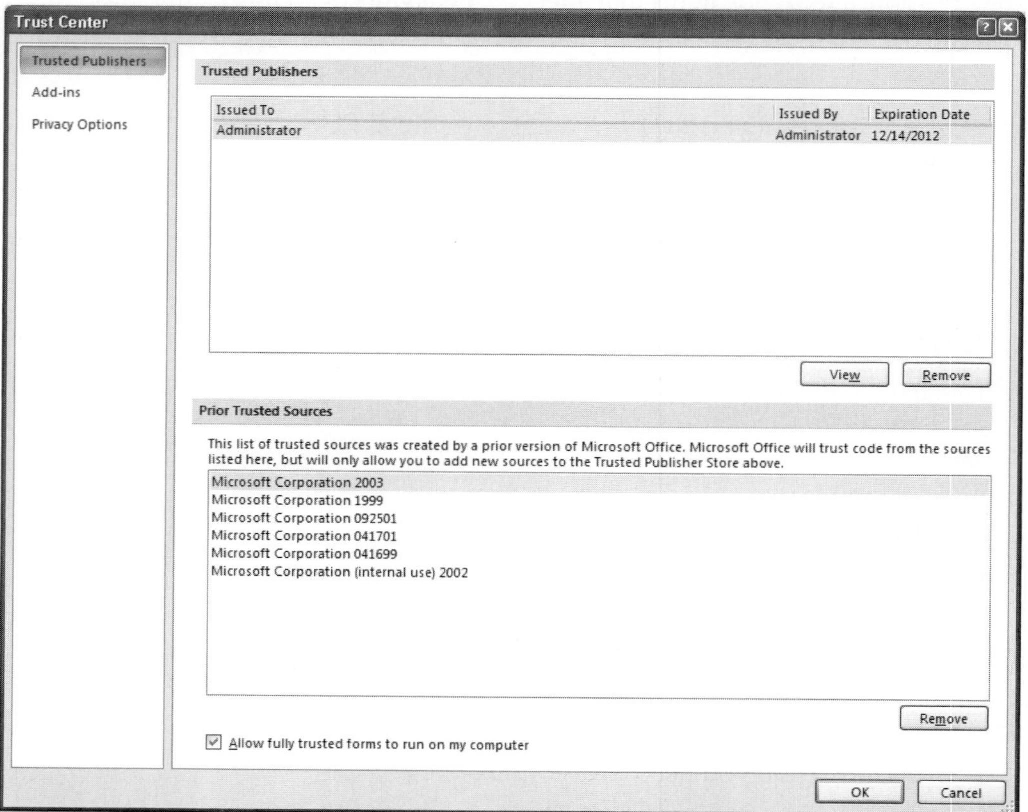

FIGURE 11.25: Trusted Publishers category of the Trust Center dialog

those publishers listed in the *Trusted Publishers* list in the Microsoft Management Console will appear in this dialog.

We covered the *Allow fully trusted forms to run on my computer* setting at the end of the previous section.

Add-ins Category

The *Add-ins* category is the control center and repository for InfoPath COM add-ins. Since these add-ins are the topic for Chapter 20, we'll save the details for then. But for now, we'll briefly explain what the settings shown in Figure 11.26 offer to the COM add-ins feature in terms of security.

When an add-in is selected in the *Add-ins* list in Figure 11.26, details such as its publisher, location, and description are shown below the list. The *Add-ins* list has four categories, but they can be broken up into two

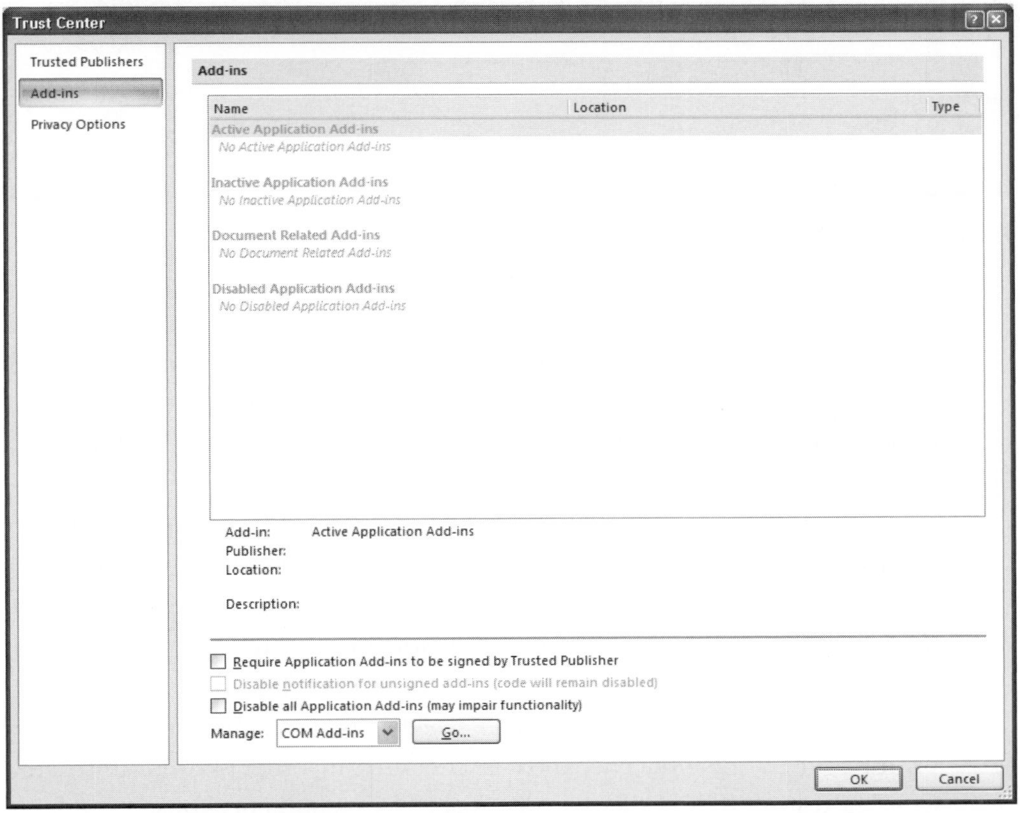

FIGURE 11.26: Add-ins category of the Trust Center dialog

parts: *Application Add-ins* and *Document Add-ins.* InfoPath does not support document extensions, so that part does not apply to us. An example of a document extension is a Smart Tag that might be useful in Outlook or Word. *Application Add-ins* lists the available COM add-ins, broken down into three subcategories: active, inactive, and disabled. Active add-ins are already trusted and used by InfoPath. Inactive add-ins are also already trusted but currently not in use. You can manage COM add-ins by using the *COM Add-Ins* dialog shown in Figure 11.27. You can access the *COM*

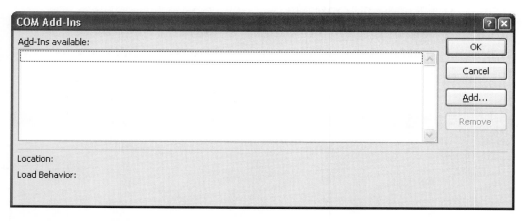

FIGURE 11.27: Dialog for adding and removing COM add-ins

Add-Ins dialog by clicking the *Go* button at the bottom of the *Trust Center* dialog. Finally, disabled add-ins are those that are not published by a trusted publisher but have already been added through the *COM Add-Ins* dialog. Add-ins can be disabled only if *Require Application Add-ins to be signed by Trusted Publisher* is checked.

The checkboxes at the bottom of the Trust Center *Add-ins* category shown in Figure 11.26 act as master switches for the COM add-in functionality. The first checkbox, *Require Application Add-ins to be signed by Trusted Publisher,* dictates whether or not untrusted add-ins are allowed to run by first asking the user with a dialog prompt. The second checkbox, *Disable notification for unsigned add-ins (code will remain disabled),* disables the dialog prompt when the first checkbox is checked; in other words, untrusted COM add-ins will just silently not work. The second checkbox is available only if the first checkbox to require trusted publishers is enabled. The third checkbox, *Disable all Application Add-ins (may impair functionality)*, is a "kill switch" to disable all COM add-in functionality. When this checkbox is checked, the previous two checkboxes are unavailable. Add-ins are discussed further in Chapter 20.

Privacy Options Category

The *Privacy Options* category consists of Microsoft Office product-wide settings that apply to the entire suite of products, not just InfoPath, as shown in Figure 11.28. Due to the nature of these settings, there's not much to discuss in this category. Each setting is self-explanatory, but you can find more information if desired on Office Online (as referenced in the Appendix).

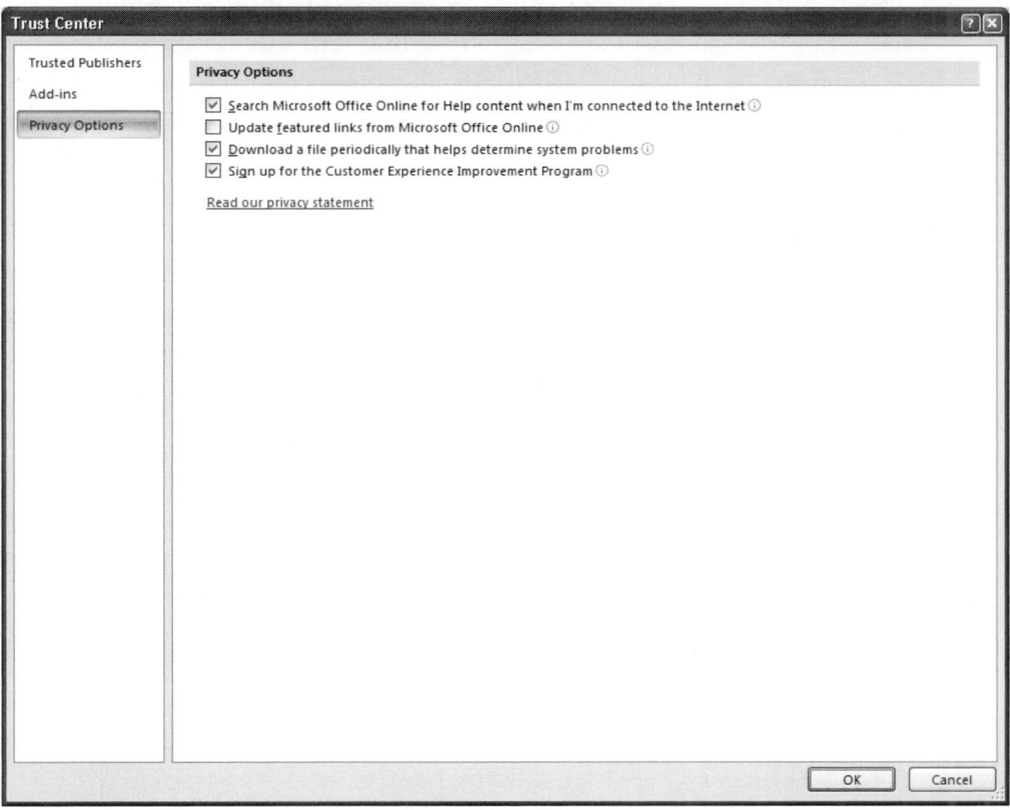

FIGURE 11.28: Privacy Options category of the Trust Center dialog

Designer Lockdown

Leave the form template designing to the designers and the form filling to everyone else, that's what we say! In a moment, we'll show you how to prevent wandering eyes from looking at your form template in design mode. But first, we must mention that the lockdown features we're about to discuss are not bulletproof. In fact, they are considered deterrents rather than actual security measures. Since the form template file format (.xsn) is just a Microsoft Cabinet (.cab) file that can be expanded by anyone, the template files are never really safe. Also remember that a user could copy the form template to a portable device or send it in e-mail, only to open it up in design mode on another computer where he or she has administrative privileges. The most secure .xsn file is one that doesn't disclose any data that you wouldn't want anyone to see.

There are two ways to lock down, or disable, the InfoPath design mode. The first option is a form-specific setting that will discourage a user from designing the form. The second setting is a more comprehensive solution: completely disable design mode as an administrative policy by using the Office Customization Tool (OCT).

Per Form Template

InfoPath can selectively discourage the user from entering design mode for certain form templates. We're careful in our choice of words by saying "discourage" because the user is not completely locked out. What will block most novice users is nothing but a short hurdle for experienced form designers. (We'll see how to circumvent this setting momentarily.) We recommend using this feature as a way to tell people they should not tamper with your form template.

To disable design mode for any form template, first enter the design mode (no joke) for that template. Under the *Advanced* category in the *Form Options* dialog, the first of a series of settings is *Protection* (Figure 11.29).

Protection

Select this option to disable the form customization commands on the Tools menu. This discourages users who are filling out the form from changing the form template.

☐ Enable protection

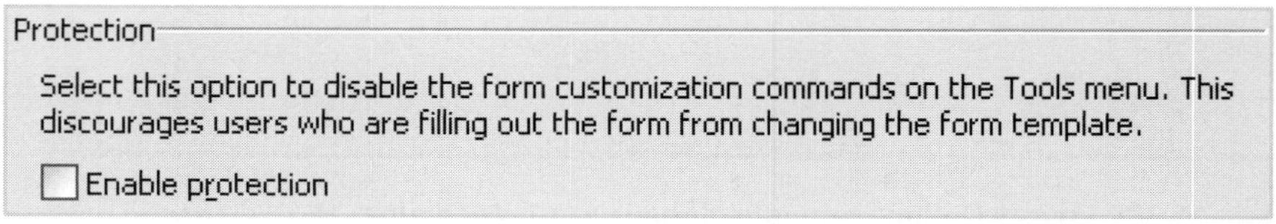

FIGURE 11.29: Enabling protection to discourage users from changing your form template

Checking the *Enable protection* checkbox will activate the mechanism that attempts to deter those folks who want to change your form template in design mode.

Turning on form protection has several effects when a user fills out the form. The *Design This Form* icon on the *Standard* toolbar as well as the menu item (with the same name) on the *Tools* menu are both disabled. However, the form template could be listed in the *Recent form templates* in the *Design a Form Template* dialog. Clicking this link will attempt to open the template using design mode.

The form protection feature isn't limited only to fill-out-a-form mode. It is expected that some users will get to design mode, as mentioned earlier. InfoPath will warn all users who try to open a protected form template and will try to scare them from continuing! The daunting dialog is shamelessly displayed in Figure 11.30.

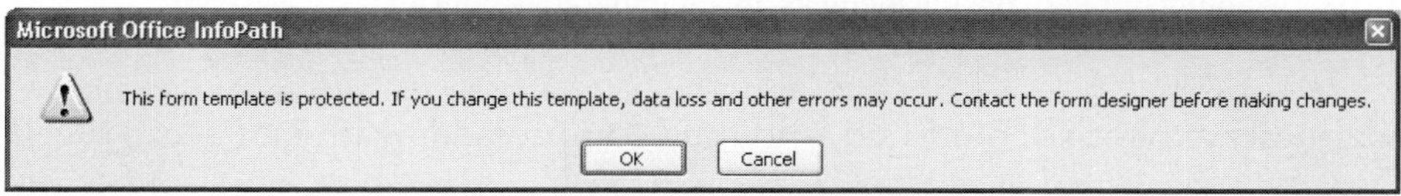

FIGURE 11.30: Warning dialog that appears when users attempt to change a protected form template

Globally Disable Design Mode

The OCT, as mentioned earlier in this chapter, is Microsoft's administration tool for enterprise deployments of Microsoft Office. It can set a policy across a single computer or an entire corporate network. In terms of security and trust, it's a very effective mechanism for applying a blanket policy to users filling out InfoPath forms. Case in point: the *Disable InfoPath Designer mode* setting (Figure 11.31).

Even the OCT is not a complete answer unless other security measures are taken. For example, a user intent on opening your form template in design mode only needs to get the .xsn file to another computer where he or she is an administrator. Then the user can make changes to the form template and copy the .xsn file back to the designer-disabled computer. The only way to truly lock down a template is to not allow any files to be copied to or from the network or computer. Moreover, the template could still be

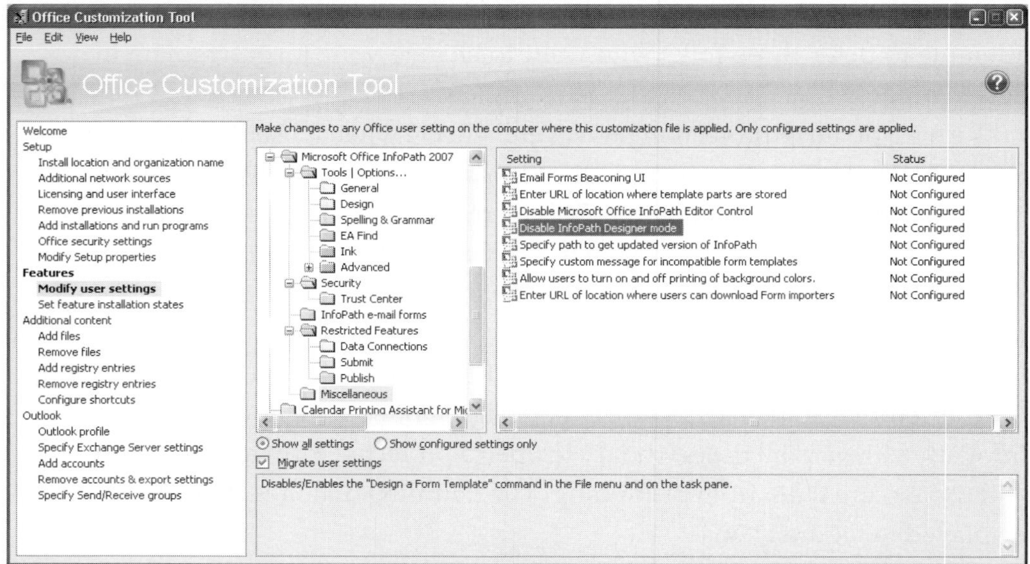

FIGURE 11.31: Disabling InfoPath design mode as an administrative policy

manually expanded, modified, and then compressed again into a .cab file. If a power user knew InfoPath very well, he or she could make all of the changes to the form template files in a simple text editor without InfoPath! To make sure that no one else can overwrite your published template, ensure that only you have write access to its location. However, if a malicious user copied your form template and made changes, he or she could essentially circumvent some of the security or validation features of your template. For example, if you have data validation that requires fields to be filled out before submit, the validation constraints may have been removed. Maybe you had a read-only view or read-only fields that become enabled only for an administrator role; yes, these fields may now be writable to a nonadministrator.

If somebody really wants to modify your form template, it's going to be pretty difficult to effectively stop that user unless you impose a very strict security policy on his or her account and computer. If your form submits data to a back-end data source, that back-end system should not trust that the form is the only mechanism that can perform the submission. For example, if the form submits data to a back-end store such as a database or

Web service, the onus should be on that external system to validate the data structure and integrity. That way, no matter what a hacker could do to change a form template or even simulate his or her own form, the data still ends up being submitted to the same place. And the hacker has no more of a privilege to submit specialized data than anyone else who filled out your form as it was intended.

Digital Signatures

How many times have you said or been told, "I didn't do that!"? We hope not too many times. But think about how that statement could play out in the real world of business. It would be very unfortunate if someone submitted an order to your company for one million units of your product but then later claimed they meant one hundred. How can you hold that customer accountable for the original order? Did he or she really request one million units, or did the order form somehow get changed after it was submitted? What if that someone refuted filling out an order form altogether?

All of these issues are solved by using digital signatures to sign documents, such as an e-mail, for example. InfoPath enables users to sign form data by using an XML Signature to sign the XML data—either in whole or just the parts that you choose as the form template designer. To sign the data with an XML Signature you use a certificate, in fact, the very same kind of certificate we used when signing the form template for full trust. For this chapter and our purposes, we'll generically define a **digital signature** as some or all form data (including the signing information) in an XML file that is signed by using a certificate (which may or may not be provided by a trusted certificate authority, as discussed earlier in this chapter). For details on the specification for XML Signature, please see the World Wide Web Consortium (W3C) Web site referenced in the Appendix.

Forms Services

Digital signatures are supported in browser-enabled form templates running in the Internet Explorer browser.

> **TIP Signing a Form Template versus Form Data**
>
> Try not to confuse digitally signing the form template (a previous topic in this chapter) with digitally signing form data (the current topic). Signing the form template uses Microsoft's Authenticode technology to associate a certificate with the form template (.xsn) file. In contrast, signing form data uses the XML Signature specification as defined by the W3C to sign a part or the whole of a form (.xml) file. Similar to how Authenticode makes it possible to sign form templates, XML Signature also uses certificates, but for signing XML form data.

If a CA is secure and trusted, and the private key of the certificate is disclosed to only the one who signs the data, InfoPath digital signatures are effective by design. This means InfoPath upholds stringent provisions for what it means to properly sign data. In some jurisdictions there may be legal implications, which could include using digitally signed data as evidence in a court of law. The actual value of digitally signed data, however, is a hotly debated topic. The value of signed data could depend on the software and other circumstantial evidence surrounding a case. Unfortunately, we cannot provide legal guidance on this matter. We recommend that you check with the governments in which you will be doing business to determine the value of digitally signed data.

InfoPath digital signatures provide a solution that partially implements the XML Signature specification as recommended by the W3C (i.e., only X509 data is supported). What this means to you is that when users fill out and sign a form, the following three document properties are guaranteed:

1. Authenticity (who filled out the form?)
2. Data integrity (has the data been changed since filled out and signed?)
3. Nonrepudiation (could the filler of the form refute filling it out?)

As you can see, digital signatures are critical mechanisms for establishing proof-positive identification and authenticity of a form. In fact, digitally signed data is the de facto standard for sending data between businesses as well as doing business with others.

Despite all of the privacy questions that InfoPath digital signatures address, they do not, however, encrypt form data. In other words, digitally signing a form does not protect the data against being viewed by unintended recipients. If your goal is to just obscure form data while in transit, digital signatures may not be right for your situation. For obscuring submitted data, we recommend using a Web-based submit solution such as HTTP submit or Web services with HTTP Security (HTTPS), as discussed in Chapter 8.

Using Digitally Signed Data in Forms

Let's turn from theory to practice and learn how to design form templates to use digital signatures. Given the power and flexibility of digital signatures, it might sound like a daunting task to add them to your form template. In fact, it's pretty easy to do.

To begin setting up your form template for digital signatures, go to the *Form Options* dialog from the *Tools* menu and select the *Digital Signatures* category. As you can see in Figure 11.32, there are three main options. The first option is always selected by default for new form templates: *Do not*

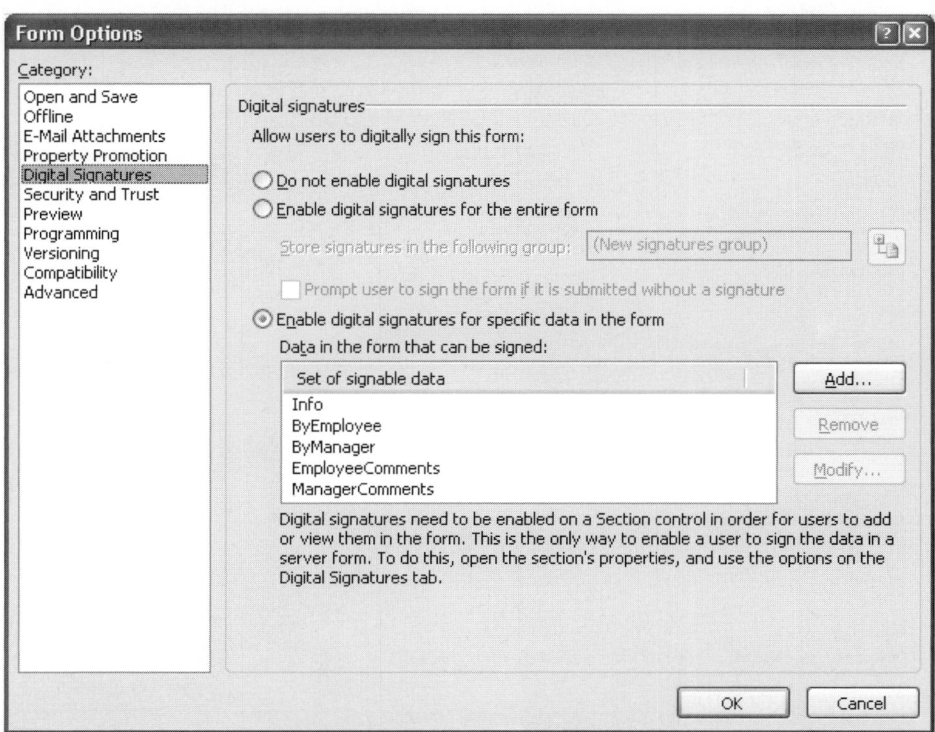

FIGURE 11.32: Configuring digital signatures for a form template

enable digital signatures. The next two options enable digital signatures for the template. The one you'll want to select will depend on your form requirements or, more importantly, business needs. The next couple of sections provide details on the two options for enabling digital signatures; at the end you will be able to choose a configuration that best meets your needs.

To show how digital signatures work in the business world, it's best to use an example form template. Throughout our discussions, we'll borrow the MOI Consulting performance review form template. (A sample form template called MOIPerformanceReview-FullSignatures is included with the samples for this chapter on the book's Web site.) MOI uses this template, as shown in Figure 11.33, for its annual reviews of employee performance.

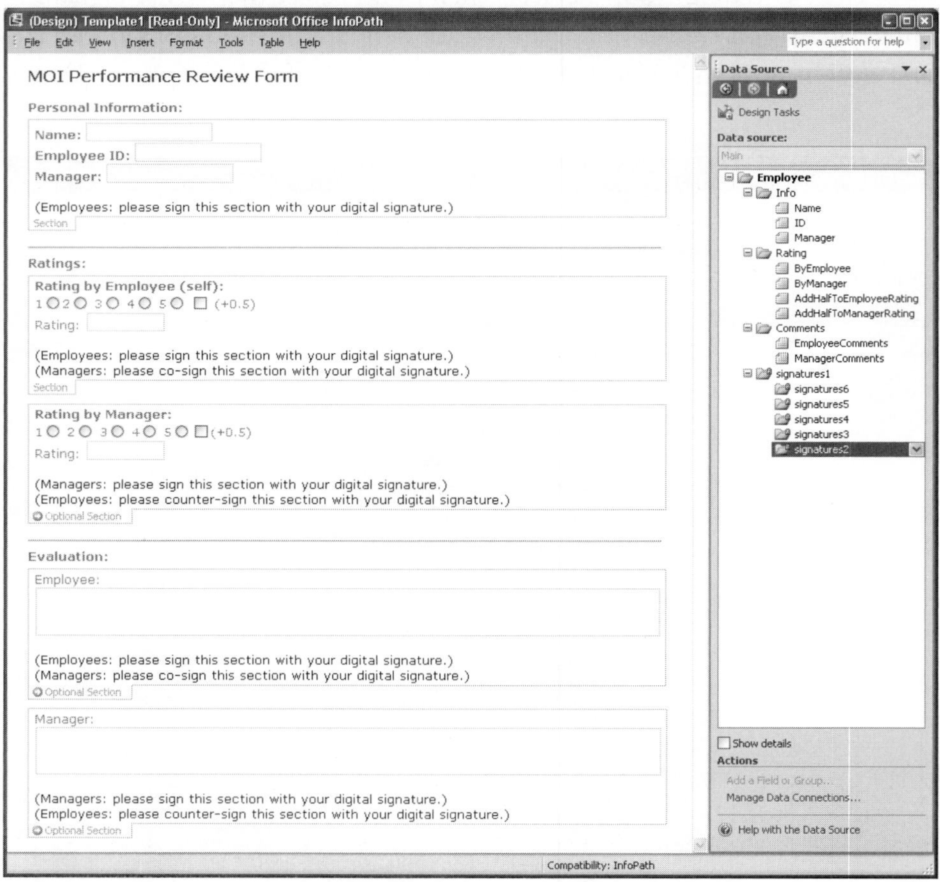

FIGURE 11.33: Our sample MOI Consulting performance review form

Since this form, when filled out, will contain sensitive data, digital signatures nicely fit its requirements. Once the performance review is filled out by an employee and manager and signed with their certificates, the form data will possess several valuable qualities that can be identified by anyone with access to the submitted form data.

- Both the employee and the manager filled out the review.
- The employee reviewed and approved the manager's portion.
- The review has not been tampered with since originally filled out.
- The review was indeed filled out by the employee who signed the form.
- The manager's review was indeed filled out by the correct manager.

Before we proceed with our examples, let's talk about several side effects, some expected and others possibly unexpected, that will reveal themselves as a byproduct of digital signatures. First, to add digital signatures to a form template, the main data source must be open for additions. If it's not open, all options in the *Digital Signatures* category shown in Figure 11.32 will be disabled. Second, signing form data makes it read-only when filling out the form. That means any controls bound to signed data cannot be modified. Leaf controls (i.e., controls that can contain text data) will show an **edit-time visual** that shows a red certificate icon.

Now that we've covered the basics, it's time to use InfoPath! Let's jump into the review form template to see how we can add digital signatures to provide a level of security to filled-out forms.

Signing All Form Data

To allow users to sign their form data, go to the *Digital Signatures* category shown in Figure 11.32 and select the *Enable digital signatures for the entire form* option. The *Store signatures in the following group* text box will be automatically populated by InfoPath. In the background, InfoPath creates a special digital signature group in the data source under the document element.

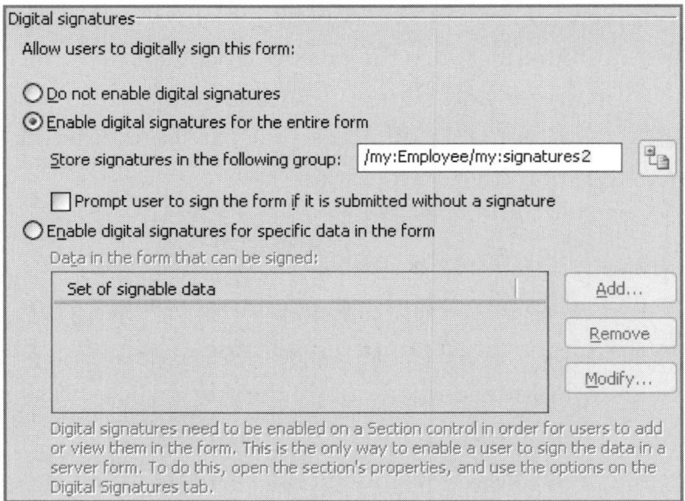

FIGURE 11.34: Setting up the template to allow signing the entire form

This group, called `my:signatures2` in our example (Figure 11.34), is where InfoPath will put the signature data generated when the form is signed.

Forms Services

Enabling digital signatures for the entire form is not available in browser-enabled form templates.

> **NOTE Selecting a Group for Signature Storage**
>
> The *Edit XPath* button adjacent to the text box in Figure 11.34 is not available if InfoPath automatically creates the signature node for you. If your data source is not editable but you already have a signature group in your data source, this button is enabled to let you choose the signature group. We'll talk about how to add a signature group to your data source later in the chapter.

In our example, we aren't submitting the form data. But if the data was to be submitted, we might want to select the *Prompt user to sign the form if it is submitted without a signature* checkbox. Checking this option will immediately open the *Submit Options* dialog. We discussed this option in Chapter 8, so we'll skip over its details for now.

After clicking *OK* to the *Form Options* dialog, take a look at the data source. Figure 11.33 shows the *Data Source* task pane with the `signatures2` group highlighted. This group was created automatically by InfoPath to hold the signature data when the user signs the form. Remember that the XML data generated as the user fills out the form must always be valid according to its XML Schema. Since the digital signatures feature needs to put the signed data somewhere in the data source, the signature group is where this data can exist without violating schema constraints.

Even though the signature group exists in the data source, there is really nothing for you to do with it. The signature group shows a lock icon, so you cannot directly delete or modify it. Dragging this group into the view doesn't insert anything into the view; instead, it shows the *Digital Signatures* category of the *Form Options* dialog (Figure 11.32). To remove the signature group, select the *Do not enable digital signatures* option button in that dialog.

There's not much excitement to be had for digital signatures in design mode, so let's try previewing and signing our form! After clicking the *Preview Form* button and filling in some data, click the *Digital Signatures* button in the *Standard* toolbar. The button is highlighted with a tool tip in Figure 11.35. Alternatively, the *Tools* menu has an equivalent *Digital Signatures* menu item.

After you click the *Digital Signatures* button (or select the *Tools* menu item), the *Digital Signatures* dialog appears (Figure 11.36). Fundamentally, this dialog lets you add or remove a digital signature. But, more importantly, it helps users understand precisely what data they're signing. Let's sign this form (which will enable the *View Signed Form* button shown in Figure 11.36) and then look at what data we signed.

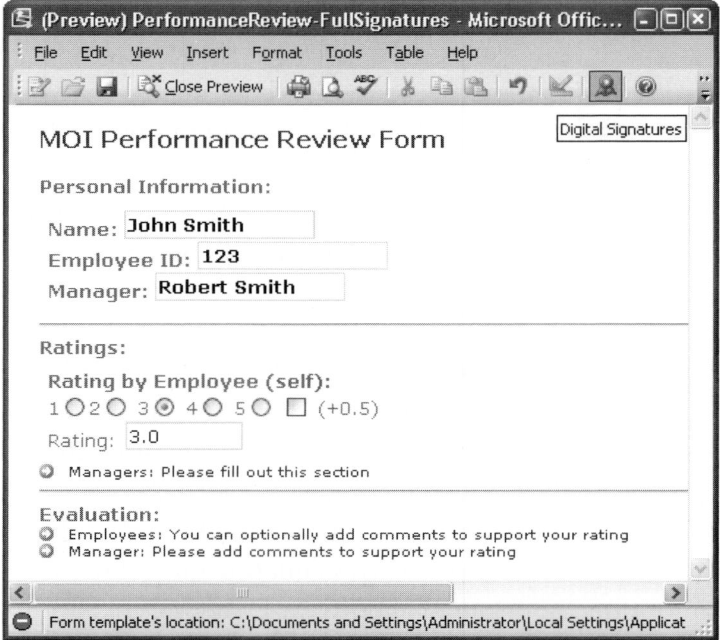

FIGURE 11.35: Filling out the MOI performance review before using a digital signature

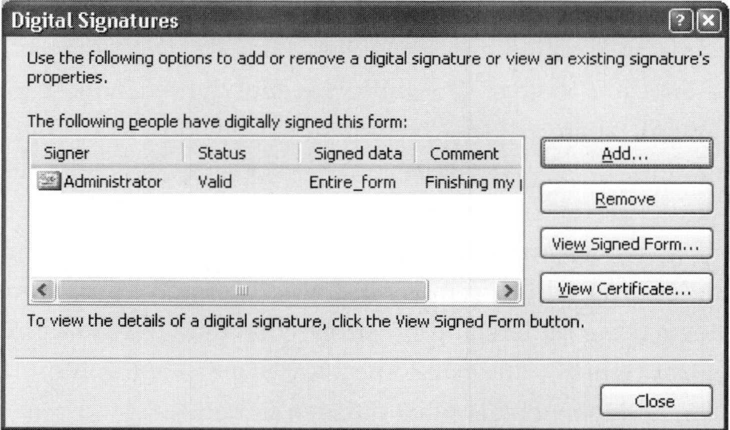

FIGURE 11.36: Digital Signatures dialog, which tracks who has signed this form

Clicking the *Add* button shows the *Select the Data to Sign* dialog Figure 11.37). Since we opted to sign the entire form when designing our form template, there's only a single option: *Entire_form*. This dialog is more useful when users need to sign specific parts of the form's data rather than the whole form.

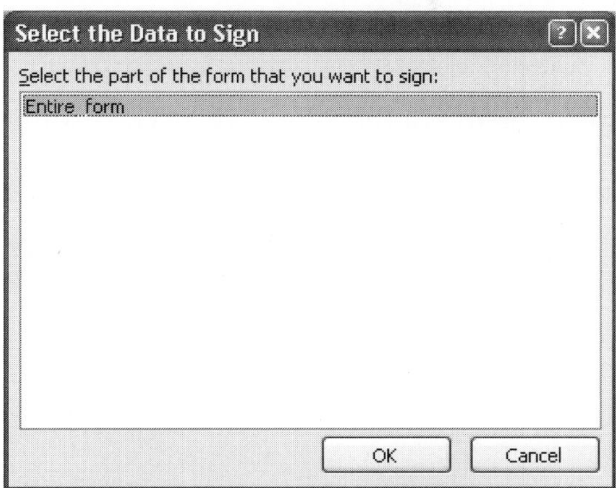

FIGURE 11.37: Selecting what form data to sign

Clicking the *OK* button takes us to the *Sign* dialog (Figure 11.38), where we can use our certificate to sign the form we've filled out.

Before clicking the *Sign* button, make sure that you've selected the proper certificate for signing. You can choose a certificate by clicking the

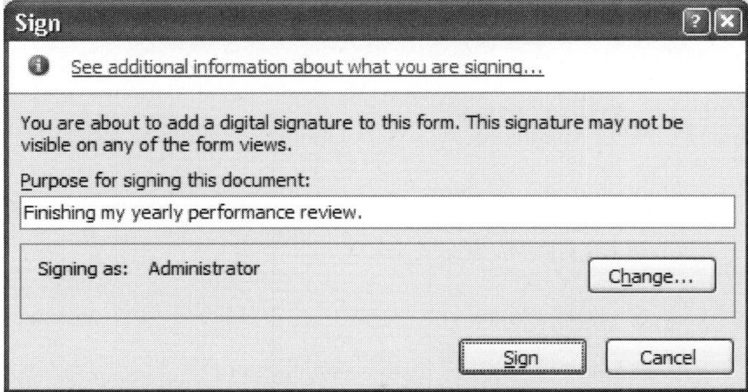

FIGURE 11.38: Clicking the Sign button to apply a digital signature to the form

Change button. Only code-signing certificates that have been issued to you can be used to sign form data. If no certificates are available, you can go back to the *Security and Trust* category on the *Form Options* dialog and click *Create Certificate* (refer back to Figure 11.18).

In the *Sign* dialog, you can also add some information to the *Purpose for signing this document* text box if you so choose—it's optional. If you do enter some text here, it will be included and signed as part of the form data.

Finally, before signing, first click the *See additional information about what you are signing* link at the top of the *Sign* dialog. The resulting dialog shows further details (Figure 11.39). It is this data (other than the form data) that

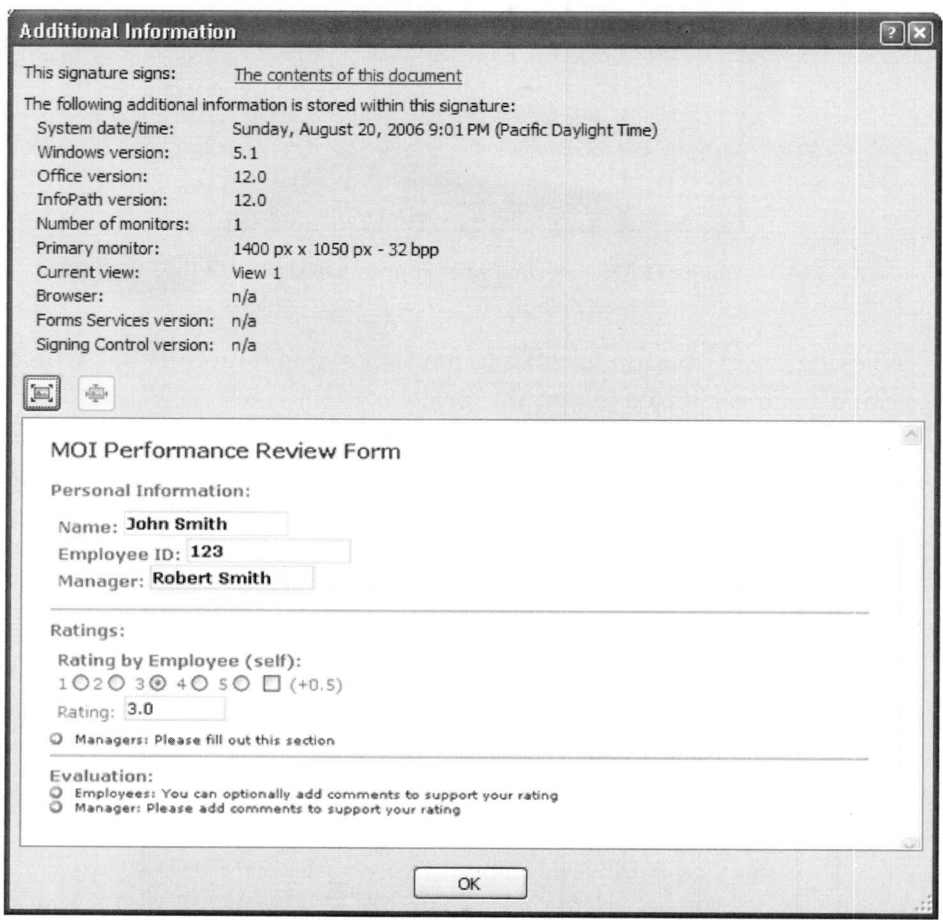

FIGURE 11.39: Additional Information dialog, which shows exactly what you're signing before you sign it

adds legitimacy to using digital signatures on InfoPath forms. As such, all of the details in the *Additional Information* dialog are included as part of the signed data. Without going into all of the properties that are captured, we'll say that the more important ones to us are the *Current view* information and a captured screenshot of that view.

Unlike signing an e-mail message or a Word document, signing an InfoPath form poses a unique problem when using digital signatures. Recall that when filling out a form, the user is actually editing an XML document in the background. But the user cannot directly see that XML document. As you know by now, the form designer completely determines what the user sees (controls bound to groups and fields) and how he or she sees it (data formatting, data validation, conditional formatting, rules, and so on). So, using digital signatures to blindly sign the form data doesn't really make sense. That's why it's important to include the visual component of the form data in the digital signature (as shown in the *Additional Information* dialog). Signing XML data is one thing, but keeping a record of what you were looking at when you signed the form is arguably more relevant. At least it would be one of the primary pieces of evidence if someone challenged what you had filled out. Remember that a picture is worth a thousand words!

After you click the *Sign* button, the *Digital Signatures* dialog appears with a signature, as we saw in Figure 11.36. When this dialog is closed, we'll be back to editing the form as we originally started. However, you might notice a few peculiarities because we're now looking at a signed form. Let's start at the top of the window shown in Figure 11.40 and work our way down. First is the title of the InfoPath window; we now see *[Signed]* appended to our form's name. This is the most dependable notification to the user that the form is signed. Next is the edit-time visual of a certificate icon that appears when we hover over or click on any text-based controls. (You see two Text Box controls with visuals in Figure 11.40 because the first one was clicked on while the second has the mouse hovered over.) It is not obvious from the figure, but all the Text Box controls are read-only because they are included in the signed data. Clicking on a Text Box does not let the cursor inside, and the data cannot be changed. What may be clearer from the same figure are the shaded Option Button and Check Box controls. Similar to the Text Box controls, hovering over these controls will also show an edit-time certificate to reiterate that this data is signed and cannot be modified.

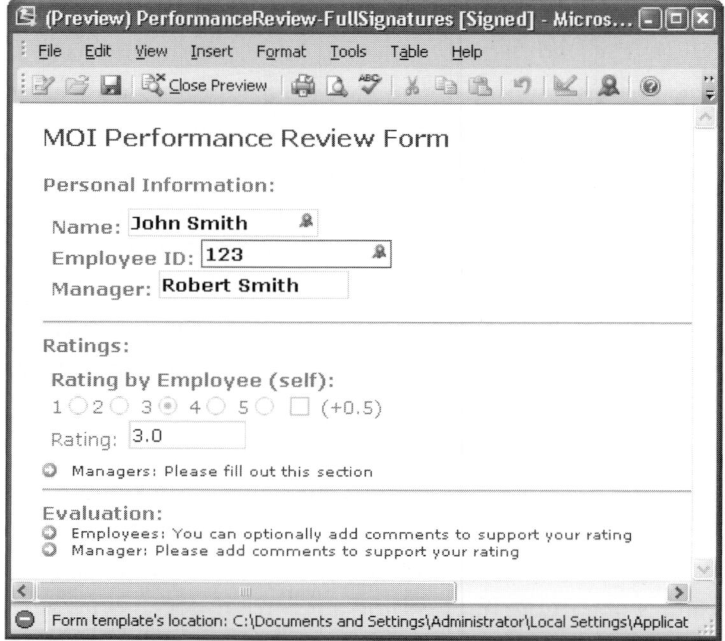

FIGURE 11.40: Digitally signed form with read-only controls

Finally, toward the bottom of the view, we have links to insert Optional Section controls. Certificate visuals are not shown when hovering over these links, and it's possible to click on one to try to insert the Section. When you click to insert, InfoPath will not allow the insertion and will show an error message: "InfoPath cannot update the data, because the form is currently read-only" (Figure 11.41).

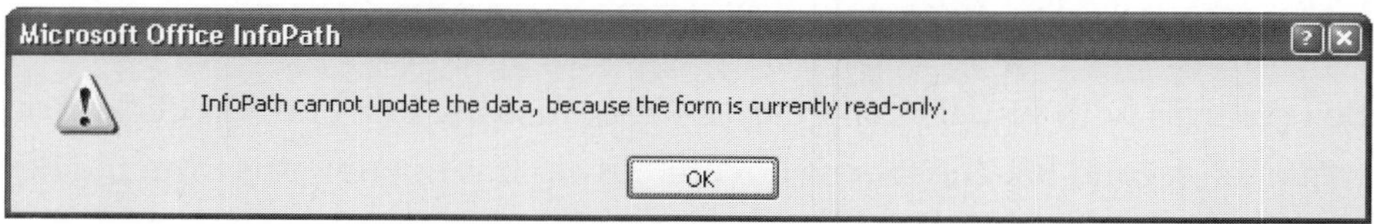

FIGURE 11.41: Error dialog that appears when trying to change signed form data

To continue editing the form as we did before signing, we must remove the digital signature. This is done by roughly reversing the process we followed to sign the form. To remove the signature, click on the *Digital Signatures* button in the *Standard* toolbar and click the *Remove* button to remove the appropriate signature.

NOTE Multiple Signatures on a Form

Multiple signatures can be used on a single form. For example, after filling out and adding the first signature to the MOI performance review, we (or someone else) could have gone through the same process to add another signature. As long as there's at least one signature, the form will be read-only. So if you sign the form, send it to others to sign (e.g., via e-mail), and then get it back with your signature still intact, you can rest assured that no one has tampered with the form data.

If others open your digitally signed form, they will immediately see a notification, shown in Figure 11.42, that the form is indeed signed. There are other ways, as we discussed earlier, to determine whether a form is digitally signed. But this dialog is obviously more explicit, which can be a helpful reminder to people who don't usually work with digitally signed forms on a regular basis.

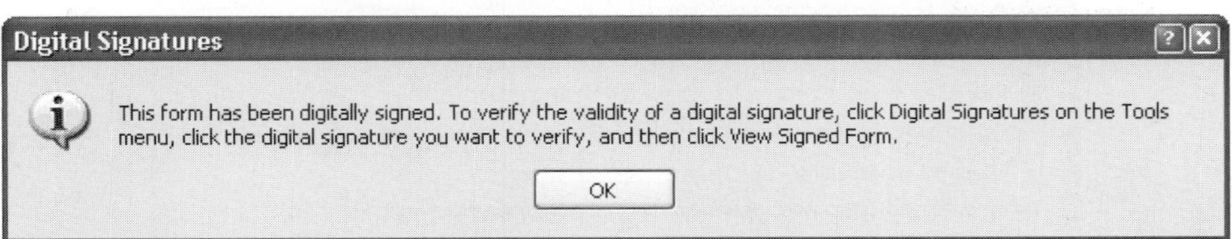

FIGURE 11.42: Friendly reminder that the form being opened is digitally signed

NOTE Signature Validation When Opening a Form

To see the dialog prompt shown in Figure 11.42, start by saving a signed form while previewing it. Then close the preview window and find the saved .xml file in Windows. Double-click on the corresponding .xml file to open the form and see the notification.

Forms Services

The notification shown in Figure 11.42 is not shown when a user fills out a form in a browser. However, he or she will see *[Signed]* in the title of the browser window.

If digitally signed forms are opened on a daily basis in your organization, the dialog in Figure 11.42 could end up being a nuisance. Thankfully, there's a setting nestled in advanced options to never show it again. Go to the *Options* menu item (not *Form Options*) under the *Tools* menu and select the *Advanced* tab. Uncheck the *Show a notification when opening forms that have been digitally signed* checkbox to disable the notification when opening digitally signed forms. Figure 11.43 shows the default settings for advanced options.

TIP Options Dialog

Unlike the *Form Options* dialog, which corresponds only to the current form template in design mode, the *Options* dialog settings apply to all forms and templates. These options are saved with the logged-in user's profile and can be changed only by that user or by an administrator.

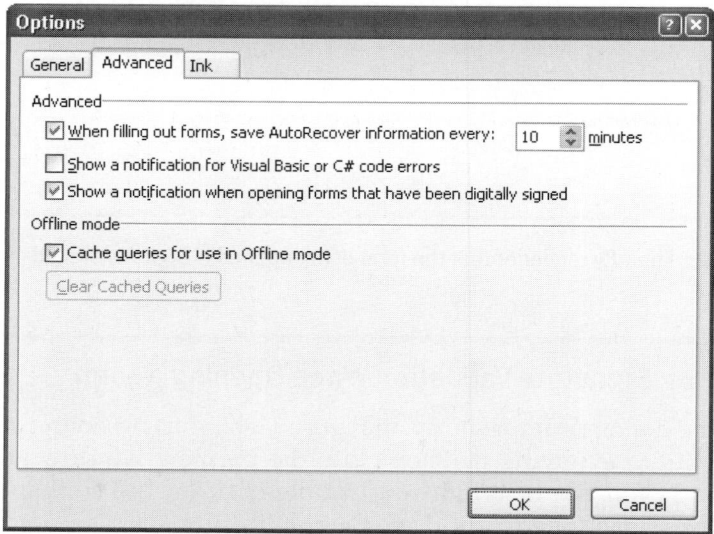

FIGURE 11.43: Choosing whether or not to show a notification when signed forms are opened

Partially Signing Form Data

A more compelling scenario for using digital signatures in business is to allow a greater degree of flexibility. In many situations, it might not make sense to sign the entire form. For example, any scenarios involving workflow are hampered by the fact that after a user adds the first signature at some stage in the workflow, subsequent users cannot modify the form because it's read-only. Furthermore, some workflow processes ask for multiple signatures across different parts of a document. To alleviate some restrictions inherent in signing the entire form, InfoPath allows for partially signing a form.

Before we switch the MOI performance review form template to use partial signing, it's beneficial to first understand a little background on how partial signing works. In contrast to signing the entire form, the flexibility in partially signing a form introduces a layer of complexity. Let's take a moment to learn about this complexity and what it means to design and fill out forms with the ability to partially sign data.

To understand partial signing, start by thinking of partial signatures in the same way as full signatures. The same concepts (controls are read-only, edit-time visuals are shown, and so on) apply. But instead of applying a signature to the entire form (i.e., the whole data source), just scope a signature to a specific group in the data source (i.e., a part of the data source). From a data source perspective, that's how partial signing differs from signing the entire form. But how does this work in the view? For a moment, try to forget about the data source concepts we just reviewed. To partially sign data in the view, InfoPath uses a Section control to delimit what is visually signed. So when designing a form, you can choose one or more Section controls that can be signed. When a user signs a Section when filling out the form, only that Section becomes read-only—the rest of the unsigned form can still be edited.

Now let's tie together our understandings of partially signing data based on groups and partially signing the view based on Section controls. When you set up partial signing for a given Section in the view, the partial signature need not point to the node in which its corresponding Section control is bound. In other words, if a Section is bound to `my:GroupThatShouldBeSigned`, it could actually sign the data that's bound to a completely different group (that may or may not be in the view) called `my:RandomGroup`. Thus, it's critical to realize that partial signing is primarily view-based. (This concept will materialize in our example.) Once we enable a Section for partial signing, then we can define what data is being signed. In most cases, the Section that is enabled for signing (in the view) is bound to the group that is being signed (in the data source). But as we mentioned, this need not be the case. As a result, a snapshot picture of the form is far more important in partial signing than in entire form signing. Since the relationship between the visually signed Section and the actually signed data could be completely different, it's critical to capture what the user really saw when signing the form.

Unlike the situation when users will sign the entire form, setting a form up for partial signatures may require changes in your form design. In fact, it's better to account for design changes due to partial signatures *before* you create your form template. Let's examine how partial signatures affect the process of designing forms.

We now know that partial signing occurs at the scope of a Section control. That means every part of your form that you want partially signed must be enclosed in a Section. Take the MOI performance review form, for example (refer back to Figure 11.33). It's visually split up into many different blocks for personal information, ratings (employee and manager), and evaluation comments (employee and manager). If you take a close look at the form in design mode, you can see that each of these visual groups is enclosed in its own Section or Optional Section. Moreover, these Section controls correspond with the following groups in the data source task pane (seen in the same figure): `Info`, `Rating`, and `Comments`.

Since the performance review form is somewhat contrived for this example, let's consider an ordinary form that doesn't have digital signatures. That form may not have groups in the data source that map nicely to the Section controls you want users to sign. This is no problem. You have a couple of options. First, you can always insert fields (elements or attributes) as a Section whose data users can sign. This is what we did with the Section controls for employee rating, manager rating, employee evaluation, and manager evaluation in the performance review form. Alternatively, you can use any arbitrary Section (where binding doesn't matter) to sign any data in the form. Our favorite example of using arbitrary Section controls is to insert the document element (top-most) group of the data source into the view simply as a Section. You can insert the document element into the view as many times as you like! Each Section, even though they're all multiply bound to the document element, can have its own partial signature by pointing to different parts of the data source that you want to sign. The bindings of the Section controls have no bearing on the signed data. Each Section can be individually configured during design time to enable signing of specific data.

Using partial signing is not as easy as just flipping a switch, as it was with signing the entire form. There are three different options when adding partial signatures; each one caters to different workflow scenarios. We'll look at each one as we change the performance review form design from one that enables signing the entire form to one that allows partial signing.

We begin the conversion by first enabling partial signing on the *Personal Information* part of the view. To do so, we first need to move the relevant controls (bound to fields `Name`, `ID`, and `Manager`) into a Section control. The Section can be bound to the `Info` group in the data source, which contains the relevant fields that we want to sign. Figure 11.44 shows a closeup of the `Info` Section and child controls.

FIGURE 11.44: Setting up the Personal Information part of the view for partial signing

The next step is to enable partial signing for this Section. We start by going to the Section's properties dialog and clicking on the *Digital Signatures* tab. (Alternatively, you could make the change from entire to partial form signing in the *Digital Signatures* category on the *Form Options* dialog shown in Figure 11.32. But doing it through Section properties is more intuitive when it comes to setting up a partial signature.) In the *Digital Signatures* tab, the *Allow users to digitally sign this section* checkbox will be unchecked. Checking it will open a dialog warning you that the form is already enabled for signing the entire form and that continuing will remove this ability and instead enable partial signatures.

After you dismiss the warning to continue, the *Sign the following data in the form when this section is signed* drop-down will be blank. Select the *Add data to be signed* item in the drop-down to choose what data will be signed for this Section. The resulting dialog, *Set of Signable Data,* will be automatically filled out, as shown in Figure 11.45.

FIGURE 11.45: Creating a new set of signable data (partial signing) on a Section control

The *Set of Signable Data* dialog has a few data points we want to call out. First is the friendly name that you want to assign to this block of data. This name will be revealed in a few places to reference this partially signed data, including in design mode and when users fill out the form. We'll see various places in the UI where this name is used as we continue our discussions.

The next text box in Figure 11.45 references the fields and groups to be signed. By default, this XPath points to the field or group bound to the Section control. But as we mentioned earlier, the data that's signed does not need to correspond with the bound field or group of the Section—but it usually will. You can select another data source node by clicking the *Select XPath* button adjacent to the text box.

You won't usually need to worry about changing the *Store signatures in the following group* setting. When your data source is unlocked, that is, when you can add and remove data source fields and groups through the *Data Source* task pane, InfoPath will disable this input and simply put *(New signatures group)* as the XPath. Since the data source is unlocked, InfoPath can create the signatures block automatically and associate it with this Section.

NOTE Signature Groups in the Data Source

When we signed the entire form, a signature group was created in the data source. For partial signing, each partial signature needs its own signature group. If your data source is open, InfoPath can create the signature groups as necessary. If not, you will need a unique signature group for every partially signed group. We'll review what it means to have signed data in the XML Schema later in the chapter.

The next item in the *Set of Signable Data* dialog is the *Signature options* region. It contains three option buttons that determine how this Section's data is to be signed. Soon we will look at these various signing options and how they affect the form from a workflow perspective.

Finally, the *Signature confirmation message* text is shown to users at the top of the *Sign* dialog when they sign a Section in the form. For this "Info" signable data, we'll ask the user to ensure that the data he or she entered is correct.

Now that we're done with the *Set of Signable Data* dialog, clicking *OK* returns us to the *Digital Signatures* tab on the *Section Properties* dialog (Figure 11.46). As you can see, the friendly name we used when creating the set of signable data appears in the drop-down. Once we add multiple sets of signable data, each one will appear in this as well as all Section properties drop-downs that show signable data.

Two settings on the *Digital Signatures* tab significantly affect how the user interacts with signed Section controls when filling out the form. If you select the *Show signatures in the section* option, users will see other signatures that have been added to the Section thus far. You may not want to show signatures if, for example, you want to keep the signers anonymous

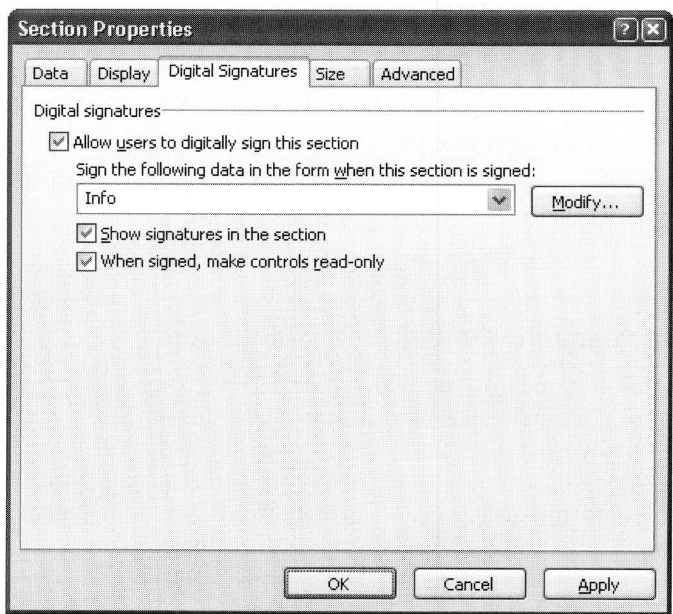

FIGURE 11.46: Setting up digital signatures on a Section control

to each other. If revealing the identities of the signers to each other is fine, it's best to leave this option enabled so it's easy to see who has signed the Section.

The second checkbox setting makes all controls in the Section read-only when the set of signable data is signed. If all of the controls in the Section are not part of the set of signable data, you will want to disable this checkbox so that the user can fill out the controls that aren't part of the signing. We highly recommend that you only include controls (that are bound to data) that are actively being signed. Otherwise, signing a Section will misrepresent what is actually being signed and the user may be confused. It's important to know that if you uncheck the *When signed, make controls read-only* setting, editing any signed data will be rejected anyway but with an error dialog. So this option does not allow users to modify signed data. It only helps enforce read-only data by disallowing editing in the control.

Let's now return to the *Signature options* portion of the *Set of Signable Data* dialog to talk about the three option buttons we mentioned.

Allowing Only One Signature

Selecting the *Allow only one signature option* allows the Section to be signed at most once. After signing, no more signatures are accepted. The Section can be signed in one of two ways. The first and most obvious way is to use the *Click here to sign this section* link under the signable Section, as shown selected in Figure 11.47.

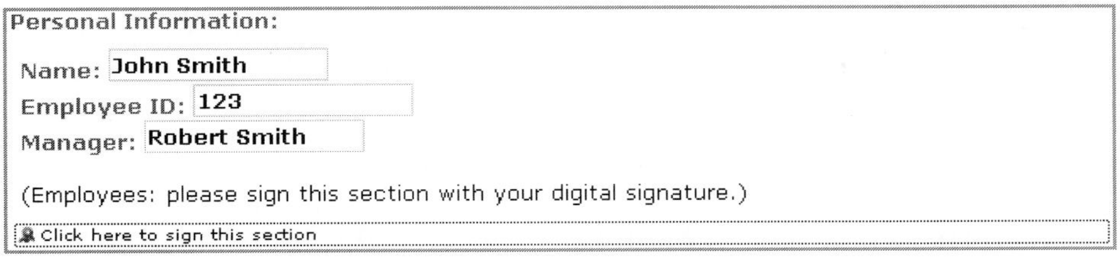

Personal Information:

Name: John Smith

Employee ID: 123

Manager: Robert Smith

(Employees: please sign this section with your digital signature.)

Click here to sign this section

FIGURE 11.47: Signing the "Info" set of signable data when filling out the form

Alternatively, we can use the *Digital Signatures* button in the *Standard* toolbar as we did earlier when signing the entire form (refer back to Figure 11.35). When partial signatures are used in a form such as ours, the *Select the Data to Sign* dialog will show all sets of signable data (Figure 11.48). Remember when we first created the set of signable data for the `Info`

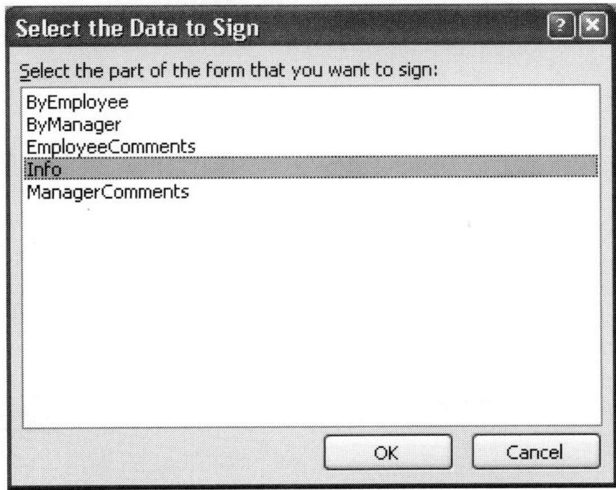

FIGURE 11.48: Using the Select the Data to Sign dialog opened by clicking the Digital Signatures button

Section? The friendly name we chose for the signable data is revealed in this dialog. In this case, "Info" might not have been the best name for the Section under the heading "Personal Information"!

Forms Services

The dialog shown in Figure 11.48 is not available when filling out a form in the browser. The only visual way to sign a Section in the browser is to click on the *Click here to sign this section* link below the Section itself. (You can also initiate form signing by calling specific InfoPath object model methods in form code, however.)

After we click the link in Figure 11.47 or select the "Info" set of signable data from Figure 11.48, the *Sign* dialog appears. The dialog is similar to the one we used when signing the entire form, but this one allows for a true signature in the form of a written name or even an image! Figure 11.49 shows the *Sign* dialog when signing a Section with "John J. Smith" as our name. Except for the area for using your own signature and the *Signature*

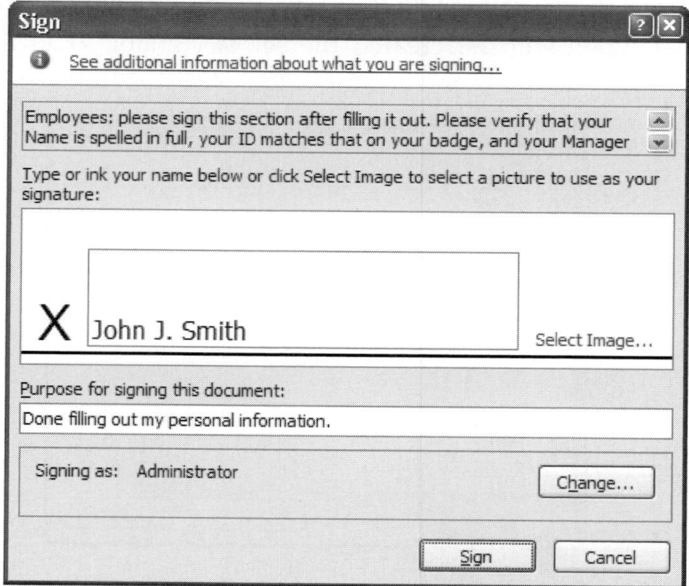

FIGURE 11.49: Signing a set of signable data when filling out the form

confirmation message text we configured (shown earlier in Figure 11.45), this dialog is identical to the one we saw when signing the entire form (refer back to Figure 11.38).

NOTE The Name (or Image) in the Sign Dialog

The name is not validated against the certificate, so you can type anything and it will be accepted when you click the *Sign* button. Similarly, any image will suffice for signing. Ideally the image embodies your handwritten signature. (A Tablet PC or scanner can capture your written signature in an electronic format.) However, you must choose whether to type your name or use an image—you can't do both when applying a digital signature.

Forms Services

Forms Services does not ask for your signature in the *Sign* dialog. Forms in the browser request only a purpose for signing.

After you enter a custom signature (or choosing an image) and optionally entering some text in the *Purpose for signing this document* text box, clicking the *Sign* button will use the chosen certificate to sign the Section. The view changes to show our typed (or selected image) signature as well as the date of signing (Figure 11.50). Our signature would not be shown if we had unchecked the *Show signatures in the section* setting (refer back to Figure 11.46). If the signature isn't visible, you can still see that the Section

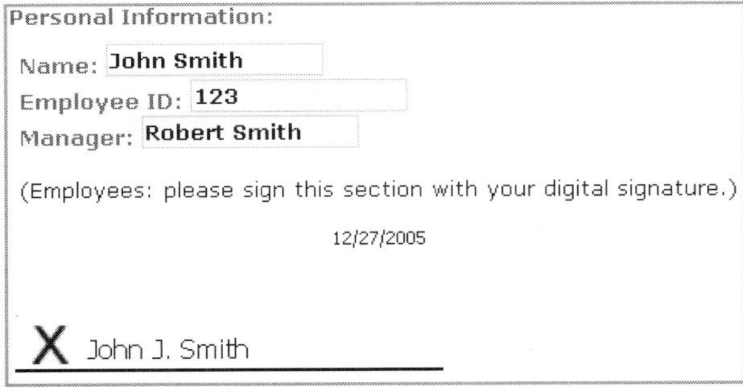

FIGURE 11.50: Form showing that the set of signable data has been signed

was signed by using the *Digital Signatures* button on the *Standard* toolbar, which opens the dialog listing all signed data in the form (presented earlier in Figure 11.36).

> **NOTE** A Signature Need Not Be Valid
>
> The existence of a signature in a form, such as that shown in Figure 11.50, does not guarantee that the certificate used for signing is actually valid.

Forms Services

After signing a section in the browser, there is no signature shown as seen at the bottom of Figure 11.50. Instead, the name of the signer is derived from the certificate.

To get more information about the signed data, including the status of signature validity, you can click on the signature shown in the form or use the *Digital Signatures* dialog. The resulting *Signature Details* dialog, shown in Figure 11.51, provides a wealth of information, such as the validity of the signature, the signer's physical signature, his or her purpose, a link to the *Certificate* dialog from the *View* button, and finally a link at the bottom for showing the *Additional Information* dialog. The *Additional Information* dialog

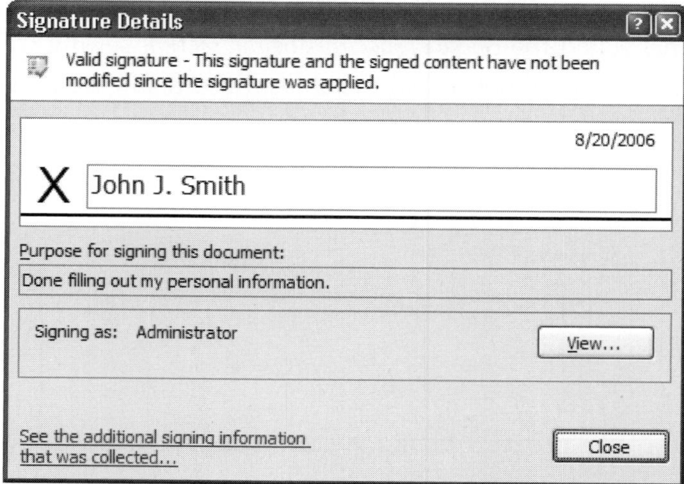

FIGURE 11.51: Signature Details dialog for a signed Section control

is the same as the one shown earlier in Figure 11.39 when we signed the entire form. It yields details such as the current view and a picture of the form when it was signed.

Using Independent Signatures (Co-signing)

Using the *All the signatures are independent (co-signing)* setting allows for an unlimited number of signatures. But similar to the case when allowing only one signature, the signed data is always read-only when a co-signed signature exists. So what's the point of co-signing data that you can't modify? An ideal example of co-signing is a petition. Every signature adds more support to the issue in question. In a petition, one signature does not override another since they're all considered parallel to each other.

The MOI performance review form uses co-signing on the Section controls for employee rating and employee comments. Before sending the review to his manager, John Smith will assign an appropriate rating for himself and add his comments to justify the rating. To prove that John indeed fill out his rating and comments, as well as to ensure that nobody else changes what he filled out, John signs those two Section controls (which correspond to the `ByEmployee` and `EmployeeComments` sets of signable data). Co-signing occurs when John's manager, Robert, acknowledges that he received and reviewed John's rating and comments. So Robert will add his signature to the same Section controls that John already filled out (Figure 11.52).

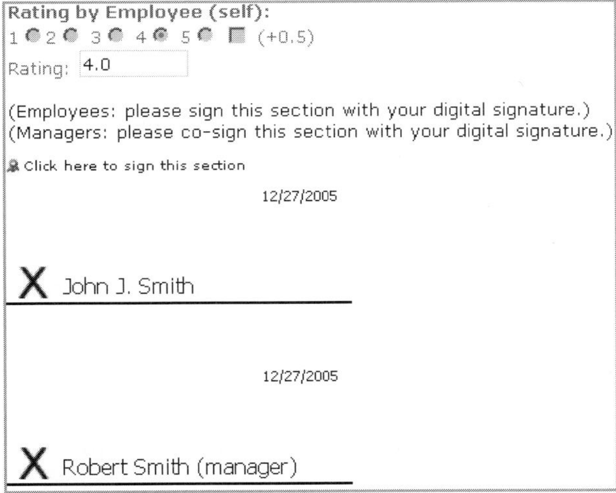

FIGURE 11.52: Form showing that Robert co-signed John's review rating

Co-signers, as with signatures on a petition, sign independently and only acknowledge the original data. When a co-signed digital signature is created in the XML data, it is created parallel to any other signatures that already exist. As a result, any signatures can be added or removed without affecting the validity of other signatures on the same signable data.

> **TIP Viewing All Signatures on a Form**
>
> Just as you can use the *Digital Signatures* dialog to see all signatures added thus far to a filled-out form, you can similarly see all sets of signed data for partial signatures. You can do so by using the *Digital Signatures* category on the *Form Options* dialog in design mode, which lists all data in the form that can be signed.

Setting Up Counter-Signatures

The last type of partial digital signature is the counter-sign, which is enabled when you select the *Each signature signs the preceding signatures (counter-sign)* option. Like co-signing, counter-signing allows for a limitless number of signatures. But the main difference between co-signing and counter-signing lies in what is being signed. In co-signing, the signer is acknowledging some data in the form, so it follows that the signature only signs that data. Counter-signing is similar in that the data is being signed, but in addition to the data, any existing signature on that data is also being signed.

Since counter-signing signs an existing signature, a hierarchy of signatures can be created, a common use within businesses. Since employees report to managers whom also report to managers (repeatedly to the top), a signature hierarchy maps nicely to a company's chain of management. A prime example of using counter-signatures would be to get executive approval for a highly funded project. Say that John J. Smith wanted to kick off a multimillion-dollar marketing campaign for a new service offered by MOI Consulting. To begin the approval process, John would fill out the MOI project proposal form and send it to his manager, Robert. If Robert likes the proposal, he'll counter-sign John's signature and send it to his own manager. As the proposal trickles up the chain of management, someone at each level would counter-sign the previous manager's signature.

Remember that a valid digital signature means the signed data has not changed. Since counter-signing applies a digital signature to an existing digital signature, any change in the signature chain will break all dependent signatures. For John's proposal, he is the "root" of the chain. If he were to remove his signature, he would effectively invalidate all dependent signatures (i.e., those by Robert, Robert's manager, and so on) because the data they signed (which included John's signature) would have changed. Counter-signatures are fragile in the sense that the last signature depends on all of the previous signatures to be valid.

In addition to using co-signing on the employee rating and comments, the MOI performance review form uses counter-signing on the Section controls for the manager rating and manager comments. (A sample for partial signatures, MOIPerformanceReview-PartialSignatures, is included with this chapter's samples.) Once Robert finishes filling out his own rating and comments for John, Robert applies his signature. John then reviews the rating and comments assigned to him by Robert and counter-signs the appropriate Section controls. In this case, counter-signing is trickling down the chain from manager to employee. This means that if Robert were to remove his signature, John's signature would become invalid. Without John's counter-signature, the review is not final. So counter-signing enforces that existing signatures should not change, and if they do, the chain of signatures will need to be reestablished by having all signers go through the signing process again.

> **NOTE** Counter-Signatures Behave Similar to Co-Signatures
>
> Counter-signatures are created and appear in the same way as co-signatures.

Digital Signatures in the XML Data and Schema

When the data source is unlocked for adding and deleting nodes, InfoPath will automatically create and manage signature groups. As we've seen so far, signing the entire form creates a single signature group, and using partial signatures creates multiple groups. But what is this so-called signature group? What does the XML data look like in a signed form? What XML

Schema is generated that allows for a signature? How about multiple signatures? And what if you start from an existing XML Schema and InfoPath disallows digital signatures? Let's explore some of these issues.

Signed Data in XML

To begin, we'll see how a digital signature looks in the data of a signed form. You can easily follow along by simply creating a new blank form, adding a Text Box control, and then enabling a signature on the entire form. (If you want, you could instead use the MOI performance review sample form.) We'll preview the form, type "Hello, world" in the Text Box, sign the form, and finally save it to a new file. Opening the file in a text editor, such as Notepad, is virtually useless because the data is incomprehensible. For your convenience, here's an outline of the XML data structure in a signed form's signature group:

```
my:signatures1 ("my" Namespace)
   Signature (Namespace = http://www.w3.org/2000/09/xmldsig#)
      SignedInfo
         CanonicalizationMethod
         SignatureMethod
         Reference+
            Transforms
            DigestMethod
            DigestValue
         SignatureValue
         KeyInfo
            X509Data
               X509Certificate
            Object
               SignatureProperties
```

> **NOTE** InfoPath Digitally Signed Data Is Enveloped
>
> A digital signature that exists within the XML data that it's signing is known as an **enveloped** signature. InfoPath generates enveloped signatures for all signed form data.

> **NOTE** Digital Signatures Standards
>
> InfoPath does not support the `PGPData`, `SPKIData`, or `MgmtData` elements for digital signing. Only the `X509Data` element is used.

The details of the XML data structure for a signature are beyond the scope of this book. The W3C has a recommendation for XML Signature Syntax and Processing (as referenced in the Appendix).

> **WARNING** **Digital Signatures and Form Performance**
>
> Signed form data is usually exponentially larger than the unsigned version. This can be directly inferred by the size of the saved .xml file. For example, when comparing signed and unsigned versions of the same form data, the signed file is on the order of 21 times (or more) larger. In a partially signed form where you can have a half dozen or more signatures, the expansion factor can be 100 times or greater! Given the blown-up sizes of signed data, it's recommended to compress the .xml files with a commercially available compression technology, which can reduce a signed file size more than 50%. This is especially crucial when sending signed data over slower network connections.

Signed Data in XML Schema

The XML data isn't so interesting; it's a little like a television box. There are really no "user-serviceable" parts inside, and everything works just fine. (Unless, of course, you were a mischievous kid who physically took apart video games!) On the other hand, the XML Schema is much more interesting for a few reasons. First, it's much simpler and easy to read. Second, and most importantly, if you created your form from an existing XML Schema, InfoPath may not allow changes to the data source. As a result, you will not be able to add digital signatures to your form template. We'll show you what the schema elements look like and how you can add them to the XML Schema in your form template to open it up for digital signatures.

Let's look at what InfoPath generates in the XML Schema to create a signatures group.

```
<xsd:element name="signatures1">
   <xsd:complexType>
      <xsd:sequence>
         <xsd:any minOccurs="0" maxOccurs="unbounded"
namespace="http://www.w3.org/2000/09/xmldsig#" processContents="lax"/>
      </xsd:sequence>
   </xsd:complexType>
</xsd:element>
```

That's simple, isn't it? The `xsd:any` schema element says that anything can exist zero or as many times as necessary in the `http://www.w3.org/2000/09/xmldsig#` namespace. This namespace completely defines a digital signature within an XML file such as an InfoPath form.

Say we started from the following fixed schema file that doesn't allow signatures.

```
<?xml version="1.0"?>
<xsd:schema xmlns:xsd="http://www.w3.org/2001/XMLSchema">
   <xsd:element name="ClosedNode">
      <xsd:complexType>
         <xsd:sequence>
            <xsd:element name="foo" type="xsd:string"/>
         </xsd:sequence>
         <xsd:attribute name="bar" type="xsd:string"/>
      </xsd:complexType>
   </xsd:element>
</xsd:schema>
```

This schema simply defines a document element called `ClosedNode` with two fields: an element `foo` and an attribute `bar`. If you create a new form template based on this schema, you will find that digital signatures cannot be added because the data source is locked. Time to do a little surgery on the schema!

> **TIP Make a Backup**
>
> Before making any hand modifications to any files, first create a backup!

To begin, open the XML Schema (.xsd) file you used to create your form template in a text editor. You should see something like our example schema just shown. (We suggest first practicing on our schema.) Next, create a new element under the document element that references a yet-to-be-defined element called `signatures1`. The changes are shown here in **bold**.

```
<?xml version="1.0"?>
<xsd:schema xmlns:xsd="http://www.w3.org/2001/XMLSchema">
   <xsd:element name="ClosedNode">
      <xsd:complexType>
         <xsd:sequence>
            <xsd:element name="foo" type="xsd:string"/>
            <xsd:element ref="signatures1"/>
```

```
            </xsd:sequence>
            <xsd:attribute name="bar" type="xsd:string"/>
         </xsd:complexType>
      </xsd:element>
   </xsd:schema>
```

Now that you've added the reference to `signatures1`, copy it from that schema snippet and put it into our schema. Changes, once again, are in **bold**.

```
<?xml version="1.0"?>
<xsd:schema xmlns:xsd="http://www.w3.org/2001/XMLSchema">
   <xsd:element name="ClosedNode">
      <xsd:complexType>
         <xsd:sequence>
            <xsd:element name="foo" type="xsd:string"/>
            <xsd:element ref="signatures1"/>
         </xsd:sequence>
         <xsd:attribute name="bar" type="xsd:string"/>
      </xsd:complexType>
   </xsd:element>
   <xsd:element name="signatures1">
      <xsd:complexType>
         <xsd:sequence>
            <xsd:any minOccurs="0" maxOccurs="unbounded"
namespace="http://www.w3.org/2000/09/xmldsig#" processContents="lax"/>
         </xsd:sequence>
      </xsd:complexType>
   </xsd:element>
</xsd:schema>
```

That's it! You're done modifying the XML Schema to support digital signatures in InfoPath. If you've already created a form template and need to update its schema, you can use the *Convert Main Data Source* option on the *Tools* menu to use the newly modified schema. If you haven't yet created a form template, you can design a new form template against this updated schema. Now you can use digital signatures with any XML Schema!

If you need multiple signatures (e.g., with partial signatures) in your form template, you will need to create multiple signature elements in the XML Schema. A one-to-one mapping should exist; for each partial signature, a new signatures element must be created. Follow the same process just shown to edit the XML Schema file; however, you will need to give each signature group a unique name. In our example, we used the name `signatures1`. The next signatures element could be called `signatures2`, and so forth. Don't forget to change both the reference name and the actual element as you add signature groups.

Information Rights Management

Information Rights Management (IRM) was introduced to the Microsoft Office suite (e.g., for Word and Excel) in version 2003. InfoPath, however, did not include IRM for its 2003 debut. Based on customer feedback, InfoPath 2007 provides IRM for both the form template and the form itself. Applying IRM permission to a form template means the form template (.xsn) file is restricted in InfoPath. Applying IRM to a form, on the other hand, is more straightforward. Clearly IRM on a form limits who can open the form to fill it out (or just to open it as read-only). In design mode, you can set default IRM permissions on a form. So when a new form is created from a form template for filling, the resulting form has those IRM permissions already defined. Let's take a closer look at how we can use IRM with our forms and templates.

IRM Is Not a Security Feature

IRM is not meant to be a complete security solution for forms and form templates. For example, a user who is denied copy and print rights can always use a camera to capture the screen. Then he or she can use optical character recognition software to get the content back into an electronic format, which then is obviously not restricted.

NOTE IRM Requires Windows Rights Management Service (RMS)

To use IRM with InfoPath, you should have access to a Windows 2003 Server running RMS. If you don't have access to RMS on your network, InfoPath will ask if you would like to use a free RMS service provided by Microsoft on the Internet.

Forms Services

Forms Services does not support IRM permission on either forms or form templates. In fact, a browser-enabled form template disallows IRM permission altogether.

Permission on Form Templates

Applying IRM permission to a template restricts the form template (.xsn) file when used with InfoPath. There is no file-based permission applied with IRM, so if a user has read access in Windows to the .xsn file, for example, IRM cannot prevent that user from expanding the .xsn file and reading the resource files. So IRM shouldn't be used as a single defense to lock users out of reading or changing a form template. However, it is an effective way to prevent unauthorized reading or changing of the form template through InfoPath design mode. Table 11.4 shows the permissions that can be granted to users through IRM and the effect on their design-time experience.

TABLE 11.4: Permissions Granted and Denied to a User Given a Form Template in Design Mode

IRM Access Level	Allowable Actions	Disallowed Actions
Read (everyone)	Filling out new forms; no design permission granted	Opening the form template in design mode
Change	Opening the form template in design mode as read-only	Modifying the form template
Full Control	Everything	Nothing

The first step to enabling IRM permission on a form template is to click on the *Permission* button on the *Standard* toolbar in design mode (Figure 11.53). The resulting *Permission* dialog appears, as shown in

FIGURE 11.53: Permission button on the Standard toolbar

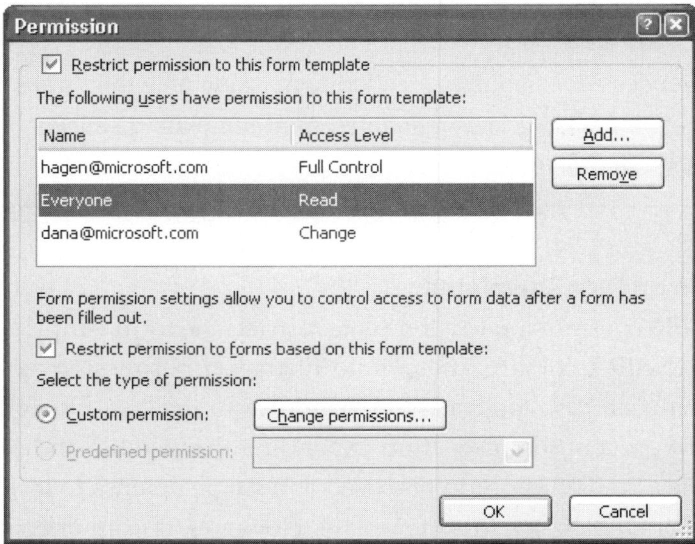

FIGURE 11.54: Defining IRM permission on a form template (top checkbox) and forms (lower checkbox)

Figure 11.54. (Note that only the top half of the dialog is relevant to permissions on the form template.) So according to our sample dialog shown in Figure 11.54, nobody can open the form template in design mode except Dana and Hagen. Only Hagen can overwrite the form template at its original location. However, everyone can fill out a new form from the form template.

There are some restrictions in how you can define permission on a form template. *Everyone* cannot be removed from the list and must have read permission. This is because users would not be able to fill out forms unless they had read access to the form template! Moreover, the user who configured permission in the first place (in this case, Hagen) must have full control. The only way to relinquish full control is to have someone else with full control open the form template in design mode. Thanks to this safety mechanism, it's impossible for you to lock yourself out of the form template unless someone else locks you out—but you gave them permission to do so!

If our friend Dana opens our form template in design mode, she may briefly see the dialog about verifying credentials, as shown in Figure 11.55. This dialog promptly disappears after checking Dana's credentials against the RMS server.

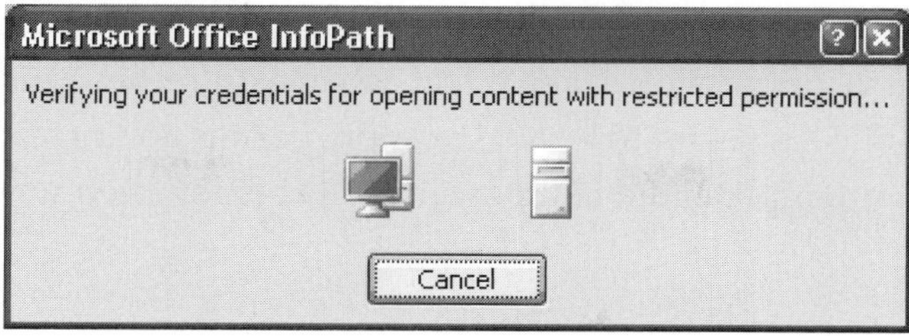

FIGURE 11.55: Dialog about verifying credentials when opening a form template

Once the form template opens in design mode, Dana can make any changes she wishes, but she will not be allowed to change IRM permission. This is because her access level is designated in the *Permission* dialog as *Change* and not *Full Control.* When Dana clicks on the *Permission* button, she is greeted by a dialog similar to the one shown in Figure 11.56. This dialog shows Dana her own permission. In fact, the permission you see in Figure 11.56 is the same for all users in design mode with *Change* permission. Dana cannot print, access the form programmatically, or assume full control. Clicking the *Request additional permissions* link opens a blank e-mail message with the owner's address in the *To* field.

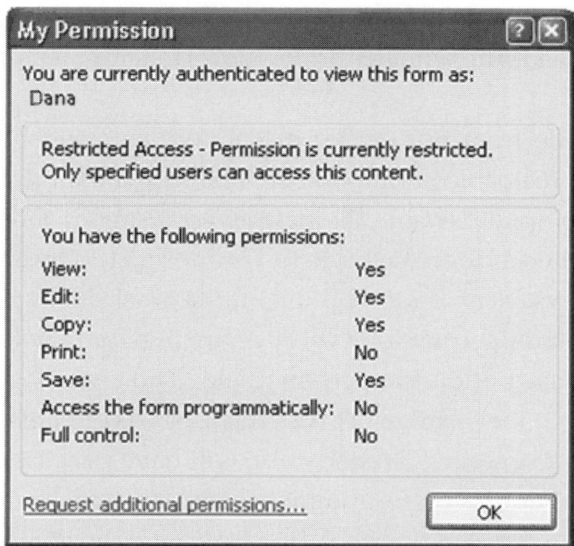

FIGURE 11.56: Restricted permission for user Dana while designing a form template

So far we've looked at what it means to apply IRM permission to a form template. Such permission takes effect when you're designing the form template. While it's useful to be able to apply permission to restrict designing your form template, the real power of IRM is revealed when users fill out forms.

Permission on Forms

Applying IRM to form filling is where most of its value is realized. You can define the following permissions to restrict individual forms.

- Read-only, read/write, or full control can be granted for specific users.
- Printing the form can be disabled.
- Copying data from the form can be disabled.
- Driving InfoPath programmatically can be disallowed.
- The contents of the resulting form (.xml) file can be encrypted.

To set up IRM for a form, you need not have IRM defined on the form template. However, for the first part of our discussion, we'll enable IRM for forms (which creates a default policy for new forms) while designing the corresponding form template. Then we'll show you how to enable IRM while filling out a form, whether or not the form template has specific form permission.

Let's continue from our earlier discussion about enabling IRM for a form template. To enable permission on all newly filled-out forms from the current form template, enable the *Restrict permission to forms based on this form template* checkbox (refer back to Figure 11.54). Once you select the checkbox, the *Custom permission* option button is selected with default form permission. Default permission is very restrictive for new forms. Click the *Change permissions* button to open the dialog shown in Figure 11.57. This dialog shows that the form owner (i.e., the user who created the new form) has the *Full Control* setting. Nobody else will have permission to open the form. To grant permission to users who can open the form, you can add them by clicking the *Add* button. You can change the access level settings for each user to either *Read*, *Change*, or *Full Control*; however, the owner's setting must be *Full Control* and cannot be altered.

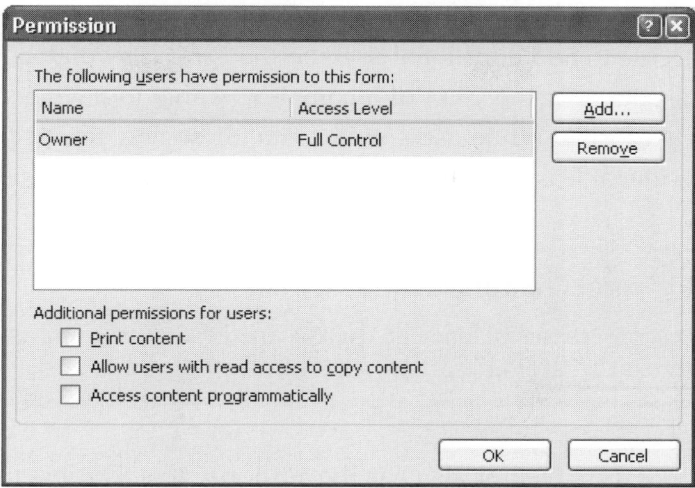

FIGURE 11.57: Specifying permission during design mode to apply when the form is filled out

> **WARNING Form Permission at Design Time Is Not Enforced**
>
> Form permission set up when the form template was designed can be circumvented by users who have the *Full Control* setting for their access level. This level is granted by default to the user who creates a new form.

In addition to granting permission to individual users or groups in the *Permission* dialog, you can also specify additional default permission to users who do not have full control. This permission includes the following settings:

- *Print content*
- *Allow users with read access to copy content*
- *Access content programmatically*

If a form template was designed with the *Restrict permission to forms based on this form template* setting enabled in the dialog shown earlier in Figure 11.54, all new forms will have IRM permission applied automatically when filled out. As mentioned, the user who created the new form has full control. As a result, the form can be opened and changed only by that user. You may decide to add additional users to the *Permission* dialog, however. Say, for example, that the CEO of a company wants to have access to all newly created forms. While users who create these new forms can revoke that permission, at least they'll see that the CEO is supposed to have access!

> **NOTE** Form Creators Must Be Owners
>
> The user who creates a form is always an owner. It is impossible to grant the form creator any other permission by default.

Similarly, a form creator also has the authority to add users to the *Read* and *Change* access control list for his or her particular form. This is easily accomplished by clicking on the *Permission* toolbar button when filling out a form. (The button's icon is the same as the one shown earlier for design mode in Figure 11.53.) Clicking on the *Permission* toolbar button brings up the *Permission* dialog, shown in Figure 11.58, which allows users with full control to this form to change IRM permission. If the current user has read or change permission instead of full control, this dialog will not be available for changes.

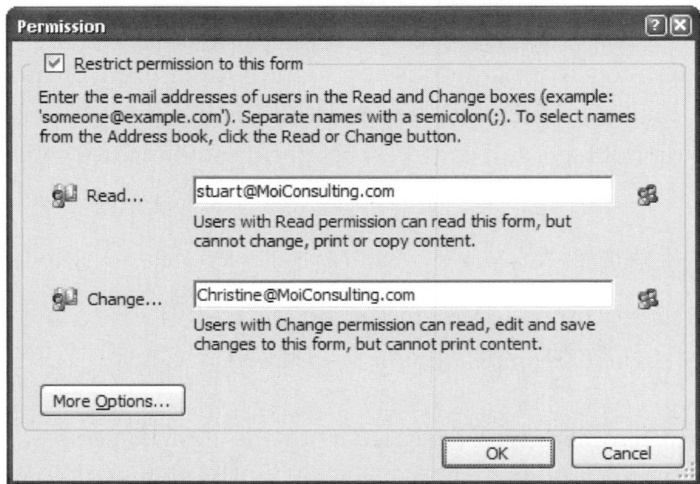

FIGURE 11.58: Specifying permission for the current form while filling it out

> **NOTE Accessing Permission When Filling Out a Form**
>
> In addition to the *Permission* toolbar button, there's an alternate entry point within the *File* menu under the *Permission* submenu.

An alternative to clicking on the *Permission* button in the toolbar is to use the *Form Permission* task pane (Figure 11.59). This task pane appears automatically when you open a form with IRM permission. Click the *Change permission* link to open the *Permission* dialog shown in Figure 11.58. The *Change User* link provides the current user the opportunity to run the form as a different user.

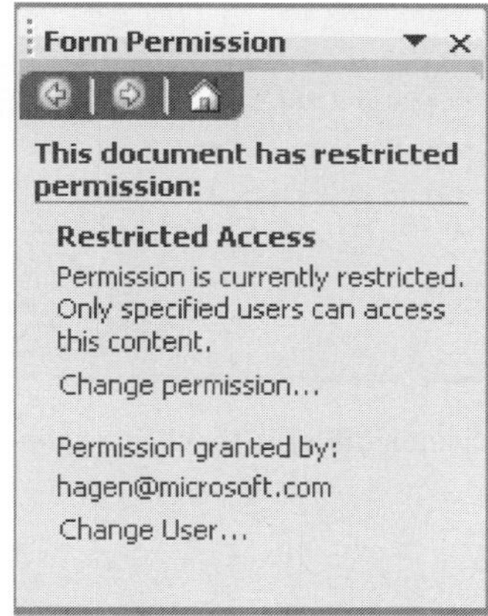

FIGURE 11.59: Form Permission task pane

> **NOTE Form Permission Task Pane**
>
> The *Form Permission* task pane shown in Figure 11.59 is for a user with full control. If a user with read or change permissions opens the form, the task pane will look a little different. The *Change permission* link will instead say *View my permission*. Also, the *Permission granted by* section is not shown.

Let's go back and look at the *Permission* dialog shown in Figure 11.58. This dialog is very straightforward in its intent. However, it's not very configurable. What if you want to allow users with read permission to copy

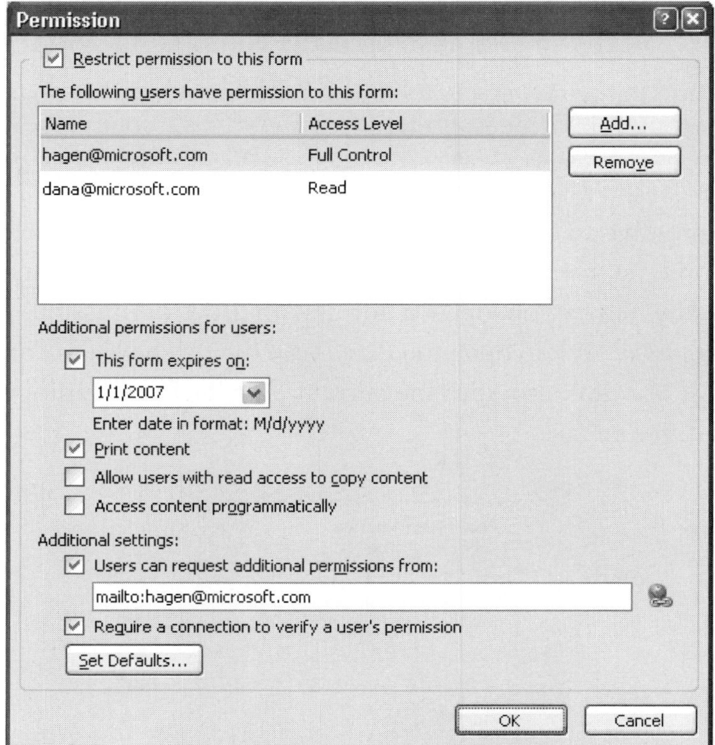

FIGURE 11.60: Permission dialog after clicking the More Options button

content? How about giving users with change permission the ability to print? Click on the *More Options* button to show a dialog with more granular control over specific permissions (Figure 11.60).

The resulting dialog offers the same level of control as the previous dialog shown in Figure 11.58. However, you will quickly notice the larger size of the dialog due to the settings below the caption *Additional permissions for users.* This dialog lets you do the following:

- Set form expiration
- Allow all users to print content and/or access content programmatically
- Allow users with read access to copy content

- Define a link to give restricted users a way to request additional permission
- Require a connection to the RMS server to verify permission

As shown in Figure 11.60, there are numerous options to control permission to your form. Let's explore each of these options to understand the impact on users. First on the list is the *This form expires on* combo box. This setting, when enabled, accepts any date between tomorrow and the last day of the year 2100. It's not possible to set form expiration any sooner, nor can you set an exact time for expiration. When the day of the form expiration occurs, all users with read and change permissions will be unable to open the form.

As is clear in Figure 11.58, users granted read and change permissions are not allowed to print the form. One of the core restrictions of IRM is to disallow the disseminating of information, so printing seems like a natural candidate for restriction. However, there are cases when you'll want to relax such stringency. For InfoPath forms, a user with full control may enable the *Print content* setting shown in Figure 11.60. Doing so permits users with at least read permission to use the *Print* command when filling out the form.

> **NOTE Additional Permission Cannot Apply to Specific Users**
>
> The settings under the *Additional permissions for users* heading (shown in Figure 11.60) cannot be scoped to specific users or groups. Enabling additional permission applies to all users with read or change permissions.

The *Allow users with read access to copy content* option is pretty self-explanatory. Enabling this setting simply gives users with read permission the ability to copy data to the clipboard. Like printing, copying to the clipboard is yet another feature that is important for IRM to restrict and thus discourage information redistribution. Enabling this checkbox will allow anyone with read access to copy and paste data from the form into another program.

The last permission-based option is *Access content programmatically.* This is an advanced setting that, when enabled, permits an external process (or even another InfoPath form) to access the current form. Since InfoPath exposes an application-based object model for opening and interacting with the form, it is yet another avenue where data can leak out. By default, external programs automating InfoPath have no access to a form with defined IRM permission. Checking this option allows programmatic access to the form data, but only as much as the user currently filling out the form has. In other words, if a user with read permission is viewing a form and the *Access content programmatically* setting is enabled, an external program is also granted read permission to the form data.

We have yet to discuss two more settings shown in Figure 11.60, those under the *Additional settings* heading. The first checkbox, *Users can request additional permission from,* has a corresponding text box. This setting, when checked, creates a *Request additional permissions* link in the dialog that appears when a user without full control clicks the *View my permission* link in the *Form Permission* task pane. You can see the *Request additional permissions* link back in Figure 11.56. The URL entered in the text box for requesting additional permissions can be any Web page or an e-mail address, as shown in Figure 11.60. When a user requests additional permissions, clicking on the *Request additional permissions* link either opens the URL (if it's a Web page) in a browser or launches the user's e-mail client with an empty message addressed to the specified address (in our example, hagen@microsoft.com).

The second setting under the *Additional settings* heading is *Require a connection to verify a user's permission.* While subtle, what this checkbox really means is that permission should not be cached. The motivation behind caching permission is for offline scenarios. Say that a user opens a form with read permission while on the corporate network in the office. Nothing should prevent the same user from opening the form that evening while on his or her flight to Boston. The only reason to check this checkbox is if permission is changing very often and you don't want IRM permission to be cached on a user's computer. Keep in mind that enabling this checkbox essentially prevents users with restricted permission from opening the form without a network connection to the RMS server.

Permission with Document Libraries

SharePoint Server 2007 allows IRM permission to apply to a document library. The purpose of using IRM with a library is to enforce the policy for all items contained in that library. While the implications of IRM on a library span beyond InfoPath scenarios, we'll limit our discussion to InfoPath forms.

IRM on a document library is meant to supplement the IRM features for InfoPath forms. Many of the IRM-specific features available when filling out a form are also offered in the library. For example, you can allow users who have restricted (i.e., read or change) permission to print documents. While there is quite a bit of parity between InfoPath and SharePoint document library IRM (as we'll soon see), library IRM does not replace form IRM. In fact, form IRM, when defined, takes precedence and supersedes IRM defined on the library. If the form does not restrict permission and the library does, IRM will apply to the form as if it were defined on the form itself.

Before you can enable IRM on a document library, you must enable IRM on the SharePoint Central Administration site. As a farm administrator, go to the Central Administration site and visit the *Operations* page. Under *Security Configuration*, click on the *Information Rights Management* link. Figure 11.61 shows the resulting page. Select the appropriate option depending on whether you want to use the default RMS server from Active Directory or specify your own server.

> **TIP Specifying an RMS Server**
>
> If you enter your own RMS server, precede the server name with "http://".

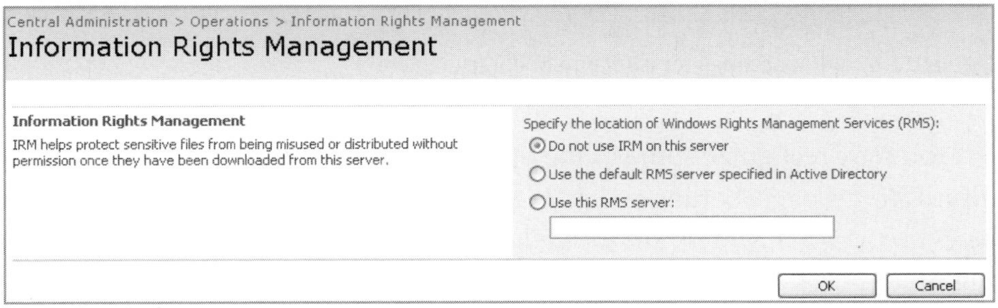

Central Administration > Operations > Information Rights Management
Information Rights Management
Information Rights Management
IRM helps protect sensitive files from being misused or distributed without permission once they have been downloaded from this server.
Specify the location of Windows Rights Management Services (RMS):
Do not use IRM on this server
Use the default RMS server specified in Active Directory
Use this RMS server:
OK Cancel

FIGURE 11.61: Enabling Information Rights Management on the SharePoint Central Administration site

After you enable IRM on the SharePoint Central Administration site, any of your SharePoint site applications and collections will be ready to define an IRM permission policy. (A policy is simply something applied to all new and even existing items in a library.) To define a policy on a document library, first visit the library. Next, select the *Document Library Settings* menu item on the *Settings* menu. Note that you must have at least a SharePoint design role to see the *Settings* menu. On the resulting *Customize* page, click on the *Information Rights Management* link to navigate to the *Information Rights Management Settings* page (Figure 11.62). If you do not see the *Information Rights Management* link on the *Customize* page, the Central Administration site was not properly configured for IRM.

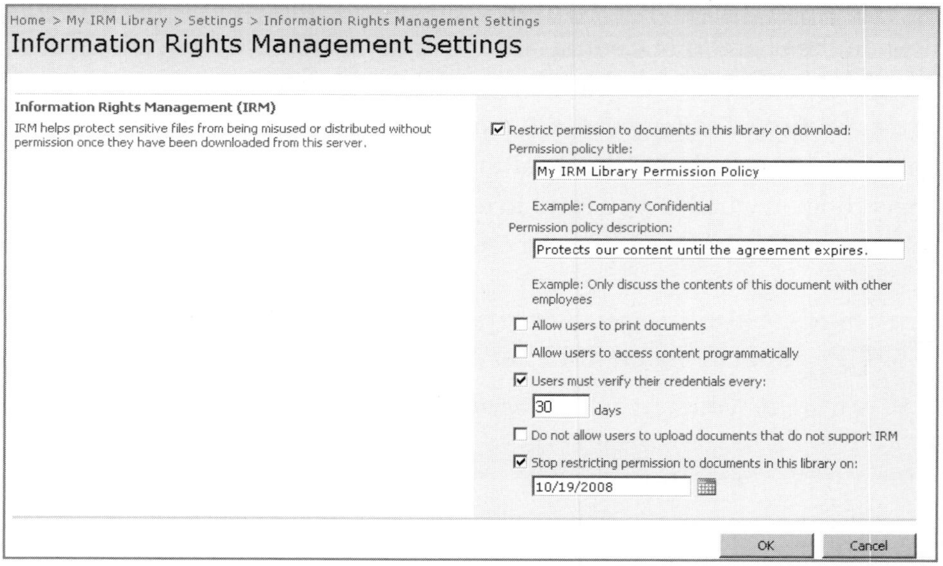

Home > My IRM Library > Settings > Information Rights Management Settings

Information Rights Management Settings

Information Rights Management (IRM)

IRM helps protect sensitive files from being misused or distributed without permission once they have been downloaded from this server.

☑ Restrict permission to documents in this library on download:

Permission policy title:

My IRM Library Permission Policy

Example: Company Confidential

Permission policy description:

Protects our content until the agreement expires.

Example: Only discuss the contents of this document with other employees

☐ Allow users to print documents

☐ Allow users to access content programmatically

☑ Users must verify their credentials every:

30 days

☐ Do not allow users to upload documents that do not support IRM

☑ Stop restricting permission to documents in this library on:

10/19/2008

OK Cancel

FIGURE 11.62: IRM settings for a document library

You may recognize some of the options in the *Information Rights Management Settings* page. Settings such as *Allow users to print documents* and *Allow users to access content programmatically* carry over from InfoPath. The remaining preferences are specific to the SharePoint document library. These extra settings are enforced by SharePoint and carry out at the library level rather than on the form itself. For example, the settings shown in Figure 11.62 specify the following permissions for this library.

- Users must verify their credentials every 30 days.
- Users are not allowed to upload documents that do not support IRM.
- SharePoint will stop restricting permission to documents in this library on October 19, 2008.

Now that you know a little about IRM with document libraries, there's one missing (and quite large) element: How can we set IRM permission for specific users? Granting or denying permission to users is yet another action that must be carried out with administrative permission on the document library. Similar to how you accessed the IRM settings page, click on the *Permissions for this form library* link on the same *Customize* page you visited earlier. The page that results from clicking *Permissions for this form library* defines users and groups with specific permissions. Table 11.5 shows the list of SharePoint roles and how they map to InfoPath form permissions. Keep in mind that Table 11.5 assumes that default permissions for SharePoint roles have not been changed from their out-of-box settings.

TABLE 11.5: Mapping of Default SharePoint Roles to IRM Permissions

SharePoint Roles	Description	IRM Permission
Full Control	Has full control.	Full Control
Design	Can view, add, update, delete, approve, and customize.	Change
Contribute	Can view, add, update, and delete.	Change
Read	Can view only.	Read
Limited Access	Can view specific lists, document libraries, list items, folders, or documents when given permission.	Read
View Only	Can view pages, list items, and documents. If the document has a server-side file handler available, these group members are limited to viewing the document using the server-side file handler.	Read

Table 11.6 shows the exact SharePoint permissions that map to IRM permissions. To see what permissions are granted, navigate to the SharePoint site in your browser. (You'll need to have *Manage Permissions* permission to do so.) Select the *Site Settings* item on the *Site Actions* button on the default page. Under the *Users and Permissions* heading, click on the *Advanced permissions* link. On the *Settings* button of the resulting permissions page, select *Permission Levels*. Clicking on an item in the *Permission Level* column will show the *Edit Permission Level* page where the permissions in Table 11.6 are defined.

TABLE 11.6: Direct Mapping of SharePoint Permissions to IRM

SharePoint Permission	IRM Permission
(Any file access)	Read
Manage Lists Edit Items Add and Customize Pages	Change
Manage Permissions Manage Web Site (WSS Search process)	Full Control

What's Next?

We've concluded our concentrated discussion about the security and trust aspects of designing InfoPath form templates. We also talked all about digital signatures and the various ways form data can be signed. Finally, we looked at how to use Information Rights Management to protect our form templates and especially our forms from prying eyes.

In the next chapter, we'll look into various real-world applications of InfoPath. You'll discover how to exploit its data-exporting capabilities by creating reports and transforming data into different formats. InfoPath is a powerful application for gathering data and participating in workflow scenarios, but it isn't always the best choice for analyzing data. The next chapter will highlight the many options for exporting and presenting your data in the ways you'll want.

12 Creating Reports

Getting Started

By now, you know a lot about designing forms with InfoPath 2007. Once you've published a form and your users start putting it to use, it's only natural that they will want to create reports based on the form. For example, let's say that you've created a status report form template. Using this form template, users can create forms that include their status for the past week, month, or quarter, for example. It's highly likely that each manager would want to receive a report that combines all the status reports for the employees on his or her team. Of course, the head of the department will probably want the same report for all the teams in the department. Finally, the vice president may want to see an aggregate report for all the departments under his or her control. This status report form template is a very simple example. However, this type of scenario also applies to other cases, such as expense or sales reports. The payroll department will probably want to receive an aggregate report of all the expenses for each department, for example. Likewise, the vice president of sales will want to receive a quarterly report of all the sales for the department.

Once people in management receive one of these aggregate reports, they will probably want to export the data to an HTML or PDF file for printing. Or, most probably, they will want to export the data to an Excel spreadsheet to analyze the data or create a fancy pivot table or chart. In all these cases, the ultimate goal is probably to print the report so that it can be distributed to all the interested parties in the company.

In this chapter, we'll show you how to design your form templates so that this process will go smoothly for users who fill out forms based on them. We'll show you how to specify in design mode how the data should be merged when creating one of these aggregate reports. We'll also show you how to customize different print settings for your form templates so they behave a certain way when users print their forms. Finally, we'll talk about how users can export your forms when filling them out so they can create professional-looking reports or analyze the data in Excel. First, though, let's talk about merging multiple forms and how you specify at design time how data in the forms should be combined.

Merging Forms

Let's take a closer look at the status report scenario we touched on in the previous section. Let's say that you are a manager of a small group of form designers. You have four employees reporting to you. You report to a team leader, Tom, who has other managers besides you reporting to him as well as other employees who are not managers. He, in turn, reports to a group manager, Andrea, who has managers from all the teams in the department reporting to her.

At the end of each week, Andrea wants to see a status report for all the employees on her team. Therefore, each Friday, every employee in the department fills out the status report shown in Figure 12.1. (We'll explain how this form template is designed shortly.) At the end of each week, Andrea must go through each status report form one by one to see the status of each employee in her department. This is extremely tedious. Therefore, Andrea asks each of the team leaders in her department to create one status report that aggregates all the status reports for each of their teams. Andrea could then merge all the status reports into one aggregate report for the entire department.

Normally, with other form tools, creating an aggregate report would be very tedious and would likely require you to write a lot of code. With

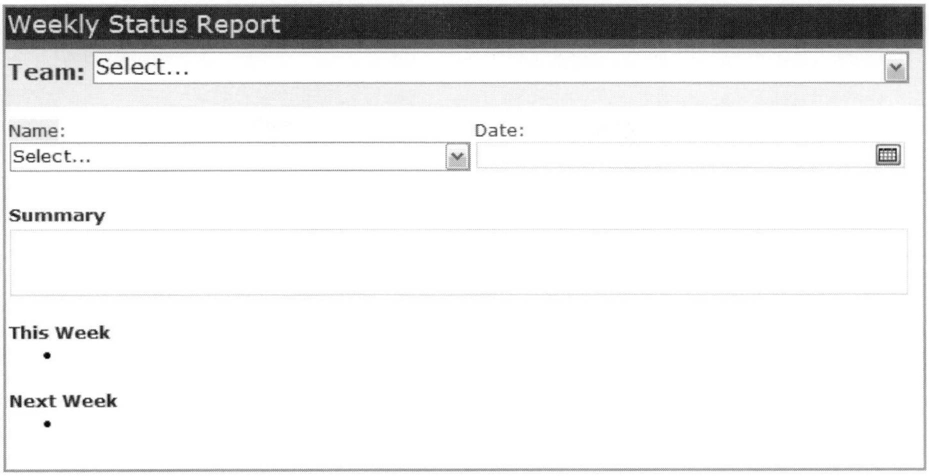

Weekly Status Report

Team: Select...

Name: Select...

Date:

Summary

This Week

Next Week

Figure 12.1: Weekly status report form

InfoPath, however, you can merge multiple forms without having to write even one line of code.

Merging Forms in InfoPath

Before we talk about how to merge multiple forms into one report, let's identify how the workflow will occur in this scenario. First, everybody in the department will fill out a status report form. The forms could be saved to a network folder, but it's likely that you'll want to save them to a Microsoft Office SharePoint Server (MOSS) 2007 document library. In fact, to make the forms easier to deal with, you'll probably want to have one SharePoint document library for each of the subteams in the department. (This will make the process of creating a merged status report much easier, as you will see shortly.)

Once your employees have filled out their status reports for the week, you will create a merged status report for all the employees on your subteam. Then your manager, Tom, will create an aggregate report that includes all the employees and subteams that report to him. This is the report that Tom will give to Andrea. Finally, Andrea may choose to create an aggregate report of the status for all the teams in her department.

Creating these aggregate reports in InfoPath is very easy. For simplicity, let's create a report that includes the status from only two employees on

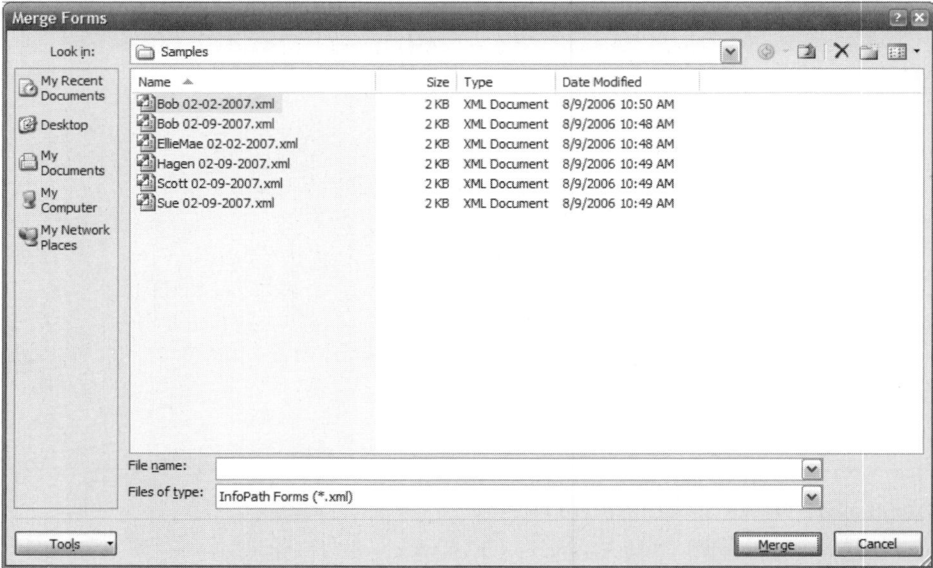

FIGURE 12.2: Merge Forms dialog

your team. There are two ways to do this. The first way is to open the status report form and then choose the *Merge Forms* item from the *File* menu. When you do, the *Merge Forms* dialog opens (Figure 12.2). From this dialog, you can choose one or more forms from your local machine, a network share, a Web site, or a SharePoint document library (just as you can when opening a form or form template). When you merge forms by using this method, we recommend that you start with a blank copy of the type of form you are going to merge. In this case, start by opening a new instance of the status report form.

Forms Services

Merging forms is not directly available in Forms Services as it is in InfoPath. As a workaround, you can merge the forms in InfoPath or just use SharePoint.

As an alternative to merging the forms from within InfoPath, you can also choose the forms to merge from a SharePoint document library. When

> **TIP Selecting Multiple Forms in the Merge Forms Dialog**
>
> If you want to choose multiple forms to merge in the *Merge Forms* dialog and you have browsed to a folder on your local machine or a network share, simply hold down the Ctrl key while clicking on each file you want to merge. However, if you browse to a SharePoint document library, this behavior is disabled by default. To enable it, click on the down arrow next to the *Views* button in the upper-right corner of the dialog, as shown in Figure 12.3. From the *Views* menu, choose anything other than *WebView.* Then just hold down the Ctrl key while clicking on each file to select multiple files to merge. Hint: When merging multiple forms, the order in which the files are merged is the reverse order of how they are selected in the *Merge Forms* dialog.

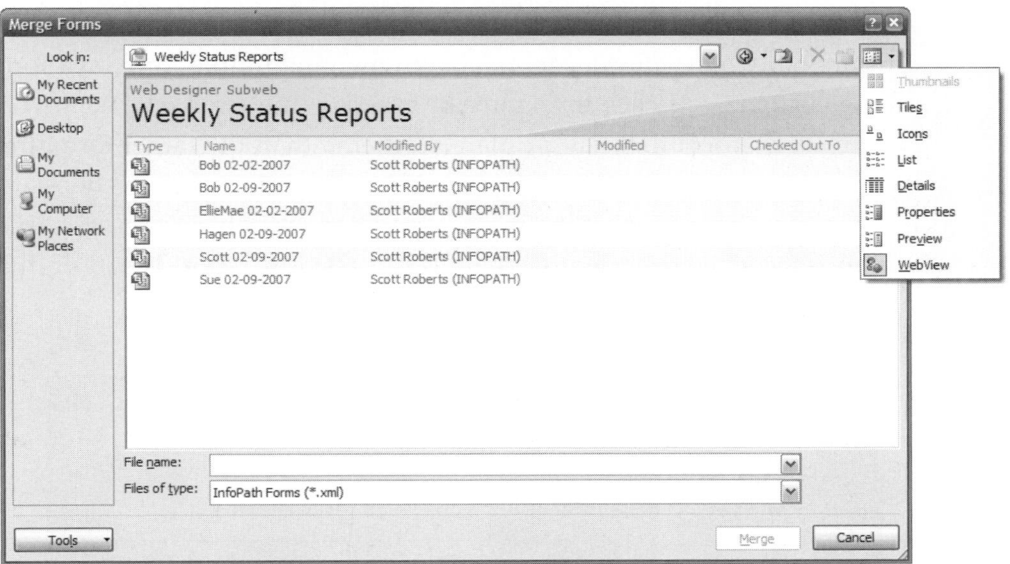

FIGURE 12.3: Merge Forms dialog showing the Views menu

you open the SharePoint document library that contains all the status reports for your team, you can merge them by clicking on the *All Documents* button at the top of the document library. Then, choose *Merge Documents.* When you do, you will see a view of your documents similar to the one shown in Figure 12.4. From here, you can select the checkbox next to each of the forms you want to merge. When you have finished choosing all the

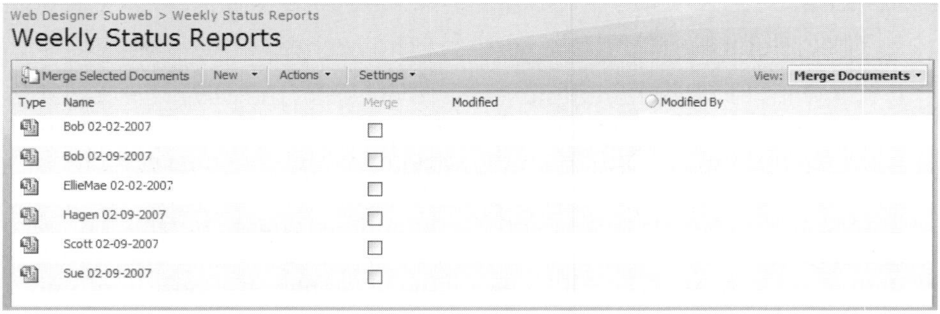

FIGURE 12.4: Weekly status report document library in Merge Forms view

forms you want to merge, just click the *Merge Selected Documents* link. InfoPath will then open, and all the chosen documents will be merged into one status report.

In either case, whether you intend to merge forms from within InfoPath or from SharePoint, in order to be able to merge multiple forms without writing custom code, each form must be based on the same schema. If you try to merge a form that has a different schema than the target form, the dialog shown in Figure 12.5 is displayed. At this point, you can choose to continue merging or cancel the merge operation entirely. In our case, this isn't an issue since every employee fills out a status report based on the

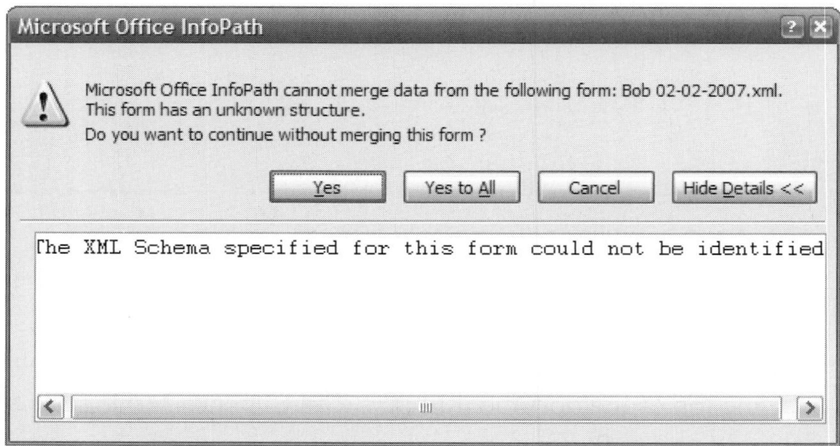

FIGURE 12.5: Merge error dialog for forms with a schema that doesn't match the target form

same form template. Therefore, all the forms we will merge will be based on the same schema.

> **NOTE Target and Source Forms**
>
> In InfoPath as well as this book, we refer to a form as a **target** when it is the target of a merge. In other words, when you open a form and merge other forms into it, the form you opened originally is the target form. **Source** forms are those forms that you are merging into the target form.

When you have finished merging all the forms, an aggregate report similar to that shown in Figure 12.6 is created. So, you can see that by using the default merge functionality in InfoPath, you can easily create a merged status report that you can give to your manager. However, in this case,

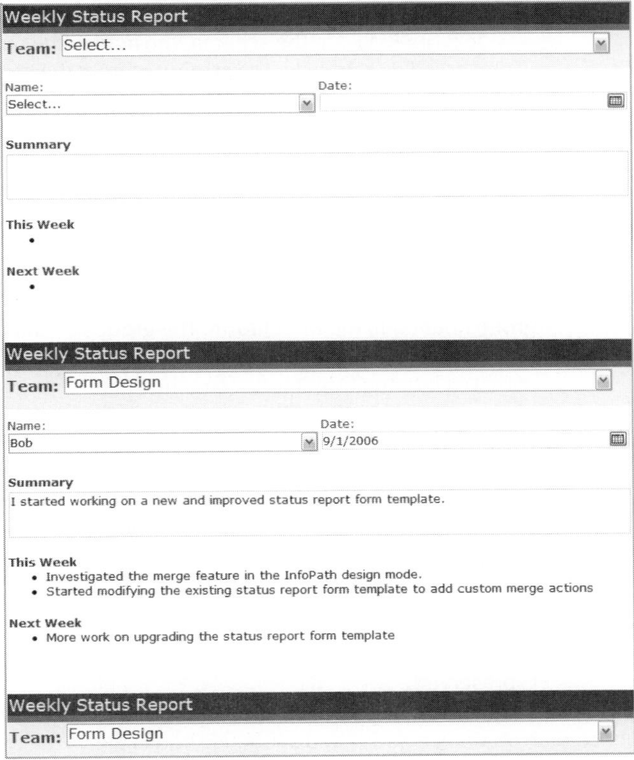

FIGURE 12.6: Merged status report form

InfoPath follows a simple set of rules to determine which action to perform when merging each of the data items in the form. These merge actions, which are listed in Table 12.1, are based on the type of node in the form. As you can see in Figure 12.6, the default action did merge the data, but it's not exactly what you want. Each employee's status report was inserted into the open form one by one. What you really want is to have the status reports for all the employees on each team combined. Also, the top of the form has an empty status report section that was there to begin with. You likely want all empty sections removed since they don't contain any data. Luckily, when designing a form template, InfoPath allows you to customize how to merge the different data items in the form.

TABLE 12.1: Default Merge Actions Based on Node Type

Node Type	Default Merge Action
Field	Preserve the value in the target form. (Note that if a node has `maxOccurs = "1"` in the schema, the field in the target form is preserved. In this case, the attributes from the source forms are merged into the target node. If `maxOccurs> "1"`, the target node is preserved.)
Group	Combine the contents of the groups in the source and target forms. (The same action applies for group nodes as for fields when it comes to the `maxOccurs` attribute.)
Repeating field or group	Insert the groups from the source forms after the corresponding group node(s) in the target form. The groups are not combined, and empty groups are preserved. Child nodes are inserted verbatim into the target form (i.e., the default merge actions are not applied to the child nodes).
Attribute	If the attribute is a child of a nonrepeating field, the value of the matching attribute in the target form is replaced with the value of the attribute from the source form. If you are merging multiple forms, the attribute in the target form will have the value of the last form merged. If the attribute is a child of a group (repeating or not) or a repeating field, the value of the attribute in the target form is preserved.
Choice/sequence	N/A. Choice nodes and sequence nodes are virtual, so they do not exist in the XML data source.

Design Recommendations for Merging Forms

When in design mode in InfoPath, you can easily customize the way data is merged when a user fills out a form. As you saw in the last section, the default merge behavior provided by InfoPath works reasonably well but will not enable you to do such things as combine similar data in the merged form based on a set of rules. For example, when we merge data from different weekly status report forms, ideally, we would like the data to be broken down first by team and then by employee name. Also, when the data is combined, we would like to customize the way that summary information is separated and also remove the empty status report item we saw in Figure 12.6.

Before we talk about how to customize the merge behavior for the different fields and groups in a form template, it's important to go over a few recommendations for designing form templates that will work well when merging multiple forms. When designing your form template, you should determine ahead of time how you want to merge the data. Since you will be combining data from multiple forms into one, the first recommendation is to make sure your form contains a repeating group node into which the data from multiple forms will be combined. For example, take a look at the data source for the status report form template (Figure 12.7). You will

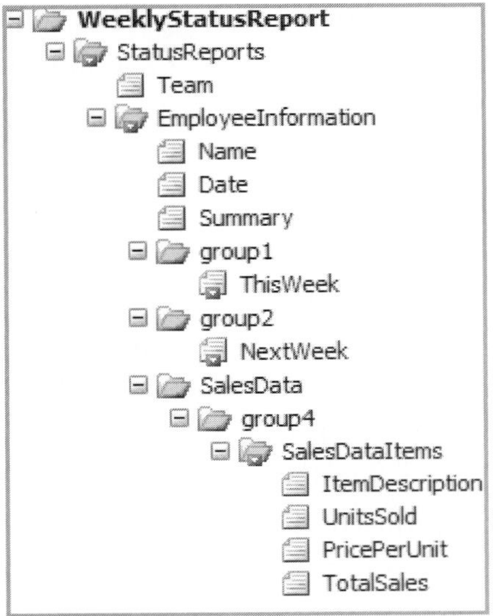

FIGURE 12.7: Data source for the status report form template

notice that the first node under the root node (`WeeklyStatusReport`) is a repeating group node named `StatusReports`. Since we will be merging multiple status report forms into one, it makes sense that our form template contains a repeating group node that will store all the status report data. If we tried to merge multiple status reports into a nonrepeating node, we would be able to store only one status report.

The second recommendation is to think ahead of time about how you want to merge the data. In our case, we want our aggregate report to be grouped by team and then by employee name. Even though this is a weekly status report form, we could merge status reports from multiple weeks into one report. Because each employee belongs to only one team (in most companies), there is a field called `Team` that is a child of the `StatusReports` group node. (You will see why this is important later when we specify the merge behavior for the `StatusReports` repeating group node.) Each employee can have multiple status reports (one for each week), so our data source also contains a repeating group node, `EmployeeInformation`, which contains the employee's status for each week.

One final recommendation is that it may be useful to create a separate view in which you will merge the status report form. This is by no means a requirement. It's a simple recommendation that may make life easier for those who are filling out the status report. Let's see why this would be useful. As we just mentioned, in order to merge the data from multiple forms, it's necessary to create a data source that contains at least one repeating group node into which the data will be merged. Normally, when you design a form template based on a schema that contains repeating group nodes, you will bind Repeating Section or Repeating Table controls to the repeating group nodes. Usually, this works fine. However, in the case of a form template such as a weekly status report, you may want to restrict your users to entering status information for only one week at a time. In that case, you would want to bind Section controls to the repeating group nodes in the data source. Figure 12.8 shows the *Weekly Status Report* view of our status report form template. This view contains Section controls bound to the repeating group nodes so that users who fill out this form can enter status information for only one week at a time. Also, one other thing to note, which will be important later, is that there is a Section control that

Weekly Status Report

Team: Select...

Name: Select...

Date:

Summary

This Week

Bulleted List

Next Week

Bulleted List

Sales Data

Item Description	Units Sold	Price Per Unit	Total

Repeating Table

Total Sales: $0.00

Section

Section

Section

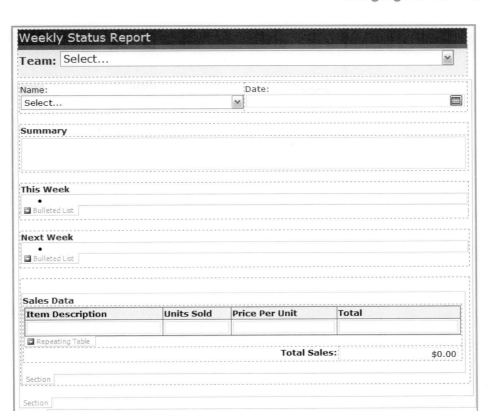

FIGURE 12.8: Weekly Status Report view in the weekly status report form template

contains sales data. When a user fills out the form, this Section is hidden (by using conditional formatting) unless the sales team is chosen from the *Team* Combo Box control.

The Section controls in the *Weekly Status Report* view certainly make it easier for you to prevent users from entering status information for more than one week at a time. However, when you merge data from multiple status reports, this design will enable you to show data from only one status report. (This is the nature of the Section control when bound to a repeating group node. The data from multiple forms will be merged into the data source but, since we are using Section controls in the view, only the first item in each repeating group node will be displayed.) So, in order to show the data that is merged from multiple forms, you can create a separate view

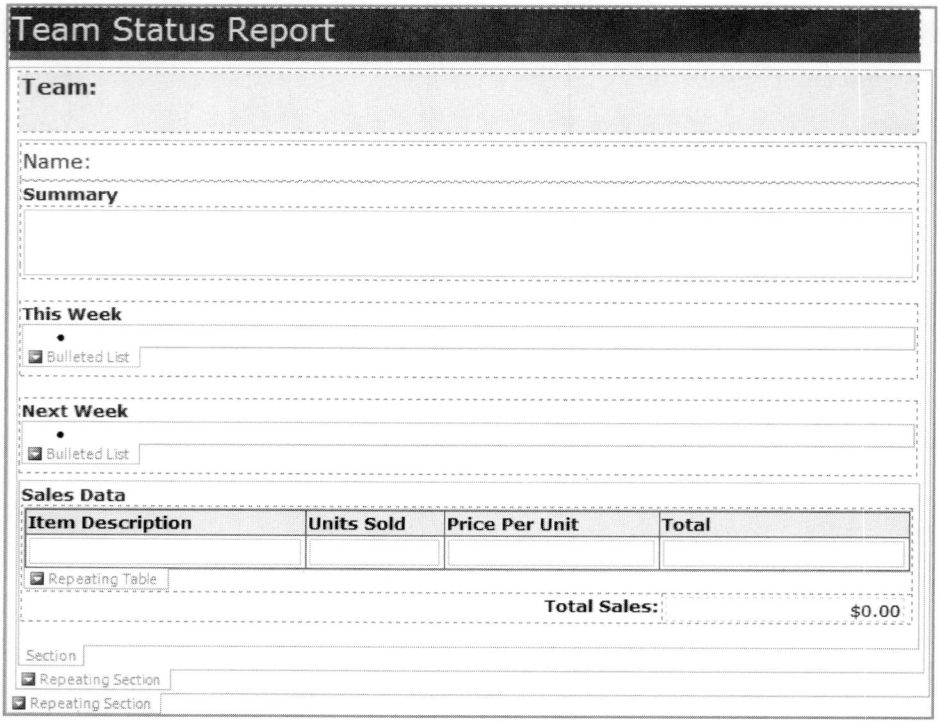

FIGURE 12.9: Team Status Report view for merging multiple status report forms

that contains Repeating Section controls bound to the repeating group nodes instead. Figure 12.9 shows the *Team Status Report* view, which we will use to view the data merged from multiple status reports. (What you can't see from the figure is that this view is marked as read-only since the data is for reporting purposes only. We've done this so our users can't use this view to enter data for multiple weeks or teams. You could further restrict this view to managers only, for example, by using roles, which we'll talk about in Chapter 13.)

Customizing Merge Behavior in Design Mode

Now that we've designed a form template that will work well when merging multiple forms, let's look at how you can customize the merge behavior for the different field and group nodes in the form template. As we mentioned earlier, the way data is merged is based on the type of each node in the form. (Refer back to Table 12.1 to see the default merge actions based on node type.) Therefore, when you customize the merge behavior for a field or group node in the data source, the different options available are based on the type of node and not the controls bound to the node. This will make much more sense if we walk through an example.

As we mentioned earlier, we want our status reports to be merged first by team name and then by employee name. The default merge behavior we saw in Figure 12.6 simply inserts each of the status report forms into the current form. The data is merged into the target form, but the data is not combined in the way we want. Obviously, we want to merge all the status report data into the target form, which is the default behavior for repeating group nodes. However, the first change we want to make to the default behavior is to combine any data in the `StatusReports` repeating group nodes in the source forms with those in the target form where their team names match.

In order to combine the `StatusReports` group nodes where the values of the `Team` nodes match, we must customize the merge behavior for the `StatusReports` group node. There are two ways to do this. Since the merge behavior is based on the node type, the first way to do this is through the *Field or Group Properties* dialog, which is available by right-clicking on a field or group in the *Data Source* pane and choosing *Properties* (or double-clicking on a field or group in the *Data Source* pane). This dialog contains a tab called *Rules and Merge* (Figure 12.10). This tab contains a *Merge Settings* button that, when clicked, allows you to customize the merge behavior for a particular node, as we'll show you shortly. Not all types of nodes support merging (e.g., choice and sequence). Therefore, the *Rules and Merge* tab is not available for every type of node supported by InfoPath.

The second way to customize the merge settings for a node is through the properties dialog for a control bound to a field or group. But wait! Didn't we just say that the merge behavior is based on the type of node and has nothing to do with any controls bound to the node? Yes, that is still true. However, remember that several data-centric properties are exposed through the properties dialog for a control, such as the field or group name and the data type. These data-centric properties are available through the control properties dialog merely as a convenience. In the case of the control

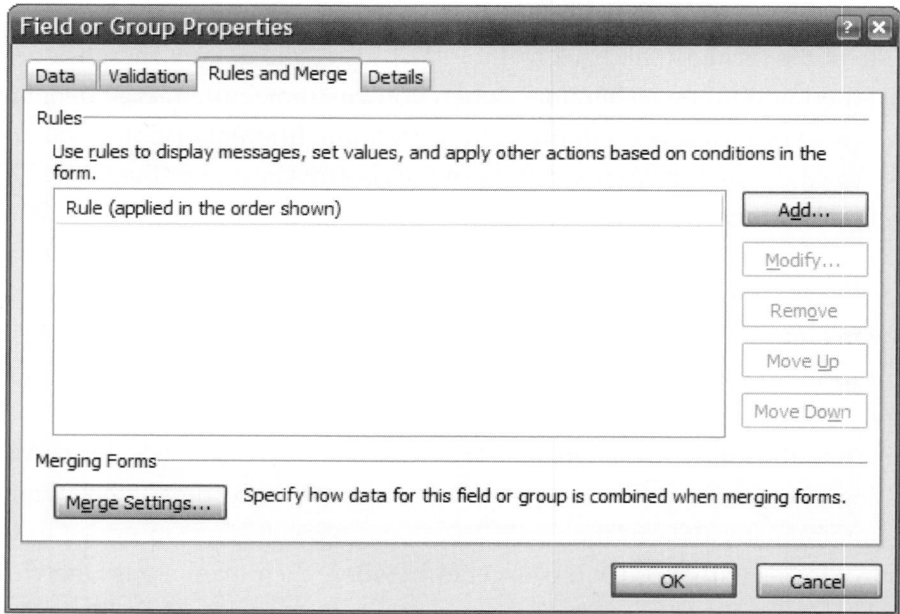

FIGURE 12.10: Rules and Merge tab on the Field or Group Properties dialog

properties dialog, the *Merge Settings* button is available on the *Advanced* tab of the dialog. (As is the case for the *Field and Group Properties* dialog, the *Merge Settings* button isn't available on the *Advanced* tab of all control properties dialog.) Figure 12.11 shows the *Advanced* tab of the *Repeating Section Properties* dialog.

You should note one thing about customizing the merge action through the control properties dialog. Since merge actions are based on the type of node to which a control is bound and not on the control itself, the type of customizations you can perform may be different for the same type of control. For example, it is possible to bind a Section control to both a repeating and a nonrepeating group node. In these cases, the customizations available from the *Merge Settings* button in the *Section Properties* dialog will be different.

Now, let's go back to our status report example and create the customizations necessary to merge the data in the `StatusReports` repeating group node based on the value of the `Team` name. Using database terminology,

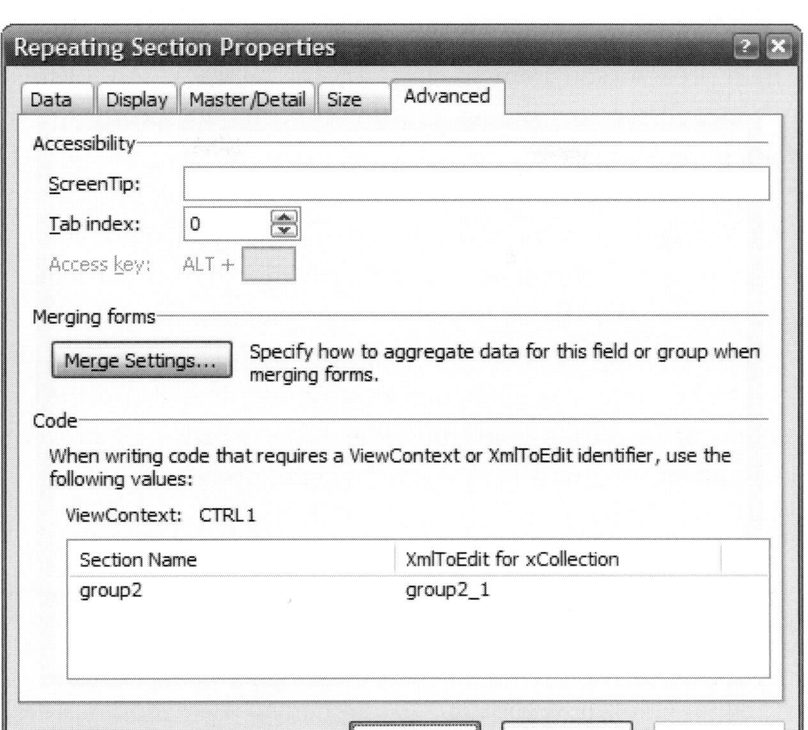

FIGURE 12.11: Advanced tab of the Repeating Section Properties dialog

you can think of the `Team` node as the key whose value will be used to perform a join (or match) between multiple `StatusReports` nodes. At first, you may be tempted to open the *Field or Group Properties* dialog for the `Team` field and click on the *Merge Settings* button, thinking that this is the correct place to specify the match criteria. When you do, however, the dialog shown in Figure 12.12 will be displayed.

Microsoft Office InfoPath

The merge settings of the parent group prevent this field from being merged directly with other fields of this type. To change merge settings for this field, first change the merge settings for the parent group.

OK

FIGURE 12.12: Merge settings error dialog

This error dialog tells you that the merge settings of the parent group for this field prevent you from customizing the merge action for this field directly. You will see this dialog any time you try to specify the merge action for a node that has an ancestor whose current merge action settings prevent you from customizing those of the current node. In order to customize the merge action for this particular node, you must change the merge settings for the parent or ancestor node first. In this particular case, the reason you see this dialog is that the merge action for the `StatusReports` repeating group node has not been specified. Therefore, because the `StatusReports` node is a repeating group node, it will use the default merge action of insert (as listed in Table 12.1), which will prevent any merge customizations on child nodes from being processed.

> **NOTE Merge Settings for a Key Field**
>
> Be careful when customizing the merge settings for a field that is used as the key for combining multiple group nodes. If you add a prefix to the key field, those fields in the source forms may not match when you perform the merge, which might result in an incorrectly merged form.

The fix for this is easy—change the merge action for the `StatusReports` repeating group node, which also happens to be the correct place to specify the match criteria that will join the group nodes based on team name. To make this customization, open the *Field or Group Properties* dialog for the `StatusReports` repeating group node, and click on the *Merge Settings* button. When you do, the *Merge Settings* dialog opens (Figure 12.13). This dialog allows you to customize the merge settings for a particular node. As we mentioned, the types of customizations you can perform are based on the type of node. Therefore, the *Merge Settings* dialog will look different

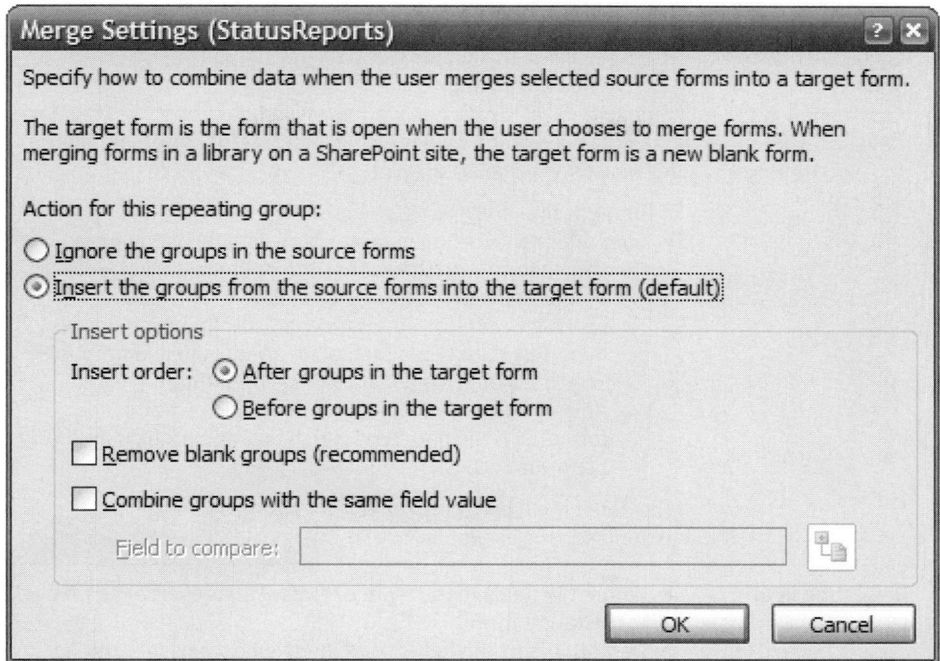

FIGURE 12.13: Merge Settings dialog for the `StatusReports` repeating group node

(sometimes radically) from one node type to the next. Table 12.2 shows the merge customizations available for each type of node supported by InfoPath.

When you first open the *Merge Settings* dialog for a node whose merge settings you've never customized, the merge action selected in the dialog will be the default for that type of node. (We've listed all the defaults in Table 12.2.) In the case of the `StatusReport` repeating group node, the default action is to insert the groups from the source forms into the target form. The default insert action is pretty simple, as you saw earlier when we merged multiple status reports using the default merge behavior. If there are any empty groups in the form, they will remain. Also, the data will not be combined in any way.

TABLE 12.2: Merge Customizations Available for Each Node Type

<table>
<tr><th>Node Type</th><th>Merge Actions Available</th></tr>
<tr><td>Field</td><td>If the data type of the field is string, rich text, or hyperlink, there are two options available:<ul><li>Default: Preserve the value in the target form.</li><li>Combine the value in the target form with the value from the source form with these possible options:<ul><li>Ignore blank fields (on by default).</li><li>Insert a separator—a single character for string or hyperlink data types (default is none), single or multiple characters for rich text (default is underline).</li><li>Add a prefix for each item (either static text or a formula). If the data type is rich text, the prefix may be formatted.</li></ul></li></ul>If the data type is anything other than string, no merge customization is available.</td></tr>
<tr><td>Repeating field</td><td><ul><li>Ignore the fields in the source forms (i.e., preserve the fields in the target form).</li><li>Default: Insert the fields from the source forms into the target form. These further customizations are possible:<ul><li>Insert order (the default insert order is after fields in the target form).</li><li>Remove blank fields (off by default).</li><li>Add a prefix for each item (either static text or a formula). If the data type is rich text, the prefix may be formatted. If the data type is not string, rich text, or hyperlink, the prefix is not available.</li></ul></li></ul></td></tr>
<tr><td>Group</td><td><ul><li>Preserve the contents of the group in the target form.</li><li>Default: Combine the contents of the groups in the source and target forms.</li></ul></td></tr>
<tr><td>Repeating group</td><td><ul><li>Ignore the groups in the source form (i.e., preserve the groups in the target form).</li><li>Default: Insert the groups from the source forms into the target form. These further customizations are possible:<ul><li>Insert order (the default insert order is after fields in the target form).</li><li>Remove blank fields (off by default).</li><li>Combine groups that have the same value for a field you choose.</li></ul></li></ul></td></tr>
</table>

Table 12.2: ***(continued)***

Node Type	Merge Actions Available

Attribute	• Preserve the value of the matching attribute in the target form.
	• **Default:** Replace the value of the attribute in the target form with the value of the attribute from the source form.
	• If the data type of the attribute is string or hyperlink, you can choose to combine the value in the target form with those from the source forms. These further customizations are available:
	  ◦ Ignore blank fields (on by default).
	  ◦ Insert a separator character.
	  ◦ Add a prefix for each item (either static text or a formula).

Choice/sequence	N/A. (See Table 12.1.)
Recursive nodes	N/A. (The merge customizations for a recursive child node are set on the outer parent node.)

For our status report example, we want to remove any empty groups and combine the groups that have the same value in their `Team` field. In the *Merge Settings* dialog, the way you specify that empty groups should be removed is fairly obvious—just check the *Remove blank groups* checkbox. In order to combine the data from the `StatusReports` nodes based on the value of the `Team` field, we simply have to specify the `Team` field in the *Field to compare* edit box. (As you have seen numerous times before, you can choose a field or group from the *Select a Field or Group* dialog. This dialog is available by clicking the button next to the *Field to compare* edit box, which becomes available after checking the *Combine groups with the same field value* checkbox.) Figure 12.14 shows the *Merge Settings* dialog after we've made these changes.

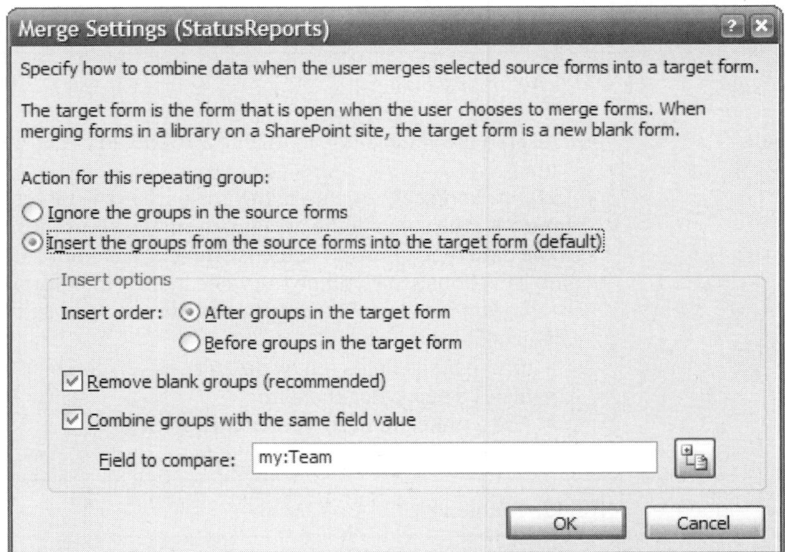

FIGURE 12.14: Merge Settings dialog with merge customizations

NOTE Blank Groups Are Removed Only If They Are Truly Empty

As we discussed, to remove blank groups, just check the *Remove blank groups* checkbox in the *Merge Settings* dialog. In order to remove a blank group from the target document, the group must be completely empty. This means that none of the children of the group can have values. It also means that none of the attributes on the group or its children can have values. (Some attributes, such as `xsi:nil`, are ignored when determining whether a group is empty.)

One "gotcha" has to do with default values. It's natural in some cases to set a default value on a node, especially if that default value is a calculation. (For example, you may want to include a default value on the `TotalSales` field in the status report form we are building that calculates the total sales based on units sold and price per unit.) If a field contains a default value, it will not be empty when you first open the form, even if you haven't made any changes. When you merge other forms into the target form, the group node that contains that field will not be removed since it has a child node with a value. Therefore, if you expect users of your form to merge multiple forms and you need to set a field's value based on a calculation, it's better to use a rule to set the field's value instead.

If you now save your changes and then merge multiple status reports, all the reports will be combined based on the name of the team. This is exactly what we want. However, we're not finished yet. If you're merging forms for your employees over multiple weeks, you probably want to combine each employee's status reports based on the employee's name as well. Remember that each employee's status report data is stored in another repeating group node called `EmployeeInformation`. Since this node repeats, if you don't customize the merge action for this node, the default insert action will be performed. That means that each employee's status information will be inserted into the target form one after another, which will make the final report very hard to read. So, in order to combine all the status reports based on the employee's name, we have to customize the merge settings for the `EmployeeInformation` group node just as we did for the `StatusReports` group node. Figure 12.15 shows the *Merge Settings* dialog after we changed the merge settings to remove blank fields and combine the data based on the `Name` field.

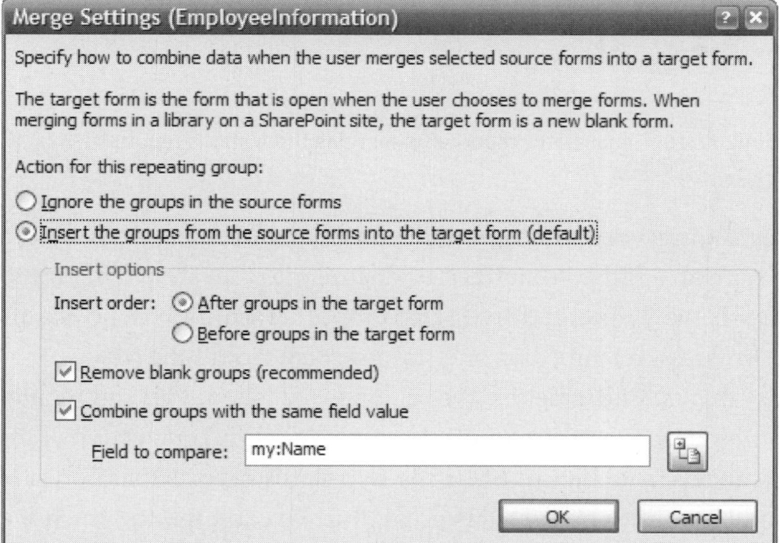

FIGURE 12.15: Merge Settings dialog for the `EmployeeInformation` node

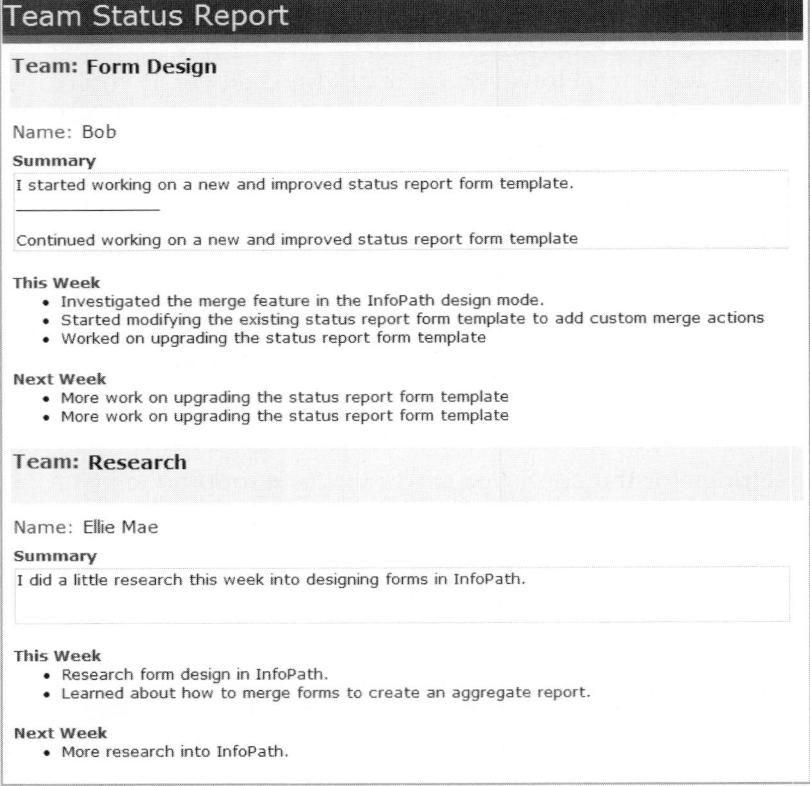

Team Status Report

Team: Form Design

Name: Bob

Summary

I started working on a new and improved status report form template.

Continued working on a new and improved status report form template

This Week

- Investigated the merge feature in the InfoPath design mode.
- Started modifying the existing status report form template to add custom merge actions
- Worked on upgrading the status report form template

Next Week

- More work on upgrading the status report form template
- More work on upgrading the status report form template

Team: Research

Name: Ellie Mae

Summary

I did a little research this week into designing forms in InfoPath.

This Week

- Research form design in InfoPath.
- Learned about how to merge forms to create an aggregate report.

Next Week

- More research into InfoPath.

FIGURE 12.16: Team status report after merging three status reports

After saving your changes and merging multiple status reports, you end up with an aggregate status report similar to that shown in Figure 12.16. In this case, we've merged two status reports from Bob, who is a member of the form design team, and one status report from Ellie Mae.

Okay, this is a little better. We're almost finished. Our aggregate report now combines reports from multiple employees into one section of the form. As you can see from Figure 12.16, the two status reports that Bob submitted were combined into one. This is great, but we can't tell to which week the status information applies. Also, the separator for the summary information is just a sequence of underline characters (_), which looks a bit ugly. So, let's fix both these issues quickly by customizing the merge actions for the nodes to which the Rich Text Box and the two Bulleted List controls are bound.

Looking back at Figure 12.7, you can see that the summary information in the status report form is stored in a node called `Summary`. (That makes

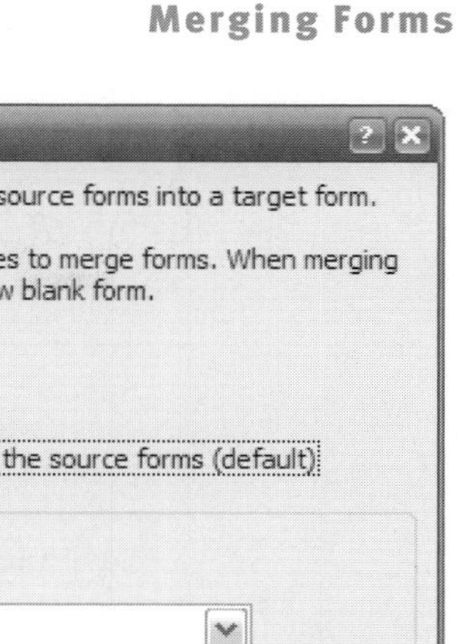

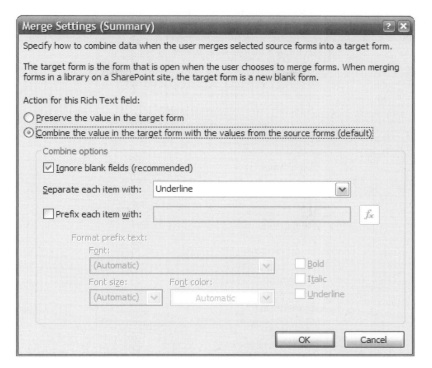

FIGURE 12.17: Merge Settings dialog for the `Summary` node

sense.) If you open the *Merge Settings* dialog for this node, the dialog shown in Figure 12.17 appears. In this case, since the `Summary` node is a field whose data type is rich text, the default action is to combine values in the target form with those from the source forms. When values are combined, blank values are ignored, and each item is separated by an underline, which is just a series of underline characters (_).

First, let's change the separator to something that looks a little better than a bunch of underline characters—a horizontal line. (Table 12.3 lists all the available separators for rich text nodes. Text fields support all the same separators as rich text fields except horizontal line. However, line break, paragraph break, and underline may not work as expected if the control bound to the text field doesn't support multiline text.)

You can see from Figure 12.17 that in addition to changing the separator, we can specify a prefix for each item. Here's where we can differentiate between the summary information for one week and another. Let's add a prefix by checking the *Prefix each item with* checkbox. When you do, a number of options become available. First, you can type in a prefix, which will

TABLE 12.3: List of Available Separators in the Merge Settings Dialog for Rich Text Fields

Available Separators (Rich Text Fields)
None
Space
Comma (,)
Semicolon (;)
Vertical line (|)
Line break
Paragraph break
Underline
Horizontal line

just be plain text, or create a formula by using the *Insert Formula* dialog you've seen many times before. In this case, we want to prefix the summary information for each week with the date that the form was filled out (which is entered by the user) and a colon with a space after it. To combine these two items, we have to use the `concat` XPath function. Also, let's make the prefix bold and change its font size to 12. Figure 12.18 shows the *Merge Settings* dialog after we've made these changes.

> **NOTE** **Prefixes When Merging into a Form That Has Data**
>
> When merging source forms into a target that already has data, prefixes are added only to the data from the source forms. When merging, the data in the target form is not updated with prefix information. Therefore, it's better to start with a blank form when merging forms so that prefix information will be correct.

Next, we want to add that same prefix to the data for this week's and last week's status. To do that, just open the *Merge Settings* dialog for both the `ThisWeek` and `NextWeek` repeating field nodes in the data source. Figure 12.19 shows the *Merge Settings* dialog after customizing the merge

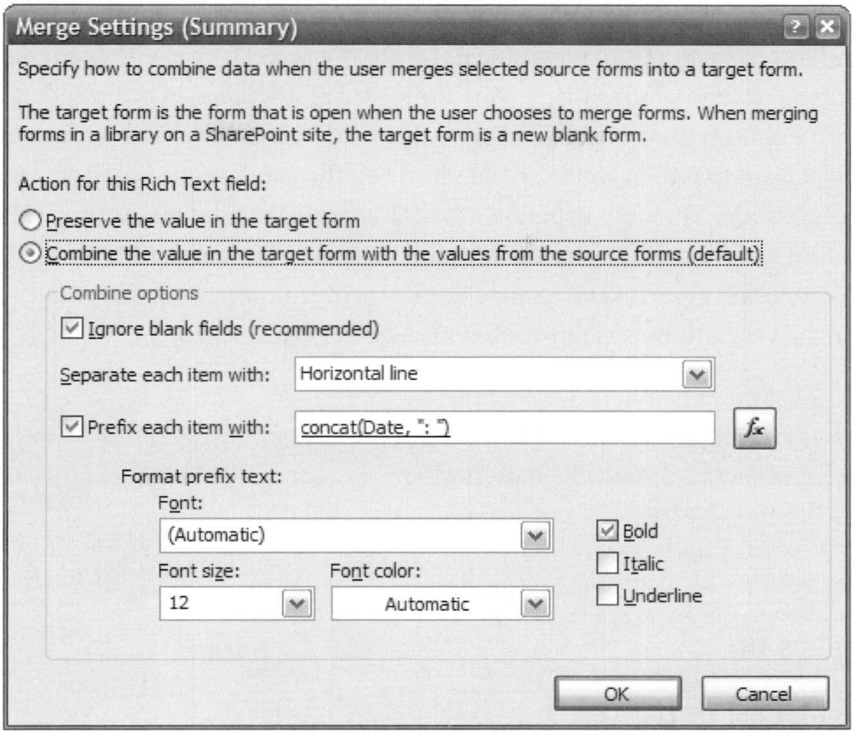

Merge Settings (Summary)

Specify how to combine data when the user merges selected source forms into a target form.

The target form is the form that is open when the user chooses to merge forms. When merging forms in a library on a SharePoint site, the target form is a new blank form.

Action for this Rich Text field:

- ○ Preserve the value in the target form
- ◉ Combine the value in the target form with the values from the source forms (default)

Combine options

- ☑ Ignore blank fields (recommended)

Separate each item with: Horizontal line

☑ Prefix each item with: concat(Date, ": ")

Format prefix text:

Font: (Automatic)

Font size: 12

Font color: Automatic

☑ Bold
☐ Italic
☐ Underline

OK Cancel

FIGURE 12.18: Merge Settings dialog for the `Summary` node after customizations are complete

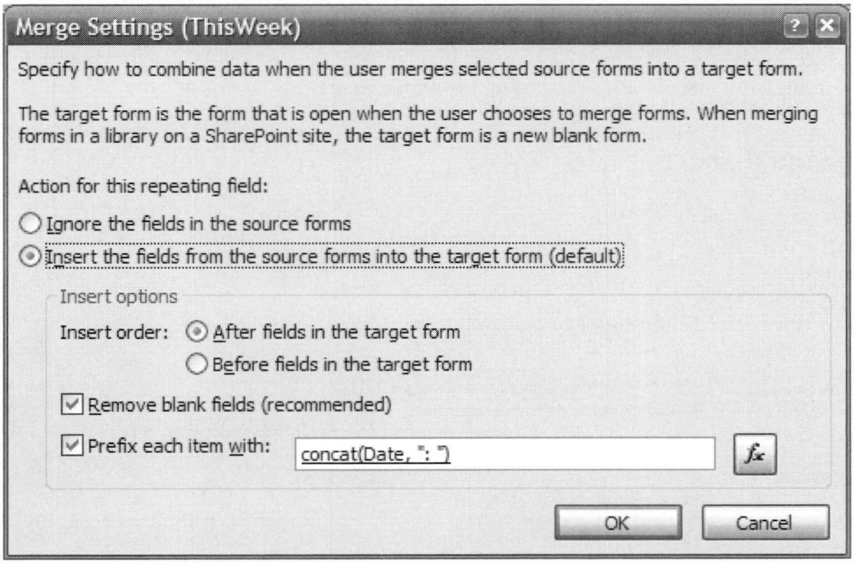

Merge Settings (ThisWeek)

Specify how to combine data when the user merges selected source forms into a target form.

The target form is the form that is open when the user chooses to merge forms. When merging forms in a library on a SharePoint site, the target form is a new blank form.

Action for this repeating field:

- ○ Ignore the fields in the source forms
- ◉ Insert the fields from the source forms into the target form (default)

Insert options

Insert order: ◉ After fields in the target form
○ Before fields in the target form

☑ Remove blank fields (recommended)

☑ Prefix each item with: concat(Date, ": ")

OK Cancel

FIGURE 12.19: Merge Settings dialog for the `ThisWeek` node after customization

action for the `ThisWeek` repeating field. Since this node is repeating, the default merge action is to insert the data into the target form, with blank fields preserved and no prefix added. We don't want blank fields in our target form, so we've chosen to remove them. Also, we want to be able to tell which status items pertain to which week, so we've added the same prefix we used for the `Summary` node. The only difference is that we can't format this prefix as bold with font size 12 since this node does not support rich text.

Now, once again, save your changes and merge a few status reports. The result should be similar to that shown in Figure 12.20.

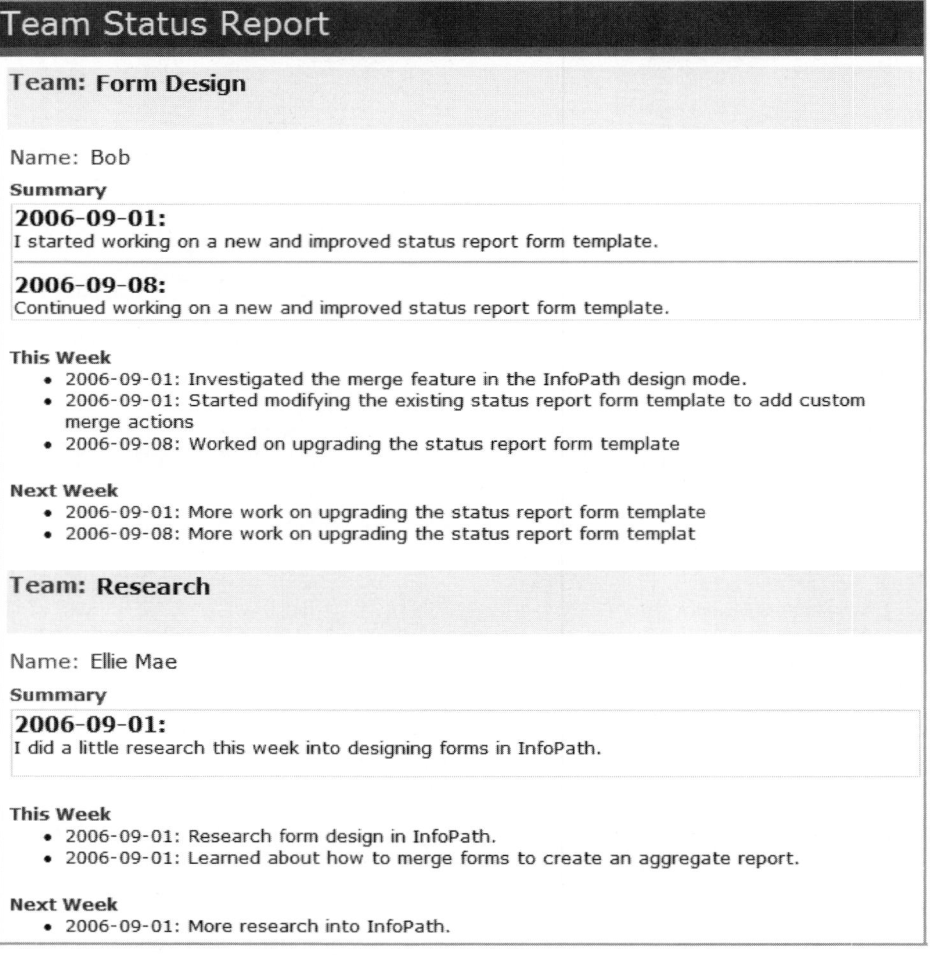

Team Status Report

Team: Form Design

Name: Bob

Summary

2006-09-01:
I started working on a new and improved status report form template.

2006-09-08:
Continued working on a new and improved status report form template.

This Week

- 2006-09-01: Investigated the merge feature in the InfoPath design mode.
- 2006-09-01: Started modifying the existing status report form template to add custom merge actions
- 2006-09-08: Worked on upgrading the status report form template

Next Week

- 2006-09-01: More work on upgrading the status report form template
- 2006-09-08: More work on upgrading the status report form templat

Team: Research

Name: Ellie Mae

Summary

2006-09-01:
I did a little research this week into designing forms in InfoPath.

This Week

- 2006-09-01: Research form design in InfoPath.
- 2006-09-01: Learned about how to merge forms to create an aggregate report.

Next Week

- 2006-09-01: More research into InfoPath.

FIGURE 12.20: Merged team status report after all customizations are complete

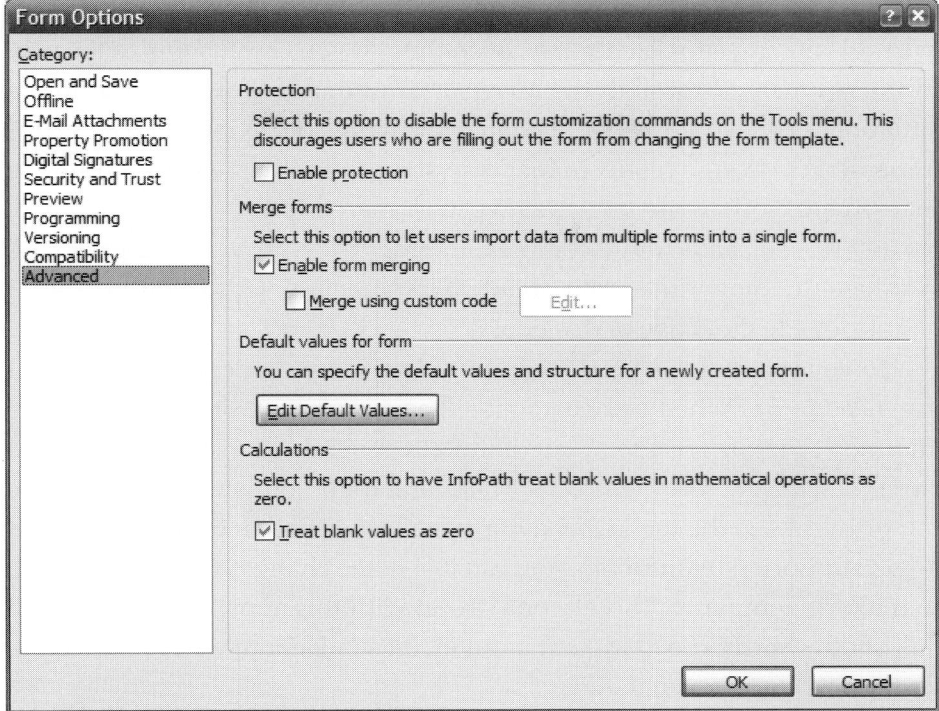

FIGURE 12.21: Advanced tab of the Form Options dialog

In addition to the fact that you can customize the merge behavior in design mode, InfoPath also gives you a couple of other ways to control the merging of forms. Figure 12.21 shows the *Advanced* tab of the *Form Options* dialog. (You can access the *Form Options* dialog from the *Tools* menu when in design mode.) In the *Advanced* tab, you can completely turn off form merging when users are filling out a form. (Of course, since this is such a useful feature, it is on by default.) Also, you can choose to write script or managed code to control the way forms are merged by selecting the *Merge using custom code* option. (We will talk more about writing script and managed code in Part II of this book.)

Forms Services

Merge using custom code is not available in browser-enabled form templates.

Custom Merge XSL (Advanced)

When designing a form template, even though you can customize the way forms are merged through the *Merge Settings* dialog, you may run into a situation where you want to customize the merge behavior in a way that is impossible in design mode. In that case, there is another way to control the merge behavior—write your own custom merge XSL. Now, writing XSL for any reason can be quite complex. In order to write custom merge XSL, you have to know quite a bit about XSL in general. (A full discussion of XSL is outside the scope of this book.)

However, it may not be as complicated as it sounds, depending on what you need to do. When you customize the merge behavior in design mode and then save the form template, InfoPath generates a merge XSL file and stores it with the form template. Therefore, if all you want to do is make minor tweaks to the merge behavior you've specified in design mode that aren't supported by InfoPath, you can just make changes to the merge XSL in the form template. (There is one caveat with this approach, which we'll talk about shortly.) So, with that in mind, let's talk about what you need to do to use a custom merge XSL.

Using InfoPath to Create the Custom Merge XSL

As we just mentioned, the easiest way to create custom merge XSL is to use InfoPath in design mode to customize the merge behavior in such a way that it does most of what you want it to do. Then just tweak the merge XSL that InfoPath generates when you save your form template. To do that, you must first save your form template as source files by using *Save as Source Files,* which is available on the *File* menu. Choosing this menu item will save the files included in the form template to a folder location you choose. Remember that a form template is just a CAB file that contains many files, including a manifest, view XSL, and schema. When you customize the merge behavior in design mode, the form template also contains a merge XSL file that is named merge.xsl by default. This merge XSL file is where you will make your modifications in order to tweak the merge settings you specified when designing the form template.

After you make the desired modifications to the merge XSL file, at this point, if you do nothing else, the modifications will work just fine when a user fills out the form. Also, when you open the form template in design mode, you will still be able to make modifications to the merge behavior by using the *Merge Settings* dialog. You may think that this is great. However, if you do make modifications to the merge settings in design mode, when you save the form template, InfoPath will regenerate the merge XSL and overwrite your changes.

Therefore, you have to tell InfoPath that you've made modifications to the merge XSL so that your changes will be protected. To do so, you have to modify the manifest file included in the form template. This is not as scary as it sounds. The manifest file (usually named manifest.xsf) is just an XML file. So, you can open it in an editor such as Notepad or Visual Studio and make the necessary modifications. In order to tell InfoPath that you've customized the merge XSL, first locate the `xsf:importSource` element that has a `transform` attribute whose value matches the name of the merge XSL file in your form template (usually `merge.xsl`). This section of the manifest usually looks like the following:

```
<xsf:importParameters enabled="yes">
  <xsf:importSource name="" schema="myschema.xsd"
  transform="merge.xsl" authoringOfTransform="automatic">
  </xsf:importSource>
</xsf:importParameters>
```

Once you locate the `xsf:importSource` element, change the value of the `authoringOfTransform` attribute from `automatic` to `manual`. `automatic` means that the XSL was generated by InfoPath. `manual` indicates that you are providing custom XSL. Once you make this change, you can open your manifest in design mode in InfoPath and choose *Save* from the *File* menu to re-create the form template (.xsn) file. (Or you can choose to leave your form template expanded as is if you wish to make more modifications in the future.)

Now, after changing the `authoringOfTransform` attribute to `manual`, you will no longer be able to change the merge behavior by using the *Merge Settings* dialog in design mode. In fact, the *Merge Settings* button in the control properties and *Field or Group Properties* dialogs will be disabled, as shown in

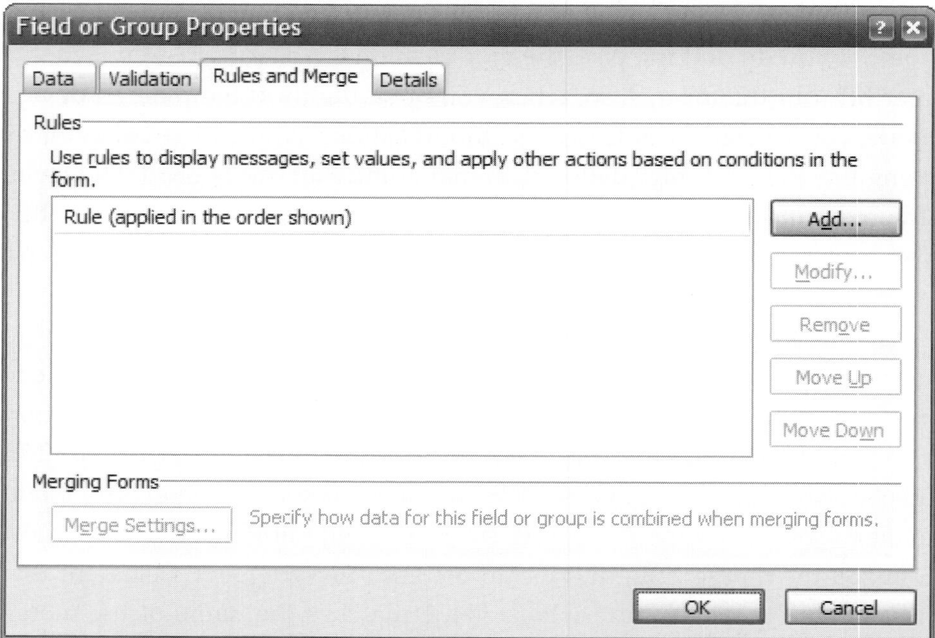

FIGURE 12.22: Field or Group Properties dialog after specifying a custom merge XSL in the manifest

Figure 12.22. This also means that the modifications you made to the merge XSL will be protected—InfoPath will not overwrite your merge XSL.

Writing Your Own Merge XSL

So far, we've talked about how to make tweaks to the merge XSL that is created by InfoPath in design mode. As we mentioned earlier, the default merge behavior in InfoPath requires the schema of the source forms to match that of the target form. If you want to merge source forms into a target form where their schemas don't match, you have no choice but to create your own custom merge XSL from scratch. This process is basically the same as customizing the merge XSL generated by InfoPath. First, you (obviously) create your merge XSL. Then, you must open the manifest file and add the `xsf:importSource` element as a child of the `xsf:importParameters` element. Finally, you need to add an `xsf:file` element under the `xsf:files` element so that InfoPath knows that your merge XSL file is part of the form template.

When you create the xsf:importSource element, there are two additional attributes of this element we haven't talked about yet that we'll mention briefly. First is the name attribute. This attribute optionally specifies the name of the source form. (This attribute is required but can be empty.) When a value exists in this attribute, the merge XSL specified in the transform attribute will be used to merge all source forms whose names match this value. (This name must match the name attribute on the mso-infoPath-Solution processing instruction in the XML of the source form. If the name of the source form does not match the name in the xsf:importSource element in the manifest for the target form, the merge XSL specified in the first xsf:importSource element is used.)

Second, the schema attribute specifies the XML Schema file that should be used to validate the source forms when merging. We've already briefly mentioned the transform attribute, which specifies the merge XSL file to use to merge the source forms into the target form. This merge XSL will be used when the schema of the source form matches that specified in the schema attribute of the xsf:importSource element. So, as you can imagine, it's possible to specify multiple xsf:importSource elements if you want to use a different merge XSL for source forms with different schemas or for different source forms based on the name of each form. (Note that, in all cases, the output of your merge XSL must be XML that matches the schema of the target form.)

As we mentioned earlier, the process of creating a custom merge XSL from scratch is quite complicated. Therefore, it's good to use the merge XSL generated by InfoPath as a starting point. We're not going to go into all the intricacies of creating XSL in this book. However, even though the merge XSL is just standard XSL, InfoPath does provide a few custom attributes in an aggregation namespace that will help you control how the forms are merged. This aggregation namespace must first be added to your xsl:stylesheet element in your merge XSL like so:

```
<xsl:stylesheet version="1.0"
xmlns:agg="http://schemas.microsoft.com/office/infopath/2003/aggregation">
```

Table 12.4 lists the merge actions that are available in the aggregation namespace. To specify one of these merge actions, add the agg:action attribute to an XML element that you output, and set the value of that attribute to one of the actions in Table 12.4. Table 12.5 lists subsequent attributes that are available for certain actions. (The merge XSL generated by InfoPath uses these attributes extensively. So, we encourage you to look at the generated merge XSL for examples of the use of these attributes.)

TABLE 12.4: Merge Actions in the Aggregation Namespace

Merge Action	Description
`insert`	Inserts a source node as the child of a node in the target form that is returned from the expression specified in the `agg:select` attribute
`delete`	Deletes the target node or nodes that are returned from the select expression (`agg:select`)
`replace`	Replaces the target node(s) that are returned from the select expression with the source node(s)
`ignore`	Ignores the target node completely
`mergeAttributes`	Merges attributes from the source node with the target node(s) returned from the select expression

TABLE 12.5: Merge Attributes Available for Merge Actions

Merge Attribute	Available for Which Merge Actions	Description	Required
`agg:select`	`insert, delete, mergeAttributes`	Selects the target nodeset to which to apply the action specified in the `agg:action` attribute	Yes
`agg:selectChild`	`insert`	Is used if `agg:select` returns a group node, to determine where in the set of child nodes the source node should be inserted	No
`agg:order`	`insert` (value can be `before` or `after` [default])	Specifies in what order (before or after) source nodes are inserted into the target	No

Note that all attributes and values in Tables 12.4 and 12.5 are case sensitive. If the case is incorrect, the attribute will be ignored.

In addition to these actions and attributes, InfoPath also provides a useful function that enables you to retrieve the DOM document of the target form—`get-documentElement`. This function is in a different namespace than the merge actions and attributes we just talked about. If you look at the merge XSL generated by InfoPath, you can see how this function is used. Listing 12.1 shows an example.

LISTING 12.1: Using the `get-documentElement` XSL Function

```
<xsl:stylesheet version="1.0"
xmlns:msxsl="urn:schemas-microsoft-com:xslt"
xmlns:agg="http://schemas.microsoft.com/office/infopath/2003/aggregation"
xmlns:mergeUI="http://schemas.microsoft.com/office/infopath/2003/
aggregation-mergeUI"
xmlns:targetDoc="http://schemas.microsoft.com/office/infopath/2003/
aggregation-target"
     xmlns:xsl="http://www.w3.org/1999/XSL/Transform"
xmlns:xdActionTable="http://schemas.microsoft.com/office/infopath/2003/
aggregation-actionTable"
     xmlns:xsi="http://www.w3.org/2001/XMLSchema-instance"
xmlns:xhtml="http://www.w3.org/1999/xhtml"
xmlns:my="http://schemas.microsoft.com/office/infopath/2003/myXSD/2005-12-
08T01:14:29"
xmlns:xd="http://schemas.microsoft.com/office/infopath/2003">
. . .    <xsl:variable
           name="targetRoot"
           select="targetDoc:get-documentElement()" />
. . .    <xsl:template
match="/my:WeeklyStatusReport/my:StatusReports/my:EmployeeInformation">
                <xsl:param name="targetParent"
                    select="$targetRoot/my:StatusReports" />
                . . .
                </xsl:template>
     . . .
</xsl:stylesheet>
```

In Listing 12.1, the `get-documentElement` function is used to get the root node of the target document, which is stored in the `targetRoot` XSL variable. This is later used to get the `my:StatusReports` node, which is used in the XSL template that merges the data from the `my:Employee-Information` nodes in the source form.

As you can probably tell just by looking at the merge XSL generated by InfoPath and by this introduction to creating custom merge XSL, although the process of creating your own merge XSL is not easy, the extensibility provided by InfoPath in this regard is quite extensive.

Printing

Now that you've created a merged status report for your team, you'll undoubtedly want to print the report. Printing in InfoPath is pretty much the same as in other Microsoft Office applications. However, when you design a form template, InfoPath allows you to specify how you would like your forms printed when users fill them out. For example, you can specify a separate view that will be used for printing, control what is displayed in the headers and footers of the printed form, indicate whether or not multiple views are printed together, and even specify a print view that will use Word for printing. Let's take a look at each of these in a bit more detail. We'll also talk a bit about printing in browser-enabled forms.

Print Views

Sometimes the view that users see may not be exactly what they want to print. For example, our status report form template contains a *Team Status Report* view that we use to view all the status reports that have been merged for our team. When we print the report for upper management, it is highly likely that those who will read the report will be interested only in the summary information for each employee and not the nitty-gritty details of each and every task performed. Therefore, when designing this form template, you'll want to create a print view for the *Team Status Report* view. Doing so is very easy.

First, switch to the *Team Status Report* view by using the *Views* task pane. At the bottom of the task pane is a link titled *Create Print Version for This View.* Clicking on this link opens the dialog displayed in Figure 12.23. Here

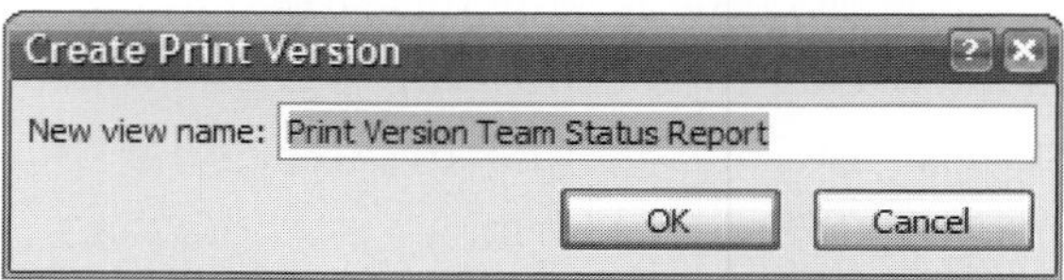

FIGURE 12.23: Create Print Version dialog

you can specify the name for your print view. (The default name is the name of the current view with "Print Version" prepended to it.) After clicking *OK*, a print view is created, and you are automatically switched to that view.

The easiest thing to do next is to copy the controls from the *Team Status Report* view, paste them into the *Print Version Team Status Report* view, and then change the view to however you want it to look when it's printed. Since we want to print only the summary information, we'll remove everything from the print view except the controls for the team name, employee name, and summary. Now when users of your form merge the status report data and are viewing it in the *Team Status Report* view, when they print the report, the print version of that view is used for printing instead of the *Team Status Report* view. Figure 12.24 shows the status report after it is printed with the print view of the *Team Status Report* view.

Of course, after merging the status reports in the *Team Status Report* view, you could always use the *View* menu to switch to the *Print Version Team Status Report* view and then print. However, that's no longer necessary since the print version will always be used for printing when the *Team Status Report* view is open.

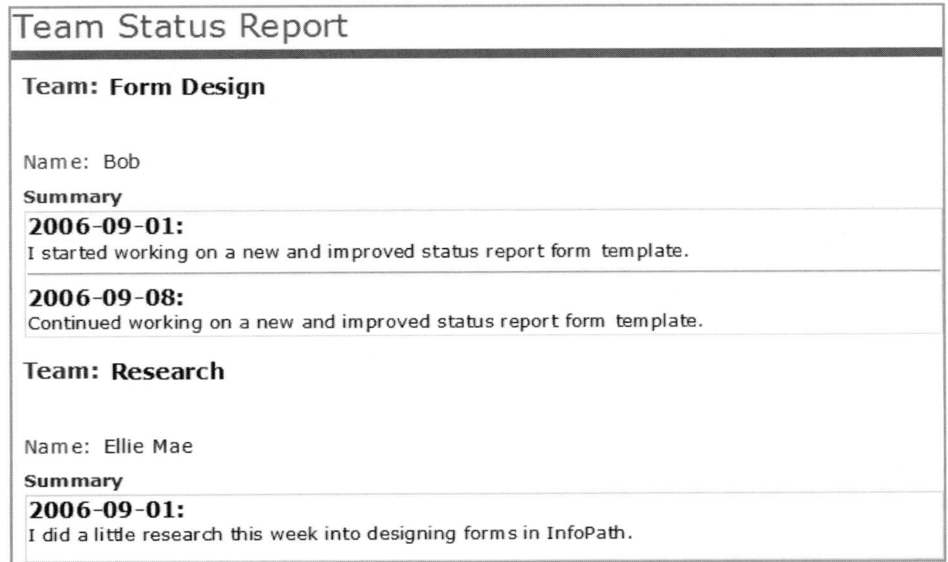

FIGURE 12.24: Printed team status report

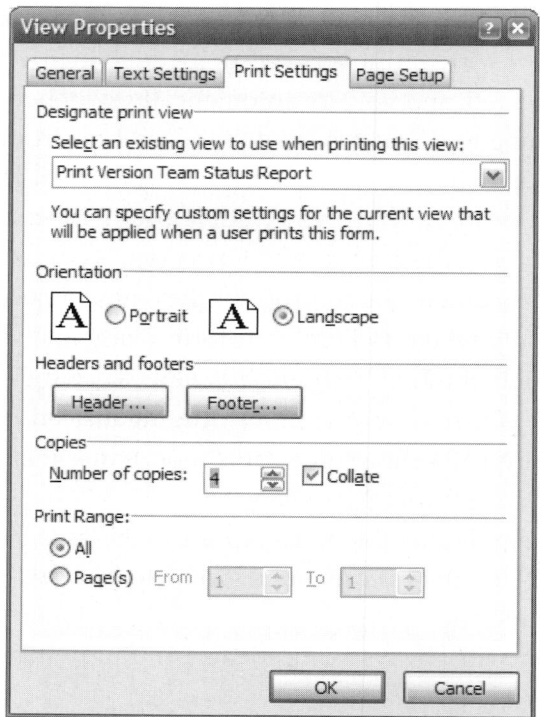

FIGURE 12.25: Print Settings tab of the View Properties dialog

If you wish to change this behavior at any time, just open the *View Properties* dialog for the *Team Status Report* view and switch to the *Print Settings* tab (Figure 12.25). The print view is designated at the top of this tab. You can designate any view as the print view (even the current view) by choosing that view from the drop-down list box. As you may have guessed, you can create as many print views as you like. You can create one for each view or even multiple print views for a particular view. However, only one print view can be used at a time for printing a particular view.

Let's leave this setting as is so the print version of the *Team Status Report* view will be used for printing. Since the print version will always be used for printing, you probably don't want the print view to show up on the *View* menu when filling out the form. You can easily remove the print view from the *View* menu by opening the properties dialog for the *Print Version Team Status Report* view and unchecking the option *Show on the View menu when filling out the form.*

Also, you will notice that in the *Print Settings* tab you can specify different printing options for each view, such as the orientation, the number of copies, or the print range. This is useful if, for example, you know that your users will most likely want to print multiple copies of the form every time they print it. (Of course, users can override your settings.) In addition to these print options, you can also specify separate headers and footers to be used when printing each view, which is the topic of our next discussion.

NOTE Specifying Print Settings for Print Views

When a view has a print view associated with it and you want to specify custom print settings such as orientation, header/footer, and so on, you should set these options on the print view itself. If you specify these settings on the view that has a print view associated with it, they will be ignored.

Headers and Footers

Printing a report without a header and/or footer can sometimes lead to confusion. "Where did the report come from?" "When was the report printed?" "In what order should the pages be?"—these are all common questions that arise when you look at a report that was printed some time ago or whose pages have gotten out of order. Adding headers and footers to your form can alleviate some of the confusion. Of course, adding headers and footers is not too difficult, but it is important enough for printed reports that we should touch on it briefly.

Forms Services

Printing headers and footers is not supported in Forms Services.

In Figure 12.25, you can see that the *Print Settings* tab contains two buttons—*Header* and *Footer.* Clicking either of these buttons opens the same basic dialog (just with a different title), as shown in Figure 12.26. The top of this dialog is where you add the header or footer information that will be added to the form when printing. (Note that any formatting you add will be applied to the entire text of the header or footer. You cannot format part of

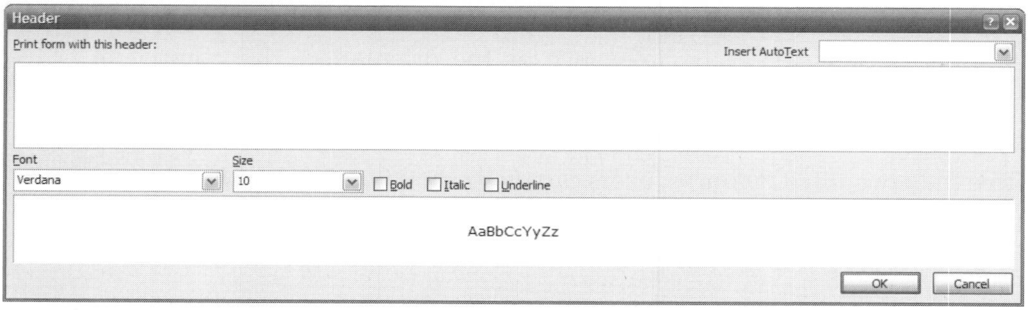

FIGURE 12.26: Header format dialog

the text using one font and another part of the text using another font, for example.) The bottom of the dialog shows a preview of how the header will look after you've added font formatting. (Unfortunately, it doesn't show a live preview of how the header text would look when printing, which would be ideal.)

In the upper-right corner of the dialog is a drop-down list box that contains **AutoText** items that you can add to the header or footer, such as the current date or current page. Also, one very useful AutoText item that you can add is a field from the form itself. Let's say that, when printing the merged status report forms, you want to print the name of the team at the top of the report. You can easily do that by adding the `Team` field to the header. To do so, just select the *Field . . .* item from the *Insert AutoText* drop-down list box. When you do, the familiar *Select a Field or Group* dialog opens, from which you can choose a field to insert into the header.

> **NOTE Inserting a Repeating Field into the Header or Footer**
>
> If you insert a repeating field or a field that is inside a repeating group node into the header and footer, only the first value will be shown. In our status report example, since the `Team` field is a child of a repeating group node, if there are multiple teams in the merged form, only the first one will appear in the header. Therefore, if you are going to create a printed report such as this, it would make sense to merge the status reports for each team separately.

In addition to the name of the team that we want to add to the header, let's add the date to the upper-right corner of the printout. Figure 12.27 shows how the *Header* format dialog looks after that change is made.

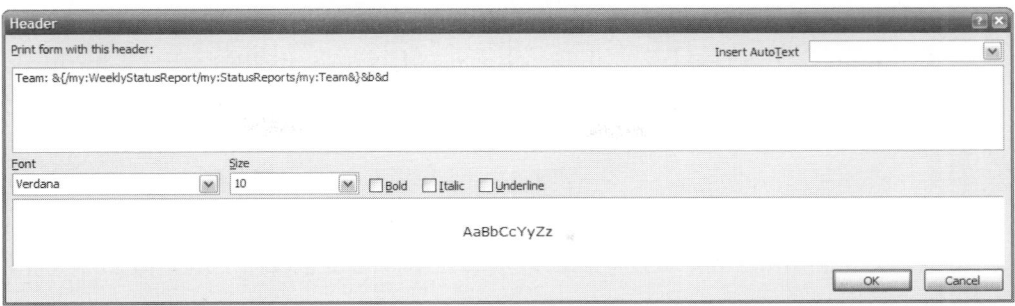

FIGURE 12.27: Header format dialog after adding `Team` field and date

In addition to adding header information, let's add the current page and total number of pages to the footer. After doing so, and after merging the status reports for the form design team, the printed report looks like that shown in Figure 12.28.

Team: Form Design 9/12/2006

Team Status Report

Team: Form Design

Name: Bob

Summary

2006-09-01:
I started working on a new and improved status report form template.

2006-09-08:
Continued working on a new and improved status report form template.

Name: Sue

Summary

2006-09-08: This week, I worked with Bob on the new InfoPath form template design. I am very excited about working with InfoPath. I also read a really good book about designing InfoPath forms.

Page 1 of 1

FIGURE 12.28: Team status report with header and footer information

Multiple View Printing

In many of the form templates you create, you will likely have multiple views. We certainly do in our status report form template. When you fill out a form and then print, normally only the current view is printed. However, you can choose to print more than one view at a time. In our status report form, we have a print view for our *Team Status Report* view that works just fine since, as it stands right now, we need to print and distribute only this one view.

However, remember that our status report form could also contain sales information from the employees in the sales department. Let's say that upper management wants not only a summary report of the employee status for the week but also a separate report that lists all the sales figures. In this case, management just wants the raw sales data for the people on the sales team. To satisfy this request, you decide to add a *Sales Report* view that will use conditional formatting to show only those employees that have sales data. (Employees that don't have any sales information in their status reports will not be shown in this view.) Figure 12.29 shows the new view in design mode. Figure 12.30 shows a sample merged report.

Since each week you need to print both the *Team Status Report* and *Sales Report* views, it would be quite an inconvenience to have to print each one separately. Fortunately, InfoPath allows you to print more than one view at a time. There are two ways to accomplish this—one when filling out the form and one when designing the form template.

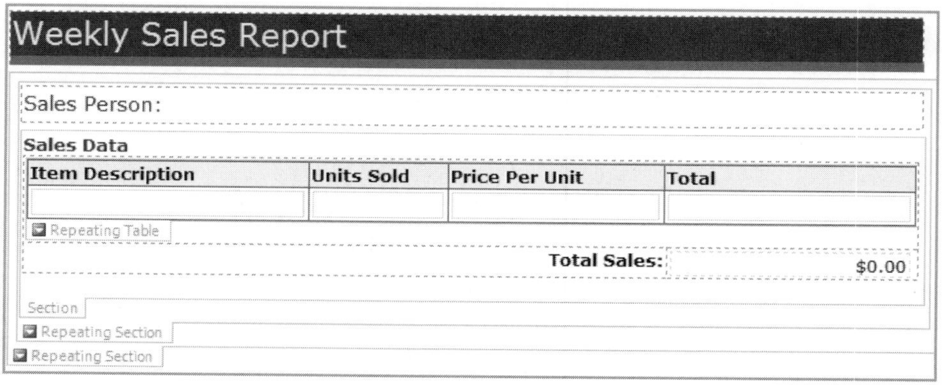

FIGURE 12.29: Sales Report view

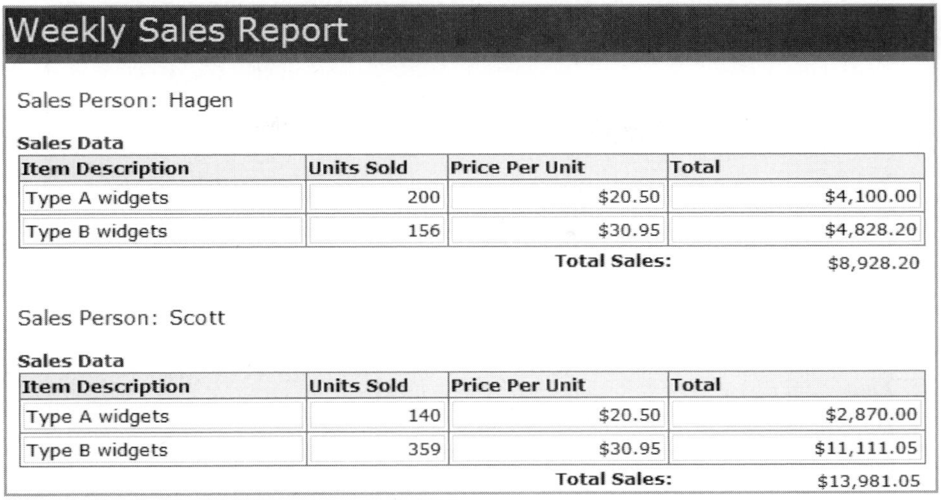

Weekly Sales Report

Sales Person: Hagen

Sales Data

Item Description	Units Sold	Price Per Unit	Total
Type A widgets	200	$20.50	$4,100.00
Type B widgets	156	$30.95	$4,828.20
		Total Sales:	$8,928.20

Sales Person: Scott

Sales Data

Item Description	Units Sold	Price Per Unit	Total
Type A widgets	140	$20.50	$2,870.00
Type B widgets	359	$30.95	$11,111.05
		Total Sales:	$13,981.05

FIGURE 12.30: Merged sales report data

When you are filling out a form that contains multiple views you want to print, printing more than one view is pretty easy. When you select *Print* from the *File* menu, the *Print* dialog opens (Figure 12.31), which contains a *Multiple Views* option.

FIGURE 12.31: Print dialog

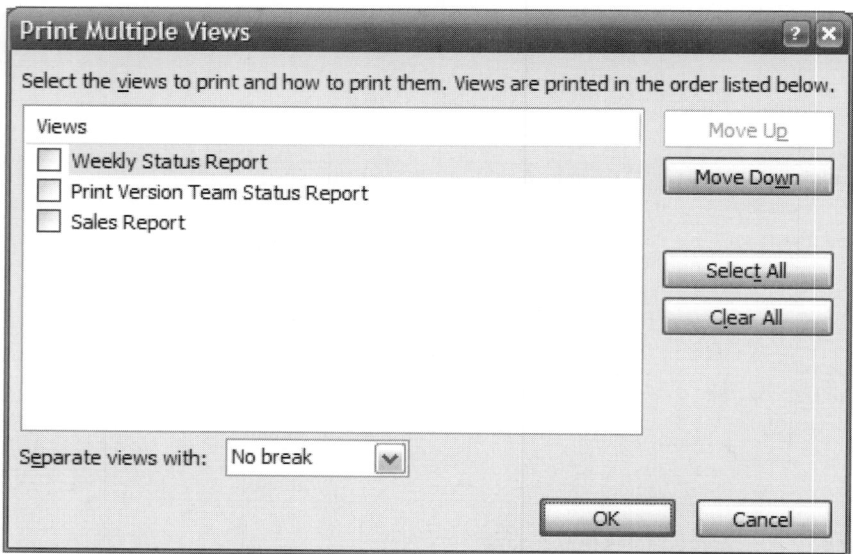

FIGURE 12.32: Print Multiple Views dialog when filling out a form

If you haven't set up multiple view printing for the form template (which we will show you how to do shortly), the checkbox for this option is initially unchecked. Checking this option immediately opens the *Print Multiple Views* dialog (Figure 12.32). From this dialog, you can choose the views to print and the order in which they are printed. Also, you can choose to separate each view with a horizontal line, a page break, or no break at all when printing. The views you select will be printed in the order they are listed in the dialog. Once you select the views you want to print and click *OK*, if you want to print again but with different settings (maybe different views), you can just click the *Settings* button (shown in Figure 12.31) to open the *Print Multiple Views* dialog again.

Forms Services

Printing multiple views simultaneously is not supported in Forms Services.

> **NOTE Print Views When Printing Multiple Views**
>
> In the *Print Multiple Views* dialog shown in Figure 12.32, notice that the *Team Status Report* view is not displayed in the list of views. Remember that we created a print view for the *Team Status Report* view called *Print Version Team Status Report.* When there is a print view associated with a view, that print view will display in the list of views in this dialog instead of the view with which it is associated. You can change this behavior by specifying the *Team Status Report* view in the list of multiple views to print when you design the form template.

As mentioned earlier, when you design the form template, you can control which views your users can print. In design mode, selecting the *Print Multiple Views* menu item on the *View* menu opens the *Print Multiple Views* dialog (Figure 12.33). This looks very similar to the dialog shown in Figure 12.32 that appears when users print while filling out a form. However, the views you choose to print in this design-mode dialog will be used

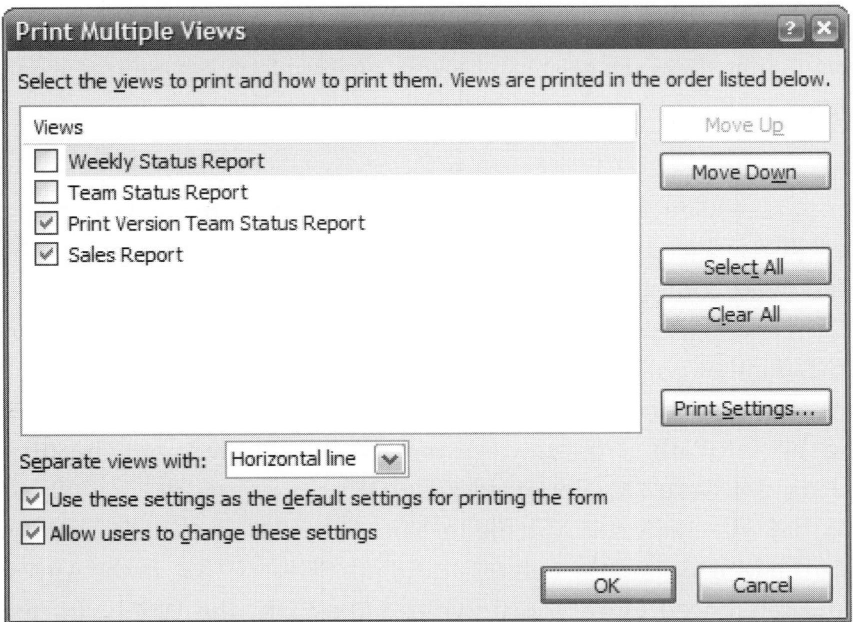

FIGURE 12.33: Print Multiple Views dialog in design mode

by default when users open the *Print* dialog, check the *Multiple Views* checkbox, and thus open the *Print Multiple Views* dialog when filling out the form. You can make printing multiple views the default by selecting that option at the bottom of the dialog. If you do, whenever a user prints one of your forms, these settings will be used automatically unless the user changes them. However, if you want to prevent the user from changing which views should be printed, just uncheck the *Allow users to change these settings* checkbox. Doing so will force users to always print the views you specified when designing the form. They cannot change the views to print or specify that only one view should be printed.

Word Print Views

Although InfoPath provides a lot of useful features when it comes to printing, it obviously doesn't provide the same level of print functionality as Word. In Word, you have support for such things as different headers and footers for different pages of your document and better print fidelity in general.

Forms Services

Word print views can exist in a browser-enabled form but are useful only when printing from InfoPath.

For that reason, InfoPath provides you with a way to create a print view that will use Word to do the printing. This may seem a bit odd, but it should make complete sense once we walk through an example.

The general idea behind the Word Print Views feature is that you create an XSL file that will take XML data as input (the data from your InfoPath form) and output a Word HTML document that will be printed through Word by InfoPath. This may seem very complicated, but, luckily, the InfoPath Software Development Kit (SDK) contains a tool called **WordPrint** that will create this XSL file for you. (The SDK is available for download from MSDN—just search for "InfoPath SDK" or look in the Appendix for the reference.) Once you download the SDK, the WordPrint tool is available in the Tools\WordPrint folder under the installation directory for the SDK. To start the application, just run the wizard.hta file.

> **NOTE Registering DLLs for the WordPrint Tool**
>
> Due to a setup issue, the WordPrint tool will not function correctly until you register all the required dynamically linked libraries (DLLs). This must be done manually. Run regsvr32 on the following DLLs: html2xhtml.dll in the Tools folder and WordPrint.dll and ImageDecode.dll in the Tools\WordPrint folder.

Once you run the WordPrint wizard, creating the XSL is fairly easy. First, you must choose the schema associated with your InfoPath form template. You can choose either the XSD file or the form template XSN file. In the latter case, the wizard will automatically extract the schema for you.

Next, you can open Word from within the WordPrint wizard in order to create a document that the wizard will use to create the XSL. This document is connected to the same schema that your form template uses. In Word, you can use the *XML Structure* task pane to insert XML nodes into the document, much like you would in InfoPath. Since creating this document in Word is not terribly straightforward, we'll create a very simple document for printing just the summary information for one employee's status report. (We're not going to go into too many details about Word's support for XML since that is outside the scope of this book.)

When you first open Word from the WordPrint wizard, the *XML Structure* task pane looks like that shown in Figure 12.34. At the bottom of the task pane, all the schema elements are listed. As in InfoPath, you can drag and drop these elements into the document. However, unlike InfoPath, there is no easy way to tell what the element hierarchy is from this task pane. As you insert elements into the document, an XML tree structure is created at the top of the *XML Structure* task pane.

When creating a document in Word that you are going to use as a Word print view in InfoPath, we first recommend that you copy the view from InfoPath you want to print and paste it into the Word document. This makes the process of creating the document much simpler.

FIGURE 12.34: XML Structure task pane in Microsoft Office Word

Second, and more importantly, we recommend that you build an XML tree structure in Word that matches the structure of the data source in InfoPath. If you don't, the document likely will not print correctly from InfoPath. In fact, it is highly probable that only a blank page will be printed. This is because the structure of the Word document is used by the WordPrint wizard to build an XSL file that will be applied against the InfoPath form data. If the XML structure in Word doesn't match the data structure of the InfoPath form, the XPaths in the generated XSL templates won't match the input data.

After doing the work to create the Word document for our weekly status report, including building the correct XML structure, the Word document we will use to generate the XSL for the Word print view looks like that shown in Figure 12.35.

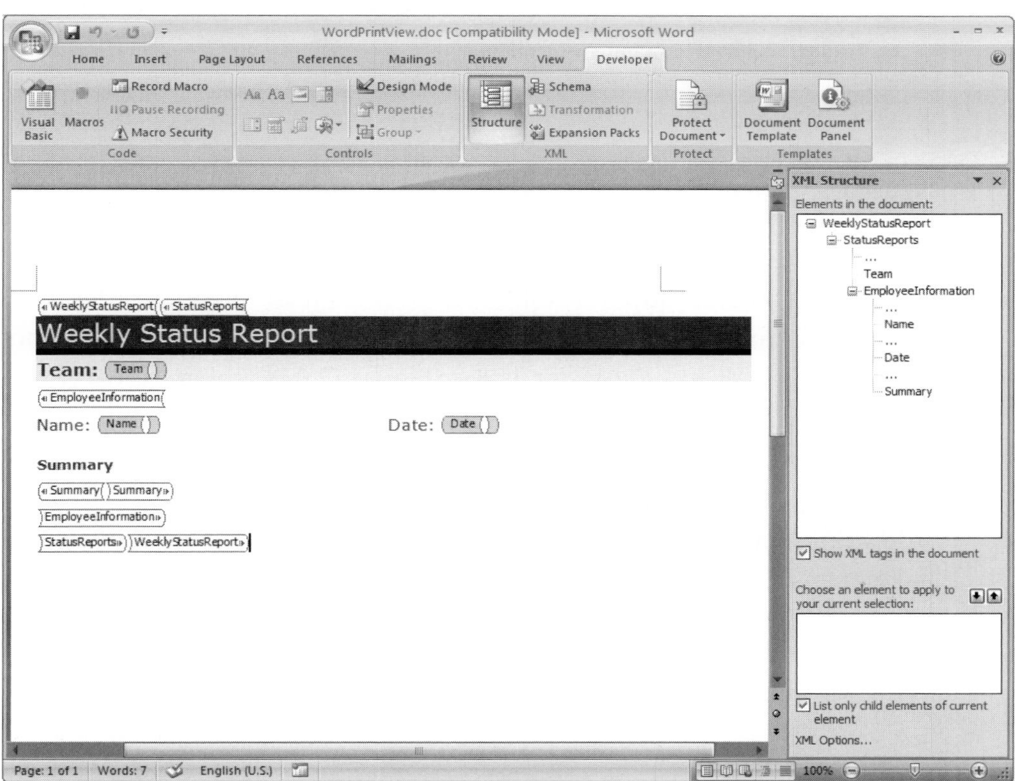

FIGURE 12.35: Word document used to generate the Word print view XSL

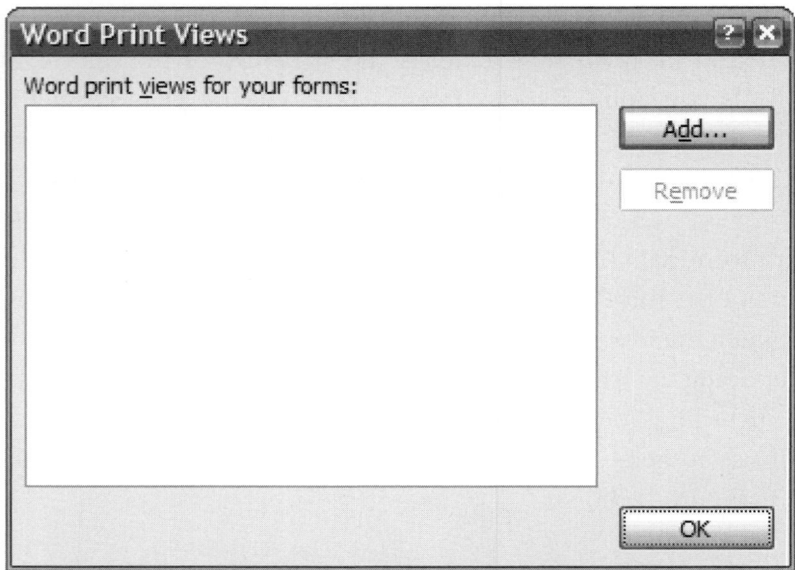

FIGURE 12.36: Word Print Views dialog

Once you have finished creating your Word document and have saved it, you give the location of this file to the WordPrint wizard, which then generates an XSL file you can use in InfoPath for printing.

Finally, you must add this XSL file to your form template. In order to do so, in design mode, click on the *Word Print Views* item on the *View* menu. This opens the *Word Print Views* dialog (Figure 12.36), which allows you to manage your Word print views. (You can also add a Word print view from the *Views* task pane.)

Clicking on the *Add* button in the *Word Print Views* dialog opens the Add Print View for Word Wizard. Clicking the *Next* button on the welcome page opens the wizard page shown in Figure 12.37. This page allows you to specify the XSL file that was just generated for you by the WordPrint wizard.

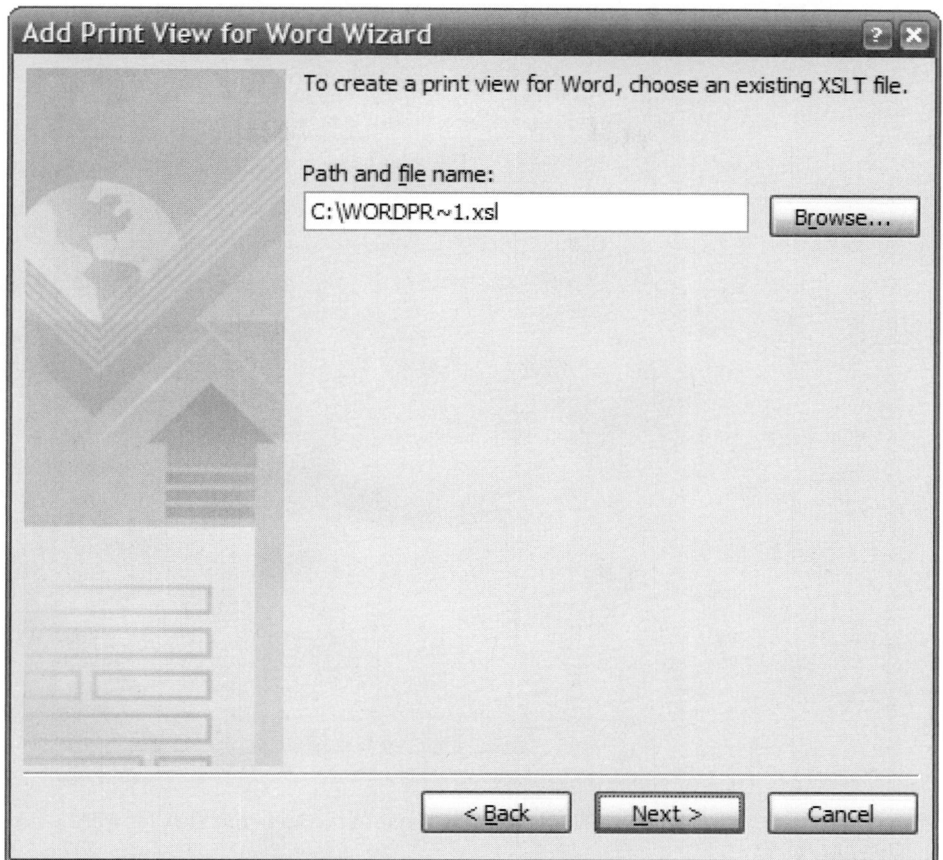

FIGURE 12.37: Choosing the path and file name from the Add Print View for Word Wizard

After you click the *Next* button again, the page shown in Figure 12.38 opens, where you can then give the print view a name. (We recommend using the name of the view in the name of the Word print view in order to identify which view it will be associated with, unless you are planning to use one Word print view for multiple views.)

After you close the dialog, you must then associate this new print view with the view that you want to use it when printing. This step is easy since

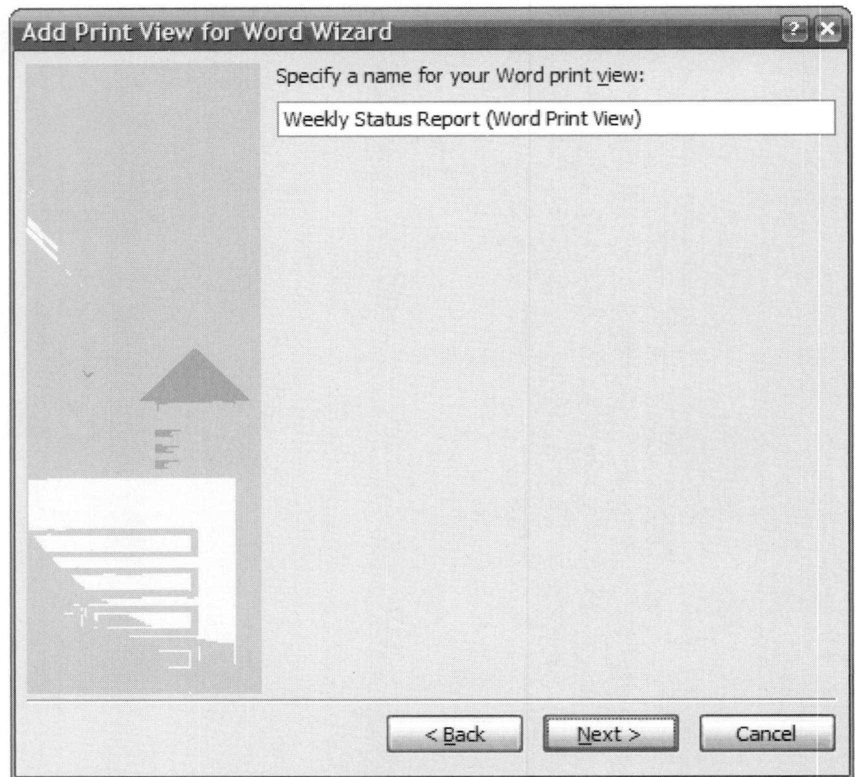

FIGURE 12.38: Specifying the Word print view name in the Add Print View for Word Wizard

you've already done this once before at the beginning of this section. In this case, we'll designate this Word print view as the view that should be used to print the *Weekly Status Report* view. (Look back at Figure 12.25 to see where you designate the print view in the *Print Settings* tab of the *View Properties* dialog.)

Now when your users are filling out their status reports in the *Weekly Status Report* view, if they print, Word will be used to print that view. More specifically, the XSL you generated in the WordPrint wizard will be applied to the data in the form. This XSL will output a Word HTML document that will be printed on the default printer using Word.

> **NOTE Word Print Views Use Default Print Settings**
>
> When you print with a Word print view, the default print settings are used. The *Print* dialog is never displayed, so you cannot specify a different printer, set printing options, or even print multiple views. This is an unfortunate limitation of an otherwise useful feature.
>
> However, if you want to print the Word print view and other views at the same time, simply switch to another view and then select *Print* from the *File* menu. In that case, the print dialog will be displayed, and you can choose multiple views to print and change other printing options. (If you want to print the Word print view but you also want to change the print settings, you can just choose the Word print view in the *Print Multiple Views* dialog. This will enable you to print only that view and also change the print settings.)
>
> As with normal print views, the Word print view will show in the *Print Multiple Views* dialog instead of the view it's associated with since we designated the Word print view as the view that should be used for printing instead of the *Weekly Status Reports* view.

Print Views in Browser-Enabled Forms

Browser-enabled forms in InfoPath Forms Services handle print views a little differently than the InfoPath client application does. Instead of having to specify one or more print views for your form, every view automatically has its own rendition of a print view. This is because someone should be able to print any view of a browser-enabled form in any supported browser. We've done the work needed to make the weekly status report a browser-enabled form template. (We'll discuss this process at length in Chapter 14. The updated sample is called WeeklyStatusReport_BrowserEnabled and is included with the samples for this chapter on the book's Web site.) Figure 12.39 shows the form being filled out.

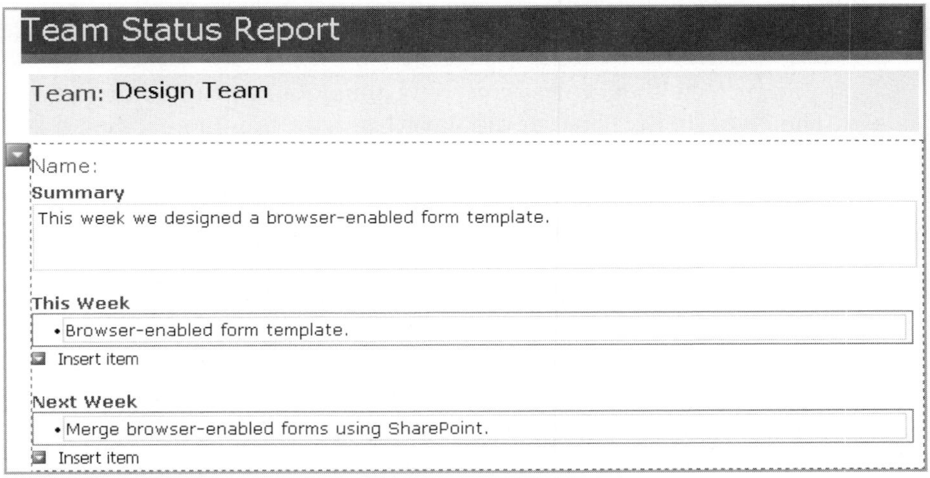

FIGURE 12.39: Filling out the Team Status Report view in the browser

To see a print view of the current view, simply click on the *Print View* toolbar button (Figure 12.40) at the top or bottom of the form. (The toolbar may not be available at the top or the bottom, depending on the design of the form; we'll discuss toolbar configuration in Chapter 14.) After you click the button, a new browser window opens so the form-filling session is preserved in the original window.

FIGURE 12.40: Print View button on the Forms Services toolbar

The *Print View* button is always available by default for browser-enabled forms. If you choose not to offer this functionality to people filling out the form in a browser, you can remove the button from the toolbar. However, removing the button is an all-or-none decision for all views on the form. Unfortunately, there is no mechanism to enable the *Print View* button for some views but not others.

Figure 12.41 shows the browser-enabled version of the print view of the *Team Status Report* view from Figure 12.39. Notice that print views in the

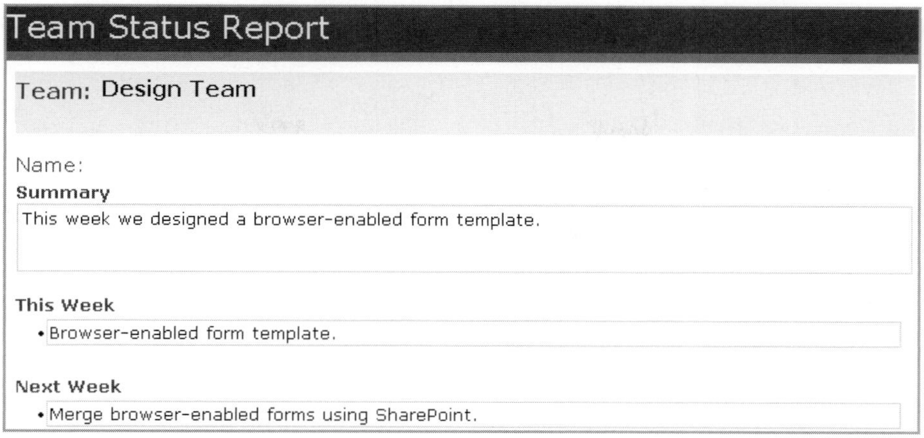

Team Status Report

Team: Design Team

Name:

Summary

This week we designed a browser-enabled form template.

This Week

- Browser-enabled form template.

Next Week

- Merge browser-enabled forms using SharePoint.

FIGURE 12.41: Team Status Report view shown as a print view in the browser

browser are always read-only. Also, any nonessential form interaction components, such as the *Insert Item* links and widget buttons on Sections and Table rows, are removed.

Exporting Forms

As we mentioned earlier, sometimes the printing functionality included in InfoPath doesn't give you everything you need. You've seen how to create a Word print view so you can print by using Word, which has more extensive printing capabilities and print fidelity. However, you have to do a bit of work to create the XSL for the Word print view. Also, this functionality is limited to Word. And sometimes you'll want to print the current view by using another application, such as Internet Explorer. Also, when you're working with data such as sales figures, you'll likely want to analyze the data using Excel.

Forms Services

The ability to export forms isn't available when filling out a form in the browser. This feature is available only from the InfoPath client application.

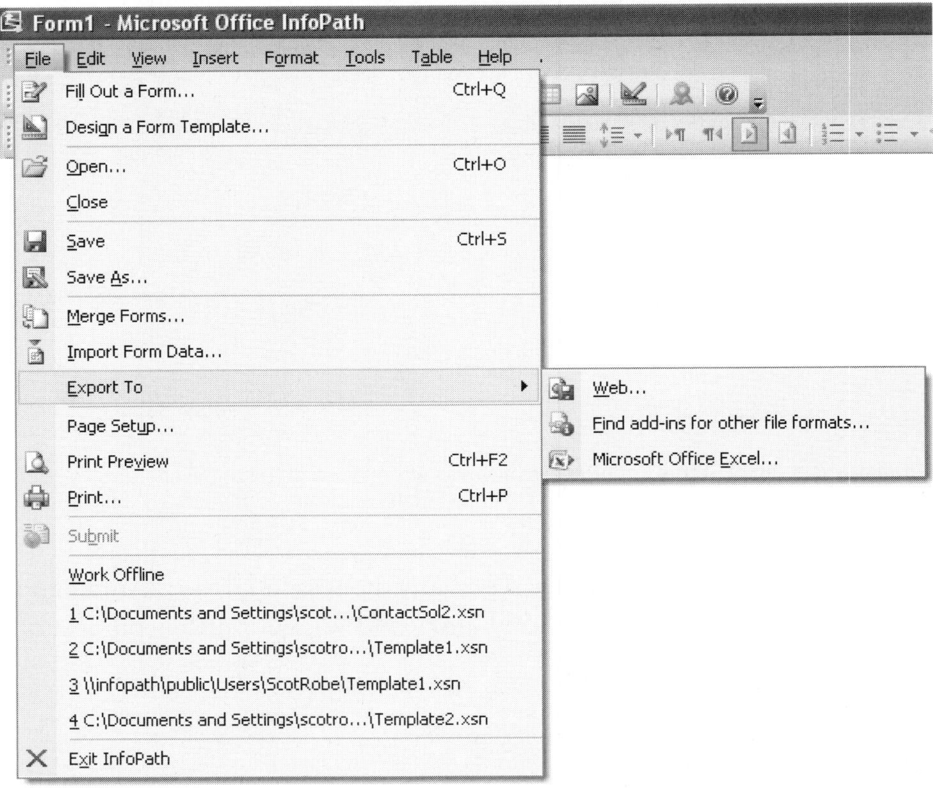

FIGURE 12.42: Export To menu item expanded

For these reasons, InfoPath allows you to export your data to other file formats. When filling out a form, the *File* menu contains an *Export To* item that offers different options for exporting your data, such as exporting to a Web format or Excel (Figure 12.42).

From this *Export To* menu, you can export the current document to a Web file. This option saves the current view as a Mime HTML file (MHT) that can be opened in other applications such as Internet Explorer, Word, or Excel. In addition to exporting to a Web file, you can also download additional importers by clicking the menu item titled *Find add-ins for other file formats.*

Whether you are exporting to an MHT or another file format (after downloading additional file exporters), you are likely doing so in order to take advantage of the printing capabilities of the applications that support these file formats. However, sometimes you want to export the data in order to perform some analysis in Excel. To do so, you can export the data in the form (or just the data in the current view) to an Excel spreadsheet. Let's look at this briefly.

Let's say that you want to analyze the sales data for the current week. You first merge the status reports from all the employees in the sales department to get the sales figures into an InfoPath form. Next, you want to export the sales data to Excel for analysis. After switching to the *Sales Report* view of the form, you click on the *Microsoft Office Excel* item on the *Export To* menu, which will launch the Export to Excel Wizard. After you click the *Next* button on the welcome page, the dialog looks like that shown in Figure 12.43.

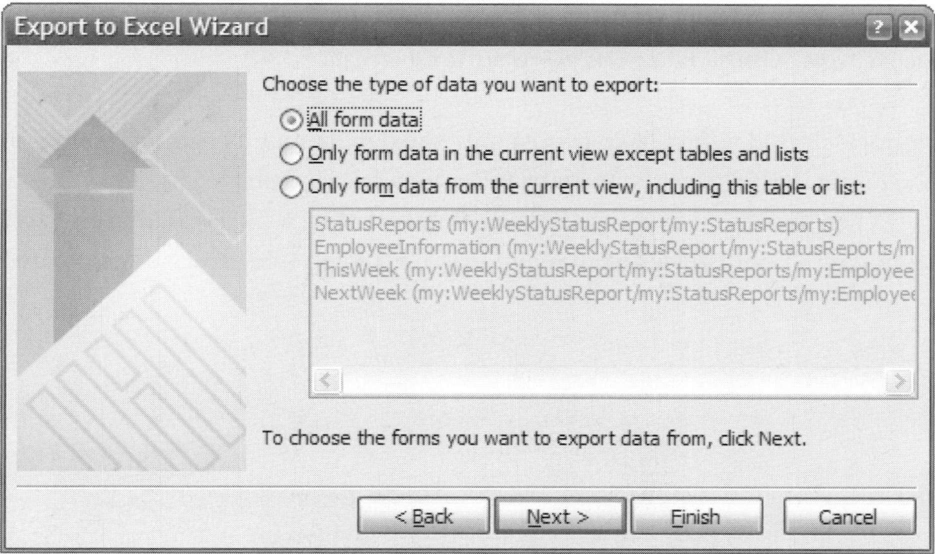

FIGURE 12.43: Choosing the type of data to export

The default option is to export all the data in the form. Clicking on the *Next* button navigates to the next step in the wizard (Figure 12.44).

From here, you can choose which forms to export. As you can see, you can choose multiple forms to export at the same time. Therefore, it's not necessary to merge the data into one form in order to export multiple forms. Since we've already merged the data into one form, we'll keep the default

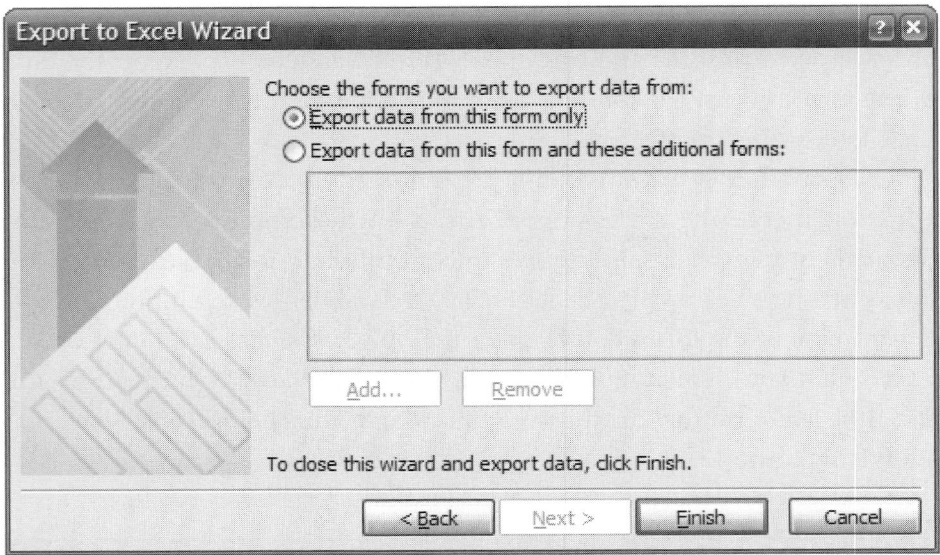

FIGURE 12.44: Choosing the forms from which to export data

option selected, which is to export only the data from this form. Clicking on the *Finish* button exports the data and opens Excel, as shown in Figure 12.45.

When the data is exported to Excel in this way, a list is created in Excel to make the data easier to manage. Also, an XML tree structure is created

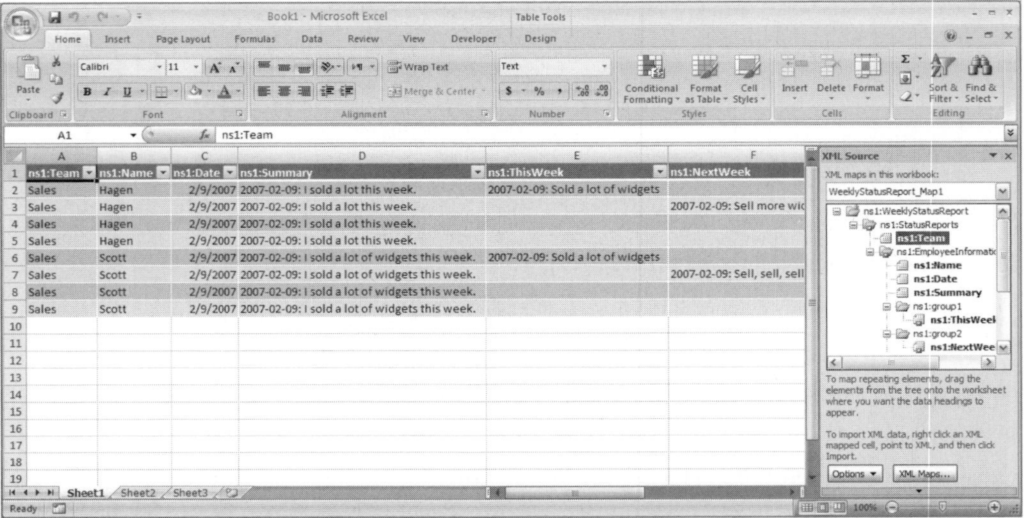

FIGURE 12.45: Status report data exported to Microsoft Office Excel

that matches the data source in the InfoPath form, and the data in the spreadsheet is linked to that XML structure. Now, since you have the data in Excel, you can sort, create charts, add calculations, or perform any of the normal operations you would do when analyzing data in Excel.

You may notice from Figure 12.45 that all the data in the InfoPath form was exported—even the team name, employee name, and employee status information. Since you want to analyze just the sales data, you probably don't want the other information. You can easily remove those columns from Excel, but ideally you would export just the sales data. To do this, when you are asked to choose the type of data to export in the Export to Excel Wizard, instead of choosing *All form data,* choose the option *Only form data from the current view, including this table or list.* Figure 12.46 shows how the wizard looks after we chose this option. In this case, we want to export just the sales data stored in the `SalesDataItems` repeating group node. Therefore, we've selected this group node from the list.

FIGURE 12.46: Export to Excel Wizard after choosing to export only the data from a specific table

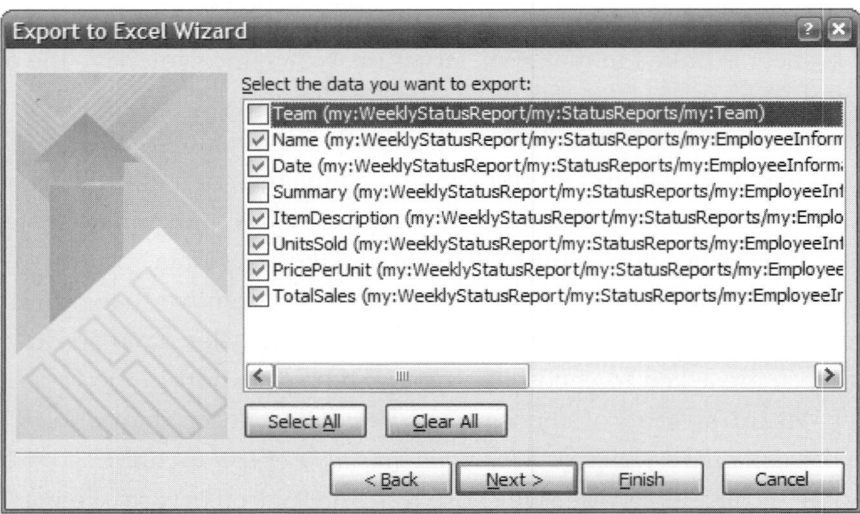

FIGURE 12.47: Selecting the data to export

When you click the *Next* button, you are asked to select the data you want to export (Figure 12.47). As mentioned, we want to export only data that is specific to the sales made and the employees who made them. Therefore, we've unchecked the `Team` and `Summary` data items.

Next, click the *Finish* button to export the data and open Excel, as shown in Figure 12.48. (Clicking *Finish* at this point skips the option to choose which forms to export. Since we want to export only data from this form, clicking *Finish* is fine.) In this case, since we are exporting the data from a specific table or list in the view, an XML tree structure and list are not created as they would be if we exported all the data. (This is an unfortunate limitation, but you can still use Excel to analyze the data.)

Looking back at Figure 12.46, you'll notice that there is one other option for exporting the data to Excel—*Only form data in the current view except tables and lists.* This option enables you to export data that is not inside a repeating group node. This is not extremely useful for the status report form since everything is inside a repeating group node. However, this could be useful if your form has a mixture of data that is and is not inside repeating groups or fields. If you wanted to export just the nonrepeating data for some reason, this is the option you would use.

So far, everything we've shown you about the export functionality can be done by a user when filling out a form. As you probably have guessed,

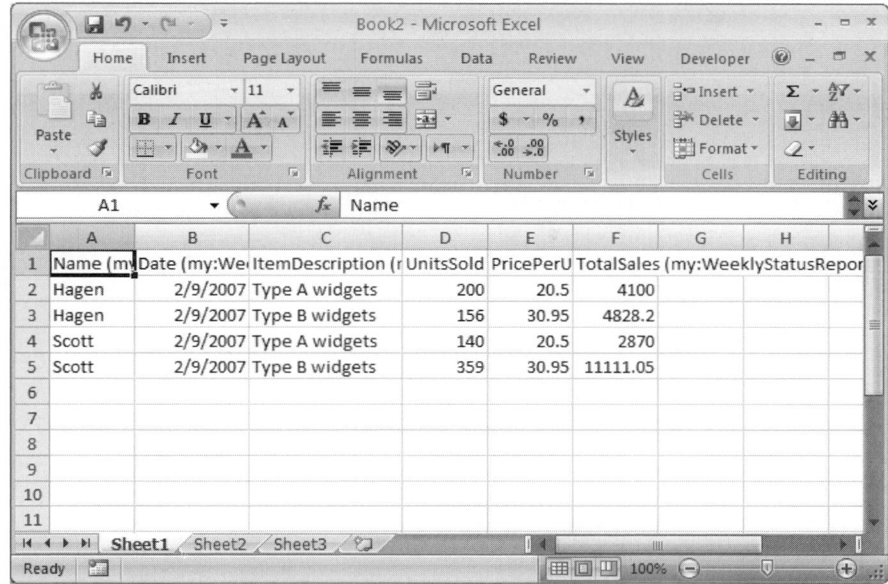
	A	B	C	D	E	F	G	H
1	Name (my	Date (my:We	ItemDescription (r	UnitsSold	PricePerU	TotalSales (my:WeeklyStatusRepor		
2	Hagen	2/9/2007	Type A widgets	200	20.5	4100		
3	Hagen	2/9/2007	Type B widgets	156	30.95	4828.2		
4	Scott	2/9/2007	Type A widgets	140	20.5	2870		
5	Scott	2/9/2007	Type B widgets	359	30.95	11111.05		

FIGURE 12.48: Sales data exported to Microsoft Office Excel

as with most other end-user features, you can control the export features when designing a form template.

As you've seen before, when designing a form, the *Form Options* dialog (available from the *Tools* menu) contains many options for customizing the behavior of the form template you are currently designing. (These options do not affect other form templates.) On the *Open and Save* tab of this dialog (Figure 12.49) is a section that allows you to enable or disable specific open and save features. From here, you can specify whether or not users who fill out forms based on your form template can export the form. You can turn off all export options or just a few. When you disable one of these options for the form template, the associated menu option becomes disabled when filling out a form.

NOTE **Exporting Form Templates**

In addition to exporting form data when filling out a form, it is also possible to export a form template. This option is available on the *File* menu in design mode. Clicking on this menu item launches the Export Wizard. We'll talk more about this wizard and how to create a form template exporter in Chapter 21.

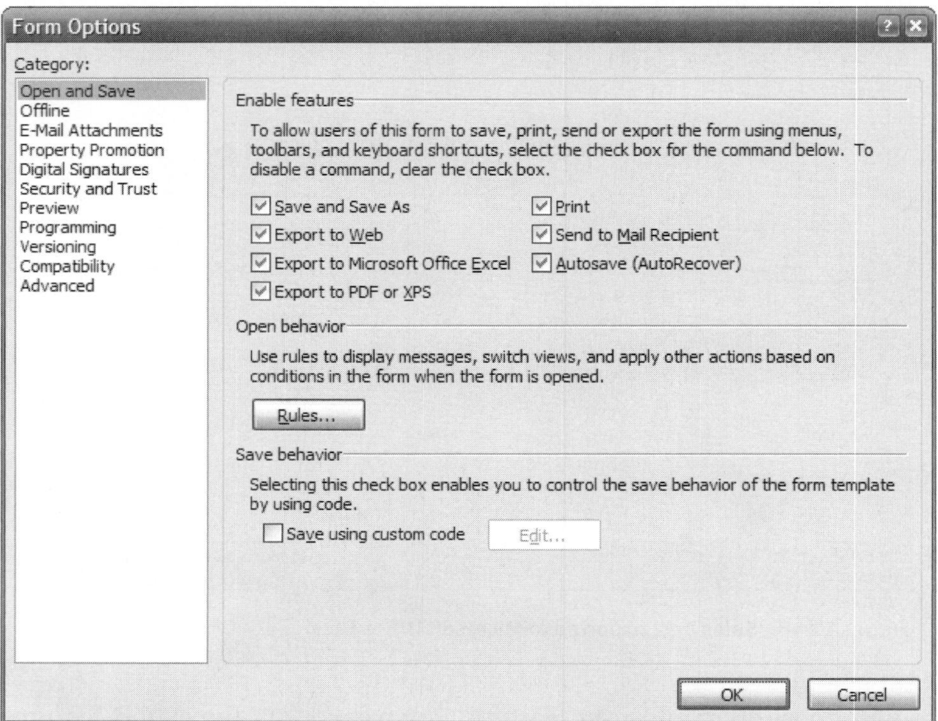

FIGURE 12.49: Open and Save tab of the Form Options dialog

What's Next?

In this chapter, we've shown you how to merge forms in InfoPath and how you can change the default merge behavior for a form when designing the form template. We then talked about how you can create professional reports by using InfoPath and Word print views. Finally, we showed you how to export data from an InfoPath form to other applications for printing or data analysis.

In the next chapter, we'll talk about integrating InfoPath into workflow processes in your company. We'll show you how to use user roles to determine who gets to see what in your form. We'll also talk about how InfoPath integrates into Outlook for a seamless e-mail experience. So, without further ado, let's move on.

13 Workflow

Getting Started

By now, you have most of the basics of designing InfoPath form templates under your belt. You can design a form template using most of the features available in InfoPath. The question that, inevitably, comes up is how to build a **workflow** process around an InfoPath form. In other words, how do you incorporate InfoPath forms into existing workflow processes that, in most organizations, consist simply of e-mail?

Let's take the status report form from Chapter 12 as an example. The status report we built can contain sales data filled out by an employee from the sales department. We can publish the status report form template to a Microsoft Office SharePoint Server (MOSS) 2007 site from which employees can open the form template and fill out their weekly status reports. The form template also contains views that management can use to create aggregate reports. Once the employees complete their status reports, management will use the same form template to create aggregate reports and analyze the sales information. The average employee usually won't use those views. Thus, in this status report form, we can incorporate **user roles**, which is an InfoPath feature that enables you to control the data that users can view in a form template. With user roles, we can show employees only the data and views that are important to them.

The scenario we just described is an example of how you can build a workflow process around an InfoPath form with user roles and MOSS 2007.

However, this particular scenario relies on all the participants in the workflow knowing what to do at each step of the workflow process. If the form is a travel request, for example, the person filling out the form needs to know about the approval process for travel requests in his or her organization. This can easily lead to extra work or errors if that person doesn't follow the process exactly. Ideally, you would like to build a formal workflow process that integrates InfoPath with MOSS 2007 in such a way that each step of the workflow process is defined ahead of time so that each person filling out a form doesn't need to understand the entire process.

So far, the scenarios we've described require you to build a workflow process from scratch. Most corporations, however, have existing workflow processes that typically consist of sending forms or other documents through e-mail. For companies that have existing status report forms, for example, after an employee enters his status information, that person will typically e-mail it to his manager. His manager, after reviewing the status report, may compile a team status report and then e-mail it to her manager, and so on.

In this chapter, we'll first show you how to incorporate user roles into your form templates, not only to control who sees what data in a form but also to make the process of data entry easier for your users. Once we've covered user roles, we'll talk about how to integrate InfoPath forms with workflows in MOSS 2007. Then we'll show you how to integrate InfoPath forms with existing e-mail workflow processes by using **InfoPath e-mail forms** in Outlook 2007. So, let's start with a discussion of user roles in InfoPath form templates.

User Roles

In every organization around the world, whether it is a small business, a large corporation, a military organization, a university, or even a family, people have different roles. In a corporation, a person can be considered a vice president, a manager, or an individual contributor. In a university, a person could be a professor or a student. In many cases, a person can even hold multiple roles. For example, in a software organization or IT department, a person is not only an employee but can be a technical manager and even a software developer or tester as well. Likewise, in a sales department, a sales manager could also be considered a salesperson. In all cases for a corporation, whether you are a manager or a vice president, you are also an employee of the company.

Forms Services

User roles are not supported in Web-enabled forms.

The role you hold in a corporation often dictates the type of data you are interested in and even the data you are permitted to access. Therefore, when designing a form template, you often must consider the roles of those who will be filling out forms based on your form template.

InfoPath provides user roles that enable you to control the data in a form based on a person's role. With user roles, you can set the values of certain fields in the form based on the team a person belongs to, for example. You can also control which views in the form a person can see based on his or her role. As you will see, with user roles, you can establish a workflow wherein participants see only the data for which they are responsible. Using the status report form template we built in Chapter 12 as an example, a possible workflow could be the following.

1. Employees fill out their weekly status reports. If an employee is in the sales department, the section of the form pertaining to sales information is available. If he or she is not in the sales department, that section of the form is hidden.
2. Next, at the end of the week, the manager of each team creates a report containing all the status information for his or her team. In this case, only the managers of each team can see the *Team Status Report* view, which they use to generate the weekly aggregate status report.
3. Finally, each week, the sales manager generates a sales report and distributes it to the vice president of the department. (In this case, the sales manager will likely also export the data to Excel and perform some data analysis.) Since the sales manager is the only team manager who needs to generate a sales report, he or she is the only person who can access the *Sales Report* view.

In this section, we'll show you how to incorporate user roles into a form template to enable the workflow scenario just described. We'll start by creating the roles we want to use in our form. Then we'll show you how to incorporate user roles with other InfoPath features such as rules, filters, data validation, and conditional formatting. Finally, we'll discuss how to specify who can access which views in a form using user roles. Let's start by creating the user roles we need for our form template.

> **WARNING** User Roles Are Not a Security Feature
>
> User roles are included in InfoPath as a convenience feature and are not a reliable way to ensure the privacy or security of data in the form. Even though a user may not be able to view the data in the form due to his or her current role, the user can still open the underlying XML in another editor (such as Notepad) to view the data. However, if the form is IRM protected, the data will be encrypted, so then users will not be able to view the underlying XML data. Therefore, if you wish to impose privacy restrictions on the data in an InfoPath form, you can combine user roles with IRM. However, we don't suggest that you rely on user roles alone as a security and/or privacy feature.

Creating User Roles

Creating user roles is a fairly straightforward process. To begin, click on the *User Roles* menu item, which is available on the *Tools* menu. The *Manage User Roles* dialog opens (Figure 13.1). This dialog lists all the user roles you

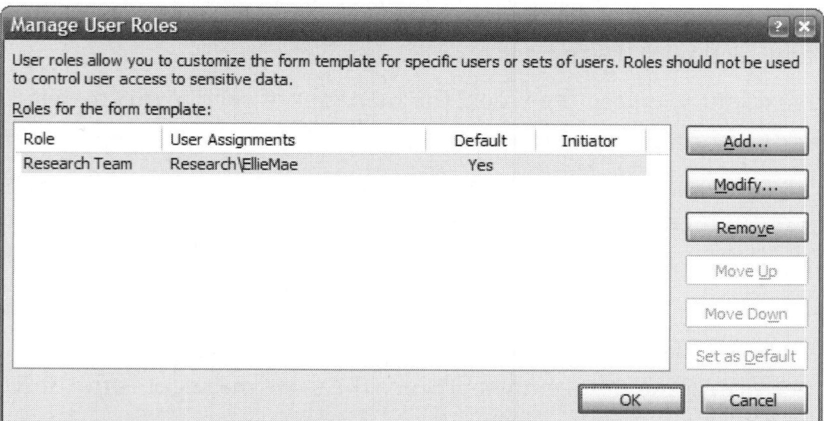

FIGURE 13.1: Manage User Roles dialog

have created. (We've already created one for the research team, as you can see.) In the *Manage User Roles* dialog, you can add new roles, modify or remove existing ones, change the ordering of roles, and set a specific role as the default.

Let's create a new user role by clicking the *Add* button. The *Add User Role* dialog opens (Figure 13.2). (If you click the *Modify* button for an existing role, this same dialog opens, but with the title *Modify User Role.*) In the *Add User Role* dialog, the first thing you should do is give your new user role a name. In this case, we're going to create a role for the employees on the sales team, so we named our user role "Sales Team".

FIGURE 13.2: Add User Role dialog

Next, we need to assign users to this role. Here we can assign individual user names or groups of users. There are two ways to assign users to a role and one way to assign a user group.

1. User names: Selecting the *User names* checkbox enables you to enter a list of the NT domain accounts of users in your organization. These account names must be in the format domain\username. Multiple

aliases must be separated by semicolons. If you know the names of the NT domains and accounts of the users you want to add to a role, you can just type them in. However, the easiest way to enter user names is by clicking the button to the right of the edit box, which brings up the *Select Users* dialog (Figure 13.3). From here, you can choose your users and even click the *Advanced* button to search for users in the address book. Also, you can click the *Locations* button to choose the location to which the user alias belongs. (Note that in InfoPath 2003, you can specify a location only under your current domain. In InfoPath 2007, you can specify a location under any domain in your corporation.)

2. Group names: Selecting specific user names for a role gives you fine-grained control. However, if you have a lot of users to add to the role, adding them can be quite tedious. In that case, instead of adding each user one by one, you can choose a group of users by selecting the *Group names* checkbox and entering the name of the groups you want to add to the role. In this case, InfoPath supports Active Directory groups only, which include Microsoft Exchange Server distribution lists for Microsoft Exchange Server 5.5 and above.

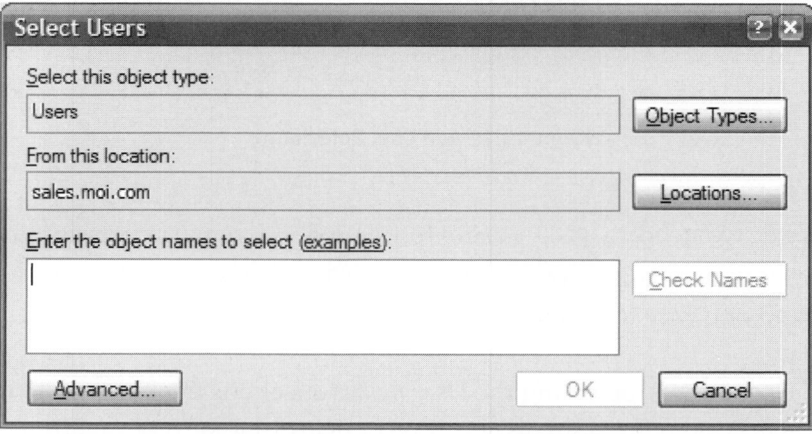

FIGURE 13.3: Select Users dialog

(InfoPath doesn't currently support NT domain groups since they are used in the context of security.) Note that, for privacy reasons, groups that contain private or hidden membership or that contain subgroups with private or hidden membership cannot be used in a user role.

3. Dynamic user names: In addition to listing user names one by one in the dialog, user names can be retrieved dynamically when the form is filled out. To do so, select the checkbox next to *User names from the form* and click the button next to the related edit box. This opens the oh-so-familiar *Select a Field or Group* dialog that we've seen many times. From here, you can choose a field from the main data source or a secondary data source. (Note that the field you choose must have a *Text (string)* data type.) One of the advantages of using this option is that it allows you to store your user names in a secondary data source that can be reused across multiple form templates. That way, there's no need to enter each user's name in each form template you create.

As you can see from the dialog shown in Figure 13.3, you have the option of selecting user names and groups for your user role from one or more of the different sources. You can choose specific users names, one or more groups, and/or user names from the form. By using this dialog, you can, for example, create a role that includes all the managers in one department (by selecting a group name) and the vice president of your company (by explicitly listing his or her user name).

One final option available in the *Add User Role* dialog is the *Set as initiator* checkbox. Selecting this option allows you to specify that this user role is the one that should be used whenever a new form is filled out. In other words, the first time you fill out this form, the user role will automatically be set to this specified role. If an existing form is opened, then the role is set as normal. (We'll talk more about how this is done shortly.)

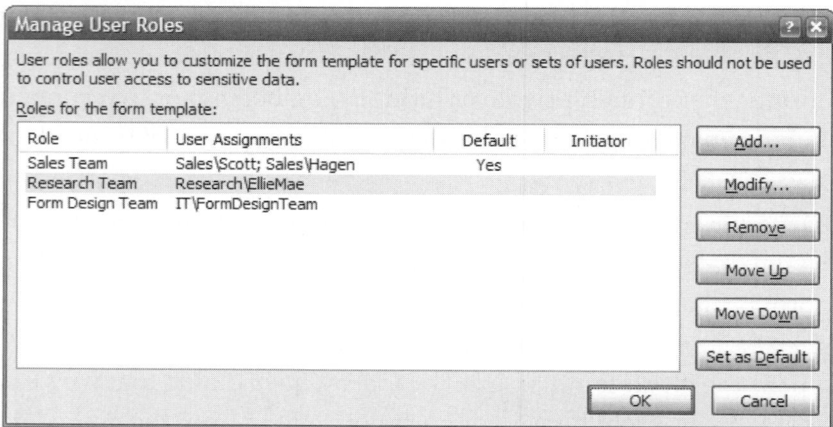

FIGURE 13.4: Manage User Roles dialog after adding a few roles

Figure 13.4 shows the *Manage User Roles* dialog for our status report form template after we've added a few more roles (including one using Active Directory groups).

Determining a User's Role When Filling Out a Form

The previous discussion of the initiator role brings up a good question: How are user roles determined when filling out a form? As just mentioned, if a role is set as the initiator, then whenever you open a blank form based on that form template, the role you specified as the initiator is set as the current role. For example, let's say that I have a purchase request form. For this form, there are two possible roles (and potentially more). One role is that of the person who is requesting to purchase something. You could call this role the "Requester" role. Another role is named the "Approver" role. This person either approves or rejects the purchase request. Whenever anyone fills out a purchase request for the first time, that person assumes the "Requester" role. However, when an existing purchase request form is opened, the role that is used depends on two things: the roles defined in the form template and who is opening the form.

For existing forms (or when there is no initiator role specified in the *Manage User Roles* dialog), each role in the form template is evaluated in the order listed in the *Manage User Roles* dialog to determine to which role the current user belongs. (Note that you can use the *Move Up* and *Move Down* buttons shown in Figure 13.4 to change the order in which the roles are evaluated.)

Since InfoPath allows a user to belong to only one role at a time, the first role that the user is found to belong to becomes the current user role. As you can tell from Figure 13.2, for each role listed in the *Manage User Roles* dialog, there are three possible ways to determine if a user belongs to a role: NT domain account, Active Directory group, or XML data in a data source. If the NT domain account of the person using the form matches one of the user names specified in the *Add User Role* dialog or in the XML field specified in this dialog, that person belongs to that role. (If a role contains user names from the form and from a list of NT domain accounts, those from the form are checked first.) Likewise, if Active Directory groups are specified in the *Add User Role* dialog and the current user belongs to one of those groups, that person belongs to that role. If the current user doesn't match any of the roles specified in the *Manage User Roles* dialog, the default role (as specified in that same dialog) is used.

> **NOTE** The `XDocument.Roles` Property
>
> The way roles are determined can be controlled further by using the `XDocument.Roles` property in the InfoPath object model. Part II of this book will explain the InfoPath object model in more detail.

User Roles in Action

Now that we've created the user roles we want to use in our form template, let's put them to use. There are many ways you can use roles in a form template. Basically, anywhere you can specify a condition in a form template, you can use a role in the condition. That means that you can use user roles with rules, filters, data validation, and conditional formatting. Each of these features allows you to specify a condition. And, as we talked about in Chapter 5 when we talked about the condition builder, one of the qualifiers you can choose from is the user's current role.

To see how this works, let's add each one of these—a rule, a filter, data validation, and conditional formatting—to our status report form template to make the process of data entry a little easier. (Each of the form templates we are about to create is included with the samples for this chapter on the book's Web site.)

User Roles in Rules

Looking back at our status report form template, remember that when an employee is filling out a status report in the *Weekly Status Report* view, the first thing he or she must do is select his or her team from the *Team* Combo Box control at the top of the view. Considering that, from week to week, a person's team name doesn't change, it's a little tedious to have to enter the same data each time he or she fills out the report. It sure would be nice to have a way to auto-populate this Combo Box control with the team name of the person filling out the form. As you know from Chapter 5, you can use rules when a form is opened in order to perform various actions—one of which is setting the value of a field in the form. Using rules together with user roles, we can set the value of the *Team* Combo Box control to the team to which the current user belongs. Let's see how.

First, we must open the *Form Options* dialog from the *Tools* menu. On the *Open and Save* tab of this dialog is a *Rules* button, as shown in Figure 13.5. (This is a review from Chapter 5.) By clicking this button, we can specify rules that will be applied when the form is opened.

As you know, when you add a rule, you can specify a condition. One of the qualifiers you can specify for the condition is the user's current role.

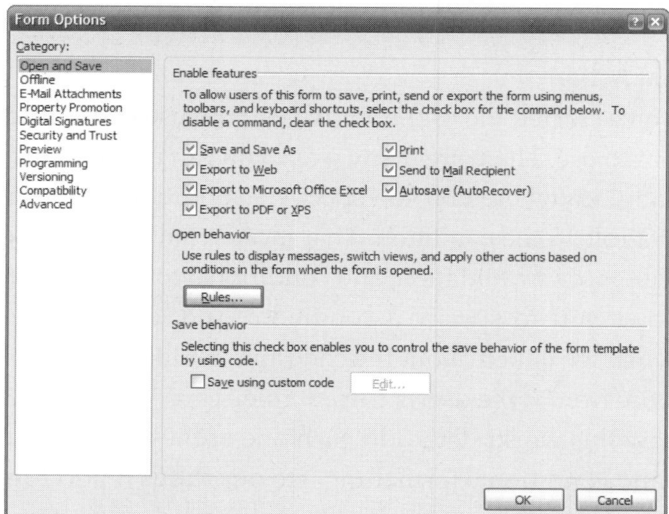

FIGURE 13.5: Open and Save tab of the Form Options dialog

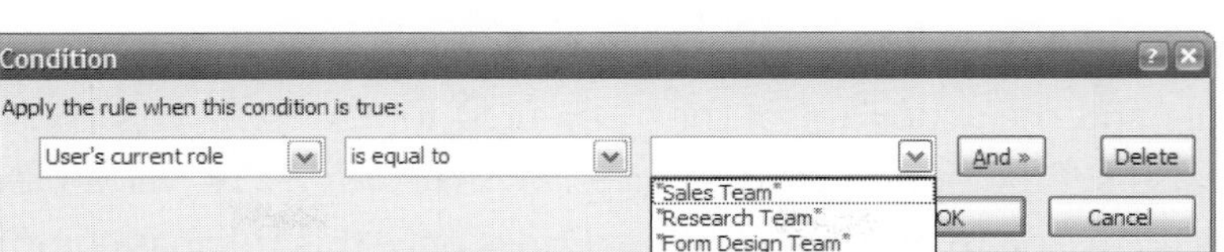

FIGURE 13.6: Selecting User's current role as the qualifier in the Condition dialog for rules

Figure 13.6 shows the *Condition* dialog after we clicked on the *Set Condition* button in the *Rule* dialog. In this case, we have selected *User's current role* as the qualifier. As you can see, you can choose one of the roles you created earlier from the value drop-down list box. (Note that you can select *Manage user roles* from this drop-down list box. Doing so opens the *Manage User Roles* dialog you saw in Figure 13.1. This way, it's not necessary to create all your user roles when you first start designing a form template.)

Now, in order to auto-populate the *Team* Combo Box control with the team name of the person filling out the form, we must create one rule for each value we wish to set. Likewise, it will be necessary to have one user role that corresponds to each team. Since we currently have three user roles—"Sales Team", "Research Team", and "Form Design Team"—let's go ahead and create one rule for each of these. For each rule, the action we will specify in the *Action* dialog is *Set a field's value.* The field we are going to set is the `Team` field, and the value will correspond to the user role. For example, for the "Sales Team" user role, the `Team` field will be set to `"Sales"`. Figure 13.7

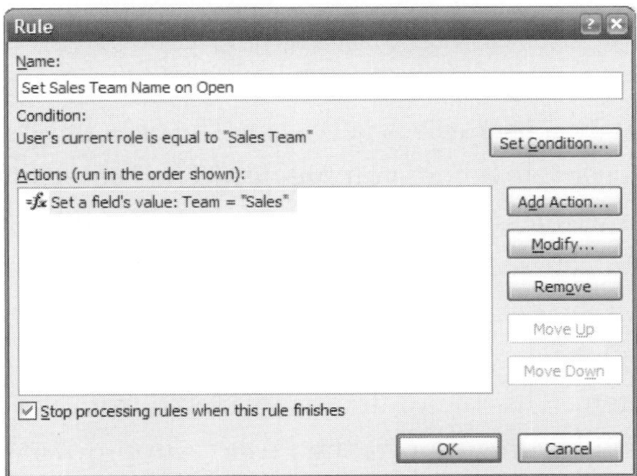

FIGURE 13.7: Rule dialog after setting the condition and action

shows the *Rule* dialog after we've set the condition to use the "Sales Team" user role and the action to set the `Team` field to `"Sales"`. (As you can see, we've also set the option to *Stop processing rules when this rule finishes* since there is no reason to process additional rules once this rule has completed.)

Figure 13.8 shows the *Rules for Opening Forms* dialog after we've added all the rules for the three user roles.

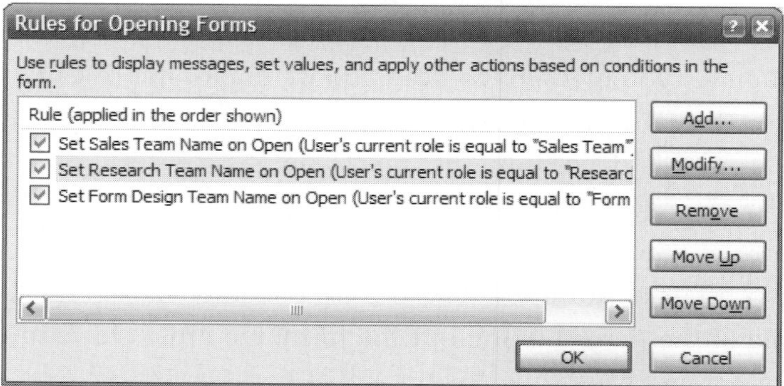

FIGURE 13.8: Rules for Opening Forms dialog after adding all rules

Previewing with a User Role

Before we continue to add more features to our form template, we should test our changes to make sure everything works. But how do you test the form template for each of the user roles? You could ask a few people around the company who have different roles to help you. Or you can just preview the form with a specific user role.

Previewing with a user role is very easy. The only thing you really need to do is set the user role before you preview. The *Form Options* dialog that you've seen many times before has a *Preview* tab (Figure 13.9).

As usual, you can access the *Form Options* dialog from the *Tools* menu and then click on the *Preview* tab. However, there is a handy-dandy way to open the *Form Options* dialog and jump directly to this tab—the *Preview Settings* menu item. This menu item is available from the *Preview* popup menu item on the *File* menu or on the *Preview* drop-down menu available on the *Standard* toolbar (Figure 13.10). Selecting the *Preview Settings* menu item opens the *Form Options* dialog directly to the *Preview* tab.

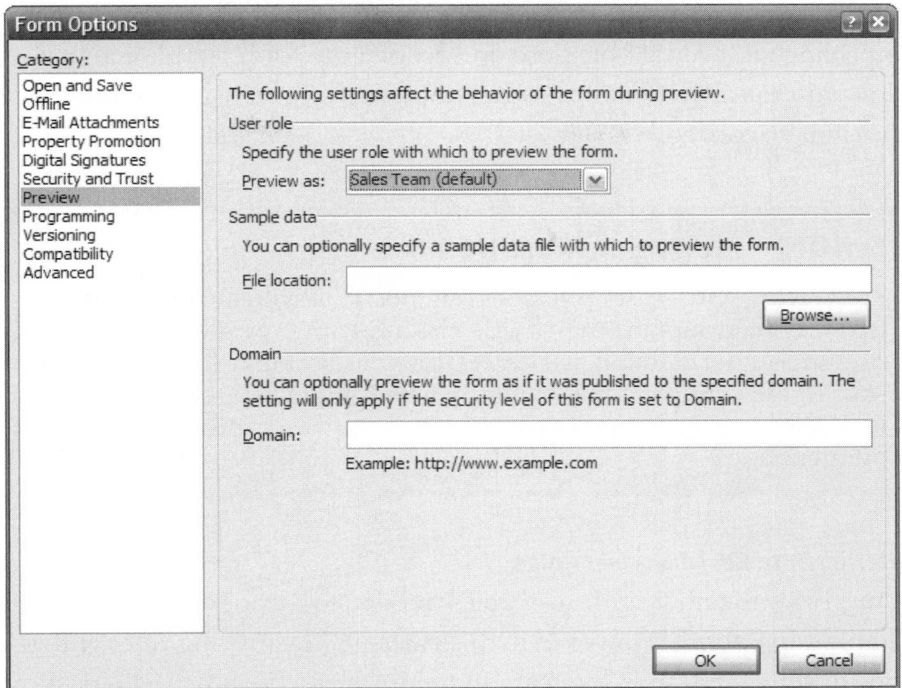

FIGURE 13.9: Preview tab on the Form Options dialog

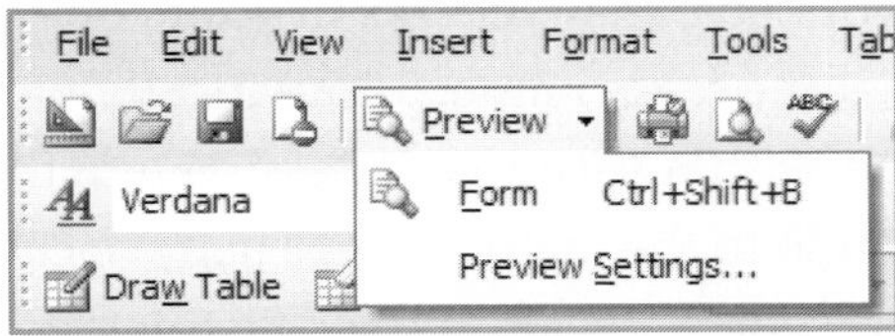

FIGURE 13.10: Preview drop-down toolbar menu

You'll notice at the top of the *Preview* tab that there is a section titled *User role*. This is where you can specify the user role that should be used when you preview the form. When you first open this dialog, if no user roles are specified for the form template, the drop-down list box is disabled. When user roles are available, they are listed in the drop-down list box, with the default user role listed first. The remaining roles are listed in the order they were created.

After you set a user role in the *Preview* tab and close the dialog, the next time you preview your form template, the current role will be set to the role that you chose in the *Form Options* dialog. (This value will remain until you change it, even if you close and reopen the form template.) This will allow you to easily test your form template while using the different user roles you've created.

> **NOTE** Previewing with a User Role
>
> Previewing with a user role does not mean that you are impersonating that user or group. In other words, the InfoPath preview window is not running under another user's NT domain account. InfoPath always runs in the context of the logged-in Windows user. Previewing with a user role simply provides a simple way to test your form template with different roles.

Filtering Data Based on User Roles

Using rules together with user roles allows you to perform some pretty complex operations. However, in this particular case, using rules with user roles to set the name of the team in the form can be quite tedious. As we mentioned, you have to create one rule for each team name in the department or corporation. This could take quite a bit of time and be a maintenance nightmare if you have many teams in your company.

A better way to set the team name automatically would be to use a calculated default value with a secondary data source that contains a mapping from each user role to the team name. Then we can add a filter with a user role to select the correct team name. Listing 13.1 contains the data from an XML file that contains the mapping from user roles to team names.

LISTING 13.1: XML Containing Mapping from User Roles to Team Names

```
<TeamData>
      <Teams>
          <Team>
               <UserRole>Sales Team</UserRole>
               <TeamName>Sales</TeamName>
          </Team>
          <Team>
               <UserRole>Research Team</UserRole>
               <TeamName>Research</TeamName>
          </Team>
```

```
        <Team>
            <UserRole>Form Design Team</UserRole>
            <TeamName>Form Design</TeamName>
        </Team>
        <Team>
            <UserRole>Development Team</UserRole>
            <TeamName>Development</TeamName>
        </Team>
        <Team>
            <UserRole>Test Team</UserRole>
            <TeamName>Testing</TeamName>
        </Team>
    </Teams>
</TeamData>
```

Let's look at how this is done. First, we must add the `TeamData` XML file shown in Listing 13.1 to our form template as a secondary data source. (Refer to Chapter 6 if you need a refresher on how to do this.) Next, since there is no longer any reason to list all the team names in the form, let's change the *Team* Combo Box control to a Text Box control by right-clicking on the Combo Box and choosing *Text Box* from the *Change To* menu. The user won't be able to choose a team name from the list, but if he or she still wants to change the value we set, the user can just type it in.

Finally, let's use a calculated default value with a user role in order to set the team name to the correct one for the current user. As you may remember from Chapter 3 when we talked about calculated default values, you can choose a field from the main data source or a secondary data source when adding a default value. In addition, you learned in Chapter 7 how to filter data obtained from a data source. Let's combine these two features with user roles to set the value of the *Team* Text Box control based on the `TeamName` field in our secondary data source. Here we want to obtain the team name that corresponds to the user's current role.

First, open the properties dialog for the Text Box control and open the *Insert Formula* dialog by clicking the *fx* button next to the *Value* edit box. Then let's choose the `TeamName` field from our secondary data source by clicking on the *Insert Field or Group* button in the *Insert Formula* dialog and choosing the `TeamName` field from the `TeamData` secondary data source.

Next we add a filter by clicking on the *Filter Data* button in the *Select a Field or Group* dialog. This filter will specify that we want to select the `TeamName` field from the secondary data source where the value of the corresponding `UserRole` field matches the user's current role. To do so, after clicking the *Add* button, we first select *User's current role* from the qualifier drop-down list box in the *Specify Filter Conditions* dialog. Then, in the value drop-down list box, choose *Select a field.* This opens the *Select a Field or Group* dialog as usual, from which we choose the `UserRole` field that corresponds to the `TeamName` field in the secondary data source, as shown in Figure 13.11.

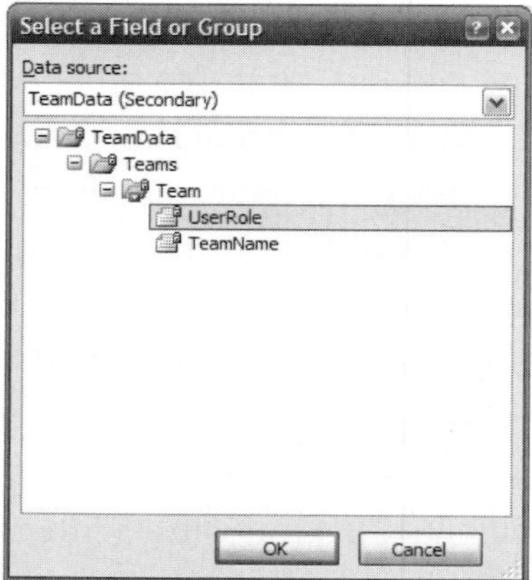

FIGURE 13.11: Selecting the `UserRole` field that corresponds to the `TeamName` field in the secondary data source

After we set the filter to the `UserRole` field in the secondary data source and close the *Filter Data* dialog, the *Insert Formula* dialog looks like that shown in Figure 13.12. Now when you preview the form using different

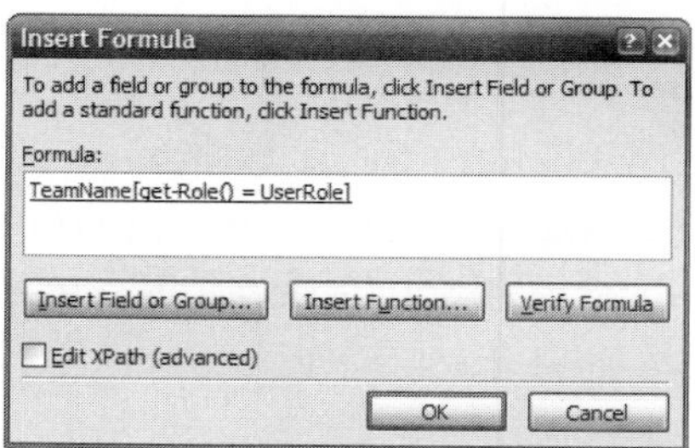

FIGURE 13.12: Insert Formula dialog after adding a calculated default value

user roles as we talked about earlier, you will see that the team name is automatically set for you.

> **NOTE** **Setting a Default Value to a User Role**
>
> You may have noticed in Figure 13.12 that the calculated default value contains a function call: `get-Role()`. This is an extension function that InfoPath uses to get the user's current role. Instead of using a secondary data source with a filter, you can simply use this function call to set the value of the field to the user's current role. To do so, simply open the *Insert Formula* dialog as usual and then add `get-Role()` to the *Formula* edit box. However, using a secondary data source that contains user role mappings allows you to change assigned user roles without having to update all the form templates that use them.

Data Validation with User Roles

As we mentioned, even though we are setting the team name when the form is opened, the user can still change it. We could prevent the user from changing it by making the *Team* Text Box control read-only. However, you may want to allow the user to change it in the off chance that the user has switched teams or the team name is otherwise set incorrectly. Remember, though, that if the user sets the team name to "Sales", he or she will be able to enter sales information. Obviously, we want to prevent any employee who is not a member of the sales team from submitting sales data. Therefore, if the user sets the team name to "Sales", we want to flag the control with a data validation error and prevent the form from being submitted. (The user will still be able to save the form, so he or she won't lose any data, but you don't want to allow the form to be submitted until this problem is corrected.) Using data validation, we can easily show users a warning and prevent them from submitting the form if the team name is "Sales" but their current user role is not in the sales team.

Just as with rules and filters, we can specify a user role in the condition for data validation. Figure 13.13 shows the *Data Validation* dialog for the `Team` field after specifying a user role in the condition. Here, if the current user entered "Sales" for the team name but is not a member of the sales team, a data validation error will be displayed along with a warning message.

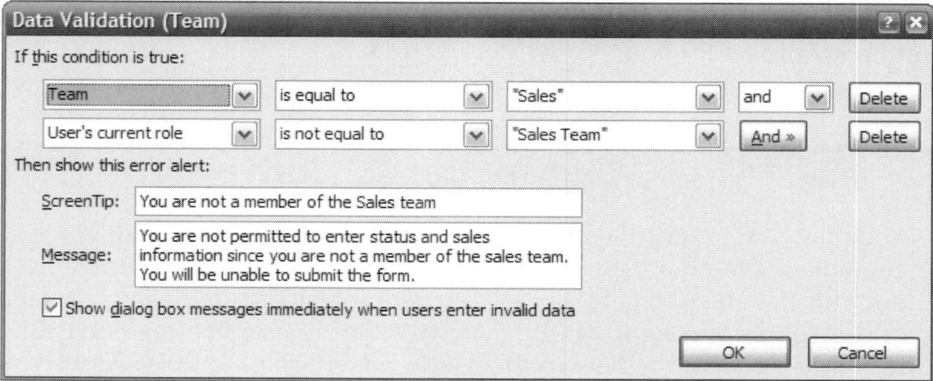

FIGURE 13.13: Specifying a user role in the condition for data validation

When this happens, the user will be able to save the form to his or her local machine but will not be able to submit it.

Conditional Formatting with User Roles

As you can see, by using data validation with user roles, you can prevent the user from entering sales information if that user is not a member of the sales team. That's very useful, but why show the sales data section of the form at all if the user is not a member of the sales team? Remember from Chapter 12, when we first designed the weekly status report form template, that when a user is filling out a status report, we use conditional formatting to hide the section of the form that contains the sales data when the value of the `Team` field is not `"Sales"`. However, users are free to enter "Sales" for the team name and then fill out sales information as they wish. Using conditional formatting with user roles, we can show the sales data section of the form only when the user is actually a member of the sales team, whether or not the team name is set to "Sales".

Hiding the sales data section based on the user's current role is very simple. First, we must open the properties dialog for the Section control that is bound to the `SalesData` group node in the form template. Then switch to the *Display* tab and click on the *Conditional Formatting* button to open the *Conditional Formatting* dialog. Since this control already uses conditional formatting, we simply need to modify the condition to use user roles

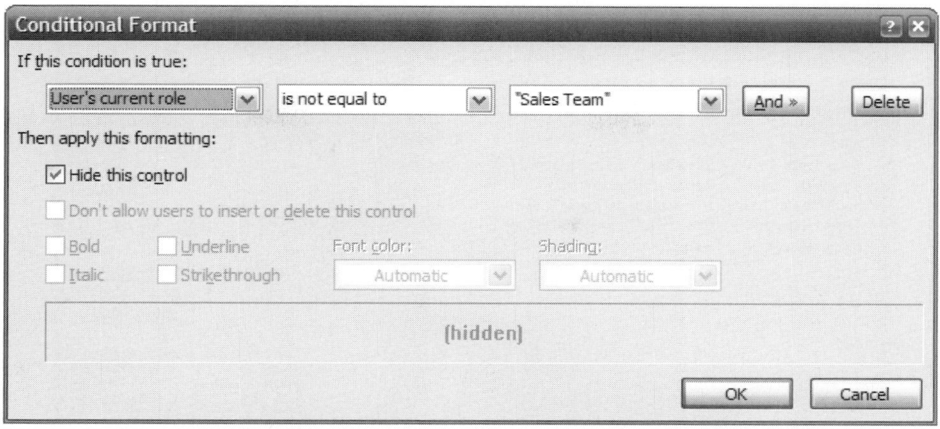

FIGURE 13.14: Conditional Format dialog after changing the condition to use a user role

instead of the value of the `Team` field. Figure 13.14 shows the *Conditional Format* dialog after we made these changes. Now when the current user is not a member of the sales team, the sales data section of the form will be hidden. Also, this means that there is no need for data validation on the *Team* Text Box. If the user changes the value of the `Team` field to `"Sales"` (and that user is not a member of the sales team), he or she can enter status information but still will not be able to enter sales data.

Role-Based Views

Now that we've put user roles to use in the first step of the status report workflow, let's incorporate them into the last two steps—creating the team status and sales reports. As we mentioned earlier, we want only team managers to be able to access the *Team Status Report* view to create the weekly team status report. Likewise, we want only sales managers to be able to access the *Sales Report* view to create the sales report for the week. To do this, we can use user roles to determine who can access which view. We accomplish this by hiding all views from the *View* menu when a user fills out a form and then using Button controls to navigate from one view to another. We use rules on each Button to determine whether the user has access to the next view. (Using Button controls to control view navigation also enables you to direct the current user to the next step in the workflow.)

The first thing we must do is create two new user roles—"Team Manager" and "Sales Manager"—by using the *Manage User Roles* dialog, as we

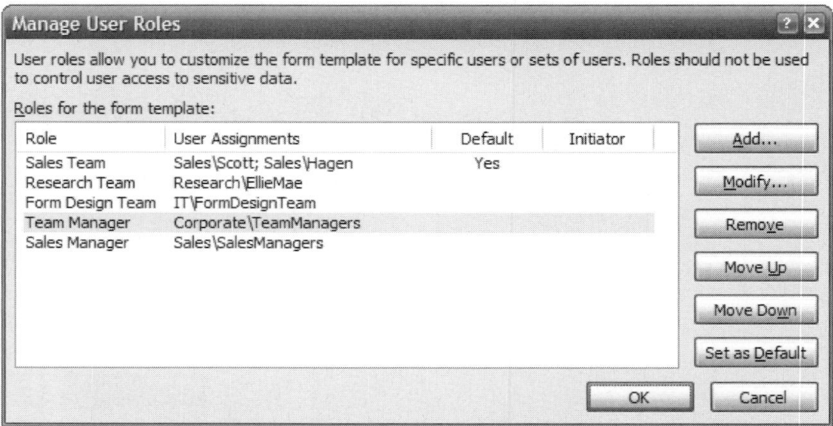

FIGURE 13.15: Manage User Roles dialog after adding "Team Manager" and "Sales Manager" roles

described how to do earlier. Figure 13.15 shows this dialog after we added the two new roles.

Next, let's hide each of the views from the *View* menu when filling out the form. To do so, just open the properties dialog for each view and uncheck the option *Show on the view menu when filling out the form.* Once you do this for all views, the user will be able to see only the default view. Next, let's add one Button control to each view to control the workflow from one view to the next and to control who can see which view.

First we add a button to the *Weekly Status Report* view, which is the default view for the form template. We'll give this button the label "Team Status Report" to indicate that pressing it will allow the user to view the *Team Status Report* view. Since we want only team managers to view the *Team Status Report* view, we will use conditional formatting together with user roles to hide this button when the user's current role is neither "Team Manager" nor "Sales Manager". Figure 13.16 shows the *Conditional Format* dialog after we made these changes.

Finally, to make this button do something useful, we'll add a rule that will switch the view to the *Team Status Report* view when the button is clicked. Figure 13.17 shows the *Rule* dialog after we added this rule.

Next, let's add a similar button to the *Team Status Report* view that will switch the view to the *Sales Report* view. However, in this case, we'll be more restrictive. Since only sales managers can view the sales report, in the

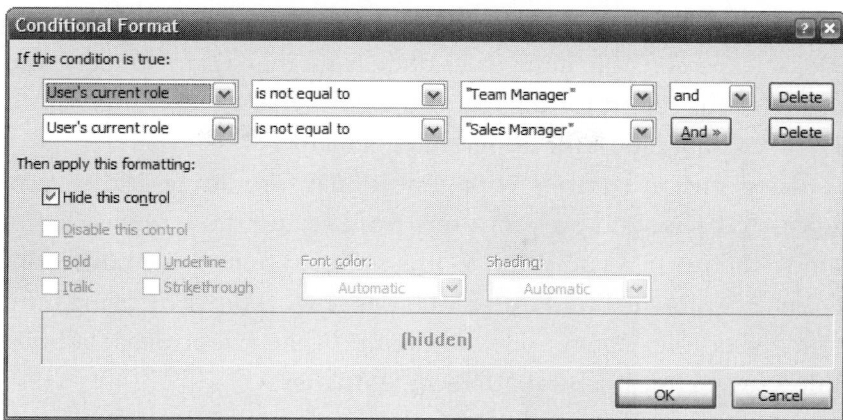

FIGURE 13.16: Conditional Format dialog after adding conditions for manager roles

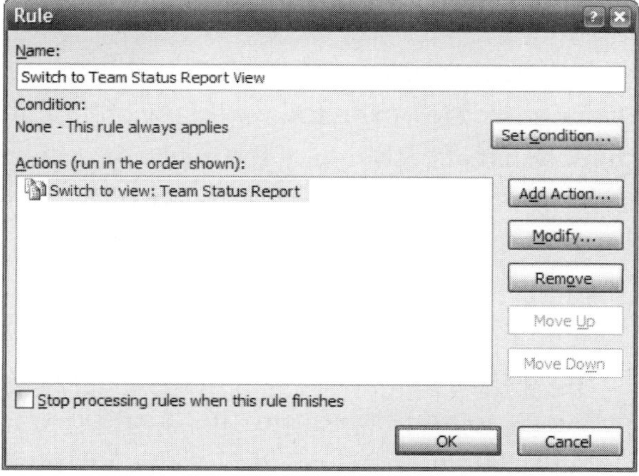

FIGURE 13.17: Rule dialog after adding a rule to switch to the Team Status Report view

Conditional Format dialog, we will specify that the user's current role must be "Sales Manager" in order to see the button. As with the first button we added, we need to add a rule to this button to switch to the *Sales Report* view. (Ideally, you will also want to add buttons to each view that will enable the user to get back to the *Weekly Status Report* and *Team Status Report* views.)

Now you're ready to publish your new status report form. As you can see, by using user roles with rules, filters, data validation, and conditional formatting, we were able to establish a workflow for our status report form. In this workflow, the user of our form needs to worry about only the data for which they are responsible. Employees can fill out their status reports, salespersons can enter sales data, team managers can generate the aggregate status report for the team, and sales managers can generate the weekly sales data report for upper management.

By using Button controls with conditional formatting and user roles, we've created a way to prevent users from seeing those views that don't pertain to their role. In addition to this scenario that we've built, you can easily imagine how to build different types of workflows by using buttons, rules, and user roles. We're sure you can think of endless ideas for building workflows with roles in InfoPath form templates.

Workflow with Microsoft Office SharePoint Server 2007

As we mentioned, with user roles, you can control who can view specific data and views in a form. However, the workflow still depends on knowing who needs to do what at each step of the way. For example, if you have a travel request form that needs to be approved by your manager, your manager still needs to know that something must be done. After you fill out the travel request form, you'll most likely need to send an e-mail to your manager to tell him or her that you have submitted a request. Then, your manager will need to know what needs to be done to approve the request and whether or not multiple approvals are needed.

By using InfoPath 2007 with MOSS 2007 (which is built on Windows SharePoint Services [WSS] 3.0), you can make this process much easier. Using these two Microsoft products, you can easily establish different types of workflow processes, as we'll show you in this section.

But first, let's talk briefly about exactly what a workflow is. A workflow is, basically, just a set of one or more activities that, together, represent some process. A workflow models a set of activities to be performed from start to finish. A workflow design usually consists of a model that groups a set of activities. This model contains not only the activities that pertain to the workflow but also the transitions between activities and the conditions (if any) that may determine which activity is next in the flow.

Workflows can contain either human or system processes. There are two types of workflow: sequential and state machine. A **sequential workflow** is ideal for operations that include a series of steps executed one after another until all the activities are completed. A **state machine workflow** consists of a set of states, transitions, and actions. In this type of workflow, there is a start state and, usually, an end state, with transitions in between. In addition, actions can be performed at each state in the workflow.

Using the Microsoft Windows Workflow Foundation, which includes a Visual Studio 2005 extension, you can create your own workflows by using a graphical designer. In addition, you can use Microsoft Office SharePoint Designer 2007 to create workflows. However, unlike Visual Studio, you cannot easily integrate InfoPath forms into the workflow when using SharePoint Designer.

MOSS 2007 includes a set of default workflows you can use right out of the box, as listed in Table 13.1. (Additional workflows available with

Table 13.1: Workflows Included with Microsoft Office SharePoint Server 2007

Workflow Name	Description
Approval	Routes the form for approval to the people you specify.
Collect Feedback	Allows you to collect feedback from various people. The form will be routed to those people you specify so they can review the form. The review feedback is compiled and sent to the owner of the form when the workflow is complete.
Collect Signatures	Routes the form to various people in order to collect signatures. This workflow allows you to obtain multiple signatures for a form or other document.
Disposition Approval	Allows participants to maintain documents. By using this workflow you can determine whether to retain or delete documents that are expired.
Group Approval	Functions similarly to the Approval workflow. However, this workflow, which is available only in East Asian versions of MOSS 2007, allows users to use a stamp control as opposed to a signature.
Translation Management	Helps you manage the translation of documents from one language to another. This workflow is available only for a Translation Management Library.

WSS 3.0 are not listed in this table. All of the workflows in Table 13.1 work with InfoPath 2007. However, not all of the workflows in WSS 3.0 will work with InfoPath.) Although a full discussion of workflow is outside of the scope of this book, we will talk a bit about the workflows built into MOSS 2007. (See the Appendix for good resources that talk about the Windows Workflow Foundation and provide information about how to build your own workflows.)

Let's look at an example to see how you can use one of the built-in workflows. Let's say that we want to create an Approval workflow for all travel requests in the department. When a person makes a travel request, he or she must first have the request approved by his or her manager and then by the head of the department. The head of the department doesn't need to see the request if the requester's manager rejects the approval.

As it happens, InfoPath includes a Travel Request sample form template that you can customize or use as is. Without changing it, let's publish this form template to a MOSS 2007 document library. (See Chapter 9 if you need a refresher about how to publish a form to SharePoint.)

Once you have finished publishing the Travel Request form template to SharePoint, creating a workflow to route the document for approval is fairly easy. First, navigate to the SharePoint form library you created when you published the Travel Request form template. Then, go to the form library settings page and click on *Workflow settings.* Since we've never created a workflow for this form library before, the *Add a Workflow* page opens (Figure 13.18). Here, we can specify the different options for the workflow, such as the type of workflow, its name, a task list, a history list, and start options. We will choose the Approval workflow and call it Travel Request Approval. We'll also specify the option to *Start this workflow when a new item is created* under the start options. This will start the workflow and, therefore, initiate the approval process each time a new travel request form is filled out. After you have finished setting the workflow options, click the *Next* button.

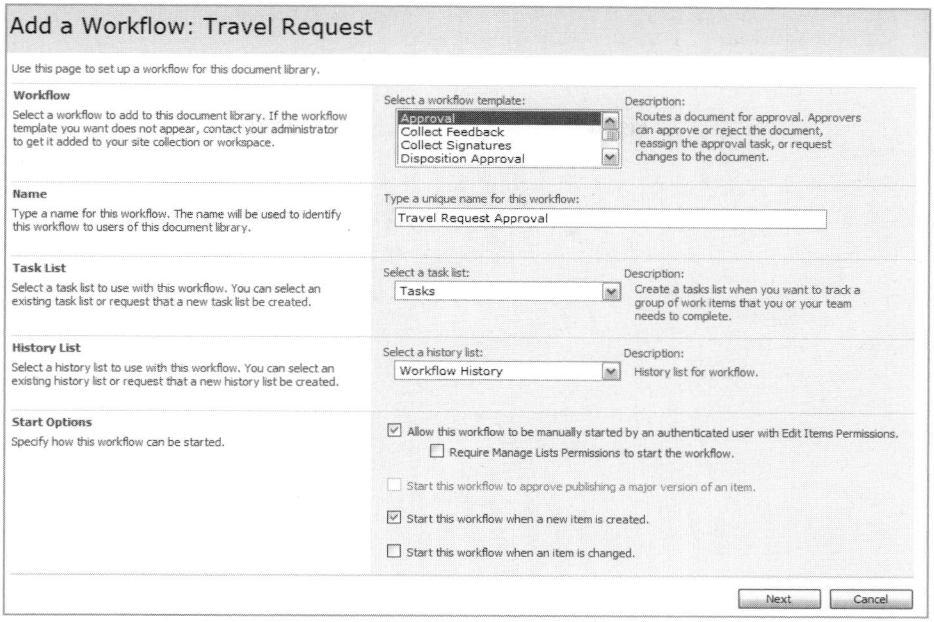

Add a Workflow: Travel Request

Use this page to set up a workflow for this document library.

Workflow
Select a workflow to add to this document library. If the workflow template you want does not appear, contact your administrator to get it added to your site collection or workspace.

Select a workflow template: Approval, Collect Feedback, Collect Signatures, Disposition Approval

Description: Routes a document for approval. Approvers can approve or reject the document, reassign the approval task, or request changes to the document.

Name
Type a name for this workflow. The name will be used to identify this workflow to users of this document library.

Type a unique name for this workflow: Travel Request Approval

Task List
Select a task list to use with this workflow. You can select an existing task list or request that a new task list be created.

Select a task list: Tasks

Description: Create a tasks list when you want to track a group of work items that you or your team needs to complete.

History List
Select a history list to use with this workflow. You can select an existing history list or request that a new history list be created.

Select a history list: Workflow History

Description: History list for workflow.

Start Options
Specify how this workflow can be started.

- [x] Allow this workflow to be manually started by an authenticated user with Edit Items Permissions.
  - [ ] Require Manage Lists Permissions to start the workflow.
- [ ] Start this workflow to approve publishing a major version of an item.
- [x] Start this workflow when a new item is created.
- [ ] Start this workflow when an item is changed.

Next | Cancel

FIGURE 13.18: Add a Workflow page

NOTE When to Choose Automatic versus Manual Initiation of a Workflow

When customizing a workflow, as we mentioned, you can specify that the workflow should be started automatically when a new item is added. The Approval workflow is the classic case where you would want to specify this option. In our example, whenever a travel request is entered, you automatically want the workflow to start so that the approval process will happen immediately. In most scenarios like the travel request, you always want a workflow to start whenever a new form is created.

There are other cases where you don't want a workflow to start automatically. The Collect Feedback workflow is one example. This workflow is ideal for those cases where you have created a document (such as a white paper or software specification) that you would like to have reviewed by multiple people. In this case, you want to allow the user to start the workflow manually. The user, therefore, can work on the document for days, weeks, or months and request feedback only when the document is complete.

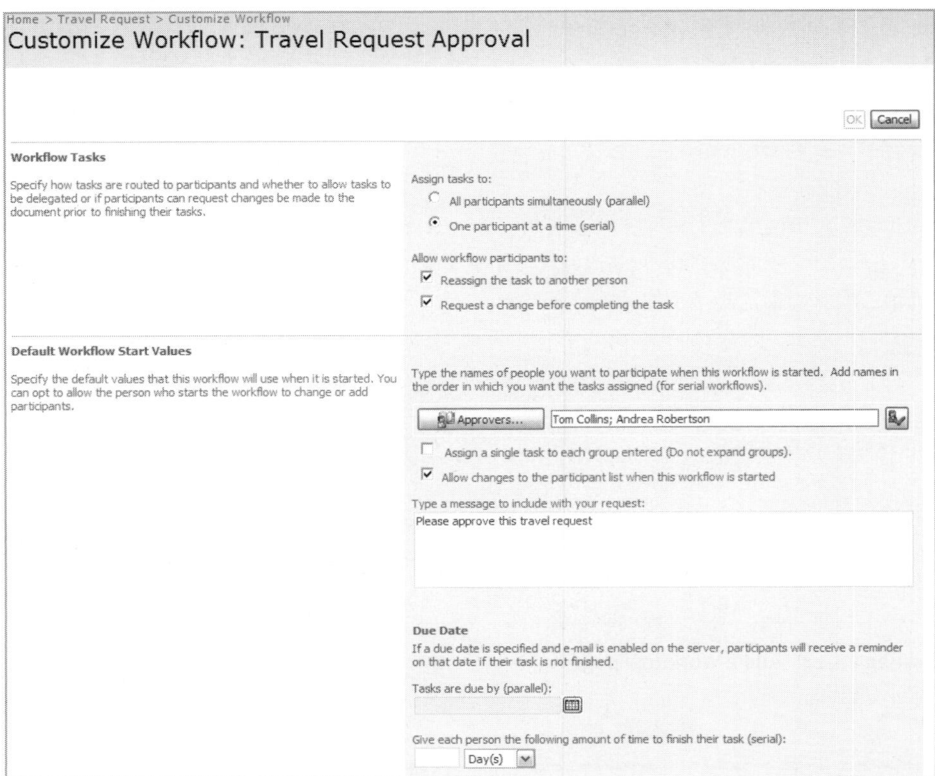

FIGURE 13.19: Customizing the Travel Request Approval workflow

Next, we can customize the Travel Request Approval workflow, as shown in Figure 13.19. Here's where you can specify the list of approvers. Since we want to have the request first approved by the manager and then by the head of the department, in that order, we'll specify to assign tasks to one participant at a time. (Tasks that are assigned to each participant are stored in the task list that you specified when creating the workflow.) Also, we must list the e-mail aliases of the approvers in the order we wish them to approve the request. Since the manager, say, Tom, must approve the request before the head of the department, say, Andrea, we will list Tom's name first. Also, in this page you can specify such options as whether or not the approvers can reassign the task to somebody else, when the workflow is considered complete, and so on. For our simple scenario, we'll just add the list of approvers and a message to include with the request. For all other options, we'll just accept the defaults. Once you finish customizing the workflow, click the *OK* button.

Next, let's see what happens when somebody fills out the Travel Request form. When a person fills out a request and saves it to the SharePoint site, the approval process is started. (The process is started whenever a new form is saved to the form library since we specified that the Approval workflow should be started whenever a new item is added.) When the Approval workflow starts, two things happen. First, the person who created the workflow in SharePoint (which is usually the same person who owns the document library) receives an e-mail similar to the one shown in Figure 13.20 that tells him or her that the workflow has started.

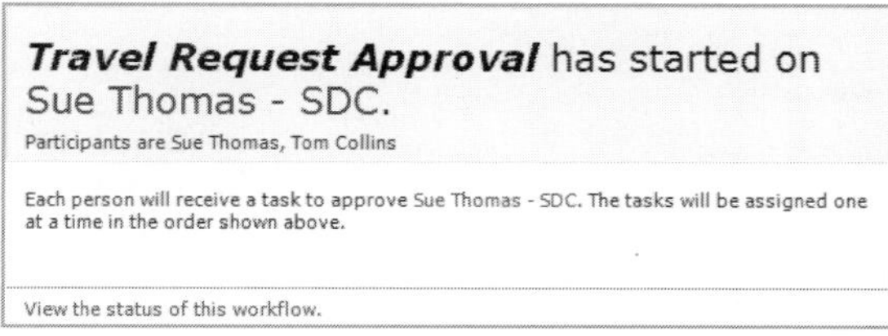

Travel Request Approval has started on Sue Thomas - SDC.
Participants are Sue Thomas, Tom Collins
Each person will receive a task to approve Sue Thomas - SDC. The tasks will be assigned one at a time in the order shown above.
View the status of this workflow.

FIGURE 13.20: Workflow initiation e-mail message

Second, the initial approver will be assigned an Outlook task and will receive an e-mail similar to the one shown in Figure 13.21. When Tom receives this e-mail, he knows that a travel request needs his approval. He can then click on the link to the form in the e-mail message to open the form in InfoPath.

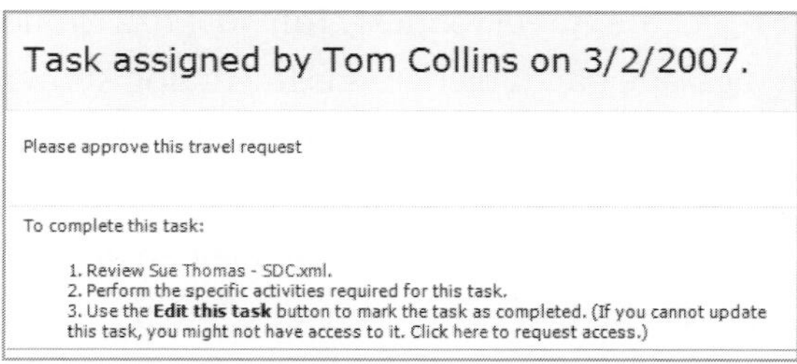

Task assigned by Tom Collins on 3/2/2007.
Please approve this travel request
To complete this task:
1. Review Sue Thomas - SDC.xml.
2. Perform the specific activities required for this task.
3. Use the Edit this task button to mark the task as completed. (If you cannot update this task, you might not have access to it. Click here to request access.)

FIGURE 13.21: E-mail task requesting approval of the travel request

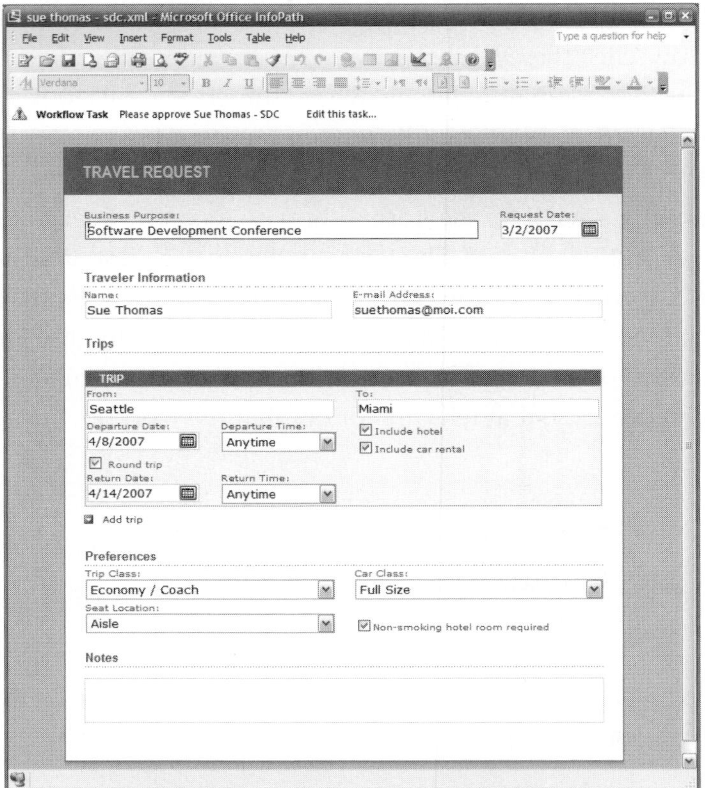

FIGURE 13.22: Travel Request form showing the Workflow Task message bar

After Tom opens the form, the *Workflow Task* message bar appears at the top of the form to tell him that there is something he has to do. Figure 13.22 shows the message bar for this travel request. (Note that you can hide or show the message bar on the *View* menu in InfoPath.)

To approve or reject the travel request, Tom just has to click on the *Edit this task* button in the message bar, which opens the dialog shown in Figure 13.23. In this dialog, he can approve or reject the task, reassign it, or request a change. If Tom approves the request, the next step in the workflow starts. For the Approval workflow, the next step is to request an approval from the next approver we specified when creating the workflow. In this case, Andrea will receive an e-mail similar to the one shown in Figure 13.21. She then must follow the same steps as Tom to approve the request. Since she is the last approver in the workflow, if she approves the form, the workflow is then considered complete.

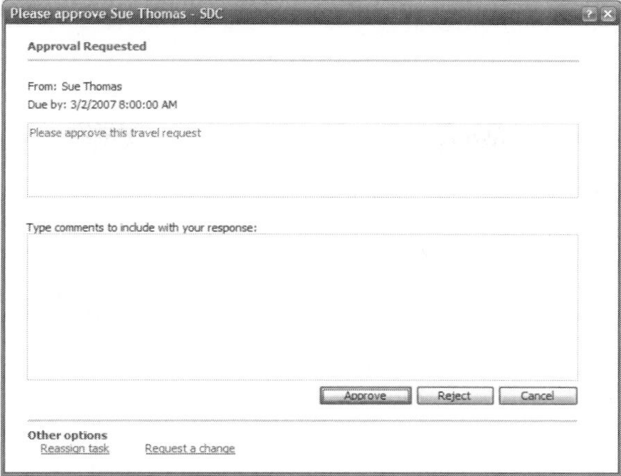

FIGURE 13.23: Workflow dialog

> **NOTE Message Bar and Workflow Dialog in Microsoft Office Applications**
>
> The *Workflow Task* message bar in Figure 13.22 and the workflow dialog in Figure 13.23 are not specific to InfoPath. Other Microsoft Office 2007 applications support workflows from MOSS 2007 in the same fashion. Word, Excel, PowerPoint, and InfoPath all support the *Workflow Task* message bar and workflow dialog. (It's interesting to note that the workflow dialog shown in Figure 13.23 is actually a dialog that is hosting the InfoPath form control, which we'll talk more about in Chapter 18.)
>
> Even though not all types of documents support these user interface features, workflows can be used with any document or item stored in a SharePoint list or document library.

One nice convenience feature included with MOSS 2007 is the ability to check on the status of your request at any point in time. When you create a workflow, WSS adds a new column to the document library that has the same name as the name of the workflow (e.g., Travel Request Approval). By looking at that column, you can easily tell the current status of the workflow, such as "In Progress". Clicking on the status opens up a detail page that lists the full detail of the approval process, including the tasks and workflow history. Using this detail page, you can easily tell the status of your request at any time.

In addition to having the workflow start automatically from SharePoint, you can also initiate a workflow from within InfoPath by choosing the *Start Workflow* item on the *File* menu. (You can also view workflow tasks by clicking on *View Workflow Tasks* on the *File* menu.) Clicking this item will open the dialog shown in Figure 13.24. Clicking on the *Start* button in the dialog will initiate the workflow.

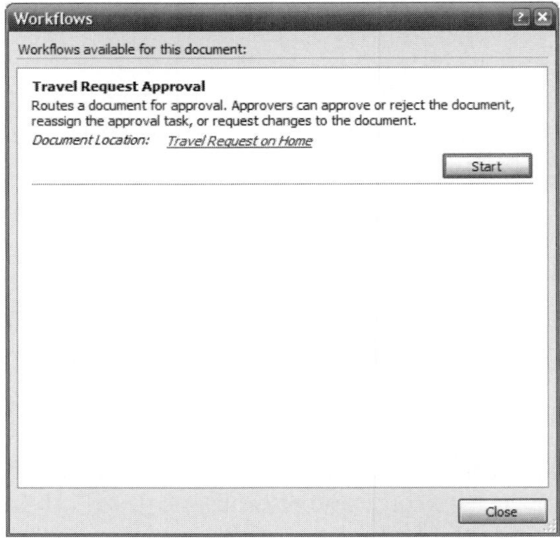

FIGURE 13.24: Workflows dialog

As we mentioned, a full discussion of workflow is outside the scope of this book. However, we hope that this simple example has sparked your interest and will prompt you to investigate workflows in MOSS 2007 a bit more. You have seen how InfoPath includes support for workflow processes from MOSS 2007 and how easy it is to create a workflow on SharePoint that includes an InfoPath form. We encourage you to read the workflow references listed in the Appendix if you are interested in learning more.

Forms Services

Browser-enabled forms can participate in workflows in MOSS 2007. However, the *Workflow Task* message bar and workflow dialog are available only in the InfoPath client application.

Workflow with InfoPath E-Mail Forms

So far, we've talked about creating new workflows with user roles and MOSS 2007. There is yet another way to establish a workflow using InfoPath forms—via e-mail. Many corporations have existing workflow processes that use e-mail, so integrating InfoPath forms into this process requires very little training on the part of your users. Also, even if your users are familiar with MOSS 2007, sometimes you just want to create a very quick form template that you can submit to your users through e-mail. For example, you may want to create a simple survey form template that will track the number of people who are going to attend the department's holiday party. In that case, you could just send an e-mail as usual. However, this makes it difficult to keep track of the number of people who will attend. It would be nice to create a simple InfoPath form template, e-mail it to those employees in the department, and then track responses in a special Outlook folder. Well, that's exactly what InfoPath e-mail forms are all about.

NOTE Disabling InfoPath E-Mail Forms in Outlook 2007

If, for whatever reason, you decide not to use InfoPath e-mail forms, you can disable them. The *Advanced Options* dialog for Outlook (*Tools -> Options -> Other* tab -> *Advanced Options*) has an option to enable or disable InfoPath e-mail forms. The option is checked by default, which specifies that it's enabled. Also, if you wish to disable this feature for all your users, you can create a `DWORD` value called `DisableInfopathForms` under the registry key HKCU\Software\Microsoft\Office\12.0\Outlook\Options\Mail. (There is also a policy key for this option in the Office Customization Tool [OCT]. Chapter 11 gives you more information about the OCT. Look for *Disable InfoPath e-mail forms in Outlook* in the OCT.) Setting the value to `"0"` disables InfoPath e-mail forms, while setting it to `"1"` enables it. This key is not present by default, which means that the e-mail forms feature is enabled.

With InfoPath e-mail forms, you, as a form template designer, can publish a form template to a number of e-mail recipients (as you've already seen in Chapter 9). Then, users can fill out, reply to, forward, and submit forms completely from within Outlook 2007 without having to directly open InfoPath. Users can open an InfoPath form in an e-mail item just as they would do with any other e-mail message. Then, when they submit the form, a reply is sent to you as the publisher of the form template. You can use Outlook to create a rule to store all the replies in a specialized **InfoPath form folder**, which will enable you to sort, filter, and group each of the replies based on content in the form itself. This will allow you to quickly track each of the forms that were submitted back to you. In addition, with InfoPath e-mail forms, you can merge multiple forms and export forms to Excel all from within Outlook.

Forms Services

Using workflows with InfoPath e-mail forms is supported only in the InfoPath 2007 client application due to its integration with Outlook 2007.

In this section, we will tell you all about InfoPath e-mail forms. We'll show you how to design form templates and publish them by using e-mail, how to fill out these forms from within Outlook 2007, and how to create custom folders in Outlook to store InfoPath forms.

NOTE InfoPath E-Mail Forms Sent to Other E-Mail Applications

If the person receiving the InfoPath e-mail form is using an e-mail application other than Outlook 2007 (including earlier versions of Outlook), the e-mail will not behave as an InfoPath e-mail form. Therefore, in that situation, you cannot take advantage of the features included in Outlook 2007 for InfoPath e-mail forms. However, those e-mail applications will receive a copy of the InfoPath form and a read-only view of the form in the body of the e-mail. If those users have InfoPath installed, they will be able to open the form and fill it out. (Whether or not users will receive a copy of the form is based on the settings of the form template. By default, this option is enabled. We will show you later in this chapter how to disable it if you so desire.)

Designing and Using InfoPath E-Mail Forms

Designing an InfoPath form template that will be used in an e-mail workflow scenario is, basically, the same as designing a form template for any other scenario. You can design your form template by using most of the features we've talked about already. Once you finish designing your form template, you simply publish it to a list of e-mail recipients. Let's walk through a complete workflow scenario from end to end. In this scenario, we will publish a form template to a list of e-mail recipients, fill out the form in Outlook 2007, store the submitted forms in an InfoPath form folder in Outlook, sort and filter the data, merge multiple forms into one from within Outlook, and export the data to Excel.

> **NOTE Restrictions of Forms Published to E-Mail Recipients**
>
> As we mentioned in Chapter 9 when we talked about publishing, only forms that have a restricted security level can be published to a list of e-mail recipients. Therefore, not all InfoPath features can be used in InfoPath e-mail forms. For example, adding user roles to a form template increases the security level to domain level. Therefore, form templates that use user roles, unfortunately, can't be published to a list of e-mail recipients. If you wish to use roles in InfoPath e-mail forms, you must publish them to a shared location first. (If you manually change the security level to restricted, you will be able to publish the form to a list of e-mail recipients. However, those features that require a domain security level will not work.)

As we mentioned, by using InfoPath e-mail forms, you can create a quick-and-dirty workflow initiated from within InfoPath. Let's look at a simple example. Say that you are a manager of a team of software developers. It has been a while since you've gotten everybody together for a team lunch and it's close to the holidays, so you decide that now is a good time. However, you're not sure what type of food each team member prefers. You know that some people like Chinese food, others like Indian food, some people like pizza, and others prefer sushi. But how do you decide what food to eat together for lunch?

Normally, you would deal with this by sending out an e-mail to the team. In the e-mail, you might use voting buttons in Outlook to gather responses from people. Or you might just ask people to send their preferences in the reply. This typically has worked well in the past, but only for very simple surveys.

You've recently heard from a colleague that this process is much easier if you use InfoPath. With InfoPath, you can create a simple form that your employees can fill out. When people respond, you can store their responses in a special InfoPath form folder you create in Outlook that allows you to sort, group, and filter the responses so you can easily see where most people would like to eat.

The first thing to do is to design a form template in InfoPath to collect the responses (Figure 13.25). As you can see, this form template is extremely

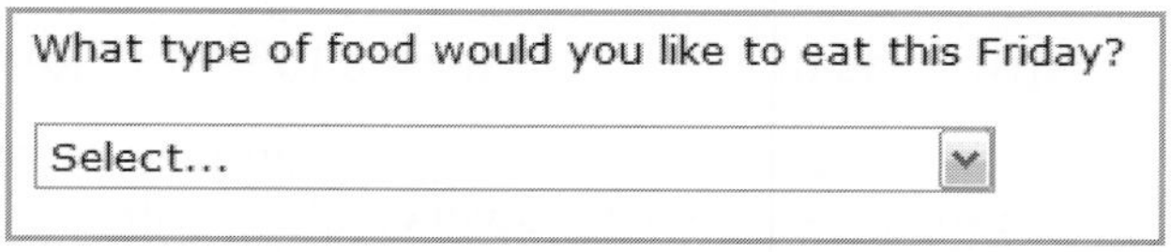

FIGURE 13.25: Food survey form template

simple. All it contains is text asking the user what food he or she would like to eat and a Combo Box control for choosing a type of food they like or typing in another preference if it doesn't exist in the list. (This control is bound to a field named `FoodPreference`.)

The next thing to do is to publish the form template to a list of e-mail recipients, as we showed you how to do in Chapter 9. To review, you first click on the *Publish* item on the *File* menu, and then choose *To a list of e-mail recipients.* After you name your form, you can choose which fields in your form you'd like to make available in Outlook folders (Figure 13.26). This step of the wizard is actually pretty important. In this step you specify which columns you would like to create in Outlook when the responses are stored in InfoPath form folders. These columns will help you group, sort, and filter your data, as you will see shortly. In Figure 13.26, we've added the "Food Preference" column (which is linked to the `FoodPreference` field to which the Combo Box control in the view is bound). We will use this column in Outlook to determine what type of food the employees would like to eat.

After you complete the Publishing Wizard, an InfoPath form based on the form template you just created is opened in an e-mail item, as shown in Figure 13.27. Here you can add the list of e-mail recipients, a subject line,

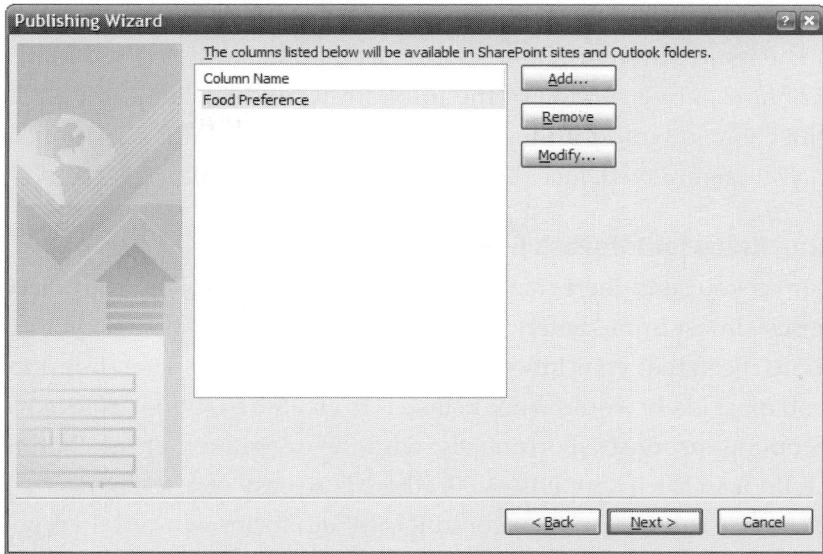

FIGURE 13.26: Choosing which properties to make available in Outlook folders

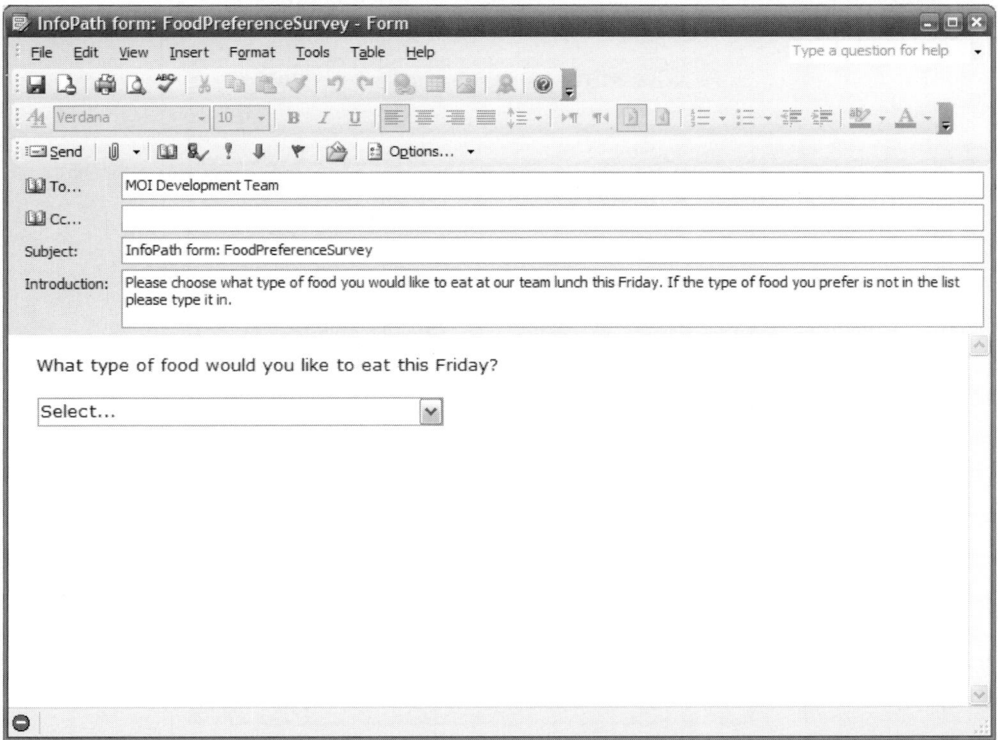

FIGURE 13.27: Sending the form to a list of e-mail recipients

and an introduction message just as you would for any other e-mail you send. The main difference here, though, is that the body of the e-mail message contains a live version of the InfoPath form. You can add data to the form just as you would if the form were open in the InfoPath application. When you are finished, just click the *Send* button as usual.

Creating Rules for InfoPath E-Mail Forms

As soon as you send the e-mail to your team, you're likely to start receiving responses almost immediately. If you have a lot of employees on your team, this could mean that your Inbox will fill up pretty quickly. Therefore, the next step you most likely would want to take is to create an Outlook rule to handle the incoming responses. Fortunately, with the integration of InfoPath forms into Outlook in Microsoft Office 2007, there is an easy way to do this.

To create a rule to handle incoming InfoPath forms of a certain type, you first must open the *Rules and Alerts* dialog by clicking on the *Rules and Alerts* menu item on the *Tools* menu in Outlook 2007. Clicking the *New Rule* button at the top of this dialog opens the Rules Wizard (Figure 13.28).

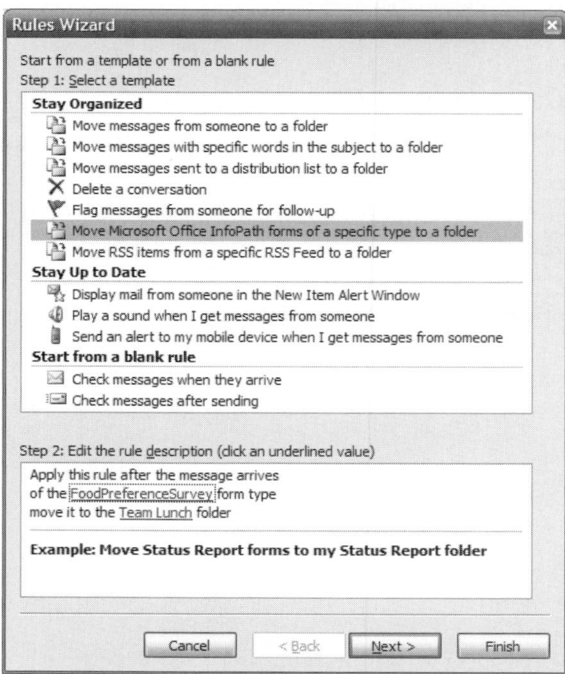

FIGURE 13.28: Rules Wizard showing the rule specific to InfoPath forms

As you can see, the Rules Wizard in Outlook 2007 contains a rule that allows you to move InfoPath forms of a specific type to a folder you choose. Once you've chosen this rule, you can click on the link titled *specific* (for specific form type) in the *Step 2* section of this dialog in order to choose the type of form to which this rule applies. Clicking this link opens the *Choose InfoPath Form* dialog (Figure 13.29). This dialog lists all the form templates

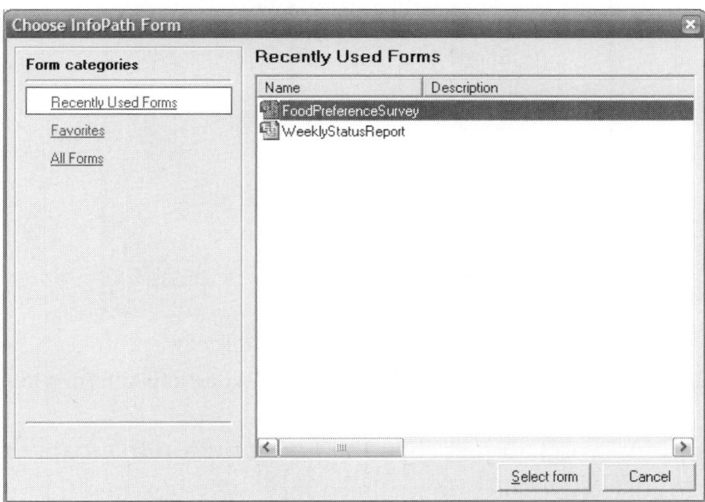

FIGURE 13.29: Choose InfoPath Form dialog

that are registered on your computer, similar to the *Getting Started* dialog in InfoPath. Since we just published the FoodPreferenceSurvey form template, this one is listed first.

Once you choose the type of form, you can then choose to which folder you would like these forms to be moved when they are received. You can see in Figure 13.28 that we first chose the FoodPreferenceSurvey form as the form type. We then clicked on the *specified* folder link in the *Step 2* section of the Rules Wizard and created the Team Lunch folder as a subfolder of our Inbox. We selected *InfoPath Form Items* to describe what it contains, as shown in Figure 13.30. Since we created the folder through the Rules Wizard in this way, the FoodPreferenceSurvey form template was automatically associated with it when we finished creating the rule. (Associating an InfoPath form with an InfoPath form folder means that the data in the form for properties that you promoted when publishing the form template will be shown in columns in the Outlook folder.)

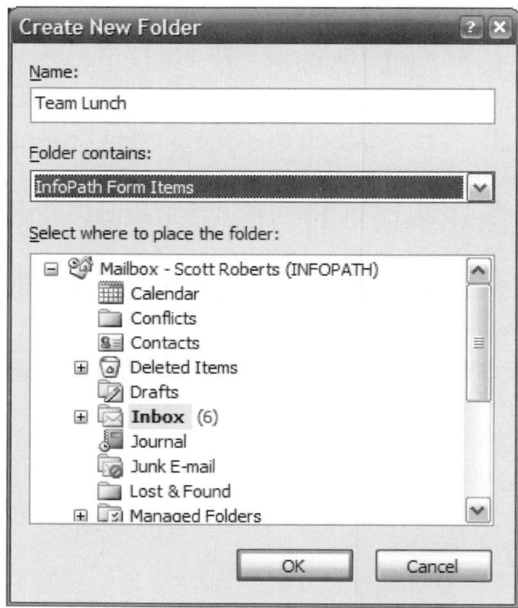

FIGURE 13.30: Create New Folder dialog after selecting InfoPath Form Items

At this point, you can just click the *Finish* button to create the rule, or click *Next* to customize the rule further. Once we've created the rule for our team lunch survey, all responses we receive will be moved to the Team Lunch folder. (Note that, when you create an InfoPath form folder while creating a rule, property promotion is turned on by default. This isn't true when you create a folder outside of the Rules Wizard, which we'll show you how to do next.)

> **NOTE** InfoPath E-Mail Forms Rules Are Client-Only
>
> The rule for handling incoming InfoPath e-mail forms is a client-only rule. This means that the rule will be processed only when Outlook is running.

Storing Received Forms in Outlook Folders

As we mentioned, when you create a rule to handle the incoming InfoPath e-mail forms, the form template you specify is automatically associated with the folder you select as long as that folder is an InfoPath form folder. But how do you create one of these folders outside of the Rules Wizard?

Creating one of these folders is as easy as creating any other folder in Outlook. To create one of these InfoPath form folders, just create a new folder as usual (e.g., by choosing *Folder* from the *New* drop-down button on the toolbar). When you do, the same *Create New Folder* dialog you used to create the Team Lunch folder in the Rules Wizard (shown in Figure 13.30) opens. From here, just create the InfoPath form folder the same way you did in the Rules Wizard.

However, whereas the Rules Wizard will associate the form template with the form folder automatically, creating an InfoPath form folder outside of the Rules Wizard will not. To associate a form template with a new form folder, open the properties dialog for the new folder by right-clicking on the folder and choosing *Properties*. The folder properties dialog contains an *InfoPath Forms* tab (Figure 13.31). From here, we can associate a form template with the folder.

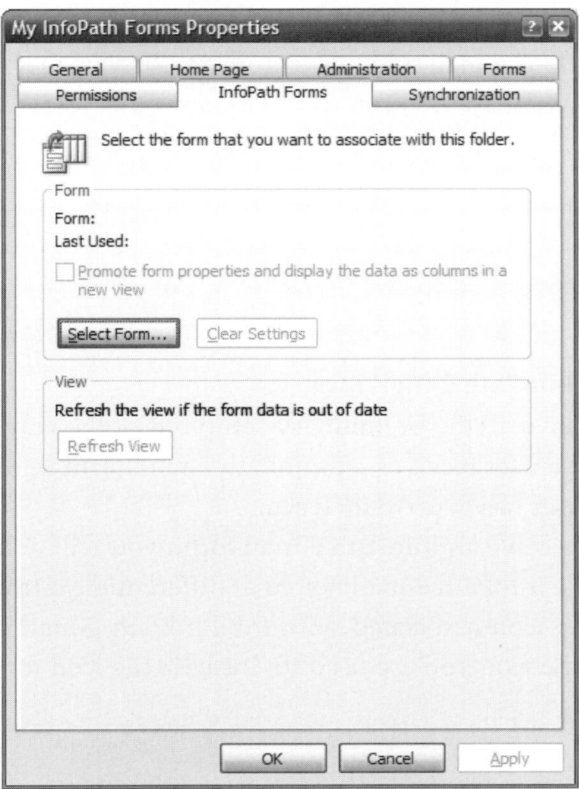

FIGURE 13.31: Folder properties dialog after clicking on the InfoPath Forms tab

In order to associate a form template with the folder, click on the *Select Form* button. This will open the *Choose InfoPath Form* dialog (shown earlier in Figure 13.29). At this point, just choose the form you would like to associate with the InfoPath form folder.

You'll notice that once you select a form template, part of the dialog that was disabled is now enabled—specifically, the checkbox *Promote form properties and display the data as columns in a new view.* This option, which is on by default, is pretty self-explanatory. Normally, you want to leave this option enabled so you can see your users' responses in the InfoPath form folder. (Note that in this dialog you can also refresh the view if you have changed the form template.)

After you close the folder properties dialog by clicking the *OK* button, the view of the folder (with which you just associated a new InfoPath form template) changes to show the columns you promoted.

If you look at the Team Lunch folder, for example, since we promoted only the "Food Preference" column, only one column is shown in addition to the normal Outlook e-mail columns (Figure 13.32). Note that you can always change these columns just as you would for any other folder in Outlook.

FIGURE 13.32: Team Lunch folder showing "Food Preference" column

Filling Out an InfoPath E-Mail Form

Now that we have all the preliminary setup out of the way, let's see what happens when a user receives an InfoPath e-mail form in his or her Inbox and what the user has to do to fill it out.

When you receive an InfoPath e-mail form, you will notice a couple of things about the InfoPath e-mail item that differentiate it from other e-mail items. First, the icon associated with the InfoPath e-mail item is not the normal envelope icon you are used to. Instead, the icon looks like a small InfoPath form.

Open form

InfoPath form: FoodPreferenceSurvey

Tom Collins

Sent: Sat 8/19/2006 4:55 PM

To: MOI Development Team

Please choose what type of food you would like to eat at our team lunch this Friday. If the type of food you prefer is not in the list please type it in.

What type of food would you like to eat this Friday?

Select...

FIGURE 13.33: InfoPath e-mail form in Outlook's reading pane

Next, when you view the InfoPath e-mail form in Outlook's reading pane, it will look like that shown in Figure 13.33. You will notice that the introduction you added when sending the InfoPath form is at the top of the body of the e-mail. Below it is a view of the actual InfoPath form. This is a simple static view of the form that cannot be changed.

You may be wondering how users will respond to your survey. That's easy. At the top of the e-mail item is a button with the title *Open form* (as you can see in Figure 13.33). Clicking this button opens this e-mail item as an editable form, as shown in Figure 13.34. This e-mail item may look like a normal e-mail but it is, in fact, an InfoPath form. (You may notice that this e-mail

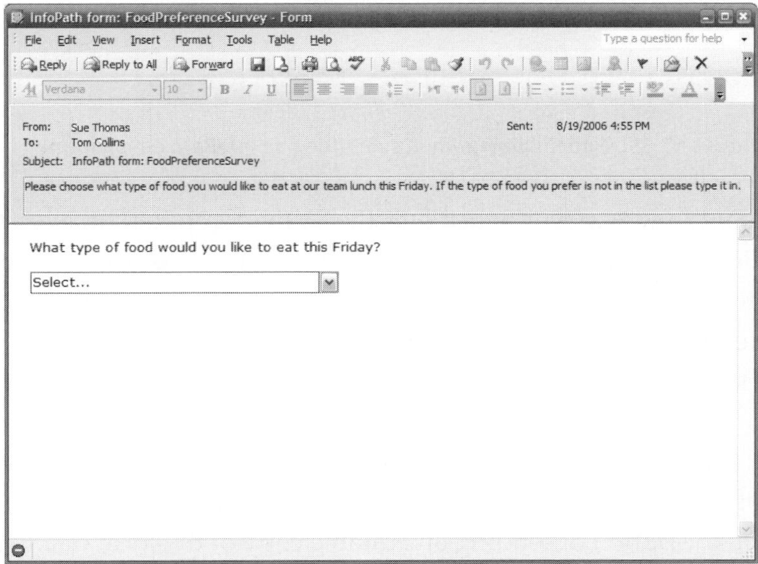

FIGURE 13.34: Filling out an InfoPath e-mail form

item is actually an instance of the InfoPath application. This is obvious the first time you open one of the menus and notice that they are the same menus as in InfoPath.)

You can fill out this InfoPath form in the body of the e-mail the same way as you would when you have the form open in the InfoPath application. Once you are finished, just click the *Reply* button to send the response to the publisher of the form template.

Or, better yet, if the publisher of the form template has set up e-mail submit (which we talked about in Chapter 8), you will then see a *Submit* button, which you can then click. This will open the submit dialog shown in Figure 13.35. Once you click the *Send* button, the InfoPath e-mail form

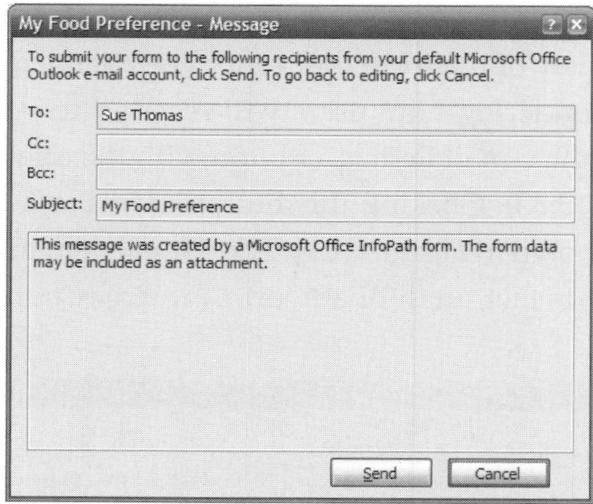

FIGURE 13.35: Submit dialog when submitting an InfoPath e-mail form

will be sent to whomever is listed in the *To* field. (Note that, even though submitting through e-mail may be most advantageous for your scenario, InfoPath e-mail forms support the same types of submit options that are available to normal InfoPath forms.)

In addition to filling out the form yourself, you may wish to pass the form on to someone else or to simply reply to the initiator. When you forward or reply to the e-mail, a new InfoPath e-mail form appears with the *Mail Options* task pane opened, as shown in Figure 13.36. This task pane gives you the option of sending an editable copy of the form or a read-only snapshot. (Note that, if you don't include the form template, the e-mail item will still be an InfoPath e-mail form when viewed in Outlook 2007. This

FIGURE 13.36: Mail Options task pane

option affects only those who are receiving the InfoPath form files as attachments. In general, you should send the form template when you aren't sure the recipients of your e-mail will have the form template already. If your users do have access to the form template, there is no need to send it. We will talk more about this later in this chapter when we talk about how to control these options when designing the form template.)

TIP Replying without Opening the InfoPath E-Mail Form

Sometimes you just want to reply to the sender of the form with a quick question without having to open the InfoPath e-mail form. In that case, all you need to do is right-click on the e-mail item (in the list of e-mail items in the InfoPath form folder) and click the *Reply with Message* menu item.

Opening the InfoPath e-mail form by clicking on the *Open form* button in the Outlook reading pane is just one way to fill out an InfoPath form from within Outlook. Let's say that you've already responded to the survey but you've changed your mind. However, you've already deleted the form from your Inbox and you can't recover it. Luckily, there are other ways to fill out this form. Of course, the form you originally sent may still be in your Sent Items folder in Outlook. You could open that one and resend it. Also, you could just open InfoPath itself and fill out the form. As long as the form has been filled out once (and, therefore, cached on your local machine), the form will be available in the *Getting Started* dialog in InfoPath.

There is yet another way. You can just fill out this form from within Outlook. To do so, just click on the *Choose InfoPath Form* item on the drop-down menu of the *New* button. This will open the *Choose InfoPath Form* dialog (shown earlier in Figure 13.29), from which you can choose a form to fill out. From there, the experience is exactly the same as when you open the form by clicking the *Open form* button in the Outlook reading pane.

Sorting, Grouping, and Filtering Responses

Once you have received all the responses to your survey, you likely want to sort, group, and maybe even filter them so you can determine which type of food the majority of people in the team prefer.

As you may remember, earlier we set up a rule that moves all the survey responses we receive to the Team Lunch folder. Figure 13.37 shows the Team

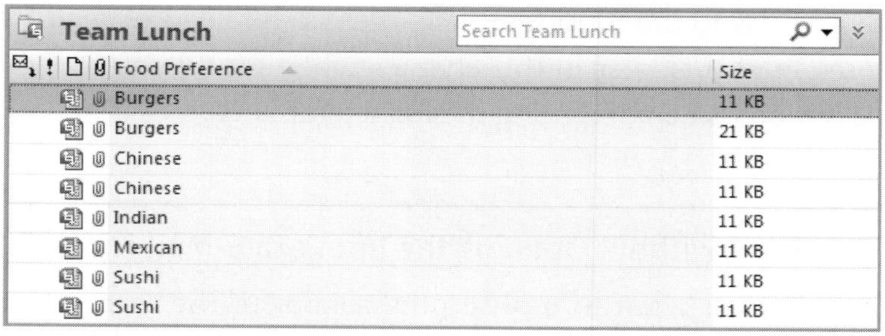

FIGURE 13.37: Team Lunch folder showing responses to the food preference survey

Lunch folder after all the responses have been received. As you can see, there is one additional column other than the columns you would normally see in Outlook e-mail folders—the "Food Preference" column. (For brevity, a few of the normal e-mail columns have been removed.) This column corresponds to the food preferences chosen by respondents who have filled out the form. (Remember that this column was added for us when we chose to promote the "Food Preference" field earlier in this chapter, as shown in Figure 13.26.) To make it easier for us to see how many people chose each type of food, we've sorted this folder by the "Food Preference" column.

Since the Team Lunch folder is simply a normal Outlook folder that just happens to have special knowledge of InfoPath forms, you can perform sorting, grouping, and filtering operations as you normally would on any

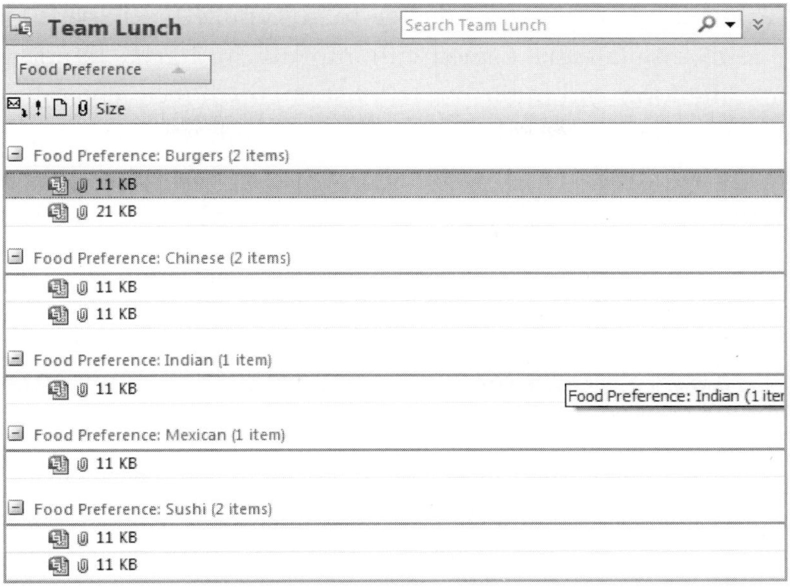

FIGURE 13.38: Team Lunch folder grouped by food preference

other folder. For example, even though we've sorted by food preference, we still need to manually count each response. It would be much easier to group the responses by the type of food preference. Figure 13.38 shows the Team Lunch folder after grouping by the "Food Preference" column. (This was done by right-clicking on the "Food Preference" column heading and then clicking *Group By This Field*.) Now, since the responses are grouped, we can easily tell how many people prefer each type of food since the number of responses in each group is listed in the group's title. Two people prefer burgers, two prefer Chinese food, one prefers Indian, one prefers Mexican food, and two prefer sushi. It looks like we'll need to send out the survey again since we have a three-way tie.

Merging and Exporting InfoPath E-Mail Forms

The food preference survey example we've talked about so far is very simple. Let's look at an example that is a little more complicated. Let's say that you are the head of the department that includes the development, form design, and research teams at MOI Consulting. You've seen how easy it is to use InfoPath 2007, so you decide that you want to have people in your organization fill out their expense reports by using an InfoPath e-mail form. To make life easier, you decide to customize the Expense Report sample form template that comes with InfoPath. You make minor modifications to the form and publish it to a list of e-mail recipients—basically, the entire department. (See the sidebar for more information about how to publish the sample form templates that come with InfoPath.) When you publish the form template, in the Publishing Wizard, you make the name, department, and total fields available as columns in Outlook.

Using a Sample Form Template as an InfoPath E-Mail Form

The sample form templates included with InfoPath are generic out-of-the-box templates that are browser-enabled form templates. This means that they can be used in both the InfoPath client application and in a browser as long as the server you are using has InfoPath Forms Services installed. (We'll talk more about InfoPath Forms Services in Chapters 14 and 17.)

Many of the sample form templates (Expense Report, Status Report, and Travel Request) include a Rich Text Box control that allows linked images. Linked images require domain-level security. Therefore, by default, these form templates cannot be published to a list of e-mail recipients.

Normally, the easy way to fix this would be to remove support for linked images in the Rich Text Box control in the form templates. However, since these are browser-enabled form templates, you cannot change this option. (Rich Text Box controls in Web-enabled form templates always support linked images.)

To enable these form templates to be published to a list of e-mail recipients, enable e-mail submit on the form template you are interested in and publish it to a network location or SharePoint document library. Then, users can open the form, fill it out as normal, and then submit it through e-mail.

Next, in Outlook, you create a rule and an InfoPath form folder (as we explained earlier) to handle the incoming expense reports. You also group the InfoPath form folder by department so you can easily see the expense reports for each department. Figure 13.39 shows the Expense Reports folder after you've received a few expense reports.

Expense Reports

Department

Name	Total	Received	Size
Department: Development (1 item)			
Tom Collins	461.68	Mon 8/21/2006 7:14 ...	49 KB
Department: Form Design (1 item)			
Sue Thomas	1,615	Mon 8/21/2006 7:23 ...	59 KB
Department: Research (1 item)			
Ellie Mae Johnson	283.45	Mon 8/21/2006 7:17 ...	49 KB

FIGURE 13.39: Expense Reports InfoPath form folder

Now that you have expense report data, you decide that you want to do some reporting with the data. You know that in InfoPath you can merge forms in order to make an aggregate report. So, you wonder if you can do the same inside of Outlook 2007. The answer is yes, you can. To merge multiple forms from within Outlook 2007, simply select all the e-mail items you want to merge by holding down the Ctrl key and clicking each one. Then right-click on the selected e-mail items to open the context menu (Figure 13.40). The context menu contains a menu item called *InfoPath actions* that contains a list of actions you can perform on InfoPath forms—*Export Forms to Excel, Merge Forms,* and *Export Forms.* (You can also access these options from the *Actions* menu in Outlook.)

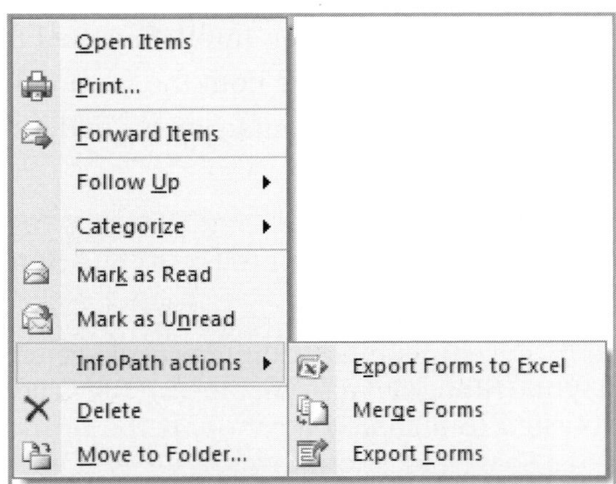

FIGURE 13.40: InfoPath actions context menu

To create your aggregate report, click the *Merge Forms* menu item. This will open the InfoPath application and merge all the forms. Once you have the aggregate report open in InfoPath, you can export the form to Excel as usual in order to perform data analysis. However, you may want to export these forms to Excel without having to open them in InfoPath. To do that, just choose the *Export Forms to Excel* menu item on the *InfoPath actions* context menu in Outlook 2007. Choosing this option exports the forms to Excel in the same way as when you choose the *All form data* option in the Export to Excel Wizard in InfoPath.

There is a third item on the *InfoPath actions* menu—*Export Forms.* Choosing this menu item allows you to export the InfoPath e-mail form to an InfoPath form file that you can later open in the InfoPath application. (Note that the name of the InfoPath form file that is saved is based on the subject line of the InfoPath e-mail form in Outlook.)

Customizing E-Mail Support for a Form Template

As is the case with many other features in InfoPath, when designing a form template, you can control how forms are sent through e-mail. As you have probably guessed, you can set these e-mail options through the *Form Options* dialog, which contains an *E-Mail Attachments* tab (Figure 13.41). Here you can control how files are attached to a message sent from within InfoPath and whether or not InfoPath e-mail forms are enabled.

As you may recall, when you send an e-mail from within InfoPath, if you haven't changed the default e-mail options for the form template, users of Outlook 2007 will receive the form as an InfoPath e-mail form. Those who are not using Outlook 2007 will receive both the form data (.xml file) and possibly the form template (.xsn file) as attachments in the e-mail message.

> **NOTE** When Is the Form Template (.xsn) File Sent in E-Mail?
>
> When you publish to a list of e-mail recipients, the .xsn file is always sent unless the form template has domain-level security. When you send an e-mail while filling out a form, the .xsn file is not sent if it was previously published to a shared location. If the form template was not published to a shared location, the .xsn file will be sent as long as the form template does not have domain-level security.

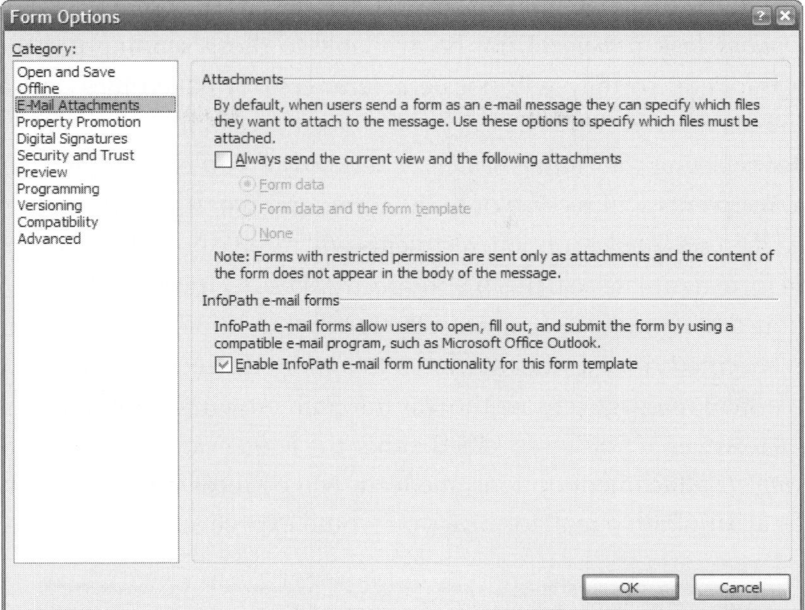

FIGURE 13.41: E-Mail Attachments tab in the Form Options dialog

By using the *E-Mail Attachments* tab of the *Form Options* dialog, you can change this default behavior. By default, the option *Enable InfoPath e-mail form functionality for this form template* is selected. If you uncheck this checkbox, the form is not an InfoPath e-mail form. E-mails sent from InfoPath will simply include the form data and form template files as attachments. In this case, even if users are using Outlook 2007, they will not receive an InfoPath e-mail form. They will receive the InfoPath files as attachments instead.

When sending the e-mail from InfoPath, whether or not support for InfoPath e-mail forms is enabled in the form template, users can change this behavior by using the *Mail Options* task pane (refer back to Figure 13.36). As we mentioned, this gives users the ability to control whether they are sending an editable copy of the form or a read-only snapshot. If they are sending an editable snapshot, they can control whether or not to send the form template. Not surprisingly, you can control this behavior when designing the form template. When sending a form through e-mail in InfoPath, if you always want just the form data file (.xml file) to be attached, the form data and form template to be attached, or neither, you can select the option *Always send the current view and the following attachments* option in the *E-Mail Attachments* tab of the *Form Options* dialog to change the default behavior. Once you do, the *Mail Options* task pane will not be available to those sending e-mail from within InfoPath, so they will not be able to control which files are sent as attachments.

After selecting the *Always send . . .* checkbox, if you choose the *Form data* option, recipients will receive only the form .xml file. If you check the *Form data and the form template* option, recipients will receive both the form .xml file and the form template .xsn file. If you specify *None,* recipients will receive neither. Note that if you specify to send the form as an InfoPath e-mail form and you've specified *None* as the attachments option, the recipient will receive a simple e-mail message and neither an InfoPath e-mail form nor any attachments. However, if you've specified either the *Form data* or *Form data and the form template* attachment options, the form will be received by Outlook 2007 users as an InfoPath e-mail form, as you would expect.

NOTE **Disabling InfoPath E-Mail Forms for InfoPath 2003–Compatible Forms**

By default, all forms sent as e-mail from InfoPath when filling out a form are sent as InfoPath e-mail forms. When designing a form template, you can control this behavior via the *Form Options* dialog. Companies that upgrade from InfoPath 2003 to InfoPath 2007, however, may want to turn off this behavior by default for forms that were created in InfoPath 2003. This will enable them to instruct their users on the use of InfoPath e-mail forms before turning on the feature.

Although there are no options to control this behavior in the *Form Options* dialog, there is a registry key that an administrator can set to disable this functionality. This registry key, however, affects only forms that are compatible with InfoPath 2003 and not forms created by using InfoPath 2007.

The registry key is the following:

```
HKEY_CURRENT_USER\Software\Microsoft\Office\12.0\InfoPath\
DisableInfoPath2003EmailForms
```

This key is a `DWORD` type that has two possible values—`0` or `1`. The value `0` indicates that InfoPath 2003 forms can be sent as InfoPath e-mail forms. The value `1` indicates that they cannot. The default value for this key is `0`. (There is also a group policy key available in the Office Customization Tool to control this setting. Look for *Disable sending InfoPath 2003 Forms as e-mail forms* in the OCT.)

What's Next?

In this chapter, you learned not only how to create workflow processes by using InfoPath but also how to incorporate InfoPath into existing processes. You added user roles to your form template in order to show only the data and views that are important to a user. You then saw how to create workflow processes by using InfoPath with Microsoft Office SharePoint Server 2007. Finally, you learned how easy it is to integrate InfoPath into existing e-mail workflow processes by using InfoPath e-mail forms and Outlook 2007.

This chapter marks the end of the basics of the InfoPath rich client application. In the next chapter, you'll have your first introduction to InfoPath Forms Services, which is InfoPath's entrance into the server domain. In addition to learning about the basics of InfoPath Forms Services, including server setup and administration, you'll also learn how you can make your form templates Web-enabled so that anyone who has a Web browser can fill out your forms. So, without any further delay, let's move on.

14

Introduction to Forms Services

Getting Started

One of the most exciting features of InfoPath 2007 is the ability to fill out a form in a Web browser. As we mentioned in Chapter 1, this answers the biggest customer request since InfoPath first hit the streets back in August 2003. Welcome to Microsoft Office InfoPath Forms Services 2007—the product that allows people to use Web browsers to fill out and manage InfoPath forms and form templates.

Before we can dive into Forms Services, it must be properly set up. To do so, we'll review the prerequisites and how to proceed through installation. We'll look at a couple Forms Services product offerings as well as the numerous ways you can configure your servers depending on your needs.

Throughout this book so far, we've explored how to design forms with InfoPath 2007. This latest version of InfoPath, as this book has hopefully shown, is the most compelling release to date. There are many new and powerful integration and form-filling features for you to leverage. While many of these capabilities are very useful, some of them do not work in the browser; that is, Forms Services does not support all the features of the rich InfoPath client program. Ideally, everyone could take advantage of the richness of InfoPath. For those who can't, Forms Services comes to the rescue. In this chapter, we'll talk about how to design a form that is compatible with Forms Services. In fact, you already know how to design a form for filling in a Web browser, thanks to the concept of **design once**. InfoPath adheres to the design once philosophy, which claims you can design a form only once and it will work with InfoPath as well as Forms Services. We'll see how to deploy the form template to the server so all of your users can participate in filling it out: InfoPath or not, Windows or not, and even computer or not (by using a mobile device)!

Forms Services offers more than just a form-filling experience for all. Built on the SharePoint Server 2007 platform, Forms Services leverages features such as document libraries, workflow, security, and administration, just to name a few. We'll look at a few ways these features help support and enhance the "Web form" experience.

This chapter is meant to familiarize you with the basics of InfoPath Forms Services. We recommend that you read it first to get started with using browser-based forms. Once you've mastered the basics you can jump, if you like, to our advanced discussion of Forms Services in Chapter 17. For your convenience, we make forward references to the advanced chapter to let you know that the topic is covered in additional detail later. We recommend reading Chapter 17, however, only after you first understand what's covered in this chapter. With that said, let's move on!

What Is InfoPath in the Browser?

In a nutshell, Forms Services is all about filling out InfoPath forms in the browser. The idea is to bring as much parity between InfoPath and Forms Services as possible. If you've ever filled out an InfoPath form (and even if you haven't), you'll have no problem with forms in the browser. In fact, you might occasionally forget that you're filling out a form in the browser instead of InfoPath! Take the status report sample form (included with InfoPath under the *Customize a Sample* link on the *Getting Started* dialog), for example. Figure 14.1 shows the form in InfoPath, while Figure 14.2 is the same form in Internet Explorer. Can you tell them apart?

Despite the visual similarities between InfoPath and Web versions of the same form, you can argue that the visual doesn't say much about the form-filling experience. As much as the Web version tries to mimic InfoPath (and does a great job doing it), it's not exactly the same. For example, some convenience features are missing, such as undo and spell checking. These

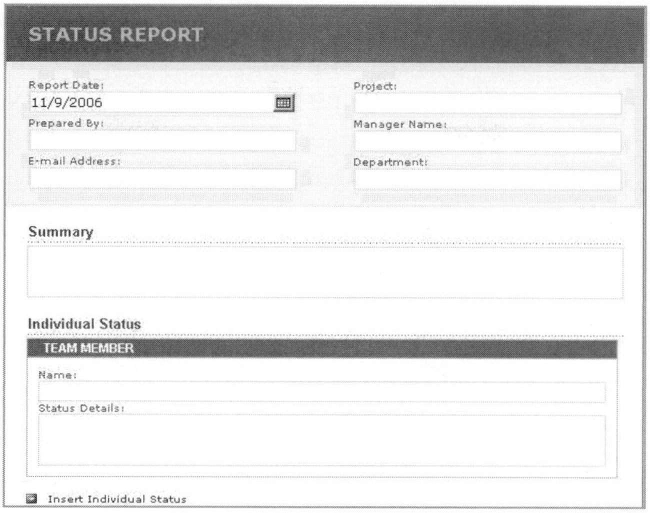

FIGURE 14.1: Filling out the status report form in InfoPath

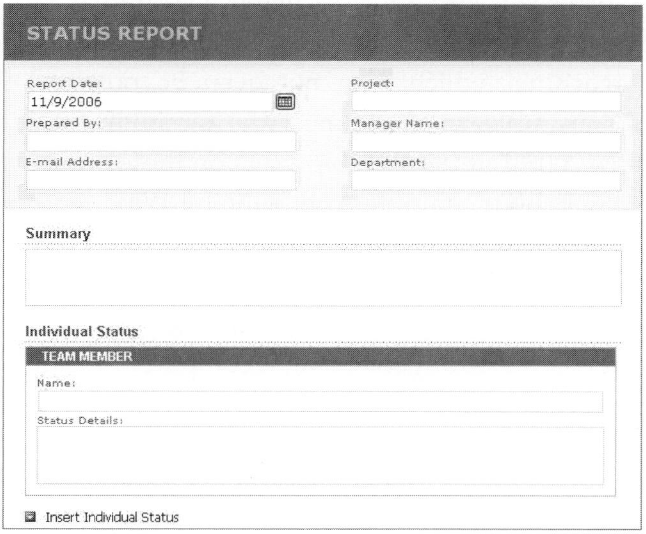

FIGURE 14.2: Filling out the status report form in the browser by using Forms Services

features aren't necessarily critical to filling out forms, but their absence is just part of the slightly degraded experience of using the browser. InfoPath and Forms Services can be likened to Outlook and Outlook Web Access (OWA). Outlook provides a wealth of additional features and upgrades compared to OWA. If you had a choice, you'd probably rather use Outlook when it's convenient. The same applies to filling out InfoPath forms: InfoPath is preferred as the form filler of choice over Forms Services. As you proceed through this chapter, you'll learn about even more differences (as well as similarities) between InfoPath and Forms Services.

Forms Services is built on and integrated with the SharePoint Server 2007 platform. As such, the ability to fill out browser-based forms takes an explicit dependency on SharePoint. Forms Services is not a plug-in, nor is it a service that installs on any Windows Web server. To use InfoPath forms in the browser, the SharePoint platform must be installed. In fact, Forms Services is bundled in the box with SharePoint. Soon we'll look at the prerequisites and setup steps for getting Forms Services running on your server.

Why Use the Browser?

Just because InfoPath provides a better experience doesn't mean it must have priority of use. There are cases when it's optimal to intentionally deploy a browser-based form template instead of installing InfoPath on every client machine—which may not even be possible! Some older computers, for example, may not meet the minimum requirements for Microsoft Office 2007, but the Web browsers on these older systems work quite nicely. What about computers not running Windows operating systems? Browser-based forms can reach Apple and UNIX systems with virtually no work on your part. What about filling out forms beyond your corporate network and firewall? You cannot realistically expect external customers, contractors, or anyone using a computer outside of your control to have InfoPath installed. With forms in the browser, there are no deployment blockers or incompatibilities to worry about. Finally, a traveling salesperson who doesn't have a laptop can even use a smart phone with basic Internet connectivity to fill out your forms! As you can see, Forms Services is a powerful way to reach out to anyone who has form-filling needs, no matter who they are.

One major part of InfoPath that Forms Services does not address is the designing of form templates. Clearly Forms Services is not meant as a standalone all-in-one solution. The process of designing forms requires that you use InfoPath's design mode. Think of Forms Services as a supplementary extension that reaches out to users who don't have the InfoPath program.

> **NOTE Designing Form Templates**
>
> The InfoPath program is required to design form templates. Forms Services only lets users fill out forms based on browser-enabled form templates.

What Is Forms Services?

Forms Services is a feature of SharePoint Server 2007 that allows for complete form filling and management. In fact, Forms Services is built and depends on SharePoint for many operations, such as form template deployment and administration. The key to successfully using Forms Services in an enterprise has less to do with filling out forms in the browser than with its integration with the SharePoint platform. We'll talk more about this when we look at forms management later in this chapter.

> **NOTE Forms Services Is Integrated with SharePoint Server 2007**
>
> Forms Services has dependencies on some parts of SharePoint's shared services and providers. Only with those parts do the scenarios around form filling become a reality. In Chapter 17, we'll look at these providers and their configuration.

Forms Services takes the InfoPath user model and rich feature set and ports it to the browser. No learning about a new program or technology is required to start using Forms Services. If you've used InfoPath before, you already know what Forms Services can do for you! Any form templates you've already created need not be redesigned for filling in the browser. The concept of design once guarantees that you can design a single form template that works the same in both the browser and InfoPath programs. This might seem confusing right now, but later in this chapter we'll explain how it works. We also look into design once and InfoPath's Design Checker feature later in this chapter.

Tidbits about Forms Services compatibility with InfoPath features are scattered throughout this book. These browser-based sidebars comment on differences in behavior when the form is filled out in a Web browser instead of in InfoPath. If there is no sidebar or mention of Forms Services, you can assume that the feature functions similarly in the browser as in InfoPath. As you read through these sidebars, it's important to differentiate between two types of browser incompatibilities: features that are not available in browser-enabled forms versus features that are not available when a user fills out the form in the browser.

When a feature isn't offered for browser-enabled form templates, it means you cannot use that specific feature at all when designing a form template compatible with Forms Services. Alternatively, when we say a feature is not available when filling out forms in the browser, the feature can still be used in the form template and works properly when a user fills out forms in the InfoPath program. If that form were opened in the browser, however, those features would not be active.

An example of a feature not available in browser-enabled form templates is user roles. The *Manage User Roles* dialog is completely disabled and shows a red "x" icon with a message about Forms Services incompatibility (Figure 14.3). User roles cannot be used in InfoPath when you design a browser-enabled form template.

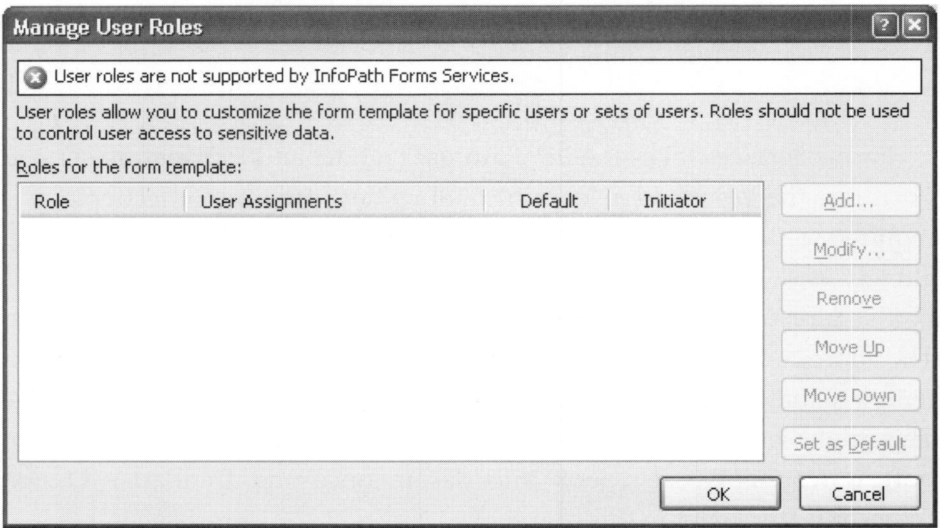

FIGURE 14.3: Message indicating that a feature cannot be used in a browser-enabled form template

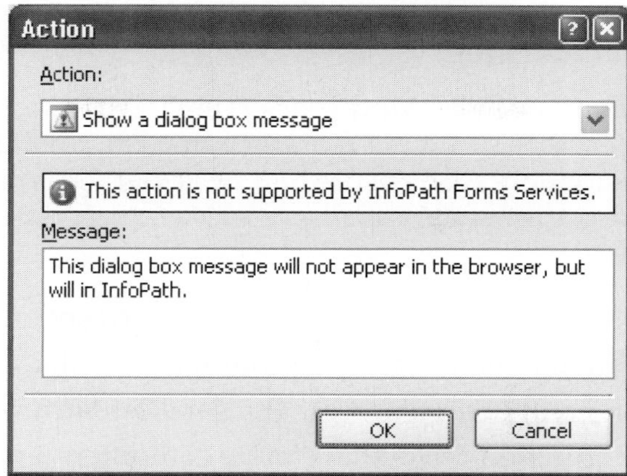

FIGURE 14.4: Message indicating that a feature can be used in a browser-enabled form template but is not active in the browser

An example of a feature that can still be used in browser-enabled templates (and works fine in InfoPath) but is not active in the browser is showing a dialog box message in a rule action. When you're designing a browser-enabled template, the *Action* dialog for rules contains a message similar to the one shown in Figure 14.3, but the icon is a blue "i" (Figure 14.4). Unlike the *Manage User Roles* dialog, however, the *Action* dialog is still enabled. You will see both the blue "i" and the red "x" icons throughout the InfoPath client application while designing form templates compatible with InfoPath Forms Services.

Installing and Configuring Forms Services

Installing Forms Services is a fairly quick process. Configuring the server, on the other hand, takes a little longer. Regardless, the configuration steps are straightforward. All of the configuration, in fact, is related to getting SharePoint up and running. Forms Services requires absolutely no up-front administrator configuration to get going. In fact, the few Forms Services settings in which you would be interested are advanced settings for controlling the ways users fill out forms. We'll look at those settings in Chapter 17.

NOTE Prerequisites

SharePoint Server requires Windows Server 2003 SP1 or later, Internet Information Services (IIS), .NET Framework 2.0, and the Windows Workflow Foundation. Also ensure that ASP.NET 2.0 is enabled in IIS.

Before you install Forms Services and the corresponding SharePoint platform, you'll want to first determine your farm topology. This is primarily based on your computer resources. The smallest farm you can create is a single-box configuration. If you have more computers, you can add them to the farm to distribute the load. SharePoint Search, for example, can use its own machine for search indexing. (Such a computer is called an application server.) This reduces the load on the actual Web server computers, or Web Front Ends (WFEs), that talk to the client computers over a network such as a corporate intranet or the Internet. While some services can be distributed on their own application servers, Forms Services has no such concept. Forms Services runs only on WFEs. Therefore, with every WFE that you add to your farm, your maximum possible load becomes theoretically higher. (But there is a point of diminishing returns. The farm is ultimately bottlenecked by a common SQL Server back end. We'll learn more about how to mitigate the bottleneck in Chapter 17.) If it's likely that your farm may run multiple services, you should set your farm up according to the best practices dictated by those individual services.

WARNING 32- and 64-Bit Architectures

SharePoint Server comes in 32- and 64-bit flavors. Installing the 32-bit version is restricted on 64-bit operating systems and vice versa.

There are two SKUs to choose from to install Forms Services. Which SKU to purchase primarily depends on your service requirements. The first option is SharePoint Server 2007. Installing SharePoint Server gives you all of the server offerings available for Microsoft Office 2007, including Excel Calculation, Search Indexing, and the Project Application services. The second option is to install Forms Server 2007. This gives you the core Windows SharePoint Services platform along with Forms Services but does not include services like Microsoft Office Server Search or Excel Calculation services. (SharePoint is a required prerequisite for Forms Services.) The latter choice is more lightweight, but you don't benefit from the other server components found in the Enterprise offering. Since we're focusing on InfoPath rather than other server options, let's take a walk through setting up Forms Server 2007.

Similar Setup

When you're installing either SharePoint Server 2007 or Forms Server 2007, you go through a similar setup wizard. The major difference is in the manual server configuration after running the SharePoint Products and Technologies Configuration Wizard. There are fewer configuration steps with Forms Server 2007.

NOTE Product Names

Forms Server 2007 is the standalone (i.e., marketing) product name that you'll find on the shrink-wrapped box. **Forms Services** is the actual server software component. Forms Services is included in SharePoint Server 2007 when Enterprise features are enabled.

Installing Forms Services

To start installation, we'll kick off the setup program. You could choose *Basic* to install a standalone version of SharePoint Server 2007 with Forms Services. A standalone installation is considered a trial version of the product because it installs and uses SQL Server Express 2005 (otherwise known as the desktop database engine). SQL Express is a throttled version of SQL Server that is not meant for more than just personal use. Moreover, the standalone version preconfigures such items as search crawls, a default Web Application, a Shared Services Provider, and a default Web site. This is fine for evaluating the product but is not ideal for enterprise deployments. In our case, we'll choose *Advanced* so we can set up a farm.

WARNING SQL Server Required for a Farm Install

SQL Server 2000 SP4 or later (including 2005) is required to set up a farm. SQL Server can reside on the same computer where you're installing Forms Server or on a different one (recommended).

The next wizard page, shown in Figure 14.5, asks what kind of server we're setting up. Select either the *Complete* or *Web Front End* options to continue. Since we're setting up Forms Server, it doesn't matter which option we choose since they're equivalent in this case. However, if we were installing SharePoint Server, choosing *Complete* would install additional services to support an application server. An application server can also be a WFE, but we'd need to manually enable the Windows SharePoint Services Web Application service after installation.

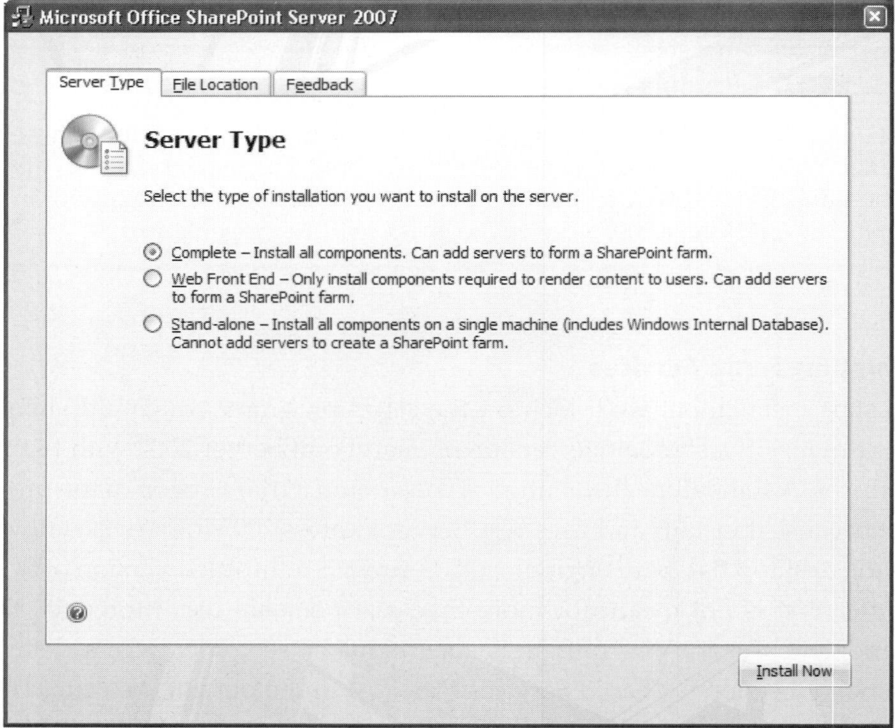

FIGURE 14.5: Choosing the type of server to install

After we click *Install Now,* the setup and installation process takes no longer than a few minutes to finish. The process is finished when a large Microsoft Office icon with the *Run the SharePoint Products and Technologies Configuration Wizard now* checkbox appears. The checkbox to run the configuration wizard is checked by default. Click the *Close* button to continue to configure the server.

Configuring Forms Services

The configuration wizard asks several questions, such as whether you want to join or create a new farm. In our case, we'll create a new farm. Any computers you add in the future can join the farm you've created. To join a farm, you just need to know the name of the SharePoint database server and its credentials to gain access. Figure 14.6 shows the dialog for configuring database settings.

At the end of the configuration wizard, the SharePoint Central Administration site opens in a new Web browser. There is a list of three

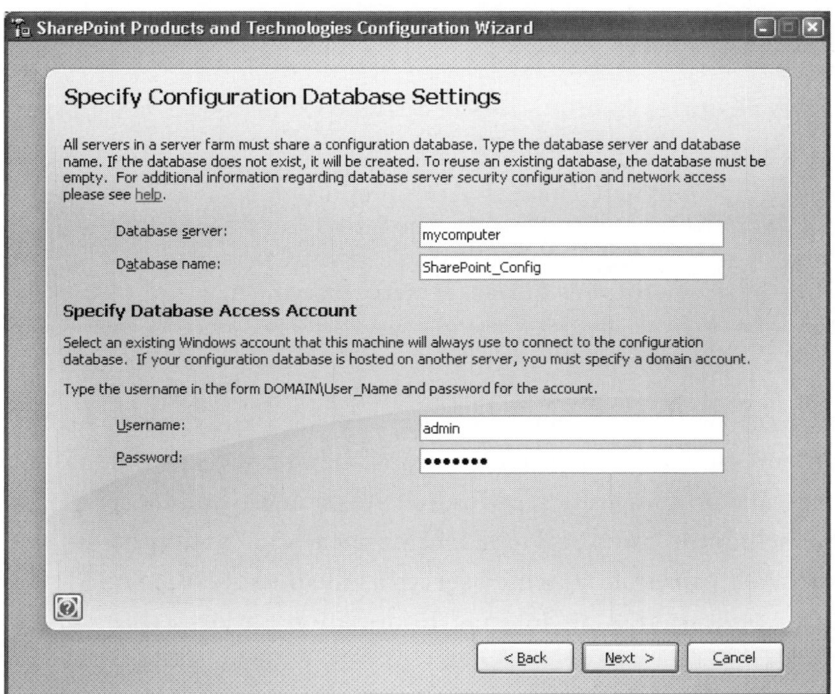

FIGURE 14.6: SharePoint database configuration settings for a farm

administrative tasks at the top of the page. If you installed SharePoint Server with Enterprise features, you'll notice it has more administrative items than listed here:

1. *Add servers to farm*
2. *Assign services to servers*
3. *Configure farm's shared services*

Unless you have additional servers to add to your farm, you can skip step 1. Remember that you can always add servers to scale out your farm at any time. If you click on the *Assign services to servers* link from step 2, above, you can assign services to a specific server. In our case, since we have only one WFE, we'll need to start the Windows SharePoint Services Web Application services. This opens up the ability to create a shared service provider, Web Application, and site, which we'll do in step 3. If we chose the *Web Front End* option in the dialog shown in Figure 14.5, the Web Application would have already been started.

TIP Central Administration Service Runs on a Specific Server

You'll notice that a Central Administration service is started by default on the server that created the farm. You can use the *Services on Server* page to configure which server in your farm runs the administration site. This applies for any service in the farm.

In step 3 we create a new Shared Services Provider (SSP). An SSP is a SharePoint concept that provides infrastructure such as databases, Web services, and administration pages that are common among server components, including Forms Services. During the SSP creation process, we also create a Web Application, which serves as the default Web site for the SSP. A Web Application is an Internet Information Services (IIS) component that represents a Web site. Then SharePoint extends that application with additional functionality. Finally, we create a site collection. A site collection creates a top-level site that you can navigate to via the browser. You can optionally choose a site theme like a wiki or blog site. A team site is the standard site type that you may be accustomed to from previous versions of SharePoint. To use Forms Services, it doesn't matter what type of site you decide to create.

That's it! There's no specific setup for Forms Services; it's all ready to use.

> **NOTE Upgrading to Forms Services**
>
> If you are already running Windows SharePoint Services 2003, upgrading to SharePoint Server 2007 or Forms Server 2007 is an option to preserve and upgrade your databases.

Is Forms Services Installed?

If you already have a SharePoint server, is Forms Services already installed? To determine whether Forms Services is available on your server, visit the server's Central Administration site. Then click on the *Application Management* tab. Next, click on the *Manage Web Application Features* link. Forms Services is packaged with the Office SharePoint Server Enterprise feature. Ensure that the feature status is set to *Active*.

> **NOTE Navigating to the Central Administration Site**
>
> You can find the SharePoint 3.0 Central Administration link in your *Start* menu under the Administrative Tools or Microsoft Office Server folders. You must be a farm administrator to gain access. Also, if you are not on the server itself, you must know the SharePoint Central Administration port number.

SharePoint Server 2007 with Enterprise Features

SharePoint Server 2007 always comes with all of the Enterprise features of the server, including Business Data Catalog, Excel Services, Report Center, Forms Services, and KPI and Filter Web Parts. Even though SharePoint has Enterprise features, they are not always enabled by default. If you are using the Microsoft Core (or Standard) Client Access License (CAL), Enterprise features are unavailable. Upgrading to the Microsoft Enterprise CAL involves purchasing licenses and then enabling Enterprise features on your server.

To begin enabling Enterprise features, go to the SharePoint Central Administration site for your server. Click on the *Operations* tab and then on the *Enable Enterprise Features* link. To really enable the Enterprise license, you must have an Enterprise Client License key to continue.

Publishing a Form Template to Forms Services

In Chapter 9, we mentioned that you can publish a form template to Forms Services via an SharePoint Server 2007 site. This is how you get an InfoPath template to the server so a user can fill it out in a browser. But in Chapter 9, we chose a non-browser-enabled form template, which, therefore, would not use Forms Services. Let's publish a browser-enabled template and then explain a little about what happens on the server as we proceed through the Publishing Wizard.

To get a form template to the server, it must first be published as compatible with Forms Services from the InfoPath program. Let's publish the status report sample form template that we looked at earlier when introducing Forms Services. To begin, start by using the *Design a Form* dialog and then click the *Customize a Sample* link. Select the *Sample–Status Report* form template. You can see that this template is already compatible with Forms Services because the status bar (the lowest and rightmost area) of the InfoPath design window shows *Compatibility: InfoPath and InfoPath Forms Services.* This form template is ready to be published!

Select *Publish Form Template* from the *Design Tasks* task pane to begin the Publishing Wizard. (You may be prompted to save. If so, save the form

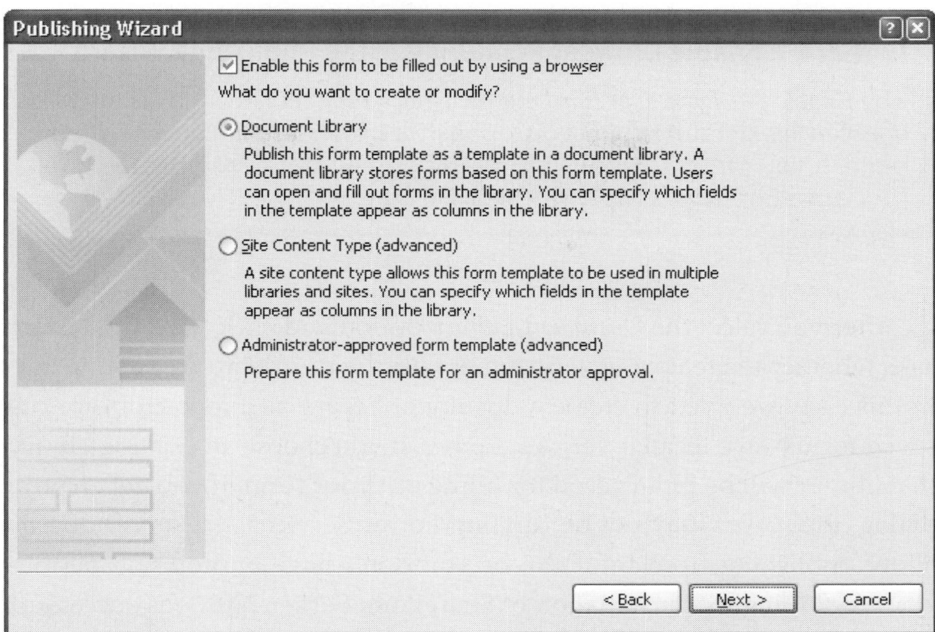

FIGURE 14.7: Choosing to publish to Forms Services via the Document Library option

template to your computer. See Chapter 9 for more information.) The default option in the wizard is to publish *To a SharePoint server with or without InfoPath Forms Services.* Since this is what we want, click *Next.*

The next wizard page asks for the location of our server. Actually, this location is the site collection in which we want to use this form template. Enter the name of your SharePoint server with Forms Services. (If you don't specify a site collection, the default, or root, site collection is used.) The next part, shown in Figure 14.7, presents three options for what to create or modify: *Document Library, Site Content Type (advanced)*, or *Administrator-approved form template (advanced).* We want to use *Document Library* for now. We'll discuss site content types later in this chapter. We'll save the last option for Chapter 17.

SharePoint Site Collection Themes

A site collection is created under a Web Application and contains a top-level SharePoint site, subsites, and various workspaces with content such as a wiki site or blog in those subsites.

> **NOTE Enable Browser Rendering in the Publishing Wizard**
>
> The *Enable this form to be filled out by using a browser* checkbox is always enabled by default when you publish a browser-enabled form template. If you prefer to publish to SharePoint without enabling the form for Forms Services, simply uncheck the box.

After you select the *Document Library* option and click *Next*, the wizard asks whether to create a new document library or update an existing one. In this case, we want to create a document library as a repository for our saved forms—we'll call it `StatusReport`. If you choose an existing library, that library will be repurposed for filling out your form. If you get an error dialog, the server may not be running Forms Services, the server doesn't allow publishing from InfoPath, or you don't have appropriate permission. Assuming that installation of SharePoint Server 2007 was successful, it's most likely that you don't have permission. If that's the case, ensure that you are classified under the designer role on the SharePoint site collection in which you're publishing. We'll look at some of the other potential problems in Chapter 17.

The next wizard page shows promoted properties that can be used as columns in the document library (as discussed in Chapter 9). The status report sample already has promoted properties, which can be changed at this point if you choose. The next and final page shows a summary and a *Publish* button (Figure 14.8). Click *Publish* to proceed with the final stage of deploying the form template to the server.

> **WARNING Gracefully Upgrading Form Templates**
>
> If you're modifying a document library or site content type, clicking *Publish* terminates any current form-filling sessions. The termination may not be noticeable immediately, and all data will be lost. To gracefully upgrade published form templates that may be in use, the specific template should first be quiesced before the upgrade. We'll discuss quiescing in Chapter 17.

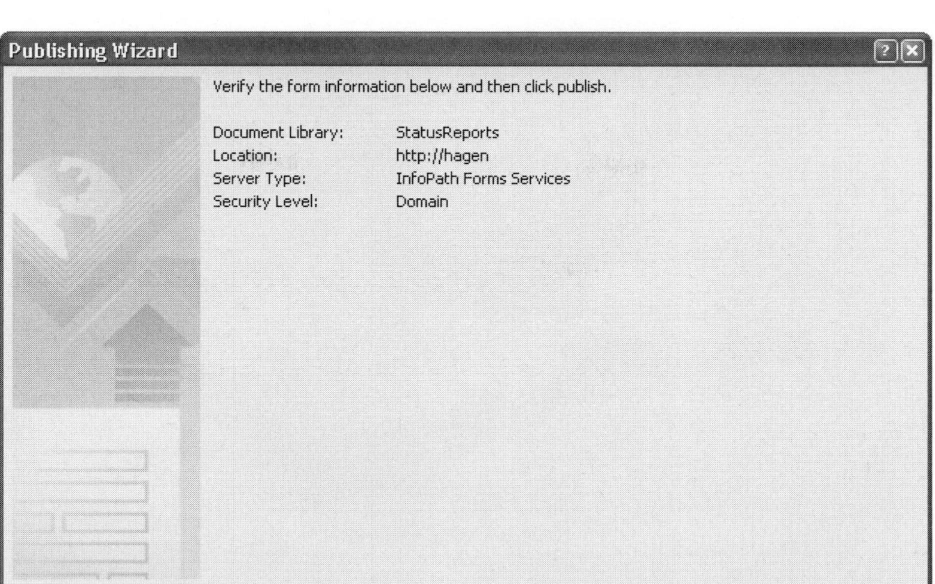

FIGURE 14.8: Last page of the Publishing Wizard before clicking the Publish button

After you click *Publish* and wait a few moments for publishing to be successful, the wizard text changes to that shown in Figure 14.9. During the moments you were waiting, a few things happened. First, the form template was uploaded to the server. The target upload location can be a new or existing document library or anywhere else within the current site collection on the server. Once uploaded, the template is thoroughly analyzed. If there are any incompatibilities or errors with the form template, they surface now. Should no problems arise, the template is converted into a special format that is consumable by Forms Services for rendering in the browser. At this point, the form template is on the server and can be filled out from within the InfoPath client application, but it's still not browser-ready. The next step is to activate the form template to a SharePoint site collection. Activation happens automatically during the publishing process from InfoPath. (It can also be done manually from the SharePoint Central Administration site. We'll explore manual activation in Chapter 17.)

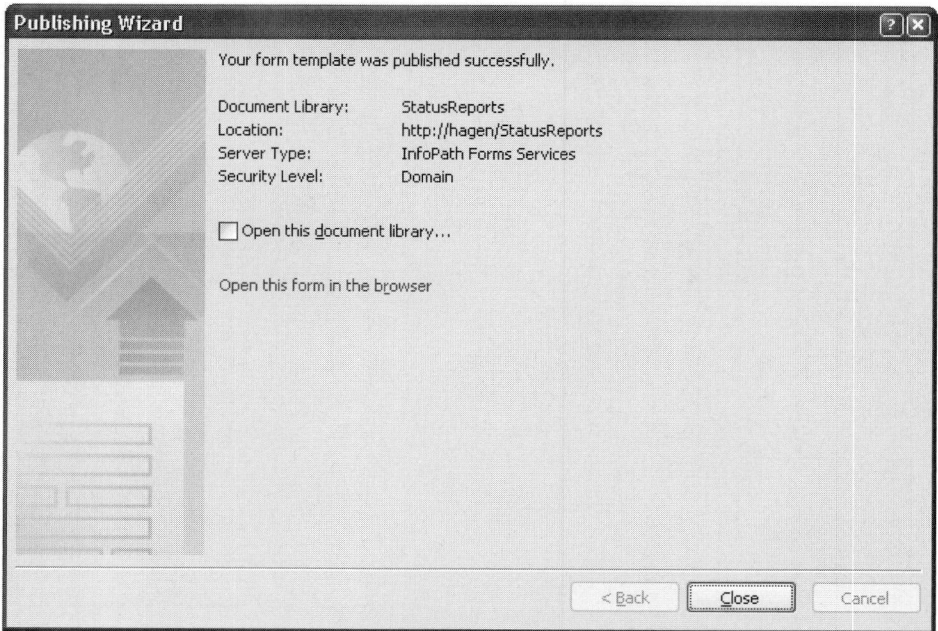

FIGURE 14.9: Last page of the Publishing Wizard after clicking the Publish button

Getting Familiar with Browser Forms

Filling out forms in the browser, as you may already perceive, is a very similar process to filling out forms in InfoPath. Forms Services strives to bring the same InfoPath experience to the Web browser. However, because filling out a form by using Forms Services is not the same as using InfoPath, there are inevitable differences. In this section, we'll cover some of the general aspects of browser-based form templates. The primary goal is to get comfortable with forms in a Web browser. By the time you finish this section, you should have a general understanding of what it means to fill out a form in environments other than InfoPath.

Creating a New Form

To create a new form for the first time, just click the *Open this form in the browser* from the last page of the Publishing Wizard (shown earlier in Figure 14.9). If you already dismissed the wizard, you can fill out the form by going to the SharePoint site where you published the form template. If you published to a new library called `MyOwnForm`, you would point your browser to http://yourserver/MyOwnForm. When the library appears, click on the *New* button to fill out a new form.

> **TIP Opening the Form in the Browser**
>
> Did the form open using InfoPath instead of the browser? Change this behavior by going to the *Settings* button and then selecting the *Form Library Settings* menu item. (You'll need at least a SharePoint designer role.) Then click on *Advanced Settings* and select the *Display as a Web page* option. We'll learn another way to open a form in the browser when we look at URL parameters in "Filling Out Browser Forms" later in this chapter.

> **WARNING A Shared Service Provider Must Exist!**
>
> Forms Services depends on session state (an important topic mostly addressed in Chapter 17). To get session state working, an SSP must first be created. Without session state, a form will fail to open in the browser. While discussing how to create an SSP is beyond the scope of this book, the SharePoint Central Administration site helps walk you through the simple process. On the home page of the Central Administration site, look at the *Administrator Task* called *Configure server farm's shared services.*

Toolbar

One of the biggest differences between the browser and its bigger sibling is the lack of a shell, primarily the shell's menus and task panes. Clearly, the browser is missing functionality without these options. To make up for this shortcoming, browser forms include a configurable toolbar at the top and bottom of the page. The toolbar, shown in Figure 14.10, contains helpful commands you can use while filling out a form. A *Submit* button appears as the first button in the toolbar if submit is enabled and you choose to show the button. This particular toolbar also contains *Save, Save As*, and *Close* buttons, which are available only when the form is being filled out in the context of a form library (more on that later). Next you can find a *View* drop-down that appears only when the form template has more than one view. Of course, there are design-configurable exceptions, such as opting not to list the view on the menu. The *Print View* button is always available by default but could be removed. The *Update* button is not added by default, but we've included it to allow forcing the form to update with the server.

FIGURE 14.10: Toolbar shown when filling out a form in the browser

> **WARNING** Properly Refreshing Form Data
>
> Clicking the *Refresh* button in your browser does not do the same thing as the *Update* toolbar button! *Refresh* clears the form and starts over. *Update* keeps the form data intact while sending the form to the server.

> **NOTE** Browser Form Toolbar
>
> The toolbar is not a browser toolbar plug-in but an HTML-based toolbar in the Web page itself.

To configure buttons on this toolbar and to decide if you even want a toolbar, look no further than the *Form Options* dialog from the *Tools* menu. The first category is *Browser*, which contains various options specific to forms opened in the browser. Among these items is a *Toolbars* section, as shown in Figure 14.11. These toolbar options don't allow you to create custom buttons but simply to include or exclude predefined buttons. Some buttons do not always appear; this depends on the context of filling out the form. (We'll see how this works when we talk about SharePoint integration.) You can also choose to have the toolbar appear at the top, bottom, both (the default setting), or neither if both options are unchecked.

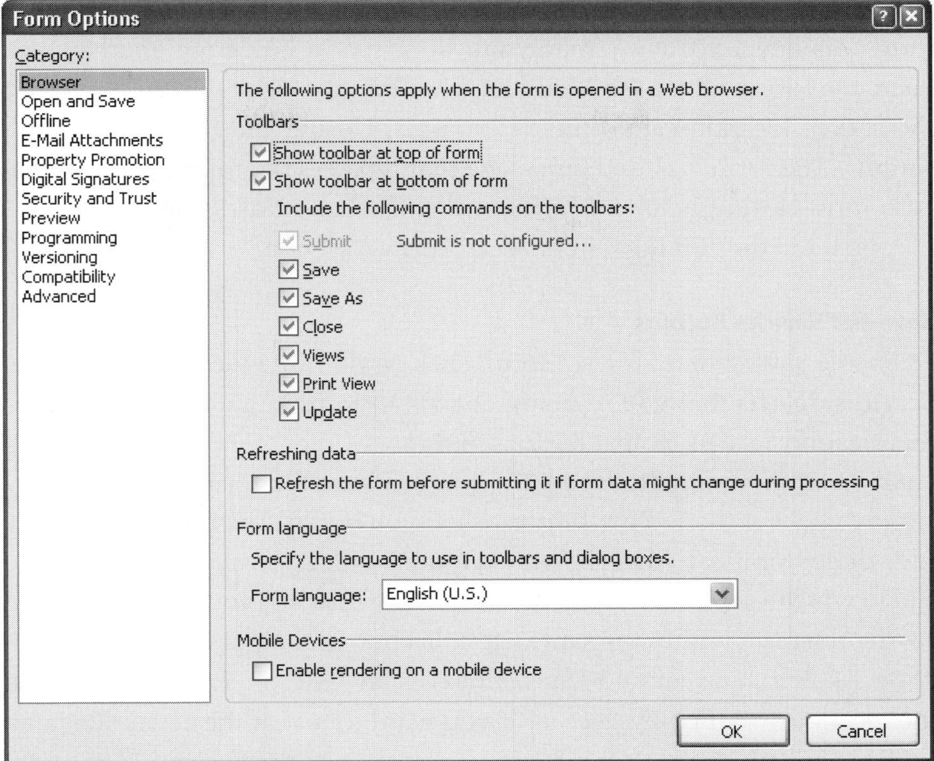

FIGURE 14.11: Configuring toolbars for a browser-enabled form template filled out in the browser

> **TIP Hiding Toolbars in Web Pages Hosting a Form**
>
> You may not want to show toolbars if your form is hosted in an ASP.NET page as it may disturb the flow of your page layout. We'll look at hosting a browser form in Chapter 18.

Submit Button

The *Submit* button may be available if you select the *Allow users to submit this form* option in the *Submit Options* dialog when you design the template. Submitting a form in the browser is a very similar experience to submitting a form using InfoPath. In fact, browser form templates support all submit options, even all of the advanced settings such as custom messages and all *After submit* actions. If *Close the form* is chosen as the *After submit* action, the form can behave in different ways depending on how it was opened. If the form was opened from a SharePoint library or a link from another Web page, the form will close by redirecting to that previous library or page. If the source location cannot be determined, closing the form results in a simple "The form is closed" message that replaces the form itself. We discuss form-closing behavior in more detail when addressing the `Source` parameter in the "Filling Out Browser Forms" section.

Save and Save As Buttons

To enable saving of a browser form, click *New* from a form library. Forms Services detects that you're filling out the form from a library and shows the *Save* and *Save As* toolbar buttons. (Of course, they'll show only if they're enabled as shown in Figure 14.11.) You can save the form at any time by simply clicking the toolbar button when you'd like. The browser shows a save dialog similar to that shown in Figure 14.12. The *Save in* location is the site in which your form is saved. For security reasons, you are restricted to saving the form within the same site collection as the published form template. Typing in a required *File name* saves an XML file with that name in the location specified by *Save in*. If you want to revisit the saved file later, simply navigate to the *Save in* location and click on the file icon. If you cannot find the file but remember where you saved it, you could enter the full location to the file in the browser address bar.

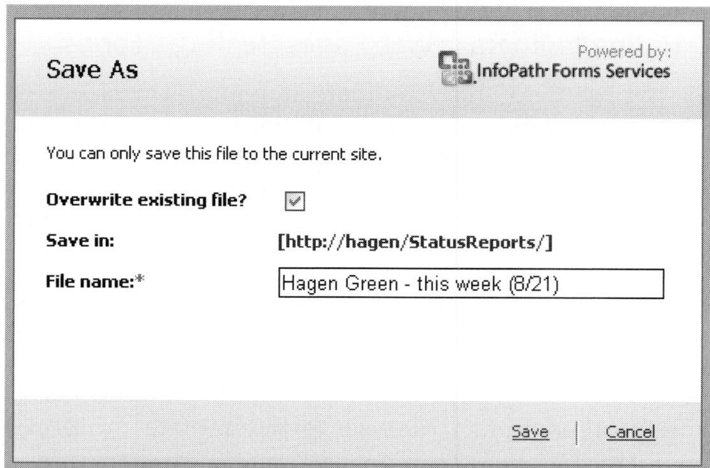

FIGURE 14.12: Saving a form in the browser

When we talk about filling out browser forms later in the chapter, we'll see how the *Save in* location is determined and how you can set it yourself.

Close Button

The *Close* button will close the form in the browser, but not the browser itself. The purpose of this button is to finalize filling of the current form by closing the session. If the *Close* button is not used to finalize form filling, the session will stay open until it times out from inactivity. While letting the session time out is fine, you should make sure that you're using a private computer with a secure connection. Not properly closing the form-filling session could lead to someone else continuing to use your session without your knowledge.

> **NOTE** Properly Closing a Form-Filling Session
>
> To ensure a form-filling session is properly closed, either click the *Close* toolbar button within the form (if the button is available) or just close the Web browser window.

View Drop-Down

The *View* drop-down in the toolbar allows the user filling out the form to switch views. This drop-down is available only if there are two or more views in the form and if the form template designer chose to show this drop-down in the toolbar. Selecting a view from the drop-down switches to the new view within the same browser window. This functionality is equivalent to what the InfoPath program offers through the *View* menu when a form is filled out.

Print View Button

The *Print View* button is useful, for example, when the user filling out the form wants to print the form for a paper record. Using the *Print View* button in browser forms is discussed at length in Chapter 12. Please refer to the "Print Views in Browser-Enabled Forms" section in that chapter for more information.

Update Button

The *Update* button gives the user filling out the form a way to force a refresh of the form's data with the server. This button is usually not needed in most forms, however. You'll learn more about update functionality in Chapter 17.

Controls

Many of the same controls available when designing InfoPath-only form templates are at your fingertips in browser-enabled mode. Only a handful of the more advanced controls are not offered, such as the Master/Detail and Combo Box controls. Table 14.1 shows a full list of the controls available in Forms Services.

TABLE 14.1: Controls Supported in Forms Services

Control	Category	Behavior Compared to InfoPath
Text Box	Standard	
Rich Text Box	Standard	A formatting toolbar appears when the box has focus.
Drop-Down List Box	Standard	
List Box	Standard	
Date Picker	Standard	A visually different date picker popup appears when the user selects a date.
Check Box	Standard	
Option Button	Standard	
Button	Standard	
Section	Standard	
Optional Section, Repeating Section	Repeating and Optional	
Repeating Table	Repeating and Optional	
File Attachment	File and Picture	Maximum file sizes are more restricted.
Hyperlink	Advanced	Clicking a Hyperlink opens a new browser window.
Expression Box	Advanced	

Of the controls listed in Table 14.1, most behave identically in the browser and the InfoPath client. Structural controls like Optional Section, Repeating Section, and Repeating Table work virtually the same as in the InfoPath client (as discussed in Chapter 2). They show an icon to the left of the control that, when clicked, brings up a context menu with actions such as *Insert* and *Remove.*

> **TIP Access Keys for Inserting and Removing Sections**
>
> If you're trying to quickly insert a repeating or optional control without fumbling through the control's menu, try hitting the Ctrl+Enter keyboard combination when the control has focus. Likewise, deleting items is quick with Ctrl+Delete.

One of the more interesting and arguably useful controls is the Rich Text Box. The Rich Text Box control has a few limitations, such as requiring all formatting options (like paragraph breaks) and not allowing embedded images. (In contrast, InfoPath provides for enabling or disabling specific Rich Text Box control formatting options.) Despite the minor restrictions, Rich Text Box has the full range of editing functionality you'd expect with a basic HTML editor. You can see the variety of editing options available when you enter text into a Rich Text Box; a toolbar appears above the control (Figure 14.13). Even some commonly used shortcut keys work, such as Ctrl+B for bold and Ctrl+I for italics!

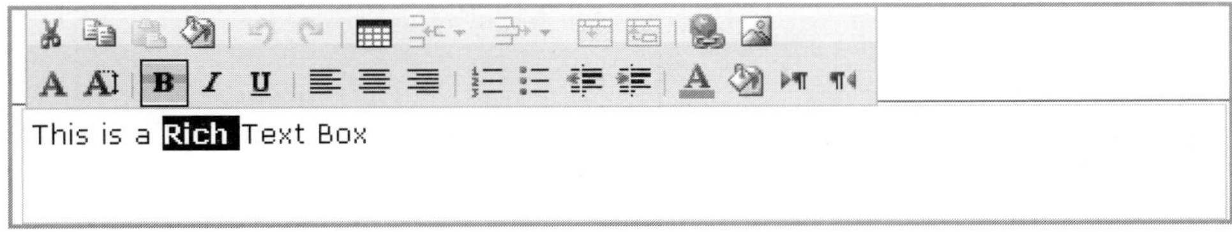

FIGURE 14.13: Editing a Rich Text Box control in the browser

Besides the slight limitation in the variety of controls, there are some subtle behavioral differences as well. One such behavior is during multiple selections. InfoPath allows users filling out a form to select multiple Section controls and Repeating Table rows. Multiple selections are handy for performing some common operations to many controls at once, such as removing them. Forms in the Web browser do not allow multiple selections. If such a selection could exist, it would simply be the browser selecting the HTML content, which would not affect the form itself.

Supported Web Browsers

As we mentioned earlier, Forms Services reaches beyond the scope of InfoPath by targeting multiple browser types. For the best experience and highest fidelity when filling out a browser form, it is recommended to use Internet Explorer 6 or later. The next best browser choices are Firefox, Mozilla, and Netscape on the Windows platform. Operating systems such as Mac OS, Linux, and UNIX variants can also be used to fill out forms. Mac OS machines can use Safari or Firefox, with Firefox providing a slightly overall better experience. On a Linux or UNIX computer, Firefox v1.5 and Mozilla v1.7 work quite nicely. Table 14.2 classifies browsers, their versions, and operating systems with comments on how well Forms Services is expected to perform. Other browsers not listed in Table 14.2 are unsupported and may not perform as expected.

The breadth of browsers and platforms enables almost anyone with a computer to fill out InfoPath forms. But what if you don't have a computer with Internet access—say, when using a laptop in a taxi? The next best thing may just be in your back pocket. Toward the end of this chapter, we'll talk about how you can use a mobile device, such as a smart phone or PDA, to fill out forms. Before we jump into mobile devices, however, let's first see how to design a browser-enabled form template.

Designing a Browser-Enabled Form Template

Earlier in the chapter, we successfully published the status report form template to Forms Services. Since the template had already been designed to be compatible with the browser (i.e., the status bar shows *Compatibility: InfoPath and InfoPath Forms Services*), there was nothing extra for us to do before publish. However, this may not be the case typically. If you're

TABLE 14.2: Matrix of Browsers Supported for Use with Forms Services

Platform	Browser	Version	Comments
Windows	Internet Explorer	6, 7	• All browser features are available and work as expected. • Internet Explorer is required for fully functional administration pages.
Windows Windows Windows Mac OS Mac OS UNIX/Linux UNIX/Linux	Firefox Netscape Mozilla Firefox Safari Firefox Netscape	1.5 8.1 1.7 1.5 2.0 1.5 7.2	• Use of digital signatures is limited to the Internet Explorer browser. • The Rich Text Box control is read-only on non-IE browsers but can be edited after the user dismisses a warning. Only plain text input is allowed. • The Date Picker control allows entering of dates, but the picker button isn't available, so this control becomes similar to a Text Box control. • Auto-complete is not available.

upgrading a form template from InfoPath 2003, it is not already compatible. Even if you designed a template starting from scratch in InfoPath 2007, it still may not be ready.

As the first step in designing a new template, you make various selections in the *Design a Form* dialog. You can choose to design a form template or template part, for example, among other options. One of the options is a checkbox at the bottom of the dialog labeled *Enable browser-compatible features only*. If you decide up front that the form template is to be compatible with the browser, then InfoPath will expose only the design-time features that maintain compatibility. This compatibility setting, however, is not a hard up-front decision. So you could choose to design a form template that is not compatible with Forms Services and later change your mind. How does InfoPath allow such a radical shift? Part of the answer lies in the concept of design once. The rest is in the Design Checker.

Design Once

Design once is not a real feature but instead a design philosophy that the InfoPath team held steadfast when creating InfoPath 2007 and Forms Services. The idea is simple: to design a form template only once that works equivalently on both InfoPath and browser clients. But since not all of the InfoPath features are available in the browser, how can design once work? InfoPath has two main design modes: (1) InfoPath client and (2) InfoPath client and Forms Services. That's why we say "browser-compatible" or "browser-enabled" when referring to such templates. When designing a compatible form template, we're maximizing the set of features available in Forms Services. That set of features is a strict subset of what is otherwise available in InfoPath. Figure 14.14 shows the approximate percentage of InfoPath features that are supported by Forms Services. When you design a browser-enabled template, both InfoPath and Forms Services subscribe to the smaller circle.

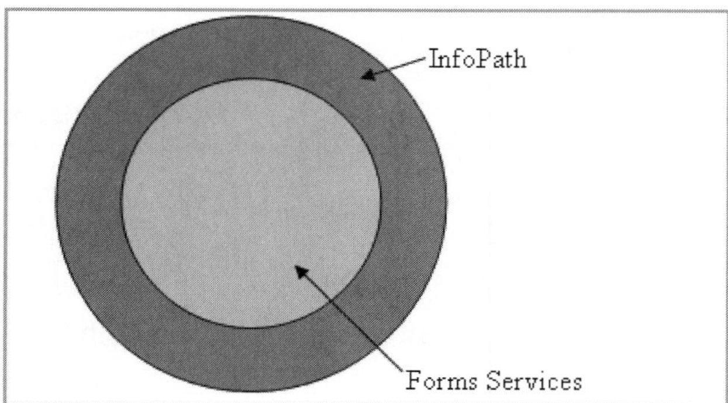

FIGURE 14.14: Commonality of InfoPath and Forms Services feature sets

> **NOTE A Form Template Is Always Designed for InfoPath**
>
> Designing a form template to work only in the browser is not possible. (You can, of course, write form code to fail loading the form if it's not in a browser.) Any form template designed for the browser will also work in InfoPath. The opposite is not always true.

Design Checker

To help make a soft transition between fundamental changes in form template design, we introduce the Design Checker (or just *checker* for short). The checker is a task pane for InfoPath 2007 that is always available while you design a form template. Its primary use is when switching template compatibility mode from *InfoPath* to *InfoPath and InfoPath Forms Services*. In doing so, the available form template features shrink from the larger circle shown in Figure 14.14 to the smaller.

It's convenient to be able to change the compatibility mode in the midst of designing a template. But it doesn't come for free: Doing so may yield a number of both messages and errors. How many issues and the difficulty involved to resolve them depends on what features are incorporated into the form template. The best way to understand what could be expected with a real-world form template is to show the MOI Consulting feedback sample form template. (The MOI feedback form template is included in this chapter's samples on the book's Web site as MoiFeedback and MoiFeedback_WebEnabled.)

The MOI feedback form template, shown in Figure 14.15, is used by the MOI Consulting firm to receive feedback from its customers. The IT department finished designing this form template by using InfoPath 2007 and rolled it out. Some folks filled out the form with no problem, but the IT department also received many phone calls from others who didn't have InfoPath. (That's some good feedback!) Quick to react, the IT pros at MOI knew that using Forms Services would be the quickest and easiest way to reach out to their customers. They heard the form template would not need a complete redesign, which was an important benefit and a factor in their decision. Let's go through the steps that the people in the IT department would take to make the feedback form template browser-enabled.

Browser-Enabling a Form Template

To begin making a form template browser-enabled, we need to change the template's compatibility mode. (Before doing this yourself, however, we recommend that you check out the various features of the MoiFeedback sample in design mode and also try filling out the form in InfoPath.) To

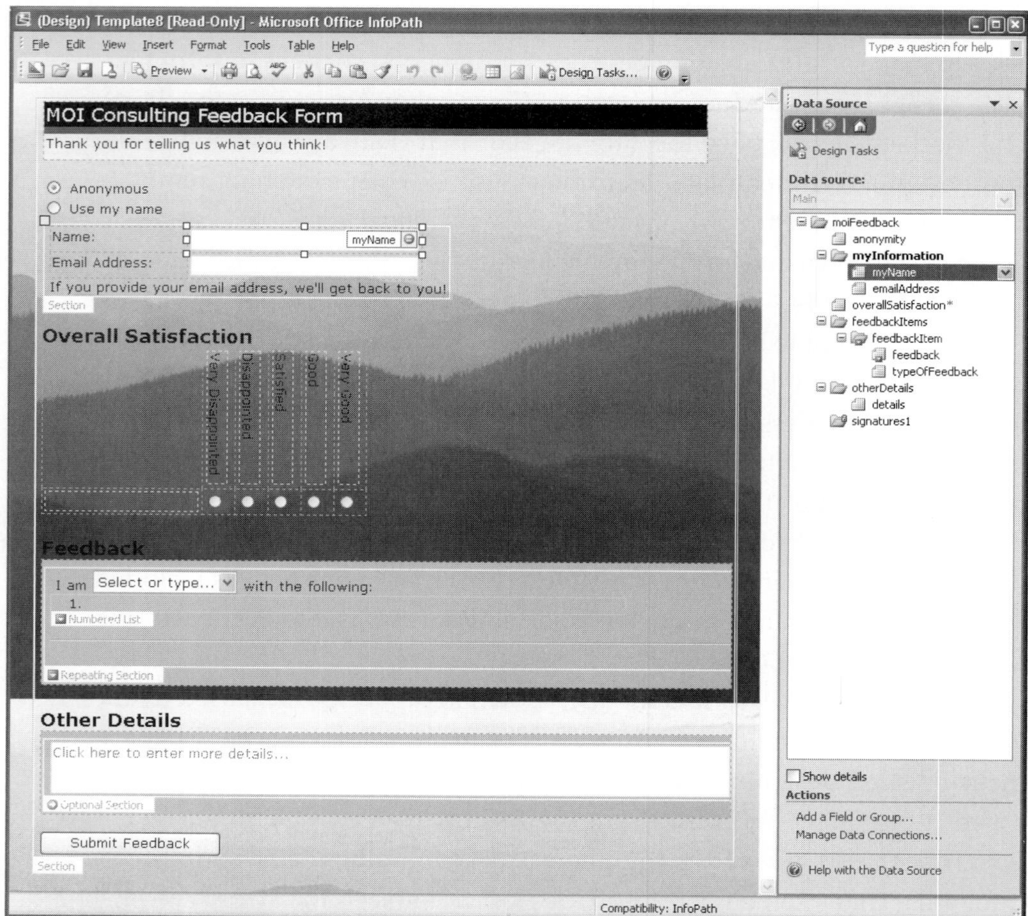

FIGURE 14.15: MOI Consulting feedback form

change the compatibility, go to the *Design Checker* task pane and click on the *Change Compatibility Settings* link. This opens the *Compatibility* category on the *Form Options* dialog (Figure 14.16).

> **TIP Shortcut to the Design Checker Task Pane**
>
> You can quickly jump to the *Design Checker* task pane by clicking anywhere in the right quadrant of the status bar. For example, clicking on the text *Compatibility: InfoPath* in Figure 14.15 shows the checker.

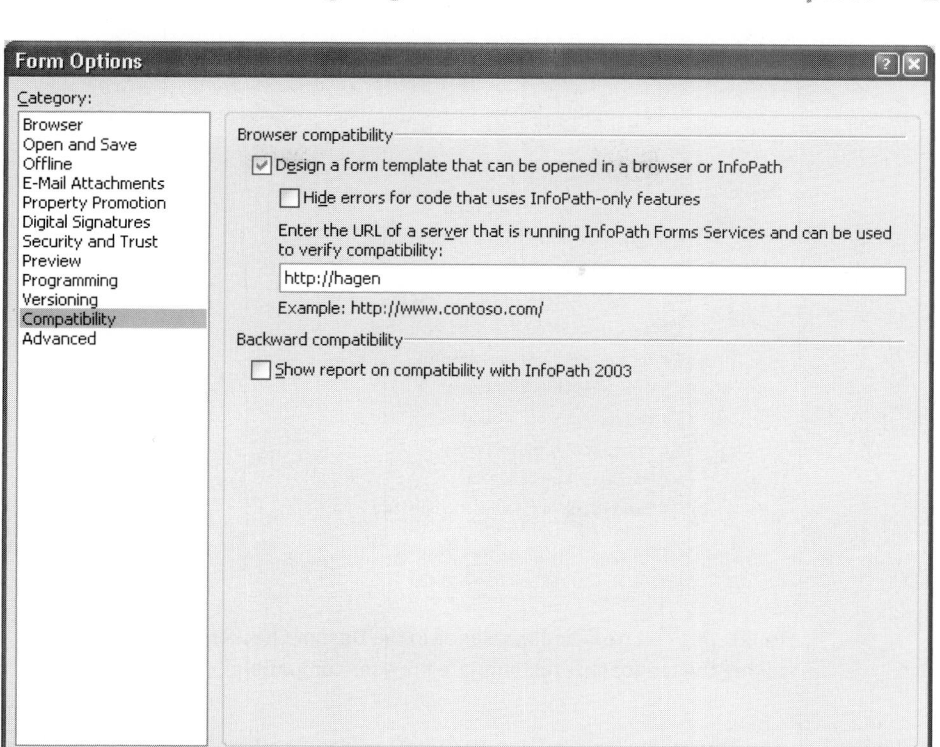

FIGURE 14.16: Compatibility settings in the Form Options dialog

Checking the *Design a form template that can be opened in a browser or InfoPath* checkbox makes the current form template compatible with Forms Services. To perform additional verification on template compatibility, we also entered the URL of our server in the text box. We'll see what benefit this buys us in a few moments. Dismissing this dialog then populates the checker with various browser-compatibility issues (Figure 14.17).

Before we can publish the form template to our server running Forms Services, we must fix all the errors listed in Figure 14.17. The checker makes it relatively easy to quickly address these design issues. When you click on an error, InfoPath either selects the control in the view that has the problem or shows you a dialog explaining what to do next. The first three browser compatibility errors relate to roles, digital signatures, and form code language. Our template defines user roles, which are not supported in browser-enabled form templates. To fix this problem, we'll remove roles

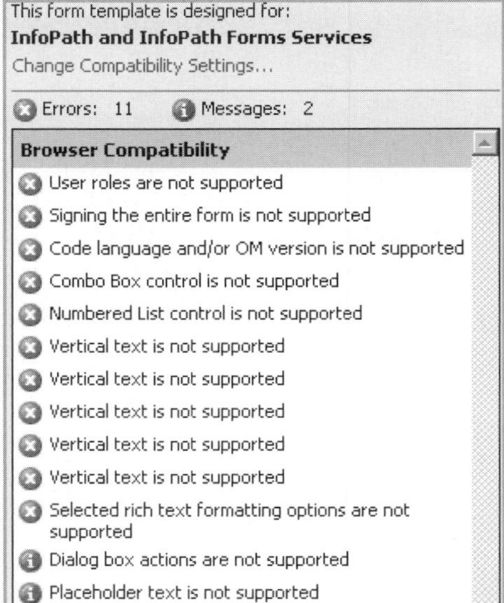

FIGURE 14.17: Errors and messages in the Design Checker after making the feedback form template browser-compatible

defined by our template as well as any references to those roles (e.g., in a conditional formatting expression). The *Manage User Roles* dialog, which we showed earlier in Figure 14.3, allows us to remove roles but not add them in this situation. If we had designed a browser-compatible form template from the start, we never would have been permitted to add roles in the first place. This philosophy applies not only to roles but also to all features that would cause errors when switching to browser-compatibility mode.

The *Signing the entire form is not supported* error does not mean digitally signing the form is not supported at all in the browser. In fact, browser-enabled form templates support signing Section controls, as evident by both the dialog that appears when you click on the error or go to the *Digital Signatures* category in *Form Options* (as shown in Figure 14.18).

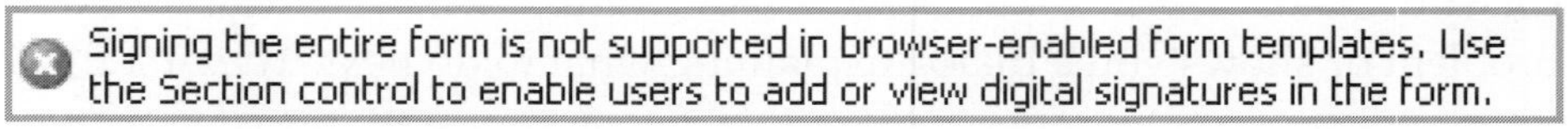

Signing the entire form is not supported in browser-enabled form templates. Use the Section control to enable users to add or view digital signatures in the form.

FIGURE 14.18: Browser-compatibility message within the Digital Signatures category under the Form Options dialog

In the *Form Options* dialog, the *Enable digital signatures for specific data in the form* option is available. Let's see how to work around the inability to digitally sign the entire form. When enabling signatures for specific data in a form, use a single forward slash (/) as the value to input in the *Fields and groups to be signed* text box. This single forward slash means "entire document" in the XPath language and is functionally equivalent (and the perfect workaround) to the *Enable digital signatures for the entire form* option that's unsupported by browser forms. It's not required, but we should visually fix our form template so that all controls become read-only when the form is signed. To do so, insert the `MoiFeedback` document element group from the data source into the view as a Section control. Then move the entire contents of our view into that control—cut and paste works nicely.

The last error in our form template (that's not in the view) is our form code language. It turns out that the MOI feedback form template has some JScript code. Unfortunately, any script and even managed code authored against the InfoPath 2003 SP1 OM is not supported in Forms Services. There is no easy way to upgrade the script code to be browser-compatible, and the only forward step you can take (without rewriting the code in the InfoPath 2007 OM, which happens to be the topic of our next chapter) is to remove the code from the template. We'll do this for the feedback form template. Go to the *Form Options* dialog's *Programming* category and click the *Remove Code* button. Script, managed code, and more about removing code from a form template are discussed in Chapter 15.

> **TIP Refreshing Design Checker Errors and Messages**
>
> You might have noticed that checker errors and messages aren't disappearing as we fix them. To update the list, click on the *Refresh* button at the bottom of the checker.

We're finished dealing with browser-compatible errors that are not related to the view. All of the errors that remain are unsupported controls or control options. These issues are usually easier to fix than the ones we just described. The first control error is the Combo Box; it is not supported in Forms Services. If you can settle for a Drop-Down List Box instead of a

Combo Box, simply right-click the control and use the *Change To* fly-out menu to do the conversion. The Drop-Down List Box preserves any options, including items, from the Combo Box. If your users still need the Combo Box capability of typing in a custom value, consider inserting a Text Box bound to the same field as the Drop-Down List Box. You can also use conditional formatting and Option Button controls to offer users a choice: predetermined or custom value.

None of the list-based controls (Bulleted List, Numbered List, and Plain List) can be used in a browser-enabled form template. A nifty way to simulate a list control is to use the *Change To* fly-out menu to convert to a Repeating Table. To keep the visual look of a list, remove the header from the Repeating Table. If you had a Bulleted List control, resize the Text Box in the Repeating Table to make enough room for a bullet symbol from the *Symbol* dialog available from the *Insert* menu. If you had a Numbered List, insert an Expression Box with XPath `concat(count(preceding-sibling::*) + 1, ".")`. This XPath generates the number, along with a period, for a given row. As a final touch, we used the *Align* button on the *Size* tab of the control properties dialogs (for both the Expression Box and Text Box). This positions the number, period, and data in the Text Box on the same vertical plane.

One error (which we mentioned earlier in this chapter) relates to the limitations of the Rich Text Box control in a browser-compatible form template: *Selected rich text formatting options are not supported.* Fixing this error is trivial. First, click on the error in the Design Checker to select the Rich Text Box control in question. Then open the *Rich Text Box Properties* dialog and click on the *Display* tab. Selecting the *Enable browser-compatible settings only* checkbox appropriately configures this Rich Text Box control for use in a Web browser. As you can see when you enable the checkbox, embedded images are disallowed (only linked images are allowed) while paragraph breaks, character formatting, and full rich text are forced requirements.

Lastly, the set of five errors is due to vertical text. It's easy to uncheck the *Display Text Vertically* option on the *Expression Box Properties* dialog, but it makes our form template quite ugly. To accommodate the lack of vertical text, it works best to lay out the *Overall Satisfaction* table again. Our vertical-to-horizontal remake is shown in Figure 14.19 from the perspective of a user filling out the form.

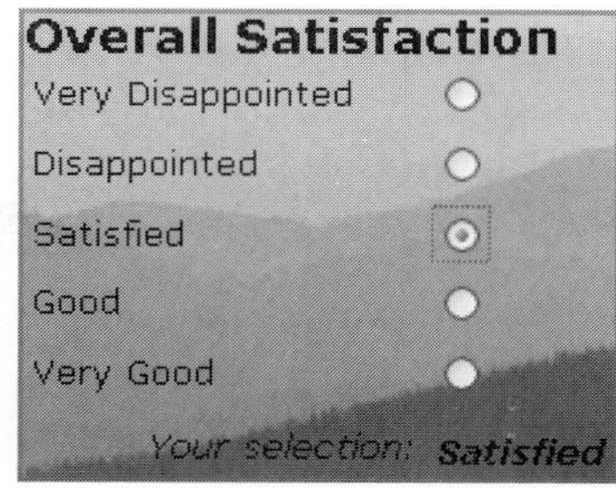

FIGURE 14.19: Remake of the Overall Satisfaction table without vertical text

The messages from the checker shown in Figure 14.17 do not need to be addressed. But it's important to know that the messages represent noticeable and degraded differences in the form template behavior when users fill out forms in the browser. Some examples of messages include placeholder text, use of dialogs (e.g., with a rule), and a custom task pane. In our sample form template, we'll leave the parts of the design that resulted in messages as they are.

As the last step in ensuring browser compatibility, let's verify our form template against the server itself. To do so, check the *Verify on Server* checkbox and click *Refresh* from the *Design Checker* task pane. Why, you may ask, should we use the server to check the form template compatibility? Since InfoPath has given us a laundry list of incompatibilities, what else could possibly be left? The answers to these questions yield good and bad news. The good news is that InfoPath catches most of the problems, especially the bigger ones. The bad news is that the server is always more strict than InfoPath. Given that publishing your form template to Forms Services performs the server verification anyway, it's just easier to deal with any errors up front. In most cases, you'll notice parity between InfoPath and Forms Services errors and messages. (Similar errors and messages between InfoPath and the server are merged, so there are no duplicates.) When we verify against the server for the MOI feedback template, you'll see that neither new errors nor messages are generated. Instead, there's a new class of message: browser optimizations.

Browser optimizations are server-generated comments on the performance of your form template when filled out in a browser. If your server may be under heavy load and form filling is a high priority for multiple users, you should consider the ramifications of these messages. The most common optimization messages are those shown in the sample feedback form template, namely, "Control sends data to server on insert or delete" and "Control sends data to server on value change." There are several reasons why data needs to be sent back to the server. In the case of this template, the first few issues relate to the fact that we're using a custom XPath expression in an Expression Box. Recall that we used this expression to generate the equivalent of a Numbered List control. If you can instead change the Expression Box to, say, a bullet symbol to simulate a Bulleted List control, you've solved the first half of the optimization problems!

> **NOTE** Advanced Forms Services
>
> You can find further discussion of browser optimizations and server performance in Chapter 17.

Other Uses for the Design Checker

The Design Checker isn't just for designing a browser-enabled form template. Its usefulness crops up occasionally as you use other InfoPath features. For example, InfoPath 2007 supports designing a template that is backward compatible with InfoPath 2003. (The setting is under the *Compatibility* category in the *Form Options* dialog.) When backward compatibility is enabled, the checker adds a *Backward Compatibility* section with any messages and errors. Other InfoPath features where the checker is useful include offline data connections and document importer messages. As you can see, its name really says it all: It checks the entire design of your form template!

> **TIP** Enabling a Form Template for Backward Compatibility
>
> To use an InfoPath 2007 form template in InfoPath 2003, set the *Save as type* drop-down in the *Save As* dialog to be *InfoPath 2003 Form Template.*

Browser-Enabled Forms without the Design Checker

In the last section, we saw how to change a form template to be browser compatible. If you are designing a new form template and already know it's going to be used with Forms Services, you can save some time. We mentioned earlier that there's a checkbox at the bottom of the *Design a Form* dialog labeled *Enable browser-compatible features only.* Checking this option restricts some features in design mode such that you should not generate errors in the Design Checker. This claim, of course, really applies only to verification of the template within InfoPath. Verifying on the server may yield minor error nuances (such as unsupported XPath expressions). Messages can still be generated for features that are supported by InfoPath, such as placeholder text, but nonfunctional in Forms Services.

> **TIP Ignoring Design Checker Messages**
>
> You can usually safely ignore Design Checker messages. However, some messages can affect the behavior or performance of your form.

Designing Browser-Enabled Template Parts

In the same way we browser-enabled a form template, you can browser-enable template parts. You can choose to make your template part compatible with Forms Services when you first design it or at any later time. We dedicated a portion of Chapter 10 to template parts.

Getting Familiar with the Browser Form Experience

So far we've published one form template to InfoPath Forms Services, and the MOI Consulting feedback template is ready for publishing. Now let's fill out a form! We'll continue with our last example and look at the form-filling experience in the browser. To fill out the MOI feedback form template, we'll use the Publishing Wizard as we did before with the status report template. Go through the wizard and click the *Publish* button at the end so you reach the final page of the wizard. This page, shown earlier in Figure 14.9, has an *Open this form in the browser* link. Clicking on it shows the Web browser, but before the form loads, you may briefly see a dialog

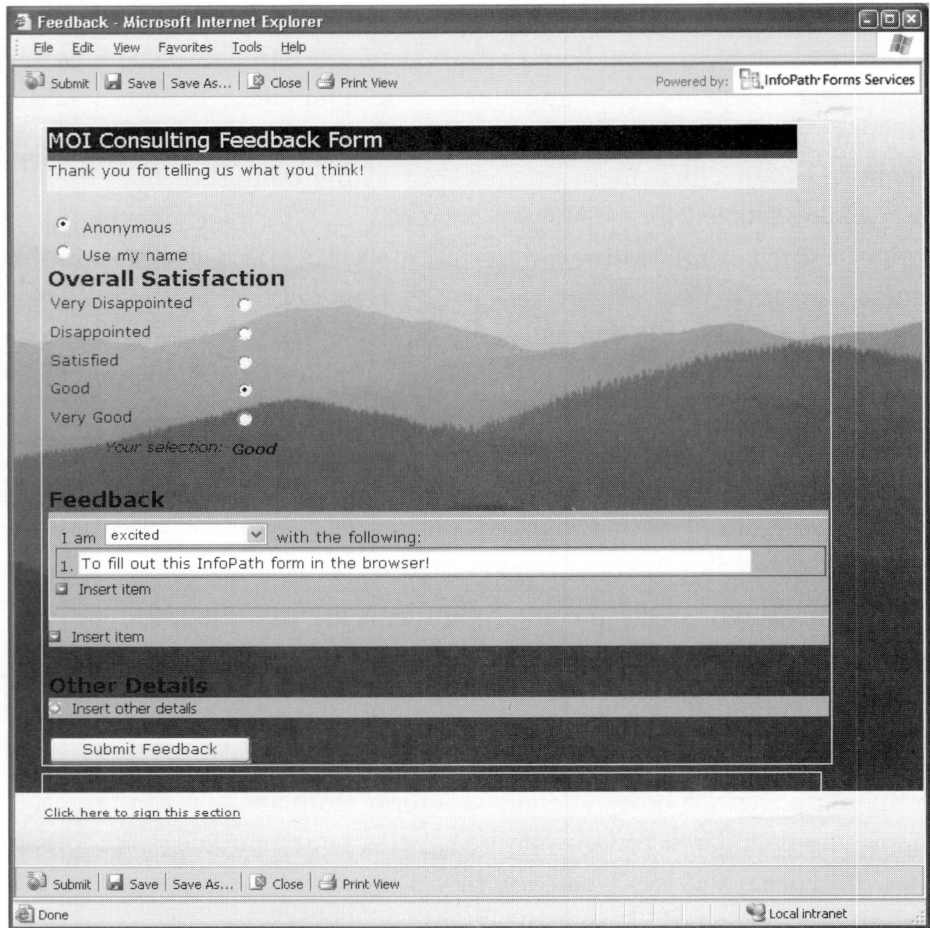

FIGURE 14.20: Filling out the MOI Consulting feedback form in the browser

that says, "Loading Form." Once the form loads, you should see a page similar to the one shown in Figure 14.20.

> **NOTE The Loading Form Dialog**
>
> The purpose of the *Loading Form* dialog is to inform the user that the server has been contacted and is processing the request. It is an especially helpful dialog on a narrowband connection such as dialup. While this dialog is showing, the browser may be asynchronously downloading script files. During this time the server may also be executing data connections or custom form code.

As you fill out the form, you may notice that it's very responsive. That's because almost all of the form "smarts" are downloaded to the browser. The technology in play behind the scenes is conceptually very similar to AJAX-style Web sites. You may find that a few parts of your form need to talk to the server. In the MOI feedback form template, for example, data is sent to and received from the server when the user inserts anything under or within the *Feedback* Repeating Section. This is because of complex XPaths used with the Expression Box control. While filling out the form, you may briefly see a dialog that says, "Sending data to the server." In Chapter 17 we'll look at how to manually suppress controls that otherwise require sending data to the server. Table 14.3 contains a list of features that may require communication with the server when users fill out the form.

> **NOTE** AJAX
>
> AJAX is an acronym for Asynchronous JavaScript and XML, which refers to a group of Web technologies that allow a Web page to display faster and be more interactive.

> **WARNING** JavaScript Must Be Enabled
>
> Scripting (specifically, JavaScript) and cookies must be enabled in the browser for browser-enabled forms to function properly.

As with any electronic form, InfoPath or not, at some point you'll want to save or submit your data. Saving typically means that the form isn't completely filled out yet. This might be the case for larger forms that take several sittings to finish, such as tax forms. When taking a break from your form, keep in mind that there's a 60-minute session timeout. This means that after 60 minutes of server inactivity, your form session is destroyed and all unsaved data is lost. When you're done filling out the form (if the form template is well designed, of course), you can click a submit button to permanently send your data.

TABLE 14.3: Form Features That May Automatically Communicate with the Server

Feature	Condition	Comments
Calculations (dynamic default values)	Certain complex calculations	Most calculations do not need to talk to the server.
Custom form code	Code behind a data source item that's bound to an edited control	Form code is run only on the server.
Controls	Out-of-context controls (B is under A in the data source, but A is inserted as a control under control B in the view)	Nontrivial control bindings or contexts require server logic.
Complex XPaths	Custom written XPaths (e.g., in an Expression Box)	
Digital signatures	Downloading of an ActiveX control and applying a digital signature to the form	
Data connections	Execution of a query or submit data connection	
Submit, *Print View*, *Save*, *Save As*, *Close*, and *Update* buttons and *View* drop-down	Use of toolbar functionality	
Field editing	Data sent to the server when a control's value changes, as can be specified to occur	Postback settings on form controls are discussed in Chapter 17.

TIP Configuring the Session State Timeout

In Chapter 17, you'll learn how to configure the timeout setting for session state.

While creating a new form is the first step in opening a form template in the browser, sometimes you will want to reopen an existing saved form. Doing so is easy. Go to the library where the form was saved and click on the link with the form name. If the form opens in the InfoPath program, there's an easy way to force rendering in the browser: Select the *Edit in Browser* command within the menu that surrounds the form link.

SharePoint Integration

Understanding SharePoint is important for succeeding with Forms Services. For example, when we published the status report to Forms Services, a document library was created for our browser-enabled form template. The second publishing option in the Publishing Wizard shown earlier in Figure 14.7, *Site Content Type (advanced),* has nothing to do with InfoPath but is rather a SharePoint-specific feature. (We'll soon see what it means for an InfoPath form template to be a site content type in SharePoint.) Finally, to publish an administrator-approved form template, you must use the SharePoint Central Administration site. No matter which route you take in publishing a form template to the server, the interaction with SharePoint is inevitable. It's clear that an important step in maximizing your productivity with browser forms is to understand how Forms Services integrates with SharePoint Server 2007. Let's take a look.

> **NOTE** Understanding SharePoint Basics
>
> Rather than spend our time discussing just SharePoint features, we'll talk about them in the context of Forms Services. If you don't have a fundamental understanding of a given SharePoint feature, consult an introductory SharePoint reference. For example, Microsoft TechNet has several introductory articles and white papers (as referenced in the Appendix).

Document Libraries

A document library is essentially a collection of files represented by its own Web page, which allows for collaboration among its users. Publishing to SharePoint (whether or not the form template is browser-enabled) creates a special library called a **form library**. A form library, which includes InfoPath XML-based forms as a primary file type, easily allows you to fill out a new or existing form. The best part about form libraries is that the concept and features are shared between InfoPath and browser-based form templates. Let's look at some of the ways form libraries can work for us when filling out our form templates.

Property Promotion, Versioning, and Permissions

Saved forms exist in the library and benefit from features such as permissions, versioning, and promoted properties. Promoted properties, as we learned in earlier chapters in the book, allow form data to be presented outside of the form. In SharePoint, this translates into custom columns in the form library. We filled out the MOI feedback form template a couple of times; you can see some of the fields' values shown in Figure 14.21.

New ▾ Upload ▾ Actions ▾ Settings ▾ View: All Documents ▾

Type	Name	Modified	Modified By	Checked Out To	Anonymity	Type Of Feedback	Details	Overall Satisfaction
	JohnFoo ! NEW	4/6/2006 9:49 PM	Hagen Green		anonymous	pleased confused		Satisfied
	MikeBar ! NEW	4/6/2006 9:49 PM	Hagen Green		anonymous	satisfied excited		Very Good

FIGURE 14.21: Promoted properties in a form library

Versioning is a SharePoint feature that saves snapshots of your data as changes are made. The primary purpose of versioning is to audit changes to a form while giving owners the ability to accept or roll back any modifications. If you are an author, a developer, or anyone who works incrementally or collaboratively on a project, you may already know how valuable versioning can be! You can enable versioning by going to the *Form Library Settings* page (from the *Settings* drop-down) and clicking on the *Versioning settings* link.

Permissions in SharePoint are further expanded with item-level granularity. That means you can restrict read and write access to specific forms within a form library. You can use SharePoint's predefined set of user roles subscribing to a set of permissions, or you can just set the permissions directly. Table 14.4 shows a list of permissions and their effects when interacting with Forms Services.

Controlling permissions goes beyond managing items in a form library. As you can see in Table 14.4, the very same permissions can be used to control who can publish a browser-enabled form template to the server.

Table 14.4: SharePoint Permissions and How They Apply to Forms Services

Permission	What It Means for the User	Impact on Forms Services
Read	Can view pages, list items, and documents	All forms viewed as read-only
Contribute	Can view pages and edit list items and documents	Same as for read permission, plus all forms can be saved
Design	Can edit lists, document libraries, and pages in the site collection	Same as for contribute permission, plus allows browser-enabling of form templates in Forms Services through InfoPath
Full control	Has full control; can manage permissions, create subsites, manage Web sites, and manage all alerts	Same as for design permission

Are Browser-Enabled Form Libraries Different?

Surprisingly, there's neither any visual nor functional difference between a browser-enabled and a "regular" form library. When the form template is published as browser-enabled, however, the template is activated with Forms Services. Only activated form templates can render their forms in the browser. (We'll explain how to manually activate a form template in Chapter 17.) The way in which a new or existing form (when its associated template is browser-enabled) is opened depends on browser form-opening logic, which can be fairly intricate. We dedicate a section, "Filling Out Browser Forms," to this topic later in the chapter.

As with any document library, a form library allows users to create new forms by clicking on the *New* button on the library's toolbar. The *New* button is not available if the user's permissions aren't sufficient. Likewise, users can upload one or more forms to the library by using the *Upload* button shown in Figure 14.21. This feature is useful, for example, when you have a form on your computer that you want to now use with the form library. The form might have been filled out offline by using InfoPath or sent to you via e-mail. If the form isn't properly associated with the form template in the library, use the *Relink Documents* view of the form library to select forms to relink. Relinking works with both InfoPath client and browser-based form templates.

Another convenience of working with a form library is that InfoPath is aware of the library location and defaults to that path when saving. That way, a user is guided to save a form in the library where it was created. However, this does not limit where the user can save. Forms Services allows a user to save the form anywhere in the current site collection. InfoPath, on the other hand, has no restrictions in place. When we talk about filling out browser form templates later in this chapter, we'll see how Forms Services determines the default save location.

WARNING **Maximum Number of Items in a SharePoint Library**

A maximum of 2,000 items may exist in a library at any given time. Attempting to create or upload more results in an error. A folder in the library can help expand the limit by another 2,000 items. See Microsoft TechNet for more information (as referenced in the Appendix).

The last interesting feature of form libraries when it comes to InfoPath and Forms Services is the behavior after a form is closed. With InfoPath, it's pretty obvious. You open a form from SharePoint, InfoPath appears for editing, and then you close the program to return to the Web browser when you're done. Forms Services has a similar model but plays out a little differently. Opening a form from a library navigates the browser away from the library for filling. Once finished, closing the form redirects the browser back to the library from which the opening originated. We'll learn more about how this redirection mechanism works when we look at filling out browser forms later in the chapter.

TIP **Closing the Form**

When we talk about closing the form in the browser, we mean clicking on the *Close* button on the form toolbar. We are not referring to the boxed "X" in the upper-right corner of the browser window.

Site Content Type

A **site content type**, or just content type for short, is a SharePoint template object that holds many pieces of data, including a document template, promoted properties metadata, and workflows. Publishing a form template as a content type opens up that template to be generically reused and filled out in any library that supports management of content types. (We'll discuss management of content types in a moment.) The real difference between a form template published as a content type versus one published to a document library is that the site content type can be added to any SharePoint library and subsequently filled out. A form template published to a form library strongly associates its forms in that library with the template. Let's explore an example to better understand when it's more appropriate to use a site content type than a form library.

Say that an automobile engineering company uses a SharePoint site to collaborate on its new designs. Each team (engine, transmission, interior, and so on) has its own document library to track schematic diagrams and archive meeting minutes. The diagrams are created in Microsoft Visio, but the meeting minutes are recorded by using InfoPath. Instead of requiring each team to create a separate form library for their minutes forms, a site content type could be added to each of the existing document libraries. Adding the content type allows the same meeting minutes form template to be shared across each of the teams' existing document libraries.

By default, multiple content types are not permitted in a library (i.e., a library does not allow for management of content types). To change this setting, go to the library settings page and click on the *Advanced settings* link. Once management of content types is allowed, a form template that was published as a content type can be added to that library. Simply click on the *Add from existing site content types* link on the settings page under the *Content Types* heading. Look for the content type name in the list, or filter the list by selecting *Microsoft Office InfoPath* from the drop-down. Once the content type is added, it is available on the *New* menu and reveals its promoted properties as columns in the library's *All Documents* view.

> **NOTE SharePoint Integration with Forms Services**
>
> The integration with SharePoint is not all specific to Forms Services. In fact, InfoPath can also take advantage of these same feature integrations. But the scenarios around Forms Services bring these points into the limelight.

Data Connections

Data connections in browser-based form templates work somewhat differently than in InfoPath. (We talked all about InfoPath query and submit data connections back in Chapters 6, 7, and 8.) When you execute a Web service query connection while filling out a form in InfoPath, for example, your computer connects directly to the Web service. When Forms Services hosts an InfoPath form, it is the server, not the browser client, that runs the Web service connection. This difference is not limited just to Web services but affects all connection types. With a shift in the initiator of the connection comes new security concerns such as the following three issues.

1. The server identity is used to make the connection.
2. Additional server resources are necessary.
3. A denial-of-service attack is possible through slow connections, receipt of large amounts of data, and so on.

Using the server identity could be an administrative nightmare. First, someone could discover what user account runs the Web Application. This information disclosure may help someone mount a more sophisticated attack. More importantly, the server's identity would have elevated privileges on the server farm. This could ultimately allow access to resources that are otherwise unavailable to a regular user. (And we haven't even started talking about points 2 and 3 yet!) Second, server administrators know how precious and scarce server resources can be during peak times. The overhead in data connections adds an additional stress to the server and network. Finally, an attacker can take advantage of the third point by leveraging intrinsic weaknesses in data connections to potentially escalate a denial-of-service attack against the server or even the browser.

To limit the potential damage a given form template can bring upon its server, Forms Services imposes a strict data connection policy: Domain trust form templates are not allowed to connect across domains. Forms can connect only to data within the same domain, which essentially limits connections to the same machine or load-balanced WFE. This goes against the inherent "domain trust" dogma, but such a departure is necessary for server security. One way to make cross-domain connections is by making your form template fully trusted. This is not always a viable option, especially since full trust form templates require publishing for administration approval. There is, in fact, a way to allow domain form templates to make cross-domain data connections. Look no further than data connection libraries and files.

Data Connection Libraries

A **data connection library** (**DCL**) is a special kind of document library in Windows SharePoint Services 3.0 (the platform of SharePoint Server 2007). In the same way a form library is a specialized document library for a form template and its saved forms, a DCL houses **data connection file** definitions. Each definition is an XML file with a .udcx or .xml extension.

> **WARNING** List-Item Permissions
>
> SharePoint list-item permissions apply to data connection definitions with .udcx or .xml extensions. Other file extensions, although they are valid definitions, do not benefit from item-based permissions.

The easiest way to create a data connection file is from within InfoPath design mode by using the *Data Connections* dialog. Select a data connection in the list, and click the *Convert* button, which opens the *Convert Data Connection* dialog (Figure 14.22). Not all connections can be converted; for example, XML document connections cannot be converted. When an unsupported connection is selected in the *Data Connections* dialog, the *Convert* button is disabled.

When converting a connection, InfoPath asks for a URL location in which to create the data connection file. To specify a valid URL to create the

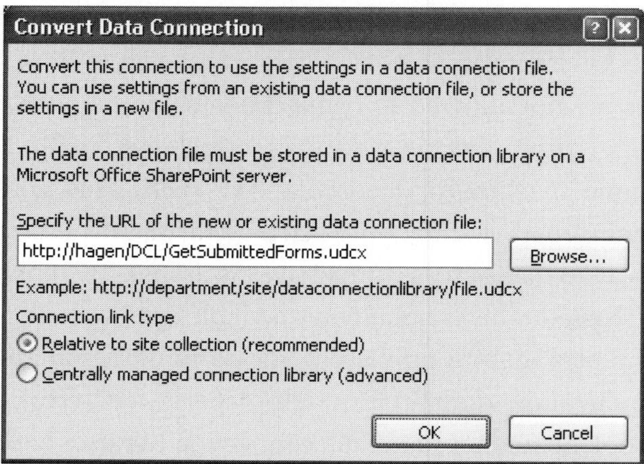

FIGURE 14.22: Converting an InfoPath data connection to use a server-defined data connection file

file, a DCL must already exist on the SharePoint server. If you have a design role on a site collection, you can create a DCL yourself by navigating to the SharePoint site in the browser. Under the *Site Actions* menu, select *Create* and click *Data connection Library*. Using a library that isn't purposed for data connections is disallowed, and if you attempt to use such a library, InfoPath shows an error. The *Relative to site collection* option is the default and recommended selection for the *Connection link type* setting. Let's explore the link type option and what it means.

> **TIP No Need to Add the File Extension to Data Connection Files**
>
> You do not need to add ".udcx" when entering a URL for a data connection file. The *Convert Data Connection* dialog will do it for you automatically when you click *OK*.

The connection link type tells InfoPath, as well as Forms Services for browser-enabled form templates, how to retrieve the data connection file. The connection file can exist in two types of locations: a DCL or the centrally managed connection library. The relative link is recommended because it requires the least administrative intervention. (We'll look at the benefits and hurdles of the *Centrally managed connection library* option in Chapter 17.) Using a relative link means that the DCL is not strongly associated with its site collection. So it doesn't matter to what site collection your form template is deployed, as long as a DCL and connection file exist with the same names within that site collection. You can compare a relative DCL link to a Web site link, for example. A relative link such as /default.htm may work on multiple Web sites (e.g., www.moiconsulting.com/default.htm). The relative Web site link (/default.htm) represents the DCL, and each Web site (www.moiconsulting.com) can be compared to a SharePoint site collection. This model allows flexibility in template deployment across site collections without the need to constantly update the form template's data connection file location.

Using a relative link for data connection files is useful when the connection specifics (e.g., for permissions) change across site collections. Say, for example, that a Web service is used as a data connection in your form template, but the authentication differs depending on which site collection it's used from. But if a form template is used across multiple site collections and essentially duplicates its DCL because the connections are the same, you'll want to consider using the connection store instead. A connection store is accessible across site collections and prevents the duplication of DCLs. We'll hold the topic of the connection store for Chapter 17.

> **WARNING** **Remote XML Document Connections Always Fail**
>
> XML document data connections created with *Access the data from the specified location* will always fail in Forms Services because of security reasons. There is no setting to change this behavior. Only use XML document connections that have the *Include the data as a resource in the form template* option selected or use an alternate connection, such as a Web service.

Security and Data Connection Libraries

When we started discussing data connections in this chapter, the focus was on security. The server's trust model for InfoPath data connections is, for the good reasons we provided, different than the one for InfoPath. For the most part, a server's security is only as good as its administrator's adherence to common sense and recommendations. For example, it should be considered a high privilege to upload items to a DCL. If you do allow a wide range of users to upload, at least require content approval by an administrator (which is a default SharePoint setting).

While we mentioned that using a DCL-based data connection allows a form to initiate cross-domain communication, this is not completely true. By default, a form cannot connect to a server in a different domain, even with a UDC-defined connection (e.g., accessing http://DataServer from http://FormsServer is not allowed). Cross-domain connections via the DCL are explicitly disallowed via a Forms Services administrative setting. While this setting can be configured easily, you may want to consider the repercussions of making such a change. Instead of using the DCL, you can have a form template request full trust permissions. A fully trusted form template has unrestricted access to cross-domain connections—DCL-based or not. Since both require administrative actions, we'll look at fully trusted templates as well as the cross-domain configuration setting in Chapter 17.

Just as important as the topics of elevated privileges for cross-domain communication is the ability to throttle data connection activity. If an attack were made against our server, it would likely involve data connections. Chapter 17 covers various available security measures a SharePoint farm administrator can take ahead of time. For example, we'll see how to preemptively mitigate damage by malicious data connections.

Filling Out Browser Forms

Assuming that a form template is published properly, a form is really easy to fill out using InfoPath: Just double-click the form template! Of course, there are other ways, too, such as clicking the *New* button in a SharePoint form library or even using the *Getting Started* dialog when you first open InfoPath. Filling out a form in the browser is also pretty simple to do but is slightly more involved due to additional moving parts. For example, how does filling out a form differ if you have InfoPath installed or not? What about InfoPath 2003 instead of InfoPath 2007? Let's examine the possibilities and learn how they work.

Configurations Supported by Forms Services

Thanks to a multitude of detection mechanisms, filling out a form is always possible with Forms Services. By determining your local system configuration when opening a form template, Forms Services offers the best form-filling experience. This is critical for cases where there may be incomplete roll-outs of InfoPath or different versions floating around. For example, what if some users are still on InfoPath 2003, most use 2003 SP1, a select few use SP2, and others have already made the jump to 2007? The situation might appear to be catastrophic at first. Let's take a closer look at how Forms Services caters to this diversity of InfoPath clients, among other scenarios.

Publishing to Forms Services is limited to browser-enabled form templates. Hence, the form templates must have been used with InfoPath 2007 to become browser-enabled in the first place. It's still possible to publish to SharePoint from InfoPath 2003 (and 2007 without browser compatibility), but the form will never render in the Web browser. In the case where the Web browser cannot render the form, it's up to the client computer to launch InfoPath. The form will not open if InfoPath is not installed.

Two InfoPath file types can be opened from the server: XML form and XSN form template. Forms Services registers both types when it's provisioned. If either type of file is opened on a server, Forms Services first determines whether or not it should handle that form or form template. (XML forms contain metadata that points to the associated XSN form template.) Forms Services resolves this decision by looking in its internal list of browser-enabled (i.e., activated) form templates. If a form template isn't available in its browser rendition, a lightweight ActiveX control launches InfoPath to open the form. If instead an XML file was opened from the server, the contents of the file itself are streamed to the client computer. This is similar to what happens when opening a Word (.doc or .docx) document from a SharePoint server.

There are cases when the InfoPath program cannot be used to fill out the form. Say, for example, that someone tries to fill out a status report form template on his or her computer from a SharePoint site with Forms Services. Since InfoPath is installed on the system, the form template first attempts to use InfoPath instead of the browser. But take the situation where the version of InfoPath on the computer is 2003 SP1, and the form template was designed with InfoPath 2007. Since InfoPath 2003 cannot open 2007-based form templates, the template fails to load. In cases like this, Forms Services is smart enough to detect that it needs to render the form template. Assuming that the form template is browser-enabled and published to Forms Services, the server takes over the responsibility of displaying the form template when the InfoPath client is not capable.

> **NOTE Opening Version 2007 Form Templates with InfoPath 2003**
>
> An InfoPath 2007 form template can be designed with the *Show report on compatibility with InfoPath 2003* option enabled (under the *Form Options, Compatibility* category). If such a form template is published as browser-enabled, it can be opened by a computer with InfoPath 2003.

Despite Forms Services being just another component of a SharePoint server, it adds tremendous value when managing InfoPath form templates across various system configurations. The best part about Forms Services is that it is very similar to filling out rich forms using the InfoPath program. As a result, there's no additional cost to an organization in terms of training or downtime to learn a new technology. This is especially true if your users are already familiar with SharePoint.

URL-Based Options

When you open a browser-enabled form template, you might be using a link such as http://myserver/mysite/forms/template.xsn for a form template or http://myserver/mysite/myform.xml for a form. But you'll notice that the URL can change to an "ugly" URL that starts with http://myserver/_layouts/FormServer.aspx and may contain several parameters. (Parameters are `name=value` pairs that start after a question mark and are separated by an ampersand, e.g., `...FormServer.aspx?param1=a¶m2=b`.) In this section, we'll look at some of these browser-specific URL parameters. Many of these parameters help to seamlessly integrate form filling into your users' typical Web-browsing experience.

`OpenIn` *Parameter*

The `OpenIn` optional parameter tells Forms Services how you prefer to open the form template. The default and preferred setting is to use the InfoPath client and otherwise fall back to the browser. This is represented by the `PreferClient` value. But you can also specify to use only the InfoPath client (`Client`) or only the browser (`Browser`). If you specify to use only InfoPath, but the program isn't available or can't open the form for whatever reason, the form will not attempt to open in the browser but will instead fail.

> **TIP URL Parameter Case Insensitivity**
>
> Despite our use of PascalCased `OpenIn` parameter values, neither they nor the `OpenIn` parameter itself are case sensitive.

In addition to `Client`, `Browser`, and `PreferClient`, you can force a mobile rendering of the form template. This is facilitated by using `OpenIn=mobile`, which redirects automatically to the MobileFormServer.aspx page. Since mobile devices should be automatically detected, you should never need to use this value. But you might find that some mobile devices may not be properly recognized. In such cases, the existence of the `OpenIn` parameter with the `mobile` value would enforce the page to be rendered appropriately for those mobile systems. Table 14.5 shows a list of `OpenIn` parameter values and their descriptions.

TABLE 14.5: `OpenIn` **Parameter Values with Brief Descriptions**

`OpenIn` Parameter Value	Description
`PreferClient`	Default to the InfoPath client; otherwise, use the browser.
`Client`	Use only the InfoPath client.
`Browser`	Use only the browser.
`Mobile`	Use mobile rendering.

> **WARNING** Rendering on a Mobile Device
>
> Unless the browser-enabled form template is enabled for mobile devices and deployed by an administrator, mobile rendering is not possible and displays an error.

`Source` Parameter

As the last action when filling out a form, you typically either save or submit the data and then close the form. Closing the form means that you either clicked on the *Close* toolbar button or submitted the form. (You can configure a form template to close the form after a successful submit operation through the *Submit Options* dialog in design mode. See Chapter 8 for details.) You may have noticed that when you close a browser form, Forms Services sends you back to where you initiated your form-filling session. Such is the case when filling out a form from a form library. However, this location may be another Web page or any document library, for example. If you started filling out the form by typing the URL directly in the browser address box or clicking on the *Open this form template in the browser* link from the Publishing Wizard, the form closes with the message, "The Form has Closed." With only the message, the obvious next step is to close the browser itself.

> **NOTE** Refreshing and Going Back to a Form Session
>
> Clicking the *Refresh* browser button when the form has been closed launches a new form-filling session for that form. Clicking the *Back* button may appear to go back to the form you were filling out (and attempt to reuse that session), but when the form is updated (either automatically or manually) a *Critical Error* dialog appears.

It's not always necessary to add the `Source` parameter when providing a URL to a form. This is typically the case when a link is clicked on a Web page. Such a link might look similar to http://myserver/mysite/form.xml?openin=browser. Forms Services leverages the `referer` HTTP header to alternatively infer the referring, or source, Web page. This header is used whenever it's available and `Source` is not provided. Explicitly using the `Source` parameter in the URL always overrides the `referer` HTTP header. You can find a link to more information about the `referer` HTTP header in the Appendix.

`XmlLocation` Parameter

The `XmlLocation` parameter is another optional parameter that tells the server to open an existing form. Its value is a path, relative to the current site collection (e.g., /mysite/myform.xml) or an absolute URL (e.g., http://myserver/mysite/form.xml), that points to a server-side .xml file. If the file isn't a real InfoPath form or the form template has since been removed, Forms Services complains that the form or template isn't valid. While `XmlLocation` can be used on its own, it also works together with the `OpenIn` or `SaveLocation` parameters.

`XsnLocation` Parameter

This parameter tells Forms Services to create a new form from an existing form template. The path to the form template is typically a relative URL from the current site collection, but it can also be an absolute location within the same site collection. The form template, obviously, must be Web-enabled to that site collection and properly published to the server.

> **WARNING Cannot Use Both `XmlLocation` and `XsnLocation` Parameters**
>
> The `XmlLocation` and `XsnLocation` parameters are mutually exclusive and cannot be used in the same URL together.

`SaveLocation` Parameter

`SaveLocation` sounds like one of the simpler parameters. Well, there's actually more to it! This parameter sets the default save folder path when the user saves the form, hence its name. (It does not actually set a default file name—that's up to the user.) However, there's another bonus when using this parameter: the *Save, Save As*, and *Close* buttons may show up on the toolbar. If they still don't appear, you need to enable them during design mode on the *Browser* category shown back in Figure 14.11. Without the `SaveLocation` parameter, the user would not actually have the option to save or close the form, even if the buttons are enabled. Creating a new or opening an existing form from a document library always sets the `SaveLocation` parameter to its library location, as shown earlier in Figure 14.12. If the `SaveLocation` parameter isn't provided, save is not available from the toolbar. In such a case, it's recommended that the form enables submit.

> **TIP A Better Form Submit Experience**
>
> When a Web-enabled form allows submit, it's suggested that you set the *After submit* option on the *Submit Options* dialog to *Close the form.* By default, the setting is *Leave the form open,* which isn't very intuitive for end users.

> **NOTE Saving Is Restricted to the Server**
>
> Save is allowed only within the form's same site collection on the server. Saving directly to the local computer, for example, is disallowed.

`Options` *Parameter*

Despite the existence of the `Options` parameter, it's seldom used. As of the first version of Forms Services, the only purpose of this parameter is to disable save by using the value `DisableSave`. Since save is disabled, the *Save, Save As,* and *Close* buttons are not shown. Even if `SaveLocation` is used, `Options=DisableSave` has precedence. The `Options` parameter primarily exists as a way to provide forward compatibility with future versions of Forms Services.

Mobile Support: Smart Phone and PDA

Going beyond the desktop Web browser, Forms Services caters to the ultra-portable class of smart phones and personal digital assistants (PDAs) via the mobile browser. Since SharePoint Server 2007 is already compatible with these mobile devices, it makes sense for InfoPath to do the same. To allow forms to be filled out in a mobile environment, Forms Services makes use of the ASP.NET mobile controls. As a result, the browser form automatically

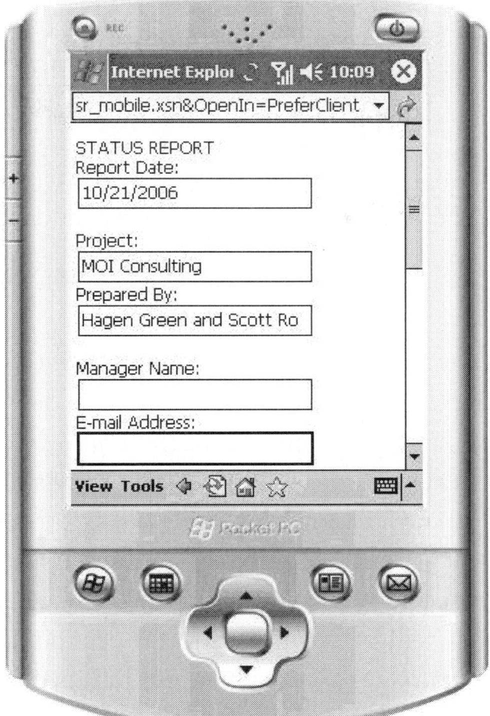

FIGURE 14.23: Filling out the status report form on a Pocket PC device

detects what format the mobile device requires (HTML, XHTML, or CHTML) to deliver an optimum experience. Moreover, there is no new URL to send your mobile users for filling out the form. The same URL used in the browser can be used on a mobile phone. Figure 14.23 shows the same status report form we filled out earlier, but this time it's on a Pocket PC device. You aren't limited to Pocket PC devices; any mobile browser will work just fine.

> **TIP SharePoint Server Has a Mobile Site**
>
> SharePoint (not Forms Services) hosts its mobile site at http://<server>/m, where <server> is the name of your server. After the server name, the URL is a single character to minimize untimely data input. SharePoint does not automatically redirect mobile clients from the fully featured site home page to the corresponding mobile site.

TIP Create a New Form in a Mobile Browser

SharePoint's mobile rendition of a document library does not allow for creating new items (such as a form). However, it's still possible to edit existing items. To create a new form and circumvent the mobile document library limitation, navigate your mobile device to the same address as the document library folder URL and append /forms/template.xsn.

By default, form templates published to Forms Services are not mobile-ready. To allow your template to be used by mobile devices, go to the *Form Options* dialog and enable the checkbox for *Enable rendering on a mobile device.* This option is at the bottom of the *Form Options* dialog (refer back to Figure 14.11). You can now publish a mobile-ready form template to Forms Services, but it is not actually enabled for mobile. For a mobile form template to work as expected, it must be administrator approved. Deploying a form template that will be administrator approved is the last option in the Publishing Wizard page (as shown earlier in Figure 14.7). We'll discuss administrator approval and deployment in Chapter 17.

WARNING Design Checker Is Not Mobile Aware

The Design Checker does not account for mobile form template limitations. In fact, besides this checkbox, InfoPath is not "aware" that the template is targeted for mobile. For example, unsupported controls and features are not flagged and are simply ignored when rendered on a mobile device.

Mobile Compatibility

In the same way that browser-enabled form templates use a strict subset of features compared to the InfoPath client, mobile-enabled templates use a strict subset of browser-enabled features. Unfortunately, design mode does not help guide you to design a mobile form template. One approach is to understand what isn't supported and then do your best to accommodate those limitations. In the next few subsections, we'll give you some guidance on what to expect with your forms in a mobile environment.

Controls

Some controls are not supported. They include Rich Text Box, Option Button, Section, Optional Section, Repeating Table, and File Attachment. In case you're wondering what's left, we'll tell you what controls *are* supported for mobile: Text Box, Drop-Down List Box, List Box, Date Picker (without the calendar button), Check Box, Button, Repeating Section, and Expression Box. Since (Optional) Section controls are not supported, neither they nor any of their contents will appear. It's also important to know that Repeating Section controls, which are supported, do not allow nesting. If another Repeating Section exists inside of a Repeating Section, it's not shown.

The Repeating Section control has a special behavior on a mobile device, so let's see how it works. All rows (which are really Section controls, but for relevance in the mobile scenario we'll call them rows) are shown in a Repeating Section, but each one has a button labeled with its ordinal row position (Figure 14.24). A part of each row's data is shown in the right half of that row. Finally, there is an extra row with only an *Insert* button.

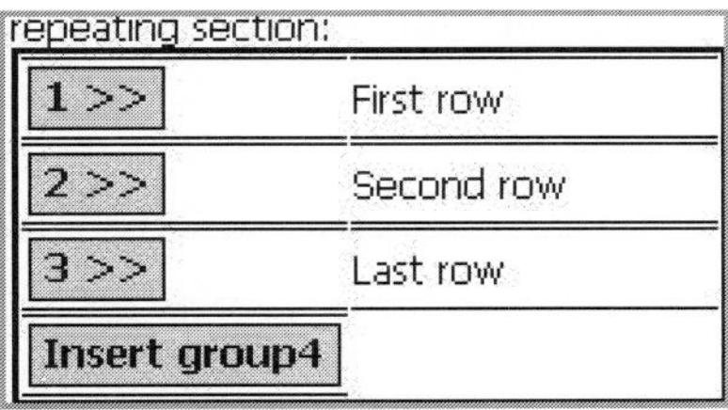

FIGURE 14.24: Repeating Section control with three items in a mobile form

When you click a row's button, a new mini-form appears (Figure 14.25). The mini-form allows you to edit any control's data within that particular row and even remove the row. At the top of this mini-form is a toolbar with

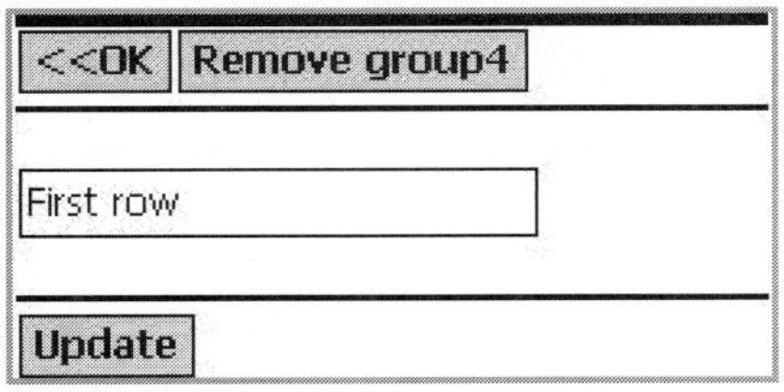

FIGURE 14.25: Editing the first row from the mobile form shown in Figure 14.24

OK and *Remove* buttons; the bottom has another toolbar with only an *Update* button. We'll learn more about the central role of the *Update* button in mobile forms in a moment.

Code

Any custom code you might have written behind the form template should work fine for mobile forms. Since the code is run on the server, there is nothing special a mobile device needs to do. We'll learn more about writing code for InfoPath in Chapter 15.

Toolbar

Earlier, we showed the toolbar that is automatically included with browser forms (refer back to Figure 14.10). Mobile forms have their own toolbar that is independent from the browser version. The mobile toolbar always appears at the bottom of mobile forms, as seen in Figure 14.26, and unlike the browser toolbar, is not configurable. A particular toolbar button is visible only if it makes sense for the current form. For example, *Submit* is available when the form has a main submit connection. The *Update* and *Close* buttons always exist.

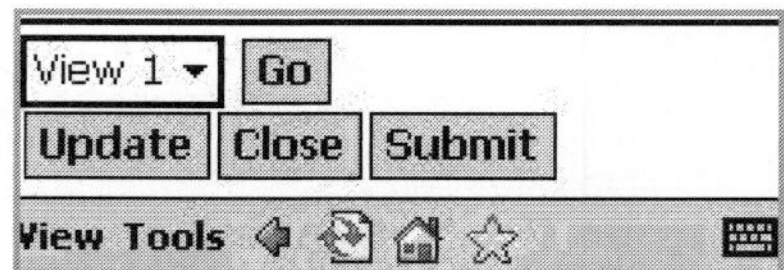

FIGURE 14.26: Mobile form toolbar with the Pocket PC Internet Explorer toolbar showing below it

Views

Mobile forms support multiple views. The view drop-down and *Go* button appear when more than one view exists in the form template. If a view is set to be read-only, that setting is respected, and none of the controls are editable. Background colors, pictures, and view layout settings are not shown.

Data Validation

Data validation is essential to InfoPath forms. As a result, mobile forms cannot, of course, go without it. To incorporate validation into the mobile experience, visible errors are called out by red text in curly braces immediately above the control in question. For example, a Text Box may be decorated with the *{ Cannot be blank. }* error.

Conditional Formatting

Some conditional formatting works in mobile forms, specifically, the ability to hide or make a control read-only. Other formatting options such as bold and strikethrough do not affect mobile controls.

Data Connections

Data connections, since they're processed solely on the server, work fine in mobile forms. They can be used in the same ways they're used in any InfoPath form, such as populating a drop-down list of states.

One class of connections is central to the mobile scenario: submit connections. Since save is not supported on a mobile form, there's only one way to get the form data from your users. By default, InfoPath sets the *After submit* action to be *Leave the form open*. Since there's no successful submit confirmation, this setting could be misleading for users. (If there's an error during submit, a warning page appears.) We suggest changing the post-submit option to *Close the form*. You can find this setting in the *Advanced* section of the *Submitting Forms* dialog; it's also discussed at length in Chapter 8.

> **TIP Mobile Users Cannot Save**
>
> The only way to get data from mobile users is by enabling submit on your form template.

Filling Out a Mobile Form

Unlike browser forms, mobile forms do not have logic to automatically update themselves. Any features that could potentially change the form state (e.g., rules, data validation, and conditional formatting) require that the form be manually updated. Without manually updating the form, you will not see these changes. An end user can manually update his or her form by clicking the *Update* button in the toolbar. If a form is never updated but just submitted, any issues that would otherwise arise when updating would appear on the attempt to submit (which then subsequently fails). If your form has logic that may require frequent updating, it benefits your users to include a tip somewhere in your form as a reminder to click the *Update* button.

What's Next?

By now you've learned the basics of browser-enabled form templates and how to publish them to a SharePoint server running Forms Services. A way to better understand how InfoPath form templates behave in Forms Services is to just publish them to the server and try them. The MOI feedback sample that we converted to be browser-enabled is meant to serve as a beginning to intermediate form template. We recommend that you try publishing your own browser-enabled form templates and going through the steps yourself.

With this introduction to Forms Services, we conclude the first part of this book. In the next part, we focus on more advanced InfoPath topics, such as writing code behind a form template. In Chapter 17, we revisit Forms Services but with a greater in-depth look at some of its advanced features, including administration and maximizing the performance of forms in the browser.

PART II
Advanced Form Design

15 Writing Code in InfoPath

Getting Started

Welcome to the first chapter in Part II! The advanced chapters are the next steps for form designers who are comfortable with creating complex InfoPath forms without code. As we venture into the facets of programming the InfoPath platform, you'll learn how to create even more dynamic and sophisticated form templates than the design-mode user interface allows. But to really take advantage of the added value these advanced topics offer, we highly recommend that you know the material presented in the first part of this book.

In this chapter, we'll start by showing you how to add code to a new or existing InfoPath form template. InfoPath supports two classes of code: script and managed code. In this chapter, we'll use **Visual Studio 2005 Tools for Applications** (VSTA) and **Microsoft Script Editor** (MSE), which are the default programming environments for writing form code. Given the prevalence and ease of use of the .NET Framework, we'll emphasize managed code (specifically, C#) over scripting. We'll also cover several options that configure the code-authoring environment.

Then we'll introduce the **InfoPath object model** (OM) and tell you how using it can enhance your form templates. Once you understand the high-level objectives of using the OM and its event-based model, we will then look at how to start using it in a form template. Our discussion will show the various ways to create event handlers through the InfoPath design mode. We'll also look at the `EventManager` object and how it hooks up the different types of InfoPath events.

Three groups of events belong to the InfoPath platform: form, control, and XML events. **Form events** include general form actions that aren't specific to any controls or data. Signing, saving, and submitting are all examples of form events. **Control events** allow your code to run when, for example, a user clicks a Button control when filling out the form. The last type of event is based on the XML data behind the form: **XML data events** (or just **XML events** or **data events**). There are three distinct states of XML data when form data is changed; each state has its own event to add custom code. We'll learn about these states and explain when you would want to use them.

After going over XML events, we'll give some helpful advice on working with the **`XPathNavigator`** class. An `XPathNavigator`, part of the .NET Framework, uses a cursor-based approach to access and modify the data source. If you are accustomed to working with the `XmlDocument` and `XmlNode` classes from .NET or Microsoft XML Core Services (MSXML), or if you're just getting started with programming XML, this section is for you.

We'll also look at **writing script** (specifically **JScript**), instead of managed code, with InfoPath. There are certain scenarios when using script is advantageous, for example, when programming a custom task pane. We take a look at the pros and cons of using script later in the chapter.

Next on the docket is a sampling of OM methods and properties commonly found in complex, real-world form templates. To show the OM in action, we'll dedicate the last third of this chapter to designing and filling out a new MOI Consulting sample form. In parallel, we'll learn some tips and tricks for working with InfoPath form code.

Finally, if you're migrating from InfoPath 2003 and are accustomed to working with its OM, there is a short learning curve to jump onto the InfoPath 2007 bandwagon. To help in this transition, we've sprinkled notes throughout this chapter when an InfoPath 2003 OM method or property has been renamed or removed or exhibits a different behavior in InfoPath 2007.

Writing Code Behind a Form

Adding code to a new or existing InfoPath form might be a big decision in the design process. But the steps to start writing code behind a form template are pretty easy. The only up-front decision concerns what programming

TABLE 15.1: Programming Languages and Available InfoPath Object Model Versions

Language	InfoPath OM Version
JScript	2003 SP1
VBScript	2003 SP1
C#	2007 managed
C# (InfoPath 2003)	2003 SP1 managed
Visual Basic	2007 managed
Visual Basic (InfoPath 2003)	2003 SP1 managed

language you prefer. Table 15.1 shows the available programming languages. Scripting languages, including JScript and VBScript, use the 2003 OM, while managed code can use the updated InfoPath 2007 OM. Since this book is focused on InfoPath 2007, we'll concentrate on the new 2007 managed OM.

Forms Services

Browser-enabled form templates support only the 2007 managed OM in C# or Visual Basic.

Terminology

Talking about code "behind" a form template isn't always very clear. That's because there are many different ways to say the same thing; that is, each way is interchangeable with another. The following terms, unless otherwise noted in the book, refer to the code included in a form template that runs when the form is filled out:

- Form code
- Form template code
- Business logic

Settings Related to Adding Code

Before adding code, let's choose the language in which we'll do our programming. The default language is Visual Basic. But if you want to choose another language, go to the *Form Options* item on the *Tools* menu and select the *Programming* category. The *Programming language* section, at the bottom of the dialog shown in Figure 15.1, lists various form template programming options.

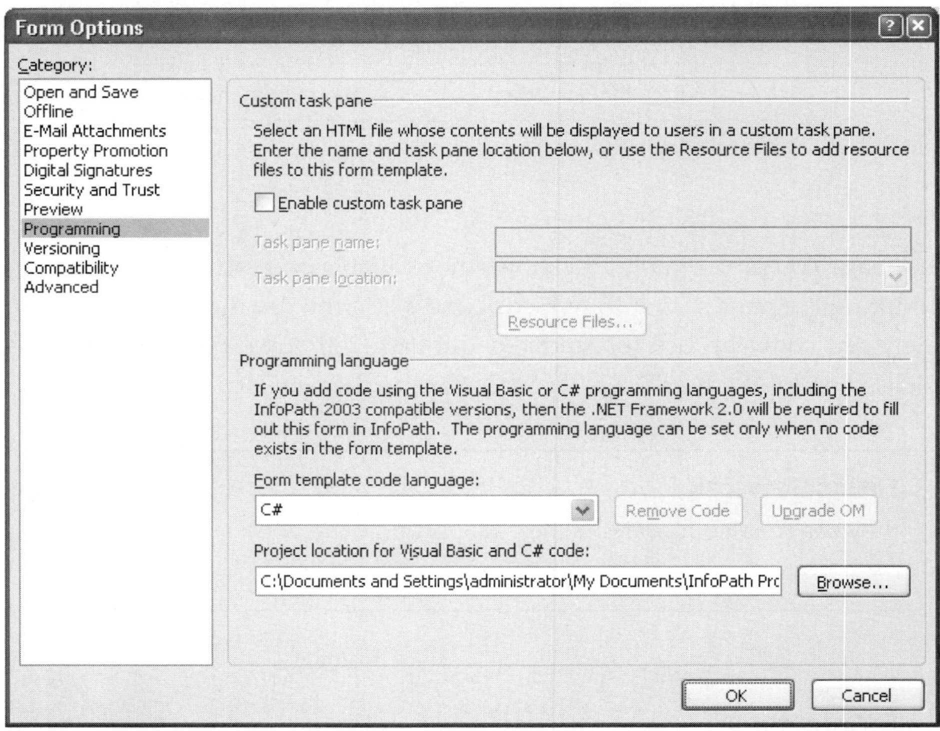

FIGURE 15.1: Programming category in the Form Options dialog

Options available in the *Programming language* section includes the *Form template code language* drop-down, *Remove Code* and *Upgrade OM* buttons, and a path for C# and Visual Basic .NET projects. When code already exists in the form, the *Form template code language* drop-down is unavailable, but the *Remove Code* button is enabled. Clicking *Remove Code* opens the dialog in Figure 15.2 so you can confirm removal.

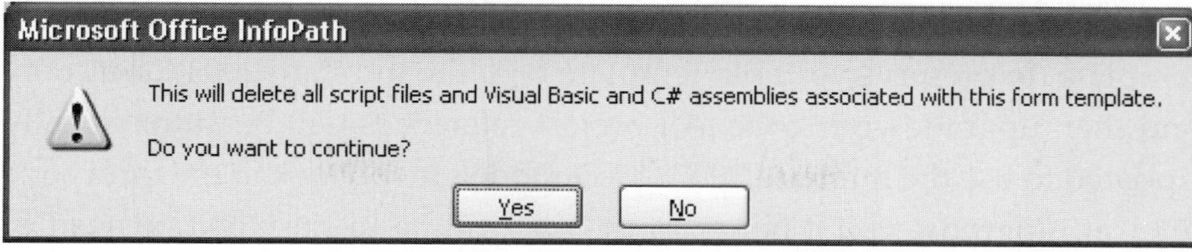

FIGURE 15.2: Confirmation dialog shown before removing code

> **WARNING Removing Code Is a One-Way Operation**
>
> You cannot undo the action of removing form code.

> **TIP Removing Managed Code**
>
> If the form template has managed code, only the assembly (.dll) and debugger (.pdb) files are removed. The Visual Studio project itself with the source code (which is not included in the form template .xsn file) is not deleted.

The *Upgrade OM* button is available when a form template with managed code was created with a version of InfoPath older than 2007. Upgrading your managed form code from an older version of InfoPath is highly recommended so you can take advantage of the much improved OM (which is also the programming focus of this book!). Since the InfoPath 2007 scripting OM is the same as older versions of InfoPath, a pre-2007 form template with script doesn't need upgrading. Clicking the *Upgrade OM* button for a template with managed code opens the dialog shown in Figure 15.3.

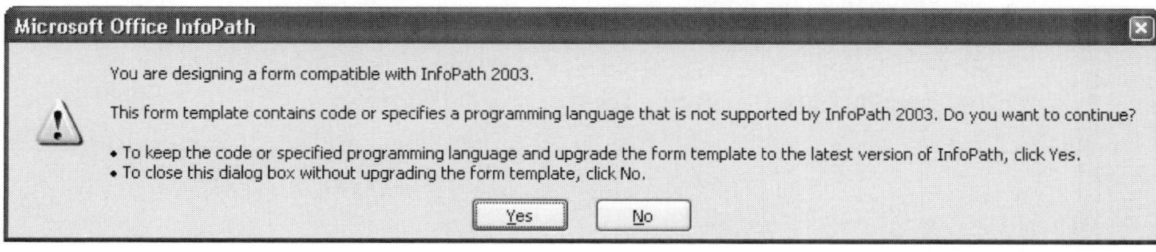

FIGURE 15.3: Upgrading code from a form template compatible with InfoPath 2003

When upgrading the OM, InfoPath will ask you to save your form template (to preserve your old template with the InfoPath 2003 form code) and then upgrade your code. All project references will be automatically updated to use the InfoPath 2007 object model. If you look at the form code after an upgrade, you'll notice most of it will be in gray text, instead of black. This is because the upgrade process essentially comments out your code by using `#if/#endif` compiler directive statements. First, the entire file's contents (within the `namespace` block) is essentially duplicated but enclosed in one large `#if/#endif` at the end of the file. (InfoPath uses the `InfoPathManagedObjectModel` symbol for the `#if` conditional directive.) Next, you'll notice that a new method called `InternalStartup` replaces the old `_Startup` and `_Shutdown` methods (there is no equivalent `_Shutdown` method in the 2007 OM). The `InternalStartup` method is automatically populated with hookups for all of the event handlers you had in your old form template. You'll also see that all of the event handlers still exist but are defined with the updated event definitions (e.g., `field3_OnAfterChange` becomes `field3_Changed`—we'll learn more about this later in the chapter) and parameters types. The code you had in each of the original event handlers is copied into the new event handler but is enclosed in `#if/#endif` compiler directives. Listing 15.1 shows the InfoPath 2003 code; Listing 15.2 shows the same code after being upgraded to the version 2007 OM.

LISTING 15.1: InfoPath 2003 C# Form Code Before Upgrading the OM Version

```
// The following function handler is created by Microsoft Office
// InfoPath. Do not modify the type or number of arguments.
[InfoPathEventHandler(MatchPath="/my:myFields/my:field1",
EventType=InfoPathEventType.OnValidate)]
public void field1_OnValidate(DataDOMEvent e)
{
   // Write your code here.
   IXMLDOMNode field1 =
thisXDocument.DOM.selectSingleNode("/my:myFields/my:field1");
   thisXDocument.UI.Alert("My foo is " + field1.text);
}
```

LISTING 15.2: Form Code from Listing 15.1 After Upgrading to the InfoPath 2007 OM Version

```
public void field1_Validating(object sender, XmlValidatingEventArgs e)
{
#if InfoPathManagedObjectModel
   // Write your code here.
   IXMLDOMNode field1 =
thisXDocument.DOM.selectSingleNode("/my:myFields/my:field1");
   thisXDocument.UI.Alert("My foo is " + field1.text);
#endif
}
```

NOTE Legacy: Hooking Up Events in Form Code

InfoPath 2003 relied on a C# attribute (specifically, the `InfoPath EventHandler` attribute) to decorate a method as an event handler. This syntax was changed in InfoPath 2007 to conform to a more recognizable .NET-standard style.

NOTE Script Code Does Not Create a Project

Adding script code does not create a project. Instead, InfoPath adds a JScript (.js) or VBScript (.vbs) file as a resource to the form template.

The final option shown in Figure 15.1 is the *Project location for Visual Basic and C# code* text box. It defaults to the InfoPath Projects folder under the current user's My Documents folder, but any path can be used. The *Project location* text box cannot be edited if a script language is chosen or if managed code is already being used in the form template.

TIP Saving a Form Template with Managed Code

If a form template already has an associated project with managed code, saving the template as a new name (not publishing) will copy the associated project folder to a folder with the same name as the newly saved form template. As a result, saving a template with a new name essentially checkpoints your entire project.

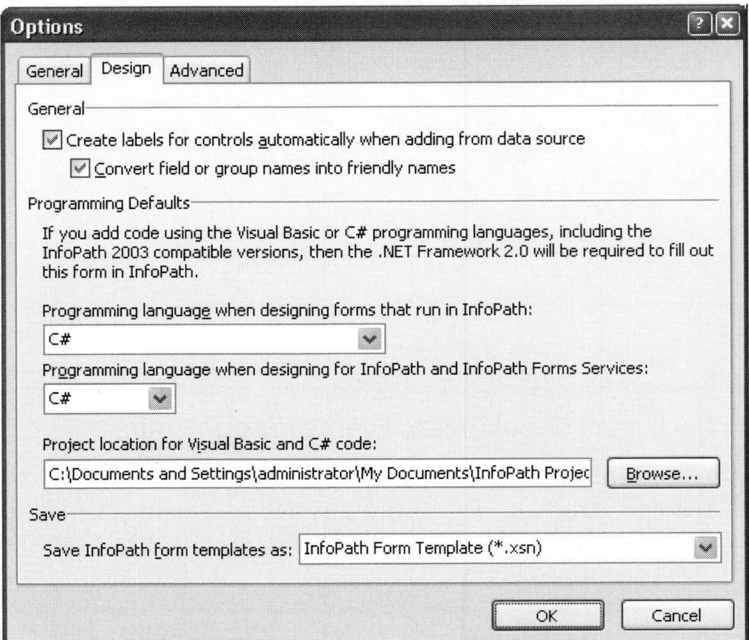

FIGURE 15.4: Programming options, which are saved as defaults for all new form templates

All of the settings shown in Figure 15.1 apply only to the current form template. If, for example, you keep changing from Visual Basic to C# as the language for your form templates, the *Options* dialog shown in Figure 15.4 offers relief. The *Programming Defaults* section contains some settings similar to those shown in Figure 15.1, but unlike those, these settings (in the *Programming Defaults* section) persist as defaults for all new form templates.

Forms Services

The *Programming language when designing for InfoPath and InfoPath Forms Services* drop-down applies when you add code to a browser-enabled form. Since Forms Services supports only the InfoPath 2007 managed code OM, *C#* and *Visual Basic* are the only available options.

Adding Code to a Form Template

To add managed code to your new or existing form, simply choose a form or data event that you want to **sink**. (Sinking an event means an event handler is created in your code that will now be invoked to handle a specific event.) You can find a list of prominent form and data events, such as *Loading Event* and *Changed Event*, on the *Programming* fly-out menu from the *Tools* menu. Alternatively, the *Programming* fly-out menu also has an entry called *Microsoft Visual Studio Tools for Applications* (or *Microsoft Script Editor* if you're using script) that will open the code editor without creating an event handler. Figure 15.5 shows the VSTA environment after we selected *Loading Event* from the *Programming* submenu.

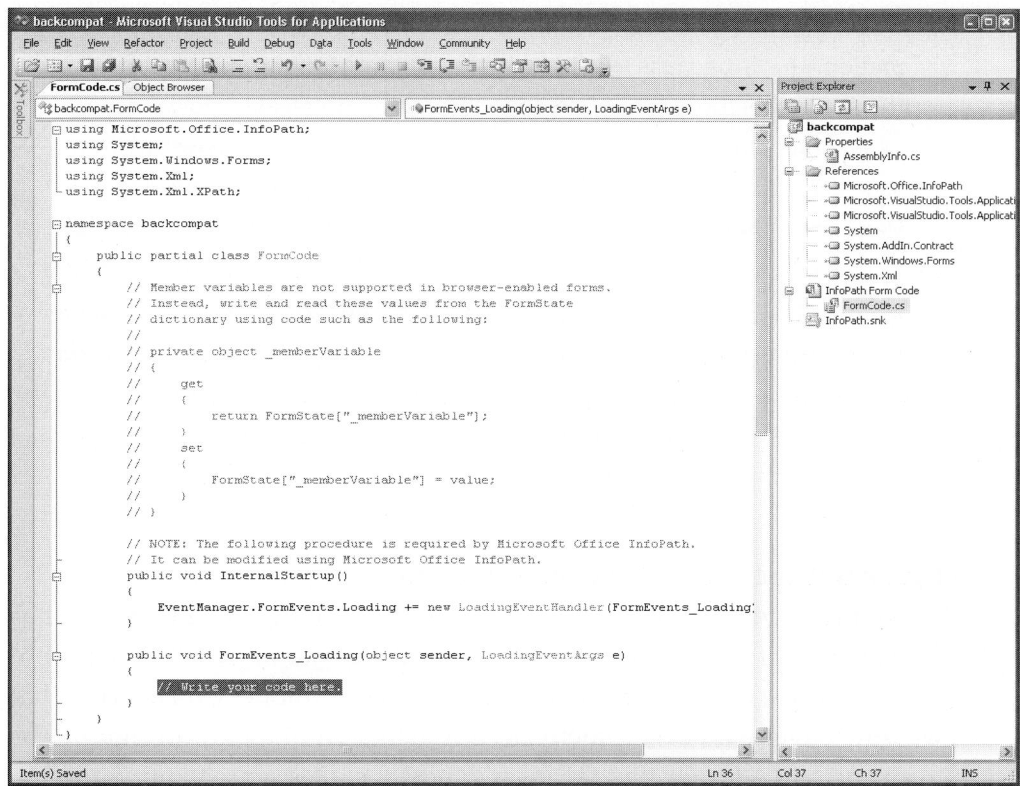

FIGURE 15.5: VSTA development environment

NOTE Save Before Adding Code

If you're adding code to a new form template, the template must first be saved. Attempting to add code to an unsaved template will result in InfoPath prompting you to save before continuing. Remember that saving is not publishing (see Chapter 9), so this is not the published form name your users will see.

No IntelliSense Information in the Object Browser or ToolTips

Selecting an InfoPath object model class, method, or property in the object browser or hovering over an object in code may not show IntelliSense information. This is because the files with information for IntelliSense are not in the same directory as the Microsoft.Office.InfoPath.dll assembly.

To fix this problem, you need to copy two files. Start by navigating to the %programfiles%\Microsoft Office\Office12 directory in Windows Explorer. Next, copy the Microsoft.Office.InfoPath.xml file in the Office12 directory to the following path: %systemdrive%\WINDOWS\assembly\GAC_MSIL\Microsoft.Office.InfoPath\12.0.0.0_71e9bce111e9429c. From the same Office12 directory, find the Microsoft.Office.Interop.InfoPath.SemiTrust.xml file, but this time copy it to %systemdrive%\WINDOWS\assembly\GAC\Microsoft.Office.Interop.InfoPath.SemiTrust\11.0.0.0_71e9bce111e9429c.

Filling Out and Debugging a Form with Code

While there's nothing particularly special about filling out a form that has code, it's helpful to become familiar with the basics of the VSTA environment and how it integrates with InfoPath design mode. Considering that we now have two development environments, InfoPath for designing the form and VSTA for writing the form's code, it makes sense to minimize the number of times we switch from one application to another.

Before we fill out our blank form that simply sinks the `Loading` event, let's add a single line of code that runs when our form is loaded. Since we've already asked InfoPath to create the method that sinks the `Loading` event (called `FormEvents_Loading` in Figure 15.5), all we need to do is put the code in the area with the comment `// Write your code here`. One of the simplest operations we can do is to show a dialog box message. Let's add this single line of form code in the `FormEvents_Loading` method:

```
MessageBox.Show("Hello, InfoPath!");
```

NOTE Legacy: XDocument.UI.Alert

The InfoPath 2003 method `XDocument.UI.Alert` no longer exists in the InfoPath OM. The .NET Framework method `MessageBox.Show` (in the `System.Windows.Forms` namespace) is its replacement.

Now that we have some code that runs when the form loads, let's look at ways we can start filling out the form. (A sample named LoadingMessageBox is included with the samples for this chapter on the book's Web site.) Since we just added code in VSTA, it would be nice to preview the form without having to go back to InfoPath. This is possible if we select the *Start Debugging* item from the *Debug* menu (the shortcut key is F5). VSTA then performs the following actions:

1. Compiles the form code and builds the assembly
2. Opens the form in a preview window
3. Attaches the debugger to the preview process to facilitate debugging

Forms Services

Showing dialogs, such as message boxes, in forms running in the browser is not supported. In fact, the `System.Windows.Forms` namespace is not automatically referenced in the form code.

NOTE What Is an Assembly?

An **assembly** is .NET code compiled and built as Microsoft Instruction Language (MSIL) in an application extension (.dll) file.

WARNING Understanding Failed Compilation

The first two steps could potentially fail for a few reasons. If compiling fails, it's likely that you have made a syntax error in your code. Should the form fail to preview, it's possible that the form template itself has problems (such as a rule or data connection that fails when the form opens) or that some code you wrote (e.g., in the `Loading` event handler) encountered an error when executing.

If you wanted only to compile your code and build the assembly, you can use the *Build* menu or hit the Ctrl+Shift+B keyboard shortcut. (You may recognize this shortcut. It's coincidently the same key combination used by InfoPath for the *Preview Form* command.) Building the form code updates the assembly that InfoPath uses when running the form. So the next time you preview the form, it will use the last successfully built assembly.

Debugging Form Code

As you would expect from a full-fledged development environment, modern conveniences of debugging are at your disposal. Features such as breakpoints, breaking on specific handled and unhandled exceptions, and variable watches are just a few of the assorted debugging options in VSTA.

To see how debugging works with code running behind an InfoPath form, let's set a breakpoint on `MessageBox.Show`. A breakpoint is a debugging mechanism used to pause execution of your code. One way to enable a breakpoint is to put your cursor on the line of code you want to pause at and hit F9. After setting your breakpoint, hit F5 to start debugging the form in a preview window. After the window appears but before the form is rendered, focus jumps to the VSTA window and highlights the line with your breakpoint. The form is running but halted until you allow execution to continue by hitting F5 or by stepping over code.

Forms Services

Debugging a form running in the browser requires debugging on the server itself (or remotely debugging to it) and attaching to the w3wp.exe process. This is conceptually similar to debugging an ASP.NET Web application. Since there is no concept of previewing a browser form, you must debug while filling out a form.

Depending on your computer's speed and the complexity of your form code, previewing while debugging with VSTA might be a little slow sometimes. And we don't blame you if you want to speed things up! However, it's not really possible to preview the form from VSTA without debugging enabled. If you want to run the form without debugging, preview the form from InfoPath instead.

> **TIP Building Is Automatic**
>
> There's no need to build the project in VSTA when previewing from InfoPath. InfoPath always asks VSTA to build the project, even if the VSTA environment isn't open!

Debugging code behind an InfoPath form is the same as debugging other types of programs, such as a Windows application or an ASP.NET Web site. With that said, we won't cover the details of debugging strategy in this book. MSDN has various articles on debugging. One such article referenced in the Appendix discusses debugging in Visual Studio, while another talks about debugging script code.

> **NOTE No Edit and Continue**
>
> Form code cannot be modified in VSTA while you're actively debugging a form.

The InfoPath Object Model

From a high level, a form template is constructed in design mode by building the contents of its views and data sources. Besides static aspects of the form (such as the color theme and number of views), many form and data-specific features are dynamic. These dynamic features reveal themselves as the user fills out the form. Examples of form features include those that allow the user to switch a view or submit the form. Invoking these features requires the user to initiate the action. Form features like changing views or submitting, of course, shouldn't affect the form's data. On the other hand, data-specific form features work directly from or on the XML data.

Some examples of data features include conditional formatting and data validation, both of which are activated depending on various data in the form. We're making the clear distinction between form and data features because this mirrors the InfoPath programming dichotomy.

Forms Services

There are actually two different object models available for writing code behind a form template. This chapter concentrates primarily on the Microsoft.Office.InfoPath.dll assembly for InfoPath forms. When you're designing a browser-enabled form template, an assembly of the same name but in a different location is used. This alternate assembly (in the InfoPathOM folder in OFFICE12) defines the browser-enabled OM to be used with both InfoPath and Forms Services. It restricts form code to a subset of the full OM normally available to the InfoPath program.

We're brushing over the concepts of form and data features because they are two main classifications of features that define the InfoPath event model. Having an event model for a programming platform means that you write your code within event handlers. An **event handler** is simply a method with a specific signature that is registered for a particular purpose with InfoPath. We'll learn about registering methods as event handlers when we look at the `EventManager` object.

Form Events

When we called `MessageBox.Show` in the earlier sample form, we wrote our code in the method sinking the Loading event. InfoPath fires this event every time our form template is loaded. We can also sink other form events. Table 15.2 presents a full list of form events, including where they are created from design mode and when they fire when a user fills out the form.

> **TIP InfoPath Programming Paradigm**
>
> InfoPath offers a pure event-based programming platform where your code runs only when something specific happens in the form.

TABLE 15.2: Form Events Exposed by InfoPath

Form Event	UI Entry Point	When Is It Fired?
`Context Changed`	*Tools | Programming*	When control focus changes the XML context
`Loading`	*Tools | Programming*	Every time the form is opened
`Merge`	*Tools | Form Options | Advanced*	When forms are merged
`Save`	*Tools | Form Options | Open and Save*	When the user saves the form
`Sign`	*Tools | Programming*	When the form is signed (entirely or partially)
`Submit`	*Tools | Submit Options*	When the main submit connection is invoked
`Version Upgrade`	*Tools | Form Options | Programming*	When an XML form is being opened whose version is earlier than that of the form template
`View Switched`	*Tools | Programming*	After switching to a different view

NOTE **Test Form Events for Yourself**

A sample form called FormEvents (included with the other samples for this chapter) sinks all form events.

Forms Services

The `Context Changed`, `Merge`, `Save`, and `Sign` events are not available in browser-enabled form templates.

Instead of providing details here about all the form events listed in Table 15.2, we'll use them in samples throughout this chapter. The events themselves aren't interesting. For example, the `Save` event is called when the form is saved. What is more exciting than the events is what code you can write when handling each event. After talking about XML data events, we'll exhibit a sample form template from our friends at MOI Consulting that shows off much of the InfoPath OM. The sample form will tie together various form events listed in Table 15.2 with properties and methods throughout the object model.

XML Data Events

Some of the most useful events to sink in a form template are those from the XML data source. Given that InfoPath is a strongly data-driven platform, it would make sense that changes in the data can be tracked at a granular level of detail. We will see in a moment that sinking data events is much more involved than one might think.

How Data Changes

Before you learn about the various events fired for XML data, you need to know *how* data can actually get changed. If you don't know how data gets changed, events will be firing all over the place for your data source, and such event notifications won't really make sense. (For a preview of this seemingly crazy behavior, see the XmlDataEvents sample form template.) The classic case of changing data is a user simply typing something into a Text Box control. Don't forget about the binding mechanics behind controls and the data source. When data is changed in a Text Box, it is not the Text Box that is changing but rather the data source field in which the Text Box is bound. Thus, the fact that some data is changing means that some item was modified in the data source.

Let's not limit ourselves to thinking only about element fields bound to a Text Box. (It doesn't matter what controls are bound to a data source node.) Attribute fields exhibit behavior similar to that of elements. And how about groups in the data source? A group can't really change, but it can be removed or inserted. Fields can be removed and inserted, too.

What about some other ways fields and groups can be changed? Here's a list of scenarios that is by no means complete:

- Inserting a row in a Repeating Table
- Removing an Optional Section

- Creating a rule action to set a field's value
- Querying a data connection, such as a Web service
- Signing form data
- Merging forms
- Running form code (which can change the data source, too!)

Event Bubbling

Our last topic prior to learning about the actual XML events is to discuss the phenomenon of **event bubbling**. You may be familiar with bubbling of events if you have scripted Internet Explorer with DHTML. In case you're not, let us provide an analogy. Picture a construction crew with crew members on each floor of a 100-story building. Their boss is on the top floor, and crew members are responsible for reporting their status to him. If a crew member on the 85th floor needs to relay a message to the boss, she'll yell it to a crew member on the 86th floor. In turn, that crew member will pass the message to someone on the 87th floor, and so on, until the boss receives the message. If someone on the 1st floor relays a message, it will need to bubble its way up every floor until it reaches the top.

Let's look at the sample form shown in Figure 15.6. The data source shows three nodes: `myFields`, `group1`, and `field1`. (You could say `myFields` is the boss of the construction crew.) To show the concept of event bubbling, we designed our form by going through each node and setting up a `Changing` event handler. InfoPath automatically creates the event handler when you right-click an item in the data source and select *Changing Event* from the *Programming* fly-out menu.

When VSTA opens, the `// Write your code here` text will be highlighted. Simply overwrite that highlighted comment by typing the code snippet shown in Listing 15.3.

LISTING 15.3: Showing a Message Box in the `Changing` XML Event

```
MessageBox.Show("Changing: Site is " + e.Site.Name + "; Source is
    "+ ((XPathNavigator)sender).Name);
```

Forms Services

The `Changing` event is not available in browser-enabled form templates.

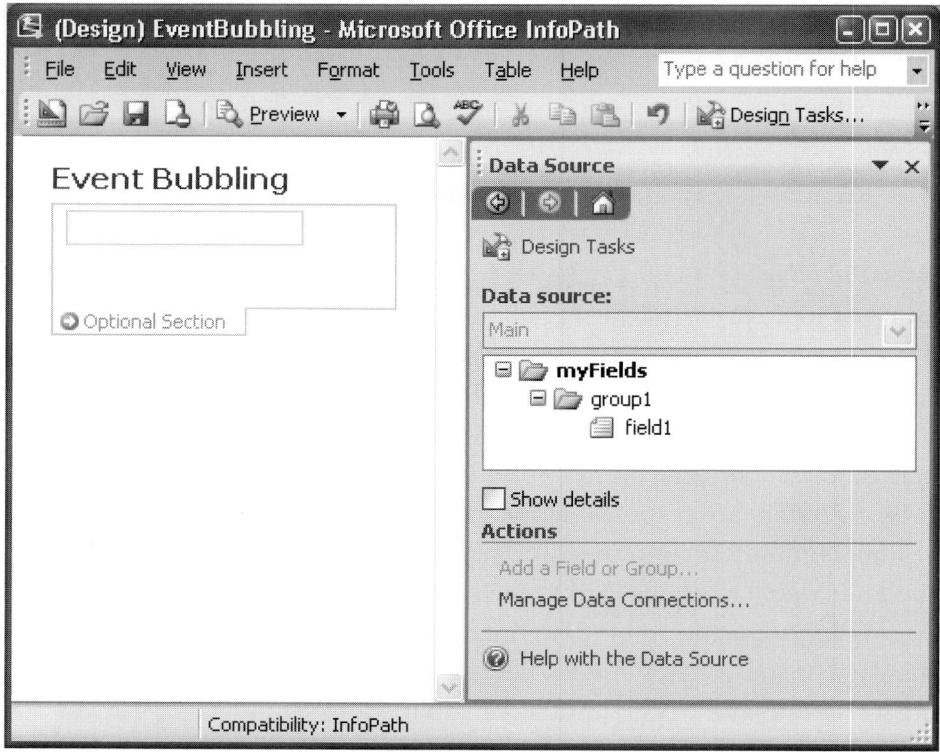

FIGURE 15.6: EventBubbling sample, which shows `Site` and `Sender` node names as events bubble up the data source

This line of code shows a dialog box message with the text "Changing:" and adds the node name of the site. The `Site` property on the `e` parameter (which is of type `XmlChangingEventArgs`; `Site` is defined in the OM on the `XmlEventArgs` parent object) yields the `XPathNavigator` of the node where the event is handled. If `field1` changes, the event handlers for `field1`, `group1`, and `myFields` will all be fired (in that order) with the `Site` being the node that's currently bubbling the event. So the `Site` for `group1` will just be `group1`, and the `Site` values for other nodes will be those same nodes. Alternatively, the `Sender` object tells an event handler who originally caused the event; in our code, we label it as the `Source`. If `field1` is changing, the `Sender` for all event handlers is `field1` no matter which node's event handler (`group1_Changing` or `myFields_Changing`) is handling the event.

What Is an `XPathNavigator`?

An `XPathNavigator` is a cursor-based reader designed for XPath-based queries to an underlying data source, such as XML. InfoPath 2007 exclusively uses `XPathNavigator` objects to programmatically traverse its data sources. The use of `XmlDocument` and `XmlNode` objects from InfoPath 2003 is essentially deprecated. We dedicate a latter part of this chapter to the `XPathNavigator` and show how to use it with the InfoPath data source.

NOTE Legacy: `Source`

The `Sender` object was exposed as `Source` on the `XmlEventArgs` object in the InfoPath 2003 OM.

TIP `Sender` as an Object Parameter

`Sender` is an object because the event handler is made generic to handle a notification from any object, not just an `XPathNavigator`. This new paradigm for `Sender` complies with .NET standards. As a result, we need to explicitly cast the object, which allows us to access `XPathNavigator` members such as the `Name` property.

As you play with the EventBubbling sample (included with this chapter's samples), some of the event notifications may surprise you. In particular, inserting or removing the Optional Section (`group1`) shows only one notification: "Changing: Site is my:myFields; Source is my:group1". This is because XML notifications are fired only for the parent of the changing node. You may ask, then, why the `field1` event handler fires when the Text Box, bound to `field1`, is changed. Isn't `group1` the parent of `field1`? Yes, but there's more to it.

To clear up the paradox, you must understand the way XML data is stored. A field (element or attribute) doesn't directly contain its own data. The data itself is considered its own separate node—specifically, a **text node**—contained within the field. It follows, then, that if the data (the text node) in `field1` is changing, the `field1` node itself will fire its `Changing` event. This upholds our assertion that the parent of the changing node fires the notification.

Data Source Field Details

Data source fields consist of two separate XML nodes: the field node itself and a text node that holds the field's data. The World Wide Web Consortium (W3C) sets the standard on node types. You can learn more about all types of nodes, including text nodes, at the W3C Web site (as referenced in the Appendix).

Sometimes event bubbling is an unwanted side effect. What if, for example, we had most of our form within the Optional Section from our EventBubbling sample? Do we really want the `group1` event firing every time some data changes? Maybe we just want to know when `group1` is inserted. Unfortunately, there's no way to directly turn off the bubbling behavior, but there is a way to circumvent it when sinking XML events on data source groups. If you want to stop event bubbling when sinking a given group notification, use the code in Listing 15.4 at the top of the event handler.

LISTING 15.4: Code to Stop XML Events from Bubbling Above the Current Event Handler

```
XPathNavigator NavSender = (XPathNavigator)sender;
  bool moveSuccess = NavSender.MoveToParent();
  if (moveSuccess && !NavSender.IsSamePosition(e.Site))
     return;
```

As you continue in the chapter and through the MOI Consulting sample form toward the latter half, you'll see other examples when we'll suppress the side effects of event bubbling.

NOTE No Nonprogrammatic Option to Cancel Bubbling

There's no built-in concept of canceling bubbling in InfoPath, such as the `cancelBubble` property serves in Internet Explorer.

Data States

Now that we've talked about the ways data can change and how event bubbling works, we're ready to tackle the three states of modified XML data. Every field or group in the main data source supports the general notions we'll discuss, so there are no special cases to call out. It's also consistent that whenever a data source node is modified, it proceeds through three states: `Changing`, `Validating`, and `Changed`.

However, just because these events fire when data changes doesn't mean that we need to concern ourselves with them. As the form template author, you can decide which events you want to sink depending on what you're trying to accomplish. Let's look at each event in turn and see when, why, and how you can use them in your form template code.

> **NOTE** Legacy: **`OnBeforeChange`**, **`OnValidate`**, and **`OnAfterChange`**
>
> `Changing`, `Validating`, and `Changed` were `OnBeforeChange`, `OnValidate`, and `OnAfterChange`, respectively.

`Changing` Event

The first event in the sequence is probably the least-used XML event, yet it offers a powerful capability: the ability to reject and roll back the changing node. Rejecting a node change in the `Changing` event will show an error dialog to the user filling out the form and make the changed control appear as if it was never modified.

> **Forms Services**
>
> The `Changing` event isn't supported by Forms Services.

> **NOTE** Cannot Hide a Rejected Change
>
> Rejecting a node change in the `Changing` event always shows an error dialog. There is no way to suppress it.

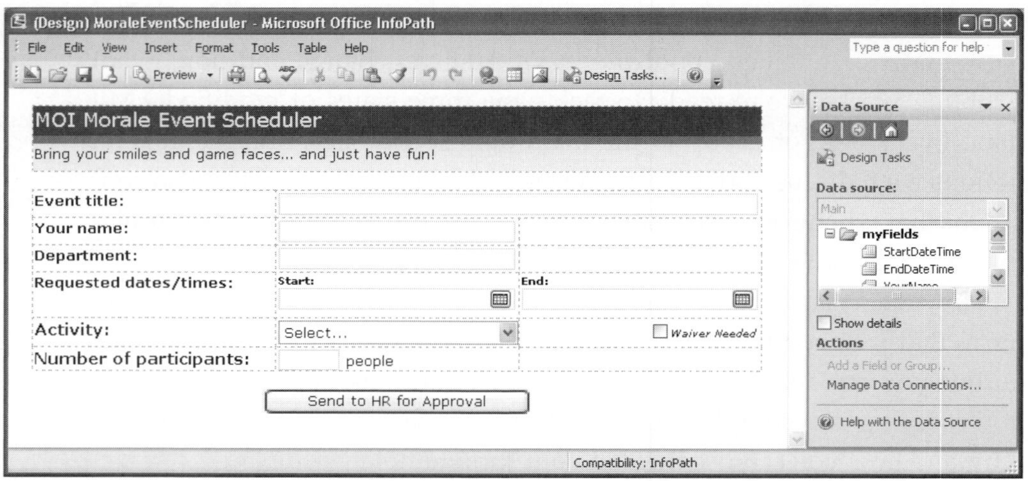

FIGURE 15.7: MOI Consulting morale event scheduler form in design mode

To exhibit the `Changing` event, we'll use the MOI Consulting morale event scheduler form. Figure 15.7 shows the form in design mode. (This sample file's name is MOIMoraleEventScheduler-Changing.)

To fill out the form, the user needs to make decisions about dates, times, and the specific activity for the morale event. Only authorized employees are allowed to fill out this form. We could just restrict access to the form altogether, but we don't want to manage the permissions at a file system level. Similarly, we don't want to just conditionally disable submit (e.g., through a rule) because someone could go through the trouble of filling out the form and then become frustrated that submit is blocked. Instead, we want to prompt for a password when someone tries to modify the form. If the password is wrong, the modification is rejected; otherwise, we grant access for the entire session. Thanks to the `Changing` event, we can use an event handler to prompt for a password and gracefully disallow changes in the form based on conditions that we include in our code.

To add a password prompt when someone tries to modify anything in the form, we can leverage event-bubbling behavior to intercept all form changes on the `myFields` document element. We begin by right-clicking on `myFields` in the data source and choosing *Changing Event* from the *Programming* submenu. Listing 15.5 shows the custom form code we use in the `myFields_Changing` event handler to prompt for a password.

LISTING 15.5: Prompting for a Password

```
public void myFields_Changing(object sender, XmlChangingEventArgs e)
{
   // Once a user is validated we won't prompt again
   if (UserIsAuthorized)
      return;

   string password = new MyPasswordDialog().Prompt();

   // This is poor security!
   if (password == "InfoPath!")
   {
      // Allow access
      e.CancelableArgs.Cancel = false;
      // Remember that this user has access
      UserIsAuthorized = true;
      MessageBox.Show("Thank you. Access has been granted for "
          + "this session.", "Access Granted");
   }
   else
   {
      e.CancelableArgs.Cancel = true;
      e.CancelableArgs.Message = "Authorized Users Only";
      e.CancelableArgs.MessageDetails = "Only authorized users "
          + " can schedule morale events.";
   }
}
```

Let's analyze this form code and figure out what it does in the `Changing` event for the document element. The first check, which we'll discuss shortly in more detail, determines whether the user has already been authorized by entering the correct password. If not, then we continue in the event handler by using the `MyPasswordDialog` class to prompt the user for a password. The code in this class uses .NET Forms library controls that aren't InfoPath-specific, so we won't discuss this code except to show what happens (Figure 15.8) when calling the `Prompt` method. You can find the code in the `MyPasswordDialog` class of the MoiEventScheduler-Changing form template (included with the samples for this chapter).

FIGURE 15.8: Password dialog prompt

WARNING Event Handlers in .NET versus InfoPath

The code in the `MyPasswordDialog` class has its own .NET form event handlers. Do not confuse these event handlers with those in InfoPath; they are different mechanisms (even though they look similar) and are not interchangeable. One such .NET form handler, for example, is registered through this code:

```
okButton.Click += new EventHandler(okButton_Click);
```

We discuss the details of registering for InfoPath events in the "Registering Event Handlers" section later in this chapter.

After the dialog prompt appears, the user can click either the *OK* or *Cancel* buttons to dismiss the dialog. If *Cancel* is clicked, an empty password is assigned to the `password` string variable. If *OK* is clicked, `password` gets whatever the user entered in the password text box. Once the password is received, we compare it against the hard-coded password `"InfoPath!"` If the password matches, access is granted for editing the form. To do so, we set the `CancelableArgs.Cancel` Boolean (on `XmlChangingEventArgs` variable `e`) property to `false`. This is the default value for the `Cancel` property, but we set it explicitly for the sake of this sample. When the `Cancel` property is `false`, InfoPath does not reject the underlying node change (whatever the change might be).

WARNING Hard-Coded Passwords Are Not Recommended

In our sample, the password is hard coded as `"InfoPath!"`, which is not a recommended practice. This is not secure code and is used here solely for demonstration.

The next line of code (`UserIsAuthorized = true;`) remembers, for the duration of this form-filling session, that the user entered the right password. As a result, we don't need to prompt the user for the password every time data in the form is changed, even though the `myFields Changing` event is fired. Checking whether the user is already authorized encompasses the first two lines of code in the `myFields Changing` event handler. Let's look at the code for the `UserIsAuthorized` property (Listing 15.6) and see how it works.

LISTING 15.6: Implementing the `UserIsAuthorized` Property Using `FormState`

```
private const string UserIsAuthorizedStr = "UserIsAuthorized";

/// <summary>
/// Remembers if this user is authorized.
/// </summary>
private bool UserIsAuthorized
{
    get
    { return (bool)FormState[UserIsAuthorizedStr]; }
    set
    { FormState[UserIsAuthorizedStr] = value; }
}
```

The `UserIsAuthorized` property uses InfoPath's **`FormState`** object to remember a Boolean value that is `true` if the user is authorized and `false` otherwise. `FormState` is the preferred means to maintaining global state in your form code. When a user enters the correct password in the morale event form, we want to remember that the user is validated so he or she doesn't need to enter the password again.

`FormState` implements the `IDictionary` interface, meaning it holds key-value pairs of any type. In the `UserIsAuthorized` property, we're storing a string (`"UserIsAuthorized"`) as the key name and a Boolean (`true` or `false`) as the value. However, we could potentially use anything as the key name despite unique strings or integers being the most common key types. The value can also be any object, but unlike the name, the value is typically a nonprimitive object such as a generic `List` (e.g., of type `string`), `DataConnection`, or any other types, which need not be InfoPath objects. To learn more about the `FormState` object as an `IDictionary` interface, see the related MSDN article referenced in the Appendix.

To get `FormState` working as expected, it must first be initialized with the name-value pair you want to use. The best place to initialize `FormState` is in the `Loading` event handler of the form. Recall that you can sink the `Loading` event by choosing *Loading Event* from the *Programming* fly-out menu of the *Tools* menu. The code snippet in Listing 15.7 shows the initialization of the `UserIsAuthorized` name (the `UserIsAuthorizedStr` variable is the constant string value of `"UserIsAuthorized"`) with a default value of `false`.

LISTING 15.7: Initializing `FormState` with `UserIsAuthorized` as `false`

```
public void FormEvents_Loading(object sender, LoadingEventArgs e)
{
    FormState.Add(UserIsAuthorizedStr, false);
}
```

An efficient and organized approach to use the `FormState` object is to expose it by wrapping it as a property. This is exactly what we did with `UserIsAuthorized`. As a property implementation, `UserIsAuthorized` appears to be a simple class-wide variable when you use it throughout your code. Another advantage is that the dictionary aspects of the `FormState` object are abstracted away. As a result, we recommend using properties (with set and get accessors) only to manage any name-value pairs stored in `FormState`.

Forms Services

Why not just use class-wide variables to store state? Browser-enabled form templates do not allow the use of class-scoped variables. Similar to an ASP.NET page or Web service, Forms Services form code does not persist state between client HTTP requests. The `FormState` object is the only way for browser-enabled templates to persist data for the duration of a given session.

Let's continue to study the code behind the `myFields Changing` event. After verifying the correct password and setting `UserIsAuthorized` to `true`, the code calls `MessageBox.Show` as positive visual feedback to the user that he or she is authorized. What happens if, instead, the user enters the wrong password or clicks *Cancel*? The code that's executed includes the `else` block of the `myFields_Changing` event code shown earlier in Listing 15.5.

This code represents the essence of the `Changing` event. Of the three XML events, this is the only time when modification to node data can be rejected. If we do not cancel the `Changing` event, the change to the data will undoubtedly occur. Setting the `CancelableArgs.Cancel` property (from the `XmlChangingEventArgs` variable `e`) to `true` will, after the `Changing` event handler has finished, cause InfoPath to reject the change of node data. Canceling the `Changing` event will kill all subsequent notifications for this node, so the `Validating` and `Changed` events will not fire. If the `Message` and/or `MessageDetails` properties are assigned, they are used in an error dialog that signifies the change was rejected. If at least the `Message` property is not set before the event handler returns, the default message is shown: "Invalid update: A custom constraint has been violated." As a courtesy to your users, you should consider providing a more informative message, such as we did for the MoiEventScheduler-Changing sample (Figure 15.9).

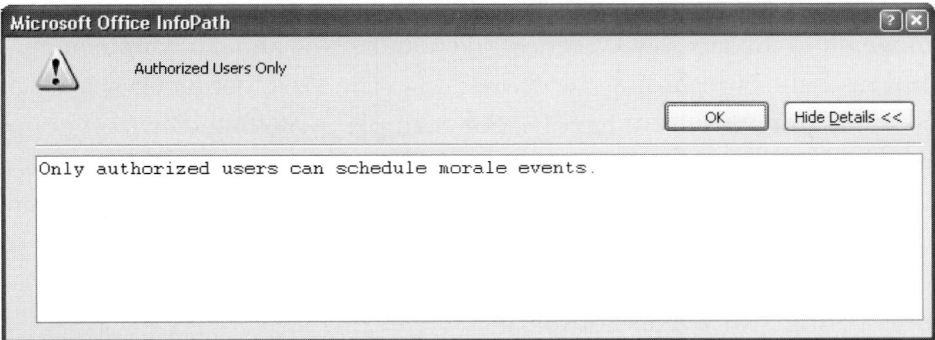

FIGURE 15.9: Custom error message that appears when a `Changing` event handler is canceled

> **NOTE Only `Changing` Is Cancelable**
>
> The `Changing` event is the only XML event that can be canceled. Canceling the `Changing` event suppresses the data change from propagating to the `Validating` and `Changed` events. Many form events are also cancelable if the event's argument inherits from the `CancelEventArgs` .NET Framework class.

Once an authorized user enters the correct password and fills out the form, the last step is to click the *Send to HR for Approval* button, which sends e-mail to the morale contacts in the human resources department.

> **TIP Watch for Bugs That Circumvent Validation in Your Form**
>
> Clicking the *Send to HR for Approval* button will not fire the `myFields` event handler, nor will it fire any event handler that we have set up. As a result, the submission is allowed even though the user doesn't have access and the form is empty. To fix this bug with our form, we can conditionally disable the button while the *Event title* field is empty. (*Event title* is convenient to use, although any field or combination of fields could have been used instead.) Later in this chapter, we'll look at how to sink a Button click event so we could handle this in code if so desired.

You now have a good understanding of the `Changing` event. Before we move on to the next XML event, you should know about a couple of general restrictions regarding the `Changing` event. First, not all OM calls can be made from this event handler. For example, switching views programmatically (which is covered later in this chapter) is disallowed. If an invalid OM call is made in a `Changing` handler, InfoPath throws an exception, which automatically cancels the event. This exception manifests itself to the user as a visual error (Figure 15.10). A complete list of unsupported OM calls during XML events appears in Table 15.3.

Another limitation of the `Changing` event is that the entire main data source is read-only. Any changes to the data using an `XPathNavigator` (or any other means) will also throw an exception similar to the one shown in Figure 15.10. The reasoning behind a read-only main data source is that the

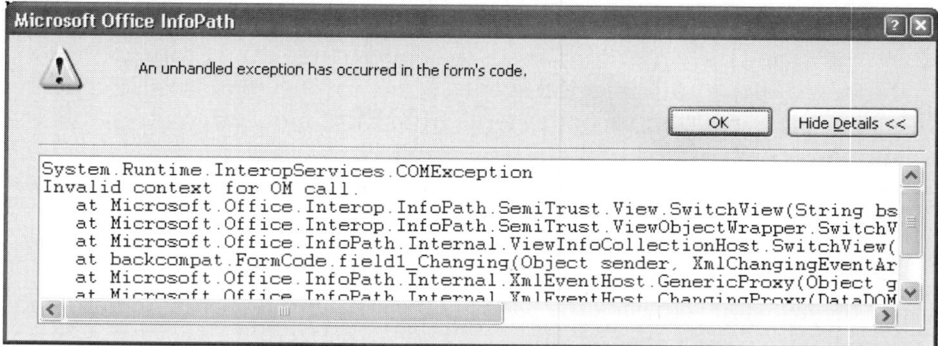

FIGURE 15.10: Error that occurs when calling unsupported OM during the `Changing` event

Table 15.3: Invalid Object Model Calls During XML Events

Event	Invalid OM	Comments
`Changing`	`SwitchView` Changing the `MainDataSource` object	`MainDataSource` is read-only.
`Validating`	`SwitchView` Changing the `MainDataSource` object	`MainDataSource` is read-only.
`Changed`	None	

`Changing` event is the first of three XML events that are fired for a node change. If the data source could be changed during this time, it would follow that two XML events may happen concurrently: Changing another node would kick off its XML events while this node still hasn't finished committing its data. As a result of disallowing changes at this time, InfoPath handles all XML operations in a synchronous, linear, and therefore predictable manner.

***`Validating`* Event**

Should the `Changing` event not be canceled, next in the XML event order is `Validating`. As its name suggests, this is the time to perform validation on the new data. Once the `Validating` event handler is called to run your code, the node's new data has already been committed. This means that the underlying main data source has assumed the new node value. Consequently, there is no way to roll back the change at this point. The role of the `Validating` event is to evaluate the new data and **report an error**, if necessary. All of the same restrictions from the `Changing` event apply to the `Validating` event (main data source is read-only, some OM cannot be called, and so on).

> **TIP The Change Is Accepted in `Validating`**
>
> Our assumption in the `Validating` event is that the change in data was allowed and supposed to occur. If the change in a node's data is to be rolled back, it should have happened in the `Changing` event.

Reporting an error does not actually affect the data. Instead, InfoPath maintains a list of nodes with data validation errors. These errors may surface visually on controls bound to the nodes with errors. Some controls, such as Section controls, do not support displaying error visuals. See Chapter 5 for more on data validation.

TIP Iterating Through Validation Errors

You can go through all validation errors, even if they aren't visible, by using the *Go to Next Error* and *Show Error Message* items on the *Tools* menu when filling out the form.

Forms Services

The *Go to Next Error* and *Show Error Message* features are also available on forms filled out in the browser. Hit Ctrl+Alt+R to go to the next error. Use Ctrl+Shift+I to show a message box with error details.

To put the `Validating` event into motion, we'll use the MOI Consulting morale event form that we used in the `Changing` event discussion. (This sample is called MoiEventScheduler-Validating.) For this sample, we want to check the dates and times of the proposed activity. We want to apply some validation rules when these values change. Here's what we want to ensure.

1. The requested start date/time is later than the end date/time.
2. The start time is between 8 A.M. and 4 P.M.; the end time is between 9 A.M. and 10 P.M.
3. An event may not last longer than one day if a waiver is necessary.

Let's begin by looking at the code that implements these validation rules by sinking the `StartDateTime` `Validating` event (Listing 15.8).

LISTING 15.8: Sinking the `StartDateTime Validating` Event

```
public void StartDateTime_Validating(
    object sender, XmlValidatingEventArgs e)
{
    // Get Start and End date-times
    XPathNavigator root = MainDataSource.CreateNavigator();
    XPathNavigator start = e.Site;
    XPathNavigator end = root.SelectSingleNode(
        "/my:myFields/my:EndDateTime", NamespaceManager);

  DateTime startDT, endDT;
    // Can we read the start?
    if (!DateTime.TryParse(start.Value, out startDT))
        return; // InfoPath handles invalid DateTime values

    const string error2a = "Start time is between 8 AM and 4 PM";
    if (startDT.Hour < 8 /*8am*/ || startDT.Hour > 12 + 4 /*4pm*/)
        e.ReportError(start, false /*siteIndepedent*/, error2a);

    // Can we read the end?
    if (!DateTime.TryParse(end.Value, out endDT))
        return; // InfoPath handles invalid DateTime values

    CheckDateTimes(e, startDT, endDT);
}
```

The first line of code in the `StartDateTime_Validating` event handler uses the `MainDataSource` and calls `CreateNavigator`, which returns an `XPathNavigator`. (We discuss the `XPathNavigator` in detail later in this chapter.) The `root XPathNavigator` is used to get the `EndDateTime` node from the main data source. We conveniently use `e.Site` to get the `StartDateTime` but could have instead used `SelectSingleNode` as we did with the `EndDateTime` field.

TIP Check Whether Changes Are Allowed

You could call `MainDataSource.ReadOnly` to check whether the main data source currently allows changes.

NOTE Legacy: `thisXDocument.DOM`

`thisXDocument.DOM` is now `this.MainDataSource` (or just `MainDataSource` since `this` object is implicit). Many of the methods that were under `thisXDocument` are now inherited from the `Microsoft.Office.InfoPath.XmlFormHostItem` class and thus available as inherited class members.

To perform validation on the start date and time, we get the `Start` field value into a .NET `DateTime` structure. The `Validating` event is called *before* InfoPath performs schema data type validation, so when our code runs we can't assume that the user entered a valid date and time value. To verify the value, we use the `TryParse` method of `DateTime` to determine whether the `Start` field is a valid date and time. If it's invalid, we simply `return` from the method and let InfoPath do the work to report the appropriate data type validation error.

.NET `DateTime` Class

`DateTime` (see the Appendix for a reference to documentation on MSDN) offers a safe and convenient way to accurately and reliably parse date/time, date, or time values.

TIP Schema and .NET Data Type Correlation

All XML Schema data types have corresponding .NET data types. Moreover, most .NET data types (except string, of course) have a `TryParse` method. See MSDN for a table of XML Schema and corresponding .NET data types (as referenced in the Appendix).

After verifying that the start date and time value is valid, we check the first part of condition 2 in our list of validation requirements. If the hour is before 8 A.M. or after 4 P.M., we call `e.ReportError` to report a data validation error. The default version of `ReportError` takes three arguments: an `XPathNavigator` where the error occurs, whether or not the error is site independent, and an error message that's shown to the user.

The one parameter that's not straightforward is the Boolean `siteIndependent` flag. Its name is somewhat of a misnomer and, in our opinion, a little confusing. You should always pass `false` to the `siteIndependent` parameter unless the error node itself is repeating. If it's repeating, passing `false` means that the error is targeting a specific node. Passing `true` tells InfoPath that all repeating instances of a node are involved in the error. InfoPath uses this information to determine when to automatically delete the error. When the error is site independent, a change in any of the nodes that repeat will remove the error; a site-dependent error, on the other hand, will not clear itself until that specific node is modified.

> **NOTE** `ReportError` Overloads
>
> The other versions of `ReportError` are similar to the `Errors.Add` method, which we'll discuss in the "Form Errors" subsection.

Since the `EndDateTime_Validating` event is almost identical to the `StartDateTime_Validating` form code in Listing 15.8, we'll omit it for brevity. You'll notice, however, that there's a call to a `CheckDateTimes` method. This code was added because both the `StartDateTime_Validating` and `EndDateTime_Validating` events call into it, thus eliminating the need for duplicate code. Listing 15.9 shows the form code for `CheckDateTimes`.

LISTING 15.9: Implementation of the `CheckDateTimes` Method

```
private void CheckDateTimes(
    XmlValidatingEventArgs e, DateTime startDT, DateTime endDT)
{
    const string error1 =
        "Requested Start date/time is later than the End date/time.";
    const string error3 =
        "An event may not last longer than 1 day if a waiver is "
            + "necessary.";
    if (startDT > endDT)
        e.ReportError(e.Site, false /*siteIndepedent*/, error1);

    if (((TimeSpan)endDT.Subtract(startDT)).Days >= 1 && WaiverNeeded)
        e.ReportError(e.Site, false /*siteIndependent*/, error3);
}
```

Remember that if a waiver is needed, the event may not last longer than one day. (The `Days` member of the `TimeSpan` class returns the number of whole days.) We use a `WaiverNeeded` property to check the `WaiverNeeded` node. Listing 15.10 shows the code.

LISTING 15.10: The `WaiverNeeded` Property

```
private bool WaiverNeeded
{
    get
    {
      XPathNavigator root = MainDataSource.CreateNavigator();
      XPathNavigator waiver = root.SelectSingleNode(
          "/my:myFields/my:WaiverNeeded", NamespaceManager);
      return waiver.ValueAsBoolean;
    }
}
```

Let's not forget to discuss what happens if someone chooses a morale event to last more than one day and then checks the *Waiver Needed* Check Box control! Checking *Waiver Needed* fires XML events on the `WaiverNeeded` node and bubbles up to the root. So our `Validating` event handlers aren't run. The result is that the violation of an event lasting longer than one day with a required waiver is not caught. While there are a few remedies to this problem, we took the approach of sinking the `Validating` event of the `WaiverNeeded` node, as shown in Listing 15.11.

LISTING 15.11: Sinking the `WaiverNeeded Validating` Event to Handle Checking of the Waiver Needed Check Box

```
public void WaiverNeeded_Validating(
    object sender, XmlValidatingEventArgs e)
{
    // Get Start and End date-times
    XPathNavigator root = MainDataSource.CreateNavigator();
    XPathNavigator start = root.SelectSingleNode(
        "/my:myFields/my:StartDateTime", NamespaceManager);
    XPathNavigator end = root.SelectSingleNode(
        "/my:myFields/my:EndDateTime", NamespaceManager);

    DateTime startDT, endDT;
    // Can we parse the Start and End values?
    if (!DateTime.TryParse(end.Value, out endDT)
        || !DateTime.TryParse(start.Value, out startDT))
      return; // InfoPath handles invalid DateTime values

    // Only do start and end common checks if date-times are both valid
    if (DateTimesAreValid())
        CheckDateTimes(e, startDT, endDT);
}
```

The code for `DateTimesAreValid` checks the `Errors` collection to see if we've already reported errors (using `ReportError`). Listing 15.12 shows the implementation.

LISTING 15.12: Checking the `Errors` Collection for Reported Start or End Errors

```
private bool DateTimesAreValid()
{
    // Are the Start and End date-times valid?
    FormError[] errs = Errors.GetErrors(FormErrorType.SystemGenerated);
    foreach (FormError err in errs)
    {
        if (err.Site.Name == "my:StartDateTime"
            || err.Site.Name == "my:EndDateTime")
        {
            return false;
        }
    }
    return true;
}
```

> **NOTE Validation Always Happens on Form Load**
>
> We mentioned that the `Validating` event is fired after `Changing` but before `Changed`. While this is true, there is one exception. Only `Validating` happens (without `Changing` or `Changed`) when the user creates a new or opens an existing form. (See the FormCodeAndRules sample for a demonstration.) If you report an error when the form is first validating, the form will still open with the validation error as expected. In previous versions of InfoPath, the form fails to load if a `Validating` event was canceled or threw an unhandled exception in its form code.

InfoPath allows for a maximum of one error per node at any given time, so it's not possible to report multiple errors on the same node simultaneously. If we report two errors on, say, the `StartDateTime` node, the first would be overwritten. As you can see from the `Validating` event and the `CheckDateTimes` shared method, our form code has the potential to report more than one error on a given node. A case where multiple errors can be reported on `Start`, for example, is when the start time is not between 8 A.M. and 4 P.M. and the start date is later than the end date. Since errors are overwritten, only the last error will be reported and seen by the user. No ill effects occur by reporting multiple errors; after the user corrects the error, the other (formally overwritten error) will be exposed. (This obviously assumes that conditions for reporting each error can be satisfied independently.)

> **TIP Accelerate Your Learning When Programming InfoPath**
>
> If you want to experiment with how this `Validating` code behaves, you can use the debugger to step through the code and use the *Immediate* debug window to run any code on-the-fly.

By the way, did you notice any bugs in our form code? If you played a little with the sample form, you might have noticed some special cases. One bug creeps in if the start time is after the end time and the valid field is modified in order to trigger the XML events for that node. Here is one way to reproduce the problem.

- Set `Start` to January 1, 2002.
- Set `End` to January 1, 2001.
- (Touch the `Start` field.) Set `Start` to January 2, 2002.

Now both `Start` and `End` have validation errors for `Start` being later than `End`. Fixing either `Start` or `End` to be valid will not remove the other error because that field was not edited. `ReportError` will remove the reported error only when the node that has the error is modified. How can we fix this case of a duplicate error? Since the main data source is read-only during the `Validating` event, it's not possible to touch the other node to force the XML events to be called. Could we go through the `Errors` collection and use the `Errors.Delete` method to remove the troublesome form error? Unfortunately, this isn't possible either. To explain, we need to talk more about InfoPath form errors as exposed via the OM.

> **NOTE "Duplicate Error" Bug**
>
> There's a way to fix our form code bug to prevent the "duplicate error" predicament. We'll leave it as an exercise for you to implement the fix. (Here's a hint: Allow only one, but not both, of the `DateTime` fields—either `Start` or `End`—to have a common error at any given time. A common error is one that involves both `Start` and `End` and could be reported on either node.)

Form Errors

From an end-user's perspective, and even from the standpoint of the form designer, a validation error is, well, just a validation error! But when you're programming InfoPath, the details of validation are essential when working with form errors. To address our question about going through the `Errors` collection and using `Errors.Delete` to remove a form error, we need to first discuss the three types of form errors.

When a validation error occurs when a user fills out a form, the error is classified as one of the following types: `SchemaValidation`, `SystemGenerated`, or `UserDefined`. `SchemaValidation` errors are reported only by the XML parsing engine (MSXML for InfoPath, `System.Xml` on Forms Services). `SystemGenerated` errors are a result of calling `ReportError`. A `UserDefined` error is generated when form code manually adds a new `FormError` to the `Errors` collection. The three error types correspond with the values of the `FormErrorType` enumeration.

Listing 15.13 shows an example of adding a `UserDefined` `FormError`.

LISTING 15.13: Adding a `UserDefined` `FormError` to the `Errors` Collection

```
XPathNavigator NumPeopleNav = MainDataSource.CreateNavigator();
NumPeopleNav = NumPeopleNav.SelectSingleNode(
    "/my:myFields/my:NumberOfPeople", NamespaceManager);
Errors.Add(NumPeopleNav, "TooManyPeople",
    "No more than 10 people can attend.");
```

This code first gets the `XPathNavigator` to the main data source root. Next, we select the `NumberOfPeople` node. Finally, an error is added by `Errors.Add`. The first parameter is the `XPathNavigator` of the node in which the error is associated, followed by the internal (unexposed to the user) error name, and finally the short error message. Override versions of this method add the following parameters: `messageDetails`, `errorCode`, and `errorMode`. The `messageDetails` parameter provides additional information to the user if he or she right-clicks the error visualization and requests to see details. `errorCode` is an arbitrary integer for your internal and personal use. Finally, the `errorMode` parameter takes a value from the `ErrorMode` enumeration: `Modal` or `Modeless`. If `Modal` is used, an error is immediately shown in an alert-style dialog that blocks the user until it's dismissed. `Modeless`, on the other hand, does not show a dialog and is the default behavior.

Calling the `Errors.Add` method can be used in any event handler (including form events) without restrictions. This is unlike the `ReportError` method, which is only available (and thus must be called) within the `Validating` XML event handler. Why, then, would anyone use `ReportError` versus `Errors.Add`? This brings us to the topic of deleting errors.

There are two ways to manually remove errors from the `Errors` collection. The first way is with the `Delete` method. An error is deleted by passing in either a `FormError` (an item from the `Errors` collection) or an error name (the internal name used in the `Add` method). Only `UserDefined` errors are allowed to be deleted. So, reporting an error using `ReportError` cannot be done easily this way. However, using the `Errors.DeleteAll` method will obliterate all form errors, no matter what their type.

> **WARNING Don't Use `ReportError` with an Arbitrary Node**
>
> When calling `ReportError` on the `XmlValidatingEventArgs` object, be sure that the error is based on the node associated with the `e.Site` `XPathNavigator`. If an error is reported on an arbitrary node with `e.ReportError`, InfoPath will not know when to remove the error, which results in it being "stuck" and your form in a bad state.

A useful mechanism for debugging form errors is to add a Button control to the view of your form that shows all errors when clicked. To set up the `ClickedEventHandler`, go to the *Button Properties* dialog and click on the *Edit Form Code* button. Listing 15.14 shows our Button event handler.

LISTING 15.14: Showing All Errors on a Button `Clicked` Event

```
public void CTRL11_5_Clicked(object sender, ClickedEventArgs e)
{
    MessageBox.Show("Number of errors: " + Errors.Count);
    string errors = string.Empty;
    foreach (FormError err in Errors)
    {
        errors += "(" + err.FormErrorType + ", "
            + err.Site.Name + ") " + err.Message
            + System.Environment.NewLine;
    }
    MessageBox.Show("Error messages: "
        + System.Environment.NewLine + errors);
}
```

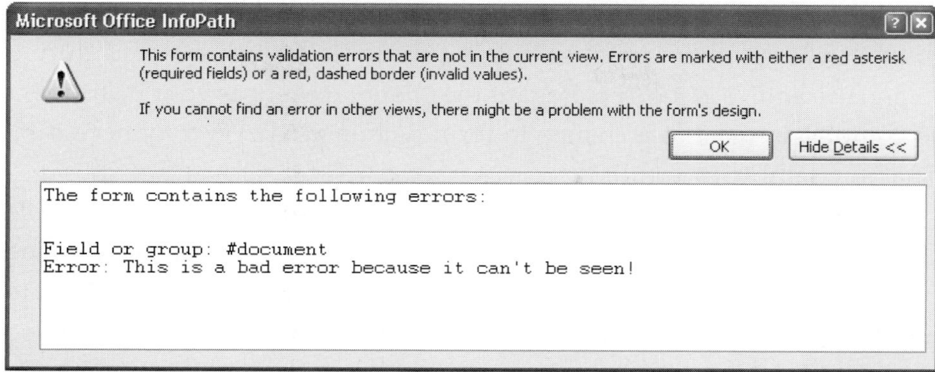

FIGURE 15.11: Show Error Message dialog

Before we move on to the `Changed` event, we have a final word about reporting custom validation errors using the OM. When using `ReportError` or `Errors.Add`, ensure that the error node exists in a view or at least that the user can sufficiently recognize the error and be able to fix it. In Figure 15.11, an error has been added to `MainDataSource.CreateNavigator()` (the root) that the user can never see. It can be seen only by using *Go to Next Error* and then *Show Error Message*. The dialog shown in Figure 15.11 appears when using the *Show Error Message* option.

This is clearly a contrived example because there is no reason to report an error on the root, but the concept remains. The code in Listing 15.15 is written behind a button `Clicked` event to reproduce the behavior shown in Figure 15.11.

LISTING 15.15: Adding an Error That the User Can Never See

```
Errors.Add(this.CreateNavigator(),
   "Error", "This is a bad error because it can't be seen!");
```

`Changed` Event

Last in the series of XML events fired on a modified node, and all of its parents, is the `Changed` event. Its name is quite representative of the state involving the modified node data: The change has already occurred. So what's the point of sinking and handling this event in custom form code? That's a good question, and we have a great answer. You can do pretty much anything your heart desires! Unlike `Changing` and `Validating`, the

`Changed` event can modify the main data source. You can also ask InfoPath to switch to another view—something that was also disallowed during `Changing` and `Validating`. Regard the `Changed` event as your instrument to completely react to a change in form data in whatever way necessary. That's certainly powerful!

Like us, you might find yourself wanting to use form code for simple things in the `Changed` event. Here are some examples: showing a dialog box, setting a node's value, querying a data source, or even switching to another view. The Rules feature was designed to cater to these scenarios so you wouldn't have to use the `Changed` event. As a matter of fact, rules fire at nearly the same time as the `Changed` event. With rules in mind, let's take another look at the order of "events" that occur when a node is modified: `Changing`, `Validating`, rules, `Changed`. (See the FormCodeAndRules sample form template.) So rules could be a direct substitution for the `Changed` event in simple scenarios.

Our recommendation is to leverage the simplistic declarative nature of rules when possible because code is harder and more expensive to maintain. If rules won't fully suffice for your needs, you can tack on a `Changed` event. If it doesn't help to split the work between rules and the `Changed` event, you could try to put some logic in the `Validating` event to precede rules. Should that not work, for example, because you need to modify the value of a node (recall that the main data source during `Validating` is read-only) before rules, you may need to reimplement the rule actions into your form code. Even though the likelihood of reimplementing rules into code is low, most rules constitute no more than about two or three lines of code.

To demonstrate the `Changed` event, we'll add some final touches to the MOI morale event scheduler form. (See the MoiEventScheduler-Changed sample.) Say that we've received feedback from the managers that we need to gather names of participants for an accurate head count. The names should be sorted in alphabetical order by last name.

Let's figure out what we need to do in our form to fulfill the managers' requirements. First we need controls in the view to capture the names of the participants. Since we'll be sorting by last name, it's easiest to separate first and last names into their own Text Box controls. The Text Box controls will be within a Repeating Table control so that multiple participant instances can be inserted and filled out.

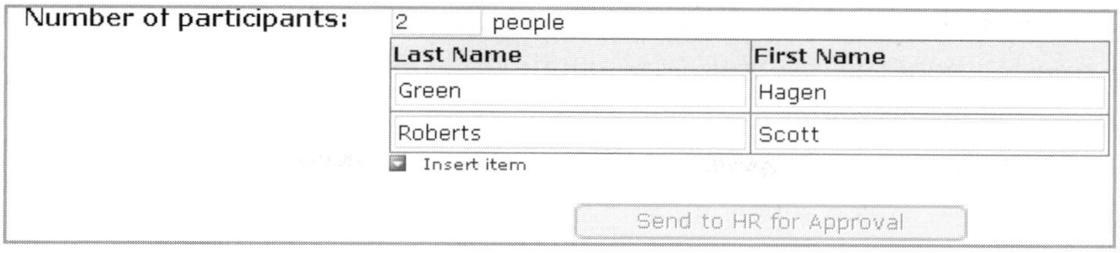

Number of participants: 2 people

Last Name	First Name
Green	Hagen
Roberts	Scott

Insert item

Send to HR for Approval

FIGURE 15.12: Supporting entry of last and first names in a Repeating Table control

With the new controls in the view, our form now supports the entry of many first and last names. Figure 15.12 shows how that part of the view appears in design mode. Now that we have the controls bound to the data source, how do we sort by the `LastName` field? Before we approach the answer, let's investigate and understand the problem.

First, there are two ways to sort data in InfoPath: in the view or in the data. Sorting content in the view simply orders the visual presentation of the data; it does not actually touch the data in the XML. With XSLT driving the presentation layer of InfoPath, you could modify the view (.xsl file) to include an `xsl:sort` directive. (See the W3Schools Web site referenced in the Appendix for specifics.) Since this is a book about using InfoPath and working with XML data, we're taking the data approach to sorting. Sometimes sorting the data is a requirement because the form XML will be used in another application that already expects the data to be sorted.

> **NOTE View-Based Sorting**
>
> Sorting in the XSL is almost always faster in terms of absolute performance. Unfortunately, sorting in the view may not always yield the results you expect. For example, if the data you're sorting is bound to more than one control, you'll need to add sorting functionality to each of the controls. Moreover, view-based sorting is not supported in browser-enabled form templates because it requires manual hand-editing of the view XSL file. Sorting the form data will work similarly in client and browser-enabled form templates.

To approach sorting the Repeating Table data containing participants, we need to first determine what will trigger the sort. Given that we're sorting by last name, it seems appropriate to fire off the sort whenever the `LastName` field is changed. Despite having `LastName` trigger the sort, we don't want to actually sort the LastName field. (If we did so, we'd move last names without the rest of the row data!) We want to sort the Participant repeating group under the Participants group. Consider the data source bound to the controls in Figure 15.12. We can see that the parent node of field LastName is a repeating group named Participant, and its parent node is a group named Participants. The code snippet listening to the LastName field is shown in Listing 15.16. To focus more on the scenario and less on the sorting algorithm, we'll use a simple bubble sort to order the Participant groups based on the LastName field. In a real-world scenario, you'd want to use the .NET Framework to efficiently sort the data.

NOTE Sinking Secondary Data Source Events

Secondary data sources allow sinking only the Changed event. Without any validation on secondary data sources, there are no equivalent concepts of the Changing or Validating events to reject or report validation errors, respectively.

LISTING 15.16: Sorting Items in the Repeating Table When the LastName Field Is Changed

```
public void LastName_Changed(object sender, XmlEventArgs e)
{
    if (e.UndoRedo)
        return;
    // resort the list
    if (e.Operation == XmlOperation.ValueChange)
    {
        XPathNavigator senderNav = sender as XPathNavigator;
        senderNav.MoveToParent(); // move to 'Participant'
        senderNav.MoveToParent(); // move to 'Participants'
        SortChildNodes(senderNav);
    }
}
```

WARNING Sorting Every Time LastName_Changed Is Called

It's very important to call SortChildNodes only when the value of LastName actually changes. Removing the if statement that checks for ValueChange will result in the LastName_Changed event firing again (within itself) when nodes are moved for the sorting operation.

The `Changed` event starts with two comments generated by InfoPath. These comments basically say that the main data source (i.e., OM property `MainDataSource`) should not be modified yet. That's because if the operation that caused the `LastName` field to change is an undo or redo, our code shouldn't handle it. InfoPath takes care of all undo and redo operations automatically. If you still wanted some code to run during an undo or redo, keep in mind that the main data source is read-only. Finally, after the check for `e.UndoRedo`, we can write our code!

Forms Services

Since there is no concept of undo or redo, the `UndoRedo` property is always `false` when a browser-enabled form template is running in the browser.

We begin by getting the `Participants` group. To get there, we could have just used `MainDataSource` to get the root and then `SelectSingleNode` with the XPath `/my:myFields/my:Participants`. Instead, we wanted to show how the `XPathNavigator` can be used as a cursor to traverse the data source. The `sender` object in all XML events will always be the `XPathNavigator` behind the specific event handler. So in this case we know that `sender` will be `LastName`. (Recall that `e.Site` is the `XPathNavigator` that initiated the event; if the event handler is sinking group XML events, `e.Site` can be any child node.) After we move to the `Participants` group, we pass the navigator to the `SortChildNodes` method, which does the actual bubble sort. Listing 15.17 shows the implementation of the sort.

The `SortChildNodes` method first needs to know the total number of participant items to sort. To get the number of `Participant` groups, we count the result of selecting all `Participant` children of the `Participants` group. The two `for` loops account for the bubble sort iterations. To compare the last names of participant `j` and participant `j+1`, we select the nodes by using XPath with a **predicate filter**. A predicate filter is signified by square brackets within an XPath expression. Passing a simple numerical value like `[1]` is a shortcut for `[position()=1]`. (You can find more on the XPath Language at the W3C site, as referenced in the Appendix.) `String.Compare` performs a culture-specific string comparison that returns `1` if `child1`'s value is lexicographically later than that of `child2`. If

Listing 15.17: Sorting Participants (by `LastName`) in the Data Source

```
public void SortChildNodes(XPathNavigator parent)
{
    const string Prtpnt = "Participant";
    XPathNodeIterator childNodes =
        parent.SelectChildren(Prtpnt, parent.NamespaceURI);
    int numberChildren = childNodes.Count;
    for (int i = 1; i <= numberChildren; i++)
        for (int j = 1; j <= numberChildren - i; j++)
        {
            XPathNavigator child1, child2;
            child1 = parent.SelectSingleNode(
               "my:" + Prtpnt + "[" + j + "]/my:LastName",
               NamespaceManager);
            child2 = parent.SelectSingleNode(
               "my:" + Prtpnt + "[" + (j+1) + "]/my:LastName",
               NamespaceManager);
            if (string.Compare(child1.Value, child2.Value) > 0)
            {
               child1.MoveToParent();
               child2.MoveToParent();
               XPathNavigator temp = child1.Clone();
               child1.ReplaceSelf(child2);
               child2.ReplaceSelf(temp);
            }
        }
}
```

that's the case, we want to swap the positions of the `child1` and `child2` parent nodes. (The parent nodes of `child1` and `child2` represent entire rows in the Repeating Table.) Since `XPathNavigator` objects are simply pointers to the underlying data source, we cannot assign new objects to them. Instead, navigators expose methods such as `Clone`, to make a deep copy, and `ReplaceSelf`, to swap out (and remove) the node for another. We use a combination of these methods to swap the positions of `child1` and `child2` `Participant` groups.

> **NOTE** XPath Is 1-Based
>
> Are you wondering why the bubble sort loops start with `1` instead of `0`? Repeating items are addressed in XPath by using a `1`-based index.

Since the `SortChildNodes` method is called only from the `LastName_Changed` event handler, it runs only when a `LastName` field is modified. What if the form template is opened with an already existing form whose underlying participants data is unsorted? Currently, it won't be sorted. However, by sinking the `Loading` form event, you could call `SortChildNodes` to ensure the data is sorted from the start. If a form is opened with a huge amount of data that's sorted in descending (Z to A) order (the worst case for the bubble sort algorithm), loading performance could be lethargic. Consider showing the user a "Please wait" message if this is a concern. However, we recommend using a more efficient algorithm such as merge or binary tree sorting, which take less time to run in their worst cases.

Forms Services

When posting data back to the server takes a long time (which includes running custom form code), Forms Services automatically shows the "Sending data to the server" busy dialog over the form in the browser.

TIP Concatenating Strings by Selecting Multiple Text Nodes

If you want to sort by last name and then by first name, you don't need to add any special code. A shortcut is to select the `Participant` itself instead of the `LastName` node. The `Value` property of a group node is the result of concatenating the `Value` of each child text node under that group. Try removing the appropriate code in the sample to see the values of `child1` and `child2`. Remember that text nodes exist *between* field nodes as white space to format the XML itself!

Multiple Event Notifications for XML Event Handlers

A single XML event handler can be fired multiple times during a data source change. In the past few examples, we didn't see this behavior because we've been using string data types. Some other data types, however, require the XML data to be decorated in particular ways. These so-called decorations require managing hidden XML on the changing element itself to accommodate its behaviors. For example, for an integer field to be blank, the hidden attribute node called `xsi:nil` must be set to `true`. (This is an XML data type requirement to which InfoPath must adhere for an integer field's data to be considered valid.) If the blank integer field is set to some value (which may or may not be a numerical value), the `xsi:nil` attribute is removed. As a result, any XML events on this integer node are fired twice: the first time for removing `xsi:nil`, the second for changing the value of the field itself. The order of notifications in this case, with the sender in parenthesis, is `Changing (xsi:nil)`, `Validating (xsi:nil)`, `Changed (xsi:nil)`, `Changing (my:integer)`, `Validating (my:integer)`, and `Changed (my:integer)`.

TIP Integer and `xsi:nil`

To witness firsthand how `xsi:nil` is involved in field changes, you can save a form with a blank integer field, and then save it again as a different name when it has a value. Open the resulting .xml file in a text editor such as Notepad to see the `xsi:nil` decoration. You can use the MultipleNotifications sample (included with the samples for this chapter) for this purpose as well as to explore other concepts involving multiple notifications.

The MultipleNotifications sample form, shown in Figure 15.13, contains several Text Box controls bound to different data types. The `String` field is the standard case; it exists only for comparison. The `Integer`, `RichText`, and `DateTime` fields all show various forms of multiple notifications. `Integer` and `DateTime` are similar in their use of `xsi:nil`, while `RichText` is a little different. The `RichText` field fires not only regular change notifications but also HTML element insertions and deletions. For example, underlining in the Rich Text Box control will fire an event from an HTML node named `u`. (The `<u>` tag in HTML represents markup for underlined content.)

Multiple notifications may cause your code to run twice or more, depending on the data source change. Running code in your XML event handlers many times may not cause any problems. You might not even know it's running a few times! But in some cases, running code several times could cause serious problems. One of the most common issues is poor performance. In our `Changed` event sample, we used a sorting algorithm to

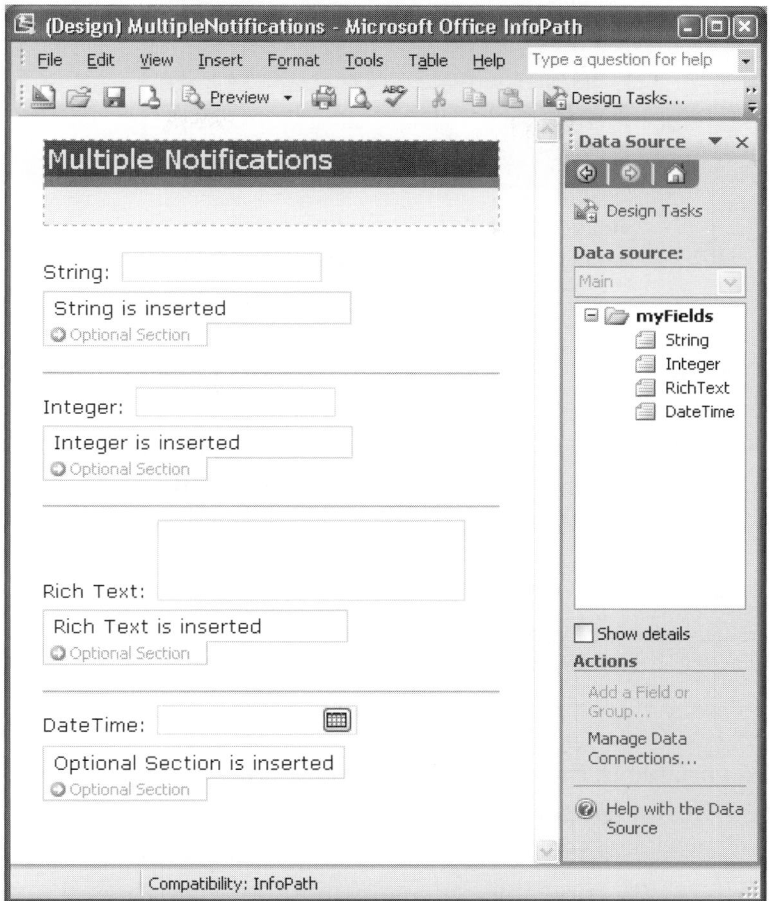

FIGURE 15.13: MultipleNotifications sample form in design mode

shuffle the main data source. If there were many items, the algorithm could take a long time to run. But without handling multiple notifications properly, the wait time can double or worse! Can we do anything to handle only the notifications we care about? Let's take another look at the MultipleNotifications sample to learn about OM that can help us make distinctions between different operations.

As you fill out the sample MultipleNotifications form, you'll notice that a message box appears after each change (Figure 15.14).

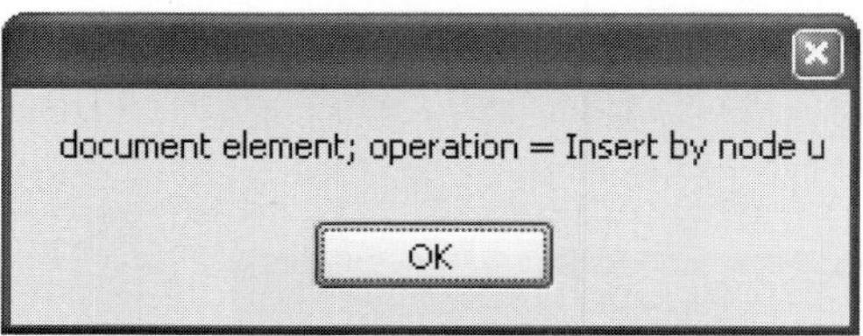

FIGURE 15.14: One of the notifications when adding underline to a rich text (XHTML) field

This dialog appears because a `Changed` event handler is listening to the document element (`myFields`) group. Because it's on the document element, this handler receives all notifications throughout the data source by the means of event bubbling. Let's look at the call to the `MessageBox` class in Listing 15.18 to see how we can get the operation by name.

LISTING 15.18: Generating Visual Notifications for Data Source Events

```
string nodeName = ((XPathNavigator)sender).Name;
MessageBox.Show("document element; operation = "
    + e.Operation + " by node " + nodeName);
```

The `e` variable in the `Changed` event is of type `XmlEventArgs`, but the same `Operation` property is also available on `XmlChangingEventArgs` and `XmlValidatingEventArgs`. `Operation` is of the `XmlOperation` enumeration type. Its allowable values include `Delete`, `Insert`, `None`, or `ValueChange`. By playing with the MultipleNotifications sample form, you will see `Delete`, `Insert`, and `ValueChange` operations. `None` is used in other cases where an event is fired for reasons other than inserts, deletes, or changes in value. (In a moment, we'll briefly look at one of the cases when `Operation` is `None`.) When writing code for any of your XML event handlers, one good approach is to handle only those `Operation` values that your code is designed to handle. Alternatively, you can reuse the code snippet shown in Listing 15.18 in your XML event handlers to show the same `MessageBox` as Figure 15.14 whenever a notification occurs. Then you can check for specific conditions and bail (by simply using `return`) from a handler if it's a multiple notification that you want to ignore.

Another out-of-band notification happens whenever a new or existing form is opened: The `Validating` event is fired on every item in the data source. This occurs to ensure that the data is in a good state before the form opens and even before the `Loading` form event fires. To handle this specific case in your `Validating` event handler, `e.Operation` will always be set to `None`.

Using `XPathNavigator` Objects

If you're aspiring to be an expert in writing form code behind InfoPath forms, the `XPathNavigator` object is absolutely crucial to understand. It is the only gateway to accessing, modifying, and working with the main and secondary data sources. In the samples and code snippets we've looked at thus far, you've learned how to do basic node selection and get a node's value. We now present advanced node selection and data modification tips and tricks that are useful when designing some form templates.

> **WARNING** Watch for Infinite Change Loops
>
> We'll discuss how to add, replace, and remove nodes in the data source. Remember that as these operations occur, the corresponding XML event handlers will fire! If you modify a node in an event handler that is also handling that node's change, your code will be in an infinite loop. Modifying a node in its own handler still fires the event handler! Consider using `OldValue` and `NewValue` from the `e` parameter to detect this case.

Finding the XPath of a Node

At a loss to figure out how to get the XPath of a node in a data source? Just find the field or group in the *Data Source* task pane, right-click, and choose *Copy XPath.* Now paste it inside double quotes as the `xpath` parameter to an `XPathNavigator Select` method.

But what about more complicated XPaths that don't represent a simple data source binding? Try using an Expression Box control. Take your time to fiddle with the XPath in design mode and see if it evaluates properly when previewing the form. Once you settle on the correct XPath in the Expression Box, you can copy and paste it into your code.

Using the `NamespaceManager` Parameter

Are you trying to use one of the various `Select` methods (such as `SelectSingleNode`), only to get an `XPathException` with the details "Namespace Manager or `XsltContext` needed"? This means the XPath you're passing uses at least one namespace prefix, such as `my:`, `dfs:`, `ns1:`, or another "prefix:name" format. You need to pass a resolver parameter (of type `IXmlNamespaceResolver`). If you aren't very familiar with using `XPathManager` and selecting nodes yet, don't worry too much about what a resolver does. This parameter is given to you by InfoPath as `NamespaceManager` (available through IntelliSense on the `this` object). It never hurts to simply pass it to node selection methods whenever it's listed as a parameter—you can still provide it even if you don't have namespace prefixes in your XPath.

> **TIP No Namespace? No `NamespaceManager`!**
>
> The `NamespaceManager` parameter is not necessary when you select nodes that don't have a namespace. They can appear as :`FirstName` (with a semicolon but without a prefix) in the data source.

Some selection methods, such as `SelectDescendants` and `SelectAncestors`, do not accept `IXmlNamspaceResolver`. Instead, they require a `namespaceURI` parameter as a string. The `namespaceURI` is the actual namespace behind the prefix. For example, the `my` prefix resolves to a namespace such as `http://schemas.microsoft.com/office/infopath/2003/myXSD/2006-01-22T20:55:55`. To figure out the namespace string in your case, go to the *Details* tab of the *Field or Group Properties* dialog for the node you want to select. If you have already selected a node (e.g., the document element) that has the same namespace prefix as a node you want to select, you can get the `namespaceURI` easily via the existing node `XPathNavigator NamespaceURI` string property. If there's no namespace listed, the node is not in a namespace, and you won't need to pass `namespaceURI`. If you must pass `namespaceURI`, use `String.Empty`.

> **TIP Don't Hard-Code the Namespace URI**
>
> Writing robust form code that doesn't hard-code the namespace URI is preferred. Using literal namespace URI strings will break your code if the underlying data source is converted to use a different namespace.

> **NOTE Secondary Data Sources Are Similar**
>
> All of the concepts discussed here also apply to secondary data sources.

Selecting Multiple Nodes

There's no need to use `SelectSingleNode` for every node you want to select. If you're working with a repeating field or group and using `SelectSingleNode`, there's no good way to determine how many of the repeating item exist. To get a set of fields or groups that are repeating, use the `Select` method of the `XPathNavigator`. In the code shown in Listing 15.19 (and in the corresponding sample form template, called SelectingMultipleNodes), we're displaying the values of every field in a Bulleted List control. The `XPathNodeIterator` object represents a collection of nodes that we can iterate through by using the `MoveNext` method and the `Current` property. The `Count` and `CurrentPosition` properties (not shown in this sample) on the iterator are useful in `for` loops.

LISTING 15.19: Selecting Multiple Nodes Using `XPathNodeIterator`

```
string message = String.Empty;
XPathNavigator root = MainDataSource.CreateNavigator();
XPathNodeIterator nodes = root.Select("/my:myFields/my:group1/my:field1",
NamespaceManager);
while (nodes.MoveNext())
{
    message += nodes.Current.Value + System.Environment.NewLine;
}
MessageBox.Show(message);
```

Deleting Nodes

You might think that you can use similar code shown in Listing 15.19 to delete multiple nodes. Could you just call `nodes.Current.DeleteSelf()` within the while loop? Yes, but you'll delete only the first node. Why? Since nodes is an XPathNodeIterator, it does not support being modified while used as an iterator. As soon as it detects itself being modified, the MoveNext method prematurely returns false.

The proper approach to deleting a series of sibling nodes is to use the DeleteRange method. By selecting the first and last nodes within a range, the DeleteRange method will remove those two nodes and all nodes in between. To determine which nodes are the first and last for a repeating field or group, we'll use a predicate filter. Recall that passing a simple number as a predicate filter indexes into the 1-based collection of nodes. The last node is found by using the XPath functions position and last. The code in Listing 15.20 shows the call to DeleteRange from the first node with the last passed as a parameter. (The sample file is named DeletingNodes.)

TIP Using DeleteRange

DeleteRange is inclusive, that is, the first and last nodes are included in the deletion.

LISTING 15.20: Deleting Node Siblings by Using DeleteRange

```
const string f1 = "/my:myFields/my:group1/my:field1";
XPathNavigator root = MainDataSource.CreateNavigator();
XPathNavigator first =
    root.SelectSingleNode(f1 + "[1]", NamespaceManager);
XPathNavigator last =
    root.SelectSingleNode(f1 + "[position()=last()]",
    NamespaceManager);
first.DeleteRange(last);
```

Learning More about XPathNavigator

Start with the article "Accessing XML Data Using XPathNavigator" on MSDN (as referenced in the Appendix). You can also search the Web for XPathNavigator to find more tutorials and references.

Registering Event Handlers

By now, we've seen that InfoPath automatically creates event handlers when you're designing a form template in design mode. Conveniently, they're also registered for us with the `EventManager` object in the `InternalStartup` method. Listing 15.21 shows an example of registering an event handler with an XML event.

Listing 15.21: Registering an XML Event Handler to the `Changing` Event of the `UseEmail` Node

```
EventManager.XmlEvents[
    "/my:myFields/my:LoginInfo/my:UseEmail"].Changing +=
        new XmlChangingEventHandler(UseEmail_Changing);
```

The `EventManager` is a class-wide member whose purpose is limited to tracking event registration. Its use is restricted to the `InternalStartup` method where all registrations must occur. Any registrations outside of `InternalStartup` will cause failures when a user fills out the form (specifically, a `SecurityException` is thrown).

TIP `InternalStartup` Is Restricted to Registration

The `InternalStartup` method is meant only for registering event handlers with InfoPath. Any calls to the InfoPath OM (in the `Startup` or `Shutdown` methods) will fail when a user fills out the form. Even though you can write other code in this method, it's strongly discouraged. The form may not be fully initialized, which could result in intermittent issues and undefined behaviors.

Form Code Is Separated into Partial Classes

The `EventManager` object is defined in the FormCode.Designer.cs file. This file, in conjunction with FormCode.cs, completely defines the partial class where your form code is written. To see FormCode.Designer.cs, enable the *Show All Files* item on the *Project* menu. This file is auto-generated by InfoPath, and manual editing of its contents is not supported.

During our discussions in this chapter, we've talked about each class of event: form, XML, and control. We briefly discussed the various form events (we'll use form events extensively later). Afterward, we thoroughly

Table 15.4: Examples of Advanced XPaths for Registering XML Event Handlers

XPath	Description
`/`	Selects the XML root; parent of the document element
`//my:field1`	Selects all descendents (including self) named `my:field1`
`//text()`	Selects all text nodes

examined each XML event. InfoPath 2007 supports a single control event: `ButtonEvent`. We used a Button control event handler when discussing form errors in the "`Validating` Event" subsection earlier in this chapter.

Registering events with the `EventManager`, for the most part, isn't particularly interesting. There is a little flexibility, however, in defining XML event handlers. InfoPath will generate the listener XPath (i.e., the string within the square brackets) based on a field or group in the data source. This is fine for most cases, but sometimes you'll need a greater level of flexibility. Table 15.4 shows some examples of XPaths that still work as expected when a user fills out the form, even though InfoPath will not generate them.

> **WARNING** **Complex XPaths for XML Events Are Not Supported**
>
> Some complex XPaths are unsupported when you register them for XML events. InfoPath throws an `ArgumentException` when attempting to run the `InternalStartup` method that registers XML events with unsupported XPaths.

Script and the Custom Task Pane

Talking about the InfoPath OM isn't complete without discussing scripting languages. In its Microsoft Office 2003 infancy, InfoPath supported scripting only with JScript or VBScript. Its object model has changed very little since then, so if you are a legacy InfoPath script writer, you'll have no problem scripting in InfoPath 2007. Not to disappoint those expert script writers, however, the motivation to use scripting over managed code is dwindling. With the InfoPath managed OM expanded and revamped in 2007, the scripting OM was kept constant. Nevertheless, one major advantage of using script over managed code is its ability to easily interoperate with the custom task pane. Communicating to and from the task pane from script code doesn't require any special permissions (besides domain trust) and is relatively easy to do.

NOTE Supported Script Languages

Our script samples will be in JScript. VBScript, however, is also supported as a scripting language for form code.

WARNING Form Code Language Must Be Homogeneous

Managed code and script cannot be mixed in an InfoPath form template. In fact, even different languages within managed code (or script) cannot be mixed.

Managed Form Code and Task Pane Script

It's possible to use managed code to communicate to the custom task pane, but it takes some .NET type trickery and a full trust assembly. (Recall from Chapter 11 that a full trust form is different than a fully trusted .NET assembly.) See the InfoPath team blog on the MSDN blogs site, referenced in the Appendix, for details.

Forms Services

Browser-enabled form templates and Forms Services do not support script code.

Custom Task Pane

In the same way InfoPath relies on its own task pane during design mode, you can use your own custom task pane. The custom task pane behaves just like any other task pane. It opens (by default) with your form to the right side of the view but can be moved anywhere or even closed by the user filling out your form. The content of the task pane, as you define it when designing the form, is essentially a Web page in a restricted instance of Internet Explorer. For example, some scripting objects, such as `WScript.Shell`, cannot be created. The task pane, unless you write custom form code, is a disconnected component of the form itself. In a moment we'll see how to tie together the form and the custom task pane.

Forms Services

A custom task pane is supported in a browser-enabled form template, but not when running in the context of a Web browser.

NOTE Custom Task Pane Cannot Sink Data Source Events

You cannot bind HTML controls in the custom task pane to the InfoPath data source.

WARNING Objects Unsafe for Scripting Are Restricted

Attempting to create restricted ActiveX objects such as `WScript.Shell` results in a "Cannot create automation object" runtime script error.

To add a custom task pane to your form, go to the *Programming* category on the *Form Options* dialog (Figure 15.15). Check the *Enable custom task pane* checkbox to enable the *Task pane name* text box and *Task pane location* drop-down. The name is used in the heading of the task pane. The task pane location can be any Web site URL (e.g., http://www.moiconsulting.com/taskpane.htm), local path (e.g., C:\taskpane.htm), UNC path (e.g., \\mycomputer\myshare\taskpane.htm), or resource file that is included in the form template. In our example, we've added a static HTML page to the form by using the *Resource Files* button.

NOTE Custom Task Pane Is Not Shown in Design Mode

The custom task pane does not appear in design mode. In fact, you might forget you have one until you fill out the form!

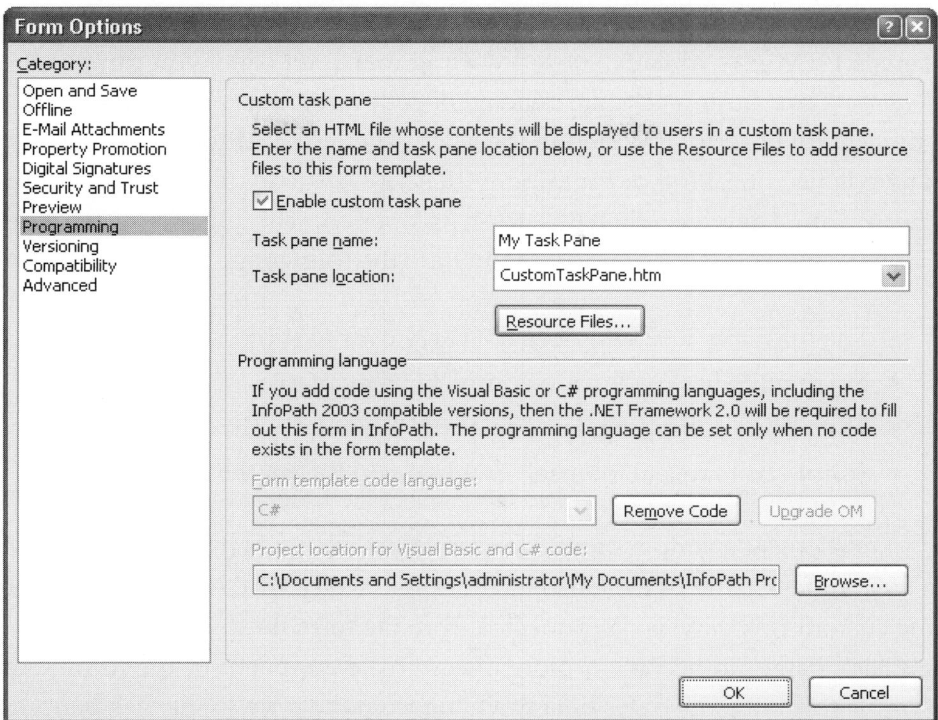

FIGURE 15.15: Setting up a custom task pane in the Form Options dialog

A very useful scenario is to use the custom task pane as an active help reference when users fill out your form. We'll show a sample later in this chapter where we use the custom task pane with the `ContextChanged` event to provide on-demand context-sensitive help.

> **WARNING Use a Task Pane from Local Resource Files**
>
> It's preferred to use a task pane that is included as part of the form template. Referencing an external page, for example, may be prohibited if the form trust level is not sufficient. Moreover, will your users even have permission to access the external site?

Scripting the Custom Task Pane

Designing a form with script is as simple as selecting a scripting language in the *Form Options* dialog's *Programming* category before editing the code.

(See "Writing Code Behind a Form" at the beginning of this chapter for details.) If you've already started writing managed code, you can use the *Remove Code* button. Unlike managed code and the VSTA project that comes with it, script is edited in the Microsoft Script Editor as a single file. There is no compiling or building with script. Instead, it is interpreted by the scripting engine when the form is opened. The biggest differences between managed code and script include the following.

- The InfoPath 2007 OM does not carry over to scripting languages.
- No IntelliSense (code auto-complete) is available.
- There is no compiling, so code errors are not caught in design mode.
- Script errors reveal themselves when you fill out the form.

Let's look at a simple sample form that uses script behind the form with a custom task pane (which also includes its own script). As we mentioned, the custom task pane is disconnected from the form itself. Using form code, the task pane can become a more interactive component of the form. Our sample form demonstrates data traveling from the form to the task pane, as well as from the task pane to the form. While we don't incorporate any specific scenario in the sample, you can picture the form populating a Drop-Down List Box control with a list of articles from a secondary data source. A click on an article in the List Box (handled by the `Changed` event) could fill in a hidden field in the custom task pane HTML and post the data to a server to get the corresponding article details. If you wanted to really tie in the interaction between the task pane and the form, the task pane can directly call in to execute and pass parameters to a method in the form's script. Let's look at how the sample, shown in a preview window in Figure 15.16, works behind the scenes. (The sample form template is named CustomTaskPaneInterop.)

The first Text Box control, labeled *Field1* in Figure 15.16, is simply bound to a field with the same name in the main data source. Nothing is particularly special about this control. However, the *Set Task Pane Text Box* Button control is hooked up to run some script when clicked. The script essentially takes the value of the *Field1* Text Box and sets the text box in the custom task pane. The code in Listing 15.22 implements this functionality.

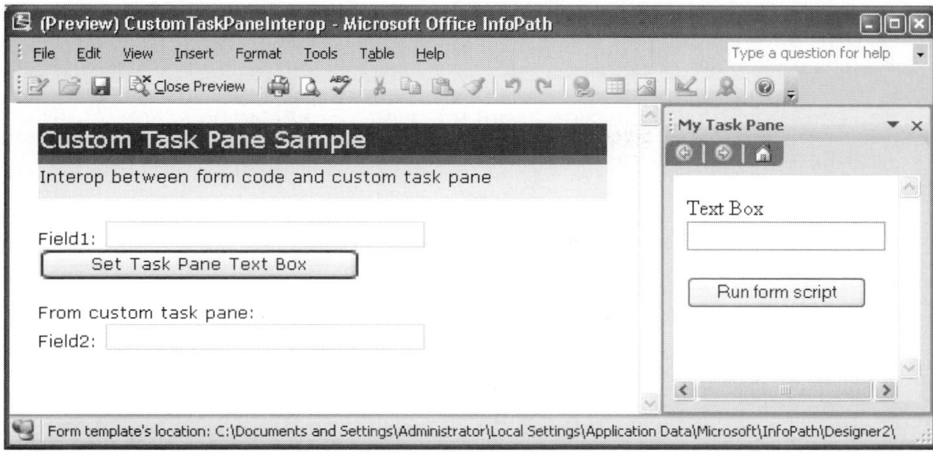

FIGURE 15.16: Filling out the CustomTaskPaneInterop sample form

> **NOTE** Setting Up Events in Script
>
> Sinking an event for a Button control, or any XML or form event for that matter, is the same process as when working with managed form code.

LISTING 15.22: Setting a Value in the Form's Data Source from the Custom Task Pane

```
function CTRL1_5::OnClick(eventObj)
{
    // get the task pane
    var taskPane = XDocument.View.Window.TaskPanes.Item(0);

    // get the html document
    var htmlDocument = taskPane.HTMLDocument;
    var textbox1 = htmlDocument.getElementById("textbox1");

    // get field1 from the main data source
    var myField1 =
        XDocument.DOM.selectSingleNode("/my:myFields/my:field1");

    // assign the value of my:field1 to the task pane text box
    textbox1.value = myField1.text;
}
```

Despite the inline comments, we'll take a closer look at the script to decipher exactly what it is doing. The first step to working with the custom task pane is to get the task pane object. You can always assume the `HTMLTaskPane` object is always the zeroth item in the `TaskPanes` collection.

HTMLTaskPane Object

You can find more information about the HTMLTaskPane object on MSDN (as referenced in the Appendix). Additionally, MSDN explains how to wait for the custom task pane to completely load (if it takes a long time loading a large page) and even call methods in the task pane HTML script from the form script.

The next step in the form script code is to get the HTMLDocument object. This returns a reference to Internet Explorer's HTMLDocument object, which implements the IHTMLDocument2 interface. We use this object in the next line of script to get the HTML element with ID textbox1. As you can probably guess, the HTMLDocument object exposes properties and methods that are not part of InfoPath.

TIP Useful HTMLTaskPane OM

The HTMLTaskPane object has some other useful properties and methods, including the Navigate method (accepts a URL), the HTMLWindow property (returns IHTMLWindow2), the Type property (enum XdTaskPaneType, which will always return 0, or xdTaskPane-HTML, for the custom task pane), and the Visible property. The HTML-Window property is level 3 OM, so it's restricted to fully trusted form templates.

The final steps include getting the data source node for my:field1 and assigning its value to the textbox1 HTML element in the custom task pane. The final result is that the text box in the task pane gets the value of the *Field1* Text Box control from the InfoPath form.

Programming Internet Explorer

We could write an entire book dedicated to programming Internet Explorer. Actually, we already did! A former publication by coauthor Scott Roberts, *Programming Internet Explorer 5*, was published in 1999 by Microsoft Press.

Let's now look at the HTML behind our custom task pane page, as shown in Listing 15.23. You can see the text box with `id=textbox1` that we're assigning in the script from Listing 15.22.

LISTING 15.23: Calling Form Script from the Custom Task Pane

```
<html>
<head>
    <title>Custom Task Pane</title>
</head>
<body>
Text Box <input id=textbox1 type=text><p>
<input type=button id=runscript onclick="CallFormCode();"
    value="Run form script">
</body>
<script>
function CallFormCode()
{
    window.external.Window.XDocument.UI.Alert(
    'Calling "SetField2" from the custom task pane.');
    window.external.Window.XDocument.Extension.SetField2(
    textbox1.value);
}
</script>
</html>
```

Now that we've witnessed InfoPath script code changing the HTML content in the task pane, let's see how the task pane can affect the form. In the task pane HTML shown in Listing 15.23, we can see the `CallFormCode` function that is executed when the user clicks the `runscript` button (visible as the *Run form script* button in the custom task pane shown earlier in Figure 15.16). The first thing that the `CallFormCode` function does is call into the InfoPath OM to show an alert dialog. If similar functionality existed in the form script instead of the task pane HTML script, the form script would simply be `XDocument.UI.Alert`. The next line of script uses the `XDocument.Extension` object to access functions in the form script. In this case, the task pane is calling function `SetField2` and passing the value of `textbox1` (the text box in the custom task pane).

> **NOTE Not All OM Is Available Via `window.external`**
>
> Not all InfoPath OM is directly callable through the `window.external.Window.XDocument` object. Access is denied to some parts of the OM for security reasons. A workaround is to use the `XDocument.Extension` object to call a function in the form script that can, in turn, call into any InfoPath OM property or method as allowed by the security level of the form.

Listing 15.24 shows how the `SetField2` function looks. Remember that this function lives in the form script. (Its simplicity may surprise you!)

Listing 15.24: Implementation of the `SetField2` Method in Form Script

```
function SetField2(val)
{
    var field2 =
        XDocument.DOM.selectSingleNode("/my:myFields/my:field2");
    field2.text = val;
}
```

This JScript code snippet is pretty simple. Despite its plainness, it shows off some of the more interesting capabilities of interacting with the task pane. Since there are no plans to further develop JScript (as well as VBScript) support in InfoPath, there's no guarantee that the script code you write today will work in the next wave of InfoPath programs. We can already see this today: Browser-enabled form templates with script code cannot be published to a server running Forms Services.

You can find more information about programming InfoPath with script languages in any resource that discusses InfoPath 2003 or SP1 scripting. We recommend that you visit MSDN for further reading and research.

Programming InfoPath . . . in Action!

By now you are familiar with the various form events, have a thorough working knowledge of XML events, and know about the single control event (`ButtonClick`). We've seen bits and pieces of the OM throughout this chapter, but we still haven't really used an overwhelming majority of what is available. Those OM objects that appear more often in form events have particularly evaded our focus. The best way to show commonly used InfoPath OM, as well as form events, is to tie everything into a real-world sample.

Forms Services

This sample form template is strictly tied to the full InfoPath object model. In Chapter 17, we'll discuss the shared InfoPath and Forms Services OM in a little more detail.

The MOI Consulting Request Form

For the remainder of this chapter, we'll demonstrate the MOI Consulting request form. This is one of the primary forms used by MOI Consulting to field requests from customers; as such, it is a complex form using a wide variety of InfoPath features including, of course, a generous amount of C# form code. Figure 15.17 shows the *Welcome* view. (This sample is named MoiConsultingRequest.)

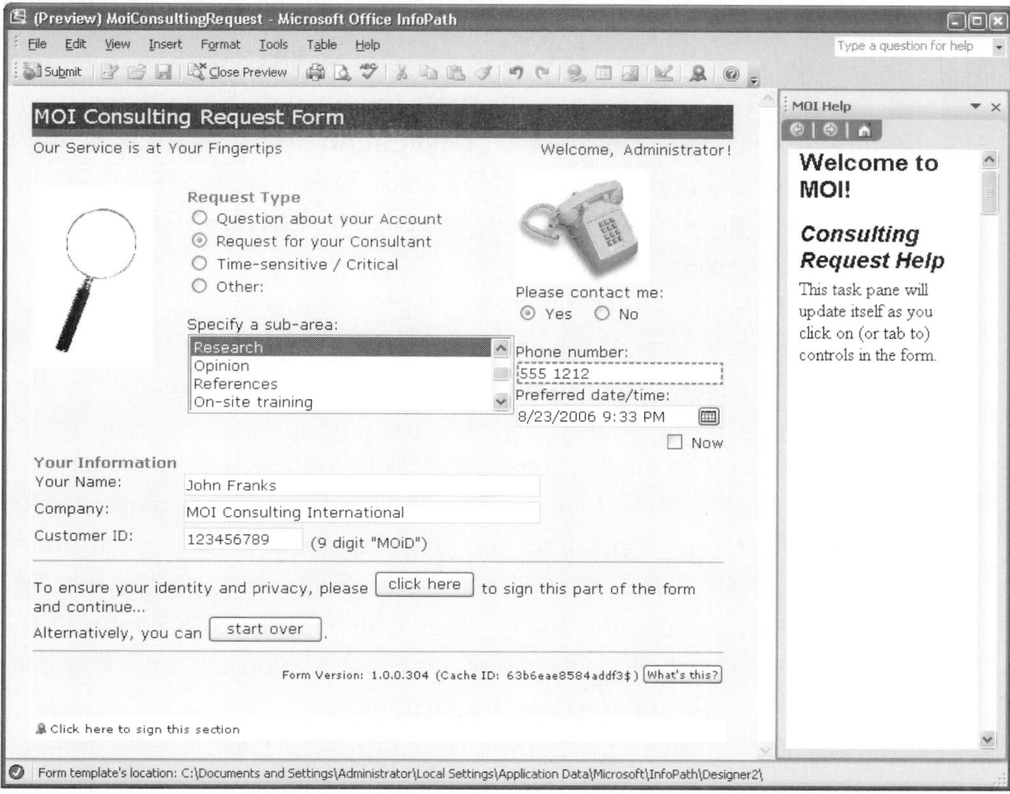

FIGURE 15.17: Welcome view of the MOI Consulting request form

Filling Out the MOI Consulting Request Form

Let's start learning about the request form by first filling it out. We'll look at the end-user experience and then, afterward, discuss how the form was designed. Since the request sample requires full trust to fill out, we can open the form template in design mode and then click *Preview.* (See Chapter 11 to read more about previewing fully trusted forms.) We'll soon see why the form needs to be fully trusted in the first place.

> **NOTE** Web Service Sample Dependency
>
> For this form to run as expected, the `GetSubAreas` Web service must exist at http://localhost:1369/MoiConsultingRequest/Service.asmx. Web service code is included in the sample files for this chapter as GetSubAreas. You can modify the service location of the sample form template by using the *Data Connections* dialog in design mode.

When the form opens, you may notice a lot of red validation rectangles and asterisks. The form doesn't contain as much validation as it appears to considering that, for example, the Option Button controls for selecting a request type are all bound to the same node. As a result, once you select one of those options, the red validation rectangles on all the Option Button controls in that group disappear.

Let's try toggling the various request type options. As you select different options, two things occur in the form: Items suddenly appear in the subarea List Box, and the custom task pane changes. The subarea List Box changes relative to the request type selected. The custom task pane, on the other hand, jumps to the "Request Type" help topic, which is constant for any request type. (The text shown in the custom task pane changes when you click on various controls in the view. As such, we'll leave it out of the immediate discussion to minimize distractions.) If you select the *Time sensitive/Critical* option, the dialog shown in Figure 15.18 confirms the high-priority request status. Clicking *Yes* in this dialog sets the *Please contact me* control to *Yes* and disables the *No* option.

When the *Please contact me* control is set to *Yes,* the *Phone number* and *Preferred date/time* fields are both required to be filled in. *Phone number* requires a particular format and will show a validation error dialog when it's not

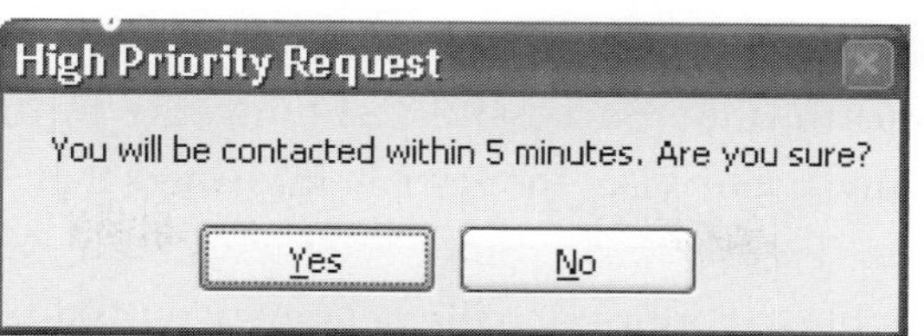

FIGURE 15.18: Dialog that results when the Time-sensitive/Critical request type is selected

satisfied. *Preferred date/time* accepts both a date (in 1/2/2007 format) as well as a time (e.g., 1:23 P.M.), with the default being two days from the current date/time. This field also has many validation constraints. For example, a date/time cannot be chosen in the past, nor can it be within five minutes of the current time. The *Now* Check Box control, situated below the *Preferred date/time* Date Picker, sets the date/time to five minutes from now while emphasizing and disabling the date/time value.

The next set of fields appears under the *Your Information* region. It includes *Your Name, Company,* and *Customer ID* Text Box controls. The only requirement for these fields is that they cannot be blank. Following the *Your Information* region are a couple of Button controls: *click here* and *start over.* Clicking *click here* first causes InfoPath to check for validation errors, but only in this view. If any errors are found, a dialog similar to the one shown in Figure 15.19 appears.

FIGURE 15.19: Dialog that appears when form errors exist in the current view

If there are no validation errors, the *Signatures* dialog appears, asking the user to sign the form data. Successfully signing the form switches to the *Request Details* view; otherwise, the user is informed that the data must be signed to continue (Figure 15.20). Since the views aren't listed on the *View* menu, it is impossible to continue to the next view without signing the form.

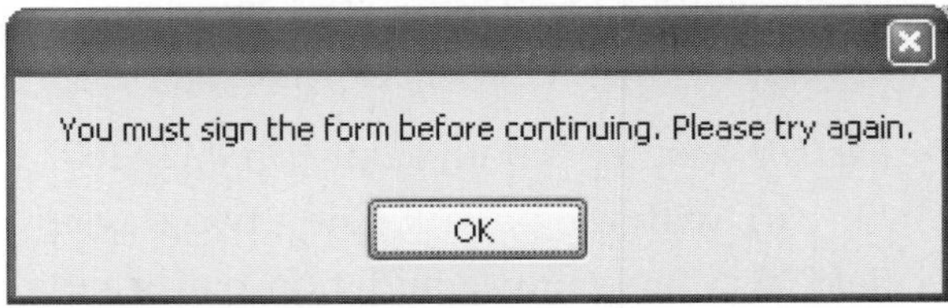

FIGURE 15.20: Informing the user that signing is required to continue

The *start over* Button control, as its name suggests, clears all form data so you can fill out the form from blank. We'll see this Button control again as we continue filling out the form and progress through its different views. When the current view isn't the *Welcome* default view, *start over* carries out the view switch automatically.

Toward the bottom of the form, we see some smaller font text, another Button control, and finally a *Click here to sign this section* link. The text reveals the form version and cache ID values of the form. The version corresponds to the version of the underlying form template. Cache ID, on the other hand, gives the folder name containing the extracted form template files kept on the user's machine. If someone encounters a problem when using the form, having the version readily available can help you determine whether the user is using the most recent template. The cache ID might be useful in rare cases. For example, if the form template cache somehow becomes corrupted, you could instruct the user to delete the cache directory. This forces InfoPath to fetch and cache a fresh copy of the original form template. The *What's this?* Button control simply shows a dialog telling the user that the form version and cache ID are helpful data points for diagnosing problems. Finally, the *Click here to sign this section* link is the standard (noncustomizable) entry point provided by InfoPath when a signable section exists in the view. Clicking it does not sign the form but instead opens the dialog shown in Figure 15.21.

FIGURE 15.21: Dialog that appears after using the Click here to sign this section link in the MOI request form

Once there are no errors, the *click here* Button control has been clicked, and signing has been successful, the view switches to *Request Details* and the task pane disappears (Figure 15.22).

The *Request Details* view contains two input fields: a Rich Text Box for the request description and a Bulleted List for additional details. The Bulleted List is included inside an Optional Section that does not exist by default. Clicking the *Add Additional Details* Button control inserts the Optional Section. Subsequent clicks on the same Button control insert new Bulleted List items. After completing this part of the form, we can click *Continue* to move forward. Clicking *Back,* however, takes you back to the *Welcome* view.

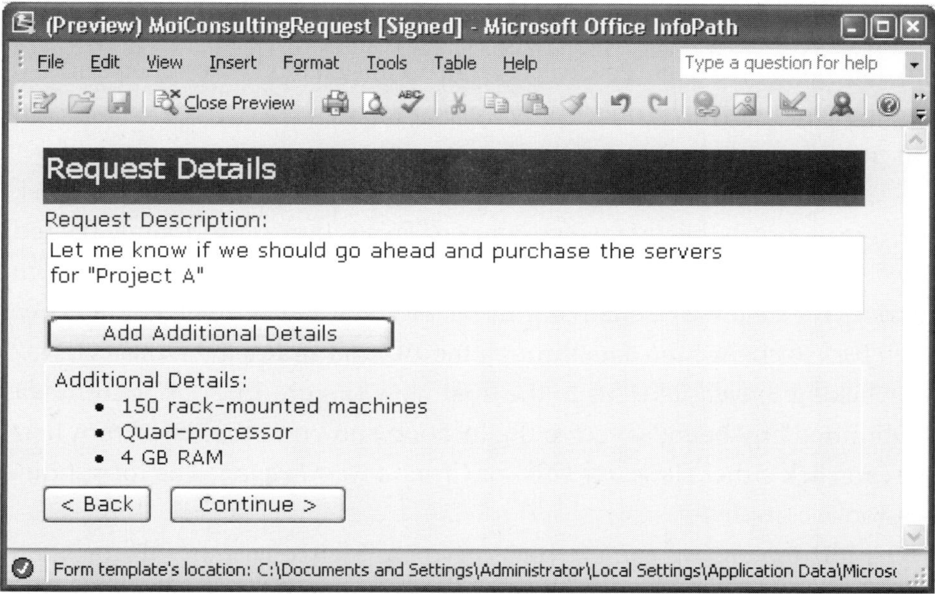

FIGURE 15.22: Request Details view of the MOI Consulting request form

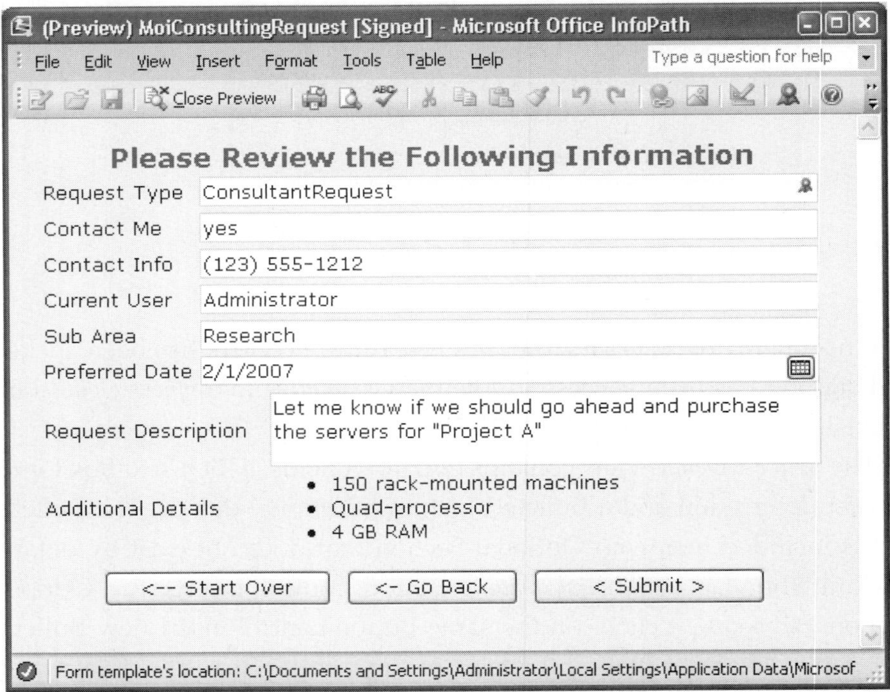

FIGURE 15.23: Confirm view of the MOI Consulting request form

No data on the *Welcome* view can change because it has been signed and, as a result, is read-only. The only options are to use the *click here* or *start over* Button controls.

After clicking *Continue* on the *Request Details* view, a dialog appears asking us to confirm the data we've entered. This is the (appropriately named) *Confirm* read-only view. Figure 15.23 shows the *Confirm* view, which summarizes the data we've entered thus far. Nothing can be changed unless we click *Back* to change the data through the *Welcome* or *Request Details* views.

Clicking *Submit* takes us to the final view (Figure 15.24). The form was "submitted" by being saved to the location shown in the link. From here, we can click either *Close this Form* or *Create a New Request*. The form-filling session is complete.

Unfortunately, we can't cover every possible scenario in this form. But we suggest that you spend some time playing with this sample and getting accustomed to its behavior. Having a better understanding of the details in

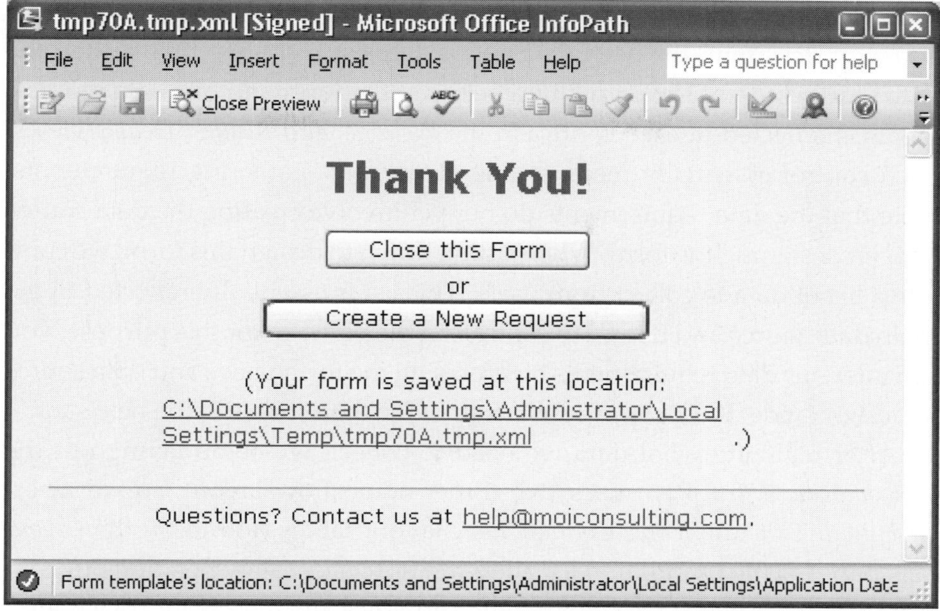

FIGURE 15.24: Thank You view of the MOI Consulting request form

this form will benefit you when we discuss its detailed design and underlying form code implementation.

Designing the MOI Consulting Request Form

Are you anxious to learn how to design this form template? For the remainder of the chapter, we'll go through many lines of form code as well as relevant thought processes used to develop and refine the form's behavior. We'll introduce new OM objects, including their properties and methods, as we encounter their use in the code behind the form.

> **NOTE** Taking a Scenario-Based Focus
>
> It's not our intention to cover the precise steps of designing this form. Our goal is to focus on the scenario and higher-level operatives that contribute to a complex template. Since this chapter is about programming InfoPath, we'll obviously dedicate more time to form code.

Gathering Requirements and Designing the Visual Layout

To begin designing the MOI Consulting request form, we first gather our data requirements. The correlation between the form and our data requirements is reflected in each control in the *Welcome* and *Request Details* views. Each control essentially maps to one of our data-gathering requirements. Note that the data requirements do not yet involve creating the data source or even designing the form. When sitting down to design this form, we compile a list of data to collect from users. This list is essentially reflected in the main data source and bound to controls in the view; so for this purpose, you can infer our data requirements by browsing the form views and data source in design mode. We'll create a first draft of the data source in the next step.

After realizing what data we need to collect, we begin laying out the *Welcome* view. InfoPath uses two-dimensional flow layout, so we insert *Table with Title* and *Three-Column Table* layout tables (found on the *Layout* task pane) as the foundation for allowing us to accurately position our content. Then we choose a color scheme to spice up the boring black-and-white form. However, we could choose the color scheme later since it can be applied at any time.

The next step in our design approach is to insert various controls from the *Controls* task pane to satisfy our data requirements. At this point, we don't necessarily care about the data source. Our goal is to visually lay out controls that correspond with our data requirements; we'll deal with the details of the data source later. As we insert controls, we try to logically group them within adjacent table cells. Some crafty work with the *Merge Cells* and *Split Cells* toolbar buttons as well as changes to the height and width of individual cells eventually give us a pleasing visual layout. To help identify controls, we type labels adjacent to them.

At this point you might realize that there are too many controls on the view, or that it's just too busy. This is where multiple views come in handy. We decide to use a wizard style of form (with *Next* and *Back* buttons) because the user should confirm the data entered across more than one view. Finally, we add a terminating view (*Thank You*) to make it very clear that the form had been filled out and submitted successfully.

Organizing the Data Source

Once we have hashed out the visual layout and end-user form-filling scenarios, the form looks like it's 90% ready for production. Truth be told, we have barely scratched the surface in terms of the total amount of work that needs to be done! The next step is determining the structure of the main data source and the names of its fields and groups. Since we've already created an unstructured version of the data source by dragging all of the controls into the view, this step is mostly a matter of moving and renaming fields. However, we need to consider some other data source changes to support the visual design of the form.

One such change in the data source, for example, is related to having a wizard-like form. We want the user to continue to the next view only if the current view is free of validation errors. (We'll see how to check for form errors in the "Adding Form Code" section later in this chapter.) The easiest way to achieve such behavior is to gather all data source fields and groups that you want to validate under a common parent. This is easiest to do by creating groups that map to the views in the form. In our case, only the *Welcome* and *Request Details* views collect data from users. Once we create groups that correspond with these views, we can move each node into its appropriate group.

Another task of data source editing involves renaming the generic node names (`field1`, `group1`, and so on) to something meaningful. Remember the text labels we created for the newly inserted controls when visually setting up the form? We've found it easiest to mimic those names in the field or group name with PascalCasing. Many benefits are realized by properly naming data source nodes. One benefit that we didn't realize until it "just worked" is displaying the raw field names to the user to identify specific errors (as shown earlier in Figure 15.19). Another big win is hooking up the context-sensitive help in the custom task pane. As you can see, naming your nodes properly can make form development easier when you add advanced form features.

> **TIP Modifying Other Data Source Properties**
>
> While you're renaming data source nodes, also consider whether they cannot be blank and whether the data type should be more restrictive. For data types such as integer, you can click the *Format* button to define a display format. If you're not sure, you can always change the properties later, but it's quicker to make changes in a single pass.

What if you want to use some data in your form but really don't have anywhere to put it (such as the form version or cache ID)? Consider adding that data node under the document element. In our case, let's add `FormVersion`, `CacheId`, and `SavedFileLocation` as attribute fields to the document element. These fields aren't edited by the user, yet they're set through form code and are displayed to the user.

> **WARNING Do Not Store Sensitive Information in the Main Data Source**
>
> Storing sensitive data in the main data source is not recommended, even if you are not displaying the fields in the view. Simply saving the form and viewing the content in a text editor (unless the form uses Information Rights Management) will reveal all form data in plain text.

This form also contains a data connection (and corresponding secondary data source) for populating the subarea List Box items. We can create a very simple Web service (whose code is available in the GetSubAreas sample file) that takes a request type as a parameter and returns an array of subarea strings. The data connection that we create to query this Web service does not have the *Automatically retrieve data when form is opened* checkbox checked. This is because we're going to set the parameter value and perform the query manually in form code.

Finally, we want to make sure that the data entered by the user on the *Welcome* view is digitally signed for proof that this person, indeed, filled out the request. We enable signing the `Welcome` group by inserting it into the view as a Section control, essentially dragging the entire view (except for the Table with Title at the top) into the Section, and turning on the option that allows the Section to be signed. Alternatively, we could have added the `Welcome` group to the set of signable data in the *Form Options* dialog. However, we want the user to get visual feedback that the data is digitally signed with his or her own certificate. The fallout from showing the digital signature in the view leads to having the *Click here to sign this section* link available for users to click. Since we want to check for form errors in the *Welcome* view before a user can sign the data and switch to the *Request Details* view, we want to block this link from doing any signing. We'll see how to handle this in the "Adding Form Code" section.

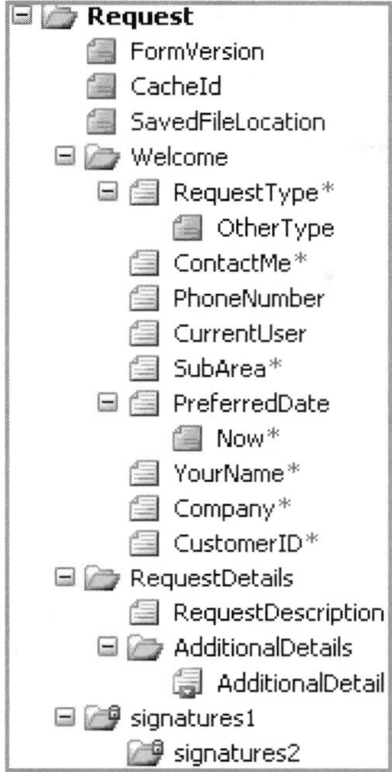

FIGURE 15.25: Main data source for the MOI Consulting request form template

Figure 15.25 shows the main data source for the MOI Consulting request form template.

Adding Logic without Code

The next major step after getting most of the data source in place is to add logic to our form. We could implement all of our form's logic by just writing code, but that's not the best approach. You might not expect us to recommend this (especially in this chapter), but you should consider using rules before form code when adding logic. Form code not only takes longer for you to implement but also is more difficult to maintain. It is prone to errors and security flaws, despite how good we think we are at programming. Rules, on the other hand, can be maintained by almost anyone and have been well tested for use in countless situations. Moreover, rules are declaratively defined as part of the form definition, so there is neither code to compile nor an assembly to build.

Here is a sampling of the rules used in the MOI Consulting request form.

- When `ContactMe` is changed, set `Now` to `false`.
- When `Now` is checked, set `PreferredDate` to `now()` plus five minutes.
- When `RequestType` is `SensitiveCritical`, set `ContactMe` to `yes`.
- Clicking the *What's this?* Button control on the *Welcome* view shows a dialog box message.
- Clicking the *Next* or *Back* Button controls takes the user to the next view or the previous view, respectively.

As you can see, rules define an "if X then do Y" behavior that can easily replace a few lines of form code. Rules can also have multiple conditions and multiple actions that may be tedious to implement using code. Writing the code isn't the only burden—there's also the need to handle special cases, for example, whether a field node exists or is just empty. If you're skeptical that rules save time and energy, we leave it as an exercise for you to reimplement all rules as form code in the MOI request form.

More logic that we can't forget to add to our form involves data validation and conditional formatting. Using InfoPath's built-in pattern builder to define data validation constraints basically defeats the purpose of doing any basic regular expression matching in the `Validating` event handler. We also use extensive data validation on the `PreferredDate` field; errors will be reported under any of these conditions:

- If `ContactMe` is `yes` and `PreferredDate` is blank
- If `PreferredDate` is within an hour of now and `RequestType` is not `SensitiveCritical` and `ContactMe` is `yes`
- If `PreferredDate` is less than five minutes from now and `ContactMe` is `yes`

Conditional formatting in this sample form makes controls read-only or hidden under certain conditions in the data. For example, we use conditional formatting to hide the `OtherType` Text Box when `RequestType` is not set to `Other`. Condition disabling is used for both the *Please contact me* (bound to field `ContactMe`) Option Button controls as well as the `PhoneNumber` and `PreferredDate` fields under certain circumstances. We didn't conditionally disable the *click here* Button control, but we could have done so by checking some field (perhaps `enableClickHere`) in the data source that does not exist in the view. In the right circumstances, we could set this field to a specific value through form code, which would allow the user to click the Button control. We won't take this approach because we believe that having a disabled control would frustrate users. Keeping the Button control enabled might tempt some users to click it too early, but we offer feedback (in this case) through data validation. That's where we show the error dialog shown earlier in Figure 15.19.

Adding Form Code

When making the decision to add code, it shouldn't only be a question of whether you already tried using rules and data validation. You should also be sure to solidify names and the structure of the data source, as we mentioned earlier. As we start to add form code, we should have already convinced ourselves that between rules and data validation we still cannot get the desired form behavior. Although this is the guidance we give to our readers, we do not completely adhere to this practice in the MOI request form. We'll call out when we're violating our own principles, but keep in mind that it's only to show the breadth of writing form code with the InfoPath OM.

Naming Your Nodes and Buttons Besides assigning real names to data source fields and groups, giving real ID values to all Button controls (in the *Button Properties* dialog) is worth the small time investment. This seemingly tedious task is important, if, of course, you want your form code to be readable and maintainable! But how do data source names, structure, and Button ID values correlate with code behind the form? Take a look at our `InternalStartup` method in Listing 15.25 and see for yourself.

Without proper field and group names in the data source, the XPath expressions used for hooking up any XML events would be meaningless. Moreover, the event handler method names are also based on the nodes whose events they're sinking. It's possible to change the names of nodes in the data source after creating XML event handlers, but InfoPath will update only the XPath expression. The method name does not change unless you do it manually. Furthermore, any code you already wrote that depends on a

Listing 15.25: `InternalStartup` **Definition for the MOI Consulting Request Form Template**

```
public void InternalStartup()
{
    EventManager.XmlEvents[
        "/my:Request/my:Welcome/my:RequestType"].Changing +=
            new XmlChangingEventHandler(RequestType_Changing);
    EventManager.FormEvents.Loading +=
        new LoadingEventHandler(FormEvents_Loading);
    ((ButtonEvent)EventManager.ControlEvents["Start_Over"]).Clicked +=
        new ClickedEventHandler(Start_Over_Clicked);
    ((ButtonEvent)EventManager.ControlEvents[
        "click_here_to_sign"]).Clicked +=
            new ClickedEventHandler(click_here_to_sign_Clicked);
    EventManager.FormEvents.ContextChanged +=
        new ContextChangedEventHandler(FormEvents_ContextChanged);
    EventManager.XmlEvents[
        "/my:Request/my:Welcome/my:RequestType"].Changed +=
            new XmlChangedEventHandler(RequestType_Changed);
    EventManager.FormEvents.ViewSwitched +=
        new ViewSwitchedEventHandler(FormEvents_ViewSwitched);
    ((ButtonEvent)EventManager.ControlEvents[
        "Add_Additional_Details"]).Clicked +=
            new ClickedEventHandler(Add_Additional_Details_Clicked);
    EventManager.FormEvents.Submit +=
        new SubmitEventHandler(FormEvents_Submit);
    EventManager.FormEvents.Sign +=
        new SignEventHandler(FormEvents_Sign);
}
```

particular data source structure (e.g., using `XPathNavigator` objects to select nodes) could break. It's easy to see that getting your data source right the first time saves time and problems in the long run!

Unlike XPath expressions that automatically update when the data source changes, Button ID values do not enjoy the same luxury. If the Button ID is changed when a `Clicked` event handler is already set up, that particular Button control will no longer fire the event handler. With default Button IDs such as `CTRL1_5` (and whatever other senseless IDs Button controls can have), looking at a method in form code such as `CTRL1_5_Clicked` is frustrating. Furthermore, if your form has many Button controls, it's not easy to determine which ID maps to a given Button. The best way to understand which `Clicked` event handlers listen to which Button controls is to give each

Button's ID value a meaningful name. We visit each Button's properties dialog in the MOI request form, copy the display label, paste it into the ID box, and then replace spaces with underscore characters. (A Button control ID must begin with a letter and contain only alphanumeric characters and underscores.) This practice, as you can see in Listing 15.25, makes the `Clicked` event handler methods easily recognizable.

Showing a Custom Dialog with Buttons One of the first form behaviors you may have noticed is a confirmation dialog (shown earlier in Figure 15.18) that appears when you select the *Time-sensitive/Critical* request type. The code that implements this behavior (Listing 15.26) shouldn't introduce anything new in terms of the `Changing` XML event. However, it does show how to use the `MessageBox.Show` static method to show buttons and get back the user's selection. The Rules feature can only show a dialog with an *OK* button. In this case, we want user feedback, which requires the use of form code.

LISTING 15.26: Using `MessageBox.Show` to Get User Feedback

```
public void RequestType_Changing(object sender, XmlChangingEventArgs e)
{
    if (e.NewValue == "SensitiveCritical"
       && e.Operation == XmlOperation.ValueChange)
    {
       DialogResult result = MessageBox.Show(
          "You will be contacted within 5 minutes. Are you sure?",
          "High Priority Request", MessageBoxButtons.YesNo);
       if (result != DialogResult.Yes)
          e.CancelableArgs.Cancel = true;
    }
}
```

Showing Read-Only Properties from the OM Another interesting form feature you may have noticed is the use of dynamic, read-only data in parts of the view. Specifically, we show the user name in the upper right, and in the lower right we show the form version and, in parentheses, the cache ID (refer back to Figure 15.17). How did we get this data? It comes straight from various InfoPath OM properties. But to show this data in the view, we need to set values of fields in the data source that are bound to Expression Box controls. We could use read-only Text Box controls, but Text Box controls have an opaque white background, which makes them stand out (and beg to be filled out) against the soft peach view background. Since these controls are not to be filled out by the user yet still need to exist in the data source, we add `FormVersion` and `CacheId` nodes under the document element as attribute fields and put `CurrentUser` within the `Welcome` group as an element field. (Refer back to Figure 15.25 for the main *Data Source* task pane.)

Since setting the `FormVersion`, `CacheId`, and `CurrentUser` fields is a one-time occurrence when the form opens, the code seems to fit nicely in the `Loading` event. We also have some other code that must be run either when the form first opens or during other one-time operations. The code that needs to run when the form opens does a check to see if the form that's opening is new from the template or an existing .xml file. In the MOI request form, we don't want existing forms to be reopened. In fact, let's disable the *Save* and *Save As* options (through the *Open and Save* category of the *Form Options* dialog) to ensure that the form can't be saved.

A Form to Be Filled Out in One Sitting Why do we go through the trouble to discourage saving and prevent opening an existing form? The request form isn't meant to be saved. Its purpose is to allow a user to quickly fill out one request during a single sitting. We can check to see whether the form is new or not by looking at the `New` property. In the form code shown in Listing 15.27, if the form is not new (i.e., it is an existing saved form— and who knows how the user got it?), we cancel the `Loading` event. Similar to canceling the `Changing` event, which we discussed earlier in this chapter, canceling the `Loading` event forces InfoPath to fail loading the form.

> **NOTE** **`UserName` versus `LoginName`**
>
> Getting the user's name with `Application.User.UserName` returns the Active Directory (AD) display name. If AD is unavailable, the nondomain portion of the login name is returned. Alternatively, `Application.User.LoginName` always returns the `DOMAIN\LoginName` identity of the user. Note that using `Application.User.LoginName` requires a fully trusted form.

LISTING 15.27: The `Loading` Event Handler for the MOI Consulting Request Form

```
const string _startOverOuterXml = "startOverOuterXml";
const string _startOverGetSubAreas = "startOverGetSubAreas";
/* . . . */
public void FormEvents_Loading(object sender, LoadingEventArgs e)
{
    // Only allow new forms (i.e., no saved forms can be opened).
    // We could add more logic to check the user role or specific data
    // in the form before rejecting it.
    if (!this.New)
    {
        e.CancelableArgs.Cancel = true;
        e.CancelableArgs.Message = "I'm sorry, you must fill out a "
            + " new request. Previous requests cannot be honored.";
        return;
    }

    XPathNavigator root = MainDataSource.CreateNavigator();
    XPathNavigator user = root.SelectSingleNode(
        "/my:Request/my:Welcome/my:CurrentUser", NamespaceManager);
    user.SetValue(Application.User.UserName);
    XPathNavigator uri = root.SelectSingleNode(
        "/my:Request/@my:CacheId", NamespaceManager);
    uri.SetValue(this.Template.CacheId);

    XPathNavigator version = root.SelectSingleNode(
        "/my:Request/@my:FormVersion", NamespaceManager);
    version.SetValue(this.Template.Version);

    // Cache the Entire data source for the "Start Over" feature.
    // The StartOverOuterXml property will return this saved data.
    XPathNavigator docElem = root.SelectSingleNode("*");
    FormState.Add(_startOverOuterXml, docElem.OuterXml);

    // Cache secondary data source.
    XPathNavigator getSubAreasRoot =
        DataSources["GetSubAreas"].CreateNavigator();
    XPathNavigator getSubAreasDomElem =
        getSubAreasRoot.SelectSingleNode("*");
    FormState.Add(_startOverGetSubAreas, getSubAreasDomElem.OuterXml);

    // Set the default view.
    ViewInfos.Initial = ViewInfos["Welcome"];
}
```

FIGURE 15.26: Error dialog that appears when user attempts to open an existing MOI request form

If a user tries to open an existing form, an error dialog appears (Figure 15.26), and then InfoPath closes the form-filling session.

"Start Over" Feature and Setting a Default View Another nifty form feature in this form is the ability to start over when filling out the form. You can find Button controls labeled *start over* or *Create a New Request* in three of the four views. All of these Button controls call into the same clicked event handler. But before we look at that particular event handler, we need to first consider a couple other one-time operations that are included in the `Loading` event. The comments in Listing 15.27 (labeled with comments `Cache the Entire data source for the "Start Over" feature` and `Cache secondary data source`) show caching of both the main and `GetSubAreas` data sources. We store the data by getting the document element's outer XML and saving it in the `FormState` object. Without doing these prerequisites, the "start over" feature would not work. This will become clearer in a moment as we see the code behind starting over. The last line in the `Loading` event sets the view that appears when the form opens. Despite setting the *Welcome* view as the default in design mode, this setting is a little redundant. But since calling the `SwitchView` method (a member of `ViewInfos`) is not supported and will throw an exception in the context of the `Loading` event, it's helpful to know how to set a default view as the form opens. (Calling `SwitchView` within the `Merge` form event is also disallowed.)

> **TIP Setting the Default View Dynamically**
>
> You could add additional logic (e.g., using `if` statements) to go to a specific view based on criteria in the form (such as a field value) or other factors (such as the user's name or role).

The "start again" feature we added to our form came out of our feeling that it's easier to start over by clicking a button than it is to manually close and reopen a form. To facilitate starting again, we should think about the various states of the form at the time it's invoked.

- We can be on any view.
- There could be validation errors.
- The form could be blank to begin with.
- The data may be digitally signed.

Since we could be on any view, starting again means we should go back to the *Welcome* view. As a result, the first OM call is to `SwitchView`. If we're already on the *Welcome* view, this code has no effect. So there's no need to check what view you're on with `this.CurrentView` before switching. We threw the next two bullet points regarding validation errors and a blank form as curve balls! These form states do not affect the ability for our "start again" code to perform as expected. Neither validation errors nor the blank form (which still has validation errors) hinders us in modifying the data source.

When we first wrote the `Start_Over_Clicked` Button handler (see Listing 15.28), we didn't check to see if the form was digitally signed. If the form is signed, clearing the main data source fails. Remember that a signed data block is always read-only after a signature is applied. Seeing as it could be a potential security issue if form code were allowed to remove a signature, we cannot do it programmatically. To accommodate this scenario, we still switch to the *Welcome* view but bail out by asking the user to manually remove the signature and try again. That's exactly what we do within the first `if` statement in Listing 15.28.

If the form isn't digitally signed, we have the green light for clearing the data sources. Remember how we cached the main and secondary data sources in the `Loading` event? Specifically, we took the document element outer XML strings and added them to the `FormState` object. As you can see in Listing 15.28, we call `ReplaceSelf` on the document element node (of both the main and `GetSubAreas` data sources) and pass our cached copy of the outer XML. Since our cached copies of the data sources are snapshots of the initial form's data sources, we can rest assured that they're valid according to the schema and that the form will appear similar to a newly created form. The code in Listing 15.29 supports the `Start_Over_Clicked` method by exposing our `FormState` data wrapped in properties for consistent data access.

LISTING 15.28: Implementation of the Start Over Button Click Event

```
public void Start_Over_Clicked(object sender, ClickedEventArgs e)
{
    // Every button ID called "Start_Over" calls into this handler
    ViewInfos.SwitchView("Welcome");

    // Tell the user to remove his or her digital signature
    if (this.Signed)
    {
        MessageBox.Show("Cannot start over because the form "
            + "data is signed. Please go to the Digital Signatures "
            + "dialog and remove your signature. Then click this "
            + "button again to continue.");
        return;
    }

    // Clear the main data source
    XPathNavigator docElem =
        MainDataSource.CreateNavigator().SelectSingleNode("*");
    docElem.ReplaceSelf(StartOverOuterXml);

    // Clear any secondary data sources
    XPathNavigator subAreasRoot =
        DataSources["GetSubAreas"].CreateNavigator();
    XPathNavigator subDocElem = subAreasRoot.SelectSingleNode("*");
    subDocElem.ReplaceSelf(StartOverGetSubAreas);
}
```

> **NOTE Using `FormState` to Persist Session Data**
>
> To recall an earlier discussion in this chapter, the `FormState` object holds name-value pairs of any serializable types. Its purpose is to maintain state in form code from the time a specific form is opened for filling until it is closed. The `Loading` event is well suited for initializing `FormState` objects.

LISTING 15.29: Persisting the Default State of XML for Main and Secondary Data Sources

```
const string _startOverOuterXml = "startOverOuterXml";
const string _startOverGetSubAreas = "startOverGetSubAreas";
/* ... */
private string StartOverOuterXml
{
    get
```

```
    {
        if (FormState.Contains(_startOverOuterXml))
            return FormState[_startOverOuterXml] as string;
        throw new Exception(
            "Form load did not load properly before Starting Over!");
    }
}

private string StartOverGetSubAreas
{
    get
    {
        if (FormState.Contains(_startOverGetSubAreas))
            return FormState[_startOverGetSubAreas] as string;
        throw new Exception(
            "Form load did not load properly before Starting Over!");
    }
}
```

Checking for Errors and Adding a Digital Signature Now that we've seen how the form can start over, we should learn about the *click here* Button control. As its surrounding text hints, clicking this Button will "sign this part of the form and continue." But that's not all. Earlier we made it a requirement that before the user can sign and switch to the next view, there must be no pending form errors within the `Welcome` group. That means all required or invalid fields with validation errors in the *Welcome* view must be fixed. To determine whether a form error exists on an item within the `Welcome` group, we use the `XPathNavigator IsDescendent` method. As you'll see in the code, we ask the `Welcome` node whether a specific node is a descendent; if so, we've found a node of interest. If errors are found, we show a dialog listing the exact errors with a corresponding corrective action. Figure 15.27 shows the dialog (which also

FIGURE 15.27: Dialog for clearly presenting to the user any form errors

appeared earlier as Figure 15.19). Generating such a detailed dialog is very easy. But ultimately, to make the dialog helpful for users, you must rely on field names that closely resemble any text labels adjacent to the corresponding controls.

As you look at the code snippet shown in Listing 15.30, you'll see that we first check whether the form data is signed. This will be true, by the way, if the form is partially or wholly signed. If signing has already occurred, we don't need to check for form errors. For signing to occur in the first place, we must have already validated that there are no errors through this same code path! Since we're also sinking and special-casing the `Signing` event (as you'll soon see), there's no other way for the form to get signed.

LISTING 15.30: Code for the Button That Starts Validation on the Default View of the MOI Consulting Request Form

```
public void click_here_to_sign_Clicked(
    object sender, ClickedEventArgs e)
{
     if (this.Signed)
     {
          ViewInfos.SwitchView("RequestDetails");
          return;
     }

     // 1. Check for errors
     XPathNavigator root = MainDataSource.CreateNavigator();
     XPathNavigator welcome = root.SelectSingleNode(
          "/my:Request/my:Welcome", NamespaceManager);

     string welcomeErrors = string.Empty;
     foreach (FormError error in Errors)
     {
          // Is this error under the "Welcome" group?
          if (welcome.IsDescendant(error.Site))
               welcomeErrors += error.Site.LocalName + ": "
                    + error.Message + System.Environment.NewLine;
     }

     // If there are errors, report them and stop
     if (!string.IsNullOrEmpty(welcomeErrors))
     {
          MessageBox.Show("Please fix these errors: "
               + System.Environment.NewLine + System.Environment.NewLine
               + welcomeErrors, "Please Fill or Fix Some Data");
          return;
     }

     // Tell the Signed event it's okay to allow signing
     SigningAllowed = true;
```

```
    // Continue with signing
    foreach (SignedDataBlock sig in SignedDataBlocks)
        // Sign only this block
        if (sig.XPath.Expression.EndsWith("my:Welcome"))
        {
            // Calling Sign requires a full trust form
            sig.Sign();

            // Was it actually signed or canceled?
            if (sig.Signatures.Count > 0)
                ViewInfos.SwitchView("RequestDetails");
            else
                MessageBox.Show("You must sign the form "
                    + "before continuing. Please try again.");
            break;
        }
    SigningAllowed = false;
}
```

The code for going through errors is quite easy. First, the `FormErrorsCollection` object is exposed by the `this.Errors` (or just `Errors`) property. Since `FormErrorsCollection` inherits from the `ICollection` interface, iterating through each `FormError` object is performed by a `foreach` loop. Of the properties on the `FormError` object, the most interesting to us are `Site` (yielding the `XPathNavigator` of the node with the error) and `Message`. `Error` will always provides a nonempty short error message, while `MessageDetails` might be more verbose. `MessageDetails` is often empty unless a specific data validation constraint provides details. In this sample, `MessageDetails` is empty for all errors except for a few that we defined through InfoPath design mode, such as the `PhoneNumber` and `PreferredDate` fields. To detect whether there are any errors to show, we start with an empty `welcomeErrors` string. If it's still empty after looping through any form errors, the code skips over showing a dialog because there are no errors.

A moment ago, we said that we're sinking the `Signing` event to programmatically determine when signing is permitted. Essentially, we want the code from Listing 15.30 (but nothing else) to initiate signing the form. Other ways to add a signature include clicking the *Click here to sign this section* link in the view as well as using the *Digital Signatures* dialog accessed from the *Tools* menu. No matter how signing is instigated, the `Signing` event is always fired, which takes over the entire signing process. For our scenario to work properly, we need to essentially block all attempts to sign the form unless the *click here* Button control is the initiator. The `SigningAllowed` Boolean property facilitates our scenario by allowing signing in the `Signing` event only when the property is set to `true`. We'll look at the `Signing` event shortly.

To sign the `Welcome` group in the form, the code iterates through the `SignedDataBlocks` collection. We look for the signed data block whose XPath ends with `my:Welcome` for brevity. The full XPath is `/my:Request/my:Welcome`. Calling the `Sign` method tells InfoPath to show the signing dialog for this specific signed data block. It is not possible to block this dialog and silently sign the form. This is for security reasons. Despite our call to `Sign`, it's up to the user to follow through with signing. Since the dialog could be closed or canceled without signing, the code must check whether a signature really exists. To perform this check, we use the `Count` property of the `Signatures` object. Instead, since there is only one signature, we could have used the `this.Signed` property as we did earlier in this method.

WARNING **Determine Which Data Block Is Signed**

The `this.Signed` property will return `true` if the form has a signature. If you have multiple signed data blocks, the `Count` property on the `Signatures` object of the `SignedDataBlock` itself is sure evidence that the specific block in question was signed.

The `Signing` event is fired immediately before the *Signatures* dialog, which signs the data, appears. We mentioned before that we need to block signing unless the user clicks the *click here* Button control. Since we just reviewed the `click_here_to_sign_Clicked` event handler sinking that Button control, we can see how to arrange this. Let's also look at the `SigningAllowed` property that maintains its Boolean status through the `FormState` object. Listing 15.31 shows the code from the sample form template.

NOTE **`Signing` Event Requires Full Trust**

Only fully trusted forms can sink the `Signing` event. As a result, you'll need to set the form template's security level to full trust.

LISTING 15.31: Code for the `Sign` Form Event

```
const string _signingAllowed = "signingAllowed";
/* . . . */
private bool SigningAllowed
{
    get
    {
        if (FormState.Contains(_signingAllowed))
            return (bool)FormState[_signingAllowed];
        return false;
    }
    set
    {
        if (!FormState.Contains(_signingAllowed))
            FormState.Add(_signingAllowed, value);
        else
            FormState[_signingAllowed] = value;
    }
}
/* . . . */
public void FormEvents_Sign(object sender, SignEventArgs e)
{
    if (SigningAllowed)
    {
        Signature thisSignature =
            e.SignedDataBlock.Signatures.CreateSignature();
        thisSignature.Sign();
        e.SignatureWizard = true;
    }
    else
    {
        e.SignatureWizard = false;
        MessageBox.Show("Please use the 'click here' "
            + "button (in the form) to proceed.");
        return;
    }
}
```

If the `SigningAllowed` property is `true`, we first create a new signature by using the `CreateSignature()` method of the `Signatures` object (which returns a `SignatureCollection`). Calling `Sign` on the newly created `Signature` shows the *Signatures* dialog, which the user can fill out. The code won't continue past `Sign` until the dialog is dismissed. In the case when the user tries to sign the form in an alternate way (such as using the *Digital Signatures* dialog), we show a dialog explaining how our form expects the user to sign the form data. Whether or not the user applied a signature or just closed the dialog is handled by the Button `Clicked` event handler we looked at in Listing 15.30.

Context-Sensitive Help in the Custom Task Pane Another major feature in the MOI request form is the context-sensitive help in the custom task pane. Before we see how the task pane is involved in the code, it's important to learn about the underlying mechanism that causes the task pane to change. The `ContextChanged` event is a form event fired whenever XML context in the current view is changed. The "context" portion of "XML context" is determined by what control in the view has focus. The "XML" part is the specific data source field or group bound to that control. So whenever control focus changes from control A to B, XML context changes if and only if controls A and B are bound to different data source nodes.

To give a concrete example, let's look at the MOI request form. As you click through the Option Button controls for the request type, you'll notice that the task pane does not change; it just stays on the "Request Type" help topic. Even though we're clicking on different controls, the data source (`RequestType`) behind those controls is the same. Now try clicking on any other control in the view; as expected, the control in which you clicked is not bound to `RequestType`, and the task pane changes its content.

> **WARNING** `Context Changed` **Event Behavior**
>
> The `ContextChanged` event is called for all sorts of contexts that you may not expect. For example, clicking in white space in the view (not on a control) results in the document element getting context! We recommend that you try repeating controls as well. The best way to see when the event is called is to put this code into the `Context Changed` event handler: `MessageBox.Show(e.Context.Name);`.

Now that we understand how the `ContextChanged` event works, let's apply it to our context-sensitive help system in the task pane. For starters, the task pane content is a single HTML file authored in Word. We used Word's Bookmarks feature to place bookmarks throughout the document. These bookmarks are simply HTML anchor tags with unique names. We're leveraging Internet Explorer's ability to jump to an anchor on an HTML page by using the # character at the end of the URL, followed by the anchor's name. Thanks to the effort we gave when properly naming the fields and groups in the data source, it's really easy to hook up the `ContextChanged` event handler to the task pane. Assuming that we use the field and group names (such as `RequestType` for the "Request Type" help topic) to bookmark content in the HTML file, the anchor name is given automatically in the `ContextChanged` event! See the implementation of the `ContextChanged` form event in Listing 15.32.

> **NOTE Custom Task Pane HTML**
>
> The HTML file included in the sample includes only simple text. InfoPath does not impose any artificial boundaries in terms of the complexity of the HTML file. A lightweight HTML file was used for the sake of this sample.

> **TIP Custom Task Pane Navigation and Pane Visibility**
>
> We use an optimization to skip navigation if the task pane is not visible. It is not a requirement to have a visible task pane to perform navigation.

LISTING 15.32: Wiring Up the `ContextChanged` Form Event for Context-Sensitive Help in the Task Pane

```
public void FormEvents_ContextChanged(object sender,
ContextChangedEventArgs e)
{
    if (e.ChangeType == "ContextNode")
    {
        HtmlTaskPane htmlTaskPane =
            (HtmlTaskPane)this.TaskPanes[TaskPaneType.Html];
        if (htmlTaskPane.Visible)
            htmlTaskPane.Navigate("MoiConsultingRequest.htm#"
                + e.Context.LocalName);
        return;
    }
}
```

Before we move on to the *Request Details* view that appears after the user clicks the *click here* Button control, let's talk about another data-rich feature you may have noticed. Selecting an Option Button in the *Request Type* region of the form automatically populates the subarea List Box. This happens via a `Changed` event handler on the `RequestType` field. We chose the `Changed` event for several reasons. First, the data in the `RequestType` field has been confirmed because it made it past the `Changing` and `Validating` XML events. Second, even though we're not doing it, the main data source can be modified. This gives us flexibility in the future if we decide to add functionality that could change other data in the form. In this particular case with the `RequestType` field, we also have a `Changing` event. (We showed this `Changing` event toward the beginning of explaining the MOI request sample form.) In the case where the `Changing` event rejects the user's selection (which is a possibility if he or she chooses the *Time-sensitive/Critical* option), our `Changed` event is never called. Listing 15.33 shows the `Changed` event handler.

> **NOTE** **Querying Via a Rule Instead of Form Code**
>
> In reality, we would have chosen to use a rule on the `RequestType` node. It would set the `requestType` query parameter on the secondary data source (using the *Set a Field's Value* action); then query the Web service connection. We wrote this code to demonstrate form code involving data connections, as well as some other OM properties and methods.

LISTING 15.33: Dynamically Populating the `RequestType` List Box Using a Data Connection

```
public void RequestType_Changed (object sender, XmlEventArgs e)
{
    // Process value changes only for the RequestType field.
    // This code also should not run when filling the OtherType field.
    if (e.UndoRedo
        || e.Operation != XmlOperation.ValueChange
        || e.Site.Name != ((XPathNavigator)sender).Name)
        {
            return;
        }

    // Request Type changed, get an updated list of Sub Areas
    DataSource getSubAreasDS = DataSources["GetSubAreas"];
    // We could have also used DataConnections["GetSubAreas"], below
    WebServiceConnection getSubAreasWSC =
        (WebServiceConnection)getSubAreasDS.QueryConnection;
```

```
    // Get the navigator for the GetSubAreas secondary data source
    XPathNavigator getSubAreasNav = getSubAreasDS.CreateNavigator();
    // Get the requestType param that will be sent to the Web service
    XPathNavigator requestTypeNav = getSubAreasNav.SelectSingleNode(
        + "/dfs:myFields/dfs:queryFields/tns:GetSubAreas"
        + "/tns:requestType", NamespaceManager);
    // Get the Request Type from the main data source
    requestTypeNav.SetValue(e.NewValue);

    // Web service timeout is 30s, increase to 60 for slow connections
    getSubAreasWSC.Timeout = 60;
    // Create a new navigator to capture errors, if any
    XmlDocument errorsXmlDoc = new XmlDocument();
    XPathNavigator errorsNav = errorsXmlDoc.CreateNavigator();
    try
    {
        // Query the Web service
        getSubAreasWSC.Execute(
            null /*input*/, null /*output*/, errorsNav /*errors*/);
    }
    // Silently fail and we'll show the message box in a moment.
    // If we didn't do this, InfoPath would show the exception.
    catch (Exception) { }

    if (errorsNav.HasChildren)
        MessageBox.Show("I'm sorry, an error occurred accessing " +
            getSubAreasWSC.ServiceUrl
            + ". Please select a Request Type again.");
}
```

The `Changed` event handler for `RequestType` (Listing 15.33) at first may appear to be a long and complicated method. But most of it merely involves comments or data source operations, which happen to take up more lines of code. Let's parse through this source code to understand what purposes it serves. We left most of the comments in the code to offer a more development-centric viewpoint (since, of course, we added them while writing the code). See the MoiConsultingRequest sample code for the entirety of comments.

As we know from studying behaviors of XML events, event bubbling is both our friend and our enemy. It's convenient to use at a higher level in the data source to handle a specific event on a variety of nodes. However, in a case like ours where we want to query via a Web service connection, it is best to restrict this code to running only when necessary. Querying an external data source is a relatively slow ordeal and should be minimized when possible. To adhere to this best practice, we are selective about whether or not our event handler continues processing. Three conditions must hold true for the event to continue with querying the Web service.

1. The user must not have incurred an undo or redo.
2. The operation must be a change in value.
3. The site (where we're listening) and sender (what actually changed) nodes must be the same.

As the comments in the code suggest, the last two conditions are very important in our effort to filter irrelevant event notifications. If the second condition ceased to exist, our code would query the Web service when the user clicks the *start over* Button control. This is because the `RequestType` node would be deleted and then inserted. Surely we wouldn't want to query because the `GetSubAreas` secondary data source will be cleared anyway in the "start over" handler. If the last condition were not in place, our code would still run because of event bubbling. This happens when the user selects the *Other* Option Button control in the *Request Type* region and thus changes the `OtherType` attribute field (bound to the associated Text Box).

In the cases where the user successfully changes the `RequestType` node by clicking on one of the Option Button controls, we want to proceed and query the Web service. The Web service method for getting the list of subareas (called `GetSubAreas`) accepts a string value that matches a `RequestType` enumeration. This enumeration is defined in the Web service itself. If a nonenumerated value is used, the query will fail. The Web service implementation is succinct for the purpose of this sample; it maps the Option Button values to an array of hard-coded strings.

> **NOTE** GetSubAreas Web Service Sample
>
> You can find the Web service code, GetSubAreas.cs, with the samples for this chapter.

Before we do the query, however, we have to take care of a few prequery setup steps. As we know from Chapter 7, secondary query data connections use corresponding secondary data sources to get data to and from the external source. In this case, the secondary data source (called GetSubAreas, which corresponds with its connection counterpart with the same name) is used to populate the List Box bound to the SubAreas secondary data source. When we query GetSubAreas, the content of queryFields is sent to the Web service. The result of the query is returned in the dataFields group. If you look in the queryFields group (Figure 15.28) of the secondary data source in the *Data Source* task pane, you will see the requestType field, which is sent as the parameter to the Web service. RequestType node values (such as AccountQuestion, ConsultantRequest, and so on) are mimicked in the Web service enumeration. As a result, we simply need to copy the value of the RequestType node from the main data source to the GetSubAreas requestType parameter.

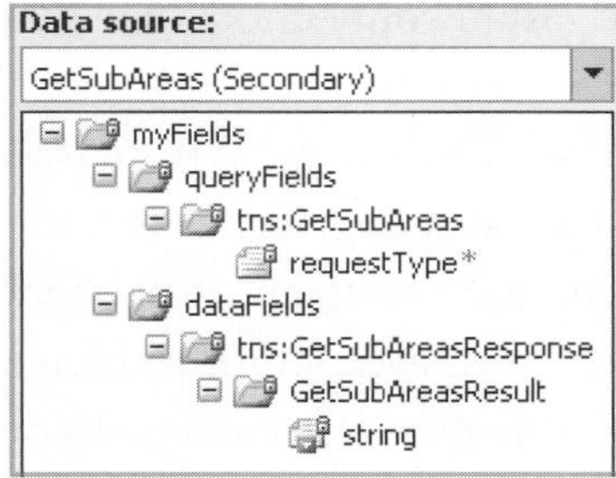

FIGURE 15.28: GetSubAreas secondary data source

> **WARNING No Validation in Secondary Data Sources**
>
> GetSubAreas is a secondary data source, so there is no data validation. As a result, neither the requirement that the field cannot be blank nor the enumerated data type of the requestType field is enforced.

To set the value of the requestType parameter, we need to get an XPathNavigator to the GetSubAreas secondary data source. We use the DataSources collection to get the secondary data source by name, and similar to the main data source, we call CreateNavigator. Selecting the requestType field and setting its value is no different than working with the main data source. If you have trouble finding the correct XPath, we suggest reviewing Chapter 3. We also discuss how to find XPaths in the

"Using XPathNavigator Objects" section earlier in this chapter. The relevant code corresponds to the code starting where we use a DataSource object to the line of code where we set the value of the request type. This code is in the RequestType_Changed method shown in Listing 15.33.

> **TIP DataSources (and DataConnections) Collections**
>
> The main data source is included in the DataSources collection as the empty string (String.Empty). Likewise, a main data connection is also included in the DataConnections collection. This is important to remember if you're iterating through these collections or using the Count property.

Subjacent to the secondary data source lines of code are the lines for getting the corresponding data connection. (See where we get the WebServiceConnection object within the RequestType_Changed method.) The easiest way to get the connection is to get it from the DataSource object that we used to create the XPathNavigator. Remember that every secondary data source, by definition, must have an associated query data connection, so the QueryConnection property should always be available. Alternatively, a reference to the Web service connection could be attained through the DataConnections collection. This happens in the same fashion in which the secondary data source was found in the DataSources collection. Getting a data connection from the collection returns a DataSource object that exposes only two useful items: the Name property and the Execute method. Since we know it's a Web service connection and we need to access some Web service–specific properties and methods, we need to cast the generic DataSource to a WebServiceConnection.

The InfoPath OM defines a specific data connection object for each connection type, as shown in Table 15.5. Some commonly used properties and methods are also listed in this table.

> **TIP Execute Override Behavior**
>
> Passing null for an XPathNavigator parameter in an Execute override method tells InfoPath to use the default XPathNavigator that it would have used without the override.

TABLE 15.5: Types of Data Connections and Their Commonly Used Properties and Methods

Connection Type	Commonly Used OM	Comments

`AdoQueryConnection`
`AdoSubmitConnection`
	`Command`
	`Connection`
	`Timeout`
		`Command` can change the SQL query statement; `Connection` modifies the connection string.

`EmailSubmitConnection`	`AttachmentFileName`
	`Introduction`
	`Subject`
	`Execute(XPathNavigator input)`
		The `Execute` override method accepts any data source, including main or secondary, to attach to the mail message.

`FileQueryConnection`	`FileLocation`	Receive data from XML document.
`FileSubmitConnection`	`Filename` `FolderUrl`	Submit data to a SharePoint document library. Sets the name of the file and folder location when using SharePoint DAV submit.
`SharePointListQueryConnection`	`SiteUrl` `Execute(XPathNavigator output)`	The `Execute` override method returns the queried data to the output `XPathNavigator` provided by form code.

`WebServiceConnection`	`ServiceUrl`
	`SoapAction`
	`Timeout`
	`Execute(XPathNavigator input, XPathNavigator output, XPathNavigator errors)`
		The `Execute` override method allows form code to specify optional `XPathNavigator` objects for providing input when sending data, getting output when receiving, or retrieving SOAP fault error output. The `Execute` override behaves similarly for both query and submit connections.

Now that we've set the `requestType` query parameter and have the Web service connection object, it's almost time to perform the query. However, we have noticed that the server hosting the Web service can sometimes get bogged down from many requests. Sometimes the server can take some time to respond. InfoPath's default 30-second timeout on data connections may not be enough time. Once the timeout is changed, it will be persisted for the life of that connection. So we could have increased the timeout in the `Loading` event instead of immediately before querying the connection. Listing 15.34 shows how to set the `Timeout` property.

LISTING 15.34: Setting the Web Service Connection `Timeout` Property

```
// Web service timeout is 30s, increase it to 60 for slow connections
getSubAreasWSC.Timeout = 60;
```

The Web service server has turned out to be quite the unreliable machine. Even with the extended timeout, we see occasional spurious errors when performing queries. InfoPath handles a data connection error by showing a dialog with server details that may not make sense to the user. To make the error case a little less confusing for our users, we want to detect errors when querying the Web service and handle the errors in our form code. We use a `try-catch` block around the Web service connection's `Execute` override method (see Table 15.5) because an exception is thrown when an error occurs. You could put any error-handling logic in the `catch` block; however, we've decided to just check the resulting errors navigator that will be nonempty when an error happens on the server. Listing 15.35 shows the code.

> **TIP Handling Web Service Connection Failures**
>
> When a Web service (or other data connection) fails to execute, the resulting server-side error message may reveal implementation details about your external data source. Using a `try-catch` and handling the error in your form code allows you to choose what error messages the user can see.

LISTING 15.35: Capturing Errors from Executing a Web Service Data Connection

```
// Create a new navigator to capture errors, if any
XmlDocument errorsXmlDoc = new XmlDocument();
XPathNavigator errorsNav = errorsXmlDoc.CreateNavigator();
try
{
    // Query the Web service
    getSubAreasWSC.Execute(
        null /*input*/, null /*output*/, errorsNav /*errors*/);
}
catch (Exception)
{
    // Silently fail for now
    // If we didn't do this, InfoPath would show the exception
}
// Did an error occur?
if (errorsNav.HasChildren)
{
    MessageBox.Show("I'm sorry, an error occurred accessing "
        + getSubAreasWSC.ServiceUrl
        + ". Please select a Request Type again.");
}
```

TIP Benefits of Using `Execute` Overrides

A `try-catch` could have been used with the no-argument `Execute()` (instead of the override version) and would have achieved the same effect as in Listing 15.35. The advantages of using the override for getting errors is to perform your own logging or send an administrative alert to track how many errors your users encounter with this particular data connection.

The *Request Details* view, shown in Figure 15.29, gives the user an opportunity to enter specifics of the request.

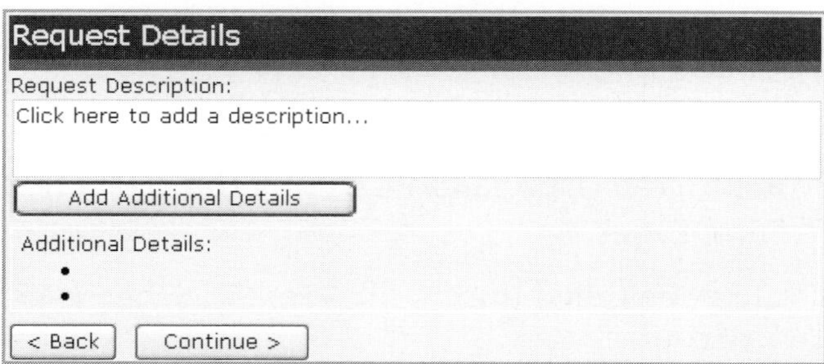

FIGURE 15.29: Request Details view

Did you notice that the task pane disappeared? We want our help task pane to be visible only on the *Welcome* view. Instead of adding logic behind Button clicks that change views, it's much easier to just get notified when the view is actually changed. To do so, we can sink and handle the `ViewSwitched` event. We can also use this event handler (shown in Listing 15.36) for other purposes, such as showing a dialog message on the *Confirm* view.

> **WARNING Hiding Does Not Disable the Task Pane**
>
> Hiding the task pane by using the `Visible` property does not block the user from deciding to show it again.

LISTING 15.36: Handling the `ViewSwitched` Form Event When Switching to Specific Views

```
public void FormEvents_ViewSwitched(
    object sender, ViewSwitchedEventArgs e)
{
    switch(this.CurrentView.ViewInfo.Name)
    {
        case "Confirm":
            MessageBox.Show("Please confirm the data and click "
                + "Submit to continue.", "Confirm Data");
            break;
        case "Welcome":
            Application.ActiveWindow.TaskPanes[
                TaskPaneType.Html].Visible = true;
            break;
        default:
            Application.ActiveWindow.TaskPanes[
                TaskPaneType.Html].Visible = false;
            break;
    }
}
```

> **NOTE Restricted OM Available During the `SwitchView` Form Event**
>
> Some OM cannot be called during the `ViewSwitched` event, such as `SwitchView`, of course.

The RequestDescription field is a Rich Text Box control, which allows unrestricted HTML input. We did not add any special logic behind this field. However, the *Add Additional Details* Button control offers a list-item approach for more structured request details. By default, the AdditionalDetails Bulleted List control does not exist. As we saw earlier when filling out this form, clicking the Button control inserts an Optional Section that contains the Bulleted List. Subsequent clicks on the same Button control insert another item in the Bulleted List. Keep in mind that these are two different controls bound to separate data source items.

The logic behind the *Add Additional Details* Button control is as follows: If the Optional Section (bound to AdditionalDetails) exists, then insert it; otherwise, insert another item at the end of the Bulleted List (bound to AdditionalDetail). We use two different approaches to facilitate the insertion of these controls. Since the Optional Section is a container control, it can benefit from view-based structural editing operations. Other structurally enabled controls include (but are not limited to) Repeating Table, Repeating Section, File Attachment, and Choice Group and Repeating Choice Group controls. View-based structural editing through the OM uses the ExecuteAction method of the CurrentView object. The nicety in using ExecuteAction over pure data source operations (as we'll use in a moment to insert an item in the Bulleted List) is not needing to concern ourselves (or our code for that matter) with inserting an entire XML subtree in the correct context. For example, if the Optional Section contained many nodes below it, either immediately below or through many depths, the ExecuteAction method will take care of inserting all necessary fields and groups. In fact, the ExecuteAction method is exactly what InfoPath uses behind the scenes when a user clicks the *Click here to insert* link. Of course, the link doesn't need to exist in the view for form code to successfully call it.

The first argument to ExecuteAction is an ActionType. This is an enumeration type, and through IntelliSense, you can find all of its enumerated values. In the case of an Optional Section, we use the xOptionalInsert ActionType. The second parameter is the xmlToEdit string. This value identifies on which control to perform the ActionType. To find the xmlToEdit string for a structurally editable control, go to the *Advanced* tab of the control's properties dialog. The *Code* region, shown in Figure 15.30, reveals the *XmlToEdit* value as well as the control's xOptional capability.

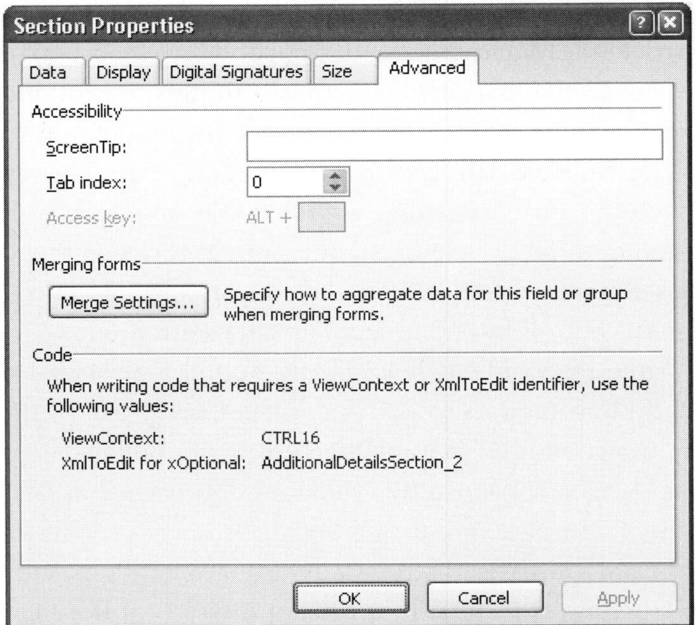

FIGURE 15.30: Finding the `xmlToEdit` and `ActionType` capability of a structurally editable control

The code snippet in Listing 15.37 shows how we use `ExecuteAction()` to insert the Optional Section if it does not already exist in the data source.

LISTING 15.37: Using `ExecuteAction` to Insert an Optional Section

```
public void Add_Additional_Details_Clicked(
    object sender, ClickedEventArgs e)
{
    // Is AdditionalDetails already inserted?
    XPathNavigator root = MainDataSource.CreateNavigator();
    XPathNavigator additionalDetails = root.SelectSingleNode(
        "/my:Request/my:RequestDetails/my:AdditionalDetails",
        NamespaceManager);

    // If it doesn't exist, we'll insert it
    if (additionalDetails == null)
        // XmlToEdit for xOptional: AdditionalDetailsSection_2
        this.CurrentView.ExecuteAction(
            ActionType.XOptionalInsert, "AdditionalDetailsSection_2");
        // If it already exists, insert an AdditionalDetail
        else
        // Bulleted List doesn't support ExecuteAction since
        // there's no XmlToEdit.
```

```
        // We'll insert it using the data source instead.
        additionalDetails.AppendChildElement(
            additionalDetails.Prefix, "AdditionalDetail",
            additionalDetails.NamespaceURI, string.Empty);
}
```

If the Optional Section control, bound to `AdditionalDetails`, already exists, the Button control will insert an `AdditionalDetail` node. Adding this node to the data source will, in turn, add an item to the Bulleted List control. Since the `AdditionalDetail` repeating field is a child of the `AdditionalDetails` group and we already have a reference to `AdditionalDetails`, we can easily use the `XPathNavigator` method `AppendChildElement`. The `AppendChildElement` method creates a new data source node and adds it to the end of children nodes relative to the context (`AdditionalDetails`) `XPathNavigator`. If you wanted to assign a value to the newly inserted item, you could pass it instead of the empty string as the last argument to `AppendChildElement`.

> **TIP Using the `XPathNavigator's` `AppendChildElement` Method**
>
> `AppendChildElement` requires the namespace prefix and URI as parameters. Since the node in which we're appending has the same prefix and URI, we can just reference their values. This lessens the chance of mistyping and is more robust if, say, the namespace or prefix change.

After the user completes the *Request Details* view, the read-only *Confirm* view (refer back to Figure 15.23) displays a summary of gathered form data. Of the three Button controls at the bottom of the view (*Start Over, Go Back,* and *Submit*), we haven't yet discussed *Submit.* As its name implies, clicking this control submits the form. You learned all about submitting forms in Chapter 8, but the MOI request form does not implement a traditional-style submit to a data connection. Instead, via the *Submit Options* dialog shown in Figure 15.31, we have chosen to submit using our own code. Clicking on the *Edit Code* button in this dialog opens VSTA, hooks up the event in `InternalStartup`, and creates the event handler method called `FormEvents_Submit`.

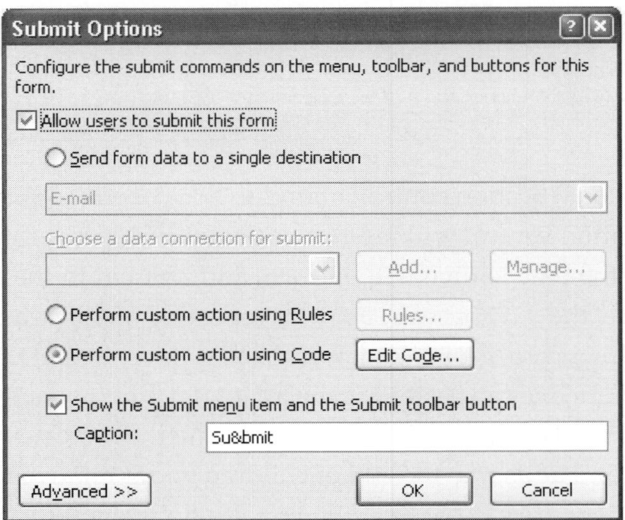

FIGURE 15.31: Setting up the form's main submit to use code

The MOI request form defines the `Submit` event as saving the form to the user's computer. Listing 15.38 shows the implementation for `Submit`. Before doing the save, however, we want to check whether the current form was recovered. We can detect a recovered form by checking the `this.Recovered` Boolean flag. A form's data is recovered if InfoPath suddenly and unexpectedly closed while the form was being filled out. This could happen, for example, if the computer turned off due to a power outage. Because InfoPath quit unexpectedly, the form could be in an indeterminate state. We'd rather be safe and ask the user if he or she wants to continue submitting recovered data. The user may choose to go back and finish filling out parts of the form that weren't completed.

LISTING 15.38: Sinking the `Submit` Form Event

```
public void FormEvents_Submit(object sender, SubmitEventArgs e)
{
    // NOTE: There are no errors if InfoPath allows submit to happen.
    // If this is recovered data, ask the user if we should continue.
    DialogResult result = DialogResult.Yes;
    if (this.Recovered)
        result = MessageBox.Show("This data is recovered. "
            + "Still continue?", "Submitting Recovered Data",
            MessageBoxButtons.YesNo);

    if (result == DialogResult.Yes)
```

```
    {
        // Save the form
        string tempFileName = System.IO.Path.GetTempFileName()
            + ".xml";
        this.SaveAs(tempFileName);
        // Fills a link to see where it saved
        XPathNavigator root = MainDataSource.CreateNavigator();
        XPathNavigator savedFileLocation = root.SelectSingleNode(
            "/my:Request/@my:SavedFileLocation", NamespaceManager);
        savedFileLocation.SetValue(tempFileName);
        // Go to the Thank You view
        ViewInfos.SwitchView("ThankYou");
    }
    else
    {
        e.CancelableArgs.Cancel = true;
        e.CancelableArgs.Message = "Submit was canceled.";
        e.CancelableArgs.MessageDetails =
            "Submit again whenever you are ready.";
    }
}
```

TIP Accounting for Performance in Form Code

When a single event handler changes both the data source and switches the view, the view switch should be the last operation. Switching the view first is more expensive if the controls bound to the changing data are only visible in the new view.

When submit proceeds successfully, a file is created on the local computer with the .xml extension. The form data is saved by calling `SaveAs` and passing the full path with file name. After saving the file, the user goes to the final *Thank You* view. A hyperlink in this view (bound to `SavedFileLocation`) shows the actual location of the saved form. If calling `SaveAs` failed, say, because the disk is full or read-only, the `Submit` event would also fail. A `try-catch` block could be used around `SaveAs` if you wanted to handle the failure in a special way, such as trying again or asking for an alternate save location.

TIP `Save` Requires Full Trust

Calling `Save` or `SaveAs` requires a fully trusted form template.

What's Next?

Now that you've been introduced to the InfoPath OM and learned about writing code behind forms, we are positioned to move forward with more advanced programming features. The OM knowledge you've garnered thus far will be used and further developed in the coming chapters. Areas such as hosting, leveraging browser-enabled form templates with Forms Services, and building custom controls using ActiveX all incorporate various aspects of the OM. In the meantime, we encourage you to have fun programming your own advanced InfoPath form templates.

16

Visual Studio Tools for Microsoft Office InfoPath 2007

Getting Started

In the last chapter we learned about writing form code using the InfoPath object model (OM) and the C# programming language. To write code, we used the Visual Studio Tools for Applications (VSTA) programming environment. As you may have noticed in Chapter 15, one of the hindrances with VSTA is that it's a separate program from InfoPath. Switching between InfoPath, VSTA, and other programs such as Visual Studio 2005 (for designing your Web services) is not only a hassle but also distracting. Ideally, everything would be accomplished in the same "place" without worrying about where you're working.

We all know developers work best in a flexible development-like environment that caters to their specific needs. InfoPath design mode is fine, for example, for information workers seeking to design relatively complicated forms. But programmers like you, on the other hand, are more accustomed to working in an environment akin to Visual Studio. With Visual Studio 2005 now the norm for Windows program and service development, there is no better place for writing code. Ideally your InfoPath forms could be designed in Visual Studio–like surroundings.

The InfoPath team knew that VSTA only partially answers the gripes from our developers. Some of the major remaining issues revolved around the disjoint development experiences just mentioned. But as a member of the Microsoft Office family, InfoPath primarily needs to be an easy-to-use component of a business-oriented productivity suite. Any other goal, such as increasing appeal to developers, takes a secondary focus. Or does it? The latest version of Office definitely breaks this mold with **Microsoft Visual Studio 2005 Tools for the 2007 Microsoft Office System** (VSTO 2005 SE, although in this chapter we'll refer to it simply as VSTO). VSTO attempts to directly tackle the hard problems we posed regarding disparate programming and form template development environments. In this chapter, we'll see what VSTO means to you as a developer and InfoPath form designer.

After learning a little about what VSTO is and how it's different from VSTA, you'll see how to set up and get VSTO running on your computer. If you already have InfoPath 2007 installed, you're a step ahead!

Once we install VSTO, we'll look at how to start by designing a form template. Then we'll get accustomed to the VSTO environment by discussing the similarities and differences between it and the InfoPath design mode. Likewise, we'll look at the advantages as well as some shortcomings associated with VSTO relative to the traditional InfoPath offering.

If you're a developer, no matter if you're new to InfoPath or a seasoned expert, this chapter is written for you. We'll look at some of the most exciting developer-focused integration InfoPath has ever seen!

What Is VSTO?

VSTO is available as a separate, add-on product to the 2007 Microsoft Office system. Its purpose is to provide a development environment for creating line-of-business applications for many programs in the Microsoft Office suite. VSTO for 2007 is based on Visual Studio 2005 and contains many of the same basic features. In the latest version of VSTO (Second Edition), extensions are included to customize the Ribbon (for those Microsoft Office applications that use it), create application-level Custom Task Panes, and support custom form regions in Outlook 2007. The VSTO package includes support for programming and extending Word, Excel, Access, Outlook, and (of course) InfoPath.

In the last chapter, you learned all about VSTA and how to use it to add code behind a form template. VSTA is bundled with InfoPath (and the larger Microsoft Office suite) and is basically the replacement for the InfoPath 2003 Toolkit for Visual Studio from the last version of InfoPath and Microsoft Office. But unlike the InfoPath 2003 Toolkit, where Visual Studio was a required prerequisite that had to be purchased separately, VSTA is free. Although VSTO (which is also free) requires Visual Studio 2005 (which is not free), it's a tantalizing offering given that the entire form template design experience is now encapsulated in the Visual Studio 2005 environment.

You can find more information about VSTO on MSDN (as referenced in the Appendix).

> **NOTE** Visual Studio 2005 Support for Both InfoPath 2003 and 2007
>
> The VSTO support for InfoPath 2007 should not be confused with the Microsoft Office InfoPath 2003 Toolkit for Visual Studio 2005. The InfoPath 2003 Toolkit enabled developers to add managed form code to InfoPath 2003 SP1 forms. The topic of this chapter is the VSTO package for Microsoft Office InfoPath 2007.

Bringing InfoPath into Visual Studio

What does a developer do when designing an InfoPath form template? Typically, he or she spends more time in the InfoPath program during the first half of form template development and then spends the latter half (or more) writing or debugging source code. But the time spent in either environment is not exclusive. Switching between InfoPath and VSTA happens whenever the developer shifts between code and any other form template design activity. As we all know by now, this switch can happen at almost any time during the design phase. With VSTO, there's no need to switch programs. Everything is now found in Visual Studio. VSTO was designed to bring you, the developer, back into your comfort zone.

Clearly, the biggest win for developers with VSTO is the integration of Visual Studio and the InfoPath design mode. As a result, it's now possible to design a form template entirely in Visual Studio. This essentially deprecates most template-designing activities using InfoPath, although you can still design in InfoPath if you like.

Installing VSTO

Installing VSTO is easy. Simply install the VSTO 2005 SE package, which includes support for all the Microsoft Office products mentioned earlier.

> **WARNING** Close InfoPath and Visual Studio
>
> Before beginning or repairing any VSTO installation, ensure that all InfoPath and Visual Studio program instances are closed.

VSTO requires one of the following versions of Visual Studio 2005 as a prerequisite:

- Microsoft Visual Studio 2005 Team System
- Microsoft Visual Studio 2005 Professional
- Microsoft Visual Studio 2005 Tools for the 2007 Microsoft Office System

There are no other prerequisites to install VSTO. You can install it with or without InfoPath 2007 already present on the computer. If you install VSTO first, Visual Studio will contain the InfoPath templates, but using them will result in an error. That's because you need to have InfoPath 2007 installed. Once InfoPath is installed, the Visual Studio templates work as expected. (We'll see exactly how they work in a moment.) See MSDN for additional details (as referenced in the Appendix).

Designing a Form Template with VSTO

VSTO for InfoPath attempts to maintain much of the InfoPath design experience while capitalizing on the benefits of Visual Studio. Now that you're a skilled form designer in the InfoPath program, making the jump to the Visual Studio bandwagon for designing forms shouldn't be a shocker. If you are new to Visual Studio, we recommend taking a tutorial so you can get familiar with its development environment before attempting to use VSTO.

Start Designing a Form Template

It doesn't matter whether you're designing a new or existing form template—the starting point is always the Visual Studio *New Project* dialog (Figure 16.1). You can click the *Create Project* link on the *Start Page*, use the *New Project* button on the *Standard* toolbar, or use the *New* fly-out menu on the *File* menu. Under the *Visual C#* or *Visual Basic* item will be an *Office* subitem containing all the Visual Studio project templates (not to be confused with form templates) corresponding to those offered by VSTO. Figure 16.1 shows the InfoPath project template in the *New Project* dialog on Visual Studio 2005 Professional with C#.

When you use VSTO to design an InfoPath form template, a new project is created. This is true for both new and existing form templates. The project maintains the form template files in an extracted format (the code behind the form template) and various other files and settings stored by the Visual

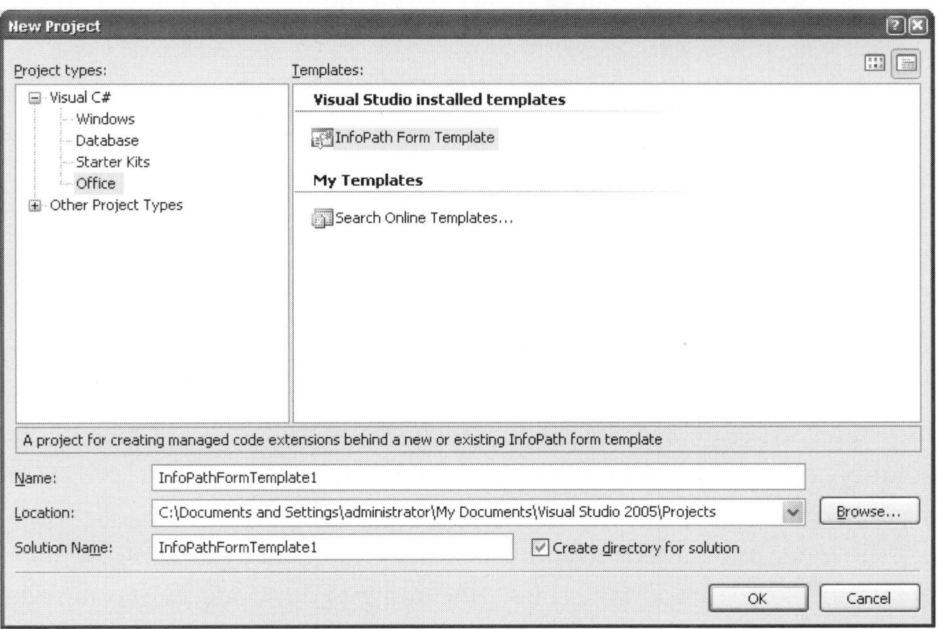

FIGURE 16.1: Visual Studio's New Project dialog

Studio environment. Once a project is created, it serves as the entry point to designing that form template in future sessions. When you close the project, you can reopen it by double-clicking either the Visual Studio Solution (.sln) or the Visual C# or Visual Basic project (.csproj or .vbproj, respectively) file.

> **TIP Missing Your Project?**
>
> If you can't find the solution or project file to continue designing your InfoPath form template, try looking under the *Recent Projects* fly-out menu on the *File* menu of Visual Studio.

The project itself will be created as a folder with the name and in the location you specify at the bottom of the *New Project* dialog. In our case, you can see the folder named InfoPathFormTemplate1 under the Projects folder in Figure 16.2 (which shows the entire tree structure for an InfoPath VSTO project).

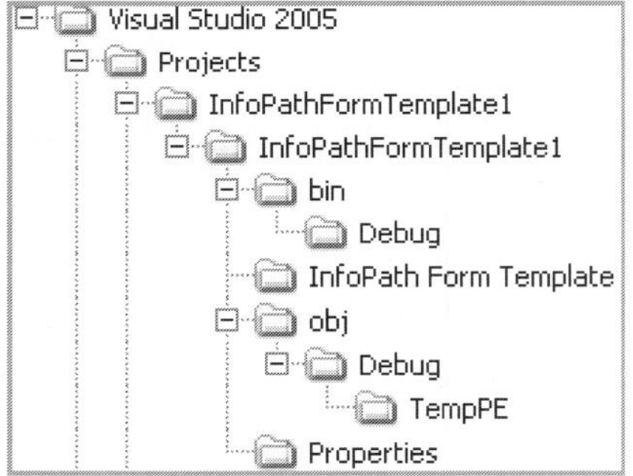

FIGURE 16.2: Structure of a VSTO InfoPath project

The outer InfoPathFormTemplate1 folder contains the Microsoft Visual Studio Solution and User Options files. (Notice that Figure 16.2 shows only the folder structure and not the files included in the project.) Opening the solution file in Windows is the preferred way to reopen this project in Visual Studio.

The inner InfoPathFormTemplate1 folder holds many folders, but there are also some important files, including FormCode.cs, FormCode.Designer.cs, FormCode.Designer.xml, and the Visual Studio Project file. The various FormCode files include your handwritten form code, as well as other supporting InfoPath auto-generated code and settings. The bin folder holds the assembly (.dll) and program debug database (.pdb) files built by the Visual Studio compiler. A custom build action from VSTO copies them into the InfoPath Form Template folder. The InfoPath Form Template folder contains the form template files for the project. The obj folder contains temporarily cached data involved in the assembly and debug file build processes. Finally, the Properties directory holds supporting code, such as assembly properties (e.g., name and versioning information) and resource mappings. The Properties directory is also shown and can be modified in the Solution Explorer of Visual Studio when the project is open.

Creating a New Project for a New or Existing Form Template

Whenever you create a new Visual Studio project for an InfoPath form template, the *Design a Form Template* dialog appears (Figure 16.3). This dialog is very similar to the *Design a Form Template* dialog in InfoPath. In fact, the right half of the dialog, under the *Design a new* caption, is the same. It serves the same purpose as it does in InfoPath: to help you create a new form template or template part. The left portion of the dialog is slightly modified to accommodate VSTO. The *Create project from existing form template* section lets you choose an existing form template from a number of places, such as

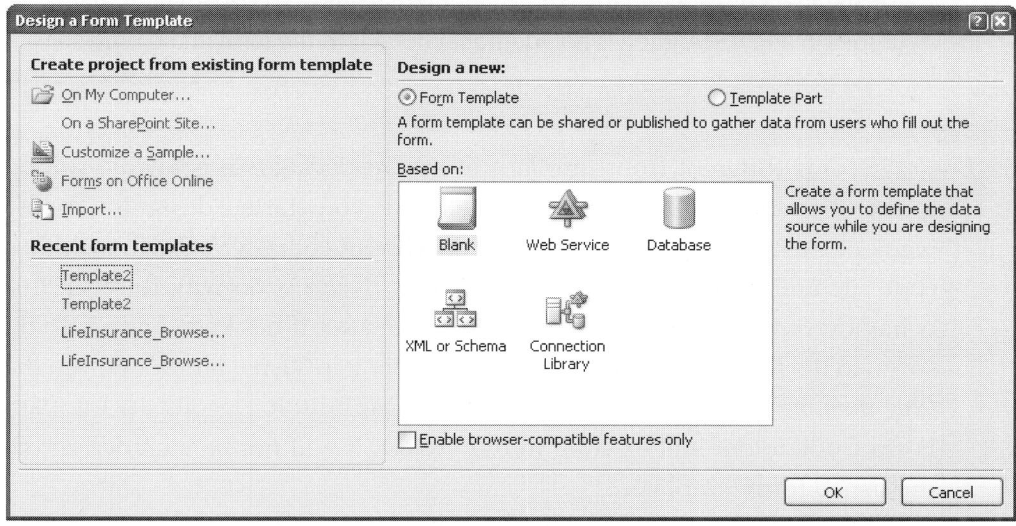

FIGURE 16.3: Design a Form Template dialog in VSTO

a SharePoint site. The links in the *Recent form templates* section come in handy if you started to design a form template in InfoPath and now want to switch to VSTO.

Designing an existing form template never modifies the original, so there's no need for you to make a backup ahead of time. Whenever a new project is created against an existing form template, the warning shown in Figure 16.4 appears. The existing form template is saved as source files to the InfoPath Form Template directory where the Visual Studio project was created. Any form code or script from the existing form template remains in the project, but it isn't used by InfoPath. You can delete these files from the Visual Studio Solution Explorer if they're no longer needed.

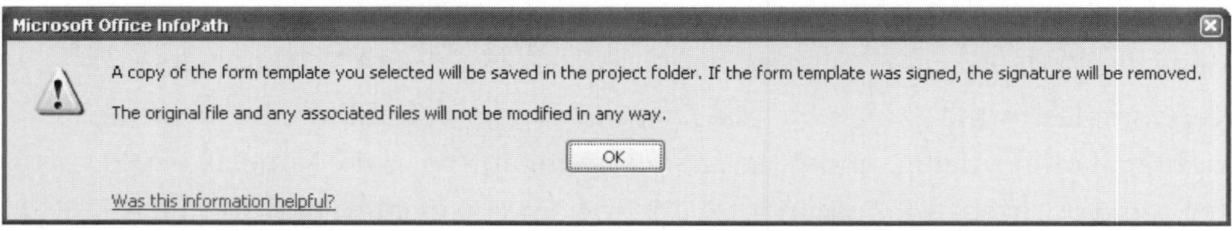

FIGURE 16.4: Dialog informing that VSTO never modifies an existing form template

---

Forms Services

Designing a browser-enabled form template using VSTO is similar to using InfoPath and VSTA; there's no additional benefit to the form in the browser.

VSTO is different from InfoPath in one respect: Code is always added to the form template. Regardless of whether you started designing a new blank or existing form template (with or without code), VSTO will include a code file and build it as part of the project. There is no way to block this behavior; however, you can remove the code after it has been added. To do so, go to the *Form Options* item on the *Tools* menu in Visual Studio. Within the *Programming* category, click on the *Remove Code* button. Despite the InfoPath Form Code folder still existing in the project, it will not be included in the published form template.

> **TIP Publishing to Forms Services**
>
> VSTO form templates always have form code by default, so form templates must be administrator approved. If you explicitly remove code from the form template, the Publishing Wizard will allow user deployment directly from VSTO.

Designing a Template Part

The experience of designing template parts in VSTO is almost the same as in InfoPath. The entry point for creating a template part is shown in Figure 16.3 under the *Design a new* heading. The difference between InfoPath and VSTO lies in how the template part (.xtp) file is generated. As we discussed earlier, VSTO keeps form templates in an extracted file format instead of in a single file. As a result, a VSTO template part cannot be used directly in its extracted state. To generate the template part (.xtp) file in VSTO, select *Publish* on the *Build* menu. This brings up the same *Save As* dialog used in InfoPath when you save a template part.

For more about template parts, see Chapter 10.

Existing Form Templates with Code

Sometimes the form template you want to design may already have associated code. The version of InfoPath OM does not matter, since VSTO is compatible with both 2003 and 2007 OMs. However, your ability to capitalize on VSTO will depend on what coding language is used. In any case, VSTO will always accept your form template; it's really a question of whether your code can come with it. Let's look at what you can do to maintain compatibility with VSTO.

Script Using an existing form template with script to create an InfoPath project in VSTO visually appears to be no different from using a template with no code. This means there is no notification of any sort that the script is about to be decoupled from the form template. The form template's script file will still be part of the InfoPath Form Template folder but will no longer function as it did before it was brought into VSTO. Only managed code is supported in the VSTO environment. If you still want to use a scripting language, you should continue using InfoPath and the Microsoft Script Editor.

We briefly discussed programming InfoPath with script in Chapter 15.

InfoPath 2003 Service Pack 1 (SP1) with Form Code If you're starting from a form template that has InfoPath 2003 SP1 managed code (managed code was not supported before SP1), you can still use VSTO to edit your code. Most likely you're migrating a form template that was created with the InfoPath 2003 Toolkit for Visual Studio .NET. If this is the case, Visual Studio will prompt you to upgrade the project. Upgrading will allow your form template to fully take advantage of the InfoPath 2007 features and revamped OM. The code associated with that project and the InfoPath form template itself, however, are not upgraded and remain unchanged.

TIP Upgrading Form Code from InfoPath 2003

If you want to upgrade your InfoPath 2003 form code, you'll first need to upgrade your form template to the InfoPath 2007 format. Only then will you also be able to upgrade the form code OM to version 2007. To allow these upgrades, you must first open the form template with InfoPath. Only then can you migrate to VSTO.

InfoPath 2007 VSTA Do you have a VSTA form template that you now want to use with VSTO? Unfortunately, VSTO doesn't offer an automatic migration path. Luckily, however, there is a workaround that will successfully convert your VSTA project to one in VSTO.

First, go to the folder of the VSTA project you want to convert. Create a new folder with the exact name InfoPath Form Template. Next, find the form template (.xsn) file and open it in InfoPath design mode. Use the *Save As Source Files* command on the *File* menu to save the form template to the InfoPath Form Template folder you created. Now open this same VSTA project in Visual Studio 2005. In the Solution Explorer for your project, right-click anywhere in the pane and select *Add,* then *Existing Item.* Find the InfoPath Form Template folder where the source files were saved. The resulting *Add Existing Item* dialog may have a filter (the *Files of type* drop-down) that blocks some file types, so make sure *All Files (*.*)* is selected. Select the manifest.xsf file in the folder and click on the arrow immediately to the right of the *Add* button to choose *Add As Link.*

That's it! Simply double-click on the manifest.xsf file in the Solution Explorer to design your form template in VSTO.

> **NOTE** VSTO Not Installed?
>
> Converting a VSTA project to VSTO will not work if VSTO is not installed.

> **NOTE** Either VSTA or VSTO
>
> Designing an InfoPath 2007 form template with code is classified as using either VSTA (with InfoPath) or VSTO (with Visual Studio), but not both.

The VSTO Design Experience

A first impression of VSTO InfoPath design mode is that it appears to be much different than the traditional InfoPath design experience. Appearances can be deceiving, however; designing the view in VSTO, for example, is very similar to doing so in InfoPath. Figure 16.5 shows how

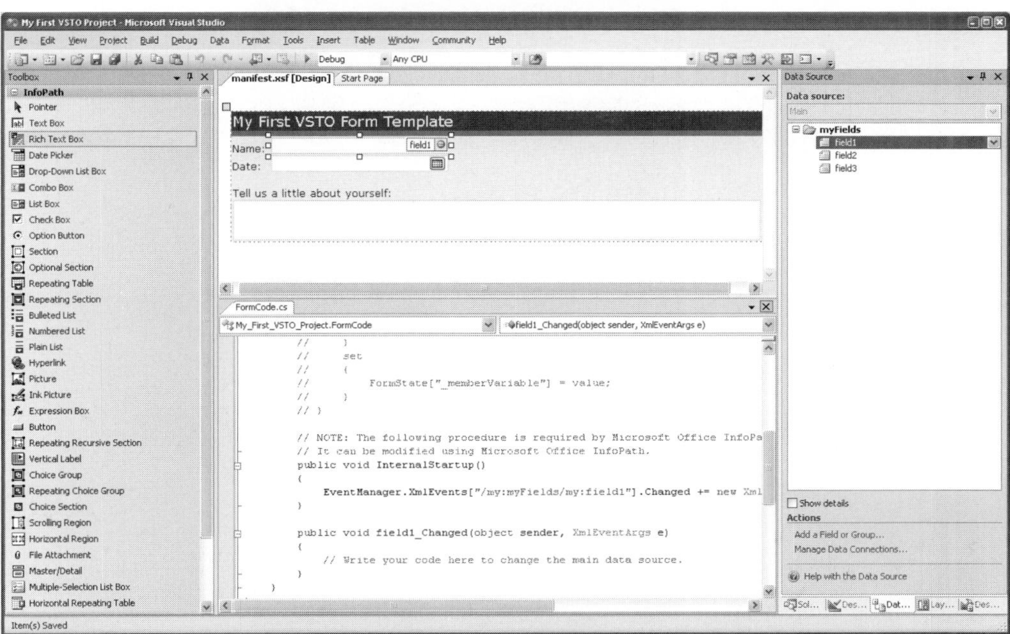

FIGURE 16.5: VSTO environment while designing a form template

VSTO looked while we designed a simple form template. (A sample called MyFirstVSTOProject is included with the samples for this chapter on the book's Web site.)

One of the most apparent differences in VSTO compared to InfoPath is the user interface. While designing the view is similar, finding and getting used to new behaviors in other features is different with VSTO. One area of dissimilarity is a critical component that InfoPath relies heavily on for many highly visible features: the task pane. Let's look at what the VSTO-integrated InfoPath task panes have to offer.

Task Panes

When creating your first VSTO InfoPath form template, you are greeted by the proverbial *Design Tasks* task pane (Figure 16.6). This pane offers the exact same capabilities as its InfoPath counterpart. However, you may notice that task panes manifest themselves differently in VSTO. For example, the top of the VSTO task pane does not offer a drop-down for selecting from the list of all task panes, as the InfoPath task pane does.

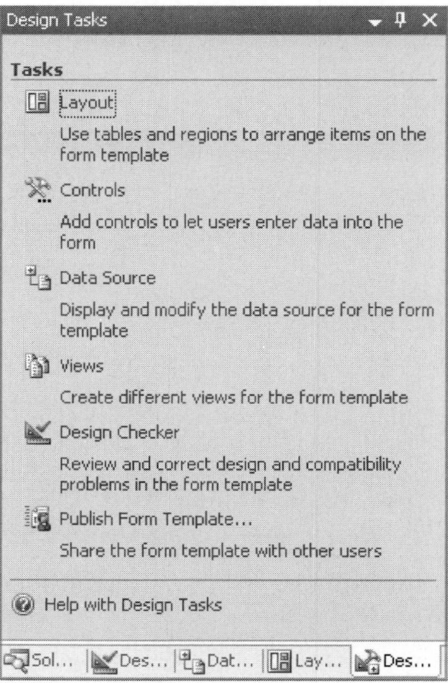

FIGURE 16.6: Design Tasks task pane in VSTO

Instead, VSTO has the downward-facing triangle and pushpin icons, which are Visual Studio–specific features. The triangle icon offers a slew of options for representing this specific *Design Tasks* pane: floating, dockable, tabbed document, auto-hide, and hide. The pushpin icon is a shortcut for switching between dockable (pushpin is in) and auto-hide (pushpin is out).

TIP Did You Lose the Design Tasks Pane?

Hiding a task pane makes it disappear. If you hide the *Design Tasks* pane, you might find it impossible to get it back! One way to fix it is to select *Design Tasks* on the *View* menu. If all else fails, the *Reset Window Layout* option is available on the *Window* menu.

From the *Design Tasks* task pane, the *Layout, Data Source, Views,* and *Design Checker* links open their corresponding task panes as expected. The *Controls* link, however, behaves a little differently. (We will look at the *Controls* task pane soon.) And as we already know from Chapter 9, clicking the *Publish Form Template* link opens the Publishing Wizard instead of a task pane. As you can see in Figure 16.6, opening a new task pane adds a tab to the bottom of the existing task pane. This is how Visual Studio organizes its panes. InfoPath developers may especially appreciate floating panes. This allows you to have as many panes as you want (such as *Layouts* and *Data Source*) simultaneously available while you design your form template. (A popular arrangement is to have the *Controls* pane on the left and the *Data Source* pane to the right.) You can change a dockable or tabbed pane to a floating one by right-clicking on the tab or, if the pane is active, using the triangle icon.

TIP VSTO Remembers Your Pane

If you're using dockable task panes (the default setting), creating a new or opening an existing InfoPath project starts by showing the last used pane. If the *Data Source* task pane was the last pane used in a project, for example, it is shown by default in the next project. On the contrary, InfoPath always starts with the *Design Tasks* pane.

The *Controls* task pane appears to be the odd one of the bunch, but there is good reason. VSTO integrates all InfoPath controls into the Visual Studio Toolbox. The Toolbox is a commonly used Visual Studio pane that groups all Visual Studio Designer controls into categories called tabs. (To find out more about the Visual Studio Designer, see MSDN for general information on Visual Studio 2005, as referenced in the Appendix.) Clicking on the *Controls* link in the *Design Tasks* pane shows the *Toolbox* pane on the left side of the Visual Studio window. InfoPath has its own tab in the Toolbox, appropriately named "InfoPath," of course. By default, only the InfoPath tab is shown, although there are over a dozen other tabs. To see the other hidden tabs, right-click in the pane and select *Show All*. If you prefer a nameless view of the controls, turn off the *List View* option (also available on the right-click menu). Figure 16.7 shows *List View* enabled, while Figure 16.8 has it turned off.

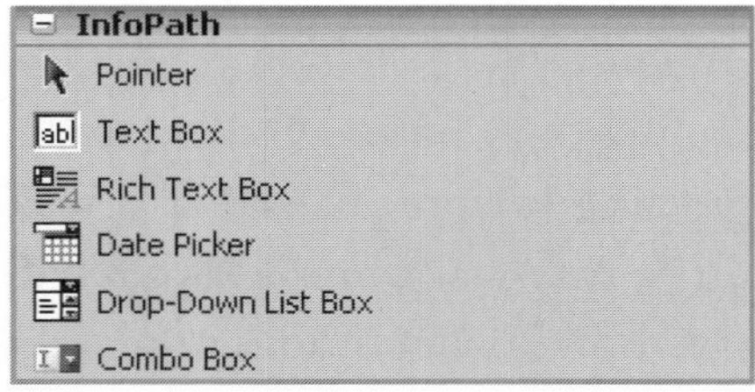

FIGURE 16.7: InfoPath controls in a list view

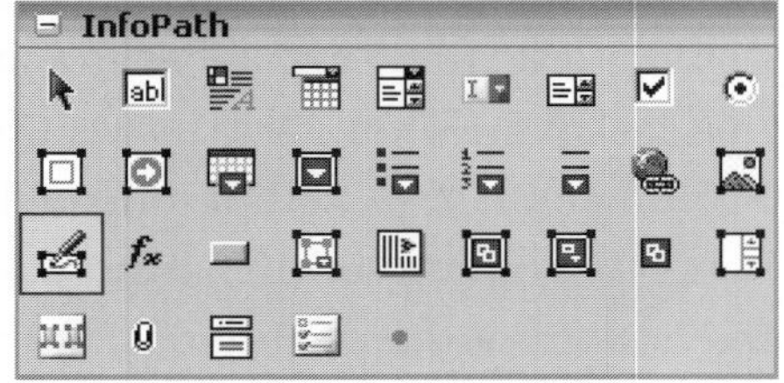

FIGURE 16.8: InfoPath controls as icons

Forms Services

Similar to InfoPath, not all controls are available when you design a browser-enabled form template with VSTO.

The *InfoPath* tab and its controls allow customization in the VSTO environment. You can rename the *InfoPath* tab to another name if you so choose. Likewise, you can rename individual controls. You can also move the tab and its controls up and down relative to other tabs and controls. Even the grouping of controls can be changed. For example, you can create and move any InfoPath controls to your own tab. However, you cannot delete any InfoPath-specific controls.

TIP Sort Menu Items

You can use the *Sort Items Alphabetically* command on the right-click menu to help you quickly find controls when you need them.

Inserting controls from the Toolbox is similar to using InfoPath's *Controls* task pane. As with InfoPath, you can drag and drop a control into the view. However, the practice of inserting a control by simply clicking on it in the *Controls* task pane does not work in VSTO. Visual Studio allows single-click selection of a control in the Toolbox, so you have to double-click to insert a new control.

By default, InfoPath automatically creates the data source when you insert controls. The option checkbox for disabling this behavior appears at the bottom of the *Controls* pane in InfoPath. The same option in VSTO has been moved to the *Data* menu.

WARNING Reset Toolbox Removes InfoPath Controls

Do not use the *Reset Toolbox* option on the *Toolbox* pane. Doing so will remove the InfoPath category of controls! To restore the controls, you can close and restart VSTO.

Have you been looking for an *Add or Remove Custom Controls* link like the one that shows in the bottom of the InfoPath *Controls* task pane? In VSTO, this option appears in the right-click menu of the Toolbox. The menu item is *Choose Items,* which brings up the *Add or Remove Custom Controls* dialog. (There is also a *Choose Toolbox Items* item in the *Tools* menu.) Both template parts and ActiveX controls are supported in the VSTO Toolbox. After you add either a template part or an ActiveX control, it will appear in the Toolbox alongside other controls.

Forms Services

Custom ActiveX controls cannot be used with Forms Services, so they are hidden from the Toolbox.

Menus

If you're familiar with either Visual Studio or InfoPath, but not both, learning the menu commands and structure of VSTO is a short matter of time. If, however, you're accustomed to using both Visual Studio and InfoPath, the merging of the menus can be a little confusing. Many of the commands in VSTO are on menus with the same names as those used in InfoPath, but that's not always the case. To add to the menu confusion, InfoPath-specific menu commands are visible only when the *manifest.xsf [Design]* tab is selected. This tab shows a view of the form template in design mode. Table 16.1 shows the InfoPath commands available in the VSTO environment when you design a form template.

TABLE 16.1: InfoPath-Specific Commands in VSTO

VSTO Menu	VSTO Menu Item	InfoPath Menu Item
File	(VSTO items similar to InfoPath)	
Edit	*Change Binding . . .* *Change To . . .*	
View	*Page Width Guide* *Design Tasks . . .* *Data Source . . .* *Views . . .* *Design Checker . . .* *Properties Windows*	
Build	*Publish Selection*	*Build | Publish*
Data	*View Sample Data* *Automatically Create Data Source* *Default Values . . .* *Data Connections . . .*	
Format	*Font . . .* *Paragraph . . .* *Bullets and Numbering . . .* *Borders and Shading . . .* *Apply Font to All . . .* *Layout . . .* *Form Background Color . . .* *Color Schemes . . .* *Data Formatting . . .*	

TABLE 16.1: *(continued)*

<table>
<tr><th>VSTO Menu</th><th>VSTO Menu Item</th><th>InfoPath Menu Item</th></tr>
<tr><td></td><td>Conditional Formatting . . .
Data Validation . . .
Control Properties . . .
View Properties . . .</td><td>Format | View Properties . . .</td></tr>
<tr><td>Tools</td><td>Spelling . . .
Set Language . . .
Form Submit Options . . .
Resource Files . . .
User Roles . . .
Logic Inspector . . .
Form Options . . .
Export Form . . .
Word Print Views . . .
Print Multiple Views . . .</td><td></td></tr>
<tr><td>Insert</td><td>Event
Picture
Hyperlink . . .
Header and Footer . . .
Horizontal Line
Page Break
Symbol . . .</td><td>Tools | Programming</td></tr>
<tr><td>Table</td><td>VSTO items similar to InfoPath</td><td></td></tr>
<tr><td>Help</td><td>Microsoft Office InfoPath Help
Developer Resources
Contact Microsoft Office Online
Check for InfoPath Updates
Office Diagnostics
Activate InfoPath
InfoPath Customer Feedback Options</td><td>Microsoft Office InfoPath Developer Resources</td></tr>
</table>

WARNING Where Are the InfoPath Menu Items?

Many InfoPath-specific menu items are neither visible nor available unless the *manifest.xsf [Design]* tab is selected.

Forms Services

Some menu items are unavailable in VSTO when you design browser-enabled form templates.

Some additional InfoPath options in VSTO are located under the *Microsoft Office InfoPath* category in the *Options* menu item of the *Tools* menu (Figure 16.9). You'll recognize these settings from the *Options* dialog's *Design* and *Advanced* tabs in InfoPath. These settings between VSTO and InfoPath are shared by the same registry keys. So any changes in this dialog will also reflect in InfoPath, and vice versa.

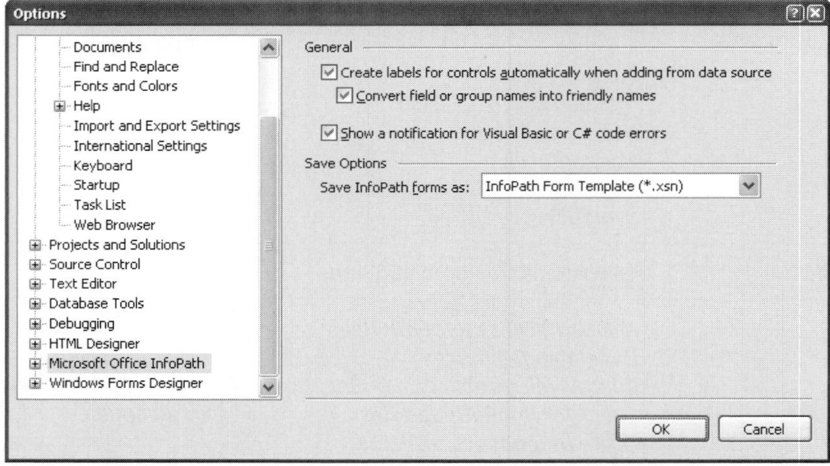

FIGURE 16.9: Microsoft Office InfoPath category options in the VSTO Options dialog

The *Show a notification for Visual Basic or C# code errors* checkbox, visible in Figure 16.9, dictates whether InfoPath exceptions are shown when a user fills out the form. When the checkbox is checked, any error in running code when the form is filled out reveals itself as a dialog, similar to that shown in Figure 16.10. This checkbox, however, applies only for real form-filling sessions; that is, previewing a form is unaffected. Previewing a form always shows notifications for code errors.

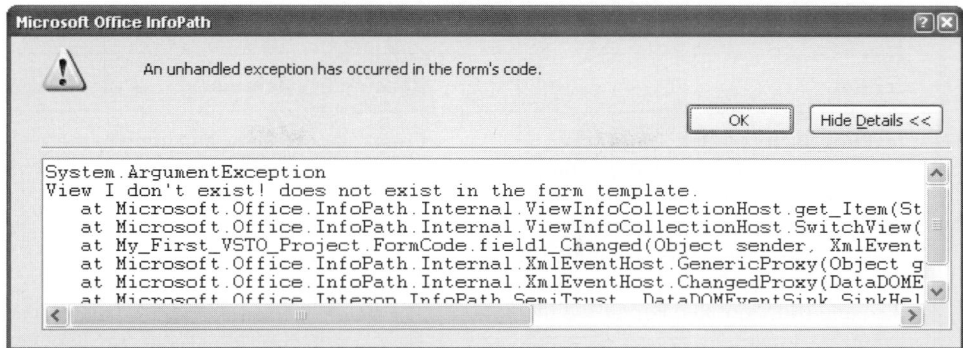

FIGURE 16.10: Notification for managed code errors, which makes debugging easier

---

Forms Services

The *Show a notification for managed code errors* checkbox does not affect forms running under Forms Services.

> **NOTE Double Notifications for Unhandled Exceptions?**
>
> When the *Show a notification for managed code errors* option is enabled or you're previewing the form, you may see two subsequent dialogs when an error occurs. The first dialog will be similar to that shown in Figure 16.10, while the second is what the user will see regardless of the *Show a notification* setting.

Working with Controls

Now that you're familiar with inserting controls and getting accustomed to the menu items that InfoPath adds to Visual Studio, let's see how to work with controls in the view. One of the biggest differences when designing a form template in VSTO lies in how a control responds when double-clicked. As we know, InfoPath shows the control's properties dialog. VSTO, on the other hand, jumps into the form code and creates a `Changed` event handler for the node bound to that control. This may feel a little odd (and sometimes annoying) at first. But in the grand scheme of using the Visual Studio Designer, that's what all controls do! Whether you're creating an HTML page, an ASP.NET Web site, or a Windows application in Visual Studio,

TABLE 16.2: InfoPath Controls' Behaviors on Double-Click

Control	Double-Click Behavior
Text Box, Rich Text Box, Date Picker, Option Button, (Optional/Repeating/Recursive) Section, (Repeating) Choice (Section/Group), File Attachment, Bulleted/Numbered/Plain List, Picture, Ink Picture, Drop-Down List Box, Combo Box, and (Horizontally) Repeating Table	Create, if necessary, and jump to the `Changed` event in form code.
All unbound controls (Button, Expression Box, Scrolling/Horizontal Region, etc.)	Open the properties dialog for the control.

double-clicking on a control in the Visual Studio Designer creates and jumps into the `OnClick` or `OnChange` handler for that control. InfoPath now conforms to the Visual Studio standard! This is a giant departure from the InfoPath design mode. But not all of the InfoPath controls jump into code. Table 16.2 documents the behaviors you can expect when double-clicking on an InfoPath control in VSTO.

> **NOTE** **`Changed` Event as Default XML Event**
>
> The `Changed` event was chosen as the default event over the `Changing` and `Validating` events because of its ubiquity in InfoPath forms. It is also the most flexible XML event because the main data source is not read-only. See Chapter 15 for details regarding XML events.

Since a double-click sends you into code, you need a quick way to get to a control's properties. There are a couple of ways to do so. One option is to use the Alt+Enter key shortcut carried over from InfoPath. An alternative is to use the shortcut key from the school of Visual Studio: F4. As always, you can still right-click on a control and get the menu, which is similar to that shown in InfoPath. The last item in the right-click menu is yet another entry point for the properties dialog. The resulting properties dialog mimics the same UI you see in InfoPath.

> **TIP Mistakenly Created an Event Handler?**
>
> Did you double-click and jump into code, but you meant to go to the control's properties dialog instead? Immediately after double-clicking and while still in the form code, perform four undo operations. (Undo the event handler formatting, remove the event handler, undo the `EventManager` hookup formatting, and finally remove the `EventManager` hookup.)

If you're versed in working with controls in the Visual Studio Designer, you might know there's a *Properties Window* menu item (accessible via the *View* menu). The *Properties Window* dialog is a modeless and dockable window that exposes quick access to read and change properties for a selected control. You can witness the *Properties Window* dialog behavior with any ASP.NET or Windows Forms controls, for example, by simply selecting the control in the Visual Studio Designer. Unfortunately, InfoPath's VSTO support does not include integrating with this dialog. As a result, it will always be empty when you select an InfoPath control. The workaround is to use the conventional InfoPath properties dialog as described earlier.

> **TIP Got Switching Sickness?**
>
> Sick of switching to and from the *FormCode* and *manifest.xsf [Design]* tabs? Try selecting *New Vertical* (or *Horizontal*) *Tab Group* from the *Window* menu.

The VSTO Feature Set

VSTO doesn't just integrate InfoPath design mode into Visual Studio, it also buys you some Visual Studio–specific features that tie into the designing experience. Some of the VSTO integration features do not give you more functionality than InfoPath. Other features, such as source control, add value when you're designing a single form template in a multideveloper setting. Let's take a look at a few feature highlights in VSTO that carry over from Visual Studio.

Find and Replace

Find is one of those features we all take for granted because it should just work. However, using find and replace while designing a form template in InfoPath wasn't always a smooth operation. InfoPath uses a task pane to find and replace text, so it can feel a little odd. VSTO doesn't reuse the *Find* and *Replace* task panes. Instead, the Visual Studio–specific *Find and Replace* dialog takes their place. Unfortunately, the find feature in VSTO is no more useful in functionality than its InfoPath counterpart. At first, the dialog appears to offer more flexibility (Figure 16.11). However, this turns out not to be the case. Only the *Current Document* option is available for the *Look in* drop-down when manifest.xsf is being designed. Other selections, such as *Entire Solution*, work only when manifest.xsf is not being designed. But the results, oddly enough, include all files in the project, except the InfoPath Form Template folder. Keep in mind that the InfoPath Form Template folder contains the form and all of its files, so everything you find won't be within the form template!

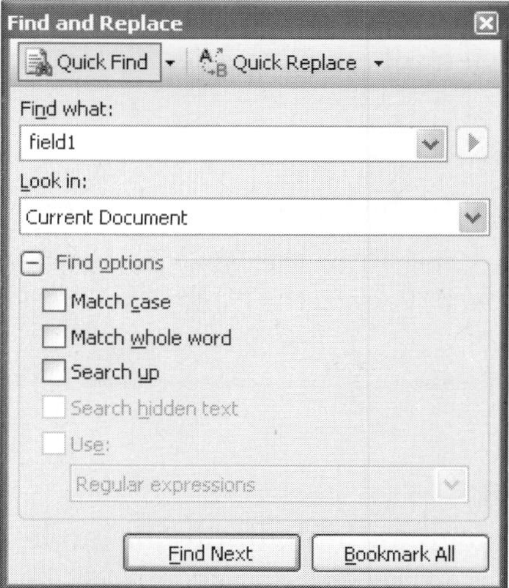

FIGURE 16.11: Quick Find in VSTO

> **NOTE** Quick Replace
>
> *Quick Replace* offers functionality similar to that of *Quick Find.*

Additional options such as *Match case, Match whole word,* and *Use* are already available in InfoPath and yield the same results. The *Search hidden text* checkbox is available but isn't useful because there's no such concept when you're designing a form template. The *Search up* option is available in VSTO and is identical to the InfoPath design mode.

> **NOTE** Find In Files
>
> The *Find* and *Replace In Files* features from Visual Studio are not supported when you're designing the manifest.xsf file.

> **TIP** Find/Replace in Code Files
>
> You can still use find and replace within some files in your project by first going to another tab (e.g., *FormCode.cs*) from the *manifest.xsf [Design]* tab and then initiating the search. When you do so, all code files will be searched. But this still won't search the InfoPath Form Template folder files, including the XSF, XSL, and XSD file types.

> **NOTE** Bookmarks
>
> Bookmarks are not available when you design InfoPath form templates in VSTO.

Source Control with Visual SourceSafe

Visual SourceSafe is compatible with designing a form template by using VSTO. However, there is a significant caveat: All form template files in the InfoPath Form Template folder are read-only while you're actively designing a form template in VSTO. As a result, you may need to perform SourceSafe operations (such as adding, checking in, or checking out form template files) while the project is closed. If a SourceSafe operation fails while the project is still open, the workaround is to perform the same operation with the project closed.

Visual Studio Project-Specific Features

If you are familiar with the Visual Studio environment, you may already know that its project management is quite extensive. VSTO takes advantage of the full breadth of the Visual Studio feature set, so you can leverage these features while designing your form templates. We'll review two specific capabilities: working with multiple projects and exporting the Visual Studio project as a template for later reuse.

Working with Multiple Projects You're probably accustomed to building a single project while working in the Visual Studio environment. While there's usually a one-to-one mapping between a Visual Studio solution and a project, that's not always the case. It's possible to have multiple projects within a single solution. There are many scenarios when multiple projects are useful. A prime example is when you're building a Windows program and a shared library. Most likely you'll want to build the shared library as an application extension (.dll) file and the program as a separate executable (.exe) file. If you are a Web developer, you might have used multiple projects to separate your Web site from the server's back-end logic. The back end may interact with a Web service or database—both of which can be separate projects!

A compelling multiproject scenario for an InfoPath form template in VSTO is hosting. (Chapter 18 looks at hosting InfoPath forms.) While we'll leave the details until our discussion in Chapter 18, the idea is simple: In addition to your InfoPath project, add a new Windows application project. The new application may have an InfoPath form control, which allows hosting of the InfoPath form template that you're designing. Don't forget to set the startup project to the Windows application in the Visual Studio Solution Explorer. Of course, you'll need to point the form control to the form template you're building. At this point, the Windows application takes an explicit dependency on the InfoPath form template. Hit F5 to start running the program with the form control. Visual Studio will automatically build all of the dependencies in the correct order. Any changes you make in the form template will automatically appear in your program!

To begin adding a new project to an open solution in Visual Studio, start by right-clicking on the solution icon at the top of the Solution Explorer. Under the *Add* fly-out menu is the *New Project* item. If you already have a project you want to include, you can also use the *Existing Project* item under the *Add* menu.

Exporting Projects as Templates Not to be confused with an InfoPath form template, a Visual Studio project template is, of course, specific to Visual Studio. It allows you to save a VSTO-based InfoPath form template in design mode and use it as a basis for creating new form templates in VSTO. It captures the state of the entire form template, including form code and project-specific settings. Visual Studio templates are handy in several cases:

- Designing many form templates that are similar but need to be different form template (.xsn) files
- Providing a common standard form template when working in a collaborative environment
- Customizing InfoPath's VSTO definition of a new, blank form template

To create a Visual Studio template from a form template at any time, select the *Export Template* option from the *File* menu. You may be prompted to close the *manifest.xsf [Design]* tab as well as save the project before continuing. When creating the template, you'll have to choose either the *Project template* or the *Item template* option. Choosing to create a project template will take your entire InfoPath VSTO project and add it to the *New Project* dialog when a new Visual Studio project is created. To find the project template you created, look under the *Visual C#* (or *Visual Basic*) item on the *New Project* dialog. Your template will appear under the *My Templates* section.

Creating an item template, on the other hand, is not so interesting for InfoPath form templates. Creating an item template requires that you select only a single file within your existing project. For example, you could create an item template based on your view.xsl or manifest.xsf file. While it's possible to create such a template, it's not plausible to reuse it. As you may know, a form template's files (.xsf, .xsl, .xml, .xsd) are strongly tied together. Copying a view file from one form template to another (which is essentially what you'd be doing by making an item template from a view.xsl file and reusing it in another VSTO InfoPath project) is really not supported.

Resource Editing

A convenient advantage of the VSTO environment is the ability to edit auxiliary resource files such as HTML files for the custom task pane and XML files. While both the VSTO and InfoPath applications use the *Resource Files* dialog (accessed from the *Tools* menu) shown in Figure 16.12 to manage files, InfoPath doesn't let you view the file. The only operations you can perform on a file are *Add, Remove, Rename,* and *Export.*

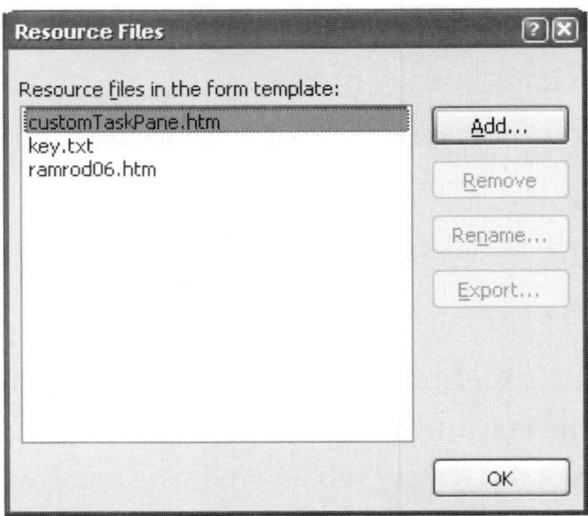

FIGURE 16.12: Resource Files dialog used in InfoPath and VSTO

In VSTO, adding a resource file to the form template lists that file in the Solution Explorer under the InfoPath Form Template folder. To edit a resource file, simply double-click the item in the Solution Explorer. While the process of adding resource files in InfoPath and VSTO is the same, VSTO offers the resource-editing experience missing from InfoPath.

> **WARNING Adding Resource Files to a Form Template**
>
> Add resources by using the *Resource Files* item on the *Tools* menu. Manually putting an existing item into the InfoPath Form Template folder in the Solution Explorer does not properly add the resource to the form template!

Code-Specific Features

Resource editing is just one of the benefits of using VSTO. While extending the experience of designing form templates is a valuable proposition, some form designers really just want a powerful code editor. Since we're working in the Visual Studio environment, this is the sweet spot of InfoPath and Visual Studio integration! Let's look at some of the advanced code-editing features at our disposal when writing form code.

Signing Code signing, or the creation of a strong-named assembly, is the process by which an assembly is uniquely identified and claimed to be published by a specific vendor (and untampered with by anyone else). Since we could spend many pages (and even a few chapters!) on code signing, we'll assume you understand the benefits and are interested in signing your form code assemblies. To sign a form code assembly using Visual Studio 2005, simply follow the step-by-step tutorial on MSDN. Another resource, including an introduction on code signing, is also on MSDN. (The Appendix lists both of these resources.)

Refactoring Writing form code for an InfoPath form template usually doesn't turn out perfectly the first time. For example, you might notice you're copying and pasting or writing similar blocks of code in many places. One such case might be getting an `XPathNavigator` to the document element of the main data source. Or maybe you want to just rename a variable so it's more representative of its purpose. Although most programmers would just do this work manually, it's really a redundant and repetitive task that can be automated by software. Why not leave the dirty work to Visual Studio? Thanks to code refactoring features available in Visual Studio 2005, numerous refactoring algorithms are a simple click away.

To use the refactoring feature in Visual Studio 2005, right-click on the code you want to refactor. The right-click could be on something as simple as a variable name or a multiline selection of code. On the right-click menu, select the *Refactor* fly-out menu item. Figure 16.13 shows the *Refactor* menu items.

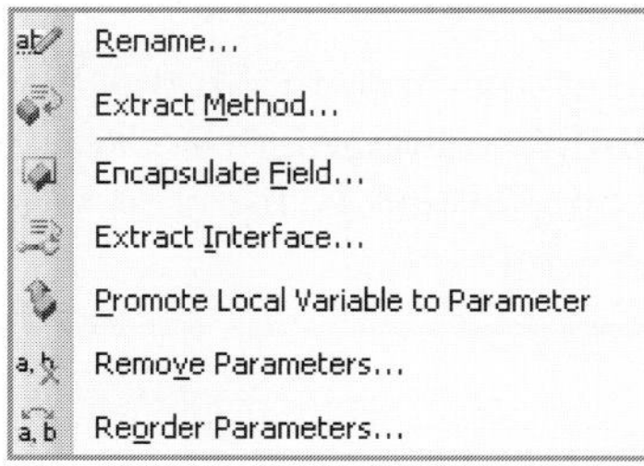

FIGURE 16.13: Visual Studio 2005 refactoring tools

NOTE Refactoring in Visual Studio 2005

Read up on the refactoring capabilities in Visual Studio 2005 on MSDN, as referenced in the Appendix.

Code Snippets Another cool code-editing feature in Visual Studio 2005 is the use of code snippets. Code snippets are a collection of ready-to-use code samples that you can insert into your source. To use a code snippet, select *Insert Snippet* on the right-click context menu. Table 16.3 shows some commonly used code snippets.

TABLE 16.3: Commonly Used Code Snippets

Snippet Name	Expanded Code
`mbox`	`MessageBox.Show("Test");`
`cw`	`Console.WriteLine();`
`try`	`try { }` `catch (Exception) { throw; }`

Another aspect of code snippets is *Surround With* functionality, also available on the context menu. Some code snippets, like the `try` snippet, are slight inconveniences if you need to cut and paste existing code. With *Surround With* it's easy: Just select the code to surround in a try-catch block and use the `try` surround snippet.

TIP Want Your Own Custom Snippets?

The *Code Snippet Manager* menu item, on the *Tools* menu of Visual Studio, offers an extensibility mechanism so you can add new, custom snippets. This could come in handy for common blocks of code when you're authoring InfoPath form code.

> **NOTE Code-Editing Features in Visual Studio 2005**
>
> For a full list of new code-editing features in Visual Studio 2005, check out MSDN, as referenced in the Appendix.

Missing Features in VSTO

An overwhelming majority of InfoPath features carry over to VSTO. Although most are congruent, some features exist in a different way, and others may not even be available. If you can't find what you're looking for in VSTO, InfoPath is there as a backup. You always have the option of designing a VSTO-based form template in InfoPath design mode if you choose.

Tables Toolbar

The *Tables* toolbar, shown in Figure 16.14, does not exist in VSTO. However, you can find the same functionality by using the items on the VSTO *Table* menu.

FIGURE 16.14: InfoPath Tables toolbar, which is not available in VSTO

If you're the type of person who must have this toolbar, there is a workaround. You can create your own toolbar by right-clicking in the toolbar region and selecting *Customize*. After creating a new toolbar, it will appear empty. You can go to the *Commands* tab of the *Customize* dialog to add table-specific commands to your toolbar via drag and drop.

> **NOTE No Eraser in VSTO**
>
> The eraser is the only table tool unavailable in VSTO.

Save and Save As Form Template Commands

InfoPath offers the *Save* and *Save As* commands from the *File* menu. Using either of these commands creates a form template (.xsn) file. VSTO instead has *Save* and *Save All* options that update the existing manifest.xsf file. In fact, the *Save As* command is explicitly disabled when you're designing a form template. But if you need to save as a form template (.xsn) file, there are several workarounds available. One option is to publish the form template by using the *Publish* command on the *Build* menu. A longer approach is to use InfoPath instead of VSTO. First, browse to the InfoPath Form Template folder associated with the form template's Visual Studio project. Next, right-click on the manifest.xsf file and select *Design* to open the form template directly into InfoPath design mode. From there you can save as usual.

> **TIP Design Using InfoPath, Too**
>
> Remember that you can edit the form template's saved source files located in the InfoPath Form Template folder by using InfoPath, and then you can reopen them in VSTO.

> **WARNING Use One Design Environment at a Time**
>
> When you're designing a form template in one environment, make sure that it's not open in another. For example, if the form template is open in VSTO, it should not be open in InfoPath design mode. Both VSTO and InfoPath place a lock on all form template files when they're in design.

Information Rights Management (IRM)

You cannot use VSTO to restrict permissions for a form template. To accommodate IRM, you must first open the form template in InfoPath. Once IRM is set up, you can save the form template source files and then reopened them in VSTO.

To learn more about IRM, see Chapter 11.

Limited InfoPath Settings on the VSTO Options Dialog

We mentioned earlier (and showed in Figure 16.9) that the *Options* dialog in VSTO has a specific *Microsoft Office InfoPath* category. But the InfoPath options offer a limited set of preferences compared with the *Options* dialog used by InfoPath. Opening InfoPath in design mode to view and edit these settings is one way to work around this limitation, but there's an easier way. In InfoPath, the *Options* dialog has two identical entry points: the *Tools* menu in design mode and also the *Tools* menu in fill-out-a-form mode (including preview). Since this dialog is not available in VSTO design mode, just fill out the form (while still in VSTO) to open the form in a preview window. Since the InfoPath *Options* dialog exists from the preview window, you won't need to go out of your way to open InfoPath design or fill-out-a-form modes. Any changes made from preview will apply to all modes and environments (whether you're designing, previewing, or filling out a form in either VSTO or InfoPath).

Print Preview

Visual Studio 2005 offers print preview (through the *Print* dialog) for most project types. Unfortunately, VSTO does not support print preview while you're designing InfoPath form templates. To print preview your form template, use InfoPath design mode instead. Print preview is still available when you're previewing from VSTO.

> **NOTE** Macro Recording
>
> Visual Studio's Macro Recording feature is unavailable when you're designing a form template in VSTO.

Previewing a Form in VSTO

VSTO buys the form designer a richer design experience in Visual Studio. However, users must still use InfoPath to fill out your forms. Similar to InfoPath, VSTO lets you preview the form directly from its environment. You can preview by selecting *Start Debugging* or *Start Without Debugging* from the *Debug* menu. Alternatively, you can hit F5 or Shift+F5, respectively. Previewing a form in VSTO is identical to doing so in InfoPath.

You can find more information on previewing forms in Chapter 9.

What's Next?

Visual Studio is undoubtedly the ultimate development environment for designing InfoPath form templates. Especially with the powerful code-editing and convenience features, VSTO makes complicated projects easier to manage. In the next chapter, we'll extend our conversation from Chapter 14 to discuss the advanced features of browser-enabled form templates and InfoPath Forms Services. In Chapter 18, we look at hosting InfoPath using custom .NET and C++ applications. You'll also learn about how to host a form in the browser by creating a custom ASP.NET page in Visual Studio. With VSTO under your belt, creating hosted forms will be easier since your development can be entirely under one solution and all in Visual Studio.

17

Advanced Forms Services

Getting Started

Since we've transitioned to the advanced part of the book, we've looked at programming InfoPath and Visual Studio integration through VSTO. We now shift back to designing forms for the server and using Forms Services. This chapter starts where Chapter 14 leaves off. We assume you have a working understanding of how to design and fill out browser-based forms. After you finish reading this chapter, you will have a deeper understanding of topics specific to Forms Services, such as form postbacks, administration, performance and monitoring, and data connections. We'll even show you how to emulate missing features from Forms Services, such as user roles and showing UI such as message boxes!

To start the chapter, we'll look at the Design Checker and the messages we encountered from our MOI feedback sample in Chapter 14. You'll learn how to make sense of the messages and what we should do to address them. The discussion will then carry over to **postbacks** (which is how the form updates its data with the server). We also include a brief section on designing accessible forms. Unfortunately, InfoPath does not always include accessibility-specific meta information on controls in a form. We'll show you how to add this information to keep all of your customers happy.

The next topic in the chapter is about **writing code for browser-enabled form templates**. Although we mentioned in Chapter 15 that the "design once" methodology of InfoPath applies to code, there are some "gotchas" that you should know about. We'll relay these important differences as well as offer tips on what object model (OM) methods and properties you can count on to be identical between InfoPath and Forms Services. We also take advantage of this section on form code to implement workarounds to browser limitations. One example is the inability to show user interface elements such as dialog boxes.

Administration for Forms Services is integrated into the SharePoint Central Administration site. We use most of this chapter to look at all the available configuration options you can use to administer your server. Included in these admin options are advanced publishing, form template management, and the session state service. Since administration is such an important topic, we give you three different approaches via Web UI, command-line, and object model interfaces. One or more of these approaches may work better depending on your specific scenario.

One of the biggest functional differences between forms that run in the browser and those that run in InfoPath is the behavior of data connections. As we mentioned in Chapter 14 and will expand on in this chapter, data connections are run on the server. Given the security implications of querying and submitting connection data from the server, there is a new set of supporting features to make connections more secure. We'll cover topics such as administration settings, the **centrally managed connection library**, and connection authentication.

We finish off the chapter with an in-depth dialogue on **performance** and **monitoring**. Putting an InfoPath form into the browser raises new performance considerations, including scalability, throughput, and latency. Server stresses occur when many people decide to fill out forms simultaneously. We'll show you how to analyze and concentrate on various aspects of the server using a feature-based approach as well as using tools such as the Windows Performance Monitor and Microsoft Operations Manager. There are also many other performance issues to address, such as the design complexity of your form template and even external factors like data connections. After finishing this chapter, you will have the knowledge to design and deploy high-performance and scalable form templates for filling out in a Web browser.

Controls and Browser Optimizations

In Chapter 14, you learned that browser-enabled form templates are pretty easy to design and deploy. By simply setting the compatibility mode to *Design a form template that can be opened in a browser or InfoPath,* you can have the Design Checker report a series of messages and errors regarding browser compatibilities. Any errors must be fixed before publishing to the server. On the other hand, messages need not be addressed. It's fine to publish and test your form template on Forms Services when messages exist. However, it's vital to understand the consequences of using such a form on the server.

While designing the MOI feedback form in Chapter 14, we encountered browser optimization messages in the *Design Checker* task pane. Figure 17.1 shows those same messages. (The MOI feedback form template is included as MoiFeedback_WebEnabled in this chapter's samples on the book's Web site.) We know it's okay to publish such templates to the server for use in the browser, but remember that optimization issues can severely hamper the performance of your form and even your server farm. In this example, we have two classes of messages: *Browser Compatibility* and *Browser Optimization.* The messages listed under *Browser Compatibility* include those form features that do not exist in the browser. There are no performance implications when compatibility issues arise, but simply a warning to the form designer that the experiences between the browser and InfoPath program may differ. Let's focus our efforts on parsing and making decisions on the *Browser Optimization* class of messages.

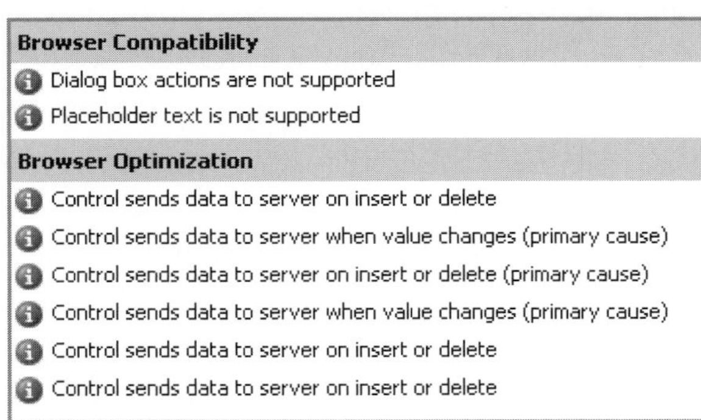

FIGURE 17.1: Design Checker messages from the MOI feedback form template

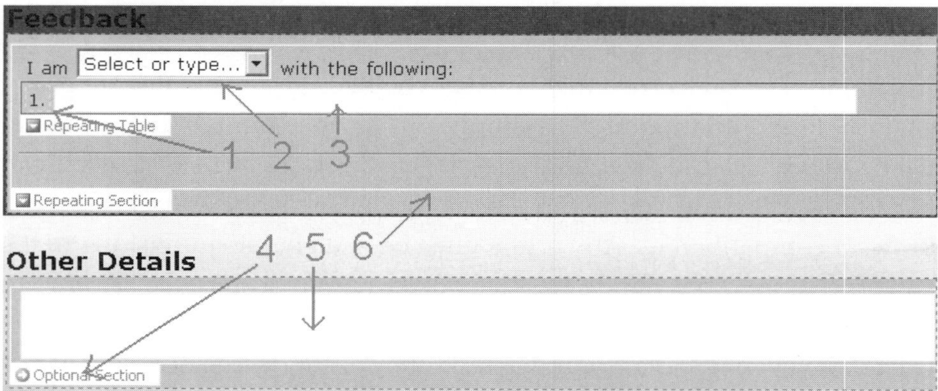

FIGURE 17.2: Controls targeted by the messages in the Design Checker for the MOI feedback form template

Although we see six different entries in the *Browser Optimization* list in Figure 17.1, there are only two core issues. The other messages are either side effects of the primary causes or separate issues. Let's take a closer look at the messages and their associated controls in the view to clarify exactly what the Design Checker is detecting. We'll use Figure 17.2 to correlate messages with the view. The numbers in Figure 17.2 may not correspond with the order of messages in Figure 17.1.

Recall from Chapter 14 the complex XPath we used for the Expression Box (shown as "1" in Figure 17.2): `concat(count(preceding-sibling::*) + 1, ".")`. We mentioned that the Expression Box (which helped us mimic a Numbered List control) was causing the majority of the messages. It should be no surprise, then, that the Expression Box is targeted as a primary cause. How, then, are the Drop-Down List Box ("2") and Text Box ("3") implicated in the optimization messages? Let's take a moment to analyze the situation. The XPath used by the Expression Box references the `preceding-siblings` axis, that is, previous items of the "current" item (i.e., the context of a given Expression Box). Recall that the "current" item is just one in potentially many of the repeating group representing the items. The count of the previous items (plus one, of course) gives us the number we'd expect to appear in the Expression Box. If you think about it, we're only counting the repeating group bound to the Repeating Table. For the sake of the calculated XPath expression in the Expression Box, we don't care about the Text Box or the Drop-Down List Box.

The Text Box, despite being within the Repeating Table (whose rows we're counting), neither is affected by nor affects the Expression Box value because there's no dependency. That is, the value of the Text Box is mutually exclusive from the XPath of the Expression Box. The same argument applies for the Drop-Down List Box control. Furthermore, the Repeating Section, represented by "6" in Figure 17.2, is a direct parent of both the Repeating Table and the Drop-Down List Box ("2"). As a result, Forms Services plays it safe and requests a postback for the Repeating Section for the proper rendering of the Section and its contents.

The Optional Section and Rich Text Box ("4" and "5", respectively) are associated with the *Control sends data to server on insert or delete* entries in the Design Checker. You might wonder why these controls require sending data to the server, and that's a good question! The two *(primary cause)* issues are associated with the Repeating Table and Drop-Down List Box. These controls and the nodes in the data source are not at all related to the Optional Section, the Rich Text Box, or their data source nodes. In fact, you're witnessing a case in which the algorithm Forms Services uses for dependency analysis is overcompensating. The Optional Section and Rich Text Box never need to send data to the server for the form to appear correctly in the browser.

> **NOTE Overcompensation in Dependency Analysis**
>
> Despite Forms Services requiring some controls to send data to the server in this sample, this is not very common. The likelihood of required but unnecessary server communication goes up with the complexity of the form template. Custom XPaths will typically cause this extra communication.

Forms Services references the Text Box, Drop-Down List Box, Repeating Table, Repeating Section, Optional Section, and Rich Text Box in its *Browser Optimization* list, giving the messages as *Control sends data to server when value changes*. Because of these messages, the form will talk to the server (referred to as a postback in ASP.NET) every time either the Text Box, Drop-Down List Box, or Rich Text Box values are changed or if the Repeating Section,

Repeating Table, or Optional Section controls are inserted or removed. There are two direct consequences of these optimization messages:

- A degraded user experience, especially with slower network connections
- Higher average server load; perceivable performance degradation under stress

Browser optimization issues typically affect both the browser client and the server. In this particular case, any editing of these controls results in a noticeable delay before form editing can proceed. In most cases, the *Sending data to the server* dialog will appear for a second or even longer, depending on connection speed and server processing time. On the server the effect is clear: It's yet another HTTP request that must be processed. Forms Services does a bit of work to process the request, too, such as reinstating the user session and processing the actions on the form. There are performance repercussions to consider—we'll analyze Forms Services form performance at the end of the chapter. Shortly, we'll also take a closer look at session and form action processing.

So far, we've figured out that all of the labeled controls, shown in Figure 17.2, require sending data to the server. We've also learned that there is a nontrivial cost associated with sending data to the server. We're witnessing a case where Forms Services is conservative in its analysis of our custom XPath expression. In fact, it's not smart enough to precisely determine which controls require updating and which do not. Its algorithm is designed to default to form correctness. This means that the browser is unable to do the required form processing. As such, the browser will send its data to the server for processing to occur.

NOTE **Sometimes the Server Must Do It**

Some form actions cannot be carried out in the browser itself, such as evaluating complex XPaths, executing business logic code, and digitally signing the form. These actions require the form to post back data to the server. A complete list appears in Chapter 14 (see Table 14.3).

While Forms Services has the first shot at warning us that extra postbacks are inevitable, it doesn't have the final word! We know that we don't want (or need) the Text Box and Drop-Down List Box to talk to the server. It's nice to know that as the form designer, you have the final word on any browser optimization issues. Let's see how we can configure our form template so that the browser does not post back when the data in these controls changes.

Postback Settings

Your options for mitigating optimization issues aren't limited to changing the XPath or just putting up with the extra postbacks. When you're designing a form with InfoPath 2007 in browser-compatibility mode, most controls have a new *Browser forms* tab in their properties dialogs. Let's start with the Text Box in the Repeating Section shown in Figure 17.2. As you can see in Figure 17.3, we changed the postback settings from the default of *Only when necessary* to *Never.*

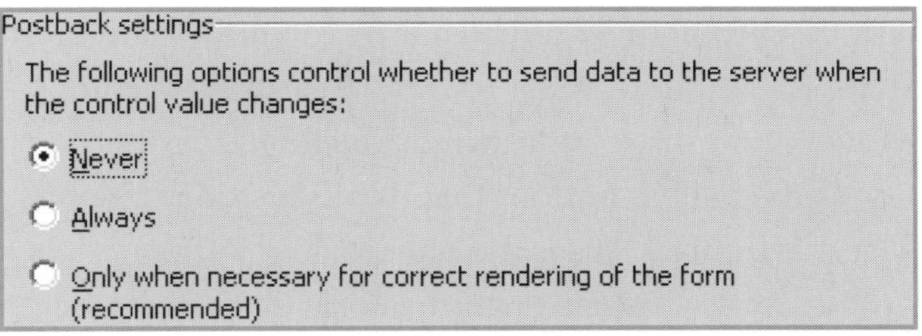

FIGURE 17.3: Postback settings for a control in a browser-enabled form template

With the simple change of overriding postback settings for the controls labeled in Figure 17.2, we effectively suppress each control from automatically posting back when the values change or an item is inserted or removed. You should ensure that suppressing control postbacks is acceptable in a form-filling experience. For example, if you suppress postback on the Repeating Table in Figure 17.2, the Expression Box will not show the correct value as new rows are inserted. It's important to thoroughly test your form using realistic scenarios after repressing any control postback actions.

TIP Use the Verify on Server Option to Get Optimization Messages

Browser optimization messages are provided only when you check *Verify on Server* on the *Design Checker* task pane.

The Update Button

While the postback algorithm is usually correct or conservative (as we saw in the MOI feedback form template), that may not always be the case. Sometimes the browser won't post back when it should. Most times, you can correct these one-off cases by selecting the *Always* option shown in Figure 17.3. However, there may be rare cases in highly complex templates where form data doesn't update as you would expect. Even with the post-back settings on a control set for *Always,* you might find that some parts of the form don't update as expected. This may happen because the browser form does not realize it needs to refresh some of its data. If you find a form template with this problem, you'll be happy to know there's a way to effectively force the form data to post back to the server. Sending data to the server is a way to guarantee your form is displayed properly.

In addition to the toolbar buttons that we discussed in Chapter 14, you can also add an *Update* button. This is the only toolbar button that is not selected by default in the *Browser* category on the *Form Options* dialog (Figure 17.4). The *Update* button, when added in this dialog, adds an *Update* button at the end of the toolbar in browser forms. This button specifically refreshes the

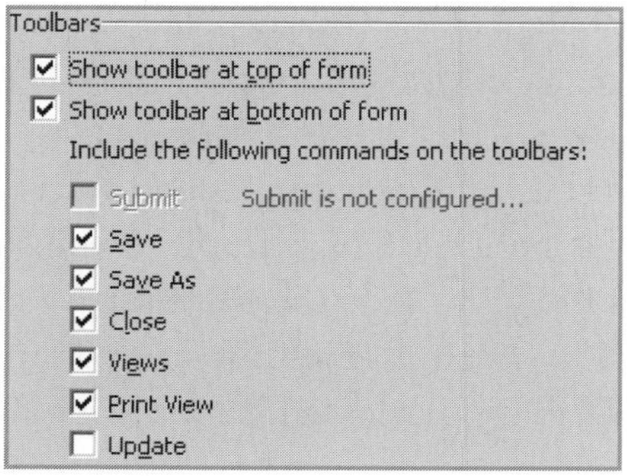

FIGURE 17.4: Customizing toolbar buttons for a browser-enabled form template

form data with the server. Clicking it at any time when filling out a form can never negatively affect your data. As we mentioned, it's useful to add this button to your form if there's a reason for the user to have manual control over the refreshing of form data. Keep in mind that it's not a "free lunch" to expose this button to your users. Despite its harmless demeanor, every click to the *Update* button results in the form passing data from the browser to the server and then the server returning the updated form back to the browser. Extra postback requests to the server potentially reduce its ability to support its otherwise maximum number of simultaneous users. We'll look more carefully at the effects of form features and behaviors, such as postbacks, toward the end of this chapter.

If your browser-enabled form template does not show toolbars (i.e., you unchecked both of the *Show toolbar* items shown in Figure 17.4), the *Update* button will obviously not be available. This may be the case if your browser-based form is hosted in an ASP.NET Web page. In hosting a form, however, the toolbars may disrupt the overall flow and layout of your page. (Hosting a browser form is a topic of Chapter 18.) If you still need update functionality but don't have a toolbar, you have another option.

A Button control can provide the same update functionality offered by the *Update* toolbar button. When you're designing a browser-enabled template, the Button control offers a new action called *Update Form* (Figure 17.5).

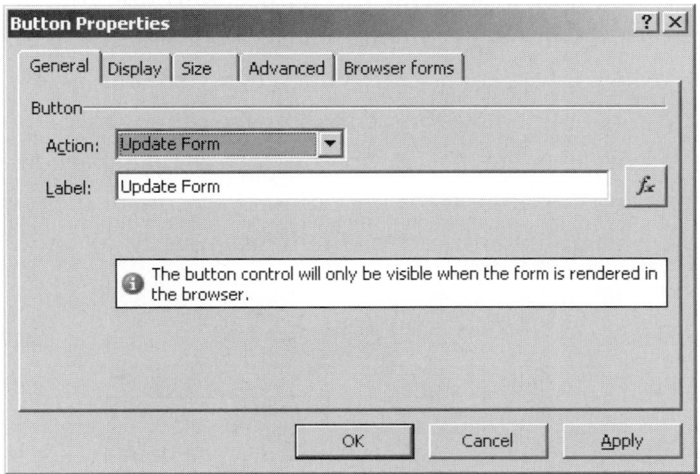

FIGURE 17.5: Configuring a Button control to use the Update Form option for a browser-enabled form template

The *Update Form* action does not apply to forms filled out in InfoPath. As a result, all Button controls with the action set to *Update Form* are not visible in InfoPath.

Designing Accessible Forms

InfoPath makes it easy to design sleek and functional forms for collecting data. Sometimes form designers get a little carried away with making their templates overcomplicated or too feature-rich. Obviously, it's important to remember your audience when designing your forms. But no matter how much effort you may dedicate to improving your template, someone is bound to complain about its usability. We think form usability is an underrated topic in design considerations, especially in forms found on the Internet. Given the wider reach of audiences with Forms Services over InfoPath, we believe that a successful browser-enabled form is one that is easy for everyone to use.

Chapter 4, in the "Control Properties" section, discusses various settings for configuring form controls. In particular, the subsection about the *Advanced* tab introduces the *ScreenTip, Tab index,* and *Access key* settings (Figure 17.6). We can't stress enough the importance of filling in these fields with accurate information to help guide users who fill out your forms. Without these fields' data, it can be particularly troublesome (or nearly impossible) for users with special needs to use your form. Some people may incorrectly believe that making a form accessible is synonymous with using only a keyboard. While keyboard-only access is a basic litmus test, a conventional keyboard and mouse cannot be assumed. Many accessibility tools leverage these properties (*ScreenTip* in particular) to help users with various disabilities or impediments. Some of them even interface with special equipment, such as Braille keyboards, to convey browser information.

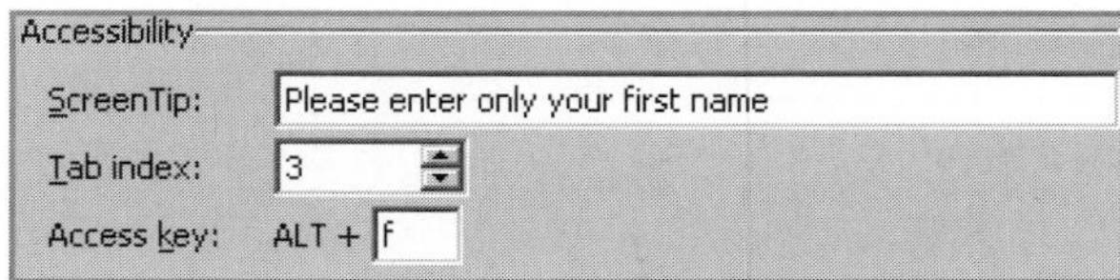

FIGURE 17.6: Accessibility control settings

NOTE Designing Accessible Forms

See Chapter 4 for more information on designing accessible InfoPath form templates.

Searching Form Data

Microsoft SharePoint Server for Search indexes all content on the SharePoint site. For InfoPath forms, Search crawls all promoted properties and goes only one level deep in the form data. You should consider promoting any properties that may be helpful when using search to query your forms for data. Remember that you will receive search results only for those items in which you have permission to at least read.

Form Code

While reading Chapter 14, you learned that JScript code is not supported on the server. This was evident by an error listed in the Design Checker when verifying the MOI feedback form template. Despite the lack of support for form templates with script, Forms Services still supports templates with code. At the beginning of Chapter 15, we mentioned that Forms Services supports only the InfoPath 2007 managed object model (OM). In fact, that's the only version of the OM we focused on. Couple your knowledge of the OM with its "design once" approach (see Chapter 14), and you can directly apply much of your InfoPath programming skills to Forms Services!

NOTE Form Code Adheres to Design Once

Recall that design once is InfoPath's design paradigm for supporting browser-enabled form templates. By virtue of the Design Checker, a template can be designed once for InfoPath and the browser.

The best approach to adding form code to a browser-enabled form is to do so *after* switching the design mode to be compatible with InfoPath Forms Services. Unlike the variety of declarative InfoPath features that the Design Checker knows (and warns you) about, form code is a different beast. The Design Checker attempts to parse your custom form code, but it cannot tell you in all cases whether or not you're using a construct that will work on the server. When the design mode is switched from InfoPath-only to browser-enabled, or vice versa, the VSTA or VSTO project's assembly references are modified. (We mentioned in Chapter 15 that a different version of the Microsoft.Office.InfoPath.dll assembly is referenced. Also, it's important to know that the System.Windows.Forms.dll reference is removed.) If you wrote code against the InfoPath-only OM and then switched to design a browser-enabled template, you'll be relying on build warnings and errors to carry you through the transition. While this is fine, it's much less of a hassle to just start writing code with the template already set as browser-enabled. Later in this chapter (see Table 17.2), we'll give you a complete list of unsupported object model classes, methods, properties, and events in Forms Services. This list will show you, before you write code, what constructs you might be using in InfoPath that aren't available in the browser.

> **NOTE** Forms Services Object Model
>
> The object model available on the server is a strict subset of that offered by InfoPath. In other words, there is no server-specific OM.

Before we jump into object model differences between programming for InfoPath and Forms Services, we want to first focus on form code for browser-enabled templates. What, exactly, does it mean to run form code in the context of a server-based browser form? We'll take a brief look at how the server executes the form code associated with a template. Of course, our discussion is not complete unless you're able to troubleshoot and debug your code, right? You may be surprised to know it's easier than you might think.

Executing Form Code in the Browser

Don't be fooled by the title of this section—it's somewhat of a misnomer! When a form template with code is deployed on Forms Services and running in a Web browser, the code itself isn't actually run in the browser. It's executed on the server. Because the server executes the code, there are some serious security implications to consider. As we'll see in a later discussion on advanced publishing, templates with code must be deployed by a server administrator and may (but are not required to) demand full trust. You can view a fully trusted form template with code as a managed executable that can run with full administrative privileges on your server. If that doesn't sound scary (which it absolutely should!), consider the fact that such a template can do utterly anything it wants to your server. In our section on advanced publishing, we'll look at various ways you, as the administrator, can effectively censor such highly privileged templates for coherence before they go live on your farm.

Data Source Events Are Lazy

Say that we have a browser-enabled form template where we sink every available data source and form event. Then we fill out the form side by side in InfoPath and the browser. How does the behavior of the form in InfoPath compare to that in the browser? You may be pleased to know that the experience is very similar in almost every respect. Of course, this is what you'd expect with design once: Write the same code once and it works in both InfoPath and Forms Services. Although the parity between the platforms exists, the browser reacts differently in response to data source events. The browser is lazy compared to InfoPath. Let's see what this means.

To better understand the difference between InfoPath and Forms Services with respect to data source events, let's take a very simple example. Say that we create a form template with a single Text Box (bound to `field1`). Then we define an event handler for `field1` to listen to either the `Validating` or `Changed` event; it doesn't matter. Do something in that event handler so you know when it runs—such as setting `field1` to `"Hello, InfoPath!"` Now fill out that form by editing the Text Box in both InfoPath and the browser. In InfoPath, you'll notice that the Text Box will immediately show `"Hello, InfoPath!"` after you click or tab away. What happens in the browser? Unlike InfoPath, the Text Box doesn't change after an edit! Forms Services, by default, does not automatically run form code on demand. Its behavior is such, as we'll see toward the end of this chapter, for performance motivations. The form code for data source events is run only when data is sent to the server on a postback. Later in the chapter, you'll learn more about how the server gets the form data from the browser on a postback.

As you can see, sinking data source events, such as `Validating` or `Changed`, does not fire event handler code immediately after the data is changed. To make this happen in the browser exactly as it does in InfoPath, you'll need to configure the control's *Postback settings* option on the *Browser forms* tab (for the control bound to the data source listening to data source events) to *Always*. Then the control will always post back whenever the value changes (refer back to Figure 17.3).

> **WARNING** Performance Issues with Extra Postbacks
>
> There is a fine balance between form correctness and performance. The more postbacks your form makes during filling, the fewer overall number of concurrent users and forms your server will be able to adequately serve. We look more closely at server and browser performance at the end of the chapter.

Circumventing Browser-Enabled Limitations

Almost everything you learned about programming InfoPath in Chapter 15 applies to Forms Services. There are some exceptions, however. One of the biggest exceptions in browser-enabled forms is the lack of UI through rules and form code. (The exception to not showing UI in the browser is the submit feature, where standard or custom submit messages show an alert dialog in the browser.)

Showing UI by Using `MessageBox`

One sorely missed feature of InfoPath in the browser is the ability to show a message box. Since the System.Windows.Forms.dll assembly isn't referenced, the `MessageBox.Show()` method is unavailable (and even if it was, showing UI is suppressed). Despite the inability to show UI in the browser, it doesn't mean we can't do something similar! With a little creativity, we're able to simulate showing a message box in a browser-based form. Figure 17.7 shows our own dialog box. (See the sample called MessageBox.)

FIGURE 17.7: Our own message box

Our dialog box is really just another view made up of a layout table, an Expression Box, and a Button control. The layout table, of course, has some fancy borders, shading, and cell merges to give it a dialog-like appearance. The Expression Box shows the dialog text; in this case, "Hello, world!" To show this pseudo-dialog (which works on both InfoPath and the browser), simply call a new method that we wrote called `MessageBox_Show()`. This method remembers the current view name and the message to show, then switches to the `MessageBox` view. Listing 17.1 shows the definition.

LISTING 17.1: Showing a Faux Message Box in the Browser

```
private void MessageBox_Show(string message)
{
   XPathNavigator root = this.MainDataSource.CreateNavigator();
   string thisViewName = this.CurrentView.ViewInfo.Name;
   root.SelectSingleNode("/my:myFields/my:ViewSender",
      NamespaceManager).SetValue(thisViewName);
   root.SelectSingleNode("/my:myFields/my:MessageBox",
      NamespaceManager).SetValue(message);
   ViewInfos.SwitchView("MessageBox");
}
```

The dialog has an *OK* button that, when clicked, runs the code in Listing 17.2 to return to the view of the `MessageBox_Show` caller.

LISTING 17.2: Clicking the OK Button on the View with the Faux Message Box

```
public void CTRL2_7_Clicked(object sender, ClickedEventArgs e)
{
   // Go back to the view that initiated the MessageBox
   XPathNavigator root = this.MainDataSource.CreateNavigator();
   string viewSender = root.SelectSingleNode(
      "/my:myFields/my:ViewSender", NamespaceManager).Value;
   ViewInfos.SwitchView(viewSender);
}
```

Simulating User Roles in the Browser

User roles are frequently used in complex InfoPath form templates. Unfortunately, roles are not natively supported on Forms Services. Furthermore, there is no easy workaround without code. If the availability of user roles in your form template is a make-or-break situation, we can help you.

Recall from Chapter 13 that a role is defined by a unique role name that includes one or more users or groups. After defining at least one role in the template, you can reference that role in conditional formatting (to show or hide a Section control), data validation (to determine when errors occur), conditions for rules (to determine when a rule may fire), and form code. As Chapter 13 concluded, roles are a very handy form feature whenever you want to customize your form template for specific users or the form is part of a workflow.

InfoPath completely removes any hint of the roles feature when you're designing a form template that is compatible with InfoPath Forms Services. Despite roles not being available while designing a form, it won't stop us from determining who is filling out the form. In a moment, we'll show you how to get the current user. But unlike InfoPath's roles feature, our workaround does not bucket users into roles with unique names. While that's possible to do (and we'll tell you exactly how), it requires another level of overhead that not all form templates do. It's worthwhile to implement mapping a one-to-many relationship between users and a role name only if you have more than a couple of users to correlate with a specific role and if the role membership list changes over time.

Getting the name of the current user isn't possible through the InfoPath design-mode user interface when designing a template to be compatible with Forms Services. In InfoPath, it's quite easy to get the user name. Simply use the `userName()` formula under the *All* category. For example, if `userName()` does not equal `"MoiExecutive"` and `totalSpent` is greater than `50`, then conditionally format the Text Box data as bold and red. When designing a browser-enabled template, using the `userName()` view extension function triggers an error in the Design Checker. Let's see how to work around this limitation.

Some parts of the InfoPath OM correspond with view extension functions. View extension functions are extensions to the XSL standard provided by InfoPath that can be used in an XPath expression. Most view extension functions provided by InfoPath simply make a call to the InfoPath OM. (Forms in the browser do not enjoy the same breadth of support for view extensions as forms in InfoPath do, but some functions are still available.) In this case, the `userName()` extension function works in InfoPath as well as Forms Services. To get the user name from the OM, just use `Application.UserName`, which requires domain trust security privileges. (If you want the user's login name instead, use `Application.LoginName`, which requires a fully trusted form template with both InfoPath and the browser.)

Now that we have the user name, how can we use it similarly to roles? The trick is to save the user name value in the data source. We suggest dedicating a field (say, an attribute under the document element) called `userName` to hold the user's name. Set the `userName` field by sinking the `Loading` form event and assigning `Application.UserName` to the value of the `userName` attribute field. Now you can make decisions in your form, for example, about conditional formatting for a field, by comparing against the `userName` field.

Say that you wanted to take the next step to more closely mimic the roles feature. The easiest way to do so is create a grouping data structure in your form code. In our case, we defined a `Role` structure. Then we created a private method (called `GetRoleForUser`) that defines all roles and its members. We include this data within the method because if it had class scope, the role data would be serialized into the session state and stored for each filled-out form. (Session state is what Forms Services uses to remember the state of the form while a user is filling it out.) But since this data never changes and we want to keep it private, we just define it as stateless in the method where we need it. The algorithm for determining the user role is simple: Search through every role for a user name match. The code, shown in Listing 17.3, returns the name of the role in which the user is a member; the empty string is returned if there is no membership match.

LISTING 17.3: A Rudimentary Implementation of Roles in the Browser

```
struct Role
{
    public string[] Users;
    public string Name;

    public Role(string name, string[] users)
    {
        Name = name;
        Users = users;
    }
}

public string GetRoleForUser()
{
    Role[] roles = new Role[2];
    roles[0] = new Role("users",
        new string[] { "Dana", "Rob", "David" });
    roles[1] = new Role("admins",
        new string[] { "Eric", "Alan", "Kevin" });

    string userName = this.CreateNavigator().SelectSingleNode(
       "/my:myFields/userName", NamespaceManager).Value;

    foreach (Role role in roles)
        foreach (string s in role.Users)
            if (userName == s)
                // assume user belongs to a single role
                return role.Name;
    return String.Empty;
}
```

To use roles in your browser-enabled form template, simply put the code from Listing 17.3 into your own `GetRoleForUser()` method. The resulting role can be saved, for example, into another attribute field called `userRole` under the document element.

Simulating a Custom Task Pane in the Browser

A common design pattern with InfoPath form templates is to use a custom task pane. As we witnessed in Chapter 15, task panes can interact directly with the form, and vice versa, through the object model. Migrating a form template to a Web browser should not mean sacrificing the existence of your task pane.

Unlike our previous workarounds that can be used in both the InfoPath application and a Web browser, accommodating a custom task pane requires plumbing specific to Web pages in a browser. In fact, if you are familiar with the HTML frame and frameset tags, you're a step ahead. You can probably imagine how a workaround is implemented. While we won't cover this specific example, we defer discussion of hosting forms in custom ASP.NET pages until Chapter 18. That chapter should give you all of the tools you need for simulating a custom task pane in the browser.

Detecting the Browser or the InfoPath Client

Most form templates designed for the browser will also work in InfoPath. However, in more complicated templates you might want fine-grained control over certain form behaviors. For example, you might want the form to submit using a different data connection in the browser than in InfoPath. Or you may just want to run some form code only in the InfoPath application because it's not compatible with the browser. Whatever the case, you'll find the ability to detect the form environment (InfoPath, Web browser, or even mobile browser) a welcome convenience.

You can detect the form environment only by writing code. So if you wanted to make decisions in your form (e.g., to show or hide a Section), you could implement this by setting a field value through form code. Let's look at what OM is at our disposal to determine the environment in which our form is running.

Two Boolean read-only properties help us determine whether we're in InfoPath, the Web browser, or a mobile browser. Both of these properties are statically exposed off of the `Environment` class (which, in turn, is on the `Application` class). The first property is appropriately named `IsBrowser`, while the second property is called `IsMobile`. The `IsBrowser` property is set to `true` only if the form is being filled out in a Web browser. We can test the `IsBrowser` property by designing a new, blank browser-enabled form template and inserting a Text Box control. Next, sink the `Loading` event (under the *Programming* submenu on the *Tools* menu) to add C# form code. Use the code shown in Listing 17.4 in the `Loading` event handler.

LISTING 17.4: Demonstrating the `IsBrowser` and `IsMobile` Environment Properties

```
XPathNavigator field1 =
   CreateNavigator().SelectSingleNode(
   "/my:myFields/my:field1", NamespaceManager);

if (Application.Environment.IsBrowser)
{
   field1.SetValue("IsBrowser");
   if (Application.Environment.IsMobile)
   {
      field1.SetValue("IsMobile");
   }
}
else
{
   field1.SetValue("IsInfoPath");
}
```

As you may expect, the Text Box shows `"IsBrowser"` when the form is filled out in a Web browser. If you happened to enable rendering on a mobile device (see Chapter 14 for details) and opened the form in a mobile browser, the Text Box would show `"IsMobile"`. You'll notice that whenever `IsMobile` is `true`, `IsBrowser` must be `true`. The association between the OM and the form environment is best expressed in a matrix, as shown in Table 17.1.

TABLE 17.1: `IsBrowser` and `IsMobile` Values in Various Environments

OM/Environment	InfoPath	Web Browser	Mobile
`IsBrowser`	`false`	`true`	`true`
`IsMobile`	`false`	`false`	`true`

Form Code Compatibility with Forms Services

We just finished talking about how to detect the form-filling environment in your form code. But you may not have a particular reason to do so. We aren't surprised if you don't have a specific scenario in mind where you would want some form code to run in either InfoPath or the browser, but not both. But with the additional details we're about to give you regarding

OM compatibility with Forms Services, you might find the `IsBrowser` property very helpful.

As we mentioned in Chapter 15, writing code for a browser-enabled form template is a little different than for InfoPath. Browser-enabled templates implement only a strict subset of the classes, properties, methods, and events that InfoPath provides. If you can write code for InfoPath (which you have been doing up until this point), it's easy to transition to Forms Services. Switching a template from InfoPath to be compatible with Forms Services changes the Microsoft.Office.InfoPath.dll assembly reference, resulting in some InfoPath OM being unavailable. This means that if you started writing code for an InfoPath-only template, making the template browser-compatible may result in build errors. If you write enough code and design enough form templates, you would eventually learn what OM is not implemented in the browser. To save you the time and hassle of designing countless form templates, we offer Table 17.2. It lists all OM that is unavailable in browser-enabled templates. Classes or events listed in Table 17.2 without any properties or methods, such as `XmlFormCollection` and `Window`, are unavailable in whole; the `XmlForm` class, on the other hand, omits only some of its properties and methods. Keep this reference close at hand when designing an InfoPath-only template that may end up being browser-compatible!

SharePoint Integration

We began touching on Forms Services integration with SharePoint when we introduced Forms Services in Chapter 14. You learned how document libraries and site content types, for example, can be used with browser-enabled forms. In this chapter, we'll look at the depth of integration between SharePoint and Forms Services by focusing on administration. The behind-the-scenes look at server management will show what you, the SharePoint server administrator, will be working with on an almost daily basis. The essence of a successful server is its upkeep and how it's managed. We'll look at how to deploy templates published for administrator approval, manage existing form templates, and configure administrative options in Forms Services. We'll also peek at shared services and their configurations. Finally, we'll show you how easy it is to integrate an InfoPath form into a page on your SharePoint site.

TABLE 17.2: Object Model Classes, Events, Properties, and Methods Not Implemented by Forms Services

Class/Event	Property/Method

`Application`	`ActiveWindow`
	`CacheFormTemplate(. . .)`
	`ComAdsIns`
	`GetFormTemplateLocation(. . .)`
	`IsDestinationReachable(. . .)`
	`LanguageSettings`
	`MachineOnlineState`
	`Quit(. . .)`
	`Un/RegisterFormTemplate(. . .)`
	`UsableWidth/Height`
	`Version`
	`Windows`
	`XmlForms`

`ContextChangedEventHandler`	
`FormError`	`ErrorCode`
`FormErrorCollection`	`Add(XPathNavigator, string, string, string, int)` `Add(XPathNavigator, string, string, string, int, ErrorMode)`
`FormTemplate`	`CacheId`
`MailEnvelope`	
`MergeEventHandler`	

`Permission`
`UserPermission`
`UserPermissionCollection`	

`SaveEventHandler`	
`SharepointListQueryConnection`	`QueryThisFormOnly`

`Signature`	`Certificate`
	`Comment`
	`SignatureBlockXmlNode`
	`Status`

`SignEventHandler`
`SignatureCollection`
`Certificate`
`SignedDataBlock`
`SignedDataBlockCollection`	

TABLE 17.2: (*continued*)

Class/Event	Property/Method
TaskPane HtmlTaskPane	
User	IsUserMemberOf(. . .)
View	DisableAutoUpdate() EnableAutoUpdate() ExecuteAction(. . .) Export(. . .) ForceUpdate() GetContextNodes(. . .) GetSelectedNodes() SelectNodes(. . . .) SelectText(. . .) ShowMailItem(. . .) Window
ViewInfo	Caption HideName
Window WindowCollection	
XmlChangingEventHandler	
XmlForm	Dirty Extension GetWorkflowTasks(), GetWorkflowTemplates() Host, HostName, Hosted MergeForm(. . .) New(. . .), NewFromFormTemplate(. . .) Open(. . .), Close() Permission Print(. . .) Recovered Save(), SaveAs(. . .) SetSaveAsDialogFilename(), SetSaveAsDialogLocation() SignedDataBlocks TaskPanes UserRole
XmlFormCollection	
XmlValidatingEventArgs	ReportError(XPathNavigator, bool, string, string, int, ErrorMode)

What Is SharePoint Integration?

Forms Services is built on SharePoint Server 2007. When we talk about integration between Forms Services and SharePoint, we are really referring to existing or new (for 2007) SharePoint feature functionality with which someone from an InfoPath-only world would not be familiar. For example, we discuss advanced publishing. An InfoPath user would think of advanced publishing as using the Publishing Wizard within the InfoPath program. Instead, advanced publishing uses the SharePoint Central Administration site to expose its functionality.

Advanced Publishing

There are essentially two types of publishing: user and administrator. In this context, a user is an individual who designs basic data entry forms using InfoPath. He or she may use highly visible features such as conditional formatting and rules but not use (or even know about) form code or digital signatures, for example. Chapter 14 stepped through the user publishing process. (Note that we didn't actually call it "user publishing" in Chapter 14.) For more feature-rich and advanced templates, user publishing is not sufficient for browser-based form templates. (You can still publish such a form template to SharePoint that's not browser-enabled.) To allow more capable and rich templates in the browser, look no further than administrator deployment (admin deployment for short).

There are two components of admin deployment: InfoPath publishing and the deployment itself. The InfoPath portion simply involves saving the browser-enabled form template in some location where the administrator can pick it up. The second part of admin deployment depends on the server administrator to take the form template and deploy it to the server. Let's go through each of the two components of admin publishing to see it in action.

WARNING The Power of Administration

Admin deployment (a manual step after publishing where the server administrator approves the form template) is the most powerful way to publish a form template to Forms Services. As the server administrator, be wary with admin deployment by knowing exactly what the template does *before* you proceed.

Publishing a Form Template for Administrator Approval

So far we've been using the Publishing Wizard from InfoPath to deploy browser-enabled forms to Forms Services. This has appropriately served our needs since we've been publishing relatively simple form templates. But how do we qualify a "relatively simple" form template? In a nutshell, it's one that does not need administrator approval. Until now, all forms we've deployed to the server have not needed approval because they've been user published directly from InfoPath. However, administrators would not want users to publish certain form templates directly to the server. One example is a form template containing code. As you've seen in previous chapters, form code is a powerful extensibility feature that is beyond the scope of novices and even most intermediate users. Clearly you (as an administrator) wouldn't want form templates with code to be published on your server without your permission!

Five distinct features qualify a form template as needing administrator approval.

1. The security level is set to *Full Trust.*
2. The form template contains managed form code (using the 2007 object model; script isn't supported).
3. The *Enable rendering on a mobile device* setting is checked.
4. Cross-domain data connections are defined in the form template (not from the data connection library).
5. Data connections are defined in the centrally managed connection library.

When you're publishing a form template to Forms Services that uses one of these features, the Publishing Wizard forces *Administrator-approved*

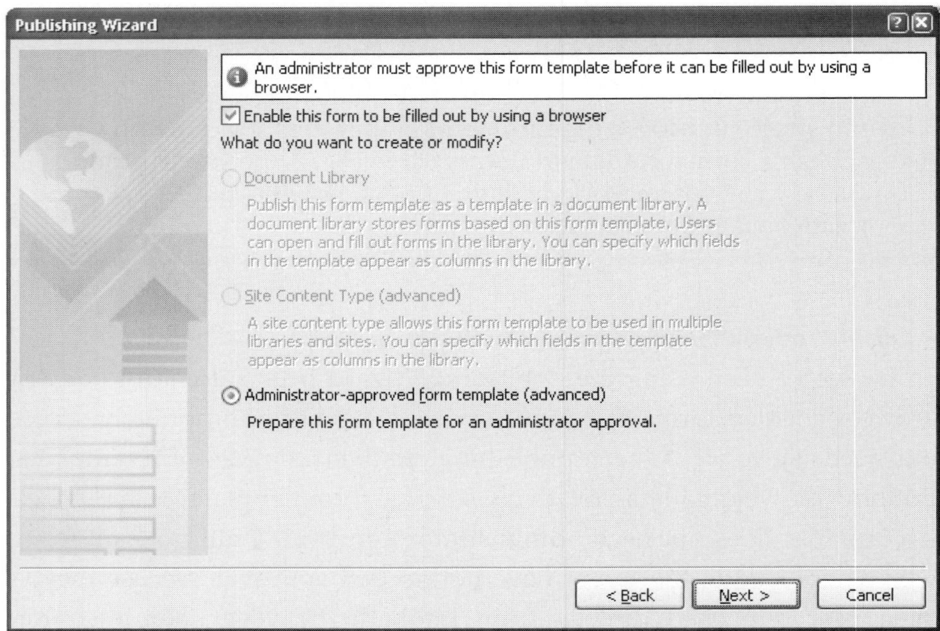

FIGURE 17.8: Publishing to Forms Services a form template that requires administrator approval

form template (advanced) as the only available option (Figure 17.8). In the particular example shown in Figure 17.8, we created a new blank browser-enabled form template and manually set the security level (in the *Form Options* dialog) to *Full Trust*.

> **NOTE Disabling Browser Rendering**
>
> Unchecking *Enable this form to be filled out by using a browser* enables the *Document Library* and *Site Content Type (advanced)* options but disables the *Administrator-approved form template (advanced)* option. This is because only InfoPath can open such a form.

After you click the *Next* button shown in Figure 17.8, the wizard prompts for a location for saving, as shown in Figure 17.9. The server administrator will go to this location to pick up your form template. As the text in Figure 17.9 suggests, you'll want to save the template somewhere where your administrator will have access. Typically this will be a drop box such

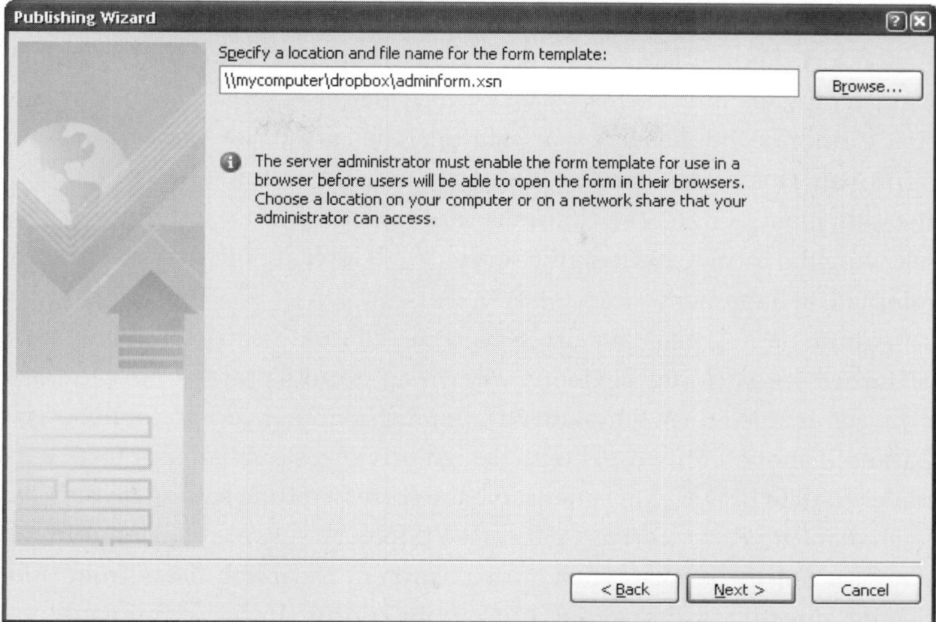

FIGURE 17.9: Specifying a path during publishing to save a form template requiring administrator approval

as a network share. Some administrators might prefer that you e-mail the form template to them. To send your template via e-mail, save the form template (.xsn) file to your computer and then attach it to the e-mail message. Unlike the access path of the templates we published in Chapter 9, the path entered in Figure 17.9 is simply to save the form somewhere. This path is not used by InfoPath or Forms Services in any other way.

> **NOTE Publishing Equivalence**
>
> Publishing a form template to Forms Services that requires administrator approval is technically the same as publishing a template to a network location without an access path.

The last wizard page has a *Publish* button that saves the file to the location you specified. At this point, the onus is on the server administrator to finish the process. Why don't we switch roles and be the administrator for a little while?

Administrative Deployment to Forms Services

As the server administrator, you're the gatekeeper to letting high-privilege form templates into Forms Services. In general, any user form template that cannot be published by a form designer is subject to administrator approval. This means the template may contain features (as we listed in the previous section) the administrator would like to scrutinize before allowing the form to exist on the server. We'll look at how to dissect a form template in a moment.

Admin deployment can also serve as an alternative to user deployment of form templates. Its flexibility allows an administrator to deploy any browser-enabled form template without restriction. If you prefer to be a bit paranoid about letting users with design privileges publish user form templates to your server, you can disable the corresponding setting on the *Configure InfoPath Forms Services* page. (We'll look closely at the configuration page for Forms Services later in this chapter.) Disabling users from publishing directly to the server puts more control in the administrator's hands. How you configure Forms Services on your farm will depend on who is using your server. If your server is facing the Internet, you'll likely want to lock down as much as possible. On the other hand, if the farm is in a controlled and trusted corporate environment, you may consider giving more flexibility to your colleagues.

You may have questioned why this subsection is within the "SharePoint Integration" topic. It's because the crux of admin deployment takes place in SharePoint! Without further delay, let's see how to deploy the form template that was published for administrator approval (\\mycomputer\dropbox\adminform.xsn) from Figure 7–9. To begin, first navigate your browser to the SharePoint Central Administration site. The address will look something like http://yourserver:12345 (or https:// . . .), with yourserver replaced with your server name and 12345 with the admin port number.

> **TIP Where's the Central Administration Site?**
>
> If you don't know the SharePoint Central Administration site URL, simply go to *Start*, then *Programs*, then *Microsoft Office Server*, and select *SharePoint 3.0 Central Administration*. This can be done on any computer that has SharePoint Server installed and is joined to the farm.

InfoPath Forms Services

- Manage form templates
- Configure InfoPath Forms Services
- Upload form template
- Manage data connection files
- Manage the Web service proxy

FIGURE 17.10: Administration links for Forms Services

Once you've browsed to the Central Administration site, click on the *Application Management* tab at the top of the page. At this point, you should see a section titled *InfoPath Forms Services* (Figure 17.10). The links within this section are the main administrative configuration options for Forms Services on the farm. For advanced publishing, we'll focus on the *Manage form templates* and *Upload form template* links. The other links shown in Figure 17.10 are covered elsewhere in this chapter.

Before we jump into deploying our form template, it's important to understand that this portion of admin deploying is not a single action. In fact, there are two steps for you, the administrator, to take in order to make the form template (in our case, the one published to \\mycomputer\dropbox\adminform.xsn, pending admin approval) work in the browser.

1. Upload the form template to the server.
2. Activate the form template to a site collection.

Let's explore those steps now.

Uploading the Form Template to the Server. Step 1 is facilitated by the *Upload form template* link shown in Figure 17.10. Clicking on that link opens the page shown in Figure 17.11. The *Upload Form Template* page is technically contained within the *Manage Form Templates* page, which is why that name appears in the path at the top of Figure 17.11. In fact, we're redirected to *Manage Form Templates* after clicking either the *Upload* or *Cancel* buttons. For now we'll just look at the *Upload Form Template* (upper) section within the *Upload Form Template* page. Later, we'll talk more about the *Upgrade* (lower) section.

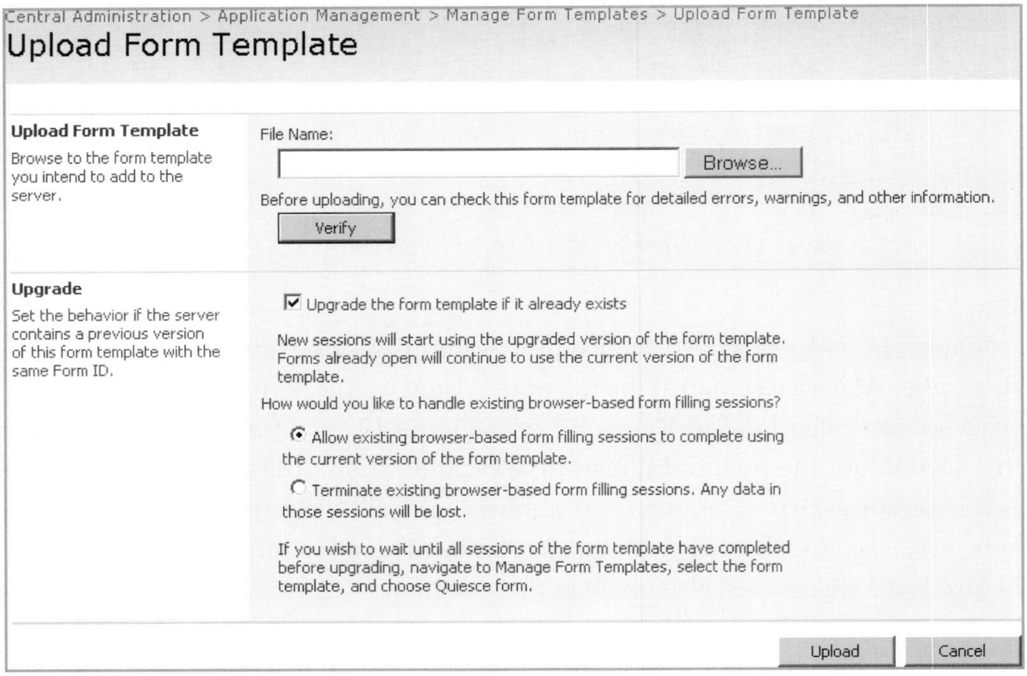

Central Administration > Application Management > Manage Form Templates > Upload Form Template

Upload Form Template

Upload Form Template

Browse to the form template you intend to add to the server.

File Name:

Browse...

Before uploading, you can check this form template for detailed errors, warnings, and other information.

Verify

Upgrade

Set the behavior if the server contains a previous version of this form template with the same Form ID.

☑ Upgrade the form template if it already exists

New sessions will start using the upgraded version of the form template. Forms already open will continue to use the current version of the form template.

How would you like to handle existing browser-based form filling sessions?

◉ Allow existing browser-based form filling sessions to complete using the current version of the form template.

○ Terminate existing browser-based form filling sessions. Any data in those sessions will be lost.

If you wish to wait until all sessions of the form template have completed before upgrading, navigate to Manage Form Templates, select the form template, and choose Quiesce form.

Upload Cancel

FIGURE 17.11: Upload Form Template page

To upload the form template, use the *Browse* button shown in Figure 17.11 to find the published .xsn file. In our case, the form template is at \\mycomputer\dropbox\adminform.xsn. Before clicking *Upload* in the *Upload Form Template* page, you may want to verify the template. Verifying the form template is equivalent to what the Design Checker does when *Verify on Server* is enabled. (Chapter 14 discusses the Design Checker.) If you have already used the checker in InfoPath, verifying the template in the *Upload Form Template* page is redundant. Click *Upload* to complete step 1 in admin deployment. Form template verification is implicitly part of the upload process.

TIP Copy the Location Before Verification

Clicking *Verify* will cause the *File Name* text box to forget what you had typed. Before clicking *Verify*, be sure to first copy the text in the *File Name* text box so you can paste it when coming back to this page to upload.

If the upload succeeds, the page will display this message: "The form template has been successfully uploaded to the farm. To make the form template available in a site collection, activate the form template from the Manage Form Templates page or from the feature activation page in the site collection."

NOTE Where Are Administrator-Approved Templates Located?

Admin-uploaded form templates physically exist on the server at %ProgramFiles%\Common Files\Microsoft Shared\Web Server Extensions\12\TEMPLATE\FEATURES under a GUID folder name.

Activating the Form Template to a Site Collection. Uploading a form template only copies it onto the server. It's actually not browser-ready until activation. There are two ways to activate a form: from the *Manage Form Templates* page or from the *Site Collection Features* page. Let's first use the *Manage Form Templates* page to activate our form template. Then we'll see how we could have done a functionally equivalent activation with the site collection.

Activation with the Manage Form Templates Page. After successfully uploading the form template and clicking *Upload,* you are automatically redirected to the *Manage Form Templates* page. A list shows which templates the administrator has uploaded to the farm (Figure 17.12). To identify the template you just uploaded, look for the item with a matching name. All admin form template names must be unique. Also ensure that the *Status* field on your form template says *Ready.* A template is not ready if it's still being processed and distributed across a farm. This is likely the case if your network or servers are particularly slow or you have a large farm.

TIP Recovering from a Hung Upload or Activation

There's a very small chance that an uploaded or activating form template could get hung for some reason. Its status may never change to *Ready.* If you're in such a case, you can delete the SharePoint timer job that is responsible for uploading or activating the form template. Visit the *Operations* tab's *Timer job status* and *Timer job definitions* pages to delete the appropriate jobs.

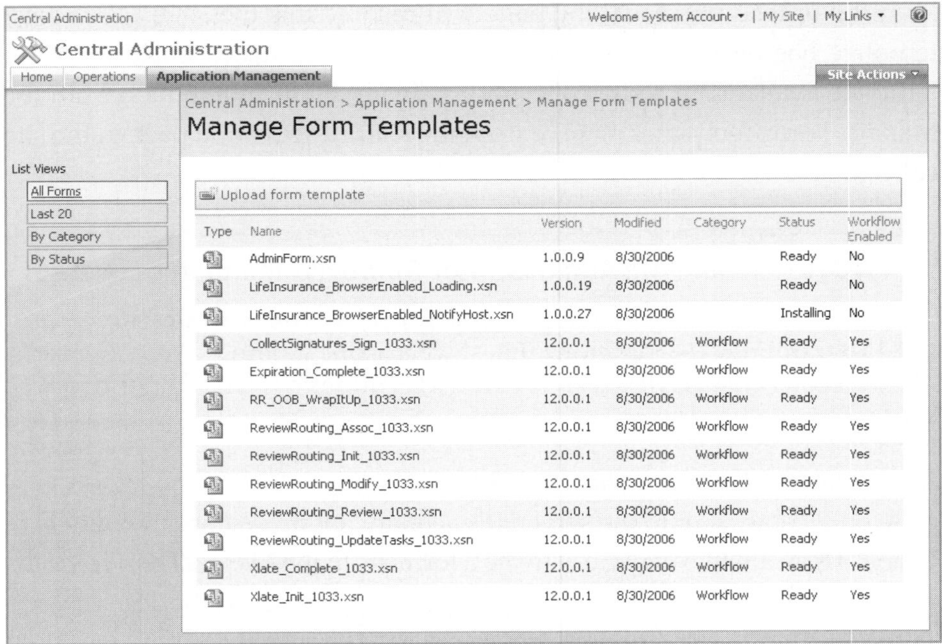

FIGURE 17.12: Manage Form Templates page

> **TIP Form Name versus File Name**
>
> The *Name* column is the file name. To see the form name, go to *View Properties* for a template in the *Manage Form Templates* list.

Once the *Status* value says *Ready,* hover over the name of the template and then left- or right-click to show the context menu. Selecting the *Activate to a Site Collection* option takes you to the *Activate Form Template* page. The only purpose of this page is for you to choose a Web application and site collection for activation. Clicking on the *Site Collection* drop-down and choosing *Change Site Collection* opens the dialog shown in Figure 17.13. The root site collection is designated by the single forward slash. To change the value listed under *Web Application,* use the drop-down shown in the upper right of Figure 17.13. After you've chosen a site collection and Web application (if necessary), click *OK* on the *Activate Form Template* page to activate the template! Once activated, the form template appears in the `FormServerTemplates` library of that site collection.

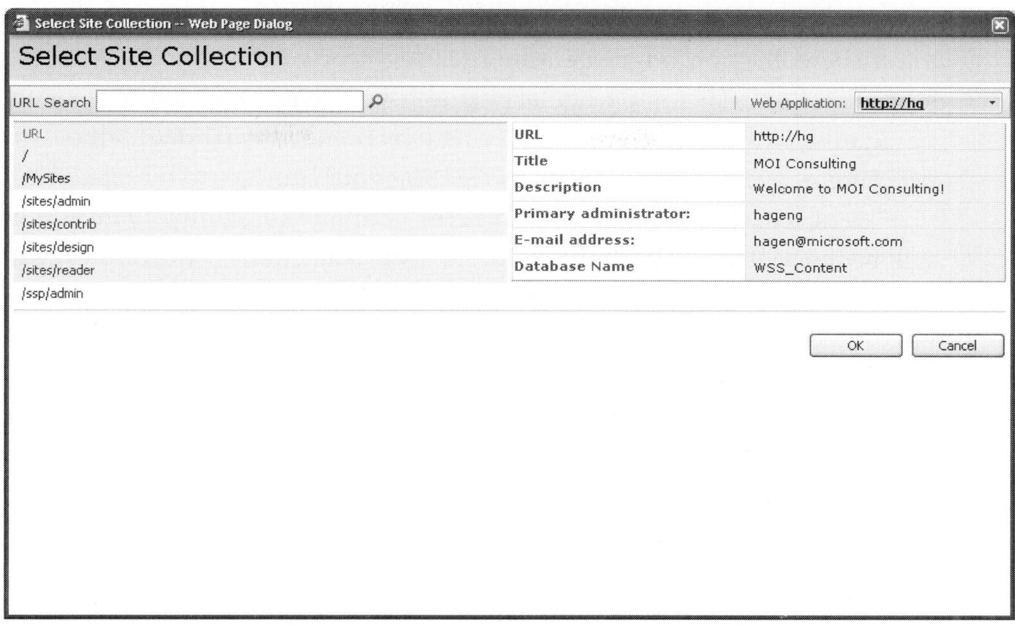

FIGURE 17.13: Choosing a site collection and Web application for activation

> **WARNING** Activation Is per Site Collection
>
> The form can render in the browser only on a site collection in which it's activated.

> **TIP** Using a Form Template Across Multiple Site Collections
>
> A form template can be activated to multiple site collections.

As an exclusive repository for admin-deployed and activated form templates, the `FormServerTemplates` library exists on all site collections where Forms Services is enabled. The location is http://myserver/formservertemplates on the root site, while another site (e.g., mysite) could be http://myserver/sites/mysite/formservertemplates. Since it is essentially a special type of SharePoint document library, you can do customizations as for any other library.

Activation with the Site Collection Features Page. Activating a form template via a site collection might be a more straightforward approach for some administrators. This is particularly true if you're accustomed to visually navigating to the site versus identifying it by name as we did with the *Activate Form Template* page. Start by navigating your browser to the site where you want to activate an uploaded form template (e.g., http://myserver will be the root site collection). If you're a site collection administrator, you should see the *Site Actions* drop-down in the upper-right portion of the page. Choose *Site Settings.* Next, go to the *Site Collection Features* page by clicking on a link with the same name. The page, similar to Figure 17.14, lists all features on the site, sorted by the value of the *Status* column. The features include InfoPath form templates, workflows, site content types, and even Forms Services itself. (Yes, you can deactivate Forms Services from this site collection!) Find the template you want to activate and click its corresponding *Activate* button.

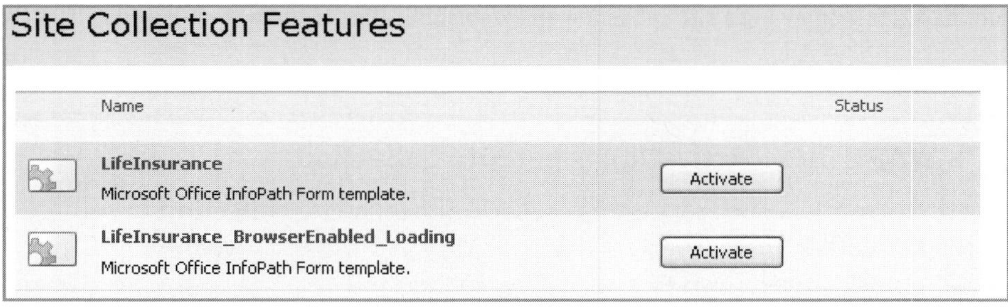

FIGURE 17.14: Activating a form template on the Site Collection Features page

> **TIP Form Template Names Listed in the Site Collections Features**
>
> The form name (not file name) is used in the *Site Collection Features* list.

Alternate Admin Deployments. The SharePoint site is arguably one of the easiest ways for an administrator to admin deploy a form. But what if you had hundreds of forms? Or what if you had a tool that would allow some users to admin deploy forms but not give them access to the entire SharePoint Central Administration site? If these scenarios (or something similar) sound familiar, we have solutions that may help you. Besides the SharePoint Web pages, there are two alternate ways to upload and deploy form templates: via the command line and programmatically.

Command-Line Admin Deployment. To facilitate command-line deployment, we introduce the stsadm.exe tool. If you've familiar with SharePoint, you might have heard of or used it before. The stsadm.exe tool allows command-line administration of your SharePoint site. Almost everything you can do with the Web site you can also do with this tool. Let's look at the Forms Services–specific functionality provided by stsadm.exe.

To start using stsadm.exe, open a Windows command shell prompt and change the directory to %CommonProgramFiles%\Microsoft Shared\Web Server Extensions\12\BIN. Table 17.3 shows a full listing of commands specific to Forms Services. Some of the more common commands include `uploadformtemplate` and `activateformtemplate`. Listing 17.5 shows sample command-line executions for stsadm.exe.

TABLE 17.3: Full List of stsadm.exe Commands Specific to Forms Services

Operation	What It Does
`activateformtemplate`	Activates a form template at a given URL
`deactivateformtemplate`	Deactivates a form template at a given URL
`enumformtemplates`	Lists all activated form templates
`getformtemplateproperty`	Gets a property (e.g., `version`) from a form template
`reconvertallformtemplates`	Converts all form templates as if they were reuploaded
`removeformtemplate`	Removes a form template
`setformtemplateproperty`	Sets a property on a form template
`upgradeformtemplate`	Upgrades a form template with a newly uploaded version
`uploadformtemplate`	Uploads a form template
`verifyformtemplate`	Behaves similar to the *Verify* button on the *Upload Form Template* page

LISTING 17.5: Sample Command Lines for Running the stsadm.exe Tool

```
stsadm.exe -o uploadformtemplate -filename c:\myforms\survey.xsn
stsadm.exe -o activateformtemplate -url http://myserver -filename
    c:\myforms\survey.xsn
stsadm.exe -o enumformtemplates
```

> **NOTE** Using the stsadm.exe Tool
>
> For more information on stsadm.exe, use `stsadm.exe /?` or see the Windows SharePoint Services administration guide.

Programmatic Admin Deployment. While command-line deployment can help you automate Forms Services administration using batch files, it might not completely suffice for your needs. The lowest level of administrative control available is to use the Forms Services object model. In fact, the OM is exactly what stsadm.exe uses behind the scenes to do its work!

To create a program that uses the object model, begin by creating a new Visual Studio project (or use your favorite development environment). Add an assembly reference to the following .dll files:

- Microsoft.Office.InfoPath.Server.dll in %ProgramFiles%\Microsoft Office Servers\12.0\Bin
- Microsoft.SharePoint.dll in %CommonProgramFiles%\Microsoft Shared\Web Server Extensions\12\ISAPI
- Microsoft.Office.Server.dll in %CommonProgramFiles%\Microsoft Shared\Web Server Extensions\12\ISAPI

We don't use it in this sample, but objects belonging to shared services and providers live in the Microsoft.Office.Server.dll assembly. These three assemblies include everything you require for all of your administration needs.

To show how the admin OM can be used, we created a sample Windows application, as shown in Figure 17.15. It provides three functions: *Verify, Upload & Activate* (to the root site collection), and *List Form Templates.* To run this sample, you need to execute the code on a server in the farm. (The code is packaged into the FormsServicesAdmin sample archive.) We'll quickly look at a few core lines of code used in the program.

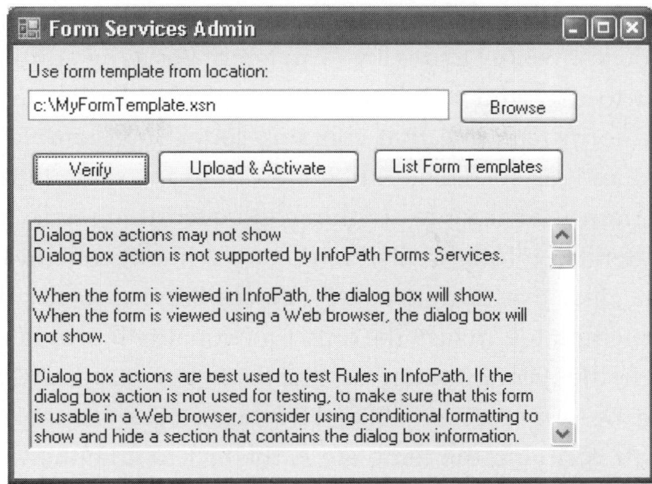

FIGURE 17.15: Forms Services Admin tool authored by using the admin object model

We used the following to verify a form template:

```
ConverterMessageCollection messages =
   FormTemplateCollection.VerifyFormTemplate(UploadLocation.Text);
```

To list form templates, we iterate through the `FormTemplates` collection:

```
foreach (FormTemplate formTemplate in formsService.FormTemplates)
```

Upload and activation is more complicated and requires more lines of code. We suggest opening, examining, and running the FormsServicesAdmin sample in Visual Studio 2005 to better understand the intricacies of the admin OM.

> **WARNING** Waiting for Upload to Complete Before Activation
>
> A caveat when using the Forms Services object model is that you must wait for the upload operation to complete before activating the same form template. If you don't wait, an exception will be thrown. Look closely at the FormsServicesAdmin sample code for the waiting time between upload and activation.

Screening Form Templates for Approval

Now that you know how to deploy form templates as an administrator, we caution you to use your privilege with vigilance. Earlier, we discussed deploying a form template that contains code. Such templates must be fully trusted and, as such, should be viewed in the same light as an executable program. They can do anything and everything with full access to your computer. Even fully trusted templates without code must be scrutinized with a close eye. Unfortunately, Forms Services really doesn't help you analyze templates. In fact, the only functionality it provides is verification through the *Verify* button on the *Upload Form Template* page (or through the Design Checker when *Verify on Server* is enabled). The big problem with verifying the template is the fact that neither InfoPath nor Forms Services looks at the form code.

> **WARNING** Verify the Form Template
>
> Trust the verification functionality to tell you only whether the template will deploy and render properly in the browser. Do not trust verification to convey malicious template behavior, such as the possibility of harming your server, for example.

The best way to screen a form template is to assume it is evil until proven innocent. We're assuming, of course, that you didn't design the template yourself, but rather that it came from someone asking you to approve it for deployment (i.e., asking you to deploy it). To prove its innocence, the best way to scavenge the form template is by opening it in InfoPath design mode. Begin by looking at the view (or views if there are more than one) for preliminary indications of what purposes the template serves. Once you get an idea of what the user interface is like, the next step and the crux of the process is to understand what's happening behind the scenes. Major areas to glance at include the following:

- All categories under the *Form Options* dialog
  - Especially *Security and Trust* for full trust permission
  - Also *Programming* for included form code

- The *Manage Resources* dialog for included files
- The *Data Connections* dialog for potential data exchange beyond the server realm
- The *Design Checker* task pane for incompatibilities or performance messages

You should be most cautious when deploying templates with code. When you receive a template with code, the source code is not included in the form template (.xsn) file. In fact, only the compiled application extension (.dll) and optionally a program debug database (.pdb) are physically included as files in the template. The form's designer may not have known that publishing pending administrator approval does not include the source code. Clearly you wouldn't want to publicly publish a template with source code. But in the case of sending the template to an administrator for approval, it's imperative that the source code be available for close inspection.

> **TIP Always Look at the Source Code**
>
> Never deploy a template with code without first reviewing the source code! If you receive a template without source code, ask the author for a copy of the Visual Studio project with the form template so you can conveniently open it through InfoPath using VSTA or VSTO. But if you don't trust that the code built into the assembly in the form template matches the code given to you, just rebuild and publish the template yourself.

As the administrator, it's up to you to judge whether or not code is worthy of running on your server. Look for any code that may take too long to run or seem malicious (e.g., excessive view switching or data connection usage, heavy data source operations, or use of the server's file system, to name a few indications). Use your best judgment and ensure that you understand what every line of code is doing. After you review the code, we recommend first running the template by filling out the form in a preview window with InfoPath. Only after you feel comfortable with the template and its code should you deploy it to the server for additional private testing before rolling it out to a larger audience.

> **NOTE** More on Deploying Administrator-Approved Form Templates
>
> You can find more information about advanced form deployment on Microsoft TechNet (as referenced in the Appendix).

Managing Form Templates

In the previous section on advanced publishing, you learned how to admin publish, upload, and activate InfoPath form templates to Forms Services. But over time, your server will accumulate templates, some of which you might want to remove or deactivate. Admin-deployed form templates can be administered by using the *Manage Form Templates* page (refer back to Figure 17.12). Click (with either the right or left mouse button) any template to show the context menu and select *Deactivate from a Site Collection* to prevent Forms Services from rendering the form in the browser. (You can also deactivate a template from the *Site Collection Features* page shown earlier in Figure 17.14.) If you want to remove the form template, select *Remove Form* from the context menu. InfoPath can still open deactivated templates that are not deleted from the server.

> **WARNING** Deactivate Before Deleting
>
> Deactivate a form template first before removing it.

User-deployed form templates are handled differently than those that are admin deployed. While all admin form templates reside in the `FormServerTemplates` library and can be managed from the *Manage Form Templates* page, user templates can live anywhere (except the `FormServerTemplates` library). User publishing to a document library saves the template as template.xsn within the Forms folder of the library. To deactivate a user-deployed form template, go to the `IWConvertedForms` library on that site collection (e.g., the root site location would be http://myserver/IWConvertedForms). Deleting an item from this list essentially deactivates, but doesn't physically delete, the form template. In other words, InfoPath can still open the form, but Forms Services cannot render it in the browser. Unfortunately there's no easy way to reactivate a form template (that was formerly user-deployed) besides republishing.

InfoPath Publishing Internals

For user deployment, InfoPath's Publishing Wizard internally uses a Web service at http://myserver/_vti_bin/FormsServices.asmx to browser-enable a form template. You could design a form against this Web service and use it to reactivate an existing template!

The other type of user deployment is publishing as a site content type. With content types, it's possible to save the form template anywhere within the site collection (but limited, of course, to where you have access). To remove a content type, begin by going to the site collection where it's activated. Then go to the *Site Settings* page and click on the *Site content types* link to visit the *Site Content Type Gallery* page. From this page you can select and delete the appropriate InfoPath content type. You can also deactivate the content type by using the `IWConvertedForms` library, as discussed for form libraries.

TIP Secure Your Sites

Locking down site permission limits the number of random locations where your users can user deploy a form template. Contributor permission is required for user deployment.

After a form template is deployed to Forms Services, it's not possible to change any of its properties. For example, you can't change the .xsn file name, form name, version, or locale. Since this information is extracted from the form definition (.xsf) file, the only way to change it is to update the form template (in design mode) and upload again.

NOTE More on Managing Form Templates

Learn more about managing templates on Microsoft TechNet (as referenced in the Appendix).

Configuring InfoPath Forms Services

As an administrator, it's imperative to have control over various features in Forms Services. In Chapter 14, you learned how to use SharePoint permission to restrict users' ability to deploy form templates or even to fill out deployed forms. In addition to SharePoint permission, there are global administrative settings to dictate what features are available (and to what extent).

To configure Forms Services, begin by going to the SharePoint Central Administration site and clicking on *Application Management*. Under the *InfoPath Forms Services* section (shown earlier in Figure 17.10), click on the *Configure InfoPath Forms Services* link. The configuration page appears with over a dozen settings to control or throttle an assortment of features. Let's begin by looking at the *User Browser-enabled Form Templates* settings (Figure 17.16).

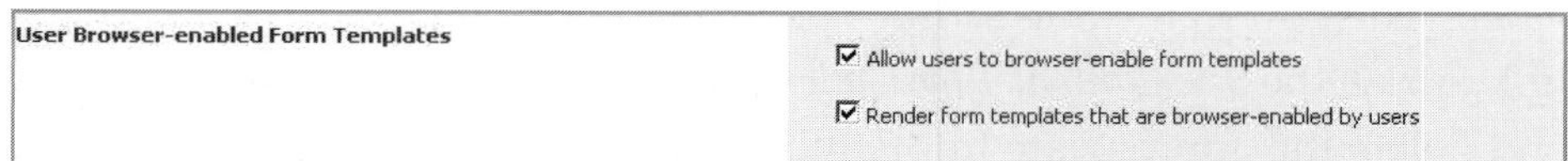

FIGURE 17.16: Some settings for configuring InfoPath Forms Services

The options shown in Figure 17.16 dictate the activation rights of end users. The first setting, *Allow users to browser-enable form templates,* directly affects the InfoPath Publishing Wizard when publishing to Forms Services. If this checkbox is cleared, the wizard unchecks and disables its *Enable this form to be filled out by using a browser* option. In some cases, you may instead see the last page of the wizard mention that the form couldn't be browser-enabled. No matter what happens in InfoPath, disabling this setting blocks all user activations of form templates. But the form can still be uploaded to the site for opening with InfoPath.

The second setting, *Render form templates that are browser-enabled by users,* is somewhat related to the first setting. If you disable user activation (the first setting), disabling user rendering (the second setting) affects only form templates that have already been user deployed. Realistically, this may not be such a useful configuration. Alternatively, you could keep user activation enabled but disable rendering. However, users may then think that your server is broken when they attempt to open the form in the browser after successfully publishing. Unfortunately, it is not possible to selectively enable user-deployed form templates with user rendering disabled.

If you prefer, you can also disable Forms Services from a specific site collection. Such a setting is not available on the *Configure InfoPath Forms Services* page, however. Earlier in the chapter we talked about activation with the *Site Collection Features* page (shown in Figure 17.14). Among the activated features for the site collection you will find Forms Services. Deactivating Forms Services disables server renderings of all forms for that site collection.

We've made only a dent so far in the *Configure InfoPath Forms Services* administration page. All of the remaining settings on the page are associated with either data connections or shared services. We're covering advanced facets of these topics in upcoming sections, so stay tuned!

Configuring Shared Services and Providers

We've looked at Forms Services and we've looked at parts of SharePoint. But we have yet to discuss some areas that are not categorized strictly as SharePoint or Forms Services. That's where shared services and providers come in. These "features" span a great variety of capabilities. Few are critical to Forms Services, and others are add-ons. Regardless, you'll learn about the shared services that cross paths with Forms Services and how to configure them according to your needs.

Session State Service

Session state is one of the critical shared services on which Forms Services depends. The session state service (SSS) serves a single purpose: to remember the state of a form, per user, while being filling out. Since SSS is, of course, a shared service, it is not specific to filling out forms; other Microsoft Office Server products, such as Excel Services, may also use SSS for their user sessions.

There is not much to do with SSS when it comes to configuration. You can find the *Configure Session State* page, shown in Figure 17.17, under the *Office SharePoint Server Shared Services* section on the *Application Management* admin page. By default, SSS is enabled, but you can turn it off. If you do, Forms Services and possibly other Microsoft Office Server services will fail to work properly. The only configuration option, besides *Enable Session*

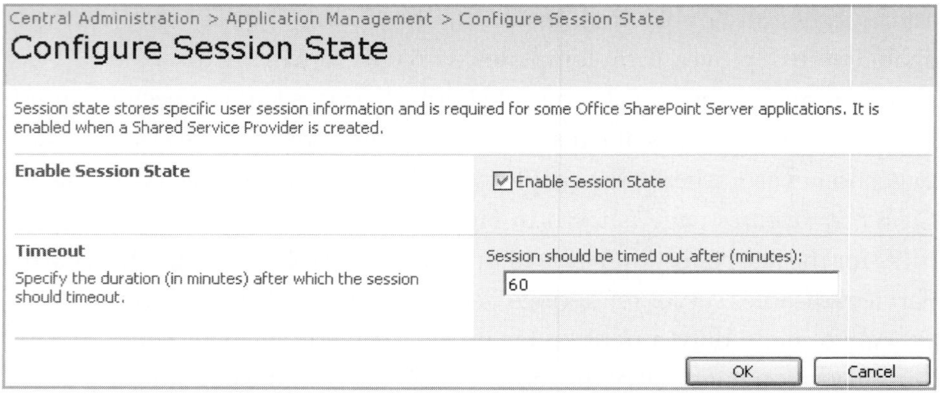

Central Administration > Application Management > Configure Session State

Configure Session State

Session state stores specific user session information and is required for some Office SharePoint Server applications. It is enabled when a Shared Service Provider is created.

Enable Session State	☑ Enable Session State
Timeout Specify the duration (in minutes) after which the session should timeout.	Session should be timed out after (minutes): 60

OK Cancel

FIGURE 17.17: Configuring the session state shared service

State, is the *Timeout* setting. The default of 60 means that after sixty minutes of server inactivity, that session is permanently destroyed. Choosing the right setting is a balance between giving your users more time versus taxing the server with too many lingering sessions. If your servers see consistently elevated server loads over long periods of time, you may consider decreasing the timeout.

Now that we know a little about the purpose of SSS and its configuration, let's see how Forms Services uses it.

Session State in Forms Services. When a new form-filling session is initiated, Forms Services tells SSS to create a new session. The session contains all sorts of information about the form (including its data and what view the user is currently on) and retains the `FormState` object used in form code (as you learned in Chapter 15).

Although it would be nice to say that the session is kept alive as long as the form is being filling out, this is more ideological than practical. As you learned in Chapter 14, Forms Services uses JavaScript quite extensively to provide as rich of a form-filling experience as possible in the browser. As a result, the need to send and receive data to and from the server is drastically reduced. This is great for server throughput and performance, but SSS will not think that the session is still in use because there's no server communication. Another topic we addressed in Chapter 14 was when a form would need to talk to the server. For example, we mentioned that form code (for, say, a node's `Changed` event) would require the browser to post back the data. Obviously, when the form is finished being filled out, the user will need to either save or submit. Either of these actions also performs a postback. Any server communications, including postbacks, reset that session's timer, which otherwise ticks until the timeout.

> **TIP Save Your Form**
>
> It's a good idea to save your form as you fill it out. If you get busy and forget about your open form session, you could lose all of the data. If the form designer disabled save, he or she should at least allow "draft" and "final" submit options.

If there's a period of inactivity longer than the SSS timeout, your session is destroyed, and any unsaved data is lost. The session state timeout isn't always obvious, however. Say that you're sure that your session timed out, but you can still fill out the form. How could that be? Remember that a form in the browser occasionally needs to send data to the server, but not always. It would simply be a matter of time before you do something (e.g., save, click a button that runs form code, switch views, and so on) that causes a postback. At that point, a critical error dialog will appear to tell you, "For your protection, the current session has been terminated due to inactivity."

> **WARNING Be Mindful of Session State Performance**
>
> The establishment and maintenance of session state is a relatively expensive operation for a farm. In the "Performance Tips and Best Design Practices" section later in this chapter, we'll look at session state and performance in detail.

How Else Can a Session Be Destroyed? Besides timing out due to inactivity during a form-filling session, there are other ways a session can be killed automatically. These mechanisms are all specific to Forms Services and are not part of SSS. Let's see how else we can control a user's session and why these session settings are important.

Number of Postbacks per Form Session State Setting. One way is to perform too many postbacks in a given session. Most forms shouldn't require more than a handful of round-trips to the server. Very few forms will require more than a couple dozen postbacks. Any more than that and you might be dealing with a malicious user or hacker trying to tax or break into the server. Forms Services allows for a maximum of 75 postbacks within a given session. The 76th postback results in a server error and logs the occurrence to the server's Windows event log for the administrator. (We'll look at server logging shortly.) If you'd like to change the number of postbacks per form session state, you can find the threshold setting on the *Configure InfoPath Forms Services* administration page. This specific setting is shown at the top right of Figure 17.18.

Thresholds
Specify the thresholds at which to end user sessions and log error messages.

Number of postbacks per form session state: 75
Number of actions per postback: 200

Form Session State
Form session state stores data necessary to maintain a user session. File attachment data in the form will receive an additional 50 percent of session state space.

Active sessions should be terminated after: 1440 minutes

Maximum size of form session state: 4096 kilobytes

Select the location to use for storing form session state:
Session State Service (best for low-bandwidth users)
Form view (reduces database load on server). If form session state is larger than the specified value, the Session State Service will be used instead.

40 kilobytes

FIGURE 17.18: Administrative session state thresholds

Number of Actions per Postback Setting. Besides posting back to the server too much, it's also possible to tax the server in a single request. Let's see how this works. As you may already know from Chapter 14, Forms Services has a rich client-side architecture that delivers an AJAX-like user experience. One of the advantages of AJAX is the drastic reduction of required communication between the client and the server. Browser forms record every action in a temporary log that's held in the browser client. When a postback is necessary (due to either clicking the *Update* button or performing an action that requires a postback, such as running business logic or submit), the recorded log data is sent and your recorded actions replayed on the server. The server defines a maximum *Number of actions per postback* threshold setting. This effectively limits the number of actions that can be replayed on the server in a single postback. Even in the largest of forms, you'll be hard pressed to generate more than 100 actions. (Switching views, by the way, causes a postback.) To protect Forms Services from dedicating too much time to any single postback, the maximum number of actions is limited to 200. For all we know, a hacker could be crafting his or her own event logs and sending them to the server in an attempt to bring it to its knees! The setting to modify this threshold appears near the top right of Figure 17.18.

Terminate Active Sessions Setting. The remaining settings in Figure 17.18 relate directly to a user's session but are specific to Forms Services (whereas the *Configure Session State* page is generic to all services that use sessions). While you can define the timeout that kills a session due to inactivity in the *Configure Session State* page, it doesn't stop a user from keeping the session alive for a long time. As long as the browser posts back to the server once an hour (the default timeout is 60 minutes), the session will persist. If the maximum number of postbacks for a given session is 75 (the default), a session can last as long as 4,500 minutes! What you really need is a way to define the maximum total time a session can be alive. In fact, this is exactly what you get with the *Active sessions should be terminated after* setting shown in Figure 17.18. As you'd expect, the value of 1,440 minutes is configurable.

Maximum Size of Form Session State Setting. This is the most critical security setting related to session state. Without a maximum size, a user's session could potentially contain so much data that the server runs out of memory or hard disk space! Since a session holds everything that relates to the state of filling out the form, the amount of storage can get quite large. This is especially true if a form's data source contains hundreds or even thousands of elements. And, as you can imagine, one of the quickest ways to grow session size is to use the File Attachment control. It's easy to see the importance of a maximum session size if a form (with a File Attachment, of course) is being filled out by thousands of people simultaneously! The *Maximum size of form session state* setting, shown in Figure 17.18, sets a ceiling on the number of kilobytes per session. The default of 4MB should be plentiful for even the most complicated form templates. But be careful with this setting; allowing larger maximum session sizes reduces the scalability of your farm under high load.

> **NOTE File Attachment Data Increases Maximum Session Size**
>
> When a File Attachment control is detected in a template, Forms Services automatically increases the maximum session size by 50%. Take this into consideration when setting the maximum size.

While session state is a global service, it's used heavily by Forms Services. Keep in mind that other services depending on it will also be affected. Unfortunately, there's no way to scope SSS changes to only Forms Services. But as we saw in the last few sections, Forms Services offers session-specific configuration options to mitigate potential abuses of server resources. Our next topic, yet another shared service, builds on the session state service to help you gracefully take forms (or even the entire farm) offline.

> **NOTE More on Session State**
>
> Learn more about session state for SharePoint Server on Microsoft TechNet. You can also find information on session state specific to Forms Services there. (See the Appendix for both references.)

Quiesce, Quiescing, Quiesced . . .

According to the *Free Online Dictionary of Computing* (http://foldoc.org), the word "quiesce" carries the following definition based in networking:

> To render quiescent, i.e., temporarily inactive or disabled. For example, to quiesce a device (such as a digital modem). It is also a system command in MAX TNT software which is used to "Temporarily disable a modem or DS0 channel".

Forms Services takes the same basic definition but extends it to form templates on the server. In essence, quiescing allows an administrator to gracefully disable a form template. The alternative is to abruptly cut off any users filling out the form, which results in lost data and unhappy users.

When a user begins filling out a new or existing form in the browser, we say that an editing session has begun. While a form is being filled out, the session is considered to be alive. The mechanism that controls the editing session, as we discussed earlier, is the SSS. Let's see how to quiesce a form template and what happens with session state.

> **NOTE Quiescing Applies to Admin-Deployed Form Templates**
>
> A form must be activated by an administrator via admin deployment to be properly quiesced.

Quiescing a Form Template. Say that you're going about your regular business filling out this week's status report form in the browser. You're a few minutes into filling out the form when an e-mail appears about immediate server downtime for maintenance. You continue filling out the form with no problem. After getting his cup of coffee, John (in the cubicle to your right) sits down to fill out his status report. After a moment, you hear a grumbling of frustration. When you ask John what's wrong, he says the status report form is down and shows you an error dialog (Figure 17.19). But you're still filling out the form with no problem! What gives? Let's see what the server administrator has been doing for the past ten minutes.

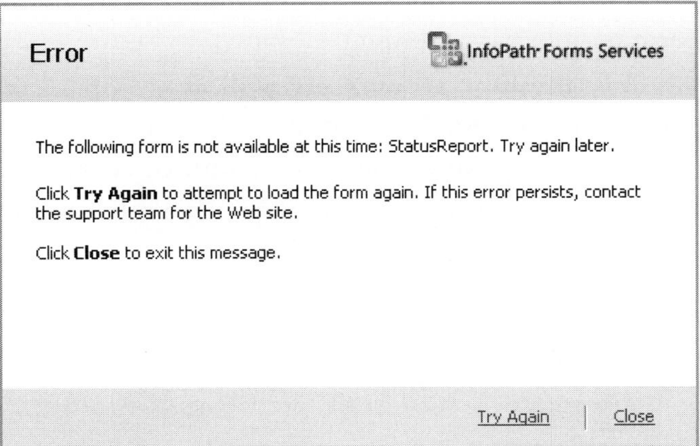

FIGURE 17.19: Quiescing error that frustrated John when creating a status report form

About ten minutes ago, Jaime, the server administrator, received a notification from her antivirus program about a new vulnerability. It required immediate attention as well as a rare reboot of the soon-to-be patched servers. Since it's Friday at 4 P.M., she figures it won't impact too many folks except for the few filling out their end-of-week status reports. Her first instinct is to send out a high-priority e-mail to notify the entire office of a short impending server downtime. The next step she takes is to quiesce the status report form using the *Quiesce Form Template* page, as shown (in part) in Figure 17.20. To quiesce, she enters the time of five minutes until the form template should be fully quiesced.

Status Normal

Quiesce the Form Template to stop accepting new user sessions for long running operations.

The Form Template should be fully quiesced after this long (Time in Minutes): 5

Start Quiescing

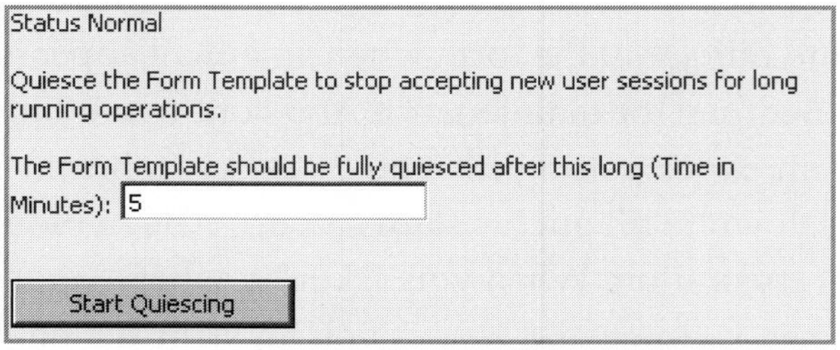

FIGURE 17.20: Configuring to quiesce a form template on the Quiesce Form Template page

After she clicks the *Start Quiescing* button and before the five minutes elapse, the form template is quiescing, as shown in Figure 17.21. Quiescing is when existing form-filling sessions are kept alive, but all new requests for form sessions are rejected. At this point, John can't fill out a new form, and you're sitting on a ticking time bomb! But, of course, Jaime kindly mentioned in the e-mail to the office that you have five minutes to save your form before the server goes down.

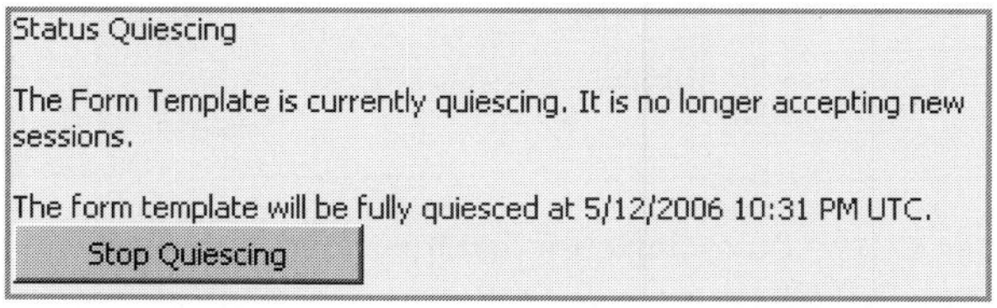

Status Quiescing

The Form Template is currently quiescing. It is no longer accepting new sessions.

The form template will be fully quiesced at 5/12/2006 10:31 PM UTC.

Stop Quiescing

FIGURE 17.21: Status of a quiescing form template

After several minutes, Jaime refreshes the page to see the status shown in Figure 17.22. Now the status report template is fully quiesced. This means any existing sessions at the end of five minutes were killed, and any pending data is lost. (Unfortunately, there are no easy ways to determine the number of active form-filling sessions.) The server can now go down for maintenance. Jaime makes a note to remember to reset the quiesced state of the status report template when she's finished.

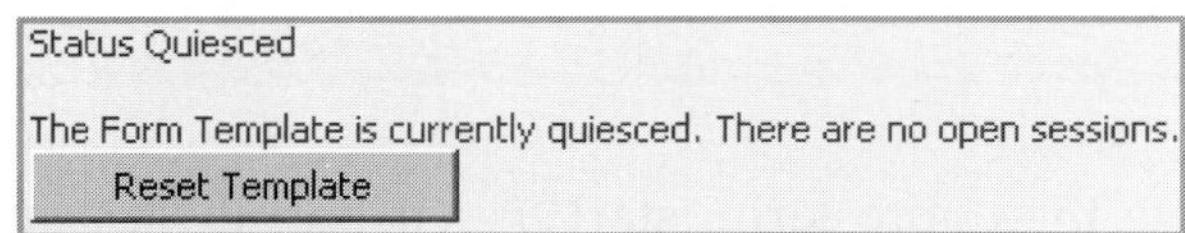

FIGURE 17.22: Fully quiesced form template

> **TIP Stop Quiescing**
>
> You can stop quiescing at any time by clicking the *Stop Quiescing* button. Likewise, you can unquiesce a quiesced template by using the *Reset Template* button.

Table 17.4 shows what happens to new and existing sessions during the three quiesce states. As you can see, quiescing is a soft landing to immobilize a form template.

Quiescing the Entire Farm. When Jaime had to take down the servers, she assumed that the only form being filled out used the status report template. What if there were dozens of form templates in use? And to make matters

TABLE 17.4: New and Existing Form-Filling Sessions During Quiescing and Quiesced Status

Quiesce Status	New Sessions	Existing Sessions
Normal	Accepted	Maintained
Quiescing	Rejected	Maintained
Quiesced	Rejected	Killed

worse, dozens of form templates across dozens of site collections? Although the `FormsServices` admin object model allows for reading and setting quiescing status, there's a much easier way to quiesce all form templates: Just quiesce the entire farm.

> **WARNING** Quiescing Is Shared
>
> Quiescing is a shared service, and thus quiescing the farm may affect other services on the farm.

To quiesce the entire farm, start by visiting the *Operations* tab on the SharePoint Central Administration site. Under the *Global Configuration* section, click on the *Quiesce Farm* link. This page uses the same structure as the *Quiesce Form Template* page shown earlier in Figure 17.20. Any new sessions created during quiescing or any new or existing sessions when a form template is quiesced show the error dialog that appears in Figure 17.19, but with this message: "The server is currently being taken down for maintenance. Check with your system administrator to see when this server is scheduled to come back online." Unfortunately, this message cannot be customized.

> **NOTE** Time to Quiesce
>
> The quiescing time for a form template or a farm can be anywhere from 0 to 1,440 minutes, inclusive. Typically, you'll want to use larger values for forms that take longer to fill out. Use 0 to immediately quiesce the form template or farm.

Despite the compelling role that quiescing plays in server downtime, that may not be its most useful purpose. In fact, quiescing goes hand in hand with form template upgrade. Let's see how it works.

Upgrading a Form Template. We mentioned earlier in the chapter (when talking about the *Upload Form Template* page) that a form template can be upgraded. This will happen quite often as you iterate over tweaking a template in InfoPath design mode, publishing, and then trying it out in the browser. User publishing from InfoPath will simply kill all existing sessions when the *Publish* button is clicked. (There is a warning in the Publishing Wizard on the last page to remind you.) Admin deployment, on the other hand, can take advantage of different flexible types of template upgrades. If you're upgrading a critical form template that's in production for business, this information may be of interest to you.

There are two options available to the administrator when uploading a newer copy of a form template (as shown earlier in Figure 17.11 in the *Upload Form Template* page):

1. *Allow existing browser-based form filling sessions to complete using the current version of the form template.*
2. *Terminate existing browser-based form filling sessions. Any data in those sessions will be lost.*

The second item is not really an option since immediate data loss is not acceptable. Option 1, although it might sound similar, is different from quiescing. With the first option, existing sessions can potentially continue indefinitely with the old version of the template. New sessions begin using the new version of the template. There are a few potential issues with this from an administrative standpoint. First, there's no point at which you can confidently know when the old form is no longer being used. Second, there are two versions of the same form running in a side-by-side configuration. This adds overhead, particularly if data connections or external dependencies have changed, because they may not work anymore!

Instead of relying on either option 1 or 2, you can simply quiesce the form template that you want to upgrade. After the template is fully quiesced, both options from the *Upload Form Template* page work the same way since there won't be any existing form-filling sessions.

Command-Line and Programmatic Quiescing. Quiescing stays inline with the philosophy that all admin features are also accessible via the command line and through code. As with all admin features, stsadm.exe is your key to command-line quiescing. Table 17.5 lists the commands you'll find useful to quiesce a form and the farm.

TABLE 17.5: Commands for stsadm.exe Specific to Quiescing

Operation	What It Does
`formtemplatequiescestatus`	Shows the quiesce status of a form template
`quiesceformtemplate`	Quiesces a form template
`unquiesceformtemplate`	Unquiesces a form template that has been quiesced
`quiescefarm`	Quiesces the farm
`quiescefarmstatus`	Shows the quiesce status of the farm
`unquiescefarm`	Unquiesces the farm

TABLE 17.6: Administration OM on the `FormTemplate` Object Specific to Quiescing

Item	Returns	Arguments
`Quiesce` method	`Void`	`maxDuration` as `TimeSpan`
`QueisceEndTime` method	`DateTime`	`Void`
`Unquiesce` method	`Void`	`Void`
`QuiesceStatus` property (read-only)	`QuiesceMode`	N/A

Table 17.6 shows a list of object model methods and one property. These OM items are available from a `FormTemplate` object on the `FormTemplates` collection. Programmatically quiescing the farm, as expected, is not available from the `FormTemplate` object. Let's take a moment to see where we can find the OM to quiesce the farm and why it's not on `FormTemplate`.

Form and farm quiescing essentially throttles new and existing form-filling sessions. As you learned in the section about the shared session state service, filling out a form is defined by a user session in the session state service. So while it makes sense for the `Quiesce()` method to exist on the `FormTemplate` object for a form template, the `Quiesce()` method for the farm is on the `SessionStateService` object. This makes sense if you think about quiescing the farm in terms of settling the session state service.

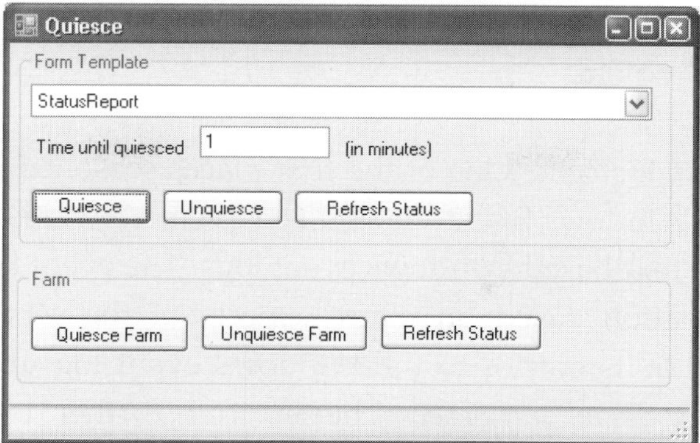

FIGURE 17.23: Quiesce tool authored by using admin object models

To help you understand how to use both the form and farm quiescing APIs, we have another Windows application sample, as shown in Figure 17.23. This sample, called Quiesce (available with this chapter's sample files), exercises the full range of quiesce features and functionality. The drop-down at the top of the program contains a full list of form templates on the farm so you can easily select a form for quiescing. The quiescing status for the form and farm are shown in the status bar and updated automatically. Clicking *Refresh Status* will force update the message for the selected form or farm.

The sample is straightforward; we encourage you to explore it further to learn its intricacies.

Logging

It's relatively easy to get a server set up and running. What makes server administration difficult is when something goes wrong. Being able to quickly and easily diagnose a server or the entire farm can be especially critical. To maintain at least a five 9s (or 99.999%) uptime—broadly considered the "high availability" standard—a system may not be unavailable for longer than 5 minutes and 15 seconds a year. Depending on the nature of your business, server downtime can account for an enormous loss in productivity. Prepare for such a potentially dire situation ahead of time. There is a set of tools available to help you detect problems before they start. Think of these tools as a means of preventive maintenance. If you're already in the red, you can use the same tools to diagnose and get to the bottom of the problem.

Windows Event Viewer. One of the first places seasoned administrators will turn is the Windows Event Viewer. The Event Viewer is a friendly user interface to the text-based Windows event logs. The event logs themselves contain information based on many aspects of the server. SharePoint Server 2007 adds its entries to the Windows event log under the *Source* column as *Office SharePoint Server.* The service is further delineated by the *Category* column. As you would expect, the category name in which you'll be most interested is *Forms Services.* But rarely will you see just *Forms Services* as the category; instead, you'll see categories such as *Forms Services Administration, Forms Services Conversion and Deployment,* and *Forms Services Runtime–Session State.*

> **NOTE Forms Services Categories**
>
> Forms Services has several category names. Each one begins with "Forms Services" but may be followed by an additional word, such as "Runtime".

Open the Event Viewer on any WFE server by running the *Event Viewer* program from the *Administrative Tools* folder form Windows. (You can also use the *Connect to another computer* command on the *Action* menu of the Event Viewer from any computer.) When looking at a server's events, pay particular attention to the error (red "X") entries. Also look near the errors for corresponding warnings. They may be responsible for the primary cause, whereas the errors might just be effects. Table 17.7 lists all of the Forms Services errors that you may see in the event log. Likewise, Table 17.8 contains all of the possible warnings you might encounter. If you see any of the errors classified as admin configurable, you have an opportunity to change the server settings—but don't change the settings unless you're absolutely certain you need to do so! Be sure someone wasn't trying to be malicious and break your server.

TABLE 17.7: Forms Services Errors That May Appear in the Windows Event Log

Error Message	Comments	Admin Configurable?
Two business logic assemblies with the same identity, X, exist.	Two form template assemblies have the same identity.	No.
Cannot persist business logic type X because it is not serializable.	Only serializable types can be saved in the `FormState` dictionary object.	No.
Calculations exceeded the maximum stack depth.	One or more form calculations results in a loop.	No, fixed size of 30.
Rules exceeded the maximum stack depth.	One or more form rules cause a loop.	No, fixed size of 30.
Business logic object model reentrance count limit was exceeded. The business logic may be in an infinite event recursion.	Form code is causing infinite recursion.	No.
Request timed out and was aborted by IIS while running business logic. The business logic may be in an infinite loop.	Form code took too long to run.	Yes. Increase the IIS timeout or reduce the time required by form code.
A memory allocation made by business logic could not be satisfied.	Low memory conditions exist.	No.
An exception occurred during loading of business logic.	Loading the form code assembly failed.	No.
The server has encountered a critical error. The database has returned a session state entry with an unrecognized version.	Session state version is unrecognized and may be corrupted.	No.

continued

Table 17.7: Forms Services Errors That May Appear in the Windows Event Log (*continued*)

Error Message	Comments	Admin Configurable?
Session state size, X bytes, has exceeded Y bytes, the maximum allowable value.	Session state is too big.	Yes.
Exception occurred during request processing.	An internal server error occurred.	No.
The form template failed to load.	An internal server error occurred when loading the form template.	No.
There was a form postback error.	Processing postback data on the server failed.	No.
Number of postbacks, X, has exceeded Y, the maximum allowable value per session.	There were too many postbacks for a given session.	Yes.
Number of form actions, X, has exceeded Y, the maximum allowable value per request.	There were too many actions in a given postback.	Yes.
Forms Services has detected a mismatch between the user's data in the browser and on the server. This may indicate the session state is not configured properly on a multiple front end farm or that a malicious user is trying to tamper with client data.	Client and server form data is out of sync.	No.
Registration of session state failed with an exception.	Session state may not be properly installed. Try recreating the Shared Service Provider (SSP).	No.
Failed to load product component ifsFileNames.xml. Web virtual root may be installed improperly.	Try recreating the Web application or site collection to fix this problem.	No.

Table 17.8: Forms Services Warnings That May Appear in the Windows Event Log

Warning Message	Comments	Admin Configurable?
Activation of form template on site collection X failed.	The form template failed to activate due to an error. Review the activation error (from the end-user's or administrator's perspective) and try again.	No.
Deactivation of form template on site collection X failed.	The form template may still be in use. You may want to wait and try again. It's also a good idea to review surrounding log entries to see if there is a separate root cause for this warning.	No.
Removal of form template failed.	The form template may still be in use.	No.
Detected converted data version mismatch.	The versions of files included in the form template did not match each other.	No.
Business logic failed due to an exception.	An exception was thrown by form code.	No.
The following query failed: X.	A query data connection failed.	No.
Form submission failed.	The form's main submit (which may not be a data connection) failed.	No.

continued

Table 17.8: Forms Services Warnings That May Appear in the Windows Event Log (*continued*)

Warning Message	Comments	Admin Configurable?
The form could not be submitted to X because this action would violate cross-domain security restrictions. The form could not retrieve data from X because it would violate cross-domain restrictions.		To allow this data connection for administrator-approved forms, enable full trust for the form template, or add the connection to a data connection library. For user forms, cross-domain connections must be enabled in SharePoint Central Administration, and all connections must be in a data connection library.
Exception occurred during request processing.	An error when processing the form. Typically happens when a user's session expires and the form attempts to post back data to the server.	No.
Form templates in the Forms Services in-memory cache are being reloaded frequently. This could indicate high memory pressure and suboptimal performance.	Low memory conditions exist, or a form is consuming large amounts of memory.	No.

> **TIP Each WFE Has Its Own Logs**
>
> If you have multiple WFE servers, the logs may vary for each computer. Just because you've looked at one computer with no errors doesn't mean the other servers are assumed to be the same. Check each WFE server event log for errors. You can also use Microsoft Operations Manager to monitor multiple computers simultaneously. We discuss Microsoft Operations Manager later in this chapter.

Tracing with Unified Logging Service. In most cases, the Windows event log is sufficient to detect and diagnose most problems. If you find that it's not helpful, you may want to increase the verbosity of the server's logging level. We'll see how to do that in a moment. But for now, let's say that even maximizing event logging didn't help us pinpoint a problem. What's an admin to do? Beyond the Windows system event log is yet another text-based proprietary logging system to SharePoint Server 2007: Unified Logging Service (ULS).

ULS supports all services on Office SharePoint Server 2007, including Search, Content Management, Excel Services, Forms Services, and various shared services such as SharePoint itself. Unlike the Windows event log, ULS serves as a high-performance scalable tracing system for recording hundreds of data points per second. It exists for the sole purpose of drilling very deeply into server performance issues or malfunctions. Similar to the Windows log, ULS has a configurable threshold for tracing verbosity. By default, the trace settings are fairly high to keep the log sizes reasonably small. If a recurring problem occurs on the server, you have the option of increasing the verbosity of logging for one or more categories. After gathering more detailed log files to capture the essence of a problem, you can analyze the data to pinpoint the culprit and hopefully turn around reasonably quickly with a fix.

The configuration page for server logging and tracing settings is found on the SharePoint Central Administration site's *Operations* tab under the *Logging and Tracing* link (Figure 17.24). Settings relevant to the Windows event log are under the *Event Throttling* section; ULS trace settings are included in the *Trace Log* section shown at the bottom of Figure 17.24.

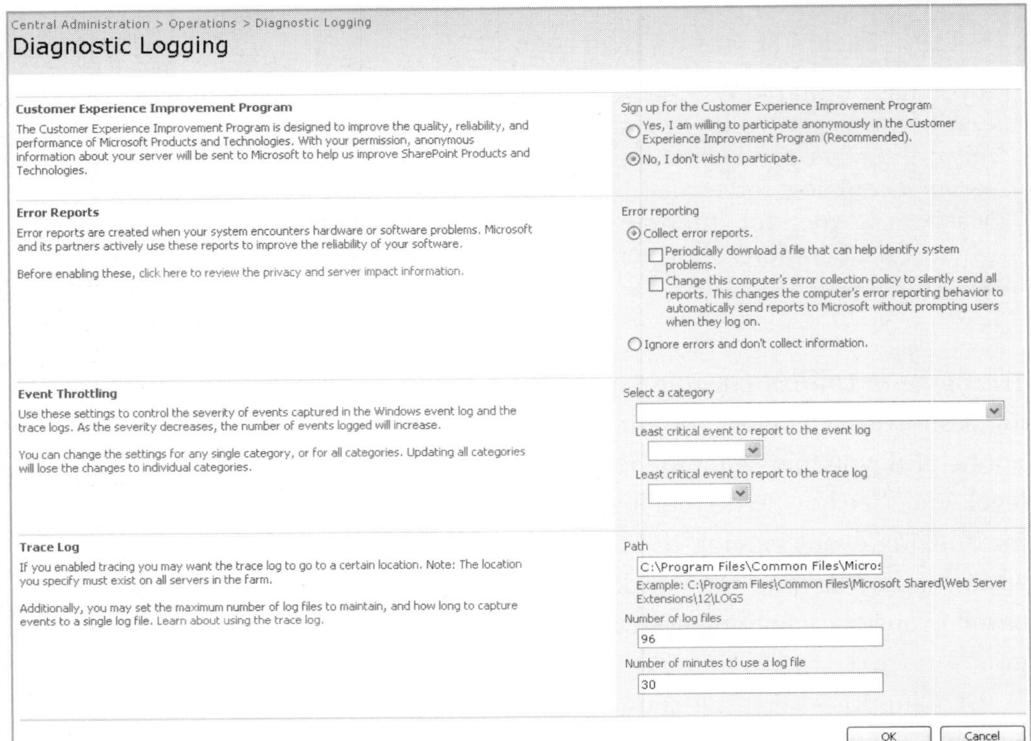

FIGURE 17.24: Diagnostic Logging administration page

ULS sends its tracing data directly to text files under the %CommonProgramFiles%\Microsoft Office Servers\Web Server Extensions\12\LOGS directory. You can change this logs directory by setting the *Path* value under the *Trace Log* settings shown in Figure 17.24. On occasion (and under specific conditions that are beyond the scope of this text), ULS creates a new log. Furthermore, it removes old logs after some time. If you are trying to find tracing data from a specific time frame, it helps to sort by and look at the last modified dates and times of the log files. Once you find the log file of interest, try opening it in your favorite text editor. If you choose a large log file (say, 1MB or larger), just be prepared to wait several minutes for it to open!

> **WARNING Too Much Verbosity Can Hurt**
>
> Use caution when increasing the verbosity of trace logs. Having more categories that trace with higher verbosity generates larger log files more quickly. Higher verbosities degrade server performance, so it's best to use this technique modestly for investigating problems.

Once you have the log data in front of you, you'll notice that it's very extensive. There are nine columns of data with all sorts of details underneath. You can look at the time stamps, product, category, and severity for each log entry. It might drive an average person insane, but it is possible to work through! To better sort, filter, and get the data you need, it's easiest to import the data into a spreadsheet program such as Excel. This is particularly important considering that there isn't a guarantee by ULS that the order of rows descends by date and time. In fact, it's quite easy to assume they're in order. This slight mistake can cost you dearly, especially when performing root cause analysis that depends on the chronological ordering of log entries.

While it's nice to know that you can dig deeply into verbose server logs to narrow down problems, it's definitely not something you'll be using (or want to use) very often. Your first defense to prevent issues will be preventive maintenance. Try filling out your server's forms occasionally to ensure that things such as data connections and form code still work as they were designed. Plus, it's wise to monitor the Windows event log for errors and warnings. If the errors or warnings in the Windows logs don't give you enough information to resolve the problem, the next step is to increase the verbosity of the event log or move to the trace logs.

Alternate Access Mappings

When invoking a form in the browser, Forms Services is configured to recognize only URLs that come from the site. In other words, a form may be properly invoked only by using the SharePoint site URL. Even though it may appear to work, using localhost from the server itself is not supported. If you're familiar with SharePoint, you may already know that access paths other than the site URL are not automatically supported.

Similar to SharePoint, any alternate access mapping (AAM) URLs must be declared via the Central Administration site. So, if you wanted to be able to access your server via an IP address instead of http://myServer, for example, it would need to be registered with SharePoint.

> **NOTE** Errors Navigating to Forms
>
> If you receive an error while trying to access a browser form using an alternate URL, you likely need to add that URL to the SharePoint alternate access mappings definition.

To register an alternate URL with SharePoint that is recognized by Forms Services, start by visiting the Central Administration site's *Operations* tab. Then click on the *Alternate access mappings* link under the *Global Configuration* section. You can define three different types of AAMs: incoming, outgoing, and external URL mappings. The most common reason to use an AAM is for Network Address Translation (NAT) or port forwarding, for example. This type of AAM requires alternate incoming and outgoing URLs that map the WFE servers to a translated address on the outside and vice versa.

You can find more information on AAM on Office Online (as referenced in the Appendix).

Filling Out a Form on a SharePoint Page

So far, we've been filling out browser-enabled form templates in the FormServer.aspx page. This is the default rendering page used by Forms Services every time a form is filled out in the browser. While we're limited to displaying a form by using this page (for now), we're not constrained by where we can show a form. Thanks to SharePoint's Page Viewer Web Part, it's possible to fill out a form within the context of any customizable SharePoint page. The Page Viewer Web Part simply lets you choose a URL for the control to navigate to. By carefully choosing a URL to the FormServer.aspx page, you can fill out a form within this Web part!

To add the Page Viewer Web Part to your SharePoint page, you first need to have a design role. If you have the appropriate permission, you'll see a *Site Settings* button on the upper-right corner of the page. Clicking the button shows a menu; select the *Edit Page* item. Once in customization mode, select *Add a Web Part* from any section (e.g., Left, Right, and so on) in the page. On the dialog listing available Web parts, choose the *Page Viewer Web Part,* and click *Add* at the bottom of the page. Once the part is added to the section, click on its *Edit* menu, and select *Modified Shared Web Part.* It's important to get the correct URL for this Web part. One of the easiest ways is to just navigate to the form in the browser. Then copy and paste the Web browser location into the Page Viewer's *Link* text box.

> **WARNING** Is InfoPath Installed?
>
> If you don't have InfoPath installed, the form always opens in the browser. But on computers with InfoPath, the form will first attempt to open in InfoPath—even in a Page Viewer Web Part! Ensure that the `OpenIn` parameter with value `browser` is present as a URL parameter.

Data Connections

Most advanced form templates will have one or more data connections to bring data in or send data out of the form. As you learned in Chapter 14, data connections on the server behave differently than in InfoPath. This is because the server runs the connections itself, which ultimately poses a security risk to the server and its users. As a result, a form template granted domain trust (which, by the way, is the minimum security level required to deploy a browser-enabled form template to Forms Services) cannot connect to data sources outside of the server's domain. InfoPath, on the other hand, prompts the user to make similar cross-domain connections. How can we enable the server to allow connections beyond the domain of the server?

There are three ways to allow cross-domain connections:

1. Fully trusted form template
2. Domain trust user form template using the data connection library
3. Domain trust form template using the centrally managed connection library

Each method has its own advantages and disadvantages. Determining which one you want to use depends on several factors, such as how much you trust your form template designers and how much time you can dedicate to administrative tasks.

For the InfoPath traditionalists out there, the easiest way to allow a cross-domain connection is to deploy a template as full trust. In our opinion, this isn't always the best option. If your form template requires full trust for a feature like form code and the connection is unique to that particular template, then full trust is the right choice. Otherwise, the other two choices are not only more viable but also easier to maintain. Let's see how to incorporate connection libraries into our form templates.

You learned about data connection libraries (DCLs) in Chapter 14. We walked through creating a DCL as well as converting an existing data connection to a .udcx file within the DCL. Despite the advantages of sharing server-defined data connections across a specific site collection, cross-domain connections fail to execute properly. The result in the browser is a generic "Cannot connect to the data source" warning. Only by examining the server's Windows event log (as discussed earlier) is it revealed that cross-domain connections are prohibited due to current security settings. So where are these security settings, and how can we change them? Before we show you these settings and how to allow user-deployed templates to make cross-domain connections using the DCL, you should seriously consider the security implications. You will be opening up your server to initiated connections (e.g., Web service, database, XML file, and so on) with any other server as defined by the DCL. As such, it's best to apply an appropriate level of security to existing DCLs and to police any new DCLs that might be created.

> **WARNING** Be Careful with User Forms and Cross-Domain Privileges
>
> Allowing user form templates to use the data connection library to make cross-domain connections can be risky. Be sure you trust every user who has write permission to existing DCLs. Also, designers can create new DCLs. Any of the users essentially have administrative rights in the Forms Services data connection department!

Data Connections Administration Settings

To allow user-deployed templates to make cross-domain connections, we revisit the *Configure InfoPath Forms Services* Central Administration site. We started looking at this configuration page earlier in the chapter with the *User Browser-enabled Form Templates* settings (refer back to Figure 17.16). While we're visiting *Configure InfoPath Forms Services,* we'll take some time to cover the remaining settings in the page. Later in this chapter, in the "Centrally Managed Connection Library" section, we will continue to look at the last of the three ways to enable cross-domain data connections.

Cross-Domain Access for User Form Templates

Domain trust user form templates are restricted, by default, from making cross-domain data connections. The motivation behind this design is a clear step in the secure-by-default ideology. Administrators will most likely not want any unapproved form templates accessing data outside the realm of the server farm. But as the administrator, you can forfeit this security restriction and allow user templates cross-domain rights. Enabling the last setting shown in Figure 17.25—*Allow cross-domain data access for user form templates that use connection settings in a data connection file*—does just that. If this setting is enabled, only those user form templates with server-defined UDC data connections may cross the domain boundary. Data connections defined within the form template itself are never allowed to go cross-domain (unless, of course, the template is fully trusted, but then it cannot be deployed as a user form template).

> **NOTE The Ideal Cross-Domain Situation**
>
> Are you looking for cross-domain benefits for domain trust form templates, but you don't want to lift the restriction on all user form templates to go cross-domain? A data connection in the centrally managed connection library will fit the bill very nicely. We discuss this third way to allow cross-domain connections in the next section.

After changing settings on the *Configure InfoPath Forms Services* page, clicking the *OK* button immediately applies them to the server. There's no need to redeploy form templates or reset any services. If you're in the

Data Connection Timeouts Specify default and maximum timeouts for data connections from browser-enabled form. The connection timeout can be changed by code in the form template, but will never exceed the maximum timeout specified.	Default data connection timeout: 10000 milliseconds Maximum data connection timeout: 20000 milliseconds
Data Connection Response Size Specify the maximum size of responses data connections are allowed to process.	1500 kilobytes
HTTP data connections If data connections in browser-enabled form templates require Basic Authentication or Digest Authentication, a password will be sent over the network. Check this box to require an SSL-encrypted connection for these authentication types.	☑ Require SSL for HTTP authentication to data sources
Embedded SQL Authentication Forms that connect to data bases may embed SQL username and password in the connection string. The connection string can be read in cleartext in the UDC file associated with the solution, or in the solution manifest. Uncheck this box to block forms from using embedded SQL credentials.	☐ Allow embedded SQL authentication
Authentication to data sources (user form templates) Data connection files can contain authentication information, such as an explicit username and password or a Microsoft Office Single Sign-On Application ID. Check this box to allow user form templates to use this authentication information.	☐ Allow user form templates to use authentication information contained in data connection files
Cross-Domain Access for User Form Templates Form templates can contain data connections that access data from other domains. Select this check box to allow user form templates to access data from another domain.	☐ Allow cross-domain data access for user form templates that use connection settings in a data connection file

FIGURE 17.25: Global administrative data connection settings for Forms Services

midst of filling out a form in the browser, simply updating the page (or posting back to the server) reflects the changes.

While we have the opportunity to enable cross-domain for user forms, there is a wealth of other data connection–specific settings at our disposal. These settings all have one theme in common: security. The out-of-the-box defaults are recommended and should not be changed unless you're willing to assume the various risks and potential security issues. Let's look at each setting, what it means, and why you might want to change it. We'll then discuss the resulting security implications.

Data Connection Timeouts

The data connection timeout settings limit the amount of time the server will wait for connections to consummate. Long-running data connection requests can create a denial-of-service situation if too many Internet Information Services (IIS) worker threads are used simultaneously. (See the Appendix for a link to the Internet Information Services 6.0 Technical Library on Microsoft TechNet for more information.) While an administrator can increase the maximum number of IIS worker threads, it will typically not solve the problem if the data connection timeout property is too large. The *Default data connection timeout* setting, shown at the top of Figure 17.25, sets the default timeout for every data connection for every form. While the default timeout will be used by most data connections, a fully trusted form template with code can change the data connection timeout on-the-fly. To prevent a form template from elevating the timeout to unrealistic levels, the *Maximum data connection timeout* setting institutes an absolute cap to which all data connection timeouts must adhere. Even the *Default data connection timeout* setting must respect the *Maximum* setting!

Data Connection Response Size

This is simply the largest amount of data, in kilobytes, that can be retrieved at any one time by a data connection. The default size of 1,500K should be plentiful for most cases. Although 1,500K might sound like a lot of data, remember that this is the total size of the payload returned by the external data source. In the case of a Web service, for example, it's possible that the majority of the data in a payload is XML structure and ultimately not the data you'll end up displaying. Even if most of a big payload is actual data, remember that it doesn't mean all of it is presented in the form. For example, you might be filtering a list of hundreds of items in a Drop-Down List Box to just a few dozen.

The purpose of this setting is to prevent tying up server resources in downloading a ton of data. As a byproduct, it also helps mitigate malicious requests to tax and ultimately take down the server. But use good judgment when modifying this setting. Remember that data connections downloading more than the prescribed limit will fail with a generic error message in the browser. Only the admin, through the system event or trace logs, can discover the underlying cause for a data connection failure.

HTTP Data Connections

There are various ways to authenticate with a server via HTTP, some of which are more secure than others. Authentication is required whenever anonymous access is disallowed. Chances are that the data source you're accessing will require some method of authentication, especially if the data is sensitive. Some authentication choices include basic, digest, Windows Integrated, and Single Sign-On (SSO). Basic is intrinsically insecure because credentials are physically included over the network. Digest, on the other hand, uses an MD5 one-way hash function to authenticate itself with the server. The problem with digest authentication is that it's subject to attack by brute force. While longer passwords mitigate this threat somewhat, simple passwords are especially vulnerable. The best advice we can give on HTTP authentication is to use a secure scheme such as Windows Integrated or SSO.

Unfortunately, you may not have control over some form data connections. This may be the case if you're querying data from an external Web site or Web service, for example. While it's not possible to disallow forms from making HTTP data connections, you can constrain such connections to use only a secure layer. Enabling the *Require SSL for HTTP authentication to data sources* checkbox in Figure 17.25 enforces all insecure HTTP connections to use Secure Sockets Layer (SSL). An insecure connection is an HTTP-based connection that uses basic or digest authentication. If a data connection defines an HTTP connection but does not use SSL, the form template can still be deployed to Forms Services but will fail when the connection is executed.

> **NOTE** Other Authentication Methods Are Not Affected
>
> HTTP connections that use authentication schemes besides basic or digest are not affected by the *Require SSL for HTTP authentication to data sources* setting.

Embedded SQL Authentication

Another example of exposed passwords is embedded SQL authentication. Unlike HTTP data connections using basic or digest authentication, embedded SQL user name and password strings are much more easily exposed.

There are two places SQL credentials can be kept: the manifest (.xsf) or UDC (.udcx) files. The manifest is used when a regular database data connection exists in the form template. (We talked about creating database connections in Chapter 6.) A UDC file is used when we convert a regular data connection to be a shared SharePoint Server–based connection residing in a data connection library. Regardless of where the credentials reside, they are readily available in plain text. Anyone who has access to the form template (.xsn) file on the server can extract its files and open the manifest.xsf file in a simple text editor to read the user name and password. The same idea applies to the UDC file.

InfoPath discourages embedding SQL credentials when you design a form template. As we discussed in Chapter 6, defining a database connection that does not use a trusted connection (e.g., Windows Authentication) prompts to make sure you want to continue before saving the user name and password as clear text. However, once the form is filled out, InfoPath runs database data connections with the saved user name and password as it normally would for any other connection. Forms Services performs similarly if the *Allow embedded SQL authentication* checkbox is checked; otherwise, executing database connections with embedded credentials always fails.

With security in mind, embedded SQL user name and password strings are not a good idea. The safe alternative is to use a trusted connection. A trusted connection uses Windows Integrated authentication to identify the client user to the SQL server. This is how Internet Explorer works (by default) when browsing intranet Web sites, for example.

Authentication to Data Sources (User Form Templates)

Data connection (.udcx) files, as we'll soon see in the "Authentication Considerations" section later in this chapter, can optionally contain information on authentication. This means a user name and account can be associated with and stored within a specific UDC file. This setting does not restrict the ability for a user form template to use a specific data connection; rather, it limits such a template from using that connection with the associated authentication information. Administratively deployed form templates are not susceptible to this setting. Enabling the *Allow user form templates to use authentication information contained in data connection files* checkbox permits such connections to connect with the user name and password as provided by the UDC file or as defined by SSO. If this setting is not checked, the connection will occur as if no explicit authentication information exists.

Centrally Managed Connection Library

The third and arguably most secure way to allow a form template cross-domain data connection rights is to use the centrally managed connection library (CMCL). The advantages of using the CMCL include the following.

- You don't need a fully trusted form template.
- Data connections are accessible by templates across site collections and the farm.
- Anyone can read a CMCL connection definition (as long as he or she has permission to a form template that is activated on the server and references that server connection).

While the flexibility of the CMCL is handy, it doesn't go without some level of security. The constraints in place to use the CMCL are the following.

- Form templates referencing the CMCL must be deployed by an administrator.
- Adding connection definitions to the CMCL is an administrative task.

Don't be fooled by the first constraint! Remember that just because the template requires administrator approval does not mean the form template must be fully trusted. This is important to understand because administratively deploying a domain trust template is much safer than admin deploying one that requires full trust. (A fully trusted form template can run form code with full control on the server.) Additionally, the CMCL is considered more secure than a DCL. While a contributor role can upload a data connection file to a DCL, a farm administrator is required to upload to the CMCL.

> **TIP Unapproved DCL Connection Definitions**
>
> A contributor can upload connection definitions to a DCL, but those uploaded definition files will not be approved. This means that only the user can see those definitions. You can turn off the approval requirement, but it's a built-in safety net that we recommend leaving enabled.

There's no better way to understand the CMCL than to see it in action. In the following sample, we'll show how to convert a normal data connection to a CMCL-defined data connection.

Designing against the Centrally Managed Connection Library

We start with a form template called Fibonacci (included with this chapter's samples). It has a single data connection to query the `Fib` Web service method. We added the data connection to the template by using the *Data Connections* dialog from the *Tools* menu. The `Fib` Web service should be deployed on a different server than the SharePoint Server running Forms Services. To make matters simple (or if you have only a single server), you can create a new Web site in IIS under an unused port. Accessing a different port under the same server is considered to be a cross-domain connection. For this sample, we chose port 81 and copied the Service.asmx Web service file to a new Web application under that site. The Fibonacci sample form template defines a connection to `Fib`, which takes a single integer parameter and returns the Fibonacci number. You can preview the form template (after modifying the data connection to point to your own Web service; the Fibonacci Web service is included with this chapter's samples), and it should work as expected.

There are a few steps to follow before the template can use the CMCL instead of the template-defined data connection.

1. Convert the connection to use an absolute reference to Fib.udcx in the data connection library.
2. Upload the resulting .udcx file from the DCL to the CMCL. (Fib.udcx is included with this chapter's samples.)
3. Optionally delete the .udcx file from the data connection library.
4. Publish the form template for administrator approval.

Converting to a Data Connection Library. The first step is replicating what you learned in Chapter 14. We have a data connection library under the root site collection called `dcl`. We use the *Convert* button on the *Data Connections* dialog to make our connection use a UDC file in that DCL. But instead of using the *Relative to site collection* option as the connection link type, we choose *Centrally managed connection library (advanced)*, as shown in Figure 17.26. Selecting this link type tells InfoPath to only use the CMCL when a user fills out a form template. In other words, converting this connection doesn't put the .udcx file into the CMCL. It puts it into the DCL as defined in the path of the *Convert Data Connection* dialog shown in Figure 17.26. InfoPath will not put a file into the CMCL for you; it must be done manually using the Central Administration site.

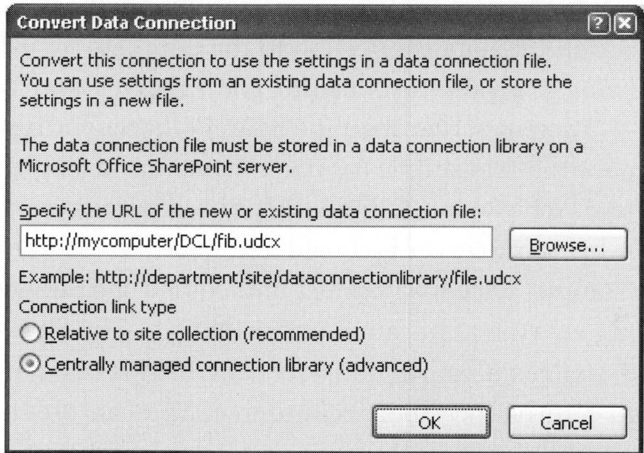

FIGURE 17.26: The Convert Data Connection dialog

Once we're finishing creating the DCL-based data connection, the *Data Connection* dialog shows (under the *Connection source* property) the *link type* as *store* instead of *relative*. The *store* link type is synonymous with the CMCL. (The sample form template is called fibonacci-cmcl.)

Instead of creating a new DCL-based data connection as we do in this sample, you may already have a DCL connection you prefer to use. If so, you can start in the *Data Connections* dialog as we did earlier. Instead of clicking the *Convert* button (which will be disabled because the connection was already converted), click the *Modify* button to open the *Connection*

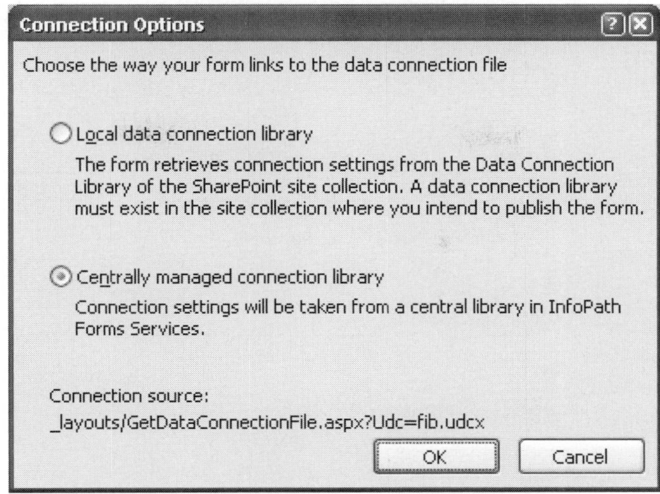

FIGURE 17.27: Connection Options dialog when modifying a server-based connection

Options dialog (Figure 17.27). Note that the *Connection source* setting is listed as *_layouts/GetDataConnectionFile.aspx?Udc=fib.udcx*. In a moment we'll take a closer look at the GetDataConnectionFile.aspx Web page.

Uploading the Resulting .udcx File to the CMCL. If we were to publish this form template to Forms Services, it would be broken. Any attempt to use it in the browser or InfoPath client would fail to query the data connection that we converted. It fails because Forms Services and InfoPath both expect the data connection to be defined in the CMCL. But it's not there yet! Let's upload our DCL-based connection to the CMCL.

The CMCL is a special library in the SharePoint Server Central Administration site. Unlike a DCL, there is neither a library to create nor any special settings to configure. To navigate to the CMCL, start by going to the Central Administration site. Click on the *Application Management* tab and look under the *InfoPath Forms Services* section for the *Manage data connection files* link.

The only option is to upload a new connection file. Clicking the button shows the *Upload Data Connection File* page (Figure 17.28). In the *File name* box, we enter the location of our .udcx file in the DCL from the previous step. In this case, we use the path C:\fib.udcx because we copied the .udcx

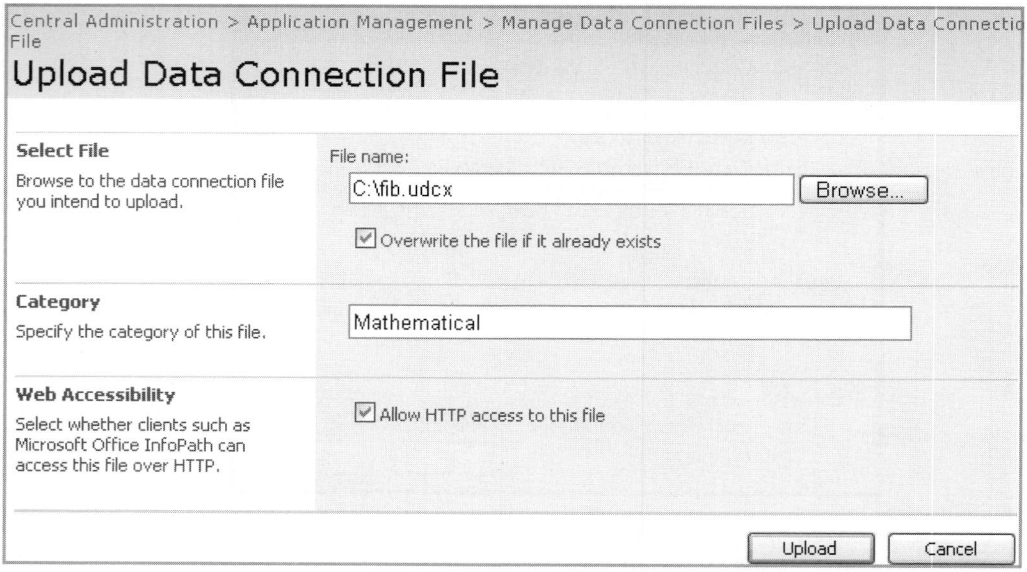

Central Administration > Application Management > Manage Data Connection Files > Upload Data Connection File

Upload Data Connection File

Select File
Browse to the data connection file you intend to upload.
File name:
C:\fib.udcx
Browse...
Overwrite the file if it already exists

Category
Specify the category of this file.
Mathematical

Web Accessibility
Select whether clients such as Microsoft Office InfoPath can access this file over HTTP.
Allow HTTP access to this file

Upload
Cancel

FIGURE 17.28: Uploading to the centrally managed connection library

file to the C drive root on the local computer. You could also reference the .udcx file directly from the DCL at http://mycomputer/dcl/fib.udcx if the file isn't already copied to your computer. The *Category* box is optional and used simply as a pivot for sorting the connections in the CMCL. You can also modify the category later. The *Web Accessibility* setting either denies (default) or allows HTTP access to get the connection file. Basically, this determines whether or not the InfoPath program can use the connection at all. InfoPath gets server-defined data connections through HTTP, while Forms Services can get the connection information directly from the server. If you do not check the *Allow HTTP access to this file* checkbox, InfoPath cannot use this connection. Clicking the *Upload* button adds the .udcx file to the CMCL.

TIP Keeping Track of CMCL References in Form Templates

Remembering which form templates reference what CMCL data connections could be a taxing process for an administrator. Go to the *Edit Properties* page of a CMCL connection to see a list of form template URN references.

Optionally Deleting the .udcx File from the Data Connection Library. We used the *Convert* button functionality to put an InfoPath data connection on our server as a data connection (.udcx) file. Since we've added the .udcx file to the CMCL from the DCL, it doesn't make sense to have two copies. Moreover, for security reasons, you won't want to leave the connection file in the less secure DCL. If you decide to not delete the DCL-based connection file for whatever reason, realize that the DCL and CMCL connections are completely independent.

> **WARNING** **Previewing Unpublished Forms with CMCL Connections**
>
> When you're previewing a form template with a CMCL-defined data connection, you cannot use the CMCL! The CMCL requires a form template published and activated in Forms Services. The act of filling out a form in a preview window automatically uses the DCL-defined connection that you configured in design mode. This is because a form preview never uses the published version of the form template.

Publishing the Form Template for Administrator Approval. Browser-enabled form templates with CMCL data connections must be administrator approved. A CMCL data connection is one of the few features mentioned in the Publishing Wizard that does not allow the user to directly activate the form template. As a result, publishing to Forms Services forces the *Administrator-approved form template (advanced)* option (with the others disabled), as we saw back in Figure 17.8.

Once the template is uploaded and activated by the administrator, the form can freely use the Fibonacci data connection. Notice that the runtime experiences of CMCL-defined and DCL-defined connection files are equivalent. The implementation of a template's data connections is insignificant when a user fills out the form.

A great selling feature of the CMCL is its ability to span the entire server farm. In other words, any form template activated on the farm—no matter what Web application or site collection the template belongs to—can share a CMCL-defined connection. Alternatively, the DCL can be referenced by templates only within its same site collection. Accessing a DCL across site collections fails. It is an inherent design decision by SharePoint to keep site collections mutually exclusive. The CMCL solves this problem because it uses the Central Administration site, which is always available.

Getting Data Connection Files from the CMCL

Slightly contrary to our understanding of the CMCL so far, typical users filling out your forms cannot access the Central Administration site. But the CMCL isn't really accessed through the Central Administration site. There are two ways that a CMCL-based data connection file can be retrieved. The first way is by Forms Services directly accessing the file in the library. Unfortunately, there is no user-exposed or administrator-exposed mechanism to replicate what Forms Services does internally. Instead, the server exposes a Web page (within any site collection) to get a connection file. The _layouts directory is the progenitor of the GetDataConnectionFile.aspx Web page; the URL to get a data connection file may look something like http://server/_layouts/GetDataConnectionFile.aspx (with URL parameters omitted; we'll look at parameters shortly).

> **NOTE** Making Connection Files Available through HTTP
>
> A data connection file isn't accessible through the GetDataConnectionFile.aspx Web page unless the *Allow HTTP access to this file* option is enabled in a connection file's settings in the CMCL.

The GetDataConnectionFile.aspx Web page allows specific access to a data connection in the CMCL for nonadministrators. Well, not everyone can just access a data connection file from the CMCL. A set of security checks must be passed before the file is returned by the Web page. The checks ensure that the following statement is true: The user requesting a specific connection file must have permission to open a particular form template that references that connection. To validate the statement, the GetDataConnectionFile.aspx Web page accepts three case-insensitive parameters in any order: `udc`, `urn`, and `version`.

The `udc` parameter determines what data connection (.udcx or .xml) file you want to retrieve from the CMCL. If the provided file name does not exist, an error will be returned from the GetDataConnectionFile.aspx Web page. Remember that the file name is different from the display name. By default, the display name is the file name. To modify the display name, click on any data connection file entry in the CMCL and select *Edit Properties.*

The `urn` parameter tells the GetDataConnectionFile.aspx Web page which form template to use. Only administrator-deployed templates are considered possible matches. For a form template to reference and use a CMCL data connection, it must have been deployed by the administrator. (This fact is made clear in the Publishing Wizard when such a connection exists.) At least one form template must use the UDC file being requested for GetDataConnectionFile.aspx to succeed. A CMCL-based data connection that is not used by any templates can never be retrieved through this Web page.

The last parameter used by the GetDataConnectionFile.aspx Web page is `version`. The value of `version` (which looks something like `1.0.0.5`) corresponds with the version of the form template as provided by the `urn` parameter. Why is the `version` parameter necessary? Multiple versions of a form template can exist simultaneously on the farm. For example, earlier we talked about upgrading form templates. An option labeled *Allow existing browser-based form filling sessions to complete using the current version of the form template* can be used when uploading a form template. While some users are still filling out the old form template, others may already be filling out the new one. A CMCL-defined data connection could potentially be in use by one version of the form template but not the other. It makes sense to permit access to a CMCL file if and only if a specific version of a form template references that server connection file.

Authentication Considerations

The server introduces new problems in data connection authentication. This was never a problem with InfoPath. Since InfoPath runs on every user's computer as his or her account, the person making the connection was always that user. Running a data connection in InfoPath is a one-hop scenario with credentials propagating directly from the InfoPath program to an external server. With Forms Services and SharePoint Server, authentication works a bit differently. Instead of one hop from the InfoPath program running on the user's computer to the data source, as shown in Figure 17.29, there is a two-hop process with Forms Services. The first hop is from the

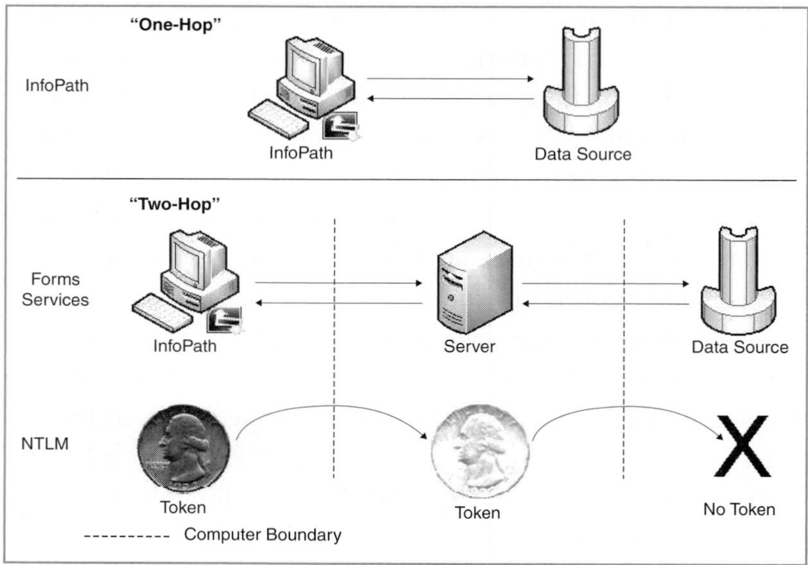

FIGURE 17.29: Passing NTLM credentials for data connections with InfoPath and Forms Services

Web browser to the server running Forms Services, and the second hop is from the server to the data source. Since NTLM authentication (a protocol of Windows Integrated authentication) tokens can be used only on a single hop, the hop from the server to the data source cannot forward the authentication token. As a result, the data source will see the data connection request as if it were from an anonymous user.

UDC Authentication

As you can see, it is not possible to authenticate yourself across more than one computer using the default authentication of NTLM. You can mitigate this problem by using another authentication technology such as basic, digest, Kerberos, or SSO. But instead of hassling with implementing a new authentication scheme across the board, consider keeping NTLM. Thanks to a special feature provided by server-defined UDCs, we can pass our NTLM token across the second computer boundary to a data source.

Every data connection converted to a server-based UDC will have a commented-out authentication block. To see this block, open any UDC file in your favorite text editor. Because it's commented out, the authentication block isn't doing anything useful. This authentication block merely exists as a convenience should you want to pass credentials (to mitigate the two-hop limitation) to the data source:

```
<!--udc:Authentication><udc:SSO AppId=''
   CredentialType=''/></udc:Authentication-->
```

To enable the authentication feature of a UDC file, uncomment the `udc:Authentication` block, add relevant information to the block, and save your changes. Subsequently, upload the file back to the library (DCL or CMCL). Now Forms Services will use the specified credentials in the .udcx file to connect to its data source every time that connection is used. Remember that the specified credentials are always used by that UDC file no matter who is using the connection. As such, you'll be prudent to limit access to this connection to only those who should use it.

> **TIP Authentication Requires a Hand-Edit**
>
> Unfortunately, there is no user interface to add, remove, or modify the authentication block in a UDC file. Open the file in a text editor to modify the authentication section and reupload it to the data connection library on the SharePoint site.

The default authentication type is `udc:SSO`. It is the recommended authentication method due to its inherent security. If you have an SSO server in your farm, simply modify the authentication block to include the application identifier (`AppId`) and `CredentialType` (`Sql`, `NTLM`, `Kerberos`, `CD`, `Basic`, or `Digest`) values. Find out more about implementing SSO in a TechNet article about Single Sign-On (as referenced in the Appendix).

If you can't use SSO, or if you just want to quickly test the authentication capability of UDC, try replacing the entire `udc:SSO` node with `udc:UseExplicit. UseExplicit` relies on hard-coded credentials in the .udcx file instead of doing a lookup using SSO. Listing 17.6 shows the `UseExplicit` structure.

LISTING 17.6: `UseExplicit` Block for a Data Connection (.udcx) File

```
<udc:UseExplicit CredentialType="Basic">
      <udc:UserId>moi\hagengreen</udc:UserId>
      <udc:Password>infopath.2007</udc:Password>
</udc:UseExplicit>
```

In this sample `UseExplicit` structure, we chose `Basic` authentication; however, we could have used any of the `CredentialType` values defined by SSO.

> **WARNING Hard-Coded Credentials**
>
> Using `explicit` credentials in a UDC file is not recommended because anyone with access to that file can get the user name and password! `SSO` is preferred over `explicit` because it uses an `AppId` that securely abstracts away all traces of credentials.

Web Service Proxy

The Web service proxy is simply a Web service that acts as a middleman between your InfoPath form (both on InfoPath and Forms Services) and the Web service to which you want to connect. Its purpose is to provide the current user's login name to the target Web service. Why do we need a proxy just to get the user's login name? Recall from the discussion about authentication that an NTLM token is good only for the first hop. This first hop is from the browser (on the user's computer) to the server running Forms Services. Any Web service data connections that connect to another computer beyond the server are considered a second hop. These connections will not (and cannot) connect as the user running the browser on the client. But sometimes all a Web service needs to know is the current user name. In such a case, the Web service proxy is just what the doctor ordered.

To use the Web service proxy, you must be using a server-defined UDC Web service connection. If you don't already have a UDC-based connection, use the *Convert* feature we covered back in Chapter 14. Once you've created the data connection (.udcx) file, you'll need to hand-edit the file in the same way we did earlier for the authentication block. Look for the following line and switch its value from `false` to `true`, so it reads:

```
<udc:ServiceUrl UseFormsServiceProxy="true">
http:// . . . <//udc:ServiceUrl>
```

Even though we've switched the `UseFormsServiceProxy` attribute to `true`, the proxy will not work properly yet. The Web service proxy feature

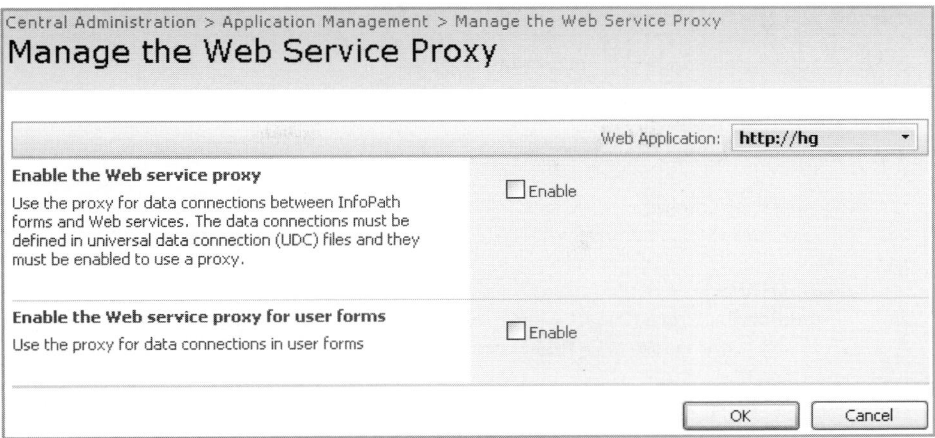
Central Administration > Application Management > Manage the Web Service Proxy
Manage the Web Service Proxy
Web Application: http://hg
Enable the Web service proxy
Use the proxy for data connections between InfoPath forms and Web services. The data connections must be defined in universal data connection (UDC) files and they must be enabled to use a proxy.
Enable
Enable the Web service proxy for user forms
Use the proxy for data connections in user forms
Enable
OK
Cancel

FIGURE 17.30: Settings on the Managing the Web Service Proxy page

first needs to be enabled. To turn on the proxy, go to the Central Administration site and click on the *Application Management* tab. Under the *InfoPath Forms Services* section, click on the *Manage the Web service proxy* link, which results in the page shown in Figure 17.30.

The proxy has two settings for enabling its use. The first is a general setting to allow the proxy to be used in the first place, but only for administrator-deployed form templates. If you want to let user forms use the proxy, enable the second setting, *Enable the Web service proxy for user forms.* Enabling the second setting without the first is the same as if you just didn't enable the second setting; basically the second setting does not matter without the first enabled.

Getting the User Login Name from the Proxy. At this point we've enabled the proxy and used it to execute either a query or a submit to a Web service. But how does the Web service retrieve the user's login name? To get the login name, you need to write special code in your Web service method to parse SOAP headers. Listing 17.7 shows a Web service method to get the user login name from the header and return it to the caller. If the caller isn't the Web service proxy, this Web method returns `"(Not specified)"`.

LISTING 17.7: Code Behind a Web Service to Get the User Name from the Web Service Proxy

```
public SoapUnknownHeader[] unknownHeaders;
[WebMethod]
[SoapHeader("unknownHeaders")]
public string GetUserLoginName()
{
    string userLoginName = "(Not specified)";
    if (unknownHeaders.Length > 0)
    {
        userLoginName =
            unknownHeaders[0].Element.CreateNavigator().SelectSingleNode(
            "//*[local-name(.)='Username']").Value;
    }
    return "Current login user:" + authorizedUser;
}
```

Say that our user login name is guest within the MOI Consulting Corporation's domain. Assume that we are filling out an InfoPath form in the browser with the following conditions:

- NTLM (default) authentication
- A UDC server-based Web service query or submit data connection
- The `UseFormsServiceProxy` attribute in the .udcx file set to `true`

In this situation, running the data connection would retrieve MOI\guest from the SOAP header. The Web service can then use the user name to perform database lookups or make any other decisions as it chooses.

E-Mail Data Connections

Sending e-mail is a common way to finish filling out a form. Most form templates send the e-mail by using an e-mail data connection as the submit action. As you may have thought, using an e-mail connection in the browser is different than in the InfoPath program. With InfoPath, submitting via e-mail shows the Outlook envelope dialog, which summarizes several properties such as To, Cc, Bcc, Subject, and Introduction. Clicking the *Send* button on the envelope dialog sends the e-mail.

In Forms Services, the e-mail model is a little different. Since the browser cannot depend on the existence of Outlook (let alone on the use of Windows as the operating system!), the e-mail is sent by the server computer. As a result, the client need not be particularly configured to send e-mail. (Even a mobile device can use an e-mail data connection, for example.) Let's see how to configure the server to send e-mail. Configuring the server allows Forms Services to send e-mail when executing an e-mail data connection.

> **WARNING Not Configuring E-Mail Settings Results in Errors**
>
> Failing to configure your server's e-mail settings will result in an error every time Forms Services attempts to send an e-mail. You will see entries in the Windows event log if such an error occurs.

To configure the server to send e-mail, start by visiting the *Application Management* tab on the Central Administration site. Under *SharePoint Web Application Management,* click the *E-mail settings* link.

> **TIP Settings Applied per Web Application**
>
> Like most administration settings, e-mail settings are applied to the specific Web application selected on the settings page.

Three properties are required for the server to send e-mail: *Outbound SMTP server, From address,* and *Reply-to address.* E-mail sent from Forms Services does not use the current user's name, but rather uses the *From address* setting. While this may seem odd, it serves the purpose of a machine account. Clients can always expect that e-mails sent by that account are actually from the server and not a real person.

An alternative to using the UI is to use the OM or the stsadm.exe tool. The example command line in Listing 17.8 shows how to use stsadm.exe.

LISTING 17.8: Sample Command Line for Configuring E-Mail

```
stsadm.exe -o email -outsmtpserver emailserver -fromaddress
   FormsServices@moiconsulting.com -replytoaddress
   FormsServicesReply@moiconsulting.com -codepage 65001
```

To use the OM, first get the `SPWebService` from the farm's `Services` collection. Then get the appropriate `SPWebApplication` and use the code in Listing 17.9 to do an operation similar to the stsadm.exe command shown in Listing 17.8.

LISTING 17.9: Configuring E-Mail Settings via the Object Model

```
webApplication.UpdateMailSettings("emailserver",
   "FormsServices@moiconsulting.com",
   "FormsServicesReply@moiconsulting.com", 65001);
```

Now that the SharePoint server's e-mail settings have been configured, Forms Services can successfully send e-mail. Simply set up a submit data connection to e-mail as you would for any other InfoPath form template. Submit using e-mail in the browser, unlike InfoPath, does not prompt before sending the e-mail. The e-mail is simply sent. A major difference between e-mails sent by InfoPath versus those sent by the server is the e-mail introduction. While you can configure the introduction in the Data Connection Wizard, browser forms add additional text. An introduction for an e-mail coming from the server will begin with the following text:

```
[Submitted by guest@moiconsulting.org]
```

Notice that the user's e-mail address is included in the introduction within square brackets. This is the case for all authenticated users. If the user is unknown (e.g., anonymous is enabled) the e-mail address is replaced with "Anonymous user".

> **NOTE "Submitted by" Introduction Line**
>
> The *[Submitted by . . .]* introduction cannot be removed or modified. It is always sent with e-mails originating from a form being filled out in a browser. The decision behind this design is to mitigate anonymous spamming or relaying of e-mail through Forms Services.

Performance Tips and Best Design Practices

One of the most essential aspects of a browser-based form is how it performs in regular use. We all know what it's like to use a system that is annoyingly slow. Sometimes a system can seem to take forever just to initialize and be ready for use. Other times a system can respond quite sluggishly during use, which can be distracting, not to mention a waste of time. A system can become slow for many reasons. In our system—Forms Services on your farm—we'll look at several aspects of your form templates that may contribute to performance gains and losses. By the time you finish reading this section, you'll have a great deal of information to better assess your form template design to optimize performance. You will be able to iterate over the design of your templates to make them more robust and scalable. The more closely you can adhere to these guidelines, the greater performance yield your farm will realize under heavy server loads.

With Forms Services, there's no silver bullet for getting performance 100% correct. For optimizations in load-time or runtime performance, you'll be giving up some server throughput. Likewise, improving server throughput tips the scales away from speedy form load and runtime. The key is balance and weighing tradeoffs to find what works best for your needs. This will depend largely on your farm configuration (both software settings and hardware), the number of users and their behaviors, and the design and features included in your form templates. Let's look at some specific form features and see how you can offer all of your users the best form-filling experience possible.

> **NOTE** InfoPath Forms Services Best Practices
>
> You can find a rudimentary list of best practices for Forms Services on Microsoft TechNet (as referenced in the Appendix).

Form Template Deployment

Administrative-deployed form templates generally exhibit slightly greater performance than equivalent user-deployed forms. Since user forms are stored in the SharePoint content database, a user form must be fetched from the database (through SharePoint) every time it's needed. While SharePoint is a performance-minded platform, retrieving the form template from the database is slower than getting it from the local disk. Admin-deployed templates have the advantage of being stored on the local disk of the WFE server. Compare the elapsed time to fetch the same form template from a SQL Server (on a *different* machine over the network) versus from a computer's local disk. While we don't have precise measurements to present, we can tell you that the network latency between the

SQL Server and WFE alone is orders of magnitude slower than local disk read access.

Views

If a speedy load time is important, consider using multiple views to separate your form data. The less data you are presenting (in controls) on the initial view, the quicker your form will load in the browser. Don't overdo it, however, and use too many smaller views. View switching is a relatively expensive operation as it requires a full postback and complete refresh and repaint of data in the browser.

A logical way to separate views is to break them apart when postbacks are required. Say, for example, that your form contains a Button control that runs a query data connection to populate a Drop-Down List Box control with a list of data. Since the Button will require a postback so the server can execute the connection, you might as well switch to another view that contains the Drop-Down List Box, along with the rest of the form data. If the Button happens to physically be around the middle of a large view, it works out particularly nicely. The first new view can include the first half of the original view including the Button. The second new view would, of course, contain the remainder of the view after the Button.

While it's easy to make arbitrary decisions as to how a large view should be broken up, there's a better methodological approach. We recommend that you fill out the form yourself. Use the same hardware and network connection as the majority of your users, and fill it out using a real scenario. If need be, ask your users for examples of how they will be using the form. Going the extra mile to put yourself in their shoes may be the best thing to help you make a view-splitting decision!

> **WARNING** Hiding Isn't Better
>
> If you've designed complex form templates for InfoPath, you may have used conditional formatting to hide parts of a view that you may not want to show at certain times. While this little trick works great in InfoPath, it doesn't drastically help performance in the browser. Even though the conditionally hidden data is not visible, it is still downloaded to the browser.

Form Code

The existence of form code in a browser form affects server stress. Even if the code isn't used (which is unlikely), the assembly containing the code is loaded into the server's application domain. This directly results in extra CPU cycles and resource usage. If you expect your server farm to scale to hundreds or even thousands of templates, all with form code and most of them used simultaneously, you may want to revisit your hardware requirements. For best results when you have many loaded templates with form code, we recommend using 64-bit architecture with the corresponding 64-bit version of SharePoint Server 2007 or Forms Server 2007.

On the other hand, the mere existence of form code in a template on the server doesn't affect overall data throughput. But throughput, as you may expect, is affected when form code is running in form-filling sessions. There are two effects of running form code. The first effect is that the server must perform extra processing as defined by the code to run. This should be a given. The second effect is slightly more obscure but directly affects throughput: Running form code requires the form to post data back to the server. Postbacks, as we'll see next, are the leading cause of limited server throughput. The more you can prevent or eliminate postbacks, the greater the number of users who can simultaneously fill out your form.

Reduction of Form Postbacks

The most important performance optimization you can make for your browser-based form template is to reduce or eliminate postbacks. There are two major reasons to reduce postbacks.

1. Throughput: Increase the maximum number of sustainable users simultaneously filling out forms.
2. Experience: A postback forces the user to wait while the form takes anywhere from a couple of seconds to over a minute (primarily depending on network speeds) to exchange data with the server.

While we've convinced you that postbacks are important to tackle, we'd like to make it easy for you to do something about them. Following is a list of tools at your disposal to better analyze and control your form template postbacks:

- Design Checker (enable the *Browser Optimizations* setting under the *Options* button)
- *Browser forms* controls setting (as we reviewed at the beginning of this chapter)
- Logic Inspector (helps trace complex form interactions resulting in postbacks)

If you are using formulas in your controls (e.g., for Expression Box controls, default values, rules conditions, conditional formatting, and so on), be wary of wildcard expressions. Such expressions are imprecise XPaths that select more data than necessary. Common culprits are the // and * operators. The double forward slashes mean to select all descendents including the current context. Using this toward the top of a large data source may have serious effects on form performance. Likewise, the asterisk selects all nodes in a given context. While not as bad as the forward slashes, it still allows a wide selection of data, which results in unnecessary postbacks.

> **TIP Forcibly Denying a Postback**
>
> Unexpected postbacks may happen due to an expression in an unrelated control. We saw such an interaction in the Design Checker at the beginning of this chapter. To suppress a control from inevitable postbacks, use the *Browser forms* tab on the affected control.

Data-Heavy Features

As you might guess, a File Attachment control adds overhead when downloading form data. If you're going to use a File Attachment on a heavy populated view, you may want to consider moving it to a separate view instead. Especially if your form template has multiple File Attachment controls in the same view, the hit on form latency may be quite noticeable. While we don't want to discourage you from using this control, we do want you to be informed of the potential performance degradation. As we mentioned earlier, there's no better gauge than for you to fill out your own forms while simulating what your users would do (i.e., by using the same hardware, connection, and realistic scenarios). Keep in mind that form load latency will increase as the simultaneous number of concurrent users increases.

Along the same lines of the File Attachment control, form templates with digitally signed sections may also slightly degrade loading performance. For absolute best performance, we recommend adding section signing to a separate view in the form. This way, downloading the necessary data from the server (for the ActiveX control and the signature-related form data) is done only when necessary and is isolated in a view that will be visited only during signing. If you had the digitally signed section on the default view, for example, it would cause the extra download of data to happen every time the form is loaded. Despite the cost of adding extra views to isolate relatively expensive operations such as digitally signing data and attaching files, this technique definitely pays off. The additional views (and extra postbacks to switch to and from the view) scale much better during peak server use than they do if you put them all on the default view.

The existence of Rich Text Box controls, even many of them, will not cause a performance problem. However, you'll start seeing performance issues when a lot of HTML is stuffed into one or more of these controls. When users enter data into a Rich Text Box, it can come from almost anywhere. A simple copy and paste can insert HTML from Word, an e-mail, or any Web page. If the content is large enough, hundreds of kilobytes or more can be inserted into a Rich Text Box, which is then sent to the server. On a full page postback (e.g., loading the form or switching views), the server needs to push that entire HTML blob back to the browser. You can probably see how this can become a performance problem. The best advice we can give is to limit the amount of HTML that's needed in any one Rich Text Box. Unfortunately, there's no UI in InfoPath to limit the amount of data a user can insert into a Rich Text Box control. The best way to validate the amount of data in a Rich Text Box is to define a `Validating` event handler for the XHTML node and get a count of characters from the field's `OuterHtml` or `Value` property. While the `OuterHtml` property will tell you how much total data has been entered, it doesn't tell you the amount of visual data that has been entered. On the other hand, the `Value` property will give you the visual data. But `Value` doesn't hint as to how much HTML tag-specific data (e.g., tables, images, and so on) exists.

Data Connections

Nothing will make your forms feel more sluggish than to execute slow data connections. The more query and submit connections used during form filling, the slower you should expect the form to load and react. This is especially true with connections beyond the farm or with slow hardware or network speeds. Instead of initializing data sources (with query connections) on form load (the last checkbox in the Data Connection Wizard for secondary data sources), consider executing them on demand when they're needed. You can do this by using a rule or by calling the `Execute()` method on the data connection in form code.

We highly recommend that you independently test all data connections outside of InfoPath. Data connections are synchronously executed by Forms Services. The total time includes the time needed to send the request from Forms Services to the external data source and then to receive the response. Remember that this total time is added to the time it takes for Forms Services to just process a postback request.

Form View State

A major bottleneck when serving hundreds of forms to browser clients is maintaining session state. Recall that the shared session state service (SSS) uses a SQL Server database to persist a single form-filling session and its data. When too many sessions are being managed by Forms Services, communicating with the SQL Server to maintain all of those sessions can become quite expensive. In fact, it becomes one of the first bottlenecks when serving and managing many forms all at the same time. Session state performance also becomes much worse as the size of sessions grows larger, but that's a secondary concern. One of the first signs that SQL Server session state is becoming a bottleneck is when the data stream between the WFE servers and SQL Server stabilizes at a high level because of the large amount of traffic.

Thanks to a special feature that pushes the session state to the client browser (instead of the SQL Server), we can alleviate the SQL Server bottleneck! The trick is to reduce the overall "chat" between the WFEs and SQL

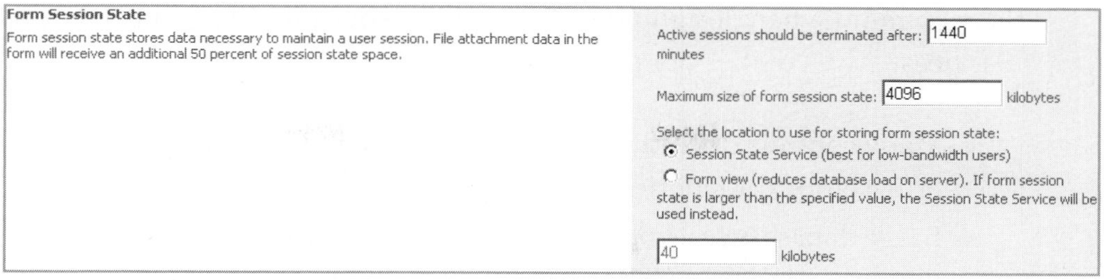

Form Session State

Form session state stores data necessary to maintain a user session. File attachment data in the form will receive an additional 50 percent of session state space.

Active sessions should be terminated after: 1440 minutes

Maximum size of form session state: 4096 kilobytes

Select the location to use for storing form session state:

- Session State Service (best for low-bandwidth users)
- Form view (reduces database load on server). If form session state is larger than the specified value, the Session State Service will be used instead.

40 kilobytes

FIGURE 17.31: Configuring Forms Services form session state

Server by eliminating the need for the database for small session sizes. To configure this feature, go to the bottom of the *Configure InfoPath Forms Services* administration page (Figure 17.31). Switch the setting from *Session State Service* to *Form view* to use form view state under circumstances when the session state size is small. As you can see in Figure 17.31, form view state is used until a session gets larger than a specified value. The default value of 40 kilobytes is recommended as it's a point of inflection for exponentially worse SQL Server session state performance when many small sessions exist in high stress situations.

Continue measuring SQL session state service performance while adjusting the threshold kilobytes value to optimize the setting. It's a good idea to start at the default value of 40 and see what happens to WFE and SQL server loads and network usage (both between WFEs and SQL Server and between WFEs and browser clients) as adjustments are made.

> **NOTE Using Session State versus View State**
>
> You can find more information about deciding between these two state mechanisms on Microsoft TechNet (as referenced in the Appendix).

Miscellaneous Performance Tips

We've discussed the biggest performance issues you may encounter in real-world InfoPath browser forms. But the list isn't complete. There are some other obvious and not so obvious aspects of form templates you should keep in mind. Here are a few tips and comments that you should keep in mind when designing and deploying your form template to Forms Services.

- Many controls (including Sections) on a single view can slow browser form-rendering times.
- Large data sources, both main and secondary, can bog down the server and form-filling experience.
- Whatever you wouldn't do in a Web page, you shouldn't do in Forms Services.
- Use InfoPath Forms Services performance counters to gauge specific metrics.

Remember: Overall server and farm performance is dictated by a vast number of factors. There is no silver bullet for fixing all issues. Bottlenecks can exist anywhere, and your system must be carefully analyzed and tested to ensure that it works as you would expect. In the next section, we'll look at performance monitoring, concentrating on performance counters to further focus our efforts on specific aspects of Forms Services.

Performance Monitoring

Server administrators know that nothing tells the truth like graphs and the numbers behind them. That's why performance-conscious admins turn to Windows Performance Monitor, otherwise known as PerfMon. In case you aren't familiar with PerfMon, we'll quickly explain its purpose. PerfMon gathers key performance indicators, called counters, from various system components. It allows you to profile resource usage and analyze areas as potential bottlenecks. You can watch these counters live on a graph as well as view the raw log data.

Forms Services installs the *InfoPath Forms Services* performance object, as shown in Figure 17.32. In Figure 17.32, we're adding specific counters for all installed form templates. If you wanted to profile only a specific form template, you could choose the *Select instances from list* option instead of *All instances*. If you click the *Explain* button, you'll see a brief explanation of the currently selected counter.

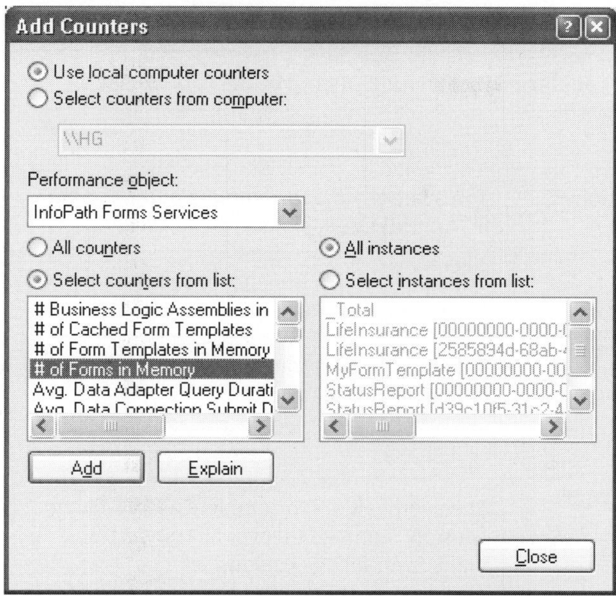

FIGURE 17.32: Adding performance counters for templates activated with InfoPath Forms Services

The *InfoPath Forms Services* performance object includes many data points that play a critical role in server-side performance. Table 17.9 shows a full list of counters and their explanations. These counters are categorized into four different areas: transaction, session, data connection, and template/document.

A transaction is any communication with the server. By using the started and completed rate counters, you can see the rate at which browsers are beginning and ending their communication (i.e., postback) with the server. The longer a postback takes, the potentially more expensive it can be for a server to handle.

The session counters, on the other hand, focus on the time during which a form is being filled out. A session is considered to be starting when a form (new or existing) is beginning to be filled out. A session ends when the form is closed after submit, when the user clicks the *Close* button in the toolbar, or when the session times out.

TABLE 17.9: Complete List of InfoPath Forms Services Performance Counters

Performance Counter	Explanation Offered by the *Explain* Button	Counter Type
Transaction		
Avg. Transaction Duration	The average time to complete a transaction in form-filling sessions.	Average Timer
Transactions Started Rate	The rate at which transactions started in form-filling sessions.	Event Rate
Transactions Completed Rate	The rate at which transactions completed in form-filling sessions.	Event Rate
Session		
Avg. Session Duration	The average time to complete a form-filling session, summed up over all transactions in the form-filling session.	Average Timer
Session Started Rate	The rate at which form-filling sessions started.	Event Rate
Session Completed Rate	The rate at which form-filling sessions completed.	Event Rate
Data Connection		
Avg. Data Connection Submit Duration	The average time to complete a data connection submit in form-filling sessions.	Average Timer
Data Connection Submit Started Rate	The rate at which data connection submits started in form-filling sessions.	Event Rate
Data Connection Submit Completed Rate	The rate at which data connection submits completed in form-filling sessions.	Event Rate
Data Connection Submit Failure Rate	The rate of failures for data connection submits in form-filling sessions.	Event Rate
Avg. Data Connection Query Duration	The average time to complete a data connection query in form-filling sessions.	Average Timer
Data Connection Query Started Rate	The rate at which data connection queries started in form-filling sessions.	Event Rate

TABLE 17.9: (*continued*)

Performance Counter	Explanation Offered by the *Explain* Button	Counter Type
Data Connection Query Completed Rate	The rate at which data connection queries completed in form-filling sessions.	Event Rate
Data Connection Query Failure Rate	The rate of failures for data connection queries in form-filling sessions.	Event Rate
Template/Document		
# of Cached Form Templates	The number of form templates that have been added to, and not yet expired out of, the ASP.NET object cache.	Raw Count
# of Business Logic Assemblies in Memory	The number of business logic assemblies currently loaded in memory. Administrator-approved form templates may contain zero, one, or more managed code assemblies.	Raw Count
# of Form Templates in Memory	The number of form templates objects that are currently loaded in memory.	Raw Count
# of Forms in memory	The number of forms that are currently loaded in memory.	Raw Count

TIP Session State Timeout

Too many active sessions on a server can bog it down. If you notice the average session duration is very high, consider decreasing the session state service timeout.

Another type of counter traces data connection performance. The connection counters are broken down into query and submit. For each type, you can see the average time for a query or submit connection to execute, the rates of connections beginning or ending, and even the rate of failure. Unfortunately, there's no direct correlation between a performance counter and a specific data connection in a form template.

Finally, the counters that track templates and documents (or instances of filling out form templates) show how many form templates are in the

ASP.NET cache and memory. These counters could help you determine whether Forms Services is part of a memory bloating problem, if such a condition exists on your server.

> **WARNING Total Server Health Monitoring**
>
> By no means is the *InfoPath Forms Services* performance object a complete monitoring solution. To accurately monitor server health, you need to consider counters in the *Processor* and *Server* performance objects, for example.

Health Monitoring

Microsoft Operations Manager, known as MOM for short, is an invaluable tool for server monitoring tasks (Figure 17.33). It's designed to scale to watch hundreds of computers simultaneously. It's the best way to monitor

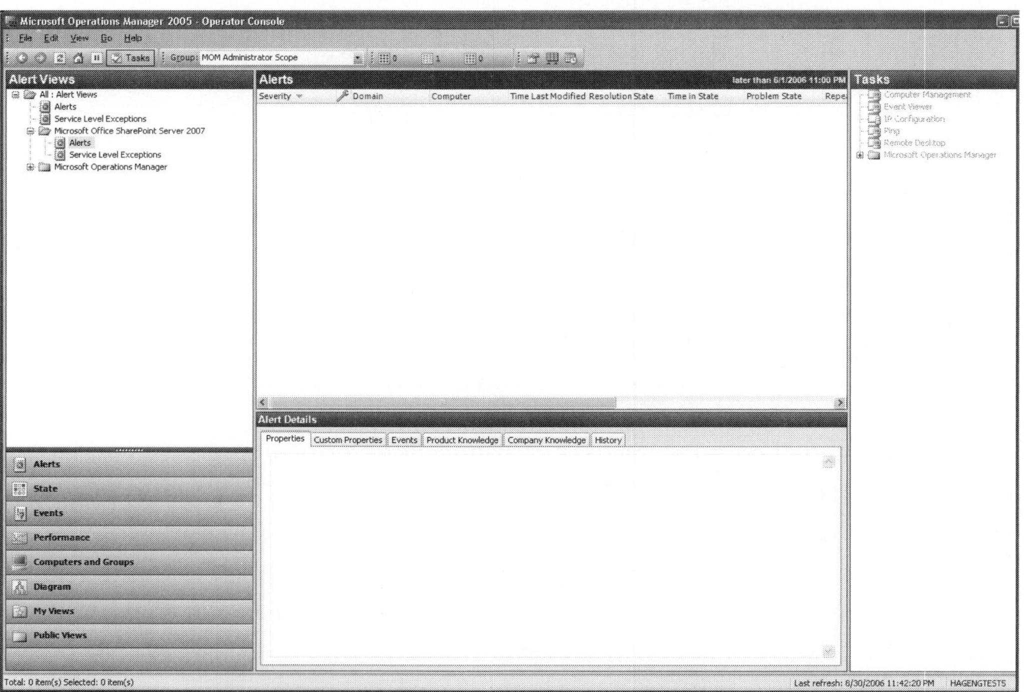

FIGURE 17.33: Microsoft Operations Manager Operator Console

your entire farm from a single operator's console without focusing on any one computer.

SharePoint Server 2007 comes with a MOM pack defining rules for every major service in the SharePoint Server offering. The InfoPath Forms Services pack defines a set of 18 basic rules to catch critical entries in the Windows event log. Errors such as a failure to load form code, an unsuccessful postback attempt, and a number of actions that exceeds the maximum allowed for a given postback are all caught by the rules defined in the MOM pack.

These rules were created to get you started, but by no means are they a complete list of everything you'd be interested in monitoring. Feel free to customize existing rules or create your own for Forms Services in cases where you'd want to be notified in the MOM console.

Learn more about MOM on Microsoft's Web site (as referenced in the Appendix).

What's Next?

You are now well versed in advanced facets of InfoPath Forms Services. We've presented a lot of information in this chapter. We hope that it makes you aware of the plethora of server features available at your fingertips. In the next chapter, we look at different ways InfoPath can be hosted. We'll show you how to host an InfoPath form in your own custom application. Afterward, we'll look at hosting a browser form by including it in your own ASP.NET Web page. Hosting is a new and exciting capability to extend the form-filling experience beyond InfoPath and Forms Services.

18 Hosting InfoPath

Getting Started

By now, you've learned how to design anything from basic form templates that use no code whatsoever to very complex solutions that use business logic to solve various business scenarios. You've seen how InfoPath provides structured editing of XML data with the ease-of-use of a Microsoft Office application.

The fact that InfoPath provides structured editing of data and such features as data validation, rules, and business logic (to name a few) is great, but what if you want to take advantage of these features in your own applications? It would be nice to be able to incorporate the form-editing features provided by InfoPath in your own applications without having to implement these features from scratch.

Luckily, you can. InfoPath 2007 is available not only as a standalone application but also as an ActiveX control. This control can be hosted in Windows applications using .NET and in standard COM ActiveX host containers. Not only that, but you can also host InfoPath Forms Services in your own Web page. In both cases, hosting InfoPath allows you to take advantage of the InfoPath form-filling experience in your own applications.

In this chapter, we'll talk about hosting the InfoPath client application. We'll first talk about scenarios in which hosting makes sense, including other Microsoft Office applications that host InfoPath. Then, we'll show how to create a Windows application using .NET that hosts InfoPath.

Afterward, we'll finish up by explaining how to host a browser-enabled form template in an ASP.NET Web page using InfoPath Forms Services.

Hosting Scenarios

The obvious answer to "When should I host InfoPath in my own application or ASP.NET page?" is whenever you want to take advantage of any of the structural data-editing features included in InfoPath. Maybe you just want to give your users the ability to fill out forms in your application without having to write a form tool like InfoPath yourself (which could take years). Maybe you want to create a consistent look-and-feel for all the applications in your company, but you still want to use InfoPath for filling out forms. Or maybe you want to create something as simple as an application that contains a repository of all the InfoPath forms in your department and also have your users fill out forms directly in that application.

Whatever your scenario may be, as long as you have experience writing a Windows application with managed code or an ActiveX control host in unmanaged code, you can include InfoPath in your applications.

Before we see how to create your own applications, let's look at a few Microsoft Office 2007 applications that directly host InfoPath.

Document Information Panel

If you are an avid user of Word, Excel, or PowerPoint, you may have at one time or another needed to change various properties associated with a document. For example, you may have changed the name of the author, added a category, or included some comments in the document properties. In Word 2003, for example, you set these properties by using the document properties dialog shown in Figure 18.1. This dialog looks suspiciously like a form, doesn't it?

This fact was not lost on the Microsoft Office team. This dialog is so much like a form that it would make sense to use InfoPath to fill it out. In Word, Excel, and PowerPoint in Microsoft Office 2007, when you open the document properties (available from the *Prepare* menu under the *Office Button* in the Ribbon), an InfoPath form opens within these applications, as shown in Figure 18.2. This **Document Information Panel** is actually an instance of the InfoPath client application hosted within Word 2007.

FIGURE 18.1: Document properties dialog in Word 2003

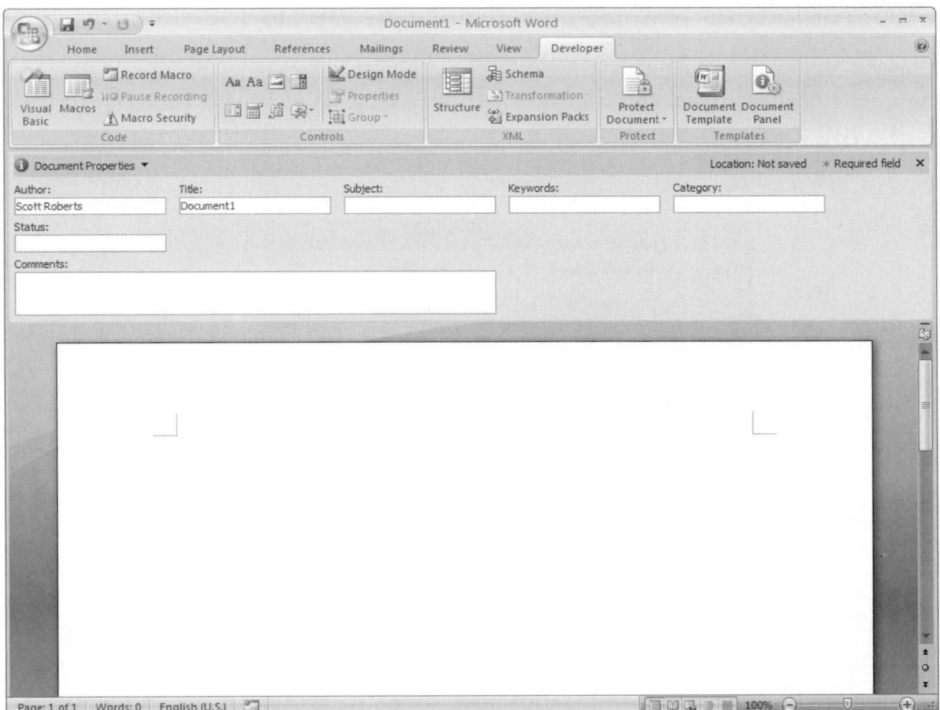

FIGURE 18.2: Document Information Panel in Word 2007

As you can see from Figure 18.2, by default the Document Information Panel contains the common properties for a document. Each of these properties is connected to a control in the panel just as in a normal InfoPath form. As you would expect, changing the values in these controls will change the corresponding property values associated with the document.

In addition to the default Document Information Panel included in Word, Excel, and PowerPoint, you can also include your own form template. Since the Document Information Panel is just an InfoPath form, it makes sense that you can include any InfoPath form in one of these types of documents. Doing so is very easy. First, however, you must turn on the *Developer* tab. In order to enable this tab, open the *Options* dialog for the application and check the *Show Developer tab in the Ribbon* checkbox. When you close the dialog, the *Developer* tab will now appear in the Ribbon, as you can see in Figure 18.2.

At the rightmost end of the Ribbon is a button named *Document Panel.* Clicking this button opens the dialog shown in Figure 18.3. From here, you can choose any form template that has been published to a URL, UNC, or URN. For security reasons, form templates saved to your local machine cannot be used. However, saving the form on your local machine as a URN (i.e., as a shared folder) instead of directly to a local folder (e.g., C:\temp) will work.

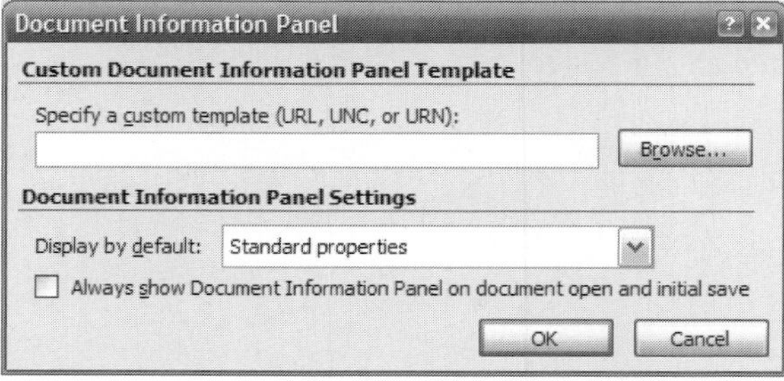

FIGURE 18.3: Document Information Panel dialog

Once you choose a form template, you can view it in the Document Information Panel by clicking on the *Document Properties* drop-down arrow at the top left corner of the panel, as shown in Figure 18.2. The standard document properties form template is shown by default until you choose otherwise from the *Document Properties* drop-down list. One interesting thing to note is that if the form template you choose has multiple views, all the views that have the *Show on the View menu when filling out the form* option set in the *View* properties dialog when designing the form template will show in the *Document Properties* drop-down menu.

Adding your own form templates to the Document Information Panel is interesting. However, what is more interesting is creating custom form templates based on SharePoint content types. A SharePoint content type basically describes the type of data stored in SharePoint. For example, when you create a SharePoint document library, the documents in the library are tied to the Document content type. (The content type may be different depending on the type of library you create in SharePoint.) This content type contains meta properties associated with each document. There are two types of properties for a document—Microsoft Office properties and SharePoint properties.

You've already seen the Microsoft Office properties for a document (Figure 18.2). The SharePoint properties are those properties you set for a document of any type from within SharePoint. You do this by simply clicking on the drop-down menu for a document in a SharePoint document library and choosing *Properties*. By default, the page shown in Figure 18.4 is displayed. Although this is useful, it would be nice to be able to use a custom InfoPath form when editing the properties from within the document itself.

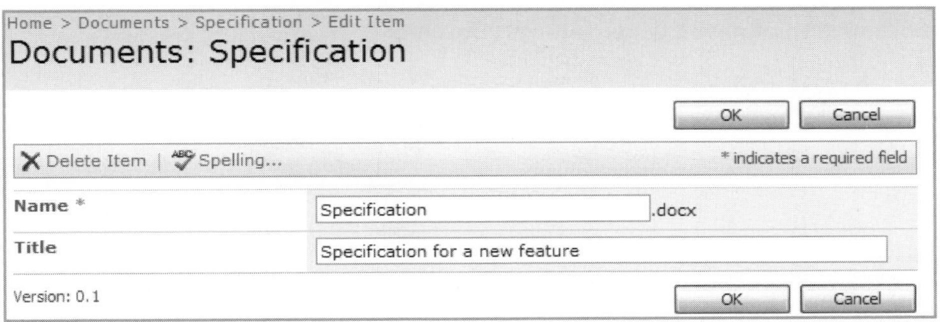

FIGURE 18.4: SharePoint Document Properties page

Just as in the *Document Information Panel* dialog in Word, Excel, and PowerPoint, in SharePoint you can also specify that an InfoPath form should be used to edit the properties for a Microsoft Office document. Before you can do that, however, you have to enable content type management for the document library. You can do this from the *Advanced Settings* page for the document library (which is available from the *Document Library Settings* page). In the *Advanced Settings* page, selecting *Yes* for the *Allow management of content types* option will do the trick.

Once you've done that, a *Content Types* section becomes available in the *Settings* page for the document library. For a document library, the content type is *Document.* Clicking on this content type in the *Settings* page will open the content type settings page. From here you can add columns to the content type. These columns are additional properties associated with the document. When you add one or more columns, these properties will now be exposed through the properties page for the document in SharePoint.

Now that you've exposed a few more properties, how do you specify that a custom InfoPath form should be used for editing the properties from within the document? To do that, from the content type settings page, simply click on the *Document Information Panel settings* link, which will open the page shown in Figure 18.5. From here you can specify the form template that should be used for editing the properties for documents in this document library and indicate whether or not the Document Information Panel should be shown when the document is opened and first saved.

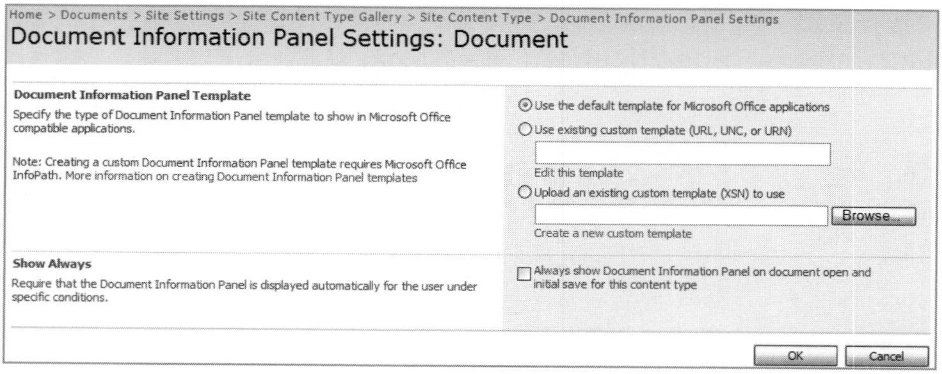

FIGURE 18.5: Document Information Panel Settings page

Being able to upload an InfoPath form template from within SharePoint is helpful, but just uploading any old form template is not very useful. What you really want to do is create a form template that can be used to edit the properties for the SharePoint content type.

There are two ways to do this. The first way is to design a form template based on the content type. To do that, start InfoPath in design mode as normal. From the *Design a Form Template* pane, choose *XML or Schema.* When the Data Source Wizard appears, enter the URL of your SharePoint site. (Make sure that you specify the URL of the site and not the URL of the default.aspx page or another page on the site. For example, if you have a Development subsite on the MOI Consulting corporate site, the URL you would enter is http://moi/Development/, not http://moi/Development/AllItems.aspx.) Once you click the *Next* button, InfoPath will retrieve a list of content types from the SharePoint site. The list of content types will look similar to that shown in Figure 18.6. Since we want to create a form template to edit the properties of the *Document* content type, we will choose that content type from the list. After choosing the content type, you simply complete the wizard as normal.

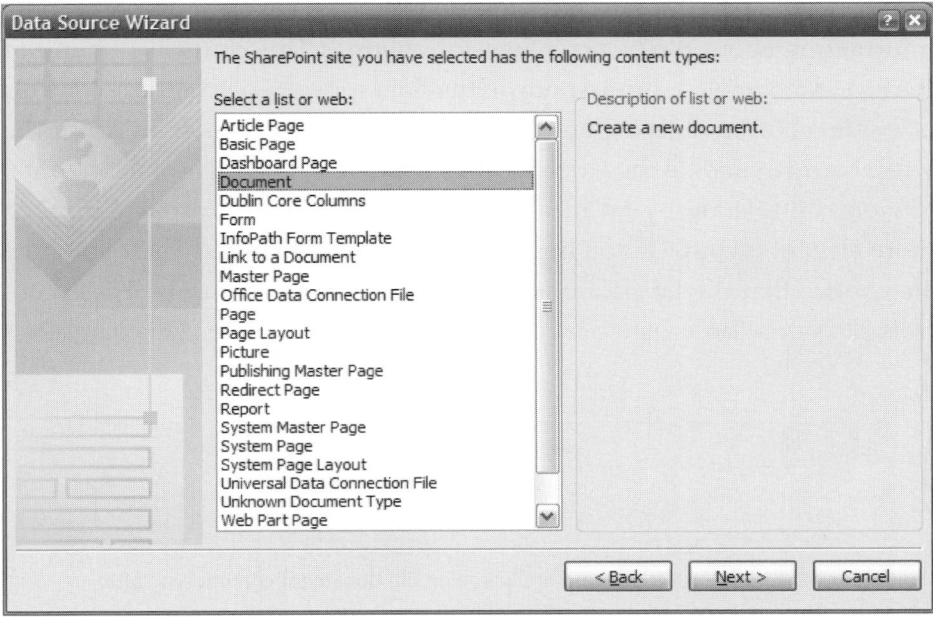

FIGURE 18.6: List of content types in the Data Source Wizard

Although you can create a form template based on a SharePoint content type by using the approach we just described, there is a second and easier way to do this. All you have to do is click on the *Create a new custom template* link in the *Document Information Panel Settings* page in SharePoint shown in Figure 18.5. This will open InfoPath in design mode and execute all but the last step of the Data Source Wizard, which is just the *Finish* page of the wizard. Basically, this is just as if you started designing a form template based on a content type. However, in this case, InfoPath completes most of the Data Source Wizard for you.

After clicking the *Finish* button in the Data Source Wizard, InfoPath will retrieve the content type definition and create a basic form template that has two views. The first view, which is the default, is named *Document Properties–Server.* You use this view to edit the SharePoint-specific properties. The controls in this view are bound to the columns that you have exposed for the Document content type in the *Document Information Panel Settings* page in SharePoint.

In Figure 18.7, you can see that we have a Text Box control bound to the `title` property. Also, we have added the Assigned To property in SharePoint in the content type settings page. Therefore, a **Contact Selector** control is also included in the form template. (See the note for more information about the Contact Selector control.) This control is bound to the `ns1:AssignedTo` group node in the data source. Each of these controls is inside a Horizontal Region control that causes the contained control to wrap correctly inside the Document Information Panel. These Horizontal Region controls are by no means required, but they do provide a much more elegant layout. (If you open the form template in InfoPath, you may also notice that the labels are within Expression Box controls. These controls also provide a better layout for the form template. This sample is

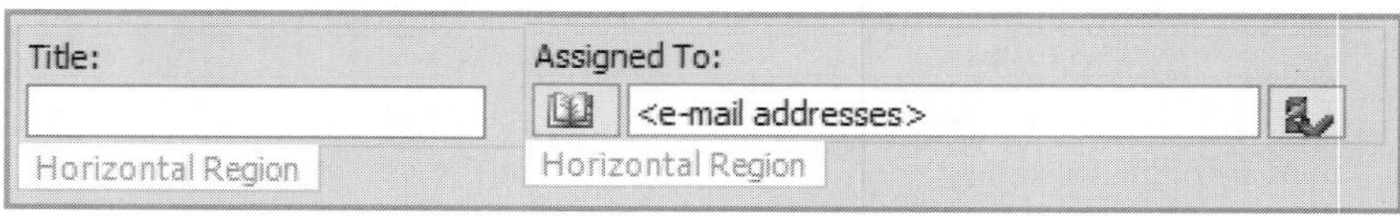

FIGURE 18.7: InfoPath form template based on the Document content type after adding the Assigned To column in SharePoint

called DocumentPropertiesTemplate and is included with the samples for this chapter on the book's Web site.)

NOTE Contact Selector Control

This may be the first time you are seeing this control. The Contact Selector is an ActiveX control that is installed with Microsoft Office 2007. This control allows you to choose e-mail addresses from the Outlook address book. Since this control is not one of the built-in InfoPath controls, when you design a Document Information Panel by clicking on the *Create a new custom template* link in SharePoint, this control will not behave the same as other controls in InfoPath when in design mode. To take advantage of the features available to other ActiveX controls, you must first add it to the *Controls* task pane by using the *ActiveX Control* option in the Add or Remove Custom Controls Wizard. When the list of ActiveX controls installed on your system is displayed, simply choose *Contact Selector.* You may choose the default settings for the remainder of the options in the wizard. However, when asked for the data type of the ActiveX control, choose *Field or Group (any data type).*

After the initial form template is created, as with any other InfoPath form template, you can add as many controls as you like. However, in this case, the schema for the content type is locked. So, when you add controls from the *Controls* task pane, you will be required to choose a node from the data source. It's just as easy to open the *Data Source* pane directly and bind controls to fields and groups in the data source. Figure 18.8 shows the data source for the Document content type. You can see that it contains a mixture of standard Microsoft Office document properties, such as the title of the document (`dc:title`) and Windows SharePoint Services properties such as the person a task is assigned to (`ns1:AssignedTo`). There will be fields or groups in the data source for any columns that we add to the content type in SharePoint through the content type settings page for the document library.

Let's add a Text Box control bound to the `dc:creator` group node in the *Data Source* pane. Of course, you probably want to follow the design of

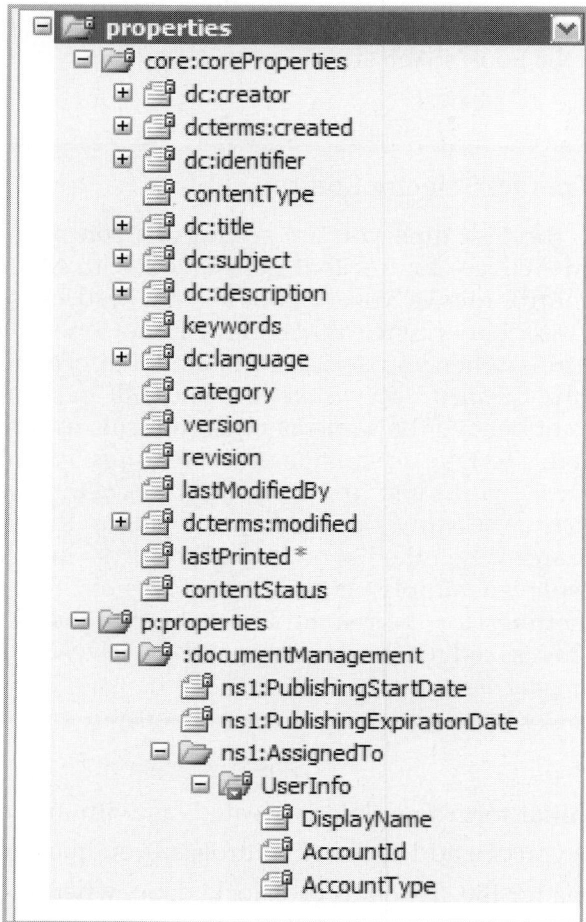

FIGURE 18.8: Data source for the Document content type

this form template and insert the Text Box inside a Horizontal Region and the label inside an Expression Box.

As we mentioned earlier, there is a second view in this form template. This view, named *Document Properties,* is the view used to edit the standard Microsoft Office document properties. Just as with the *Document Properties–Server* view, you can customize the *Document Properties* view to meet your own needs. Let's remove the *Category* Horizontal Region and add one for the document version. (The Text Box control inside the Horizontal Region will be bound to the `version` field in the data source.) Figure 18.9 shows the final view after we made these changes.

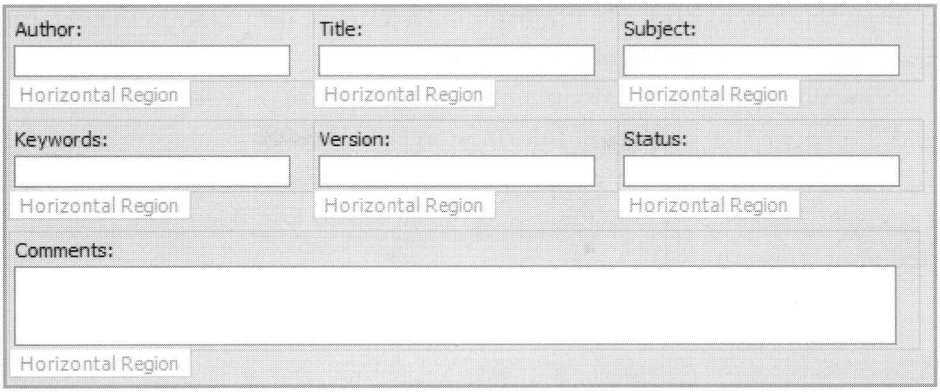

FIGURE 18.9: Customized Document Properties view for editing standard document properties

When you are finished designing the form template, in order to use it in documents created from SharePoint, you must publish it back to SharePoint. Publishing it back to SharePoint is done the same way as you would for any other type of form template. When you open the Publishing Wizard, however, the last option, *As a Document Information Panel template for a SharePoint site content type or list content type*, is selected by default (Figure 18.10).

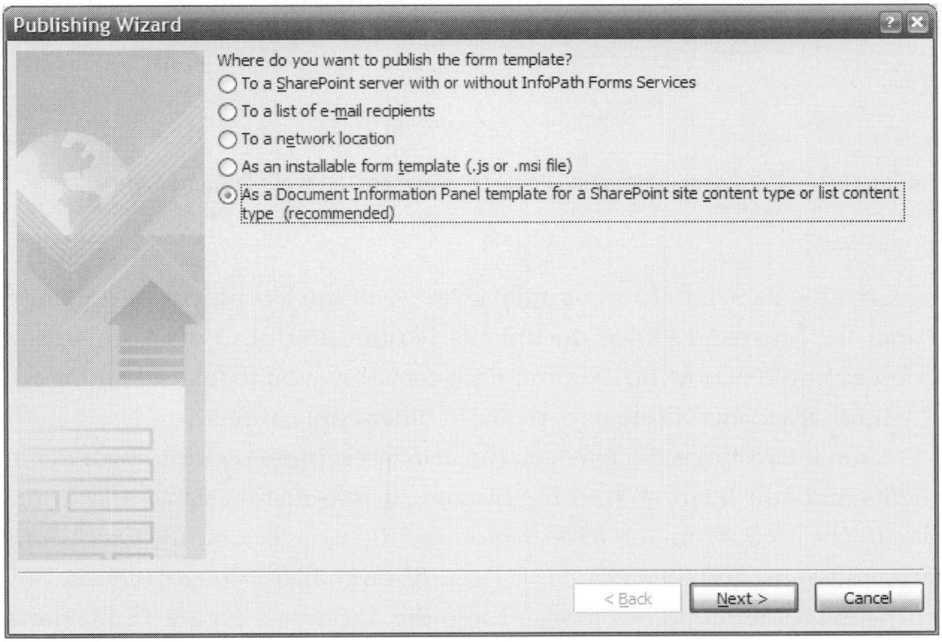

FIGURE 18.10: Publishing the new form template as a Document Information Panel template for SharePoint

Completing the wizard will publish the Document Information Panel template back to the SharePoint document library.

Now when you open a document from the SharePoint document library and then open the Document Information Panel, the custom form template you created will be used to edit the document properties. By default, the *Document Properties–Server* view will be shown in the Document Information Panel (Figure 18.11).

FIGURE 18.11: Document Information Panel showing the Document Properties—Server view

Switching to the *Document Properties* view allows you to edit the standard Microsoft Office document properties (Figure 18.12).

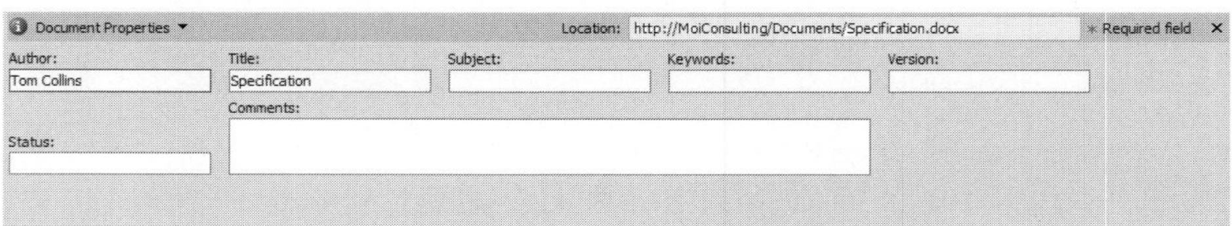

FIGURE 18.12: Document Information Panel showing the Document Properties view

Creating a custom form template for use in the Document Information Panel for Microsoft Office documents is quite useful. It also provides a good example of how hosting InfoPath can allow you to take advantage of the InfoPath form-editing experience in other applications.

As an interesting side note, you can also insert properties into your documents and edit them both in the Document Information Panel and in the document itself. From the *Insert* tab on the Ribbon, click on the *Quick Parts* drop-down list and then *Document Property*. From there, you can choose any of the available properties to insert into the document. Figure 18.13 shows

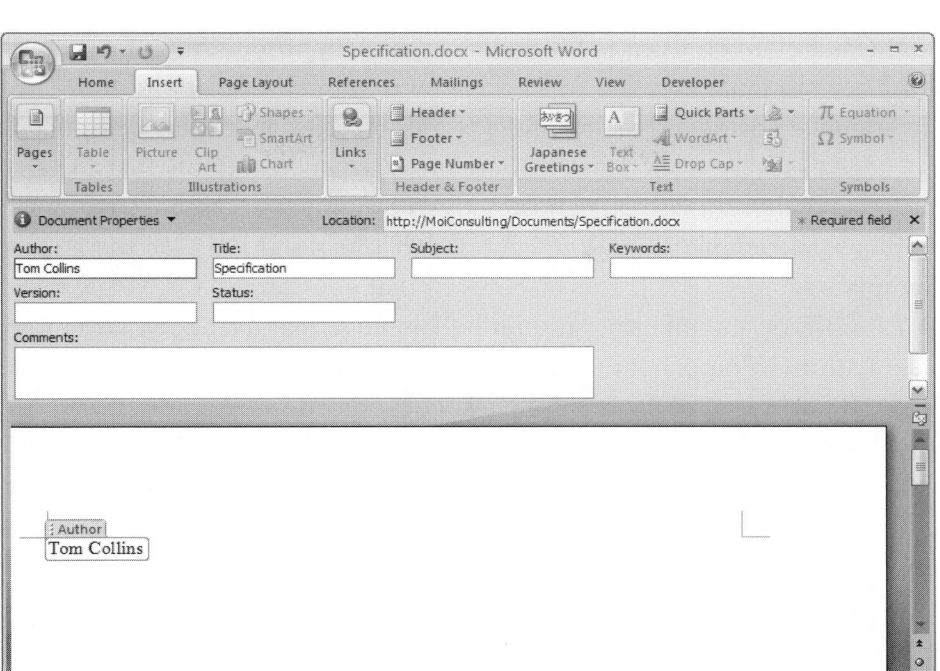

FIGURE 18.13: Word document showing the Document Information Panel and the `Author` property in the body of the document

a Word document with the Document Information Panel open and the `Author` property inserted into the document content. Now, when you change the name of the author in the Document Information Panel, the value in the document will be changed as well, and vice versa. In addition, any rules, calculations, or data connections in the Document Information Panel will run (since InfoPath is being hosted) and could affect data in the document.

Now that we've shown you how other applications can host InfoPath, you're probably wondering how you can host InfoPath in your own application. Well, that happens to be our next topic.

Creating an InfoPath Host Application

As we mentioned earlier, there are many reasons that you may want to host InfoPath within your own application. The main reason comes down to the fact that you want to take advantage of the form-editing features in InfoPath without having to create your own form-editing application.

To make hosting possible, InfoPath 2007 includes its editing component packaged as an ActiveX control. Therefore, you can host InfoPath using any technology that allows you to host ActiveX controls, such as .NET Windows Forms applications, Microsoft Foundation Classes (MFC), or the Active Template Library (ATL). This also means that you can use C#, Visual Basic .NET, C++, or any other programming language that enables you to interface with the Component Object Model (COM). (As a side note, InfoPath does not include a redistributable package for the form-editing ActiveX control. Users of your application will still need to have InfoPath 2007 installed.)

> **NOTE Common Language Runtime 2.0 Is Required**
>
> Note that at least version 2.0 of the Common Language Runtime (CLR) is required in order to host the InfoPath ActiveX control in a managed (.NET) application. Version 2.0 of the CLR is installed by Visual Studio 2005 or can be obtained by downloading the .NET Framework 2.0 from MSDN (as referenced in the Appendix).

Since building a full-blown ActiveX hosting application in C++ can be quite complicated (especially if you don't use MFC or ATL), we will focus on creating a .NET Windows Forms application using C#. Along the way, we will talk about the interfaces exposed by the InfoPath ActiveX control that are available to host applications. Therefore, if you wish to create a hosting application using another programming language or technology, you will be able to apply the same concepts we will use in the Windows Forms application in this chapter.

In this part of the chapter, we're going to create an insurance forms application for a fictional company named IP Insurance. This company has various forms that its agents use on a daily basis—forms for auto, homeowners, and life insurance, for example. The main problem that agents at IP Insurance have is locating the forms they need. There are too many forms, and they're stored in too many places. Therefore, we're going to create an application that allows agents to choose from a list of forms.

There is a second problem, though. We want to enable our agents to use InfoPath to fill out the forms. However, the company has a general requirement that all applications used by the corporation must follow a standard set of user interface guidelines. Following a standard set of UI guidelines for applications helps the company cut down on training costs. So, not only will our application allow the agents to locate all their forms, it will also allow them to fill out those forms from within the same application. Of course, since InfoPath is available as an ActiveX control, we will host InfoPath in our application so that we don't have to create our own form-editing tool. Also, since our developers are familiar with .NET and C#, we will use these technologies to cut down on development costs.

Creating an InfoPath Host Application in .NET

Creating a .NET Windows Forms application that hosts InfoPath is as easy as creating any other Windows Forms application. So, if you are familiar with that process, some of this may be a review for you. If you have never done this before, you will want to follow this part of the chapter very closely. (We will assume, however, that you are already familiar with Visual Studio 2005.)

To create a Windows Forms application to host InfoPath, you'll first need to open Visual Studio and create your project. The application we want to create is a Visual C# Windows application. So, we'll choose that project type from the *New Project* dialog in Visual Studio.

As usual, after closing the *New Project* dialog, a new project is created and an empty Windows form is opened in design mode. Before we do anything else, we'll set the title of our Windows form to "IP Insurance–Form Library". Once we've done that and set any other properties that we'd like (such as the size of the dialog), we'll add the InfoPath form control to the Windows form. However, before we can do that, we have to add it to the Toolbox in Visual Studio.

To add the InfoPath control to the Toolbox, first click on *Choose Toolbox Items* on the *Tools* menu. Then, make sure that the *.NET Framework Components* tab is selected, and scroll down until you see a component named `FormControl` in the `Microsoft.Office.InfoPath` namespace. If you don't see this component (which will be the case if you haven't added it before), click the *Browse* button, change to the installation folder for InfoPath 2007 (e.g., C:\Program Files\Microsoft Office\Office12), and select the Microsoft.Office.InfoPath.FormControl.dll file. This will add the form control to the list in the *.NET Framework Components* tab. Finally, check the box next to the `FormControl` component, and then close the dialog by clicking the *OK* button. After you close the dialog, the `FormControl` component is added to the *General* section of the Visual Studio Toolbox (Figure 18.14).

FIGURE 18.14: Visual Studio Toolbox after adding the InfoPath `FormControl` control

Once the control is in the Toolbox, you can drag it to your form like any other control. After adding the InfoPath `FormControl` component to a Windows form, you will see that, in design mode, the control appears as a simple disabled window. If you look at the properties for the control, you will see that, by default, the name of the control is `formControl1`. For simplicity, we'll keep that name for our control.

If you look at the code that is auto-generated when you insert the form control, which is stored in the Form1.Designer.cs file, you will notice that the `formControl1` object has a type of `Microsoft.Office.InfoPath.FormControl`. (In C++ this is basically equivalent to the `IInfoPathEditor` interface). As you would imagine, this object provides many methods and properties that enable you to interact with the InfoPath form control and any InfoPath forms loaded into the control. Table 18.1 lists all the methods available in the `FormControl` class (or on the `IInfoPathEditor` interface in C++), and Table 18.2 lists all the properties. We'll use a lot of these methods in the IP Insurance application.

Now that we've added the InfoPath form control to our Windows application, let's take care of a few more of the basic requirements before we do more with the InfoPath form control. Remember that we want to give our insurance agents a single repository for all their insurance forms. Therefore,

Table 18.1: InfoPath Form Control Methods

Managed Code (`FormControl`)	Unmanaged Code (`IInfoPathEditor`)	Description
`AttachInterfaces`	N/A	Is inherited from the `AxHost` base class.
`Close`	`CloseDocument`	Closes the form.
`FormControl`	N/A	Is a constructor.
`NewFromFormTemplate`	`NewFromSolution` `NewFromSolutionWithData`	Loads a new form from the specified form template. There are two overloads of this method (in managed code). One simply takes the URL of the form template. The second takes the URL, a stream containing XML data to be loaded into the form, and the open mode, which allows you to specify whether the form is initially read-only, among other things. (The two overloads in managed code map to the two `NewFromSolution`* methods listed in the Unmanaged Code column.)
`Open`	`Load` `LoadFromStream`	Opens an InfoPath form from a URL or a stream that contains XML data. In managed code, there are two overloads of the `Open` method, which map to the `Load` and `LoadFromStream` methods in the `IInfoPathEditor` interface.

continued

Table 18.1: InfoPath Form Control Methods (*continued*)

Managed Code (`FormControl`)	Unmanaged Code (`IInfoPathEditor`)	Description
`SetInitEventHandler`	`SetInitEventHandler`	Sets the event handler to call when a form is initialized. The object specified as the handler must implement the `IInitEventHandler` interface, which contains one `method`–`InitEventHandler`. (`InitEventHandler` is equivalent to the `OnLoad` event in code that is part of a form template.)
`SetNotifyHostEventHandler`	`SetNotifyHostEventHandler`	Sets the event handler called when form code calls the `NotifyHost` method. The object specified as the handler must implement `INotifyHostEventHandler`.
`SetSubmitToHostEventHandler`	`SetSubmitToHostEventHandler`	Sets the event handler called when a form is submitted to the host. (We'll talk about what this means later in this chapter.) The object specified as the handler must implement `ISubmitToHostEventHandler`.
`SyncLastChange`	`FlushDocument`	Flushes all changes that have been made to the form.

TABLE 18.2: InfoPath Form Control Properties

Managed Code (`FormControl`)	Unmanaged Code (`IInfoPathEditor`)	Description
`DataConnectionBaseUrl`	`DataConnectionBaseUrl`	Sets the base URL to use for relative data connections.
`EventManager`	N/A	Gives the hosting application access to the event manager for the form. This allows managed hosting applications to sink events from the form. Hosting applications written in unmanaged code can use connection points to sink events from the form.
`Host`	`Host`	Is a property that the host can set that can be accessed from form code. This enables form code to interact with the host.
`HostName`	`HostName`	Sets the name of the host that will be used in the title bar for dialogs displayed from the InfoPath form control. If this property is not set, "Microsoft Office InfoPath" will show in the title bar of dialogs by default.
`XmlForm`	`XDocument`	Provides access to the hosted form. Through this property, you can access most of the InfoPath object model in the same way that we explained in Chapter 15. Certain objects, such as the `Application` and `Window` objects, are not available.

it makes sense that we will need a way for them to choose any of the forms they need. So, let's add a Combo Box control to the form. In this Combo Box, we'll list all the forms we want to expose to our agents and an item called *None* that, when selected, will close the current form. We will expose three basic forms in this application: auto insurance, homeowners insurance, and life insurance. (In a real-world application, you would likely want to retrieve the list of forms and their URLs from a database or Web service.) Also, let's add some GroupBox controls to the form in order to group our controls nicely. Our Windows form at this point looks like that shown in Figure 18.15.

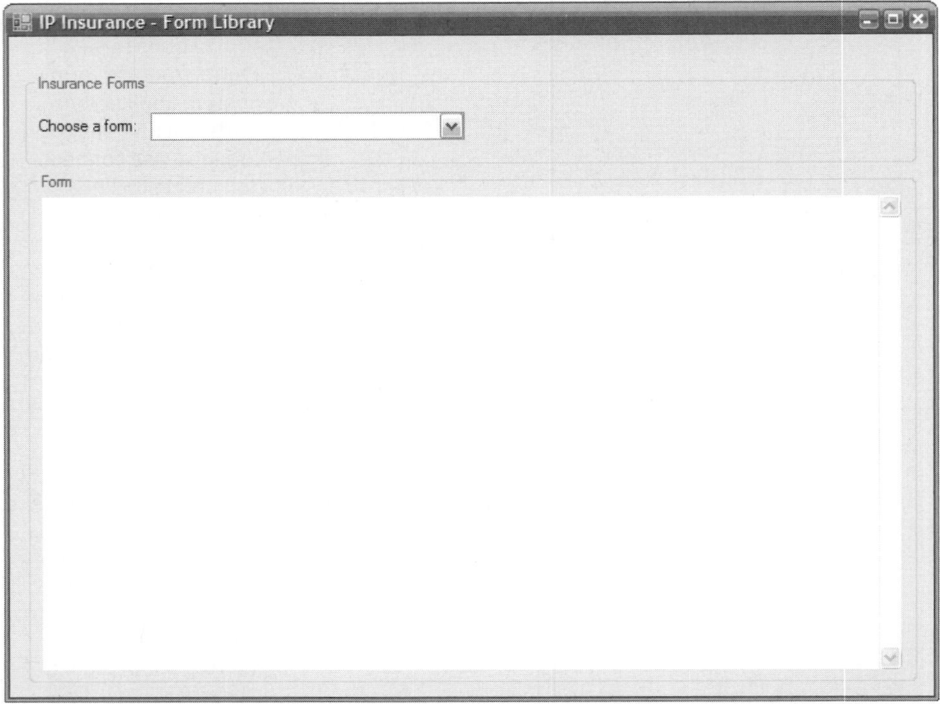

FIGURE 18.15: IP Insurance application after adding Combo Box and GroupBox controls

Now that we have the basic controls we need, we'll obviously need to add some code to do something interesting. (Otherwise, our application might be just a little boring.) When the user chooses a form from the Combo Box control, we want to load the form into the InfoPath form control. To do that, we're going to handle the `SelectedIndexChanged` event on the Combo Box control and then call the `NewFromFormTemplate` method on `formControl1`. (In this example, we're assuming that all forms exist in a

Forms folder that is in the same folder as the executable application. Of course, in the real world, your forms would likely live on a SharePoint [or other] server that is accessible to everyone in your department or corporation.) Listing 18.1 shows the code for the `SelectedIndexChanged` event handler at this point. (Note that `AutoInsurance`, `HomeOwnersInsurance`, and `LifeInsurance` are constants that are defined as `1`, `2`, and `3`, respectively. These equate to the indices of these forms in the Combo Box control.)

LISTING 18.1: `SelectedIndexChanged` **Event Handler**

```
private void comboBox1_SelectedIndexChanged(object sender, EventArgs e)
{
    ComboBox comboBox = (ComboBox)sender;
    string formTemplate = null;

    switch (comboBox.SelectedIndex)
    {
        case AutoInsurance:
            formTemplate = "AutoInsurance.xsn";
            break;

        case HomeOwnersInsurance:
            formTemplate = "HomeOwnersInsurance.xsn";
            break;

        case LifeInsurance:
            formTemplate = "LifeInsurance.xsn";
            break;
    }
    if (formTemplate != null)
    {
        // NewFromFormTemplate will throw an exception if the
        // form cannot be opened.
        try
        {
            formControl1.NewFromFormTemplate (
                _currentDir + "\\Forms\\" + formTemplate);
                _currentlySelectedForm = comboBox.SelectedIndex;
        }
        catch (Exception ex)
        {
            MessageBox.Show(ex.Message, HostDisplayName);
        }
    }
    else
    {
        // If the "None" entry is selected, no form is selected.
        // In this case, simply hide the form control.
        formControl1.Visible = false;
    }
}
```

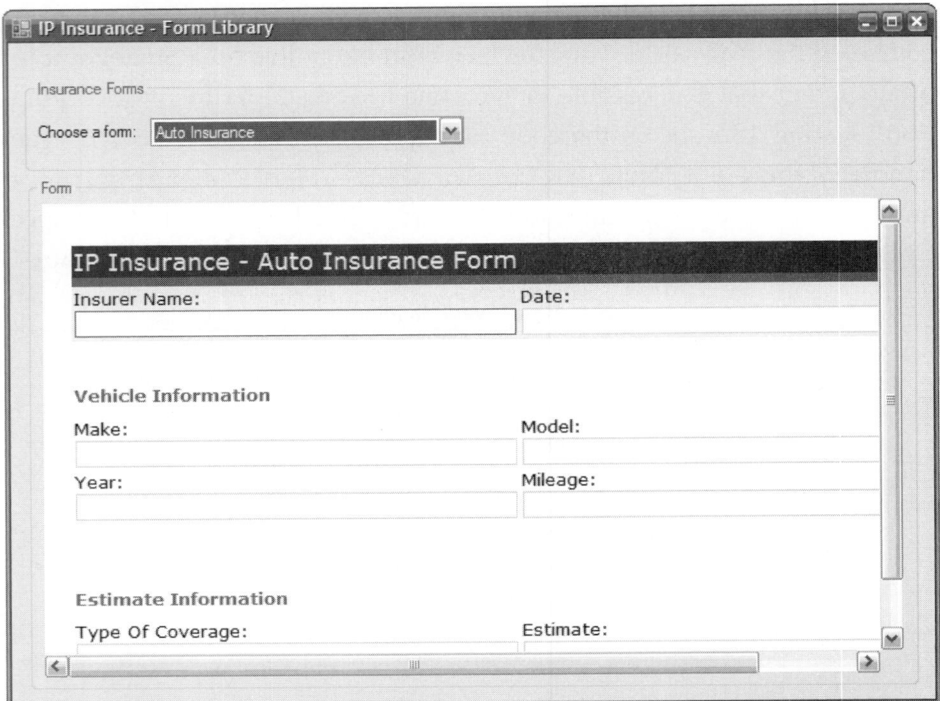

FIGURE 18.16: IP Insurance application after loading the auto insurance form

At this point, if you compile the code, run it, and choose *Auto Insurance* from the drop-down list of the Combo Box control, the form will be loaded into the InfoPath form control and will look like that shown in Figure 18.16.

As the code is currently written, if you now select another form from the Combo Box, the call to `NewFromFormTemplate` will throw an exception of type `System.Runtime.InteropServices.COMException`. The exception gives you additional information that tells you that the current document must be closed before opening a new one. Fixing that is very easy. Just call `formControl1.Close()` before calling `NewFromFormTemplate`. In fact, since we always want the current document to close when choosing an item from the list in the Combo Box even if that item is *None*, we'll call the `Close` method before the `if` statement that checks whether the `formTemplate` variable is `null`.

Now we have a fairly functional application. The insurance agents can use our form library application to find all the forms they need and can fill them out within our application as well. However, one thing is missing. When users of our application enter data and then close the application, the application just closes. That means all the data that was entered is lost! Obviously, an application that cannot save the user's data is not complete. So, we need to add this functionality. When closing the application, if the user has entered some data, we want to ask whether he or she would like to save the data. We also want to do the same if the user has made some changes and then switches to another form. Since we've already seen the code that opens the form, let's look at the changes to the `SelectedIndexChanged` event handler that are needed to support this. Listing 18.2 shows the section of code that will change to ask the user whether or not to save the form.

LISTING 18.2: `SelectedIndexChanged` Event Handler After Adding Code to Support Saving the Current Form If Dirty

```
private void comboBox1_SelectedIndexChanged(object sender, EventArgs e)
{
    . . .
    bool shouldClose = SaveIfDirty();
    if (shouldClose)
    {
        // Close the form before opening a new one.
        formControl1.Close ();
        _currentlySelectedForm = NoSelection; // "None" option (0)

        if (formTemplate != null) // Note: try/catch removed for brevity
        {
            formControl1.NewFromFormTemplate(
                _currentDir + "\\Forms\\" + formTemplate);
                _currentlySelectedForm = comboBox.SelectedIndex;
        }
        else
        {
            // Otherwise, hide the form control.
            formControl1.Visible = false;
        }
    }
    else
    {
        // Reset the previous selection.
        comboBox.SelectedIndex = _currentlySelectedForm;
    }
}
```

Before we look at the code that prompts the user to save, let's take a closer look at the code in Listing 18.2. You can see that we have a method called `SaveIfDirty`. This method, as its name implies, will check to see whether the currently loaded form is dirty and then prompt the user to save. It returns a `bool` that indicates whether or not the user chose to cancel the save operation and, therefore, wants to keep the current form open. If the return value is `true`, then we won't close the current form and won't open a new one. Because the Combo Box control in the .NET Framework doesn't have an event that allows us to cancel the selection before it happens, we must store the currently selected item in the `_currentlySelectedForm` member variable and reset the selected index if the user chooses not to close the form.

In addition to prompting the user to save when changing to a new form, if he or she closes the application and the currently loaded form is dirty, we'll have to prompt to save then as well. The code that handles closing the application is quite simple:

```
private void Form1_Closing(object sender,
                           System.ComponentModel.CancelEventArgs e)
{
    bool shouldClose = SaveIfDirty();
    e.Cancel = !shouldClose;
}
```

As you would expect, in the `Closing` event handler, we simply call `SaveIfDirty` and then set the `Cancel` property of `CancelEventArgs` to the return value of the `SaveIfDirty` method.

Next, let's look at the code that will prompt the user to save (Listing 18.3). This code snippet contains two methods—`SaveIfDirty` and `SaveForm`. The `SaveIfDirty` method is very simple. First, we check to ensure that there is a form loaded. If there isn't, `formControl1.XmlForm` will be `null`. (Remember from Table 18.2 that the `XmlForm` property gives you access to the InfoPath object model.) If a form is loaded, we then check to see whether the user has entered data by querying the `Dirty` property. If the form is dirty, we then ask if the user would like to save the form. If he or she chooses *Yes*, we call the `SaveForm` method. If he or she chooses *Cancel*, we return `false` to indicate that the form shouldn't be closed. If the user chooses *No*, we simply return `true`, which will cause the form (or the application) to close without saving the data.

LISTING 18.3: Code to Save the Currently Loaded Form

```
private bool SaveIfDirty()
{
    if (formControl1.XmlForm != null && formControl1.XmlForm.Dirty)
    {
        DialogResult result = MessageBox.Show(
            "Would you like to save your changes?",
            "IP Insurance",
            MessageBoxButtons.YesNoCancel);

        if (result == DialogResult.Yes)
            SaveForm();
        else if (result == DialogResult.Cancel)
            return false;
    }
    return true; // No form open or the form isn't dirty
}

private void SaveForm()
{
    if (formControl1 != null)
    {
        if (_currentFileName != null)
            formControl1.XmlForm.Save();
        else
        {
            SaveFileDialog saveFileDialog = new SaveFileDialog();

            saveFileDialog.Filter =
        "All InfoPath Forms (*.xsn; *.xsf; *.xml)|*.xsn;*.xsf;*.xml";

            saveFileDialog.FilterIndex = 1;

            if (saveFileDialog.ShowDialog() == DialogResult.OK)
            {
                formControl1.XmlForm.SaveAs(_currentFileName);
                _currentFileName = saveFileDialog.FileName;
            }
        }
    }
}
```

The bulk of the work to save the form is done in the `SaveForm` method. In this method, we save the form by using the InfoPath object model. Two methods can be used to save the data—`Save` and `SaveAs`. The `Save` method assumes that you have saved the data before and have associated a file name with the form. The first time we attempt to save, there is no file name associated with the form, so we must call `SaveAs` to indicate the file name. Before calling the `SaveAs` method, we show the *Save As* dialog by using the `SaveFileDialog` class to allow the user to choose a file to save to. Once the user chooses a file name (as long as he or she doesn't cancel the dialog), we'll call the `SaveAs` method to save the form data and then store the current file name in the `_currentFileName` member variable. We store this file name in a member variable so we can call the `Save` method instead of `SaveAs` the next time the user tries to save this particular form. (Since we are closing the form, you may be wondering why this is necessary. This will become necessary later when we add buttons to the form that will allow the user to save the form at will.)

Host to InfoPath Communication

So far, the way the host application has communicated with the InfoPath form control is through the `FormControl` class (or the `IInfoPathEditor` interface in unmanaged code). This class provides methods and properties that give you most of the basic functionality you need—loading a form, closing the document, and accessing the InfoPath object model, to name a few.

However, not all functionality is available through the `FormControl` class. In fact, as you might imagine, not all the features available in the InfoPath client application are provided free to hosting applications. For example, the menus, toolbars, and task panes you are accustomed to using in the InfoPath client application are not available when hosting the InfoPath form control. The InfoPath form control simply provides the form-editing functionality you get when filling out a form.

Even though these UI features are not present when hosting the form control, that doesn't mean that the underlying functionality isn't there. In fact, you can access most of the underlying functionality present in the InfoPath client application. However, you will need to create the user interface to access the features in which you are interested.

Let's look at an example. Most applications, including InfoPath, include one or more toolbars that contain buttons to do various things—open a file, save, cut/copy/paste, undo/redo, and perhaps find a string, for example. So, let's add one of these toolbars to our application. Visual Studio 2005 includes a control called **ToolStrip**. This control is, basically, a toolbar to which you can add buttons. Let's add one of these ToolStrip controls to our application and

FIGURE 18.17: Standard toolbar for the IP Insurance application

add buttons that will be used to open a file, save, cut/copy/paste, and undo/redo. We'll also add a Text Box control and a *Find* button that can be used to search for text in the hosted form. Figure 18.17 shows how this toolbar will look. The *Open* button will simply display the *Open File* dialog and allow the user to choose an InfoPath file, as is the case in the InfoPath client application. Once the user chooses a file, either `formControl1.Open` or `formControl1.NewFromTemplate` will be called, depending on whether the file is a form (.xml) or a form template (.xsf or .xsn). The *Save* button in the toolbar will simply call our own `SaveForm` method.

Writing the code for the *Open* and *Save* buttons is pretty easy because the `FormControl` class offers methods that will allow us to load and save a form. However, if you look closely at the `FormControl` class, you will see that there are no methods to cut, copy, or paste data and no methods to undo or redo changes. So, how do we implement these features?

Fortunately, as we mentioned, there is a way to access most of the features available in InfoPath even if the functionality isn't available through the `FormControl` class. You can access these features through the `IOleCommandTarget` interface. This interface, which may be familiar to you if you have done any COM programming, allows you to query for the status of various commands and then execute these commands if they are available. Since this interface isn't part of the .NET Framework, when you are developing a managed code application that hosts the InfoPath form control, you have to use COM interop in order to access it and send commands to the InfoPath form control. Fortunately, doing so is relatively straightforward.

Let's look at how we can implement the other features of our application toolbar by using the `IOleCommandTarget` interface. First, we must define the `IOleCommandTarget` interface and its dependencies. Listing 18.4 shows the code that defines the `IOleCommandTarget` interface. The interface and the corresponding `OLECMD` structure and `OleCmdf` enumeration are exactly what you would see if you looked up this interface in MSDN.

Listing 18.4: `IOleCommandTarget` Interface and Its Dependencies

```
[StructLayout(LayoutKind.Sequential)]
struct OLECMD
{
    public uint cmdID;
    public uint cmdf;
}
private enum OleCmdf
{
    Supported = 1, // The command is supported
    Enabled = 2, // The command is available and enabled
    Latched = 4, // The command is a toggle and is currently on
    Ninched = 8 // Reserved for future use
}

// Note that the GUID created using guidgen tool that comes
// with Visual Studio 2005
[
ComImport,
Guid("B722BCCB-4E68-101B-A2BC-00AA00404770"),
InterfaceType(ComInterfaceType.InterfaceIsIUnknown)
]
interface IOleCommandTarget
{
    void QueryStatus(ref Guid pguidCmdGroup, uint cCmds,
                     [MarshalAs(UnmanagedType.LPArray), In, Out]
                     OLECMD[] prgCmds, IntPtr pCmdText);
    void Exec(ref Guid pguidCmdGroup, uint nCmdID, uint nCmdExecOpt,
              ref object pvaIn, ref object pvaOut);
}
```

Now let's look at the methods we will use to query and execute commands using the `IOleCommandTarget` interface. Listing 18.5 shows three methods—two overloaded `ExecuteCommand` methods and one `QueryStatusCommand` method. As you can probably guess from the names of these methods, the execute methods pass a command to the form control for execution, and the query status method checks to see if a command is available. (The first `ExecuteCommand` method does the actual work of executing the command, while the second one is added merely for convenience.) As you can see from the code in Listing 18.5, the main execute method first queries the form control to see if the command to execute is available before passing it to the form control for execution.

LISTING 18.5: Methods to Query and Execute Commands

```
private void ExecuteCommand(Editor.UICommand cmd,
                            object parameters, ref object output)
{
    // Don't do anything if the command is not available
    if (QueryStatusCommand(cmd))
    {
        // Get the command target object from the form control
        IOleCommandTarget cmdTarget = formControl1.GetOcx()
                                      as IOleCommandTarget;

        cmdTarget.Exec(ref Editor.CommandGroup,
            Convert.ToUInt16(cmd), 0, ref parameters, ref output);
    }
}

private void ExecuteCommand(Editor.UICommand cmd)
{
    object output = null;
    ExecuteCommand(cmd, null, ref output);
}

public bool QueryStatusCommand(Editor.UICommand cmd)
{
    // Get the command target object from the form control
    if (formControl1 != null)
    {
        IOleCommandTarget commandTarget = formControl1.GetOcx()
                                          as IOleCommandTarget;
        OLECMD[] oleCommands = new OLECMD[1];
        oleCommands[0].cmdID = Convert.ToUInt16(cmd);
        oleCommands[0].cmdf = 0;
        commandTarget.QueryStatus(ref Editor.CommandGroup, 1,
                                  oleCommands, IntPtr.Zero);

        return (((oleCommands[0].cmdf & (uint)OleCmdf.Supported)
                != 0)
                && ((oleCommands[0].cmdf & (uint)OleCmdf.Enabled)
                != 0));
}
    return false;
}
```

In either case, whether querying or executing, we must first access the `IOleCommandTarget` interface through the form control. To do this, we call `formControl1.GetOcx()` and cast it to the `IOleCommandTarget` interface. Once you have this interface, you call its methods as you would for any other interface. When calling the `QueryStatus` method, we pass the ID of the command in which we are interested. (The IDs for each of the commands supported by InfoPath are in the `CommandIds` enumeration in the `FormControlCommandIds` class.) The current status of the command is returned in the `cmdf` member variable of the `OLECMD` structure that we pass to the method. The status of the command will be one of the values listed in the `OleCmdf` enumeration. When calling the `Exec` method, we pass in the ID of the command as usual and any parameters the command may require. (Note that not all commands require parameters.) If the command returns data, which not all do, it will be returned in the `output` object.

Making the Buttons Work

Now that we have the supporting methods we need in order to query and execute commands, let's see how we can put them to use. Let's look at the *Cut* button first. When the *Cut* button is pressed, we will handle the button press in a `Click` event handler called `cutButton_Click`. When this event handler is called, we simply have to call our `ExecuteCommand` method as follows:

```
ExecuteCommand(FormControlCommandIds.CommandIds.Cut)
```

That's it. Now users can click this button to cut text out of the hosted form. The *Copy, Paste, Undo,* and *Redo* buttons are all equally as simple. The only difference is that, in each of these cases, you pass a different command ID from the `CommandIds` enumeration in the `FormControlCommandIds` class.

As we mentioned, the `CommandIds` enumeration contains all the commands supported by InfoPath. You can see the full list of commands by looking at the `FormControlCommandIds.CommandIds` enumeration in `Microsoft.Office.InfoPath.FormControl` assembly in the Object Browser in Visual Studio 2005 or by looking at the documentation available in MSDN. Most of the commands are self-explanatory and easy to use.

Others, especially those that require additional parameters, will require you to look at the MSDN documentation to see the supported parameters and how to use the command. (Unfortunately, there are far too many commands to list in this chapter.)

Let's look at one of the commands that requires additional parameters—the find command. Using this command, we can find text within the hosted form. When the text is found, it will be selected. Unlike the simple commands like cut, copy, and paste, which can all be executed in one step, find is normally at least a two-step process. First, you must set the find string by calling the `Exec` method with the `SetFindString` command. This command ID requires one parameter—the find string—that InfoPath will use for each find operation until the `Exec` method is called again with the `SetFindString` command. Once you've told InfoPath what you want to find, you then call Exec one more time with the `FindReplaceFindNext` command to start the find operation. Executing these two commands will give you very basic search functionality. However, if you use only these two commands, you will only be able to find the first occurrence of the string in the hosted form. The basic problem is that, when you execute the `SetFindString` command, it resets the search. Another issue is that if the string you are looking for appears before the current location of the cursor, it won't be found. Fortunately, there are commands that enable you to work around these limitations.

Take a look at Listing 18.6 which shows the code for the `Click` event handler for the *Find* button. In this code, we first execute the `GetFindString` command. This command will return the search string currently being used. If the value returned in the `output` parameter does not match the string in the find text box, we execute the `SetFindString` command, passing in the new string to find. (Checking the state of the search criteria before resetting it allows us to search for multiple occurrences of a string in the form. If we know that we have already set the search criteria, not setting it again will prevent the problem of being able to find only one occurrence of a string.)

LISTING 18.6: Code to Find Text in the Hosted Form

```
private void findButton_Click(object sender, EventArgs e)
{
    object output = null;

    ExecuteCommand(FormControlCommandIds.CommandIds.GetFindString,
                   null, ref output);

    if (output.ToString() != findTextBox.Text)
    {
        ExecuteCommand(FormControlCommandIds.CommandIds.SetFindString,
                       findTextBox.Text, ref output);
    }

   ExecuteCommand(
   FormControlCommandIds.CommandIds.SetFindReplaceOptionSearchDirection,
                  FindDirection.entireDocument, ref output);

    if (ExecuteCommand(
            FormControlCommandIds.CommandIds.FindReplaceFindNext)
        == false)
    {
        ExecuteCommand(FormControlCommandIds.CommandIds.SetFindString,
                       findTextBox.Text, ref output);

        if (ExecuteCommand(
            FormControlCommandIds.CommandIds.FindReplaceFindNext)
            == false)
        {
            MessageBox.Show(findTextBox.Text + " could not be found.",
                            "InsuranceForms");
        }
    }
}
```

After calling `ExecuteCommand` with `SetFindString` to specify the text to find, we then execute the `SetFindReplaceOptionSearchDirection` command. This command allows us to set the direction of the search—up, down, or entire document. Since we want to find multiple occurrences of a string, we set it to `FindDirection.entireDocument`. (`FindDirection` is an enumeration we created ourselves in order to make the code more readable. The `entireDocument` value is defined as `3`. The other available values are `up` [`1`] and `down` [`2`].)

Finally, we execute the `FindReplaceFindNext` command, which will start the find operation. If the text is found, InfoPath will select it. If we press the *Find* button a second time, we will find the next occurrence of the string, and so on. If the text is not found, it could be that we've reached the end of the document. So, we reset the search string by executing the `SetFindString` command and then try to find the string once again. If it fails a second time, we know that the string doesn't exist in the form.

We hope this small example gives you some idea of how you can use the various commands available to you via the `IOleCommandTarget` interface. As you can see, some of the commands are very easy to use, and others require a bit more work. However, by using the commands in the `CommandIds` enumeration, you can add most of the functionality included in InfoPath to your own applications.

Updating Toolbar Buttons During Application Idle State

Now we know how to execute commands so that our buttons will work. However, there is one small issue. Our buttons are always enabled. In the `ExecuteCommand` method we do check the state of each command first by calling `QueryStatusCommand` and then execute the command only if it is enabled. However, why should the buttons be enabled at all if the commands are disabled? Obviously, any application with one or more toolbars will want to enable or disable toolbar buttons depending on the current state of the document. For example, you want the *Cut* and *Copy* buttons to be enabled only if some text in the form is selected. Likewise, the *Paste* button should be enabled only if there is something on the clipboard. The *Undo* and *Redo* buttons should be enabled only if there is something to undo or redo. Finally, the *Save* button should be enabled only if the form is dirty. (The *Open* button is always enabled since you always want to allow the user to open a new form.)

Typically, an application would perform such toolbar updates during the application's idle state. Our application is no different. Implementing this is relatively straightforward. First, we need to set up an event handler for the `Idle` event of the `System.Windows.Forms.Application` class. The following code shows how we would do this:

```
_lastIdleTime = DateTime.Now;
System.Windows.Forms.Application.Idle +=
    new EventHandler(Application_Idle);
```

The first thing we do in this code is save the current time in a member variable called `_lastIdleTime`, which is a `DateTime` type. You'll see why this is needed shortly. Then we create a new `EventHandler` object, passing in our event handler method `Application_Idle`, and set the `Application.Idle` property to this new `EventHandler` object.

Next, we need to implement the `Application_Idle` method. This method, shown in Listing 18.7, first will determine whether one second has passed since the last time this method is called before setting the state of the buttons. (This is the reason for the `_lastIdleTime` member variable.) We don't want to set the enabled/disabled state of the buttons every time this method is called since it will be called a lot.

LISTING 18.7: Implementation of the `Application_Idle` Method

```
void Application_Idle(object sender, EventArgs e)
{
    // Don't update the UI on every idle call. Wait at least
    // one second between each update.
    if (DateTime.Now > _lastIdleTime.AddSeconds(1))
    {
        this.SuspendLayout();
        SetToolBarButtonStates();
        this.ResumeLayout();

        _lastIdleTime = DateTime.Now;
    }
}
```

Then, we suspend the layout of the Windows form temporarily so layout doesn't occur while we're checking the state of the buttons. Finally, we call `SetToolBarButtonStates` to enable or disable the buttons in the toolbar. Let's look at this method (Listing 18.8).

LISTING 18.8: `SetToolBarButtonStates` Method

```
public void SetToolBarButtonStates()
{
    if (formControl1 != null)
    {
        ToolStripButton[] buttons =
        {
            cutButton,
            copyButton,
            pasteButton,
            undoButton,
            redoButton
        };
```

```
        IOleCommandTarget commandTarget =
            formControl1.GetOcx() as IOleCommandTarget;

        commandTarget.QueryStatus(
            ref FormControlCommandIds.CommandGroup,
            Convert.ToUInt16(_commands.Length),
            _commands,
            IntPtr.Zero);

        for (int i = 0; i < _commands.Length; i++)
        {
            bool enabled =
                (((_commands[i].cmdf & (uint)OleCmdf.Supported) != 0) &&
                 ((_commands[i].cmdf & (uint)OleCmdf.Enabled) != 0));
            buttons[i].Enabled = enabled;
        }

        saveButton.Enabled = (formControl1.XmlForm != null)
                            && formControl1.XmlForm.Dirty;
    }
}
```

The main purpose of the SetToolBarButtonStates method is to enable or disable the toolbar buttons based on the state of the document. In order to determine the current state of the buttons, we have to call the QueryStatus method of the IOleCommandTarget interface of the form control object. You've already seen how we can do this when we called QueryStatusCommand earlier. However, when we called that method, we checked the state of a single command. Since the SetToolBarButton-States method is called during idle time, calling QueryStatus (via a call to QueryStatusCommand) could kill the performance of your application—especially if you have a lot of toolbar buttons.

Therefore, in order to improve the performance of toolbar updates, you can pass an array of commands that you want to check to the QueryStatus method. The array of commands you pass in is an array of OLECMD objects. Each object has its cmdID member variable set to the command you want to check. QueryStatus will return the state of each command in the same array by setting the cmdf member variable for each command. Let's take a closer look at this.

In Listing 18.8, notice that we are passing an array called _commands to the QueryStatus method. This is an array of OLECMD objects, as we mentioned. This array is populated in the application class's constructor by calling the EnsureCommandsArray method shown in Listing 18.9. If you

LISTING 18.9: `EnsureCommandsArray` Method

```
public void EnsureCommandsArray()
{
    FormControlCommandIds.CommandIds[] formControlCommands =
    {
        FormControlCommandIds.CommandIds.Cut,
        FormControlCommandIds.CommandIds.Copy,
        FormControlCommandIds.CommandIds.Paste,
        FormControlCommandIds.CommandIds.Undo,
        FormControlCommandIds.CommandIds.Redo,
    };

    _commands = new OLECMD[formControlCommands.Length];

    for (int i = 0; i < formControlCommands.Length; i++)
    {
        _commands[i].cmdID = Convert.ToUInt16(formControlCommands[i]);
        _commands[i].cmdf = 0;
    }
}
```

look at this method, you'll notice that we create a variable called `formControlCommands`, which is an array of `FormControlCommandIds.CommandIds` objects. This array contains each of the commands whose state we want to check—`Cut`, `Copy`, `Paste`, `Undo`, and `Redo`. Then, we create a new `OLECMD` array called `_commands` that is the same size as the `formControlCommands` array. Finally, we loop over the length of the array and populate the `_commands` array with the different commands from `formControlCommands`.

Now that you understand how the `_commands` array is populated, let's look back at the `SetToolBarButtonStates` method. After `QueryStatus` returns, as we mentioned, the `cmdf` member of each `OLECMD` object in the `_commands` array will contain the state of each corresponding command. So, since we've set up an array of the `ToolStripButton` objects (in the `buttons` array), we can just loop over the `_commands` array and set the state of each button based on the value of the `cmdf` member variable.

Once we've enabled or disabled the *Cut, Copy, Paste, Undo,* and *Redo* buttons, we have one more button to enable or disable—*Save.* For the *Save* button, we enable it only if the form itself is dirty, which we can tell by checking the `Dirty` property on the `XmlForm` object. Of course, we will disable the button if the `XmlForm` object is `null`, which will be the case if a form is not opened.

Handling Events from the Form

So far, we've talked about how the hosting application can access the different methods and properties of the form control. What if you want to handle different events from the form so that you know when certain things have happened, such as when the form is loaded or when data has changed? In addition to being able to interact with the form itself through the InfoPath form control, hosting applications can also receive events from the form.

The most obvious event that a hosting application would like to know about is when the form has loaded. In order to know when the form has loaded, the host application can implement the `IInitEventHandler` interface and then call the `SetInitEventHandler` method on the `FormControl` object to designate the host as an init handler, like so: `formControl1.SetInitEventHandler(this);`

The `IInitEventHandler` interface has one method—`InitEventHandler`—which corresponds to the `Loading` event in form code and is fired basically at the same time. When this event is fired, the `XmlForm` object has not yet been initialized, so you cannot interact with the form. However, this event does give you a good place to perform general initialization of data that you may later use in the hosted form. Also, you can set the initial view mode of the form when it is open—default, noneditable, or frozen. For example, the following code sets the initial state of the form to noneditable (read-only):

```
public void InitEventHandler(object sender,
                             XmlForm xmlForm,
                             out XdReadOnlyViewMode viewsReadOnlyMode)
{
    viewsReadOnlyMode = XdReadOnlyViewMode.xdNonEditable;
}
```

As you can see from this code snippet, the `InitEventHandler` method takes the following three parameters:

1. `sender`: a reference to the InfoPath form control that initiated the event. This is useful if you are hosting multiple instances of the form control. In that case, this object can be used to differentiate between each of the form controls being hosted.
2. `xmlForm`: the XML form (corresponds to the `XmlForm` object).

3. `viewsReadOnlyMode`: the read-only view mode, which can be one of three possible values:
   a. `xdDefault`: The view functions as normal.
   b. `xdNonEditable`: The view is read-only. You cannot change the values of controls in the form. However, you can still click on buttons.
   c. `xdFrozen`: The view is frozen. This is a superset of `xdNonEditable`. The view is read-only and all controls (including buttons) are disabled.

> **WARNING** Do Not Store a Reference to the **`XmlForm`** Object
>
> When `InitEventHandler` is called, it may be tempting to store a reference to the `XmlForm` object as a data member of the class. Doing so, however, could result in an exception being thrown when you try to access it. This is because the `XmlForm` object is reset at different points in the form's lifetime. Instead, whenever you need to access the `XmlForm` object, do so through the `XmlForm` property of the `FormControl` class.

The `InitEventHandler` event will alert the hosting application when the hosted form is loading, which is very useful. But how do you tell when other events are occurring in the form, such as the `Changed` or `Validating` events? Fortunately, the `FormControl` object exposes the `EventManager` object so you can receive events from the form. In order to hook up events using the `EventManager`, you must first handle the `InternalStartup` event. To do so, in your application's form constructor or `Form_Load` method, you must first set the `InternalStartup` event handler like so:

```
formControl1.InternalStartup
    += new FormControl.EventHandler<EventArgs>(
           formControl1_InternalStartup);
```

Then, implement the `InternalStartup` method and hook up the form events you care about. (Trying to use the `EventManager` object to hook up events anywhere but in `InternalStartup` will result in an exception being thrown by InfoPath.) The following code shows a sample implementation of the `InternalStartup` method that hooks up an event handler for the `Changed` event of the `InsurerName` field so that we're alerted whenever this field has changed.

```
void formControl1_InternalStartup(object sender, EventArgs e)
{
    formControl1.EventManager.XmlEvents[
            "/my:myFields/my:InsurerName"].Changed
        += new XmlChangedEventHandler(InsurerNameChanged);
}
```

`NotifyHost` Method

Being able to handle form events using the `EventManager` object allows you to know when most things are happening in the form—when the data is changed, when the view switches, and so on. However, sometimes you want your form code to notify the hosting application in a customized way. For example, even though your hosting application can handle the `ViewSwitched` event for any form, you may need to perform certain form-specific processing in the `ViewSwitched` event in the form itself before the form is truly ready to be used. If the host application handles the `ViewSwitched` event, it will receive the event before this form-specific processing can be performed. In that case, you really want the form to tell the host application when it is truly ready.

The `XDocument` object includes a `NotifyHost` method that can be called from form code to pass a string to the hosting application. The host application can register to receive these notifications by implementing the `INotifyHostEventHandler` interface and then calling the `SetNotifyHostEventHandler` on the `FormControl` object: `formControl1.SetNotifyHostEventHandler(this);`

Next, in the host application, simply implement the `NotifyHostEventHandler` method to handle the notification:

```
public void NotifyHostEventHandler(object sender, string notification)
{
    if (notification == "FormReady")
    {
        // Do something special here.
        MessageBox.Show("The form is ready");
    }
}
```

As you can see from this code, the `NotifyHostEventHandler` method receives the following two parameters:

1. `sender`: a reference to the InfoPath form control that initiated the event
2. `notification`: the string sent from the form code

In our NotifyHostEventHandler method, we are planning to receive a notification from form code that the form has completely finished loading, as we mentioned earlier. In this case, the form is completely loaded after the ViewSwitched event occurs and we have done some special form-specific processing. Notifying the host from code in the form is just a matter of calling the NotifyHost method, as shown in the following code snippet:

```
public void FormEvents_ViewSwitched(object sender,
                                    ViewSwitchedEventArgs e)
{
    // Do some advanced processing here.
    if (this.Hosted)
        this.NotifyHost("FormReady");
}
```

As you can see in this code, in the ViewSwitched event handler, we first check the Hosted property to see if the form is being hosted by an application other than InfoPath. If that is the case, we call the NotifyHost method, passing it a string that tells the host that the form is ready. It's that simple. You can use this method to notify the host of other specialized events or for any other reason you choose.

Using the Host Property

The NotifyHost method is useful, but only in the case where you want to pass a string to the hosting application. What if you want to pass more data to the host? For example, the forms we are loading in our host application all contain an estimate for the cost of the insurance. Let's say that we want to perform custom validation on the estimate, but we don't want to write code in each of the form templates (or create rules in each form). Instead, we'd prefer to write the code once—in the host—and then call methods on the host to validate the date. This is just what the Host property is used for.

Let's create a new assembly that will hold any host utilities we want to call from form code. First, open Visual Studio 2005 and create a new project. In the New Project Wizard, we'll add a new Class Library project and call it HostClassLibrary. Then, let's add an interface called IHostUtilities that we will use in form code to call utility methods. The interface is defined as follows:

```
public interface IHostUtilities
{
    bool IsValidEstimate(XPathNavigator navigator,
                         out string errorMessage);
}
```

The IHostUtilities interface contains one method—IsValidEstimate. This is the method we'll call from form code to determine whether the estimate is correct. Next, let's create a class to implement this interface. This class, HostUtilities, and the implementation of the IsValidEstimate method are shown in Listing 18.10. There is one point to keep in mind about this code. Since the InfoPath form control is an ActiveX control, it uses COM interop to work in managed code. Therefore, it is necessary to specify two attributes on the HostUtilities class—ComVisible(true) and Serializable. If you don't specify these attributes, you will not be able to access methods of this class from form code.

LISTING 18.10: HostUtilities **Class**

```
[ComVisible(true)]
[Serializable]
public class HostUtilities : IHostUtilities
{
   public bool IsValidEstimate(XPathNavigator node,
                               out string errorMessage)
   {
       bool isValid = true;
       errorMessage = null;
       if (node != null
           && node.NodeType == XPathNodeType.Element
           && node.Value != "")
       {
                double estimate = node.ValueAsDouble;
                if (estimate <= 0)
                {
                    errorMessage =
                        "The estimate must be greater than 0";
                    isValid = false;
                }
                else if (estimate > 10000)
                {
                    errorMessage = "The estimate is too high. "
                               + "Ensure that the estimate is correct.";
                    isValid = false;
                    }
                }
       }
       return isValid;
   }
}
```

Once we've compiled this code into its own assembly—HostClass-Library.dll—we need to add it as a reference to our main `InsuranceForms` project so that we can access the `HostUtilities` class. Once that is done, we simply need to set the `Host` property on the InfoPath form control to an instance of the `HostUtilities` class by adding the following code to the `Form1_Load` event handler of the Windows Forms application: `formControl1.Host = new HostUtilities();`

Now we're ready to put this utility class to work in code included in our InfoPath form templates. As with our main Windows form project, in order to access the `HostUtilities` class or the `IHostUtilities` interface from form code, we first need to add a reference to the assembly in our form code. Once that is done, we can call methods on the `IHostUtilities` interface through the `Host` property in the form. (Note that accessing the `Host` property from form code requires the form to be full-trust. So, you must either sign the form or install it on your users' machines.)

Listing 18.11 shows the event handler for the `Validating` event of the `Estimate` field in form code. In this method, we first check to make sure that the form is hosted and that the `Host` property is not `null`. Then, we cast the `Host` property to `IHostUtilities`. If that succeeds, we call the `IsValidEstimate` method on the `IHostUtilities` interface, passing it the node corresponding to the `Estimate` field. `IsValidEstimate` is very

LISTING 18.11: `Validating` Event Handler for the `Estimate` Field in Form Code

```
public void Estimate_Validating(object sender,
                                XmlValidatingEventArgs e)
{
    // Store the current value of the field in the host's property bag.
    if (this.Hosted && this.Host != null)
    {
        IHostUtilities hostUtils = this.Host as IHostUtilities;
        if (hostUtils != null)
        {
            string errorMessage;
            XPathNavigator node = sender as XPathNavigator;

            if (!hostUtils.IsValidEstimate(node, out errorMessage))
                e.ReportError(node, false, errorMessage);
        }
    }
}
```

simple. It just validates that the estimate is greater than 0 and less than or equal to 10,000. If it's not, it fills in the `errorMessage` parameter with the correct error message and returns `false`. In form code, when `IsValidEstimate` returns `false`, we call the `ReportError` method on the event parameter, which will flag the field as having a data validation error. The string specified in the `errorMessage` parameter will be used for the screen tip for the data validation error in the form itself. Of course, this data validation can easily be done using rules, but, as we mentioned earlier, by using these host utilities, we have to write the validation code only once and can use it in multiple forms.

Submitting a Form to the Host

Back in Chapter 8, when we talked about submitting forms, we talked briefly about how you can submit a form to a hosting environment. There are various reasons you may want to do this. For example, you may want to perform similar validation on all your forms before submitting to a back-end database. (In this case, you want to perform the validation when submitting the form as opposed to doing so when the data changes, as in the last scenario.) Instead of adding the same validation code to all your forms, you can simply perform the common validation inside the hosting application and then use one of the other InfoPath submit adapters to submit the data to the back-end system.

Let's look at how you can design a form template to submit to a hosting application and then how you can set up the host to receive the submitted data.

The first thing you must do, as we discussed in Chapter 8, is to specify the submit data connection for the form template. You can do that by using the *Submit Options* dialog available from the *Tools* menu in design mode. When you specify the submit data connection in this way, by default, a menu item and toolbar button are added to the InfoPath user interface. When using the InfoPath client application, this is fine. However, remember that the InfoPath UI is not available to hosting applications. So, let's add a *Submit* button to our form. After adding a Button control to the form, open the *Button Properties* dialog and change the *Action* item to *Submit*. This will cause the button's label text to automatically change to "Submit". Next, click on the *Submit Options* button in the properties dialog. This

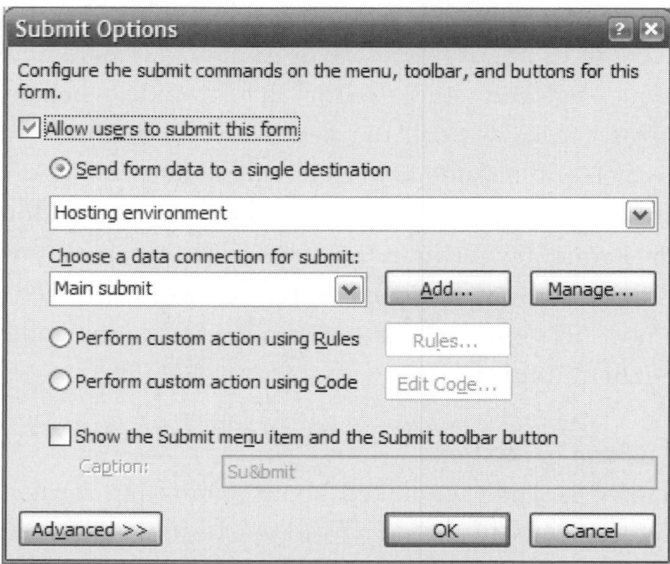

FIGURE 18.18: Submit Options dialog with Hosting environment as the destination

opens the dialog shown in Figure 18.18. From here, you can specify *Hosting environment* as the destination. Next, if you haven't already, you must add a data connection; by default, it is called `Main submit`. For hosting, this is usually the data connection you will want to specify. Also, uncheck the option *Show the Submit menu item and the Submit toolbar button* at the bottom of the dialog. Once you are finished adding the submit data connection, close the *Submit Options* dialog and save your form template.

That's it. Now when you submit the form, the form is submitted to the hosting environment. If you submit from within InfoPath, nothing will actually be submitted. (However, unless you've changed the *Advanced* submit options in the *Submit Options* dialog, a dialog will appear to tell you that the form was submitted successfully even though nothing really happened.) Likewise, if you open this form in a hosting application and submit, and you haven't done anything else, nothing will be submitted.

Let's look at what needs to be added to the host in order to receive a notification that the form is being submitted. As you might have guessed, the code we need to add is similar to that which we added for the init and notify host event handlers. First, the host form needs to implement the `ISubmitToHostEventHandler` interface and then call the `SetSubmit-ToHostEventHandler` method on the `FormControl` object to designate the host as the submit handler:

```
formControl1.SetSubmitToHostEventHandler(this);
```

The `ISubmitToHostEventHandler` interface has one method that the host must implement—`SubmitToHostEventHandler`. This method takes the following three parameters:

1. `sender`: a reference to the InfoPath form control that initiated the event
2. `adapterName`: the adapter name specified in the *Submit Options* dialog
3. `errorMessage`: an error message to display when the submit has been canceled

The `SubmitToHostEventHandler` method returns an integer that specifies whether or not the submit operation succeeded. Return `1` if the submit succeeded and `0:` otherwise. If the submit operation fails, a default message is displayed to the user along with the error message passed back in the `errorMessage` parameter.

Let's look at a simple example. The code in Listing 18.12 shows the implementation of the `SubmitToHostEventHandler` method. This method will perform some custom validation of the form data. Basically, it will ensure that the insurer name has been entered. (Of course, you can do this in the InfoPath form, but this example is meant to demonstrate how you can centralize your submit validation code.) If the insurer name has been entered, the code will submit the form using an e-mail submit connection defined in this form. (In this example, each of the form templates that we load in the host application has an e-mail submit data connection called `Email Submit`.) Even though this example uses an e-mail submit data connection, you could just as easily use another data connection, such as the ADO.NET submit connection we talked about in Chapter 8.

LISTING 18.12: `SubmitToHostEventHandler` **Method**

```
public int SubmitToHostEventHandler(object sender,
                                    string adapterName,
                                    out string errorMessage)
{
    bool formIsValid = true;
    errorMessage = null;

    if (formControl1.XmlForm != null)
    {
        XPathNavigator navigator =
            formControl1.XmlForm.MainDataSource.CreateNavigator();

        XPathNavigator insurerNameNode =
            navigator.SelectSingleNode(
                "my:myFields/my:InsurerName",
                formControl1.XmlForm.NamespaceManager);

        if (insurerNameNode != null && insurerNameNode.Value == "")
        {
            formIsValid = false;
            errorMessage = "The insurer name cannot be empty";
        }
    }

    if (formIsValid)
    {
        EmailSubmitConnection emailSubmit =
            formControl1.XmlForm.DataConnections["Email Submit"]
                as EmailSubmitConnection;

        if (emailSubmit != null)
            emailSubmit.Execute();
    }
    return formIsValid ? 1 : 0;
}
```

As you can see, hosting InfoPath allows you to extend and customize the user experience of filling out forms in InfoPath. You can use InfoPath for the structured form editing that it provides while extending it to meet your own needs. You can host InfoPath to do anything from simply creating a repository for your forms to customizing the entire form-editing experience.

> **NOTE** Submit Event Will Occur First in the Form Code
>
> If the form opened in the hosting application handles the submit event, the event will be fired to the form first before being sent to the hosting application's `SubmitToHostEventHandler`. Therefore, if the submit event handler in form code cancels the event, the host will never receive the event.

Hosting the InfoPath Form Control in a Web Browser

At this point you know how to host InfoPath forms in your own applications. The IP Insurance sample showed how a form can be integrated into a custom application while maintaining a seamless user interface and experience. We learned all about the InfoPath form control and wrote code to communicate between the form and the host application. In this section, we're going to do something very similar, but instead of using a Windows Forms application, we'll be working in the context of a Web page.

As you may have guessed, the browser version of the form control is powered by InfoPath Forms Services. Given that the browser-based form control is based on Forms Services, we're back to working with InfoPath Forms Services and browser-enabled form templates. As such, you can't use just any InfoPath form and fill it in the browser by using the browser form control. Everything we learned back in Chapters 14 and 17 now applies. If you haven't yet looked at those chapters, we highly recommend that you at least understand the material presented in Chapter 14.

Hosting the InfoPath form control in the browser is quite different than hosting it in a .NET Windows Forms application. In fact, the browser version is a completely different control with a different interface. Instead of the `FormControl` class as we used for hosting InfoPath, we'll be using the **`XmlFormView`** class. The `XmlFormView` component is really just an ASP.NET control. If you've authored an ASP.NET page before, you'll know that ASP.NET controls can be used when designing a Web form (i.e., an ASP.NET Web page) in Visual Studio 2005. Since we're using an ASP.NET control, we want to call out a few differences from the `FormControl` control we used earlier.

- `XmlFormView` must be used within the context of an ASP.NET (not ASP) page.
- As an ASP.NET control, the `XmlFormView` control resides on the server.
- C# and Visual Basic are the only supported languages.

Without further ado, let's see how to build a custom ASP.NET Web form to host a browser-enabled form template.

> **WARNING `XmlFormView` Requires a Server and Site Running InfoPath Forms Services**
>
> Before you rush out and start inserting the `XmlFormView` control into your ASP.NET pages, you should know that the control must be used within the context of a SharePoint Server running InfoPath Forms Services. The page hosting the control must also be within a SharePoint site.

Before we can build an ASP.NET Web form with the `XmlFormView` control, we need to set up our environment. First and foremost, you should be working on a Web Front End (WFE) server running InfoPath Forms Services. That means you need to have Visual Studio 2005 installed on the server. (Although it's possible to open the site remotely, you'd need to add several references to Forms Services and SharePoint assemblies that exist only on the server.) Once you're on the WFE server with Visual Studio, you'll continue to set up your environment by creating a project that maps to the SharePoint Web site with InfoPath Forms Services and adding the `XmlFormView` control to the Visual Studio 2005 Toolbox.

Before creating a project for the SharePoint site on your server running InfoPath Forms Services, you first need to get the physical path of the site where you want your browser form to live. For example, if you want to host the page on the root site collection, the URL would look something like http://yourserver/mypage.aspx or http://yourserver/yourfolder/mypage.aspx. To get the physical path of the root site collection, open the

Internet Information Services (IIS) Manager item on the WFE. (The entry point is under the Administrative Tools folder within the Control Panel.) Right-click the site labeled *SharePoint—80* and select *Properties.* On the *Home Directory* tab of the resulting dialog (Figure 18.19), copy the text from the *Local path* text box to the clipboard.

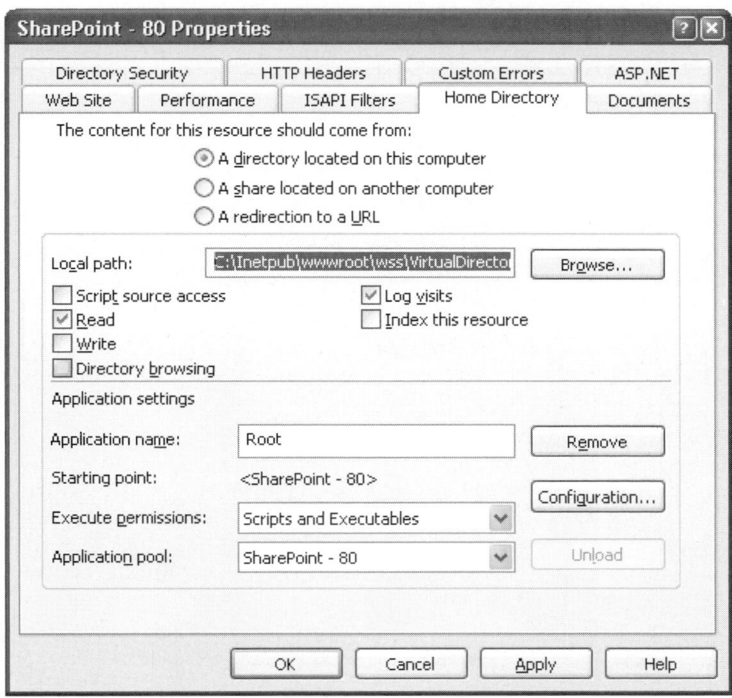

FIGURE 18.19: Copying the physical path for the SharePoint root site collection from IIS Manager

> **NOTE SharePoint Site Names**
>
> The SharePoint site need not be at port 80 and using the root site collection. While port 80 is the default site, you can use any SharePoint site. Likewise, the site collection can be anywhere and is not limited to the root.

Now that you have the physical path to the root SharePoint site, let's kick off Visual Studio 2005 and create the project. Start by going to the *File* menu and then the *Open* submenu, and select *Web Site.* On the resulting *Open Web Site* dialog, select the *File System* button, and then paste the physical path for the SharePoint site collection into the *Folder* text box. You should see something similar to Figure 18.20. Clicking *Open* will take a few moments to open the site and create the project.

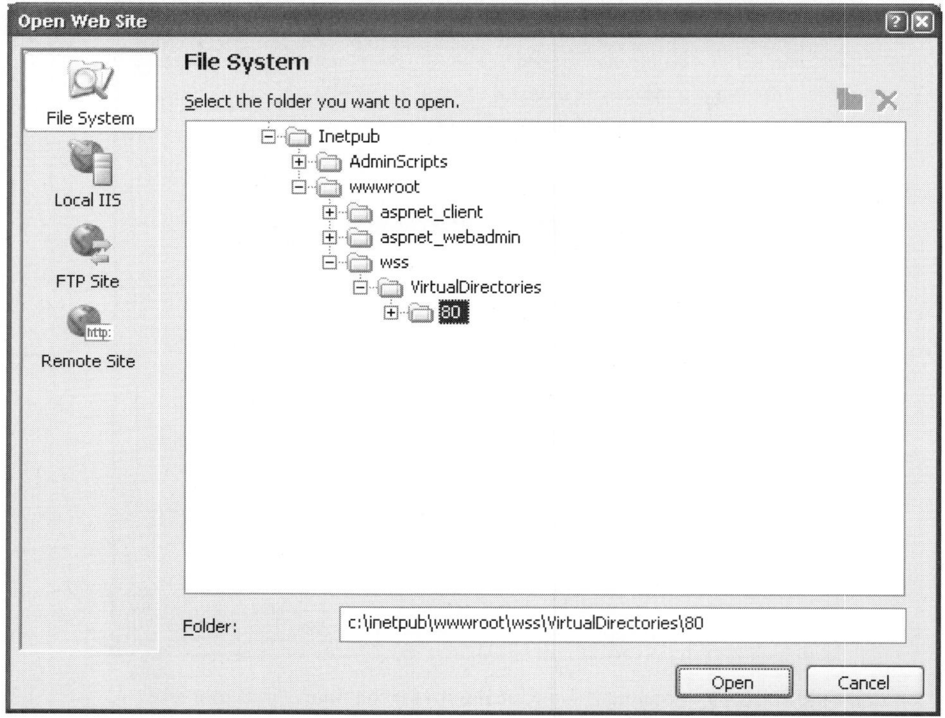

FIGURE 18.20: Opening the SharePoint site by using the file system path

At this point, you've successfully created the project. The next step is to decide where you want your ASP.NET page to live within the SharePoint site. For this example, we created a new folder under the *C:\. . . \80* root called *XmlFormView.* Below this folder, we added a new Web form called *MyPage.aspx.* To add an item in the Solution Explorer, right-click on the parent of where you want to add the item. Commands such as *New Folder* and *Add New Item* are available from the right-click menu. Figure 18.21 shows the result of adding the folder and page.

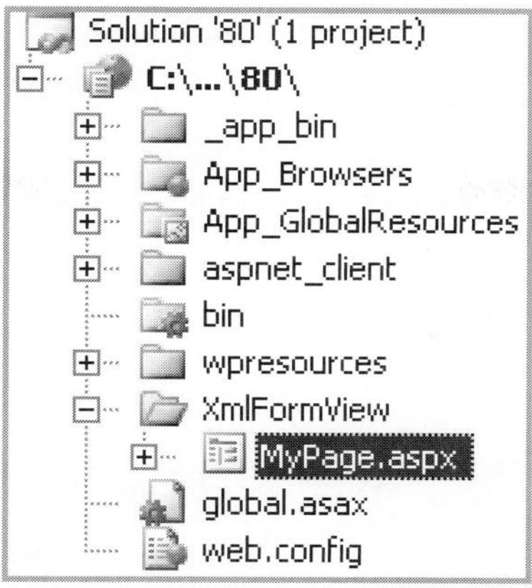

FIGURE 18.21: Solution Explorer after adding the XmlFormView folder and MyPage.aspx Web form

The next step is to start designing your ASP.NET (.aspx) page. To do so, double-click *MyPage.aspx.* This will show the source code of the page; select the *Design* button at the bottom-left of the page to switch to the design view. You can use this view as an alternative to writing code for authoring the page. Once in the design view, you can just drag and drop controls from the Toolbox into the page. (If you can't see the Toolbox, select *Toolbox* from the *View* menu.) At this point, you can design your page however you please. For learning purposes, we're going to start with a trivial example: a page with only the `XmlFormView` control.

> **NOTE Mimicking the Default Rendering Page for InfoPath Forms Services**
>
> The ASP.NET Web page we're about to design is basically mimicking the FormServer.aspx page that Forms Services uses to render its forms in the browser.

You might have noticed that `XmlFormView` is not present in the list of available controls. If that's the case, you'll need to first add the control. Similarly to how we added the `FormControl` control to the Toolbox earlier in this chapter, start by selecting *Choose Toolbox Items* from the *Tools* menu of Visual Studio 2005. If the `XmlFormView` class doesn't already exist under the *.NET Framework Components* list that appears, browse to the Microsoft.Office.InfoPath.Server.dll assembly on the server at %ProgramFiles%\Microsoft Office Servers\12.0\bin. After adding the assembly, enable the checkbox to add the component, and click *OK*. (Notice that the control itself is defined within the `Microsoft.Office.InfoPath.Server.Controls` namespace.) You'll see the control in the Toolbox, as shown in Figure 18.22.

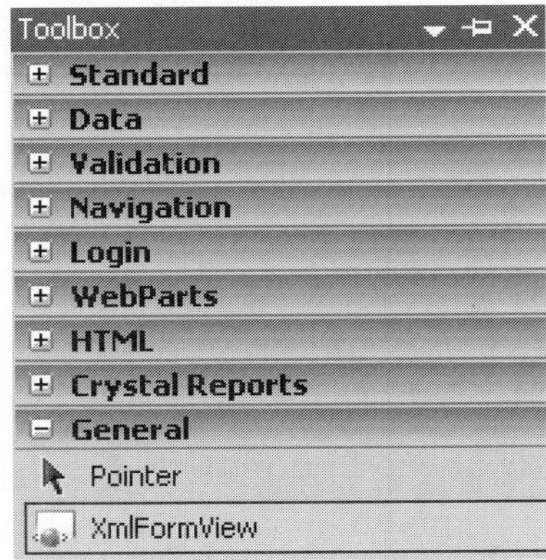

FIGURE 18.22: Toolbox after adding the `XmlFormView` control

Go ahead and insert the `XmlFormView` control into the design view of the MyPage.aspx page. The control appears as a plain rectangle with the text "The form will appear here". The ID of the control will be `XmlFormView1`, which we'll keep for simplicity. Click anywhere in the rectangle and select the *Properties Window* item on the *View* menu to look at the properties of the `XmlFormView` control. As you may know from ASP.NET control development in Visual Studio 2005, the properties shown in the *Properties* window reflect the various attributes that the control supports. Think of these settings as defaults or initializing values for the control when it first appears in the browser. If you use the *Categorized* button to sort within the *Properties* window, pay particular attention to the *Data Binding* and *Features* categories. The most commonly used properties are explained in Table 18.3. We'll be using some of these properties to configure the `XmlFormView` control to render the form template of our choice, for example.

Table 18.3: Commonly Used Properties of the `XmlFormView` Control

Property	Purpose	Notes	Sample Value
`SaveLocation`	Sets the default document library for when the user decides to saves the form.	The path must be relative to the site collection in which the form is running.	`/MyStatusReports`
		Use `~site collection` to cross-reference a site collection.	`~sitecollection/ name`
`XmlLocation`	Points to an existing form (.xml) file on the server for displaying in the control.	The form must have an associated form template that has been activated with InfoPath Forms Services on the same site collection.	`/MyStatusReports/ Feb.xml`
`XsnLocation`	Points to an existing form template (.xsn) file on the server for displaying in the control.	The form template must be activated with Forms Services on the same site collection.	`/FormServer Templates/Status Report.xsn`
`EditingStatus`	Sets the editing state of the `XmlFormView` control.	This property accepts values of `Init` and `Editing;` `Closed` cannot be set, but only received.	`Editing`
`Options`	Allows disabling of the *Save* button in the form.	Set to `Disable Save` to disable the *Save* button.	(Empty string)
`ShowHeader`	Determines whether the top toolbar is shown in the form.	Accepts Boolean values of `true` and `false`.	`true`
`ShowFooter`	Determines whether the bottom toolbar is shown in the form.	Accepts Boolean values of `true` and `false`.	`true`

> **TIP One Instance of XmlFormView per Page**
>
> Forms Services supports only one `XmlFormView` control on an ASP.NET page. To display more than one form in the browser, considering using HTML frames or an IFRAME for another .aspx page.

Before we can try using MyPage.aspx in the browser, there are a few more settings to address. First we need to tell the `XmlFormView` control what form or form template to use. We can do this by setting either the `XmlLocation` or `XsnLocation` property. For a form template, let's use the IP Insurance form template for life insurance that we used earlier in the chapter. We took that form template and, by using the Design Checker in InfoPath design mode, browser-enabled the form template. (This sample, LifeInsurance_BrowserEnabled, is included with the samples for this chapter on the book's Web site.) The process was really easy since there were no messages or errors in the Design Checker as a result of browser-enabling the form template. The next step is to publish the form template to your SharePoint server running Forms Services. We'll use the Publishing Wizard in InfoPath design mode to publish the form template to InfoPath Forms Services. In this example, we published to a document library with the name `LifeInsurance`. On the last page of the Publishing Wizard, click on the *Open this form in the browser* link. When the browser opens with the form, look carefully at the Web page URL. You should see an `XsnLocation` parameter with a value that looks similar to the following: `XsnLocation=http://localhost/LifeInsurance/forms/template.xsn`

Take that value (`http://localhost/LifeInsurance/forms/template.xsn`) and set the `XsnLocation` property of our `XmlFormView1` control in the *Properties* window of Visual Studio 2005. The next step before we can preview our form is to enable session state on our ASP.NET page. As you learned in Chapter 17, forms running in the browser use the session state service. To enable session state, click anywhere outside of the `XmlFormView1` control in the design view of MyPage.aspx in Visual Studio. In the *Properties* window, you should see *DOCUMENT* listed in the drop-down at the top of the window. You will see the `EnableSessionState` property, which you can set to `True`.

The last step to successfully preview your `XmlFormView` control is to set the URL that Visual Studio will launch when you run the project. By default, Visual Studio creates a temporary Web site for debugging. However, this temporary site is not a SharePoint site, so the `XmlFormView` will fail to load. To set the URL, go to the *Start Options* item under the *Website* menu. Select the option button adjacent to the *Start URL* text and use the following URL: http://localhost/XmlFormView/MyPage.aspx. After clicking *OK* to the dialog, you now can run the page just created. Click the *Start Debugging* button on the toolbar in Visual Studio, or just hit F5 to run. The browser will open with the URL you specified, which shows the life insurance form (Figure 18.23)!

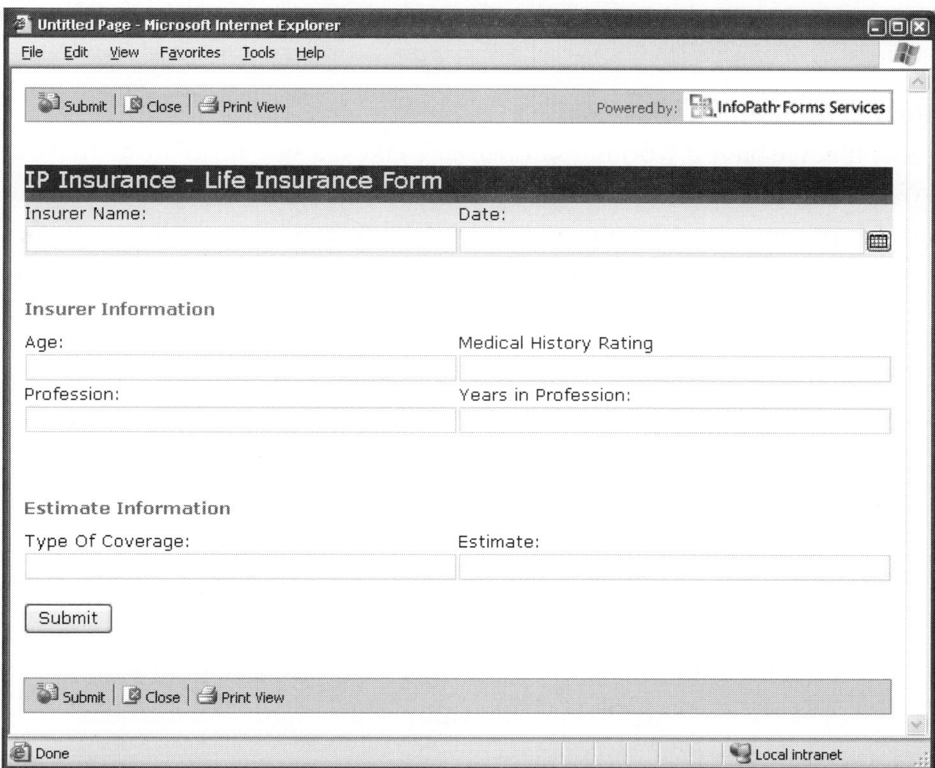

FIGURE 18.23: Hosting the life insurance form in MyPage.aspx

> **TIP Missing Icons in the Toolbar?**
>
> You may notice that icons are missing in the toolbars, among other stylistic oddities in the form itself. The problem lies in the HTML in the custom ASP.NET page. Removing the `<!DOCTYPE...>` declaration (which will exist toward the top of the page source code) solves the problem.

> **TIP File Attachments Require Additional Work**
>
> A File Attachment control in your form will not upload properly unless you add `enctype="multipart/form-data"` to the `<form>` HTML tag in the ASP.NET page source code.

Host to InfoPath Communication

Now that we have a working sample, let's take it a step further. Say that our ASP.NET page doesn't initially show the form. Instead, we ask for the insurance applicant's name in our own ASP.NET Text Box control. Only clicking a button will show the form and automatically set the *Insurer Name* Text Box in our form. To add this functionality, we carry out a few simple steps.

1. Set the `XmlFormView1` control's `Style` property to `visibility:hidden` in the *Properties* window in design mode in Visual Studio.
2. Insert a Text Box and a Button control from the Toolbox into the design view of the page.
3. Double-click on the Button control to write code that executes when the Button is clicked.
4. The code behind the Button sets the `Style` property to `visibility:visible` and also sets the value of the `InsurerName` field.

Listing 18.13 shows the code behind the Button control to make the `XmlFormView1` control visible. It also gets the insurer's name from the ASP.NET Text Box in MyPage.aspx and sets it to the `InsurerName` field in our form.

LISTING 18.13: Code Behind the ASP.NET Button Control in MyPage.aspx

```
XmlFormView1.Style["visibility"] = "visible";
XPathNavigator root =
        XmlFormView1.XmlForm.MainDataSource.CreateNavigator();
XPathNavigator insurerName =
        root.SelectSingleNode("/my:myFields/my:InsurerName",
        XmlFormView1.XmlForm.NamespaceManager);

insurerName.SetValue(TextBox1.Text);
```

> **NOTE Why Not Use `XmlFormView.EditingStatus` to Hide the Control?**
>
> When `EditingStatus` is set to `Init`, the `XmlFormView` control is not properly initialized. As a result, the `XmlForm` member, which gives us access to a great majority of the InfoPath object model, is `null`. Even if we set `EditingStatus=Editing` in the Button handler, it does not work properly. The `DataBind()` method on the `XmlFormView` control must first be called. (Note that `DataBind()` is called automatically in the `PreRender()` ASP.NET page event if it's not called explicitly by your page code.) This involves a postback after setting `EditingStatus` for the `XmlFormView` to be fully initialized. Instead of troubling ourselves with an extra postback, we can use the `visibility` CSS style to mimic similar behavior without the risk of the control being uninitialized.

> **NOTE Adding References to the Project**
>
> You may need to add `using` references to various namespaces as you write code for your ASP.NET page. For example, to use the `XPathNavigator` objects exposed from the `CreateNavigator()` method of the `MainDataSource` property, you'll need to add `using System.Xml.XPath` at the top of your code.

Passing Parameters from the Host to the Form

Say that you have a site where some pages call other pages and pass parameters. One convenient way to send parameter data to a page is to use URL parameters. InfoPath Forms Services automatically passes URL parameters to the form template, which the form template can use through

Timeline of `XmlFormView` Initialization

Initializing the `XmlFormView` control revolves around the `DataBind()` method. Before `DataBind()` is called, you can set some initialization properties. These properties include all of those listed in Table 18.3. Once `DataBind()` is called, these properties may not be changed. Some other properties, however, cannot be used at all until `DataBind()` is called. These properties include `SubmitStatus` and `XmlForm`. Recall that `DataBind()` is implicitly called in the page `PreRender` event, but it can be called explicitly by the host page.

the `Loading` event (in the form template code) or the `Initialize` event (in the ASP.NET host page code). In this example, we'll show you how to map custom parameters to a form from a host page as well as how to handle them in the InfoPath form code. Our goal is to map the passed `InsurerName` parameter from the MyPage.aspx URL in the InfoPath form. In other words, instead of just using the `InsurerName` parameter in the form, we will map it to another name such as `InsName`. The purpose of this hidden mapping is to shield the actual form parameter name from the user so our InfoPath form is less susceptible to a direct input parameter attack. We'll also write some code within the InfoPath form template to handle the parameters. To begin, let's look at how to add parameters to the form.

ASP.NET exposes URL parameters through the `Request` object's `QueryString` property. The `Request` object is globally available in our host page, so there's nothing special we need to do to get parameters from our host page. Now we just need to determine how to set additional form parameters. The `Initialize` event on the `XmlFormView` control provides an `InitializeEventArgs` object that exposes an `InputParameters` property. A similar property (called `LoadingEventArgs`) is passed to the `Loading` event in the form's code (which we'll edit momentarily) that exposes the same `InputParameters` object. To sink the `XmlFormView Initialize` event, click on the *Events* button in the properties dialog for `XmlFormView1`, and double-click in the box adjacent to the *Initialize* text. Figure 18.24 shows the *Properties* window for `XmlFormView1:` after adding the `Initialize` event.

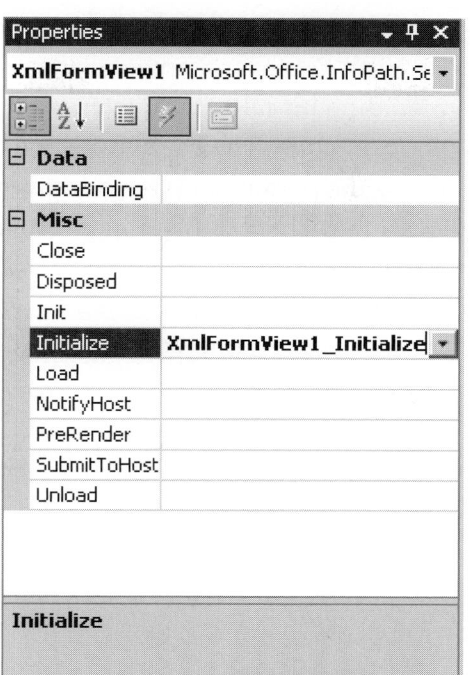

FIGURE 18.24: Adding the `Initialize` event handler in the host page for the `XmlFormView1` control

Now that we are sinking the `Initialize` event for the `XmlFormView1` control, it's time to write the code to pass the parameters to the form. Listing 18.14 shows the code for adding form parameters to the form from within the ASP.NET host page.

LISTING 18.14: Sinking the `XmlFormView1`: Control's `Initialize` Event to Pass a Parameter to the Form

```
protected void XmlFormView1_Initialize(
   object sender, InitializeEventArgs e)
{
   string insurerName = Request.QueryString["InsurerName"];
   e.InputParameters.Add("InsName", insurerName);
}
```

The form is now receiving our own `InsName` parameter from the ASP.NET page. However, the form template isn't actually using the parameter! To use the parameter, we'll write code in the form's `Loading` event handler to set the InsurerName field. It's important to know that both the InsurerName and InsName parameters are available to the form, but since we're masquerading the URL parameter, we want to use our own InsName parameter in form code. The code in Listing 18.15 is within the form template itself to use the parameter passed from the host page. You'll find a form template with the name LifeInsurance_BrowserEnabled_Loading in the samples for this chapter.

LISTING 18.15: Sinking the Loading Event in the Form Template to Use the Parameters

```
public void FormEvents_Loading(object sender, LoadingEventArgs e)
{
    string insurerNameParam = e.InputParameters["InsName"];
    if (!string.IsNullOrEmpty(insurerNameParam))
    {
        XPathNavigator root = this.CreateNavigator();

        XPathNavigator insurerName =
                root.SelectSingleNode("/my:myFields/my:InsurerName",
                NamespaceManager);

        insurerName.SetValue(insurerNameParam);
    }
}
```

WARNING Do Not Assume the Existence of Parameters

In Listing 18.15 we first check for a missing parameter by using the IsNullOrEmpty static method of the String class. This is a safety check that should always be performed when reading parameters in your form. If the parameter doesn't exist, you may want to cancel the Loading event (e.CancelableArgs.Cancel = true), which will fail loading of the form.

Since we've added form code to our form template, it can no longer be user activated through the InfoPath Publishing Wizard to a document library. Our only option is to use the Publishing Wizard to publish an administrator-approved form template. (Chapter 17 discusses publishing and activating form templates for administrator approval.) Once the form template is activated with InfoPath Forms Services, it will have a different

XsnLocation than our previous form template without code. Be sure to update the XsnLocation of the XmlFormView1 control with the new URL. You may also want to reset the visibility style on the control to be visible so we can see our form when we first navigate to the host page.

To see how our host page and form now work, navigate your browser to http://localhost/XmlFormView/MyPage.aspx?InsurerName=Tom%20 Collins, and you'll see that the insurer name appears as "Tom Collins".

Writing InfoPath Form Code in the Host Page Using `XmlFormView`

In these last few examples, you've had a taste of InfoPath form code in the host page. So far we've used the MainDataSource, NamespaceManager, and InputParameters objects to communicate to the InfoPath form in the browser. These properties are all members of the InfoPath object model (OM) that you would normally use within the code of a form template. In fact, almost the entire InfoPath OM is at your disposal through the XmlForm property of the XmlFormView control! You can apply any of the same browser-enabled form code concepts from Chapters 15 and 17 to writing code using the InfoPath OM in a host page.

Before we discuss the XmlForm property exposed by the XmlFormView control, let's first look at all of the properties (there are no useful public methods) that are specifically exposed by the XmlFormView control. Keep in mind that IntelliSense will list much more than what we show in Table 18.4. This is because the XmlFormView class inherits from the System.Web.UI.WebControls.WebParts.WebPart class. Some of these properties are useful for customizing the look of the form, while others let you configure specific aspects of the behaviors of the XmlFormView control or even the form.

> **NOTE** `EditingStatus` **Cannot Be Set to** `Closed`
>
> While it's tempting to set EditingStatus to Closed, it does not work as you would expect. The form is considered closed (and is reflected as such by the EditingStatus) only when one of the following actions occurs.
>
> - The form is closed by clicking the *Close* button in the toolbar.
> - Form submit is configured to close the form after a successful submit.

Table 18.4: All Properties of the `XmlFormView` Control (Includes Properties from Table 18.3 but No Inherited Properties)

`XmlFormView` Property	Returns	Comments
`ShowHeader`	`Boolean`	Sets or gets the visibility of the top toolbar
`ShowFooter`	`Boolean`	Sets or gets the visibility of the bottom toolbar
`PrintWindow`	`Boolean`	Returns the visibility status of the print view window
`EditingState`	`EditingStatus` enumeration	Sets or gets the editing state of the `XmlFormView` control; cannot set `EditingStatus` to `Closed`
`SubmitState`	`SubmitStatus` enumeration	Gets the resulting submit status after main submit finishes
`XsnLocation`	`String`	Gets or sets the form template location

`DataConnectionBaseUrl`
 	
`BaseUrl`
	`Uri`	Gets or sets the server portion (base) of the URL for all subsequent Web service data connections

`XmlLocation`	`String`	Gets or sets the form location
`XmlForm`	`XmlForm`	Returns the `XmlForm` object; similar context as code behind a form template
`SaveLocation`	`String`	Gets or sets the default save location for when the form is saved
`Options`	`String`	Sets to `DisableSave` to disable the *Save* toolbar button

While it's great to have the entire `XmlForm` object at our disposal, it's very important to understand that not all of its members are accessible. For example, you can try to reference the errors in the form by using `XmlFormView1.XmlForm.Errors`. While the ASP.NET host page will build fine in Visual Studio 2005, you may be surprised to see what happens when that code runs. An exception is thrown by InfoPath Forms Services with the message "Calling this property or method from a hosting page is not supported." Unfortunately, there's no good way to tell which properties and methods are supported and which are not without trying to use them. Luckily, we've done the dirty work to get you a list of properties and methods that cannot be called from the host page. See Table 18.5 for a complete list of

TABLE 18.5: Properties and Methods Not Available to the ASP.NET Host Page

Object	Property/Method	Returns
XmlForm	Template	FormTemplate
XmlForm	Errors	FormErrorCollection
XmlForm	ViewInfos	ViewInfoCollection
XmlForm	CurrentView	View
XmlForm	SignedDataBlocks	SignedDataBlock Collection
XmlForm	DataConnections	DataConnection Collection
XmlForm	QueryData Connection	DataConnection
XmForm	NotifyHost(string)	void
DataObject	QueryConnection	DataConnection
DataObject	GetNamedNode Property(xmlNode, name)	String
DataObject	SetNamedNode Property(xmlNode, name)	void

TABLE 18.6: Events the ASP.NET Host Page May Not Sink

Event Type	Event Name	Comments
`Form`	`Loading`	Use the ASP.NET Page `Load` or `Form Initialize` events instead.
`Form`	`VersionUpgrade`	Should be handled by the form template.
`Form`	`Submit`	Should always be directly handled by the form template. `Submit` can be configured to call the hosting environment.
`Form`	`ViewSwitched`	Should be handled by the form template.
`Xml`	`XmlEvent[xpath]`	Should be handled by the form template.
`Xml`	`XmlEvent[xpath, dataObjectName]`	Should be handled by the form template.
`Button`	`Clicked`	Should be handled by the form template.

restricted OM methods and properties. In the next section, we'll show you a workaround to get the errors from InfoPath to the `XmlFormView` control.

In addition to the properties and methods listed in Table 18.5, the host is not permitted to attach event handlers. You are accustomed to having the `Form`, `Xml`, and `Button` event handlers attached for you by InfoPath in the `InternalStartup` method. While the host is not allowed to attach to the events listed in Table 18.6, it does not really stop the host from doing something during any of these events. By writing form code behind the form template for any of the events listed in Table 18.6, you can have the form code call into the host by using the `InvokeHost` method. We'll look at an example that uses the `InvokeHost` method to call into the host in the next section.

InfoPath to Host Communication

It's easy to see that many Web sites on the Internet (and intranet sites as well) use forms. Many of those forms do not (quite yet) leverage the power of

InfoPath Forms Services. Assume that our fictitious IP Insurance company has its own custom ASP.NET forms for customers to use when applying for life insurance. But the life insurance form isn't a standalone ASP.NET page. This page is part of a series of pages that collects information from customers and returns a custom response in HTML that can be easily processed by some of the company's own legacy systems. (And these systems date before the XML days!) The idea is that the customer can save this HTML page to his or her system and simply upload it to one of the legacy systems when he or she needs to file a claim.

Here is a case where it would be nice to use a browser-enabled InfoPath form. It's a perfect fit for collecting data from other sources (from URL parameters, data connections in the form template, and so on), presenting the data, and having the customer fill out the form. While it seems like a match made in heaven, how can InfoPath return a custom HTML response? From an InfoPath traditionalist point of view, this may seem impossible. And in an InfoPath-only world, it actually is not possible! But in a hosted ASP.NET page, we can leverage the flexibility of ASP.NET to do the work. And as a bonus, the ASP.NET life insurance page that IP Insurance already uses has this custom HTML logic already written. Using an InfoPath form might not be so bad after all. In this case, we'll consider submitting to the hosting environment, otherwise known as `SubmitToHost`.

Submitting to the Hosting Environment Using `SubmitToHost`

We already know how to receive data using data connections in InfoPath. In the last section, we looked at passing parameters through ASP.NET to the form. In this section, to fulfill the needs of IP Insurance, our goal is to use ASP.NET by calling into the host page as the submit action for our form template. Since we're reusing the life insurance form from earlier in the chapter, you may recall that the main form submit is already configured to send data to the hosting environment. To confirm, open the form template in design mode and visit the *Submit Options* item under the *Tools* menu. *Allow users to submit this form* should be checked, along with *Send form data to a single destination.* The drop-down should have *Hosting environment* selected. Since the form is all set up for submitting to the hosting environment, the next step is to sink the `SubmitToHost` event in the host page.

In Visual Studio 2005, go back to the `XmlFormView1` *Properties* window (refer back to Figure 18.24) and select the *Events* button. Double-click in the box adjacent to the `SubmitToHost` event name. Visual Studio will create a method named `XmlFormView1_SubmitToHost` to sink the `SubmitToHost` event. This method is called by the form when the form is submitted. Since it's in the context of the host page, you can use any ASP.NET code (including the InfoPath object model through the `XmlFormView1:` control) as necessary. In this example, we take over the ASP.NET response stream from Forms Services and cut it off with `Response.End()` before the form can render itself again. Listing 18.16 shows the source code for the `SubmitToHost` event handler in the host page.

LISTING 18.16: Handling Submit in the Host Page with `SubmitToHost`

```
protected void XmlFormView1_SubmitToHost(
    object sender, SubmitToHostEventArgs e)
{
   Response.Write("<h2>Thank you for your submission!</h2><br>");
   Response.Write("<h5> Please select 'Save As' on the 'File' menu in
              your browser to save this for future claims.</h5><p>");

   Response.Write("<span id=formdata style='visibility:hidden'>");
   XPathNavigator root =
         XmlFormView1.XmlForm.MainDataSource.CreateNavigator();

   Response.Write(root.OuterXml);
   Response.Write("</span>");
   Response.End();
}
```

Figure 18.25 shows the effect of clicking the *Submit* toolbar button in the form.

Thank you for your submission!

Please select 'Save As' on the 'File' menu in your browser to save this for future claims.

FIGURE 18.25: Host page handling the form submit by sending a custom response

In more complex forms that have multiple submit connections, you may want to have more than one submit connection for `SubmitToHost`. This is easy to do: Just add a new connection (as many times as you need) within the *Data Connections* dialog. (Access the dialog from the *Data Connections* menu item on the *Tools* menu in InfoPath design mode.) When choosing a submit connection in the Data Connection Wizard, select the *To a hosting environment, such as an ASP.NET page or a hosting application* option. Every `SubmitToHost` connection you create will be given a name that you choose. We suggest naming each connection appropriately so you can handle them in your host page when that submit connection is executed. Notice that there is only one `SubmitToHost` event handler in your ASP.NET host page to handle any number of `SubmitToHost` connections by the form. The best way to handle this many-to-one mapping is to look at the name of the `SubmitToHost` connection and run whatever code should be associated with that connection name. Listing 18.17 shows one possible example of how you might handle this mapping, which should clarify this concept.

LISTING 18.17: How to Handle Multiple `SubmitToHost` Form Connections in a Host Page

```
switch (e.AdapterName)
{
    case "NewCustomerData":
        // write code here to handle SubmitToHost
        // by the "NewCustomerData" connection
        break;

    case "UpdatedProfile":
        // handles the connection named "UpdatedProfile"
        break;

    // handle more SubmitToHost connections as necessary
    default:
        throw new NotImplementedException(
            "This SubmitToHost connection is not implemented: "
            + e.AdapterName);
}
```

Using `NotifyHost` for Nonsubmit Cases

There are several cases when the form needs the host page to do something, but it shouldn't be considered a submit action. A key example of using such functionality is when you're trying to do something that InfoPath Forms Services doesn't support, such as showing a message box dialog. We mentioned in Chapter 14 that you cannot show a dialog box message using rules when a form is filled out in the browser. However, you can use a host page to work around that limitation and show a dialog! In this sample, we'll show you how to show a dialog box with a custom message. Although this

Submit Is Asynchronous

Submitting a browser-enabled form, including by using `SubmitToHost`, is always asynchronous. Let's explain what this means and give a simple example. Recall from Chapter 17 that Forms Services records the form-editing actions within the browser. Only occasionally will the form require a postback to communicate the changes with the server. Say, for example, you have a Button control in your form template that runs form code. The code behind the Button may do something similar to the following: switch views, submit the form, and set a data source field to a value. Notice that submit is not the last action. When the Button click is replayed on the server, the order of operations is the following: switch views, set a data source field to a value, and finally send data back to the browser with a pending submit action. No matter what actions happen before submit, submit is always added as a pending action when data is sent back to the form. Ultimately, the pending submit action requires another (automatic) postback to actually execute.

is just a simple example, you can take the ideas we present and let your imagination run wild with possibilities!

Earlier in this chapter we introduced the `NotifyHost` method. You'll be glad to know that this method also works with hosted browser forms. Simply call it within your InfoPath form code, and Forms Services fires the `NotifyHost` event handler in the ASP.NET page. For this example, we're going to call `NotifyHost` behind a Button control in the LifeInsurance_BrowserEnabled_NotifyHost sample form template. The purpose of the Button is to check the form for errors and pass them as a string to the host. However, if there aren't any errors, the button still shows a dialog as a proof-of-concept. The code behind the new Button (called *Validate Form*) is shown in Listing 18.18. (Notice the escaping of the backslash characters so the JScript code properly decodes the carriage return and newline characters.)

LISTING 18.18: Code Behind the Validate Form Button in the Life Insurance Form Template

```
public void ValidateForm_Clicked(object sender, ClickedEventArgs e)
{
    string errorString = string.Empty;
    foreach (FormError error in Errors)
    {
        errorString += error.Site.Name + ": "
                     + error.Message + "\\r\\n";
    }

    if (string.IsNullOrEmpty(errorString))
        errorString = "No errors exist in the form!";
    else
        errorString = Errors.Count
                     + " errors found:\\r\\n\\r\\n"
                     + errorString;

    this.NotifyHost(errorString);
}
```

To handle the `NotifyHost` call in the host page, simply create the event handler using the *Properties* window for the `XmlFormView1` control. The process is similar to what we did with the `Initialize` and `SubmitToHost` event handlers. Once the event handler is created in the host page, the next step is to implement showing a dialog in the browser. We're going to do it in JScript code within the HTML of the browser. To inject the JScript into the page, we'll use the ASP.NET `Literal` control. (You can find more information on the `Literal` control in MSDN.) We inserted a `Literal` control from the Toolbox into the MyPage.aspx page with a default ID of `Literal1`. The `NotifyHost` event handler, shown in Listing 18.19, populates `Literal1` with JScript code that the browser executes after the `NotifyHost` event handler completes.

LISTING 18.19: Using the Host Page to Display a Dialog Box Message in the Browser

```
protected void XmlFormView1_NotifyHost(
    object sender,
    NotifyHostEventArgs e)
{
    Literal1.Text = "<script lang='jscript'>"
            + "alert('" + e.Notification + "');"
            + "</script>";
}
```

FIGURE 18.26: Clicking the Validate Form button shows a dialog box message in the browser

Figure 18.26 shows a sample dialog.

Did you notice the state of the form when the message box (from Figure 18.26) appeared? If you've written script in Internet Explorer before, you know that global JScript code is one of the first things that runs when the page is loaded in the browser. While there's nothing wrong with using global JScript in general, the problem with injecting JScript code into the host page is that InfoPath Forms Services runs its own script code after a postback or after the form is fully loaded in the browser. Figure 18.27 shows how the form looks while the dialog box has top-level focus.

As you can probably see, running arbitrary script in a host page may be disruptive to the form. In fact, any JScript defined by the host page (including

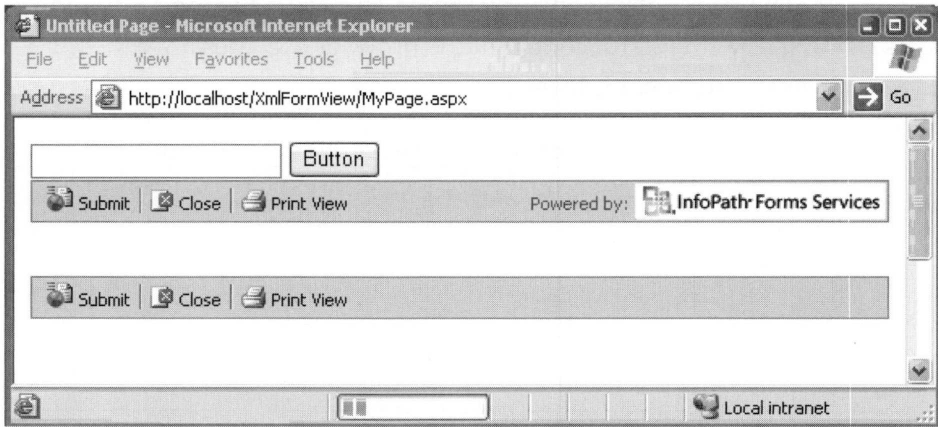

FIGURE 18.27: State of the life insurance form while the dialog box still has focus

script injected by ASP.NET, as in this example) may run asynchronously relative to the form JScript. This may surface as intermittent race conditions that could cause script errors and leave the form in an indeterminate state.

> **WARNING** Use Body `onload` Event Instead of Global Script
>
> It's a safer bet to use the `onload` event of the HTML body tag instead of global script. While this example just happens to "work" in this case, we don't recommend it as a best practice. Its purpose is to demonstrate interacting with the form from the host and its effects (albeit ill) on the form. If using `onload`, you may need to chain your `onload` handler to the existing document `onload` handler. Whether or not chaining is necessary will depend on when your `onload` handler is actually assigned. The exact determination is beyond the scope of this book (since it relies on details of ASP.NET and HTML document processing); we recommend thoroughly testing any `onload` handlers for proper behavior and correctness in form rendering.

In our case with Figure 18.27, rendering by Forms Services has been temporary halted to show the dialog. If our JScript code depended on any HTML in the form, it would fail in this specific case because nothing yet exists. To let the form fully render and mitigate most race conditions, consider wrapping your JScript code by using `window.setTimeout`. The `setTimeout` method (provided by Internet Explorer) waits a specified number of milliseconds before running your script on a separate thread. Its use is as follows:

```
window.setTimeout(function() { alert('your code goes here'); }, 500);
```

The exact wait time (500 milliseconds in this example) will depend on the results of extensive testing of your form. As you can see, using JScript in the host page is a delicate balancing act, and the host page developer should take measures to ensure it does not affect the state of the form in the HTML.

> **NOTE** Host OM Properties Are Not Available from Forms Services
>
> The `HostName`, `Hosted`, and `Host` properties are not available from the code of a browser-enabled form template to communicate to the host.

What's Next?

In this chapter, you learned about hosting InfoPath in order to take advantage of many of the features available in the InfoPath client application in your own applications. We first showed you how other Microsoft Office applications take advantage of InfoPath in their Document Information Panels. We also showed you how to create your own forms based on SharePoint content types in order to create your own custom Document Information Panel. Next, we showed you how easy it is to host the InfoPath form control in a managed code Windows application. Finally, we looked at hosting a browser form in a custom ASP.NET Web page by using the `XmlFormView` control.

Hosting InfoPath is just one way you can reuse and extend the features available in InfoPath. In the next chapter, we'll expand on this by showing you another way that InfoPath allows you to customize the user experience—by creating your own custom controls using ActiveX technology.

19 Building Custom Controls Using ActiveX Technologies

Getting Started

When designing form templates, you've seen that InfoPath provides an abundance of built-in controls. The types of built-in controls range from simple ones, such as the Text Box, Drop-Down List Box, and Check Box, to more complicated controls, such as the Repeating Table, Choice Group, and Choice Section. Also, as you learned in Chapter 10, you can create your own custom controls by combining other controls into template parts. This is all well and good, but what if you need a control that InfoPath doesn't provide and you can't build by using other InfoPath controls? The answer is simple (relatively speaking)—just build your own.

In addition to template parts, InfoPath supports other types of custom controls—those built using ActiveX technologies. Since ActiveX controls have been around for over ten years, there are hundreds, even thousands, of them to choose from. In fact, you probably have a few hundred ActiveX controls already installed on your computer. Many of these controls come preinstalled with Windows; others are installed by various other applications, such as the 2007 Microsoft Office system. Although not all of the controls installed on your computer can be used with InfoPath, many can. So, if you happen to need a slider control, an up/down control, or a calendar control, it's likely that you can find an existing one that can be used with InfoPath without any modification whatsoever. And, because InfoPath supports controls built by using ActiveX technologies, if you can't find a control that suits your needs or doesn't work quite right with InfoPath, you can always create your own ActiveX control that does what you need or wraps an existing control to make it work in InfoPath.

In this chapter, we'll first show you how to use existing ActiveX controls in InfoPath. We'll talk about what types of controls are supported, how you can install them into the *Controls* task pane, and how to put them to use in your form templates. Then we'll show you how to create your own ActiveX controls that will work well in InfoPath forms. When we show you how to create your own controls, we'll first talk about how to do so in unmanaged code using C++ and then how to do the same in managed code using C#.

Installing and Using ActiveX Controls

As with template parts, before you can use an ActiveX control in a form template, you have to install it. However, whereas the process of installing a template part is very easy—you just specify the location of the .xtp file—installing an ActiveX control is slightly more difficult, but not by much.

Adding an ActiveX Control to the Controls Task Pane

The first step is to click on the *Add or Remove Custom Controls* link at the bottom of the *Controls* task pane. As you've seen before, this opens the *Add or Remove Custom Controls* dialog, which lists all the controls installed in the *Custom* category of the *Controls* task pane—both template parts and ActiveX controls. Clicking on the *Add* button opens the Add Custom Control Wizard. The *Select a Control Type* page is opened initially, as you've seen before. By default, the *Template Part* option is selected. To install an ActiveX control, as you can probably guess, you must first select the *ActiveX Control* option and then click the *Next* button.

At this point, a list of all the ActiveX controls on your computer is retrieved from the registry. As mentioned earlier, you likely have hundreds of controls installed on your system, but not all of them will work in

InfoPath. (You may wonder why InfoPath shows ActiveX controls that don't work in InfoPath. As you'll learn shortly, it's not possible to tell which controls will work in InfoPath without instantiating them. As you might guess, instantiating each and every control on your system would be quite costly.)

The main requirement for using an ActiveX control in InfoPath is that the control must be safe for scripting and initialization. (More information about safe initialization and scripting of ActiveX controls is available in MSDN, as referenced in the Appendix.) If you choose a control that is not specified as safe and then click the *Next* button, an error message will appear, and the wizard will not proceed to the next step. However, if you choose a safe control, such as the `Microsoft UpDown Control` 6.0, as shown in Figure 19.1, you will proceed to the next step in the wizard after you click the *Next* button. (Note that, depending on which software applications you

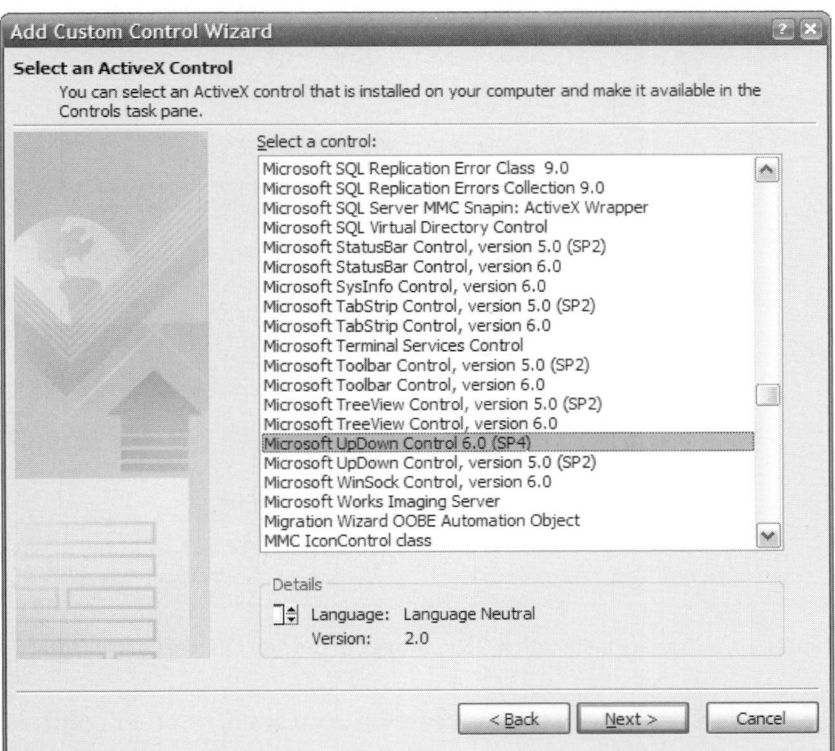

FIGURE 19.1: Add Custom Control Wizard showing the `Microsoft UpDown Control` 6.0 (SP4) selected in the list of ActiveX controls

have installed on your computer, you may not see the `Microsoft UpDown Control` in the list of controls. However, the information in this chapter applies to any of the controls in the list.)

This brings you to the *Specify Installation Options* page (Figure 19.2), where you can specify a CAB (.cab) file that can be used to install the control onto your users' machines. If you know the control you chose will already be installed (either by Microsoft Windows, Microsoft Office, or other means), this step isn't necessary. In the case of the `Microsoft UpDown Control` 6.0, which is installed by Microsoft Office, we know that our users will have this control installed, so we don't need to specify a CAB file.

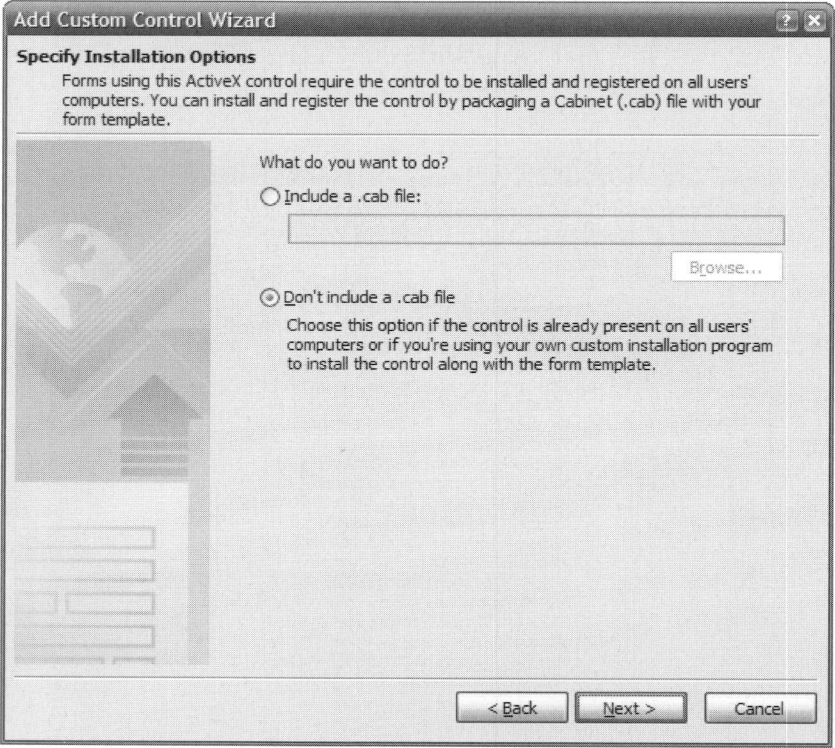

FIGURE 19.2: Specify Installation Options page of the Add Custom Control Wizard

For ActiveX controls that you create on your own, or other controls that are not installed by default, you need to install the ActiveX control on all your users' computers before they can use the control in your form. (If a user tries to use a form that contains an ActiveX control that isn't installed on the computer, he or she will receive an error from InfoPath and won't be able to open the form.) One way to install an ActiveX control on a user's computer is to use a custom installation program. However, if you have a CAB file for your ActiveX control, you can specify it during this step of the wizard. The CAB file will then be packaged with your form template, and the control will automatically be installed by InfoPath the first time the control needs to be used. However, in order to use a CAB file in InfoPath to install your control, you will need to digitally sign your CAB file using a certificate from a trusted authority such as VeriSign. (Explaining how to create CAB files is outside the scope of this book. You can find information about creating CAB files on MSDN, as referenced in the Appendix.)

When you click the *Next* button, the *Specify a Binding Property* page opens (Figure 19.3). In this page of the wizard, you specify the property you want to use for binding the control to fields or groups in the data source.

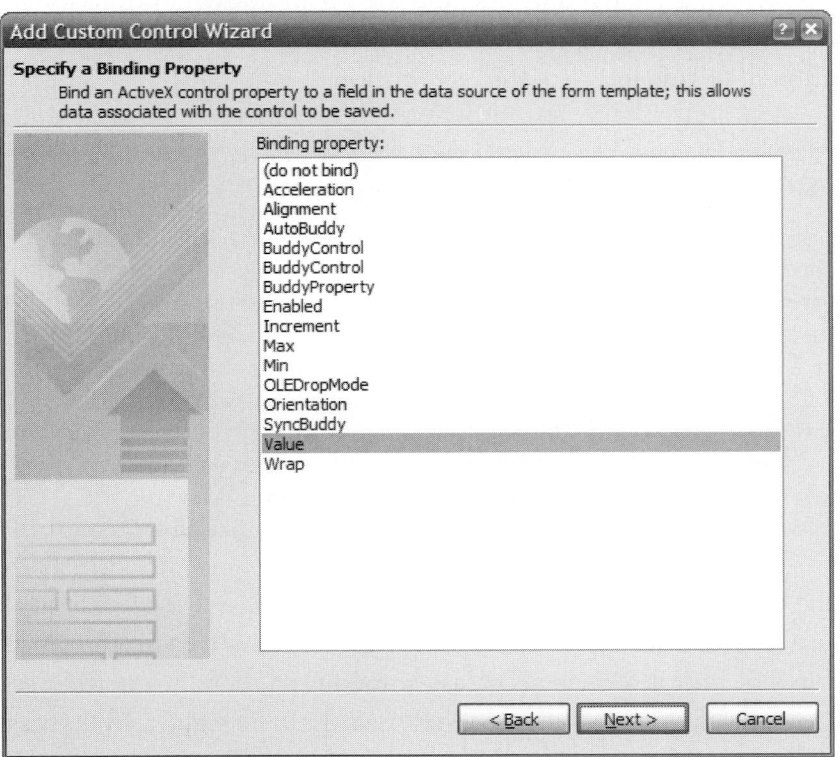

FIGURE 19.3: Specify a Binding Property page of the Add Custom Control Wizard

Like the built-in InfoPath controls, ActiveX controls can be bound to data in the data source. However, this is not a requirement. Sometimes you might not want to bind an ActiveX control to data in the form, such as when a control displays a video or music clip. If this is the case, choose the *(do not bind)* option from the list.

In most cases, however, you will want to bind values from the control to data in the data source. Any properties exposed by the ActiveX control can be used for binding. The `Microsoft UpDown Control`, for example, exposes quite a few properties, as you can see in Figure 19.3. You can bind any one of the properties shown in the list to the data in the data source. If a control exposes a property named `Value`, this will be the property selected by default in the list. (If the `Value` property doesn't exist, the *(do not bind)* item will be selected.) In most controls that expose it, the `Value` property contains the value of the data in the control. In the case of the UpDown control, for example, the `Value` property contains the current value stored in the control, which is changed by clicking the up and down buttons. Since this is exactly what we want, we'll leave the binding property set to the default selection of `Value` and click the *Next* button.

NOTE Controls That Can't Be Aggregated

In order for an ActiveX control to be bound correctly to data when a user fills out a form, the control must be able to be aggregated. (For more information about aggregation, please refer to MSDN.) Since most controls normally can be aggregated, this doesn't usually present a problem. Although you will be able to install and insert them into a form template, those controls that can't be aggregated may not work correctly in InfoPath when a user fills out the form. Normally, you won't need to worry about this since ActiveX controls created with Visual Studio have aggregation turned on by default.

The next page of the wizard, the *Specify an Enable or Disable Property* page (Figure 19.4), allows you to specify a property that will be used to enable or disable the control. This is necessary sometimes when the control needs to be disabled, such as when the entire form is digitally signed. In that case, all controls in the form are disabled. If the ActiveX control cannot be disabled,

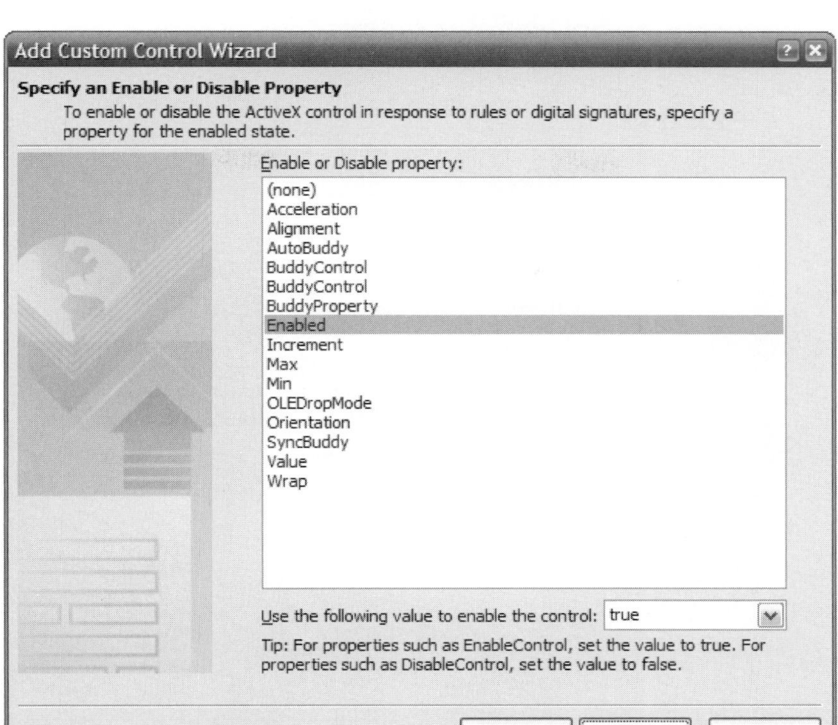

FIGURE 19.4: Specify an Enable or Disable Property page of the Add Custom Control Wizard

it will not work well in these situations. Similar to the `Value` binding property just mentioned, if the control exposes an `Enabled` property, that property will be selected by default in the list on this page. If the `Enabled` property doesn't exist, the *(none)* item will be selected. If you don't choose a property other than *(none)*, the control cannot be disabled. In our example, the `Microsoft UpDown Control` does expose an `Enabled` property, so we'll keep that one selected.

This page of the wizard also allows you to choose the value that should be passed to the control to enable it. Since the property is called `Enabled`, it makes sense to keep the default value set to *true* to enable the control. However, if the property were called `Disabled`, we would want to change this value to *false.*

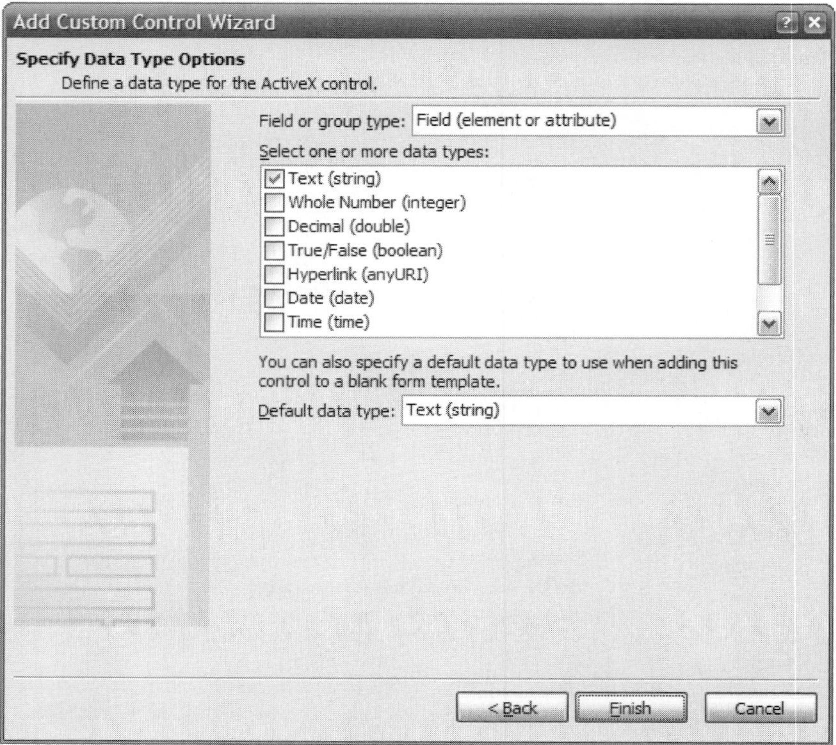

FIGURE 19.5: Specify Data Type Options page of the Add Custom Control Wizard

Clicking the *Next* button then opens the *Specify Data Type Options* page (Figure 19.5). Besides the binding property specified earlier, the options you set in this page of the wizard are the most important. The options you select here tell InfoPath what type of elements to create in the XML Schema when you insert a control (with the *Automatically create data source* option checked in the *Controls* task pane) and which types of data the control can be bound to. Unfortunately, there's no way for InfoPath to tell you in the wizard what type of data binding the control supports—that's up to the developer of the control. The control author is responsible for publishing documentation that explains how to use the control. However, in most cases, especially for existing controls that weren't built specifically for InfoPath, the default data type options should suffice.

TABLE 19.1: Field or Group Types

Type	Description
Field (element or attribute)	The control can be bound to a field or attribute.
Field (element with custom data type)	The control can be bound to a field. The data will contain XML from a custom namespace that you specify. This is similar to the `Rich Text Box` control in InfoPath, which is bound to a field that can contain XHTML.
Field or Group (any data type)	The control can be bound to a field or group node of any type. This type is typically used when a control can be bound to an XML subtree. (A group node is created in the data source when you insert a control that supports this type and have the *Automatically create data source* option selected in the *Controls* task pane.)

Let's look at the various data type options available. The first data type option you need to specify is the type of field or group. The *Field or group type* drop-down lists three options that specify what types of XML elements are supported by the control (Table 19.1). In most cases, unless you know that the control supports data from a custom namespace or that it binds to an XML tree, you want to choose the default option—*Field (element or attribute).* For existing controls, this is the most common type of data type binding supported and is akin to InfoPath's field-level controls, such as the Text Box and Drop-Down List Box.

Depending on which type of field or group data you choose, you can specify further data type options. In the case of the *Field (element or attribute)* type, you can specify which data types are supported and the default data type to use should you choose more than one.

If you choose *Field (element with custom data type)* as the field or group type, you will be required to enter the namespace URI (as shown in Figure 19.6) that will be used to validate the elements and attributes

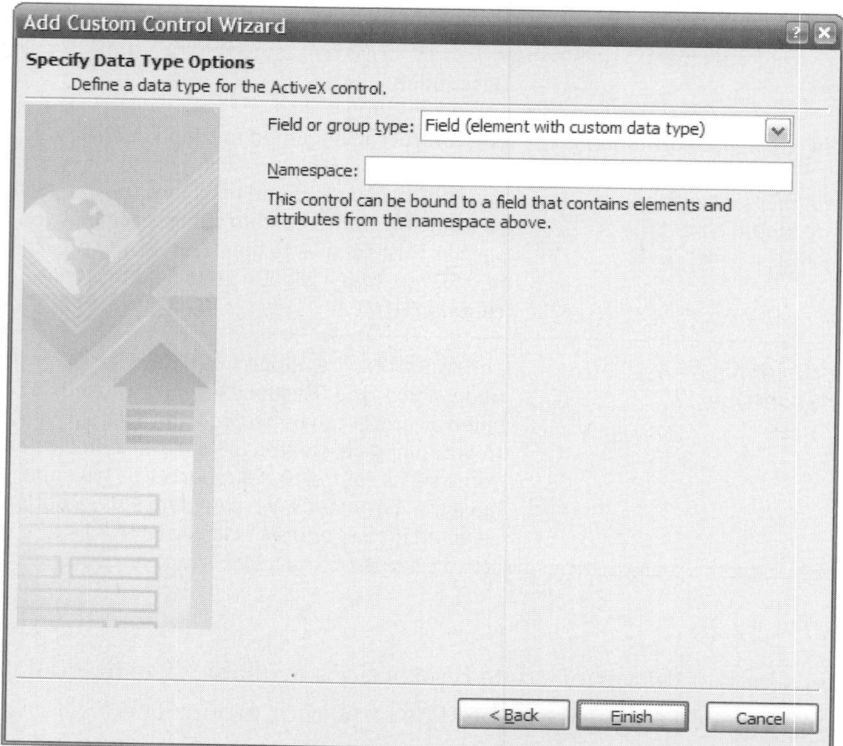

FIGURE 19.6: Specify Data Type Options page showing the Field (element with custom data type) option

contained in the data. (Note that validation is lax, which means that if the schema for the namespace can be located, it will be used to validate any elements from that namespace. If the schema cannot be located, no validation will occur.)

TIP Adding an ActiveX Control That Consumes Rich Text Data

You will notice that when you choose *Field (element or attribute)* as the field or group type, there is no Rich Text (XHTML) data type as there is in the *Field or Group Properties* dialog for a field. If you wish to add an ActiveX control that consumes XHTML, choose *Field (element with custom data type)* as the field or group type in the *Specify Data Type Options* wizard page. For the namespace, enter the URI of the XHTML namespace: http://www.w3.org/1999/xhtml.

You will notice that, in the *Specify Data Type Options* page, if you choose *Field or Group (any data type)* as the field or group type, there are no additional options. In this case, the control can be bound to any type of field or group element in the data source. You normally specify this option when you want to use a control that understands XML and will be bound to an XML subtree in the data source.

For the `Microsoft UpDown Control`, let's just accept the default options on the *Specify Data Type Options* page. After clicking the *Finish* button, you'll see the *Custom Control Added* wizard page, which tells you that the control has been added to the *Controls* task pane. Similar to template parts, the new control will be available in the *Custom* section of the *Controls* task pane.

Now you can use this ActiveX control like any other control. When you insert the new control into a form template while the *Automatically create data source* option is selected in the *Controls* task pane, either a field or a group will be created in the data source, just like when you add any of the built-in controls to your form template. The type of data created depends on the options you chose in the *Specify Data Type Options* page when adding the custom control. If you open the data source and right-click on an existing field or group, the control may be recommended as a possible control to bind to the current data type. Again, whether or not the ActiveX control is suggested depends on the data type options you specified when adding the control. (In the case of ActiveX controls, as with template parts, when you right-click on a field or group in the data source, the custom control may not appear in the immediate list of suggestions. You may have to click on the *More* menu item to find the custom control you want.)

Property Pages

Once you insert an ActiveX control into a form template, the next logical thing you will probably want to do is customize various properties of the control. When working with built-in controls in InfoPath, you're used to opening the properties dialog for a control to customize various aspects of the control, such as size, conditional formatting, and even the screen tip for the control. Customizing properties for an ActiveX control is no different.

If you open the properties dialog for an ActiveX control, you will see the familiar *Data, Display, Size,* and *Advanced* tabs. However, you may notice something different. Some ActiveX controls have additional tabs in their

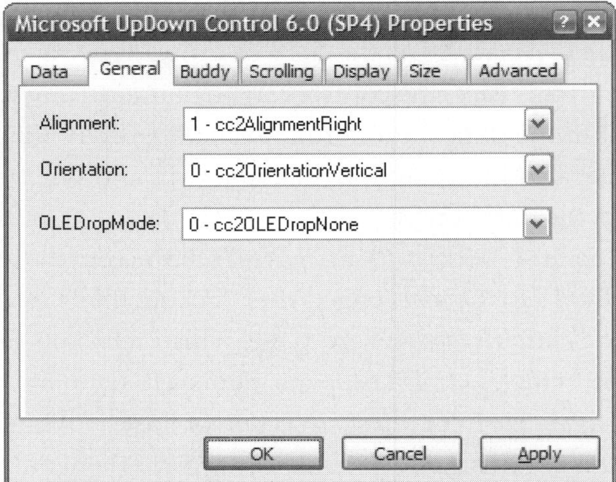

FIGURE 19.7: Properties dialog for the `Microsoft UpDown Control`

properties dialogs. If a control exposes custom property pages to allow you to customize the control, InfoPath will include those property pages in the control properties dialog. For example, Figure 19.7 shows the properties dialog for the `Microsoft UpDown Control`. This control exposes three additional property tabs—*General, Buddy,* and *Scrolling*—that enable you to customize various aspects of the control.

> **NOTE** **Sharing the Development of Form Templates Containing ActiveX Controls**
>
> You may work in a development environment where more than one person works on a form template (e.g., one person designs the layout and another adds the code). If that is the case, and a form template you are designing uses an ActiveX control, each form designer must add the ActiveX control to his or her *Controls* task pane. (The control must be installed and registered on the machine as well.) Otherwise, InfoPath will not recognize the ActiveX control in the form template as a control and will not treat it as such. Certain control features, such as the properties dialog, will not work.

Building Custom Controls for InfoPath Using ActiveX

The `Microsoft UpDown Control` is one example of an existing ActiveX control that works well in InfoPath. You can insert it into a form template to increase or decrease the value of a field by using up and down buttons. This control wasn't built specifically for InfoPath but works quite well nonetheless. Many other existing controls also work well in InfoPath form templates. But what do you do if you can't find a control that satisfies your requirements? In that case, your only option may be to build your own.

Implementing an ActiveX control is nothing new. In fact, there are many books available that will tell you everything you need to know about creating ActiveX controls. Therefore, we won't show you the process of building a control step by step. We'll mainly concentrate on those aspects of implementing ActiveX controls that pertain to InfoPath. First, we'll talk about building ActiveX controls for InfoPath in C++. (Although we are using C++, the concepts we will discuss apply to Visual Basic 6 as well.) Then, we'll tell you what you need to know to do the same in managed code with C#.

However, whether you create an InfoPath control using C++, C#, or any other technology, the control must provide certain functionality to work well in InfoPath. Table 19.2 lists the different features that a control should implement. There is only one required interface that the control must implement—`IObjectSafety`. However, if your control implements only this one interface, you will not be able to bind it to data, among other things. Therefore, as you'll see, you'll want your control to implement one or more of the other interfaces and properties.

Building an ActiveX Control for InfoPath Using C++

To demonstrate how to implement ActiveX controls for InfoPath using C++, we've included two ActiveX controls with the samples for this chapter on the book's Web site—`SimpleInfoPathActiveX` and `InfoPathChart`. The `SimpleInfoPathActiveX` control is a simple control (as its name implies) that basically is just a `Rich Edit` control. Although this isn't very useful since InfoPath already includes the `Rich Text Box` control, the `SimpleInfoPath-ActiveX` control shows you how to build a control that binds to a simple field. When installing this control, choose the *Field (element or attribute)* type on the *Specify Data Type Options* page of the Add Custom Control Wizard.

Table 19.2: Interfaces and Properties That Controls Should Implement to Work Well in InfoPath

Feature	Description
`IObjectSafety` interface	Controls must implement this interface and specify that the control is safe for scripting and initialization in order to be included in InfoPath forms.
`Binding` property	This property must be implemented by the control if the control is bound to data in the data source.
`Enabled` property	This property is needed if you want to enable and disable the control when necessary. (However, it is not necessary for a control to implement this property if it implements the `InfoPathControl` interface.)
`IPropertyNotifySink` interface	The control must call into InfoPath's `IPropertyNotifySink` interface in order to alert InfoPath of changes to the control.
`InfoPathControl` interface	This interface allows the control to receive calls from InfoPath when the control is being initialized/uninitialized or enabled/disabled and when the control should save its state.
`IViewObject` interface	This interface is required if the control needs to display its data when printing or in the snapshot of the view created when digitally signing the form. This interface is also necessary if you want the control to display its view representation when the form is exported to MHT (see Chapter 12).

The process of implementing a control that binds to the *Field (element with custom data type)* type is very similar to the way that `SimpleInfoPathActiveX` control is implemented. Therefore, we have not included a separate control that binds to this data type. We will, however, talk about the differences as we go.

The second control—`InfoPathChart`—shows you how to implement a control that binds to an XML subtree. This control will use the data in the data source to draw a pie chart. When installing this control, choose the *Field or Group (any data type)* type on the *Specify Data Type Options* page. (We will focus mainly on the `SimpleInfoPathActiveX` control when talking about how to implement an ActiveX control for InfoPath. `InfoPathChart` is included with the samples to give you an idea of how to deal with an XML subtree. When necessary, however, we will talk about those things that are important to know when implementing a control of this type.)

Although these two controls bind to different types of data, the process of implementing them is basically the same. If you've ever built an ActiveX control using C++ before, you likely have used the Active Template Library (ATL) to do so. ATL greatly simplifies the process of building ActiveX controls. Therefore, we will use ATL to implement our ActiveX controls for InfoPath. Let's get started.

Obviously, after creating the basic ATL project for your control, you'll need to add the actual ActiveX control to the project by using the ATL Control Wizard. There's nothing really unusual about this wizard when you're creating controls to use in InfoPath. However, keep a couple of things in mind. First, when you get to the *Interfaces* page of the wizard, you will most likely want to have your control implement the `IPropertyNotifySink` interface. If you want to communicate changes in your control to InfoPath, which will definitely be the case if your control is editable and binds to data, you need to include this interface. Through this interface, the control alerts InfoPath that the data has changed, causing InfoPath to update the data source.

Second, if you want your control to include property pages for stock properties, such as background color, border color, or font, when you get to the *Stock Properties* page of the wizard (Figure 19.8), you should choose the properties that you want your control to implement. When you complete the wizard, the necessary code will be added to your control to support these properties and to include property pages for properties that have corresponding stock property pages. As we discussed earlier, these property pages will be included in the properties dialog for the control in InfoPath when designing a form template. Of course, you aren't limited to only property pages for stock properties. You can easily build and expose your own property pages using ATL.

Also, when choosing the stock properties to include in your control, you'll notice that there is an `Enabled` property. Remember that when you're installing an ActiveX control into the InfoPath *Controls* task pane, if the control includes an `Enabled` property, that property will be selected by default in the *Specify an Enable or Disable Property* page of the Add Custom Control

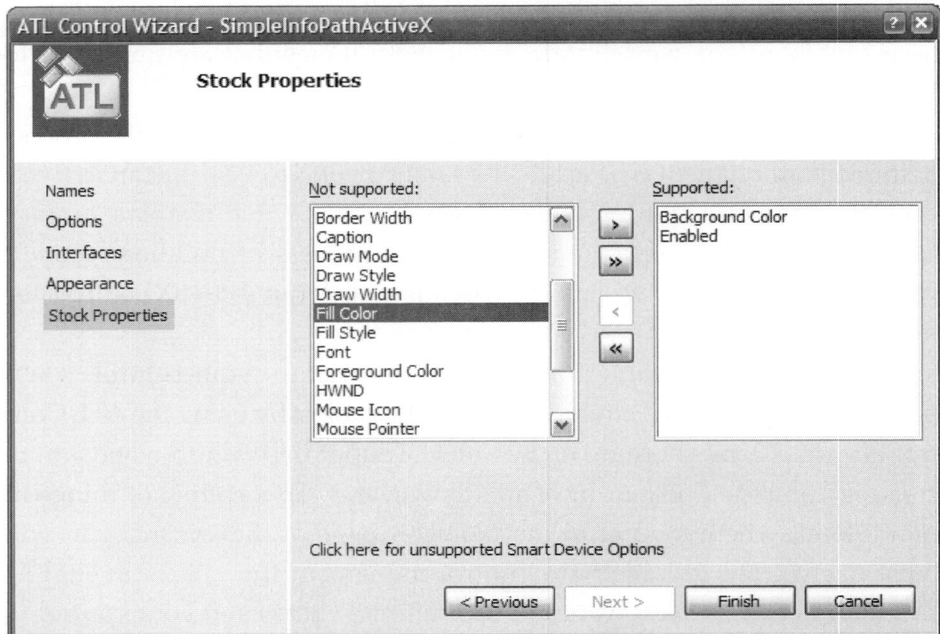

FIGURE 19.8: Stock Properties page of the ATL Control Wizard for the `SimpleInfoPathActiveX` control

Wizard (refer back to Figure 19.4). Therefore, you will want to include this property when choosing the stock properties. Otherwise, InfoPath won't be able to disable your control. (Of course, you can always use another property for this purpose if you like.)

You will also notice in the *Stock Properties* page of the ATL Control Wizard that there is no `Value` property. (Remember that InfoPath will automatically choose this property when you get to the *Specify a Binding Property* page, as shown earlier in Figure 19.3.) You could instead use the `Text` stock property, which is included in the list of properties, and require that your users choose that one when installing your control. However, for our controls, we'll go ahead and implement our own `Value` property, which we'll show you how to do shortly.

Once you are done choosing the stock properties you want to include in your control, just click the *Finish* button to complete the wizard. At this point, you can build your control, but you won't be able to use it in InfoPath. Let's talk about the code changes we need to make to install this control into the InfoPath *Controls* task pane and use it in our form templates.

> **NOTE** **Why Can't I Rebuild My ActiveX Control After Using It in InfoPath?**
>
> Each time you test your ActiveX control and need to make a change, you will need to close InfoPath completely to rebuild your control. When a form contains an ActiveX control, a lock is placed on the DLL and is not released until InfoPath is shut down.

Specifying That an ActiveX Control Is Safe

The main reason that your control won't work in InfoPath at this point is that it doesn't register itself as being safe for scripting and initialization. Remember, earlier we mentioned that InfoPath requires that a control be registered as being safe before you can install it or use it in a form. Luckily, specifying that your control is safe is fairly easy.

> **NOTE** **Is an ActiveX Control Really Safe?**
>
> The simple fact that a control registers itself as being safe for scripting and initialization does not, necessarily, mean that it is indeed safe. It is up to the developer of the control to ensure that the control is actually safe when registering it as such. InfoPath, and other applications such as Internet Explorer, for that matter, trust that if the control is registered as safe, the control's developer is being honest. Therefore, we recommend that you never use an existing ActiveX control unless you have obtained it from a trusted source.

A control can specify that it is safe for scripting and initialization in two ways. The first and easiest method is for the control to implement the `IObjectSafety` interface. If you are using ATL, implementing this interface is a snap. Just add the following line of code to the inheritance list for the ActiveX control class:

```
public IObjectSafetyImpl<SimpleInfoPathControl,
    INTERFACESAFE_FOR_UNTRUSTED_CALLER |
    INTERFACESAFE_FOR_UNTRUSTED_DATA>
```

The `IObjectSafetyImpl` class implements the `IObjectSafety` interface for you. The code as it is shown here specifies that the control is safe for scripting (INTERFACESAFE_FOR_UNTRUSTED_CALLER) and initialization (INTERFACESAFE_FOR_UNTRUSTED_DATA).

The second, and less common, method is to register two category IDs in the registry when the control class is registered using a tool such as regsvr32. The two category IDs to register are CATID_SafeForScripting and CATID_SafeForInitializing, both defined in the objsafe.h file included in the Windows Platform SDK with Visual Studio 2005. To register these categories, include these two category IDs under the Implemented Categories key when registering the control. (For more information about category IDs, refer to the MSDN article "Safe Initialization and Scripting for ActiveX Controls" referenced in the Appendix.)

Now that you've done the work to register your control as safe for scripting and initialization, once you've built it, you can install it into the InfoPath *Controls* task pane in design mode and add it to your form. Once the control is inserted into a form template, it acts just like a built-in InfoPath control. For example, since we chose to implement the background color property when creating our control, it will even include additional property pages when you open the properties dialog for the control, as shown in Figure 19.9.

At this point, however, unless your control doesn't do anything specific with the data in the form, it won't completely function as a normal InfoPath

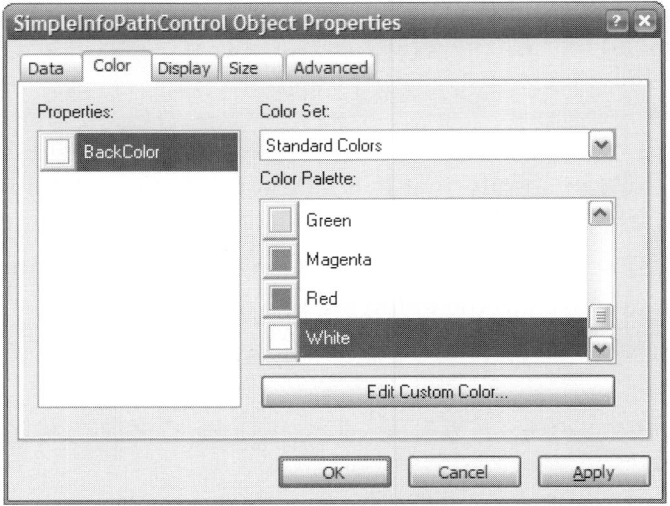

FIGURE 19.9: Color property page for the SimpleInfoPathControl object

control. It will work, but you won't be able to bind data to the control (unless you've chosen to use a stock property for binding). Also, changes to the data in your ActiveX control won't be saved back to the data source in the InfoPath form. So, let's look now at the code changes we need to make to complete the basic functionality needed to have our control function like a built-in InfoPath control.

Implementing the `Enabled` Property

Back when we first created our control, remember that we included the `Enabled` stock property. When the control is inserted into a form and users are filling out that form, InfoPath will use this property (or another property you can choose when installing the control) to enable and disable the control. This becomes particularly important in certain situations, such as when the form is read-only or when it is digitally signed. If your control doesn't implement a property that can be used to enable or disable it, the control will always remain enabled. In that case, it's likely that other form template designers won't insert your control into form templates if they need it to work like the built-in InfoPath controls.

When we chose the `Enabled` property in the *Stock Properties* page, the wizard included the basic code for that property. This code includes an event handler—`OnEnabledChanged`—that is called when InfoPath sets the property. However, this event doesn't do anything special. To disable our control when needed, we'll need to add some code to this event handler. This code obviously will differ depending on how the control is implemented but will typically look something like the following:

```
STDMETHODIMP_(void) InfoPathChartControl::OnEnabledChanged()
{
    if (IsWindow())
    {
        EnableWindow(m_bEnabled);
    }
}
```

When InfoPath needs to enable or disable your control, it will set the `Enabled` property on the control accordingly. When the property is set, the `m_bEnabled` data member will set to `TRUE` or `FALSE`, and the `OnEnabledChanged` method will be called by the base ATL control code. This will cause our control to enable or disable its window.

Implementing the `Value` Property

Now let's look at what we need to do in order to have our control participate in binding in InfoPath forms. As mentioned earlier, when you create the control in the ATL Control Wizard, you may just decide at that point to use a stock property for binding, such as the `Text` property. If you do, the wizard will create the basic code to implement this property. The one disadvantage of this approach is that when other form template designers install your control into the InfoPath *Controls* task pane, they have to know which property to use for binding. This problem can typically be solved through documentation, but it's much simpler just to implement the `Value` property. In that case, when you install your control, InfoPath will choose that property by default in the Add Custom Control Wizard. Form template designers who are accustomed to installing ActiveX controls in InfoPath will know that the `Value` property is the correct one to use for binding.

Implementing this property in ATL is fairly straightforward. When you created the ATL control class for your ActiveX control, the ATL Control Wizard created an interface for your control. In the case of the `SimpleInfoPathControl` object included in the `SimpleInfoPathActiveX` project, this interface is named `ISimpleInfoPathControl`. All you need to do to implement the `Value` property is to add a new property to this interface and name it `Value`.

There are a couple of things to keep in mind, however, when adding this property to the interface. First, you must implement both get and put methods for this property. InfoPath will use the get method to retrieve the current value of the data in the control and the put method to set the data in the control. Second, you must decide on the type of data ahead of time. If your control will bind to either the *Field (element or attribute)* or the *Field (element with custom data type)* data types, your `Value` property must be implemented as a `BSTR`. If your control binds to the *Field or Group (any data type)* type (as is the case with the `InfoPathChart` sample control), it must be implemented as either an `IDispatch` or an `IUnknown` property type.

Once you've added your property, you obviously will need to implement the code for the `get_Value` and `put_Value` methods. Again, how you implement these methods completely depends on the type of data your control will bind to. If your control binds to the *Field (element or attribute)* type, for example, the `put_Value` method will receive a `BSTR` that contains the text of the field to which the control is bound. If instead your control was implemented to bind to the *Field (element with custom data type)* type, the `put_Value` method will still receive a `BSTR`, but that string will contain XML that you can then parse or, more likely, load into an XML DOM.

The `put_Value` method will be called anytime that the data changes in the field so you can keep the data in your control up to date. (This could happen, for example, if another control is bound to the same field or the data is changed through form code.) For example, Listing 19.1 shows the implementation of the `put_Value` method for the `SimpleInfoPathControl` class.

LISTING 19.1: Implementation of the `put_Value` Method

```
STDMETHODIMP SimpleInfoPathControl::put_Value(BSTR newVal)
{
    m_bstrValue = newVal; // Save the current value in a data member
    if (m_ctlRichEdit.IsWindow()) // Has the control been created?
    {
        // Set the value of the Rich Edit control to the new value.
        m_ctlRichEdit.SetWindowTextW(newVal);
    }
    return S_OK;
}
```

In this case, since the `SimpleInfoPathControl` class is implemented in terms of the `Rich Edit` control, when the `put_Value` method is called, we set the value of the control by calling the `SetWindowTextW` method on the `m_ctlRichEdit` data member. (For an example of how to implement the `Value` property for controls that bind to the *Field or Group (any data type)* type, look at the `InfoPathChart` sample.)

The `get_Value` method, which is called by InfoPath anytime it needs to update the data in the underlying data source, simply retrieves the data from the inner control by calling `GetWindowTextW` and setting the given `BSTR` pointer to that value. InfoPath will automatically call this method when the form is first opened and when the form is closed to ensure that the data source is up to date.

However, when data in the control is changed, the `get_Value` method won't be called unless you tell InfoPath that the data in the data source needs to be updated. Fortunately, since we're using ATL, doing this is simple. When we initially implemented the ATL control class, we specified in the wizard that we wanted our control to implement the `IPropertyNotifySink` interface. Through this interface, an ActiveX control alerts InfoPath of property changes in the control.

When the data in your control changes, you simply need to call the `FireOnChanged` method of the `CComControl` base class to alert InfoPath that it needs to update the data. When InfoPath receives the notification, it will call the control's `get_Value` method again to update the data. For example, in the `SimpleInfoPathControl` class, when the focus leaves the control, we call the `FireOnChanged` method, passing the dispatch ID of the `Value` property like so:

```
FireOnChanged(DISPID_EDIT_VALUE);
```

Now that you've implemented the `Enabled` and `Value` properties, your control is ready to be used. You can install it into the *Controls* task pane and insert it into your form templates. When users fill out forms that contain your control, the control will work like the built-in InfoPath controls.

> **NOTE** ActiveX Controls Must Be Installed and Registered
>
> Before users can fill out forms that contain your ActiveX control, it must be installed and registered. This is a basic ActiveX concept that we want to reiterate. If a control is not installed and registered on a user's machine, the control simply won't run at all. (If the control is installed by Microsoft Windows or some other application, this is not an issue. However, when creating your own ActiveX control, you must implement this functionality yourself.) You can create a separate installation application to install your control or create a CAB file that you then include with your form template.

Implementing the InfoPathControl Interface

In addition to the basic support for control properties and property pages, InfoPath also includes two custom interfaces that your control can use to interact with the InfoPath form.

The first interface is the `InfoPathControl` interface. This interface, which can be implemented by the ActiveX control, provides methods that enable your control to know when certain events occur in the form, such as when the control is being initialized or uninitialized by InfoPath, when the control should persist any internal state, and when the control should enable or disable itself. Table 19.3 lists the methods included in the `InfoPathControl` interface.

The methods listed in Table 19.3 give you a little better integration with the InfoPath form. Two methods are particularly interesting. The `Enable` method is called by InfoPath to enable or disable your control. You may wonder why this is needed since your control can just expose an `Enabled` property. Besides the fact that there may be scenarios in which you don't want to expose this property, implementing this method instead actually makes it easier for other form template designers to install your control. When an ActiveX control implements the `InfoPathControl` interface, the *Specify an Enable or Disable Property* page of the Add Custom Control Wizard will be skipped since InfoPath knows that your control should be enabled or disabled by calling the `Enable` method on the `InfoPathControl` interface.

TABLE 19.3: `InfoPathControl` **Interface Methods**

Method	Description
`Init`	Is called when the control is being initialized. The control receives a pointer to the `InfoPathControlSite` interface implemented by InfoPath.
`Uninit`	Alerts the control that it is about to be destroyed. The control should perform any necessary cleanup when this method is called.
`SaveState`	Is called to tell the control to persist any internal state. Certain changes in the form will cause the ActiveX control to be destroyed and recreated. In the `SaveState` method, the control should persist data that it wishes to save from one instance of the control to another. When `Init` is called, the control can reload the saved data. (Tip: Your control can use the `SetNamedNodeProperty` and `GetNamedNodeProperty` methods in the InfoPath object model to store state.)
`Enable`	Specifies whether the control should be enabled or disabled.

One of the other interesting methods of the `InfoPathControl` interface is the `Init` method. By using this method as an indicator that your control is hosted in InfoPath, you can disable your control completely until `Init` is called. Therefore, you can make your control a little safer by ensuring that it will never be used in another application. (The `Init` method is called only when a user fills out a form. Therefore, you probably will want to disable your control only if it is not running in design mode. For a control written using ATL, the `m_bInPlaceActive` member variable is set to `FALSE` when the control is running in design mode.)

When the `Init` method is called, your control is given a pointer to the `InfoPathControlSite` interface, which is implemented by InfoPath. This interface has two properties—`XDocument` and `Node`. (Of course, in C++ you access these properties by calling `get_XDocument` and `get_Node`, respectively.) By using the `XDocument` property, you can access the DOM of the InfoPath form in which your control is being hosted. This gives you full access to the data in the form. The `Node` property gives you direct access to the XML node to which your control is bound. Be careful not to change the value of the node when InfoPath calls your `get_Value` method, however. Doing so could result in an infinite loop if you're not careful.

NOTE Where Are the InfoPath Interfaces Defined?

InfoPath doesn't ship any header files for its interfaces. However, the interfaces are included in the type library of the ipeditor.dll file, which exists in the same location as the InfoPath.exe application file. Therefore, to use any of the InfoPath interfaces in your projects, you must use the `#import` directive to import the type library from the ipeditor.dll file.

After you implement the `InfoPathControl` interface in your ActiveX control and rebuild, the control is ready to be used in form templates. There is one additional point you should keep in mind when making major changes to your control. If you've changed the data type of the binding property, for example, and you have existing form templates that use your control, you will need to reinstall the control into the *Controls* task pane and update the existing form templates with the new control. InfoPath caches some information about the control, so if you make major structural changes, you will need to update the control so InfoPath will update its cache with the new control information.

Using ATL, the process of creating an ActiveX control in C++ isn't too difficult. Most of the functionality you need, including support for interfaces such as `IObjectSafety` and `IViewObject`, is built into ATL. However, writing managed code is typically much easier than writing unmanaged code. So, it's inevitable that you would want to create your controls using managed code, which just happens to be our next topic.

Building an ActiveX Control for InfoPath Using C#

The process of creating a .NET control for InfoPath is pretty straightforward. There are two main issues to keep in mind when creating a managed code control for InfoPath. First, InfoPath doesn't natively support .NET controls. InfoPath supports plain vanilla ActiveX controls through COM. So, to use .NET controls in InfoPath, you must use COM interop to make your control look like an ActiveX control. That's fairly simple, as you'll see shortly. The second issue to deal with involves installing your control. Your managed code control must be installed in the global assembly cache (GAC) before it can be used in an InfoPath form.

Let's discuss how to create a managed code control using C# that we'll then use in our InfoPath forms. We'll show you how to implement the control so it can be installed into the InfoPath *Controls* task pane and used in form templates. Then, we'll show you how to ensure that your control is registered when your users fill out forms that contain your control.

You already know that InfoPath includes a Text Box control and that you can use a pattern in conditional formatting or data validation to ensure that the user's input matches a specified structure. However, customers have often requested a control that visually indicates the pattern that must be entered—such as a phone number (e.g., 1-111-111-1111) or social security number (e.g., 111-11-1111). You may already know that the .NET Framework includes such a control—the masked text box. Unfortunately, we can't use this control in InfoPath as is. To use it, we have to create our own `UserControl` class in .NET that wraps this common control. Let's look at how to do this.

Implementing the Basics

First, you will need to create a class that inherits from the `UserControl` class. To do this, create a new Windows Control Library project in Visual Studio 2005. We will name our project InfoPathControlLibrary. (This file is included with the samples for this chapter.) Once you complete the New Project Wizard, Visual Studio will create the basic template code for the new user control. Before continuing, let's rename our user control class to `InfoPathMaskedTextBox`.

Next, let's add the `MaskedTextBox` control to the design surface of our user control by dragging and dropping it from the Visual Studio Toolbox. And, just for purposes of this demonstration, let's open the properties for the control and set the `Mask` property to *Social security number.* At this point, if we build the control, it is usable in applications that natively support .NET controls but not in InfoPath.

To make this control work in InfoPath, we first need to make it look like a normal ActiveX control by using COM interop. This isn't nearly as difficult as it sounds. We just need to add a few attributes to the class to specify that the control is visible to COM, has a GUID, and has a class interface. Listing 19.2 shows the `InfoPathMaskedTextBox` class after we added the attributes needed to make the class appear to InfoPath as an ActiveX control. Note that the `ClassInterface` attribute must be set to `ClassInterfaceType.AutoDual` for the control to work within InfoPath. Also, the CLSID specified in the `Guid` attribute was obtained by running the guidgen.exe tool, which is included with Visual Studio 2005.

LISTING 19.2: `InfoPathMaskedTextBox` **Class After Adding COM Interop Attributes**

```
[ComVisible(true)]
[Guid("F24E3AC4-3987-4a62-9DDC-AB56CE896301")]
[ClassInterface(ClassInterfaceType.AutoDual)]
public partial class InfoPathMaskedTextBox : UserControl
{
. . .
}
```

Next, once you've added the necessary attributes to make your class look like an ActiveX control, you will want to expose a couple of properties to InfoPath—namely, the `Value` and `Enabled` properties. Let's create an interface called `IInfoPathMaskedTextBox` that will define these properties

(Listing 19.3). There are a couple of things to note about this code. First, we have to use the `InterfaceType` attribute and set it to `ComInterfaceType.InterfaceIsIDispatch` to expose this interface through COM. This attribute specifies that this interface supports `IDispatch`, which is necessary when using the control in InfoPath. Next, since this is a dispatch interface, we have to specify dispatch IDs for the two properties it supports using the `DispId` attribute. The IDs we use are defined in the `InfoPathMaskedTextBox` class—`DispidValue` and `DispidEnabled`. These IDs can be defined as any value you like, but, as you'll see later, if your binding property is `Value`, you should set `DispidValue` to `0`.

LISTING 19.3: `IInfoPathMaskedTextBox` Interface

```
[InterfaceType(ComInterfaceType.InterfaceIsIDispatch)]
public interface IInfoPathMaskedTextBox
{
    [DispId(InfoPathMaskedTextBox.DispidValue)]
    string Value { get; set; }

    [DispId(InfoPathMaskedTextBox.DispidEnabled)]
    bool Enabled { get; set; }
}
```

The `IInfoPathMaskedTextBox` control interface is then added to the inheritance list for the `InfoPathMaskedTextBox` class. The `Value` property is implemented to get and set the value of the nested masked text box object. The `Enabled` property simply enables or disables the masked text box control. Listing 19.4 shows the code to implement the `IInfoPathMaskedTextBox` interface.

LISTING 19.4: Implementation of the `IInfoPathMaskedTextBox` Interface Methods

```
public string Value
{
    get { return maskedTextBox1.Text; }
    set { maskedTextBox1.Text = value; }
}

public new bool Enabled
{
    get { return maskedTextBox1.Enabled; }
    set { maskedTextBox1.Enabled = value; }
}
```

Now, if you build your control, it will act as an ActiveX control and will expose the `Value` and `Enabled` properties, which can be used in InfoPath. However, the control still won't work in InfoPath until we implement the `IObjectSafety` interface.

Implementing `IObjectSafety`

The `IObjectSafety` interface is a standard COM interface that has no equivalent in the .NET world. However, that doesn't mean that you can't use it in your managed code controls. To use it, you simply need to define the interface, as you would any other interface, and then expose it to COM applications using COM interop. The code in Listing 19.5 shows the definition of the `IObjectSafety` interface in C#. (The original definition of this interface is in the objsafe.idl file in the Platform SDK. The CLSID specified in the `Guid` attribute comes from this definition.) Since this is a COM interface, we've specified the typical `ComImport`, `Guid`, and `InterfaceType` attributes on the interface declaration, as well as the `PreserveSig` attribute on the method declarations in order to preserve the return value of each method.

LISTING 19.5: Definition of the `IObjectSafety` Interface

```
[ComImport]
[Guid("CB5BDC81-93C1-11CF-8F20-00805F2CD064")]
[InterfaceType(ComInterfaceType.InterfaceIsIUnknown)]
interface IObjectSafety
{
    [PreserveSig]
    int GetInterfaceSafetyOptions(
            ref Guid riid,
            out int pdwSupportedOptions,
            out int pdwEnabledOptions);

    [PreserveSig]
    int SetInterfaceSafetyOptions(
            ref Guid riid,
            int dwOptionSetMask,
            int dwEnabledOptions);
}
```

After declaring the `IObjectSafety` interface, the obvious next step is to implement it. First, we must add it to the inheritance list for the `InfoPathMaskedTextBox` class and then implement both its methods, as shown in Listing 19.6. As you can tell from the code, the more important method is `GetInterfaceSafetyOptions`. This method is called by InfoPath to determine whether the control is safe for scripting and initialization. When this method is called, we must return both the supported and the enabled safety options. Typically, these are the same. In order for our control to work in InfoPath, it must be safe for scripting and initialization. Therefore, we set both the supported and the enabled options to `INTERFACESAFE_FOR_UNTRUSTED_CALLER`, which indicates that the control is safe for scripting, and `INTERFACESAFE_FOR_UNTRUSTED_DATA`, which indicates that it is safe for initialization. (Note that the values for both of these constants come directly from the objsafe.idl file.)

LISTING 19.6: Implementation of the `IObjectSafety` Interface Methods and Constants

```
private const int INTERFACESAFE_FOR_UNTRUSTED_CALLER = 1;
private const int INTERFACESAFE_FOR_UNTRUSTED_DATA = 2;
private const int S_OK = 0;

int IObjectSafety.GetInterfaceSafetyOptions(
    ref Guid riid,
    out int pdwSupportedOptions,
    out int pdwEnabledOptions)
{
         pdwSupportedOptions = INTERFACESAFE_FOR_UNTRUSTED_CALLER
                             | INTERFACESAFE_FOR_UNTRUSTED_DATA;
         pdwEnabledOptions = INTERFACESAFE_FOR_UNTRUSTED_CALLER
                             | INTERFACESAFE_FOR_UNTRUSTED_DATA;
    return S_OK;
}

int IObjectSafety.SetInterfaceSafetyOptions(
    ref Guid riid,
    int dwOptionSetMask,
    int dwEnabledOptions)
{
    return S_OK;
}
```

Adding a Managed Code Control to a Form Template

Now that we've completed all the prerequisites to use a control in InfoPath, after building it, we're ready to put it to use in our form templates. First, however, as you learned earlier, we have to register the control with InfoPath. Normally, we do that by using the *Add or Remove Custom Controls* dialog from the *Controls* task pane. But wait! If you look at the controls included in the list of ActiveX controls in the *Add or Remove Custom Controls* dialog, the InfoPathMaskedTextBox control isn't there. But why? The reason is that this list includes only controls that are listed in the *Controls* category in the registry. Controls created by using .NET, whether or not they use COM interop, are not registered as ActiveX controls. Therefore, they won't be included in the list of ActiveX controls in the *Add or Remove Custom Controls* dialog in InfoPath.

All is not lost, however. We can still make this work, and doing so is surprisingly easy. All you have to do is register the control in the same way as an ActiveX control. The easiest way to do this is by using a setup program. Since the InfoPathControlLibrary project includes a setup project, we'll just use that one. In the setup project, go to the registry view of the project and add a key named `CLSID` under `HKEY_CLASSES_ROOT`. Next, create a new key under the `CLSID` key that corresponds to the GUID for your control. This is the same GUID we specified earlier for the `InfoPath-MaskedTextBox` class—`"F24E3AC4-3987-4a62-9DDC-AB56CE896301"`. Finally, create a new key as a child of this key and name it `Control`. The value of the key is the name of the class—`"InfoPathMaskedTextBox"`. The setup program will take care of adding any additional keys needed to register the InfoPathMaskedTextBox control as an ActiveX control. Once you build the setup program and install it, your control will look like a standard ActiveX control and will appear in the list of controls in the *Add or Remove Custom Controls* dialog.

Once the InfoPathMaskedTextBox control is installed, you can insert it into your form templates as usual. And it will work like a normal InfoPath control in that it can be bound to fields in the data source and can be enabled and disabled. However, once you fill out a form that uses your managed control, you will immediately discover a problem. When you change data in the control, the data source is not updated with your changes. That is because the control doesn't alert InfoPath of data changes through the `IPropertyNotify-Sink` interface.

Calling into InfoPath's `IPropertyNotifySink` Interface

Remember that, earlier, when we showed you how to implement an ActiveX control in C++, we talked about the fact that, in order for a control to alert InfoPath of changes to the control's data, it has to call into the host's `IPropertyNotifySink` interface. Specifically, the control calls the `OnChanged` method, which in ATL was done by calling the `FireOnChanged` method. Well, for managed code, there's no difference. We just need to set up an event source for the `IPropertyNotifySink` interface.

As you probably have guessed, since the `IPropertyNotifySink` interface is a COM interface, which coincidentally is defined in the OCIdl.idl file in the Platform SDK, we need to use COM interop in order to use this interface in our managed code control. First, we need to declare this interface using the standard COM interop attributes, as shown in Listing 19.7.

LISTING 19.7: Declaration of the `IPropertyNotifySink` Interface

```
[ComImport]
[Guid("9BFBBC02-EFF1-101A-84ED-00AA00341D07")]
[InterfaceType(ComInterfaceType.InterfaceIsIUnknown)]
public interface IPropertyNotifySink
{
    [PreserveSig]
    int OnChanged(int dispId);

    [PreserveSig]
    int OnRequestEdit(int dispId);
}
```

Next, to expose the `IPropertyNotifySink` interface as an event source to InfoPath, we need to add another COM interop attribute to the `InfoPathMaskedTextBox` class—`ComSourceInterfaces`. This attribute specifies which interfaces are exposed as COM connection points. Therefore, to expose `IPropertyNotifySink` as an event source, we must specify the `ComSourceInterfaces` attribute on the class as follows:

```
[ComSourceInterfaces(typeof(IPropertyNotifySink))]
public partial class InfoPathMaskedTextBox :
    UserControl,
    IInfoPathMaskedTextBox,
    IObjectSafety
```

Once that is completed, we must define a delegate so we can call the `OnChanged` method in InfoPath. The signature of this delegate must match that of the `OnChanged` method and is declared is as follows:

```
public delegate int OnChangedDelegate(int dispID);
```

Now we just need to fire the event whenever we want to alert InfoPath of changes to the data in the control. To fire the event, let's create a helper method to do the work. This helper method, called `FireOnChanged`, is shown in Listing 19.8. As you can see, this method takes the dispatch ID of the property that changed, which is then passed to the `OnChanged` method in InfoPath. Usually, this dispatch ID will match that of the binding property, which in the case of our control is set to `0`. Note that passing `0` to `OnChanged` will work if your binding property is named `Value`. However, if you name the property something other than `Value`, you should pass `-1:` as the dispatch ID to InfoPath, which will tell it to update all the control properties. Also, you'll notice in the code in Listing 19.8 that we are ensuring that the `OnChanged` method is not `null` before calling it. This is necessary because the `IPropertyNotifySink` event sink will be detached and reattached when the data in the main data source for the form has changed. If you don't perform this check, your control will throw an exception, which will cause InfoPath to crash. (Also, remember earlier that we mentioned that the `ClassInterface` attribute must be set to `ClassInterfaceType.AutoDual`. If you set this attribute to anything but `ClassInterfaceType.AutoDual`, the `OnChanged` and `OnRequestEdit` delegates will be `null`.)

LISTING 19.8: `FireOnChanged` Helper Method

```
private int FireOnChanged(int dispID)
{
    if (OnChanged != null)
    {
        return OnChanged(dispID);
    }

    return 0;
}
```

Typically, for performance reasons, you wouldn't want to fire the `OnChanged` event each time the user types a character in the masked text box. Instead, you probably want to fire the event when focus leaves the control. That's just what we'll do. When the masked text box loses focus (i.e., the user presses the Tab key or clicks to move focus out of the control), we'll call the `FireOnChanged` method, passing it the dispatch ID of the binding property if `Value` is the binding property or `-1` otherwise. Of course, you probably want to call the `FireOnChanged` method only if the data has actually changed.

Implementing the InfoPathControl Interface

Now you have a fully functional .NET control that works in InfoPath. Your control can bind to data in a form's data source and be enabled and disabled when necessary. However, just as when we created the C++ ActiveX control earlier in this chapter, you probably want to have your control do other things such as interact with the data in the form. As you learned earlier, in order to do so, your control has to implement the `InfoPathControl` interface.

Since the `InfoPathControl` interface and the corresponding `InfoPath-ControlSite` interface are both COM interfaces, normally we would have to use COM interop to define them in our managed code project. However, InfoPath ships two primary interop assemblies that we can just reference in our project to implement the `InfoPathControl` interface.

The first interop assembly is `Microsoft.Office.Interop.InfoPath`. This assembly contains a namespace of the same name that includes both the `InfoPathControl` and `InfoPathControlSite` interfaces, as well as others needed to do such things as access the data source.

The second interop assembly that we want to reference in our project is `Microsoft.Office.Interop.InfoPath.Xml`. This assembly contains a namespace of the same name that includes definitions for all the MSXML interfaces we'll need in order to directly access the XML nodes in the data source.

So, once we've referenced these assemblies in our project and added the corresponding `using` statements to the top of the InfoPathMasked-TextBox.cs file, we'll need to implement the `InfoPathControl` interface.

First, as usual, we'll add the interface to the inheritance list of the `InfoPathMaskedTextBox` class. After adding this interface, the class definition looks like that shown in Listing 19.9.

LISTING 19.9: `InfoPathMaskedTextBox` **Class Definition**

```
[ComVisible(true)]
[Guid("F24E3AC4-3987-4a62-9DDC-AB56CE896301")]
[ClassInterface(ClassInterfaceType.AutoDual)]
[ComSourceInterfaces(typeof(IPropertyNotifySink))]

public partial class InfoPathMaskedTextBox :
      UserControl,
      IInfoPathMaskedTextBox,
      IObjectSafety,
      InfoPathControl
```

The rest is simple. We just need to provide the implementation of the `InfoPathControl` methods, as shown in Listing 19.10.

LISTING 19.10: `InfoPathControl` Methods

```
public void Init(InfoPathControlSite controlSite)
{
    _controlSite = controlSite;
}

public void Uninit()
{
    _controlSite = null;
}

public void SaveState()
{
}

public void Enable(bool enabled)
{
    this.Enabled = enabled;
}
```

As you can see, we are storing a reference to the `InfoPathControlSite` object that is passed to the `Init` method. This will allow us to do such things as access the node to which this control is bound, as shown in the following line:

```
IXMLDOMNode boundNode = _controlSite.Node;
```

Then, we can access the XML of the node with this code:

```
string xml = boundNode.xml
```

Deploying the Managed Code Control

Now that we have completed the development of an InfoPath .NET control, the next obvious step is to deploy it to our users. As with unmanaged ActiveX controls, we could create a CAB file in order to have our control installed when the form opens. However, the process for creating a CAB file to install a .NET control is much more complicated than doing so for a normal ActiveX control. In order for a .NET control to work in an InfoPath form, it must first be installed in the GAC, as we mentioned earlier. To do so from a CAB file, you will have to first create a setup application for your control and then use a setup hook in the CAB file.

A full discussion of creating setup applications and CAB files is outside the scope of this book. However, MSDN is a great resource for information about creating CAB files (see the reference in the Appendix). Also, Visual Studio includes a wizard to help you create a setup application. We have created one for the InfoPathMaskedTextBox control that even registers it as an ActiveX control in the registry so that you can install it into the *Controls* task pane in InfoPath by using the Add Custom Control Wizard. (This is included with the InfoPathControlLibrary sample.) The main point to remember is that, as with any other ActiveX control, the control must be installed on your users' machines before it can be added to form templates or used in existing forms.

Final Thoughts about Using .NET Controls in InfoPath

Getting a .NET control to work in InfoPath is a little more complicated than building an ActiveX control, but it is not impossible. We've shown you how to implement the necessary COM interfaces in .NET so that the control will function as a normal ActiveX control in InfoPath. Adding additional interfaces, such as `IViewObject`, is equally as easy.

However, we haven't really talked about how to implement property pages so that other form template designers can customize your control in InfoPath when designing form templates. Unfortunately, this is the one case where .NET controls won't work the same as normal ActiveX controls. The interfaces needed to implement property pages don't work well through COM interop. One option is to create your control in managed C++. Using managed C++, you can mix managed and unmanaged code, which will allow you to implement the property pages in unmanaged C++.

There are other less drastic ways to deal with this, though, if you want to allow other form template designers to customize your control at design time. For example, you could provide a custom context menu that contains a menu option to set custom properties on the control. You probably don't want to show this context menu when the form template designer right-clicks on the control since it will override the standard InfoPath context menu. Instead, you could show your context menu when the form template designer presses the Ctrl key and then right-clicks the control. Also, you'll want to show this context menu only in design mode. If you have implemented the `InfoPathControl` interface, the `Init` method is called only when filling out the form. Therefore, when you want to show the context menu, if `Init` hasn't been called, you know you're in design mode and, therefore, can show the menu.

What's Next?

In this chapter, we have talked about using ActiveX controls in InfoPath as well as implementing your own. We have shown you how to implement InfoPath controls in both C++ and C#. Hopefully, after reading this chapter, you have all the information you need to create controls that work very much like the built-in InfoPath controls. This will allow you to extend the set of InfoPath controls as you see fit.

In the next chapter, we'll show you another way you can extend the functionality of InfoPath—by using add-ins. Using these components, you can customize the way that InfoPath behaves as a whole instead of just affecting a particular form, as with ActiveX controls.

20 Add-ins

Getting Started

In the previous chapter, we showed you how to extend InfoPath's built-in collection of controls by creating your own custom ActiveX controls for InfoPath. Creating your own custom controls is just one way to extend the basic set of features included in InfoPath. In this chapter, we'll show you another way to enhance the InfoPath feature set—through the use of COM add-ins.

By using COM add-ins you can add functionality that is not included in the core InfoPath application. Whether you create your own or purchase them from a third-party retailer, COM add-ins allow you to provide a customized experience for your users. And, because COM add-ins are supported by most Microsoft Office applications (Access, Excel, FrontPage, InfoPath, Outlook, PowerPoint, Project, Publisher, Visio, and Word), you can create one COM add-in that can be used in multiple applications.

In addition to the added support for COM add-ins, InfoPath 2007 (as well as certain other Microsoft Office applications) includes support for Custom Task Panes. These task panes, which are implemented by using a combination of a COM add-in and an ActiveX control, allow you to create your own task panes that can be shared across multiple Microsoft Office applications. (InfoPath already includes support for HTML task panes, but these can be used only in InfoPath and not in other Microsoft Office applications.)

In this chapter, we'll first tell you a little about COM add-ins. Then, we'll show you how to create your own add-in that will enable you to copy XML data from one form and paste it into another. Once you have a good understanding of the basics, we'll show you how to combine a COM add-in with an ActiveX control to create your own Custom Task Pane that will show you the XML structure and data in the currently opened InfoPath form. Finally, we'll show you how to create managed add-ins with Visual Studio 2005 Tools for the 2007 Microsoft Office System (VSTO 2005 SE).

Introduction to COM Add-ins

As we mentioned, COM add-ins provide a way for you to extend an application in order to include your own features. COM add-ins have been a standard way to extend the functionality of various applications for some time. Therefore, as you would imagine, this technology is well documented in MSDN. However, to understand the process of creating a COM add-in, it is necessary to understand a little about the technology. Before we show you how to create your own COM add-in, let's start with a little background that will help move things along. This introduction will give you a very brief overview of COM add-ins. A full drill-down into all the intricacies of COM add-ins is outside the scope of this book. To acquire a deeper understanding of the technology, please refer to the MSDN online documentation for add-ins (referenced in the Appendix).

As the name implies, the COM add-in technology is based on the Component Object Model. As such, COM add-ins are typically written in unmanaged code such as C++, but, through the use of COM interop, you can write your COM add-ins in managed code as well.

A COM add-in is compiled into a dynamically linked library (DLL) that is then registered to load in one or more applications such as Excel, InfoPath, or Word. Depending on how it is registered, your add-in can be used in a single application or in multiple applications. Therefore, you can easily create one add-in that can add similar functionality to many applications at once.

Although each application that supports COM add-ins may have its own object model (OM), some objects are common across the different OMs. (The list of shared objects is available in the MSDN online documentation.

See the MSDN articles referenced in the Appendix for more information.) Therefore, if you want to create an add-in to work in multiple applications, you should write code that accesses only those shared objects, unless, of course, you want to provide different functionality for each individual application.

Since this is a book about InfoPath 2007, however, we will concentrate only on those aspects of COM add-ins specific to InfoPath. Also, since InfoPath has its own OM, we won't limit our add-ins to the shared object model.

`IDTExtensibility2` Interface

In order for a component to be considered a COM add-in, it must implement the `IDTExtensibility2` interface (see the MSDN reference listed in the Appendix). Through this interface, the add-in is alerted of various events that occur in the application, such as when the application is started, when it is shut down, when the add-in is loaded, and so on. Table 20.1 lists the methods of the `IDTExtensibility2` interface.

It is through the `OnConnection` method of the `IDTExtensibility2` interface that the COM add-in obtains access to the application object of the hosting application. The application object is one of those shared

TABLE 20.1: `IDTExtensibility2` **Interface Methods**

Method Name	Description
`OnAddInsUpdate`	Is called when a change occurs to the add-in
`OnBeginShutdown`	Is called when the application is being shut down
`OnConnection`	Occurs when the add-in is loaded by the host application
`OnDisconnection`	Occurs when the add-in is unloaded by the host application
`OnStartupComplete`	Is called when the application has completed its startup procedure as long as the add-in is set to load at application startup

objects we mentioned that is common to all applications that support COM add-ins. Through the application object, the COM add-in can access the OM of the host application, as we'll show you shortly.

Adding User Interface Items

To be useful, most COM add-ins add some custom buttons, menu items, or other items to the user interface of the application that is hosting the add-in. These UI elements give your users a way to interact with your COM add-in. Adding UI elements in InfoPath 2007 is typically done by using the **`CommandBars`** collection and **`CommandBar`** object. Therefore, as we show you how to create COM add-ins for InfoPath, along the way, we'll also show you how to use the `CommandBars` collection to add your own UI.

However, there is one thing you should keep in mind if you plan to create a COM add-in to be shared by multiple applications. As we're sure you've noticed by now, certain applications in the 2007 Microsoft Office system now include a new user interface—the Ribbon. Certain other applications, including InfoPath, do not. Therefore, the process of creating user interface elements for add-ins that are shared across multiple applications is a little more difficult. Since our discussion of COM add-ins is limited to InfoPath 2007, however, we will only show you how to add UI using the `CommandBars` collection. As we've mentioned, since a full discussion of creating UI, whether you're using command bars or the Ribbon, is outside the scope of this book, we will once again refer you to the MSDN online documentation. However, once we walk through the samples together, you should have enough knowledge to add any user interface elements to InfoPath that you like. Now, without further ado, let's create our first COM add-in for InfoPath.

Building a COM Add-in for InfoPath

Let's start by creating a COM add-in that will allow us to copy the entire data from one InfoPath form and paste it into another form of the same type (i.e., both forms are based on the same form template and, therefore, the same schema). You can certainly write all the code for your add-in from scratch. However, why do that when Visual Studio 2005 includes an add-in wizard that greatly simplifies this process?

To create a COM add-in for InfoPath, after firing up Visual Studio and opening the New Project wizard, click on the *Extensibility* project type (under the *Other Project Types* branch). Then, click on the *Shared Add-in* project template type, as shown in Figure 20.1. After you enter the name of the project (FormUtilities, in this case) and click the *OK* button, the Shared Add-in Wizard begins. (The FormUtilities sample project is included with the samples for this chapter on the book's Web site.) After you see the welcome page, click *Next* to start to specify the different options for your new add-in.

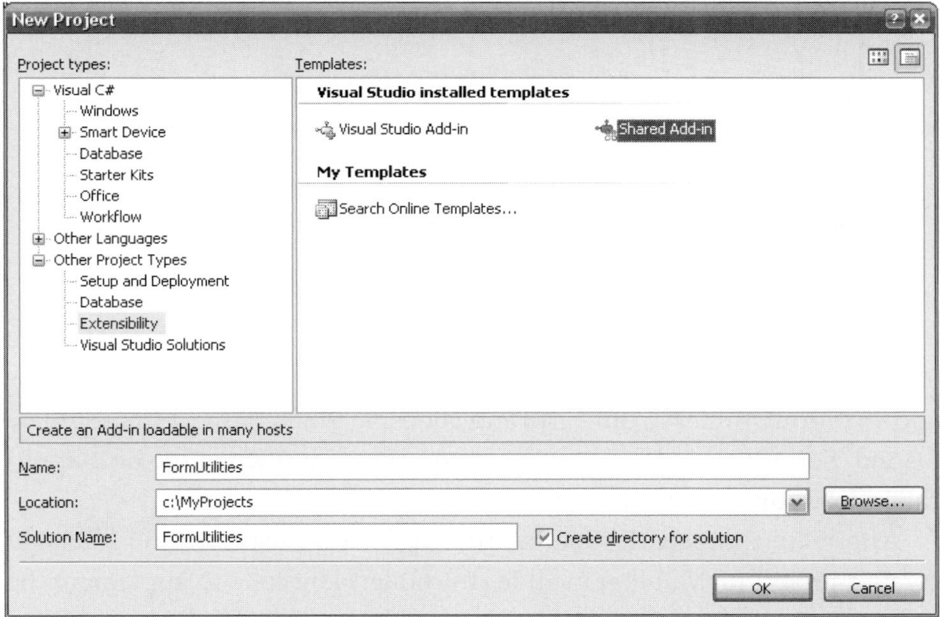

FIGURE 20.1: New Project wizard showing the Shared Add-in project template type

Most pages of the wizard are self-explanatory. For example, on the first page of the wizard, you can choose which language the wizard should use when generating the boilerplate code for your add-in—C#, Visual Basic, or C++/ATL. For this project, let's use C#.

On the second page of the wizard, you choose which applications are supported by your COM add-in. You can choose one application or many different applications. Since our COM add-in is specific to InfoPath, we'll uncheck the checkboxes next to all applications except InfoPath, as shown

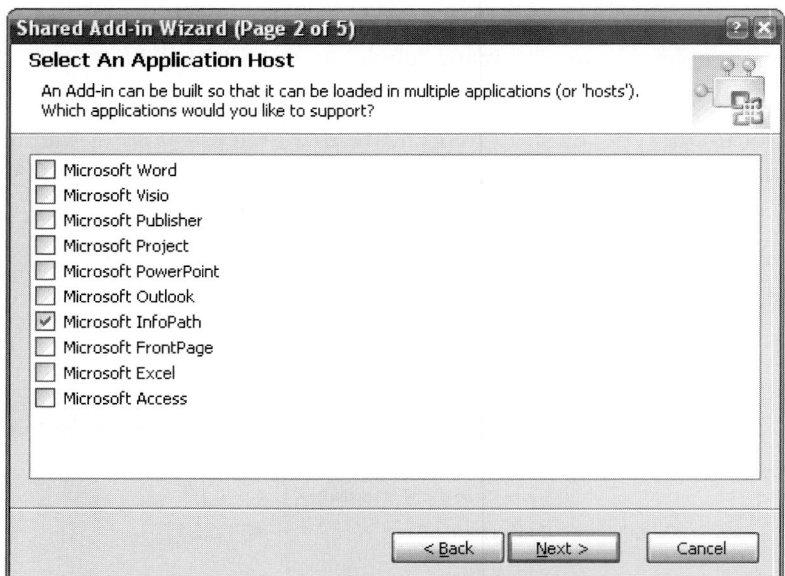

FIGURE 20.2: Selecting InfoPath as the supported application in the Shared Add-in Wizard

in Figure 20.2. After completing step 2 of the wizard, just follow the instructions for the remaining steps, which include giving a name to your add-in (FormUtilities in our case) and choosing when the add-in should be loaded. For our add-in, we've chosen to have it load when the host application loads and to have the add-in be available to all users.

After you complete the Shared Add-in Wizard, Visual Studio 2005 will create a project for you that includes the boilerplate code to implement the `IDTExtensibility2` interface (including the attributes needed for COM interop if you are using managed code), any code needed to register your add-in, and a setup project that you can deploy to your users so they can install your COM add-in. Listing 20.1 shows the basic code for the namespace and class created by the wizard, excluding any comments and class members. By default, the namespace is the same as the project name, and the name of the class is `Connect` (which you can change if you wish). As you can also see from Listing 20.1, the wizard has added the `GuidAttribute` and `ProgId` attributes so that this managed code add-in can participate in COM interop.

Listing 20.1: Namespace and Class Created by the Shared Add-in Wizard

```
namespace FormUtilities
{
    using System;
    using Extensibility;
    using System.Runtime.InteropServices;

    [GuidAttribute("29D8627D-71C3-4D0A-8249-DB1434F039FF"),
        ProgId("FormUtilities.Connect")]
    public class Connect : Object, Extensibility.IDTExtensibility2
    {
    }
}
```

Before we do anything else, we need to add a few references to our project that we'll need when we add some code later. First, let's add a reference to the `Microsoft.Office.Interop.InfoPath` and `Microsoft.Office.Interop.InfoPath.Xml` assemblies and then add `using` statements to our class for each of the associated namespaces. The first assembly contains the objects in the InfoPath object model that we'll need later to access the application, window, and form that is loaded into InfoPath. The second assembly contains the definition of the MSXML object model that we'll need to access the data in the form. Finally, let's add a reference to the `Microsoft.Office.Core` assembly. This assembly contains the definitions of the classes and interfaces we'll need to add user interface items (e.g., `CommandBars`, and so on). We will show you the rest of the code for the class as we move on.

`OnConnection` Method

Now that you've created the project for your add-in, you'll want to add some code to make it do something interesting. Figure 20.3 shows the data flow for our add-in. The data flow for each add-in will differ depending on the activities it performs. Of course, every add-in has a similar data flow that is defined by the COM add-in architecture and implemented via the `IDTExtensibility2` interface. However, Figure 20.3 shows only the data flow for our FormUtilities add-in. This diagram will be useful as a reference as we talk about each of the different methods in turn.

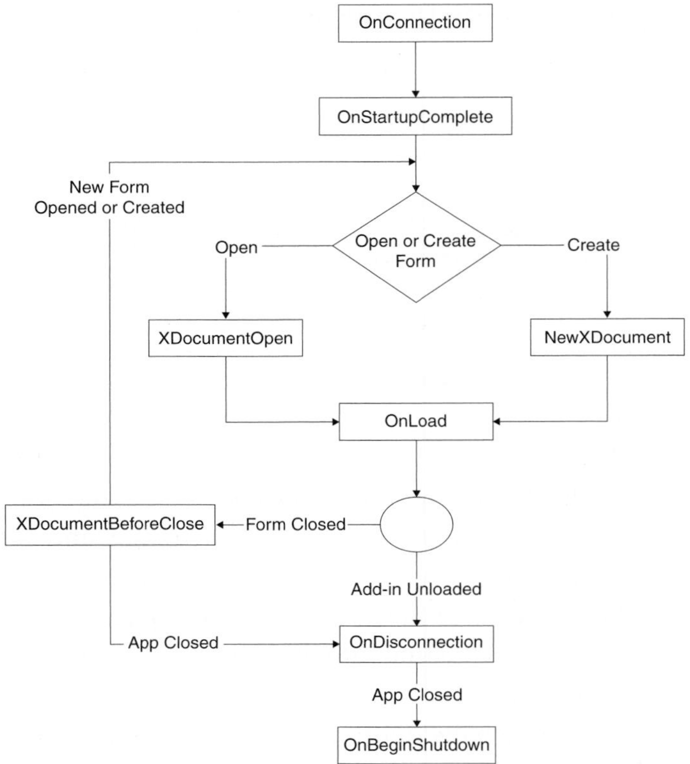

FIGURE 20.3: Data flow for the FormUtilities add-in

When the add-in is loaded by the host application, obviously, the first thing the add-in should do is initialize itself. Even though the add-in class has a constructor, typically you want to initialize your add-in when the `OnConnection` method is called since this is where the add-in is first given access to the `application` object corresponding to the host. In most cases, you'll want to store a reference to the `application` object as a data member of the class. Since we know that our COM add-in will be loaded only by InfoPath, we can cast the `application` object to `ApplicationClass`, which is the class type of the application object in the InfoPath OM. (In unmanaged code, the `ApplicationClass` object is equivalent to the `IApplication` interface.) Listing 20.2 shows the code for the `OnConnection` method at this point.

LISTING 20.2: Initial Code for the `OnConnection` Method

```
public void OnConnection(object application,
                         Extensibility.ext_ConnectMode connectMode,
                         object addInInst,
                         ref System.Array custom)
{
    _applicationObject = (ApplicationClass)application;
}
```

As you can see from Listing 20.2, besides the `application` object, three other parameters are passed to the `OnConnection` method.

1. connectMode
   a. ext_cm_AfterStartup
   b. ext_cm_Startup
   c. etc
2. addInInst
3. custom

`connectMode`: This parameter describes how the add-in is being loaded. The `Extensibility.ext_ConnectMode` enumeration has the following values (full details of each of these values are available in MSDN):

`ext_cm_AfterStartup`: The add-in was loaded after the host application started.

`ext_cm_Startup`: The add-in was loaded when the host started.

`ext_cm_External`: An external client loaded the add-in.

`ext_cm_CommandLine`: The add-in was loaded from the command line.

`ext_cm_Solution`: The add-in was loaded by a solution.

`ext_cm_UISetup`: The add-in was loaded during user interface setup.

`addInInst`: This parameter is the current instance of this add-in.

`custom`: This parameter is an array that contains additional data about the add-in.

Besides your standard initialization, such as storing a reference to the `application` object, in the `OnConnection` method you also want to set up any events that are specific to the host application. InfoPath 2007 just happens to expose a few new events specifically for COM add-ins. These

TABLE 20.2: Application Events Available to COM Add-ins

Event Name	Description
`NewXDocument`	Fired when a new form is created.
`Quit`	Called when the InfoPath application is closed.
`WindowActivate`	Fired when an InfoPath window is activated.
`WindowDeactivate`	Fired when a window is deactivated.
`WindowSize`	Called when a window is resized or moved.
`XDocumentChange`	Fired when a new form is created, when an existing form is opened, or when another form is set as the active form (e.g., when switching between different InfoPath windows that have forms loaded).
`XDocumentBeforeClose`	Called before a form is closed. This event can be canceled. Note that this event is not fired if you close the application without first closing the form. It is fired only when you close the form. Since this event can be canceled, if it were fired when the application is shut down, a COM add-in could prevent the application from closing.
`XDocumentOpen`	Fired when an existing form is opened.
`XDocumentBeforePrint`	Occurs right before a form is printed. This event can be canceled.
`XDocumentBeforeSave`	Fired immediately before a form is saved. This event can be canceled.

events are part of the `ApplicationEvents` object, which can be accessed through the `Events` property of the `ApplicationClass` object in the InfoPath object model. Table 20.2 lists and explains these events.

For the purpose of our add-in, we simply want to hook up event handlers for three of the events: `XDocumentOpen`, `NewXDocument`, and `XDocument-BeforeClose`. We want to handle the first two events so the add-in is alerted when an existing form is opened or a new form is created. We handle the `XDocumentBeforeClose` event so we can perform any necessary cleanup when a form is closed. Listing 20.3 shows the code to hook up the event handlers in the `OnConnection` method. We'll show you the event handlers for each of these later in this chapter.

LISTING 20.3: Code in the `OnConnection` Method to Hook Up the Application Event Handlers

```
_applicationEvents = (ApplicationEvents)_applicationObject.Events;
_applicationEvents.XDocumentOpen +=
    new _ApplicationEvents_XDocumentOpenEventHandler(
          _applicationEvents_XDocumentOpen);
_applicationEvents.NewXDocument +=
    new _ApplicationEvents_NewXDocumentEventHandler(
          _applicationEvents_NewXDocument);
_applicationEvents.XDocumentBeforeClose +=
    new _ApplicationEvents_XDocumentBeforeCloseEventHandler(
          _applicationEvents_XDocumentBeforeClose);
```

`OnStartupComplete` Method

The `OnStartupComplete` method, which occurs after `OnConnection`, is called when the host application has completed loading and the COM add-in is set to load at application startup time, which is the case for the add-in we are creating. (If the add-in is not set to load at startup, this method does not occur.) Here's where things get a little interesting. In the `OnStartup-Complete` method, you'll want to create any toolbars, buttons, menus, and so on that you need for your COM add-in.

In our case, we want to create a *Form Utilities* toolbar that contains two buttons—*Copy Form Data* and *Paste Form Data*. When clicked, these buttons will do exactly what their names imply—copy or paste the data in the form. Listing 20.4 shows the code for the `OnStartupComplete` method (minus comments and error handling). Let's look at this method and its helper methods in detail.

The `OnStartupComplete` method is relatively simple. First, it creates a toolbar (if it doesn't already exist) by calling the `CreateToolbar` method. Next, it will check to see if the copy and paste buttons have already been created on the toolbar. If they haven't, the two subsequent calls to the `AddButton` method will create them. If they already exist, `AddButton` will simply initialize them, as we'll see later. Notice that `AddButton` is called first for the paste button and second for the copy button, but the copy

LISTING 20.4: `OnStartupComplete` **and Associated Helper Methods**

```
public void OnStartupComplete(ref System.Array custom)
{
    CreateToolbar();

    CommandBarButton copyButton = GetButton(CopyButtonTag);
    CommandBarButton pasteButton = GetButton(PasteButtonTag);

    AddButton(ref pasteButton,
              "Paste Form Data",
              "Paste data copied from another form",
              PasteButtonTag,
              true /*beginGroup*/,
              OnPasteClick);

    AddButton(ref copyButton,
              "Copy Form Data",
              "Copy all data from this form",
              CopyButtonTag,
              false /*beginGroup*/,
              OnCopyClick);

copyButton.Enabled = false;
pasteButton.Enabled = false;
}
```

button is the first button in the toolbar. Buttons are added to the toolbar in reverse of the order in which they appear.

Finally, `OnStartupComplete` will disable both the copy and paste buttons. Since these buttons are not useful without an opened form, they are enabled only when a new form is created or an existing one is opened, as you'll soon see.

`CreateToolbar` and `GetCurrentToolbar` Methods

As we mentioned, the `CreateToolbar` method is called to create the *Form Utilities* toolbar if it doesn't already exist. You need to create the toolbar only once. As long as the user doesn't remove it from the UI through the *Customize Toolbars* dialog (by right-clicking on the toolbar and choosing *Customize*), the toolbar will persist from one instance of InfoPath to the next. If the toolbar has been removed, the COM add-in will need to create it again when `OnStartupComplete` is called.

Listing 20.5 shows the code for the `CreateToolbar` and `GetCurrentToolbar` methods. The first thing the `CreateToolbar` method does is try to determine whether a toolbar already exists by calling `GetCurrentToolbar`.

The latter method is a common helper method used by other methods through our `Connect` class to retrieve the toolbar `CommandBar` object.

LISTING 20.5: Implementation of the `CreateToolbar` and `GetCurrentToolbar` Methods

```
void CreateToolbar()
{
    Window window = _applicationObject.Windows[0];
    CommandBar toolbar = GetCurrentToolbar();
    if (toolbar == null)
    {
        CommandBars commandBars = (CommandBars)window.CommandBars;
        // Note that ToolbarName is a constant defined
        // as "Form Utilities", which is the name of the toolbar
        // for the COM add-in.
        toolbar = commandBars.Add(
                        ToolbarName,
                        MsoBarPosition.msoBarTop,
                        false /*replace*/,
                        false /*temporary*/);
    }
    toolbar.Visible = true;
}
CommandBar GetCurrentToolbar()
{
    Window window = _applicationObject.ActiveWindow;
    if (window == null)
    {
        window = _applicationObject.Windows[0];
    }
    CommandBars commandBars = (CommandBars)window.CommandBars;
    CommandBar toolbar = null;
    try
    {
        toolbar = commandBars[ToolbarName];
    }
    catch (ArgumentException)
    {
        // An exception is thrown if the toolbar doesn't exist
    }
    return toolbar;
}
```

The first thing that `GetCurrentToolbar` does is attempt to obtain the active window through the `ActiveWindow` property of the `_applicationObject` object. When the application first starts and `OnStartupComplete` is called, the active window hasn't been set yet. So, when `GetCurrentToolbar` is called for the first time, if the `ActiveWindow` property is `null`, the window is obtained from the first object in the `Windows` collection since there is only one window when the application first starts. However, `GetCurrentToolbar` is a common helper method called from multiple places—it could be called when multiple windows are open at the same time. Therefore, we can't always access the first window in the `Windows` collection but must instead access the toolbar of the active window.

Once we obtain the window object, we then must try to get the toolbar by name from the `CommandBars` collection on the window. You'll notice from the code that, if the toolbar doesn't exist, accessing it from the `CommandBars` collection using the array syntax will cause an exception of type `ArgumentException` to be thrown. In that case, we handle the exception and simply return `null` from the `GetCurrentToolbar` method.

> **NOTE** COM Add-in Lifetime and Command Bars
>
> It's important to note that there is never more than one instance of a particular COM add-in loaded for the application. However, multiple windows can be open at any time. Therefore, if you need to add or update a toolbar (or button, menu item, and so on), you must obtain these UI objects dynamically through the `CommandBars` collection on the currently active window. If you instead store a reference to a user interface object as a data member of the class, you will most likely not see the behavior you expect. The object reference you store in the class will not be the reference of the current window unless your users never open more than one window.

Back in `CreateToolbar`, if the `GetCurrentToolbar` method returns `null`, we know that we need to create a toolbar. So, we simply call the `Add` method on the `CommandBars` object, passing it the name of the toolbar (`ToolBarName` is a constant defined as `"Form Utilities"`), the position of the toolbar, whether or not to replace an existing one of the same name, and whether or not the toolbar is temporary.

`GetButton` and `AddButton` Methods

After creating the toolbar, `OnStartupComplete` will add the copy and paste buttons if they don't already exist. Listing 20.6 shows the code for the `GetButton` and `AddButton` methods.

LISTING 20.6: Implementation of the `GetButton` and `AddButton` Methods

```
CommandBarButton GetButton(string tag)
{
    return (CommandBarButton)GetCurrentToolbar().FindControl(
                MsoControlType.msoControlButton,
                Missing.Value,
                tag,
                true /*Visible*/,
                false /*Recursive*/);
}

void AddButton(ref CommandBarButton button,
               string caption,
               string tooltip,
               string tag,
               bool beginGroup,
               _CommandBarButtonEvents_ClickEventHandler clickHandler)
{
    if (button == null)
    {
        button = (CommandBarButton)GetCurrentToolbar().Controls.Add(
                        MsoControlType.msoControlButton,
                        Missing.Value,
                        Missing.Value,
                        1,
                        false /*temporary*/);

        button.BeginGroup = beginGroup;
}

    button.Visible = true;
    button.Caption = caption;
    button.Style = MsoButtonStyle.msoButtonCaption;
    button.Tag = tag;
    button.TooltipText = tooltip;

    button.Click +=
        new _CommandBarButtonEvents_ClickEventHandler(clickHandler);
}
```

The `GetButton` method is another one of those very useful helper methods that we call from different places in the code. Its job is simply to return a button if it already exists. This is done by calling `GetCurrent-Toolbar` to retrieve the current toolbar. Then, the `CommandBar` object's `FindControl` method is called to locate the control. When calling this method, we pass the control type as `msoControlButton`, which comes from the `MsoControlType` enumeration. We also pass a tag that is a string that uniquely identifies the button. The tag is either `"Copy"` for the copy button or `"Paste"` for the paste button and is set on the button in the `AddButton` method, as you'll see shortly.

If the button doesn't exist on the toolbar, the `GetButton` method will return `null`. The only time we expect it to return `null` is when this method is called the very first time in `OnStartupComplete`. Looking back at `OnStartupComplete` in Listing 20.4, you'll see that after `GetButton` is called in `OnStartupComplete` for both the copy and paste buttons, the `AddButton` method will then be called. If the reference to the button that is passed in is `null`, `AddButton` will call the `Add` method of the `Controls` collection for the current toolbar in order to add the button. Also, if we pass in `true` for the `beginGroup` parameter, a new group will be started. This will insert a separator between the two buttons.

Finally, whether or not we add a new button, `AddButton` will initialize the button by making it visible and setting its caption text, style, and tool-tip text. Also, here is where we specify a tag for the button that will uniquely identify it. In our case, we're just using a string as the identifier. And, last but not least, we must specify an event handler for the `Click` event on the button. Otherwise, our button won't do anything when the user clicks on it. Shortly, we'll talk about the click event handlers, which add the functionality that makes this COM add-in interesting. But first, let's continue with the next step of the load process—what happens when a form is created or opened.

Event Handlers for Loading a Form

Remember that when `OnConnection` was called, we hooked up three InfoPath event handlers—`XDocumentOpen`, `NewXDocument`, and `XDocumentBeforeClose`. After `OnStartupComplete` is called, the add-in basically goes into idle state until a form is created or opened. (Now is a good time to refer to the data flow diagram shown earlier in Figure 20.3 if you need a refresher.)

Since we've hooked up event handlers for the `XDocumentOpen` and `NewXDocument` events, our add-in will be alerted when a form is opened or created. When the event handlers are called, you can hook up other event handlers that are specific to the InfoPath OM for the form, such as the `OnSwitchView` event. Listing 20.7 shows how to hook up an event handler for the `OnSwitchView` event of the form. The code for the `NewXDocument` event handler is exactly the same. As you know, the `OnSwitchView` event is fired any time the view is switched. However, it's also called the first time a form is opened at the point where the form is finished loading. By hooking up an event handler for the `OnSwitchView` event, you can add initialization code for your COM add-in or code to access the InfoPath object model.

LISTING 20.7: Implementation of the `XDocumentOpen` Event Handler

```
private void _applicationEvents_XDocumentOpen(_XDocument pDocument)
{
    ((XDocument)pDocument).OnSwitchView +=
            new _XDocumentEventSink2_OnSwitchViewEventHandler(
                    Connect_OnSwitchView);
}
```

`OnSwitchView` will be called after either `XDocumentOpen` or `NewXDocument` is called. Listing 20.8 shows the code for this method, which is the standard InfoPath `OnSwitchView` event handler called in business logic for a form. When `Connect_OnSwitchView` is called, we know that the view is ready. So, we can now enable our copy and paste buttons. First, we call `GetButton`, passing the tag for the copy button in order to retrieve the copy button for the current window. Once we obtain the copy button, we just set its `Enabled` property to `true`. Enabling the paste button is almost the same. We first obtain the paste button and then call its `Enabled` property. However, we want to enable the paste button only if we've previously copied some data. The copied data is stored in a member variable named `_copiedNode`, which is set when the copy button is pressed, as you'll see next. (You may be wondering why we check to see whether we have data that has been copied when the form is opened. Remember that there is only one instance of our COM add-in for the application. We store the copied data in a data member so that we can paste the data into multiple forms, even if those forms are in different windows.)

LISTING 20.8: `OnSwitchView` Event Handler

```
void Connect_OnSwitchView(DocEvent pEvent)
{
    CommandBarButton copyButton = GetButton("Copy");
    copyButton.Enabled = true;

    CommandBarButton pasteButton = GetButton("Paste");
    pasteButton.Enabled = (_copiedNode != null);
}
```

Copy and Paste Button Event Handlers

So far, we've talked about what happens when the COM add-in is loaded and how to initialize the toolbar and copy and paste buttons. Now that we've added the user interface for the add-in, what's next? Well, obviously, we want something to happen when the user clicks one of the buttons.

Listing 20.9 shows the code for the click event handler for the copy button. Remember that we hooked up this event handler (as well as the handler for the paste button) when we initialized the buttons in `OnStartupComplete`.

LISTING 20.9: Copy Button Event Handler and `EnabledAllPasteButtons` Method

```
public void OnCopyClick(CommandBarButton Ctrl, ref bool CancelDefault)
{
    try
    {
        XDocument document = _applicationObject.ActiveWindow.XDocument;
        IXMLDOMNode rootNode =
            document.DOM.selectSingleNode(
                "*[not(self::processing-instruction())]");
        _copiedNode = rootNode.cloneNode(true /*deep*/);
        EnableAllPasteButtons();
}
    catch (Exception e)
    {
        MessageBox.Show(e.Message);
    }
}
private void EnableAllPasteButtons()
{
    Windows windows = _applicationObject.Windows;
    int numWindows = windows.Count;
    for (int i = 0; i < numWindows; i++)
    {
        Window window = windows[i];
        CommandBar toolbar =
            ((CommandBars)window.CommandBars)[ToolbarName];
        CommandBarButton pasteButton =
            (CommandBarButton)toolbar.FindControl(
                    MsoControlType.msoControlButton,
                    Missing.Value,
                    PasteButtonTag,
                    true,
                    false);
        pasteButton.Enabled = true;
    }
}
```

Let's look at this event handler in detail. When the copy button is clicked, the `OnCopyClick` method is called. This method receives a copy of the `CommandBarButton` that was clicked, as well as a `bool` parameter that can be set to cancel the default action, if any.

When the copy button is clicked, we want to store the root node of the document in the `_copiedNode` member variable so that we can paste it into other documents later. Therefore, we must first get the root node from the `DOM` property of the current document. The current document is stored in the `XDocument` property on the `Window` object. Obviously, we want to access that document from the current window, so we get it from the `ActiveWindow` property of the `_applicationObject` object.

Once we have the document, we have to get the root node. To get the root node, we call the `selectSingleNode` method of the DOM, passing an XPath that will return the first node that is not a processing-instruction node. (Of course, this will return only the first node, which may or may not be the root, depending on the complexity of the schema. For the purposes of this sample, we're assuming that the first node that is not a processing instruction is the root.) Once we have the root, we clone it and store it in `_copiedNode` for later.

We're almost finished. Remember that the `OnSwitchView` method is where we enable the buttons. We always enable the copy button, but we enable the paste button only if `_copiedNode` is not `null`. Therefore, the first time that `OnSwitchView` is called after the COM add-in is loaded, the paste button will be disabled. So, when the copy button is clicked, we want to enable the paste button.

To do so, we simply call `EnableAllPasteButtons`. But wait—why is this called `Enable`**`All`**`PasteButtons`? Don't we have only one paste button? That's true, but remember that there could be multiple InfoPath windows open at any given time. So, when the copy button is pressed, we want to enable the paste button in each of the opened windows. To do that, `EnableAllPasteButtons` loops through all the windows in the `Windows` collection, gets the *Form Utilities* toolbar, finds the paste button, and enables it. It's that simple.

So, now you see how the add-in copies the data in the form. However, what do we do when we want to paste the data into a new form? When the paste button is pressed, the `OnPasteClick` event handler is called, as shown in Listing 20.10. Similar to the event handler for the copy button, this method first gets the current document and then finds the root node. However, before pasting, we check to make sure that the namespace URI of the root node of the current document matches that of the copied node. If the namespaces don't match, we show an error message and prevent the paste from occurring. (We're assuming that if the namespace URIs match, the schema for each of the nodes is the same. You may want to do a more robust check to ensure that they are the same beyond a reasonable doubt.)

LISTING 20.10: Paste Button Event Handler

```
public void OnPasteClick(CommandBarButton Ctrl, ref bool CancelDefault)
{
    XDocument document = _applicationObject.ActiveWindow.XDocument;

    IXMLDOMNode targetRootNode =
        document.DOM.selectSingleNode(
            "*[not(self::processing-instruction())]");

    if (targetRootNode.namespaceURI == _copiedNode.namespaceURI)
    {
        document.View.DisableAutoUpdate();

        targetRootNode.ownerDocument.replaceChild(
            _copiedNode, targetRootNode);

        document.View.EnableAutoUpdate();
    }
    else
    {
        MessageBox.Show(
            "You cannot paste into this document. The " +
            "namespace of the target document does not match " +
            "that of the source document.");
    }
}
```

If the namespace URIs match, the root node of the current document is replaced with the copied node by calling the `replaceChild` method on the owner document of the root node in the current form.

That's it. Once you compile the code, you now have a fully functional COM add-in that will allow you to easily copy data from one InfoPath form to another.

Custom Task Panes

In addition to the ability to host COM add-ins, InfoPath 2007 introduces support for a new feature available in other Microsoft Office 2007 applications—Custom Task Panes. You're already familiar with task panes in InfoPath, so you can probably guess that Custom Task Panes are those you can create yourself and add into certain Microsoft Office applications such as Access, Excel, InfoPath, Outlook, PowerPoint, and Word in order to add your own behavior to these applications. Custom Task Panes are built as a combination of a COM add-in and an ActiveX control, so you can add just about any behavior you want.

You may be wondering why you need support for this new Custom Task Pane technology when InfoPath already includes support for custom task panes implemented with HTML and script. The new Custom Task Pane technology has three main advantages over the existing HTML task panes in InfoPath.

1. Custom Task Panes can be shared among multiple Microsoft Office applications. This allows you to create a consistent user experience across a wide range of applications.
2. HTML task panes live with the form template, while Custom Task Panes are installed on the user's machine. This allows you to add functionality to forms one time without having to add your task pane to each and every form template.
3. Since Custom Task Panes are installed on your users' machines, they have full access to the entire InfoPath OM, whether or not the form template has a security level of full trust. HTML task panes, on the other hand, can access the full-trust object model only if the form template is installed or digitally signed.

Creating a Custom Task Pane

Now that you see the advantages of Custom Task Panes, let's look at how to create one. Since you already know a bit about COM add-ins, creating a Custom Task Pane should be relatively easy.

Let's create a Custom Task Pane that will allow us to view the XML data in a form. We'll call this pane the *Form Data View* pane. To open our *Form*

Data View pane, we'll create a COM add-in that creates a toolbar and two buttons—one to show the Custom Task Pane and one to refresh the XML data shown in the task pane. As we mentioned, Custom Task Panes are implemented by using a combination of a COM add-in and an ActiveX control. The COM add-in is the driver of the task pane. As you'll see, it is through the COM add-in that the task pane is created, displayed, and so on.

To get started, the first thing you must do is follow the first part of this chapter and create a COM add-in in Visual Studio. Of course, this time around, you'll want to give it a different name. In this case, let's name our project FormDataTaskPane and name our add-in FormDataTaskPaneAddIn. (This sample, called FormDataTaskPane, is available with the other samples for this chapter.)

The process of creating this add-in is exactly the same as we explained earlier. You'll want to implement `OnConnection` to set up the necessary event sinks, `OnStartupComplete` to create and initialize the toolbar and the two buttons we talked about, and `OnSwitchView` to enable the buttons when a form is loaded. Figure 20.4 shows how our toolbar and Custom Task

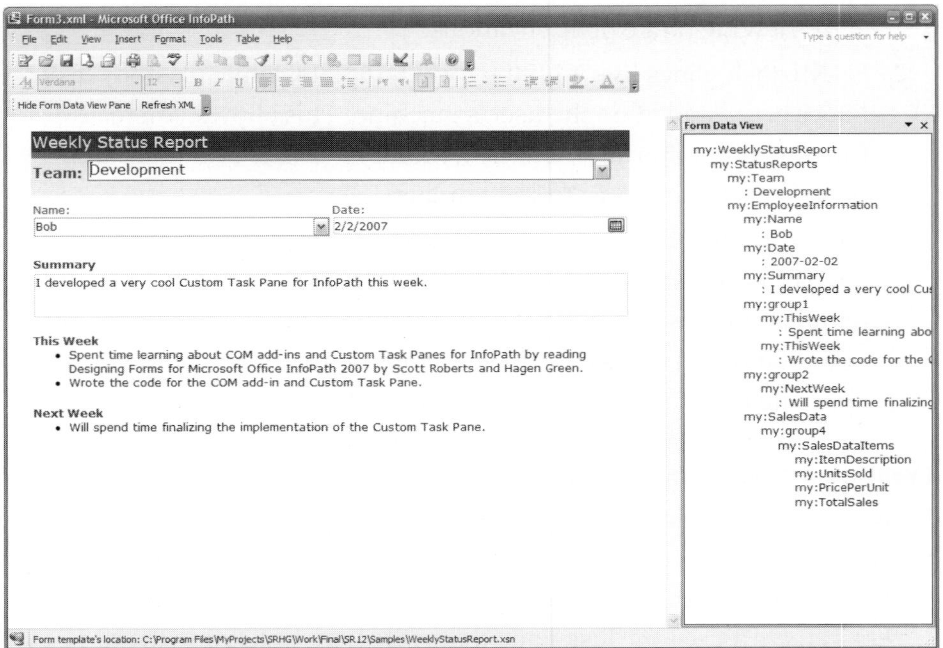

FIGURE 20.4: Form Data View task pane

Pane look after we're finished. As you can see, the *Form Data View* task pane shows the XML structure of the form as well as the data entered by the user.

As we mentioned, the implementation of the FormDataTaskPane COM add-in is pretty much the same as the FormUtilities add-in we implemented earlier. However, to tell InfoPath that our COM add-in is the driver for a Custom Task Pane, we must implement a new interface—`ICustomTaskPaneConsumer`. This interface includes one method—`CTPFactoryAvailable`—which is called after `OnConnection` but before `OnStartupComplete`. Our implementation of this method, which is shown in Listing 20.11, receives an `ICTPFactory` object. This object, as its name implies, is the Custom Task Pane factory object. It contains one method—`CreateCTP`—which can be used to create as many Custom Task Panes as you like.

LISTING 20.11: `CTPFactoryAvailable` **Method**

```
public void CTPFactoryAvailable(ICTPFactory CTPFactoryInst)
{
    _ctpFactory = CTPFactoryInst;
}
```

As you can see in Listing 20.11, we are storing a reference to the Custom Task Pane factory object in a member variable. When the user presses the button to show the task pane, at that point we will create the task pane using the `_ctpFactory` object. Of course, once the task pane is created, we'll want to show it. The code for the button click event handler, which is called `OnToggleClick` since we are toggling the visibility of the task pane, is shown in Listing 20.12.

The code in `OnToggleClick` is doing quite a bit of work, so let's look at it in detail. First, notice that we are getting the hash code of the window and using it as a key into a collection of task panes stored in a member variable called `_taskPanes`. This member variable is just a `ListDictionary` type that holds a collection of `CustomTaskPane` objects pertaining to all the task panes we've created.

You may be wondering why we have to do this instead of just storing the created task pane as a member variable. The reason is simple. Remember that there is one instance of a COM add-in per application. However, there can be one or more instances of each task pane you create in each

Listing 20.12: `OnToggleClick` Event Handler for the Show/Hide Task Pane Button

```
private void OnToggleClick(CommandBarButton Ctrl,
                           ref bool CancelDefault)
{
    int hashCode = _applicationObject.ActiveWindow.GetHashCode();
    CustomTaskPane taskPane = (CustomTaskPane)_taskPanes[hashCode];

    if (Ctrl.Caption == "Show Form Data View Pane")
    {
        if (taskPane == null)
        {
            taskPane = _ctpFactory.CreateCTP(
                            "FormDataTaskPaneActiveX.FormDataTPAxCtl",
                            "Form Data View",
                            Missing.Value);

            taskPane.VisibleStateChange +=
                new CustomTaskPaneEvents_VisibleStateChangeEventHandler(
                        taskPane_VisibleStateChange);

            _taskPanes.Add(hashCode, taskPane);
        }

        taskPane.Visible = true;
        Ctrl.Caption = "Hide Form Data View Pane";
    }
    else
    {
        CommandBarButton refreshButton = GetButton(RefreshButtonTag);

        taskPane.Visible = false;
        Ctrl.Caption = "Show Form Data View Pane";

        refreshButton.Enabled = false;
    }
}
```

application window. For example, if you open two InfoPath windows, you will have only one COM add-in. However, if you click the show task pane button on the toolbar for your add-in in each window, you will have two instances of your Custom Task Pane—one in each window.

Once you create a task pane, there is no way to access it from the `CommandBars` collection as you can for a toolbar or button. So, once you create the task pane, you need some way to store a reference to it. We chose to do that by adding each instance we create to the `_taskPanes` collection.

When the show task pane button is clicked, we first try to retrieve the task pane from the `_taskPanes` collection. Then, if the text of the button is currently set to `"Show Form Data View Pane"` and the task pane doesn't exist in our collection, we create it and add it to the collection, using the window's hash code as the key into the collection. Next, we show the task pane by setting its `Visible` property to `true`, and finally, we set the text of the toolbar button to `"Hide Form Data View Pane"`. Likewise, when the button is pressed, if the text of the button is `"Hide Form Data View Pane"`, we hide it and reset the text of the button to `"Show Form Data View Pane"`.

Creating the task pane is very straightforward. As you can see in Listing 20.12, to create the task pane, we call the `CreateCTP` method on the `_ctpFactory` member variable. The `CreateCTP` method has three parameters, as shown in Table 20.3. In Listing 20.12 we are passing `"FormDataTaskPaneActiveX.FormDataTPAxCtl"` as the ID of the control. This is the ProgID of the ActiveX control that will show the XML tree representation of the form. This is a standard ActiveX control that we created with Visual Studio in much the same way we did in the last chapter. (However, in this case, our control does not implement the `InfoPathControl` interface. This interface is supported by InfoPath only for ActiveX controls that are in the actual form itself.)

`CreateCTP` will return an instance of a `CustomTaskPane` object if the task pane could be created. The task pane creation will fail if the ID of the ActiveX control is not provided or is invalid or if the ActiveX control failed to be created for any reason.

TABLE 20.3: `CreateCTP` Parameters

Parameter	Description
`CTPAxID`	The CLSID or ProgID of an ActiveX control to load into the task pane.
`CTPTitle`	The title to use for the task pane.
`CTPParentWindow`	The window to use to host the task pane (optional). If this parameter is not specified, the active window will be used.

Once the task pane is created, you can use the returned `CustomTaskPane` object to show or hide the task pane, set its height and width, or set its docking position. You can even hook up event handlers to know when the dock position or visibility state has changed. (Table 20.4 shows all the methods, properties, and events of the `CustomTaskPane` object.)

In Listing 20.12, you can see that we are hooking up an event handler for the `VisibleStateChange` event. This event, which is fired when the `Visible` property is changed or when the user closes the task pane manually, allows us to set the enabled state of the refresh XML button in our toolbar. We want the refresh button to be enabled only when the task pane is displayed. As you can see in Listing 20.12, we can set the enabled state of the button when the user presses the show/hide task pane button. However, we need to know when the user manually closes the task pane so we can disable the refresh button and reset the text of the show/hide button. Listing 20.13 shows the code for the `VisibleStateChange` event handler. You can see that, when this event is fired, if the Custom Task Pane is not visible, we set the text of the show/hide button to "`Show Form Data View Pane`" and then disable the refresh button. (The refresh button will be enabled again the next time the task pane is shown.)

TABLE 20.4: `CustomTaskPane` Methods, Properties, and Events

Member	Type	Description
`Delete`	Method	Deletes the Custom Task Pane and frees the instance of the ActiveX control.
`Application`	Property	The application object of the host application. This property is read-only.
`ContentControl`	Property	The instance of the ActiveX control in the task pane. Through this property, your COM add-in can communicate with the ActiveX control. This property is read-only.
`DockPosition`	Property	The dock position of the task pane. The position comes from the `MsoCTP DockPosition` enumeration.

Table 20.4: *(continued)*

Member	Type	Description
`DockPositionRestrict`	Property	Allows you to set a restriction on the orientation of the dock position. Setting this property will fail if this value conflicts with the value of the `DockPosition` property. The valid values for `DockPosition Restrict` come from the `MsoCTPDockPositionRestrict` enumeration.
`Height`	Property	The height in pixels of the task pane. This value can be changed but will have no effect if the dock position is `msoCTPDockPositionLeft` or `msoCTPDockPositionRight`.
`Title`	Property	The title for the Custom Task Pane. This value can be set only when creating the task pane. This property is read-only.
`Visible`	Property	Shows or hides the Custom Task Pane.
`Width`	Property	The width in pixels of the task pane. This value can be changed but will have no effect if the dock position is `msoCTPDockPositionTop` or `msoCTPDockPositionBottom`.
`Window`	Property	The parent window of the host application. This property is read-only.
`DockPositionStateChange`	Event	Fired whenever the value of the `DockPosition` property is changed.
`VisibleStateChange`	Event	Fired when the visible state changes due to either setting the `Visible` property or manually closing the task pane by clicking the *Close* button.

LISTING 20.13: `VisibleStateChange` **Event Handler**

```
private void taskPane_VisibleStateChange(
        CustomTaskPane CustomTaskPaneInst)
{
    if (!CustomTaskPaneInst.Visible)
    {
        CommandBarButton toggleButton = GetButton(ToggleButtonTag);
        toggleButton.Caption = "Show Form Data View Pane";

        CommandBarButton refreshButton = GetButton(RefreshButtonTag);
        refreshButton.Enabled = false;
    }
}
```

Communicating between the COM Add-in and the ActiveX Control

Since Custom Task Panes are built with a combination of a COM add-in and an ActiveX control, it's inevitable that you will want to have the COM add-in communicate with the ActiveX control and vice versa. For example, when you click the show/hide button in the toolbar, you want it to not only show the task pane but also actually do something—show the XML structure and data of the form. Likewise, when you press the refresh button, you'll want to update the task pane with any changes from the document. The obvious way to do this is to obtain a reference (or pointer in unmanaged code) to an interface implemented by the ActiveX control and then call a method or set a property on the control. But how do you get to the ActiveX control from within the code for the COM add-in?

That's where the `ContentControl` property of the `CustomTaskPane` object comes in handy. The `ContentControl` property is set to the instance of the ActiveX control created when the `CreateCTP` method is called. This property gives your COM add-in access to the ActiveX control instance loaded in the task pane. You can cast this property (in managed code) or call `QueryInterface` for it (in unmanaged code) to obtain any interface supported by the control. Then, just call methods or access properties on the interface as usual. Let's see how to do this in our COM add-in that we've implemented in C#.

First, we must build the ActiveX control and then set a reference to its DLL in our COM add-in project. In the case of our FormDataTaskPane solution, the ActiveX control DLL is named FormDataTaskPaneActiveX.dll. Setting a reference to this DLL in our C# project will automatically generate an interop assembly that we can use in C#. Next, we add a `using` statement to the top of the `FormDataTaskPane` namespace (for the COM add-in) so that we can easily access type information from the ActiveX control's namespace, which in this case is `FormDataTaskPaneActiveX`.

Now, we just cast the `ContentControl` property of the `CustomTaskPane` object to an interface supported by the control. Our ActiveX control implements an interface called `IFormDataTPActiveXCtl` that has one property—`Application`. This property represents the InfoPath `Application` object. When this property is set, the ActiveX control will retrieve the `XDocument` object from the active window and display the XML structure and data in the Custom Task Pane.

To see this in action, take a look at the click event handler for the refresh button (Listing 20.14). When the refresh button is clicked, the first thing we do is obtain the task pane object we created previously from the collection of task panes. (Obviously, this could fail if the task pane failed to be created for some reason. This code does not show any error handling being done in the full sample.) Next, we cast the `ContentControl` property to `IFormDataTPActiveXCtl`. Finally, we set the `Application` property of the ActiveX control to the `Application` property of the task pane. This will cause the ActiveX control to grab the XML from the form and update the task pane with the new information. (The `OnToggleClick` method also sets the `Application` property when showing the task pane and clears it when hiding the task pane. This bit of code is not shown in Listing 20.12 in order to keep things simple, but it does exist in the full sample.)

LISTING 20.14: `OnRefreshClick` Event Handler

```
private void OnRefreshClick(CommandBarButton Ctrl,
                            ref bool CancelDefault)
{
    CustomTaskPane taskPane =
        (CustomTaskPane)_taskPanes[
            _applicationObject.ActiveWindow.GetHashCode()];
    // Setting the Application property refreshes the XML in
    // the Custom Task Pane
    IFormDataTPActiveXCtl ctpActiveXCtrl =
            (IFormDataTPActiveXCtl)taskPane.ContentControl;
    ctpActiveXCtrl.Application = taskPane.Application;
}
```

As you can see, it's very easy for the COM add-in to communicate with the ActiveX control. But how can the ActiveX control communicate with the COM add-in? When the `Application` property is set on the ActiveX control, the control will walk the XML DOM of the form; obtain the XML elements, attributes, and data; format them nicely; and display them in the task pane. This process, as you can imagine, could take a while depending on the size of the form. So, you probably want to have the ActiveX control alert the COM add-in when the operation is complete. At that point, the COM add-in can do such things as enable the refresh button. (If the ActiveX control does the work to retrieve and format the XML synchronously, this obviously doesn't need to be done. However, for such a long operation, you probably will want to do this work asynchronously, in which case you will need a way to tell the add-in that the work is complete.)

To make this work, you'll first want to create an interface that can be implemented by the COM add-in and used by the ActiveX control. This interface, which we'll call `IFormDataViewAddIn`, is shown in Listing 20.15. (Since this interface will be called from unmanaged code, we have to specify the attributes needed for COM interop—`ComVisible`, `InterfaceType`, and `Guid`.)

LISTING 20.15: `IFormDataViewAddIn` Interface

```
[ComVisible(true)]
[InterfaceType(ComInterfaceType.InterfaceIsIUnknown)]
[Guid("3995A8BB-7B96-450a-AC72-E2C46F2315D4")]
public interface IFormDataViewAddIn
{
    void OnTaskPaneReady();
}
```

The `IFormDataViewAddIn` interface, which is then implemented by the `FormDataViewAddIn` class, includes one method, `OnTaskPaneReady`, which will be called by the ActiveX control after rendering is complete. The implementation of this method is very simple—it just enables the refresh button, which was previously disabled.

Once we've created this interface and rebuilt our COM add-in, Visual Studio will export a type library containing this interface that we can then include in the header file for our ActiveX control by using the `#import` statement. This type library will include the `IFormDataViewAddIn` interface. But how do we get a pointer to the COM add-in object and then obtain the `IFormDataViewAddIn` interface? Doing so is pretty straightforward.

InfoPath's object model includes a property called `COMAddins`, which is available on the `Application` object. The `COMAddins` object is a collection of all the COM add-ins currently loaded for the application.

Listing 20.16 shows the code for a method called `FireTaskPaneReady`, which is implemented by the ActiveX control. This method loops through

LISTING 20.16: Accessing the `IFormDataViewAddIn` Interface

```
void CFormDataTPActiveXCtl::FireTaskPaneReady()
{
    _Application3Ptr spApplication3;

    // Get the add-in object from the COMAddIns collection and
    // fire the OnTaskPaneReady event.
    HRESULT hr = _spApplication.QueryInterface(
                    __uuidof(_Application3), &spApplication3);

    if (SUCCEEDED(hr))
    {
        CComDispatchDriver spdispCOMAddIns;

        hr = spApplication3->get_COMAddIns(&spdispCOMAddIns);
        if (SUCCEEDED(hr))
        {
            COMAddInsPtr spCOMAddIns;

            hr = spdispCOMAddIns->QueryInterface(
                     __uuidof(COMAddIns), (void**)&spCOMAddIns);
                if (SUCCEEDED(hr))
                {
                    COMAddInPtr spCOMAddIn;

                    hr = spCOMAddIns->Item(
                             &CComVariant(L"FormDataTaskPane.Connect"),
                             &spCOMAddIn);
                    if (SUCCEEDED(hr))
                    {
                        CComDispatchDriver spdispCOMAddIn;

                        hr = spCOMAddIn->get_Object(&spdispCOMAddIn);
                        if (SUCCEEDED(hr) && spdispCOMAddIn != NULL)
                        {
                            IFormDataViewAddInPtr spFormDataViewAddIn;

                            hr = spdispCOMAddIn->QueryInterface(
                                     __uuidof(IFormDataViewAddIn),
                                     (void**)&spFormDataViewAddIn);
                            if (SUCCEEDED(hr))
                            {
                                spFormDataViewAddIn->OnTaskPaneReady();
                            }
                        }
                    }
                }
        }
    }
}
```

all the COM add-ins that are currently loaded and queries for the `IFormDataViewAddIn` interface. When the method finds an add-in that supports this interface, it calls the `OnTaskPaneReady` method to let the COM add-in know that the rendering process is complete. (Of course, if multiple COM add-ins support this interface, they will all be alerted.)

As you can see, the process of creating COM add-ins and Custom Task Panes is relatively simple. Visual Studio includes wizards that greatly simplify the process of creating both COM add-ins and ActiveX controls. In addition, you can easily combine the two technologies to create very powerful Custom Task Panes that can be used in many different Microsoft Office applications.

NOTE Building the Custom Task Pane Sample

In the implementation for the Custom Task Pane sample, the COM add-in references an interface in the ActiveX control. Also, the ActiveX control imports a type library that is exported when the COM add-in is built. This creates a circular build dependency. You won't be able to build the COM add-in until the ActiveX control is built, but you can't build the ActiveX control until the COM add-in is built.

One way to work around this is to comment out all references to the `IFormDataTPActiveXCtl` interface (and objects of that type) in FormDataViewAddin.cs and then build just the COM add-in project—FormDataTaskPane.

Once the COM add-in is built, you can build the ActiveX control—FormDataTaskPaneActiveX. Finally, uncomment the code that references the `IFormDataTPActiveXCtl` interface in FormDataViewAddin.cs and build the add-in project again. This should be a problem only the first time you build the sample.

In the FormDataTaskPane project, you may need to reset the references to the Microsoft Office 12 Object Library (`Microsoft.Office.Core`), the InfoPath interop assembly (`Microsoft.Office.Interop.InfoPath`), and the FormDataTaskPane DLL.

Also note that the code for the ActiveX control includes `#import` statements that reference Microsoft Office DLLs directly. You may need to change the paths to those files in order to build. See the ReadMe.txt file included with the sample for more information.

Writing Add-ins and Custom Task Panes Using VSTO 2005 SE

We've shown you how to create COM add-ins and Custom Task Panes using Visual Studio 2005. The examples presented so far demonstrate how to implement these components using Visual Studio without Visual Studio Tools for Office (VSTO). If you install the latest version of VSTO, Visual Studio 2005 Tools for the 2007 Microsoft Office System (or VSTO 2005 SE for short), there is an even easier way to create add-ins and Custom Task Panes. In fact, you don't need to know much or anything about COM. These add-ins use pure managed code!

Besides using managed code, the new managed add-ins also have another advantage—they are loaded into their own application domains. This means that if one add-in crashes (i.e., throws an exception), neither the application nor other add-ins are affected. Let's take a look at how easy it is to implement these new managed add-ins. The samples for this chapter include a managed add-in project called TrackBarTaskPane. This sample is a managed add-in that implements a Custom Task Pane. In this task pane is simply a TrackBar control (otherwise known as a slider control). When the task pane is loaded and you load a form in InfoPath that has at least one field, the value of the field will change as you position the track bar in the task pane. This is a very simple example that demonstrates how to implement a managed add-in and Custom Task Pane using VSTO 2005 SE.

To implement this sample, we're going to perform the following steps.

1. Create the managed add-in using VSTO 2005 SE.
2. Create a User Control that will be hosted in the Custom Task Pane.
3. Add a TrackBar control to the User Control.
4. Add the User Control to the `CustomTaskPanes` collection.
5. Show the Custom Task Pane.

Let's discuss in more detail how this is implemented.

Implementing a Managed Add-in

The first thing you must do (after installing VSTO 2005 SE) is create a new project in Visual Studio as you normally would. When you open the New

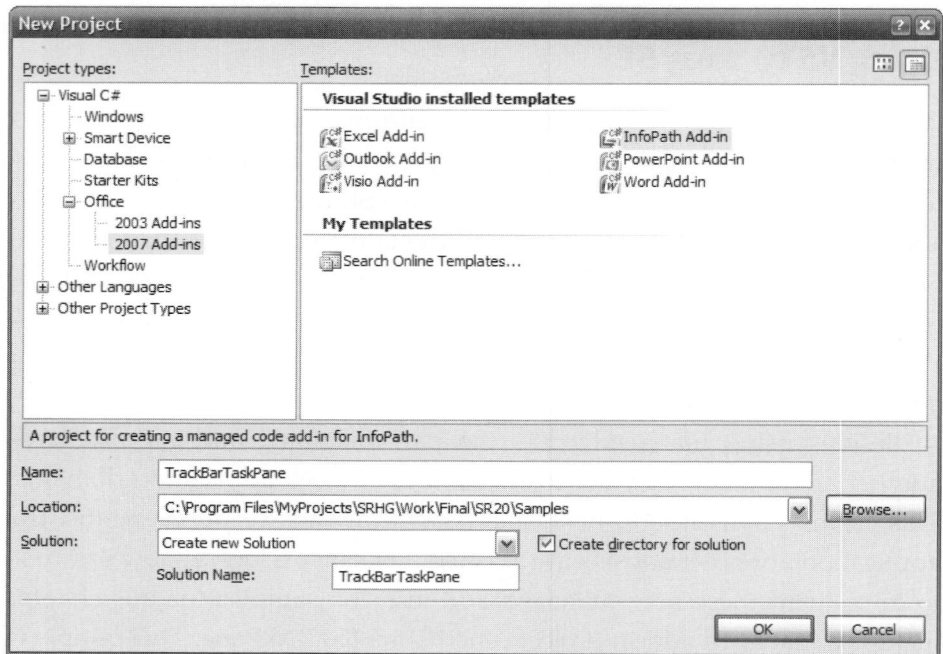

FIGURE 20.5: New Project wizard showing the InfoPath Add-in project type

Project wizard, you'll notice an *Office* branch under the *Visual C#* and *Visual Basic* project types. Under the *Office* branch are two project categories—*2003 Add-ins* and *2007 Add-ins*. Since add-ins for InfoPath are supported only for InfoPath 2007, let's select the *2007 Add-ins* category. After you click this category, the *New Project* dialog looks like that shown in Figure 20.5.

Once you select the *InfoPath Add-in* project type and complete the wizard, Visual Studio will create an add-in project. This project will contain a file called ThisAddIn.cs (or ThisAddIn.vb if you are using Visual Basic) that contains the template code for the managed add-in. The code is very simple. There are only two methods—`ThisAddIn_Startup` and `ThisAddIn_Shutdown`. Obviously, the former is called when the add-in is loaded, which happens when the hosting application is opened. The latter is called when the add-in is unloaded, which happens when the application is closed. Each of these methods receives a `sender` parameter of type `object` and an `EventArgs` parameter. The `sender` parameter is a reference to the add-in object itself.

Accessing the InfoPath Object Model from a Managed Add-in

In COM add-ins, when `OnConnection` is called, the add-in receives a reference to the application object that has loaded the add-in. In the case of InfoPath, this is the InfoPath `Application` object in the InfoPath OM.

However, in the case of a managed add-in, when `ThisAddIn_Startup` is called, the object passed in is not the application object, it's the add-in itself. You can still access the InfoPath object model, though, and do everything that we discussed earlier for COM add-ins—create toolbar buttons and other UI, access the data in the form, sink application and form events, and so on.

The add-in you create includes a partial class that is called `ThisAddIn` by default. When you created the project, in addition to ThisAddIn.cs (or ThisAddIn.vb), VSTO creates a file called ThisAddIn.Designer.cs/.vb that contains the rest of the class definition. (Note that you will not see this file in the Solution Explorer in Visual Studio by default. However, it does exist in the project folder.) This class contains two data members (among other methods and properties)—`Application` and `CustomTaskPanes`. (We'll talk about the latter shortly.)

The `Application` data member is a reference to the `Application` object of the application that is hosting the add-in—in this case, InfoPath. You can cast this property to `InfoPath.ApplicationClass` in order to have access to the full `Application` object in the InfoPath OM. Take a look at Listing 20.17, which shows the implementation of the `ThisAddIn_Startup` method in our sample add-in.

In the implementation of `ThisAddIn_Startup`, we first cast the `Application` data member to `InfoPath.ApplicationClass`. Then, just as we did with the COM add-in we built earlier, we obtain a reference to the `ApplicationEvents` object so that we can sink the `XDocumentOpen`, `NewXDocument`, and `XDocumentBeforeClose` events.

So, as you can see, just as with COM add-ins, you can access the InfoPath object model in a managed add-in. We'll leave it up to you to implement the toolbar buttons and additional functionality that we discussed earlier for COM add-ins.

LISTING 20.17: Implementation of the `ThisAddIn_Startup` Method

```
private void ThisAddIn_Startup(object sender, System.EventArgs e)
{
    _application = (InfoPath.ApplicationClass)this.Application;

    _applicationEvents =
        (InfoPath.ApplicationEvents)_application.Events;

    _applicationEvents.XDocumentOpen
        += new InfoPath._ApplicationEvents_XDocumentOpenEventHandler(
               _applicationEvents_XDocumentOpen);

    _applicationEvents.NewXDocument
        += new InfoPath._ApplicationEvents_NewXDocumentEventHandler(
               _applicationEvents_NewXDocument);

    _applicationEvents.XDocumentBeforeClose
    += new InfoPath._ApplicationEvents_XDocumentBeforeCloseEventHandler(
           _applicationEvents_XDocumentBeforeClose);
}
```

Adding a Custom Task Pane in a Managed Add-in

Now that we have the basic code for our add-in and we can tell when a form is opened, we obviously want to do something interesting. Let's create a Custom Task Pane that will appear as soon as a form is opened and hidden when the form is closed.

Earlier, when we talked about creating a Custom Task Pane, we mentioned that these task panes were implemented by using ActiveX controls. Wouldn't it be much easier to use managed code? Fortunately, with VSTO 2005 SE, this is now possible.

To create a Custom Task Pane with managed code, simply add a User Control to your project. Once you do, you can add any controls from the Visual Studio Toolbox to your User Control as normal. In this case, let's add a TrackBar control.

Once we've created the User Control, which we've named `TrackBarUserControl`, and added the TrackBar control to it, we need to create an instance of the User Control in our add-in and add the User Control to the collection of Custom Task Panes owned by the `ThisAddIn` class. (This will cause the Custom Task Pane to be created and is equivalent to the `CreateCTP` method we used when we created a Custom Task Pane in our earlier COM add-in example.) Doing these two things is easy. Just add the following lines of code to the bottom of the `ThisAddIn_Startup` method:

```
_userControl = new TrackBarUserControl();
this.CustomTaskPanes.Add(_userControl, "TrackBar Task Pane");
```

The data member `_userControl` is an instance of the `TrackBarUserControl` class. After creating this object, we add it to the collection of Custom Task Panes by calling the `Add` method on the `CustomTaskPanes` collection. The first parameter passed in is the User Control we want to host in the task pane. The second parameter is the title that will show at the top of the task pane.

Now we've created the task pane and hosted the User Control inside it. However, even though the add-in will be created when the application starts, the task pane will be hidden until we make it visible. As we mentioned earlier, we want to show the task pane when a form is opened and hide it when that form is closed. Therefore, we want to show the task pane when either the `XDocumentOpen` or `NewXDocument` events are fired and hide it when `XDocumentBeforeClose` occurs. When the form is opened (and the two former events are handled by the add-in), we call a common helper method called `OnFormOpened`, which is shown in Listing 20.18.

LISTING 20.18: `OnFormOpened` **Method**

```
private void OnFormOpened()
{
    if (pDocument.DOM != null)
    {
        IXMLDOMNode rootNode =
            pDocument.DOM.selectSingleNode(
                "*[not(self::processing-instruction())]");
        if (rootNode != null)
        {
            _node = rootNode.selectSingleNode("*");
            if (_node != null)
            {
                _userControl.TrackBar.ValueChanged
                    += new EventHandler(TrackBar_ValueChanged);
                _userControl.TrackBar.Enabled = true;
            }
        }
    }
    this.CustomTaskPanes[0].Visible = true;
}
```

In the OnFormOpened method, we're going to obtain a reference to the first field in the form so that we can update its value when the track bar's value changes in the task pane. To do that, after ensuring that the DOM is not null, we obtain a reference to the root node of the form. If you've created a blank form in InfoPath, the root node will be my:myFields.

Next, we select the first node that is a child of the root node. (This sample includes a sample form template—TrackBarSample—that has a single field. The first child node of the root node in this case is my:field1.)

Once we have a reference to the node that we're going to update, we create a new event handler for the ValueChanged event for the TrackBar control in the User Control. (The TrackBar property is a simple property we created that exposes the TrackBar control hosted in the User Control.) This event handler simply sets the value of the node to the current value of the TrackBar control:

```
void TrackBar_ValueChanged(object sender, EventArgs e)
{
    _node.text = _userControl.TrackBar.Value.ToString();
}
```

Back in the OnFormOpened method, after establishing the event handler, we enable the TrackBar control, which is disabled by default in the User Control in case we don't find a node to update.

After all this work is completed, we show the Custom Task Pane by setting its Visible property to true. (This sample, as it's currently written, works only for Custom Task Panes in one InfoPath window. Back when we talked about Custom Task Panes written with ActiveX controls, we mentioned that there is no easy way to obtain the task pane for the current window. We also showed you a way to deal with this that you can incorporate into this sample.)

At this point, we have a fully functional task pane that opens when a form loads and in which you can move a track bar to change the value of a field in the form. Figure 20.6 shows the task pane in action.

Now that our task pane displays when a form is opened, the only thing left for us to do is hide it when the form is closed. That part is easy. We just set the Visible property to false in the event handler method for the XDocumentBeforeClose event.

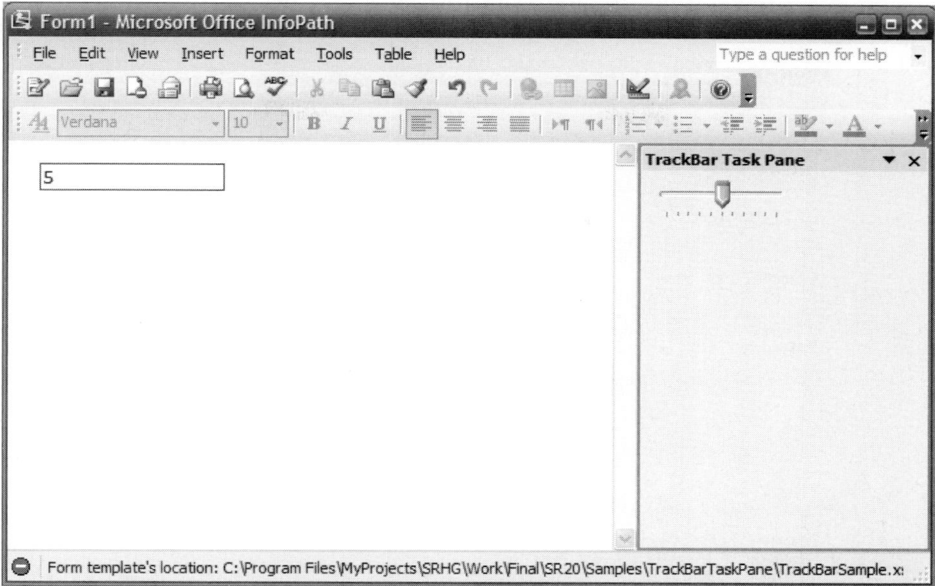

FIGURE 20.6: TrackBar task pane

It's easy to see that, by using VSTO 2005 SE, you can build managed add-ins and Custom Task Panes very rapidly. And, on top of that, hosting other controls is extremely simple. You don't need to write an ActiveX control or use COM at all to build add-ins and Custom Task Panes. Now that you know how to create your own add-ins, whether you do so using COM or managed code, you inevitably will want to be able to manage them from within InfoPath.

Managing InfoPath Add-ins

In Chapter 11, we showed you the *Trust Center* dialog, which you can use to manage options related to security and privacy. The Trust Center just happens to be the same place where you can manage add-ins. Figure 20.7 shows the *Trust Center* dialog after we selected the *Add-ins* tab. The two COM add-ins we created in this chapter, Form Data Viewer and Form Utilities, as well as the managed add-in TrackBarTaskPane, are listed under the *Active Application Add-ins* category. The dialog will also list inactive and disabled application add-ins. Note that there is also a category for document

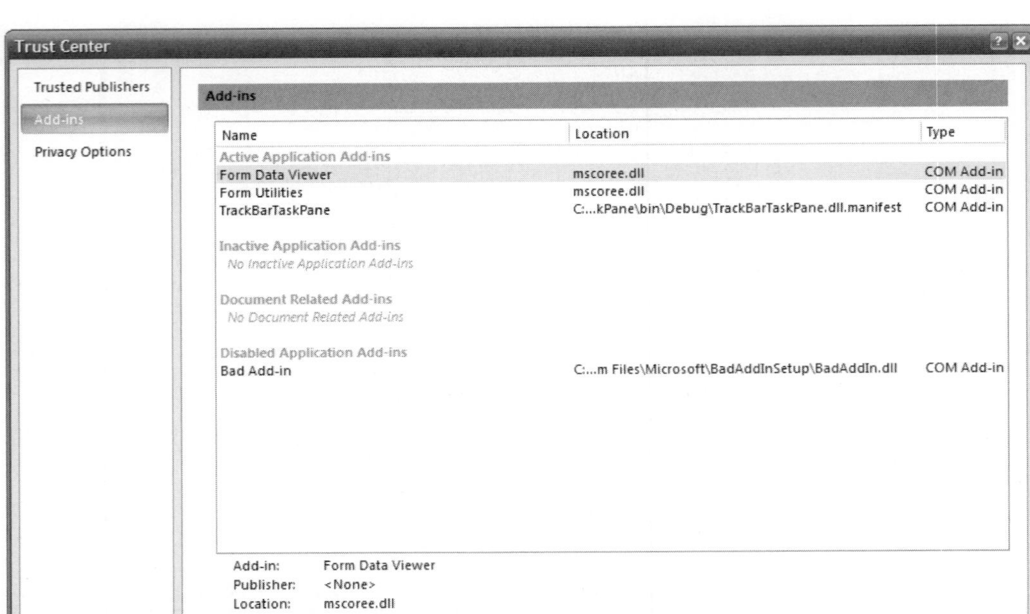

FIGURE 20.7: Trust Center dialog showing the Add-ins tab

add-ins, which are add-ins hosted inside documents. InfoPath 2007 doesn't support document add-ins. Other Microsoft Office applications do, however. (This dialog is shared among many Microsoft Office applications, so this category appears, although it is not supported by InfoPath 2007.)

The location of each add-in listed in the dialog is specified as well. This location is the DLL in which the add-in resides. Since our COM add-ins were written in managed code and use COM interop to work inside InfoPath, they will all be listed as residing in the mscoree.dll file, which is the Microsoft Component Object (.NET) Runtime Execution Engine DLL. The managed add-in resides in the TrackBarTaskPane.dll.manifest file.

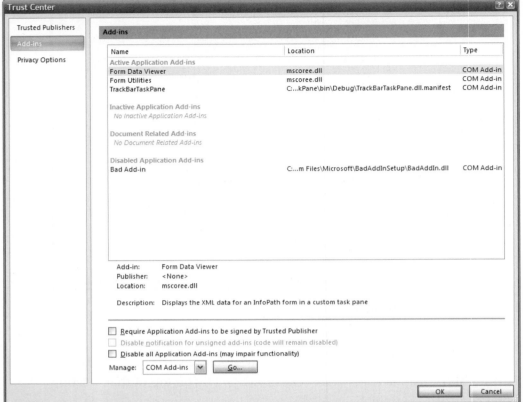

In the *Trust Center* dialog, you can specify certain options for add-ins, such as whether or not they must be signed by a trusted publisher. Also, you can disable all add-ins at once by selecting that option at the bottom of the dialog. (Note that some changes you make in this dialog will not take effect until you close InfoPath and restart.)

The Trust Center also allows you to manage each add-in individually. Just choose *COM Add-ins* from the *Manage* drop-down list box, and then click the *Go* button. When you do, the dialog shown in Figure 20.8 appears. From this dialog, you can deactivate one or more add-ins by unchecking the box next to the name of the add-in. Then the add-in will be listed under the *Inactive Application Add-ins* category in the *Add-ins* tab of the *Trust Center* dialog.

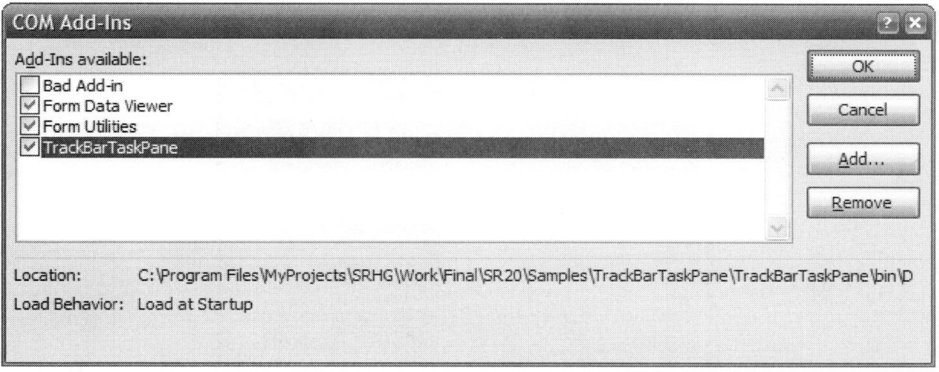

FIGURE 20.8: COM Add-ins dialog

You can also add an add-in manually by clicking the *Add* button and selecting the DLL of the add-in, or you can completely remove an add-in from InfoPath by clicking the *Remove* button. If you remove an add-in from InfoPath, to add it back you either need to add it manually from the *COM Add-ins* dialog or rerun the setup application for the add-in.

Whenever a COM add-in prevents InfoPath from functioning correctly (e.g., it causes InfoPath to crash) during a call to one of the methods in the `IDTExtensibility2` interface, the add-in will be listed under the *Disabled Application Add-ins* category in the *Trust Center* dialog. For example, if an add-in causes a crash during a call to `OnConnection`, the next time you start InfoPath, you will be presented with a warning dialog (Figure 20.9). If you choose to disable the add-in, it will be disabled and listed under the *Disabled Application Add-ins* category. (Note that for managed add-ins, exceptions will not cause the add-in to be disabled. Exceptions will be handled, and the add-in will be set to inactive.)

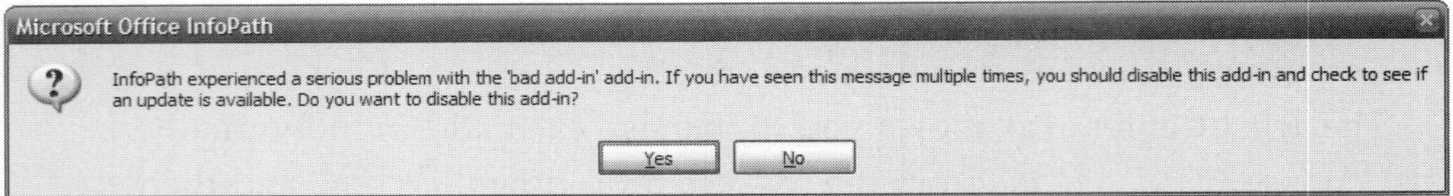
Microsoft Office InfoPath
InfoPath experienced a serious problem with the 'bad add-in' add-in. If you have seen this message multiple times, you should disable this add-in and check to see if an update is available. Do you want to disable this add-in?
Yes
No

FIGURE 20.9: Warning dialog shown after an add-in causes a serious error

After you've resolved any issues with your add-in, you can reenable the add-in by selecting the *Disabled Items* option from the *Manage* drop-down list box in the *Trust Center* dialog and then click the *Go* button. This opens the *Disabled Items* dialog (Figure 20.10). From here, to reenable an add-in, just select it and click the *Enable* button.

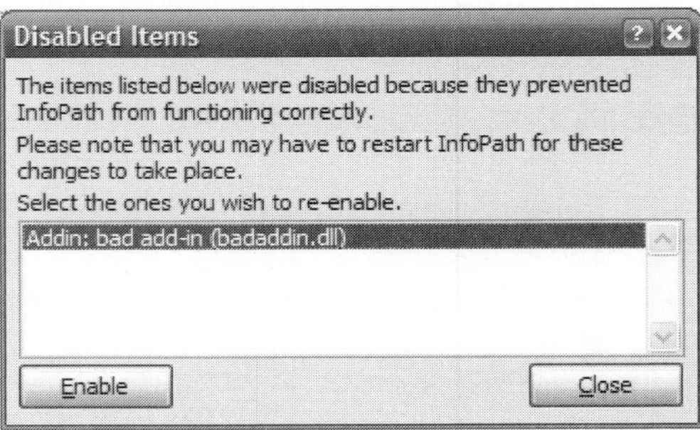
Disabled Items
The items listed below were disabled because they prevented InfoPath from functioning correctly.
Please note that you may have to restart InfoPath for these changes to take place.
Select the ones you wish to re-enable.
Addin: bad add-in (badaddin.dll)
Enable
Close

FIGURE 20.10: Disabled Items dialog

What's Next?

Add-ins, especially when combined with Custom Task Panes, give you a relatively easy way to customize the user experience in InfoPath. In a matter of a few hours or less, you can easily put together an add-in and a Custom Task Pane in Visual Studio that can enhance the user interface, add help context information, customize the form-filling experience, or do anything else you can dream up.

In the next chapter, which happens to be the final chapter in this book, we'll talk about importers and exporters. We'll discuss the two built-in form template importers in InfoPath 2007 that enable you to import Word and Excel documents into InfoPath as form templates. We'll also show you how to create your own form importers and exporters as well as how to create a form data importer.

21 Importers and Exporters

Getting Started

If you're like most people, you probably have used forms that were created in Word, Excel, or any number of other applications. Filling out forms with these applications works well, but as you've seen, InfoPath is the ideal application to use for designing and filling out forms. However, before InfoPath came along, many other applications had to be used to create and fill out forms. Now that you have InfoPath, you'll likely want to convert those existing forms into InfoPath form templates so you can start collecting the data as structured XML and use that data with back-end processes that consume XML data.

In this chapter, we'll show you how to use the new Word and Excel **form importers** included with InfoPath 2007 to convert existing Word and Excel forms into InfoPath form templates. Even though InfoPath includes only these two built-in importers, that doesn't mean you can't import forms created with other applications. Also, what if you want to export an InfoPath form template to some other type of form? To help you import forms from applications other than Word and Excel (or implement your own importers for Word and/or Excel) and export InfoPath form templates to another format, InfoPath provides an **import/export framework** with which you can create your own importers and exporters. We'll talk about this framework as well.

As we mentioned, you probably have forms created by other applications that have been in use for quite some time. Being able to import these forms into InfoPath to create form templates is great, but what do you do with all the data you've collected by using these other applications? Ideally, you want to import the data into InfoPath forms so you don't need to reenter it by hand. Luckily, InfoPath also includes a **data importer framework** that enables you to create your own importer to move the data from existing forms into InfoPath. Later in this chapter we'll introduce this framework.

Built-in Form Importers

InfoPath 2007 includes two built-in importers, one to import Word forms and another for Excel forms. In this section, we will show you how to use these two built-in importers and how they not only import the layout of the form but create controls and a data source structure as well. The built-in form importers for Word and Excel are quite simple to use, as we'll show you shortly.

Whether you are filling out a form created in Word or in Excel, forms fall into one of two classifications: printable or electronic forms. Forms meant to be printed and filled out by hand are, obviously, classified as printable forms. These forms typically indicate places to fill in data by using visual cues such as underlines or tables. For example, if the creator of the form wants you to insert your name, you might see something like this in the form:

Name: ______________________

Electronic forms are meant to be filled out by using a computer instead of paper and pencil. Electronic forms usually, but not always, contain form fields instead of visual cues to tell users where to enter data.

In either case, whether your form is meant to be filled out electronically or printed out and filled out by hand, you can still import it into InfoPath (as long as you have the form in an electronic document format). When you import the form, if it contains visual cues that indicate where to fill in the data, in most cases the built-in importers will detect these cues and insert controls and their corresponding data source elements. If the form contains form fields, the importers will detect those as well and also convert them to controls and data source elements.

This is very powerful. Importing just the layout of the form is much easier than having to create the form in InfoPath from scratch. However, if that were all the importers did for you, you would still need to create the controls and data source structure yourself to take advantage of the real power of InfoPath—the ability to collect data. The fact that the built-in importers will create controls for you greatly simplifies the process of converting forms from Word and Excel to InfoPath form templates.

Let's see how to import a Word form. The process for importing Excel forms is pretty much the same. We will point out those few places where there are differences.

> **NOTE** **Application Version Requirement for the Built-in InfoPath Form Importers**
>
> The built-in importers for Word and Excel forms both require that you have the 2007 version of these applications installed. You can still import documents created in previous versions of these applications, but, in order for the importers to work, the 2007 versions must be installed.

Let's start by trying to import the form shown in Figure 21.1. This form is an expense report form for MOI Consulting that was created in Word. (This document is named MOIConsulting.doc and is included with the samples for this chapter on the book's Web site.) Let's look at this form in detail to see what it contains.

First, you'll notice that there is a picture at the top as well as the name of the company and the title of the form. What you can't see is that these items are within a table (with no borders) that is being used for layout. Next, the form has a place to fill out your name. We use underlines to indicate where you should enter this information. Then, we use a form field to capture the e-mail address. So, you can see that this form is meant to be filled out electronically. However, nothing keeps you from printing it and

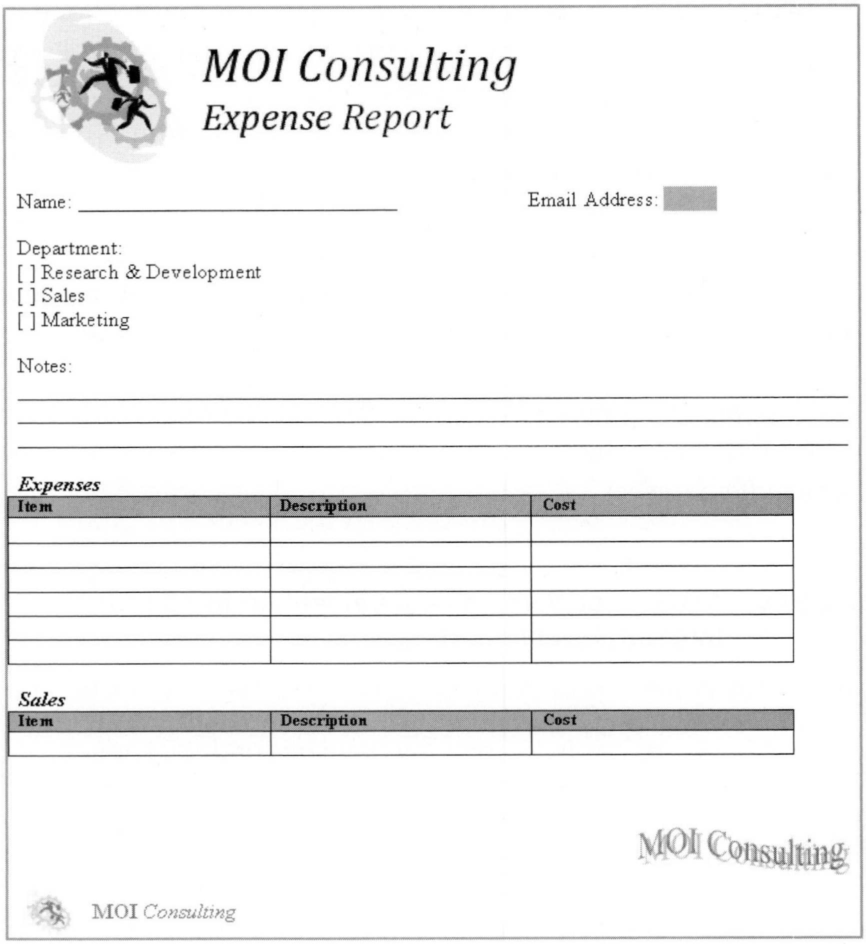

MOI Consulting
Expense Report

Name: ______________________ Email Address:

Department:
[ ] Research & Development
[ ] Sales
[ ] Marketing

Notes:

Expenses

Item	Description	Cost

Sales

Item	Description	Cost

MOI Consulting

MOI *Consulting*

FIGURE 21.1: MOI Consulting expense report form created in Word

filling it out by hand. (The simple fact that the form contains the text "Email Address:" lets you know that you are meant to fill in your e-mail address after this text, even if you can't see the form field when printed.)

Next, there are three checkbox-like areas of the form for you to check your department name. Here you simply put an X or checkmark next to the appropriate department. However, what prevents you from marking multiple departments?

Then comes an area in which you can enter additional notes that describe your expense report in more detail. However, you are limited to three lines. If you want to add additional information, you need to include a secondary document (if you are filling out the form electronically) or write on the back of the paper.

A table included in the form provides space in which you can enter all the expense report information, including the expense item, description, and cost. However, you are limited to six expense items. This is the same problem as with the notes section. How do you enter more expense items? Also, how do you know the total expenses? Well, you could just whip out your handy-dandy pocket calculator, but what a pain that can be.

After the table for expenses is a table for sales information. In addition to the same problems we have with the expense table (no room for additional items and no easy way to calculate the total), there is one more issue. If you aren't in the sales department, you likely won't need to fill out this section of the form. It sure would be nice to hide this part if it's not needed. Hmmm, is there an application we can use that will allow us to do that?

Finally, there are a few items at the bottom of the form to make the form look nice. (We added them mainly to demonstrate a few features of the built-in importers, as you'll see soon.) A bit of Word art at the bottom displays the MOI Consulting logo. The footer contains a picture and branding for the company. Notice that the text "MOI Consulting" contains mixed formatting. The first part sets in bold, the second part in italics. What you can't see is that this footer also contains a layout table to help position the picture and text.

Importing a Form into InfoPath

Now that we've seen the form, let's see how we can import it into InfoPath. As you've probably guessed, importing forms into InfoPath is very easy. First, from the *Getting Started* dialog, click on the *Import a Form* link under the *Design a Form* category. This will open the first page of the Import Wizard (Figure 21.2). If you've never installed an importer before, you'll see only the two default importers in this start page of the wizard.

Next, since we want to import a Word document, let's choose the second option and then click the *Next* button. The wizard page shown in Figure 21.3

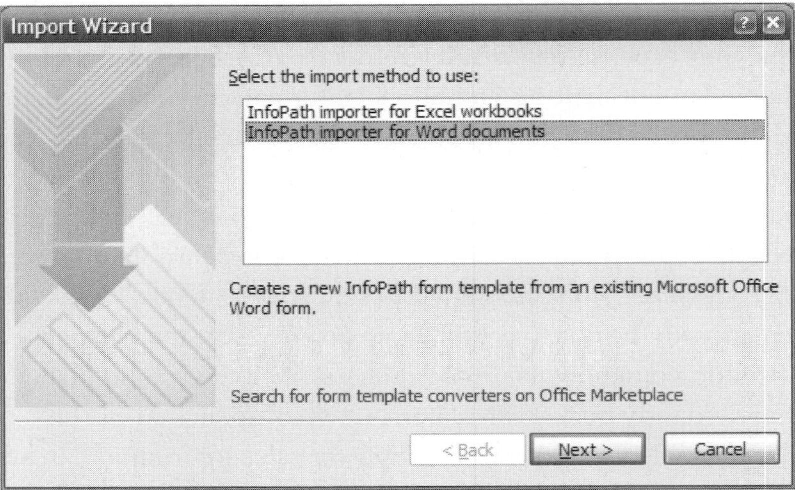

FIGURE 21.2: Import Wizard page for selecting the importer to use

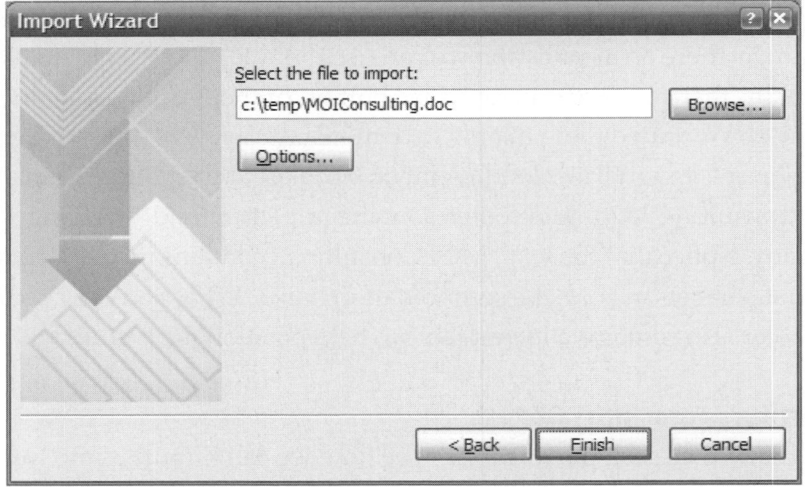

FIGURE 21.3: Import Wizard page for selecting the file to import

opens. If you choose a file and then click the *Finish* button, the Word document will be imported. In this case, InfoPath will use a default set of rules to determine how to convert parts of the document into controls. For example, if InfoPath sees text that looks like "[ ]", it will convert that text to a Check Box control that is bound to a field in the data source.

TIP Make Sure the File to Be Imported Is Not in Use

If the file you are trying to import is opened in its corresponding application (e.g., Excel or Word), you may not be able to import it. Some applications lock opened files, which will prevent the importer from accessing the file. If this is the case, when you try to import the file, you will receive an error that tells you that the specified file cannot be accessed. Therefore, make sure the file isn't being used before you try to import it.

You can see all the rules that will be applied and control how the document is imported by clicking on the *Options* button in this step of the Import Wizard. When you do so, the *Import Options* dialog opens (Figure 21.4). The *Import Options* dialog is not actually an InfoPath dialog; it is displayed by the importer itself. (It just so happens that the Word and Excel importers are implemented by InfoPath, however. But other importers implemented outside of InfoPath are responsible for showing this dialog, as you'll see later in this chapter.)

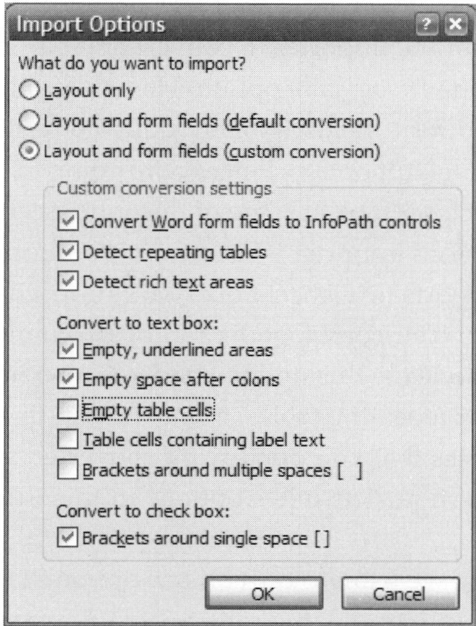

FIGURE 21.4: Import Options dialog for importing Word documents

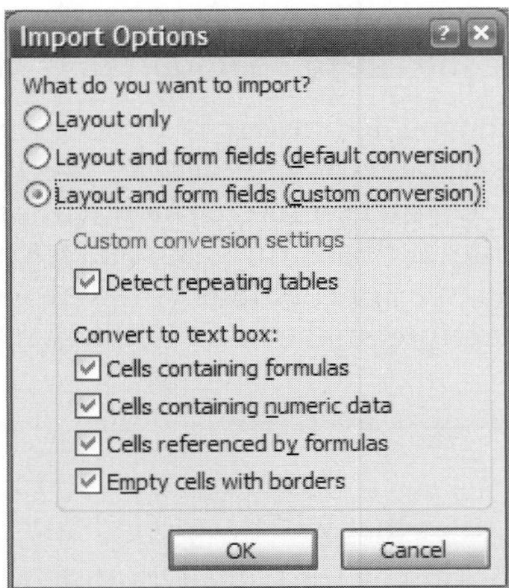

FIGURE 21.5: Import Options dialog for importing Excel workbooks

Figure 21.5 shows the *Import Options* dialog for importing Excel workbooks. In both cases, the default option is to import the layout of the form and form fields by using the default conversion rules. (In the figures, we've selected *Layout and form fields (custom conversion)* just to show all the rules that are available.)

If you don't want the importer to convert any part of the document to form fields, select the *Layout only* option. However, since converting parts of the document to form fields is really quite convenient, you probably want to choose the default option. Since we're going to import a Word document, let's take a closer look at some of the options shown in Figure 21.4.

By default, the Word importer will convert Word form fields to InfoPath controls. Word supports text, checkboxes, and drop-down form fields that will map directly to their corresponding InfoPath counterparts. Therefore, you'll likely want to leave this option checked. Also notice that the Word importer will detect repeating tables. In most cases, this is what you want, but if you have tables that you don't want converted to a repeating table, just uncheck this option. The other options in this dialog are pretty self-explanatory.

For our example, we want to turn on one option that is off by default—the option to convert empty table cells to Text Box controls. One table in our expense report is used to collect data but has only a single row—the sales table. A repeating table typically has multiple rows, and if it doesn't, it's usually used for layout. In that case, you most likely don't want the empty table cells to be converted to Text Box controls. However, in the case of our expense report, we do want to be able to enter multiple rows of data into the sales table, so we'll turn on the *Empty table cells* option.

Now, let's complete the wizard and import the Word document. Depending on the size of your document, the import process could take a while. There is a progress dialog, though, so you won't get too bored. When the document has been completely imported, the final page of the wizard appears (Figure 21.6). If there were no issues, you will simply see a success message. However, as shown in Figure 21.6, in our example we'll need to look into some issues that were identified while importing the form.

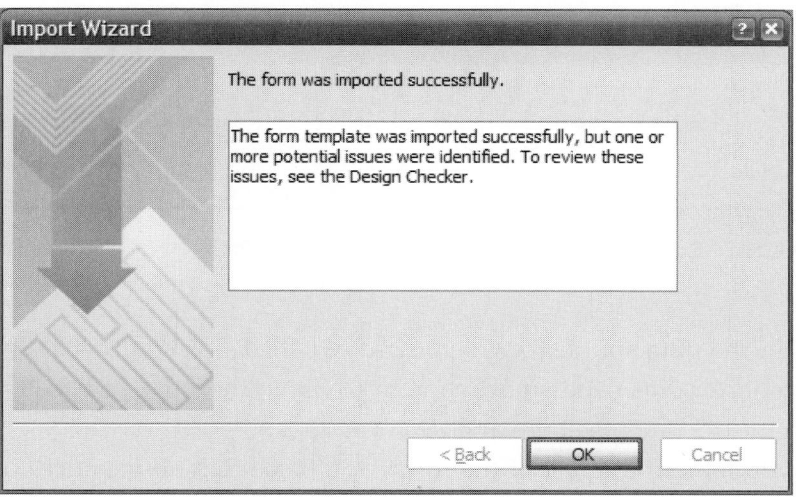

FIGURE 21.6: Final page of the Import Wizard

Let's close the wizard and look at the imported form (Figure 21.7). Notice that the *Design Checker* task pane is open and lists three warnings. We'll discuss those warnings soon, but first let's look at the form itself.

The form shown in Figure 21.7 looks almost exactly like the original Word form. The layout table at the top of the form was imported, as well as the picture and text inside the table cells. The Word importer detected the underlines next to the text "Name:" and the form field next to "Email Address:" and converted those to Text Box controls. In addition, if you open the *Data Source* task pane, you'll notice that the importer created text

FIGURE 21.7: Expense report form after importing into InfoPath

fields in the data source to which these two Text Box controls are bound. The importer was even smart enough to name those fields based on the text in the document—`Name` and `EmailAddress`.

If you look at the rest of the form, you'll see that all instances of "[ ]" were converted to Check Box controls, and the multiple underlines were converted to a Rich Text Box control. The repeating table for expenses was correctly detected and converted to a Repeating Table control, and the empty table cells inside the sales table were converted to Text Box controls.

Now that you've imported the Word form, you can add some features to the form template that you couldn't easily do with Word. For example, you can add Expression Box controls to calculate the total expenses and sales. You can also put the sales table inside a Section control and use conditional formatting to hide it unless the person filling out the form is in the sales department (which you might detect through user roles). First, though, we need to take care of a few issues in the form.

Fixing the Imported Form

Although the Word importer was able to import the layout of the form and convert parts of the document to form fields, there are a few issues. First, there is a Text Box control next to the text "Department:". That text was really supposed to be used as the label for the department checkboxes below it. However, the importer saw the colon character and assumed this text was supposed to be a field. Fixing this is easy. Simply delete the Text Box and its corresponding field in the data source, which is easy to find since it has the same name as the label text—`Department`.

Next, as we mentioned, the Word importer correctly converted each occurrence of "[ ]" to a Check Box control. However, in most companies, an employee can be in only one department. The problem with the original Word document is that there was no way to prevent somebody from checking multiple departments. Now that the form has been imported into InfoPath, enforcing that requirement is easy. We just need to convert these Check Box controls to Option Button controls so that only one department can be chosen. However, if you change each Check Box control to an Option Button one by one, you have changed the control type but not its behavior. You'll still be able to choose multiple departments. The easiest way to fix this is to select all the Check Box controls for all the departments (by holding down the Ctrl key while selecting each Check Box). Then from the *Edit* menu, click on the *Change To* fly-out menu and then click *Option Button.* When you do this, InfoPath will convert all the selected Check Box controls to Option Button controls and bind them to a new field in the data source. The fields to which the original Check Box controls were bound will remain in the data source, so you'll need to remove them manually.

Next, our sales table was imported and the empty cells were converted to Text Box controls. However, our original intention was for this table to contain multiple sales items even though we didn't include space for more than one. Since there was only one row in the table, the Word importer didn't import this table as a Repeating Table control. Luckily, we can easily convert this table to a Repeating Table. Just select the entire table (or place your insertion point anywhere inside the table but without selecting one of the Text Box controls), click on the *Change To* fly-out menu from the *Edit* menu, and then choose *Repeating Table.* When you do, you'll see the dialog shown in Figure 21.8.

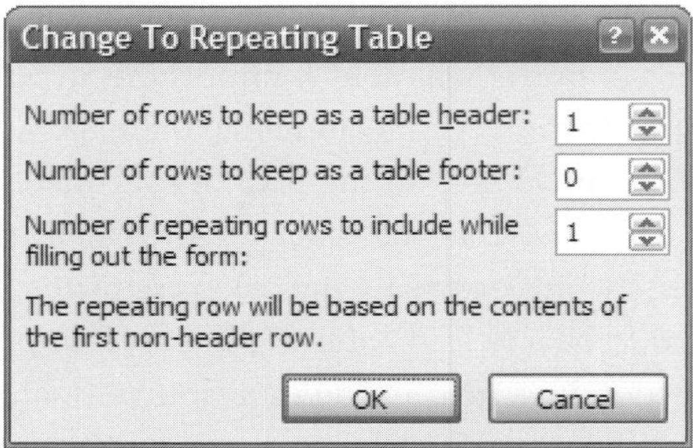

FIGURE 21.8: Change To Repeating Table dialog

From this dialog, you can choose the number of rows to be used as the header. By default, this value is 0, but we'll set it to 1 (as shown in Figure 21.8) since our table has a header row. If you leave the value as 0, InfoPath will assume that the first row is the data row and will display an error since the first row doesn't contain any controls. (For a Repeating Table to work, it must contain at least one control that is bound to data in the data source.) So, if you have a header row, make sure you change this value to 1 in the dialog. You can also choose the number of rows to use as the footer and the number of repeating rows to include by default when filling out the form.

Once you click the *OK* button in this dialog, the table is converted to a Repeating Table. As was the case when converting Check Box controls to Option Button controls, when you convert from a layout table to a Repeating Table control, InfoPath will create the correct elements in the data source for you. In this case, InfoPath creates a new group node and moves the fields to which the Text Box controls are bound below the new group node.

Post-Import Warnings

So, we've made a few changes to our form to clean it up a bit. We're almost done. Remember that we pointed out that some issues were identified when importing the form. The *Design Checker* task pane lists these issues. For our form, we have three warnings. The first one tells us that some formatting was removed from the footer text. (As with any such error or warning, if you click on it in the *Design Checker* task pane, you will be given more information about the issue, or focus will shift to the control in the view that has the problem.) Remember that we had mixed formatting in our footer. (Part of the footer text has bold text while another part has italics.) InfoPath doesn't support mixed formatting in headers and footers, so the formatting was removed, but the text was preserved. If you have uniform formatting in a header or footer (e.g., all bold and italic or all underline and italic), that formatting will be preserved.

Remember that we also had a layout table and a picture in our footer. InfoPath doesn't support these constructs in headers and footers either, so they were also removed. There are no *Design Checker* warnings about these issues, but any text in the footer is preserved.

The next warning in the *Design Checker* task pane is that one or more drawings were discarded. Clicking on this warning tells us that InfoPath doesn't support drawings and that any drawings in the form were replaced with placeholders to preserve the layout of the form. If you look at the bottom of the form, you'll notice the Word art we created for the MOI Consulting logo in the original document was replaced with a placeholder. However, the Word importer did preserve the original text. To fix this, we can remove the placeholder and replace it with either a picture or text that is formatted with a fancy font.

The final warning simply tells us that our original document had bookmarks, comments, and/or tracked changes, which InfoPath doesn't support. We can't do anything about that, so we'll just ignore it.

These are just three of the many warnings that may arise when importing a form. The warnings shown are specified by the importer itself, so they will differ from one importer to the next.

NOTE **Removing Post-Import Warnings**

It's not possible to remove individual import warnings from the *Design Checker* task pane. However, you can remove all post-import warnings by opening the *Resource Files* dialog from the *Tools* menu. In the dialog that opens, select the ImportErrors.xml file and then click the *Remove* button.

Creating Your Own Form Importers and Exporters

Now you have a taste of what it's like to import a form from another application into InfoPath. You can see how InfoPath makes it simple for you to import forms and to fix up your forms after importing.

InfoPath 2007 includes only the two default importers for Excel and Word documents. What if you want to import a form that was created by a totally different application? You may have noticed on the first page of the Import Wizard that there is a link to *Office Marketplace* at the bottom. If you browse to *Office Marketplace*, you can download and install additional importers. You can certainly download them from other places as well.

However, how do you go about creating your own importer? You may have your own application that creates forms that you want to be able to import into InfoPath. Or maybe you want to export an InfoPath form template into another format. (Unfortunately, InfoPath 2007 doesn't include any built-in exporters.)

InfoPath 2007 includes a framework for importing and exporting form templates. Next, we'll show you how to take advantage of this framework to create your own importers and/or exporters.

InfoPath Import/Export Framework

Taking advantage of the import/export framework is relatively easy. If you know how to create a COM object (which you should if you read the chapters on ActiveX and COM add-ins), you can easily create an importer or exporter.

Follow these three main steps when creating an importer or exporter:

1. Create a COM object.
2 Register the object as either an importer or an exporter (or both).
3. Implement the `IFormTemplateConverter2` interface.

Obviously, you must create your COM object first, but you can do steps 2 and 3 in either order. You've already seen how to create a COM object in previous chapters. So, let's dive into the other two requirements in detail.

Registering Your Importer/Exporter

Once you create your COM object, the next logical step is to register it with InfoPath so that it will be recognized as either an importer or an exporter or both. You can choose to have the control register itself or have it registered via a setup application.

To register your object as an importer, you must first create a registry key under `HKEY_LOCAL_MACHINE\SOFTWARE\Microsoft\Office\InfoPath\Converters\Import`. The new key that you create should have the same name as the ProgID of your COM object. For example, if you are creating an importer/exporter named SimpleImporterExporter whose ProgID is `IPImporterExporter.SimpleImportExport`, that is the name you should give to the new key you create. (If you are creating an exporter, everything we'll talk about here applies as well. However, the keys and values we're going to talk about should be created under the `HKEY_LOCAL_MACHINE\SOFTWARE\Microsoft\Office\InfoPath\Converters\Export` key instead.)

Next, you should create one key under this newly created ProgID key for each of the languages supported by the importer. The name of the key should be the locale ID (LCID) for the supported language. For example, if the importer supports U.S. English and Japanese, you'll create two keys—`1033` (U.S. English) and `1041` (Japanese). (Figure 21.9 shows the registry key structure for a sample importer/exporter.) The key for each locale contains a list of strings that InfoPath will show to the user in the Import Wizard, so it's important to have different localized versions of each string. We'll talk about the contents of the LCID keys shortly.

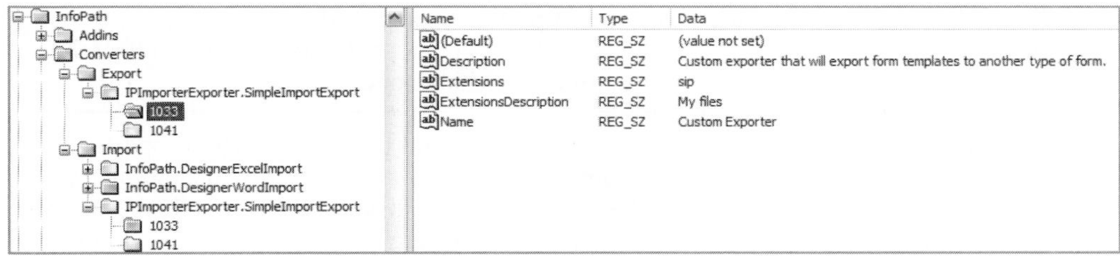

FIGURE 21.9: Registry key structure for importers and exporters

You'll next want to create a DWORD value called **DefaultLCID** under the ProgID key you created earlier. Set the value of this DWORD to be the LCID to use when the current LCID is not supported by the importer. For example, if you set DefaultLCID to 1033 in decimal (U.S. English), the user's current LCID is 1031 (German), and the importer doesn't support German, InfoPath will look at the 1033 key in the registry for the strings to show to the user in the Import Wizard.

Finally, under each key for each LCID that the importer supports, create the string values listed in Table 21.1. (Figure 21.9 shows the string values in the registry for our sample importer.)

Once you've registered your importer or exporter, even though you haven't implemented the IFormTemplateConverter2 interface, the importer/exporter will show up in the Import Wizard and/or the Export Wizard. (You can access the Export Wizard by clicking *Export Form* from the

TABLE 21.1: String Values to Be Added Under Each LCID Key

Name	Description
Name	The name of the importer. This name will be shown in the first page of the Import Wizard. The maximum length of the name is 64 characters.
Description	The description of the importer that will be shown in the first page of the Import Wizard. The maximum length of the description is 128 characters.
Extensions	The file extensions that are supported by the importer. These extensions are shown in the *Browse* dialog when you choose a file to import. Each extension is separated by a space. For example, if the importer supports text and XML files, the list of extensions will be "txt xml". The maximum length of the extensions string is 64 characters.
Extensions-Description	A description of the extensions that the importer supports. The extensions description is shown in the *Browse* dialog when you choose a file to import. This will typically be something like "My files" (as shown in Figure 21.9) or "MOI Consulting files". The maximum length of the extensions description is 64 characters.

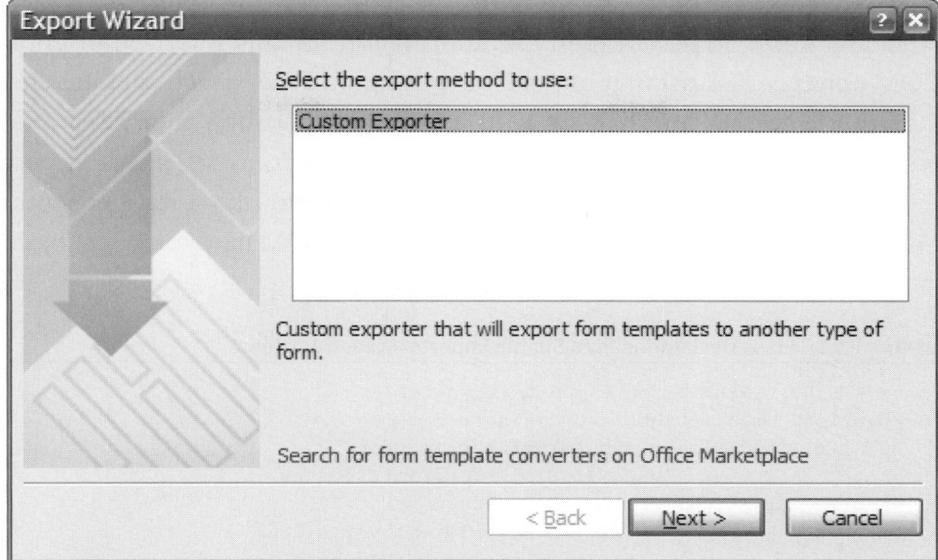

FIGURE 21.10: Export Wizard showing a custom exporter

File menu when a form template is opened in design mode.) Figure 21.10 shows the Export Wizard after we registered a custom exporter.

Implementing the `IFormTemplateConverter2` Interface

We now have registered a custom importer or exporter. However, if we click the *Next* button in either wizard after selecting the importer/exporter that we just registered, we will receive an error since we haven't yet implemented the `IFormTemplateConverter2` interface.

> **NOTE** Why Not Implement `IFormTemplateConverter`?
>
> You may wonder why the interface we suggest that you use is `IFormTemplateConverter2` and not `IFormTemplateConverter`. The latter interface, which was created in InfoPath 2003 SP1 (and is now deprecated), does not contain much of the functionality of the newer `IFormTemplateConverter2` interface. The first version of this interface is still supported by InfoPath 2007 for backward compatibility. However, to take advantage of the new import/export framework, you must implement `IFormTemplateConverter2`.

Implementing this interface is no different than the process for any other interface. To access the type information for this interface in your COM object, you must first import the ipdesign.dll file, which contains the definition for this interface as well as other supporting interfaces and types. Since `IFormTemplateConverter2` inherits from `IDispatch`, you will need to implement that interface as well. If you have created your COM object using ATL, the class declaration and COM map for your object may look similar to that shown in Listing 21.1.

LISTING 21.1: Class Declaration for a Simple Importer/Exporter Object

```
class ATL_NO_VTABLE CSimpleImporterExporter :
    public CComObjectRootEx<CComSingleThreadModel>,
    public CComCoClass<CSimpleImporterExporter,
                       &CLSID_SimpleImporterExporter>,
    public IDispatchImpl<IFormTemplateConverter2,
                       &IID_IFormTemplateConverter2,
                       &LIBID_SimpleInfoPathImporterExporterLib,
                       /*wMajor =*/ 1, /*wMinor =*/ 0>
{
public:
    BEGIN_COM_MAP(CSimpleImporterExporter)
      COM_INTERFACE_ENTRY(IFormTemplateConverter2)
      COM_INTERFACE_ENTRY2(IDispatch, IFormTemplateConverter2)
    END_COM_MAP()
. . .
. . .
};
```

Now you just need to implement each of the interface methods of `IFormTemplateConverter2`. That's simple enough, right? Table 21.2 lists and describes each of the methods of this interface.

Figure 21.11 shows the process flow for an importer/exporter indicating when each `IFormTemplateConverter2` method is called. Let's look at this diagram in more detail.

When the user first opens the Import Wizard (or Export Wizard), InfoPath will look in the registry for all the registered importers/exporters. It will list them all in the first page of the wizard. When the user chooses one and then clicks the *Next* button, InfoPath will create an instance of the importer/exporter using the ProgID under which the component is registered.

TABLE 21.2: Methods of the `IFormTemplateConverter2` Interface

Method	Description
`Initialize`	Called to initialize the importer/exporter. This method is passed a pointer to the `IUnknown` interface of the conversion manager.
`UnInitialize`	Called right before the importer/exporter is unloaded.
`Import`	Called to import a form into InfoPath.
`Export`	Called to export a form template from InfoPath to some other format.
`ShowOptionsDialog`	Called when the user presses the *Options* button in the Import or Export Wizards so the importer/exporter can show its options dialog.
`SetLcid`	Called by InfoPath to tell the importer/exporter what locale ID is being used.

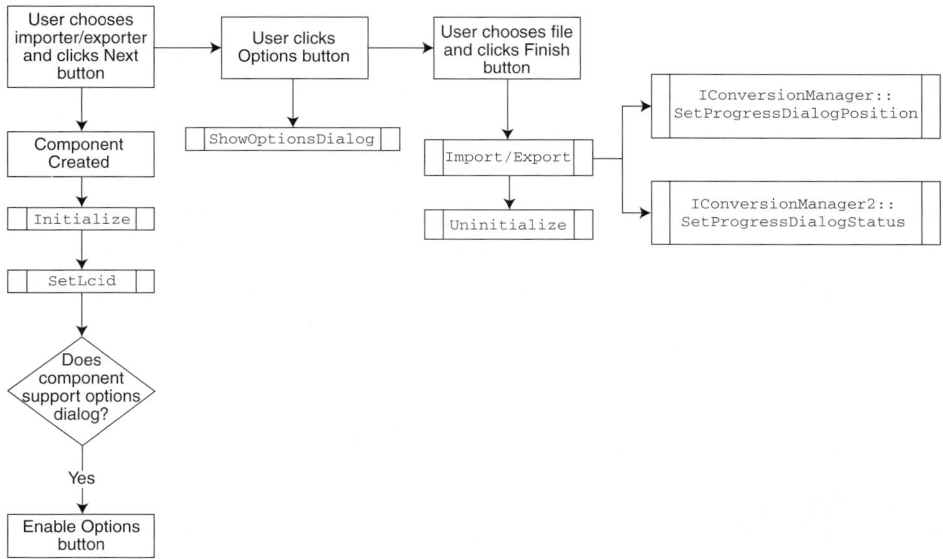

FIGURE 21.11: Importer/exporter process flow

TABLE 21.3: Methods of the `IConversionManager` Interface

Method Name	Description
`get_ProductVersion`	Returns the current version of InfoPath.
`SetPreference`	Sets various preferences for the importer/exporter. Besides `prefNil`, which specifies no preferences, there are two options that can be set. The `prefSupportProgressDialog` option specifies that the importer/exporter supports a progress dialog and will update it at various points during the conversion process. If this preference isn't set, only a wait cursor will be shown. The other option, `prefSupportOptionsDialog`, specifies that the importer/exporter supports an options dialog.
`SetProgressDialogPosition`	Sets the position of the progress bar in the progress dialog. The number passed in must be between 0 and 100.
`SetProgressDialogCaption`	Sets the title of the progress dialog.

Next, InfoPath will call the `Initialize` method, passing a pointer to the `IUnknown` interface of the conversion manager. You can call `QueryInterface` on this interface to access either the `IConversionManager` or `IConversionManager2` interface. These interfaces, whose methods are listed in Tables 21.3 and 21.4, respectively, enable the importer/exporter to set specific preferences (such as whether or not the options or progress dialogs are supported) get the product version, and set various information in the progress dialog.

TABLE 21.4: Method of the `IConversionManager2` Interface

Method Name	Description
`SetProgressDialogStatus`	Specifies informational text about the current progress of the importer/exporter. An example of this could be "Exporting document" or "Converting controls."

Listing 21.2 shows an example implementation of the `Initialize` method. In this case, we've specified that our component supports both the options and progress dialogs.

LISTING 21.2: `Initialize` **Method**

```
STDMETHOD(Initialize)(IUnknown* pUnkConversionManager)
{
    CComQIPtr<IConversionManager> spConversionManager;
    spConversionManager = pUnkConversionManager;
    if (spConversionManager != NULL)
    {
        spConversionManager->SetPreference(
            (xdPreference)(prefSupportProgressDialog
                         | prefSupportOptionsDialog));
    }
        return S_OK;
}
```

After `Initialize` is called, InfoPath will call `SetLcid`, passing in the current locale identifier. If the LCID is supported by the importer/exporter or you want InfoPath to use the LCID specified by the `DefaultLCID` value in the registry, then just return `S_OK`. You can return a failure code to indicate that the specified locale is not supported, at which point the import or export process will be aborted.

After initialization is complete, the second page of the wizard appears. When `Initialize` was called, if the component specified that it supported the options dialog, the *Options* button in the second page of the wizard will be enabled. If the user clicks the *Options* button, the `ShowOptionsDialog` method is called, at which time it is up to the importer/exporter to show its own dialog. Any options set in the dialog must be persisted by the component itself. InfoPath will not save this data for you.

On the second page of the dialog, in order to continue, the user must specify a file to import or export. If the user clicks the *Browse* button, InfoPath looks at the `Extensions` and `ExtensionsDescription` string values under the key for the current LCID to populate the browse dialog with a list of supported file types.

Importing and Exporting

After the user chooses a file and then clicks the *Finish* button, the fun begins. Now the form from the other application is imported or the current

TABLE 21.5: Parameters for the `Import` and `Export` Methods

Parameter Name	Description
`srcPath`	Specifies the path to the source file to import or the form template files to export.
`destPath`	Specifies the path to the destination location for the imported form template or the file to which to export.
`vfShowUI`	Specifies whether or not the importer/exporter can show any UI such as dialog messages. If this is `VARIANT_FALSE`, the importer/exporter should not show any UI while importing or exporting. When the converter is being run by InfoPath, this parameter will always be `VARIANT_TRUE`. However, it could be `VARIANT_FALSE` if `Import` or `Export` is called in automation scenarios.
`pMessage`	When the import or export process is complete, the component can specify additional details about the operation in this parameter. This string will be shown in the last page of the Import or Export Wizards.

form template opened in InfoPath design mode is exported. In the former case, the `Import` method is called. In the latter, as you might have guessed, the `Export` method is called. Whether you're importing or exporting, the process is basically the same. In fact, the signatures of the `Import` and `Export` methods are exactly the same. Table 21.5 shows the parameters for both of these methods. The only difference between the `Import` and `Export` methods is the meaning of `srcPath` and `destPath`.

When `Import` is called, `srcPath` specifies the location of the file that the user wants to import into InfoPath. The `destPath` parameter specifies a temporary location to which the importer should save the form template files. When `Import` is called, it is the responsibility of the importer to open the file specified in the `srcPath` parameter and then create all the files that are normally included in a form template.

Normally, as you know, when you create a form template in InfoPath, one file is saved—a .xsn file. Earlier in this book, we talked about how this .xsn file is just a CAB file that contains other files that define different parts of the form. If you create a blank form template and then select *Save as*

Source Files from the *File* menu, you'll notice that the form template is made up of the following files:

- `manifest.xsf` defines the contents of the form template and how it should be edited (e.g., rules, calculations, data connections, and so on).
- `myschema.xsd` defines the schema for the form template. The name of this file will be different if you have designed your form from an existing schema.
- `sampledata.xml` includes sample data that will be shown in design mode.
- `template.xml` contains default data for the form.
- `view1.xsl` defines the controls and other view constructs shown to the user in the form. There is one `.xsl` file for each view.

When importing a form, the importer must create each of the files listed here and any additional resource files, such as pictures, that need to be included in the form template. These files should be saved to the location specified by the `destPath` parameter. (When importing the form, since this process could take some time depending on the size of the form being imported, don't forget to call the `SetProgressDialogPosition` and `SetProgressDialogStatus` methods to let the user know what the importer is doing.)

For exporters, the process is simply reversed. The `srcPath` parameter specifies the location of the files included in the form template, and the `destPath` parameter specifies the location and file name of the form to which the form template is being exported. The exporter must analyze the files contained in the form template and convert any of the InfoPath constructs (view, data, editing behavior) into the appropriate constructs in the target file type.

Understanding Form Templates

The fact that InfoPath doesn't provide any interfaces or helper functions to make the conversion process easier means that you, as the developer of the importer or exporter, need to understand how form templates are built. This may seem daunting at first, but it's really not as difficult as it sounds. The best way to handle this is to look at examples in InfoPath. For example, you can tell immediately by opening up the manifest.xsf file that it contains a list of all the files in the form template, as shown in Listing 21.3.

LISTING 21.3: Package Section of manifest.xsf

```
<xsf:package>
  <xsf:files>
    <xsf:file name="myschema.xsd">
      <xsf:fileProperties>
        <xsf:property name="namespace" type="string"
value="http://schemas.microsoft.com/office/infopath/2003/myXSD/2006-06-
25T23:47:44">
        </xsf:property>
      <xsf:property name="editability" type="string" value="full">
      </xsf:property>
      <xsf:property name="rootElement" type="string" value="myFields">
      </xsf:property>
      <xsf:property name="useOnDemandAlgorithm" type="string"
                  value="yes">
        </xsf:property>
      </xsf:fileProperties>
    </xsf:file>
    <xsf:file name="template.xml"></xsf:file>
    <xsf:file name="sampledata.xml">
      <xsf:fileProperties>
        <xsf:property name="fileType" type="string" value="sampleData">
        </xsf:property>
      </xsf:fileProperties>
    </xsf:file>
    <xsf:file name="view1.xsl">
      <xsf:fileProperties>
        <xsf:property name="lang" type="string" value="1033">
        </xsf:property>
      </xsf:fileProperties>
    </xsf:file>
  </xsf:files>
</xsf:package>
```

What if you want your importer to create controls when importing the form? Well, that's easy to do, too. Just insert the controls you want your importer to create into a blank form, and look at what InfoPath does when you save the form template as source files. InfoPath will create elements in the schema file, XSLT constructs in the XSL file that pertains to the view, sample data in the sampledata.xml file, and XML elements in the template.xml file. Depending on the type of control and properties that you may have set, InfoPath might even add some information to the manifest.xsf file. The guidance here is to look at what InfoPath is doing and have your importer do the same.

Let's take a quick look at an example. Let's say that we want our importer to convert underlines to a Text Box control. What do we need to add to the form template to create a Text Box control? Well, after opening a blank form template, inserting a Text Box control, and saving the form template as source files, here's what we end up with. First, InfoPath added an element in the schema below the root node (which happens to be `myFields` in this case). The `myFields` element in the schema after inserting the new field looks like the following (the new elements are underlined).

```
<xsd:element name="myFields">
    <xsd:complexType>
        <xsd:sequence>
            <xsd:element ref="my:field1" minOccurs="0"/>
        </xsd:sequence>
        <xsd:anyAttribute processContents="lax"
            namespace="http://www.w3.org/XML/1998/namespace"/>
    </xsd:complexType>
</xsd:element>
<xsd:element name="field1" type="xsd:string"/>
```

Next, XSLT was added to the view to render the control. The following is the XSLT that was added to the .xsl file that pertains to the view. This XSLT was added directly below the `BODY` element since that is where we inserted the Text Box control in the view. As you can see from this code, most of it looks like standard HTML with some XSLT mixed in. Since InfoPath 2007 uses HTML to render the view, this makes sense. However, we highlighted in bold some important items to discuss.

```
<span class="xdTextBox" hideFocus="1" title="" xd:binding="my:field1"
        tabIndex="0" xd:xctname="PlainText" xd:CtrlId="CTRL1"
        style="WIDTH: 130px">
    <xsl:value-of select="my:field1"/>
</span>
```

First, the **`xd:binding`** attribute specifies which field in the data source this control is bound to. In this case, that field is `my:field1`. Next, the **`xd:xctname`** attribute specifies the type of control this HTML pertains to. In this case, the name of the control is `PlainText`, which indicates to InfoPath that this is a Text Box control. If this attribute isn't set correctly, several of the control-specific features in InfoPath won't work. Next, the **xd:CtrlId** attribute specifies the ID of the control. This is used for such things as business logic for the control. Finally, the **xsl:value-of** statement inside the `span` element is used to render the actual data in the control.

In addition to the changes to the schema and view files, InfoPath also inserts an XML element into the sampledata.xml and template.xml files. So, to recap, since InfoPath doesn't supply an object model to enable you to generate form templates, the best way to build them is to look at what InfoPath is doing and have your importer do the same.

For exporters, understanding the construction of a form template is equally important. You must understand how a form template is built before you can export one to a different file type. Our guidance here is the same. Since there is no object model for working with an existing form template in design mode, look at what InfoPath is doing to build each of the constructs you care about and convert them one by one into the constructs that exist in the file type to which you are exporting.

How Post-Import Warnings Work

Earlier, when we introduced the Word and Excel importers, we showed you how the importers will report warnings that show up in the *Design Checker* task pane. It's possible for your importer to display its own warnings as well.

When the import process is complete, InfoPath looks for a file called **ImportErrors.xml** in the location specified by the `destPath` parameter of the `Import` method. If this file exists, InfoPath will parse the file contents and show the warnings listed in this file in the *Design Checker* task pane. (Note that, even though this file is called ImportErrors and the constructs inside this file refer to "errors", importer errors are shown only as warnings in the *Design Checker* task pane.)

So, in order for your importer to display its own warnings, it simply needs to generate this XML file. Listing 21.4 shows the ImportErrors.xml file for the MOI Consulting expense report form we imported earlier. You can see that the format of this file is very straightforward. The warnings are based on the view, so there is a `view` element that specifies the view to which these warnings apply. Although the Word importer imports only a single view, the Excel importer can import multiple views, as might be the case for your own importer. If you have multiple views, you would include one `view` element for each view that has warnings to show. The `name` attribute of each `view` element is set to the name of the view, as you might expect.

LISTING 21.4: ImportErrors.xml File for the Imported MOI Consulting Expense Report

```
<importErrors
xmlns="http://schemas.microsoft.com/office/infopath/2006/ImportErrors">
 <view name="View 1">
   <errorCategory categoryId="0" name="">
     <importError shortErrorString="Some formatting was removed from
the footer text">InfoPath cannot display a combination of character
formatting, such as a combination of bold and italic formatting, in
footer text. Therefore, some formatting was removed from the footer
during the conversion process.
     </importError>
     <importError shortErrorString="One or more drawings were
discarded">InfoPath does not support drawings. Therefore, drawings
were replaced with placeholders during the conversion process.
     </importError>
     <importError shortErrorString="Tracked changes and comments were
discarded">InfoPath does not support tracked changes and comments.
Therefore, tracked changes and comments were removed during the conversion
process.
      </importError>
    </errorCategory>
  </view>
</importErrors>
```

Next, there is an `errorCategory` element that is not currently used by InfoPath but could be used in the future to specify the error category. Inside the `errorCategory` element is one `importError` element for each warning you want to list in the *Design Checker* task pane. Only the first 200 warnings specified will be listed in the *Design Checker* task pane. Each `importError` element contains a `shortErrorString` attribute that lists the string that will be shown in the *Design Checker* task pane. This string can have a maximum of 512 characters. The text inside the `importError` element appears in the dialog displayed when the user clicks on the warning in the *Design Checker* task pane. This text can be of any size.

As you can see, the ImportErrors.xml file allows you to give very useful information to users about issues encountered during the import process. These warnings will help users fix problems in the form template after the import process is complete.

Importing Form Data

Now that you've imported a form from another application and created an InfoPath form template, you'll probably want to import the data from existing forms created with that application into InfoPath forms. Even if you haven't created a form template importer, maybe you just want to import some unstructured data into a structured InfoPath form. That's where the **data importer framework** comes into play.

Although InfoPath doesn't include any built-in data importers, there's nothing keeping you from creating your own. In this section, we'll explain the data importer framework in detail so you'll have all the information you need to create your own data importers.

Data Importer Framework

Building a data importer is somewhat analogous to building a form importer. You must first register your data importer with InfoPath and then build a COM object that implements a specific interface (`IInfoPath-DataImporter`) in order to interact with the InfoPath form. (Of course, as we mentioned earlier, you can do these two steps in reverse order. Also, you could have the importer register itself.)

Registering the data importer is very similar to doing so for form importers and exporters. First, you must create a registry key that has the same name as the ProgID of the COM object that implements the importer code. This key should be created under the following key in the registry: `HKEY_LOCAL_MACHINE\SOFTWARE\Microsoft\Office\12.0\InfoPath\Data Importers`. (Note that the `Data Importers` key may not exist, so you may need to create it.)

Then, just like the form importers, you should create a `DWORD` value called `DefaultLCID` under the ProgID key. The value of this string should be the default locale identifier to use for strings if the data importer doesn't support the current user interface language of InfoPath.

Finally, create one key under the ProgID key for each LCID that the data importer supports. InfoPath will attempt to read strings from the LCID key that corresponds to the user interface language of InfoPath. If such an LCID doesn't exist, InfoPath will look for strings under the LCID that is specified in the `DefaultLCID` string value under the ProgID key.

Each LCID key should have two string values—`Name` and `Description`—which specify the name of the importer and a description. These strings will be listed in the *Import Form Data* dialog, as you'll see shortly. (Note that the name of the data importer is limited to 64 characters, while the description is limited to 255 characters.)

Once you've registered your importer, you can test to see whether it's registered correctly even before you implement the `IInfoPathDataImporter` interface and even before you implement the COM object. To do so, first open an existing form or a new instance of a form template into which you'll eventually want to import form data. Then click on the *Import Form Data* menu item on the *File* menu, which will open the *Import Form Data* dialog (Figure 21.12). Finally, select the data importer you want and click the *OK* button to start the data importer and import the data into your form.

FIGURE 21.12: Import Form Data dialog

`IInfoPathDataImporter` Interface

After registering the data importer, the next logical step (besides creating the COM object itself) is to implement the `IInfoPathDataImporter` interface. This interface has three methods, as shown in Table 21.6. To reference this interface, as well as the other data importer interfaces, you should import the ipeditor.dll file into your C++ header file.

TABLE 21.6: Methods of the `IInfoPathDataImporter` Interface

Name	Description
`Initialize`	Called to initialize the importer. This method receives one parameter, which is the LCID of the current user interface language of InfoPath. Returning an error from this method will stop the import process and cause InfoPath to display an error.
`Import`	Called to start the import process.
`Uninitialize`	Called to uninitialize the data importer.

Of the three methods listed in Table 21.6, obviously the most interesting one is the `Import` method. This method is called to perform the actual import of the data into the InfoPath form. This method has the following signature:

```
HRESULT Import(
        [in] IPropertyBag* pPrintSettings,
        [in] IEnumUnknown* punkViewControls);
```

The first parameter is a pointer to a read-only property bag object used to pass print settings to the importer. Table 21.7 lists the print settings that are exposed, which are available only if a printer is installed.

TABLE 21.7: Print Settings Supplied to the Data Importer

Print Setting Value	Description
`PageSize`	A string that indicates the current page size (e.g., A3, A5, Legal, Tabloid)
`TopMargin`	The size of the top margin
`BottomMargin`	The size of the bottom margin
`LeftMargin`	The size of the left margin
`RightMargin`	The size of the right margin
`MarginUnitsType`	The type of units used in each of the margin sizes

TABLE 21.8: Controls Included in the Controls Collection

Control	Control Type (Specified by the IInfoPathViewControl Interface)
Text Box	`PlainText`
Rich Text Box	`RichText`
Drop-Down List Box	`dropdown`
Combo Box	`PlainText`
List Box	`ListBox`
Date Picker	`DTPicker_DTText`
Check Box	`CheckBox`
Option Button	`OptionButton`
Bulleted List, Numbered List, Plain List	`ListItem_Plain` (if bound to a text field) or `ListItem_Formatted` (if bound to a rich text field)
File Attachment	`FileAttachment`
Picture	`InlineImage` or `LinkedImage`
Ink Picture	`inkpicture`
ActiveX controls	The CLSID of the ActiveX control

The second parameter passed to the `Import` method is an enumerator for a collection of all the controls in the current view. The collection of controls is created when the view first opens. This collection is static and does not change as the form is updated.

Although this collection contains controls in the current view, it does not contain all the controls in the view. Only the types of controls listed in Table 21.8 are included in the collection. In addition, if the node to which the control is bound is read-only, disabled, or hidden, it will not be included in the collection.

Listing 21.5 presents a sample implementation of the `Import` method and shows how to enumerate through the controls collection passed to the

`Import` method. When enumerating through the collection of controls, as you can see in Listing 21.5, you can query each control for the `IInfoPathViewControl` interface. This interface, whose properties are listed in Table 21.9, enables you to get positional information about each control, which could be useful if your data importer supports optical character recognition (OCR) for scanning paper forms and importing the data into InfoPath forms. In addition to positional data, you can use this interface to get the data type (XML Schema type) or name of the node to which the control is bound or the type of the control itself. The values for the different control types are listed in the "Control Type" column in Table 21.8.

LISTING 21.5: Sample Implementation of the `Import` Method

```
STDMETHOD(Import)(
    IPropertyBag* pPrintSettings,
    IEnumUnknown* punkViewControls)
{
    HRESULT hr;
    CComPtr<IUnknown> spunk;
    while(SUCCEEDED(punkViewControls->Next(1, &spunk, NULL))
          && (spunk != NULL))
    {
        CComPtr<IInfoPathViewControl> spViewControl;

        hr = spunk->QueryInterface(__uuidof(IInfoPathViewControl),
                                   (void**)&spViewControl);
        if (SUCCEEDED(hr))
        {
            CComBSTR bstrValue;
            CComBSTR bstrDataType;
            CComBSTR bstrNodeName;
            CComBSTR bstrControlType;

            spViewControl->get_ControlType(&bstrControlType);
            spViewControl->get_DataType(&bstrDataType);
            spViewControl->get_NodeName(&bstrNodeName);
            spViewControl->get_Value(&bstrValue);

    AtlTrace("ControlType:%S\tNodeName:%S\tDataType:%S\t Value:%S\n",
             bstrControlType, bstrNodeName, bstrDataType, bstrValue);

            spunk = NULL;
        }
    }
    return S_OK;
}
```

TABLE 21.9: Properties of the `IInfoPathViewControl` Interface

Property Name	Description
`Top`	The offset (in pixels) of the control from the top of its parent container in the view.
`Bottom`	The offset (in pixels) of the control from the bottom of its parent container in the view.
`Left`	The offset (in pixels) of the control from the left of its parent container in the view.
`Right`	The offset (in pixels) of the control from the right of its parent container in the view.
`ControlType`	The type of control, as listed in the "Control Type" column in Table 21.8.
`DataType`	The XML Schema (XSD) type of the node to which the control is bound.
`NodeName`	The XML local name of the node to which the control is bound
`Value`	The XML value of the node to which the control is bound. This property, which returns a `BSTR`, is read/write.
`InputScopes`	Returns input scope information. (We talked about input scope in Chapter 4.)

Most importantly, you can retrieve or set the XML value of the node to which the control is bound by accessing the `Value` property. This is the main method a data importer will use to import the data into an InfoPath form.

As far as the position information in Table 21.9 is concerned, the offsets may differ for controls that are inside a Scrolling Region or Horizontal Region control. If the control for which you are retrieving offset information is scrolled out of view, the positions may be incorrect. Also, note that when setting the value of the control, the values that can be set are based on the data type of the node to which the control is bound, just as if a user was manually entering the data. So, entering invalid data will result in a schema validation error.

As you can see, by using the data importer framework, you can create a data importer to import data from existing forms created in applications other than InfoPath. This also enables you to import data from other unstructured data sources into a structured InfoPath form.

What's Next?

You've finally made it. If you've reached this point, and you've read every single chapter, you're an InfoPath expert. Congratulations! Go tell your friends and colleagues. Put "InfoPath Expert" on your business cards or in your e-mail signature.

Most importantly, take the knowledge you've learned in this book and put it to use. Design many InfoPath forms, use template parts to help speed up the design process, incorporate your InfoPath forms into SharePoint workflows, and deploy your forms to InfoPath Forms Services so people can fill out your forms even if they don't have the InfoPath client application installed.

We hope you've enjoyed the ride. We know that we have.

Appendix
Further Reading

Introduction

This appendix includes supplemental reading that will give you more details about topics that are outside the scope of this book. The reading materials are listed by chapter to help you easily find reading material that pertains to the topic that interests you. Some reading material is referenced in the chapters, and some is extra material. Not all chapters include supplemental reading, but most do. In addition to the reading material for each chapter, we include some general references that may be of use to you as well.

Further Reading

Chapter 2: Basics of InfoPath Form Design

"Attaching Files in InfoPath 2003":
http://msdn.microsoft.com/library/default.asp?url=/library/en-us/odc_ip2003_ta/html/odc_InfoPath_attaching_files.asp

Microsoft Windows XP Tablet PC Edition Software Development Kit:
http://msdn2.microsoft.com/en-us/library/ms950406.aspx

Chapter 3: Working with Data

"Naming and Addressing: URIs, URLs, . . .":
http://www.w3.org/Addressing

"XML Schema Part 2: Datatypes Second Edition":
http://www.w3.org/TR/xmlschema-2/

"XSD Inference Utility":
http://msdn.microsoft.com/library/default.asp?url=/library/en-us/dnxmlnet/html/xsdinference.asp

"XSD: The <any> Element":
http://www.w3schools.com/schema/schema_complex_any.asp

Chapter 4: Advanced Controls and Customization

"Custom Input Scopes with Regular Expression":
http://msdn.microsoft.com/library/default.asp?url=/library/en-us/tpcsdk10/lonestar/inkconcepts/custominputscopes.asp

"`InputScope` Enumeration":
http://msdn.microsoft.com/library/default.asp?url=/library/en-us/tpcsdk10/lonestar/inkconcepts/inputscopeenumeration.asp

"Programming the Tablet PC":
http://msdn.microsoft.com/library/default.asp?url=/library/en-us/tpcsdk10/lonestar/unmanaged_ref/tbconprogrammingthetabletpc.asp

Chapter 6: Retrieving Data from External Sources

"A Proxy-Based Approach to Secure Web Services":
http://www.developer.com/services/article.php/3320851

"IIS Authentication":
http://msdn.microsoft.com/library/default.asp?url=/library/en-us/vsent7/html/vxconIISAuthentication.asp

"Web Services Specifications":
http://msdn.microsoft.com/webservices/webservices/understanding/specs/default.aspx

XMethods Web site:
http://www.xmethods.net

Chapter 7: Extended Features of Data Connections

"Introduction to Datasets":
http://msdn.microsoft.com/library/en-us/vbcon/html/vbcondatasets.asp

"Overview of ADO.NET":
http://msdn.microsoft.com/library/default.asp?url=/library/en-us/cpguide/html/cpconoverviewofadonet.asp

Chapter 8: Submitting Form Data

HTTP version 1.1 Status Code Definitions:
http://www.w3.org/Protocols/rfc2616/rfc2616-sec10.html

Using DataSets in InfoPath:
http://msdn.microsoft.com/library/default.asp?url=/library/en-us/odc_ip2003_ta/html/Office_InfoPath_using_datasets.asp

Chapter 9: Saving and Publishing

InfoPath Team Blog: "Relinking Forms and Form Templates":
http://blogs.msdn.com/infopath/archive/2006/11/01/relinking-forms-and-form-templates.aspx

Microsoft Windows SharePoint Services:
http://www.microsoft.com/technet/windowsserver/sharepoint/default.mspx

PJ Hough's Blog: "Windows SharePoint Services etc.":
http://blogs.msdn.com/pjhough/

"The Build Process: Team Development with Visual Studio.NET and Visual SourceSafe":
http://msdn.microsoft.com/library/en-us/dnbda/html/tdlg_ch5.asp

Chapter 11: Security and Deployment

"Code Access Security":
http://msdn.microsoft.com/library/en-us/cpguide/html/cpconcodeaccesssecurity.asp

"Configuring Security Policy Using the Code Access Security Policy Tool (Caspol.exe)":
http://msdn2.microsoft.com/en-us/library/a0ke3k86.aspx

"Find Out What's New with Code Access Security in the .NET Framework 2.0":
http://msdn.microsoft.com/msdnmag/issues/05/11/CodeAccessSecurity/default.aspx
"Introduction to Code Signing":
http://msdn.microsoft.com/library/default.asp?url=/workshop/security/authcode/intro_authenticode.asp
Microsoft Trustworthy Computing:
http://www.microsoft.com/mscorp/twc
Security and privacy options for Microsoft Office:
http://office.microsoft.com/en-us/ork2003/CH011480831033.aspx
"XML-Signature Syntax and Processing":
http://www.w3.org/TR/2002/REC-xmldsig-core-20020212
XML Signatures:
http://www.w3.org/Signature

Chapter 12: Creating Reports

InfoPath Software Development Kit:
http://msdn2.microsoft.com/en-us/library/aa662321(office.11).aspx

Chapter 13: Workflow

Microsoft SharePoint Products and Technologies Team Blog: "Introduction to SharePoint Workflow!":
http://blogs.msdn.com/sharepoint/archive/2006/06/07/621210.aspx
Windows Workflow Foundation (MSDN):
http://msdn.microsoft.com/winfx/technologies/workflow/default.aspx

Chapter 14: Introduction to Forms Services

"HTTP Request Fields" (request headers in the HTTP protocol):
http://www.w3.org/Protocols/HTTP/HTRQ_Headers.html
Microsoft Windows SharePoint Services:
http://www.microsoft.com/technet/windowsserver/sharepoint
Office SharePoint Server 2007 Administration:
http://technet2.microsoft.com/Office/en-us/library/ed7378c1-4add-49c7-b215-76a25df1dedf1033.mspx

Chapter 15: Writing Code in InfoPath

"Accessing XML Data Using `XPathNavigator`":
http://msdn2.microsoft.com/en-us/library/yy355fzd.aspx

"Data Type Support between XML Schema (XSD) Types and .NET Framework Types":
http://msdn.microsoft.com/library/en-us/cpguide/html/cpcondatatypesupportbetweenxsdtypesnetframeworktypes.asp

"`DateTime` Structure":
http://msdn2.microsoft.com/en-us/library/System.DateTime.aspx

Debugging in Visual Studio:
http://msdn.microsoft.com/library/en-us/vsdebug/html/_asug_How_Do_I_Topics3a_Debugging.asp

Debugging Script Code in InfoPath:
http://support.microsoft.com/?scid=kb;en-us;827002&spid=2515&sid=229

"`HTMLTaskPane` Object":
http://msdn.microsoft.com/library/en-us/ipsdk/html/xdobjHTMLTaskPane_HV01024620.asp

"`IDictionary` Interface":
http://msdn.microsoft.com/library/en-us/cpref/html/frlrfSystemCollectionsIDictionaryClassTopic.asp

InfoPath Team Blog: "Problems When Calling into Script Functions in a Task Pane from Managed Code":
http://blogs.msdn.com/infopath/archive/2004/09/27/234911.aspx

"XML DOM Node Types":
http://www.w3schools.com/dom/dom_nodetype.asp

XPath language reference:
http://www.w3.org/TR/xpath

"XSLT `<xsl:sort>` Element":
http://www.w3schools.com/xsl/el_sort.asp

Chapter 16: Visual Studio Tools for Microsoft Office InfoPath 2007

"ClickOnce Manifest Signing and Strong-Name Assembly Signing Using Visual Studio Project Designer's Signing Page":
http://msdn.microsoft.com/library/default.asp?url=/library/en-us/dnvs05/html/RS_VSSign.asp

Microsoft Visual Studio 2005 Tools for the Microsoft Office System:
http://msdn.microsoft.com/vstudio/products/vsto/details

Microsoft's Visual Studio 2005 MSDN site:
http://msdn.microsoft.com/vstudio/

"Refactoring C# Code Using Visual Studio 2005":
http://msdn.microsoft.com/vcsharp/default.aspx?pull=/library/en-us/dnvs05/html/vs05_refac.asp

"Security Briefs: Strong Names and Security in the .NET Framework":
http://msdn.microsoft.com/netframework/default.aspx?pull=/library/en-us/dnnetsec/html/strongNames.asp

Visual Studio Tools for Office Developer Portal:
http://msdn.microsoft.com/office/tool/vsto

"What's New in Code Editing":
http://msdn2.microsoft.com/en-us/library/ms165082(VS.80).aspx

Chapter 17: Advanced Forms Services

"Alternate Access Mapping":
http://office.microsoft.com/en-us/assistance/HA100240231033.aspx

"Configure Session State for InfoPath Forms Services":
http://technet2.microsoft.com/Office/en-us/library/3c4e8fb1-c3ce-4d27-8c65-6c4ab140f7051033.mspx

"Deploy Administrator-Approved Form Templates":
http://technet2.microsoft.com/Office/en-us/library/8285b82e-19db-4408-859f-1430830fe0fb1033.mspx

"InfoPath Forms Services Best Practices":
http://technet2.microsoft.com/Office/en-us/library/0e9966df-e374-4df5-b3be-9848c78f9ca71033.mspx

Internet Information Services (IIS) 6.0 Technical Library:
http://technet2.microsoft.com/WindowsServer/en/library/10135f7a-144b-4ec6-9ad0-d6d441e50bd01033.mspx

"Manage Form Templates":
http://technet2.microsoft.com/Office/en-us/library/8dfcffcb-fa3c-4314-a644-184f9c2ce25e1033.mspx

"Manage Session State" (for Microsoft Office SharePoint Server 2007):
http://technet2.microsoft.com/Office/en-us/library/ffa4a256-6885-4295-a712-537ce82b9a0c1033.mspx
Microsoft Operations Manager site:
http://www.microsoft.com/mom
Single Sign-On in SharePoint Portal Server:
http://www.microsoft.com/technet/prodtechnol/sppt/reskit/c2661881x.mspx

Chapter 18: Hosting InfoPath

"Hosting the InfoPath 2007 Form Editing Environment in a Custom Windows Form Application":
http://msdn2.microsoft.com/en-us/library/ms406041.aspx
.NET Framework Developer Center:
http://msdn2.microsoft.com/en-us/netframework/default.aspx

Chapter 19: Building Custom Controls Using ActiveX Technologies

"Creating a CAB File":
http://msdn.microsoft.com/library/default.asp?url=/library/en-us/vccore/html/_vccore_creating_a_cab_file.asp
"Safe Initialization and Scripting for ActiveX Controls":
http://msdn.microsoft.com/library/default.asp?url=/workshop/components/activex/safety.asp

Chapter 20: Add-ins

COM Add-ins—`IDTExtensibility2`:
http://msdn.microsoft.com/library/default.asp?url=/library/en-us/vsintro7/html/vxlrfIDTExtensibility2Interface.asp
"Isolating Office Extensions with the COM Shim Wizard Version 2.0":
http://msdn2.microsoft.com/en-us/library/aa537166(office.11).aspx
Office Developer Center: "Add-ins":
http://msdn.microsoft.com/office/tool/addin/

General Reference Material

"Designing Form Templates with the New Features of InfoPath," *MSDN Magazine,* August 2006, by Scott Roberts and Hagen Green: http://msdn.microsoft.com/msdnmag/issues/06/08/InfoPath2007/default.aspx

InfoPath Team Blog:
http://blogs.msdn.com/infopath

InfoPath Public Newsgroup:
microsoft.public.infopath

Index

Italicized page locators indicate figures; tables are noted with a lower-case italicized *t;* monofont terms are in **bold**.

A

AAM. *See* Alternate access mappings
Absolute addresses, 406
Access
 COM add-ins supported by, 1073
 connecting to databases other than, 256
 Custom Task Panes added into, 1093
 VSTO package and, 834
Access 2003, unsupported data type and, 343*t*
Access 2007, unsupported data type and, 343*t*
Access content programmatically permission-based option, 547
Accessibility control settings, 874, *874*
Accessible forms, designing, 874, 875
"Accessing XML Data Using **XPathNavigator**," 780
Access keys, for inserting and removing sections, 689
Access key text box, 194
Access paths
 defining, 468
 domain trust form templates and, 467
 error dialog that appears when opening a form from path not related to, *403*
 for installable form templates, 486
 publishing via e-mail and, 416
 on restricted form templates, 464, 465
 security designed into form templates and, 459
 setting in Publishing Wizard, 462, *463*
 updates and, 463
Action dialog, for rules, 671
Actions, for rules, 232, 233*t*
Actions menu (Outlook), 659
ActionType enumeration type, finding, for a structurally editable control, 827, *828*
Activate Form Template page, 896, 898
Activation
 choosing site collection and Web application for, *897*
 with Manage Form Templates page, 895–897
 publishing process and, 681
 recovering from, 895
 with Site Collection Features page, 898
 waiting for upload to complete before, 901
Active add-ins, 502
Active Data Objects, 256
Active Directory group, 621
Active sessions setting, terminating, 911
Active Template Library
 basic, creating for control, 1051
 hosting InfoPath and, 978
ActiveX control(s), 79, 173, 847, 1073
 Add Custom Control Wizard showing Microsoft UpDown Control 6.0 selected in list of, 1039, *1039*

ActiveX control(s) (*cont.*)
adding to Controls task pane, 1038–1047
aggregation and, 1042
binding values from, to data in data source, 1042
building custom controls for InfoPath with use of, 1049–1072
building for InfoPath using C#, 1061–1072
building for InfoPath using C++, 1049–1061
CAB files for, 1041
classification of, 471
communicating between COM add-in and, 1100–1104
customizing various properties of, 1047–1048
FireTaskPaneReady method implemented by, 1103 (listing)
hosting InfoPath and, 978
implementing, 1049
inability to rebuild, after using in InfoPath, 1053
InfoPath 2007 available as, 965
InfoPath support for, 438, 439
installing and registering, 1058
installing and using, 1038–1048
property pages and, 1047–1048
rich text data and, 1046
safe initialization and scripting of, 1039
sharing development of form templates containing, 1048
specifying safety of, 1053–1055
ActiveX objects, script and, 497
ActiveX technologies, 24
building custom controls with, 174, 1037–1072
adapterName parameter, **SubmitTo-HostEventHandler** method and, 1009
Adapters, XML file, 247
Add Additional Details Button control, logic behind, 827
Add a Workflow page, *637*
AddButton method, 1083, 1088
implementation of, 1086, 1087 (listing)
Add Custom Control Wizard, 442, 1038, 1056, 1071
Custom Control Added page, 441, *441*
with Microsoft UpDown Control 6.0 selected in list of ActiveX controls, 1039, *1039*
Select a Control Type page, *439*
Specify a Binding Property page, *1041*, 1042
Specify an Enable or Disable Property page, 1042, *1043*, 1051–1052
Specify Data Type Options page, 1044, *1044*
Specify Installation Options page, 1040, *1040*
Add-ins
COM add-ins, 1073–1092, 1105–1106
Custom Task Panes, 1093–1104
InfoPath 2007 and support for, 23
initializing, 1080
learning more about, 1074
managed, accessing InfoPath object model from, 1107–1111
managing in InfoPath, 1111–1114
reenabling, 1114
warning dialog after serious error caused by, *1114*
writing add-ins and Custom Task Panes using VSTO 2005 SE, 1105–1106
Add-ins category, in Trust Center dialog, 499, 501–503
Add-ins tab in, Trust Center dialog, 1111, *1112*
Additional Information dialog, 517, 530–531
showing exactly what you are signing before you sign it, *516*, 516–517
Additional permission, enabling, 547
Add operation, 86
Add or Remove Custom Controls dialog, *439*, 441, 1038, 1065, 1066
Add Print View for Word Wizard, 600
choosing path and file name from, *601*
specifying Word print view name in, 601, *602*
Add/Remove Programs dialog, 417
Address block
after pasting into the view, *437*
creating, 437
Address block section, of MOI employment application form, *432*
AddressBlock template, custom category of Controls task pane after addition of, *441*
AddressBlock template part, 447
with cascading Combo Box controls, 448, *448*
data source for, 432, *433*
design-time visual for new version of, 449, *450*
inserting into blank form, *444*
inserting into new form template, 443–447

installing new version of, 449
more details for, *450*
updating, 448
updating form template containing, 449–451
Address information, controls for adding to employment application form, 46
Add to Favorites link, 16
Add User Role dialog, 617, *617*, 619, 621
Add View dialog, opening, 75, *75*
Administration
for Forms Services, 866
power of, 889
Administrative (admin) deployment
alternative, 898–901
command-line admin deployment, 899
to Forms Services, 892–901
activating form template to a site collection, 893, 895–898
uploading form template to server, 893–895
programmatic admin deployment, 900–901
template upgrades and, 917
two components of, 888
Administrative policy, disabling InfoPath design mode as, *506*
Administrative session state thresholds, 910, *910*
Administrator, InfoPath installed as, 457
Administrator approval
publishing form templates for, 889–891, *890*, 941–942
specifying a path during publishing to save a form template requiring, 891, *891*
Administrator-approved templates, location of, 895
admin object models
Forms Services Admin tool authored by, 900, *901*
quiesce tool authored by, 919, *919*
ADO. *See* Active Data Objects
ADO.NET, 256, 297, 350
submitting data with use of, 344
ADO.NET **DataSet** object, 344
designing view of form receiving and submitting to, *374*
rules and, 388–389
Web service support for, 12
AdoNetDataSet sample, 374
ADO.NET **DataSet** submit, 369–392
ADO.NET datasets and rules, 388–389
custom submit using form code, 383–384
custom submit using rules, 384–388
designing form template with a dataset, 370–374
disadvantages with rules, 389–391
filling out the dataset form, 375–377
submitting to a hosting environment, 391–392
submitting to a SharePoint library, 377–380
submitting to a Web server via HTTP, 380–383
ADO.NET dataset Web service, configuring change tracking for, *371*
ADO.NET Web services, 300–307
example Customers and Orders Web service, 302–307
typed and untyped DataSets, 301
ADOXML, 256
Advanced controls, 25, 156–174
Choice Group control, 167–171
Choice Section control, 167–171
custom controls, 172–173
Expression Box control, 158–163
Horizontal Region layout element, 164–167
Hyperlink control, 156–158
Repeating Choice Group control, 167–171
Repeating Recursive Section control, 171–172
Scrolling Region layout element, 164–167
Vertical Label control, 163–164
Advanced formatting, 76–82
control formatting, 78–79
Format Painter, 79–80
for multiple controls, 80–82
Advanced Forms Services, 865–963
controls and browser optimizations, 867–875
designing accessible forms, 874
postback settings, 871
Update button, 872–874
data connections, 929–950
administrations settings, 931–936
authentication considerations, 943–948
centrally managed connection library, 936–943
e-mail, 948–950
form code, 875–885
circumventing browser-enabled limitations, 878–879

Advanced Forms Services (*cont.*)
compatibility of, with Forms Services, 884–885
detecting the browser or InfoPath client, 883–884
executing in browser, 876–878
simulating a custom task pane in browser, 882–883
simulating user roles in browser, 880–882
getting started with, 865–866
performance tips and best design practices, 950–963
data connections, 956
data-heavy features, 954–956
form code, 953
form template deployment, 951–952
form view state, 956–957
health monitoring, 962–963
miscellaneous tips, 957–958
performance monitoring, 958–959, 961–962
reduction of form postbacks, 953–954
views, 952
SharePoint integration, 885–929
advanced publishing, 888–903
configuring InfoPath Forms Services, 906–907
configuring shared services and providers, 907–920, 925–928
filling out a form on a SharePoint page, 928–929
managing form templates, 904–905
Advanced section, of Submit Options dialog, 393, *393*
Advanced tab, 193–198
of Form Options dialog, 579, *579*
of Repeating Section Properties dialog, 566, *567*
After submit option, 394
agg:action attribute, 583
agg:order attribute, for merge actions, *584*
Aggregated status report, 574, *574*
Aggregate reports, 553, 554, 555, 613, 660
design and merging of, 562
merged, 559, *559*
Aggregation, ActiveX controls and, 1042
Aggregation namespace, merge actions in, 583, *584*
agg:select attribute, for merge actions, *584*
agg:selectChild attribute, for merge actions, *584*
Airline form
with default value for **FlightType** as "**Roundtrip,**" *106*
XML Schema for, 109 (listing)
AirlineReservation document element, 120 (listing)
Airline reservations
NumberOfChildren attribute as nonexistent in form and XML data, *147*
NumberOfChildren attribute field, *146*
NumberOfChildren attribute field inserted in the form and XML with default value of 1, *147*
AJAX (Asynchronous JavaScript and XML), 703, 910
Alerts, 405
Aliases, user roles and, 617–618
Allow fully trusted forms to run on my computer checkbox, 498
Allow only signature option, 527
AllowPartiallyTrustedCallersAttribute. *See* APTCA
Allow users to change these settings checkbox, 596
Allow users to edit data in this field by using a datasheet or properties page option, cautionary note about, 413
Allow users to fill out this form if data is unavailable checkbox, 313
Allow users with read access to copy content permission-based option, 547
All the signatures are independent (co-signing) setting, using, 531
Alphabetic characters, XML, naming nodes and, 104
Alphanumeric characters, XML, naming nodes and, 104
Alternate access mappings, 927–928
defining three types of, 928
Ambiguous schemas, 129 (listing), 135
converting to, 134
first prompt related to starting from, *129*
Ampersand (&) character, submit keyboard shortcut and, 335
And button, specifying conditions with, 218
Anonymous access, authentication and disallowance of, 934

Appeals process, evaluations and, 281
AppendChildElement method, using, 829
Apple systems, browser-based forms and, 668
Application class, 883
ApplicationClass object, **Events** property of, 1082
Application data member, 1107
ApplicationEvents object, 1082
Application_Idle method, implementation of, 998 (listing)
Application idle state, updating toolbar buttons during, 997–1000
Application.LoginName, 881
application object, casting to **Application-Class,** 1080
_applicationObject object, 1091
Application review form, with Scrolling Region control when filling out the form, *166*
Application server, 672
Application.UserName, 881
Apply Font to All Controls
  controls providing support for, 82*t*
  selecting from Format menu, 81
Approval workflow, 637
"Approver" role, 620
APTCA, allowable list, 498
Arbitrary Section controls, 522–523
ArgumentException, 1086
Artificial domains, testing form template with, 482
Asian language forms, Vertical Label control and, 163
ASP.NET, 853
ASP.NET controls, use of, for Web form design, 1011
ASP.NET mobile controls, 720
ASP.NET page
  beginning design for, 1015
  events that host page may not sink, 1028*t*
  host to InfoPath communication and, 1020–1028
  InfoPath to host communication and, 1028–1035
  properties and methods not available to, 1027*t*
  session state enabled on, 1018
  setting destination option for, *381*
  storage for, 1014
ASP.NET page load event handler, to read data submitted by Web server (HTTP) connection, 383 (listing)
ASP.NET Web service, new Web site dialog with template for, 274, *274*
Assembly, 739
ATL. *See* Active Template Library
ATL Control Wizard
  adding ActiveX control to project with use of, 1051
  implementing **Value** property and, 1056
  Stock Properties page of, for Simple-InfoPathActiveX control, 1051, *1052*
Atomic controls, 444, 445, 450
Attached files, XML format for, 70
"Attaching Files in InfoPath 2003" (MSDN Web site), 68, 70
Attribute nodes, adding, 116
Attribute node type, merge customizations available for, 571*t*
Attributes
  database data types and, 269
  designing music collection form's data source with and without, *117*
  elements *vs.*, 118
  with fields and groups, 94
  as nodes, 94
  use of, 117
Authentication
  basic, 934, 944
  to data sources, 935–936
  digest, 934, 944
  disallowance of anonymous access and, 934
  embedded SQL, 934–935
  Kerberos, 944
  Single Sign-On, 934, 944
  UDC, 944–946
  Windows Integrated, 934
Authenticity, 508
Authenticode, 493
Author property, in body of document, and Word document showing Document Information Panel, 976, *977*
Auto insurance form, after loading in IP insurance application, 986, *986*
Automatically create data source, 91
  dialog prompt for, 139, *139*
Automatically create data source checkbox, 41
Automatically determine security level (recommended) feature, 482, 483

Automatically retrieve data when form is opened checkbox, 251, *251*, 314
Automatic security level, 482–483
AutoText items, 590

B

"Backdoor" network share, publishing MeetingRequest template to a Web server via, 401, *401*
Background color
adding to view, 76
for SimpleInfoPathActiveX control, 1051, *1052*
for stock tracking Text Box, 219, 220, 221
Backup copies, modifying existing form templates and, 447
Backups, creating, before making any hand modifications, 536
Backward compatibility, enabling form template for, 700
Bad sorting conditions, disabling of Finish button and, 265
Basic authentication, 934, 944
BasicDataFormTemplate sample, 285
Binding mechanics, behind controls and the data source, 744
Binding(s)
ActiveX control to fields or groups in data source, 1041–1042
changing, 140, 142
changing via context menu, *140*
choosing data source node for, 139
customizing new, 142–144
field or group types and, 1045, 1045*t*
multiple, 145–147
multiple, details of, 147–149
of newly inserted controls to newly created data source, 9
odd, 145
secondary data source, 307–312
Binding section, of Data tab, 176, 180
Binding style, 288
Binding visuals, 65
Bin folder, contents of, 839
Blank form
creating, 30*t*
new, 32, *33*
Blank groups, removal of, only if empty, 571, 572
Bookmarks, unavailability of, when designing InfoPath form templates in VSTO, 855
Bookmarks feature, 816
Border color, for SimpleInfoPathActiveX control, 1051, *1052*
Borders
in layout tables, 36
for Plain List control, 66
Borders and Shading dialog, 36
Bound controls, 86
clicking on control in the view for selection of, in data source, *87*
Breakpoints, enabling, 740
Browse button, 440
Browse dialog, 440
Browse for Folder dialog, for selecting location to save template source files, 421–422, *422*
Browser
detecting, 883–884
filling out InfoPath forms in, 666–668
form code executed in, 876–877
form opened in, 683
matrix of, for use with Forms Services, 690, *691*
rudimentary implementation of roles in, 882 (listing)
seeing forms in, 49
showing faux message box in, 879 (listing)
simulating custom task pane in, 882–883
Team Status Report view filled out in, 604, *604*
Team Status Report view shown as a print view in, 604, *605*
user roles simulated in, 880–882
using host page to display dialog box message in, 1033 (listing)
Browser-based forms, performance tips and best design practices, 950–963
Browser-based form templates, data connections in, 710–714
Browser category, on Form Options dialog, 872
Browser-compatible errors, 695, *696*, 697
Browser-enabled form libraries, "regular" form libraries and, 707
Browser-enabled forms
form code added to, 876
print views in, 603–605
sending e-mail from browser in, 339

Browser-enabled form template design, 690–701
Design Checker and, 693–701
design once philosophy and, 692
Browser-enabled form templates
Changing event not available in, 745
configuring Button control to use the Update Form option for, 873, *873*
customizing toolbar buttons for, 872, *872*
designing with VSTO, 840
message indicating feature can be used in, but is not active in browser, 671, *671*
message indicating feature cannot be used in, 670, *670*
postback settings for control in, 871, *871*
URL-based options for opening of, 716–720
Browser-enabled limitations, circumventing, 878–883
Browser forms
Close button, 687
closing, 708
controls, 688–690
creating, 682–683
filling out, 714–720
Print View button, 687
reopening, 704–705
Save and Save As buttons, 686–687
Submit button, 685–686
toolbar and, 683–684
Update button, 687
View drop-down, 687
Browser forms controls setting, form template postbacks and, 954
Browser forms tab, 198
Browser incompatibilities, two types of, 670–671
Browser optimizations, 699–700
in Advanced Forms Services, 867–874
issues with, 868–870
Browser rendering
disabling, 890
enabling in Publishing Wizard, 680
Browser test form, for **SaveItem** Web service method, *280*
Browser value, 717
Bubbling, lack of nonprogrammatic option for canceling of, 748
Buddy tab, in Properties dialog for Microsoft UpDown Control, 1048
Bugs
circumventing validation in forms, watching for, 756
"duplicate error," 764
Build menu, 740
Build scripts, 419
Bulleted List control, 7, 65, 66
binding behavior of, 90*t*
Bulleted List Properties dialog, 307
secondary data source-bound controls with little customization allowed, *308*
Business Data Catalog, 678
Business logic, 731
ButtonClick event, 790
Button control, 45*t*, 88
binding behavior of, 89*t*
sinking an event for, 787
specifying action for rule to run when user clicks on, *231*
Button control (ASP.NET), code behind, in MyPage.aspx, 1021 (listing)
ButtonEvent, 782
Button event handler, 766 (listing)
Buttons, MOI Consulting request form code and, 803–805
By key field option, 202

C

CA. *See* Certificate authority
CAB files
creating, 1071
form templates stored in, 26
.NET control installation process and, 1070
specifying, ActiveX controls and, 1040, 1041
Cache, Getting Started dialog with form templates in, 465, *465*
Cache conflict, occurrence of, when different version of same form template is opened, *464*
Cached form template files, 424
Cached queries
offline, 316
saving, time span and, 314
CacheId field, 800, 806
Cache ID nodes, 805, 806
Cache ID values, of MOI Consulting request form, 794
Cache queries, for use in Offline mode checkbox, 314

CAL. *See* Client Access License
Calculated default data, 86
Calculated default values, 107
 updating template parts and, 451
Calculated Default Values section, in Logic Inspector dialog, 238
Calendar year, Horizontal Repeating Table control and forms based on, 60
CallFormCode function, 789
CancelableArgs.Cancel property, 754
Cannot be blank property, 101–102
 optional field *vs.*, 105–106
 validation error for, *102*
CAS, form code permission and, 497
Cascading, updates and deletes, 305, 306
CAS permission set, for **LocalIntranet,** 496*t*
Category box, in Upload Data Connection File page, 940, *940*
Category filters, grocery form filled out with, *325*
Category IDs, registering in registry, safe initialization and scripting for ActiveX controls and, 1054
CATID_SafeForInitializing, 1054
CATID_SafeForScripting, 1054
CComControl base class, 1058
Cells
 merging and splitting, 37, 38
 splitting rows into, 37
Central Administration site, navigating to, 677
Centrally managed connection library, 866, 936–943
 advantages and constraints with use of, 936
 data connection in, 931
 designing against, 937–942
 domain trust form templates and, 461
 domain trust user form template and use of, 929
 retrieving data connection files from, 942–943
 uploading .udcx file to, 939–940, *940*
Certificate authority, 487, 488, 489, 499
Certificate dialog, 530
 general tab of, which shows whether the publisher of certificate is trusted, *491*
Certificate properties dialog, 493
Changed Event, 737
Changed event, 767–777
 as default XML event, 852
Change permissions button, 542
Change To menu item, 58, *58*
 use of, for most controls, 59
Change to Repeating Table dialog, choosing number of rows used in header in, 1125, *1126*
Change tracking, configuring for ADO.NET dataset Web service, *371*
Changing event, 749–757
 canceling, 755, *755*
 error that occurs when calling unsupported OM during, *756*, 756–757
 exhibiting, 750
 lack of availability for, in browser-enabled form templates, 745
 showing message box in, 745 (listing)
Changing event handler, error message for canceling of, 755, *755*
Chat programs, 392
Check Box control, 7, 45*t*, 1037
 binding behavior of, 89*t*
 converting to Option Button control, 1125
CheckDateTimes method, implementation of, 761 (listing)
Child tables, defining relationships between parent tables and, *263*
Choice controls, 167–171
Choice Group control, 14, 167–171, 827, 1037
 binding behavior of, 90*t*
 in design mode, *168*
 employment application form with, *170*
 in InfoPath 2003 SP1, 14
Choice Section control, 14, 167–171, 1037
 binding behavior of, 91*t*
 default commands for, when filling out a form, 212, *212*
Choose InfoPath Form dialog, 649, *649*, 656
C# language, 833
 building ActiveX control for InfoPath with use of, 1061–1072
 form code, before upgrading the OM version, 734*t*
 hosting InfoPath and, 978
C++ language
 building ActiveX control for InfoPath with use of, 1049–1061
 COM add-ins written in, 1074
 hosting InfoPath and, 978
Classes, not implemented by Forms Services, 886–887*t*

ClassInformation group, 379
submitting to **XmlNodeToString** Web method, 358
Class Information view, start date and start time in, 352
Click event handler, code for, 995
Click here to insert link, optional controls after clicking on, 51, *51*
Client Access License, 678
Client-only rules, InfoPath e-mail forms as, 650
Client value, 717
Clone method, 772
Close button, on browser form toolbar, 683, 687
ClosedNode document element, 536
Close the form action, 394
Close the form rule action, 234
CLR. *See* Common Language Runtime
CLSID KEY, 1066
CMCL. *See* Centrally managed connection library
Code
adding logic without, 215–240
addition of, to form template in VSTO, 840
addition of, to form templates, 737–738
behind ASP.NET Button control in MyPage.aspx, 1021 (listing)
behind a Web service to get user name from Web service proxy, 948 (listing)
confirmation dialog before removal of, *733*
editing with InfoPath, 384
existing form templates with, in VSTO, 841–842
filling out and debugging form with, 738–740
to find text in hosted form, 995, 996 (listing)
fully trusted form templates without, 902
mobile compatibility and, 724
MOI Consulting request form template and addition of logic without, 801–803
multiple notifications and, 774
removal of, as one-way operation, 733
to save currently loaded IP insurance form, 989 (listing)
saving before addition of, 738
settings related to addition of, 732–736
for **Sign** form event, 815 (listing)
for stopping XML events from bubbling above current event handler, 748 (listing)
for **UserIsAuthorized** property, 752, 753 (listing)
using to submit forms, 337
writing, for Web service sample, 276 (listing)
writing behind a form, 730–741
Code Access Security (CAS) model, 496
Code editing in Visual Studio 2005, 858–860
features, 861
code snippets, 860
refactoring, 859
signing, 859
Code group, creating, 497
Code language, homogeneity of, 783
Code signing, 859
creating self-signed certificate for, 490, *490*
Code-signing certificates, 487–488
for signing form templates, 490
Code snippets
commonly used, 860*t*
customizing, 860
in Visual Studio 2005, 860
Collect Feedback workflow, 637
Color, for stock tracking Text Box, 219, 220, 221
Color properties, for SimpleInfoPathActiveX control, 1051, *1052*
Color property page, for SimpleInfoPath-Control object, 1054, *1054*
Color schemes, 7
for forms, 39
in Repeating Table control, 57
Color Schemes task pane, 39, *40*
Columns
adding, published templates and, 408
as attributes, in database data sources, 269
inserting in layout tables, 37
promoting properties to make them available as, in Outlook, 415, *415*
COM. *See* Component Object Model
COM add-ins, 1073–1092, 1105–1106
adding user interface items and, 1076
application events available to, 1082*t*
building for InfoPath, 1076–1092
communicating between ActiveX control and, 1100–1104
dialog for addition and removal of, 502, *502*
introduction to, 1074–1076
lifetime and command bars, 1086
support for, 1073
COM Add-Ins dialog, 502, *502*, 1113, *1113*
COMAddins object, 1102

Combo Box control, 45*t*
binding behavior of, 89*t*
country data and, 46
in InfoPath 2007 Controls task pane, 22
IP insurance application after addition of, 984, *984*
Combo Box controls, cascading, Address-Block template part with, 448, *448*
COM interop, writing COM add-ins in managed code with, 1074
COM Interop attributes, **InfoPathMasked-TextBox** class after addition of, 1062 (listing)
CommandBar object, 1076, 1085
CommandBars collection, 1076, 1086, 1096
CommandIds enumeration, 997
in **FormControlCommandIds** class, 994
Command-line admin deployment, 899
Command-line quiescing, 917–919
Commands
customizing, 210–212
shortcut keys assigned to, 211
Comments group, 522
Common Language Runtime, hosting InfoPath and version 2.0 of, 978
Compatibility category, on Form Options dialog, 694, *695*
Compatibility mode, changing, in midst of designing template, 693
Compatibility setting, changing, 405
Compatible form template design, design once philosophy and, 692
Compiling, failure in, 740
Complex script, support for, with InfoPath SP1, 14
complexType data type, 99, 99*t*
Component Object Model, 23
COM add-in technology based on, 1074
hosting InfoPath and, 978
Compound built-in controls, 445
ComSourceInterfaces attribute, 1067
ComVisible (true) attribute, 1005
concat function, 338, 576
Conditional Format dialog, 216, *217*
after adding conditions for manager roles, 632, *633*
after changing condition to use a user role, *631*
with multiple conditions, *219*
with specifications showing conditions needed to set background color to yellow, *221*
Conditional formatting, 6, 11, 18, 19, 118, 215–222, 426, 562, 742
in mobile forms, 725
on MOI Consulting request form, 802
referencing user role in, 880
Sales Report view with, 592
updating template parts and, 451
with user roles, 621, 630–631
Conditional Formatting button, 182, 630
Conditional Formatting dialog, 216, *216*, 630
accessing, 215
with condition, where **StockPrice** is less than or equal to $18.00, *220*
conditions added to, 216–217
with one condition, *220*
showing all three conditions, for stock tracking, *222*
Condition dialog for rules, selecting user's current role as qualifier in, 623, *623*
Conditions
comparison operands for, 217–218
hiding or disabling of, 216, 222
specifying, 217
user roles and specification of, 622
Configuration wizard, configuring Forms Services and, 675
Configure InfoPath Forms Services administration page, 957
threshold setting on, 910
Configure InfoPath Forms Services page, 931
Configure Session State page, 907
Configuring a Button control, to use the Update Form option for a browser-enabled form template, 873, *873*
Confirmation dialog, before removing code, *733*
Confirm view, 829
of MOI Consulting request form, 796, *796*
Connect class, 1078
Connection authentication, 866
Connection counters, 961
Connection library, form template design and, 30*t*
Connection Library option, in Design a Form Template dialog, 245
Connection Options dialog, modifying a server-based connection in, 938–939, *939*

Connection store, 713
Connection timeouts, InfoPath Web service, 360
Contact Selector control, 972, 973
Container controls, 169
changing from one type to another, 59
rebinding, 142
selecting, 78
Container nodes, 87, 94
ContentControl property, 1101
of **CustomTaskPane** object, 1100, 1101
Content type management, enabling for document library, 970
Content types
list of, in Data Source Wizard, 971, *971*
management of, 709
ContextChanged event, 785
behavior of, 816
wiring up, for context-sensitive help in custom task pane, 817 (listing)
Context menu
of most popular control bindings, *143*
for Optional Section control when filling out a form, 52, *52*
for Repeating Section control when previewing form, *54*
Context-sensitive help in custom task pane
MOI Consulting request form code and, 816–822, 824–831
wiring up **ContextChanged** form event for, 817 (listing)
Control bindings
changing, 140, 142
popular, context menu of, *143*
Control events, 730
Control formatting, 78–79
Control inserting, 91
Control properties, 174–203
changing/resetting of, after rebinding, 141*t*
Control properties dialog, customizing merge action through, 566
Controls. *See also* Advanced controls
binding behaviors for, 89–91*t*
binding mechanics behind, 744
binding to data source, 138–139
bound, 86
Bulleted, 65, 66
conditional formatting of, 216
custom, 173–174
data fit to, 353
design-time visual icons over, to indicate potential binding issues, *149*
File and Picture, 67
File Attachment, 68–70
formatting multiple, 80–82
Forms Services and, 867–874
Horizontal Repeating Table, 60–61
hybrid, 88
Hyperlink, 88
Ink Picture, 72–73
inserting, 41, 43
list, 65–66
Master/Detail, 62–65
mobile compatibility and, 723–724
Multiple-Selection List Box, 67
Numbered List, 65, 66
Optional Section, 49–51
Picture, 70–72
Plain List, 65, 66
purpose of, 44
Repeating Section, 52–55
Repeating Table, 56–60
seeing name of, 65
Selected Text Box, 78
for settings for a control in browser-enabled form template, *871*
standard, 43–44, 45–46*t*, 46–48
structurally enabled, 827
support for, in Forms Services, 688*t*
template parts without, 447
that are not bound, 88
using, 41–73
virtual, 168
when design-time visuals appear on, *150*
working with in VSTO, 851–853
XML Schema created "behind" data source in XSD file and, 111–115*t*
Controls collections, controls included in, 1145*t*
Control selection, 78
Controls link, in Design Tasks pane, 41
Controls task pane, 34*t*, 41, *42*, 86, 155, 158, 1047
ActiveX controls added to, 1038–1047
Choice Section control in, 169
custom category of, after adding the AddressBlock template, *441*
custom controls support, with InfoPath 2003 SP1, 14
default data types and, 43

Controls task pane (*cont.*)
File and Picture category in, 67
in InfoPath 2003, *8*
list controls in, 65–66
new controls, in InfoPath 2007, 22
new controls for, in InfoPath 2003 SP1, 14
template parts added to, 438–441
template parts inserted into the view from, 445
Control text, aligning with adjacent text labels, 354
Convert Data Connection dialog, 712, *712*, 938, *938*
Convert feature, using Web service proxy and, 946
Convert Main Data Source option, 132–135
benefits with, 132
for query connections, 357
on Tools menu, 537
_copiedNode member variable, 1091
Copy button
enabling/disabling, 1000
hosted form and, 994, 997
Copy button event handler, **EnabledAll-PasteButtons** method and, 1090 (listing)
Copy Form Data button, 1083
Copying to clipboard, Information Rights Management and, 547
Co-signed signatures, using, 531–532
Co-signing, 15
counter-signing *vs.*, 532
Counters
connection, 961
InfoPath Forms Services performance counters, 960–961*t*
rate, 959
for tracking templates and documents, 961–962
Counter-signatures, setting up, 532–533
Counter-signing, 15
co-signing *vs.*, 532
Crash recovery, 12
Create a new blank form action, 394
CreateCTP method, 1095, 1100, 1108
CreateCTP parameters, 1097*t*
Create New Folder dialog, 651
after selecting InfoPath form items, 649, *650*
CreateObject method, 471
Create Print Version dialog, *586*
CreateToolbar method, 1084
implementation of, 1084, 1085 (listing)
CredentialType values, 946
Cross-domain access, 471, 473
security prompt for, 474, *474*
for user form templates, 931–932
Cross-domain data connections, 711
allowing, 929–930
Cross-domain privileges, 930
CTPFactoryAvailable method, 1095 (listing)
CurrentUser field, 806
Custom (complexType) data type, 99, 99*t*
Custom Control Added wizard page, 1047
Custom controls, 14, 173–174
building with ActiveX technologies, 1037–1072
InfoPath 2003 SP1 and support for, 14
InfoPath support for, 438, 439
Custom dialog with buttons, showing, 805
Customers and **Orders SqlDataAdapter** objects, creating typed dataset from, *304*
Customers and **Orders** tables, adding a relationship to, in the dataset, *305*
Customers and **Orders** Web service, example, 302–307
Customers data, displaying, *271*
CustomersOrders sample, 270
Customers parent table, **Orders** child table added to, *262*
Customers secondary data source, 268, *268*
Customers table, 375
in Northwind database, 258
structure of, for MOI Consulting firm, 369*t*
Custom exporter, in Export Wizard, *1131*
Custom form code, 18
"Custom Input Scopes with Regular Expression," 198
Customizations (advanced), 204–212
customizing commands, 210–212
editing default values, 204–208
Customize Commands buttons, 181, 210, *210*
Customizing
aspects of Microsoft UpDown Control, 1048
code snippets, 860
data source, 116
Document Properties view, 974
e-mail support for a form template, 660–662
existing template parts, 452–454
layout, 39
layout tables, 37

merge behavior in design mode, 564–569, 571, 573–576, 578–579
new bindings, 142–144
properties of ActiveX controls, 1047–1048
sample form templates, 28
submit functionality, 285
toolbar buttons for a browser-enabled form template, 872, *872*
Travel Request Approval workflow, 638, *638*
view properties, 75–76
workflow, 637
Customizing Expense Report sample form template, 658–660
Customizing Ribbon, 834
Custom merge XSL (advanced), 580–586
InfoPath used in creation of, 580–582
writing own merge XSL, 580, 582–586
Custom pattern box, 229, *229*
Custom patterns, 228–229
Custom permission option button, 542
Custom submits
defining, 337
with form code, 383–384
with rules, 384–388
Custom task pane factory object, 1095
Custom task pane HTML, 817
CustomTaskPaneInterop sample form, filling out, *787*
CustomTaskPaneInterop sample form template, 786
CustomTaskPane methods, properties, and events, 1098–1099*t*
CustomTaskPane object, 1097, 1098
Custom task panes, 783–790, 834, 1093–1104
add-ins and support for, 23
addition of, to forms, 784
advantages with, over existing HTML task panes in InfoPath, 1093
calling form script from, 789 (listing)
communicating between COM add-in and ActiveX control, 1100–1104
context-sensitive help in, 816–822, 824–831
creating, 1093–1100
InfoPath 2007 support for, 1073
navigation and pane visibility, 817
script and, 782–790
setting a value in Form's data source from, 787 (listing)
simulating in browser, 882–883
writing, using VSTO 2005 SE, 1105–1106
Custom Task Pane sample, building, 1104
CustomTaskPanes data member, 1107
Cut button
enabling/disabling, 1000
hosted form and, 994, 997

D

Data, 7
controls fit to, 353
how it changes, 744–745
performance and large amounts of, 264
retrieval of, from external sources, 241–296
sorting and filtering, 272
working with, 85–154
Data adapters, 244
role of, 241
Database connection
Data Connection Wizard for, 258, *259*
submitting data with form template based on, 342–344
Database data types, unsupported, for submit, 343*t*
Database option, in Design a Form Template dialog, 245
Databases, 256–271, 297
forms created from, 30*t*
integrating database connection into form template, 268–271
setting up connections to, 257–267
submitting forms to, 336, 341–344
ubiquity of, 256
Database tables, nested, 270, *270*
Data binding, 25, 85, 86–94
advanced, 137–151
creating data source automatically, 86–88, 91–92
template parts and, 443, 445
understanding, 138–139
understanding data source details, 93–94
DataBind method, 1021
Data connection authentication, server and, 943–948
Data Connection dialog, after finishing the XML file Data Connection Wizard, 252
Data connection files, retrieval of, from centrally managed connection library, 942–943
Data connection library(ies), 711–714, 930
converting to, 938–939

Data connection library(ies) (*cont.*)
domain trust form templates and, 461
domain trust user form template and use of, 929
optionally deleting .udcx file from, 941
security and, 713–714
Data connections, 242–246, 929–950
administration settings, 931–932
authentication considerations, 943–948
authentication to data sources, 935–936
in browser-based form templates, 710–714
centrally managed connection library, 936–943
conceptual understanding of, 242–243
creating, 245–246
cross-domain, 711, 929–930
e-mail, 948–950
embedded SQL authentication, 934–935
extended features of, 297–325
HTTP, 934
issues with, when inserting multiple instances of same template part, 446
mobile forms and, 725
need for, 242
performance tips, 956
response size, 933
security notices and, 255
security prompt with, 290
template parts and replacement of, 447
timeouts, 933
types of, and their commonly used properties and methods, 823*t*
unused, deleting, 380
updating template parts and, 451
various types of, 244
DataConnections collection, 822
Data Connections dialog, 711
screening for potential data exchange beyond server realm, 903
SubmitToHost and, 1030–1031
Data Connection Wizard, 342, 344
added **Customers** and **Orders** tables shown in, *262*
choosing submit connection in, 1031
configuring attachment options for submitting via e-mail, *340*
for database connection, 258, *259*
Data Connection dialog after finishing XML file, *252*
final page of, for XML file, *251*
first page of, for setting properties of e-mail when users submit form, *338*
paying attention to last page of, 343
specifying how form works with Web service, *346*
on a submit-only main connection, 347
Data Entry Pattern dialog, 228, *228*
Data features, examples of, 742
Data field labels, 58
dataFields group
within data source, 342
student sign-in form and, 347
Data flow, for FormUtilities add-on, 1079, *1080*
Data formatting, settings for, 352
Data-heavy features, performance tips, 954–956
Data importer
print settings supplied to, 1144*t*
registering, 1142
Data importer framework, 1142–1143, 1148
Data integrity, 508
Data loss, changing field or group names and, 95
Data requirements
controls and, 43
defining, 31
for employment application form, 44
for MOI Consulting employment application, 32*t*
DataSet, Web service code for return of, 306 (listing)
Data set data, submitting, 301
Dataset form
filling out, 375–377
filling out with default data, *375*
DataSet form data, submitting, 369
DataSet object, setting up parameter mapping for, *372*
DataSet object data, Web service code for getting and setting, 370 (listing)
DataSet objects, 300
types of, 301
Datasets
form templates designed with, 370–374
support for only one at a time, 373
Dataset serialization, 373
Dataset structure, data source representative of, *373*
Data source, 26
for address block template part, 432, *433*

automatic creation of, 86–88, 91–92
binding control to, 138–139
binding mechanics behind, 744
binding values from ActiveX control to data in, 1042
clicking on control in the view to select bound control in, *87*
creation of, from XML document, *136*
disambiguation of, by use of Edit Settings dialog, *130*
for Document content type, 973, *974*
for expense report example, *161*
inserting **field1** in, 144, *144*
manual edit of, 110, 116–137
meanings related to, 94
namespaces in, 135–137
organizing for MOI Consulting request form, 798–801
sample, for Master/Detail example, 199–200, *200*
saving user name value in, 881
shaping and customizing, 116
signature groups in, 525
sorting participants by **LastName** in, 772 (listing)
for status report form template, *561*, 561–562
understanding details about, 93–94
DataSource collection, 822
Data source details, 108–110
showing, 106
Data source enhancements, InfoPath 2003 SP1 and support for, 14
Data source events, 877–878
custom task pane and sinking of, 784
generating visual notifications for, 776 (listing)
Data source field and group properties, 95–110
cannot be blank property, 101–102
optional field *vs.*, 105–106
data source details, 108–110
data type property, 98–101
default value property, 106–107
calculated default values, 107
static default values, 106
name property, 95–97
repeating property, 102–105
Data source field details, 748
Data source field or group, warning dialog when changing name of, for published form, 96–97, *97*
Data Source link, in Design Tasks task pane, 845
Data source nodes
choosing for binding, 139
extra, manual clean-up of, 91
icons in Data Source task pane for various types of, *87*
naming, 92
optional, in XML Schema, 205
types of, 86–87
DataSource object, 822
Data sources
authentication to, 935–936
conceptual understanding of, 242–243
populating list box control with, 317
recursive, 123
secondary, 241
Data Source task pane, 9, 34*t*, 85, 86, 94, 845
binding template part to node in, 443
in InfoPath 2003, *9*
name property and, 95
prefixes in, 135
secondary data source in, 253, *253*
Data Source Wizard, list of content types in, 971, *971*
Data states, 749–764
Changing event, 749–757
Validating event, 757–764
Data tab, 176–182
diverse properties available with, 182
Data type binding, field or group types and, 1045, 1045*t*
Data type errors, 100
Data type limitations, Web service with ADO.NET **DataSet** object and, 343
Data type property, 98–101
Data type validation error, invalid data in field and, *100*
Data validation, 6, 11, 18, 19, 118, 222–229, 426, 742
adding to form template, 223–227
description of, 222–223
mobile forms and, 724–725
pattern matching, 227–229
on **PreferredDate** field, 802
referencing user role in, 880
secondary data sources and, 311–312
specifying a user role in condition for, *630*
submitting forms and, 331–334
updating template parts and, 451
user roles in, 621, 629–630

Data Validation condition builder, 224, *225*
Data Validation dialog, 223, *223*, 629
with listing for two conditions to validate total number of guests, 226–227, *227*
Data validation errors
full error description for, 226, *226*
inline alert for, *225*
DataValidation node, detailed view of, *239*
Data Validation section, in Logic Inspector dialog, 238
Data View pane, 1093
Date data type, 99*t*
Date Picker control, 45*t*, 311
binding behavior of, 89*t*
DateTime class, 760
DateTime data type, 99*t*
DateTime field, 774
DateTime type, 997
Days member, of **TimeSpan** class, 761
DCL. *See* Data connection library
DCL connection definitions, unapproved, 937
Deactivation, of user-deployed form templates, 904
Debugging
form code, 740–741
previewing and, 741
Web service project in Visual Studio, 277
Decimal (double) data type, 99*t*
Declarative data validation, 98
Decorations, XML data and, 773
Default Choice Section
with context menu commands, *170*
employment application form after replacement of, *170*
Default data
calculated, 86
static, 85–86
Default data connection timeout setting, Maximum setting and, 933
Default data types, for controls, 43
Default formatting styles, setting for controls, 82
Default insert action, target form and, 569
DefaultLCID DWORD value, 1130
Default merge actions, 561, 565
node type and, 560*t*
Default permission, 542, 543
Default print settings, Word print views and, 603
Default submit messages, overriding, 394
Default template data, editing, 151–154
Default value calculation button, *107*
Default value property, 106–107
calculated default values, 107
static default values, 106
Default values
calculated, 107
editing, 204–208
removal of empty groups and, 572
setting to a user role, 629
static, 106
Default Value section, of Data tab, 180
Default value text box, 154
Default view
MOI Consulting request form code and setting of, 808–810
setting dynamically, 808
Delete method, manually removing errors from **Errors** collection with, 766
Delete operation, 86
DeleteRange, using, 780
Deletes, cascading, 305, 306
Deleting
nodes, 88, 121–122, 779–780
unused data connections, 380
Denial-of-service attack, data connections in browser-based form templates and, 710
Deployment
of digitally signed template, 487–493
of installable template, 486–487
of restricted form template, 462, 464–466
security and, 455–552
Description field
fully structured *vs.* semistructured documents and flexibility in, 93
Description field, in Publishing Wizard, 407
Description string value, LCID key and, 1143
Design
of form template dialog, 27–30
of form templates with VSTO, 836–863
for merging forms, 561–564
partial signatures and changes in, 522
Design a Form dialog, making selections in, 691
Design a Form link, 16
Design a Form Template dialog, *28*, 342, 435
creation of main query connection and, *245*
in InfoPath 2007, 20–21, *22*
opening, 28

with Template Part option selected, 433, *433*
VSTO, *839*
Design a new category, on Design a Form Template dialog, 29
Design Checker (checker), 691, 693–701, 1018
browser-enabled forms without, 701
browser-enabling a form template, 693–700
controls targeted by the messages in, for MOI feedback form template, 868, *869*
designing browser-enabled template parts and, 701
errors and messages in, after making the feedback form template browser-compatible, 695, *696*
form template postbacks and, 954
ignoring messages in, 701
in InfoPath 2007, 19
other uses for, 700
refreshing errors and messages in, 697
warning about Checker not being mobile aware, 722
Design Checker item, on Tools menu, 405
Design Checker link, in Design Tasks task pane, 845
Design Checker task pane, 34*t*, 694, 867
post-import warnings in, 1126, 1127
report warnings in, 1140
shortcut to, 694
showing template parts needing updating, 451, *452*
specified warnings listed in, 1141
Verify on Server option on, 872
Designer lockdown, 504–507
globally disable design mode, 505–506
per form template, 504–505
trust and, 499–507
Design form, Scrolling Region control in, *165*
Designing layout of form, 34–40
color schemes, 39, *40*
Layout task pane, 34–35, *35*, 37–39
Design mode, 25, 26
after finishing Data Connection for submitting student sign-in data to Web service, *348*
changing form files outside of, 423–424
Choice Group control in, *168*
customizing merge behavior in, 564–569, 571, 573–576, 578–579, 580
custom task pane not shown in, 784
data connection file creation in, 711
default IRM permissions on form set in, 538
diagnosing problems with Web services (InfoPath) in, 288, 289
disabling, for form template, 504
discouraging and disabling, 455
File Attachment control in, *68*
gridlines in, 36
Horizontal Region controls in, *167*
Horizontal Repeating Table control in, *61*
Hyperlink control in, *158*
InfoPath usage in, 27–30
list controls in, *66*
master and detail controls in, *63*
MOI Consulting morale event scheduler form in, 750, *750*
MultipleNotifications sample form in, *775*
permissions granted and denied to user given form template in, 539, *539*
previewing form in, 48
Print Multiple Views dialog in, 595, *595*
Repeating Recursive Section in, *172*
Repeating Table control in, *57*
resizing controls in, 54
Resources Files menu item on Tools menu in, 27
Section control selected in, *47*
seeing data source in, 86
specifying permission during, to apply when form is filled out, *543*
template part, 434–435, 437–438
Design once philosophy, 666, 692
form code adherence to, 875
Design surface, 33
Design targets, 434–435
Design Tasks task pane, 435
accessing from anywhere, 39
Controls link in, 41
designing a template part in, *434*
tasks within, 33, *33*, 34*t*
in VSTO, 844, *844*, 845
Design this Form link, 16
Design-time visual, 47
for new version of AddressBlock template part, 449, *450*
Design-time visual icons, over controls to indicate potential binding issues, *149*
Design-time visuals, 10, 65, 149–151
for Master/Detail controls, 201
when they appear on controls, *150*
Desktop database engine, 673

destPath parameter, 1136, 1136*t*, 1137, 1140
Developer tab, enablng, 968
Diagnostic Logging administration page, 925, *926*
Diffgram serialization, 374
Digest authentication, 934, 944
Digitally signed data
  controlling whether or not to display prompt giving user chance to digitally sign form before submission, *368*
  dialog giving user chance to digitally sign form before submission, *367*
  reminder about signing, 367
  submitting, 365–368
Digitally signed form templates
  deploying, 487–493
  digitally signed form data *vs.*, 508
  high privileges and, 417
  reasoning behind, 493
Digital signatures, 15, 19, 217, 455–456, 507–538, 552
  allowing only one signature, 527–531
  defining, 507
  enabling for specific data in a form, 697
  flexibility and, 521
  form performance and, 535
  MOI Consulting request form code and addition of, 811–816
  removing, 518–519
  setting up counter-signatures, 532–533
  standards, 534
  using digitally signed data in forms, 509–526
  using independent signatures (co-signing), 531–532
  valid, 533
  in XML data and Schema, 533–538
Digital Signatures button, 513
Digital Signatures category, browser-compatibility message within, under Form Options dialog, *696*
Digital Signatures dialog, 517, 530, 813, 815
  tracking who has signed form in, *514*
Digital Signatures tab, signed Section controls and settings on, 525–526
Digital signing, selecting certificate to use for, 490, *490*
Dirty property, 988, 1000
Disabled add-ins, 502
Disabled commands, previewing a form and, *425*
Disabled Items dialog, 1114, *1114*
Disable InfoPath Designer mode setting, 505, *506*
Disabling, of Save and Save As, 330
Disambiguated schemas, 130
DispidEnabled ID, 1063
DispidValue ID, 1063
Display tab, 182–188, 215
  checkboxes in, 183, *183*
  for Rich Text Box control, *186*
  of Text Box Properties dialog, *183*
Display text vertically checkbox, 188
DLLs. *See* Dynamically linked libraries
Dockable task panes, 845
Document content type, data source for, 973, *974*
Document element, 103
Document Information Panel, 966–977
  with Document Properties view, 976, *976*
  in InfoPath 2007, 24
  Settings page in, 970, *970*
  in Word 2007, 966, *967*
  Word document showing **Author** property in body of document and, 976, *977*
Document Information Panel dialog, 968, *968*
Document library(ies), 705–708
  adding site content types to, 409, *410*
  defining policy on, 550
  Include data for the active form only option for, 294
  IRM settings for, 550, *550*
  permissions on, 548–552
  property promotion, versioning, and permissions, 706
Document Library option, 406
  choosing to publish to Forms Services via, 679, *679*
Document/literal Web services, 288
Document Object Model, 367
Document properties dialog, in Word 2003, 966, *967*
Document Properties drop-down menu, 968, 969
Document Properties-Server view, 972, 974
  shown in Document Information Panel, 976, *976*
DocumentPropertiesTemplate sample, 973
Document Properties view, customized, for editing standard document properties, 974, *975*

DOM. *See* Document Object Model
Domain, defining, 467
Domain forms
identification of, 467
restricted flexibility with, 463
running of, in local machine zone, 478
Domain form templates, as most common type, 469
Domain option, 428
Domain security level, 459, 467–482
Internet zone, 475
local intranet zone, 470–474
local machine zone, 478
moving published domain trust form, 479–481
restricted sites zone, 470
restricting Internet domain forms through the OCT, 476
simulating a publish domain for testing, 481–482
trusted sites zone, 477
Domain simulation, previewing form templates and, 428–429
Domain trust forms, 475
Forms Services and, 461
published, moving, 479–481
Domain trust form templates, 711
Domain trust level, list of any settings or features resulting in form template being at, *484*
Do not include the section in the form by default, buttons enabled with, 181–182
Double-clicking, on InfoPath control in VSTO, 851–852, 852*t*
Drop-Down List Box control, 7, 10, 44, 45*t*, 53, 59, 446, 1037
binding behavior of, 89*t*
views and, 952
Drop Down List Box Properties dialog, 318, *319*
DSN-less database connection, 257
DSP. *See* Data Source task pane
Due Date, **When** data source field promoted as, 411, *413*
"Duplicate error" bug, 764
Dynamically linked libraries
COM add-ins compiled in, 1074
registering for WordPrint tool, 597
Dynamic features, 741
Dynamic user names, 619

E

Editable schema, simple, 137 (listing)
Edit Default Values button, 181
in Section Properties dialog, 205
Edit Default Values dialog, 151–152, *152*, 204
cutaway of, when Choice exists in data source, *153*
Edit Formula button, 158, 159
Editing. *See also* Manually editing data source
code with InfoPath, 384
default template data, 151–154
default values, 204–208
demoted properties, 412
standard document properties, customized Document Properties view for, 974, *975*
structural, 308, 310
EditingStatus, note on closing, 1025
Edit Settings dialog, disambiguating data source by use of, *130*
Edit SQL dialog, Test SQL Statement button in, 266
Edit-time visual, 511
Edit Values dialog, for Optional Section control, *206*
Edit XPath button, 512
Electronic forms, 1116
Elements
attributes *vs.*, 118
with fields and groups, 94
layout, 164
as nodes, 94
Elevated privileges, 401, 403
e-mail
access paths and opening form templates in, 464
form template deployment to, 413–416
restrictions related to publishing via, 415–416
resulting e-mail in Outlook after finishing Publishing Wizard for, 415, *416*
sample command line for configuring, 949 (listing)
sending form template via, 397, 403, 891
submit forms via, 336, 337–341
e-mail addresses, controls for, on employment application form, 44
E-mail Attachments tab, in Form Options dialog, 660, *661*

e-mail data connections, 948–950
e-mail forms (InfoPath), workflow with, 643–662
e-mail introduction, configuring, 950
e-mail properties, formulas for, 339
e-mail publishing, in InfoPath 2003 SP1, 16
e-mail settings, errors and failure in setting of, 949
e-mail submit connections, for restricted form templates, 466–467
e-mail submits, disadvantages with, 340–341
EmailSubmit sample, 338
e-mail task, requesting approval of travel request, *639*
Embedded images checkbox, 187
Embedded SQL authentication, 934–935
EmployeeInformation group, setting, for repeating and referencing itself, *123*
EmployeeInformation repeating group node, Merge Settings dialog for, 573, *573*
Employment application form template
  after adding standard controls, *46*
  after replacing the default Choice Section, *170*
  with cells for first and last names, 37, *38*
  changing Repeating Section control with job information to a Repeating Table control, 57
  with Choice Group control, *170*
  controls added to, 44
  creation of, 30–33
  with Optional Section controls, *50*
  preview of, 48, *48*
  with Repeating Section control, 53, *53*
  with row for address information, 38, *38*
  with title added by using Table with Title, *36*
Empty groups, removing, 571, 572
EnabledAllPasteButtons method, 1091
  Copy button event handler and, 1090 (listing)
Enabled property, 1043, 1059
  building custom controls for InfoPath using ActiveX and implementation of, 1055–1056
  stock properties for SimpleInfoPathActiveX control and, 1051
Enable method, 1059
Enable protection checkbox, 505
EnableSessionState property, 1018
EnsureCommandsArray method, 999, 1000 (listing)
Enterprise Client License key, 678
Enterprise features
  enabling, 678
  Forms Services and, 673
  with SharePoint Server, 676, 678
Enterprise Search, 19
Enveloped signature, 534
Environment class, 883
e parameter, **OldValue** and **NewValue** from, 777
Eraser, unavailability of, in VSTO, 861
Error cases, multiple rules and, 232
errorCategory element, post-import warnings and, 1141
errorCode parameter, 765
Error dialog
  appearance of, when trying to change signed form data, *518*
  when domain form is not opened from its access path and published template is unavailable, 480, *480*
  when opening restricted form template attempting to query external data source, 461, *461*
Error handling, rules and, 389–391, 390
errorMessage parameter, **SubmitTo-HostEventHandler** method and, 1009
errorMode parameter, 765
Error (red "X") entries, server events and, 920
Error reporting
  Validating event and, 757
  validation and, 763
Errors. *See also* Data validation errors
  adding those that user never sees, 767 (listing)
  capturing, from execution of Web service data connection, 825 (listing)
  in Design Checker after making feedback form template browser-compatible, 695, *696*, 697
  failure to configure e-mail settings and, 949
  full trust form template and, 494
  MOI Consulting request form code and checking for, 811–816
  in navigating to forms, 928
  red asterisk for, 228, *228*
  refreshing, in Design Checker, 697
  rules and, 234
  showing on a button **Clicked** event, 766 (listing)

Errors collection
adding **UserDefined FormError** to, 765 (listing)
checking, for reported start or end errors, 763 (listing)
manually removing errors from, 766
Errors.DeleteAll method, manually removing errors from **Errors** collection with, 766
EventArgs parameter, 1106
Event bubbling, 745–748
querying and, 819–820
EventBubbling sample, 747, 748
showing **Site** and **Sender** node names as events bubble up the data source, 745, *746*
EventHandler object, new, 998
Event handlers, 742
for loading a form, 1088–1089
mistaken creation of, 853
in .NET *vs.* in InfoPath, 752
registering, 780–782
Event logs
Forms Services errors in, 920, 921–924*t*
Windows, 920
EventManager object, 730, 742
definition of, in FormCode.Designer.cs file, 781
Events, sinking, 737
Events property, of **ApplicationClass** object, 1082
Event Viewer program, running, 920
Example sample data, 154
Excel, 3, 4, 605
COM add-ins supported by, 1073
Custom Task Panes added into, 1093
default Document Information Panel in, 966, 968, 970
exporting InfoPath form data to, 12
form importing and, 28, 29
Mime HTML file opened in, 606
status report data exported to, *608*, 608–609
Trust Center dialog and, 499
VSTO package and, 834
Excel Calculation, 672
Excel documents, InfoPath default importers for, 1128
Excel forms, built-in importer for, 1116
Excel Services, 678
Excel workbooks, Import Options dialog for importing, 1122, *1122*
Exclamation point, red, meaning of, 149–150
Exec method, hosted form and, 994, 995
ExecuteAction, using to insert an Optional Section control, 828–829 (listing)
ExecuteAction method, of **CurrentView** object, 827
ExecuteCommand method, hosted form and, 992, 993 (listing), 996
Execute overrides, benefits of, 825
Executive approval, counter-signatures and, 532
Expense report example, data source for, *161*
Expense report form
Expression Box control and, 161
during preview, *163*
Expense Report sample form template, customizing, 658–660
Expense Reports InfoPath form folder, 658, *659*
Expiration, setting, 314
explicit credentials, UDC file and use of, 946
Exporters
process flow, *1133*
registering, 1129–1131
registry key structure for, 1129, *1129*
steps in creation of, 1128
understanding construction of form template and, 1140
Export Forms to Excel menu item, on InfoPath actions context menu in Outlook 2007, 660
Exporting forms, 605–612
choosing forms from which to export data, 607, *608*
choosing type of data to export, 607, *607*
InfoPath e-mail forms, 657–660
selecting data to export, 610, *610*
Export method, parameters for, 1136, 1136*t*
Export to Excel Wizard, after choosing to export only the data from a specific table, 609, *609*
Export To menu item, expanded, 606, *606*
Export Wizard, 611, 1132
accessing, 1130–1131
custom exporter shown in, *1131*
Expression, of qualifier, 217

Expression Box controls, 7, 158–163, 972
binding behavior of, 90*t*
changing to Vertical Label control, 188
data fit to, 353
finding XPath of node and, 777
Extensible Stylesheet Language Transformations, 6
External data sources
error dialog for failed connection to, *315*
examples of, 241
relationships between forms and, 243, *243*
External sources, data retrieved from, 241–296
External URL mappings, 928
Extracted source files, templates saved as, 421–424

F

Failed compilation, 740
False Boolean value, form submits and, 350, 351
Farm install, SQL Server required for, 674
Farms
entire, quiescing, 915–916
joining, 675
quiescing, 918–919
quiescing time for, 916
SharePoint database configuration settings for, 675, *675*
Farm topology, determining, 672
Faux message box
clicking OK button on the View with, 879 (listing)
showing in browser, 879 (listing)
Favorites link, 16
fibonacci-cmcl sample form template, 938
Fibonacci data connection, 941
Fibonacci form template, 937
Fib Web service method, 937
Field (attribute), 94
Field (element), 94
Field (element with custom data type) type, implementing control that binds to, 1050
Field names
changing, 95
dialog warning about data loss and, *177*
Data tab and, 176
Field node type, merge customizations available for, 570*t*
Field option, Specify Data Type Options page with, 1045, *1046*
Field or Group Properties dialog, 176
after specifying a custom merge XSL in the manifest, 581, *582*
namespaces in, 108, *108*
Rules and Merge tab on, *566*
updating node names and, 92
validation tab on, 224, *224*
Field(s), 86, 94
changing, 744
in Data Source task pane, 9
data type property and, 98
groups and, 143–144
InfoPath submit behaviors for, projected over Include setting, 361, *362*
of qualifier, 217
representation of, in data source, 87
File and Picture controls, 67
File Attachment control, 12, 14, 52, 68–70, 169, 827, 1020
binding behavior of, 90*t*
commands, *69*
in design mode, *68*
for filling out a form, *68*
growing session size and, 911
performance tips, 954–955
with résumé file attached, 69, *69*
File attachment data, increase in maximum session size and, 912
File attachments, large, adding to form, 71
File name, form name *vs.*, 896
File name box, in Upload Data Connection File page, 939, *940*
File server, local intranet forms and, 471
FileSystemObject, 473
File system path, opening SharePoint site with use of, 1014, *1014*
Filling out a form
control behavior, structural selection and, 51–52
File Attachment control for, *68*, 68–69
list controls for, *66*
Master/Detail control and, 63–65
Master/Detail control in application review form and, *64*
Multiple-Selection List Box control for, *67*
Picture control for, *72*
secondary data sources and, 310–312
on a SharePoint page, 928–929

in Web browsers, 665
Fill out a form category, on Design a Form Template dialog, 29
Fill out a Form dialog, in InfoPath 2003 SP1, 16, *17*
Fill-out-a-form mode, 25, 26
Filter Data button, 628
Filtering
of data based on user roles, 626–629
List Box items, 323–324
survey responses, 656–657
Filters, 298
specification of, to show only grocery items from a selected category, *324*
user roles in, 621
Filter Web Parts, 678
Find and Replace dialog, 854
Find button, code for **Click** event handler and, 995
find command, hosted form and, 995
FindControl method, 1087
Find feature, from Visual Studio, 855
FindReplaceFindNext command, hosted form and, 995, 996
Firefox, Forms Services and, 690
FireOnChanged method, 1058, 1069 (listing)
FireTaskPaneReady method, code for, 1103 (listing)
Folder properties dialog, after clicking on InfoPath Forms tab, 651, *651*
Font, for SimpleInfoPathActiveX control, 1051, *1052*
Font task pane, 77, *77*
FoodPreferenceSurvey form, 649
sending to a list of e-mail recipients, *647*
Food survey form template, 646, *646*
Footer button, 589
Footers
for printed reports, 589–591
repeating field inserted into, 590
team status report with, 591, *591*
Formative evaluation, 273
Format menu
Apply Font to All Controls selected from, 81
Borders and Shading dialog accessed from, 36
Format Painter, 79–80
in InfoPath 2003 Service Pack 1 (SP1), 12, 13
on Standard toolbar, 79, *79*
Format Painter cursor, *80*
Formatting
advanced, 76–82
conditional, 215–222
control, 78–79
multiple controls, 80–82
FormCode.cs, 838
FormCode.Designer.cs, 838
EventManager object defined in, 781
FormCode.Designer.xml, 838
FormCode files, 838
Form code (MOI Consulting request form)
adding, 803–831
checking for errors and adding digital signature, 811–816
context-sensitive Help in custom task pane, 816–822, 824–831
form to be filled out in one sitting, 806, 808
naming your nodes and buttons, 803–805
showing a custom dialog with buttons, 805
showing read-only properties from OM, 805–806
"start over" feature and setting a default view, 808–811
Form code permission, CAS and, 497
Form codes, 731, 875–885
accounting for performance in, 831
after upgrading to InfoPath 2007 OM version, *735t*
compatibility of, with Forms Services, 884–885
custom submit with, 383–384
debugging, 740–741
design once philosophy and, 875
execution of, in browser, 876–877
hooking up events in, 735
InfoPath 2003 Service Pack 1 with, 842
performance tips, 953
querying via a rule instead of, 818
referencing user role in, 880
separation of, into partial classes, 781
upgrading from InfoPath 2003, 842
Form conflicts, 466
FormControl class, 990, 991
methods available in, 981–983*t*
FormControlCommandIds class, **CommandIds** enumeration in, 994
FormControl control, 1015
Visual Studio Toolbox after addition of, 980, *980*
XmlFormView control *vs.*, 1012

Form Control methods, in InfoPath, 981–983*t*
Form creators, as owners, 544
Form data
 digitally signing, 511–520
 importing, 1142–1148
 partially signing, 521–526
 proper refreshing of, 684
 saving, 429
 searching, 875
 submitting, 327–395
FormDataTaskPaneActiveX, 1101
FormDataTaskPaneActiveX.dll, 1100
FormDataTaskPaneAddIn, 1094
FormDataTaskPane namespace, 1100
FormDataTaskPane sample, 1094
Form Data Viewer COM add-in, 1111
Form Data View task pane, *1094,* 1095
Form definition file, 27
Form deployment, advanced, 904
Form design
 Design a Form Template dialog and, 28–29
 starting points for, 30*t*
Form Error dialog, 403
FormError object, 813
Form errors, 765–767
 dialog for clear presentation of, *811,* 811–812
 types of, 765
FormErrorsCollection object, 813
FormErrorType enumeration, 765
Form events, 730, 742–744
 testing by yourself, 743
FormEvents_Loading method, 739
FormEvents sample, 743
FormEvents_Submit method, 829
Form filling, security and, 461
Form-filling sessions
 new and existing, three quiesce states for, 915*t*
 proper closure of, 687
Form ID
 Form Properties dialog for setting, 460, *460*
 publishing via e-mail and, 416
 security designed into form templates and, 459
Form importer framework, 29
Form importers, 1115
 built-in, 1116–1127
  application version requirements for, 1117
 third parties and creation of, 29
Form library(ies), 705–706
 behavior of, after form is closed, 708
 property promotion, versioning, and permissions, 706
 on SharePoint, *409*
 specific creation of, for templates, 405
Form loading
 event handlers for, 1088–1089
 validation and, 763
Form load latency, 955
Form name
 e-mail deployment and, 414
 file name *vs.,* 896
 in Site Collection Features list, 898
"Form-only" features, accessing, 330
"Form-only" model, disabling save and, 329–331
Form options
 settings for enabling/disabling certain features for users, such as ability to save a form, *330*
Form Options dialog, 513, 611, 626, 662
 Advanced tab of, 579, *579*
 Browser category in, 872
 browser-compatibility message within Digital Signatures category under, *696*
 Compatibility category in, 694, *695*
 configuring toolbars for browser-enabled form template filled out in browser, 684, *685*
 E-mail Attachments tab in, 660, *661*
 Enable digital signatures for specific data in the form option in, 697
 Open and Save tab of, 611, *612,* 622, *622*
 Preview tab in, 624, *625*
 Programming category in, 732, *732,* 784
 screening all categories under, 902
 Security and Trust category in, 468
 Security and Trust tab of, *485*
 setting up custom task pane in, 784, *785*
 from Tools menu, 684
Form performance, digital signatures and, 535
Form Permission task pane, 545, *545,* 548
Form postbacks, reduction of, 953–954
Form Properties dialog for setting form ID, 460, *460*
Form Registration Tool, 417
Forms. *See also* Browser forms; Domain forms; Filling out a form; Submitting forms

accessible, designing, 874
browser-enabled, print views in, 603–605
classifications of, 1116
with code, filling out and debugging, 738–740
controlling permissions to, 547–548
controls inserted into, 41, 43
creating in mobile browser, 722
custom task pane added to, 784
defined, 4
defining IRM permission on, *540*
determining user's role when filling out, 620–621
digitally signed data used in, 509–526
errors navigating to, 928
full use of, without Internet connection, 312
importing into InfoPath 2007, 1119–1124
Information Rights Management applied to, 538
inserting large file attachments and pictures to, 71
layout design for, 34–40
local intranet, 471
merging, 554–586
multiple records displayed in, 265
opening in browser, 683
partial signatures and design of, 522–526
permissions on, 542–548
permission with document libraries and, 548–552
previewing in VSTO, 863
relationships between external data sources and, 243, *243*
source, 559
submitting to host, 1007–1010
target, 559
viewing all signatures on, 532
watching for bugs that circumvent validation in, 756
writing code behind, 730–741
Forms dialog, digital Signatures category in, 509, *509*
FormServer.aspx page, 928
FormServerTemplates library, 896, 897
Form session, refreshing and going back to, 718
Form session state setting, maximum size of, 911–912
Forms on Office Online link, 16
Forms Server 2007, 953
Forms Services *vs.*, 673
installing, 673–675
Forms Services, 413, 461, 665–726, 678. *See also* Advanced Forms Services
administration links to, 893, *893*
administrative deployment to, 892–901
best practices for, 951
browser-based form control based on, 1011
browser-enabled forms in, 603
category names for, 920
configurations for filling out a form supported by, 715–716
configuring, 671, 675–677, *906*, 906–907
controls supported in, 688*t*
data connection authentication and, 943
data connections synchronously executed by, 956
description of, 669–671
determining availability of, on server, 677
form code compatibility with, 884–885
full list of stadm.exe commands specific to, 899*t*
global administrative data connection settings for, 931, *932*
host OM properties unavailable from, 1035
installation prerequisites, 672
installing, 671–675
integration of, with SharePoint Server 2007, 668, 669, 885, 888, 925–929
lack of support for **Changing** event in, 749
matrix of browsers supported for use with, 690, *691*
mimicking default rendering page for, 1015
object model classes, events, properties and methods not implemented by, 886–887*t*
passing NTLM credentials for data connections with, 944, *944*
publishing form template to, 678–681
publishing VSTO form templates to, 841
quiescing and, 912
session state and, 683, 908–909
SharePoint permissions and how they apply to, 707*t*
status report form filled out in browser with, *667*
supported Web browsers, 690
upgrading to, 677
URL parameters automatically passed to form template in, 1021
FormsServices admin object, 916

Forms Services Admin tool, authored by admin object model, 900, *901*
Forms Services errors, in Windows event log, 920, 921–924*t*
Forms Services features sets, commonality of InfoPath feature sets and, 692, *692*
Forms Services form session state, configuring, 957, *957*
Forms Services site
 flowchart for determining whether form publishes to SharePoint server or, *404*
 publishing form template to, 404–409
 specifying server location for publishing to, *406*
 uploading to, 397
Forms Services toolbar, Print View button on, 604, *604*
FormState object, 908
 exposing, by wrapping it as a property, 754
 initializing, 753
 for persist session data, 810
Form template code, 731
Form Template Conflict prompt, 464, *464*
Form template definition **.xsf** file, buttons in, 151
Form template deployment
 in InfoPath 2003 SP1, 16
 performance tips, 951–952
Form template designers, permissions and, 458
Form template dialog, designing, 27–30
Form template files
 cached, 424
 design mode lock and, 424
FormTemplate object, administration OM on, specific to quiescing, 918*t*
Form template resource files, XML data included in, 250
Form templates, 458
 activating on Site Collection Features page, 898, *898*
 activating to site collection, 895
 associating previewed forms with, 430
 beginning design for, in VSTO, 837–842
 best submit methods for, 335–337
 browser-enabling, 693–700
 changing number of, 29
 code added to, 737–738
 code-signing certificates for signing, 490
 configuration of, for offline mode queries, *313*
 configuring digital signatures for, 509, *509*
 configuring security and trust settings for, 459, *459*
 creating Visual Studio templates from, 856
 customizing e-mail support for, 660–662
 custom widths for, 76
 database connections integrated into, 268–271
 data validation added to, 223–227
 deactivation of, before removal of, 904
 defined, 4
 defining IRM permission on, *540*
 description of, 26–27
 designing, 669
  with a dataset, 370–374
  entirely in Visual Studio, 835
  with VSTO, 836–863
 dialog about verifying credentials when opening, 541, *541*
 digital signing of, 493
 domain trust and features in, *484*
 enabling for backward compatibility, 700
 existing with code, in VSTO, 841–842
 exporting, 611
 external data source and design of, 245
 extracting XML Schema from, 102
 fully quiesced, 915, *915*
 gracefully upgrading, 680
 hiding, 952
 installable, 417–420
 location for publishing tip for, 401
 for Logic Inspector sample, 236, *236*
 lookups and opening of, 479
 managed code control added to, 1065–1066
 managing, 904–905
 moving by republishing, 481
 new blank, creation of, 30–33
 new or existing, creating new Visual Studio project for, 839–840
 opening existing forms, 28
 permissions on, 539–542
 previewing, 424–429
 primary key field in, 376
 programming options, which are saved as defaults for, 736, *736*
 publishing, 11
  for administrator approval, 889–891, *890*, 941–942

equivalence, 891
to Forms Services, 678–681
quiescing, 913–915
status of, 14, 914
time for, 916
upgrading of and, 916–917
requirements definitions and design of, 31
resource files added to, 858
restricted, 460
restricted permission for user during design of, 541, *541*
restrictions on defining permissions on, 540
saving
as extracted source files, 421–424
with managed code, 735
publishing with InfoPath and, 398–420
screening for approval, 902–903
secondary data source binding and design of, 307–309
secondary query connection created for, 245–246, *246*
security designed into, 459–460
seeing form files in, 421
submitting data with those based on database connection, 342–344
template parts inserted into, 442–447
testing, 48
with artificial domains, 482
tracking CMCL references in, 940
two different object models available for writing code behind, 742
understanding, 1137–1140
uploading to server, 893–895
user roles used in, 621
verification of, 902
VSTO environment during design of, 843, *843*
FormTemplates collection, 901
Form template size, processing time and, 419
FormTemplates library, 904
Form template target, 435
Formula edit box, 629
Formulas, for e-mail properties, 339
FormUtilities add-on, data flow for, 1079, *1080*
Form Utilities COM add-in, 1111
FormUtilities sample project, 1077
Form Utilities toolbar, 1083, 1084, 1091
FormVersion attribute field, 800, 806
Form view state, performance tips, 956–957
Form Warning dialog, 235, 390
Forward slash, enabling signatures for specific data in a form and use of, 697
Fragment commands, 210
Friendly labels, 119
Friendly names
in Set of Signable Data dialog, 524
signable data and, 525, 528
FrontPage, COM add-ins supported by, 1073
Full Rich text checkbox, 187
Full trust forms
previewing, 792
restricted flexibility with, 463
restricting, 495–498
Full trust form templates, 417, 480, 902
cross-domain connections and, 929, 930
designing, 485–486
errors with, 494
error that occurs when opening template that is neither digitally signed nor installed, 494, *494*
Save and **SaveAs** and, 831
Full trust security level, 459, 484–498
deploying digitally signed template, 487–493
deploying installable template, 486–487
full trust form template errors, 494
restricting full trust forms, 495–498
Fully quiesced form templates, 915, *915*
Fully structured documents, 93
Function drop-down list box, 411, 412
Fx button, 158

G

GAC. *See* Global assembly cache
General tab, in Properties dialog for Microsoft UpDown Control, 1048
Generic node names, renaming, 799
Genre field, 93
GetButton method, 1088
function of, 1087
implementation of, 1086, 1087 (listing)
GetCurrentToolbar method, 1086, 1087
implementation of, 1084, 1085 (listing)
GetDataConnectionFile.aspx Web page, case-insensitive parameters accepted by, 942–943
get-documentElement function, using, 585 (listing)

GetInterfaceSafetyOptions method, 1065
GetRoleForUser method, 881, 882
GetSavedItems method
 Web service response from running of, *280*
 Web service sample, 275, 276, 277*t*, 279, 282, 286
GetSubAreas.cs sample, 820
GetSubAreas sample file, 800
GetSubAreas secondary data source, *821*
 querying, 821
GetSubAreas Web service, 792
GetTile Web service method, designing TerraServer form with, *290*
Getting Started dialog, *27*, 494, 655, 1119
 with form templates in InfoPath cache, 465, *465*
 in InfoPath 2007, 16, 20, *21*
get_Value method, 1057, 1058, 1060
Global assembly cache, 498, 1061
Globally disable design mode, 505–507
Global script, using body **onload** event instead of, 1035
Go to Next Error feature, 758
Grab handles, for resizing controls, 78
Graceful upgrades, of form templates, 680
Gridlines, 36
Grocery items, in XML file to populate a data connection, 317 (listing)
GroceryItemsData sample, 317
Grocery list form
 creating, 208
 filling out
  after adding note-taking feature, 322, *322*
  with category filters, *325*
  when items are retrieved from a data connection, *320*
 note-taking capability added to, 322, *322*
Grocery list form template, *318*
Grocery shopping list
 filling out, *209*
 three sections of, in Repeating Section Properties dialog, *209*
GroceryShoppingList sample, 208, 317
GroupBox control, IP insurance application after addition of, 984, *984*
Group names
 changing, 95
 selecting, for a role, 618–619
Group names checkbox, 618
Group nodes, binding template part to data in form template and, 443, 445
Group node type, merge customizations available for, 570*t*
Groups, 87, 94
 changing, 744
 in Data Source task pane, 9
 as elements, 94
 fields and, 143–144
 InfoPath submit behaviors for, projected over Include setting, 361, *362*
GuidAttribute attribute, 1078

H

Hackers
 globally disable design mode and, 506, 507
 postbacks per form session state setting and, 910
Handwriting, improving recognition of, 195
Hard-coded credentials, in UDC file, 945, 946
Hard-coded passwords, 752
Header button, 589
Header format dialog, 589–590, *590*, *591*
 after adding **Team** field and date, *591*
Header information, team status report with, 591, *591*
Header rows, choosing number of, in Change to Repeating Table dialog, 1125, *1126*
Headers
 for printed reports, 589–591
 repeating field inserted into, 590
Health monitoring, server and, 962–963
Hello, world! message box, 879, *879*
HelloWorld: FilePath method, Web service sample, 275, 277*t*, 278
HelloWorld definition, in Web service WSDL, 279 (listing)
HelloWorld method, Web service sample and, 275
Helpdesk request, submitting, dialog prompt in which user must click Send for, *341*
Hide Gridlines button, in Tables toolbar, 36
High-level summary, in employment application form, 31
HKEY_CLASSES_ROOT, CLSID key added under, 1066
Horizontal Region control, 972, 1147
 binding behavior of, 90*t*
 in design mode, *167*
 in InfoPath 2007 Controls task pane, 22
Horizontal Region layout element, 164, 166–167

Horizontal Repeating Table control, 60–61
  binding behavior of, 89*t*
  in design mode, *61*
  filling out a form and, *62*
  in InfoPath 2007 Controls task pane, 22
HostClassLibrary, 1004
HostClassLibrary.dll, 1006
Hosting, 856
Hosting environment
  as destination, Submit Options dialog with, 1008, *1008*
  submit connection, 336, 337
  submitting to, 391–392, 1007–1010
Hosting InfoPath, 965–1036
  creating InfoPath host application, 977–980, 984–1010
  Document Information Panel, 966–977
  hosting InfoPath control in a Web browser, 1011–1016, 1018–1025, 1027–1035
  hosting scenarios, 966
Host page
  handling multiple **SubmitToHost** form connections in, 1031 (listing)
  running arbitrary script in, 1034
Host property, using, 1004–1007
HostUtilities class, 1005 (listing), 1006
"How to Use the ADO SHAPE Command," 267
HTML, custom task pane, 817
HTMLDocument object, 788
HTMLTaskPane object, 787, 788
HTTP
  data connections, 934
  making connection files available through, 942
  Submit Options dialog for Web server submit via, *381*
  submitting form to Web server via, 380–383
HTTPS, secure submit with, 383
HTTP status codes, submit and, 351
Hung upload, recovering from, 895
Hybrid controls, 88
Hyperlink control, 7, 88, 156–158
  Advanced tab for, 193, *193*
  binding behavior of, 90*t*
  in design mode, *158*
Hyperlink data type, 99*t*
Hyperlinks, 156
Hyperlink sample file, 88
Hyphens, XML, naming nodes and, 105

I

Icons
  changing, template parts and, 448
  in Data Source task pane for various types of data source nodes, *87*
  InfoPath controls ad, *846*
  InfoPath e-mail item, 652
  missing, in toolbars, 1020
IConversionManager interface, methods of, 1134*t*
IConversionManager2 interface, method of, 1134*t*
ICTPFactory object, 1095
ID, template part, 453, 454
IDictionary interface, 753
IDispatch property type, 1056
Idle event, setting up event handler for, 997
Idle state, updating toolbar buttons during, 997–1000
IDTExtensibility2 interface, 1075–1076, 1078, 1113
  methods of, 1075*t*
ID values, giving to all Button controls, in Button Properties dialog, 803–805
IE. *See* Internet Explorer
#if/#endif compiler directive statements, 734
IFormDataTPActiveXCtl interface, 1101
IFormDataViewAddIn interface, 1102 (listing)
  accessing, 1103 (listing)
IFormTemplateConverter, InfoPath 2007 support for backward compatibility and, 1131
IFormTemplateConverter2 interface
  implementing, 1131–1135
  methods of, 1133*t*
IHostUtilities interface, 1004, 1005, 1006
IInfoPathDataImporter interface
  importing form data and, 1143–1148
  methods of, 1144*t*
IInfoPathEditor interface, 990
IInfoPathMaskedTextBox interface, creating, 1062, 1063 (listing)
IInfoPathMaskedTextBox interface methods, implementation of, 1063 (listing)
IInfoPathViewControl interface
  properties of, 1147*t*
  querying controls for, 1146
IInitEventHandler interface, 1001

IIS. *See* Internet Information Services
Immediate debug window, running any code on-the-fly in, 764
Impersonation, previewing as user role and, 428
Imported forms, fixing, 1125–1126
Importer/exporter object, simple, class declaration for, 1132 (listing)
ImportErrors.xml file, 1141
 for MOI Consulting expense report form, 1140, 1141 (listing)
ImportErrors.xml file, 1140
Importers
 process flow, *1133*
 registering, 1129–1131
 registry key structure for, 1129, *1129*
 steps in creation of, 1128
 understanding construction of form template and, 1138–1140
Import/export framework, 1115
Import Form Data dialog, 1143, *1143*
Importing
 locked open files and, 1121
 post-import warnings and, 1126–1127
Importing form data, 1142–1148
 data importer framework, 1142–1143
 IInfoPathDataImporter interface, 1143–1148
Import link, on Design a Form Template dialog, 29
Import method, 1140, 1145
 parameters for, 1136, 1136*t*
 sample implementation of, 1146 (listing)
 signature for, 1144
Import Options dialog
 for importing Excel workbooks, 1122, *1122*
 for importing Word documents, 1121, *1121*
#import statement, 1102
Import Wizard, 1132
 final page of, 1123, *1123*
Import Wizard page
 for selecting file to import, 1119, *1120*
 for selecting importer to use, *1120*
Improvement plans, 278
Inactive add-ins, 502
Include data for the active form only option, for document libraries, 294
Include setting, InfoPath submit behaviors for fields and groups projected over, 361, *362*
Incoming alternate access mappings, 928
Independent properties, changing/resetting of, after rebinding, 141*t*
Independent signatures (co-signing), using, 531–532
Indeterminate state, 331
Industry-defined schemas, 128
Infinite change loops, 777
Info group, 522
InfoPatch, global cached queries setting in CK spell for main, 314, *315*
InfoPath. *See also* Hosting InfoPath
 ActiveX controls and building custom controls for, 1049–1072
 advantages with, 11
 advantages with Custom Task Panes over existing HTML task panes in, 1093
 bringing into Visual Studio, 835–836
 building
  ActiveX control for, with use of C#, 1061–1072
  COM add-in for, 1076–1092
  XML tree structure in Word to match structure of data source in, 599
 classes of code supported by, 729
 closing before beginning or repairing VSTO installation, 836
 COM add-ins supported by, 1073
 custom merge XSL created in, 580–582
 Custom Task Panes added into, 1093
 default merge functionality in, 559
 description of, 3–4
 editing code with, 384
 event handlers in .NET *vs.*, 752
 formatting options with, and those in Word, 77
 form events exposed by, 743*t*
 form template always designed for, 692
 form templates in, 26–27
 installing as an administrator, 457
 interfaces and properties that controls should implement to work well in, 1050*t*
 managing add-ins in, 1111–1114
 merging forms in, 555–560
 object model in, 729, 741–790
 Office Configuration Tool security settings for, *477*
 passing NTLM credentials for data connections with, 944, *944*
 preview feature and, 425

programming paradigm, 742
Resource Files dialog in, 858, *858*
saving and publishing form templates with, 398–420
searching for Web services by using UDDI in, *300*
security and, 455
summary thoughts on use of .NET controls in, 1071–1072
TerraServer Web service used in, 289–290
two-dimensional flow layout in, 798
two modes for running of, 25
using in design mode, 4
using Web service data connection in, 273
value to, 5
VSTA bundled with, 834
Web service compatibility with, 288–289
InfoPath actions context menu, 659, *659*
InfoPath.ApplicationClass, 1107
InfoPathChart control, implementing control that binds to XML subtree and, 1050–1051
InfoPath client, detecting, 883–884
InfoPathControl interface, 1071
building custom controls for InfoPath using ActiveX and implementation of, 1058–1061
implementing, 1069–1070
InfoPathControl interface methods, 1059, 1059*t*
InfoPathControlLibrary project, 1066
InfoPathControl methods, 1070 (listing)
InfoPath controls
as icons, *846*
XML Schema created "behind" data source in XSD file and, 111–115*t*
InfoPath data connection
converting to use a server-defined data connection file, 711, *712*
My Data Sources connection *vs.*, 260
InfoPath design mode, data types available in, and their value ranges, 99*t*
InfoPath e-mail forms, 22, 614
creating rules for, 648–650
customizing e-mail support for a form template, 660–662
designing and using, 644–648
disabling for InfoPath 2003-compatible forms, 662
disabling in Outlook 2007, 643
filling out, 652–656, *653*, 654
merging and exporting, 657–660
in Outlook reading pane, 653, *653*
replying to, without opening, 655
restrictions of those published to e-mail recipients, 645
sending to other e-mail applications, 644
sorting, grouping, and filtering responses, 656–657
storing received forms in Outlook folders, 650–652
submitting, in Submit dialog, 654, *654*
using sample form template as, 658
workflow with, 643–662
INFOPATH.EXE program, in OFFICE12 installation directory, 495
infopath.exe program, preview feature and, 425
InfoPath feature sets, commonality of Forms Services features sets and, 692, *692*
InfoPath form code, writing in host page with use of **XmlFormView,** 1025, 1027–1028
InfoPath form control, hosting in Web browser, 1011–1035
InfoPath Form Control methods, 981–983*t*
InfoPath form design, basics of, 25–83
InfoPath form folder, 644
InfoPath forms, filling out, in the browser, 666–668
InfoPath Forms Services, 17
success of, 18–19
InfoPath Forms Services pack, 963
InfoPath Forms Services performance counters, list of, 960–961*t*
InfoPath Forms Services performance object
installing, 958
server-side performance and, 959
InfoPath form template cache, 480
InfoPath Form Template folder, 854
InfoPathFormTemplate1 folder, files within, 838
InfoPath Form Templates code group, 472
InfoPath host application
creating, 977–980, 984–1010
creating, in .NET, 979–980, 984–990
handling events from the form, 1001–1004
host to InfoPath communication, 990–1000
submitting a form to the host, 1007–1010
using **Host** property, 1004–1007

InfoPath import/export framework, 1128–1140
implementing **IFormTemplateConverter2** interface, 1131–1135
importing and exporting, 1135–1137
registering your importer/exporter, 1129–1131
understanding form templates, 1137–1140
InfoPath interfaces, location for defining of, 1060
InfoPathManagedObjectModel symbol, 734
InfoPathMaskedTextBox class, 1064
after addition of COM Interop attributes, 1062 (listing)
InfoPathMaskedTextBox class definition, 1069 (listing)
InfoPathMaskedTextBox control, installation of, 1066
"InfoPath Restricted," as not "Internet Explorer Restricted," 470
InfoPath schema inference, 126
InfoPath settings, limited, on VSTO Options dialog, 863–863
InfoPath Team Blog, 429
InfoPath 2003, 7–12
C# form code before upgrading the OM version, 734*t*
controls task pane in, *8*
Data Source task pane in, *9*
opening version 2007 form templates with, 716
pulling external data into, 10
upgrading code from form template compatible with, *733*
upgrading form code from, 842
Visual Studio 2005 support for, 835
InfoPath 2007, 17–24
application version requirements for built-in form importers in, 1117
building reusable components with, 431
built-in form importers in, 1116–1127
controls and their binding behaviors, 89–91*t*
custom task panes supported by, 1073
default importers for Excel and Word documents in, 1128
importing form into, 1119–1124
Information Rights Management with, 538
managed code and, 731
richness of, 665
sample form templates with, 28
saving forms during preview in, 429
Visual Studio 2005 support for, 835
Visual Studio Tools for, 833–863
InfoPath 2007 form template, opening with InfoPath 2003, 716
InfoPath 2003 Service Pack 1 (SP1), 12–16
controls added in, 14
with form code, 842
release of, 12
InfoPath 2003 Toolkit for Visual Studio, 835
InfoPath 2007 VSTA, 842
InfoPath Web service, connection timeouts, 360
InfoPath Web services, 280–287
Information Rights Management, 456, 538–552
direct mapping of SharePoint permissions to, 552*t*
enabling, on SharePoint Central Administration site, 549, *549*
in InfoPath 2007, 23
note on not using as security feature, 538
permission(s)
with document libraries, 548–552
on forms, 542–548
on form templates, 539–542
mapping default SharePoint roles to, 551*t*
policy, 550
setting for individual users, 551–552
VSTO and, 862
Information technology, 3
InitEventHandler event, 1002
InitEventHandler method, three parameters taken by, 1001–1002
Initialization, safety of ActiveX controls and, 1039, 1053–1055
InitializeComponent method, uncommenting, 306–307
InitializeEventArgs object, 1022
Initialize event handler, adding in host page for **XmlFormView1** control, *1023*
Initialize method, importer/exporter and, 1134, 1135 (listing)
Initiator roles, 620
Init method, 1060, 1070, 1071, 1072
Ink-entry mode, in InfoPath 2003 SP1, 16
Ink Picture control, 14, 72–73, 79
binding behavior of, 90*t*
in InfoPath 2003 SP1, 16
with text entered with a Tablet PC stylus, *73*
Inline alert, for data validation error, *225*
InnerXml property, 365

InputParameters property, 1022
Input scope, 195
controls providing support for, 195*t*
standard, Input Scope dialog with, *196*
Input Scope button, 194, 195
Input Scope dialog
with custom input scopes, *197*
new, showing Phrase List option, *197*
with standard input scopes, *196*
InputScope enumeration, in MSDN, 196
Insert AutoText drop-down list box, 590
Insert Expression Box dialog, 158, *159*
Insert Formula button, 154
Insert Formula dialog, 159, 576, 627, 629
after adding a calculated default value, 628, *628*
after checking the Edit XPath checkbox, *160*
after choosing a field, *159*
after inserting **sum** function, *162*
with formula setting this field's default value to today's date plus 45 days, 107, *107*
Insert Function button, 161
Insert Function dialog, 160, *160*
Insert Horizontal Repeating Table dialog, 61
Insert Hyperlink dialog, 156, *157*
Insert layout controls section, in Layout task pane, 39
Insert Layout Table button, in InfoPath 2003 SP1, 12–13
Insert Layout Table toolbar item, in InfoPath 2003 SP1, *13*
Insert Master/Detail dialog, *63*
Insert Picture Control dialog, *71*
Insert Picture dialog, *187*
Insert Vertical Label dialog, 164, *164*
Installable form templates
access path for, 486
creating, 479
deploying, 486–487
final page of Publishing Wizard during creation of, 419, *419*
first page of Publishing Wizard during creation of, 417, *418*
publishing, 417–420
reasons for not wanting to publish form as, 420
Install Certificate button, 493
Installed form, error that occurs when attempting to remove form from dialog, *495*
Installed form templates
listing of, in registry, 487
removing, 494
Installer file, choosing a location for saving, 418, *418*
Installing Forms Services, 671–675
Insufficient security privilege error, 403
Integer field, 774
Integer Format dialog, for Whole Number (integer) data types, *179*
IntelliSense information, lack of, in object browser or ToolTips, 738
INTERFACESAFE_FOR_UNTRUSTED_CALLER, 1054, 1065
INTERFACESAFE_FOR_UNTRUSTED_DATA, 1054, 1065
InternalStartup definition, for MOI Consulting request form template, 804 (listing)
InternalStartup method, 734, 1002
restriction of, to registration, 781
Internet, 892, 1028
Internet domain forms, restricting through Office Customization Tool, 476
Internet Explorer
filling out a browser-enabled form template in, *18*
InfoPath and use of settings in, 476
Mime HTML file opened in, 606
programming, 788
security settings, 467
Internet Explorer 6, Forms Services and, 690
Internet Explorer Web content zones, 468
with security levels, *469*
Internet Information Services, 676
Internet Information Services Manager, copying physical path for SharePoint root site collection from, 1013, *1013*
Internet Information Services worker threads, data connection timeouts and, 933
Internet zone, 475
InvokeHost method, 1028
IObjectSafety interface, 1049, 1061
definition of, 1064 (listing)
implementing, 1064–1065
safety of ActiveX controls for scripting, initialization and, 1053–1054
IObjectSafety interface methods and constants, implementation of, 1065 (listing)

IOleCommandTarget interface, 997
accessing through form control, 993
calling **QueryStatus** method of, 999
defining, 991
dependencies of, 991, 992 (listing)
ipdesign.dll file, 1132
ipeditor.dll file, importing into C++ header file, 1143
IP Insurance (fictional company), insurance forms application for, 978–979
IP insurance form application
after loading the auto insurance form, 986, *986*
creating in .NET, 797–980, 984–990
standard toolbar for, 991, *991*
IP life insurance form
hosting in MyPage.aspx, 1019, *1019*
state of, while dialog box still has focus, 1034, *1034*
IP life insurance form template, code behind Validate Form button in, 1033 (listing)
IPropertyNotifySink interface, 1051, 1058
calling into, 1066–1068
declaration of, 1067 (listing)
IRM. *See* Information Rights Management
IsBrowser property, 883
demonstrating, 884 (listing)
in various environments, 884*t*
ISimpleInfoPathControl interface, 1056
IsMobile property, 884
demonstrating, 884 (listing)
in various environments, 884*t*
IS_NUMBER input scope, 195
Issuer Statement button, 493
ISubmitToHostEventHandler interface, 1009
IsValidEstimate method, 1005
IT. *See* Information technology
Item-level granularity, permissions in SharePoint and, 706
IUnknown property type, 1056
IViewObject interface, 1061, 1071

J

JavaScript, 908
functioning of browser-enabled forms and enabling of, 703
Job application form, 331–333
first view of, *332*
last page of, *333*
JobApplication sample, 332
JScript, 10, 11, 497, 697, 730, 731, 782, 783, 790
global, 1034
inserting into host page, 1033–1035

K

Kerberos authentication, 944
Key field, merge settings for, 568
KPI, 678

L

Labels
data field, 58
friendly, 119
Language settings, Microsoft Installer file and, 417–418
Large file attachments, adding to forms, 71
Latency, 866
form load, 955
Layout
customizing, 39
elements, 164
Layout link, in Design Tasks task pane, 845
Layout of form
designing, 34–40
importing, 1117
Layout tables, 7
color schemes and, 39
customizing, 37
gridlines in, 36
selecting entire, 38
use of, *vs.* use of Section controls, 47
Layout task pane, 34, 34*t*, *35*, 39
merge and split cells category of, 37, *37*
LCID. *See* Locale ID
LCID keys, string values to be added under, 1130*t*
Leaf nodes, 86–87
Leave the form open action, 394
Level 3 OM, access to, 484
LifeInsurance_BrowserEnabled_NotifyHost sample form template, calling **NotifyHost** method behind, 1032
LifeInsurance_BrowserEnabled sample, 1018
Linked images checkbox, 187
Linux, Forms Services and, 690
List Box controls, 7, 44, 45*t*

binding behavior of, 89*t*
connections between secondary data sources and, 316–324
duplicate items in, 324
secondary data showing in, 317–321
secondary data sources and populating of, 298
type-ahead support in, 44
List Box entries, selecting secondary data source node from XML file connection that provides data for, *319*
List Box items
filtering, 323–324
main data source used for, 321–322
List controls, 65–66
in design mode, *66*
for filling out a form, *66*
simulating, 698
List Form Templates function, 900
List-item permissions, 711
Lists, SharePoint libraries and, 292–295
List view, InfoPath controls in, 846, *846*
Literal control, finding more information on, 1033
LMZ. *See* Local machine zone
Loading event, 737, 738, 739, 742
canceling, 806
sinking, 753, 881, 883
in form template to use the parameters, 1024 (listing)
LoadingEventArgs property, 1022
Loading event handler, for MOI Consulting request form, 807*t*
Loading Form dialog, 702
Locale ID, registering importer/exporter and, 1129
LocalIntranet, CAS permission set for, 496*t*
Local intranet forms, 471
LocalIntranet permission, 496, 497
LocalIntranet trust assembly, 496
Local intranet zone, 470–474
settings for defining, 470, *470*
Local machine zone, 469
types of domain forms run in, 478
Location
of administrator-approved templates, 895
alternative, for template parts, 442
of template parts needing updating, 451–452
Location field, promoting, 408, 410
Logging, 919–927
Unified Logging Service, 925–927
for WFE servers, 925
Windows Event Viewer, 920
Logic
behind Add Additional Details Button control, 827
MOI Consulting request form template and addition of, without code, 801–803
Logic added without code, 215–240
conditional formatting, 215–222
data validation, 222–229
Logic Inspector, 235–239
rules, 229–235
Logic Inspector, 235–239, 446
form template postbacks and, 954
showing logic for entire form template, 236–238, *237*
LogicInspector sample, 236
LoginName, UserName *vs.*, 806
Loss of data, changing field or group names and, 95

M

MacOS, Forms Services and, 690
Macro Recording feature, in Visual Studio, 863
Mail Options task pane, 654, *655*, 661, 662
Main database connections, availability of query and submit through, 342
Main data connections, secondary data sources *vs.*, 244
Main data query connections
Design a Form Template dialog and creation of, *245*
types of, 246*t*
Main data source, 297
database data connection used on, 258
DataSet object submitted from, 369
form templates and, 26
keeping sensitive information out of, 800
for MOI Consulting request form template, 801, *801*
persisting default state of XML for, 810–811 (listing)
using for List Box items, 321–322
XML or Schema for, 255
Main data source extensibility, Web services and, 353
MainDataSource.ReadOnly, 759

Main data source submit connection, setting up, 345
Main query connections, creating, 245
Main query data connection, 389
Main submit connection
dialog shown when submit using rules fails on, 391, *391*
generic failure dialog for, *393*
generic success dialog for, *393*
secondary submit connection *vs.*, 390
Main submit data connection, 389
Make Compatible with InfoPath Forms Services checkbox, 188
Make New Folder button, 423
Malicious full trust forms, 495
Managed add-ins
accessing InfoPath object model from, 1107–1111
implementing, 1105–1106
Managed code
InfoPath 2007 and use of, 731
InfoPath 2003 SP1 and support for, 15
InfoPath support for, 729
removing, 733
saving a from template with, 735
script *vs.*, 786
Managed code control
addition of, to a form template, 1065–1066
deploying, 1070–1071
Managed code errors, notification for, *851*
Managed form code, task pane script and, 783
Manage Form Templates page, 893, 895
activation with, 895–897
Manage Permissions permission, 552
Manage Resources dialog, screening for included files, 903
Manager roles, Conditional Format dialog after adding conditions for, 632, *633*
Manage User Roles dialog, 616, *616*, 617, 621, 623, 631, 670, *670*
after adding a few roles, 620, *620*
after adding "Team Manager" and "Sales Manager" roles, 632, *632*
Managing the Web Service Proxy page, settings on, 946–947, *947*
Manifest, 73
information in, 27
SQL credentials in, 935
Manifest information, about controls, 43
manifest.xsf, 581
Package section of, 1138 (listing)
manifest.xsf[Design] tab, 848, 849
Manually editing data source
adding nodes, 116–119
deleting nodes, 121–122
moving nodes, 119–121
referencing nodes, 122–123
starting with own data source, 124, 126–137
Convert Main Data Source feature, 132–137
potential complications of starting from XML Schema, 129–132
starting from XML data, 126–127
starting from XML Schema, 128–129
Map databases, TerraServer project, 289
Margins, 190
Master/Detail control, 12, 14, 62–65, 199
applicant data and, *64*
in application review form when filling out a form, *64*
binding behavior of, 89*t*
defining one-to-many relationships and, 271
design-time visuals for, 201
filling out a form and, 63–65
Scrolling Region control used with, 165
when filling out a form, *204*
Master/Detail relationships, creating, 198–203
Master/Detail tab, 199
for Repeating Section set as detail control, *202*
for Repeating Table set as the master control, 200, *200*
Maximum size of form session state setting, security and, 911–912
MeetingRequest form, 407, 408
MeetingRequest template, publishing, to a Web server via a "backdoor" network share, *401*
Merge actions
in aggregation namespace, 583, *584*
node type and, 560*t*
Merge attributes, for merge actions, 584, *584*
Merge Cells toolbar button, 798
Merge customizations
Merge Settings dialog after, 571, *572*
for node types, 570–571*t*
Merged sales report data, *593*
Merged status report form, 558–559, *559*
Merged status reports, creating, 555–560
Merged team status report, after all customizations are complete, 578, *578*

Merge error dialog, for forms with a schema that doesn't match the target form, *558*
Merge Forms dialog, 556, *556*
selecting multiple forms in, 557
with Views menu, 557, *557*
Merge Forms view, weekly status report document library in, *558*
Merge settings, for key field, 568
Merge Settings button, 566
Merge Settings dialog, 580
with merge customizations, 571, *572*
separators in, for rich text fields, 575, *576*
Merge settings error dialog, *567*, 567–568
Merge Table Cells, in Layout task pane, 38
Merge Table cells item, 37
Merging
cells, 37, 38
InfoPath e-mail forms, 657–660
Merging forms, 554–586
customizing merge behavior in design mode, 564–579
custom merge XSL (advanced), 580–586
design recommendations for, 561–564
in form library, 405
in InfoPath, 555–560
MessageBox class, 776
showing UI by using, 878–879
MessageBox sample, 878
MessageBox.Show, 740, 742
using to get user feedback, 805 (listing)
messageDetails parameter, 765
Methods, not implemented by Forms Services, 886–887*t*
MFC. *See* Microsoft Foundation Classes
MHT. *See* Mime HTML file
Microsoft, TWC initiative Web site, 456
Microsoft Authenticode technology, 508
Microsoft Component Object (.NET) Runtime Execution Engine DLL, 1112
Microsoft Exchange Server 5.5, 618
Microsoft Foundation Classes, hosting InfoPath and, 978
Microsoft Installer, 486
Microsoft Installer file
building, 419
languages supported by, 417–418
processing time and, 419
Microsoft Instruction Language, 739
Microsoft Management Console, 488, 491, 492, 499
Microsoft Office applications
COM add-ins supported by, 1073
message bar and Workflow dialog in, 641
Microsoft.Office.Core assembly, reference added to, 1079
Microsoft Office Excel, sales data exported to, 610, *611*
Microsoft Office InfoPath. *See* InfoPath
Microsoft Office InfoPath Security Notice dialog, 255
Microsoft Office InfoPath 2003 Toolkit for Visual Studio .NET, 23
Microsoft.Office.InfoPath.XmlFormHost-Item class, 759
Microsoft.Office.Interop.InfoPath assembly, reference added to, 1079
Microsoft.Office.Interop.InfoPath.Xml assembly, reference added to, 1079
Microsoft.Office.Server.dll assembly, objects belonging to shared services and providers in, 900
Microsoft Office SharePoint Server (MOSS) 2007, workflow with, 634–642, 635*t*
Microsoft Office SharePoint Server (MOSS) 2007 document library, status report forms saved to, 555
Microsoft Office SharePoint Server (MOSS) 2007 site, status report form template published to, 613
Microsoft Office system (2007), 17
Microsoft Office Word, XML Structure task pane in, 597, *598*
Microsoft Operations Manager, 866, 925, 962
learning more about, 963
Operator console, *962*
Microsoft Script Editor, 10, 23, 729, 737, 786
scripting language and, 841
Microsoft TechNet, 904, 905, 912
best practices for Forms Services on, 951
Microsoft TerraServer, Web service for, 273
Microsoft TerraServer Web site, using in InfoPath, 289–290
Microsoft UpDown control, 1042, 1043, 1047, 1049
Properties dialog for, 1048, *1048*
Microsoft UpDown Control 6.0, in Add Custom Control Wizard, selected in list of ActiveX controls, 1039, *1039*, 1040
Microsoft Visual Studio Solution file, 838

Microsoft Windows Workflow Foundation, 635
Microsoft Windows XP Tablet PC Edition Software Development Kit, Ink Picture control and, 73
Microsoft XML Core Services, 730
Mime HTML file, 606
Minimum salary desired, field for, and formatting as currency, *179*
minLength feature, 101
Mobile browser, 720
  creating new form in, 722
Mobile devices
  filling out forms with, 690, 720–726
  rendering on, 718
Mobile forms, 722–725
  code, 724
  conditional formatting, 725
  controls, 723–724
  data connections, 725
  data validation, 724–725
  editing first row from, 723, *723*
  filling out, 25–726
  toolbar, 724
  views, 724
Mobile form toolbar, with Pocket PC Internet Explorer toolbar showing below it, *724*
mobile value, 717
Modal value, 765
Modeless value, 765
Modify Table button, role of, 264
MOI Consulting Company (fictional)
  data requirements for employment application, 31, 32*t*
  filling out employee information form, *124*
  structure of **Customers** table for, 369*t*
MOIConsulting database, 369
MOI Consulting expense report form
  after importing into InfoPath, 1123, *1124*
  created in Word, importing, 1117–1119, *1118*
  ImportErrors.xml file for, 1140, 1141 (listing)
MOI Consulting IT department, technical issues form sent to, 338–341
MOI Consulting morale event form
  in design mode, 750, *750*
  Validating event and, 758–764
MOI Consulting performance review form, sample, 510, *510*
MOI Consulting request form
  code for the button that starts validation on default view of, 812 (listing)
  Confirm view of, 796, *796*
  demonstration of, 791–831
  designing, 797–831
    adding form code, 803–831
    adding logic without code, 801–803
    gathering requirements and designing visual layout, 798
    organizing data source, 798–801
  existing, error dialog that appears when user attempts to open, *808*
  filling out, 792–797
  Loading event handler for, 807 (listing)
  Request Details view of, 795, *795*
  rules used in, 802
  Thank You view of, *797*
  toggling request type options in, 792
  Welcome view of, 791, *791*
MOI Consulting request form template
  InternalStartup definition for, 804 (listing)
  main data source for, 801, *801*
MoiConsultingRequest sample, 791
MoiConsultingRequest sample code, 819
MOI employment application form, 437
  address block section of, 432, *432*
MoiEventScheduler-Changing form template, **MyPasswordDialog** class of, 751
MoiEventScheduler-Changing sample, 755
MoiEventScheduler-Validating sample, 758
MoiFeedback document element group, 697
MOI feedback form template, 693, *694*
  controls targeted by the messages in Design Checker for, 868, *869*
  Design Checker messages from, 867, *867*
  filling out, in the browser, 701–703, *702*
MoiFeedback sample, 693
MOI morale event scheduler form, final touches added to, 768
MOI performance review form
  co-signing and, 531, *531*, 533
  filling out, before using a digital signature, *514*
  partial signing and, 522
MOIPerformanceReview-FullSignatures sample, 510
MOM. *See* Microsoft Operations Manager
Monitoring, 866
Move command, 120

Move Field or Group dialog, for moving an existing field or group, *119*
Move operation, 86
Mozilla, 17
Forms Services and, 690
mscoree.dll file, COM add-ins in, 1112
MSE. *See* Microsoft Script Editor
MS Forms, 494
MSIL. *See* Microsoft Instruction Language
msoControlButton, 1087
MsoControlType enumeration, 1087
MSXML. *See* Microsoft XML Core Services
Multi-line checkbox, in Display tab, 184
Multi-line property, 184
Multiple binding, 145–147
details of, 147–149
Option buttons and, 150
Multiple conditions, Conditional Format dialog with, *219*
Multiple controls
formatting, 80–82
Properties dialog for resizing of, 192, *192*
resizing, 191–193
Multiple forms
selection of, in Merge Forms dialog, 557
showing data merged from, 563–564
Multiple nodes, selecting, 779
MultipleNotifications sample form, 774
in design mode, *775*
Multiple projects, working with, in Visual Studio environment, 856
Multiple records, display of, in forms, 265
Multiple rules, error cases and, 232
Multiple-Selection List Box control, 67
binding behavior of, 90*t*
for filling out a form, *67*
in InfoPath 2007 Controls task pane, 22
Multiple signatures, on a form, 519
Multiple status report forms, merging, Team Status Report view for, 564, *564*
Multiple text nodes, concatenating strings by selection of, 773
Multiple top-level elements
prompt indicating a start from schema with, *131*
schema with, 131 (listing)
starting from schema with, 130–132
Multiple view printing, 592–596
Multiple views, 19
creating, 73–76
Music collection form, designing data source for, with and without attributes, *117*
My Data Sources connection, InfoPath data connection *vs.*, 260
MyMusicAndPhotos sample, 292, 295
MyPage.aspx page, 1016
code behind the ASP.NET Button control in, 1021 (listing)
hosting life insurance form in, 1019, *1019*
MyPage.aspx Web form, 1014
Solution Explorer after addition of, 1014, *1015*
my prefix, 778

N

name attribute, 583
Name changes
matching XML data and schema and, *96*
mismatched XML data and schema and, *96*
Name field, in Publishing Wizard, 407
Name of controls, seeing, 65
Name property, 95–97
Names
for print view, 601, *602*
SharePoint site, 1013
template part, 453, 454
user, assignment of, 617–618
NamespaceManager parameter, using, 778
Namespaces
in data source, 135–137
in Field or Group Properties dialog, 108, *108*
prefixes, 778
Namespace URI, hard-coding and, 779
Name string value, LCID key and, 1143
Naming
data source nodes, 92
repeating field, 103–104
NAT. *See* Network Address Translation
Nested database tables, 270, *270*
.NET
creating InfoPath host application in, 979–980, 984–990
event handlers in, *vs.* in InfoPath, 752
.NET controls
creating for InfoPath, 1061
summary on use of, in InfoPath, 1071–1072
Netscape, Forms Services and, 690
.NET Windows Forms applications, hosting InfoPath and, 978

Network Address Translation, alternate access mappings and, 928
Network locations
saving and publishing form template on, 400–403
saving to, 397
new ActiveXObject method, 471
New bindings, customizing, 142–144
Newline characters, replacing, 361
New Project dialog, 838
in Visual Studio 2005, 837, *837*
New Project Wizard, 1004
InfoPath Add-in project type shown in, 1106, *1106*
Shared Add-in project template type shown in, 1077, *1077*
New Rule button, 648
New Web Site dialog, with template for New Web, 274, *274*
NewXDocument event, 1107, 1109
hooking up event handlers for, 1082
NewXDocument event handler, 1088, 1089
nillable feature, removing, 101
Node changes, rejecting in **Changing** event, 749
Node names
changing, 95
updated, for readability, *105*
updating, 92
Node properties, changing/resetting of, after rebinding, 141*t*
Node property, 1060
Nodes
adding in data source, 116–119
analyzing namespaces relative to their immediate ancestors, 136*t*
customizing merge settings for, 565–566
data source, 86
deleting, 88, 779–780
deleting in data source, 121–122
finding XPath of, 777
in InfoPath data source during design mode, 94
leaf, 86–87
MOI Consulting request form code and, 803–805
moving in data source, 119–121
multiple, selecting, 779
nillable, 101
nonrepeating, *87*
referencing in data source, 122–123
repeating, *87*
in XML, 93–94
Node siblings, deleting, by using **DeleteRange,** 780 (listing)
Node types
default merge actions based on, 560*t*
merge customizations available for, 570–571*t*
Nonrepeating node, *87*
Nonrepudiable partial signatures, 15
Nonrepudiation, 508
Nonsubmit cases, using **NotifyHost for,** 1031–1035
Normal quiesce status, new and existing form-filling sessions during, 915*t*
Northwind customers and orders data, preview of modified form layout with, *272*
Northwind database, 258, 260, *261*
Customers and **Orders** table in, 258
Customers and **Orders** Web service example, 302–307
Notepad, opening schema in, 133
notification parameter, **NotifyHostEventHandler** method and, 1003
NotifyHostEventHandler method, 1004
parameters received by, 1003
NotifyHost method, 1003–1004, 1032
using for nonsubmit cases, 1031–1035
NT domain account, 621
NTLM authentication, 948
for data connections with InfoPath and Forms Services, 944, *944*
Null values, translation of, as missing nodes, 374
Numbered List control, 7, 65, 66
binding behavior of, 90*t*
repeating nodes and, 103

O

Object browser, lack of IntelliSense information in, 738
Object model, 4, 729, 741–790, 833, 866, 875
accessing from a managed add-in, 1107–1111
COM add-ins, shared objects and, 1074–1075

configuring e-mail settings via, 949, 950 (listing)
form events, 742–744
programming languages and versions of, 731*t*
registering event handlers, 780–782
reporting custom validation errors with use of, 767
script and the Custom task pane, 782–790
showing read-only properties from, 805–806
two types of, for writing code behind a form template, 742
upgrading, 734
using **XPathNavigator** objects and, 777–780
view-based structural editing through, 827
XML data events, 744–777

Object model classes, not implemented by Forms Services, 886–887*t*

Object model (OM) security level, 471
definitions, 471–472, 472*t*
form and IE security level impacts on, 473*t*
setting for template with managed code, 472

obj folder, 839

objsafe.h file, in Windows Platform SDK with Visual Studio 2005, 1054

OCR. *See* Optical character recognition

OCT. *See* Office Customization Tool

ODBC DSN, 257

ODC files, 257

Odd bindings, 145

"Off-box" connections, domain trust form templates and, 461

Office Configuration Tool security settings, for InfoPath, *477*

Office Customization Tool, 455, 505
design lockdown and, 504
disabling InfoPath e-mail forms for InfoPath 2003-compatible forms and, 662
restricting Internet domain forms through, 476

Office Marketplace, 1128

Office Online, 503
alternate access mappings information on, 928
forms downloaded from, 16
form templates available on, 28

Office Resource Kit, 455

Office Server connection, with Web server (HTTP) submit, 382

Offline cached queries, 316

Offline mode queries, configuring form template for, *313*

Offline mode query support, 312–316
for data connections, 298
enabling, for offline mode when adding or modifying secondary data connection, *313*

OLECMD objects, 999, 1000

OLE DB, 257, 300

OM. *See* Object model

"On-box" connections, domain trust for, 461

OnChanged method, 1067, 1068

OnConnection method, 1079–1083, 1088
code in, to hook up the application event handlers, 1083 (listing)
of **IDTExtensibility2** interface, 1075
initial code for, 1081 (listing)
parameters passed to, 1081

OnCopyClick method, 1091

OnEnabledChanged event handler, 1055

One-to-many relationships, Master/Detail control and, 271

On failure option, 394

OnFormOpened method, 1109 (listing), 1110

onload event, use of, instead of using global script, 1035

Only when the user inserts this section button, 207, 208

OnPasteClick event handler, 1091

OnRefreshClick event handler, 1100 (listing)

OnStartupComplete method, 1083–1088
associated helper methods and, 1084 (listing)

On success option, 394

OnSwitchView event, 1088, 1089, 1091

OnSwitchView event handler, 1089 (listing)

OnTaskPaneReady method, 1102, 1104

OnToggleClick event handler, 1095
for Show/Hide task pane button, 1095, 1096 (listing)

Open a form template category, within Design a Form Template dialog, 28

Open and Save tab, of Form Options dialog, 611, *612*, 622, *622*

Open a new form to fill out rule action, 234

Open button (ToolStrip toolbar), 997
writing code for, 991

OpenIn optional parameter values, with brief descriptions, 717*t*

OpenIn parameter, 717, 719
Operand, comparison, choosing for condition, 217
Operation values, 776
Optical character recognition, data importer and, 1146
Optional controls
after clicking on Click here to insert link, *51*
for previewing employment application form, *51*
Optional Section control, 7, 49–51
binding missing nodes to, 153
Edit Values dialog for, *206*
employment application form template with, *50*
inserting, using **ExecuteAction** for, 828–829 (listing)
Properties dialog for, with minimum salary desired, 180, *181*
Section Properties dialog for, *205*, 205–206
Option Button controls, 7, 45*t*
binding behavior of, 89*t*
converting Check Box controls to, 1125
Option buttons, multiple binding and, 150
Options dialog, 520
choosing whether or not to show a notification when signed forms are opened, *520*
Options dialog (VSTO), limited InfoPath settings on, 863–863
Option Section control, context menu for, when filling out a form, 52, *52*
Options parameter, 720
Oracle, 300
Orders child table, adding to **Customers** parent table, *262*
Orders data, displaying, *271*
Orders table, in Northwind database, 258
ORK. *See* Office Resource Kit
OuterHtml property, 955
Outgoing alternate access mappings, 928
Outlook, 667, 668
COM add-ins supported by, 1073
Custom Task Panes added into, 1093
InfoPath e-mail form in reading pane, 653, *653*
promoting properties to make them available as columns in, 415, *415*
resulting e-mail in, after finishing the Publishing Wizard for e-mail, 415, *416*
security feature, 467
Outlook 2007, 413
custom form regions in, 834
disabling InfoPath e-mail forms in, 643
e-mail submits and, 340
Rules Wizard in, *648*, 649
using InfoPath e-mail forms in, 614
Outlook folders
choosing which properties to make available in, *647*
storing received forms in, 650–652
Outlook Web Access, 20, 667, 668
Overall Satisfaction table, vertical-to-horizontal remake of, 698, *699*
Override behavior, executing, 822
OWA. *See* Outlook Web Access

P

Package section, of manifest.xsf, 1138 (listing)
Padding, 190
Page Viewer Web Part
adding to SharePoint page, 928–929
checking on InfoPath installation and, 929
Paragraph breaks property, 185
Parameter mappings
to any data source, 359
defining for Web service submit, *356*, 356–358
setting, 347
setting up, for **DataSet** object, *372*
submit and, 345
Parameter mappings dialog, configuration of, for submitting entire form, 363, *363*
Parameters
warning about assuming existence of, 1024
Web service, 364
Parent tables, defining relationships between child tables and, *263*
Partial signatures, adding, 523
Partial signing
of form data, 521–526
setting up Personal Information part of the view for, 523, *523*
PartyPlanner sample, 224
Party-planning form template
data validation for, 224–227
pattern matching for, 227–229
PascalCasing, 799
Password dialog prompt, 751, *751*

Password prompts, adding, 750
Passwords, 259
  hard-coded, 752
  prompting for, 751 (listing)
Paste button
  enabling/disabling, 1000
  hosted form and, 994, 997
Paste button event handler, 1092 (listing)
Paste Form Data button, 1083
Pattern matching, 218, 227–229
Patterns, custom, 228–229
PDAs. *See* Personal digital assistants
Performance, 866
  accounting for, in form code, 831
  extra postbacks and, 878
  large amounts of data and impact on, 264
  monitoring, 958–962
  optimizing, 951
  session state, 908, 909
Performance counters
  addition of, for templates activated with InfoPath Forms Services, 958, *959*
  InfoPath Forms Services, 960–961*t*
Performance Monitor (PerfMon), purpose of, 958
Performance tips
  data connections, 956
  data-heavy features, 954–956
  form code, 953
  form template deployment, 951–952
  form template design, 950–963
  form view state, 956–957
  miscellaneous, 957–958
  reduction of form postbacks, 953–954
  views, 952
Periods, XML, naming nodes and, 105
Permission button, 541
  on Standard toolbar, 539, *539*
Permission dialog, 539, *540*, 544, 545–547
  after clicking More Options button, 546, *546*
Permissions, 406
  accessing, when filling out a form, 545
  additional, enabling, 547
  controlling, to your form, 547–548
  defining, to restrict individual forms, 542
  form libraries and, 706
  on form templates, 539–542
  granted, viewing of, 552
  granting, 457, 458
  insufficient, Form Error dialog and, 403
  publishing via e-mail and, 415–416
  requesting, 458
  specifying, for current form while filling it out, *544*
  XML files and, 247
Permissions dialog, 541
Personal digital assistants, filling out forms with, 690, 720
Personal Information part of the view, setting up, for partial signing, 523, *523*
Phone numbers, controls for, on employment application form, 44
Phrase List option, 196, 198
  new Input Scope dialog with, *197*
Physical path, to root SharePoint site, 1013, *1013*
Picture control, 70–72, 79
  binding behavior of, 90*t*
  File Attachment control *vs.*, 70
  for filling out a form, *72*
  with picture inserted, *72*
Picture files, large, adding to form, 71
Picture or File Attachment (base64) data type, 99*t*
Pictures, form templates and, 27
Pictures library (SharePoint site), 292, *293*, 293–294
  filling out music and photos form, with list of photos from, *295*
Placeholder field, in Text Box Properties dialog, 83
Placeholder text, in Text Box control, *184*
Plain List control, 7, 65, 66
  binding behavior of, 90*t*
Plain text, SharePoint columns and support for, 411, 412
PlainText control, 1139
Pocket PC device, filling out status report form on, 721, *721*
Port forwarding, alternate access mappings and, 928
Postbacks, 865
  extra, performance issues with, 878
  forcible denial of, 954
  number of, per form session state setting, 910
  rate counters and, 959
  reduction of, 953–954
  resetting session's timer and, 909
  separating views and, 952
  view switching and, 911

Postback settings
Forms Services and, 871
number of actions per, 910–911
Post-import warnings
functioning of, 1140–1141
removing, 1127
Post-submit actions, warning about, 394
PowerPoint
COM add-ins supported by, 1073
custom task panes added into, 1093
default Document Information Panel in, 966, 968, 970
Predicate filter, 770, 771
PreferClient value, 717
PreferredDate field, data validation on, 802
Prefix each item with checkbox, 575
Prefixes
in Data Source task pane, 135
for merging into a form that has data, 575, 576
namspaces, 778
Preventive maintenance, server downtime and, 919–920, 927
Preview as drop-down, enabling, 428
Preview button, 424
on Standard toolbar, 48
Preview drop-down toolbar menu, *625*
Preview feature, 398, 425
Preview Form command, 740
Previewing
debugging and, 741
employment application form, 48, *48*
forms in VSTO, 863
fully trusted forms, 485, 792
unpublished forms, with CMCL connections, 941
with a user role, 624–626
Previewing form
context menu for Repeating Section control and, *54*
Repeating Section control for, *54*
Repeating Table control for, *60*
Previewing form templates, 424–429
disabled commands and, *425*
domain simulation, 428–429
error message related to attempting to open form that was saved during previewing, *429*
with sample data, 426–427
saving form data and, 429
with user roles, 427–428
Preview settings, configuring, 425, *426*
Previews options, persisted information and, 427
Preview tab, on Form Options dialog, 624, *625*
Preview window, 424
Primary key field, in form templates, 376
Printable forms, 1116
Print command, 547
Print content setting, enabling, 547
Print dialog, 593, *593*, 596
Printing reports, 586–605
headers and footers, 589–591
multiple view printing, 592–596
print views, 586–589
in browser-enabled forms, 603–605
Word print views, 596–603
Print Multiple Views dialog, 596, 603
in design mode, 595, *595*
for filling out a form, 594, *594*
Print preview, in Visual Studio 2005, 863
Print settings, specifying for print views, 589
Print Settings tab, of View Properties dialog, 588, *588*, 589
Print View button, 604
on browser form toolbar, 684, 687
on Forms Services toolbar, 604, *604*
Print views, 586–589
specifying print settings for, 589
Print Views feature, in Word, 596–605
Prior Trusted Sources list, 500
Privacy
group names and, 619
saving form templates and, 399
submitting digitally signed form data and, 365–368
Privacy Options category, of Trust Center dialog, 503, *503*
Private roles, assigning users to, in InfoPath 2003 SP1, 15
Privileges, user form and cross-domain, 930
Processing instructions, XML, 364
ProgId attribute, 1078
ProgID key
creating **DefaultLCID DWORD** value under, 1142
registered importers/exporters and, 1132
Programmatic admin deployment, 900–901
Programmatic quiescing, 917–919
Programming category, in Form Options dialog, 732, *732*

Programming Internet Explorer 5, 788
Programming language section, options available in Form Options dialog, 732, *732*
Programming language when designing for InfoPath and InfoPath Forms Services drop-down, 736
Programming section, in Logic Inspector dialog, 238
Progress dialogs, canceling, 23
Project Application services, 672
Projects
 COM add-ins supported by, 1073
 new, for new or existing form templates, 839–840
Promoted properties
 form libraries and, 706
 maximum number of, 412
 on Publishing Wizard page, which appear as columns in SharePoint libraries and lists, 408, *408*
Prompt method, 751
Properties, not implemented by Forms Services, 886–887*t*
Properties dialog
 for Microsoft UpDown Control, 1048, *1048*
 for resizing multiple controls, 192, *192*
 for Text Box control, 174, *175*
Properties directory, 839
Properties Window dialog, 853
Property demotion, 405, 412–413
Property pages, ActiveX controls and, 1047–1048
Property promotion, 405, 410–413
 outside of Publishing Wizard, 410
Protected form template, warning dialog for when users attempt to change template, *505*
Protection, enabling, to discourage users from changing your form template, *504*
Providers
 configuring, 907–912
 searching UDDI by, 299
Proxy Web service, creating, 288
Public roles, assigning users to, in InfoPath 2003 SP1, 15
Publish button, 402
 last page of Publishing Wizard, before clicking, 680, *681*
Publish domain, simulating for testing, 481–482
Published domain trust form, moving, 479–481
Published form template, data source operations on, and affect on saved forms, *97*
Publishers
 COM add-ins supported by, 1073
 trusted, 489
Publishing, 398
 to Forms Services, 715
 form template as a content type, 709
 form templates, 11, 397
  for administrator approval, 941–942
  to Forms Services, 678–681
 four types of, 397
 new form template as a Document Information Panel template for SharePoint, 975, *975*
 saving comes with, 399
 two types of, 888
 via e-mail, 397
 VSTO form templates to Forms Services, 841
Publishing (advanced), 888–903
 administrative deployment to Forms Services, 892–901
 managing form templates, 904–905
 publishing form templates for administrator approval, 889–891
 screening form templates for approval, 902–903
Publishing Wizard, 658, 678, 845, 889, 1018, 1024
 Company Name and Language text boxes, 417, *418*
 conveniences built in to, 420
 enabling browser rendering in, 680
 filling out MOI feedback form template with, 701
 final page of in creation of installable form template, 419, *419*
 first page of, 399, *400*
 first wizard page for publishing form to e-mail recipients, 414, *414*
 internal use of Web service by, 905
 last page of, 402, 403
 last page of, before clicking Publish button, 680, *681*
 page showing promoted properties from template's data source, *408*
 promoting properties to make them available as columns in Outlook, 415, *415*

Publishing Wizard (*cont.*)
property promotion outside of, 410
setting access path in, 462, *463*
verifying document library name, document library location, and status of Forms Services in, 409
Publish locations, standard paths for, 402
publishUrl attribute, access path definition and, 468
Purchase request forms, 620
Pushpin icons, in VSTO, 845
put_Value method, implementation of, 1057 (listing)

Q

Qualifier, of condition, 217
Query Builder, 302
Query data connection, 242
queryFields group
within data source, 342
student sign-in form and, 347
Querying
event bubbling and, 819–820
via a rule instead of with form code, 818
QueryStatusCommand method, 992, 993 (listing), 994, 997
QueryStatus method, calling, 999
QueryString property, 1022
Query support, enabling, for offline mode when adding or modifying a secondary data connection, *313*
QueryXmlFile sample, 254
Quick Find, in VSTO, *854*
Quiesced status, new and existing form-filling sessions during, 915*t*
Quiesce Farm link, 916
Quiesce Form Template page, 916
configuring to quiesce a form template on, 14, 914
Quiesce method, 918
Quiesce sample, 919
Quiescing, 680
administration OM on the **FormTemplate** object specific to, 918*t*
command-line, 917–919
commands for stsadm.exe specific to, 918*t*
definition of, 912
entire farm, 915–916
farm, 918–919
form templates, 913–915
programmatic, 917–919
as shared service, 916
stopping, 915
upgrading form templates and, 916–917
Quiescing errors, occurrence of, when creating status report forms, 913, *913*
Quiescing status, new and existing form-filling sessions during, 915*t*
Quiescing time, for form template or a farm, 916

R

Rate counters, postbacks and, 959
Readability, data with updated node names for, *105*
Reading pane (Outlook), InfoPath e-mail form in, 653, *653*
Read-only controls, digitally signed form with, *518*
Rebinding, 140
container controls, 142
Control, Node, and other unrelated properties that change/get reset after, 141*t*
reverting, 142
Receive and submit data option, 345
Receive and Submit Data Wizard, differences between Submit Data and Receive Data Wizards and, *346*
Receive Data Wizard, *346*
Recent form templates category, on Design a Form Template dialog, 29
Recently Used Forms link, 16
Recently Used Forms list, e-mailed forms in, 414
Recent Projects fly-out menu, on File menu of Visual Studio, 838
Recognize non-matching input checkbox, 196
Records, multiple, displaying in forms, 265
Recovered forms, detecting, 830
Recursion, 14–15, 122–123
Recursive data sources, support for, 123
Recursive Section control, 14, 172
in InfoPath 2003 SP1, 14, 15
Red asterisk error, 228, *228*
Red exclamation point, meaning of, 149–150
Redistribution, creating installable form for, 397
Redo button

enabling/disabling, 1000
hosted form and, 994, 997
Redo operation, 771
Red validation rectangles, in MOI Consulting request form, 792
Refactoring, in Visual Studio 2005, 859, 860
Reference operation, 86, 122
recursion, 122–123
Referer HTTP header, 718, 719
Refresh button, 684
Refresh (or requery), data, 251
Regular Expression option, 198
Relationships
defining, between child and parent tables, *263*
defining, between tables, 261, 263
Relative links, for data connection files, 712, 713
Relinking, form libraries and, 707–708
Relink tool, using, 429
Remove blank groups checkbox, 571, 572
Rendering, on mobile device, 718
Repeating a Section control, 51
Repeating Choice Group control, 14, 167–171, 827
binding behavior of, 91*t*
Repeating container
sample form XML Data with and without, *104*
Repeating control, removing, 56
Repeating field, *147*
inserting into header or footer, 590
Repeating field node type, merge customizations available for, 570*t*
Repeating fields, renaming, 104–105
Repeating group node, merging data and, 561, 562
Repeating group node type, merge customizations available for, 570*t*
Repeating nodes, *87*
in data source, 103
inserting new instances of, 153
Repeating property, 102–105
Repeating Recursive Section
in design mode, *172*
for filling out employee information form, *173*
Repeating Recursive Section control, 171–172
binding behavior of, 91*t*
Repeating Section controls, 7, 52–55, 827
binding behavior of, 89*t*
binding to repeating group nodes, 561, 562
employment application form template form with, 53, *53*
inserting new, 55
Master/Detail tab for, set as a detail control, *202*
for previewing form, *54*
setting as detail control, 201
three instances of, inserted into form, 55, *55*
with three items in a mobile form, 723, *723*
XML fragments for, 207
Repeating Section fragment, Section Properties dialog for, *208*
Repeating Section Properties dialog, 207
Advanced tab of, 566, *567*
three sections of grocery shopping list in, *209*
Repeating Table control, 7, 52, 56–60, 827, 1037
adding to grocery form template, 321–322, *322*
after changing from Repeating Section control, *58*
binding behavior of, 89*t*
binding to repeating group nodes, 561, 562
color schemes and, 39
in design mode, *57*
for expenses, *161*
nested database table (**Orders**), which is hard to represent when parent table (**Customers**), is in view as, *270*
for previewing form, *60*
Repeating Section control changed to, 57, 58
Repeating Section control *vs.*, 56–57
setting as master control, 201
supporting entry of last and first names in, 768, *769*
replaceChild method, 1092
Replace In Files feature, from Visual Studio, 855
ReplaceSelf method, 772
Replace With action, Choice Section control and, 212
Report Center, 678
ReportError method, 1007
default version of, 760
warning regarding use of, with arbitrary node, 766
ReportError overload, 761
Reporting errors, **Validating** event and, 757, 758

Reports
creating, 553–612
exporting, 605–611
printing, 586–605
Republishing, form template moved by, 481
ReqeustType field, **Changed** event handler for, 818–819
Request Details view, 825, *825*
completing, 829
of MOI Consulting request form, 795, *795*, 798, 799
Request object, 1022
RequestType List Box, dynamically populating, by using a data connection, 818–819 (listing)
requestType query parameter, setting, 821–823, 824
Require a connection to verify a user's permission setting, 548
requiredString data type, 101
Requirements
defining, new form creation and, 31
defining specifications for, 31
gathering for MOI Consulting request form, 798
Require SSL for HTTP authentication to data sources checkbox, enabling, 934
Reset Toolbox option, on Toolbox pane, 847
Resizing, multiple controls, 191–193
Resizing controls
in design mode, 54
grab handles for, 78
Resolver parameters, 778
Resource editing, in VSTO, 858
Resource files, adding to a form template, 858
Resource Files dialog
files accessible by all form templates shown in, 466, *466*
in InfoPath and VSTO, 858, *858*
Resource Files menu item, on Tools menu in design mode, 27
Resource Manager, 27
Resources, in form templates, 27
Response size, data connection, 933
Restricted form templates
access paths on, 464, 465
data connections types for, 466
deploying, 462, 464–466
error dialog that appears when opening one that attempts to query external data source, 461, *461*
flexibility with, 464
Restricted permission, for user, while designing a form template, 541, *541*
Restricted security level, 459, 460–467
deploying restricted form templates, 462, 464–466
more restrictions with restricted forms, 466–467
Restricted sites zone, 470
Restrict permission to forms based on this form template checkbox, 542
Reusable components
building, 431–454
creation of, in two ways, 432
Reuse, locating template parts for, 438
Ribbon, 1076
customizing, 834
Developer tab appearing in, 968
Rich text, use of, as a promoted property, 411, 412
Rich Text Box control, 7, 45*t*, 53, 79, 184
appropriate configuration of, for use in Web browser, 698
binding behavior of, 89*t*
in browser, 689, *689*
display tab for, *186*
inside Optional Section, 50
validating amount of data in, 955
Rich text data, adding ActiveX controls and, 1046
RichText field, 774
Rich text fields, separators in Merge Settings dialog for, 575, *576*
Rich text (HTML) field, one of the notifications when adding underline to, 775, *776*
Rich text (XHTML) data type, 99, 99*t*, 178
Rights Management Service
Information Rights Management and, 538
specifying server, 549
Right-to-left languages, 185, 186
support for, with InfoPath SP1, 14
RMS. *See* Rights Management Service
Role-based views, 631–634
Roles, 426, 564
in InfoPath 2003 SP1, 15
Role structure, 881
Roots, 87
Rows, inserting in layout tables, 37, 38
RPC/encoded Web services, 288

RSS feeds, 405
Rule dialog
after adding a rule to switch to Team Status Report view, 632, *633*
after setting the condition and action, *623*, 623–624
Rules, 19, 118, 229–235, 426
actions available for, 233*t*
actions for actual submit to the Web services, *387*
adding, 230–231
adding or modifying, so that four actions are always run when form is submitted, *230*
ADO.NET **DataSet** object and, 388–389
creating, 230–231
creating for InfoPath e-mail forms, 648–650
custom submit with, 384–388
dialog displayed for action failing to execute when user fills out the form, 234, *234*
disadvantages with, 389–391
errors and, 234
in MOI Consulting request form, 802
multiple, 232
no error handling for, 390
setting up, when user opens form, 232
setting up submit with use of, 385, *385*
simulating user roles and, 880
template parts and replacement of, 447
updating template parts and, 451
user roles in, 621, 622–624
using to submit forms, 337
Rules and Alerts dialog, 648
Rules and Merge tab, on the Field or Group Properties dialog, *566*
Rules button, 181, 182, 229, 230
Rules feature, 229–230
entry points and structure of, 232, *232*
in InfoPath 2003 SP1, 15
secondary data source field and, 308–309
Rules for Opening Forms dialog, after adding all rules, 624, *624*
Rules for Submitting Forms dialog, 385
Rules section, in Logic Inspector dialog, 238
RulesSimpleExample sample, 231
Rules Wizard
creating folder outside of, 650–652
with rule specific to InfoPath forms, 648, *648*
Run As command, 495
Run Query button, 375

S

Safari, 17
Forms Services and, 690
"Safe Initialization and Scripting for ActiveX Controls," 1054
Safety, of ActiveX controls, for scripting and initialization, 1053–1055
Sales data, exporting to Microsoft Office Excel, 610, *611*
Sales Report view, 592, *592*, 615
Sample data, previewing forms with, 426–427
Sample data connection
clicking on Button and querying of, *254*
rule for querying of, 254
Sample data files, creating, 427
Sample form templates
customizing, 28
using as InfoPath e-mail form, 658
Save, full trust and, 831
Save and Save As, InfoPath prompt that appears when choosing either for new form template, *399*
Save As button, on browser form toolbar, 683, *686*, 686–687
SaveAs method
full trust and, 831
saving IP insurance method and, 989, 990
Save as Source Files option, 397, 398
files making up form template and, 1137
Save button
on browser form toolbar, 683, 686–687
enabling, only if form is dirty, 997
enabling/disabling, 1000
using "form-only" model for disabling of, 329–331
writing code for, 991
Save event, 744
SaveForm method, 989
SaveIfDirty method, 988
SaveItems Web service method, 344
choosing data source node to submit to, *285*
setting up parameter to, which involves selecting which data source node provides its value, 284, *284*

SaveItems Web service method (*cont.*)
Web service form sample and, 275, 277*t*, 279, 282, 283, 284, 287
SaveItem Web service method
browser test form for, *280*
Web service form sample and, 275, 277*t*, 279, 282, 283, 284
SaveLocation parameter, 719–720
Save method, saving IP insurance method and, 989
Saving
before adding code, 738
browser forms, 703
form data, 429
form templates, purpose of, 398
to network location, 397
publishing comes with, 399
templates as extracted source files, 421–424
Saving and publishing, 397–430
Saving and publishing form template, 398–420
common conveniences with Publishing Wizard, 420
e-mail deployment, 397, 413–416
with InfoPath, 398–420
installable form templates, 397, 417–420
to network locations, 397, 400–403
to SharePoint or Forms Services, 397, 404–413
Saving forms, *330*
submitting forms *vs.*, 328
Scalability, 866
schema element, 583
SchemaValidation errors, 765
Screening, form templates for approval, 902–903
Screen readers, ScreenTip property and, 193
ScreenTip text box, 193
Script, 497
custom task pane and, 782–790
InfoPath support for, 729
managed code *vs.*, 786
using existing form template with, to create InfoPath project in VSTO, 841
Script code, debugging, 741
Scripting
of ActiveX controls, 1039
custom task pane, 785–790
restriction of objects unsafe for, 784
safety of ActiveX controls for, 1053–1055
Scripting languages, 731
Scrolling Region control, 14, 203, 1147
application review form with, when filling out the form, *166*
binding behavior of, 90*t*
in design form, *165*
Scrolling Region layout element, 164–166
Scrolling tab, in Properties dialog for Microsoft UpDown Control, 1048
SDK. *See* Software Development Kit
Search crawls, 673
Search Indexing, 672
Search UDDI button, 299
Search Web Service dialog, 299, *300*
Secondary data, showing in list box control, 317–321
Secondary database connections, 258
Secondary data connection, inability to submit form to database via, 341–342
Secondary data connection query, 310
Secondary data source
Customers, 268, *268*
in Data Source task pane, 253, *253*
persisting default state of XML for, 810–811 (listing)
Secondary data source binding, 307–312
data validation, 311–312
designing form template, 307–309
filling out the form, 310–312
Secondary data source events, sinking, 770
Secondary data sources, 10, 241, 297, 298, 779
available and unavailable features for, 309*t*
form templates and, 26
list box controls connected to, 316–324
main data connections *vs.*, 244
no validation in, 821
populating of List Box family of controls and, 298
query data connection associated with, 822
secondary query data connections and, 820–821
SharePoint connections supported as, 292
Secondary query connections
creating, 245–246
types of, 246*t*
Secondary submit connection, main submit connection *vs.*, 390
Section, Optional control, binding behavior of, 89*t*

Section Commands dialog, 210, *210*
Section controls, 7, 46*t*
address information and, 46
arbitrary, 522–523
binding behavior of, 89*t*
creating new set of signable data (partial signing) on, 524, *524*
in design mode, *47*
partial signing and, 522
setting up digital signatures on, *526*
use of, *vs.* use of layout tables, 47
in Weekly Status Report view, 563
Section Properties dialog
for Optional Section control, *205*, 205–206
for Repeating Section fragment, *208*
Sections
access keys for inserting and removal of, 689
enabling for partial signing, 522
Section signing, loading performance and, 955
"Secure by default," 15, 931
Secure submit, with HTTPS, 383
Security, 456, 552
accessing data connection files from CMCL and, 942
centrally managed connection library and, 936
configuring into form templates, 459, *459*
cross-domain connections using the DCL and, 930
data connection libraries and, 713–714
data connections in browser-based form templates and, 710
deployment and, 455–552
designing into form templates, 459–460
domain simulation and, 428, 429
embedded SQL authentication and, 934–935
form filling and, 461
form template publishing and, 401–402
HTTP data connections and, 934
introduction to, 456–458
local intranet zone and, 471
publishing via e-mail and, 415–416
setting up connection to database and, 257
signed data blocks and, 814
submitting digitally signed form data and, 365–368
Security and Trust category, on Form Options dialog, 468
Security and Trust category settings, for signing a form template, 489, *489*
Security and Trust tab, of Form Options dialog, *485*
Security levels
automatic, 482–483
designing security into form templates, 459–460
domain, 467–482
full trust, 484–498
with InfoPath, 458–498
request on demand for, 462
restricted, 460–467
Security levels for this zone setting, 468–469, *469*
Security notices, data connections and, 255
Security privilege error, insufficient, 403
Security prompt, with data connections, 290
Security settings spillover warning, 468
Security zone, determining, 468
Select a Control dialog, *143*
Select a Field or Group dialog, 157, *157*, 158, 590
Filter Data button in, 628
SelectAncestors method, 778
Select Certificate dialog, 490
Select Database and Table dialog, 261, *261*
SelectDescendants method, 778
SelectedIndexChanged event handler, 985 (listing)
after code to support saving the current form if dirty, 987 (listing)
Selected Text Box control, 78
Select methods, 778
selectSingleNode method, 1091
Select the Data to Sign dialog, *515*
using, *527*
Select Users dialog, 618, *618*
Select XPath button, 157
Self-signed certificates, 489
creating for code signing, 490, *490*
in Select Certificate dialog, *491*
trusting, 491, 492
Semicolons, multiple aliases separated by, 617–618
Semistructured documents, 5, 93
Sender object
exposure of, as **Source** on **XmlEventArgs** object in InfoPath 2003 OM, 747
as object parameter, 747

sender parameter, 1106
  InitEventHandler method and, 1001
  NotifyHostEventHandler method and, 1003
  SubmitToHostEventHandler method and, 1009
"Sending data to the server" busy dialog, 773
Send to HR for Approval button, 755
Sensitive information, keeping out of main data source, 800
Separators
  for multiple view printing, 594
  for rich text nodes, 575, *576*
Sequential workflow, 634–635
Serializable attribute, 1005
Serialization, 366
  dataset, 373
  diffgram, 374
Server
  configuring, to send e-mail, 949
  data connection authentication and, 943–948
  disabling user from publishing directly to, 892
  form features that automatically communicate with, 704*t*
  uploading form template to, 893–895
Server downtime
  preventive maintenance and, 919–920, 927
  quiescing and, 913–916
Server health, monitoring, 962–963
Server identity, data connections in browser-based form templates and, 710
Server location, specifying, for publishing to a SharePoint site or Forms Services site, *406*
Server stress, form code in browser form and, 953
Server throughput, tradeoffs related to, 951
Service, searching UDDI by, 299
Session state, 881
  enabling on ASP.NET page, 1018
  Forms Services and, 683
  learning more about, 912
  view state *vs.*, 957
Session state performance, paying attention to, 909
Session state service, 907–908, 1018
  configuring, *908*
  in Forms Services, 908–909
  turning off, 907
SessionStateService object, 918
Session state setting, number of postbacks per, 910
Session state timeout, 961
SetFindReplaceOptionSearchDirection command, hosted form and, 996
SetFindString command, hosted form and, 995, 996, 997
SetLcid, 1135
Set of Signable Data dialog, 524, 525
  Signature options portion of, 526
SetProgressDialogPosition method, 1137
SetProgressDialogStatus method, 1137
SetSubmitToHostEventHandler method, 1009
Settings Page, in Document Information Panel, 970, *970*
SetToolBarButtonStates method, 998–999
  (listing), 1000
  main purpose of, 999
Shape command (ADO), 267
Shape query, 266
Shared Add-in project template type, shown in New Project wizard, 1077, *1077*
Shared Add-in Wizard
  namespace and class created by, 1078, 1079 (listing)
  selecting InfoPath as supported application in, 1078, *1078*
Shared services, configuring, 907–912
Shared Services Provider, 676
Shared session service, 918
Shared session state service, performance tips, 956, 957
SharePoint
  form library on, *409*
  InfoPath form template based on Document content type after adding Assigned To column in, 972, *972*
  publishing new form template as a Document Information Panel template for, 975, *975*
  registering alternate URLs with, 928
  understanding basics of, 705
SharePoint 2007, Microsoft Operations Manager pack with, 963
SharePoint Central Administration site, 20, 675
  configuration page for server logging and tracing settings on, 925

enabling Information Rights Management on, 549, *549*
SharePoint Central Administration site URL, 892
SharePoint document library
merging forms from, 556–558
submit connection to, 336, 337
Submit Options dialog configured to submit to, *379*
with submitted form data, *380*
SharePoint Document Properties page, *969*
SharePoint integration, 705–710, 885, 888, 925–929
advanced publishing, 888–903
configuring InfoPath Forms Services, 906–907
configuring shared services and providers, 907–920, 925–928
document libraries and, 705–708
filling out a form on a SharePoint page, 928–929
with Forms Services, 710
form templates management, 904–905
site content type and, 709
SharePoint library(ies), 297
lists and, 292–295
maximum number of items in, 708
property promotion and, 410
submitting forms to, 377–380
SharePoint list, 26, 467
choosing fields from, to use for data connection, *294*
SharePoint page, filling out a form on, 928–929
SharePoint permissions
direct mapping of, to IRM, 552*t*
Forms Services and, 707*t*
SharePoint Products and Technologies Configuration Wizard, 673
SharePoint roles, mapping of, to IRM permissions, 551*t*
SharePoint root site collection, copying physical path for, from Internet Information Services (IIS) Manager, 1013, *1013*
SharePoint server
data connection authentication and, 943
entering address of site collection of, 405
flowchart for determining whether form publishes to Forms Services site or, *404*
libraries and lists available for querying from, *293*
local intranet forms and, 471
mobile site for, 721
publishing form template to, 404–409
saving template somewhere on, when creating a site content type, *407*
specifying server location for publishing to, *406*
in 32- and 64-bit architectures, 672
SharePoint Server 2007, 953
choosing type of server to install, 674, *674*
with Enterprise features, 678
installing, 672
SharePoint Server 2007 platform, 19
Form Services built on and integrated with, 668, 669
SharePoint Services, 19
Web Application service, 674
SharePoint site
collection themes, 679
form templates published to, and lack of access paths, 467
opening, by using file system path, 1014, *1014*
uploading to, 397
using published site content type on, 409
SharePoint site names, 1013
SharePoint Web site, opening form template from, 28
Shortcut keys, assignment of, to commands, 211
Shortcut menu (or context menu), 211
Show a notification for Visual Basic or C# code errors checkbox, in VSTO Options dialog, 850
Show a success or failure message, 394
Show dialog box messages immediately when users enter invalid data action, 226
Show Error Message dialog, 767, *767*
Show Error Message feature, 758
Show only entries with unique display names checkbox, 320
Show Trust Center entry point, under Tools menu, 498
Sidebars, Forms Services, 669, 670
Signable data
form showing the set of, with signature, *529*
for qualifier, 217
signing when filling out the form, *528*

Signature confirmation message text, 529
in Set of Signable Data dialog, 525
Signature Details dialog, for a signed Section control, *530*
Signature groups
creation and management of, 533
in data source, 525
Signature options region, in Set of Signable Data dialog, 525
Signatures dialog, 794, 814, 815
Signatures group, XML Schema and, 535–536
Signature storage, selecting a group for, 512
Signature validation, opening a form and, 519
Sign button, clicking, to apply a digital signature to a form, 515, *515*
Sign dialog, 516
name (or image) in, 529
Signed data
in XML data, 534–353
in XML Schema, 535–538
SignedDataBlocks collection, 814
Signed form templates, updating, 493
Sign form event, code for, 815 (listing)
SigningAllowed Boolean property, 814, 815
Signing event
full trust required for, 814
sinking and special-casing, 812, 813–814
Sign method, 814
SimpleInfoPathActiveX control, 1050
Stock Properties page of ATL Control Wizard for, 1051, *1052*
SimpleInfoPathControl class, 1058
put_Value method for, 1057 (listing)
SimpleInfoPathControl object, 1056
Color property page for, 1054, *1054*
Single Sign-On
additional implementation information about, 945
authentication, 934, 944
CredentialType values defined by, 946
Sinking, 737
form events, 742
Loading event, 753
Loading event in form template to use the parameters, 1024 (listing)
Loading form event, 881, 883
secondary data source events, 770
Signing event, 812, 813–814
Submit form event, 830–831 (listing)
XmlFormView Initialize event, 1022
XmlFormView1 control, 1023
Site Collection Features list, form name in, 898
Site Collection Features page, 895
activation with, 898, *898*
Site collections
activating form template to, 895
multiple, using form template across, 897
Site content types, 709
adding to document library, 409, *410*
promoting properties with, 411
publishing as, 905
siteIndependent parameter, 760
Site permission, locking down, 905
Size tab, 189–193
resizing multiple controls, 191–193
setting text alignment, 190–191
of Text Box Properties dialog, *189*
SKUs, Forms Services installation and, 672–673
Smart phones, 18
filling out forms on, 690, 720
Software, trustworthy, 456–457
Software Development Kit, 417
WordPrint tool in, 596
Solution Explorer, after adding the XmlFormView folder and MyPage.aspx Web form, 1014, *1015*
SortChildNodes method, 771, 773
Sorting
survey responses, 656–657
view-based, 769
Sorting conditions, bad, 265
Sort Items Alphabetically command, 847
Sort Order dialog, for setting three levels of sorting order, *265*
Source code, reviewing, 903
Source files, warning that appears when saving to a folder already containing existing source files, *423*
Source forms, 559
Source parameter, 718–719
SourceSafe operation, 855
Specify a Binding Property page, of Add Custom Control Wizard, *1041*, 1042
Specify an Enable or Disable Property page, of Add Custom Control Wizard, 1042, *1043*, 1051–1052
Specify Data Type Options page, 1047
of Add Custom Control Wizard, 1044, *1044*

with Field option, 1045, *1046*
installing InfoPathChart control and Field or Group type on, 1050
Specify Filter Conditions dialog, 628
Specify Installation Options page, of Add Custom Control Wizard, 1040, *1040*
Speech input, improving recognition of, 195
Split Cells toolbar button, 798
Split Table Cells Vertically, in Layout task pane, 37
Splitting, cells, 37
SP1. *See* InfoPath 2003 Service Pack 1 (SP1)
SQL authentication, embedded, 934–935
SQL Server, 300
alleviating bottleneck in, 956–957
connecting to, after clicking Select Database, *260*
connecting to databases other than, 256
SQL Server Express 2005, 673
SQL server login credentials, warning about, 257
SQL Server 2000, unsupported data type and, 343*t*
SQL Server 2005
unsupported data type and, 343*t*
XML data type, 269
SQL session state service performance, measuring, 957
Square brackets, user's e-mail address within, 950
srcPath parameter, 1136, 1136*t*, 1137
SSP. *See* Shared Services Provider
SSS. *See* Session state service
Standard category
controls in, 43
in Controls task pane, 44
Standard controls, 43–44, 45–46*t*, 46–48
employment application form template after addition of, *46*
Standard toolbar, Format Painter on, 79, *79*
Start mode, changing, 25
"Start Over" feature, MOI Consulting request form code and, 808–810
State machine workflow, 635
Static default data, 85
Static default values, 106
Status report data, exporting to Microsoft Office Excel, *608*, 608–609
Status report forms, 555, 613
filling out
in browser by using Forms Services, *667*
on Pocket PC device, 721, *721*
merging, 558–559, *559*
quiescing error and, 913, *913*
Status report form template, 553, 554
workflow and, 615
Status reports
merging by team name and then by employee name, 561, 565
merging into one, 561–562
Status report sample form template, publishing to Form Services, 678–681
StatusReports group node, customizing merge behavior for, 565–566
StatusReports repeating group node
Merge Settings dialog for, 568, *569*
merging data in, based on value of **Team** name, 566–569, 571, 573–576, 578
Stock Properties page, of ATL Control Wizard for SimpleInfoPathActiveX control, 1051, *1052*
Stock tracking Text Box control, conditional formatting applied to, 219–222
String data types, 99, 99*t*, 773
String field, 774
string field, explanation behind name for, 287
String values, addition of, under each LCID key, 1130*t*
Structural editing, 7, 308, 310
Structural selection, 52
Structural validation, 311
stsadm.exe commands
full list of, specific to Forms Services, 899*t*
specific to quiescing, 918*t*
stsadm.exe tool, 899
command-line quiescing and, 917
configuring e-mail and, 949 (listing)
sample command lines for running of, 900 (listing)
using, 900
Student sign-in form
configuring conditional formatting to hide **LateReason** section if start time is later than now, *354*
configuring SharePoint document library submit for, 378, *378*
creating, 347–361
custom submit using rules and, 384–388
data source for, *362*

Student sign-in form (*cont.*)
 design mode after finishing Data Connection Wizard for submitting data to Web service, *348*
 dialog that appears when student signs in tardy, *388*
 expression shown in popup message when student signs in late to class, *387*
 including text and child elements only in, 358–361
 with instructor's Class Information view with default data, 352, *352*
 matrix of submit possibilities among fields, groups, and the Include setting, 362*t*
 partial submit and, 351–358
 during preview, *350*
 previewing, 380
 selecting Web service method for submit, *348*
 submitting entire form, 352–365
 tardy student signs in to philosophy class, 357, *357*
Student sign-in form view, designing, *354*
Student SignIn Library document library, 379
StudentSignIn method, parameter mapping and, 357
StudentSignIn-Rules sample, 385
StudentSignIn sample, 347
StudentSignIn1 sample, 351
Subject field, 93
Submit, unsupported database data types for, 343*t*
Submit button, 390
 on browser form toolbar, 683, 685–686
Submit data connections, 327
 specifying for form template, 1007
Submit data option, 345
Submit Data Wizard, differences between Receive and Submit Data and Receive Data Wizards and, *346*
Submit dialog, submitting InfoPath e-mail form in, 654, *654*
Submit error, dialog about, when user clicks Submit button after not filling in name in first view, 332, *333*
Submit failures, browser alert dialog and, 333, *333*
Submit form event, sinking, 830–831 (listing)
Submit functionality, customizing, 285
Submit keyboard shortcut, assigning, 335
Submit-only forms, creating, 347–361
Submit Options dialog, 334, *335*, 337, 390, 513
 Advanced section of, 393, *393*
 configuration of, to submit to a SharePoint document library, *379*
 with Hosting environment as the destination, 1008, *1008*
 setting up form's main submit to use code in, 829, *830*
 setting up submit using rules, 385, *385*
 for Web server submit via HTTP, *381*
"Submitted by" subject line, in e-mail introduction, 950
Submitted data, obscuring, 509
Submitting forms, 327–395
 best methods for, 335–337
 custom submit with form code, 383–384
 custom submit with rules, 384–388
 to database, 341–344
 data validation and, 331–334
 dialog asking whether user wants to save form or to submit form, *329*
 dialog confirming that submit succeeded, *350*
 dialog that appears when submit with rules fails on a secondary connection, *390*
 digitally signed form data, 365–368
 in entirety, 352–365
 generic success dialog for main submit connection, *393*
 to host, 1007–1010
 to hosting environment, 391–392
 limiting amount of submitted data, 363
 options for, 392–395
 post-submit actions warning, 394
 query may not get newly submitted data warning, 389
 reasons for doing, 328–329
 running list of rules and, *386*
 set up for, 334
 to SharePoint library, 377–380
 successful operations, 345
 via e-mail, 337–341
 to Web server via HTTP, 380–383
 to a Web service, 344–368
Submitting to a Web service, 344–368
 including text and child elements only, 358–361
 main submit, 344–345, 347, 349–351
 partial submit, 351–358
 submit parameter options, 358
SubmitToHost

asynchronous nature of, 1032
handling submit in host page with, 1030 (listing)
submitting to hosting environment using, 1029–1031
SubmitToHostEventHandler method, 1010 (listing)
three parameters taken by, 1009
Summary node, 574
Merge Settings dialog for, 575, *575*
Merge Settings dialog for, after customizations are complete, *577*
Surround With functionality, with code snippets, 860
Survey-style forms, sending data as e-mail and, 336
Switching sickness, 853
SwitchView form event, restricted OM available during, 826
System.Data.OleDb.NET Framework classes, 256
SystemGenerated errors, 765
System.Runtime.InteropServices.COM Exception, 986
System.Windows.Forms.Application class, 997
System.Windows.Forms namespace, 739

T

Tab characters, replacing, 361
Tab index property, 194
Table cells, empty, converting to Text Box controls, 1122–1123
Table-drawing tool, in InfoPath 2003 Service Pack 1 (SP1), 12
Table formats, in Layout task pane, 34–35, *35*
Table menu, 39
Tables
defining relationships between, 261, 263
inserting, in InfoPath 2003 SP1, *13*
Tables toolbar, 39
Hide Gridlines button in, 36
in InfoPath 2003 SP1, 13, *13*
unavailability of, in VSTO, 861, *861*
Tablet PCs, 16
Ink Picture control and form design with, 72
Input Scope button and, 195
Input Scope feature and, 198
Tablet PC stylus, Ink Picture control showing text entered with, *73*
Table with Title, employment application form template and title added with, *36*
Tabs, Visual Studio Designer controls grouped into, 846
Tampered forms, 366
Target documents, removing blank groups from, 572
Target forms, 559
default insert action and, 569
merging status report data into, 565
Targeting, form templates, 434–435
targetRoot XSL variable, 585
Task panes
dockable, 845
hiding, in VSTO, 845
using from local resource files, 785
in VSTO, 844–847
TaskPanes collection, 787
_taskPanes collection, 1096, 1097
Task pane script, managed form code and, 783
TCS. *See* Trusted Certificate Store
Team Combo Box control, 622
auto-populating with team name of person filling out the form, 623
TeamData XML file, 626–627 (listing)
Team field and date, Header format dialog after addition of, *591*
Team Lunch folder
"Food Preference" column shown in, 652, *652*
grouping of, by food preference, *657*
with responses to food preference survey, 656, *656*
TeamName field, selecting **UserRole** field corresponding to, in secondary data source, *628*
Team names, merging data in **StatusReports** repeating group node based on value of, 566–569, 571, 573–576, 578
Team names, XML file containing mapping from user roles to, 626–627 (listing)
Team status report
after merging three status reports, 574, *574*
with header and footer information, 591, *591*
merged, after all customizations are complete, 578, *578*
printed, 587, *587*

Team Status Report view, 586, 587, 595, 615, 631, 632
filling out, in the browser, 604, *604*
for merging multiple status report forms, 564, *564*
as a print view in the browser, 604, *605*
Team Text Box control, 629
Template compatibility, performing additional verification on, 695
Template data, default, editing, 151–154
Template Part Properties dialog, 448, *449*
after changing name and ID, 453, *453*
Template parts, 22, 29, 173, 174
adding to Controls task pane, 438–441
browser-enabled, designing, 701
data connections issues and inserting multiple instances of, 446
designing in VSTO, 841
existing, customization of, 452–454
icon and version number for, 440
identification of, in the view, 444
InfoPath support for, 438, 439
inserting into form template, 442–447
list of features not supported by, 435–436*t*
locating for reuse, 438
with no controls, 447
specifying alternative location for, 442
updating, 447–452
using, 438–447
Template parts designing, 432–438
template part design mode, 434–435, 437–438
Template part target, 435
Template source files, Browse for Folder dialog for selecting location for saving of, *422*
Temporary file (.tmp extension), sample Web service saving InfoPath form data to, 365
TerraServer, querying, for section of the San Francisco Bay near Highway 80, *291*
TerraServer project, 289
Testing
form templates, 48
form template with artificial domains, 482
full trust form, 485
simulating a publish domain for, 481–482
Test page, Web service, 280
Test SQL Statement button, in Edit SQL dialog, 266
Text alignment, setting with Size tab, 190–191
Text Box Binding dialog, appearance of, when Automatically create data source is disabled or Change Binding is used from a control, *139*
Text Box control, 7, 45*t*, 59, 169, 1037
address data and, 46
binding behavior of, 89*t*
conditional formatting set on, 216
converting empty table cells to, 1122–1123
importer and converting underlines to, 1139
with inner text aligned to outer text, *191*
with inner text not aligned to outer text, *190*
inserting into form template, 44
placeholder text in, *184*
Properties dialog for, 174, *175*
read-only, 805–806
unbound, critical design-time visual on, *150*
Text Box Properties dialog
Advanced tab of, showing input recognition section, *194*
Display tab of, *183*
Size tab of, *189*
Text labels, adjacent, control text aligned with, 354
Text nodes, 747
multiple, concatenating strings by selection of, 773
Text selection, multiple controls selected with, 80–81
Text stock property, 1052
Thank You view, 831
of MOI Consulting request form, *797*
ThisAddIn.cs file, 1106, 1107
ThisAddIn.Designer.cs/.vb, 1107
ThisAddIn partial class, 1107
ThisAddIn_Shutdown method, 1106
ThisAddIn_Startup method, 1106
implementation of, 1107, 1108 (listing), 1109
ThisAddIn.vb file, 1106, 1107
This form expires on combo box, 547
this.MainDataSource, 759
thisXDocument.DOM, 759
Throughput, 866
postback reduction and, 953
Time data type, 99*t*
Timeout property, setting, 824 (listing)
Timeouts
data connection, 933
session state, 909, 961
setting, 908

Time-sensitive/Critical request type, dialog resulting from selection of, *793*
To all occurrences of this section button, 206
To a network location deployment option, on Publishing Wizard, 400
Toolbar, browser form, 683–684, *684*
  configuring buttons on, 684
Toolbar buttons, customizing, for a browser-enabled template, 872, *872*
Toolbars
  hiding in Web pages hosting a form, 685
  missing icons in, 1020
  mobile forms and, 724
Toolbar updates
  during application idle state, 997–1000
  improving performance of, 999
Toolbox, after addition of **XmlFormView** control, 1016, *1016*
Toolbox pane, Reset Toolbox option on, 847
ToolStrip control, adding, to IP insurance application, 990–991
ToolTips, lack of IntelliSense information in, 738
Tracing, with Unified Logging Service, 925–927
TrackBar control, 1108
TrackBar property, 1110
TrackBarSample sample form template, 1110
TrackBar task pane, 1110, *1111*
TrackBarTaskPane.dll.manifest file, managed add-ins in, 1112
TrackBarTaskPane managed add-in project, 1105
TrackBarUserControl class, 1108
transform attribute, 581, 583
Travel request approval, workflow initiation e-mail message, *639*
Travel request approval workflow, 636
  customizing, 638, *638*
Travel request forms, 634
  with Workflow Task message bar, 640, *640*
Travel requests, 614
  approval or rejection of, 640
Travel Request sample form template, 636
Triangle icons, in VSTO, 845
True Boolean value, form submits and, 350, 351
True/false (Boolean) data type, 99*t*
Trust, 455, 456, 552
  designer lockdown and, 499–507
Trust Center, 489, 498, 499–503
Trust Center dialog, 1111, 1112, 1113, 1114
  Add-ins category of, 501, *501*, 501–503
  Add-ins tab shown in, 1111, *1112*
  availability of, 499
  categories in, 499
  Privacy Options category of, 503, *503*
  Trusted Publishers category of, 499–501, 500, *500*
Trusted Certificate Store, updating, 488
Trusted publishers, list of, 489
Trusted Publishers category, in Trust Center dialog, 499–501, 500, *500*
Trusted root certification authorities, for the current user, 488, *488*
Trusted Root Certification Authorities folder, 488, *488*
Trusted sites zone, 477
Trusting, untrusted certificates, 492
Trust levels, domain simulation and, 429
Trust settings
  configuring into form templates, 459, *459*
  publishing via e-mail and, 416
Trustworthy Computing, 455, 456, 457
  two sides to, 456–457, 458
try-catch block, using around Web service connection's **Execute** override method, 824
TryParse method, of **DateTime,** 760
try snippet, 860
Try to Connect, error dialog resulting from clicking on, if data connection is unavailable, 316, *316*
TWC. *See* Trustworthy Computing
Two-dimensional flow layout, 798
Type-ahead support, in list box controls, 44
Typed dataset, creating from **Customers** and **Orders SqlDataAdapter** objects, *304*
Typed dataset objects, 301
Type property, 788

U

UDC authentication, 944–946
UDC files, SQL credentials in, 935
udc parameter, data connections from CMCL and, 942
udc:SSO authentication type, 945
.udcx extension, list-item permissions and, 711

.udcx file
optionally deleting from data connection library, 941
uploading to centrally managed connection library, 939–940, *940*
UDDI. *See* Universal Description, Discovery, and Integration
UI. *See* User interface
Unbound control, 150, *150*
UNC network path, local intranet forms and, 471
Underscores, XML, naming nodes and, 104
Undo button
enabling/disabling, 1000
hosted form and, 994, 997
Undo operation, 771
UndoRedo property, 771
Unhandled exceptions, double notifications for, 851
Unified Logging Service, tracing with, 925–927
Uniform Resource Locators
domain form identified by, 467
form template's access path and, 460
registering alternate, with SharePoint, 928
Uniform Resource Names, 459
for template parts, 454
Universal Description, Discovery, and Integration, 291, 297
searching with, 299
UNIX systems, browser-based forms and, 668
UNIX variants, Forms Services and, 690
Unpublished forms, previewing, with CMCL connections, 941
Unstructured documents, 93
Untrusted certificate authority, InfoPath prompt for, *492*
Untrusted certificates, trusting, 492
Untrusted Root Authority dialog, 488
Untyped dataset objects, 301
Unused data connections, deleting, 380
Update button
adding, 872–874
on browser form toolbar, 684, 687
Update Form action, 873
Updates/updating
access path and, 463
cascading, 305, 306
publishing form templates and, 407
signed form templates, 493
template parts, 447–452
locating all template parts needing to be updated, 451–452
updating form template containing AddressBlock template part, 449–451
Update this value when the result of the formula is recalculated checkbox, 154
Upgrade OM button, 733
Upgrading
form code from InfoPath 2003, 842
to Forms Services, 677
form templates, quiescing and, 916–917
Object Model, 734
Upload & Activate function, 900
Upload Data Connection File page, 939, *940*
Upload Form Template page, 893, *894*, 917
URL-based options, for opening browser-enabled form templates, 716–720
URL parameters, passing, from host to the form, 1021–1025
URLs. *See* Uniform Resource Locators
urn parameter
data connections from CMCL and, 942, 943
URNs. *See* Uniform Resource Names
UseExplicit block, for data connection (.udcx) file, 945, *945*
Use (literal or encoded) part, 288
UseMail node, registering XML event handler to **Changing** event of, 781 (listing)
User Control, 1108
UserControl class, creating in .NET, for wrapping Text Box control, 1061
UserDefined errors, 765
User feedback, **MessageBox.Show** and, 805 (listing)
User form templates, cross-domain access for, 931–932
User groups, assigning, 617–618
User interface, 4
showing by using **MessageBox,** 878–879
User interface (UI) items, COM add-ins and addition of, 1076
UserIsAuthorized property, code for, 752, 753 (listing)
User login name, retrieval of, from Web service proxy, 947–948
UserName, LoginName *vs.*, 806

User names, assignment of, to roles, 617–618
User names checkbox, 617
User Options file, 838
User publishing, 888
UserRole field, selection of, that corresponds to **TeamName** field in secondary data source, *628*
User roles, 613, 614–634, 670, 865
in action, 621
conditional formatting with, 630–631
creating, 616–620
current, 217
data validation with, 629–630
determination of, when filling out a form, 620–621
filtering data based on, 626–629
new, creating, 617
previewing forms with, 427–428
previewing with, 624–626
role-based views, 631–634
rudimentary implementation of, in browser, 882 (listing)
in rules, 622–624
setting default value to, 629
simulating in the browser, 880–882
specifying, in condition for data validation, *630*
warning about use of, as security feature, 616
XML containing mapping from, to team names, 626–627 (listing)
User role section, at top of Preview tab, 625
Users, setting IRM permissions for, 551–552
Users' access path, specifying, 401, *402*
Users can request additional permission form setting, 548
User's current role qualifier, 217
using references, adding to ASP.NET project, 1021

V

Validate Form button
clicking on, to show dialog box message in the browser, 1034, *1034*
code behind, in life insurance form template, 1032, 1033 (listing)
Validating event, 757–764, 776, 955
changes accepted in, 757
Validating event handler, 802
for **Estimate** field in form code, 1006 (listing)
Validation
data, 222–229
on form load, 763
structural, 311
Validation and Rules section, of Data tab, 180
Validation error messages, *100*
Validation errors, 413
for cannot be blank property, delineated by red asterisk, *102*
error dialog related to submitting form with, in current view, *349*
iterating through, 758
for opening a form created before the **FlightType-FlightDate** node swap, *121*
submitting forms and, 331
warning when saving form with, *100*
Validation tab, on Field or Group Properties dialog, 224, *224*
Valid digital signatures, 533
Value, of condition, 217
Value binding property, 1042
ValueChanged event, 1110
Value property, 955–956, 1052, 1147
building custom controls for InfoPath using ActiveX and implementation of, 1056–1058
Variable watches, 740
VBScript, 10, 497, 731, 782, 783, 790
Verbosity
increasing, for server's logging level, 925
server performance and increases in, 927
Verification
of form template, 902
of form template, copying location before, 893
Verify Formula button, 162
Verify function, 900
Verify on Server option, in Design Checker task pane, 872
VeriSign, 489, 492, 1041
Versioning, form libraries and, 706
Version numbers, automatic setting of, 440
version parameter, data connections from CMCL and, 942, 943
Version upgrade feature, 96
Vertical Label control, 14, 163–164, *164*
binding behavior of, 90*t*
Expression Box control changed to, 188

Vertical text
errors due to, 698
remake of Overall Satisfaction table without, 698, *699*
View-based sorting, 769
View-based structural editing, through object model, 827
View drop-down, on browser form toolbar, 684, 687
view element, post-import warnings and, 1140, 1141
View extension functions, 881
View menu, removing print view from, 588
View properties, customizing, 75–76
View Properties dialog
opening, 75, *75*
Print Settings tab of, 588, *588*, 589
Text Settings tab in, 82, *83*
View representation, of controls, 41
Views
in form templates, 26
merged status report forms in, 562
mobile forms, 724
multiple, creation of, 73–76
performance tips, 952
Views link, in Design Tasks task pane, 845
viewsReadOnlyMode parameter, **InitEventHandler** method and, 1002
Views task pane, 34*t*, 74, *74*, 586
View state, session state *vs.*, 957
ViewSwitched event, 1003
ViewSwitched form event, handling, when switching to specific views, 826 (listing)
View switching, 952
postbacks and, 911
Virtual controls, 168
Visible property, 788, 1098
hiding task pane and, 826
VisibleStateChange event handler, 1098, 1100 (listing)
Visio, COM add-ins supported by, 1073
Visual Basic, 732
custom controls and, 174
project file, 838
Visual Basic .NET, 4
custom controls and, 174
hosting InfoPath and, 978
Visual C#, custom controls and, 174
Visual C++, custom controls and, 174
Visual C# project file, 838
Visual C# Windows application, 979
Visual flair, adding to forms, 85
Visual layout, designing for MOI Consulting request form, 798
Visuals
design-time, 47
showing all, 151
Visual SourceSafe, source control with, 855
Visual Studio, 288
building Installer package and, 419
debugging in, 741
debugging Web service in, 277, 359, *359*
graphical schema editor with, 133
installable form templates and, 417
Visual Studio Designer, 853
Visual Studio Designer controls, grouping of, into tabs, 846
Visual Studio Project file, 838
Visual Studio project-specific features, 856–857
exporting projects as templates, 857
working with multiple projects, 856
Visual Studio schema editor, *305*
Visual Studio Solution Explorer, deleting files from, 840
Visual Studio Solution (.sln), 838
Visual Studio Toolbox
after addition of **FormControl** control, 980, *980*
InfoPath controls integrated into, 846
Visual Studio Tools for Microsoft Office InfoPath 2007, 833–863
Visual Studio 2005, 23, 344, 833, 834, 835, 1076, 1105
closing before beginning or repairing VSTO installation, 836
code signing in, 859
creating new Windows Control Library project in, 1062
creating simple Web service with, 274–279
New Project dialog in, 837, *837*
objsafe.h file in Windows Platform SDK with, 1054
panes organized in, 845
Print preview in, 863
refactoring tools in, 859, *859*
versions of, as prerequisites to VSTO installation, 836

Web service created in, 296
Visual Studio 2005 Tools for Applications. *See* VSTA
Visual Studio 2005 Tools for the 2007 Microsoft Office System. *See* VSTO
VSTA, 29, 737, 834
building the project and, 741
debugging options in, 740
preview feature and, 425
switching between InfoPath and, 835
VSTA development environment, after selecting Loading Event from Programming submenu, 737, *737*
VSTO, 23, 834
Design a Form Template dialog in, *839*
designing browser-enabled form template with, 840
Design Tasks task pane in, 844, *844*
dialog informing user that VSTO never modifies existing form template, *840*
form template design with, 836–863
InfoPath-specific commands in, 848–849*t*
InfoPath *vs.*, 840
installing, 836
integration of Visual Studio and InfoPath design mode and, 835
missing features in, 861–863
preview feature and, 425
previewing a form in, 863
purpose of, 834–835
Quick Find in, *854*
Resource Files dialog in, 858, *858*
Save and Save All options in, 861–862
start designing form template in, 837–842
template parts designed in, 841
using existing form template with script, to create InfoPath project in, 841
warning about using one design environment at a time, 862
VSTO design experience, 843–853
menus, 848, 850
task panes, 844–847
working with controls, 851–853
VSTO feature set, 853–860
code-specific features, 858–860
code snippets, 860
refactoring, 859
signing, 859
Find and Replace, 854–855
resource editing, 858
source control with Visual SourceSafe, 855
Visual Studio project-specific features, 856–857
exporting projects as templates, 857
working with multiple projects, 856
VSTO InfoPath project, structure of, 838, *838*
VSTO Options dialog, Microsoft Office InfoPath category options in, 850, *850*
VSTO 2005 SE, writing add-ins and Custom Task Panes with use of, 1105–1106

W

Web, publishing InfoPath from template to, 17
Web Accessibility setting, in Upload Data Connection File page, 940, *940*
Web browsers
designing forms users can fill via, 29
forms filled out in, 665
hosting InfoPath form control in, 1011–1035
Web-enabled forms, submit and, 720
Web Front Ends, 672, 676
Web Front End servers
building ASP.NET Web form with **XmlFormView** control and, 1012
logs for, 925
SQL Server and, 956, 957
Web server, 273
submitting form to, via HTTP, 380–383
Web server (HTTP), submit connection to, 336, 337
Web server (HTTP) connection, ASP.NET page load event handler to read data submitted by, 383 (listing)
Web server (HTTP) submit
how it is not considered real data connection, 382
how it works, 382
Office Server connection with, 382
Web service connection **Timeout** property, setting, 824 (listing)
Web service data connections, 467
capturing errors from execution of, 825 (listing)
Web Service Definition Language, 10, 273
displaying Web service method description from, 282

entering an address to, *281*
portability of, 282
use of, 279
Web service form, querying and submitting during preview, 287, *287*
Web Service option, in Design a Form Template dialog, 245
Web service parameters, 364
Web service project, debugging in Visual Studio, 277
Web service proxy, 946–948
code behind a Web service to get user name from, 947, 948 (listing)
getting user login name from, 947–948
turning on, 947
Web service repository, 291
Web services, 10, 273–291, 297
ADO.NET, 300–307
compatibility of, with InfoPath, 288–289
description of, 273
design after finishing Data Connection Wizard for submitting data to, *348*
designing student sign-in form based on, 347
extended features of, 298–307
form templates created from, 30*t*
handling connection failures, 824
main data source extensibility and, 353
querying, 820
returning data from, 349
searching with UDDI, 299
selecting method for submitting student sign-in data, *348*
sending digitally signed form data to, 366
specifying how form works with, *346*
submitting forms to, 336, 344–368
UDDI and searches for, 291
Web service sample dependency, 792
Web service (simple)
creating with Visual Studio 2005, 274–279
InfoPath design mode after finishing Data Connection Wizard for, *286*
InfoPath Web services and, 280–287
list of methods from, for receiving data, *283*
part of browser-friendly test page for navigation in, *278*
using, 279–280
warning: sample code not production-ready, 275
writing code for, 276 (listing)
Web Service Submit, 384, 385, 386
Web service submit, parameter mappings defined for, *356,* 356–358
Web Service Submit connection, in list on Data Connection dialog, 379
Web service test page, 280
WeeklyStatusReport_BrowserEnabled sample, 603
Weekly status report document library, in Merge Forms view, *558*
Weekly status report form, *555*
Weekly status report form template, Weekly Status Report view of, 562, *563*
Weekly Status Report view, 602, 622, 632
Welcome view, 808, 809
of MOI Consulting request form, 791, *791,* 798, 799, 800
WFEs. *See* Web Front Ends
Whole number (integer) data type, 99*t,* 178
Widths, custom, for forms, 76
Wildcard expressions, form performance and, 954
window.external.Window.XDocument object, not all OM is available via, 790
Windows Authentication, 259
window.setTimeout method, 1035
Windows Event Viewer, 920
Windows Explorer, finding template file location with, 422
Windows Integrated authentication, 934
Windows Performance Monitor, 866, 958
Word, 3, 4
COM add-ins supported by, 1073
custom task panes added into, 1093
default Document Information Panel in, 966, 968, 970
form importing and, 28, 29
InfoPath formatting options and those in, 77
Mime HTML file opened in, 606
Print Views feature in, 596–605
Trust Center dialog and, 499
VSTO package and, 834
Word documents
importing into InfoPath, 1119–1124
Import Options dialog for importing of, 1121, *1121*
InfoPath default importers for, 1128
Word forms, built-in importer for, 1116

WordPrint tool, 596
registering dynamically linked libraries for, 597
Word print view, default print settings and, 603
Word Print Views dialog, 600, *600*
WordPrint wizard, 597, 600
Word 2003, Document properties dialog in, 966, *967*
Word 2007, Document Information Panel in, 966, *967*
Workflow, 613–663
automatic *vs.* manual initiation of, 637
browser-enabled forms and, 642
checking on status of, 641
with InfoPath e-mail forms, 643–662
InfoPath 2003 SP1 and support for, 16
with Microsoft Office SharePoint Server 2007, 634–642
sequential, 634–635
state machine, 635
user roles, 614–634
Workflow dialog, *641*, 642
Workflow Services, 19
Workflow Task message bar, 640, *640*, 641
World Wide Web Consortium, 5, 507, 508
Wrap text property, 185
Writing
own merge XSL, 582–586
script, 730
W3 Schools Web site, 137, 769
WScript.Shell, 784
WSDL. *See* Web Service Definition Language
WSDL URL, creating Web service data connection while designing a form and, 273
W3C. *See* World Wide Web Consortium

X

xd:binding attribute, 1139
xd:CtrlId attribute, 1140
xdDefault value, **viewsReadOnlyMode** parameter and, 1002
xdFrozen value, **viewsReadOnlyMode** parameter and, 1002
xdNonEditable value, **viewsReadOnly-Mode** parameter and, 1002
XDocumentBeforeClose event, 1107, 1109, 1110
hooking up event handlers for, 1082
XDocumentBeforeClose event handler, 1088
XDocumentOpen event, 1107, 1109
hooking up event handlers for, 1082
XDocumentOpen event handler, 1088, 1089
implementation of, 1089 (listing)
XDocument property, 1060
XDocument.Roles property, 621
XDocument.UI.Alert, 739
xd:xctname attribute, 1139
XHTML data type, 99, *99t*
XMethods Web site, 291
XML
element and attribute fields in, 95
persisting default state of, for main and secondary data sources, 810–811 (listing)
processing instructions, 364
recursion in, 122
XML-based technologies, rapid adoption of, 3
XML data, 621
co-signed digital signature created in, 532
digital signatures in, 533–535
entering file location to use when creating a secondary connection to, *249*
in form template resource files, 250
signed, warning about, 367
signed data in, 534–353
starting new blank form from, 126–127
XML data and schema
matching of, before changing field or group name, *96*
mismatched, after name change, *96*
XML data connection, for restricted form templates, 466
XML data events, 730, 744–777
Changed event, 767–773
data states, 749–764
event bubbling, 745–748
form errors, 765–767
how data changes, 744–745
XmlDataEvents sample form template, 744
XML data file adapter, data to fill into a form and save to Sample.xml, to be read later with, *248*
XML document
data source created from, *136*
Type drop-down menu, with option for addition of, *134*
XmlDocument, loading data into, 367

XmlDocument class, 730
XML document connections, remote, 713
XML document or schema
existing, designing form from instead of creating data source from scratch, *125*
selecting location of, *125*
XML event handlers
examples of advanced XPaths for registration of, 782*t*
multiple event notifications for, 773–777
registering to **Changing** event of **UseMail** node, 781 (listing)
XML events, no support of complex XPaths for, 782
.xml extension, list-item permissions and, 711
XML file connection settings, to opt in or out of including the data as a file in your template, *249*
XML file data adapter, 247
XML files, 247–255, 297
choosing whether to include data from, as form template default data, *127*
final page of Data Connection Wizard for, *251*
inferring, 127
with mapping from user roles to team names, 626–627 (listing)
permissions and, 247
XML file secondary data connection, form after querying, *310*
XML form, opening from the server, 715
XML format, for attached files, 70
XmlForm object
checking **Dirty** property on, 1000
warning against storing references to, 1002
xmlForm parameter, **InitEventHandler** method and, 1001
XmlFormView class, 1011, 1015
XmlFormView control
all properties of, 1026*t*
commonly used properties of, 1017*t*
one instance of, per page, 1018
requirements for, 1012
Toolbox after addition of, 1016, *1016*
writing InfoPath form code in host page with use of, 1025, 1027–1028
XmlFormView1 control
Initialize event handler added in host page for, *1023*
sinking, 1023
visibility of, 1020
XmlFormView.EditingStatus, hiding **XmlFormView** control and, 1021
XmlFormView folder, Solution Explorer after addition of, 1014, *1015*
XmlFormView initialization, timeline of, 1022
XmlFormView1_SubmitToHost method, 1030
XML fragments, 206, 207, 317
XmlLocation parameter, 719
XmlNode class, 730
XmlNodeToString Web method, submitting **ClassInformation** group to, 358
XML Path Language, 6, 133, 771
XML Schema, 4, 5, 7, 14, 124, 513
for airline form template, 109 (listing)
data source details and, 93–94
extraction of, from form template, 102
form template created from, 30*t*
inferring, 127
InfoPath controls and, created "behind" data source in XSD file, 111–115*t*
for main data source, 255
potential complications with starting new blank form from, 129–132
signed data in, 535–538
starting new blank form from, 128–129
Type drop-down menu, with option for addition of, *134*
XML Signature, 507, 508
XML Signature Syntax and Processing, 535
XML Structure task pane, in Microsoft Office Word, 597, *598*
XML subtree, including the selected element option, 361
XML subtree, InfoPathChart control and implementing control that binds to, 1050–1051
XML technologies, 4
xmlToEdit string, finding, for a structurally editable control, 827, *828*
XML tree structure in Word, building, to match structure of data source in InfoPath, 599
XPath. *See* XML Path Language
XPathException, 778
XPathNavigator class, 730
description of, 747
learning more about, 780
XPathNavigator IsDescendent method, 811

XPathNavigator objects, 312
deleting nodes and, 779–780
finding XPath of node, 777
selecting multiple nodes, 779
using, 777–780
using **NamespaceManager** parameter, 778
XPathNavigator parameter, passing **null** for, in **Execute** override method, 822
XPathNavigator Select method, 777
XPathNodeIterator, selecting multiple nodes with, 779 (listing)
Xpath parameter, 777
XSD. *See* XML Schema
xsd:any extensibility element, 133
xsd:any schema element, 137, 292
XSD file, InfoPath controls and XML Schema created "behind" data source in, 111–115*t*
.xsf file, buttons in, 151
xsf:importSource element, 581, 583
xsf namespace, 108
xsi:nil, field changes and, 774
XSL, 580
for Word print view, 599, *599*
xsl:sort directive, 769
XSLT. *See* Extensible Stylesheet Language Transformations
xsl:value-of statement, 1140
.xsn file, 398
.xsn file extension, for form templates, 26
XSN form template, opening from the server, 715
XsnLocation, updating, 1025
XsnLocation parameter, 719

Z

Zones, 467
Internet, 475
local intranet, 470–474
local machine, 478
restricted sites, 470
trusted sites, 477

Microsoft .NET Development Series

.NET Framework Standard Library Annotated Reference
Volume 1: Base Class Library and Extended Numerics Library
Microsoft .net Development Series
Brad Abrams

0321154894

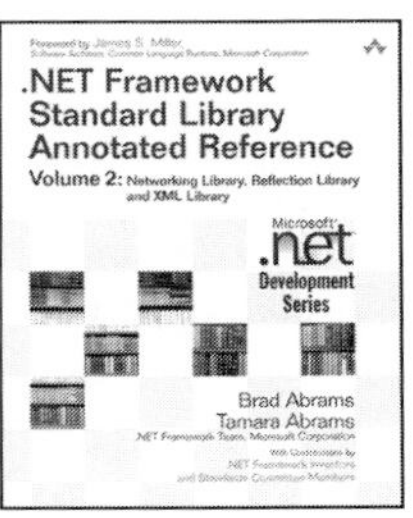

.NET Framework Standard Library Annotated Reference
Volume 2: Networking Library, Reflection Library and XML Library
Microsoft .net Development Series
Brad Abrams
Tamara Abrams

0321194454

.NET Web Services
Architecture and Implementation
Keith Ballinger

0321113594

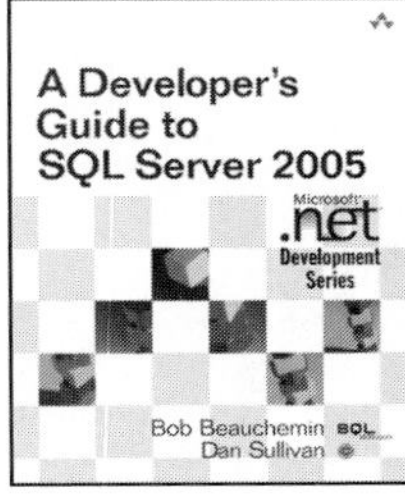

A Developer's Guide to SQL Server 2005
Microsoft .net Development Series
Bob Beauchemin
Dan Sullivan

0321382188

Visual Studio Tools for Office
Using C# with Excel, Word, Outlook, and InfoPath
Microsoft .net Development Series
Eric Carter
Eric Lippert

0321334884

Visual Studio Tools for Office
Using Visual Basic 2005 with Excel, Word, Outlook, and InfoPath
Microsoft .net Development Series
Eric Carter
Eric Lippert

0321411757

0321160770

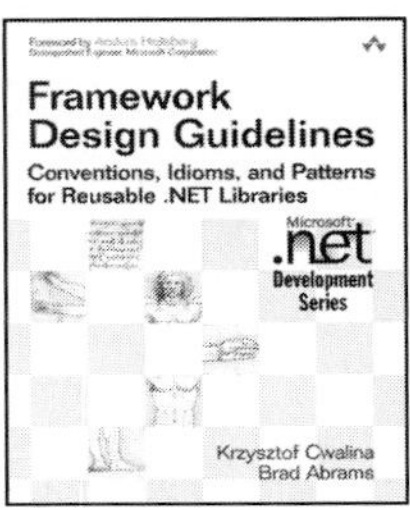

Framework Design Guidelines
Conventions, Idioms, and Patterns for Reusable .NET Libraries
Microsoft .net Development Series
Krzysztof Cwalina
Brad Abrams

0321246756

0321418344

The .NET Developer's Guide to Directory Services Programming
Microsoft .net Development Series
Joe Kaplan
Ryan Dunn

0321350170

0321150775

The Common Language Infrastructure Annotated Standard
Microsoft .net Development Series
James S. Miller
Susann Ragsdale

0321154932

Essential ASP.NET with Examples in C#
Microsoft .net Development Series
Fritz Onion

0201760401

Essential ASP.NET with Examples in Visual Basic .NET
Microsoft .net Development Series
Fritz Onion

0201760398

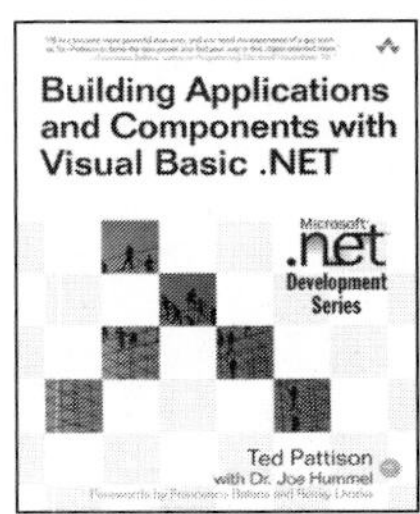

Building Applications and Components with Visual Basic .NET
Microsoft .net Development Series
Ted Pattison
with Dr. Joe Hummel

0201734958

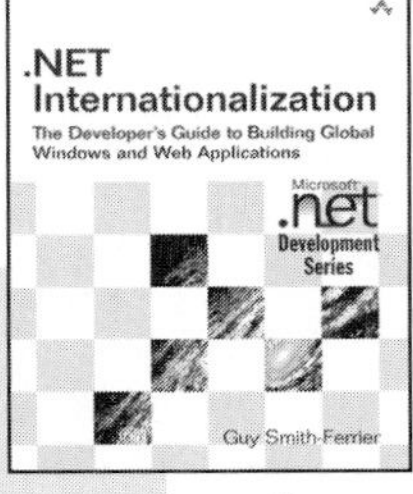

.NET Internationalization
The Developer's Guide to Building Global Windows and Web Applications
Microsoft .net Development Series
Guy Smith-Ferrier

0321341384

0321169514

For more information go to www.awprofessional.com/msdotnetseries/

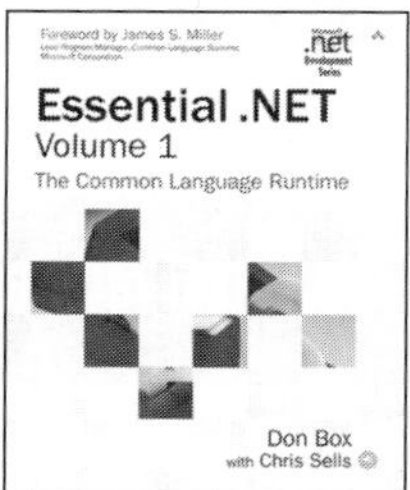

0201734117

0321228359

0321334213

0321278720

0321334434

032124673X

032126892X

0321197690

0321237706

0321410599

0321303636

0321267966

0321399838

0201770180

0201745682

0321174038

0321174046

THIS BOOK IS SAFARI ENABLED

INCLUDES FREE 45-DAY ACCESS TO THE ONLINE EDITION

The Safari® Enabled icon on the cover of your favorite technology book means the book is available through Safari Bookshelf. When you buy this book, you get free access to the online edition for 45 days.

Safari Bookshelf is an electronic reference library that lets you easily search thousands of technical books, find code samples, download chapters, and access technical information whenever and wherever you need it.

TO GAIN 45-DAY SAFARI ENABLED ACCESS TO THIS BOOK:

- Go to **http://www.awprofessional.com/safarienabled**
- Complete the brief registration form
- Enter the coupon code found in the front of this book on the "Copyright" page

If you have difficulty registering on Safari Bookshelf or accessing the online edition, please e-mail customer-service@safaribooksonline.com.